Contemporary Developments in International Law

Contemporary Developments in International Law

Essays in Honour of Budislav Vukas

Edited by

Rüdiger Wolfrum
Maja Seršić
Trpimir M. Šošić

BRILL
NIJHOFF

LEIDEN | BOSTON

Library of Congress Cataloging-in-Publication Data

Contemporary developments in international law : essays in honour of Budislav Vukas / Edited by Rüdiger Wolfrum, Maja Seršić, Trpimir M. Šošić.
  pages cm
  Includes bibliographical references and index.
  ISBN 978-90-04-24531-0 (hardback : alk. paper) -- ISBN 978-90-04-24562-4 (e-book : alk. paper) 1. International law. I. Vukas, Budislav, honouree. II. Wolfrum, Rüdiger, editor. III. Seršić, Maja, editor. IV. Šošić, Trpimir M., editor.

KZ3410.C668 2015
341--dc23

2015035250

This publication has been typeset in the multilingual "Brill" typeface. With over 5,100 characters covering Latin, IPA, Greek, and Cyrillic, this typeface is especially suitable for use in the humanities. For more information, please see www.brill.com/brill-typeface.

ISBN 978-90-04-24531-0 (hardback)
ISBN 978-90-04-24562-4 (e-book)

Copyright 2016 by Koninklijke Brill NV, Leiden, The Netherlands.
Koninklijke Brill NV incorporates the imprints Brill, Brill Hes & De Graaf, Brill Nijhoff, Brill Rodopi and Hotei Publishing.
All rights reserved. No part of this publication may be reproduced, translated, stored in a retrieval system, or transmitted in any form or by any means, electronic, mechanical, photocopying, recording or otherwise, without prior written permission from the publisher.
Authorization to photocopy items for internal or personal use is granted by Koninklijke Brill NV provided that the appropriate fees are paid directly to The Copyright Clearance Center, 222 Rosewood Drive, Suite 910, Danvers, MA 01923, USA.
Fees are subject to change.

This book is printed on acid-free paper.

Contents

Introduction XI
Bibliography of Budislav Vukas XV

PART 1
Subjects of International Law

1 La Ville libre de Dantzig devant la Cour permanente de Justice internationale 3
   Philippe Couvreur

2 Macedonian-Greek Relations and the ICJ Judgment of 5 December 2011 26
   Toni Deskoski

3 When Can Property of a State be Attached to Enforce a Foreign Judgment Given against It in Another Country? Some Guidance in the ICJ Judgment in the *Jurisdictional Immunities* Case 46
   Hazel Fox

4 Controversial Subjects of Contemporary International Law: IGO-like Entities as Participants in International Legal Relations – Do We Need a 'Reparation Case II'? 56
   Davorin Lapaš

5 La controverse sur le statut de la Palestine 102
   Djamchid Momtaz

6 The Treaty-Making Capacity of International Organizations: Practice *vs.* Codification Efforts 116
   Obrad Račić

7 Suspension of a Member State in an International Integration Organization: Mercosur 138
   Ernesto J. Rey Caro

8   Due Diligence: Fault-Based Responsibility or Autonomous
    Standard?   151
       Maja Seršić

PART 2
Law of the Sea

9   A Succinct Historical Overview of the Status of Straits in
    International Law   173
       Hugo Caminos

10 Modern Piracy off the Coast of Somalia: A Test-Bed for Old and
    New International Prevention and Repression Instruments   188
       Maria Clelia Ciciriello and Federica Mucci

11 Le régime des baies et des golfes dans la Mer Méditerranée   206
       Umberto Leanza

12 ITLOS's Approach to the Delimitation of the Continental Shelf
    beyond 200 Nautical Miles in the *Bangladesh/Myanmar* Case:
    Theoretical and Practical Difficulties   230
       Alex G. Oude Elferink

13 The Status of Islands in the International Law of the Sea:
    Megisti Island   250
       Nicholas M. Poulantzas

14 Theorizing about Conventional Environmental Sea Regimes
    as International Trusts: The Case of the Barcelona Convention
    System   263
       Evangelos Raftopoulos

15 Harlequin and the Mediterranean   291
       Tullio Scovazzi

16 The 24-Mile Archaeological Zone: Abandoned or Confirmed?   305
       Trpimir M. Šošić

17 Fisheries Disputes: Judicial and Arbitral Practice since the Entry into Force of UNCLOS   328
    Tullio Treves

18 Forgotten Rights? Landlocked States and the Law of the Sea   337
    Helmut Tuerk

19 Military Vessel Protection Detachments under National and International Law   360
    Rüdiger Wolfrum

20 En Route to the Final Shape of the UNCLOS Dispute Settlement System: Some Pivotal Negotiating Procedural Steps Worthy of Consideration by Future Treaty-Makers and Leaders in Treaty-Making   369
    Sienho Yee

PART 3
Protection of Human Rights

21 Minority Protection and the Prohibition of Discrimination   391
    Elena Andreevska

22 Precarious Times, Precarious Work: Lessons from Flexicurity   405
    Nada Bodiroga-Vukobrat, Ana Pošćić and Adrijana Martinović

23 The Iraqi Cases: Further Elements and Thoughts concerning 'Jurisdiction' under Article 1 of the European Convention on Human Rights   431
    Lucius Caflisch

24 Some Reflections on the Right of Access to Justice in Its Wide Dimension   458
    Antônio Augusto Cançado Trindade

25 Nation et minorités en Europe   467
    Giorgio Conetti

26 Protection of Croatian as a Minority Language
    in Europe   477
    Vesna Crnić-Grotić

27 Some Considerations on the Legal Role of the Sentences and
    Recommendations of International Bodies Created for the Protection
    of Human Rights   500
    Zlata Drnas de Clément

28 Doctrinal Views *versus* State Views on Humanitarian Assistance in the
    Event of Disasters: Comparing the Work of the *Institut de Droit
    International* with That of the International Law Commission   520
    Gerhard Hafner

29 Application of Article 20 of the 1989 Convention on the Rights of the
    Child in the Republic of Croatia   540
    Mira Lulić

30 Social Rights and International Law   564
    Bernd v. Maydell

31 Les droits de l'homme aujourd'hui   574
    Tafsir Malick Ndiaye

32 Sovereignty of State *v.* Protection of Persons in the Case of
    Disasters   583
    Ernest Petrič

33 Avoiding Plurality of International Proceedings in the European
    Court of Human Rights   614
    Nina Vajić and Vadim Pak

34 The Role of Provisions on Human Rights Protection in Constructing
    Croatian-Italian (Formerly Yugoslav-Italian) Relations   636
    Budislav Vukas Jr.

35 The Role of the Committee of Experts in the ILO's Supervisory
    Mechanism: Reflections on Ten Years' Experience as a Member   652
    Yozo Yokota

PART 4
Settlement of Disputes

36 International Arbitration: A Judicial Function?   677
   Chittharanjan F. Amerasinghe

37 Flexibility in the Award of Reparation: The Role of the Parties and the Tribunal   690
   James Crawford

38 The International Court of Justice and Diplomatic Settlement of Disputes: Could ICJ Judgments Play an Effective Role in the Negotiation of Interstate Disputes?   709
   Sašo Georgievski

39 Wrong Address? Advisory Opinion of the ICJ on the Judgment No. 2867 of the ILOAT upon a Complaint Filed against the International Fund for Agricultural Development   729
   Dražen Petrović

40 Asia and Dispute Settlement: The Law of the Sea   755
   M.C.W. Pinto

41 The State as a Party in Arbitral Proceedings on Settlement of Private Law Disputes – Miscellaneous   770
   Krešimir Sajko

42 Of Courts and Competition: Dispute Settlement under Part XV of UNCLOS   789
   Philippe Sands

PART 5
Miscellaneous

43 Le prétendu caractère « primitif » du droit international public   801
   Robert Kolb

44 The United Nations Charter, Chapter VII, Non-Use-of-Force and Non-Intervention in Contemporary International Law: The Sisyphean Labours of the *Institut de Droit International* on Defining and Controlling 'Use of Force' Today   821
    Edward McWhinney

45 Some Remarks on Soft Law and Some Specific Forms of Treaty Making   840
    Robert Mrljić

46 The Ancient Origins of General Principles in International Law   851
    Marko Petrak

47 Fraudulent Treaties: The Covenant with the Gibeonites in the Biblical Book of *Joshua*   860
    Maurizio Ragazzi

48 The Notion of Sources of International Criminal Law   879
    Mirjam Škrk

49 Passage from Natural Resources Law to Environmental Law to Sustainable Development Law   906
    Amado S. Tolentino Jr.

Introduction

Professor Budislav Vukas was born on 1 January 1938 in Rijeka/Sušak, Croatia. He completed his law studies at the University of Zagreb, Faculty of Law in 1961; an LLM followed in 1965 as well as a Doctor of Laws in 1974. Already in 1961 he was admitted to and attended courses at the Hague Academy of International Law (1961).

His professional career started early and focused on an academic career in international law right from the beginning. He became an assistant in 1963, a lecturer in 1970, an assistant professor in 1974 and a professor since 1977. Budislav Vukas was and still is a much sought after lecturer. He lectured at many very prestigious universities such as Belgrade, Bologna, Boston, Brest, Ljubljana, Milan, Paris, Parma, Rome, Split, Thessaloniki, Tilburg and Valletta. His lectures covered various subjects of public international law. The fact that he was called to lecture at so many different universities showed that he was accepted broadly and he had the fame of a lecturer who attracted student interest. Further he directed courses on various subjects such as on the law of the sea at the Dubrovnik Inter-University Centre (1984–2001) and the Rhodes Academy of Oceans Law and Policy (1999–2001 and 2004), on "States, Peoples and Minorities" at the Hague Academy of International Law (*Recueil des cours*, Vol. 231, 1992), on intervention in contemporary international law at the Bancaja Euromediterranean Courses of International Law (Castellón, 2003). In particular his involvement in the law of the sea course at the Inter-University Centre of Dubrovnik was important since he transformed the annual sessions of this course into an attractive meeting point for younger public international law scholars. His lecture on states, peoples and minorities at the Hague Academy is one of the standard publications on this subject.

Budislav Vukas participated in various conferences, in particular the Third United Nations Conference on the Law of the Sea (1975–1982), the Preparatory Commission for the International Seabed Authority and for the International Tribunal for the Law of the Sea (1984–1990 and 1994), the International Seabed Authority (1994–1996), the Meeting of the States Parties to the United Nations Convention on the Law of the Sea (1994–1996). He was also involved in more general negotiations such as in the Sixth Committee of the United Nations General Assembly (1990, 1991, 1995), in the Working Group on the United Nations Decade of International Law of the UN General Assembly's Sixth Committee (Chairman, 1990), in the CSCE Conference on the Human Dimension, Copenhagen Meeting (1990), in the CSCE Meeting of Experts on National Minorities, Geneva (1991), in the World Conference on Human Rights, Vienna (1993) and in the 26th

International Conference of the Red Cross and Red Crescent (1995). All these political/diplomatic activities showed the deep understanding of Budislav Vukas in law of the sea matters and international human rights issues. The practical experience he gained in these conferences was later reflected in his writings.

This broad academic and diplomatic background is matched by his involvement in international dispute settlement mechanisms. Budislav Vukas is member of the Permanent Court of Arbitration (1989–1991 and since 1999), he was member of the International Tribunal for the Law of the Sea (1996–2005) and its Vice-President (2002–2005). He was member of the Arbitral Tribunal constituted on the basis of the Arbitration Agreement between the Republic of Croatia and the Republic of Slovenia (2012–2015), the Committee of Experts on the Application of Conventions and Recommendations of the International Labour Organization (1985–2006), and the Commissions of Inquiry formed under Article 26 of the Constitution of the International Labour Organization to examine the observance by Romania of the Discrimination (Employment and Occupation) Convention, 1958 (No. 111) (1989–1991) and the observance by Belarus of the Freedom of Association and Protection of the Right to Organize Convention, 1948 (No. 87) and the Right to Organize and Collective Bargaining Convention, 1949 (No. 98) (President, 2004). He is member of the Court of Conciliation and Arbitration within the OSCE (since 1995). Finally he was Judge *ad hoc* in two cases before the International Court of Justice – the Case concerning Application of the Convention on the Prevention and Punishment of the Crime of Genocide (Croatia *v.* Serbia) (1999–2015) and the Case concerning Application of the Interim Accord of 13 September 1995 (the former Yugoslav Republic of Macedonia *v.* Greece) (2003–2011). He left his marks in all these institutions; he is, in particular, well remembered, in the International Tribunal for the Law of the Sea.

Budislav Vukas is member in the most prestigious international law associations. Early in his career he became Associate Member (1991) and Member (since 1997) of the *Institut de Droit International*; he was *Rapporteur* on "The Humanitarian Assistance", and the resolution on the topic was unanimously adopted at the Bruges Session of the Institute in 2003. He is member of the Croatian Society of International Law (since 1961) and President (since 2010); the Argentine Society of International Law (since 2002); the Croatian Academy of Legal Sciences (established in 2001); and the International Council of Environmental Law, Bonn (since 1978). He was furthermore appointed to the Scientific Council of the European Institute for Marine Studies, Brest, France (1997–2005); and the Scientific Council of the *Institut de droit économique de la mer*, Monaco (2000–2006).

He is author of numerous books, monographs, articles and papers in nearly all fields of public international law, in particular law of the sea, international environmental law, international protection of human rights, national minorities, international humanitarian law and the international law of treaties. In a period where the tendency seems to prevail to concentrate on particular issues of public international law Budislav Vukas sticks out as one of the few remaining generalists. It is this wide horizon that made him the internationally sought after lecturer and organizer of conferences.

In spite of his many academic and international achievements Budislav Vukas always tried to find time for his hobby – football – and remained interested in many issues not related to international law. He was always dedicated to his family, and in recent years his three grandchildren – Lara, Korina and Ante – have become the focus of his life.

The reputation and regard Budislav Vukas enjoys among his colleagues is reflected by the overwhelming response that we, as Editors of this volume, received when sending out the initial invitations. We thank all of Professor Vukas's friends, colleagues and former students who, by contributing their essays, would not miss the opportunity to honour an esteemed friend, colleague and teacher and pay tribute to his distinguished and long-lasting academic and international career. The contributions in the *Liber Amicorum* deal with a wide variety of current developments in international law, but mainly in fields that were the focus of Professor Vukas's academic interest. The first part of the book, thus, contains contributions on various legal aspects involving the subjects of international law. The number of essays in the second part, dedicated to the law of the sea, demonstrates the particular importance of this field of international law in Professor Vukas's career. The same may be said of the third part, which brings together essays on international legal issues concerning the protection of human rights, including minority rights. The fourth part is devoted to dispute settlement. The contributions in the fifth part cover diverse topics not falling under the other four headings, thus mirroring Professor Vukas's wide-ranging interest for questions of general international law beyond particular fields of specialization. These essays tackle fundamental issues concerning the nature and the sources of international law, including treaties and general principles of law, but also the use of force in international law.

This project in honour of Professor Budislav Vukas could not have been realized without the support of Brill. We are particularly indebted to Ms Ingeborg van der Laan for all her insightful help and patience during the editing process which is not always easy to handle in the case of edited volumes such as this one.

We hope that Professor Vukas will be satisfied with the result and that he will take pleasure in reading the essays written by his friends, colleagues and former students. We wish him success with his future endeavours in the realm of international law, but above all good health and many friendly gatherings.

The Editors

Bibliography of Budislav Vukas

I   Books/Monographs

1. *Međunarodnopravna pitanja koegizstencije* [*International Legal Issues of Co-existence*], Zagreb, 1964, vii, 75 pp. (master's thesis).
2. *Korištenje morskog dna i podmorja izvan granica nacionalne jurisdikcije* [*Uses of the Seabed and Its Subsoil beyond National Jurisdiction*] (with B. Sambrailo), Zagreb, 1968, 22 pp.
3. *Iskorištavanje morskog dna i podzemlja u velikim dubinama* [*The Exploitation of the Seabed and Subsoil at Great Depths*] (with J. Andrassy and E. Pallua), Zagreb, 1970, 43 pp.
4. *Međunarodnopravna osnova položaja hrvatske manjine u susjednim zemljama i Čehoslovačkoj* [*The International Legal Basis for the Status of the Croatian Minority in Neighbouring Countries and in Czechoslovakia*], Zagreb, 1971, 78 pp.
5. *Načelo* pacta tertiis nec nocent nec prosunt *u međunarodnom pravu* [*The Prinicple* Pacta Tertiis Nec Nocent Nec Prosunt *in International Law*], Zagreb, 1973, xxxvii, 535 pp. (doctoral dissertation).
6. *Relativno djelovanje međunarodnih ugovora* [*The Relativity of International Treaties*], Zagreb, 1975, 179 pp.
7. *Epikontinentalni pojas* [*The Continental Shelf*] (with D. Rudolf *et al.*), Split, 1976, 237 pp.
8. *Sredozemlje i novo međunarodno pravo mora* [*The Mediterranean and the New International Law of the Sea*], Zagreb, 1977, 79 pp.
9. *Etničke manjine i međunarodni odnosi* [*Ethnic Minorities and International Relations*], Zagreb, 1978, 251 pp.
10. *Novo pravo mora* [*The New Law of the Sea*] (ed.), Zagreb, 1982, ii, 308 pp.
11. *Gradišćanski Hrvati 1553–1983* [*The Burgenland Croats 1553–1983*] (ed. with V. Belaj *et al.*), Zagreb, 1984, xxii, 298 pp.
12. *Essays on the New Law of the Sea* (ed.), Zagreb, 1985, x, 556 pp.
13. *Konvencija Ujedinjenih naroda o pravu mora (1982); sa Završnim aktom Treće konferencije UN o pravu mora i komentarskim bilješkama* [*The United Nations Convention on the Law of the Sea; with the Final Act of the Third UN Conference on the Law of the Sea and Commentarial Annotations*] (with D. Rudolf *et al.*), Split, 1986, 221 pp.
14. *Međunarodnopravni problemi tumačenja i primjene Konvencije Ujedinjenih naroda o pravu mora* [*International Legal Problems regarding the Interpretation and Application of the United Nations Convention on the Law of the Sea*] (with collaborators), Zagreb, 1987, 44, xii pp.; Part II, Zagreb, 1988, 48, xiii pp.; Part III, Zagreb, 1989, 50 pp.; Part IV, Zagreb, 1990, 36 pp.

15. *The Legal Regime of Enclosed or Semi-enclosed Seas: The Particular Case of the Mediterranean* (ed.), Zagreb, 1988, vi, 515 pp.
16. *Essays on the New Law of the Sea 2* (ed.), Zagreb, 1990, v, 450 pp.
17. *Povelja Ujedinjenih naroda i Statut Međunarodnog suda* [*The Charter of the United Nations and the Statute of the International Court of Justice*], (ed. with B. Bakotić and N. Vajić), Zagreb, 1992, 81 pp.
18. *Međunarodno pravo* [*International Law*], Vol. I (with J. Andrassy and B. Bakotić), Zagreb, 1995 (reprinted 1998), xix, 348 pp.
    ———, 2nd edn. (with J. Andrassy, B. Bakotić and M. Seršić), Zagreb, 2010, xxi, 475 pp.
19. *Essays on the New Law of the Sea 3* (ed.), Zagreb, 1996, 235 pp.
20. *Hrvatska i Ujedinjeni narodi* [*Croatia and the United Nations*] (ed. with I. Šimonović and B. Vukmir), Zagreb, 1996, xii, 596 pp.
21. *The Law of the Sea – Selected Writings*, Leiden, 2004, viii, 359 pp.
22. *Međunarodno pravo* [*International Law*], Vol. III (with J. Andrassy, B. Bakotić and M. Seršić), Zagreb, 2006, xxi, 230 pp.
23. *International Law: New Actors, New Concepts – Continuing Dilemmas; Liber Amicorum Božidar Bakotić* (ed. with T.M. Šošić), Leiden, 2010, xiv, 614 pp.
24. *Međunarodno pravo* [*International Law*], Vol. II (with J. Andrassy, B. Bakotić, D. Lapaš and M. Seršić), Zagreb, 2012, xix, 262 pp.

II Articles/Book Chapters/Notes

1. "Problem neškodljivog prolaska ratnog broda" ["Problem of Innocent Passage of Warships"], *Jugoslovenska revija za međunarodno pravo* [*Yugoslav Review of International Law*], Vol. 9, 1962, pp. 86–102.
2. "Međunarodni ugovori Jugoslavije o ribarstvu u graničnim vodama rijeka, jezera i mora" ["Yugoslavia's Treaties regarding Fisheries in Boundary Rivers, Lakes and Maritime Waters"], *Jugoslovenska revija za međunarodno pravo* [*Yugoslav Review of International Law*], Vol. 10, 1963, pp. 400–411.
3. "Neki problemi režima teritorijalnog mora u vezi s korištenjem nuklearne energije" ["Some Problems of the Territorial Sea Regime with Respect to the Use of Nuclear Energy"], in: *Pravni problemi miroljubivog korišćenja nuklearne energije: referati i diskusije sa Savjetovanja održanog 13. i 14. decembra 1963.* [*Legal Problems regarding Peaceful Uses of Nuclear Energy: Papers and Discussions of the Symposium held on 13 and 14 December 1963*], Beograd, 1964, pp. 117–123.
4. "Kodifikacija načela međunarodnog prava o aktivnoj miroljubivoj koegzistenciji" ["The Codification of International Law Principles on Active Peaceful Coexistence"], *Politička misao* [*Croatian Political Science Review*], Vol. 3, No. 4, 1966, pp. 124–139.

5. "Konvencije Evropskog savjeta o zaštiti prava čovjeka" ["The Council of Europe Conventions on the Protection of Human Rights"], *Politička misao* [*Croatian Political Science Review*], Vol. 4, No. 3, 1967, pp. 438–450.
6. "Pravila međunarodnog ugovornog prava o političkim izbjeglicama" ["International Treaty Law Relating to Political Refugees"], *Zbornik Pravnog fakulteta u Zagrebu* [*Collected Papers of the Zagreb Faculty of Law*], Vol. 19, 1969, pp. 152–164.
7. "Ugovor o prijateljstvu, suradnji i uzajamnoj pomoći između Narodne Republike Albanije, Narodne Republike Bugarske, Madžarske Narodne Republike, Njemačke Demokratske Republike, Poljske Narodne Republike, Rumunjske Narodne Republike, Saveza Sovjetskih Socijalističkih Republika i Čehoslovačke Republike, potpisan u Varšavi 14. svibnja 1955." ["Treaty of Friendship, Co-operation and Mutual Assistance between the People's Republic of Albania, the People's Republic of Bulgaria, the Hungarian People's Republic, the German Democratic Republic, the Polish People's Republic, the Romanian People's Republic, the Union of Soviet Socialist Republics and the Czechoslovak Republic, signed at Warsaw on 14 May 1955"] (translation and commentary), *Politička misao* [*Croatian Political Science Review*], Vol. 6, No. 2, 1969, pp. 223–232.
8. "Pravila o morskom dnu i podzemlju" ["Rules regarding the Seabed and Its Subsoil"], *Međunarodna politika* [*International Politics*], Vol. 21, No. 476, 1970, pp. 32–33.
9. "Zaštita prava čovjeka u Ujedinjenim narodima" ["The Protection of Human Rights within the United Nations"], in: *Ujedinjene nacije i savremeni svet* [*The United Nations and the Contemporary World*], Beograd, 1970, pp. 171–187.
10. "Djelomična demilitarizacija podmorja" ["The Partial Demilitarisation of the Seabed and Subsoil"], *Pravnik* [*Lawyer*], Nos. 1–2, 1971, pp. 4–5.
11. "Oružja za masovno uništavanje i međunarodno pravo" ["Weapons of Mass Destruction and International Law"], *Međunarodni problemi* [*International Problems*], Vol. 23, No. 1, 1971, pp. 39–53.
12. "Zabrana rasne diskriminacije po općim aktima o pravima čovjeka usvojenim u Ujedinjenim narodima" ["The Prohibition of Racial Discrimination According to the General Acts on Human Rights Adopted within the United Nations"], *Jugoslovenska revija za međunarodno pravo* [*Yugoslav Review of International Law*], Vol. 18, 1971, pp. 208–220.
13. "Zagrebačko zasjedanje Instituta za međunarodno pravo (rujan 1971.)" ["The Zagreb Session of the Institute of International Law (September 1971)"] (with B. Bakotić, Ž. Matić and K. Sajko), *Zbornik Pravnog fakulteta u Zagrebu* [*Collected Papers of the Zagreb Faculty of Law*], Vol. 21, 1971, pp. 487–508.
14. "International Instruments Dealing with the Status of Stateless Persons and of Refugees", *Revue belge de droit international*, Vol. 8, 1972, pp. 143–175.

15. "Nekoliko napomena o nedostacima novijeg međunarodnog javnog prava" ["Some Remarks on the Deficiencies of Contemporary Public International Law"], *Zbornik Pravnog fakulteta u Zagrebu* [*Collected Papers of the Zagreb Faculty of Law*], Vol. 22, 1972, pp. 233–246.
16. "La situation juridique de l'individu dans la société d'aujourd'hui – Yougoslavie", *Prinosi za poredbeno proučavanje prava i međunarodno pravo* [*Contributions to the Study of Comparative Law and International Law*], Vol. 5, 1972, pp. 43–73.
17. "Djelo profesora Milana Markovića o međunarodnopravnoj zaštiti čovjeka" ["The Writings of Professor Milan Marković on the International Protection of Human Rights"], *Jugoslovenska revija za međunarodno pravo* [*Yugoslav Review of International Law*], Vol. 20, 1973, pp. 85–96.
18. "Međunarodni ugovori i unutrašnji pravni akti SFR Jugoslavije o moru i bibliografija jugoslavenskih pisaca o međunarodnom pravu mora" ["Treaties and Internal Legal Acts of the SFR Yugoslavia concerning the Sea and Bibliography of Yugoslav Authors on the International Law of the Sea"] (with D. Dugošević,), *Zbornik Pravnog fakulteta u Zagrebu* [*Collected Papers of the Zagreb Faculty of Law*], Vol. 23, 1973, pp. 371–395.
19. "Nekoliko napomena o načinima neformalne izmjene Povelje Ujedinjenih naroda" ["Some Remarks on the Ways to Informally Amend the United Nations Charter"], in: *Razvoj i perspektive Ujedinjenih naroda* [*The Evolution and Perspectives of the United Nations*], Zagreb, 1973, pp. 172–194.
20. "Prihvaćanje Ženevskih konvencija o pravu mora od strane međunarodne zajednice" ["The Acceptance of the Geneva Conventions on the Law of the Sea by the International Community"], in: *Problemi međunarodnog prava mora s obzirom na saziv III. Konferencije UN o pravu mora* [*International Law of the Sea Problems with Respect to the Convocation of the Third UN Conference on the Law of the Sea*], Zagreb, 1973, pp. 41–62.
21. "National Procedures for Giving Effect to Governmental Obligations Undertaken and Agreements Concluded by Governments", in: *Yugoslav Reports for the Ninth International Congress of Comparative Law, Tehran, 1974*, Beograd, 1974, pp. 151–160.
22. "Odnos unutrašnjeg pravnog poretka prema pravilima međunarodnog prava po Ustavu SFR Jugoslavije od godine 1974." ["Yugoslav Internal Legal Order and Its Relation to the Rules of International Law According to the Federal Constitution of 1974"], *Zbornik Pravnog fakulteta u Zagrebu* [*Collected Papers of the Zagreb Faculty of Law*], Vol. 24, 1974, pp. 241–252.
23. "Pregled osnovnih pravila međunarodnog javnog prava o problemu zagađivanja mora" ["An Overview of the Basic Rules of International Law regarding the Issue of Maritime Pollution"], in: *Konferencija o zaštiti Jadrana: zbornik referata; Opatija, 21., 22. i 23. studenog 1974.* [*Conference on the Protection of the*

Adriatic: Collected Papers; Opatija, 21, 22 and 23 November 1974], Zagreb, 1974, pp. 55–77.

24. "Some Comments on the Draft Convention on Territorial Asylum", *Revue égyptienne de droit international*, Vol. 30, 1974, pp. 98–119.
25. "Suverenost nad tršćanskim područjem nakon Drugog svjetskog rata" ["Sovereignty over the Trieste Area after the Second World War"], *Pravnik* [*Lawyer*], Nos. 8–9, 1974, pp. 65–67.
26. "General International Law and the Protection of Minorities", *Revue des droits de l'homme*, Vol. 8, No. 1, 1975, pp. 41–49.
27. "Izbor gledišta jugoslavenskih pisaca o međunarodnopravnim pitanjima vezanim za tršćansko područje nakon drugog svjetskog rata" ["Select Views of Yugoslav Authors on International Law Issues regarding the Trieste Area after the Second World War"], *Časopis za suvremenu povijest* [*Journal of Contemporary History*], Vol. 7, No. 1, 1975, pp. 297–319.
28. "Napomena o odnosu ustavnih zabrana pristanka na okupaciju i kapitulaciju i međunarodnog prava" ["Remark on the Relationship between the Constitutional Prohibitions to Acquiesce in Occupation and Capitulation and International Law"], *Jugoslovenska revija za međunarodno pravo* [*Yugoslav Review of International Law*], Vol. 22, 1975, pp. 78–84.
29. "Nekoliko napomena o budućim pravilima međunarodnog prava o prolasku stranih ratnih brodova teritorijalnim morem" ["Some Remarks on the Prospective Rules of International Law concerning the Passage of Foreign Warships through the Territorial Sea"], *Jugoslovenska revija za međunarodno pravo* [*Yugoslav Review of International Law*], Vol. 22, 1975, pp. 186–190.
30. "'Tršćansko pitanje' u 1974. godini s gledišta međunarodnog prava" ["The 'Trieste Issue' in the Year 1974 from the Perspective of International Law"], *Časopis za suvremenu povijest* [*Journal of Contemporary History*], Vol. 7, No. 1, 1975, pp. 241–252.
31. "Ženevsko zasjedanje Treće konferencije Ujedinjenih naroda o pravu mora" ["The Geneva Session of the Third United Nations Conference on the Law of the Sea"], *Pomorstvo* [*Maritime Affairs*], Vol. 30, 1975, pp. 454–458.
32. "Novi razvoj međunarodnog prava mora (Treća Konferencija Ujedinjenih naroda)" ["The Recent Development of the International Law of the Sea (Third United Nations Conference)"], *Radio Sarajevo – Treći program* [*Radio Sarajevo – Third Programme*], Vol. 5, No. 14, 1976, pp. 213–238.
33. "Obilježja novog razvoja mirnog rješavanja međunarodnih sporova" ["Peaceful Settlement of International Disputes: Some Features of the Latest Developments"], *Jugoslovenska revija za međunarodno pravo* [*Yugoslav Review of International Law*], Vol. 23, 1976, pp. 96–115.
34. "Prava slovenske i hrvatske manjine u Austriji na temelju međunarodnog prava", in: *Sodobna vprašanja slovenske in hrvaške manjšine v Avstriji/Suvremena pitanja*

slovenske i hrvatske manjine u Austriji, Ljubljana, Zagreb, 1976, pp. 17–20/"The Rights of Slovene and Croatian Minorities in Austria in the Light of International Law", in: *Actual Questions of the Slovene and Croat Minorities in Austria*, Ljubljana, Zagreb, 1976, pp. 17–21 (published in Croatian, English and German).

35. "Pravila međunarodnog prava o pravnom položaju gradišćanskih Hrvata u Austriji" ["The Rules of International Law concerning the Legal Status of the Burgenland Croats in Austria"], *Razprave in gradivo* [*Treatises and Documents*], Nos. 7–8, 1976, pp. 49–68.

36. "Solution définitive de la 'question de Trieste' par la conclusion des accords entre l'Italie et la Yougoslavie à Osimo (Ancona), le 10 novembre 1975", *Annuaire français de droit international*, Vol. 22, 1976, pp. 77–95.

37. "Bilješka o sudbini ugovornih odredaba o zaštiti manjina iz vremena Lige naroda" ["A Note on the Fate of Treaty Provisions on Minority Protection Dating from the Time of the League of Nations"], *Zbornik Pravnog fakulteta u Zagrebu* [*Collected Papers of the Zagreb Faculty of Law*], Vol. 27, 1977, str. 273–283.

38. "The Mediterranean and the New International Law of the Sea", *Jugoslovenska revija za međunarodno pravo* [*Yugoslav Review of International Law*], Vol. 24, 1977, pp. 115–126.

39. "Međunarodnopravna zaštita narodnih manjina u Austriji – položaj Gradišćanskih Hrvata" ["The International Legal Protection of National Minorities in Austria – The Status of the Burgenland Croats"], *Časopis za suvremenu povijest* [*Journal of Contemporary History*], Vol. 9, No. 1, 1977, pp. 47–68.

40. "Međunarodnopravna zaštita prava čovjeka u poretku Ujedinjenih naroda" ["The Protection of Human Rights under International Rules Adopted in the United Nations"], *Zbornik Pravnog fakulteta u Zagrebu* [*Collected Papers of the Zagreb Faculty of Law*], Vol. 27, 1977, pp. 145–155.

41. "Međunarodnopravni položaj Hrvata u Mađarskoj" ["The International Legal Status of Croats in Hungary"], in: *Hrvatska narodna manjina u Mađarskoj* [*The Croatian National Minority in Hungary*], Zagreb, 1977, pp. 15–43.

42. "Odredbe o nacionalnim manjinama iz Završnog akta Konferencije o sigurnosti i suradnji u Evropi i njihovo provođenje u međunarodnim odnosima SFR Jugoslavije" ["Provisions on National Minorities in the Final Act of the Conference on Security and Cooperation in Europe and Their Implementation in International Relations of Yugoslavia"], *Godišnjak Pravnog fakulteta u Sarajevu* [*Yearbook of the Sarajevo Faculty of Law*], Vol. 25, 1977, pp. 379–386.

43. "Osimski sporazumi Jugoslavije i Italije" ["The Osimo Agreements between Yugoslavia and Italy"], *Prinosi za poredbeno proučavanje prava i međunarodno pravo* [*Contributions to the Study of Comparative Law and International Law*], Vol. 10, 1977, pp. 1–12.

44. "Provođenje odredaba Državnog ugovora u odnosu prema hrvatskoj manjini u Gradišću", in: B. Osolnik (ed.), *Problem manjina u jugoslovensko-austrijskim*

odnosima, Beograd, 1977, pp. 70–76/"State Treaty Implementation in Relation to the Burgenland Croat Minority", in: B. Osolnik (ed.), *Minority Problems in Yugoslav-Austrian Relations*, Beograd, 1977, pp. 81–88 (published in Croatian, English, French, German and Slovenian).

45. "Enclosed and Semi-enclosed Seas", *Iranian Review of International Relations*, Nos. 11–12, 1978, pp. 171–196.
46. "Manjine i međunarodno pravo – najnoviji razvoj" ["Minorities and International Law – Contemporary Developments"], *Jugoslovenska revija za međunarodno pravo* [*Yugoslav Review of International Law*], Vol. 25, 1978, pp. 274–291.
47. "Juraj Andrassy o pravu mora" ["Juraj Andrassy and the Law of the Sea"], *Jugoslovenska revija za međunarodno pravo* [*Yugoslav Review of International Law*], Vol. 26, 1979, pp. 199–211.
48. "Le projet de déclaration sur les droits des personnes appartenant à des minorités nationales, ethniques, religieuses et linguistiques", *Annuaire français de droit international*, Vol. 25, 1979, pp. 281–294.
49. "Najnoviji razvoj međunarodnopravne zaštite mora od zagađivanja" ["Contemporary Developments concerning the International Legal Protection of the Sea from Pollution"] (with B. Bohte), in: *Druga Konferencija o zaštiti Jadrana – zbornik referata* [*Second Conference on the Protection of the Adriatic Sea – Collected Papers*], Vol. I, Zagreb, 1979, pp. 7–16.
50. "O nekim oblicima utjecaja međunarodnih organizacija na međunarodne ugovore" ["Some Impacts of International Organization on Treaties"], in: B. Babović, O. Šuković (eds.), *Nove tendencije u razvoju međunarodnog prava* [*New Trends in the Development of International Law*], Beograd, 1979, pp. 77–98, 127–131 (discussion).
51. "International Law and the Pollution of the Sea" (with B. Bohte), in: C.C.A. Voskuil, J.A. Wade (eds.), *Hague-Zagreb Essays 3*, The Hague, Alphen aan den Rijn, 1980, pp. 143–169.
52. "Međunarodnopravna osnova položaja naših manjina u Rumunjskoj" ["The International Legal Basis for the Status of Our Minorities in Romania"], in: *Hrvatska narodna manjina u Rumunjskoj* [*The Croatian National Minority in Romania*], Zagreb, 1980, pp. 1–29.
53. "Pristup moru država bez morske obale" ["Access of Land-Locked States to the Sea"], *Godišnjak Pravnog fakulteta u Banjaluci* [*Yearbook of the Banjaluka Faculty of Law*], Vol. 4, 1980, pp. 181–190.
54. "Promjene u međunarodnom poretku na moru u svjetlu rada Treće Konferencije UN o pravu mora" ["The Changes in the International Order of the Sea in Light of the Third UN Conference on the Law of Sea"], *Morsko ribarstvo* [*Sea Fisheries*], Vol. 32, 1980, pp. 80–84.
55. "Tito i aktivna miroljubiva koegzistencija" ["Tito and the Active Peaceful Co-existence"], *Zbornik Pravnog fakulteta u Zagrebu* [*Collected Papers of the Zagreb Faculty of Law*], Vol. 30, 1980, pp. 261–276.

56. "Il nuovo diritto internazionale del mare, la gestione e la salvaguardia delle risorse ittiche del Mediterraneo", in: *Il nuovo diritto internazionale del mare, la C.E.E., la salvaguardia e la gestione delle risorse ittiche del Mediterraneo – Atti del X Convegno internazionale sui problemi della pesca*, Bologna, 1982, pp. 32–44.
57. "Odnos člana 27. Međunarodnog pakta o građanskim i političkim pravima i deklaracije o pravima manjina" ["The Relation of Article 27 of the International Covenant on Civil and Political Rights and the Declaration on the Rights of Minorities"], *Razprave in gradivo* [*Treatises and Documents*], Nos. 13–14, 1981, pp. 45–51.
58. "Provisions of the Draft Convention on the Law of the Sea Relating to the Protection and Preservation of the Marine Environment and the UNEP's Involvement in Their Implementation", *United Nations Environment Programme*, UNEP/IG.28/Background Doc. No. 5, 10 August 1981, 45 pp. (also published in French).
59. "Zajednička baština čovječanstva" ["The Common Heritage of Mankind"], *Godišnjak Instituta za međunarodnu politiku i privredu* [*Yearbook of the Institute of International Politics and Economics*], 1981–1982, pp. 191–211.
60. "La CEE et la prévention de la pollution de la Méditerranée", in: *La Communauté économique européenne élargie et la Méditerranée: quelle coopération?*, Paris, 1982, pp. 406–421.
61. "Pristup moru država bez morske obale" ["Right of Access of Land-Locked States to and from the Sea"], in: B. Vukas (ed.), *Novo pravo mora* [*The New Law of the Sea*], Zagreb, 1982, pp. 158–169.
62. "Zaštita i očuvanje morske okoline" ["Protection and Preservation of the Marine Environment"] (with B. Bohte), in: B. Vukas (ed.), *Novo pravo mora* [*The New Law of the Sea*], Zagreb, 1982, pp. 232–245.
63. "Zatvorena ili poluzatvorena mora" ["Enclosed or Semi-enclosed Seas"], in: B. Vukas (ed.), *Novo pravo mora* [*The New Law of the Sea*], Zagreb, 1982, pp. 138–157.
64. "La cooperazione tra Jugoslavija ed Italia per la protezione del mare Adriatico dall'inquinamento", in: V. Starace (ed.), *Diritto internazionale e protezione dell'ambiente marino*, Milano, 1983, pp. 297–321.
65. "Evropska ekonomska zajednica i Konvencija o pravu mora" ["The European Economic Community and the Convention on the Law of the Sea"], *Godišnjak Pravnog fakulteta u Banjaluci* [*Yearbook of the Banjaluka Faculty of Law*], Vol. 7, 1983, pp. 123–133.
66. "The Impact of the Third United Nations Conference on the Law of the Sea on Customary Law", in: C.L. Rozakis, C.A. Stephanou (eds.), *The New Law of the Sea*, Athens, 1983, pp. 33–54.
67. "Jadran – zatvoreno ili poluzatvoreno more"/"The Adriatic: An Enclosed or Semi-enclosed Sea", in: *I problemi del mare Adriatico: Atti del convegno internazionale, Trieste, 26/27 settembre 1983*, Trieste, [1983], pp. 3–11 (published in Croatian and English).

68. "Jugoslavija i Konvencija Ujedinjenih naroda o pravu mora" ["Yugoslavia and the United Nations Convention on the Law of the Sea"], *Zbornik Pravnog fakulteta u Rijeci* [*Collected Papers of the Law Faculty of the University of Rijeka*], Vol. 4, 1983, pp. 210–212.

69. "Međunarodni ugovori u odnosu prema Ustavu SFR Jugoslavije, saveznim i republičkim zakonima" ["The Relation of Treaties with the Constitution of the SFR Yugoslavia, the Federal Laws and the Laws of the Socialist Republics"], *Jugoslovenska revija za međunarodno pravo* [*Yugoslav Review of International Law*], Vol. 30, 1983, pp. 90–102.

70. "The New Law of the Sea and the NIEO", *VITE Bulletin*, Vol. 4, No. 3, 1983, pp. 6–8.

71. "Pritisak zemalja bez morske obale i država u nepovoljnom geografskom položaju na eksploataciju izvora u ekonomskoj zoni susjednih zemalja" ["The Pressure of Land-Locked and Geographically Disadvantaged States with Respect to Resource Exploitation in the Exclusive Zones of Neighbouring States"], in: *Ekonomske posljedice Konvencije o pravu mora na zemlje u razvoju i Jugoslaviju* [*The Economic Effects of the Convention on the Law of the Sea on Developing Countries and Yugoslavia*], Zagreb, 1983, pp. 22–31.

72. "Problemi pravnog uređenja ribolova s Italijom" ["Problems regarding the Legal Regulation of Fisheries with Italy"], in: *Pravno uređenje ribolova na Jadranu u odnosima s Italijom* [*The Legal Regulation of Fisheries in the Adriatic Sea in the Relations with Italy*], Zagreb, 1983, pp. 17–31.

73. "Uređenje međunarodne plovidbe po Konvenciji Ujedinjenih naroda o pravu mora" ["The Regulation of Navigation in the United Nations Convention on the Law of the Sea"], *Pomorski zbornik* [*Collected Maritime Papers*], Vol. 21, 1983, pp. 43–71.

74. "Alcuni commenti sul nuovo diritto del mare", in: *Atti del Seminario internazionale di studio Mare e territorio, Agrigento, 9-10-11 dicembre 1983; Quaderno n. 8*, Palermo, 1984, pp. 405–406.

75. "Jadran – zatvoreno ili poluzatvoreno more" ["The Adriatic – An Enclosed or Semi-enclosed Sea"], *Morsko ribarstvo* [*Sea Fisheries*], Vol. 36, 1984, pp. 9–11.

76. "Konvencija Ujedinjenih naroda o pravu mora i plovidba Otrantom" ["The United Nations Convention on the Law of the Sea and Navigation through the Strait of Otranto"], *Uporedno pomorsko pravo i pomorska kupoprodaja* [*Comparative Maritime Law and Maritime Contracts of Sale*], Vol. 26, Nos. 103–104, 1984, pp. 515–532.

77. "Neighbourly Relations Between Italy and Yugoslavia and the Establishment of a New Type of Regional Co-operation in the Mediterranean", in: A.M. Calamia, P. Mengozzi, N. Ronzitti (eds.), *I rapporti di vicinato tra Italia e Jugoslavia*, Milano, 1984, pp. 21–55.

78. "Protezione dall'inquinamento e pesca nel mare Adriatico con particolare riferimento ai rapporti Italo-Jugoslavi", in: *L'area Mediterranea: Atti del 2° Convegno internazionale Mare e territorio, Agrigento, 13-14-15 dicembre 1984; Quaderno n. 12*, [1984], pp. 86–94; also published in: *Il Gazzetino della pesca*, Vol. 32, 1985, pp. 4–6.

79. "Savjetovanje o položaju, pravima i interesima Jugoslavije koji proizlaze iz Konvencije Ujedinjenih naroda o pravu mora (1982.)" ["Symposium on the Status, Rights and Interests of Yugoslavia Arising from the United Nations Convention on the Law of the Sea (1982)"], *Pomorski zbornik [Collected Maritime Papers]*, Vol. 22, 1984, pp. 579–586.

80. "Isključiva ekonomska zona u Jadranu i Mediteranu i stav Jugoslavije" ["The Exclusive Economic Zone in the Adriatic and the Mediterranean and the Position of Yugoslavia"], in: *Primjena Konvencije o pravu mora – jugoslavenska gledišta [Application of the Convention on the Law of the Sea – Yugoslav Viewpoints]*, Zagreb, 1985, pp. 51–57.

81. "The LOS Convention and Sea Boundary Delimitation", in: B. Vukas (ed.), *Essays on the New Law of the Sea*, Zagreb, 1985, pp. 147–185.

82. "Međunarodna definicija manjina" ["International Law and the Definition of the Term 'Minority'"], *Jugoslovenska revija za međunarodno pravo [Yugoslav Review of International Law]*, Vol. 32, 1985, pp. 433–438.

83. "Neki problemi u izradi poslovnika Skupštine i Vijeća Međunarodne vlasti za morsko dno" ["Some Problems concerning the Elaboration of the Rules of Procedure for the Assembly and Council of the International Seabed Authority"], in: *Primjena Konvencije o pravu mora – jugoslavenska gledišta [Application of the Convention on the Law of the Sea – Yugoslav Viewpoints]*, Zagreb, 1985, pp. 36–42.

84. "Novo pravo mora i pristup neobalnih država morskim lukama" ["The New Law of the Sea and Access of Land-Locked States to Maritime Ports"], in: J. Mutak (ed.), *Uloga i značenje luka u gospodarskom razvitku zemlje [The Role and Significance of Ports for the Country's Economic Development]*, Vol. I, Zagreb, 1985, pp. 163–168.

85. "The United Nations Law of the Sea Convention and the Regional Legal Instruments for the Protection of the Mediterranean Sea against Pollution", *United Nations Environment Programme*, UNEP/IG.56/INF.5, 3June 1985, 25 pp.; also published in: *Zbornik Pravnog fakulteta u Zagrebu [Collected Papers of the Zagreb Faculty of Law]*, Vol. 38, 1988, pp. 531–552.

86. "L'utilisation pacifique de la mer, dénucléarisation et désarmement", in: R.-J. Dupuy, D. Vignes (eds.), *Traité du nouveau droit de la mer*, Paris, Bruxelles, 1985, pp. 1047–1093.

87. "Vladimir Ibler – osvrt na život i djelo"/"Vladimir Ibler – A Review of His Life and Work" (with B. Bakotić), *Zbornik Pravnog fakulteta u Zagrebu [Collected Papers of the Zagreb Faculty of Law]*, Vol. 35, 1985, pp. 531–545 (published in Croatian and English).

88. "Common Heritage of Mankind: A Legal Concept for Survival of Humanity", in: M. Bulajić, D. Pindić, M. Marinković (eds.), *The Charter of Economic Rights and Duties of States, Ten Years of Implementation*, Beograd, 1986, pp. 209–214.

89. "Osnovne promjene u međunarodnom pravu mora" ["The Main Changes in the International Law of the Sea"], *Pravnik* [*Lawyer*], Nos. 1–2, 1986, pp. 103–111.

90. "Transboundary Co-operation between Yugoslavia and Its Neighbouring States", in: C. Flinterman, B. Kwiatkowska, J.G. Lammers (eds.), *Transboundary Air Pollution*, Dordrecht, 1986, pp. 199–204.

91. "Concluding Observations on General International Law and New Challenges in the Field of Transboundary Air Pollution", in: C. Flinterman, B. Kwiatkowska, J.G. Lammers (eds.), *Transboundary Air Pollution*, Dordrecht, 1986, pp. 347–354.

92. "L'Adriatico, il diritto del mare ed i rapporti Italo-Jugoslavi", *Studi marittimi*, Vol. 10, No. 31, 1987, pp. 51–55.

93. "Conventional Provisions on Insurance and Compensation for Damages Caused by Pollution", in: *Atti del quarto Convegno internazionale Mare e territorio, Agrigento, 23–25 ottobre 1986; Quaderno n. 21*, Palermo, 1987, pp. 127–135.

94. "The New Law of the Sea and the International Economic Order: Comments on A.W. Koers & B. Kwiatkowska's Paper", in: P. van Dijk et al. (eds.), *Restructuring the International Economic Order: The Role of Law and Lawyers*, Deventer, 1987, pp. 213–221.

95. "The Protection of the Mediterranean Sea against Pollution", in: U. Leanza (ed.), *Il regime giuridico internazionale del Mare Mediterraneo*, Milano, 1987, pp. 413–435.

96. "Uz Zakon o obalnom moru i epikontinentalnom pojasu SFR Jugoslavije od godine 1987." ["The 1987 Law on the Coastal Sea and the Continental Shelf of the SFR Yugoslavia"], *Jugoslovenska revija za međunarodno pravo* [*Yugoslav Review of International Law*], Vol. 34, 1987, pp. 199–220.

97. "Authority to Manage Fisheries and Mineral Resources of the Southern Ocean – Commentary", in: T.A. Clingan Jr. (ed.), *The Law of the Sea: What Lies Ahead?*, Honolulu, 1988, pp. 404–407.

98. "Violence at Sea – Commentary", in: T.A. Clingan Jr. (ed.), *The Law of the Sea: What Lies Ahead?*, Honolulu, 1988, pp. 445–449.

99. "The Mediterranean: An Enclosed or Semi-enclosed Sea?", in: B. Vukas (ed.), *The Legal Regime of Enclosed or Semi-enclosed Seas: The Particular Case of the Mediterranean*, Zagreb, 1988, pp. 49–66.

100. "Le projet du protocole relatif à la protection de la mer Méditerranée contre la pollution résultant de l'exploration du fond de la mer et de son sous-sol", in: J.-Y. Chérot, A. Roux (eds.), *Droit méditerranéen de l'environnement*, Paris, 1988, pp. 147–155.

101. "Protection of the Mediterranean from Off-Shore Activities", in: *Mediterraneo – mare da preservare; Atti del Convegno dei Lions del Mediterraneo, Giardini*

Naxos, 7–9 maggio 1987, Catania, 1988, pp. 215–221; also published in: *Jugoslovenska revija za međunarodno pravo* [*Yugoslav Review of International Law*], Vol. 35, 1988, pp. 93–97.

102. "The Protection of the Mediterranean Sea from Pollution", *Indian Journal of International Law*, Vol. 28, 1988, pp. 104–113.

103. "Rad Bogdana Babovića na području međunarodnog prava mora" ["The Work of Bogdan Babović in the Field of the International Law of the Sea"], *Jugoslovenska revija za kriminologiju i krivično pravo* [*Yugoslav Review of Criminology and Criminal Law*], Vol. 35, 1988, pp. 326–344.

104. "The 1982 United Nations Convention on the Law of the Sea and the Protection of the Living Resources of the Sea", in: J. Kregar, I. Šimonović, (eds.), *Yugoslavia: Legal Framework, Social, Political and Economic Aspects*, Zagreb, 1989, pp. 164–175.

105. "Međunarodna organizacija rada i zaštita prava čovjeka" ["International Labour Organisation and the Protection of Human Rights"], *Jugoslovenska revija za međunarodno pravo* [*Yugoslav Review of International Law*], Vol. 36, 1989, pp. 91–122.

106. "Međunarodna zaštita prava čovjeka: granice rasta" ["International Protection of Human Rights: Limits of Growth"], *Zbornik Pravnog fakulteta u Zagrebu* [*Collected Papers of the Zagreb Faculty of Law*], Vol. 39, 1989, pp. 671–678.

107. "Report on the Seventh Session of the Preparatory Commission 1989", *Marine Policy Reports*, Vol. 1, 1989, pp. 247–253.

108. "The UNCLOS Provisions on Navigation and Customary International Law", in: *Maritime Transport and International Shipping: Legal and Economic Aspects*, Valetta, 1989, pp. 549–550.

109. "La coopération CEE – pays tiers dans le domaine de la protection de l'environnement marin en Méditerranée", in: J. Lebullenger, D. Le Morvan (eds.), *La Communauté Européenne et la mer*, Paris, 1990, pp. 403–408.

110. "Generally Accepted International Rules and Standards", *Zbornik Pravnog fakulteta u Zagrebu* [*Collected Papers of the Zagreb Faculty of Law*], Vol. 39, 1989, pp. 537–549; also published in: A.H.A. Soons (ed.), *Implementation of the Law of the Sea Convention through International Institutions*, Honolulu, 1990, pp. 405–421.

111. "Military Uses of the Sea and the United Nations Law of the Sea Convention", in: B. Vukas (ed.), *Essays on the New Law of the Sea 2*, Zagreb, 1990, pp. 401–429.

112. "The CSCE and the Protection of National Minorities", in: D. Bardonnet (ed.), *The Peaceful Settlement of International Disputes in Europe: Future Prospects*, Dordrecht, 1991, pp. 567–579.

113. "The New Law of the Sea and Navigation: A View from the Mediterranean", in: *The Law of the Sea with Emphasis on the Mediterranean Issues*; *Thesaurus Acroasium*, Vol. 17, 1991, pp. 401–431; also published in: R.S. Pathak, R.P. Dhokalia (eds.) *International Law in Transition: Essays in Memory of Judge Nagendra Singh*, Dordrecht, 1992, pp. 65–86.

114. "Peaceful Uses of the Sea, Denuclearization and Disarmament", in: R.-J. Dupuy, D. Vignes (eds.), *A Handbook on the New Law of the Sea*, Vol. II, Dordrecht, 1991, pp. 1233–1320.
115. "Opća načela prava kao izvor prava Evropskih zajednica" ["General Principles of Law as a Source of Law in the European Communities"], *Zbornik Pravnog fakulteta u Zagrebu* [*Collected Papers of the Zagreb Faculty of Law*], Vol. 42, 1992, pp. 253–265.
116. "Settlement of Disputes under the UN Law of the Sea Convention and the Protection of the Marine Environment", in: A. Postiglione (ed.), *Tribunale internazionale dell'ambiente*, Roma, 1992, pp. 293–297.
117. "Protection of the Marine Environment – Questions Related to State Boundaries", in: M. Vivod (ed.), *Harmonization of Frontier Controls of Goods*, New York, 1993, pp. 303–306.
118. "Prava i slobode etničkih i nacionalnih zajednica/manjina" ["The Rights and Freedoms of Ethnic and National Communities/Minorities"] (with M. Domini), in: Lj. Čučić (ed.), *Ocjena stanja demokratskih sloboda u Republici Hrvatskoj* [*Evaluating the Status of Democratic Freedoms in the Republic of Croatia*], Zagreb, 1995, pp. 22–32.
119. "Croatia and the Law of the Sea", in: B. Vukas (ed.), *Essays on the New Law of the Sea 3*, Zagreb, 1996, pp. 13–22.
120. "The Diverse Supervisory Procedures in a Comparison", in: B. von Maydell, A. Nußberger (eds.), *Social Protection by Way of International Law*, Berlin, 1996, pp. 105–132.
121. "Protecting the Polar Marine Environment: Aspects of 1982 LOS Convention", in: Polar Oceans and the Law of the Sea Project (POLOS), *Polar Oceans Reports; No. 1*, Lysaker, 1996, 20 pp.
122. "Ujedinjeni narodi i zaštita manjina" ["The United Nations and Minority Protection"], in: I. Šimonović, B. Vukas, B. Vukmir (eds.), *Hrvatska i Ujedinjeni narodi* [*Croatia and the United Nations*], Zagreb, 1996, pp. 171–182.
123. "The Establishment of the International Tribunal for the Law of the Sea", *IJO Newsletter*, Vol. 9, No. 1, 1997, pp. 13–14.
124. "Hrvati u Sloveniji: etnička (nacionalna) manjina?" ["The Croats in Slovenia: An Ethnic (National) Minority?"], in: M. Domini (ed.), *Hrvati u Sloveniji: zbornik radova/znanstveni skup, Zagreb, 20.–21. lipnja 1996* [*The Croats in Slovenia: Collected Papers/Scientific Conference, Zagreb, 20–21 June 1996*], Zagreb, 1997, pp. 227–233.
125. "The International Tribunal for the Law of the Sea: Some Features of the New International Judicial Institution", *Indian Journal of International Law*, Vol. 37, 1997, pp. 372–387; also published in: P.C. Rao, R. Khan (eds.), *The International Tribunal for the Law of the Sea: Law and Practice*, The Hague, 2001, pp. 59–72.

126. "Republika Hrvatska i međunarodna zaštita prava čovjeka" ["The Republic of Croatia and the International Legal Protection of Human Rights"], *Zbornik Diplomatske akademije* [*Diplomatic Academy Yearbook*], Vol. 2, 1997, pp. 167–169.

127. "The Law of the Sea Convention and the Law of Treaties", in: V. Götz, P. Selmer, R. Wolfrum (eds.), *Liber Amicorum Günther Jaenicke – Zum 85. Geburtstag*, Berlin, 1998, pp. 631–652.

128. "Međunarodni sud za pravo mora" ["The International Tribunal for the Law of the Sea"], *Zbornik radova Pravnog fakulteta u Splitu* [*Collected Papers of the Faculty of Law in Split*], Vol. 35, 1998, pp. 701–704.

129. "Međunarodno pravo i zaštita ljudskih prava" ["International Law and Human Rights Protection"], *Zbornik Pravnog fakulteta u Zagrebu* [*Collected Papers of the Zagreb Faculty of Law*], Vol. 48, 1998, pp. 713–715.

130. "Protection of Minorities", in: M.I. Glassner (ed.), *The United Nations at Work*, Westport, Connecticut, 1998, pp. 75–102.

131. "Recognition of States – European Practice in the Nineties", in: M. Prieur, C. Lambrechts (eds.), *Les hommes et l'environnement: Quels droits pour le vingt-et-unième siècle?; Etudes en hommage à Alexandre Kiss*, Paris, 1998, pp. 97–108.

132. "Règlement du Tribunal international du droit de la mer – questions choisis", *Espaces et ressources maritimes*, No. 12, 1998, pp. 15–23.

133. "Some Recent Aspects of the Implementation of the Right of Peoples to Self-determination", in: L.O. Baptista, J.R. Franco da Fonseca (eds.), *O direito internacional no terceiro milênio; Estudos em homenagen ao professor Vicente Marotta Rangel*, São Paulo, 1998, pp. 166–177.

134. "International Law and the Definition of Minorities", in: R.-J. Dupuy (ed.), *Mélanges en l'honneur de Nicolas Valticos; Droit et justice*, Paris, 1999, pp. 233–242.

135. "The Legal Status of Minorities in Croatia", in: S. Trifunovska (ed.), *Minorities in Europe: Croatia, Estonia and Slovakia*, The Hague, 1999, pp. 39–63.

136. "Possible Role of the International Tribunal for the Law of the Sea in Interpretation and Progressive Development of the Law of the Sea", in: D. Vidas, W. Østreng (eds.), *Order for the Oceans at the Turn of the Century*, The Hague, 1999, pp. 95–104.

137. "States, Peoples and Minorities", *Recueil des cours de l'Académie de droit international de La Haye*, Vol. 231, 1999, pp. 263–524.

138. "International Protection of Minorities: Limits and Growth", in: *Human Rights and Democracy for the 21st Century; Thesaurus Acroasium*, Vol. 29, 2000, pp. 17–36.

139. "Odbor stručnjaka Međunarodne organizacije rada za nadzor nad primjenom konvencija i preporuka Organizacije" ["The International Labour Organization's Committee of Experts on the Application of Conventions and

Recommendations"], in: K. Rožman, V. Ribić (eds.), *Zbornik radova sa skupa: Zakon o radu – četiri godine poslije* [*The Labour Act – Four Years Later; Collected Conference Papers*], Zagreb, 2000, pp. 27–30, 112–113.

140. "United Nations Convention on the Law of the Sea and the Polar Marine Environment", u: D. Vidas (ed.), *Protecting the Polar Marine Environment*, Cambridge, 2000, pp. 34–56.

141. "Za ustavne odredbe nije isključivo mjerodavna struka ustavnog prava" ["The Provisions of the Constitution Are Not the Exclusive Domain of Constitutional Law Experts"], *Zbornik Pravnog fakulteta u Zagrebu* [*Collected Papers of the Zagreb Faculty of Law*], Vol. 50, 2000, pp. 617–618.

142. "The Croatian Model of Organisation and Operation of Minority Associations", *Zbornik Pravnog fakulteta u Zagrebu* [*Collected Papers of the Zagreb Faculty of Law*], Vol. 51, 2001, pp. 991–1006.

143. "Flags of Convenience and High Seas Fisheries: The Emergence of a Legal Framework" (with D. Vidas), in: O. Schram Stokke (ed.), *Governing High Seas Fisheries: The Interplay of Global and Regional Regimes*, Oxford, 2001, pp. 53–90.

144. "General Principles of Law regarding the Protection of Minorities", in: Sienho Yee, Wang Tieya (eds.), *International Law in the Post-cold War World: Essays in Memory of Li Haopei*, London, 2001, pp. 348–356.

145. "Main Features of Courts and Tribunals Dealing with the Law of the Sea Cases", in: M.H. Nordquist, J.N. Moore (eds.), *Current Marine Environmental Issues and the International Tribunal for the Law of the Sea*, The Hague, 2001, pp. 217–222.

146. "Il caso delle bombe NATO in Adriatico", in: *Il diritto internazionale del mare: fra usi antichi e nuove forme di utilizzazione*, Napoli, 2002, pp. 107–111.

147. "The Definition of the Law of the Sea", in: N. Ando, E.W. McWhinney, R. Wolfrum (eds.), *Liber Amicorum Judge Shigeru Oda*, Vol. II, The Hague, 2002, pp. 1303–1310.

148. "Droit de la mer et droits de l'homme", in: G. Cataldi (ed.), *La Méditerranée et le droit de la mer à l'aube du 21e siècle*, Bruxelles, 2002, pp. 85–95.

149. "The Legal Status of National Minorities in the Republic of Croatia", in: Z. Drnas de Clément (ed.), *Estudios de derecho internacional en homenaje al profesor Ernesto J. Rey Caro*, Vol. II, Córdoba, 2002, pp. 887–891.

150. "Décision *ex aequo et bono* et différends relatifs au droit de la mer", in: V. Coussirat-Coustère et al. (eds.), *La mer et son droit: Mélanges offerts à Laurent Lucchini et Jean-Pierre Quéneudec*, Paris, 2003, pp. 689–694.

151. "The Exclusive Economic Zone and Other International Legal Regimes at Sea", *Croatian International Relations Review*, Vol. 9, No. 32, 2003, pp. 2–3.

152. "The Humanitarian Assistance", *Annuaire de l'Institut de Droit international*, Vol. 70-I, 2002–2003, pp. 457–492, 541–576 (provisional report, final report); Vol. 71-II, 2004, pp. 262–277 (adopted resolution).

153. "Interference with Navigation: Modern Challenges; Concluding Remarks at the Symposium", *International Journal of Marine and Coastal Law*, Vol. 18, 2003, pp. 441–443.

154. "Opća i posebna međunarodna zaštita manjina" ["General and Special (Regional) Protection of Minorities"], *Zbornik Pravnog fakulteta u Zagrebu* [*Collected Papers of the Zagreb Faculty of Law*], Vol. 53, 2003, pp. 291–307.

155. "Le choix de procédés prévus par l'article 287 de la Convention de 1982 sur le droit de la mer", in: *Le processus de délimitation maritime: étude d'un cas fictif*, Paris, 2004, pp. 318–322.

156. "Complexity of the International Protection of Minorities", in: *Studi di diritto internazionale in onore di Gaetano Arangio-Ruiz*, Vol. III, Napoli, 2004, pp. 2311–2322.

157. "Some Remarks concerning the Commissions of Inquiry Established under the Constitution of the International Labour Organization", in: J.-C. Javillier, B. Gernigon (eds.), *Les normes internationales du travail: un patrimoine pour l'avenir; Mélanges en l'honneur de Nicolas Valticos*, Genève, 2004, pp. 75–79.

158. "The Extension of the Jurisdiction of the Coastal States in the Adriatic Sea", in: N. Ronzitti (ed.), *I rapporti di vicinato dell'Italia con Croazia, Serbia-Montenegro e Slovenia*, 2005, pp. 251–268.

159. "Humanitarian Intervention and International Responsibility", in: M. Ragazzi (ed.), *International Responsibility Today: Essays in Memory of Oscar Schachter*, Leiden, 2005, pp. 235–240.

160. "Povelja Ujedinjenih naroda – zastarjeli ustav Svjetske organizacije" ["Charter of the United Nations – the Outdated Constitution of the World Organisation"], *Nova prisutnost: časopis za intelektualna i duhovna pitanja* [*New Presence: Review for Intellectual and Spiritual Issues*], Vol. 3, 2005, pp. 189–198.

161. "Sea Boundary Delimitation and the UN Law of the Sea Convention", in: L. Caflisch *et al.* (eds.), *El derecho internacional: normas, hechos y valores; Liber amicorum José Antonio Pastor Ridruejo*, Madrid, 2005, pp. 455–465.

162. [Commentaries to Articles 98–106], in: P.C. Rao, P. Gautier (eds.), *The Rules of the International Tribunal for the Law of the Sea: A Commentary*, Leiden, 2006, pp. 279–298.

163. "Maritime Delimitation in a Semi-enclosed Sea: The Case of the Adriatic Sea", in: R. Lagoni, D. Vignes (eds.), *Maritime Delimitation*, Leiden, 2006, pp. 205–222.

164. "State Practice in the Aftermath of the UN Convention on the Law of the Sea: The Exclusive Economic Zone and the Mediterranean Sea", in: A. Strati, M. Gavouneli, N. Skourtos (eds.), *Unresolved Issues and New Challenges to the Law of the Sea: Time Before and Time After*, Leiden, 2006, pp. 251–258.

165. "A Quarter of a Century after UNCLOS III: A Personal Recollection", in: M.G. Kohen (ed.), *Promoting Justice, Human Rights and Conflict Resolution through International Law: Liber Amicorum Lucius Caflisch*, Leiden, 2007, str. 799–807.

166. "Sea Boundary Delimitation and Internal Waters", in: T.M. Ndiaye, R. Wolfrum (eds.), *Law of the Sea, Environmental Law and Settlement of Disputes: Liber Amicorum Judge Thomas A. Mensah*, Leiden, 2007, pp. 553–565.

167. "Pomorski zakonik Republike Hrvatske i međunarodno pravo mora" ["The Maritime Code of the Republic of Croatia and the Law of the Sea"], *Zbornik Pravnog fakulteta u Zagrebu* [*Collected Papers of the Zagreb Faculty of Law*], Vol. 58, 2008, pp. 181–203.

168. "The Application of the Law of the Sea to the Marine Areas along the Coasts of Croatia", in: M.C. Ciciriello *et al.* (eds.), *Studi in onore di Umberto Leanza*, Vol. III, Napoli, 2008, pp. 1895–1904.

169. "Some Provisions of the Statute of the International Court of Justice which Deserve Amendments", in: Sienho Yee, J.-Y. Morin (eds.), *Multiculturalism and International Law: Essays in Honour of Edward McWhinney*, Leiden, 2009, pp. 277–283.

170. "Humanitarian Aid and Humanitarian Intervention", in: *International Challenges to Peace and Security in the New Millennium; Thesaurus Acroasium*, Vol. 33, 2010, pp. 249–268.

171. "States, Peoples and Minorities as Subjects of International Law", in: F. Johns (ed.), *International Legal Personality*, Farnham, 2010, pp. 79–104.

172. "The Vagueness of the International Rules on the Continental Shelf", in: B. Vukas, T.M. Šošić (eds.), *International Law: New Actors, New Concepts – Continuing Dilemmas; Liber Amicorum Božidar Bakotić*, Leiden, 2010, pp. 351–358.

173. "The Origins and Some Main Problems of the International Protection of Minorities", in: M. Pogačnik (ed.), *Challenges of Contemporary International Law and International Relations: Liber Amicorum in Honour of Ernest Petrič*, Nova Gorica, 2011, pp. 423–430.

174. "Nepreciznosti kodifikacije pravila o međunarodnim ugovorima" ["Some Vague Solutions in the Codification of the Law of Treaties"], *Zbornik Pravnog fakulteta u Zagrebu* [*Collected Papers of the Zagreb Faculty of Law*], Vol. 62, 2012, pp. 753–762.

175. "Self-Determination of Peoples – A Chronic Problem of Humankind", in: H.P. Hestermeyer *et al.* (eds.), *Coexistence, Cooperation and Solidarity: Liber Amicorum Rüdiger Wolfrum*, Vol. II, Leiden, 2012, pp. 1543–1552.

176. "The Composition of the International Court of Justice", in: N. Boschiero *et al.* (eds.), *International Courts and the Development of International Law: Essays in Honour of Tullio Treves*, The Hague, 2013, pp. 213–218.

177. "The 1995 Interim Accord and Membership of the Republic of Macedonia in International Organizations", in: E.J. Rey Caro, M.C. Rodríguez de Taborda (eds.), *Estudios de derecho internacional: En homenaje a la Dra. Zlata Drnas de Clément*, Vol. II, Córdoba, 2014, pp. 1015–1023.
178. "Croatian Writers and State Practice in the Law of the Sea", in: M.W. Lodge, M.H. Nordquist (eds.), *Peaceful Order in the World's Oceans: Essays in Honor of Satya N. Nandan*, Leiden, 2014, pp. 208–217.

III   Contributions in Encyclopaedias

1. "More; More s pravnog gledišta" ["The Sea; The Sea from the Legal Perspective"] (with V. Brajković), in: V. Brajković (ed.), *Pomorska enciklopedija* [*Maritime Encyclopaedia*], 2nd edn., Vol. V, Zagreb, 1981, p. 105.
2. "Otvoreno more" ["High Seas"] (with J. Andrassy), in: V. Brajković (ed.), *Pomorska enciklopedija* [*Maritime Encyclopaedia*], 2nd edn., Vol. V, Zagreb, 1981, pp. 652–653.
3. "Podmorje; Podmorje izvan granica nacionalne jurisdikcije" ["Seabed and Subsoil; Seabed and Subsoil beyond the Limits of National Jurisdiction"], in: V. Brajković (ed.), *Pomorska enciklopedija* [*Maritime Encyclopaedia*], 2nd edn., Vol. VI, Zagreb, 1983, pp. 137–138.
4. "Pravo mora; Konvencija Ujedinjenih naroda o pravu mora" ["Law of the Sea; United Nations Convention on the Law of the Sea"], in: V. Brajković (ed.), *Pomorska enciklopedija* [*Maritime Encyclopaedia*], 2nd edn., Vol. VI, Zagreb, 1983, pp. 410–411.
5. "Rat na moru" ["War at Sea"] (with J. Andrassy), in: V. Brajković (ed.), *Pomorska enciklopedija* [*Maritime Encyclopaedia*], 2nd edn., Vol. VI, Zagreb, 1983, pp. 640–642.
6. "Ratna kontrabanda" ["Contraband of War"], in: V. Brajković (ed.), *Pomorska enciklopedija* [*Maritime Encyclopaedia*], 2nd edn., Vol. VI, Zagreb, 1983, pp. 642–643.
7. "Režim otoka" ["Regime of Islands"], in: V. Brajković (ed.), *Pomorska enciklopedija* [*Maritime Encyclopaedia*], 2nd edn., Vol. VI, Zagreb, 1983, p. 697.
8. "Sigurnosne zone" ["Safety Zones"], in: V. Brajković (ed.), *Pomorska enciklopedija* [*Maritime Encyclopaedia*], 2nd edn., Vol. VII, Zagreb, 1985, pp. 272–273.
9. "Sueski kanal; Međunarodni položaj" ["Suez Canal; International Status"] (with J. Andrassy), in: V. Brajković (ed.), *Pomorska enciklopedija* [*Maritime Encyclopaedia*], 2nd edn., Vol. VII, Zagreb, 1985, str. 593–594.
10. "Tehnologija, morska; Transfer morske tehnologije" ["Marine Technology; Transfer of Marine Technology"], in: V. Brajković (ed.), *Pomorska enciklopedija* [*Maritime Encyclopaedia*], 2nd edn., Vol. VIII, Zagreb, 1989, p. 105.
11. "Teritorijalno more" ["Territorial Sea"] (with N. Katičić), in: V. Brajković (ed.), *Pomorska enciklopedija* [*Maritime Encyclopaedia*], 2nd edn., Vol. VIII, Zagreb, 1989, pp. 121–123.

12. "Tranzitni prolazak" ["Transit Passage"], in: V. Brajković (ed.), *Pomorska enciklopedija* [*Maritime Encyclopaedia*], 2nd edn., Vol. VIII, Zagreb, 1989, p. 198.
13. "Tranzitni promet; Sloboda tranzita" ["Traffic in Transit; Freedom of Transit"], in: V. Brajković (ed.), *Pomorska enciklopedija* [*Maritime Encyclopaedia*], 2nd edn., Vol. VIII, Zagreb, 1989, pp. 198–199.
14. "Umjetni otok" ["Artificial Island"] (with J. Andrassy), in: V. Brajković (ed.), *Pomorska enciklopedija* [*Maritime Encyclopaedia*], 2nd edn., Vol. VIII, Zagreb, 1989, p. 310.
15. "UNEP", in: V. Brajković (ed.), *Pomorska enciklopedija* [*Maritime Encyclopaedia*], 2nd edn., Vol. VIII, Zagreb, 1989, p. 335.
16. "Unutrašnje morske vode" ["Internal Waters"] (with J. Andrassy), in: V. Brajković (ed.), *Pomorska enciklopedija* [*Maritime Encyclopaedia*], 2nd edn., Vol. VIII, Zagreb, 1989, pp. 344–345.
17. "Vode, arhipelaške" ["Archipelagic Waters"], in: V. Brajković (ed.), *Pomorska enciklopedija* [*Maritime Encyclopaedia*], 2nd edn., Vol. VIII, Zagreb, 1989, p. 505.
18. "Zatvorena ili poluzatvorena mora" ["Enclosed or Semi-enclosed Seas"], in: V. Brajković (ed.), *Pomorska enciklopedija* [*Maritime Encyclopaedia*], 2nd edn., Vol. VIII, Zagreb, pp. 598–599.
19. "Znanstveno istraživanje mora" ["Marine Scientific Research"], in: V. Brajković (ed.), *Pomorska enciklopedija* [*Maritime Encyclopaedia*], 2nd edn., Vol. VIII, Zagreb, 1989, pp. 610–611.
20. "Ženevska konvencija i Statut o morskim lukama" ["Geneva Convention and Statute on Maritime Ports"] (with U. Štanger), in: V. Brajković (ed.), *Pomorska enciklopedija* [*Maritime Encyclopaedia*], 2nd edn., Vol. VIII, Zagreb, 1989, p. 643.
21. "Ženevske konvencije o pravu mora" ["Geneva Conventions on the Law of the Sea"], in: V. Brajković (ed.), *Pomorska enciklopedija* [*Maritime Encyclopaedia*], 2nd edn., Vol. VIII, Zagreb, pp. 643–644.
22. "Ženevske konvencije o zaštiti žrtava rata" ["Geneva Conventions for the Protection of War Victims"], in: V. Brajković (ed.), *Pomorska enciklopedija* [*Maritime Encyclopaedia*], 2nd edn., Vol. VIII, Zagreb, p. 644.
23. "Pravo mora" ["Law of the Sea"], in: S. Ravlić (ed.), *Hrvatska enciklopedija* [*Croatian Encyclopaedia*], Vol. VIII, Zagreb, 2006, pp. 736–738.
24. "Adriatic Sea", in: R. Wolfrum (ed.), *The Max Planck Encyclopedia of Public International Law*, Vol. I, Oxford, 2012, pp. 89–96.
25. "Enclosed or Semi-enclosed Seas", in: R. Wolfrum (ed.), *The Max Planck Encyclopedia of Public International Law*, Vol. III, Oxford, 2012, pp. 415–423.
26. "Humanitarian Assistance in Cases of Emergency", in: R. Wolfrum (ed.), *The Max Planck Encyclopedia of Public International Law*, Vol. V, Oxford, 2012, pp. 39–47.
27. "Treaties, Third-Party Effect", in: R. Wolfrum (ed.), *The Max Planck Encyclopedia of Public International Law*, Vol. X, Oxford, 2012, pp. 31–38.

PART 1

Subjects of International Law

∴

CHAPTER 1

La Ville libre de Dantzig devant la Cour permanente de Justice internationale

Philippe Couvreur [*]

Les noms de Dantzig et de la Cour permanente de Justice internationale (CPJI) sont, aujourd'hui encore, étroitement associés aux prononcés de cette dernière touchant au statut des individus dans l'ordre juridique international, notamment à leur capacité à se voir reconnaître directement des droits et obligations par la voie de traités,[1] aux rapports entre le droit international et l'ordre juridique interne,[2] ou encore à certains principes généraux de droit public.[3]

Notre propos ici est plutôt de jeter un regard rétrospectif sur la question du statut international, entre les deux guerres mondiales,[4] de la Ville libre de Dantzig, à la lumière du traitement réservé à celle-ci par la CPJI. Le statut

---

[*] Greffier de la Cour internationale de Justice ; Membre correspondant de l'Académie royale des sciences morales et politiques d'Espagne ; Maître de conférence invité à la Faculté de droit de l'Université Catholique de Louvain. Les vues ici exprimées sont strictement personnelles. L'auteur remercie M. Antoine Ollivier, juriste au Greffe de la CIJ, pour sa précieuse assistance.

[1] *Compétence des tribunaux de Dantzig* (*Réclamations pécuniaires des fonctionnaires ferroviaires dantzikois passés au service polonais contre l'Administration polonaise des chemins de fer*), *avis consultatif du 3 mars 1928, Série B n°15*, pp. 17–18 : « On peut facilement admettre que, selon un principe de droit international bien établi, [un] accord international ne peut, comme tel, créer directement des droits et des obligations pour des particuliers. Mais on ne saurait contester que l'objet même d'un accord international, dans l'intention des Parties contractantes, puisse être l'adoption, par les Parties, de règles déterminées, créant des droits et obligations pour des individus, et susceptibles d'être appliquées par les tribunaux nationaux ». Pour un réexamen récent de ce passage de l'avis de la Cour permanente, et des analyses divergentes qui en ont été faites, v. K. Parlett, « The PCIJ's Opinion in *Jurisdiction of the Courts of Danzig*. Individual Rights under Treaties », *Journal of the History of International Law*, 2008, pp. 119–145.

[2] *Traitement des nationaux polonais à Dantzig, Série A/B n°44*, p. 24. Sur la portée de cet avis, concernant la nature étatique de la Ville libre, v. *infra* I.

[3] Dans son avis relatif à la *Compatibilité de certains décrets-lois dantzikois avec la constitution de la Ville libre*, la Cour permanente s'est notamment penchée sur les principes de « l'Etat de droit (*Rechtsstaat*) », les « droits fondamentaux » de l'individu et les principes de droit pénal *Nullum crimen sine lege* et *Nulla poena sine lege*, *Série A/B n°65*, p. 41.

[4] Sur le statut de Dantzig après la seconde guerre mondiale, jusqu'au règlement de la question allemande lors de la réunification, v. C. Whomersley, « The International Legal Status of

juridique de la Ville comme telle ayant déjà été largement débattu, tant d'un point de vue historique que du point de vue de l'évolution des théories et doctrines relatives aux sujets du droit international, l'accent sera exclusivement mis, ci-après, sur les six avis consultatifs rendus par la Cour permanente à propos de la Ville libre de Dantzig, en plusieurs points remarquables.

De manière générale, le recours à la CPJI, en vue du règlement de différentes questions touchant à Dantzig, a constitué une expérience singulière pour la juridiction internationale permanente : par la voie de demandes d'avis consultatif, émanant du Conseil de la Société des Nations (SDN), la Cour permanente a en effet été directement associée au mécanisme, prévu par le Traité de Versailles, de « protection » du statut de Dantzig par la SDN et de « garantie », par l'organisation internationale, de la constitution de la Ville libre. La CPJI n'a jamais été invitée, dans ce contexte, à déterminer la nature de cette entité juridique; elle n'en a pas moins été confrontée, afin de répondre à certaines des demandes d'avis qui lui furent adressées, à la question du « statut juridique spécial de la Ville libre »[5] (I).

Par ailleurs, la pratique de la CPJI à l'égard de Dantzig a donné lieu à plusieurs innovations ou développements en ce qui concerne tant le traitement spécifiquement réservé à la Ville libre que des aspects plus généraux de la procédure suivie devant la Cour en matière consultative (II).

I

Fruit de nécessités historiques et de compromis politiques, l'institution, après la première guerre mondiale,[6] de la « Ville libre de Dantzig » a répondu aux revendications concurrentes de l'Allemagne et de la Pologne sur ce territoire et, plus largement, à la recherche d'un règlement de la question satisfaisant l'équilibre entre les Puissances alliées et associées sur le continent européen.[7] Dantzig fut

---

Gdansk, Klaipeda and the Former East Prussia », *International and Comparative Law Quarterly*, 1993, pp. 919–928.

5 *La Ville libre de Dantzig et l'Organisation internationale du travail*, Série B n°18, avis consultatif du 26 août 1930, p. 9.

6 Pour bref un résumé de l'histoire de Dantzig, jusqu'en 1919, v. C. Hattenhauer, « Danzig (Free City of) », *Max Planck Encyclopedia of Public International Law*, (ed. R. Wolfrum), Oxford University Press, Oxford, 2012, vol. II, pp. 1018–1026, spéc. pp. 1018–1020.

7 Sur l'évolution des positions des principales puissances alliées à ce sujet, v. la présentation sommaire *in* C. Berezowski, « Les sujets non souverains du droit international », *Recueil des Cours de l'Académie de Droit international de La Haye (RCADI)*, vol. 65, 1937, p. 54; v. aussi J. Hostie, « Questions de principe relatives au statut international de Dantzig », *Revue de droit international et de législation comparée*, 1933, pp. 572–574.

ainsi érigée en Ville libre, par le Traité de Versailles, de manière à respecter la composition quasi exclusivement allemande de la population dantzikoise, tout en assurant à la Pologne, compte tenu de sa situation géographique et suivant le principe proclamé dans le treizième des « 14 points » du Président Wilson, un « accès libre et sûr à la mer ».[8] En vue de ce double objectif, les dispositions du Traité de Versailles ont substitué à la souveraineté exercée jusqu'alors par l'Allemagne sur le territoire de Dantzig[9] l'établissement de cette dernière en « Ville libre », placée sous la « protection de la Société des Nations ».[10]

Cette solution reposait sur la reconnaissance de l'autonomie des autorités dantzikoises, à travers notamment l'adoption d'une constitution « par des représentants de la Ville libre régulièrement désignés »,[11] en même temps qu'elle assurait à la Pologne une série de droits à l'égard de Dantzig, touchant à divers aspects de l'administration de la Ville, incluait celle-ci dans les limites de la frontière douanière polonaise et conférait au Gouvernement polonais la responsabilité de « conduire ses affaires extérieures ».[12]

---

8   Assurer un tel accès fut « le motif en vertu duquel Dantzig a été séparée de l'Allemagne par le Traité de Versailles et constituée en Ville libre », CPJI, *Accès et stationnement des navires de guerre polonais dans le port de Dantzig*, avis consultatif, Série A/B n°43, p. 132.

9   Suivant l'article 100 du Traité de Versailles, « [l]'Allemagne renonc[çait], en faveur des Principales Puissances alliées et associées, à tous droits et titres sur le territoire compris dans les limites [définies dans cet article et dont la fixation sur place devait revenir à une Commission prévue à l'article 101] ». Les articles 105–107 du Traité de Versailles fixaient les principes régissant la nationalité des ressortissants allemands domiciliés sur le territoire en question et le sort des biens leur appartenant ou appartenant à l'Empire ou à des Etats allemands.

10 Article 102 du Traité de Versailles: « Les Principales Puissances alliées et associées s'engagent à constituer la Ville de Dantzig [...] en Ville libre. Elle sera placée sous la protection de la Société des Nations ». Les principales Puissances alliées et associées ont constitué la Ville libre de Dantzig par une décision de la Conférence des ambassadeurs datée du 27 octobre 1920, acceptée le 9 novembre 1920 par les représentants de Dantzig et entrée en vigueur le 15 novembre 1920.

11 Article 103 du Traité de Versailles.

12 Article 104 du Traité de Versailles. Aux termes de cette disposition, et suivant les principes qui y étaient posés, l'organisation des relations entre Pologne et la Ville libre devait faire l'objet d'une convention entre les deux parties concernées, dont les Puissances alliées et associées négocieraient les termes. La convention entre la Pologne et la Ville de Dantzig (connue sous le nom de « Traité » ou de « Convention » de Paris) fut conclue le 9 novembre 1920 et entra en vigueur le 15 novembre 1920 ; l'historique des travaux relatifs à l'élaboration de la convention est récapitulé dans l'avis consultatif de la Cour permanente relatif au *Traitement des nationaux polonais et des autres personnes d'origine ou de langue polonaise dans le territoire de Dantzig*, Série A/B n°44, 4 février 1932, pp. 13–16 (le texte de la convention est reproduit in CPJI Série C n°8, pp. 25–33). Cette convention fut elle-même

Ainsi établi dans ses grandes lignes par le Traité de Versailles, le statut de la Ville libre de Dantzig conférait à la Société des Nations certaines responsabilités qui allaient au-delà de la seule « défense » de la Ville libre qu'impliquait son placement sous la « protection » de la SDN.[13] Traduction concrète de ce devoir de protection compris au sens large, le Traité de Versailles avait en effet placé la future Constitution de Dantzig « sous la garantie de la Société des Nations ».[14] D'un point de vue formel, la Constitution de la Ville libre, comme toute modification ultérieure y apportée, devait ainsi être adoptée après approbation de la Société des Nations.[15] En substance, et plus généralement, il revenait à la Société des Nations « de se préoccuper [...] de la bonne application [de la Constitution] » et des « devoirs touchant, entre autres matières, l'application effective de la Constitution », notamment celui « d'intervenir dans le cas d'une mauvaise application par Dantzig de sa Constitution ».[16]

---

complétée, pour en régler les détails d'exécution, par une autre convention dantziko-polonaise, signée à Varsovie le 24 octobre 1921 (« la Convention de Varsovie »).

13 « Il résulte de [l'article 102 du Traité de Versailles] que la Société, et en conséquence le Conseil, agissant en son nom, a le droit et le devoir d'assurer la protection et par conséquent la défense de la Ville libre de Dantzig », CPJI Accès et stationnement des navires de guerre polonais dans le port de Dantzig, avis consultatif, Série A/B n°43, p. 134. Dans son rapport au Conseil de la SDN, en vue de l'établissement de la Ville libre et des responsabilités du Conseil à cet égard, le représentant du Japon, le Vicomte Ishii, précisait que « la "protection" de la Ville libre par la Société des Nations parai[ssait] signifier que la Société des Nations s'engage[rait] à respecter et maintenir contre toute agression extérieure l'intégrité territoriale et l'indépendance politique de la Ville libre de Dantzig de la même manière qu'elle le fai[sait] pour tous les Membres de la Société des Nations, aux termes de l'article 10 du Pacte », rapport du 17 novembre 1920, reproduit in Série C n°8, pp. 193–203, spéc. p. 194.

14 Article 103, premier alinéa, du Traité de Versailles. Les idées de « protection » de la Ville libre et de « garantie de [s]a Constitution », bien qu'étroitement liées, ne se recoupaient pas entièrement. Quoi qu'il en soit, « [l]a portée précise de la protection de la Ville libre par la Société des Nations et celle de la garantie de [s]a constitution n'[étaient] pas [...] définies d'une façon complète », v. La Ville libre de Dantzig et l'Organisation internationale du travail, Série B n°18, p. 12.

15 Élaborée et adoptée par une Assemblée constituante en 1920, la Constitution fut approuvée par le Conseil de la SDN en 1922, après que certaines modifications eurent été apportées au texte ; sur les différentes étapes de l'élaboration et de l'adoption de la Constitution, v. l'avis relatif au Traitement des nationaux polonais et des autres personnes d'origine ou de langue polonaise dans le territoire de Dantzig, CPJI Série A/B n°44, pp. 12–13. Elle fut modifiée en 1930, v. CPJI Série C n°56, pp. 49–69 (en allemand ; v. le texte en français in SDN, Journal officiel, XIe année, n°12, déc. 1930).

16 CPJI, Traitement des nationaux polonais et des autres personnes d'origine ou de langue polonaise dans le territoire de Dantzig, avis consultatif, CPJI Série A/B n°44, p. 21;

Il s'agissait, à différents égards, d'un des premiers exemples « d'administration internationale d'un territoire ».[17] Au titre des responsabilités de la SDN vis-à-vis de la Ville libre de Dantzig figurait notamment sa contribution au mécanisme de règlement des différends institué par le Traité de Versailles et aux termes duquel le Haut-Commissaire de la SDN était chargé de « statuer en première instance sur toutes les contestations qui viendraient à s'élever entre la Pologne et la Ville libre au sujet du [Traité de Versailles] ou des arrangements et accords complémentaires ».[18] C'est précisément dans ce cadre que furent présentées trois des six requêtes pour avis consultatifs adressées à la Cour permanente, à la suite de l'appel de l'une des parties formé devant le Conseil de la SDN contre une décision du Haut-Commissaire.[19]

***

---

v. également *Compatibilité de certains décrets-lois dantzikois avec la constitution de la Ville libre*, Série A/B n°65, pp. 49–50.

17   Pour une mise en perspective, en ce sens, du précédent de Dantzig avec les missions entreprises plus récemment par les Nations Unies, v. R. Wilde, « From Danzig to East Timor and Beyond : The Role of International Territorial Administration », *American Journal of International Law*, 2001, pp. 583–606.

18   Article 103, second alinéa, du Traité de Versailles. La Cour permanente a souligné, lors de la première demande d'avis consultatif concernant Dantzig, qu'il ressortait de cette disposition, considérée conjointement avec l'article 39 de la Convention de Paris, que les fonctions du Haut-Commissaire étaient « d'ordre judiciaire », *Service postal polonais à Dantzig, avis consultatif,* Série B n°11, p. 26. A cette occasion, la Cour a notamment recherché si certaines décisions du Haut-Commissaire revêtaient le caractère et l'autorité de la chose jugée (*res judicata*) à l'égard des droits en litige sur lesquels portait la demande d'avis consultatif.

19   *Service postal polonais à Dantzig, avis consultatif,* Série B n°11 (à l'initiative de la Pologne) ; *Compétence des tribunaux de Dantzig, avis consultatif,* Série B n°15 (à l'initiative de la Ville libre) ; *Traitement des nationaux polonais et des autres personnes d'origine ou de langue polonaise dans le territoire de Dantzig, avis consultatif,* CPJI Série A/B n°44 (à l'initiative de la Pologne). S'agissant de la procédure relative à la *Participation de la Ville libre à l'OIT*, la demande avait été présentée par le Conseil de la SDN, à la requête du Conseil d'administration de l'OIT, et faisait suite à une démarche du Sénat de Dantzig tendant à l'acquisition, par la Ville, de la qualité de Membre de cette Organisation, v. Série B n°18, pp. 7–9. L'avis relatif aux *Navires de guerre polonais dans le port de Dantzig* trouvait son origine dans une revendication récurrente de la Pologne, remontant à l'institution de la Ville libre, qui n'avait jamais pu être définitivement réglée et dont le Conseil avait finalement saisi la Cour permanente en 1931. Enfin, la question de la *Compatibilité de certains décrets-lois dantzikois avec la Constitution de la Ville libre* fut soumise à la Cour permanente après que le Haut-Commissaire eut transmis au Conseil la pétition y afférente des partis minoritaires de l'Assemblée populaire (*Volkstag*) de Dantzig.

Le caractère inédit et complexe de la situation juridique de Dantzig a nourri une abondante littérature, sans que la CPJI elle-même n'eut à se prononcer directement au fond sur la question de savoir si la Ville libre constituait un Etat au sens du droit international.[20] Il est certes probable que, posée en ces termes, la question ne pouvait appeler de réponse tranchée. Certes, qualifier d'« étatique » la Ville libre de Dantzig permettait de répondre commodément à la difficulté de caractériser autrement une entité juridique relevant du droit international.[21] De surcroît, dénier toute qualité « étatique » à la Ville libre, en raison des limitations apportées à l'indépendance politique de celle-ci, en particulier s'agissant de la « conduite de ses relations extérieures »,[22] pouvait se heurter à l'observation que de telles limitations et restrictions n'excluaient pas nécessairement que constitue un Etat une entité satisfaisant par ailleurs aux différents critères de définition de l'Etat au sens du droit international.[23] Certains auteurs ont ainsi présenté la Ville libre de Dantzig comme un Etat d'une nature spéciale,

---

20 Pour les passages pertinents des différents avis de la Cour sur cette question, v. *infra*. En ce qui concerne la qualification d'« Etat » retenue expressément par la Cour permanente aux fins de l'application du Règlement de la Cour, v. le point II ci-après.

21 V. par ex. la qualification incertaine donnée par L. Delbez, « Le concept d'internationalisation », *Revue générale de droit international public* (RGDIP), 1967, p. 18 : « Nous pensons [...] que la Ville libre était un « Etat », avec son drapeau, ses armoiries, sa monnaie, sa police, son administration, sa nationalité et sa souveraineté territoriale. Seulement, c'était un Etat artificiel, créé de toutes pièces par un traité, et un Etat hétéronome, dont la souveraineté subissait un certain nombre de limitations : protection des droits de la minorité polonaise, interdiction de fabriquer du matériel de guerre, limitation du Sénat dans la conduite des affaires extérieures, approbation des révisions constitutionnelles par le Conseil, etc. [...] La Ville libre restait donc, en dépit des obligations qui pesaient sur elle, une personne internationale. Elle était, bien que sa capacité internationale fut limitée, un membre de la communauté internationale et un sujet du droit des gens ».

22 En ce sens, par ex., Ch. Rousseau, *Droit international public* (Tome II : Les sujets de droit), Sirey, Paris, 1974, pp. 425–426. V. aussi P. Daillier, M. Forteau, A. Pellet, *Droit international public* (*Nguyen Quoc Dinh †*), LGDJ, Paris, 8e éd., p. 508.

23 Le cas de la Ville libre de Dantzig a été utilisé par D. Anzilotti aux fins d'illustrer la situation des Etats protégés, le protectorat international supposant, précisément, un rapport de droit international entre deux sujets souverains, *Cours de droit international*, trad. G. Gidel (1929), rééd. LGDJ, Paris, 1999, pp. 231–232. L'éminent juriste italien voyait dans la Ville libre un Etat protégé à l'égard de la Pologne, et distinguait, d'autres situations, la « protection » attribuée à la SDN par article 102 du Traité de Versailles comme relevant « plutôt [d']un contrôle des rapports intervenant entre la Ville libre et la Pologne », *ibid.*, p. 232. Dans le même sens, H. Lauterpacht (ed.), *Oppenheim's International Law*, vol. I: *Peace*, Longmans, London, 8th ed., 1967, p. 194.

créé sur la base d'un traité.[24] Les débats relatifs à la nature étatique de la Ville de Dantzig renvoyant aux interrogations sur la définition même de l'Etat au sens du droit international, une solution médiane pouvait consister à reconnaître dans la Ville libre de Dantzig un nouveau type de sujet de droit international.[25] Il échet toutefois de noter, à cet égard, que classer la Ville libre de Dantzig parmi un ensemble de Villes ou territoires « internationalisés » ne pouvait suffire à en préciser le statut juridique dès lors que ces entités ne constituaient pas en elles-mêmes une catégorie définie ou un genre particulier de sujets de droit international.[26] Certains commentateurs ont ainsi renoncé à vouloir ranger le statut de Dantzig dans une typologie des sujets du droit international, le régime mis en place sur le fondement du Traité de Versailles ne se prêtant, selon eux, qu'à une description, non à une définition juridique.[27]

*

24 A. Verdross, « Règles générales du droit international de la paix », RCADI, vol. 30, 1929, p. 324 : « La Ville libre de Dantzig [...] forme un Etat souverain d'une catégorie spéciale. Car il s'agit d'un Etat qui se gouverne bien lui-même sur la base directe du droit des gens, mais qui dépend en certaines matières de la Société des Nations ». Cet auteur est toutefois revenu sur la qualification étatique de la Ville libre de Dantzig, pour y voir un nouveau genre de sujet du droit international, v. *Völkerrecht*, Springer Verlag, Vienne, 1955, 3ᵉ éd., pp. 153–154. Pour P. Guggenheim, une distinction devait être établie entre les « Etats souverains », qui « relèvent *directement* du droit international *coutumier* » (p. 85), et d'autres Etats devant leur existence au droit conventionnel (« Les principes de droit international public », RCADI, vol. 80, 1952, pp. 80 et s.), la Ville libre de Dantzig rentrant dans cette dernière catégorie (*ibid.* pp. 95–96 : « Les restrictions que le droit international impose aux territoires sous mandat et sous tutelle ne leur enlève pas plus le caractère d'Etat au sens du droit international que ce n'est le cas pour les Etats constitués en vertu d'un traité et qui, comme Cracovie ou Dantzig dans le passé, Tanger dans le présent, ne sont pas arrivés au degré d'indépendance réalisé par les Etats souverains dont le fondement juridique immédiat est le droit international coutumier »).
25 V. par ex. C. Berezowski, « Les sujets non souverains du droit international », *op. cit.*, pp. 54 et s., spéc. p. 57 : « Nous pensons que la Ville libre de Dantzig a pour nature juridique d'être une organisation territoriale non souveraine, placée sous la protection de la Société des Nations ».
26 En ce sens, L. Delbez, « Le concept d'internationalisation », *op. cit.*, p. 12 ; J. Crawford, *The Creation of States in International Law*, Clarendon Press, Oxford, 2006, 2nd ed., p. 233. En témoigne la comparaison de la situation de Dantzig avec des exemples très différents de territoires ou Villes « internationalisés », à la même époque, aux seules fins de constituer un territoire autonome au sein d'un Etat souverain (tels Memel (Lithuanie) ou la Sarre (Allemagne)).
27 V. par ex. I. Morrow, « The International Status of the Free City of Danzig », *British Yearbook of International Law (BYIL)*, vol. 18, 1937, pp. 114–126, spéc. p. 126. On sait, au demeurant, que la Cour internationale de Justice, en reconnaissant, formellement, en

Les avis consultatifs de la CPJI ont pu donner lieu à diverses interprétations, et il paraît difficile de dégager de leur lecture une position absolue, ou du moins constante, de la Cour permanente à l'égard de la nature exacte de la Ville libre de Dantzig. Selon que tel ou tel avis de la Cour est examiné, des conclusions contradictoires ont parfois pu, en effet, être tirées à ce sujet.

Dans le contexte de la procédure consultative relative au *Service postal polonais à Dantzig*, la Ville libre et la Pologne s'étaient opposées sur l'incidence que pouvait avoir la nature de Dantzig sur la réponse à donner par la CPJI à la question concrète dont elle était saisie.[28] La Cour statua sur le droit de la Pologne de tenir un service postal sur le territoire de Dantzig en se fondant sur les seules dispositions des accords conclus entre les deux parties concernées, sans tirer des conséquences, extensives ou restrictives, quant à ce droit, du régime juridique de Dantzig au regard du droit international.[29]

S'agissant de l'avis consultatif rendu au sujet de l'*Accès et stationnement des navires de guerre polonais dans le port de Dantzig*, certains auteurs ont conclu que la Cour permanente avait implicitement considéré la Ville libre comme un

---

1949 la personnalité juridique de l'Organisation des Nations Unies et, partant, l'existence de sujets du droit international autres que les Etats, a consacré le principe selon lequel « [l]es sujets de droit, dans un système juridique, ne sont pas nécessairement identiques quant à leur nature ou à l'étendue de leurs droits ; et leur nature dépend des besoins de la communauté », *Réparation des dommages subis au service des Nations Unies, avis consultatif*, CIJ Recueil 1949, p. 178.

28 Le débat est apparu au cours de la procédure écrite, la Ville libre de Dantzig ayant souhaité rectifier, dans son mémoire complémentaire, les qualificatifs employés par la Pologne dans son mémoire, qui se référait à « l'autonomie politique » de Dantzig et à son caractère de « communauté *sui generis* », v. *Série C n°8*, p. 435 (Mémoire complémentaire du 15 avril 1925). C'est à cette occasion que les autorités de Dantzig ont défendu le plus directement, devant la Cour, le caractère d'Etat souverain de la Ville libre ; sur la série d'arguments invoqués en ce sens, v. *ibid.*, pp. 435–437. En réponse à ces développements, le Gouvernement polonais répliqua, dans ses observations complémentaires, que la question était de nature politique et qu'il n'était pas dans son intention d'examiner la situation de la Ville libre de Dantzig au point de vue du droit international. Non seulement le Gouvernement polonais ne voyait « aucune connexité entre la question politique de la situation internationale de la Ville libre et les questions [adressées à la Cour] », « la définition de la situation internationale de la Ville libre [étant] complètement indifférent[e] pour l'interprétation des clauses des Traités et Conventions ayant trait aux relations de la Pologne et de Dantzig dans la matière postale », mais il faisait également valoir que le Conseil de la SDN lui-même, saisi d'un appel contre une décision du Haut-Commissaire reconnaissant la qualité étatique de Dantzig, avait exprimé le vœu de ne pas être saisi de la question du statut international de la Ville libre, *ibid.*, pp. 454–455.

29 *Série B n°11*, pp. 39–40.

Etat en indiquant que les droits revendiqués par la Pologne sur le territoire de Dantzig devaient « reposer sur une base bien claire », au motif que « [l]e port de Dantzig n'[était] pas territoire polonais et, par suite, [que] les droits que revendiqu[ait] la Pologne s'exerceraient par dérogation aux droits de la Ville libre ».[30]

Dans son avis consultatif relatif à la *Ville libre de Dantzig et l'OIT*, la Cour permanente a détaillé le « statut juridique spécial » de la Ville libre, et conclu que ce dernier ne lui permettait pas de devenir membre de l'Organisation internationale du Travail tant qu'un arrangement n'était pas conclu avec la Pologne.[31] Si cet avis consultatif est parfois présenté comme ayant exclu implicitement la qualité d'Etat dans le chef de Dantzig,[32] il a apporté des précisions significatives sur la capacité internationale de la Ville libre. La Cour permanente a en effet noté qu'il était « communément admis par la Pologne et la

---

30   Série A/B n°43, p. 142 ; v. J. Crawford, *The Creation of States in International Law, op. cit.*, p. 240 (« *the Lotus presumption applied in Danzig's favour, in cases of doubt* »), et, pour une discussion plus large, dans cette perspective, des avis consultatifs relatifs à Dantzig, O. Spiermann, *International Argument in the Permanent Court of International Justice. The Rise of the International Judiciary*, Cambridge University Press, 2004, pp. 332 et s.

31   Série B n°18, pp. 4 et s. La Cour n'a examiné que la question de savoir ce qui, dans le « statut juridique spécial » de Dantzig, pouvait faire obstacle à la participation de la Ville libre à l'OIT Elle a refusé de se pencher sur la question plus large des conditions de participation à l'OIT d'un « Etat ou [d']une communauté » non membre de la SDN, et d'examiner dans quelle mesure la Ville libre pouvait, le cas échéant, les remplir. V. à cet égard les opinions individuelles des juges Anzilotti (*ibid.*, p. 18 et s.) et Huber (*ibid.*, pp. 29–30).

32   P. Daillier, M. Forteau, A. Pellet, *Droit international public (Nguyen Quoc Dinh †), op. cit.*, pp. 508. *Contra*, J. Crawford, « The Criteria for Statehood in International Law », *BYIL*, 1976–1977, vol. 48, p. 139, pour qui la Cour n'a pas exclu la qualification d'Etat pour Dantzig, cet auteur se référant notamment au passage de l'avis dans lequel la Cour permanente dit « n'[avoir] » trouvé dans la Partie XIII du Traité de Versailles aucune disposition qui dispense[rait] *un Etat faisant partie de l'Organisation internationale du Travail* de s'acquitter de ses obligations de Membre ou qui lui permette de ne pas participer aux activités normales de l'Organisation s'il ne peut, au préalable, obtenir le consentement d'un autre Membre de l'Organisation », et en infère que Dantzig ne pourrait dès lors pas participer aux travaux de l'Organisation tant qu'un arrangement ne serait pas conclu afin de garantir d'avance qu'aucune objection ne serait faite par le Gouvernement polonais à une action quelconque que la Ville libre pourrait désirer entreprendre en qualité de Membre de cette Organisation, *Série B n°18*, p. 15 (italiques ajoutés). Cet auteur reconnaît par ailleurs expressément la qualité d'« Etat » à Dantzig, compte tenu du régime souple attaché par le droit international à cette qualification, *ibid.* et *The Creation of States in International Law, op. cit.*, p. 240, 253.

Ville libre que les droits de la Pologne en matière de conduite des relations extérieures de la Ville libre n['étaient] pas absolus » :

> Le Gouvernement polonais n'a pas le droit, contrairement à la volonté de la Ville libre, de lui imposer une politique déterminée, ni de prendre contre sa volonté des mesures visant ses relations extérieures. En revanche, la Ville libre ne peut inviter la Pologne à prendre, relativement aux relations extérieures de la Ville libre, des mesures opposées à la politique propre de la Pologne. [...] Il en résulte que, pour ce qui est des relations extérieures de Dantzig, ni la Pologne ni la Ville libre ne sont complètement maîtresses de la situation. La Ville libre a le droit de s'occuper de ses propres intérêts et de veiller à ce que rien ne soit fait qui leur porte préjudice. La Pologne a le droit de veiller à ses propres intérêts et de refuser de prendre toute mesure qui leur serait contraire.[33]

Ce passage rend compte très précisément de ce que la « conduite des relations extérieures de la Ville libre » par la Pologne ne devait ni se réduire à une simple représentation des intérêts de la Ville libre dans la sphère des rapports internationaux ni, à l'opposé, conférer une compétence discrétionnaire de la Pologne en la matière. A cet égard, et au-delà de la conduite des relations extérieures, l'intérêt de la question d'une qualification précise et constante de la Ville libre comme sujet de droit international paraissait donc pouvoir être relativisé au profit d'une qualification, objective, du territoire de Dantzig comme une « situation juridique internationale » dans laquelle divers acteurs s'étaient vus reconnaître des droits et obligations, ainsi que les charges et facultés qui en découlaient, à la mesure de leurs intérêts respectifs.

Il est permis, de la sorte, de reconnaître « le fait que le statut juridique de Dantzig [était] *sui generis* », dans le sens où la Ville libre n'était pas entièrement, et à tous points de vue, assimilable à un Etat au sens du droit international, bien qu'à certains égards puissent lui être appliqués « les principes généraux du droit international » et notamment, dans ses relations avec la Pologne, « les principes usuels qui régissent les relations entre les Etats ».[34] Ces passages bien connus de l'avis consultatif relatif au *Traitement des nationaux polonais à Dantzig*, parfois cités à l'appui de la qualification étatique de la Ville libre,[35] rendraient ainsi plutôt compte, en réalité, de la nature complexe

---

33 *Série B n°18*, p. 13.
34 *Traitement des nationaux polonais et des autres personnes d'origine ou de langue polonaise dans le territoire de Dantzig, avis consultatif, Série A/B n°44*, pp. 23–24.
35 V. par ex., P. Guggenheim, « Les principes de droit international public », *op. cit.*, p. 92.

de cette entité, placée sur un pied d'égalité à l'égard de la Pologne pour certaines matières, et subordonnée à la Société des Nations dans d'autres.[36]

Il est néanmoins tout autant possible de considérer que la qualification d'Etat revêt, en droit international, un caractère fonctionnel, indépendamment de la question de savoir ce que recouvre l'essence même du « concept » d'Etat.[37] A ce titre, la qualification d'une entité juridique comme « Etat » serait relative aux règles dont l'application concrète est en question, compte tenu des buts et finalités que celles-ci poursuivent, et pourrait ainsi varier d'une branche du droit à une autre, selon la norme appliquée, ou encore suivant l'institution devant laquelle ces règles devraient être mises en œuvre.[38] En ce sens, la Ville libre de Dantzig a pu être considérée comme un « Etat », indépendamment de toute prise de position quant à sa nature intrinsèque, aux fins de l'application du Statut et du Règlement de la Cour dans l'organisation de la procédure

---

36   « Le caractère particulier de la Constitution de Dantzig [...] n'affecte que les relations entre la Ville libre et la Société des Nations », *Traitement des nationaux polonais et des autres personnes d'origine ou de langue polonaise dans le territoire de Dantzig, avis consultatif,* Série A/B n°44, p. 24. V. aussi *Ville libre de Dantzig et Organisation internationale du Travail,* Série B n°18, p. 11 : « le statut juridique spécial de la Ville libre comprend deux éléments : un rapport spécial avec la Société des Nations [...] et un rapport spécial avec la Pologne ». *Cf.* également J. Hostie, « Questions de principe relatives au statut international de Dantzig », *Revue de droit international et de législation comparée,* 1933, pp. 613–614.

37   Une approche plus pragmatique de la question pourrait consister à tenir les conséquences de la qualification d'Etat au sens du droit international comme étant suffisamment larges ou peu rigides pour s'appliquer à des entités dites « sui generis » ; en ce sens, à propos notamment de la Ville libre de Dantzig, v. J. Crawford, « The Criteria for Statehood in International Law », *op. cit.,* p. 139 : « The denomination '*sui generis*' often applied to entities which, for some reason, it is desired not to characterize as States, is of little help. On the one hand the regime of rules concerning States provides a flexible and readily applicable standard; on the other, the induction of the multitude of necessary (and usually unexpressed) rules regarding a '*sui generis* entity' is both laborious and, usually, unnecessary. The assumption that, for example, 'internationalized territories' are *a priori* excluded from statehood in the legal sense is unwarranted, since it exaggerates the importance and rigidity of the international legal regime of statehood ».

38   Cette idée de l'Etat comme « figure à géométrie variable » a été notamment exposée par R. Higgins, « The Concept of the 'State' : Variable Geometry and Dualist Perceptions », *in* L. Boisson de Chazournes, V. Gowlland-Debbas (dir.), *L'ordre juridique international. Un système en quête d'équité : liber amicorum Georges Abi-Saab,* Martinus Nijhoff, La Haye, 2001, pp. 547–561. V. également M. Forteau, « L'Etat selon le droit international : une figure à géométrie variable ? », *RGDIP,* 2007, pp. 737–768 ; A. Pellet, « Les effets de la reconnaissance par la Palestine de la compétence de la Cour pénale internationale », *in* S. Doumbé-Billé ; H. Gherari & R. Kherad (dir.), *Droit, liberté, paix, développement. Mélanges en l'honneur de Madjid Benchikh,* Pedone, Paris, 2011, pp. 327 et s., spéc. pp. 329–333.

consultative.[39] La pratique suivie à l'égard de Dantzig par la Cour permanente se révèle alors instructive, moins au regard de la question de principe de la nature exacte de la Ville libre, que du point de vue de l'esprit et du but dans lesquels les règles de procédure pertinentes ont été mises en œuvre par la CPJI.

II

Compte tenu des incertitudes planant sur la nature juridique abstraite de la Ville libre de Dantzig, telle que celle-ci fut instituée par le Traité de Versailles, la CPJI devait nécessairement se trouver confrontée au point de savoir quel traitement réserver à Dantzig devant elle.

La question s'est certes posée tout d'abord d'une façon générale, en ce qui concerne l'accès de Dantzig à la Cour permanente en matière contentieuse. Mais elle a pris tout son relief, dans la pratique, à l'occasion de chacune des demandes d'avis consultatif adressées à la Cour. Eu égard au silence initialement gardé dans le Statut quant au déroulement de la procédure consultative, il est revenu à la Cour de déterminer quelle application donner aux dispositions pertinentes de son Règlement s'agissant de la participation de la Ville libre à la procédure, notamment quant à la désignation par la Ville d'un juge *ad hoc*.

En ce qui est de la procédure contentieuse, il échet de rappeler que la Cour permanente eut à décider à quels « Etats », autres que les Etats membres de la Société des Nations ou mentionnés à l'annexe du Pacte, il convenait de communiquer la résolution prise par le Conseil, le 17 mai 1922, en vertu de l'article 35, paragraphe 2, du Statut de la Cour.[40] Le Conseil s'en était remis à celle-ci pour

---

39   V. J. Crawford, *The Creation of States in International Law, op. cit.*, p. 31 : la nature d'Etat de Dantzig a été établie aux fins de l'article 71 du Règlement de la Cour (relatif à la désignation d'un juge *ad hoc* dans la procédure consultative, *cf. infra*), mais est demeurée controversée à d'autres égards.

40   Dans sa rédaction initiale, l'article 35, paragraphe 2, du Statut de la CPJI énonçait que « [l]es conditions auxquelles [la Cour était] ouverte aux autres Etats [que ceux déjà Membres de la Société des Nations ou mentionnés à l'annexe au Pacte] étaient, sous réserve des dispositions particulières des traités en vigueur, réglées par le Conseil, et dans tous les cas, sans qu'il puisse en résulter pour les parties aucune inégalité devant la Cour ». La Cour permanente discuta, au cours de sa session préliminaire, en 1922, de la façon dont le Conseil devait exercer ses pouvoirs conformément à cette disposition, et appela l'attention du Conseil sur ce point, par une lettre du Président de la Cour en date du 21 février 1922, v. *Série D n°2 (Préparation du Règlement de la Cour)*, pp. 63, 69–72, 76 et 345–347. V. aussi M. Hudson, *The Permanent Court of International Justice 1920–1942*, (1943), rééd. Garland Publishing, New York & London, 1973, p. 386. Le texte de la résolution prise à cet

« donner effet » à sa résolution,[41] et il a été souligné que les décisions qu'elle avait à prendre dans ce contexte étaient susceptibles de la mêler à des questions politiques.[42] La Cour décida de rendre la Ville libre destinataire d'une telle communication. Cette décision, en date du 28 juin 1922, fut mise en œuvre, initialement, avec beaucoup de prudence, ainsi qu'il est relaté dans le premier rapport annuel de la Cour permanente.[43] La Ville libre en a tiré un argument en faveur de sa qualité d'Etat au regard du droit international.[44] Quoi qu'il en soit, Dantzig n'a jamais déposé de déclaration sur la base de la résolution du Conseil, et la question de sa capacité à ester devant la Cour en matière contentieuse ne s'est pas posée dans la pratique.[45]

Dans le cadre des divers arrangements administratifs qu'il y avait lieu de prendre dès après l'installation de la CPJI, un accord fut conclu entre le Greffe de la Cour et la légation de Pologne aux Pays-Bas au sujet des communications que la Cour aurait à faire à la Ville libre de Dantzig.[46] Cet accord prévoyait, dans le respect de la disposition du Traité de Versailles relative à la « conduite des relations extérieures » de la Ville libre, que les communications destinées

---

égard par le Conseil le 17 mai 1922 est reproduit *in* CPJI *Série E n°1*, pp. 139–140. Selon cette résolution, les Etats non membres ou non mentionnés à l'annexe au Pacte devaient déposer une déclaration par laquelle ils acceptaient la juridiction de la Cour, « conformément au Pacte de la Société des Nations et aux termes et conditions du Statut et du Règlement de la Cour, en s'engageant à exécuter de bonne foi les sentences rendues et à ne pas recourir à la guerre contre tout Etat qui s'y conformera[it] ». *Cf.* l'article 35, paragraphe 2, du Statut de la CIJ et la résolution 9 (1946) prise par le Conseil de sécurité le 15 octobre 1946, CIJ *Actes et documents n°6*, pp. 186–187.

41 M. Hudson, *The Permanent Court of International Justice 1920–1942, op. cit.*, p. 388.
42 *Ibid.*, p. 389.
43 *Série E n°1*, pp. 140–141 : « Le 28 juin 1922, la Cour décida de communiquer la Résolution (1°) aux Etats non Membres de la Société et mentionnés à l'annexe aux Pacte ; (2°) aux Etats suivants : [...] Pologne (pour transmission à la Ville libre de Dantzig) [...]. La liste complète est donc la suivante : [...] Pologne (pour transmission à la Ville libre de Dantzig) [...] ». Cependant, dès le deuxième rapport annuel (1925), il fut indiqué que le destinataire de la communication était « la Ville libre de Dantzig (par l'intermédiaire de la Pologne) », *Série E n°2*, p. 89. V. également, *Série E n°4*, p. 123, note 1, où il est signalé que « la Ville libre, [avait] été, dès 1922, formellement reconnue par la Cour comme une entité juridique admise à ester devant elle ».
44 V. la procédure consultative relative au *Service postal polonais*, *Série C n°8*, p. 436.
45 Le paragraphe 5 de la résolution du Conseil indiquait que « [l]a Cour [devait connaître] de toute question relative à la validité ou à l'effet d'une déclaration faite aux termes de [ladite] Résolution ».
46 Echange de notes des 3 et 6 novembre 1922, non publié. *Cf.* par ex. la lettre, en date du 24 mars 1925, du Greffier au Ministre de Pologne à La Haye, *Série C n°8*, p. 501.

à cette dernière seraient adressées à la légation de Pologne à La Haye, pour transmission par le Ministère des affaires étrangères à Varsovie aux autorités compétentes de la Ville. Peu problématique pour les communications « circulaires » de la Cour, effectuées par le Greffe, conformément au Règlement, aux fins d'information des Etats parties au Statut de la Cour, ou aux autres Etats auxquels celle-ci était ouverte, une telle voie de communication aurait pu se révéler peu commode pour les communications à partie dans le contexte d'une éventuelle affaire contentieuse. Une difficulté de cet ordre s'est présentée à l'occasion de la première demande d'avis consultatif intéressant la Ville libre de Dantzig, et fut résolue avec pragmatisme. Dans la procédure consultative relative au *Service postal polonais à Dantzig*, le Greffier, s'agissant de la notification de la requête et de l'invitation à fournir des renseignements, suivit la voie indiquée par l'accord conclu en 1922 avec la Légation de Pologne, tout en adressant directement à la Ville libre de Dantzig un double de la communication, compte tenu du caractère urgent de l'affaire.[47] Il précisa en outre dans sa lettre au Ministre de Pologne que « [l]e fait que dans la présente affaire la Cour adopte, pour ses communications à la Ville libre, la voie convenue dans l'échange de notes visé ci-dessus, ne saurait [...] être interprété comme préjugeant son droit d'entrer, en matières semblables, en rapports directs avec les entités juridiques susceptibles de lui fournir des renseignements sur les questions dont elle se trouvera saisie ».[48] Sur ce point, c'est en effet à la Cour permanente elle-même qu'il revenait d'interpréter les règles applicables et de déterminer l'étendue de ses pouvoirs et obligations aux fins de l'exercice de ses fonctions. Ce précédent a été suivi dans les procédures consultatives ultérieures.[49]

---

47   Lettre du 24 mars 1925 au Ministre de Pologne à La Haye, *Série C n°8*, p. 501 (« Le Conseil ayant fortement souligné le caractère urgent de cette affaire, et la transmission à la Ville libre par Votre intermédiaire et celui de Votre Gouvernement comportant nécessairement des retards très considérables, j'ai été chargé d'expédier directement à la Ville libre un double de la communication dont il s'agit »).

48   *Ibid.*

49   *Compétence des tribunaux de Dantzig (Réclamations pécuniaires des fonctionnaires ferroviaires dantzikois passés au service polonais contre l'Administration polonaise des chemins de fer)*, Série C n°14, pp. 518–520 (lettres du Greffier au Ministère des affaires étrangères de Pologne et au Sénat de Dantzig, 30 septembre 1927) ; *La Ville libre de Dantzig et l'Organisation internationale du Travail*, Série C n°18, p. 232 et pp. 233–234 (lettres du Greffier au Sénat de Dantzig, au Ministre de Pologne à La Haye, et au Président du Sénat de Dantzig, 20 mai 1930) ; *Accès et stationnement des navires de guerre polonais dans le port de Dantzig*, Série C n°55, p. 417 (lettres du Greffier au Ministre de Pologne à La Haye et au Président du Sénat de Dantzig, 1er octobre 1931) ; *Traitement des nationaux polonais et des autres personnes d'origine ou de langue polonaise dans le territoire de Dantzig*, Série C n°56, pp. 423–424 (lettres du

Lors de la première demande d'avis consultatif intéressant Dantzig, la requête fut « communiquée au Sénat de la Ville libre de Dantzig, comme étant susceptible de fournir des renseignements sur les questions posées à la Cour ».[50] La Cour se fondait à cet égard sur l'article 73, alinéa 2, du Règlement de 1922, prévoyant que « [l]es *organisations internationales* susceptibles de fournir des renseignements sur la question [...] reçoivent communication » de la requête demandant l'avis consultatif.[51] A partir de la deuxième demande d'avis consultatif relatif à Dantzig, la Cour fit application de l'article 73, tel qu'il avait été révisé en 1926, en adressant « aux Gouvernements de la Pologne et de la Ville libre de Dantzig, considérés comme susceptibles de fournir des renseignements sur la question au sujet de laquelle l'avis de la Cour [était] sollicité, une communication spéciale et directe portant que la Cour était disposée à recevoir de leur part des exposés écrits et, le cas échéant, à entendre des exposés oraux faits en leur nom et au cours d'une audience publique tenue à cet effet ».[52] On ne pouvait inférer d'une telle formule à quel titre précis la Ville libre de Dantzig entrait dans les prévisions de l'article 73, paragraphe 1, second alinéa, du Règlement.[53] En revanche, dans l'avis consultatif relatif à la

---

Greffier au Ministre de Pologne à La Haye et au Président du Sénat de Dantzig, 1er juin 1931) ; *Compatibilité de certains décrets-lois dantzikois avec la Constitution de la Ville libre*, Série C n°77, pp. 249, 250–251 et 252 (lettres du Greffier au Président du Sénat de Dantzig, au Sénat de Dantzig et au Ministre de Pologne à La Haye, 1er et 2 octobre 1935).

50 Série B n°11, p. 9. Le Sénat de la Ville libre était, aux termes de la Constitution de Dantzig, l'organe collégial exerçant le pouvoir exécutif.

51 Italiques ajoutés.

52 *Compétence des tribunaux de Dantzig (Réclamations pécuniaires des fonctionnaires ferroviaires dantzikois passés au service polonais contre l'Administration polonaise des chemins de fer)*, avis consultatif du 3 mars 1928, Série B n°15, p. 7. V. aussi : *La Ville libre de Dantzig et l'Organisation internationale du Travail*, avis consultatif du 26 août 1930, Série B n°18, pp. 5–6 (communication spéciale et directe adressée « au Sénat de Dantzig, au Gouvernement polonais et au Directeur du Bureau international du Travail ») ; *Accès et stationnement des navires de guerre polonais dans le port de Dantzig*, avis consultatif du 11 décembre 1931, Série A/B n°43, p. 130 (communication spéciale et directe adressée « aux Gouvernements de la République polonaise et de la Ville libre de Dantzig ») ; *Traitement des nationaux polonais et des autres personnes d'origine ou de langue polonaise dans le territoire de Dantzig*, avis consultatif du 4 février 1932, Série A/B n°44, pp. 6–7 (idem).

53 L'article 73, paragraphe 1, du Règlement de la Cour révisé en 1926 se lisait comme suit : « Le Greffier notifie immédiatement la requête demandant l'avis consultatif aux Membres de la Société des Nations par l'entremise du Secrétaire général de la Société ainsi qu'aux Etats admis à ester en justice devant la Cour. En outre, *à tout Membre de la Société, à tout Etat admis à ester devant la Cour, et à toute organisation internationale jugée, par la Cour ou par le Président si elle ne siège pas, susceptible de fournir des renseignements sur la*

Compatibilité de certains décrets-lois dantzikois avec la Constitution de la Ville libre, il fut expressément fait référence à la Ville libre de Dantzig comme à un « Etat admis à ester devant la Cour ».[54] La Ville avait toutefois déjà été qualifiée d'Etat dans certains avis précédents, aux fins de lui reconnaître le droit de désigner un juge *ad hoc*, conformément à l'article 71 du Règlement de la Cour.

C'est par un amendement au Règlement de la Cour, adopté en 1927 sur une proposition de D. Anzilotti, que l'article 31 du Statut fut reconnu applicable en matière consultative « lorsque l'avis est demandé sur une question relative à un différend actuellement né entre deux ou plusieurs États ou Membres de la Société des Nations ».[55] La possibilité pour un Etat de désigner un juge « national », à l'occasion d'une procédure consultative, avait été déjà discutée, au moment de l'élaboration du Statut de la Cour permanente,[56] et rejetée lors de la première révision du Règlement de la CPJI en 1926.[57] L'amendement

---

question, le Greffier fait connaître, par communication spéciale et directe, que la Cour est disposée à recevoir des exposés écrits dans un délai à fixer par le Président, ou à entendre des exposés oraux au cours d'une audience publique tenue à cet effet. [...] » [italiques ajoutés].

54 *Avis consultatif du 4 décembre 1935, Série A/B n° 65*, p. 43 : « le Greffier a, par note datée du 4 octobre 1935, adressée à la Ville libre de Dantzig, jugée par le Président – la Cour ne siégeant pas – *comme un Etat admis à ester devant la Cour* et susceptible de fournir des renseignements sur la question soumise pour avis consultatif, la communication spéciale et directe prévue par l'article 73, n°1, alinéa 2, du Règlement » [italiques ajoutés].

55 Les textes relatifs à cette modification ont été publiés dans le quatrième rapport annuel de la Cour permanente, *Série E n°4*, pp. 68–74.

56 Comité consultatif de juristes, *Procès-Verbaux*, pp. 730–732. Lors de l'examen, par l'Assemblée de la Société des Nations, du projet de Statut présenté par le Comité, il fut décidé de ne pas adopter la disposition prévoyant que la Cour statue, « lorsqu'elle donne son avis sur une question qui fait l'objet d'un différend actuellement né », « dans les mêmes conditions que s'il s'agissait d'un différend porté devant elle » (une commission de trois à cinq membres devant en revanche être constituée dans le cas d'une demande d'avis sur un « point » indépendamment de tout différend actuellement né). La Sous-Commission de l'Assemblée chargée d'examiner le projet avait estimé qu'il n'y avait pas lieu de maintenir la distinction entre avis demandé sur un « différend » et avis demandé sur un « point », au motif notamment que cette distinction n'était pas nette et pouvait donner lieu à des difficultés pratiques, et que le projet entrait dans des détails qui concernaient plutôt le Règlement de la Cour. C'est pour ces raisons qu'aucune règle relative à la procédure consultative ne figura finalement dans le Statut initialement adopté. V. B. Schenk van Stauffenberg, *Statut et Règlement de la Cour permanente de Justice internationale, Eléments d'interprétation*, Carl Heymans Verlag, Berlin, 1934, pp. 454–456.

57 *Série D n°2, Add.*, pp. 184–193 (v. aussi pp. 267–268 et 288–293 (proposition de D. Anzilotti), p. 277 et pp. 298–299 (proposition de M. Beichmann), et pp. 253–259 (proposition de M. Huber)). Une majorité des membres de la Cour fut alors d'avis que la question touchait

apporté au Règlement en 1927 devait cependant compléter l'assimilation, déjà largement réalisée, de la procédure consultative à la procédure contentieuse, compte tenu de l'importance prise par la fonction consultative de la Cour et des risques apparus en pratique que des Etats parties à un différend sur lequel eût porté une demande d'avis pussent se retrouver dans une situation d'inégalité au regard de la composition de la Cour.[58] En effet, jusqu'alors, l'usage avait été d'exclure l'application de l'article 31 du Statut dans la procédure consultative,[59] mais cette exclusion avait été sans effet pratique pour les Etats directement concernés, soit que ceux-ci eussent déjà compté un juge national sur le siège,[60] soit qu'aucun d'entre eux n'en eût compté un.[61] En 1927, la Cour réexamina la question du droit des Etats de désigner un juge *ad hoc* dans le cadre d'une demande d'avis consultatif, comme suite aux difficultés qui s'étaient présentées dans la procédure relative à la *Compétence de la commission européenne du Danube* : celles-ci n'avaient pu être résolues que du fait de l'empêchement fortuit d'un juge titulaire et de son remplacement par un juge suppléant de la nationalité de l'Etat qui ne disposait initialement pas d'un juge de sa nationalité sur le siège.[62]

à la constitution de la Cour et ne relevait pas du domaine de la compétence réglementaire de cette dernière, v. également *Série E n°3*, p. 226.

58 V. le rapport du comité (composé de MM. Loder, Moore et Anzilotti), chargé d'examiner la question en 1927, *Série E n°4*, pp. 71 et s.

59 V. la réponse apportée en ce sens par le Greffier de la Cour à la notification par la Turquie de la désignation d'un juge national dans la procédure relative à *l'Echange des populations grecques et turques*, *Série C n°7*, pp. 238–239. C'est le seul cas dans lequel la Cour (en l'espèce le Président, la Cour ne siégeant pas) eut à statuer sur la question, *cf.* les observations du Greffier *in Série D n°2, Add.*, p. 191. Le point fut toutefois également discuté par la Cour, à l'occasion de la demande d'avis consultatif dans l'affaire de Mossoul (*Interprétation de l'article 2, paragraphe 3, du Traité de Lausanne, Série B n°12*), « de savoir si la Turquie ne devait pas être invitée à désigner un juge *ad hoc*, puisque l'autre Partie intéressée, la Grande-Bretagne, comptait au sein de la Cour un juge de sa nationalité. Le débat qui suivit montra que la Cour, sans préjuger en rien des changements qui pourraient par la suite être apportés au Règlement, ne désirait pas modifier l'usage suivi jusque là et notamment lors de l'Avis consultatif n°10 », *Série E n°3*, p. 226.

60 Tel était le cas de la France et du Royaume-Uni dans la procédure relative aux *Décrets de nationalité promulgués en Tunisie et au Maroc*, avis consultatif du 7 février 1923, *Série B n°4*, p. 7.

61 V., par exemple, *Statut de la Carélie orientale*, avis consultatif du 23 juillet 1923, *Série B n°5* et *Série E n°3*, pp. 225–226.

62 V. *Série E n°4*, p. 73. Dans cette procédure, la Roumanie compta en effet sur le siège, dans la personne du juge suppléant Négulesco, un juge de sa nationalité, à l'instar de la France, du Royaume-Uni et de l'Italie, *Série B n°14*, avis consultatif du 8 décembre 1927.

La Ville libre de Dantzig et la Pologne furent les premières à bénéficier de l'introduction, dans le Règlement, d'une disposition rendant possible la désignation d'un juge *ad hoc* dans une procédure consultative, sans que la Cour ne motive particulièrement l'application du nouvel article 71 dans le cas d'espèce.[63] A la suite du renouvellement de la composition de la Cour en 1930, et de l'élection comme membre de la Cour du comte Rostworowski, de nationalité polonaise, seule la Ville libre désigna, dans les procédures ultérieures, un juge *ad hoc*; elle y fut autorisée en étant expressément qualifiée dans ce contexte d'« Etat » au sens du Règlement.[64]

La reconnaissance à Dantzig de la faculté de désigner un juge *ad hoc* n'appelait, dans ces affaires, guère de discussion, dans la mesure où l'existence d'un « différend », relatif à l'étendue des droits et obligations internationales réciproques de la Pologne et de la Ville libre, était manifeste. Aux fins de l'application du Règlement en matière consultative, la pratique de la Cour permanente a constamment témoigné d'une approche réaliste, conforme à l'esprit dans

---

63   *Compétence des tribunaux de Dantzig (Réclamations pécuniaires des fonctionnaires ferroviaires dantzikois passés au service polonais contre l'Administration polonaise des chemins de fer), avis consultatif du 3 mars 1928, Série B n°15*, p. 4. Le Greffier appela l'attention des deux parties sur la possibilité de désigner un juge *ad hoc* à la suite de la modification apportée au Règlement, v. *Série C n°14*, pp. 516–517, 519. Sous l'empire du Statut de 1920 et du premier Règlement de la CPJI, les juges *ad hoc* (alors dénommés « juges nationaux ») devaient être de la nationalité de l'Etat les désignant (cette exigence fut formellement abandonnée à la suite de la révision du Règlement en 1936). Il est intéressant de relever que, dans le cas d'espèce, la Ville libre désigna initialement un ressortissant dantzikois, M. Crusen, qui fut empêché pour raison de santé, quelques jours avant l'ouverture des audiences, d'exercer ses fonctions. La Ville libre désigna alors en remplacement un juge de nationalité allemande (M. Bruns), v. *Série C n°14*, p. 529 et pp. 549–550. La Pologne désigna un juge de nationalité polonaise (M. Ehrlich). Dans la procédure relative à *La Ville libre de Dantzig et l'Organisation internationale du Travail*, la Pologne et la Ville libre de Dantzig ne firent l'objet que de la communication spéciale et directe, prévue à l'article 73 du Règlement, et ni l'une ni l'autre ne demandèrent à désigner un juge *ad hoc*, avis consultatif du 26 août 1930, *Série B n°18*, p. 4.

64   *Accès et stationnement des navires de guerre polonais dans le port de Dantzig, avis consultatif du 11 décembre 1931, Série A/B n°43*, p. 128 : « La Cour a estimé que la question à elle soumise pour avis consultatif visait un différend actuellement né entre la Ville libre de Dantzig et la Pologne au sens de l'article 71, alinéa 2, du Règlement. *Comme un seul de ces Etats – la Pologne – comptait sur le siège un juge de sa nationalité*, le Sénat de la Ville libre de Dantzig s'est prévalu de son droit, conformément à l'article 71 du Règlement, de désigner, pour siéger dans l'affaire, un juge *ad hoc* » [italiques ajoutés] ; *Traitement des nationaux polonais et des autres personnes d'origine ou de langue polonaise dans le territoire de Dantzig, Série A/B n°44*, p. 8 (*idem*). La Ville libre a également désigné M. Bruns pour siéger en qualité de juge *ad hoc* dans ces deux procédures consultatives.

lequel ces questions de nature préalable et procédurale paraissaient devoir être tranchées.[65] De la sorte, indépendamment de la qualification abstraite et générale de la Ville libre de Dantzig au regard du droit international, la Cour a privilégié l'égalité des « parties » se trouvant effectivement en litige sur le fond des questions faisant l'objet des demandes d'avis consultatif.

C'est pour un tel motif, précisément, que la Cour permanente a rejeté la demande de la Ville libre de Dantzig de pouvoir désigner un juge *ad hoc* dans l'affaire de la *Compatibilité de certains décrets-lois dantzikois avec la Constitution de la Ville libre*.[66] Dans l'ordonnance rendue sur cette question, la Cour permanente souligna le fait qu'aux termes de l'article 31 du Statut « la présence éventuelle de juges *ad hoc* [était] exclusivement prévue pour le cas où il y a[vait] des parties devant la Cour » et considéra « que tel n'[était] pas le cas dans la présente affaire ».[67] La CPJI précisa en outre que l'application de l'article 31 du Statut à la procédure en matière consultative, conformément à l'article 71, alinéa 2, du Règlement, « constitu[ait] la seule exception à la règle générale [concernant la composition de la Cour] » et qu'en conséquence elle ne « saurait être étendue au-delà des limites qui lui [avaient] été réglementairement fixées ».[68] Les arguments d'opportunité avancés par le représentant de la Ville libre, qui avait invoqué les avantages que pouvait représenter la participation

---

65   Le comité chargé d'examiner la question de la désignation d'un juge *ad hoc* dans le cadre d'une procédure consultative souligna à cet égard la différence « purement nominale » qui pouvait exister entre les affaires contentieuses et les affaires consultatives, *Série E n°4*, p. 72.

66   *Série A/B n°65*, p. 44 (avis consultatif du 31 octobre 1935) et pp. 70–71 (ordonnance du 31 octobre 1935). La Ville libre de Dantzig fut invitée à exposer les motifs de sa demande à l'ouverture des audiences tenues sur la requête pour avis consultatif. Le jour suivant, le Président déclara à l'audience que la Cour avait décidé qu'il n'y avait pas lieu de faire droit à cette demande et que cette décision ferait l'objet d'une ordonnance dont la rédaction serait établie ultérieurement.

67   *Ibid.*, p. 70.

68   *Ibid.*, p. 71. Dans la procédure consultative relative à la *Namibie*, la Cour actuelle s'est référée à cette décision et a estimé, de la même manière, « ne pas être en mesure d'exercer un pouvoir discrétionnaire » aux fins d'accéder à la demande de l'Afrique du Sud de désigner un juge *ad hoc*, *Conséquences juridiques pour les Etats de la présence continue de l'Afrique du Sud en Namibie (Sud-Ouest africain) nonobstant la résolution 276 (1970) du Conseil de sécurité*, avis consultatif, CIJ Recueil 1971, pp. 23–27, par. 39. La question s'est à nouveau posée dans le cadre de la procédure consultative relative au *Sahara occidental*. Il s'agissait de savoir si, dès lors que la requête pour avis consultatif ne portait pas sur « une question juridique actuellement pendante » entre l'Espagne et la Mauritanie rendant applicable l'article 31 du Statut conformément à l'article 89 [actuel 102, paragraphe 3] du Règlement de la Cour, la Cour avait néanmoins le pouvoir d'autoriser la désignation par la Mauritanie

d'un juge *ad hoc* qui soit entièrement au courant du droit constitutionnel dantzikois,[69] n'y changeaient rien.

Dans le cas d'espèce, la demande d'avis consultatif présentée à la Cour permanente ne portait pas sur l'un des « différends » entre la Ville libre et la Pologne, visés par le Traité de Versailles, qu'il revenait aux organes de la Société des Nations (Haut-Commissaire et Conseil) de régler.[70] Saisie d'une question juridique « abstraite » de compatibilité entre, d'une part, deux décrets adoptés par le Sénat de la Ville libre, relatifs au droit pénal et à la procédure pénale, et, d'autre part, la Constitution dantzikoise,[71] la Cour permanente se trouvait en réalité placée, plus largement, devant la contestation, par les partis minoritaires composant l'Assemblée populaire de la Ville libre, de la politique mise en œuvre à travers ces décrets par le parti national-socialiste devenu majoritaire au sein de cette Assemblée. Dans ce contexte, le rôle de la Cour ne consistait pas à donner un avis au sujet d'un différend international, mais participait du mécanisme de garantie de la Constitution de Dantzig par la Société des Nations.[72] Aussi bien, du point de vue de l'organisation de la procédure, la principale question soulevée ne touchait-elle pas à l'égalité entre la Pologne et la Ville libre de Dantzig,[73] mais à l'éventuelle participation des différentes entités politiques composant cette dernière.

Sur ce dernier point, la CPJI a implicitement distingué la qualité officielle en vertu de laquelle la Ville libre était autorisée, conformément au Règlement, à participer à la procédure tant écrite qu'orale, et la faculté octroyée à titre spécial

---

d'un juge *ad hoc*. La Cour a rejeté la demande présentée à cette fin par la Mauritanie, *Sahara occidental*, CIJ *Recueil 1975*, pp. 6–8.

69 *Série A/B n°65*, p. 70. V. sur ce point l'exposé préliminaire de l'agent de la Ville libre, *Série C n°77*, pp. 171–179.

70 Article 103, second alinéa, du Traité de Versailles. V. *supra* note 18.

71 Dans la résolution adoptée le 23 septembre 1935, le Conseil de la SDN avait prié la Cour de donner un avis consultatif « sur la question de savoir si lesdits décrets [étaient] compatibles avec la Constitution de Dantzig ou si, au contraire, ils viol[ai]ent une des dispositions ou un des principes de ladite Constitution », *Série A/B n°65*, p. 42.

72 *Ibid.*, pp. 49–50 : « Encore que l'interprétation de la Constitution de Dantzig soit essentiellement une question d'ordre interne, il est clair que cette interprétation peut engager la garantie de la Société des Nations [...]. Il s'ensuit qu'une pétition, telle [que celle présentée au Haut-Commissaire par certains partis politiques de Dantzig] met nécessairement en jeu la garantie, par la Société des Nations, de la Constitution de Dantzig. Ceci suffit à établir l'existence d'un élément international dans le problème posé par la pétition qui a abouti à la demande d'avis du Conseil ». V. sur ce point l'opinion dissidente du Juge Anzilotti, *ibid.*, pp. 60–63.

73 Seule Dantzig fit l'objet, dans cette affaire, de la communication spéciale et directe prévue par l'article 73 du Règlement, v. *supra* note 54.

par la Cour aux auteurs de la pétition de pouvoir compléter celle-ci par le dépôt d'une « note explicative ».[74] Si le Sénat de la Ville libre et les partis politiques minoritaires de Dantzig ne se trouvaient pas ainsi sur un pied d'égalité dans la procédure devant la CPJI, cette dernière n'a pas pour autant considéré qu'il était de ce fait porté atteinte à une règle fondamentale de procédure et que la Cour n'aurait dès lors pas été en mesure de répondre à la demande d'avis.[75] A cet égard, en effet, les différents partis politiques intéressés ne pouvaient être placés sur le même plan que la Ville libre de Dantzig, dont l'existence internationale, quelle qu'en fût la qualification exacte, était directement fondée sur le Traité de Versailles.

Les précédents afférents au traitement de Dantzig ont certainement constitué une étape importante dans l'évolution de la pratique et des règles concernant la participation à la procédure consultative devant la Cour permanente. Comme on le sait, les dispositions de l'article 73 du Règlement de la Cour, tel que révisé en 1926,[76] furent transférées à l'article 66 du Statut, lors de la révision de ce dernier, opérée en 1929 et entrée en vigueur en 1936. Alors que le projet préparé par le Comité de juristes ne faisait plus mention des « organisations internationales » susceptibles de fournir des renseignements à la Cour, sans que des explications eussent été données sur cet abandon, les termes de l'article 73 furent réintroduits lors de la Conférence de révision, à la suite d'importantes discussions,[77] avec un seul changement : la communication spéciale et directe, en vue du dépôt d'exposés écrits et de la présentation d'exposés oraux, devait être effectuée « à tout Membre de la Société, à tout Etat admis à ester

---

74   *Série A/B n°65*, p. 43.

75   Telle était en revanche la position adoptée par le Juge Anzilotti, v. son opinion dissidente sur ce point, *ibid.*, pp. 63–66. Selon le juge dissident, la question mettait en réalité en jeu un différend relevant de l'ordre constitutionnel dantzikois, et la procédure suivie conduisait en conséquence nécessairement à enfreindre la règle fondamentale de l'égalité des parties, ce qui renforçait sa conclusion selon laquelle la Cour permanente ne pouvait donner l'avis demandé.

76   V. *supra* note 53.

77   Le Directeur du Bureau international du Travail avait exprimé, dans une lettre adressée au Secrétaire général de la Société des Nations, sa préoccupation que soit remise en cause, par cette suppression, une procédure qui s'était avérée utile par le passé. Au cours de la Conférence, il fut proposé d'accorder un traitement différencié au Bureau international, d'une part, et aux organisations non gouvernementales, d'autres part ; il fut en particulier soutenu que la formule utilisée dans le Règlement de la Cour « était trop large et pouvait donner lieu à certains abus » (v. *Procès-verbal de la Conférence concernant la révision du Statut de la Cour permanente de Justice internationale, tenue à Genève du 4 au 12 septembre 1929*, Société des Nations, p. 43 et s.).

devant la Cour et à toute organisation internationale *jugés* [et non plus jugée] [...] susceptibles de fournir des renseignements sur la question ».[78] Si les termes choisis reflétaient l'exigence d'une décision de la Cour quant aux Membres, Etats ou organisations internationales dont la participation à la procédure pouvait être autorisée dans chaque cas d'espèce, ils laissaient néanmoins toujours à la Cour une certaine marge d'appréciation quant à la nature des « organisations internationales » susceptibles d'être invitées sur la base de l'article 66 du Statut, tenant ainsi compte d'une pratique antérieure assez flexible.[79,80]

***

---

78   Italiques ajoutés. V. *Série D n°2, 3ᵉ Add.*, pp. 376 et 926. Sous réserve de l'abandon de la référence aux Membres de la Société des Nations, l'article 66 est demeuré inchangé dans le Statut de la Cour actuelle.

79   Sur le fondement de l'article 73, alinéa 2, tel qu'initialement rédigé (v. *supra* note 51), comme ultérieurement, la Cour permanente a notamment invité plusieurs associations, fédérations et syndicats de caractère international, intéressés dans les questions soumises pour avis consultatif, à présenter des exposés écrits et à être entendus lors d'audiences publiques, v. *Désignation du délégué ouvrier néerlandais à la troisième session de la Conférence internationale du Travail, Série B n°1*, avis du 31 juillet 1922, p. 9 ; *Compétence de l'OIT pour la réglementation internationale des conditions du travail des personnes employées dans l'agriculture, Série B n°2*, avis du 12 août 1922, p. 9 ; *Compétence de l'OIT pour réglementer accessoirement le travail personnel du patron, Série B n°13*, avis du 23 juillet 1926, p. 8 ; *Interprétation de la convention de 1919 concernant le travail de nuit des femmes, Série A/B n°50*, avis du 15 novembre 1932, p. 367. La reconnaissance par la Cour de la qualité d'« organisations internationales », au sens du Règlement de la Cour, à ces diverses entités, pouvait être reliée au statut consultatif dont jouissaient ces dernières auprès de l'OIT, conformément à l'article 12, par. 3, de la Constitution de l'OIT Cette pratique ne couvrait pas « les organismes purement nationaux », v. la lettre du Greffier en réponse à l'Union syndicale des techniciens de l'industrie, du commerce et de l'agriculture, *Série C n°1*, p. 449 (lettre du 23 juin 1922).

80   La Cour actuelle continue d'exercer une certaine discrétion en mettant en œuvre l'article 66 du Statut. V. à ce sujet, par exemple, les mesures prises à l'effet de permettre la participation de la Palestine dans la procédure consultative relative aux *Conséquences juridiques de l'édification d'un mur dans le territoire palestinien occupé* (ordonnance du 19 décembre 2003, *CIJ Recueil 2003*, p. 428) ou des auteurs de la déclaration d'indépendance du Kosovo dans la procédure relative à la *Conformité au droit international de la déclaration unilatérale d'indépendance relative au Kosovo* (ordonnance du 17 octobre 2008, *CIJ Recueil 2008*, p. 409). Bien qu'ayant une fois, par le passé, autorisé la participation d'une organisation non gouvernementale dans une procédure consultative (la Ligue internationale des droits de l'homme, dans la procédure consultative relative au *Statut international du Sud-Ouest africain*, v. *Mémoires, Plaidoiries et documents*, pp. 327 et 346), la Cour a depuis

Les observations qui précèdent n'auront certainement fait qu'effleurer l'ensemble des questions juridiques, parfois complexes, qui se sont posées au regard de l'histoire et du statut particulier de Dantzig. Ces quelques lignes n'avaient en effet d'autre objet que de rappeler succinctement comment les spécificités de la Ville libre se sont manifestées dans la pratique, notamment consultative, de la Cour permanente de Justice internationale. Au terme de cette brève entreprise, il est intéressant de noter combien certaines préoccupations actuelles continuent de faire écho à des interrogations présentes dès les débuts de la juridiction internationale permanente, notamment en ce qui concerne la nécessité d'élaborer des règles de procédure qui puissent répondre, avec flexibilité, aux exigences générales de la bonne administration de la justice dans le contexte d'une société internationale donnée.

---

adopté une attitude plus restrictive à cet égard (voir l'Instruction de procédure XII adoptée par la Cour en 2004, CIJ Actes et documents n°6, p. 170). Sur les modalités arrêtées par la Cour pour permettre aux fonctionnaires intéressés de « participer » aux procédures de réformation des jugements des tribunaux administratifs, v. par exemple l'ordonnance du 29 avril 2010 dans la procédure relative au *Jugement n°2687 du Tribunal administratif de l'Organisation internationale du Travail sur requête contre le Fonds international de développement agricole*, CIJ Recueil 2010, p. 298 ; la Cour a exprimé à cet égard son souci de voir respectée l'égalité des « parties » dans la procédure, *id.*, avis consultatif du 1er février 2012, paragraphes 44–47.

CHAPTER 2

Macedonian-Greek Relations and the ICJ Judgment of 5 December 2011

*Toni Deskoski**

I Introduction

On 5 December 2011 the International Court of Justice (hereinafter: ICJ), delivered a Judgment which declared that Greece had violated Article 11, paragraph 1, of the Interim Accord of 1995, when it objected to the extending of an invitation to Macedonia to proceed to NATO membership under the provisional reference of 'the former Yugoslav Republic of Macedonia' at the Bucharest Summit in April 2008.[1] The Judgment also declared that the Greek veto at the Bucharest Summit cannot be justified by the failure of the two parties to reach an agreement on the name difference for more than 16 years.[2]

This article addresses the possible influences of the ICJ Judgment of 5 December 2011 on the improvement of the relations between the two countries in the future, by virtue of interpretation of the vital provisions of the 1995 Interim Accord, and the obligations of the parties provided therein. Although the case resolved by the ICJ was not on the 'difference over name', still the Court ruled on several issues which are inextricably connected to this issue, and will most likely have a direct impact on the future developments. The main focus will be on determining if and to what extent the Court has contributed towards the final settlement of the 'difference over the name', which is the only unresolved issue between the two countries. An attempt will be made to provide answers to several questions: can the factual situation as established by the Court identify the errors and misinterpretations on which the parties had built their positions on the 'difference over the name' for a long time, thereby enabling them to depart from those errors and misinterpretations?

---

* Associate Professor at the Ss. Cyril and Methodius University, 'Iustinianus Primus' Faculty of Law, Skopje, Republic of Macedonia.
1 Application of the Interim Accord of 13 September 1995 (the former Yugoslav Republic of Macedonia v. Greece), Judgment of 5 December 2011, *ICJ Reports 2011*, p. 644 (hereinafter: the Judgment), paragraph 168; the text of the Judgment is available at: <http://www.icj-cij.org/docket/files/142/16827.pdf>.
2 The Judgment, paragraph 134.

Also, can the Judgment of the Court contribute towards achieving a substantial breakthrough that would lead to the final resolution of the 'name difference'?

II   The Background of the 'Difference over the Name'

When the process of dissolution of the former Socialist Federal Republic of Yugoslavia (hereinafter: Yugoslavia) reached its mature phase in mid-1991, it was clear that new states would emerge on the map of Europe. One of them was Macedonia, the most southerly member of the Federation. From the very beginning of this process, Greece had vigorously opposed the establishing of the new state on its northern border. It relied on the explanation that the newly emerged state would jeopardize peace and stability in the region. From the very moment that Macedonia declared its independence in late 1991, it lived in the shadow of the bilateral difference over its name imposed by Greece.[3] The country suffered a lot of injuries because of this difference, one of them being the unlawful Greek veto of extending to Macedonia the invitation to NATO membership at the Bucharest Summit, held on 2–4 April 2008,[4]

---

3   The Foreign Ministry of Greece summarized its concerns in the following manner:
"The issue of the name of the *Former Yugoslav Republic of Macedonia* is not just a dispute over historical facts or symbols. It concerns the conduct of a UN member state, the *Former Yugoslav Republic of Macedonia*, which contravenes the fundamental principles of international law and order; specifically, respect for good neighbourly relations, sovereignty and territorial integrity.
    The name issue is thus a problem with regional and international dimensions, consisting in the promotion of irredentist and territorial ambitions on the part of the *Former Yugoslav Republic of Macedonia*, mainly through the counterfeiting of history and usurpation of Greece's national and historical heritage." – see: "FYROM Name Issue", available at: <http://www.mfa.gr/en/fyrom-name-issue> (29 March 2013).
4   The Bucharest Summit Declaration, paragraph 20 provided:
"We recognise the hard work and the commitment demonstrated by the former Yugoslav Republic of Macedonia to NATO values and Alliance operations. We commend them for their efforts to build a multi-ethnic society. Within the framework of the United Nations, many actors have worked hard to resolve the name issue, but the Alliance has noted with regret that these talks have not produced a successful outcome. Therefore *we agreed that an invitation to the former Yugoslav Republic of Macedonia will be extended as soon as a mutually acceptable solution to the name issue has been reached.* We encourage the negotiations to be resumed without delay and expect them to be concluded as soon as possible." (emphasis added) – see: NATO Press Release (2008) 049, *Bucharest Summit Declaration Issued by the Heads of State and Government participating in the meeting of the North Atlantic Council in*

and the blocking of the opening of the accession negotiations between Macedonia and the EU since 2009.

Back in 1992, Greece had articulated its concerns through the EC Council of Foreign Ministers, which adopted the Declaration on Yugoslavia and the Declaration on the Guidelines on the Recognition of New States in Eastern Europe and the Soviet Union ('the Guidelines').[5] It was not a secret that only upon the insistence of the then Greek Foreign Minister, Andonis Samaras, were three additional conditions for recognition included in the Declaration for Yugoslavia[6]: first, a commitment from the Yugoslav Republics "prior to recognition, to adopt constitutional and political guarantees ensuring that it has no territorial claims towards a neighbouring community State"; second, that they would "conduct no hostile propaganda activities versus a neighbouring community State"; and, third, not to use "a denomination which implies territorial claims." Greek commentators emphasised that "the wording confirms that the Greek position was focused specifically on security concerns, in particular that their northern neighbour should not constitute a base for interests hostile to Greece; that any possibility of stirring up and promoting irredentist demands and visions should be nipped in the bud; and that specific commitment should be given not to engage in 'hostile propaganda'."[7]

One would have expected that upon transposition of the Greek demands in the Declaration for Yugoslavia, Greece would have no problems with accepting the opinion of the Badinter Arbitration Commission,[8] which was mandated to assess claims for recognition. However, when the Badinter Commission issued

---

Bucharest on 3 April 2008 (3 April 2008), available at: <http://www.nato.int/docu/pr/2008/p08-049e.html>.

5   Declaration on the 'Guidelines on the Recognition of New States in Eastern Europe and the Soviet Union', annexed at Annex II to a letter dated 17 December 1991 from the Representatives of Belgium, France and the United Kingdom of Great Britain and Northern Ireland addressed to the President of the United Nations Security Council, UN Doc. S/23293 (17 December 1991).

6   See P. Pazartzis, "La reconnaissance d' 'une république yougoslave': la question de l'ancienne République yougoslave de Macédoine (ARYM)", 41 *Annuaire français de droit international*, 1995, pp. 281–297; see also M. Wood, "Participation of Former Yugoslav States in the United Nations and in Multilateral Treaties", 1 *Max Planck Yearbook of United Nations Law*, 1997, pp. 231–257, p. 237, note 19.

7   E. Kofos, "The Unresolved 'Difference over the Name', A Greek Perspective", in: E. Kofos, V. Vlasidis (eds.) *Athens-Skopje: An Uneasy Symbiosis (1995–2002)*, ELIAMEP, Athens, 2005, pp. 125–223, p. 127.

8   Arbitration Commission of the Peace Conference on the Former Yugoslavia, established by the EC and comprised of the Presidents of the Constitutional Courts of France, Germany, Italy and Spain and the President of the Belgian Court of Arbitration. It was chaired by Robert Badinter, the President of the French Constitutional Court.

its Opinion No. 6 of 14 January 1992 (hereinafter: Badinter Opinion No. 6),[9] determining that Macedonia had fulfilled all the conditions for recognition as determined by the EC, emphasising explicitly that "the use of the name 'Macedonia' cannot therefore imply any territorial claim against another State",[10] Greece resolutely refused to accept it and directly caused the EC Member states to decline to grant recognition to Macedonia. The two amendments to the Constitution of the Republic of Macedonia which were adopted on 6 January 1992,[11] where it was explicitly provided that Macedonia had no territorial claims against neighbouring states, confirmed the inviolability of the state borders, and declared that Macedonia would not interfere in the sovereign rights of other states or in their internal affairs, although evaluated in a positive manner by the Commission, turned out to be insufficient for Greece to change its position of firm resistance to the recognition.[12] Badinter Opinion No. 6 had actually revealed that whatever the Greek concerns of that time were, they did not concern any stability and security issues.

Although the EC countries at that time officially demonstrated solidarity with Greece, they were working behind the scenes to overcome Greek resistance towards recognition of Macedonia and its integration into the international community. In early 1993, the three EU members of the Security Council – the United Kingdom, France and Spain – took the lead in putting together a new package with which both Greece and Macedonia were prepared to live.[13] This enabled the admission of Macedonia to membership of the United Nations (UN). The Security Council adopted Resolution 817 (1993) of 7 April 1993, which recommended to the General Assembly that the state be admitted to membership of the UN. The Resolution therefore differed from the standard Security Council resolution recommending admission of a state. The name of the state appeared nowhere in the resolution, but it was identified as "the state whose application is contained in document S/25147" or simply as "the State".

---

9   Arbitration Commission of the Conference on Yugoslavia, *Opinion No. 6 on the Recognition of the Socialist Republic of Macedonia by the European Community and its Member States* (14 January 1992) annexed at Annex III to the letter dated 26 May 1993 from the United Nations Secretary-General to the President of the Security Council, UN Doc. S/25855 (28 May 1993).

10 Badinter Opinion No. 6, paragraph 5.

11 Amendments I and II to the Constitution of the Republic of Macedonia, *Official Gazette of the Republic of Macedonia*, No. 1/1992.

12 It is awkward that Greece claimed in its written submissions to the Court that the amending of the constitution was agreed in 1995 by the conclusion of the Interim Accord – See: Counter-Memorial, Vol. I, paragraph 2.28.

13 M. Wood, *op. cit.*, p. 238.

It recommended that admission was to be granted, "this State being provisionally referred to for all purposes within the United Nations as 'the former Yugoslav Republic of Macedonia' pending settlement of the difference that has arisen over the name of the State." Such recommendation was agreed by the General Assembly, which passed Resolution 225 on the following day, 8 April, using virtually the same language as the Security Council.

1   The Conclusion of the 1995 Interim Accord

The admission of Macedonia to UN membership led to a vast number of recognitions from other states all over the world, including from EC member states. Still, it did not lead to the immediate normalisation of relations between Macedonia and Greece. Instead, Greece imposed an economic embargo on Macedonia on 16 February 1994 and continued to hinder Macedonia's efforts to obtain membership of international organisations and institutions, especially in the OSCE and the Council of Europe. Greece also opposed the newly adopted national flag of Macedonia, which depicted the historical symbol of a 'Sixteen Rayed Sun', known in Greece as a 'Vergina star' or in Macedonia as a 'Sun from Kutlesh' (hereinafter: Sixteen Rayed Sun).

In the first week of September 1995, the United States assistant secretary of state, Richard Holbrooke, stated that an agreement had been formulated to put an end to the dispute between Macedonia and Greece in which both countries had agreed to reach a compromise in the name of peace in the Balkans.[14]

As a result of the pragmatic approach, in order to exclude the name issue as an obstacle for the designation of the parties to the Interim Accord, the Parties to the Accord are referred to as 'the party of the First Part' (Greece) and 'the Party of the Second Part' (Republic of Macedonia). Although Macedonia had never disputed the name of its southern neighbour, it agreed to remain nameless in the Accord, under condition of the reciprocal treatment of Greece. This gave an impression of equality between the Parties, which was so necessary for the Macedonian side.

The Interim Accord of 1995 settled many bilateral issues with reciprocal compromises, while permitting the postponement of any final resolution of the name dispute. This sensitive and critical issue seemed to be gradually drifting towards the political margins, particularly in Greece.[15] Greece undertook to

---

14   J. Shea, *Macedonia and Greece: The Struggle to Define a New Balkan Nation*, Jefferson, North Carolina, 1997, p. 304.
15   A. Tziampiris, "The Name Dispute in the Former Yugoslav Republic of Macedonia after the Signing of the Interim Accord", in: E. Kofos, V. Vlasidis (eds.), *Athens-Skopje: An Uneasy Symbiosis (1995–2002)*, ELIAMEP, Athens, 2005, pp. 225–252, p. 229.

put an end to the economically painful embargo (Article 8) and committed itself not to hinder Macedonia's efforts to obtain membership of international organisations and institutions (Article 11, paragraph 1). Macedonia agreed to change its national flag and to abandon using the 'Sixteen Rayed Sun' (Article 7, paragraph 2), and made a clarification and interpretation of a number of provisions in its constitution which were deemed satisfactory for Greece (Article 6). Both parties agreed to continue negotiations on the name difference under the auspices of the Secretary-General of the United Nations (Article 5, paragraph 1).

III The Dispute Submitted to the Court

Macedonia's expectations of receiving an invitation to accede to NATO during the 2–4 April Bucharest Summit of NATO were not met, due to Greece's resistance to extending such an invitation, without having the difference over the name resolved first. Therefore, Macedonia unilaterally took to the Court the case concerning the violation of the 1995 Interim Accord, under Article 36, para. 1 of the Statute of the Court. As an Applicant state, it was under an obligation to indicate the subject of the dispute in its Application, pursuant to Article 40 of the Statute and Article 36 of the Rules of the Court.

Applicants can take advantage of their obligation to indicate the subject of the dispute by having the right to choose the formulation of the subject.[16] The Macedonian Application narrowed the case brought before the ICJ to the most possible extent. It concerned the breach of only one Treaty obligation by Greece, the one provided in Article 11, paragraph 1 of the Interim Accord,[17] which was in violation of the *pacta sunt servanda* principle.[18] The jurisdiction

---

16 M. Kawano, "The Role of Judicial Procedures in the Process of the Pacific Settlement of International Disputes", 346 *Collected Courses of the Hague Academy of International Law (Recueil des Cours)*, 2009, p. 64.

17 Article 11, paragraph 1 of the Interim Accord provides:
"Upon entry into force of this Interim Accord, The Party of the First Part agrees not to object to the application by or the membership of the Party of the Second Part in international, multilateral and regional organizations and institutions of which the Party of the First Part is a member; however, the Party of the First Part reserves the right to object to any membership referred to above if and to the extent of the Party of the Second Part is to be referred to in such organization or institution differently than in paragraph 2 of the United Nations Security Council resolution 817 (1993)."

18 See: Application instituting proceedings filed in the Registry of the Court on 17 November 2008, paragraph 23, available at: <http://www.icj-cij.org/docket/files/142/14879.pdf>.

of the Court was invoked on the compromissory clause in Article 21, paragraph 2 of the Interim Accord.

However, despite the simplicity of the Application, the Greek response was to develop a very complex procedural and substantive defence strategy. It was set on three levels: first, that the Court lacked jurisdiction to resolve the dispute; second, even if the Court found that it had jurisdiction to hear the case, that Greece was not in breach of Article 11, paragraph 1 of the Interim Accord; and, third, even if it had breached Article 11, paragraph 1 of the Interim Accord, it was excused from liability by virtue of the procedural defences provided in international law. As is emphasised by some authors, "in its most simplified form, Greece's line of defence can be understood as a series of no less than nine hierarchical propositions, each subsidiary to all preceding ones..."[19] Eventually, they were all rejected by the Court.

1   Compromissory Clause as a Basis for the Jurisdiction of the Court

The Interim Accord is a treaty between one powerful and economically developed state on the one hand, and a small one which was at the beginning of the road of independence, was economically fragile and located in a very troubled region, on the other. In international relations "effective legal procedures for dispute settlement are especially important for small countries and for economically weak States. While the larger and more powerful countries can apply extra-legal, political and economic pressures, it is safer for smaller and weaker ones to have the dispute directed into legal channels where the principle of equality before law prevails."[20] Less powerful states in particular require assurances that the promises of powerful states are credible. The remedies available to them if they win a case may provide some bargaining leverage, but they rely much more on the prospect that the court process and eventual decision will help mobilise other major states to put pressure on the powerful state in order to maintain the rule governed system and respect for its institutions.[21] For all the third parties that were involved in assisting the negotiating process it must have been crystal clear that an effective dispute

---

19   F. Messineo, "Maps of Ephemeral Empires: The ICJ and the Macedonian Name Dispute", 1 *Cambridge Journal of International and Comparative Law*, 2012, pp. 169–190, p. 178.

20   L.B. Sohn, "Settlement of Disputes Relating to the Interpretation and Application of Treaties", 150 *Collected Courses of the Hague Academy of International Law (Recueil des Cours)*, 1976/II, p. 205.

21   B. Kingsbury, "International Courts: Uneven Judicialisation in Global Order", in: J. Crawford, M. Koskenniemi (eds.), *The Cambridge Companion to International Law*, Cambridge, 2012, pp. 203–227, pp. 217–218.

settlement procedure had to be provided. The International Court of Justice was a logical choice for the two countries, since "the procedural system of the Court is, in principle, designed to settle bilateral disputes."[22] A compromissory clause was inserted in Article 21, paragraph 2 of the Interim Accord which provides:

> Any difference or dispute that arises between the Parties concerning the interpretation or implementation of this Interim Accord may be submitted by either of them to the International Court of Justice, except for the differences referred to in Article 5, paragraph 1.

For many, jurisdiction has the reputation of being a technical matter and thus of having a rather dry appeal, and not without cause.[23] At the time of the conclusion of the Interim Accord and during the entire period until early 2008, the Macedonian authorities did not pay any attention to the compromissory clause of Article 21, paragraph 2. According to the then Foreign Minister, Antonio Miloshoski, the Macedonian Ministry of Foreign Affairs had not previously considered the triggering of the compromissory clause as a possible reaction to eventual Greek veto.[24]

a   Greek Objections to Jurisdiction and Admissibility

As a compromissory clause enables the contracting parties to submit the dispute regarding that convention unilaterally, the filing of the Application essentially lacks prior consent from the other party with regard to the contents or scope of the 'dispute' alleged by the Applicant. The lack of such prior consent may result "in objections from the respondent to the fulfilment of the conditions provided in the compromissory clause invoked."[25]

Greece raised objections as to the ICJ's jurisdiction and the admissibility of the case, but decided to address them together with the merits, rather than raising preliminary objections.[26] The objection on jurisdiction claimed, first, that the dispute before the Court concerned the difference over the name of

---

22   M. Kawano, *op.cit.*, p. 34.
23   B. Simma, A.T. Müller, "Exercise and Limits of Jurisdiction", in: J. Crawford, M. Koskenniemi (eds.), *The Cambridge Companion to International Law*, Cambridge, 2012, pp. 134–157, p. 134.
24   A. Miloshoski, "Our justice may be slowed down, but it is not forgotten", Interview in the daily newspaper *Nova Makedonija*, 7 December, 2011, available at: <http://www.novamakedonija.com.mk/NewsDetal.asp?vest=12711845121&id=9&prilog=0&setIzdanie=2245>.
25   M. Kawano, *op. cit.*, p. 178.
26   Greece informed the Court of its decision not to raise preliminary objection by a Letter dated 5 August 2009.

the Republic of Macedonia referred to in Article 5, paragraph 1 of the Interim Accord, and that consequently it was excluded from the Court's jurisdiction by virtue of the exception provided in the compromissory clause of Article 21, paragraph 2. Second, it claimed that the dispute, even if found to be different from the name difference, would still be excluded from the Court's jurisdiction by Article 22 of the Interim Accord. Third, the Court could not exercise its jurisdiction since the dispute concerned conduct attributable to NATO. Fourth, Greece claimed that there were two inherent limitations that restrained the Court from exercising its judicial function: first, the Court's judgment would be incapable of effective application, and second, the Judgment would interfere with the on-going diplomatic negotiations on the name difference.[27]

Raising the jurisdictional objection gave Greece an opportunity to raise an issue that appeared to be its major concern, namely, what would be the influence of the ICJ's Judgment on the public perception of the international community of the Greek positions in the on-going UN mediated negotiations on the name difference. According to Greece, through a Judgment in favour of Macedonia, the Court would have endorsed the Republic of Macedonia's "attempt to unilaterally impose for international use a name that would not have been negotiated and agreed upon,"[28] or in other words to secure the name it wanted by a *fait accompli*.[29]

The Court rejected the Greek objections and found that it had jurisdiction over the legal dispute submitted to it, and that the Application was admissible.[30] It emphasised that "had the Parties considered that a future ruling by the Court would interfere with diplomatic negotiations mandated by the Security Council, they would not have agreed to refer to it disputes concerning the interpretation or implementation of the Interim Accord."[31]

IV   Greek Violation of Article 11, Paragraph 1 of the Interim Accord

Article 11, paragraph 1 of the Interim Accord was at the centre of the Republic of Macedonia's Application. This provision comprises two clauses: the first establishes the obligation on Greece 'not to object' to the Republic of

---

27   Rejoinder of the Respondent, Volume I, 27 October 2010, Chapters 3 and 4, pages 35–76, available at: <http://www.icj-cij.org/docket/files/142/16360.pdf>.
28   *Ibid.*, paragraph 4.26.
29   *Ibid.*, paragraph 4.28(i).
30   The Judgment, paragraph 61.
31   The Judgment, paragraph 59.

Macedonia's membership of international organisations and institutions of which Greece is already a member, and the second specifies the sole circumstance in which Greece reserved the right to object notwithstanding the obligation from the first clause, namely if the Republic of Macedonia were referred to in such organisation or institution differently than in Paragraph 2 of UN Security Council Resolution 817 (1993) (the former Yugoslav Republic of Macedonia).

So far as the merits of the case were concerned, the Greek defence was constructed on several alternative levels. First, Greece stated that it had not objected to Macedonian admission to NATO at the Bucharest Summit. Second, even if there was a Greek objection at the Bucharest Summit, Greece was allowed to make it by virtue of the second clause of Article 11, paragraph 1 of the Interim Accord. Third, as a subsidiary defence, even if the Greek objection in Bucharest was not permitted under the provisions of the Interim Accord, Greece was excused from responsibility for breach of Article 11, paragraph 1 on no fewer than three separate grounds under international law: (a) *exceptio non adimpleti contractus* (exception of an unperformed contract) under 'general principles of international law'[32]; (b) countermeasures under the law of state responsibility[33]; and (c) suspension of a treaty for material breach under Article 60 of the 1969 Vienna Convention on the Law of the Treaties.[34]

In brief, the Court rejected the entire Greek defence on the merits, and ruled that Greece had unlawfully objected to extending an invitation to the Republic of Macedonia to accede to NATO at the Bucharest Summit in 2008, and that that objection was not excusable.

Although the defence on the merits of both Parties raises a lot of interesting questions, the relations between the countries are especially triggered by the Court's findings on Greece's subsidiary defences. By raising the *exceptio non adimpleti contractus*, Greece asserted that Republic of Macedonia was in breach of the bulk of its obligations arising from the Interim Accord, and that Greece's conduct at the Bucharest Summit was a mere response to those breaches. If those assertions were true, the situation would be that the Interim Accord was not functioning at all for Greece.

On the other hand, Greece had serious problems in the availability of its subsidiary defences. This was thoroughly elaborated by the Macedonian

---

32 Counter-Memorial, Chapter 8, paragraphs 8.1–8.41, available at: <http://www.icj-cij.org/docket/files/142/16356.pdf>.
33 Rejoinder, Vol. I, paragraphs 8.24–8.40.
34 Verbatim Record, CR 2011/10, p. 28, paragraph 13 (Pellet), available at: < http://www.icj-cij.org/docket/files/142/16382.pdf> (29 March 2013).

counsels, which posed two lines of defence against the Greek positions: first, the *exceptio non adimpleti* was/is not adopted as a general principle of international law,[35] and that the formal conditions for suspension of a treaty under Article 60 of the 1969 Vienna Convention or for countermeasures under the law of state responsibility were not fulfilled. Second, in the alternative, even if the Court found that Greece was formally allowed to trigger any of the three subsidiary defences, still the substantive requirements were not fulfilled, since the record contained no evidence that would support breaches of the Interim Accord by the Republic of Macedonia.[36]

The Court was put in a very difficult position. Had it ruled positively on the first line of the Macedonian defence and decided that none of the three subsidiary defences were available to Greece, it would have allowed the Macedonian side to avoid confronting very serious Greek allegations that it had violated practically the entire set of its obligations under the Interim Accord, and it could still win the case. And if that had happened, Greece would have been enabled to claim that the Republic of Macedonia was in constant violation of the Interim Accord, but the Court was unable to establish it.

It seems that that was the main concern which led the Court to a different approach. It simply grouped all the subsidiary defences and identified 'certain minimum conditions that are common to all three arguments': (a) the existence of a prior breach of the Interim Accord on the part of the Republic of Macedonia; (b) a connection between that breach and Greece's objection to Macedonian admission to NATO in violation of Article 11, paragraph 1 of the Interim Accord.[37] With these conditions in mind, the Court then turned to examine the evidence submitted by Greece regarding the alleged breaches by the Republic of Macedonia. It recalled that, in general, it is the duty of the party that asserts certain facts to establish the existence of such facts.[38] Thus, it was Greece that bore the burden of establishing the facts that supported its allegation that Macedonia had failed to comply with its obligations under the Interim Accord. And it failed to prove its case.

---

35   Judge Brunno Simma issued a Separate Opinion, stating that the answer that the Court should have given to the question whether the *exceptio non adimpleti contractus*, "put forward by the Respondent as a 'defence' against the accusation of treaty breach separate, and to be distinguished, from reliance on Article 60 of the 1969 Vienna Convention or on a justification of Greece's objection...qualifying it as a countermeasure, still has a right of place in international law" – is an unqualified "no." – Judge Simma, Separate Opinion, available at: <http://www.icj-cij.org/docket/files/142/16829.pdf> (29 March 2013), the Preamble.
36   Memorial, Vol. I, paragraphs. 5.1.-5.69; Reply, Vol. I, paragraphs 5.1.-5.105.
37   The Judgment, paragraph 123.
38   The Judgment, paragraphs 123 and 72.

1 ICJ's Findings on the Greek Allegations of Violations of the Interim Accord and Their Impact on Greek-Macedonian Relations

In the proceedings before the ICJ, Greece was for the first time put in a position where an independent judicial authority was to assess the evidence by which the Greek allegations against the Republic of Macedonia for breaches of the Interim Accord were supported. The ICJ's findings on the facts were important not only for the proceedings themselves, but also for the political relations between the two countries. Both before the Court and on a diplomatic level, Greece relied on the alleged violations when claiming that the Republic of Macedonia's violations were part of a "pattern of conduct that has persisted for several years",[39] in pursuing 'irredentist aspirations' against Greece.[40] If the Court had found that the evidence before it supported the allegations of Macedonian breaches of the Interim Accord, Greece would have had very strong grounds for its claims of the existence of an irredentist pattern of behaviour.

Greece raised allegations of Macedonian breaches of 6 relevant provisions of the Interim Accord.

a   Greek Allegation of Breach of the Second Clause of Article 11, Paragraph 1

Greece invoked the second clause of Article 11 paragraph 1 of the Interim Accord twice in the proceedings before the ICJ: first as part of its defence on the main issue of the application, where it asserted that an excuse existed against the allegation that it had breached the obligation from the first clause of the said provision of the Accord; second, as part of its subsidiary defence, claiming that this was one of the provisions of the Accord establishing an obligation that was breached by Macedonia.

The foundation of this interpretation was the assumption that Macedonia was admitted to UN membership under the provisional name of 'the Former Yugoslav Republic of Macedonia', which would be mandatory for Macedonia 'for all purposes' in international organisations,[41] until a settlement was reached on the 'name difference'. In addition, Greece asserted that since Article 11 of the Interim Accord incorporated and extended the requirement of UN Security Council Resolution 817 (1993), *this provision of the Accord established an obligation* on Macedonia to use the 'provisional name' in international organisations which it adhered to under Article 11 of the Interim Accord.

---

39 Rejoinder, Vol. I, paragraph 7.8.
40 "FYROM name issue", available at: <http://www.mfa.gr/en/fyrom-name-issue/> (29 March 2013).
41 Counter-Memorial, Vol. I, paragraph 1.8 and paragraphs 8.60–8.62.

Having considered that it was indisputable between the parties that Macedonia was referring to itself under its constitutional name within the UN and every international organisation it had joined since 1993, the Court had to interpret the phrase "this State being provisionally referred to" in Paragraph 2 of the Security Council Resolution 817 (1993). In other words, did the phrase "this State being provisionally referred to" purport to determine a provisional name for the State?

The Court ruled against the Greek assertions, and accepted the interpretation that the second clause of Article 11, paragraph 1 covered only how the organisation was to refer to the Republic of Macedonia, but it did not cover the way in which the Republic of Macedonia was to refer to itself.[42] The Judgment of the ICJ confirmed the Macedonian position that the 'provisional designation' was not the 'provisional name' of Macedonia within the UN. Furthermore, the ICJ ruled that the provision of the second sentence of Article 11, paragraph 1 *did not impose any obligation* on the Republic of Macedonia, so there could not be a Macedonian breach of the second sentence of Article 11, paragraph 1 of the Interim Accord.[43]

b   Alleged Breach by the Republic of Macedonia of Article 5, Paragraph 1

Facing the impossibility to reach an agreement on the key issue that divided them, Macedonia and Greece agreed to bypass it by entering into the Interim Accord under the condition of continuing the negotiations on the name difference, with the explicit reservation of their positions. At the same time, they provided for a whole series of mutual obligations which were intended to allow for the normalisation of day-to-day relations, especially the lifting of the Greek economic embargo. As is correctly noted, "the Interim Accord was the starting point for a rapid development in peaceful relations..." between the two countries in various areas.[44]

The obligation to continue the negotiations on the name difference is stipulated in Article 5, paragraph 1 of the Interim Accord, which provides:

> The Parties agree to continue negotiations under the auspices of the Secretary-General of the United Nations pursuant to Security Council

---

42   The Judgment, paragraph 92.
43   The Judgment, paragraph 126.
44   N. Zaikos, "The Interim Accord: Prospects and Developments in Accordance with International Law", in: E. Kofos, V. Vlasidis (eds.), *Athens-Skopje: An Uneasy Symbiosis (1995–2002)*, ELIAMEP, Athens, 2005, p. 51.

resolution 845 (1993) with a view to reaching agreement on the difference described in that resolution and in Security Council resolution 817 (1993).

General international law provides for the sovereign right of states to determine their own names. By agreeing on the obligation to negotiate with Greece about its name, the Republic of Macedonia "chose to pay a considerable price in terms of its legal rights", which was the reason for some authors to conclude that "this was perhaps not such a good deal for Makedonija – albeit a necessary one at the time."[45] On the other hand, the Republic of Macedonia gained an implicit Greek admission that it could not unilaterally impose a name on its Northern neighbour and acceptance of the extension of the solution of Resolution 817 (1993) to other international organisations, where the Republic of Macedonia would apply for membership under the provisional designation (those are all international organisations admission to membership of which was previously blocked by Greece). One must have in mind that in 1995, at the time of the conclusion of the Interim Accord, there was a well-established practice of two years in the UN by which the Republic of Macedonia was able to call itself by its constitutional name while being referred to by the other members and the Organisation as 'the former Yugoslav Republic of Macedonia'.[46]

The Court noted that the obligation of the parties to negotiate in good faith was implicit under Article 5, paragraph 1 of the Interim Accord.[47] Greece asserted that the Republic of Macedonia had breached this obligation by its conduct within the negotiating process where it was allegedly attempting to redefine the scope of the ongoing negotiations by pursuing the strategy of depriving the negotiations of their object and purpose, and that it was in violation of an obligation of result.[48] The Court rejected those Greek assertions by observing that *"whether the obligation has been undertaken in good faith cannot be measured by the result obtained"*[49] (emphasis added). What is even more important is that the Court had fully destroyed the Greek assertion of

---

45 F. Francesco, *op. cit.*, p. 175.
46 See, for example, a Letter dated 17 February 1994 from the Macedonian Permanent Representative to the United Nations to the President of the Security Council, UN Doc. S/1994/194 (18 February 1994), Reply, Vol. II, Annex 15.
47 The Court relied on Article 26 of the 1969 Vienna Convention on the Law of the Treaties, and on a large number of cases in its jurisprudence: see paragraph 131 of the Judgment.
48 Rejoinder, Vol. I, paragraphs 7.53 to 7.70.
49 The Judgment, paragraph 134.

Macedonian intransigence[50] by accepting that it had shown a 'degree of openness' in the negotiations, just as Greece had departed from its initial positions.

It is awkward that even after the Judgment of the Court was delivered, the Greek Foreign Ministry still maintains its positions that the failure to achieve substantial progress in the negotiations on the name difference under the auspices of UN is a result of the intransigent insistence of the Republic of Macedonia on its initial position.[51]

c   Alleged Breach by the Republic of Macedonia of Article 6, Paragraph 2

Article 6, paragraphs 2 and 3 of the Interim Accord provide:

> 2. The Party of the Second Part hereby solemnly declares that nothing in its Constitution, and in particular in Article 49 as amended, can or should be interpreted as constituting or will ever constitute the basis for the Party of the Second Part to interfere in the internal affairs of another State in order to protect the status and rights of any persons in other States who are not citizens of the Party to the Second Part.
>
> 3. The Party of the Second Part furthermore solemnly declares that the interpretations given in paragraph 1 and 2 of this Article will not be superseded by any other interpretation of its Constitution.

In addition to the Constitutional Amendments of 1992, which were assessed positively by the Badinter Commission, the Republic of Macedonia went one step further in 1995 by adopting an interpretation of its Constitution in Article 6, paragraph 2 of the Interim Accord. It was undisputed among the commentators on the Interim Accord that this provision provided merely an interpretation of the Macedonian Constitution.[52] The obligation of Macedonia was only not to interpret its Constitution in a manner different from the one provided in Article 6, paragraph 2 of the Interim Accord. And the Court confirmed that it had not, rejecting the Greek interpretation of Article 6, paragraph 2.[53] The Court found that Greek allegations about the Republic of Macedonia

---

50   Counter-Memorial, Vol. I, paragraphs 4.2–4.26; Rejoinder of Greece, Vol. I, paragraphs 7.53–7.70.
51   See: "The FYROM Name Issue", available at: <http://www.mfa.gr//en/fyrom-name-issue/> (29 March 2013).
52   P. Pazartzis, *op. cit.*, p. 296; N. Zaikos, *op. cit.*, p. 32.
53   See: Counter Memorial, Vol. I, paragraph 8.45.

'promoting and condoning irredentism',[54] "*appear to be divorced* from the text of Article 6, paragraph 2"[55] (emphasis added).

d   Alleged Breach by the Republic of Macedonia of Article 7, Paragraph 1 (Prohibition of Hostile Activities of Propaganda)

From the very beginning of the process of the international recognition of the independence of the Republic of Macedonia, Greece raised its concern that the new country would pursue 'hostile propaganda' against it. As was noted above, this concern was transposed into conditions for recognition assessed by the Badinter Commission.

In Article 7, paragraph 1 of the Interim Accord, the same commitment was confirmed, this time as a reciprocal obligation of both parties:

> Each Party shall promptly take effective measures to prohibit hostile activities or propaganda by State-controlled agencies and to discourage acts by private entities likely to incite violence, hatred or hostility against each other.

Greece asserted before the ICJ that Macedonian authorities had allegedly failed to take effective measures to prohibit hostile activities by State-controlled agencies. The most important of them concerned historic textbooks used in the Republic of Macedonia's schools that depicted historic 'Greater Macedonia' and that presented historical figures like Alexander the Great or Philip II of Macedonia as the ancestors of the current Macedonian population. Greece asserted that "through historical inaccuracies in the school textbooks..." the people of the Republic of Macedonia were "...induced in feeling the injustice of living in a partitioned State and thus hatred for their neighbours."[56]

Assessing these Greek allegations, the Court ruled that "the textbook content described above does not provide a basis to conclude that the Applicant has failed to prohibit 'hostile activities of propaganda'."[57] In that way, the Court removed another point of friction between the two countries. Now, it should be undisputed that the contents of history textbooks published and used in Macedonian schools on which Greek historians disagree could not be claimed to represent acts of hostile propaganda.

---

54   See: Counter Memorial, Vol. I, paragraph 8.45.
55   The Judgment, paragraph 142.
56   Counter-Memorial, Vol. I, paragraph 8.50.
57   The Judgment, paragraph 147.

On the other hand, the Greek Government still claims that the Republic of Macedonia bases "its existence as an independent state on the artificial and spurious notion of the 'Macedonian nation', which was cultivated systematically through the falsification of history and the exploitation of ancient Macedonia purely for reasons of political expediency."[58] Sending a message to a neighbouring country that its existence as an independent state is based on the artificial and spurious notion of the 'Macedonian nation' cannot be considered as anything but as a hostile activity.

e   Alleged Breach by the Republic of Macedonia of Article 7, Paragraph 2

One of the major concessions of the Republic of Macedonia towards Greece in the Interim Accord was the undertaking to remove the 'Sixteen Rayed Sun' which was displayed on its national flag at that time. Article 7, paragraph 2 of the Interim Accord provides:

> Upon entry into force of this Interim Accord, the Party of the Second Part shall cease to use in any way the symbol in all its forms displayed on its national flag prior to such entry into force.

It was/is undisputed between the Parties that immediately upon the signing of the Interim Accord the Republic of Macedonia had removed the disputed symbol from its flag. Greece asserted that the Republic of Macedonia continued to use the symbol in other ways throughout the years. And indeed, the Court established one minor breach of the obligation of Article 7, paragraph 2, which occurred in 2004, and it was immediately repaired.[59]

It is very important that the Court rejected the Greek interpretation that the provision of Article 7, paragraph 2 included a prohibition on private entities (such as the 'Philip II' Cardio Surgery Clinic in Skopje) using the disputed symbol.[60]

f   Alleged Breach by the Republic of Macedonia of Article 7, Paragraph 3

Article 7, paragraph 3 of the Interim Accord provides:

> If either Party believes one or more symbols constituting part of its historic or cultural patrimony is being used by the other Party, it shall

---

58   See: "The FYROM Name Issue", available at: <http://www.29.gr//en/fyrom-name-issue/> (29 March 2013).
59   The Judgment, paragraph 151.
60   The Judgment, paragraph 153.

bring such alleged use to the attention of the other Party, and the other Party shall take appropriate corrective action or indicate why it does not consider it necessary to do so.

This provision does not contain any prohibition on either of the parties to use the symbols which the other party considers part of its historic and cultural patrimony. Therefore the Greek commentators on the Interim Accord have qualified the acceptance of this provision of the Interim Accord as a "serious error of the Greek negotiating team",[61] because it only provided for a mechanism where "the offended party was simply left with the possibility of pointing out to the other what it deemed to be inappropriate use...of certain symbols."[62] If either party believes that any such symbols are being used by the other Party, it can only bring such alleged use to the attention of the other Party.

The Court confirmed such interpretation of Article 7, paragraph 3 of the Interim Accord. It explicitly ruled that "Article 7, paragraph 3, does not contain any prohibition on the use of particular symbols...,"[63] because such a prohibition would have had to be expressly provided, just like the one in Article 7, paragraph 2. Therefore it rejected the Greek allegation that the renaming of Skopje Airport as 'Alexander the Great' in 2006, could not in itself constitute a breach of Article 7, paragraph 3.

One of the largest misconceptions of Greece in its positioning towards Macedonia was its attempt to monopolise the cultural heritage from Ancient Macedonia, which then led to another misconception that such cultural heritage was appropriated by its northern neighbour. The cultural heritage from the ancient civilizations which existed in the Southern Balkans belongs not only to the states that exist in those territories today, but also to the rest of the world as a part of a common cultural heritage. The world's historic and cultural heritage cannot, and should not, be treated as intellectual property.

2 *The Effects of the ICJ's Findings on the Alleged Macedonian Breaches of the Interim Accord*

The ICJ rejected the Greek allegations of violation of the Interim Accord by the Republic of Macedonia in their entirety. What is more important, the Court made it crystal clear that those findings were not only an issue of fact, but also an issue of law, and that Greek interpretations of the provisions of the Interim Accord were so distorted that they were actually 'divorced' from the text of that Treaty. Furthermore, this part of the Judgment confirmed that

---

61   E. Kofos, *op. cit.*, p. 138.
62   *Ibid.*
63   The Judgment, paragraph 157.

the provisional designation 'the former Yugoslav Republic of Macedonia' is not a provisional international name of the state, but that the state is allowed to use its constitutional name even within the UN. Unlike Badinter's Opinion No. 6, this time the unpleasant findings for Greece are contained in a Judgment binding on both of the parties. Such an outcome appears to be very frustrating for the Greek public, so some prominent Greek figures have expressed the opinion that "the Interim Accord, by the interpretations of the International Court of Justice, can no longer fulfill the purpose for which it was concluded," and therefore Greece "no longer has interest to continue to be obliged by it."[64] In any case, it is clear that Greece has "scored a number of own goals in the process."[65]

By deciding on the Greek allegations of breaches of the Interim Accord, the Court has provided the Parties with authoritative interpretations of the key provisions of that Treaty, and therefore with clear guidance for their future conduct. Only by abiding by their mutual legal obligations will the efforts in overcoming the only unresolved issue between them have a positive result. As the Co-Chairman of the Steering Committee of the International Conference on the Former Yugoslavia, the late Cyrus Vance, described the Interim Accord, it is a "comprehensive agreement with every detail arranged, with all elements of the dispute settled, except for the name issue."[66]

V Concluding Remarks

The Interim Accord enabled the normalisation of relations between the Republic of Macedonia and Greece 17 years ago. The ICJ Judgment of 5 December 2011 has confirmed that the Interim Accord is still in force and therefore binding on both of the Parties.

In the future, relations between the parties may be substantially improved if full abidance to the obligations imposed by the Interim Accord is achieved. The dispute resolution mechanism established by Article 21, paragraph 2 of the Interim Accord will only then have any sense.

---

64   A. Mallas, "You have been cutting the branch that you were sitting on" *Gragjanski* (weekly magazine), Saturday, 15 September 2012, p. 37 (in Macedonian).

65   A. Tzanakopoulos, "Legality of Veto to NATO Accession: Comment on the ICJ's Decision in the Dispute between fYR Macedonia and Greece", *EJIL: Talk!*, 7 December 2011, available at: <http://www.ejiltalk.org/author/atzanakopoulos/>.

66   J. Shea, *op. cit.*, p. 304.

The Greek veto on the extension of an invitation to Macedonia to join NATO at the Bucharest Summit in 2008 disrupted the balance of the negotiating process on the name difference, established by the Interim Accord. The negotiations can proceed in a successful manner only if such balance is restored. The ICJ's Judgment of 5 December 2011 indicated that Greece is liable for such interruption, and therefore it must take the necessary action to correct its wrongdoing. Otherwise, a continued stalemate is the most likely outcome of this situation.

The ICJ's Judgment of 5 December 2011 revealed two things concerning the relations between Greece and Macedonia: first, Greece is the party that violated and is still in violation of its obligations under Article 11, paragraph 1of the Interim Accord and, second, the Greek allegations about Macedonia's systematic violation of the Interim Accord are inaccurate. Since those violations are claimed to be the exclusive constitutive elements of the alleged Macedonian irredentist pattern of behaviour, no doubt is left that such irredentist pattern also does not exist. Without the irredentist component as its main pillar, the difference over the name of Macedonia loses its substance and turns out to be absurd and obscure. For the first time, Greece and Macedonia have a binding Judgment of the ICJ that resolves Greece's major concern arising out of the 'difference over the name'. Although this was not the main issue of the ICJ proceedings, it appears to be the major contribution of the ICJ that is paving the way to the resolution of the 'difference over the name'.

CHAPTER 3

When Can Property of a State be Attached to Enforce a Foreign Judgment Given against It in Another Country? Some Guidance in the ICJ Judgment in the *Jurisdictional Immunities* Case

*Hazel Fox**

Professor Vukas and I were members of the study on which I served as Special Rapporteur undertaken in the *Institut de Droit International* of the extent to which the jurisdictional immunities of States infringed the protection of human rights; and in the course of our study I came to know Professor Vukas and admire his work. Whilst State immunity from measures of constraint was not the immediate issue which we studied together, I hope this discussion may be of interest to him, namely the extent to which a judgment debt given against a foreign State in the national court of one State may be recognized and enforced by the courts of a third State.

The general position regarding situations of State insolvency, particularly in respect of the still unresolved widespread debt crisis dating from 2008, continues today unregulated by international law; there is no accepted international law or any international procedure for an orderly resolution of the situation arising from State insolvency or a State's general inability to meet its financial commitments; rescheduling of State debts remains largely a political process. Even a generally accepted legal definition of State insolvency is lacking. The situation today, as in the past, as Waibel, after providing a historical review of sovereign insolvency, acknowledges, largely continues as one in which "sovereign defaults are legion and...governments rarely repay their debts in full."[1]

Immunity from enforcement and measures of constraint in national courts has in consequence inevitably become the focus of creditor activism at a time of sovereign default, and consequently may be of particular interest to less

---

* CMG, QC; Member of the *Institut de Droit International*, Bencher of Lincoln's Inn; formerly Director of the British Institute of International and Comparative Law and General Editor of the International and Comparative Law Quarterly.

1 Waibel *Sovereign Defaults before International Courts and Tribunals* (Cambridge Univ Press 2011) 13.63.

bona fide purchasers who, by purchasing at a reduced price sovereign debt in the expectation of default, seek to profit from suing the debtor country to recover the full amount owed. In large part it is due to the claims of such international investment traders as *Elliott* and NML, pejoratively seen as speculator 'vulture funds', that national courts have been required to examine the scope of immunity from enforcement. In such cases the maintenance of the full validity of the law, in particular the 'sanctity of the contract' on which the terms of the bond are based, competes with the effective maintenance of the restructuring achieved by debtor and creditor States in the Paris Club supported by a majority of private creditors. In effect, the 'sanctity of the contract' in law on which the terms of the bond held by the bondholders are based is at odds with the politically negotiated revaluation of defaulted sovereign debt by States.

Though not yet in force (16 of the 30 ratifications required have so far been made[2]), the 2004 United Nations Convention on Jurisdictional Immunities of States and Their Property (UNSCI) provides a comprehensive regime of rules covering immunity from adjudication and measures of constraint of a State and its property from the jurisdiction of another State. Recently, in the concluding Parts IV and V of its *Jurisdictional Immunities* judgment,[3] the International Court of Justice (ICJ) referred to this Convention's Part IV as regards post judgment proceedings and applied the third exception to immunity in article 19(c) which allows post judgment enforcement measures against State property in use by the State for other than government non-commercial purposes. Although careful not to endorse article 19 in all respects the ICJ shaped, by reference to that article's exception (c), the standards to be applied by a third State's court in proceedings for recognition of a judgment given against a foreign State in the national court of another State.[4]

Whilst it has long been established in State practice and is set out in Part IV of the UN Convention, that international law requires immunity from enforcement to be accorded to the foreign State and its property as the general rule to be observed by national courts – that is that forcible measures of constraint against the property of a foreign State, by attachment, third part debt order,

---

2   Austria, Finland, France, Iran, Italy, Japan, Kazakhstan, Latvia, Lebanon, Norway, Portugal, Romania, Saudi Arabia, Spain, Sweden, Switzerland.
3   *Jurisdictional Immunities of the State (Germany v. Italy, Greece Intervening)*, Judgment of 3 February 2012, ICJ Reports 2012, p. 99 (hereafter *Jurisdictional Immunities*).
4   The Court also referred to the Convention's territorial tort exception in article 12, noting that, despite US, Chinese and German opposition, there was considerable State practice in its support. *Jurisdictional Immunities*, paras. 62–65.

sale, are barred by the State's enforcement immunity – there is lack of clarity as to its application. There are many areas of uncertainty – whether enforcement immunity is a distinct regime subject to different rules from that of an adjudication regime or the extent to which property of the foreign State other than in use for sovereign purposes may be subject to measures of constraint. It is here that the innovative nature of the ICJ's judgment in Parts IV and V of the *Jurisdictional Immunities* case provides a new understanding of the extent to which a State's property enjoys immunity from the jurisdiction of national courts enforcing a judgement of a national court given in another country in respect of acts of the State held to enjoy no immunity. Even more innovatively the ICJ lays down the standard which applies in Part IV of the UN Convention when enforcing a judgment given against a foreign State.

Although the *Jurisdictional Immunities* case and hence the ICJ has excited some academic criticism and recently come under challenge by the Italian Constitutional Court's decision no. 238/2014 that, by virtue of article 134 of the Italian Constitution, the Italian Constitutional Court, and not the ICJ, is the appropriate court to determine the extent to which State immunity bars a claim in Italian courts, I think it probable that the ICJ's application of the 2004 UN Convention's Part IV as regards post-judgment proceedings will remain unchallenged and continue to stand. I accordingly will proceed on that basis in examining the International Court's application of enforcement law.

From the written and oral proceedings so far as they are reported[5] it appears that there was very little discussion of customary international law's provisions relating to enforcement and little help to the ICJ provided as to the standard to be applied by the enforcing national court with regard to a judgment given against a foreign State in the national court of another State; all the parties' reported arguments were directed to Germany's immunity from adjudication in time of international armed conflict. It was accordingly left to the ICJ and its 15 judges in the process of drafting the judgment to declare, largely unaided by the parties and their counsel, the customary international law relating to the property of a foreign State with regard to the State's immunity from enforcement.

The facts in the case relevant to enforcement were as follows: Italy was alleged by Germany to be in breach of international law by the Italian court's recognition and grant of *exequatur* in respect of a judgment of the Greek Court of Cassation setting aside German immunity in respect of a massacre of inhabitants of a Greek Village, Distomo, as a military reprisal. A further breach was

---

5 Replies of the parties to questions of individual judges made on the last day of the oral proceedings have been published but do not relate to the issues here discussed.

also alleged by reason of the Florence Court's imposition of a legal charge by way of enforcement of the reparation due in consequence of the Greek judgment in *Distomo* on a German-owned property, the Villa Vigoni used for cultural purposes located on the Italian Lake Como.[6]

In Part V of its judgment the International Court made some general introductory remarks contrasting the two types of immunity from adjudication and enforcement: "the rules of customary international law governing immunity from enforcement are distinct from and go further than those governing jurisdictional immunity, and must be separately applied" (para. 131).[7] The ICJ then applied this distinction between the two regimes to the claims presented to it in a straightforward manner: as regards the first, the adjudication stage, it formulated the issue as "whether the Italian judgments declaring enforceable in Italy the pecuniary awards pronounced in Greece, did themselves – independently of any subsequent measure of enforcement – constitute a violation of the Applicant's immunity from jurisdiction." As regards the second stage, that of enforcement, the question was "…to determine whether a measure of constraint – such as the legal charge on Villa Vigoni – violated Germany's immunity from enforcement" (para. 124).

Although noting there to be a link between the two stages "…since the measure of constraint against Villa Vigoni could only have been imposed on the basis of the judgment of the Florence Court of Appeal according *exequatur* in respect of the judgment of the Greek court in Livadia" – the ICJ treated the two regimes as distinct and relied, with one caveat,[8] almost solely with regard to the second issue on the UN Convention article 19 with its three exceptions of

---

6   Although Italy by Decree-Law suspended this charge pending the proceedings, the ICJ noted that it might be reactivated and hence a decision as to its legality as a measure of constraint was necessary. *Jurisdictional Immunities*, paras. 109–112.
7   The ICJ stressed that "even where a judgment had been lawfully rendered" so that the foreign State could not claim immunity from jurisdiction it did not follow that the foreign State could be "the subject of measures of constraint on the territory of the forum State or on that of a third State, with a view to enforcing the judgment in question." It went on to explain the distinction by a reference to "any waiver by a State of its jurisdictional immunity before a foreign court does not of itself mean that that State has waived its enforcement as regards property belonging to it situated in the foreign territory" (para. 113).
8   "The Court considers that it is unnecessary for purposes of the present case for it to decide whether all aspects of Article 19 reflect current customary international law" (para.117). Apart from four decisions which the ICJ cited, no reference was made to the US Foreign Sovereign Immunities Act (FSIA) s. 1609 and the UK State Immunity Act (SIA) s. 13, despite both containing provisions dealing specifically with enforcement, nor to the extensive relevant State practice.

express consent, express allocation of State property, and property in use for non-government non-commercial purposes.[9]

Although on the facts of the 2012 case the application of the distinction between the two phases was a simple matter, it is to be noted that it has not always proved a straightforward task to determine whether a particular proceeding or the type of relief sought relates to adjudication or enforcement; proceedings, such as the administration of trusts, bankruptcy, review of subordinate legislation, may contain elements of both adjudicative and enforcement jurisdiction.[10] Though logically the existence of an obligation regarding an unpaid debt precedes its enforcement, in practice the location of State assets in the forum territory which can be seized is almost always the first concern of the unsatisfied creditor.[11]

It was, therefore, not surprising that the ICJ chose to address the second stage of enforcement first. Given that Villa Vigoni was the seat of a cultural centre intended to promote cultural exchanges between Germany and Italy and hence used solely for governmental non-commercial purposes, the legality of the restraint imposed by the Florence Court on German property was clearly in violation of Germany's immunity from enforcement which it enjoyed in respect of property used for sovereign purposes,[12] and in consequence the ICJ had little difficulty in ruling that the registration of a land charge on Villa Vigoni constituted a violation by Italy of its obligation to respect Germany's immunity (para.120). It would seem that on the facts of the *Jurisdictional*

---

9 The wording of UNSCI article 19(c) reads: "it has been established that the property is specifically in use or intended for use by the State for other than government non-commercial purposes and is in the territory of the State of the forum, provided that post-judgment measures of constraint may only be taken against property that has a connection with the entity against which the proceeding was directed."

10 *Re International Tin Council* [1987] 1 *All ER* 890.

11 The uncertainty of where the line for the distinction is to be drawn is illustrated by US proceedings brought by 'holdout' speculators having purchased bonds on which Argentina had defaulted at a much discounted value but seeking to enforce them at full value; *Republic of Argentina v. NML Capital, Ltd.*, 134 S.Ct. 2819 (2014).

12 One of the four national decisions related to the immunity accorded to a cultural institute of a foreign State; the Swiss Federal Tribunal of 30 April 1986 in *Kingdom of Spain v. Société X* (*Annuaire suisse de droit international*, Vol. 43, 1987, p. 158). The other three decisions related to immunity of diplomatic premises; the German Constitutional Court (*Bundesverfassungsgericht*) of 14 December 1977 (*BVerfGE*, Vol. 46, p. 342; *ILR*, Vol. 65, p. 146); the UK House of Lords of 12 April 1984 in *Alcom Ltd v. Republic of Colombia* ([1984] 1 AC 580; *ILR*, Vol. 74, p. 170); the Spanish Constitutional Court of 1 July 1992 in *Abbott v. Republic of South Africa* (*Revista española de derecho internacional*, Vol. 44, 1992, p. 565; *ILR*, Vol. 113, p. 414).

Immunities case an English court would itself have arrived at the same rulings as that of the ICJ. So far as the immunity from enforcement of the German-owned property in Italy, the UK State Immunity Act (SIA) s. 13(2)(b) bars "any process for the enforcement of a judgment" against property of a foreign State, unless "in use or intended use for commercial purposes" (SIA s. 13(4)); consequently, as the Villa Vigoni, the subject of enforcement by the Italian court, was barred from enforcement as in sole use as a cultural centre and hence property in use for the exercise of sovereign authority (in the words of UNSCI article 19(c) "for government non-commercial purposes"), it continued to enjoy immunity from enforcement, regardless of the validity of the judgment on which it was based. This outcome,[13] is likely to be supported in most other national jurisdictions which may, in addition to requiring the State property to be in use for commercial purposes, require a connection of the property to the subject matter of the claim (US Foreign Sovereign Immunities Act (FSIA) s. 1010) or with the entity against which the proceeding was directed (UNSCI article 19(c)).

In paragraph 130 the International Court of Justice then turned its attention to the second issue, that is whether Germany's immunity from adjudication had been infringed by the Italian courts' proceedings; that is whether or not the immunity of the foreign State, set aside by the first adjudicating court, the Greek court, could serve as a bar to the jurisdiction of the court in the second State – Italy. This question relating to a review of the merits/substance of the case, which the ICJ accepted to be of some complexity, might well have required a consideration of the extent to which the judgment of the originating court was to be adopted by the recognizing court in the second State taking into account a variety of issues: the facts based on the evidence, the status of the defendant claiming immunity, waiver, the applicability of an exception to immunity, including any requirement of a jurisdictional link necessary for such an exception. In short, the question which arose for the ICJ was whether the task of the court in the recognizing State was merely to 'rubberstamp' the original judgment and recognize it without any further examination, or did that court enjoy an independent jurisdiction to determine any or all of these matters by reference to the recognizing court's national law or to that law's understanding of the relevant international law?

Here, preparing the ground for its formulation of the recognizing court's task, the ICJ was careful to distinguish the 'split' nature of the case before it

---

13   Which UNSCI article 21(d) recognizes immune as "property forming part of the cultural heritage of the State" and consequently not to be considered as property in use for "government non-commercial purposes".

where judgment of the merits was given by the court of one State (Greece) and its enforcement sought in the court of another State (Italy), from the more usual case where both judgment and its enforcement were sought from the court of a single State. This difference the ICJ seized on as permitting the recognizing court to adopt without re-examination the rulings of the judgment court as to the merits stating "it was not the role of the *exequatur* [recognizing] court to re-examine in all its aspects the substance of the case which had been decided" (para. 128); but then to qualify as partial in the subsequent paragraph 130 this acceptance of the judgment court's ruling. This 'partial endorsement' enabled the ICJ to avoid any independent assessment of the facts relating to the German massacre at Distomo and any possible distinction between those facts and those complained of by Germany in the Italian cases and further as set out in paragraph 131 to apply without further discussion its rulings in Part III that Italy had disregarded Germany's immunity.

The ICJ justified this split between 'the merits' and the application of State immunity to the case, because the effects of a decision to recognize or not the original judgment constituted the exercise of a jurisdictional power by the recognizing court corresponding to that of the judgment court and consequently required them to be regarded as being conducted against the third State which was the subject of the foreign judgment (para. 128).[14]

In paragraph 130 the ICJ finally sets out the nature of the enquiry regarding State immunity which a recognizing court must conduct:

> [T]he court seised of an application for *exequatur* of a foreign judgment rendered against a third State has to ask itself whether the respondent State enjoys immunity from jurisdiction – having regard to the nature of the case in which that judgment was given – before the courts of the State in which *exequatur* proceedings have been instituted. In other words, it has to ask itself whether, in the event that it had itself been seised of the merits of a dispute identical to that which was the subject of the foreign judgment, it would have been obliged under international law to accord immunity to the respondent State (see to this effect the judgment of the Supreme Court of Canada in *Kuwait Airways Corp. v. Iraq* [2010] SCR, Vol. 2,

---

14 As the third State is always likely to be a party to the recognition proceedings opposing the judgment's enforcement, there is no risk of the recognizing court making a decision in its absence. On the facts it enabled the ICJ to avoid any review of the Greek proceedings and may well hide the ICJ's unwillingness to envisage that the recognizing court's applicability of the rule of State immunity might depend on differences both as to relevant facts and the categorisation of the merits in terms of the relevant law.

p. 571, and the judgment of the United Kingdom Supreme Court in *NML Capital Limited* v. *Republic of Argentina* [2011] UKSC 31).

In this important passage a number of elements in the original judgment are identified: the jurisdictional issue of immunity, the nature of the case as determinative of that issue, 'the merits of the dispute' on which the original court's seisin is based, the identical nature of those 'merits' before the recognizing court. Further the international law applicable to recognition is stated to be international law as applied in the recognizing court; the *lis* or matter to be decided by the recognizing court was "whether the Italian courts did themselves respect Germany's immunity from jurisdiction in allowing the application for *exequatur*, and not whether the Greek court having rendered the judgment of which *exequatur* is sought had respected Germany's jurisdictional immunity" (para. 128).[15]

This rejection of any 'rubberstamping' of the original judgment and emphasis on the independent applicability of the law of the recognizing State is a significant aspect of the ICJ's standard for recognition and one which the English and Canadian cases, referred to in its judgement, support. The review of the ICJ, however, was partial; it held that it was not necessary "to re-examine in all its aspects the substance of the case which has been decided" nor "… to rule on the legality of the decisions of the Greek courts" (para. 132). In fact the ICJ confines itself solely to the single jurisdictional issue of immunity and to whether the international law as applied by the recognizing Italian court "would have required the Italian courts to grant immunity to Germany relating to the Distomo massacre as established by the Greek courts." Since in the earlier sections of the judgment the ICJ had upheld the immunity of Germany and dismissed the three lines of attack mounted by the Italian defence, the answer to this question was clear. The International Court of Justice accordingly reasoned as follows: since, "for the reasons set out in Section III above of the present Judgment, the Italian courts would have been obliged to grant immunity to Germany if they had been seised of the merits of a case identical to that which was the subject of the decisions of the Greek courts which it was sought to declare enforceable (namely, the case of the Distomo massacre)…, they could not grant *exequatur* without thereby violating Germany's jurisdictional immunity" (para. 131).

In so deciding, the ICJ laid down a rule of customary international law for application by a national recognizing court when assessing the enforceability

---

15   The recognizing court having no power to make such a determination because Greece was not a party to the proceedings before the Italian recognizing court.

of a judgment given against a foreign State. It did so on the basis of a fundamental assumption that all national jurisdictions adopt the ICJ's categorisation of the customary rule and in determining immunity will look to the underlying transaction on which the claim to immunity is based. The International Court treated "the merits of a dispute identical to that which was the subject of the foreign judgment" as the subject matter to which the immunity enjoyed by Germany in international law as determined by the recognizing court was to be applied. The ICJ required the recognizing court in the Germany/Italy proceedings "to ask itself whether, in the event that it had itself been seised of the merits of a dispute identical to that which was the subject of the foreign judgment, it would have been obliged under international law to accord immunity to the respondent State."

On this aspect, however, differences can exist. English law adopts a different categorisation. Controversially and in contradiction to the ICJ standard, despite the International Court's citing the English Supreme Court in its support, English law distinguishes the recognition of a judgment as a different legal exercise from adjudication of an exception to State immunity. In the very case cited by the ICJ, on facts similar to the Germany/Italy case, rather than having regard to the underlying transaction on which the original judgment was given, the English Supreme Court, on a construction of the State Immunity Act – its absence of any explicit exception from immunity for judgments, and no waiver by the defendant third State – held that an English court would have been obliged to rule the US adjudicating court's judgment, for which its recognition was sought, to come within the general immunity from the courts of the United Kingdom provided in SIA Section 1(1).

One significant common element in the ICJ and English rulings, however, is that both treat the law of the recognizing State as the applicable law. Indeed, although the English court in *NML* construed the judgment as a legal act distinct from the underlying non-immune cause of action as held by the original US court, it would seem that on the facts of the *Jurisdictional Immunities* case by reason of a written submission to the English court's jurisdiction, it would itself have arrived at the same rulings as that of the ICJ.[16]

---

16   Whilst this may seem to introduce a technical English conflicts-of-law rule to govern the construction of a law on State immunity, it possibly permits a more flexible application of State immunity across frontiers. After all both the ICJ and the English decisions accord recognition to a foreign judgment for which there may well be no reciprocal treaty of enforcement of judgments between the two countries of the judgment court and the recognizing State. One is well advised to remember the comment in *Dicey, Morris and Collins on the Conflict of Laws* (14th edn. (Sweet and Maxwell 2006) para 14–019) that such

To conclude, the standard set by the ICJ to determine recognition of a judgment given against a foreign State by a court of another country is a useful one where the applicable law is clear, as was the case on the facts, once the ICJ had held the absence of any exception to State immunity for war damage to be supported by State practice and likely, however rephrased in national law, to be recognized as a bar to a national court's exercise of jurisdiction. The ICJ's decision was welcomed, and treated as a straightforward matter. Consequently no discussion of controversial issues was required.

However more complicated discrepancies may arise in future with regard to a national court's recognition of a judgment given against a foreign State by another national court. The ICJ itself acknowledged the possibility of variance between rulings of the two courts in that a waiver applicable in the original court might not apply in the recognizing State (para. 132). Similarly, though not mentioned, a jurisdictional requirement for the application of an exception to State immunity might differ between the two jurisdictions (the UK SIA allows an exception for commercial transactions entered into abroad without requiring a territorial link whereas the US law stipulates a *nexus* requirement)[17]; or the status as a sovereign State might be accorded in one State and not another, as with Kosovo in respect of the recognition by the USA and Russia.

Should this sort of discrepancy arise in subsequent disputes it may require further elucidation in the formulation of the standard which international law requires to be applied. No doubt over time either by means of the International Court of Justice or by international treaty that standard will be formulated in sufficient detail to take account of the diversity of situations requiring solution. Might there be, however, a simpler course? Might one treat the two immunities as one, abandon a separate rule of immunity from enforcement and treat immunity from adjudication both as incorporating and determining immunity from enforcement?

But this is another topic for another day!

---

recognition is "singularly generous" given that the State for whose judgment enforcement is sought, may not apply such common treaty rules of jurisdiction in its own courts. It is, therefore, not surprising to find the English court as a national supreme court reserving to its own law the power to recognize or not a foreign judgment given against a foreign State.

17   Or the territorial tort exception may be applied pursuant to SIA s. 5 without, as required by UNSCI article 12, the author of the act or omission having been present in the forum State territory at the time of the act or omission.

CHAPTER 4

Controversial Subjects of Contemporary International Law: IGO-like Entities as Participants in International Legal Relations – Do We Need a 'Reparation Case II'?

*Davorin Lapaš**

1   Introduction

In the concluding remarks to his lecture delivered at the Hague Academy of International Law in 1991 Budislav Vukas, my professor of Public International Law to whom I dedicate this paper, quite bravely asserted: "[T]he supremacy of States is an illusion, which may only temporarily conceal the reality. The history of States confirms their fragility in comparison with the groups of human beings who compose their population."[1] At first sight, the evidence for this conclusion could be found in the political processes that followed very soon, having changed the political map of the world. In fact, the dissolution of the three multinational federations – Yugoslavia, Czechoslovakia and the USSR – at the beginning of the 1990s took place mostly because those States were not accepted by the nations that lived within their borders. However, these processes were not isolated phenomena in international relations at that time. The dissolution of these multinational federations resulted in the creation of several new national States, while at the same time the process of integration in Western Europe, initiated in the early 1950s, led in 1992 to the establishment of a new type of supranational inter-governmental organization – the European Union (EU). It may be ironic, but most of these newly independent national States have very soon become extremely eager to apply for membership of this supranational organization. Therefore, the conclusion on the supremacy of States as an 'illusion' in the context of international relations characterized at the same time by the processes of dissolution and integration could be as much confirmed as denied. Nevertheless, we chose it as a starting point of this paper to indicate the temporary character of a particular form of international

---

* Professor of Public International Law at the University of Zagreb, Faculty of Law.
1 Vukas, B., "States, Peoples and Minorities", *Recueil des cours de l'Académie de droit international de La Haye* (hereinafter: RCADI), vol. 231, 1991-VI, p. 509.

legal personality as dependent on the needs of the international community and international relations in the particular epoch. After all, the International Court of Justice (ICJ) expressed a similar attitude more than half a century ago in its well-known Advisory opinion in the 'Reparation case': "The subjects of law in any legal system are not necessarily identical in their nature or in the extent of their rights, and their nature depends upon the needs of the community."[2] Thus, unlike the international law doctrine at the beginning of the previous century that considered States the only subjects of international law,[3] doctrine in the second half of the 20th century turned primarily to the postulations of general theory of law. Such approach has abstracted the notion of international legal personality from any particular entity, defining it by the general elements of legal personality in theory – legal capacity (*capacitas iuridica*) and the ability of an entity to produce legal consequences on its own (*capacitas agendi*).[4] This being so, the door of international legal personality was opened to any international entity whose *de facto* participation in international relations had become important enough for its legal regulation to provide it with rights and duties, i.e. with the necessary element of legal personality – legal capacity. Consequently, international legal personality became a pure factual category independent of any additional recognition by other, already 'indisputable' subjects of international law. Thus, the international law doctrine in the 1980s finally identified the subjects of international law as participants in legally regulated international relations.[5]

---

2   Reparation for injuries suffered in the service of the United Nations, Advisory Opinion, *ICJ Reports 1949*, p. 178.

3   Thus, for example, in his Manual on International Law in 1902 Liszt began the Chapter on subjects of International Law with the following words: "Nur die Staaten sind Subjekte des Völkerrechts: Träger von völkerrechtlichen Rechten und Pflichten." Liszt, F. von, *Das Völkerrecht – systematisch dargestellt*, Berlin, Verlag von O. Haering, 1902, p. 34. Similar attitude was expressed by the Permanent Court of International Justice in the Case concerning the SS 'Lotus' in 1927; see: Judgment No. 9, 1927, *PCIJ Series A*, No. 10, p. 18.

4   *Cf. e.g.*: Eustathiades, C.Th., "Les sujets du droit international et la responsabilité internationale. Nouvelles tendances", *RCADI*, vol. 84, 1953–III, pp. 414–415; Capotorti, F., "Cours général de droit international public", *RCADI*, vol. 248, 1994–IV, p. 42; Brownlie, I., *Principles of Public International Law*, Oxford, Clarendon Press, 1973, p. 60; Jennings, R., Watts, A. (eds.), *Oppenheim's International Law*, vol. 1, London, Longman, 1995, pp. 119–120.

5   *Cf. e.g.*: Higgins, R., "Conceptual Thinking about the Individual in International Law", in: Falk, R., Kratochwil, F., Mendlowitz, S.H. (eds.), *International Law – A Contemporary Perspective*, Boulder, London, Westview Press, 1985, p. 480. Shaw, however, finds a difference between legal personality and the participation of an entity in international relations. For him, "international personality is participation plus some form of community acceptance."

Such development has neither deprived States of their international legal personality, nor put in question their place in the contemporary international community. However, States had to find their place among the other participants in international legal relations. The functionality of international relations that followed with the technological development in the previous century has considerably facilitated co-operation across States' borders, as well as its institutionalization. Such co-operation has resulted not only in establishing of inter-governmental organizations (IGOs), but also in the appearance of specific IGO-like entities – organizations composed of central or local States' organs, sometimes even including private entities. While IGOs today are unanimously accepted as subjects of international law, those IGO-like entities still wait for their place in international law doctrine, being from time to time just topics of research and analysis in papers like this one.

II Development of International Legal Personality – From Territoriality to Functionality, and Back?

As we have already mentioned, from the beginning of classic international law in the second half of the 17th century until the beginning of the 20th century, only States were accepted as subjects of international law, including their sovereigns – emperors, kings, princes or other rulers.[6] A similar restrictive approach to international legal personality can be found in the works of some East European, and particularly Soviet authors in the second half of the 20th century. However, neither these authors, nor the ancient manuals of international law could neglect some of the entities like the Holy See, the Sovereign Order of Malta, the Catholic Church or even IGOs, that have been completely at odds with such a strictly State-centred approach.[7]

The development of the concept of international legal personality concerning IGOs was much accelerated even in the first half of the 20th century, due both to their founding members – States – and to their increasing number. Thus, the result was consensus in the doctrine recognizing IGOs' objective

---

Shaw, M.N., *International Law*, 5th edn., Cambridge, Cambridge University Press, 2007, pp. 177 and 245–246.

6 For more details on the development of international legal personality in this period see: Nijman, J.E., *The Concept of International Legal Personality – An Inquiry into the History and Theory of International Law*, The Hague, TMC Asser Press, 2004, pp. 29–84.

7 See *e.g.* Tunkin, G.I. (ed.), *International Law*, Moscow, Progress Publishers, 1986, pp. 101–104, and 120–122.

(*i.e. erga omnes*) legal personality. On the other hand, many IGO-like entities that participated in legal relations within the international community remained in an undetermined status *sui generis*, accepted in the doctrine just as *de facto* participants in international relations.

However, it should be remarked that although legal personality in theory has always been dependent on acquiring the rights and duties given out by the rules of a particular legal order (legal capacity), the journey of an entity from *de facto* participant in international (even legal) relations to a wider acceptance of its international legal personality has never been easy. International law doctrine has rarely recognized legal personality in all the new kind of participants in international relations. On the contrary, such process of recognition has always developed gradually until the 'critical mass' of these '*de facto* accepted entities' became sufficient to ensure the recognition of objective international legal personality for all entities of the same kind, including for those in the future. The acceptance of international legal personality for IGOs can be a very illustrative example here.

Although the first modern international organizations appeared in the second half of the 19th century (like the International Telegraphic Union – ITU in 1865, and the Universal Postal Union – UPU in 1874), the above-mentioned Advisory opinion of the ICJ in the 'Reparation case' in 1949 has usually been considered a turning-point for the recognition of IGOs' legal personality in international law. However, the Court accepted objective international legal personality only for the United Nations, and on the basis of the argument "that fifty States, representing the vast majority of the members of the international community, had the power, in conformity with international law, to bring into being an entity possessing objective international personality..."[8]

Soon after that, it became impossible to deny the same recognition to other universal IGOs like the UN specialized agencies. All this led international law doctrine to the acceptance of the 'objective international personality' of IGOs in general,[9] no matter how numerous or universal their membership. After all, the same attitude can be found in the ICJ's Advisory opinion concerning the Interpretation of the Agreement between the WHO and Egypt, in 1980.[10]

---

8   ICJ Reports 1949, *supra* (note 2), p. 185.
9   Thus, Seyersted considered intergovernmental organizations '*general* subjects of international law'. Seyersted, F., *Objective International Personality of Intergovernmental Organizations – Do Their Capacities Really Depend upon Their Constitutions?*, Copenhagen, 1963, p. 100.
10 The ICJ clearly stated: "International organizations are subjects of international law and, as such, are bound by any obligations incumbent upon them under general rules of

Therefore, today every newly established IGO acquires international legal personality *ipso facto* based on general customary international law, in basically the same manner as States, having fulfilled the objective criteria, *i.e.* the constitutive elements required in legal doctrine for its existence.[11] Thus, according to Fitzmaurice, "the term 'international organization' means a collectivity of States established by treaty, with a constitution and common organs, having a personality distinct from that of its member-States, and being a subject of international law with treaty-making capacity."[12]

Such development was important not only because of the enlargement of the set of international law subjects, but also for the fact that the acceptance of the 'objective international personality' of IGOs has confirmed at the same time the ability of non-territorial entities to acquire international legal personality. Thus, the element of 'territoriality', primarily proper to States, in the case of IGOs has been replaced by the element of 'functionality' as the *ratio* for the existence of those organizations as institutionalized forms of co-operation among their member States.

However, such co-operation and consequently its institutionalization have not always resulted in the creation of homogenous international organizations gathering formally in their membership States, other IGOs, or the other sovereign subjects of international law (*e.g.* the Holy See as a member of the FAO, IFAD, UPU *etc.*). Sometimes, the purpose of such co-operation led directly to its institutionalization in the form of IGO-like entities. Their membership is sometimes composed of the central State organs having legal personality in the public law of their respective States, but not in international law (*e.g.* 'official police bodies' in the International Criminal Police Organization – INTERPOL, or the parliaments in the Inter-Parliamentary Union – IPU). Because of such differences in membership in comparison with the 'classic' IGOs, as well as because their legal personality is still disputable in international law doctrine, these organizations are sometimes called 'transgovernmental organizations' (TGOs).[13]

---

international law, under their constitutions or under international agreement to which they are parties." Interpretation of the Agreement of 25 March 1951 between the WHO and Egypt, Advisory Opinion, *ICJ Reports 1980*, pp. 89–90.

11 See: Seyersted, *op. cit.* (note 9), p. 100.
12 Report on the Law of Treaties by Mr. G.G. Fitzmaurice; Art. 3, para. b), A/CN.4/101, *Yearbook of the International Law Commission*, vol. II, 1956, p. 108.
13 See *e.g.* Archer, C., *International Organizations*, 3rd edn., London, New York, Routledge, 2001, p. 40. However, Archer considers TGOs just a part of the broader category of international organizations that he calls the 'transnational organizations' (TNOs). According to his classification, the 'genuine INGOs', 'hybrid INGOs' (QUANGOs), and business INGOs (BINGOs) are also sorts of TNOs. *Ibid.*, pp. 38–40.

On the other hand, the functional logic of co-operation across States' borders has sometimes resulted in institutionalized co-operation among the local and regional authorities or other sub-State entities with legal personality in the public law of their States, but not in international law. The activities of these heterogeneous organizations, so-called 'interregional organizations' (IROs), are usually territorially determined. However, this should not put in question these organizations as non-territorial entities, bearing in mind the existence of some IGOs (*e.g.* the International Commission of the Rhine, or the Commission for the Danube) which are equally characterized by the territorially defined purpose of co-operation among their member States.

Finally, in contemporary international relations it is hard to neglect the presence of (international) NGOs. Some of them, usually called 'hybrid' or 'quasi-NGOs' (QUANGOs), even have both categories of entities as members: States, IGOs and other sovereign subjects of international law, as well as those entities belonging to the non-governmental sector. Thus, while Nicolas Politis almost a century ago described State sovereignty as a cage,[14] the accelerated technological development in the last decades has stimulated direct cross-border co-operation between public and private subjects (almost) independent of the diplomatic activities of 'their' States. Due to the institutionalization of such co-operation through the creation of various permanent international bodies, international relations and their participants have today become more heterogeneous than ever before. Of course, the functionality of international relations has not always followed the doctrinal 'types' of the 'recognized' subjects of international law. All through history, the subjects of international law have usually been created by the needs of the international community and not by scholars. Consequently, one should not be surprised to see the role of international law doctrine as similar to that of natural sciences, trying to understand and describe the processes and their participants in the international community rather than to shape international relations according to its own – legal – logic. This being so, we will meet a myriad of hybrid forms of entities participating in contemporary international (legal) relations.

Therefore, being aware of the complexity of these relations and their participants, we will try to offer at least an attempt to systematize such IGO-like entities participating in legally regulated relations in the contemporary international community, starting, as we have already mentioned, from their objective characteristics and various forms of their participation in those relations. For the

---

14   According to Politis, "[L]'État souverain était pour ses sujets une cage de fer d'où ils ne pouvaient juridiquement communiquer avec l'extérieur qu'au travers de très étroits barreaux." Politis, N., *Les nouvelles tendances du droit international*, Paris, Librairie Hachette, 1927, p. 91.

purpose of this paper we will analyse as 'IGO-like entities' primarily the organizations whose membership, although seemingly composed of States, formally consists of States' central, regional or local authorities participating on their own behalf (TGOs and IROs), while the last sections will focus on the 'hybrid' organizations gathering the public or private law subjects of different States' legal orders, together (and with equal rights and duties) with States, IGOs or other sovereign subjects of public international law (QUAIROs and QUANGOs).

1   *Transgovernmental Organizations (TGOs)*

Unlike IGOs whose membership is formally composed of States or other generally accepted, sovereign subjects of public international law on the one hand, and 'classic' international non-governmental organizations (INGOs) gathering the subjects of private law in domestic legal orders (like NGOs, and even the individuals from different States) on the other, some international entities that appeared in international (legal) relations more than a century ago could not easily be classified in this way. Some of these IGO-like entities have included in their membership various States' central organs as the public law subjects in those States' legal orders. However, these organs, not being subjects of international law, have participated in such membership in their own capacity, and not as representatives of their States.

Thus, unlike international law a few centuries ago that accorded international legal personality not only to States, but also to their sovereigns (emperors, kings, princes or other rulers),[15] the contemporary international law doctrine considers even the highest State organs just as representatives of States, *i.e.* deprived of any international legal personality of their own. Therefore, it is necessary to draw a distinction between some IGOs where the member States act through their organs (such as *e.g.* the competent national administrations,[16]

---

15   See: Nijman, *op. cit.* (note 6), pp. 29–84.

16   Thus, for example Article 11 of the Constitution of the World Health Organization regulating the composition of the World Health Assembly provides that each member State "shall be represented by not more than three delegates. ...These delegates should be chosen from among persons most qualified by their technical competence in the field of health, preferably representing the national health administration of the Member." The Constitution was adopted by the International Health Conference held in New York from 19 June to 22 July 1946, signed on 22 July 1946 and entered into force on 7 April 1948. For the original text see: *United Nations Treaty Series* (hereinafter: *UNTS*), vol. 14, 1948, pp. 186 *et seq.* Amendments adopted by the Twenty-sixth, Twenty-ninth, Thirty-ninth and Fifty-first World Health Assemblies (resolutions WHA26.37, WHA29.38, WHA39.6 and WHA51.23) came into force on 3 February 1977, 20 January 1984, 11 July 1994 and 15 September 2005 respectively.

State services,[17] Governors of central national banks,[18] *etc.*), and the organizations having the States' central organs (like the parliaments, ministries or other central bodies) formally in their membership as full members.

We are going to mention here two such organizations having been understood by international law doctrine and practice for decades as INGOs, despite the public law character of their members in their domestic States' legal orders. Today, it seems to us necessary to take into account the distinctive features of these IGO-like entities, analysing them as belonging to a specific category of participant in international (legal) relations – the TGOs.

a The Inter-Parliamentary Union (IPU)

The Inter-Parliamentary Union was established in 1889 as an organization of individual parliamentarians of mostly European States. Since then, it has developed into a global organization, which today has 163 Member Parliaments.[19] Its basic act – the Statutes of the Inter-Parliamentary Union – defines it in Article 1 as follows: "The Inter-Parliamentary Union is the international organisation of the Parliaments of sovereign States."[20]

Although having all the earlier-mentioned constitutive elements of IGOs, the IPU differs from these organizations primarily concerning their membership, and consequently the legal nature of their constituent instruments. According to Article 3 of the Statutes of the Inter-Parliamentary Union, the parliaments of sovereign States, and not the States themselves, may become members of the IPU.[21] This being so, according to contemporary international

---

17 See *e.g.* Article 7, para. b) of the Convention of the World Meteorological Organization regulating the composition of the World Meteorological Congress which provides that each member State "shall designate one of its delegates, who should be the Director of its Meteorological or Hydrometeorological Service, as its principal delegate at Congress." For the original text of the Convention see: *UNTS*, vol. 77, 1950–1951, pp. 143 *et seq.* The Convention was last amended in 2007.

18 See *e.g.* Article XII, section 2 of the Agreement of the International Monetary Fund regulating the composition of the Board of Governors, which provides that the Board shall consist of one Governor and one Alternate appointed by each member State in such manner as it may determine. The governor is usually the minister of finance or the governor of the central bank. For the original text of the Agreement see: *UNTS*, vol. 2, 1947, pp. 39 *et seq.*

19 For the list of IPU Member Parliaments see: <http://www.ipu.org/english/membshp.htm> (14 October 2013).

20 See the Statutes of the Inter-Parliamentary Union, as revised and amended in October 2011. For the text see: <http://www.ipu.org/strct-e/statutes-new.htm>(24 May 2013).

21 Equally, according to Art. 3, para. 2 of the IPU Statutes, even the parliament of a territorial entity whose aspirations and entitlement to statehood are recognized by the United

law doctrine, the Statutes of the IPU are not understood as a treaty since the parties – the IPU members – have neither international legal personality nor, as a consequence, treaty-making capacity in public international law. Starting from such differences, international law doctrine has defined the IPU for decades in a negative way – putting it in an undifferentiated group of 'non-IGOs', without taking into account the specific features existing among the entities which have found their place within such a residual group.[22] Thus, according to Article 71 of the UN Charter, the IPU was granted consultative status in the UN Economic and Social Council (ECOSOC) in 1947 as provided primarily for NGOs. However, in the next half-century the IPU's activities have shown many differences compared to those of NGOs. The IPU has concluded agreements with numerous States, *e.g.* the Headquarters agreement with Switzerland,[23] but also similar agreements with other States giving it privileges and immunities similar to those of IGOs.[24] Moreover, the IPU has concluded various co-operation agreements with many IGOs. Thus, the Cooperation Agreement between the United Nations and the Inter-Parliamentary Union was signed at New York on 24 July 1996.[25] Soon after that, the UN General

---

Nations, and which enjoys the status of Permanent Observer to that Organization may also become a member of the IPU. *Ibid.*

22   Thus, *e.g.* Bettati states: "Ainsi, l'Union interparlementaire n'est pas une organisation internationale dans la mesure où elle est créée par des parlements nationaux." See: Bettati, M., "Création et personnalité juridique des organisations internationales", in: Dupuy, R.J. (ed.), *Manuel sur les organisations internationales/A Handbook on International Organizations*, 2nd edn., The Hague, Martinus Nijhoff, 1998, p. 34.

23   For the text of the Agreement on the juridical status of the Inter-Parliamentary Union in Switzerland see: <http://www.ipu.org/finance-e/siege.pdf>(5 January 2013).

24   Thus, for example, see the Agreement between the IPU and the United States: Exchange of notes constituting an Agreement concerning the reimbursement of income tax of 1981. It should be mentioned that the Agreement was published in the United Nations Treaty Series; for the text see: *UNTS*, vol. 1549, 1989, pp. 383 *et seq.* Moreover, the United States, by the Executive Order 13097 of President Clinton in 1998, recognized the Inter-Parliamentary Union as a public international organization entitled to enjoy the privileges, exemptions, and immunities conferred by the International Organizations Immunities Act. See: Executive Order 13097 of August 7, 1998, Inter-Parliamentary Union, *Federal Register*, vol. 63, 1998. For the text see also: <http://www.presidency.ucsb.edu/ws/index.php?pid=54754> (5 January 2013).

25   The text of the Agreement can be found in the Annex to the UN General Assembly Resolution A/Res./51/402 of 25 September 1996. Thus, paragraph 5 of the Resolution provides: "The Agreement aims at strengthening relations between the two organizations by substantially facilitating their effective exercise of mutually complementary activities and allowing them to cooperate more closely in undertaking joint efforts in particular

Assembly called on the UN specialized agencies to conclude similar agreements with the IPU. Consequently, in 1999 a co-operation agreement was concluded between the ILO and the IPU. Article 3, para. 2 of the Agreement provides that: "The IPU shall be invited to participate in meetings of the International Labour Conference with the status of an official international organization...."[26]

Similarly, the UN Secretary-General in his Report of 2001 concluded that the classification of the IPU as an INGO with consultative status with ECOSOC was obsolete.[27] Therefore, the UN General Assembly has encouraged the IPU "to strengthen further its contribution to the work of the General Assembly, including its revitalization, and in relation to the process of United Nations reform and system-wide coherence."[28] Thus, the UN General Assembly in its Resolution A/57/32 of 19 November 2002 recognized observer status to the IPU, thereby concluding its consultative status with ECOSOC. Moreover, the General Assembly by its Resolution A/57/47 of 21 November 2002 invited the UN specialized agencies "to consider adopting similar modalities for cooperation with the Inter-Parliamentary Union."

All this led some authors to the conclusion that the IPU has become an IGO.[29] However, all the above-mentioned differences as compared with IGOs seem to us much more an argument for the conclusion that the IPU, as an organization still very different from IGOs, has achieved international legal

---

areas of their activities for the benefit of mankind." This Agreement was also published in the United Nations Treaty Series; for the text see: *UNTS*, vol. 1929, 1996, pp. 333 *et seq.*

26 For the text of the Agreement see: *Official Bulletin of the ILO*, vol. LXXXII, 1999, Series A, no. 1. Also available at: <http://www.ilo.org/public/english/bureau/leg/agreements/ipu.htm> (5 January 2013).

27 According to this Report, the IPU's consultative status "dates back to 1947 and no longer corresponds to the status of the world organization of parliaments, a unique inter-State organization representing 141 parliaments." See: Cooperation between the United Nations and the Inter-Parliamentary Union, Report of the Secretary General (A/55/996) of 26 June 2001, pp. 1–2.

28 See: Interaction between the United Nations, national parliaments and the Inter-Parliamentary Union; A/Res./66/261 of 7 June 2012, para. 3.

29 See for example: Brownlie, I., Goodwin-Gill, G.S., Joint Opinion on the international legal personality of the IPU, its status as an international organization in international law, and the legal implications of such status for the IPU's relations with governments and other international organizations; Reform of the Inter-Parliamentary Union, IPU-Doc. EX/229/9-Inf.1, of 5 October 1999; <http://www.ipu.org/finance-e/opinion.pdf> (5 January 2013). See also: Williams, R.V., *The Information Systems of International Inter-governmental Organizations: A Reference Guide*, Stamford, Ablex Publishing Corporation, 1998, pp. 325–327.

personality through its participation in legally regulated international relations, without changing its features or its nature.

b   The International Criminal Police Organization (ICPO/INTERPOL)

The International Criminal Police Organization (ICPO/INTERPOL) was created "[t]o ensure and promote the widest possible mutual assistance between all criminal police authorities within the limits of the laws existing in the different countries and...to establish and develop all institutions likely to contribute effectively to the prevention and suppression of ordinary law crimes."[30] Established in 1923 as 'the International Criminal Police Commission (ICPC)', INTERPOL has developed through the decades into an organization gathering in its membership 'official police bodies' from different States.[31] Therefore, the members of INTERPOL are not formally States, but their 'official police bodies' whose functions come within the framework of the activities of the Organization.[32] Consequently, INTERPOL differs from IGOs also by the fact that its basic act – 'Constitution' – is not considered in international law to be a treaty since its parties, although legal persons of public law in their States, are not accepted as subjects of international law.

For these reasons, some authors identified INTERPOL as an INGO,[33] denying it any international legal personality.[34] However, INTERPOL has some characteristics distinguishing it significantly from 'classic' INGOs. Beside the fact that its membership is composed of entities having legal personality within States' *public* law, INTERPOL, like the IPU, has also achieved some treaty-making capacity (*ius contrahendi*) directly on the international level, having participated in treaty relations not only with States, but also with IGOs. After all, the very provision of Article 41 of the INTERPOL Constitution envisaged the possibility of its participation in legal relations with IGOs. Thus, for example, we can mention here the Cooperation Agreement between the United Nations

---

30   ICPO-INTERPOL Constitution, Art. 2, paras. 1 and 2. The text of the Constitution is available at: <http://www.interpol.int/About-INTERPOL/Legal-materials/The-Constitution> (23 September 2013).
31   *Ibid.*, Art. 4, para. 1.
32   In spite of that, the official INTERPOL website uses the term 'member countries'; see: <http://www.interpol.int/Member-countries/World> (15 January 2013).
33   See *e.g.*: Shermers, H.G., "International organizations membership", in: Bernhardt, R. (ed.), *Encyclopedia of Public International Law*, vol. 2, Amsterdam, Lausanne, New York, Oxford, Shannon, Tokyo, North-Holland Elsevier, 1995, p. 1321.
34   Thus, Gallas stated: "Interpol is not an international organization. It is therefore not a subject of international law and has no jurisdiction of its own." Gallas, A., "INTERPOL", in: Bernhardt (ed.), *ibid.*, p. 1414.

and INTERPOL of 8 July 1997, as well as the Arrangement on Co-operation between the International Criminal Police Organization – INTERPOL – and the United Nations in relation to the United Nations Security Council Sanctions Committees Supplementary to the Cooperation Agreement between the International Criminal Police Organization-INTERPOL and the United Nations of 2009. In the later Agreement the "Parties agree to exchange information and documents to achieve the best use of available information related to issues of common interest..." (Section 2).

Furthermore, INTERPOL was recognized as having legal capacity within the domestic legal orders of various States, not only by their unilateral legal acts (*e.g.* in the United States),[35] but also in bilateral treaties (*e.g.* the INTERPOL Headquarters Agreement with France).[36] Thus, INTERPOL has concluded similar agreements with some other States in which it performs its activities, *e.g.* with Argentina, Cameroon, Côte d'Ivoire, El Salvador, Kenya, Thailand, and Zimbabwe.[37] By these agreements, as well as by the earlier-mentioned unilateral acts of States, INTERPOL in these States has gained not only the recognition of its legal personality, but also the privileges and immunities analogous to those of IGOs and their officials, such as the immunity from legal process in respect of all acts performed in connection with its official duties; immunity from seizure, confiscation, requisition, expropriation, or any other form of administrative or judicial constraint; the inviolability of the Organization's premises, official correspondence, archives and all documents; exemption

---

35   Thus, according to the Executive Order 12425, INTERPOL is designated as "a public international organization entitled to enjoy the privileges, exemptions and immunities conferred by the International Organizations Immunities Act; except those provided by Section 2(c), the portions of Section 2(d) and Section 3 relating to customs duties and federal internal-revenue importation taxes, Section 4, Section 5, and Section 6 of that Act." See: Executive Order of President Ronald Reagan, No. 12425 of 16 June 1983. For the text see: <http://www.presidency.ucsb.edu/ws/index.php?pid=41483> (6 March 2013). In 2009, President Obama amended this Executive Order by lifting limitations of diplomatic immunities set down in the above-mentioned exceptions. See: Executive Order of President Barack Obama, No. 13524 of 16 December 2009. For the text see: <http://www.presidency.ucsb.edu/ws/index.php?pid=87003> (2 April 2013).

36   Article 2 of the Headquarter Agreement between INTERPOL and France provides:
     "The Government of the French Republic recognizes the Organization's legal personality and, in particular, its capacity to: (a) enter into contracts; (b) acquire and dispose of movable and immovable property connected with its activities; (c) be party to judicial proceedings." The text of the Agreement is available at: <http://www.interpol.int/About-INTERPOL/Legal-materials/Fundamental-texts> (15 January 2013).

37   The texts of the above-mentioned Agreements are available at: <https://secure.interpol.int/Public/ICPO/LegalMaterials/constitution/hqagreement/Default.asp> (8 April 2013).

from all direct taxation for the assets, income and other property of the Organization, *etc*. Moreover, it should be mentioned here that, starting from 2010, INTERPOL officials, analogously with those of some IGOs (*e.g.* UN), can use the INTERPOL Travel Document – *i.e.* the 'INTERPOL Passport' accepted by the countries whose 'official police bodies' are its members.

In addition, INTERPOL has concluded numerous agreements on co-operation with various IGOs, including some of the specialized agencies of the UN.[38] Finally, in the context of this paper the fact that INTERPOL is among the Contracting Parties to the Vienna Convention on the Law of Treaties between States and International Organizations or between International Organizations of 1986 seems particularly worth mentioning, taking into account that according to the Final Provisions of the Convention only States and IGOs, which have the capacity to conclude treaties (Art. 84), can become Parties thereto.[39]

On the other hand, like the IPU, INTERPOL from 1949 enjoyed consultative status with the UN ECOSOC as provided for NGOs by Article 71 of the Charter. However, the status of INTERPOL within the UN has been changing since 1971 when ECOSOC in its Resolution 1579(L) approved the 'Arrangement for co-operation, between the United Nations and the International Criminal Police Organization (INTERPOL)' set out in the Annex of the mentioned Resolution.[40] Finally, the UN General Assembly in its Resolution 51/1 of 1996 invited INTERPOL to participate in the sessions and the work of the General Assembly in the capacity of observer.[41] Thereby, INTERPOL has been included among the intergovernmental organizations having received a standing invitation

---

38   *E.g.* Memorandum of Understanding on Co-operation between the International Criminal Police Organization – INTERPOL and the Universal Postal Union (UPU); Co-operation Agreement between the International Criminal Police Organization – INTERPOL and the World Intellectual Property Organization (WIPO); Co-operation Agreement between the International Criminal Police Organization – INTERPOL and the United Nations Educational, Scientific and Cultural Organization (UNESCO), Memorandum of Understanding on Co-operation between the International Criminal Police Organization – INTERPOL and International Civil Aviation Organization (ICAO); *etc.* Texts available at: <http://www.interpol.int/About-INTERPOL/Legal-materials/International-Cooperation-Agreements> (6 March 2013).

39   The above-mentioned provisions also included Namibia, which, at the time when the Convention was signed, was represented by the UN Council for Namibia. For the text of the Convention see: Official Records of the United Nations Conference on the Law of Treaties between States and International Organizations or between International Organizations, vol. II (United Nations publication, Sales No. E.94.V.5).

40   See: ECOSOC Resolution 1579(L) of 20 May 1971.

41   See: A/Res./51/1 of 22 October 1996.

for such participation.⁴² This being so, the ILOAT clearly stated in its Judgment of 1996: "Interpol is an independent international organisation…"⁴³ Also, the similar examples of some other UN specialized agencies could be mentioned here recognizing INTERPOL as an IGO, *e.g.* WIPO,⁴⁴ or ICAO.⁴⁵

All these facts have been interpreted by some authors as pointing to the fact that INTERPOL has been transformed from an INGO to an IGO.⁴⁶ However, having in mind the earlier-mentioned substantial differences between the INTERPOL and IGOS, such a conclusion seems oversimplified. On the contrary, it is much more plausible to accept that a peculiar international entity, composed of public law subjects from different States (just like the IPU), has achieved some elements of international legal personality through its participation in legally regulated international relations, than to equate it at any rate with IGOs, ignoring the differences which obviously exist between IGOs and TGOs.

2 *Interregional Organizations (IROS)*

The development of technology in the previous decades, as we have mentioned above, enabled not only public but also private law subjects including individuals from different States to co-operate directly across States' borders. At the same time, the enlargement of the scope of international issues has meant that central governments have been faced with internationalized activities that have made the centralized decision-making process harder than ever.

---

42   For the list of intergovernmental organizations having received a standing invitation to participate as observers in the sessions and the work of the UN General Assembly and maintaining permanent offices at Headquarters, see: <http://www.un.org/en/members/intergovorg.shtml> (14 March 2013).

43   ILOAT Judgment No. 1080 of 29 January 1991, para. 12; available at: <http://www.ilo.org/dyn/triblex/triblexmain.fullText?p_lang=en&p_judgment_no=1080&p_language_code=EN> (21 March 2013).

44   Thus, the Assemblies of the member States of WIPO in 1999 admitted INTERPOL as an IGO to attend the meetings of the Assembly as observer; see: Assemblies of the member States of WIPO, Thirty-Fourth Series of Meetings, Geneva, September 20 to 29, 1999 (A/34/10 Rev.), paras. 5–6, p. 2; available at: <http://www.wipo.int/edocs/mdocs/govbody/en/a_34/a_34_10_rev-main1.pdf> (21 March 2013).

45   See: ICAO, 48th ICAO Familiarization Course, p. 2; available at: <http://legacy.icao.int/icao/en/osg/epo/fam/48/summaries_en.pdf> (22 January 2013).

46   See *e.g.*: Osmańczyk, E.J., *Encyclopedia of the United Nations and International Agreements*, vol. 2, New York, London, Routledge, 2003, p. 1102; Rutsel Silvestre, J.M., *The Legal Foundations of INTERPOL*, Portland, Hart Publishing, 2010, pp. 22–23, 138–154; Schermers, H.G., Blokker, N.M., *International Institutional Law*, Leiden, Martinus Nijhoff Publishers, 2003, pp. 29–30.

This situation has necessarily led to co-operation on the sub-State, *i.e.* interregional level. Gradually, such co-operation has become more and more institutionalized, having resulted in some new international entities – *i.e.* organizations substantively different from IGOs. Such a process can be particularly visible in the field of transregional co-operation that led in recent decades to the appearance of IROs gathering formally in their membership the various sub-State entities of different States. Consequently, these organizations differ from IGOs primarily in respect of their membership. Instead of States or other sovereign subjects of public international law, their membership consists of regions, sub-national, even federal units and other local authorities from different States. Therefore, according to contemporary international law doctrine, the constituent instruments of these organizations are not accepted as treaties in terms of Article 5 of the Vienna Conventions on the Law of Treaties of 1969 and 1986.[47] On the other hand, the main difference between the above-mentioned TGOs and IROs lies in the fact that in TGOs the central States' organs formally participate in their membership, acting on their own behalf although their activities directly affect the international co-operation of their States. Membership of IROs, however, formally consists of territorially determined sub-State entities[48] having legal personality in the public law of their States. Therefore, the organs of the sub-State entities which are members of such IROs will never act on their own behalf, but in the name of the sub-State entities as the formal members of such organizations. Sometimes these IROs obtain the recognition of their legal personality in the States whose sub-State entities participate in their membership as a result of those States' treaty

---

47 For the text of the Vienna Convention on the Law of Treaties of 1969 see: *UNTS*, vol. 1155, 1980, pp. 331 *et seq.* For the text of the Vienna Convention on the Law of Treaties between States and International Organizations or between International Organizations see: *supra*, note 39.

48 In this context, several organizations seem to be exceptions. Thus, for example, we can mention here the International Union of Local Authorities (IULA), an organization established in 1913 in the Netherlands with the intention of promoting democratic local self-government all over the world. Although the IULA has as its members local authorities from different countries and even different continents, its goals and activities are not territorially determined. In its work the IULA concentrates on encouraging decentralization, municipal international co-operation and promoting democratic local government worldwide. Equally, some other, sometimes called 'sectoral' IROs, participating in the AER's membership, can be noted here as well, such as the Assembly of European Wine-Producing Regions – AREV, the Assembly of European Fruit and Vegetable Growing and Horticultural Regions – AREFLH, the Association of Local Democracy Agencies – ALDA, and the Federation of Local Authority Chief Executives in Europe (UDiTE). See: *infra*, note 84.

obligations. Nevertheless, although quite absurdly, sometimes the very Statutes of these organizations deny their legal personality in spite of their participation in legal relations with States, IGOs or other indisputable subjects of international law. That said, having in mind the nature of legal personality as a *de facto* category, we are going to analyse these organizations starting from their actual participation in legally regulated international relations.

a   European Groupings of Territorial Cooperation (EGTCs) and Euroregional Co-operation Groupings (ECGs)

In contrast to almost unlimited State sovereignty as understood at the beginning of the 20th century, in recent times some profound changes have taken place in the world, threatening to defy States' borders. Of course, this does not mean that sovereignty has become an obsolete concept. However, as Pascual and Benner correctly remarked, "sovereignty premised on borders serving as inviolable boundaries simply does not function in a world where money, ideas, capital, labour and even pollution know no bounds."[49] Having in mind the proliferation and diversity of contemporary international relations and their participants, some authors came to a conclusion on the appearance of 'post-national law'.[50] Although one could consider that "the term post-nationalism goes too far",[51] few would deny a strong transnational character to contemporary international relations characterized not only by the co-operation of individuals and private entities across States' borders, resulting in hundreds of thousands INGOs all over the world, but also by the institutionalized co-operation of regions and other sub-State entities from different, mostly neighbouring States relating to questions of their common interest. The institutionalization of such co-operation has resulted in the creation of a new type of 'transfrontier organism' (*organismes transfrontaliers*) – IROs. Though cross-border co-operation can also be found in other continents,[52] this process had

---

49   Pascual, C., Benner, H., "Sovereignty's Evolution: The Role of Regions – Regional Convergence in a Transnational World", in: De Lombaerde, Ph., Baert F., Felício, T. (eds.), *The United Nations and the Regions: Third World Report on Regional Integration*, United Nations University Series on Regionalism, vol. 3, Dordrecht, Heidelberg, Springer, 2012, p. 17.

50   For more details see: Krisch, N., *Beyond Constitutionalism: The Pluralist Structure of Postnational Law*, Oxford, Oxford University Press, 2010, pp. 5–14.

51   See: Shaffer, G., "A Transnational Take on Krisch's Pluralist Structure of Postnational Law", *European Journal of International Law*, vol. 23, no. 2, 2012, pp. 577–579 and 582.

52   See: Cornago, N., "On the Normalization of Sub-State Diplomacy", in: Criekemans, D. (ed.), *Regional Sub-State Diplomacy Today*, Leiden, Boston, Martinus Nijhoff Publishers, 2010, p. 29.

its culmination exactly at the heart of Europe, as Vedovato interestingly remarked: "[L]à où sont apparues les premières identités nationales."[53] Thus, the European Parliament in 1960 mentioned for the first time the notion of a 'Europe of regions' , thereby beginning the process of interregional co-operation in Europe aiming at reducing disparities in development among the European regions and making Europe polycentric.[54] Furthermore, in 1985 the member States of the Council of Europe (CoE) signed the European Charter of Local Self-Government with the aim of improving "the right and the ability of local authorities, within the limits of the law, to regulate and manage a substantial share of public affairs under their own responsibility and in the interests of the local population" (Art. 3(1)).[55] On the other hand, Regulation 1082/2006 of the European Parliament and the Council of 5 July 2006 in its Preamble correctly stated that the increase in the number of land and maritime borders in the Community following its enlargement made it necessary to facilitate the reinforcement of territorial co-operation in the Community (i.e. within the EU).[56] One of the most significant forms of such co-operation in Europe today is the European Grouping of Territorial Cooperation (EGTC). Moreover, this Regulation creates EGTCs as a new type of international entity

---

53 Vedovato, G., "La coopération transfrontalière, les eurorégions et le Conseil de l'Europe", *Annuaire Européen*, vol. XLIII, 1995, p. 1. Such a phenomenon of direct co-operation between the regions or other sub-State entities of different States today is often described as 'paradiplomacy' or 'sub-State diplomacy'; see *e.g.*: Wolff, S., "Paradiplomacy: Scope, Opportunities and Challenges", *Bologna Center Journal of International Affairs*, vol. 10, 2010, available at: <http://bcjournal.org/volume-10/paradiplomacy.html> (22 May 2013). Although this phenomenon can be found under different names such as 'micro-diplomacy', 'multilayered diplomacy', or 'constituent diplomacy', paradiplomacy has usually been defined as "...sub-state governments' involvement in international relations, through the establishment of formal and informal contacts, either permanent or ad hoc, with foreign public or private entities, with the aim to promote socio-economic, cultural or political issues, as well as any other foreign dimension of their own constitutional competences." Cornago, *op. cit.* (note 52), p. 13.

54 For more details of this process, particularly through the INTERREG I, II and III Programmes, see: Garcia-Duran, Huet, P., "Vers l'Europe des eurorégions? L'objectif de 'cohésion territoriale'", *Revue du Marché commun et de l'Union européenne*, no. 491, septembre 2005, pp. 499–502. Also, for the INTERREG IV Programme see: <http://www.interreg-fwvl.eu/fr/page.php?pageId=204> (4 October 2013).

55 European Charter of Local Self-Government, signed in Strasbourg on 15 October 1985; *European Treaty Series* (hereinafter: ETS), No. 122.

56 See: Regulation 1082/2006 of the European Parliament and the Council of 5 July 2006 on a European grouping of territorial cooperation (EGTC); Preamble, para. 3; *Official Journal of the European Union*, L210 of 31 July 2006.

– *i.e.* IROs, providing that the tasks and competences of an EGTC are to be set out in a convention and its statutes, together with its organs and rules for its budget and for the exercise of its financial responsibility.[57] Moreover, the Regulation has envisaged the possibility of participation in an EGTC even for entities from third countries where the legislation of a third country or agreements between the Community (*i.e.* the EU) member States and third countries so allow.[58] At the same time, "the Regulation has allowed subnational units to conclude a cross-border convention with homologous foreign counterparts for a cross-border co-operation body establishment, no matter if such a possibility was previously granted according to the relevant domestic legal order."[59] However, Article 1, paragraph 3 of the Regulation seems to be the most important in the context of this paper, providing that "an EGTC shall have legal personality." An EGTC acquires legal personality on the day of registration in its EU member State, or the publication of its Statutes, whichever occurs first,[60] while the EGTC members shall thereafter inform the member States concerned as well as the Committee of the Regions about the registration of an EGTC and publication of its statutes.[61] Nevertheless, in the context of the EGTCs' legal personality this provision is not much different from those of Article 47 of the Lisbon Treaty on European Union,[62] or Article 104 of the UN Charter, which

---

57   *Ibid.*, paras. 10 and 14.
58   *Ibid.*, para. 16.
59   Strazzari, D., "Harmonizing Trends *vs.* Domestic Regulatory Frameworks: Looking for the European Law on Cross-Border Cooperation", *European Journal of Legal Studies*, vol. 4, no. 1, 2011, p. 154. Thus, Strazzari considers the *Groupement local de coopération transfrontalière* (GLCT), as provided by the Karlsruhe Accord, a legal model that anticipated the following treaties concerning cross-border co-operation, and even the EGTC Regulation. See: *ibid.*, p. 165. See Art. 11 of the *Accord de Karlsruhe sur la coopération transfrontalière entre les collectivités territoriales et organismes publics locaux*. The text of the Karlsruhe Accord of 23 January 1996 is available at: <http://www.ge.ch/legislation/rsg/f/s/rsg_A1_11.html> (23 September 2013).
60   Regulation 1082/2006, Art. 5, para. 1. Also, Article 2 of the Regulation provides that "where it is necessary under Community or international private law to establish the choice of law which governs an EGTC's acts, an EGTC shall be treated as an entity of the Member State where it has its registered office." *Ibid*.
61   For the List of 37 EGTCs whose establishment was notified to the Committee of the Regions of the European Union on 25 June 2013 see: <https://portal.cor.europa.eu/egtc/en-US/Register/Pages/welcome.aspx> (23 September 2013). For the map of the EGTCs by November 2013 see: <http://cesci-net.eu/tiny_mce/uploaded/Europa_EGTC_ENG1_9.png> (4 December 2013).
62   Thus, Article 47 of the Lisbon Treaty on European Union does not mention expressly the EU's *international* legal personality, providing just that: "The Union shall have legal

provides: "The Organization shall enjoy in the territory of each of its Members such legal capacity as may be necessary for the exercise of its functions and the fulfilment of its purposes." In both cases, the international legal personality of these organizations derives from the international legal obligation of States to recognize their legal personality primarily in their own domestic legal orders. Thus, according to Article 1 of the Regulation the EU member States accept the international legal obligation to recognize the legal personality of an EGTC by allowing their regions to be members of it. In fact, such a situation is very much like to the notion of *pactum in favorem tertii, i.e.* 'third-party beneficiary contract' common not only to Roman law, or civil law in many States, but also to general legal theory. Hereby, States accept the legal obligation comprising at the same time the right of the third party – an EGTC – to obtain recognition of legal personality in these States' legal orders according to the provisions of the Regulation. Similarly, even today the legal capacity of an individual in international law derives to a certain degree from the States' international legal obligations in respect of human rights, where an individual often appears as 'the third party beneficiary'. Thus, although primarily directed to the recognition of the EGTCs' legal personality in the domestic legal orders of the EU member States, the same provision indirectly contributes to the acquiring of their international legal personality, being a derivation of the international treaty obligation of those States, particularly having in mind the provisions of Article 288 of the Lisbon Treaty on the Functioning of the European Union.[63] This being so, the States' international obligation to recognize the legal personality of the EGTCs that fulfilled the conditions required by the Regulation appears at the same time to be the EGTCs' *international right* to such recognition, providing these organizations (although as the third party) with the necessary element of international legal personality – legal capacity deriving from a treaty as a source of international law.

Furthermore, according to Article 3 of the Regulation, the membership of an EGTC may include the EU member States,[64] regional authorities, local authorities, as well as other bodies governed by public law provided by Directive

---

personality." For the text of the Lisbon Treaty on European Union, see: *Official Journal of the European Union*, C83/01, vol. 53, 30 March 2010.

63 Thus, Article 288, para. 2 of the Lisbon Treaty on the Functioning of the European Union states as follows: "A regulation shall have general application. It shall be binding in its entirety and directly applicable in all member States." For the text of the Lisbon Treaty on the Functioning of the European Union see: *ibid.*

64 Bearing in mind the possibility of States' membership in EGTCs as provided for by Article 3 of the Regulation, such EGTCs, by analogy with so-called 'hybrid or quasi-NGOs' (QUANGOS), could be equally understood as 'hybrid or quasi-IROs' (QUAIROS); see: *infra*, II.3.

2004/18/EC of the European Parliament and of the Council of 31 March 2004.[65] In addition, according to the same Article, associations consisting of bodies belonging to one or more of these categories may also become members of an EGTC. However, according to paragraph 2 of this Article, an EGTC shall be made up of members located on the territory of at least two EU member States.

Moreover, an analogy between EGTCs and IGOs can be found in Article 10, paras. 1 and 2 of the Regulation providing that an EGTC shall have its organs – at least an assembly, which is made up of representatives of its members; and director who represents the EGTC and acts on its behalf, while the statutes may provide for additional organs with clearly defined powers.

However, as an IRO, the EGTC is unique in the sense that it enables public authorities of various EU member States to team up and deliver joint services without requiring a prior specific international agreement to be signed and ratified by national parliaments. The EU member States must however agree to the participation of potential members in their respective countries.

Finally, Article 10, para. 3 of the Regulation seems also to be particularly important in this context, providing that "an EGTC shall be liable for the acts of its organs as regards third parties, even where such acts do not fall within the tasks of the EGTC". By this provision EGTCs' liability seems to be regulated more strictly than IGOs'. Pursuant to Article 8 of the Draft articles on the responsibility of international organizations adopted by the International Law Commission (ILC) in 2011 the conduct of an organ or agent of an international organization shall be considered an act of that organization under international law only provided that such an internationally wrongful act falls "within the overall functions of that organizations..."[66] On the contrary, as we have

---

65 According to the Directive, it includes the bodies established for the specific purpose of meeting needs in the general interest, not having an industrial or commercial character, having legal personality, and being financed, for the most part, by the State, regional or local authorities, or other bodies governed by public law; or being subject to management supervision by those bodies; or having an administrative, managerial or supervisory board, more than half of whose members are appointed by the State, regional or local authorities, or by other bodies governed by public law. Directive 2004/18/EC of the European Parliament and of the Council of 31 March 2004 on the coordination of procedures for the award of public works contracts, public supply contracts and public service contracts, Art. 1(9); *Official Journal of the European Union*, L134 of 30 April 2004. The non-exhaustive lists of bodies and categories of bodies governed by public law, which fulfill these criteria, are set out in Annex III to the Directive.

66 Report of the International Law Commission, Sixty-third session (26 April to 3 June and 4 July to 12 August 2011), General Assembly Official Records, Sixty-sixth session, Supplement No. 10, A/66/10, p. 53.

seen, the Regulation does not contain such limitation. What is more, apart from the obligations *ex delicto*, the Regulation in its Article 12(2) provides for the EGTCs' liability *ex contractu* envisaging that "an EGTC shall be liable for its debts whatever their nature." On the other hand, according to its Article 15, third parties who consider themselves wronged by the acts or omissions of an EGTC shall be entitled to pursue their claims against the EGTC generally before the courts of the EU member State where the EGTC has its registered office, by which provision the Regulation, following the above-mentioned logic, has indirectly recognized a kind of international *ius standi in iudicio* for EGTCs. Moreover, such extensive wording of the Regulation does not exclude at least a hypothetic possibility of the commission of an internationally wrongful act by an EGTC violating the international rights of an EU member State.

For all these reasons one can hardly deny the increasing presence of the EGTCs in international legal relations which led authors such as Ramirez and Gabbe to the conclusion that positive experiences with EGTCs have emphasized the clear need to create and further develop visible and permanent legal structures for territorial co-operation in Europe.[67]

On the other hand, EGTCs are not the only form of such institutionalized transfrontier co-operation in Europe. Beside the EGTCs, a similar type of IROs has appeared more recently at the level of the CoE in the form of Euroregional Co-operation Groupings (ECGs). In fact, the possibility of acquiring legal personality for 'transfrontier co-operation groupings' was envisaged much earlier in the Model interstate agreement (bilateral or multilateral) on transfrontier co-operation groupings having legal personality, contained in Appendix 1.14 to the European Outline Convention on Transfrontier Co-operation between Territorial Communities or Authorities, signed in Madrid on 21 May 1980 (hereinafter the Madrid Convention).[68] Of course, the Madrid Convention had no intention of using international law in the regulation of cross-border co-operation between sub-State entities. Moreover, the Convention in its Article 3 clearly states that the arrangements and agreements concluded between 'territorial communities and authorities' have no treaty value.[69] However,

---

67 Ramirez, M.G., Gabbe, J., "AEBR and EGTC – a long way to success", *Interact*, Winter 2013, p. 6.
68 For the text of the Madrid Convention see: ETS, No. 106.
69 Thus, the Explanatory report on the Madrid Convention states as follows: "In no event are the central government's powers in general policy-making or the conduct of international relations affected by the Convention. The Convention does not have the effect of conferring an 'international' character on transfrontier relations." (para. 35a). For the text of the Report see: <http://conventions.coe.int/Treaty/en/Reports/html/106.htm> (26 August 2013).

transfrontier co-operation as conceived by the Convention very soon turned into a dynamic process followed by evolving international legal regulation. In this regard, Pierre-Marie Dupuy anticipated this development in his article of 1977 on regional transfrontier co-operation, considering that international law should not be an obstacle to regional transfrontier co-operation. On the contrary, international law is supposed to be at its service.[70] Thus, the legal personality of 'transfrontier co-operation bodies' has expressly been provided for in Article 3 of the Additional Protocol to the Madrid Convention, signed in Strasbourg on 9 November 1995.[71] Later, in 1998 Protocol No. 2 to the Madrid Convention concerning interterritorial co-operation extended transfrontier co-operation to 'interterritorial co-operation', meaning "any concerted action designed to establish relations between territorial communities or authorities of two or more Contracting Parties, other than relations of transfrontier co-operation of neighbouring authorities, including the conclusion of co-operation agreements with territorial communities or authorities of other States" (Art. 1). Although Protocol No. 2 does not mention either the 'interregional co-operation bodies' or the question of legal personality, it is worth pointing out its Article 4 providing that the Contracting Parties to this Protocol, which are also Contracting Parties to the Additional Protocol to the Madrid Convention "shall apply, *mutatis mutandis*, the aforesaid Protocol to interterritorial co-operation."[72]

Finally, some of the CoE member States in 2009 signed in Utrecht Protocol No. 3 to the Madrid Convention, concerning Euroregional Co-operation Groupings (ECGs).[73] According to Article 1 of the Protocol, the territorial communities or authorities of the States Parties to the Protocol may set up a 'transfrontier co-operation body' in the form of an ECG on the territory of the member States of the CoE, Parties to this Protocol, with the objective of promoting, supporting and developing transfrontier and interterritorial co-operation between the ECG's members. Besides the territorial communities or authorities of a State Party, the membership of the ECG "may also include the respective member State concerned of the Council of Europe" (Art. 3). According to the Protocol, the ECG shall have legal personality governed by the

---

[70] Thus, Dupuy said: "Le droit international, loin d'apparaître un obstacle, serait alors au service de la coopération régionale transfrontalière." Dupuy, P.-M., "La coopération régionale transfrontalière et le droit international", *Annuaire français de droit international*, vol. XXIII, 1977, p. 854.
[71] For the text of the Additional Protocol see: ETS, No. 159.
[72] For the text of the Protocol No. 2 see: ETS, No. 169.
[73] For the text see of the Protocol No. 3 see: ETS, No. 206.

law of the CoE member State in which it has its headquarters. What is more, the Protocol provides that "the ECG shall have the most extensive legal capacity accorded to legal persons under that State's national law" (Art. 2(2)). Thereby, by analogy with the previously described situation concerning EGTCs, the Protocol, although regulating ECGs' legal personality in the domestic legal orders of the States Parties, creates a treaty obligation for those States on recognition of such legal personality, turning it, at the same time, into a right established for those organizations as the third party beneficiaries. The ECG's constituent instruments are the agreement between its founding members and the statutes as an integral part of the agreement establishing the ECG. Furthermore, as in the case of EGTCs, the Protocol has envisaged the liability of ECGs, not only with regard to third parties, but also to its members for any breach of the law to which it may be subject (Art. 9). However, some authors point out that while the Protocol and the Regulation seem to be very similar, the Protocol takes into account the fact that due to the broader membership of the CoE in comparison to that of the EU, an ECG could, at the same time, be an EGTC. Therefore, the range of possibilities opened up by the Protocol is broader and more flexible than the solutions offered by the EU Regulation.[74]

b   Association of European Border Regions (AEBR)

The Association of European Border Regions (AEBR) is one of the oldest IROs in Europe, founded in September 1971. The representatives of eight European regions from different European States signed in Bonn and Strasbourg the Statutes for the Association of European Border Regions (AEBR).[75] Today, the AEBR network is composed of approximately 100 members from the EU and

---

74 See: Mătuşescu, C., "European Juridical Instruments of Territorial Cooperation – Towards a Decentralized Foreign Policy in Europe?", *AGORA International Journal of Juridical Sciences*, no. 2, 2012, p. 92, <http://www.juridicaljournal.univagora.ro> (30 June 2013). On the other hand, Strazzari points out that "although the CoE and the EU legal instruments concerning cross-border co-operation are deeply different in their nature and function (with the CoE aimed to provide a minimal common regulation, according to international law standards, and the EU aimed to provide substantial legal harmonization of EU Member States legislations), they share nonetheless the common goal of harmonizing European national legislation and they highlight common legal developments." Strazzari, *op. cit.* (note 59), pp. 154–155.

75 These were the following regions: Regione Autonoma Friuli Venezia Giulia, Conseil Régional de Lorraine, Euregio Kommunalgemeinschaft Rhein-Ems, Sønderjyllands Amt, Ems-Dollart-Region, Castilla y León, Extremadura, and Euregio Scheldemond. The AEBR's General Assembly amended the Statutes in 1994 (in Trieste), and in 1997 (in Salamanca). For the text of the Statutes see: <http://www.aebr.eu/files/publications/Statutes_EN_signed.pdf> (18 March 2013).

beyond.[76] Thereby, the AEBR differs from EGTCs whose membership is limited to the EU member States' regions. In paragraph 2 of its Statutes the AEBR is defined as "a registered association" with the headquarters in Gronau (Westphalia, Germany). The same paragraph provides that the headquarters can be moved to another location by decision of the AEBR's General Assembly. This being so, if the AEBR's headquarters moved to another State, the Association would acquire legal personality according to the law of that State. In that case, the AEBR would continue its legal existence even in the event of the withdrawal of its legal personality by the State where its headquarters had been situated. Thus, one can conclude that the AEBR's legal personality, although subject to the law of a particular State, in some measure goes beyond the mere level of its domestic legal order. After all, the argument in favour of this conclusion can be found in paragraph 14 of the AEBR Statutes, providing that the termination of the AEBR "can only take place through a specially convened General Assembly for this purpose", *i.e.* not by the decision of any State. Moreover, according to the Statutes, the decision on termination shall be made by a two-thirds majority of the AEBR members present.

Among the aims of the AEBR as set out in paragraph 3 of its Statutes are to represent the interests of the European border and cross-border regions to national and international parliaments, organs, authorities and institutions, as well as to initiate, support and coordinate their co-operation throughout Europe. For this purpose, the AEBR's tasks are to implement programmes and projects directed to cross-border co-operation, to apply for funds and to receive and dispose of them; to organize events regarding cross-border problems; to help to solve cross-border problems and to support special activities; to prepare and implement common campaigns; to extend the Centre for European Border and Cross-border Regions in close co-operation with the EU and the CoE; and to inform European political bodies and the public about cross-border questions (para. 3(2)).

The European border and cross-border regions in the member States of the EU or CoE can be full members of the AEBR with the right to vote. Also, according to paragraph 4(1) of the Statutes, full membership of the AEBR is open to large-sized amalgamations of border regions within several countries provided not all their members join the AEBR individually.[77]

---

76 Thus, some members of the AEBR come from Armenia, Belarus, Moldova, Norway, the Russian Federation, Serbia, Switzerland, Turkey and Ukraine; see: Ramirez, Gabbe, *op. cit.* (note 67), p. 7.

77 Besides full members, the AEBR membership includes members with observer status and honorary members, as well as advisory members, all of them without the right to vote (para. 4(2–3)). Today, the AEBR has more than 60 border and cross-border regions as full

In principle, the rights and duties of AEBR members do not differ much in comparison with those of members of IGOs. Along with the right to vote, to contribute to the work of the AEBR and to use its services, programmes and facilities, they are required to support the AEBR's activities including through the payment of their contributions according to the decisions of the General Assembly and provisions of paragraph 13 of the AEBR Statutes.

Furthermore, even the AEBR's institutional structure is not very different from that of IGOs. According to Article 6 of its Statutes the organs of the AEBR are a General Assembly as the highest and plenary organ in which every full member participates with at least one vote.[78] Also, similarly to Article 19 of the UN Charter, the Statutes provide for the suspension of the right to vote for a member which is in arrears with the payment of its contribution for the previous and current calendar years (para. 7(2)). Besides, among the AEBR's principal organs the Statutes provide for an Executive Committee that includes the President, the first Vice-President and at least three further Vice-Presidents, the Treasurer, and at least 20 members as representatives from the border and cross-border regions (para. 8(2)). Finally, the Statutes also provide for a Secretary General as the head of the Secretariat General. According to paragraph 10, the AEBR is represented in its international relations by the President, First Vice-President and Secretary General.[79]

Analysing the establishment and work of the AEBR, it seems that this IRO has initiated the process of the institutionalization of interregional cooperation in Europe, having anticipated the latter IROs such as EGTCs and Euroregions with all their variety of names and structure.

On the other hand, among the more recent of the AEBR's legal activities it should be mentioned that the AEBR has actively participated in the process of reforming the place and role of EGTCs within the EU system. Thus, in November 2011 the AEBR made the 'Statement', as a kind of 'soft law' document, on the Proposal for a Regulation of the European Parliament and of the Council amending the aforementioned Regulation 1082/2006 on a European grouping of territorial cooperation as regards the clarification, simplification and improvement

---

members. For the Member Regions List see: <http://www.aebr.eu/en/members/list_of_members.php> (19 November 2012).

78 According to paragraph 7(2) of the AEBR Statutes the number of votes is regulated by the contribution regulation.

79 Beside these main organs, the Statutes provide for the possibility of creating of various committees including the Advisory Committee for Cross-border Co-operation appointed by the Executive Committee (para. 11).

of the establishment and implementation of EGTCs.[80] Similarly, in 2010 the AEBR issued another 'soft law' document delivered to the EU Commission: the AEBR Position Paper on the Future EU Strategy 2020 (Post-Lisbon Strategy).[81]

Finally, in the context of this paper it is worth noting that on 18 March 2010 the AEBR signed a Co-operation Agreement with one IGO – the CoE represented by its organ, the Congress of Local and Regional Authorities. The Agreement seeks to combine the forces of both organizations for more effective initiatives in favour of regional authorities and, in particular, in favour of European border regions.[82]

c   Assembly of European Regions (AER)

The Assembly of European Regions (AER) is a specific IRO established in 1985 in order, as defined in its Statutes, "to act as the political voice of the Regions of Europe..."[83] According to the Statutes, the AER is founded as a non-profit-making association whose full members are the regions of the member States of the CoE, as well as other European regions under the condition that they respect the fundamental principles of the CoE. Moreover, even the other IROs may become the AER's consultative members (Art. 2).[84] The organizational structure of the AER is analogous to that of other similar IROs, but also many

---

80   AEBR Statement KOM(2011)610 final; 1 November 2011. For the text of the 'Statement' see: <http://www.aebr.eu/files/publications/111129_statement_proposal_EGTC_regulation _EN_clean.pdf> (23 September 2013).

81   For the text of the AEBR Position Paper see: <http://www.aebr.eu/files/publications/ 10_01_12_AGEG_Stellungnahme_Europa_2020_EN_def.pdf> (3 September 2013).

82   See: <http://www.aebr.eu/files/publications/100330_20AEBR_20Newsflash_206_20EN _20final.pdf> (30 May 2013).

83   For the text of the AER Statutes of 12 October 2012 see: <http://www.aer.eu> (26 April 2013).

84   From its beginning in 1980s, the AER has functioned as a so-called 'umbrella organization' with the other IROs as its members. Thus, among the IROs, which are AER members today, we can mention the AEBR, the Alps-Adriatic Working Community, Eurorégion Alpes Méditerranée, the Working Community of the Danube Countries – ARGE Donauländer, the Working Community Pyrenees (Comunidad de Trabajo de los Pirineos – CTP), the Working Community of the Alps – Arge Alp, the Transjurasian Conference – CTJ, the Working Community Galice – North Portugal, the Baltic Sea States Subregional Cooperation – BSSSC, Channel Art Manche, the World Mountain People Association (WMPA). Together with the above-mentioned territorially determined IROs, the AER's membership includes some organizations based on their specific activities such as the Assembly of European Wine-Producing Regions – AREV, the Assembly of European Fruit and Vegetable Growing and Horticultural Regions – AREFLH, the Association of Local Democracy Agencies – ALDA, and the Federation of Local Authority Chief Executives in

IGOs. The AER's main organs are a General Assembly convened at least once a year and consisting of the representatives of all the AER members; a Bureau as the executive body that ensures the implementation of the decisions of the General Assembly; and a Secretary General who is in charge of the General Secretariat and responsible for implementing the decisions of the other AER bodies, presenting an annual report before the General Assembly. Also, the Statutes provide for a President as the highest authority of the AER who represents the organization in all external relations, Vice-Presidents, Committees and Standing Committees,[85] and a Treasurer. Today, the AER participates in interregional relations in Europe as one of the most significant IROs, having in mind not only its large membership composed of nearly 230 regions from 35 States and 15 IROs, but also its activities in promoting cross-border co-operation among the CoE member States. The work of the Organization is complementary to the activities of the CoE, as well as of the EU in the realization of their common policies, particularly in consideration of its 'Positions' adopted by its General Assembly. Thus, for example, it is worth mentioning here the AER Position on the European Neighbourhood Policy Reform, adopted by the AER's General Assembly in November 2011, which initiated the process of redefining the objectives of future European Neighbourhood Policy (ENP). Moreover, the need for co-operation between the EU and the IROs was recently mentioned by EU Commissioner Stefan Füle concerning the "need for...joint work with the Committee of the Regions" in which context "the interregional organisations should not be ignored."[86] Consequently, among the objectives of such IGO-IRO co-operation the AER Position states that the place of interregional and cross-border co-operation in future ENP should be strengthened. Thus, the AER Position calls for multilevel governance and partnership, as well as for paying more attention to territorial diversity in the ENP, pointing out at the same time the importance of the decentralization processes in Europe.

Europe (UDiTE). See: <http://www.aer.eu/members-and-partners/member-organisations.html> (13 January 2014).

[85] These Committees are the Executive Committee, Committee 1 for Economy and Regional Development, Committee 2 for Social Policy and Public Health, Committee 3 for Culture, Education, Youth and International Co-operation, as well as the Standing Committees for monitoring and evaluation, for institutional affairs and for equal opportunities.

[86] See: the AER Position on the European Neighbourhood Policy Reform adopted at the AER General Assembly, Ponta Delgada (Azores), 24 November 2011. The text is available at: <http://www.aer.eu> (26 April 2013). For the Letter by Commissioner Stefan Füle on the AER ENP position 2011 see: <http://www.aer.eu/en/knowledge-centre/thematic-expertise-thematic-issues/neighbourhood-policy-and-aer-in-the-world/european-neighbourhood-policy.html> (24 September 2013).

Finally, a similar attitude can be found within the EU as well. The EU Committee of the Regions in its Mission Statement clearly confirmed the need for the involvement of regional and local authorities in the European decision-making process encouraging co-operation between those authorities of different EU member States.[87]

Among the similar 'soft law' documents adopted by the AER, one should not forget the Declaration on Regionalism in Europe. Adopted in 1996, the Declaration, among other things, provides in Article 10 that "regions shall have the capability to act at an international level. They may conclude treaties, agreements or protocols which are international in scope, subject to approval by the central government where is required by national legislation."[88]

However, perhaps one of the most important steps that the AER has made towards the acquiring of personality in international legal relations is the Memorandum of Understanding signed with Tunisia in May 2011.[89] Formally, 'the undersigning parties' thereof are the AER and the Ministry for regional development of Tunisia. For this reason, one could conclude that the 'Parties' to the Memorandum are actually an IRO and the Ministry as a public law subject of domestic, but not international, law, whereby this Memorandum would stay out of the sphere of interest of public international law. Nevertheless, viewed from within, things could seem different. Starting from the Preamble, the Tunisian Ministry accepts the obligation "to encourage and support the process of decentralisation in Tunisia..." Using the teleological interpretation it seems obvious that the Ministry did not act on its own behalf, but as an organ of Tunisia as a State, particularly bearing in mind that the above-mentioned obligation does not belong to the sphere of *iure gestionis*, but in *iure imperii* activities of States. What is more, Article III of the Memorandum expressly provides that "*Tunisia* will be granted observer status at the AER" (emphasis added). Understood in this way, it seems that the Memorandum

---

87 European Union Committee of the Regions, Mission Statement of 21 April 2009; CdR 56/2009 fin FR/JP/nm/ss. The text of the Statement is available at: <http://www.cvce.eu/content/publication/2009/5/20/12b5c770-984f-4b36-8154-e3709a14170f/publishable_en.pdf> (3 September 2013).

88 For the text of the Declaration see: <http://www.aer.eu/fileadmin/user_upload/PressComm/Publications/DeclarationRegionalism/DR_GB.pdf> (24 September 2013). Also, in November 2011 the AER General Assembly adopted the Declaration on Culture and Health. The text of the Declaration is available at: <http://www.aer.eu/fileadmin/user_upload/GoverningBodies/GeneralAssembly/Events/AG2011-Acores_Adopted/EN-declaration-culture-health.pdf> (24 September 2013).

89 The text of the Memorandum is available at: <http://www.aer.eu/events/governing-bodies/2011/general-assembly-2011-regions-master-globalisation.html> (24 September 2013).

could be considered a treaty, subject to public international law, or more precisely to the customary international law of treaties.

On the other hand, the AER concluded a similar agreement, also called a Memorandum of Understanding, with the United Nations Development Programme (UNDP). In its Part 2 (called 'Agreement') the Memorandum provides that its purpose is "to establish a basis for cooperation between the UNDP and the AER" (para. 2.1). According to paragraph 2.2., the Memorandum "represents the initial stage in fostering of a concrete partnership between the UNDP and the AER. Both parties undertake to work together and to decide on concrete methods of cooperation."[90]

In this context it seems appropriate to remember the provision of Article 2 of the Vienna Convention on the Law of Treaties, which clearly states that "'treaty' means an international agreement...whatever its particular designation." A similar provision can also be found in the Vienna Convention on the Law of Treaties between States and International Organizations or between International Organizations. Of course, the Conventions leave outside their scope international agreements to which one or more States or one or more international organizations and one or more subjects of international law other than States or organizations are parties. However, in their Preambles both Conventions affirm that the rules of customary international law will continue to govern questions not regulated by their provisions. Equally, in their common Article 3 the Conventions provide among other things that the fact that their provisions do not apply to international agreements concluded between States or IGOs and other subjects of international law shall not affect the legal force of such agreements.[91] Therefore, these agreements, such as for example those concluded with the Sovereign Order of Malta, various international territorial administrations (ITAs), insurgents, or liberation movements, will be subject to the customary international law of treaties sharing mostly the same legal regulation as contained in the Vienna Conventions that resulted from the codification work of the ILC. This being so, all these treaties fulfill the above condition to be 'governed by international law'. Consequently, following Aust, a fundamental characteristic of a treaty is its binding character, even if

---

90   The text of the Memorandum is available at: <http://www.aer.eu/en/knowledge-centre/thematic-expertise-thematic-issues/neighbourhood-policy-and-aer-in-the-world/aer-and-undp.html> (23 September 2013).
91   For the text of the Vienna Convention on the Law of Treaties, see: *supra*, note 47. For the text of the Vienna Convention on the Law of Treaties between States and International Organizations or between International Organizations, see: *supra*, note 39.

called a 'Memorandum of Understanding' (MOU).⁹² On the other hand, the designation of a treaty as an MOU is not as unusual in international practice as it may seem. One of the well-known examples could be the Memorandum of Understanding between the Governments of Italy, the United Kingdom of Great Britain and Northern Ireland, the United States of America and Yugoslavia regarding the Free Territory of Trieste, signed in London in 1954.⁹³ After all, according to Aust, by August 2006 over 880 instruments called 'Memorandum of Understanding' had been registered with the UN Treaty Section and "most of them are probably treaties."⁹⁴

d   Euroregions

In his analytical article concerning transfrontier co-operation in Europe, Vedovato defined 'Euroregions' as political territorial organizations that appeared as a symbiosis of the continuing evolution of the historical and cultural, as well as the administrative space in Europe.⁹⁵ According to him, such evolving process of transfrontier co-operation was determined by social, economic, political, cultural, and other interests, including the protection of the environment as questions of common interest to the populations in many cross-border regions.⁹⁶

At first impression, this process could seem rather contradictory, setting the supranational character of European integration in opposition to so-called 'micro-integration' as equally institutionalized processes of co-operation, but on the sub-State level. However it may be, according to some authors, such process of institutionalized transfrontier co-operation in Europe is not only irreversible, but it also continues to require more detailed institutional, i.e. primarily legal, regulation.⁹⁷ Therefore, one should not be surprised at the increasing number of institutionalized forms of transfrontier co-operation in Europe

---

92   See: Aust, A., *Modern Treaty Law and Practice*, 2nd edn., Cambridge, Cambridge University Press, 2007, p. 27.
93   For the text of the Memorandum of Understanding, see: *UNTS*, vol. 235, 1956, pp. 100 *et seq.*
94   Aust, *op. cit.* (note 92), p. 344. In his valuable work, Aust precisely elaborates terminological distinctions that can be found between treaties and 'non legally binding instruments' sometimes called MOUS. However, although MOUS are usually characterized, for example, by terms like 'paragraphs' or 'participants', the above-mentioned Memorandum of Understanding between the AER and Tunisia used the terms 'articles' and 'parties' typical for treaties. *Cf. ibid.*, p. 496.
95   See: Vedovato, *op. cit.* (note 53), p. 1.
96   *Cf. ibid.*, p. 2.
97   *Ibid.*, pp. 20–21.

that have not always been easily distinguishable one from another. Thus, 'euroregions' sometimes seem to be understood as a residual group of IROs, heterogeneous not only in their names and structure, but also in their legal status. Usually having as members border regions of neighbouring States interested in cross-border co-operation, the euroregions can be found all over Europe and under different names such as 'euregios', 'euregions', 'cross-border or transfrontier associations', 'communautés d'intérêts', 'working communities', *etc.*[98]

Some of the earliest 'transfrontier associations' in Europe can be found in the middle of the 20th century, dealing with various cross-border activities such as fishery, tourism, traffic, culture co-operation *etc.*, anticipating the future 'Euroregions'. Thus, in the 1960s the first euroregions were established, such as the Communauté d'intérêts Alsace moyenne-Brisgau, and the Akershus-Hedemark Working Community which had gathered as members the regions along the Norwegian-Swedish border. Soon afterwards, the Danish and Swedish regions established the Øresund Region,[99] while at the same time the Euregio Rhine-Waal was formed alongside the German-Dutch border.[100] In addition, we can mention here a series of similar euroregions that appeared in the

---

[98] Among the European regions, it is important to mention the Baltic Sea Region established by the Baltic Sea Strategy of the EU, comprising around 100 million citizens, *i.e.* 20 per cent of the EU. It was the beginning of the initiative within the EU for creating so-called 'macro-regions' as a new model for regional co-operation that later inspired the creation of similar 'macro-regions' in areas such as the Mediterranean and Danube basin. However, these 'macro-regions' have not yet achieved a sufficient stage of institutionalization to be considered IROs in the above-mentioned meaning. Therefore, we differentiate here between a region as a geographically determined area in which the co-operation of the States or their sub-State entities takes place, and IROs that are established as a result of the institutionalization of such co-operation. For more details on macro-regions in Europe see: Schewe, Ch., "Legal Aspects of the Baltic Sea Strategy – International Law in a European Macro-Region", *Baltic Yearbook of International Law*, vol. 10, 2010, pp. 189 and 191.

[99] The main organs of the Region are: the Øresund Committee, the Øresund Commission, and the Øresund Committee's Secretariat established in order to handle activities decided on by the Committee and the Commission. For more details see: <http://www.oresund.com/oresund/welcome2.htm> (11 April 2013).

[100] The organizational structure of the Euregio Rhine-Waal is composed of the Euregio Council as a plenary organ consisting of 142 representatives of all member regions, who meet at least twice a year. Three committees have been established to prepare the decisions of the Council: Committee of Cross-Border Communication, Committee of Commerce, and Committee of Finance and Projects. Moreover, the Euroregio has its Chairman and the Board as an executive body. For more details see: <http://euregio.org/seiten/index.cfm> (11 April 2013).

following years, characterized by a highly developed institutionalized structure, like the Meuse-Rhine Euregion (composed of the Belgian regions of Liège and Limbourg, the Dutch region of Limbourg and the German region of Aachen),[101] Regio Basiliensis,[102] Conseil parlementaire interrégional (CPI),[103] Euroregion 'Neisse-Nisa-Nysa' (composed of German, Czech and Polish regions), etc.[104]

It is not infrequently the case that some euroregions can be found under the name of 'Working Communities', like the Galice-North Portugal Working Community, the Working Community of the Alps (Arge Alp), the 'Eurorégion Alpes Méditerranée' (formerly Communauté de travail des Alpes Occidentales – COTRAO), as well as the Alps-Adriatic Working Community. The last one is important for anticipating, although on the interregional level, the participative process in Central Europe starting from 1978, i.e. during the Cold

---

101 The main bodies of this Euroregion are the Committe of Directors, Euregional Council, Economic and Social Council, Strategic Groups, and Bureau. For more details see: <http://www.euregio-mr.com/fr/euregiomr/organisation> (11 April 2013).

102 The main governing bodies of the Regio Basiliensis are the General meeting, the Board of directors and the Monitoring group. The Board of directors is the supreme executive body; it approves the budget, annual accounts and annual report under the auspices of the General meeting as the plenary organ. The Monitoring group is a consultative body consisting mainly of representatives from cantonal parliaments and administrative departments. For more details see: <http://www.regbas.ch/d_Information_in_English.cfm> (11 April 2013).

103 The basic document of the Conseil parlementaire interrégional is the Convention relating to the creation of the Conseil Parlementaire Interrégional (CPI), signed in 1986 by the representatives of the Grand Duchy of Luxembourg, Landtag de Rhénanie-Palatinat, Landtag de la Sarre, Conseil Régional de Lorraine, and Conseil Provincial du Luxembourg Belge. According to the Convention, the principal organs of the CPI are: Presidency, Permanent Committee, and the Secretariat. In addition, the organizational structure of the CPI is composed of six Commissions (Commission 1 for economic affairs; Commission 2 for social affairs; Commission 3 for transport and communication; Commission 4 for environment and agriculture; Commission 5 for education, training, research and culture; and Commission 6 for internal security, civil protection and assistance service). For more details see: <http://www.cpi-ipr.com/fr/Conventions/conv_cre.asp> (11 April 2013).

104 Among the euroregions with significantly developed institutionalized structure Vedovato mentions also the euroregions of 'Benego', 'Creno' (Conférence des régions de l'Europe du Nord-Ouest), 'Comregio', Institut régional intercommunal, Association transfrontalière du bassin supérieur de l'Alzette, etc. Equally, in the Rhine basin the same author mentions the series of similar IROs being provided with legal personality, such as the 'Regio' gathering the Swiss region of Jura, the German region of Schwarzwald and the French region of Vosges; as well as the euroregions like the 'Groupe de consultation franco-allemand'; 'Cimab'; and the 'Jura Working Community'. See: Vedovato, op. cit. (note 53), pp. 8–10.

War period when the States whose regions had participated in its membership were still divided by the 'iron curtain'.[105] Moreover, the Alps-Adriatic Working Community is even more interesting in the context of this paper since, following the dissolution of ex-Yugoslavia in 1991, two of its former federal units – Croatia and Slovenia have continued their membership of the Community as independent States, turning this organization into a hybrid or quasi-IRO (QUAIRO).[106]

These euroregions, pursuant to Article 3 of the Additional Protocol to the Madrid Convention "may, or may not have legal personality".[107] However, the very Statutes of some of these euroregions sometimes deny their legal personality, often leading to legally absurd situations. Thus, for example, Article 3 para. 2 of the Statutes of the Danube-Drava-Sava Euroregional co-op[108] clearly states that the Euroregion does not have legal capacity, providing at the same time in paragraph 3 of the same Article the *legal duty* for the Euroregion to respect in its work the provisions contained in international legal documents, as well as in its member regions' States' legal orders. Having determined legal capacity as a quality of an entity to possess legal rights and duties, it seems indisputable that the Euroregion in question legally exists not only with respect to the duties provided by these domestic legal orders, but also with regard to international law obligations. After all, Article 15 of its Statutes speaks in favour of this argument providing, like the majority of IGOs' constitutions, for a series of rights and duties between the Euroregion and its member regions. In addition, Articles 10 and 11 of the Statutes precisely define the scope of activities of this Euroregion including cross-border co-operation,[109] while

---

105 In this context Vedovato has mentioned the 'Egrensis' euroregion that was enrolling as members the cross-border regions of the former Czechoslovakia and the Federal Republic of Germany; see: *ibid.*, p. 10.

106 See: *infra*, 11.3.

107 For the text see: *supra*, note 71.

108 The Danube-Drava-Sava Euroregional co-operation has as its members regions from Croatia, Hungary, and Bosnia and Herzegovina. However, its membership is open also to the regions of other States that gravitate towards the rivers Danube, Drava and Sava. The Euroregion was founded by the signing of its Statutes in Pecs (Hungary) on 28 November 1998. The official name of the Euroregion in Croatian and Hungarian is 'Euroregionalna suradnja Dunav-Drava-Sava'/ 'Duna-Dráva-Száva Euroregionális Együttműködés'. For the revised text of the Statutes see: <http://www.ddseuro.org/portal/images/pdf/dokumenti/Statut%20%20DDS%20-%20prosciceni%20tekst%20_hr_.pdf> (4 April 2013).

109 Thus, Articles 10 and 11 of the Statutes define the activities of the Euroregion such as organizing common activities to promote common values; preparing, financing and realization of common development programmes; organizing and developing of programmes in

Article 15 regulates the Euroregion's business activities. These provisions not only introduce recognize the legal capacity of such an IRO, but also its capacity and the legal consequences by its actions, in regard to both its regulates the third parties, including States. Consequently, Article 5 of the other subjects, entrusting this function to its President or vice-presidents, confirming again the legal personality of that entity. Furthermore, in Article 1 of the Statutes this Euroregion is defined as an 'organization'. Thereby, it is expressly established as an institutionalized, *i.e.* not *ad hoc*, form of co-operation among its members. Such institutionalization is particularly visible in the existence of permanent bodies as provided for by Articles 18–36 of the Statutes, such as the Assembly, President, Executive Committee, Auditing Committee and Secretariat. Besides, the analogy with some of the IGOs is also present in the fact that Article 4 of the Statutes defines even the emblem, flag and the official seal of the Euroregion.

Furthermore, one could find the additional argument that speaks in favour of the existence of another constitutive element common to IROs and IGOs – a personality of the organization, which is distinct from that of its members,[110] particularly having in mind that the will of the organization will not always necessarily be identical to that of each and every one of its members. After all, it is visible in the fact that the decisions within this and many other euroregions, as well as in most IROs, are made by majority vote. However, these decisions will be equally binding for all their members, including for those that have not voted in favour of them.

Anyhow, the Danube-Drava-Sava Euroregional co-operation shows one more peculiarity in relation to its membership. Its constituent instrument (the Statutes) not only provides for the possibility of other regions of the States gravitating to these rivers acquiring observer status,[111] but in Article 12 it also opens the membership of this euroregion up to non-territorial and non-governmental subjects of those States' legal orders, such as industrial, trade or economic chambers and other commercial subjects acting in those States.

Finally, Article 14 of the mentioned Statutes is noteworthy here, regulating as it does succession in the membership of this euroregion as an entity that,

---

the field of environmental protection, development of cross-border co-operation in the field of traffic, communication, economy, tourism, science, education, culture, sport, *etc.* According to Article 11, these activities should primarily be directed to the establishment and promotion of such co-operation between the border regions. See: *ibid.*

110 *Cf. supra*, note 12.
111 See: Art. 16 of the Statutes. For the text see: *supra*, note 108.

according to the wording of its own Statutes – i.e. its ...ic legal document – legally should not have existed!

3   Hybrid or Quasi-IROS (QUAIROS)

When talking about EGTCs we already mentioned the possibility in Article 3 of Regulation 1082/2006 that opened EGTCs' membership not only to regional and local authorities as subjects having legal personality in the public law of their States, but also to the EU member States themselves. Thus, for example, an EGTC – Eurométropole Lille-Kortrijk-Tournai has as its members two States: Belgium and France.¹¹² Also, the same possibility can be found in Article 3 of Protocol No. 3 to the Madrid Convention,¹¹³ concerning ECGs. By analogy with the quasi-NGOs (QUANGOS) whose membership includes non-governmental, private organizations together with States or IGOs as subjects of public international law,¹¹⁴ the organizations having as their members subjects of public law from different States (like the earlier-mentioned various kinds of sub-State entities) and States or IGOs will be designated here as quasi-IROS (QUAIROS). Understood in this way, it could be interesting to apply this criterion to some organizations almost unanimously accepted as IGOs, today with indisputable international legal personality. Thus, for example, the Nordic Council has as its members not only States (Denmark, Finland, Iceland, Norway and Sweden), but also some of their dependant territories such as Åland, the Faroe Islands, and Greenland. By the same logic, some other IGOs like the WMO, WTO, or the Asian Development Bank, could also be understood as QUAIROS, having as members States including the People's Republic of China, together with Hong Kong as today a kind of its sub-State entity. Furthermore, beside Hong Kong, five more 'territories' – British Caribbean Territories, French Polynesia, Macao, Curaçao and Sint Maarten, and New Caledonia – participate in WMO membership together with the member

---

112   Article 1 of the Eurométropole Lille-Kortrijk-Tournai Statute states as follows: "Un Groupement européen de coopération territoriale (GECT) est constitué entre les membres suivants, signataires de la Convention de coopération: Côté français: l'Etat, la Région Nord-Pas-de-Calais, le Département du Nord, Lille Métropole Communauté urbaine, Côté belge: l'Etat fédéral, la Région et la Communauté flamande, la Province de Flandre occidentale,..." For the text see: <http://www.cncd.fr/doc/convention_statuts_reglement _ELKT.pdf> (25 December 2013). On the other hand, Strazzari interestingly remarked: "[T]he direct involvement of the State in an EGTC is more difficult to put in place: such a move might be seen as a threat to the regional self-government rights." Strazzari, *op. cit.* (note 59), p. 203.

113   See: *supra*, note 73.

114   See: *infra*, III.

States. Finally, we could here go a step further, understanding even the UN in the same way in the period from 1945 to 1991 when two 'sub-State entities' of the former USSR – Belarus and Ukraine – were full members.

On the other hand, due to the historical circumstances a similar situation happened with one euroregion – the Alps-Adriatic Working Community in which two former republics of ex-Yugoslavia (Croatia and Slovenia) have continued their membership as independent States following the dissolution of Yugoslavia in 1991. As we have earlier mentioned, the Alps-Adriatic Working Community was founded in 1978 in Venice. Its founder members were Bavaria, Friuli-Venezia Giulia, Carinthia, Croatia, Upper Austria, Salzburg, Slovenia, Croatia and Veneto, i.e. the regions from four States at that time: Austria, Germany, Italy and Yugoslavia. By signing the 'Joint Declaration' interregional co-operation between the border regions was transformed into an organization with its organs, organizational and procedural rules, and clearly defined tasks and aims.[115] Today, the Alps-Adriatic Working Community has six members: the regions of Burgenland, Carinthia, Styria, Vas, and two States – Croatia and Slovenia.[116] According to its constitutional instrument the 'Organisational and procedural rules of the Alps-Adriatic Working Community',[117] the main organs of the Community are the Plenary Assembly, the Commission of Executive Officers, the Steering Committee and the General Secretariat. The Plenary Assembly and the Commission may set up expert groups in accordance with the goals of the Community. The Plenary Assembly is the highest-ranking organ of the Community. Each member delegates one representative to the Assembly. Among its duties, the Assembly makes decisions on political matters that affect the Community, establishes the income to common funds and controls the financing of the particular projects within the field of activities of the Community (Rule 6.2). The Plenary Assembly meets at least once a year for a formal session, whereas an extraordinary session of the Assembly can be convened by a minimum of one quarter of its members (Rules 6.4. and 6.7). The Commission of Executive Officers is the executive and coordinating body of the Assembly composed of one representative from each member of the Community (i.e. the two States and the four sub-State entities) having

---

115 Beside its organs, the Community has its Logo, as well as its anthem – the first 41 seconds of Mendelssohn Bartholdy's 4th Symphony, 1st movement. See: para. 5.4. of the 'Organisational and procedural rules of the Alps-Adriatic Working Community' of 2007. For the text see: see: <http://alpeadria.org/english/index.php?page=595301927&f=1&i=595301927> (10 April 2013).
116 For more details see: <http://www.alpeadria.org> (4 April 2013).
117 For the text see: *supra*, note 115.

equal rights and duties. The Commission makes technical preparations for the sessions of the Assembly and authorizes the founding or dissolution of expert groups and their project proposals, supporting and monitoring the realization of these projects. Also, the Commission has the duty to supervise and coordinate the work of the General Secretariat (Rule 7.4). The Steering Committee's duties include in particular coordination between the Plenary Assembly and the Commission supporting the executive officers in the implementation of the political mission of the Community, as well as in supp... activities in the work of the Assembly (Rule 8.6). Finally, th... the Commission's is an administrative and technical body of the Community. ...ral Secretariat administrative support for and the coordination of the activities of t... Commission, and expert groups; as well as of the coordination of pu...arge of tions of the Community (Rule 10.1–12).

According to the Preamble to the Organisational and procedural rules, the aims of the Working Community are to contribute to the consolidation of a peaceful, collective, democratic and pluralistic Europe; to promote friendship and wide-ranging collaboration between different peoples; as well as to build up its bridging functions between the regions of the member States of the EU and accession countries. In this context it is worth noting that the Plenary Assembly of the Heads of Governments of the Alps-Adriatic Working Community in 2005 passed the Resolution 'A Way Forward to Europe' in order, among other things, to support Croatia's EU entry which was achieved in July 2013.[118]

Furthermore, some of the European river commissions, usually accepted as IGOs, according to their membership could also be understood as QUAIROs. Thus, for example, according to the Treaty of Ghent of 2002, the members of the International Scheldt Commission are Belgium, France, the Netherlands, and three Belgian regions: the Walloon Region, the Flemish Region and the Brussels Capital Region.[119] Similarly, the International Commission for the Meuse has as members five States (Belgium, France, Germany, Luxembourg and the Netherlands) together with the three above-mentioned Belgian regions.[120] The tasks of the Commissions are similar and include multilateral coordination regarding matters of common interest concerning the utilization, flood

---

118   The Resolution is available at: <http://www.alpeadria./org/english/index.php?page=4078 96983&f=1&i=733044516&s=407896983> (14 September 2013).
119   The Treaty was signed on 3 December 2002 by the representatives of all the above-mentioned subjects and registered with the UN Secretariat pursuant to Article 102 of the UN Charter. The text of the Treaty was published in the *UNTS*, vol. 2351, 2009, pp. 13 *et seq.*
120   Accord international sur la Meuse, Art. 5. For the text see: <http://www.cipm-icbm.be/files/files/FR1.pdf> (3 October 2013).

...on of these rivers. For that purpose both Commissions prevention and ... recommendations to their members, *i.e.* equally to the formulate a... ate entities.

... ve already mentioned another specific QUAIRO in the AER's member States a... the Working Community of the Danube Countries – ARGE ...länder.[121] This being so, even the AER itself could be understood as a ...AIRO. Thus, beside the Danube regions, three States are members of this Working Community: Moldova, Serbia and Slovakia.[122] The Working Community was established in 1990 with the objective of promoting co-operation among its members for the development of the Danube area to serve the interests of its inhabitants and to foster peaceful co-operation in Europe. Among its most important achievements and the most significant projects are also some 'soft law' documents such as the 'Study about the development of smaller harbours – Portino', 'Cultural Itinerary Danube', the 'Study on Traffic Development', the 'Cooperation between Danube Cities and Harbours – Donauhanse', as well as the Projects 'Portino II' and 'Donauhanse II'.[123]

In addition, talking about QUAIROs one more organization should be mentioned as well – the Pyrenees Working Community (Comunidad de Trabajo de los Pirineos – CTP). Its Members are three French regions (Aquitaine, Midi-Pyrénées, Languedoc-Roussillon); four Spanish Autonomous Communities (Catalonia, Aragon, Navarra, the Basque Country) all located in the Pyrenees mountain range; and one State – the Principality of Andorra. The organizational structure of the CTP is composed of several main organs also by analogy with IGOs. The General Assembly is the plenary organ, being in charge primarily of making political decision for the Community. The Assembly consists of the representatives of each member of the Community and it meets in regular sessions every year. In its international relations the CTP is represented by the Presidency, headed successively by the presidents of each Community member who serve for a term of two years.

The Executive Committee is responsible for the coordination and realization of the action programmes and other decisions adopted by the General Assembly, usually on the basis of previous proposals by the Presidency. The Committee as an executive organ is supported in its work by the four 'thematic Commissions': Commission I for infrastructure and communication; Commission II for

---

121 See: *supra*, note 84.
122 See: <http://www.argedonau.at/neu/arge/mitglieder/start_f.html> (21 January 2014).
123 See: <http://www.land-oberoesterreich.gv.at/cps/rde/xbcr/ooe/ARGE_KURZINFO_E.pdf> (21 January 2014).

training and technical development; Commission III for culture, youth and sport; and Commission IV for sustainable development.

The Community is provided with its administrative organ — the General Secretariat – which is responsible for the preparation of the work of the Executive Committee, as well as for the coordination of its activities and the work of the General Assembly. The Secretariat is headed by the Head of the General appointed by the president at the time with the agreement of the other members of the Community.[124]

As with some other IROs, the CTP's participation in international law-making process is mostly visible in the form of 'soft-law' documents intending to influence the policy of regional IGOs like the CoE and EU. In this context it is worth mentioning at least two 'soft law' documents: *Contribution de la CTP au Livre Vert sur la cohésion territoriale*[125] and *Contribution au Livre Vert de la Commission Européenne sur les réseaux transeuropéens de transports*.[126] Notwithstanding their 'soft law' nature, all the activities and objectives contained in these documents do not differ much from those, which are often subjects of treaties concluded between States or IGOs.

III   Hybrid or Quasi-NGOs (QUANGOs) – Has Functionality Prevailed?

Hybrid or quasi non-governmental organizations (QUANGOs),[127] as can be concluded from their very name, find their place somewhere in between IGOs

---

124   For more details on the CTP see: <http://www.ctp.org> (17 April 2013).
125   In the same document the objectives of the CTP are defined as follows: "Les objectifs de la Communauté de Travail des Pyrénés sont: améliorer la qualité de vie de nos concitoyens en élargissant l'offre de transport; renforcer l'intégration transfrontalière; développer les complémentarités en matière économique pour les entreprises et les jeunes en formation; constituer une zone d'échanges au Sud de l'Europe capable de compter face aux pôles économiques du Nord; privilégier l'innovation, la recherche et la coopération inter-universitaire; et mettre en valeur nos territoires riches d'histoire et notamment notre patrimoine culturel et développer un tourisme durable." For the text see: <http://www.ctp.org/documentacion/contribution_ctp_livre_vert_cohesion_territorial_fres.pdf> (3 September 2013).
126   The activities of the CTP as defined in its *Bilan d'activités 2009-2010 et perspectives* include, among other things: "développement de l'aviation générale et du transport…; coopération en matière d'industrie aérodynamique; améliorer la sécurité des communications en zone de montagne transfrontalière; promouvoir et accompagner la mobilité transfrontalière; proposer des axes de travail commun dans le domaine de la formation professionnelle sur la base de projets existants dans chaque territoire de la CTP; *etc*." For the text of the documents see: <http://www.ctp.org/documentacion.php?Id=1> (3 September 2013).
127   The acronym QUANGOS was already used in the 1990s, *e.g.* in: Willetts, P. (ed.), *"The Conscience of the World" – The Influence of Non-Governmental Organizations in the UN*

and INGOs. As has already been mentioned, these organizations have as members on the one hand private, non-governmental entities (mostly so-called single-country NGOs and sometimes even individuals from different countries), and on the other subjects of public international law such as States or IGOs. The main characteristic of QUANGOs is a functional symbiosis in which both categories of their members – governmental and non-governmental – participate in the work of the organization having, according to its constituent instrument, equal rights and duties. However, such QUANGOs should be clearly distinguished from some IGOs in which the delegations of their member States, although including the representatives from the non-governmental sector, participate in the work of the organization on behalf of their States. Thus, for example, Article 3 of the ILO Constitution provides that the delegation of each member State shall be composed of four representatives, "of whom two shall be Government delegates and the two others shall be delegates representing respectively the employers and the workpeople of each of the Members." However, in spite of this solution, every delegation participates in the work of the ILO General Conference formally representing its member State. For that reason, the ILO should be considered an IGO.[128]

On the other hand, the International Union for the Conservation of Nature and Natural Resources (IUCN) undoubtedly deserves to be mentioned here as today one of the most important QUANGOs, particularly having in mind its influence on the development of international environmental law. According to its Statutes,[129] the IUCN is constituted in accordance with Article 60 of the Swiss Civil Code as an international association of governmental and non-governmental members, having legal personality in conformity with its objectives.[130] States that are members of the United Nations, or any of its specialized agencies, as well as the members of the IAEA, or the States parties to the Statute of the ICJ may become members of the IUCN by notifying the Director General

---

System, Washington DC, The Brookings Institution, 1996, p. 7.

128 On the contrary, according to Archer, the reason for counting the ILO as an IGO is the fact that it was established by a treaty between governments. Archer, *op. cit.* (note 13), p. 39. For the text of the Constitution of the ILO see: <http://www.ilo.org/dyn/normlex/en/f?p=1000:62:0::NO:62:P62_LIST_ENTRIE_ID:2453907:NO> (22 May 2013). See also: *UNTS*, vol. 15, 1948, pp. 35 *et seq.*

129 The IUCN Statutes of 5 October 1948, revised on 22 October 1996 and 13 October 2008, and last amended on 14 September 2012.

130 Part I, para. 1 of the IUCN Statutes. According to Part II of the Statutes, "the objectives of the IUCN shall be to influence, encourage and assist societies throughout the world to conserve the integrity and diversity of nature and to ensure that any use of natural resources is equitable and ecologically sustainable." *Ibid.*

of their adhesion to the IUCN Statutes. Also, government agencies,[131] political and/or economic integration organizations, as well as national non-governmental organizations and INGOs may become the members of the IUCN,[132] with the rights and obligations as set out in para. 12 of its Statutes.[133] Among the IUCN's main components there is the World Conservation Congress composed of the delegates of States and government agencies, political and economic integration IGOs, and national non-governmental organizations and INGOs. Also, according to para. 15 of the Statutes, other main components of the IUCN are the Council; the National and Regional Committees, and Regional Fora of Members; the Commissions established by the World Congress; and the Secretariat headed by the Director General. In its work the IUCN covers eight world regions: Africa; Meso and South America; North America and the Caribbean; South and East Asia; West Asia; Oceania; East Europe, North and Central Asia; and West Europe.

Due to its wide and heterogeneous membership, the IUCN actively participates in the development of international environmental law, primarily in the phase of initiative, pointing to the necessity for the international legal regulation of certain environmental issues, as well as in the phase of the creation of standard-setting resolutions, declarations and other proposals on the legal regulation of these issues. Among the important recent IUCN achievements in this field, the 'Save our Species' (SOS) Programme undoubtedly deserves to be mentioned here. The SOS Programme is a global NGO-IGO-States coalition initiated in 2011 by the IUCN, the Global Environment Facility (GEF) and the

---

131   Part III of the IUCN Statutes determines that "government agencies shall be organizations, institutions and, when applicable, government departments, which form part of the machinery of government in a State, including those agencies of the components of federal States or of States having an analogous structure"; *ibid*. The above-mentioned membership structure of the IUCN can be compared not only with QUANGOs, but also with TGOs; *cf. supra*, II.1.

132   The IUCN Statutes, Part III, para. 4; *supra*, note 129. However, in spite of these specific characteristics concerning its membership, the IUCN is by many authors, even in the most recent works, still considered an INGO; see for example: Rossi, I., *Legal Status of Non-Governmental Organizations in International Law*, Antwerp, Oxford, Portland, Intersentia, 2010, p. 20.

133   Thus, according to para. 12, the rights of IUCN Members are to participate in the World Congress and in National and Regional Committees and Regional Fora of Members; to express an opinion on applications for admission of new Members; to be informed regularly about the budget and activities of the IUCN; to communicate their views to the components of the IUCN; as well as to receive the copies of the IUCN publications and records of the official meetings. See: The IUCN Statutes, *supra*, note 129.

...ed at ...ding a species conservation fund supporting the protection of threatened species. The SOS was launched during the 10th meeting of the Conference of the Parties to the Convention on Biological Diversity, but the whole initiative has been mostly based on the findings of another important IUCN document, the IUCN Red List of Threatened Species,[134] and its network of experts around the world. Based on this starting point, the EU adopted the EU Biodiversity Strategy to 2020, which calls for "halting the loss of biodiversity and the degradation of ecosystem services in the EU by 2020, and restoring them in so far as feasible, while stepping up the EU contribution to averting global biodiversity loss."[135]

IV   Concluding Remarks

Today, more than a decade after we entered the 21st century, one could perhaps rightly question dealing with a topic such as legal personality in international law. This doubt seems even more convincing, bearing in mind on the one hand the historical verdict in the ICJ's famous 'Reparation case' mentioned at the beginning of this paper,[136] and on the other the attitude that the subjects of international law are basically nothing more than the participants in legally regulated international relations.[137] Of course, we could here go much further, dealing with, for example, the gendered approach to international legal personality,[138] or even with some of the quite extreme theories concerning the 'fragmentation of the self', and Foucault's 'anti-subject approach' that announced the 'end of the subject'.[139]

However, no matter how extensively some theoreticians define the concept of legal personality in international law, the consensus in international law doctrine seems to be much more difficult in recognizing that personality to a new kind of participant in international legal relations, even if some of them have obviously achieved international rights and duties, *i.e.* legal capacity in

---

134   For the IUCN Red List of Threatened Species see: <http://www.iucnredlist.org/> (23 September 2013).

135   For the text of the EU Biodiversity Strategy to 2020 see: <http://ec.europa.eu/environment/nature/info/pubs/docs/brochures/2020%20Biod%20brochure%20final%20lowres.pdf> (23 September 2013).

136   See: *supra*, note 2.

137   *Cf.* Higgins, *op. cit.* (note 5), p. 480.

138   See: Charlesworth, H., Chinkin Ch., Wright, Sh., "Feminist Approaches to International Law", *American Journal of International Law*, vol. 85, no. 4, 1991, pp. 621–622.

139   See: Nijman, *op. cit.* (note 6), pp. 365–378.

international law. On the other hand, such an approach in international law doctrine should not surprise anybody, taking into account that the recognition of international legal personality of a new kind of participant in international legal relations has always started with a few particular, *sui generis* entities 'that broke the ice' for all the future subjects of the same kind.

Analysing the IGO-like entities, it seems to us that the same logic of functionality in the institutionalization of international co-operation has been the common denominator for the appearance of IGOs, as well as of such IGO-like entities this paper is dealing with. Consequently, any formal recognition of international legal personality for both of these kinds of organizations would never have had anything but a declaratory meaning. Therefore, the 'Reparation case' Advisory opinion by the ICJ just confirmed the legal presence, *i.e.* the legal personality of the UN at that time. However, it also anticipated the concept of objective, *i.e. erga omnes* legal personality for all other organizations of the same kind (IGOs), including future ones.[140]

Unfortunately, although the definition of subject of international law determined by elements like legal capacity (*capacitas iuridica*) and/or the capacity of an entity to produce legal consequences on its own (*capacitas agendi*) including treaty-making capacity (*ius contrahendi*), the right of legation (*ius legationis*) or even the capacity to sue or be sued for breach of an international legal obligation (*ius standi in iudicio*) could seem very clear, their application in relation to every new participant in legal relations within the international community has often been faced with inconsistencies in international law theory.

First, international law doctrine has never determined the 'quantity' of rights and/or duties required for acquiring legal capacity as the basic element of legal personality in the international or any other legal system. On the other hand, if in domestic legal orders, as well as in general legal theory, rights and obligations were sometimes acquirable for a third party, why would international law be an exception here? Moreover, the earlier-mentioned Vienna Conventions on the Law of Treaties expressly provide for this possibility.[141]

Anyhow, IROs and particularly TGOs have achieved much more in acquiring international rights and duties through their participation, sometimes even directly, in international legal relations with States and IGOs (and other international law subjects) on their own. Moreover, Strazzari interestingly remarked

---

140   See: *supra*, note 9.
141   Thus, for example, treaties providing for obligations and rights for third States, as well as for third organizations are provided for in Articles 35 and 36 of the Vienna Conventions on the Law of Treaties, see: *supra*, notes 47 and 39.

...d favouring public nature of cross-border co-operation on the increasi... ational documents such as EU Regulation 1082/2006 con... by means o... ...rd, the argument that States are still 'the masters of the game',[143] cerni... n for *a priori* denying international legal personality to EGTCs or ...os does not seem very convincing to us. Following the same logic, one ... equally deny the international legal personality of IGOs, and even more ...t of the individual. Similarly, there is no reason for denying the possibility of acquiring international legal personality for IGO-like entities using the argument that contemporary international law doctrine (still)[144] has not accepted the same personality for their members. Such an argument would mislead us to the negation of some other widely accepted international law subjects like the Sovereign Order of Malta.

Furthermore, a few words should also be said concerning *capacitas agendi* of IROs and particularly TGOs. With regard to *ius legationis*, TGOs like the IPU and INTERPOL concluded a series of bilateral agreements with numerous States and IGOs that guarantee diplomatic privileges and immunities for their officials, similar to those provided by the Vienna Convention on Diplomatic Relations. Although the IROs themselves have not yet achieved much in this respect, the same cannot be said for some of their members, mostly the European regions and the US federal States.[145] Having in mind the participation

---

142 Strazzari, *op. cit.* (note 59), p. 156.
143 *Cf.* Mătușescu, *op.cit.* (note 74), p. 92.
144 It should be noted here that in contemporary international law doctrine there are already a number of valuable books and articles dealing with the international legal personality of sub-State entities; see *e.g.*: Michelmann, H.J., Soldatos, P. (eds.), *Federalism and International Relations: The Role of Subnational Units*, Oxford, Clarendon Press, 1990, 322 pp.; Duchacek, I.D., Latouche, D., Stevenson, G. (eds.), *Perforated Sovereignties and International Relations: Trans-Sovereign Contacts of Subnational Governments*, New York, Greenwood Press, 1988, 234 pp.; Paquin, S., "Les actions extérieures des entités subétatiques: quelle signification pour la politique comparée et les relations internationales?", *Revue international de politique comparée*, vol. 12, no. 2, 2005, pp. 129–142; Di Marzo, L., *Component Units of Federal States and International Agreements*, Alphen aan den Rijn, Sijhoff & Nordhoff, 1980, 244 pp.
145 Thus, for example, in 2010 Catalonia had five representations abroad. Scotland has representations in Washington DC, in Brussels (at the EU) and in Beijing, while the political representatives of the Belgian regions of Flanders and Wallonia have an official diplomatic status holding a diplomatic passport. Quebec probably has the most experience in this regard, having established its first representation abroad as early as in 1882 in Paris. Criekemans, D., "Regional Sub-State Diplomacy from a Comparative Perspective: Quebec, Scotland, Bavaria, Catalonia, Wallonia and Flanders", in: Criekemans, *op. cit.* (note 52),

of some of the European regions in the membership of IROs, the IROs' passive *ius legationis* as the right to receive the representatives of their member regions does not seem too hypothetical, particularly in conclusion on with IGOs' status with regard to the rules contained in the Vienna Convention of the Representation of States in their Relations with International Organizations of a Universal Character of 1975.¹⁴⁶

Finally, we have seen that IGO-like entities have influenced the law-making process in the international community, sometimes indirectly through 'Statements', 'Positions', 'Position Papers', 'Red Lists' and other kinds of 'soft-law' instruments, but sometimes even by concluding international agreements no matter what they are called (*e.g.* Memorandum of Understanding, Co-operation Agreement, Headquarters Agreement, *etc.*). Although the international law doctrine hesitates to accept their treaty character, one cannot ignore the rights and duties that result from some of these instruments, not only for those entities but also for IGOs and States acting in their *iure imperii* capacity. Despite their formal distinction, the content of the agreements mentioned often does not differ much from those concluded between States and/or IGOs. Bearing in mind the Vienna Conventions on the Law of Treaties and their explicit recognition of legal force in international law for the agreements concluded with or between 'other subjects of international law', one could easily conclude that such treaty-making capacity (*ius contrahendi*) of IGO-like entities offers undeniable evidence of their international legal personality. However, due to the inconsistency in international law theory, the way to this conclusion is not that simple. Considering treaty-making capacity as evidence of international legal personality we are faced with a situation similar to that of questioning what came first: the chicken or the egg, since, according to the international law rules regulating treaties, only 'subjects of international law' can be parties thereto. Then where to cut the Gordian knot? Maybe significantly, Shaw is less restrictive here in defining a treaty as "an agreement between parties on the international scene."¹⁴⁷ Such an approach leads us again to the hypothesis from the beginning of this paper: neither international legal personality, nor international law can be the purpose in itself. They serve

---

p. 47. Equally, in the US, for instance, only four States had representative offices in other countries in 1970, in comparison with 42 States with 233 representative offices in 30 countries in 2001. Also, in Germany, the *Länder* have established some 130 representative offices since 1970. Paquin, S., "Federalism and Compliance with International Agreements: Belgium and Canada Compared", in: Criekemans, *op. cit.* (note 52), p. 174.

146 For the text of the Convention see: UN Doc. A/CONF.67/16.
147 Shaw, *op. cit.* (note 5), p. 811.

the needs of the international community and vary with it. Therefore, TGOs, IROS, QUAIROS, INGOs or other new participants in international legal relations do not have to wait for some new 'Reparation case' Advisory opinion to obtain international legal personality. After all, even the UN did not have to in 1949. The subjects of international law appear, exist and die following the meta-juridical logic of functionality in international relations, and not due to legal doctrines. Someone could perhaps rightly consider that the thesis on international legal personality of these IGO-like entities (still today) goes too far. Maybe it leaves us with more questions than answers. However, writing such a dynamic topic as international legal personality is supposed to deal with tendencies rather than with pure facts. Otherwise, it might happen that our work had become out of date before it was completed.

Zagreb, 10 June 2014

CHAPTER 5

La controverse sur le statut de la Palestine

Djamchid Momtaz*

Certains font remonter la controverse sur le statut de la Palestine à la dissolution de l'Empire ottoman, plus précisément au choix du Royaume-Uni comme mandataire de la Palestine par la Société des Nations (SDN) sans que soit tenu compte des « vœux des communautés » vivant sur ce territoire comme l'exigeait le Pacte.[1] D'autres, plus réalistes, considèrent comme point de départ de cette controverse la décision d'avril 1947 du Royaume-Uni de se retirer de la Palestine et de remettre le dossier à l'Organisation des Nations Unies (ONU). Le 29 novembre 1947, l'Assemblée Générale, sur recommandation de la « Commission spéciale des Nations Unies pour la Palestine », adoptait une résolution intitulée « Le gouvernement futur de la Palestine »,[2] plus connue sous le nom de « plan de partage ». Y étaient prévues la création, sur le territoire sous mandat, d'un Etat juif et d'un Etat arabe et la mise en place d'un régime international de tutelle pour administrer la ville de Jérusalem.

Le rejet du plan par les Etats arabes et leur refus de reconnaître l'Etat d'Israël, dont l'existence fut proclamée le 14 mai 1948, allaient largement contribuer à envenimer la situation. Le conflit armé qui éclata suite à l'entrée des troupes de certains Etats arabes en Israël devait tourner à son avantage. Les acquisitions territoriales qui en résultèrent furent délimitées par les « lignes vertes » incluant l'ouest de Jérusalem et une partie des territoires alloués à l'Etat arabe. Ils resteront sous le contrôle d'Israël en vertu des conventions d'armistice.[3] Le 11 mai

---

* Professeur de droit international à l'Université de Téhéran ; Membre de l'Institut de droit international ; Ancien président de la Commission du droit international.
1 Article 22, al. 3 du Pacte de la Société des Nations. Le 25 avril 1920 la Conférence de San Remo confie le mandat de la Palestine au Royaume-Uni. La SDN incorpore dans le mandat la Déclaration Balfour exprimant l'appui du Royaume-Uni à l'établissement en Palestine du « foyer national pour le peuple juif en Palestine ». *Cf.* H. Cattan, *Palestine and International Law. The Legal Aspect of the Arab-Israeli Conflict*, Longman, London, 1974, pp. 25 ss.
2 Rés. 181(II) – 29 novembre 1947.
3 À partir de janvier 1949, les discussions sur la conclusion d'armistices s'engageaient à Rhodes. Dans les mois qui suivirent, Israël concluait avec quatre Etats arabes des conventions d'armistice séparés : le 24 février 1949 avec l'Egypte, le 23 mars 1949 avec le Liban, le 3 avril 1949 avec la Transjordanie et le 20 juillet 1949 avec la Syrie. Israël n'a pas estimé nécessaire de signer de tels accords avec l'Irak et l'Arabie saoudite, qui avaient pourtant participé au conflit. P.M. Martin, *Le conflit israélo-arabe*, LGDIP, Paris, 1973, p. 80.

1949, Israël était ad[mis] aux Nations Unies sans que le Conseil de Sécurité exige qu'il se retire [...]vant de ces territoires.[4] Le reste des territoires sous mandat, alloué à [...]abe, était annexé le 24 avril 1959 par la Jordanie, à l'exclusion de la b[...]aza qui passait sous administration de l'Egypte.

[...]nd conflit armé opposant les Etats arabes et Israël, qui éclata en juin [...] permit à ce dernier de consolider ses acquis territoriaux, et même de les [é]tendre. On assiste alors à l'occupation de l'ensemble des territoires autrefois sous mandat revenant à l'Etat arabe conformément au plan de partage, territoires que le Conseil de Sécurité qualifiera de « territoires occupés » au lendemain du conflit.[5] Toutefois, en étaient étrangement exclus ceux qu'Israël avait occupés lors du premier conflit armé. Exclusion confirmée par cet organe[6] après la fin du troisième conflit armé opposant Israël aux Etats arabes en octobre 1973. C'est l'assise territoriale que l'Organisation de la libération de la Palestine (OLP) revendique dans sa Proclamation de l'Etat palestinien, émise le 15 novembre 1988 après que la Jordanie ait renoncé, le 31 juillet précédent, aux territoires qu'elle avait annexés. Il convient ici de rappeler que, par cette Proclamation, l'OLP reconnaissait le droit d'Israël à exister.[7] Prenant acte de cette Proclamation, l'Assemblée Générale se réfère elle aussi aux territoires occupés depuis 1967 en tant que territoires du futur Etat dont la Proclamation est, selon cet organe, « dans la ligne du plan de partage », contradiction qui mérite d'être relevée.[8] Le fait accompli par Israël en 1949 semble ainsi avoir été entériné par tous les organes de l'ONU, y compris par la Cour internationale de Justice (CIJ) qui, dans son avis consultatif sur « les conséquences juridiques de l'édification d'un mur dans le territoire palestinien occupé »,

---

4 La Résolution 273(III) de l'Assemblée Générale, sur recommandation du Conseil de Sécurité (Rés. 62 du 16 novembre 1949), admettait Israël au sein des Nations Unies.

5 Rés. 242 du 22 novembre 1967, § 1(i).

6 Rés. 338 du 22 octobre 1973 se référant à la Résolution 242.

7 Il existe une abondante littérature sur cette Proclamation : J. Crawford, « The Creation of the State of Palestine. Too much too soon », 1 *European Journal of International Law* (*EJIL*), 1990, pp. 307–311 ; F.A. Boyle, « The Creation of the State of Palestine », 1 *EJIL*, 1990, pp. 301–306 ; V. Gowlland-Debbas, « Collective Responses to the Unilateral Declarations of Independence of Southern Rhodesia and Palestine : An Application of the Legitimizing Function of the UN », 61 *British Year Book of International Law*, 1990, pp. 135–153 ; M. Flory, « Naissance d'un Etat palestinien », 93 *Revue générale de droit international public*, 1989, pp. 385–415 ; J. Salmon, « La proclamation de l'Etat palestinien », 34 *Annuaire français de droit international* (*AFDI*), 1988, pp. 37–62 ; A. Pellet, « La destruction de Troie n'aura pas lieu », 4 *Palestine Yearbook of International Law*, 1987/1988, pp. 44–84.

8 Rés. 43/177 – 15 décembre 1988.

se réfère aux territoires occupés par Israël depuis 1967. La seule note discordante vient d'Israël, qui continue à revendiquer des « frontières défendables », ce qui présuppose une nouvelle délimitation de son territoire pour permettre une meilleure protection de sa population, y compris celle établie dans les colonies de peuplement en territoire occupé, arme « à double tranchant » susceptible de mettre en question son propre titre territorial, qui va bien au-delà de celui qui lui avait été attribué par le plan de partage,[10] à savoir les lignes septembre.

Le processus de paix lancé à Madrid le 30 octobre 1991, fondé sur le principe « paix contre la terre » allait faire naître l'espoir qu'Israël serait prêt à régler le conflit sur la base des résolutions pertinentes du Conseil de Sécurité. La « Déclaration de principe sur des arrangements intérimaires d'autonomie »,[11] signée entre Israël et l'OLP le 13 septembre 1993 prévoyait la mise en place d'une Autorité palestinienne dotée d'autonomie pour l'administration de certains territoires occupés. Cette Déclaration fut suivie d'intenses négociations qui aboutirent à l'accord du 4 mai 1994 puis à celui du 25 septembre 1995, concrétisant en partie les buts y figurant.[12] Ce processus, soutenu par le Conseil de Sécurité[13] ne put être, malgré les progrès accomplis, mené à bien après le déclenchement de la seconde Intifada le 29 septembre 2000.[14]

En vue de relancer le processus de paix, une « feuille de route »[15] sera élaborée conjointement par les Etats-Unis, l'Union européenne, la Fédération de Russie et les Nations Unies et présentée aux deux protagonistes qui l'entérineront. En contrepartie de l'engagement de mettre fin au terrorisme et à la violence, Israël s'engage à geler toutes les activités d'implantation de colonies sur les territoires occupés. Contrairement au processus de Madrid, la « feuille de route » envisageait clairement la création d'un Etat palestinien

---

9   Avis consultatif sur « les conséquences juridiques de l'édification d'un mur dans le territoire palestinien occupé », CIJ Rec. 2004, 9 juillet 2004, § 78.
10 Opinion individuelle du juge Al-Khasawneh jointe à l'avis de la CIJ sur les conséquences juridiques de l'édification d'un mur..., *op. cit.*, § 11.
11 A. Cassese, « The Israel-PLO Agreement and Self-Determination », 4 *EJIL*, 1993, pp. 564–571 ; N.K. Calvo-Goller, « L'accord entre Israël et l'OLP. Le régime d'autonomie prévu par la Déclaration de principes du 13 septembre 1993 », 39 *AFDI*, 1993, pp. 435–450.
12 A. Bockel, « L'autonomie palestinienne. La difficile mise en œuvre des accords d'Oslo-Washington », 40 *AFDI*, 1994, pp. 261–286.
13 Rés. 904 du 18 mars 1994 et Rés. 1073 du 28 septembre 1996.
14 A. Bockel, « Le pari perdu d'Oslo : le règlement du conflit israélo-palestinien dans l'impasse », 46 *AFDI*, 2000, pp. 131–138.
15 « Feuille de route axée sur les résultats en vue d'un règlement permanent du conflit israélo-arabe prévoyant deux Etats ». Annexe à la lettre adressée par le Secrétaire Général des Nations Unies au Président du Conseil de Sécurité, S/2003/529 – 7 mai 2003.

indépendant doté de droits souverains dont les frontières définitives seront fixées une fois réglée la question de Jérusalem et des réfugiés. Se trouve ainsi confirmée et concrétisée la vision du Conseil de Sécurité en faveur de la création d'un Etat palestinien à côté d'Israël désormais doté de frontières reconnues et sûres.[16]

Une nouvelle fois, le refus d'Israël de geler la colonisation et la poursuite de la violence devaient faire échouer la mise en œuvre du processus de paix. La décision d'Israël de se retirer de la bande de Gaza, menée à son terme le 12 septembre 2005,[17] fut considérée comme une alternative à sa décision d'ignorer la « feuille de route ». Les droits qu'Israël retient sur ce territoire n'offrent en fait qu'un semblant d'effectivité à l'Autorité palestinienne. L'échec de la « feuille de route » amena l'Autorité palestinienne à adopter une diplomatie plus offensive dont l'un des aboutissements aura été la demande d'admission de l'Etat de Palestine à l'ONU.[18]

Ces soubresauts et l'historique semé d'embûches des négociations israélo-palestiniennes à l'issue encore incertaine permettent tout de même de dégager l'existence de points d'accord dont la réalisation reste conditionnée par le retrait d'Israël des territoires qu'il occupe depuis 1967. Il est en effet désormais acquis que le peuple palestinien a le droit de disposer de lui-même et qu'il a vocation à former un Etat.

1   Le droit du peuple palestinien à disposer de lui-même

Si l'existence du peuple palestinien ne fait désormais plus débat, de graves obstacles continuent à entraver l'exercice par ce peuple de son droit à l'autodétermination.

1   *L'existence du peuple palestinien*
L'absence de toute référence au peuple palestinien dans le plan de partage se justifiait par le fait que l'Assemblée Générale visait à créer un Etat juif et un Etat arabe dont les territoires respectifs seraient délimités en tenant compte des lieux d'implantation principaux des Juifs tout en garantissant les droits des

---

16   Rés. 1397 du 12 mars 2002. La « feuille de route » prévoyant la création d'un Etat palestinien à côté d'Israël sera à son tour cautionnée par le Conseil de Sécurité. Rés. 1515–19 novembre 2003.
17   A. Bockel, « Le retrait israélien de Gaza et ses conséquences sur le droit international », 51 *AFDI*, 2005, p. 16.
18   Demande d'admission en tant que membre des Nations Unies adressée par le Président de l'Autorité palestinienne au Secrétaire Général le 21 septembre 2011.

minorités religieuses sur le territoire de chacun de ces Etats.[19] Ainsi, la référence au peuple de Palestine dans le rapport de la Commission spéciale pour la Palestine soumis à l'Assemblée Générale visait l'ensemble des habitants vivant sur le territoire sous mandat.[20] Après la création d'Israël, on assista à un exode massif, consécutif aux hostilités, des populations arabes et à l'expropriation de leurs biens. C'est à partir de ce moment que toute référence au peuple palestinien disparaît des documents des Nations Unies. Les Palestiniens seront alors qualifiés de réfugiés et c'est à ce titre qu'une protection leur sera offerte dans le cadre de l'« Office de secours et de travaux des Nations Unies pour les réfugiés de Palestine dans le Proche-Orient ».[21] Même au lendemain du second conflit armé opposant Israël aux Etats arabes, le Conseil de Sécurité persiste à croire que la question palestinienne se limite au « problème des réfugiés » et qu'« en vue de parvenir à l'instauration d'une paix juste et durable au Moyen-Orient » il serait nécessaire de « réaliser un juste règlement du problème ».[22]

La référence au peuple de Palestine ne fait son apparition dans les résolutions de l'Assemblée Générale qu'à partir de 1970, par ailleurs dans un cadre général consacré à la lutte des peuples sous domination coloniale et étrangère, à côté de ceux d'Afrique australe et des territoires administrés par le Portugal.[23] En admettant l'OLP en tant qu'observateur, l'Assemblée Générale reconnaissait enfin que cette Organisation représente « le peuple palestinien, principale partie intéressée à la question de la Palestine ».[24] Depuis, on retrouve une référence au peuple palestinien dans toutes les résolutions de l'Assemblée Générale consacrées à cette question, dont celle prenant acte de la Proclamation d'indépendance de la Palestine.[25]

Longtemps, la thèse officielle d'Israël consistait à dénier aux Palestiniens toute existence propre distincte du peuple jordanien.[26] Le fait qu'Israël accepte

---

19 D'après le chapitre 2 du point C du plan de partage, « il ne sera fait aucune discrimination, quelle qu'elle soit, entre les habitants, du fait des différences de race, de religion, de langage ou de sexe ». Cette disposition du plan prévoit par ailleurs qu'avant la reconnaissance de l'indépendance, le gouvernement de chacun des Etats adressera à l'ONU une déclaration qui devrait contenir une clause sur le droit des minorités, arabe ou juive, présentes sur leurs territoires respectifs. Déclaration qu'Israël s'est toujours abstenu de faire.

20 Rapport soumis le 11 novembre 1947, A/AC.14/32, add. 1, § 18.

21 Rés. 302(IV) de l'Assemblée Générale – 19 décembre 1949.

22 Rés. 242 du 22 novembre 1967.

23 Rés. 2649 du 30 novembre 1970 et Rés. 2787 du 6 novembre 1971.

24 Rés. 3210 du 14 octobre 1974.

25 Rés. 43/177 du 15 décembre 1988.

26 Déclaration du représentant d'Israël à la plénière de l'Assemblée Générale lors de sa 35ème session, GAOR XXXV, Plenary Meeting, p. 1318.

d'inclure dans les Accords de Camp David, signés avec l'Egypte le 17 septembre 1978 afin de fixer les bases des futures négociations, une vague référence aux « droits légitimes du peuple palestinien ainsi que ses justes revendications » constituait une première.[27] Suite à la Proclamation de l'Etat palestinien, Israël reconnaît qu'il est possible de trouver une solution aux « problèmes et aux aspirations des parties » dans le cadre des négociations de paix.[28] Formule vague et pour le moins timide qui n'engage nullement Israël. Le pas sera franchi avec la signature de la Déclaration de principes. Israël reconnaissait alors non seulement l'existence du peuple palestinien mais envisageait aussi l'éventualité où les Palestiniens pourraient disposer d'eux-mêmes.[29]

Dans la mesure où il n'est nulle part question d'un futur Etat palestinien, on pourrait se demander si cette référence ne vise pas uniquement la dimension interne du droit des peuples à disposer d'eux-mêmes, les élections prévues à cette fin constituant, selon les termes de la Déclaration, une étape importante dans la réalisation des droits et revendications légitimes des Palestiniens. Cette évolution ne fait que confirmer l'existence d'un peuple qui, par la constance de son combat contre l'occupant,[30] s'est forgé une véritable identité tout au long de cette période.

2 L'exercice par le peuple palestinien de son droit à la libre détermination

Les modalités de l'exercice du droit du peuple palestinien à la libre détermination seront fixées dans le cadre d'accords conclus entre Israël et l'OLP Ils prévoient le transfert d'un ensemble de compétences de portée limitée sur certaines portions des territoires occupés à l'Autorité palestinienne, organe subsidiaire de l'OLP Ces dispositions doivent permettre à Israël de préserver le plus longtemps possible le « gage territorial ».

L'autonomie la plus poussée sera accordée à la bande de Gaza et Jéricho, territoires qu'Israël s'engage à évacuer conformément à la Déclaration de principes,[31] dont les détails sont stipulés dans un Protocole annexe. L'accord du 4 mars 1994, consacré à ces deux enclaves distantes de 100 km et dont la superfi-

---

27 J. Le Morzellec, « Les accords de Camp David (17 septembre 1978) et le Traité de paix israélo-égyptien (26 mars 1979) », 26 *AFDI*, 1980, p. 179.

28 Déclaration du délégué d'Israël à la troisième Commission de l'Assemblée Générale lors de sa 43ème session, C.3/43/SR 23.

29 Al. 1 de l'article 3 de la Déclaration de principes, consacré aux conditions d'organisation des élections, dans les territoires palestiniens occupés, ceci dans l'exercice de leur droit à l'autodétermination.

30 A. Pellet, *op. cit.*, p. 60.

31 Articles V, VI et XIV de la Déclaration de principes.

cie représente à peine le quart de la superficie totale des territoires palestiniens occupés, concède quelques bribes de souveraineté à l'Autorité palestinienne. Conformément à cet accord, la souveraineté palestinienne est reconnue sur le sol et le sous-sol de ces enclaves et s'exercerait sur une zone maritime large de 20 miles contiguë aux côtes de Gaza. Sur ces étendues, l'Autorité palestinienne fera flotter son emblème, délivrera des titres de voyage aux Palestiniens et entretiendra certaines relations extérieures qu'on a évité de qualifier de diplomatiques. Si Israël renonce à la gestion de ces territoires, il n'en prend pas moins soin de maintenir la prééminence de l'autorité militaire qui continuera à contrôler l'espace aérien et maritime tout en continuant à superviser le transit des marchandises et des personnes. Ainsi, dans la rédaction de cet accord inégal, les intérêts d'Israël ont été sauvegardés. De plus, la minutie et la précision avec lesquelles ses dispositions sont rédigées évoquent un « acte notarié où le propriétaire cède, avec la plus extrême réticence, un bien limité à un légataire mineur dont il se méfie ».[32]

Le reste des territoires occupés, à l'exception de Jérusalem-est, est divisé, conformément à l'accord israélo-palestinien du 26 septembre 1995, en trois zones sur lesquelles l'Autorité palestinienne a des compétences d'attribution dont l'étendue sera déterminée en fonction des seuls intérêts d'Israël et ses craintes en matière de sécurité. La Zone A est composée d'enclaves non contiguës sur lesquelles l'Autorité sera responsable du maintien de l'ordre public. Sur la zone B, la compétence de l'Autorité en matière de maintien de l'ordre ne s'exercera qu'à l'égard des Palestiniens, Israël continuant de disposer d'une compétence exclusive pour la protection de ses nationaux et la lutte contre le terrorisme. Enfin, la zone C, qui couvre plus de la moitié de la Cisjordanie, restera sous le contrôle de l'autorité militaire israélienne, l'Autorité palestinienne ne disposant que de compétences résiduelles limitées aux questions de santé, d'éducation et d'économie.[33]

Ainsi, l'autonomie accordée par Israël aux zones B et C ne concerne pas tous les habitants de ces territoires puisque les citoyens israéliens qui y résident continueront de bénéficier d'une immunité de juridiction vis-à-vis de l'Autorité palestinienne. Qui plus est, l'enclave de Jéricho, qui jouit de l'autonomie la plus poussée, exclut les colonies juives de peuplement avoisinantes. L'inégalité de fait qui existe entre les parties prenantes a permis à Israël d'imposer sa

---

32 A. Bockel, *op. cit.*, AFDI, 1994, pp. 267–268.
33 G. Bastid-Burdeau, « Les références au droit international dans la question des titres de compétence dans les territoires de l'ancienne Palestine sous mandat : incertitudes et confusion » *in* Société française pour le droit international, *Colloque de Rennes : Les compétences de l'Etat en droit international*, A. Pedone, Paris, 2006, pp. 169 *ss*.

volonté à l'Autorité palestinienne en ce qui concerne la question de l'implantation de colonies de peuplement sur les territoires occupés. L'Autorité a finalement accepté qu'elle soit résolue dans le cadre du futur règlement « final » du conflit en contrepartie d'une vague promesse de ne plus étendre leur emprise.[34] Ce qui, en attendant, a permis à ces colonies de jouir d'un statut d'exterritorialité. La violence qui embrasa ce territoire après l'éclatement de la seconde Intifada devait servir à Israël de prétexte pour poursuivre et étendre la politique de colonisation, au mépris des engagements pris dans le cadre de la « feuille de route »[35] et en flagrante violation des dispositions de la quatrième Convention de Genève du 12 août 1949.

L'implantation des colonies juives menée à partir de 1977 est en contradiction avec la prescription du sixième alinéa de l'article 49 de cette Convention, lequel dispose que « la puissance occupante ne pourra procéder à la déportation ou au transfert d'une partie de sa propre population civile dans le territoire occupé par elle ». Le Conseil de Sécurité s'empressa de dénoncer « la validité en droit » des mesures prises par Israël dans ce sens et en vue de modifier « la composition démographique, la structure ou le statut constitutionnel des territoires palestiniens ».[36] Israël persiste pourtant à soutenir que cette implantation n'est pas contraire au droit international.[37] C'est pour

---

34 A. Bockel, *op. cit.*, AFDI, 1994, p. 281.

35 Conformément à la phase I de la « feuille de route », Israël s'engageait à geler toutes ses activités d'implantation de colonies juives dans les territoires palestiniens. Le Quatuor s'est déclaré, le 11 avril 2012, préoccupé par la poursuite des activités d'Israël en vue d'étendre ces implantations.

36 Rés. 446 du 22 mars 1979 et Rés. 465 du 1er mars 1980.

37 D'après la Cour suprême d'Israël, le statut final des implantations sera réglé sur le plan politique et, en attendant, l'armée israélienne est tenue de protéger les civils qui s'y trouvent : Yosef Muhammad Gosin v. The IDF Gaza Strip Military Commander, Jugement du 30 mai 2002. *Cf.* D. Momtaz, « Israel and the Fourth Geneva Convention : On the ICJ Advisory Opinion concerning the Separation Barrier », 8 *Yearbook of International Humanitarian Law*, 2005, pp. 351–352. Le 9 juillet 2012, une commission composée de juristes nommés par le gouvernement israélien se prononçait sur la légalité des implantations. D'après cette commission, l'alinéa 6 de l'article 49 s'oppose aux transferts forcés de population tels que pratiqués au cours de la Seconde Guerre mondiale, ce qui n'est pas le cas des transferts de Juifs dans les territoires occupés qui excluent la contrainte. *Cf.* I. Scobbie, « Justice Levy's Legal Tinsel : The Recent Israeli Report on the Status of the West Bank and Legality of the Settlements », *EJIL : Talk!*, publié le 9 septembre 2012, accessible sur : <http://www.ejiltalk.org/justice-levys-legal-tinsel-the-recent-israeli-report-on-the-status-of-the-west-bank-and-legality-of-the-settlements/> (16/01/2014) ; J. Salmon, « Les colonies de peuplement israéliennes en territoire palestinien occupé au regard de l'avis consultatif de la CIJ du 9 juillet 2004 » *in* A. Fischer-Lescano *et al.* (éd.), *Paix en*

mieux la protéger qu'Israël a entrepris l'édification d'un mur dans les territoires occupés. Son tracé, qui s'écarte par endroits de plus de 7 km des lignes établies par les armistices de 1949, a permis d'englober le plus grand nombre de colonies. La CIJ, dans son avis consultatif, qualifie cet acte de « fait accompli qui pourrait fort bien devenir permanent » et aboutir à « une annexion de facto ».[38] D'après la Cour, « cette construction s'ajoutant aux mesures prises antérieurement » – allusion à l'installation des colonies – « dresse un obstacle grave à l'exercice par le peuple palestinien de son droit à l'autodétermination et viole de ce fait l'obligation incombant à Israël de respecter ce droit »[39] aussi bien dans sa dimension interne qu'externe.

II La vocation du peuple palestinien à créer un Etat

Dans le cas où un peuple est soumis à la subjugation étrangère, le principe du droit des peuples à disposer d'eux-mêmes peut avoir pour corollaire le droit de se constituer en Etat. Dans le cas de la Palestine, ce droit ne lui est guère contesté. Néanmoins, la poursuite de l'occupation par Israël du territoire qu'elle revendique constitue le principal obstacle à son indépendance.

1 *Le droit du peuple palestinien à l'indépendance*

Le Pacte de la SDN entrevoyait déjà l'indépendance de la Palestine dans un futur proche. Selon le Pacte, « certaines communautés, qui appartenaient autrefois à l'Empire ottoman, ont atteint un degré de développement tel que leur existence comme nations indépendantes peut être reconnue provisoirement, à la condition que les conseils et l'aide d'un mandataire guident leur administration jusqu'au moment où elles seront capables de se conduire seules ».[40] Ainsi, l'Etat palestinien aurait pu naître sans aucune difficulté au lendemain de l'adoption du plan de partage. Sans vouloir faire un procès d'intention, les revendications de certains Etats arabes sur le territoire que le plan lui avait alloué firent obstacle à sa création. La Transjordanie, appuyée par

---

Liberté : Festschrift für Michael Bothe zum 70. Geburtstag, Nomos, Baden-Baden, 2008, pp. 285–295.

38 § 121 de l'avis consultatif sur les conséquences juridiques de l'édification d'un mur.
39 *Ibid.*, § 122. *Cf.* R. Rivier, « Conséquences juridiques de l'édification d'un mur dans le territoire palestinien occupé, Cour internationale de justice, avis consultatif du 9 juillet 2004 », 50 *AFDI*, 2004, pp. 302–304.
40 Art. 22 du Pacte de la SDN.

l'Irak, préconisait son annexion,⁴¹ thèse soutenue paradoxalement par le représentant spécial du Secrétaire Général⁴² tandis que la Syrie le considérait comme partie intégrante de son territoire.⁴³ Il aura fallu attendre presque trois décennies pour que l'Assemblée Générale réaffirme une nouvelle fois le droit inaliénable du peuple palestinien « à l'indépendance et à la souveraineté nationale ».⁴⁴ La rupture par la Jordanie des liens juridiques qu'elle avait établis avec les territoires palestiniens occupés laissait la voie libre à la Proclamation de l'Etat palestinien, immédiatement reconnu par un grand nombre d'Etats, alors que l'Assemblée Générale se contentait d'en prendre acte.

La Déclaration de principes et les accords israélo-palestiniens conclus par la suite ne prévoient pas expressément la création d'un Etat palestinien. Néanmoins, la référence au « statut final »⁴⁵ de la Palestine n'exclut pas pour autant la possibilité de la création d'un commun accord, à la fin de période intérimaire, d'un Etat palestinien. Il semble qu'Israël ne s'oppose pas à une telle éventualité si ses préoccupations sécuritaires sont satisfaites.⁴⁶ L'échec du processus de paix lancé à Madrid renforce l'idée selon laquelle la création d'un Etat palestinien est inéluctable et qu'elle sera de nature à faciliter le règlement du conflit. C'est ainsi que le Conseil de Sécurité se dit désormais « attaché à la vision d'une région dans laquelle deux Etats, Israël et la Palestine, vivent côte à côte », formule reprise dans la « feuille de route », dont la finalité est la création d'un Etat palestinien, et endossée une nouvelle fois par le Conseil. Il est vrai que, dans les deux cas, la création de cet Etat est conditionnée par l'existence de « frontières reconnues et sûres »,⁴⁷ référence incluse à la demande d'Israël, ce qui implique, dans certaines circonstances, un nouveau tracé de frontières, différentes de celles héritées des conventions d'armistice. De telles rectifications, effectuées sans compensation territoriale pour la Palestine, violerait le principe de l'interdiction de l'acquisition de territoires par la force. Ceci dit, on peut affirmer que la Palestine dispose désormais d'un titre juridique à créer un

---

41 B. Boutros-Ghali, « La crise de la Ligue arabe », 14 *AFDI*, 1968, p. 116.
42 A/648 – 16 septembre 1948.
43 P.M. Martin, *op. cit.*, p. 60.
44 Rés. 3237 – 22 novembre 1974.
45 Article v de la Déclaration de principes.
46 *Cf. Le Monde* du 11 décembre 1999. D'après Ehoud Barak, l'Etat palestinien existe déjà *de facto* et le problème est de savoir comment ne pas en faire un ennemi ou une menace pour Israël. De même, Benjamin Netanyahou, interviewé le 14 juin 2009 à l'Université Bar Ilan, mentionnait pour la première fois la création conditionnelle d'un Etat palestinien.
47 Rés. 1397 du 12 mars 2002. Référence incluse dans la « feuille de route » et reprise par la Rés. 1515 du Conseil de Sécurité à la demande d'Israël.

Etat mais que l'effectivité continue à lui faire défaut en raison de la persistance de l'occupation de son territoire.

2 La poursuite de l'occupation de la Palestine, obstacle à son indépendance

En prenant acte de la Proclamation de l'indépendance de la Palestine, l'Assemblée Générale affirmait qu'« il est nécessaire de permettre au peuple palestinien d'exercer sa souveraineté sur le territoire occupé en 1967 », se référant implicitement à l'absence d'effectivité de la Palestine sur son territoire. C'est l'argument qui fut invoqué par certains Etats pour justifier leur refus de reconnaître la Palestine comme nouvel Etat,[48] l'Union européenne envisageant la reconnaissance de l'Etat palestinien « le moment venu »,[49] c'est-à-dire lorsque la Palestine exercera la plénitude des compétences étatiques sur son territoire.

Pour l'heure, l'Autorité palestinienne ne constitue qu'un embryon d'Etat disposant de certaines compétences d'attribution dans le cadre du régime d'autonomie dont elle dispose, compétences qui lui permettent même d'entretenir des relations avec certains Etats, dont la Jordanie et les Etats membres de l'Union européenne avec laquelle elle a conclu des accords de coopération dans les domaines monétaire et financier.[50] Il est vrai que dans la zone A, ainsi que la CIJ ne manque pas de le relever, l'Autorité palestinienne s'est vu reconnaître certains « pouvoirs et responsabilités » mais, d'après la Cour, ces transferts de compétences sont restés « partiels et limités » en conséquence d'événements ultérieurs,[51] autant d'obstacles à la création de l'Etat de Palestine. D'après la Cour, sa consécration reste conditionnée par la mise en œuvre de bonne foi de toutes les résolutions pertinentes du Conseil de Sécurité exhortant Israël à se retirer des territoires occupés ainsi que des prescriptions de la « feuille de route ».[52]

Le retrait unilatéral d'Israël de la bande de Gaza pose la question de savoir si l'obstacle d'absence d'effectivité n'a pas été levé pour ce territoire, rendant désormais possible une reconnaissance en bonne et due forme de

---

48   *Cf.* Interview de F. Mitterrand, qui se réfère, suite à la Proclamation de l'Etat de Palestine, au « principe de l'effectivité, qui implique l'existence d'un pouvoir responsable et indépendant s'exerçant sur un territoire et une population. Ce n'est pas encore le cas. » *Le Monde* du 24 novembre 1988.
49   Déclaration de Berlin des Etats de l'Union européenne le 26 mars 1999.
50   G. Bastid-Burdeau, *op. cit.*, p. 173.
51   § 77 de l'avis consultatif sur les conséquences juridiques de l'édification d'un mur.
52   *Ibid.*, § 162.

l'Etat palestinien. Alternative au refus d'Israël de suivre la « feuille de route », le retrait israélien est loin d'assurer aux Palestiniens l'effectivité qui leur fait défaut. En effet, Israël continue de bloquer le périmètre terrestre extérieur à la bande de Gaza et d'exercer sa compétence exclusive tant sur l'espace aérien de ce territoire que sur sa mer territoriale. Qui plus est, Israël persiste à s'opposer à la remise en état de l'aéroport de Gaza ainsi qu'à la construction d'un port en eaux profonde sur ses côtes. Il se réserve enfin le droit d'exercer son droit à la légitime défense à la fois préventive et réactive en riposte aux actes qu'il considère comme menaçant sa sécurité. Il s'agit en fait d'un redéploiement des forces israéliennes, la bande de Gaza se trouvant de ce fait toujours sous le contrôle effectif d'Israël.[53] C'est pourquoi, lors du sommet de septembre 2005 aux Nations Unies, ses efforts en vue de faire reconnaître la fin de l'occupation militaire de Gaza n'ont pu aboutir. Le communiqué du 2 septembre 2005 du ministre des Affaires étrangères de l'Autorité palestinienne allait dans le même sens en insistant sur le principe de l'unité territoriale de la Palestine et le retrait d'Israël de tous les territoires occupés. En attendant, la responsabilité d'Israël en tant que puissance occupante perdure.

Dans ces conditions caractérisées par l'absence d'effectivité de l'Autorité palestinienne sur son territoire, certains estiment que la reconnaissance de la Palestine en tant qu'Etat est prématurée. Il a été soutenu qu'il est difficile de concevoir l'idée d'un Etat dont la totalité de son territoire est sous occupation.[54] De même, une proclamation ne suffit pas en soi pour fonder un Etat. Ceci dit, il n'en reste pas moins que l'effectivité dont Israël jouit dans les territoires qu'il occupe et qu'on invoque pour s'opposer à la reconnaissance de l'Etat palestinien est par essence « illégale ». Elle résulte en effet de la poursuite de l'occupation militaire de ces territoires par ce dernier, et ce malgré les injonctions du Conseil de Sécurité de la faire cesser et sa condamnation par la quasi unanimité des Etats. On pourrait dès lors se demander si les nombreuses reconnaissances dont la Palestine a fait l'objet à ce jour[55] ne devraient pas être jugées hâtives et contraires au droit international. On est cependant en droit d'exprimer de sérieux doutes à ce sujet. En effet, dans ce cas, la reconnaissance

---

53 M. Mari, « The Israeli Disengagement from the Gaza Strip : An End of the Occupation ? », 8 *Yearbook of International Humanitarian Law*, 2005, pp. 366-367.

54 J. Crawford, *The Creation of States in International Law*, 2nd edition, Clarendon Press, Oxford, 2006, pp. 446-447.

55 Fin novembre 2012, pas moins de 132 Etats avaient reconnu l'Etat palestinien. Déclaration de Mahmoud Abbas devant l'Assemblée Générale des Nations Unies. Communiqué de presse, AG/11317 – 29 novembre 2012.

ne saurait être considérée comme une intervention dans les affaires intérieures d'un autre Etat attentatoire à sa souveraineté pour être condamnée.[56] Ces reconnaissances doivent être considérées comme légitimes dans la mesure où elles sont destinées à consacrer le triomphe d'une valeur.[57] Elles s'inscrivent par ailleurs dans la ligne tracée par la CIJ qui affirme que, vu les droits et obligations en cause, « les Etats sont tenus de mettre fin aux entraves à l'exercice par le peuple palestinien de son droit à l'autodétermination ».[58] L'admission de la Palestine à l'UNESCO, le 31 octobre 2012, allant dans ce sens, on ne peut que s'en féliciter.

En revanche, il est regrettable que le Procureur de la Cour pénale internationale (CPI) ait refusé de donner effet à la déclaration de l'Autorité palestinienne par laquelle elle consentait à ce que la Cour puisse exercer sa compétence à l'égard des crimes commis sur son territoire.[59] Cette décision est d'autant plus regrettable que les accords intérimaires d'autonomie reconnaissaient la compétence palestinienne en matière judiciaire, y compris pénale. En se fondant sur cette réalité et en adoptant une approche fonctionnelle évitant tout positionnement sur la qualité étatique de l'Autorité palestinienne,[60] la Cour aurait du se contenter de s'assurer que les conditions d'exercice de sa compétence étaient remplies. Accepter la déclaration de la Palestine aurait permis à la Cour de s'acquitter de sa mission, qui est de lutter contre l'impunité.

***

Un sort identique fut réservé à la demande d'admission à l'ONU de la Palestine, présentée le 21 septembre 2011, en raison de l'opposition d'Israël et des Etats-Unis

---

56   J. Salmon, *op. cit.*, AFDI, 1988, pp. 60–61.
57   V. Gowlland-Debbas, *op. cit.*, p. 143.
58   § 159 de l'avis consultatif de la CIJ sur les conséquences juridiques de l'édification d'un mur.
59   Déclaration du 21 janvier 2009. La demande de l'Autorité palestinienne fut rejetée par le procureur de la CPI le 3 avril 2012 sans qu'il ait demandé au préalable l'avis de la Chambre préliminaire. D'après le Procureur, il faut être membre des Nations Unies pour pouvoir reconnaître la compétence de la Cour. Tel ne fut pourtant pas le cas des Iles Cook dont la déclaration d'acceptation de la compétence de la Cour fut pourtant acceptée...
60   Opinion rédigée par A. Pellet à la demande de Maître W. Bourdon, avocat à la Cour de Paris, datée du 14 février 2010 sur « les effets de la reconnaissance par la Palestine de la compétence de la CPI », § 28, disponible sur le website de la CPI A. Pellet, « Les effets de la reconnaissance par la Palestine de la compétence de la Cour pénale internationale » *in* S. Doumbé-Billé *et al.*, *Droit, liberté, paix, développement. Mélanges en l'honneur de Madjid Benchikh*, A. Pedone, Paris, 2011, pp. 327–344.

lors de la réunion consacrée par le Conseil de Sécurité à cette question le 21 juillet 2011, avant même qu'elle ne soit officiellement déposée.[61] Ces Etats estiment que la création de l'Etat palestinien ne pourrait se faire au moyen d'un « raccourci ». Le 28 juin 2011, le Sénat américain, suivi le 7 juillet de la même année par la Chambre des Représentants, menaçait de suspendre l'aide financière prodiguée à l'Autorité palestinienne si elle ne retirait pas sa demande.

C'est ainsi qu'elle a du revoir ses ambitions à la baisse et se contenter d'un statut d'Etat observateur à l'ONU. L'Assemblée Générale le lui accordera par une résolution adoptée à une large majorité[62] soixante-cinq ans après avoir voté le plan de partage de la Palestine.

Cette promotion du statut de la Palestine aux Nations Unies constitue certes une victoire diplomatique pour la Palestine dans sa lutte pour l'indépendance mais laisse entière la responsabilité de l'Organisation à son égard, ce que l'Assemblée Générale n'a pas manqué de rappeler à cette occasion. Les Nations Unies, en tant que successeur de la SDN, se trouvent en effet dans l'obligation de poursuivre ses efforts en faveur de la création d'un Etat palestinien indépendant.[63] En attendant, il appartiendra aux organes des Nations Unies de rappeler à Israël que la poursuite de l'occupation ne réduit en rien sa responsabilité à l'égard du peuple palestinien et que la reprise de la colonisation juive, décidée en représailles à la récente décision de l'Assemblée Générale, constitue une flagrante violation de ses obligations en vertu du droit international humanitaire.

---

61 S/PV.6590.
62 A/RES/67/19 du 29 novembre 2012 adoptée avec 138 voix pour, 41 abstentions et 9 voix contre, dont celles des Etats-Unis, du Canada et d'Israël.
63 J. Crawford, *The Creation of States in International Law, op. cit.*, p. 448.

CHAPTER 6

The Treaty-Making Capacity of International Organizations: Practice *vs.* Codification Efforts

*Obrad Račić**

I

There is no doubt that international organizations in domestic laws of states possess the status of legal persons. Without such status, international organizations would not be able to function as independent units. They would not be in a position to conclude contracts, to rent buildings, own cars, or to pay bills, *etc*. In other words, they would simply not exist in the legal sphere.[1] The status of international organizations in *national* laws has been less controversial – if at all – than in *international* law.

Quite a few international conventions establishing international organizations contain succinct provisions: the Charter of the United Nations:

> The Organization shall enjoy in the territory of each of its Members such legal capacity as may be necessary for the exercise of its functions and the fulfilment of its purposes.[2]

The Statute of the International Monetary Fund, however, is more specific: it provides that the Fund shall possess full juridical personality, and in particular, the capacity: (i) to contract; (ii) to acquire and dispose of immovable and movable property; and (iii) to institute legal proceedings.[3] It seems safe to conclude that both of them have the same idea in the mind. The Treaty Establishing the European Community[4] seems to be on the same line. Thus, Article 281 provides that "[t]he Community shall have legal personality", and Article 282 adds the following:

---

* Professor of International Law (retired), University of Belgrade, Faculty of Political Sciences, Serbia.
1 Henry G. Schermers, Niels M. Blokker, *International Institutional Law*, Martinus Nijhoff Publishers, Boston/Leiden, 2003, para. 1669.
2 Article 104.
3 Articles of Agreement (1944), Article IX, Section 2: Status of the Fund.
4 *Official Journal* C 325, 24 December 2002.

> In each of the Member States, the Community shall enjoy the most extensive legal capacity accorded to legal persons under their laws; it may, in particular, acquire or dispose of movable and immovable property and may be a party to legal proceedings...

Yes, the question of personality will in the first instance depend on the terms of the instrument establishing the organization. But this actually occurs only in a minority of cases. Personality on the international plane may be inferred from the powers or purposes of the organization and its practice.[5] However, the status of international organizations in *international* law emerged on the international agenda as a result of two irreversible developments: first, by providing a special status and protection to individual international organizations and to persons involved in their official business and, second, by providing them with the ability to open up capacity to enter into *international* agreements. In this way, international organizations were connected with the existing international legal order. And yet, the constituent instruments establishing international organizations, as a general rule, continued to avoid the problem of their international legal personality.

Article 7 of the Covenant of the League of Nations laid the foundations on the global plane:

> Representatives of the Members of the League and officials of the League when engaged on the business of the League shall enjoy diplomatic privileges and immunities. The buildings and other property occupied by the League or its officials or by Representatives attending its meetings shall be inviolable.[6]

On the sub-regional plane, European and International Commissions on the Danube (1856) and the Act of Navigation for the Congo (1885) provided for the privileges and immunities of international sub-regional organizations. Article 18 of the latter reads:

> The members of the International Commission, as well as its appointed agents, are invested with the privilege of inviolability in the exercise of

---

5 Malcolm N. Shaw, *International Law*, 6th edition, Cambridge University Press, 2008, pp. 1296–1297.
6 Peace Treaty concluded by Austria, France, the United Kingdom, Prussia, Russia, Sardinia and Turkey (Paris, 30 March 1856) regarding the European and International Commissions on the Danube and the General Act of the Berlin Conference on West Africa, 26 February 1885 regarding the Congo River. According to both, members of the Commission, officials, as well as bureaus and archives, enjoy privileges and immunities.

their functions. The same guarantee shall apply to the offices and archives of the Commission.

Today, the UN Charter is concise:

1. The Organization shall enjoy in the territory of each of its Members such legal capacity as may be necessary for the exercise of its functions and the fulfilment of its purposes.
2. Representatives of the Members of the Organization shall similarly enjoy such privileges and immunities...[7]

The Articles of Agreement establishing the International Monetary Fund are more specific. They provide for immunity from judicial process and other action, from taxation, of archives, freedom of assets from restrictions, privilege for communications, and immunities and privileges of officers and employees.[8]

The Statute of the Council of Europe contains a general provision and one with the aim of elaborating the principle in a future convention:

a. The Council of Europe, representatives of members and the Secretariat shall enjoy in the territories of its members such privileges and immunities as are reasonably necessary for the fulfilment of their functions. These immunities shall include immunity for all representatives to the Consultative Assembly from arrest and all legal proceedings in the territories of all members, in respect of words spoken and votes cast in the debates of the Assembly or its committees or commissions.
b. The members undertake as soon as possible to enter into agreement for the purpose of fulfilling the provisions of paragraph above...[9]

However, the statutory provisions concerning the treaty-making capacity of international organizations seem to be more diversified.

First of all, quite a few international organizations are not authorized to conclude international agreements at all. The constituent instruments that provide for their treaty-making capacity are far from identical: some of them contain a general authorization, while others list the types of agreements the organization is authorized to conclude.

---

7   Article 105 of the Charter.
8   Articles of Agreement (1944), Article IX, Status, Immunities, and Privileges.
9   Article 40 of the Statute.

The Articles of Agreement of the International Monetary Fund are of a very general nature: the Fund shall cooperate within the terms of this Agreement with any general international organization and with public international organizations having specialized responsibilities in related fields.[10]

The UN Charter is quite specific. It provides for a number of agreements the Organization may enter into. The Security Council may conclude special agreements concerning armed forces, assistance, and facilities, including rights of passage, necessary for the purpose of maintaining international peace and security (Article 43(1)); the Economic and Social Council may enter into agreements with any of the agencies referred to in Article 57 (Article 63), as well as suitable arrangements for consultation with non-governmental organizations (Article 71); the trusteeship agreement shall in each case include the terms under which the trust territory will be administered and designate the authority which will exercise the administration of the trust territory (Article 81).

The founding Treaties ('primary law') empower the European Union to conclude agreements with 'third' States and international organizations:

1. The Union may conclude an agreement with one or more third countries or international organisations where the Treaties so provide or where the conclusion of an agreement is necessary in order to achieve, within the framework of the Union's policies, or of the objectives referred to in the Treaties, or is provided for in a legally binding Union act or is likely to affect common rules or alter their scope.
2. Agreements concluded by the Union are binding upon the institutions of the Union and of its Member States.[11]

Particular problems have arisen from the status of an international organization as a legal person, not of domestic but of international law. The question whether international organizations are international legal persons arose from the fact that their statutes – apart from recognizing their status as a legal person – also mention their privileges and immunities as well as their capacity to enter into international agreements. International organizations are, therefore, legal persons under the national laws of the member states, but they are also something else: they are persons that are accorded special treatment, be it envisaged by their very statutes, conventions on privileges and immunities or

---

10 Article x: Relations with Other International Organizations.
11 Consolidated Version of the Treaty on the Functioning of the European Union, *Official Journal* C 325, 24 December 2002, Art. 216.

by their agreements with the states in which they are headquartered. International organizations are thus linked with the international legal order, whilst, simultaneously, the statutes of international organizations avoid explicitly addressing the issue of the international legal personality of the organizations they are creating.

The question of the international legal personality of international organizations remains open. So does the problem of the definition of the term 'international organization'.

There is a general understanding that international organizations are different from states.[12] They do not possess 'attributes of sovereignty'. In many respects, international organizations remain fundamentally different from states. States are reluctant to elevate the rights of international organizations to include 'attributes of sovereignty', even where this may seem tenable.[13]

What are the key criteria for identifying whether an entity is an international organization? There is the question whether such an entity must be composed only of states – or predominantly of states and/or other international organizations. Of course, it must be established under international law. But, although international organizations are usually created by a treaty, can they also be created by other means, such as a resolution of another international organization or by joint unilateral acts by states?[14]

Given the lack of consensus on a definition of an 'international organization', and the fact that such a definition was not provided by the Vienna Convention on the Law of Treaties, the Vienna Convention on the Representation of States in their Relations with International Organizations of a Universal Character or the Vienna Convention on the Law of Treaties between States and International Organizations or between International Organizations, the problem remains wide open.

But, what are they? Is an international convention – a legally binding instrument – a condition for an international organization to be recognized as such? Or, in some cases, may international organizations be established by a decision of an existing international organization or by a political declaration? To recall,

---

12   The State as a person of international law should possess the following qualifications: (a) a permanent population; (b) a defined territory; (c) government; and (d) capacity to enter into relations with other States. Colin Warbrick, "States and Recognition in International Law", in: Malcolm D. Evans (ed.), *International Law*, 2nd edition, Oxford University Press, 2006, p. 231.

13   Schermers, Blokker, *op. cit.*, para. 1876.

14   *Cf.* Dapo Akande, "International Organizations", in: Malcolm D. Evans (ed.), *International Law*, 2nd edition, Oxford University Press, 2006, p.279.

the UN Industrial Development Organization (UNIDO) was set up as an independent *organ* of the General Assembly in 1966. The decision to transform UNIDO into an international organization (a specialized UN agency) was taken subsequently. In April 1979, a diplomatic conference adopted a treaty constituting the UNIDO as an independent international organization. In seems that the UNIDO was reformed into an international organization only after the relevant international convention had been concluded.

Let us take a look at two important cases.

The Conference on Security and Co-operation in Europe (CSCE) was created by a political document[15] as a system of international conferences of states. No agreement was reached among its members (officially named 'participating States') to grant it status in international legal order at the time. One of the reasons for the resistance to such a decision lay in the fear that this would change the nature of the CSCE from a flexible framework for cooperation of the 'participating States' into a more traditional international organization.[16]

The decision to rename the CSCE into the *Organization* for Security and Co-operation in Europe (OSCE) was taken at the 1994 Budapest Summit. It was pointed out at the time that this change did not have the effect of changing the character of the obligations or the status of its institutions. The idea was thereafter the subject of serious reconsideration regarding some practical implications. If the OSCE should become a 'regional arrangement' provided for by Chapter VIII of the UN Charter, it would mean that the OSCE would undertake the responsibilities with regard to the maintenance of international peace and security (UNSC authorization with regard to enforcement actions; duty to inform it of activities undertaken or in contemplation under regional arrangements or by regional agencies, *etc.*). It was realized that this 'practical implication' would imply a serious change in the CSCE's flexible character. No final decision has been taken.[17]

In sum, the *Organization* for Security and Co-operation in Europe was only formally renamed. In fact, it is still a *Conference* – a system of periodic meetings of the representatives of the participating States at different levels.

On the other hand, is there really any doubt that the European Union (including the European Community and Euratom) – which was, by the way,

---

15 Final Act on Security and Co-operation in Europe (1975).
16 Schermers, Blokker, *op. cit.*, para. 1569.
17 The only legally binding document adopted within the framework of the OSCE is the Convention on Conciliation and Arbitration within the OSCE (1992), which was subject to ratification of the participating States willing to accept it.

invited to attend the UN Conference on the Law of Treaties between States and International Organizations or between International Organizations – is an international organization? It was established by *states*, by means of an *international convention*. However, it is much more than an ordinary organization: the elements of supra-nationality have been evolving systematically. Is it, perhaps, a federation or a confederation of States?

A case decided by the European Court of Justice[18] seems to be to the point. The EU Court of First Instance had decided that

> resolutions adopted by the Security Council under Chapter VII of the Charter of the United Nations are binding on the Member States of the Community which must therefore, in that capacity, take all measures necessary to ensure that those resolutions are put into effect and may, and indeed must, leave unapplied any provision of Community Law, whether a provision of primary law or a general principle of Community law, that raises any impediment to the proper performance of their obligations under that Charter.[19]

After the *Kadi and Al Barakaat* appeal, the European Court of Justice set aside the judgment of the Court of First Instance and annulled the Council Regulation imposing specific restrictive measures against the appellants. According to the judgment of the ECJ, 'smart' sanctions against the appellants were taken on the ground of the proceedings in the United Nations Security Council Sanctions Committee where, among others, the right to be heard and the right to effective judicial review were breached. The Court held that Article 300(7) EC provided that agreements concluded under the conditions set out in that Article were to be binding on the institutions of the Community and on Member States. By virtue of that provision, supposing it to be applicable to the Charter of the United Nations, the latter would have primacy over acts of

---

18   *Yassin Abdulah Kadi and Al Barakaat International Foundation v. Council of the European Union and Commission of the European Communities*, Joined Cases C-402/05 and C-415/05 P. The case concerned UNSC Resolution 1390 (2002), which lays down the measures to be applied against Usama bin Laden, members of the Al-Qaeda network and the Taliban and other associated individuals, groups, undertakings and entities. Taking the view that action by the Community was necessary in order to implement that resolution, the EU Council adopted Common Position 2002/402/CFSP concerning restrictive measures against Usama bin Laden and members of the Al-Qaeda organization – and the Council subsequently adopted Regulation (EC) No 561/2003 concerning exceptions to the freezing of funds and economic resources.

19   Kadi, paragraphs 189 and 190, and Yusuf and Barakaat, paragraphs 239 and 240.

secondary Community law. However, that primacy at the level of Community law would not extend to *primary* law, in particular to the general principles which include fundamental rights.[20] And finally, an international agreement cannot affect the allocation of powers fixed by the Treaties or, consequently, the autonomy of the Community legal system, the observance of which is ensured by the Court by virtue of the exclusive jurisdiction.

In contrast to 'ordinary' international organizations, it is difficult to argue that the European Union is fundamentally different from states.

II

The rich and diversified practice of the conclusion of treaties between the international organizations themselves and between them and the states is rarely based on express provisions of the constituent instruments of those organizations. In many instances that practice has reached far beyond the provisions of those instruments. Even without constitutional authorization, many international organizations have concluded agreements the legality of which has not been disputed. Today, the right to conclude agreements relating to the headquarters and the privileges and immunities of international organizations, their premises and staff can probably be seen as inherent to any international organization.

Headquarters agreements, concluded by international organizations and respective host states, reflect a necessity.[21] They have relations of specific importance regarding the issues every international organization is confronted with: the supply of several public services such as public transport, power, drainage and fire protection, as well as garbage and snow removal. Of course, privileges and immunities of international organizations as such, of representatives of states attending their conferences, and staff of the organizations follow as well.

Apart from headquarters agreements, mention needs to be made also of the extremely widespread practice of international organizations (not only the UN) to conclude agreements on the organization of international conferences

---

20 Especially paragraphs 306, 307 and 308 of the Judgment.
21 Agreement between the United Nations and United States of America regarding the Headquarters of the United Nations, signed in Lake Success on 26 June 1947; Interim Agreement on Privileges and Immunities of the United Nations Concluded between the Secretary-General of the United Nations and the Swiss Federal Council, signed at Bern on 11 June 1946 and at New York on 1 July 1946.

under their auspices and meetings of their bodies outside the organizations' headquarters.[22]

Even the OSCE – which can hardly be seen as an international organization – seems to be developing the practice of concluding agreements regarding its missions in the participating states. The Memorandum of Understanding between the OSCE and the FRY[23] stated that "[t]his Memorandum shall enter into force upon signature", with the exception of Article 5(2) and (3)(a), which "shall enter into force after the FRY informs the OSCE that necessary legislative changes enabling the entry into force of these provisions have been adopted."

Agreements on privileges and immunities may also be regarded as a precondition for the smooth operation of the diplomacy of international conferences and organizations.

It is widely believed that the treaty-making capacity of international organizations is upheld by their practice of concluding international treaties with states on these issues. However, the basic agreements on privileges and immunities of international organizations are negotiated, signed and ratified by the *states*.[24] These have been followed by agreements between international *organizations* and the host states.[25] Finally, some states have enacted their own national laws on privileges and immunities.[26] It should be recalled that a considerable proportion of headquarters agreements contain provisions on privileges and immunities as well.

As the provision of technical assistance has become an important element for rectifying inherited injustices, the number of international agreements[27]

---

22 For example, the Agreement between the UN and the Government of Yugoslavia concerning the Arrangements for the 1965 World Population Conference, signed in New York on 27 February 1964 – *Yearbook of the United Nations*, 1964 – testifies to the abundant practice of the United Nations and its specialized agencies.

23 Signed on 16 March 2001 by Ambassador Stefano Sannino, the Head of OSCE Mission to the FRY and Ambassador Branislav Milinković, the Head of the FRY Mission to the OSCE in Vienna.

24 Convention on the Privileges and Immunities of the United Nations, signed on 13 February 1946, and Convention on the Privileges and Immunities of the Specialized Agencies, signed on 13 February 1946, *etc.*

25 Interim Agreement on Privileges and Immunities of the United Nations Concluded between the Secretary-General of the United Nations and the Swiss Federal Council, signed at Bern on 11 June 1946 and in New York on 1 July 1946.

26 International Organization Immunity Act (USA, 1948).

27 *E.g.* Agreement between the Government of the Republic of South Africa and UN Development Program on Establishing a Service Center in South Africa, New York, 1 October 2007.

between international organizations (or groups of international organizations) and the states receiving their assistance has flourished; these agreements are now concluded in a typical format. These agreements, with negligible variations, govern the forms of technical assistance provided, the inputs of the recipient governments, the administrative and financial obligations of the parties, the privileges and immunities of the organizations and officers engaged in providing the technical assistance, pursuant to the 'agreement' between the organizations and the governments.

The efforts made by the UN to achieve a degree of uniformity of the relationship agreements between the United Nations and a number of international organizations provided for by the UN Charter and the constituent instruments of several international organizations met with partial success. The relationship agreements follow the customary pattern of inter-state agreements. They contain introductory provisions, the dispositions, and the final provisions. Their validity is made subject to approval by the main organs of the UN and each individual specialized agency. The fulfilment of this condition is stated in a separate protocol concerning the entry into force of the given agreement.

As noted, talks between the representatives of these organizations have highlighted a new factor in international relations – the 'sovereign awareness' of international organizations insisting on protecting their own independence. Interestingly, the introductory provisions of these agreements usually specify that the contracting parties 'agreed' the text of the following agreement, thus highlighting the agreement of the wills of the contracting parties.[28]

The trusteeship agreements, provided for by the UN Charter, represent a special category of international agreements, concluded by the UN and the states responsible for the development of some former colonial territories. The administering states have assumed obligations to administer the territory in such a manner as to achieve the basic objectives of the international trusteeship system as laid down in Article 76 of the UN Charter. They have to provide for peace, order, good government, and shall have full powers of legislation, administration and jurisdiction in the territory, and shall be responsible for the defence of the territory, and for ensuring that it shall play its part in the maintenance of international peace and security.

Agreements on peace-keeping are of a very special nature. Solutions had to be found for the problems the UN founding fathers had been unable to foresee.

---

28   See more (in Serbian, with summary in English): Obrad Račić, *Odnos između Ujedinjenih nacija i specijalizovanih ustanova* [*The Relationship between the United Nations and the Specialized Agencies*], Belgrade, 1966, p. 303.

The deployment of UN peace-keeping forces was a major novelty by which one international organization (the UN) assumed major responsibility in an important segment of international relations, without an explicit provision in its Charter. But the UN is the *only* international organization vested with these substantial powers, which international organizations customarily do not have.

One very important issue was raised by the deployment of peace keeping/making operations: how to regulate the privileges and immunities of the armed troops – which arms they are entitled to use under their mandate. This issue was deliberated extremely seriously at the very outset of this mode of peace-keeping – at the time the United Nations Emergency Forces were deployed to monitor the Israeli-Egyptian border.[29] The status of the assets of the member states taking part in this campaign was regulated separately. The agreement comprised detailed provisions on the movement of the UN Emergency Forces in UAR territory, its powers in civil and criminal matters, communications, the use of the UN flag, *etc.* It needs to be noted here that agreements were also signed with Lebanon on the UN Leave Centre and the work of the transit centre at the Beirut International Airport.

Individual agreements with the respective states governing each particular case followed[30] – or general references were made to the agreement on UN privileges and immunities. The latter sometimes went without saying.

The practice of concluding similar agreements has continued to this day, albeit not in all cases, as the deployment and activities of UN operations in the former Yugoslavia corroborate. UNSC Resolution 1244 governs the UN Mission in Kosovo (UNMIK) and Kosovo Force (KFOR) in principle, almost implicitly, while the specific issues of the activities of the International Force (IFOR) in Bosnia-Herzegovina were governed by the Dayton Accords, a document adopted outside the United Nations, which the UNSC soon supported, calling on the parties to fulfill the obligations they had assumed under it in good faith.

Therefore, the international organizations' abundant and diverse practice of concluding agreements, either among themselves or with states, is only partly based on explicit statutory provisions. Practice has evolved much more than the written text.

---

29   Exchange of letters constituting an Agreement between the United Nations and the Government of Egypt concerning the status of the United Nations Emergency Force in Egypt, New York, 8 February 1957.

30   *E.g.* Exchange of letters constituting an Agreement between the United Nations and the Government of the Republic of Cyprus concerning the status of the United Nations peace-keeping force in Cyprus, New York, 31 March 1964.

The categories of international agreements concluded between international organizations and states clearly do not coincide with the provisions of the statutes of the organizations at issue.[31] The UN has gone the furthest in concluding the types of international agreements not envisaged by the UN Charter (headquarters agreements; agreements with host states on the territory of which international conferences under the Organization's auspices or meetings of the specific organs of the Organization are to be held; technical assistance agreements; agreements on privileges and immunities and – most importantly – UN agreements with states on peace-keeping operations).

The frequent practice of various international organizations, universal and regional alike, dictated by the powers vested in them by the constituent instruments should not be disregarded either, of course.

III

There are several international conventions that have been concluded between *states*. One of them, the Convention on the Privileges and Immunities of the United Nations (1946) governs the privileges and immunities of the United Nations, while another one, which is very similar in content – the Convention on the Privileges and Immunities of the Specialized Agencies (1946) – governs the immunities and privileges of the system of UN organizations. It needs to be highlighted that these instruments indirectly allow those organizations to seek the 'quasi judgments' of the International Court of Justice. These two Conventions indicate the UN's right to be a 'party in disputes' before the ICJ: all differences arising out of the interpretation or application of the present convention shall be referred to the International Court of Justice, unless in any case it is agreed by the parties to have recourse to another mode of settlement. If a difference arises between the United Nations on the one hand and a Member on the other hand, a request shall be made for an advisory opinion on any legal question involved in accordance with Article 96 of the Charter and Article 65 of the Statute of the Court. The opinion given by the Court shall be *accepted as decisive* by the parties (Section 30).

The third Convention, the Convention on the Safety of United Nations and Associated Personnel (1994), endeavours to at least partly rectify some of the shortcomings in the UN Charter. The UN Charter focuses on inter-state conflicts, whereas various forms of intra-state conflicts predominate today,

---

31   *Cf.* Schermers, Blokker, *op. cit.*, para. 1559.

resulting in the need to deploy civilian and military components for UN operations in the conflict stricken countries.

The Convention on the Safety of the United Nations and Associated Personnel was adopted in order to protect 'United Nations personnel' ('Persons engaged or deployed by the Secretary-General of the United Nations as members of the military, police or civilian components') and 'Associated personnel' ('Persons assigned by a Government or an intergovernmental organization with the agreement of the competent organ of the United Nations'). However, according to Article 2, this Convention *shall not apply to* "United Nations operations authorized by the Security Council as an enforcement action under Chapter VII of the Charter of the United Nations in which any of the personnel are engaged as combatants against organized armed forces and to which the law of international armed conflict applies."

This Convention is relevant to the discussion in this article because it expands the UN's right to conclude international agreements in an area neglected by the UN Charter. The Convention provides that the host State and the United Nations shall conclude as soon as possible an agreement on the status of the United Nations operation and all personnel engaged in the operation including, *inter alia*, provisions on privileges and immunities for military and police components of the operation (Article 4).

To recapitulate, all three Conventions were signed by *states* and they expand the right of the respective international organizations *themselves* to conclude international agreements.

The three international conventions that will be discussed now can contribute to the debates on the international legal personality of international organizations and, at least, strengthen the arguments of those talking about the creation of international customary law on the right of international organizations to conclude *international* agreements.

Therefore, this part of the article does not deal with the treaty-making capacity of international organizations they create through their own practice, but the inter-state agreements strengthening this right of theirs: the Vienna Convention on the Law of Treaties, the Vienna Convention on the Law of Treaties between States and International Organizations or between International Organizations and the Vienna Convention on the Representation of States in their Relations with International Organizations of a Universal Character.

However, only the Vienna Convention on the Law of Treaties – indifferent to the problems of the international legal personality of international organizations and their treaty-making capacity – is in force. Article 3 simply states:

The fact that the present Convention does not apply to international agreements concluded between States and other subjects of international law or between such other subjects of international law, or to international agreements not in written form, shall not affect:

(a) The legal force of such agreements;
(b) The application to them of any of the rules set forth in the present Convention to which they would be subject under international law independently of the Convention;
(c) The application of the Convention to the relations of States as between themselves under international agreements to which other subjects of international law are also parties.

The Vienna Convention on the Law of Treaties (1969) gives a short definition of an 'international organization' which is unlikely to resolve the existing controversies among scholars. It simply states the following: "'[i]nternational organization' means an intergovernmental organization" (Article 2(1)(i)). A number of questions arise: does the notion of an 'international organization' cover institutions established by an instrument other than an international convention (*i.e.* a legally binding instrument) like the OSCE? Secondly, does it include international institutions whose members include non-state entities as well? Finally, does it include organizations possessing considerable elements of supra-nationality (such as the EU)?

The Vienna Convention on the Representation of States in their Relations with International Organizations of a Universal Character (1975) follows this short definition: "'international organization' means an intergovernmental organization". For the purposes of this Convention, an additional element of definition has been added: an 'international organization of a universal character' "means the United Nations, its specialized agencies, the International Atomic Energy Agency and any similar organization whose membership and responsibilities are on a worldwide scale" (Article 1).

Accordingly, the Convention on the Representation of States in their Relations with International Organizations of a Universal Character applies "to the representation of States in their relations with any international *organization* of a universal character," but also to their representation at *conferences* (also of an universal character) convened by or under the auspices of such an organization, on the condition that the Convention has been accepted by the host State (Article 2(1)).

Only states are invited to ratify this Convention. Although 38 years have passed since its adoption, it has been ratified by 34 (of the requisite 35) states.

The greatest problem lies in the fact that it has not been ratified by any of the states in which the leading international organizations are headquartered – including Austria, China, France, Great Britain, Italy, Canada and the USA.

The most important Convention for the subject discussed in this article – the Vienna Convention on the Law of Treaties between States and International Organizations or between International Organizations (1986) – follows the wording of the Vienna Convention on the Law of Treaties (1969): "'[i]nternational organization' means an intergovernmental organization" (Article 2(1)(i)). There is no doubt that it applies to the treaties of both an 'international organization of a universal character' and to the treaties of *all* intergovernmental organizations.

This Convention has not come into force either. Although it was adopted 27 years ago, it has been signed by 35 states and international organizations invited to take part in the conference and deposit their acts of formal confirmation (the international organizations are not reckoned in the number of requisite ratifications). Brazil, China, France, India, Russia, USA and South Africa are among the major states that have not ratified the Convention. Acts of formal confirmation were deposited by the United Nations and a number of its specialized agencies. The following have failed to do so: the Council of Europe, the European Union, the Food and Agriculture Organization, the International Telecommunication Union and UNESCO.

A few more words should be said about the provisions more or less closely linked to the status of international organizations in international law. The treaty-making capacity of international organizations "is governed by the rules of that organization" (Article 6). But, what are the rules of the organization? The "'rules of the organization' means, in particular, the constituent instruments, decisions and resolutions adopted in accordance with them, and the established practice of the organization" (Article 2(1)(j)).

Whereas the Convention on the Law of Treaties may have allowed the *possibility* of different interpretations, the Convention on the Law of Treaties between States and International Organizations or between International Organizations (Vienna, 1986) is very explicit both with respect to the right of international organizations to conclude international treaties and with respect to the legal effects of those treaties.

The capacity of international organizations to enter into international treaties is explicitly recognized. As opposed to the Convention on the Representation of States in their Relations with International Organizations of a *Universal* Character, which was concluded earlier, the Convention on the Law of Treaties does not limit its application to a specific category of international organization. The treaty-making capacity of an international organization to conclude international treaties is governed by the 'rules of the organization'. Therefore, it is regulated not only by the constituent instrument, but by the *rules* of the organization as well. What is undoubtedly at issue is the entirety of the decisions and practices developed in the manner generally envisaged by the statute and with the majority it envisages. The 'rules' of the organization therefore need to be perceived as a dynamic category.

IV

The ICJ's jurisprudence demonstrates that there is no hesitation in recognizing the treaty-making capacity of international organizations.

In its most frequently cited advisory opinion[32] the Court said, *inter alia*:

> The subjects of law in any legal system are not necessarily identical in their nature or in the extent of their rights... The Charter has equipped that centre with organs, and has given it special rights... By giving the Organization legal capacity and privileges and immunities in the territory of each member State and by providing for the conclusion of agreements between the Organization and its Members; and by providing the Organization for the conclusion of agreements between the organization and its Members...

In the opinion of the Court, the Organization was intended to exercise and enjoy

> the rights which can only be explained on the basis of the possession of a large measure of international personality and the capacity to operate on an international plane. ... Accordingly, the Court has come to the conclusion that the Organization is an international person...

However, the Court hastened to say:

> That is not the same thing as saying that it is a State which it certainly is not. Or that its legal personality and rights and duties are the same as those of the State. Still less, it is the same as saying that it is a supra-state.

---

[32] *Reparation for Injuries Suffered in the Service of the United Nations*, Advisory Opinion of 11 April 1949, *ICJ Reports 1949*, p. 174.

Yes, this advisory opinion focused on the United Nations. And yet, the reasoning of the Court – *mutatis mutandis* – seems to be applicable to other international (intergovernmental) organizations.

Indeed, in two cases on which it delivered Advisory Opinions, the ICJ recognized the right of international organizations within the UN system to conclude agreements with member states without hesitation. The (inter-state) conventions on privileges and immunities of specialized agencies at the same time opened up the possibility for them to appear before the ICJ in disputes on the interpretation and application of the Convention – albeit in the advisory opinion procedure. However, as opposed to the UN Charter and the ICJ Statute, they are under the obligation to accept these *advisory* opinions as *binding*.

In its advisory opinion concerning the fulfilment of an obligation contained in the Agreement concerning the UN Headquarters in New York City,[33] the Court unanimously stated that it "is of the opinion that the United States of America, as a party to the Agreement between the United Nations and the United States of America regarding the Headquarters of the United Nations of 26 June 1947, is under an obligation, in accordance with Section 21 of that Agreement, to enter into arbitration for the settlement of the dispute between itself and the United Nations."

In its other advisory opinion, regarding the Agreement between the WHO and Egypt,[34] by twelve votes to one the Court held that

> in the event specified in the request, the legal principles and rules, and the mutual obligations which they imply, regarding consultation, negotiation and notice, applicable as between the World Health Organization and Egypt are those which have been set out in paragraph 49 of this Advisory Opinion and in particular that: (a) their mutual obligations under those legal principles and rules place a duty both upon the Organization and upon Egypt to consult together in good faith as to the question under what conditions and in accordance with what modalities a transfer of the Regional Office from Egypt may be effected...

The ICJ has considered that "IOs are subjects of IL and, as such, are bound by an obligations incumbent upon them under general rules of IL...."

---

[33] *Applicability of the Obligation to Arbitrate under Section 21 of the United Nations Headquarters Agreement of 26 June 1947*, ICJ Reports 1988, p. 12.

[34] *Interpretation of the Agreement of 25 March 1951 between the WHO and Egypt*, Advisory Opinion, ICJ Reports 1980, p.73.

In two advisory opinions,[35] the ICJ was of the view that it went without saying that international organizations had the right to appear in disputes before the ICJ pursuant to the *inter-state* Convention on the Privileges and Immunities of the United Nations – within the advisory opinion procedure and provided that they accepted the advisory opinions as binding.

V

In view of the different opinions voiced by scholars regarding the international legal personality of international organizations, the unwillingness of states to regulate it by a legally binding instrument needs to be noted. The Vienna Convention on the Law of Treaties between States and International Organizations or between International Organizations was negotiated, signed by many states but has not entered into force to this day.

Do the views states voiced during the diplomatic conference that resulted in the adoption of the text of this Convention explain their visible reluctance to ratify it, although the International Law Commission (ILC) had earlier decided not to enter the debate on international legal personality?

Let us start with the draft submitted by the International Law Commission.[36]

The ILC explained its decision to avoid giving an answer to this controversial question in the following way:

> Attention should be drawn to a further very important consequence of the definition proposed. The present draft articles are intended to apply to treaties to which international organizations are parties, whether the purpose of those organizations is relatively general or relatively specific, whether they are universal or regional in character, and whether admission to them is relatively open or restricted. ... The fact is that the main purpose of the present draft is to regulate, not the status of international organizations, but the regime of treaties to which one or more international organizations are parties...

---

35 *Application of Article VI, Section 22, of the Convention on Privileges and Immunities of the United Nations*, Advisory Opinion of 15 December 1989 (Mr Dumitru Mazilu), *ICJ Reports 1989*, p. 177; and *Difference Relating to Immunity from Legal Process of a Special Rapporteur of the Commission on Human Rights*, Advisory Opinion of 29 April 1999 (Mr Dato' Param Cumaraswamy), *ICJ Reports 1999*, p. 62.

36 Draft Articles on the Law of Treaties between States and International Organizations or between International Organizations adopted by the International Law Commission at its Thirty-Fourth Session, Document A/CONF. 129/4*.

The proposed text on the capacity of international organizations to conclude treaties seems to be aimed also at excluding any idea of trying to decide the question of the status of international organizations in international law. It simply says, "The capacity of an international organization to conclude treaties is governed by the relevant rules of that organization". Obviously, the ILC considered that it was useful to follow the definition that had recently been given in the Vienna Convention on the Representation of States in their Relations with International Organizations of a Universal Character. The Commission accordingly adopted the present subparagraph given in that Convention.

The written observations on the Draft Articles presented by the International Law Commission,[37] submitted by the governments of states and a number of international organizations, testified to the fact that the dilemmas were far from being unfounded.

The following point was raised at the Conference on Treaties between States and International Organizations: whether some intergovernmental organizations listed with the Union of International Associations in Brussels were to be included within the scope of the proposed definition. The following view was heard: the draft articles should be concerned only with intergovernmental organizations possessing the capacity to assume rights and obligations under international law and thus to enter into treaties.[38]

In the view of another participant, "the draft articles should reflect in a sufficient degree the differences between the international legal capacity of States, which stems from their sovereignty, and the legal capacity of international organizations which is always secondary to and derivative from the concerted will of the States parties to the constitutive instrument of a particular international organization."[39]

Another participant voiced a slightly different view, stressing that international organizations were composed of sovereign States and that it followed from their composition that when they concluded treaties with other States, endowed by their member States with powers to do so, "they should receive the same treatment as States as far as this is feasible." This principle – equality of all contracting parties – ought to form the basis of the draft articles. In consequence, "in continuing its work, the Commission should adhere to its approach of not revising but adopting the rules of the Vienna Convention by merely adapting its provisions to the requirements of the subject-matter under consideration."[40]

---

37   A/CN.4/339 and Add.1–8.
38   The view expressed by Canada.
39   The view expressed by Bulgaria.
40   The view expressed by Germany.

In another opinion, some doubts were expressed about the necessity of drafting a separate legal instrument dealing with treaties to which international organizations are parties. "An analogous application of the 1969 Vienna Convention would presumably be a satisfactory way of solving many of the legal problems that may arise in connection with such treaties."[41]

As far as 'rules of the organizations' were concerned, the views expressed by the governments of States were similar – and supported the opinion that instruments of very different legal force should be included. It was argued that instruments, including "constituent instruments, relevant regulations, resolutions, decisions, and established practices, both of the organization itself and of its organs, should be included."[42]

In its written observations on the draft presented by the ILC, the Secretariat of the Council of Europe simply stated that the practice of the Council of Europe with regard to agreements between States and international organizations or between international organizations was limited, and that nothing in the statute expressly established the capacity of the Council of Europe to conclude treaties.

The European Economic Community was more specific:

> The Community considers that the spirit, if not the letter, of most of the rules established in the Vienna Convention on the Law of Treaties applies fully to both types of treaties. In the Community's view, it is important that international organizations, which increasingly participate in treaty relations, should be placed on the same footing as States as regards the conclusion and implementation of treaties, in so far as the subject matter can justify this.

And the International Agency for Atomic Energy was resolute: both States and international organizations are subjects of international law, upon which the law bears equally in almost all respects, and it would not be helpful to introduce distinctions of terminology or practice other than the ones which necessarily flow from general deficiencies of capacity in international organizations, as compared with the sovereign capacities of States.

VI

The adopted international conventions did not give rise to any relevant arguments that could help to answer the question about the international legal

---

41 The view expressed by Sweden.
42 The view expressed by Mexico and China.

personality of international organizations or their treaty-making capacity. Of course, the problem of defining the notion of an 'international organization' remained open as well.

According to the Vienna Convention on the Law of Treaties, the Vienna Convention on the Law of Treaties between States and International Organizations or between International Organizations and the Vienna Convention on the Representation of States in their Relations with International Organizations of a Universal Character, an 'international organization' means an intergovernmental organization.

The last Convention, for the purposes of that Convention, defines an 'international organization of a universal character' so as to mean the "United Nations, its specialized agencies, the International Atomic Energy Agency and any similar organization whose membership and responsibilities are on a worldwide scale." Again, a wide margin of uncertainty remains: what does 'and any similar organization' mean?

The Vienna Convention on the Law of Treaties between States and International Organizations or between International Organizations resolves the problem of the treaty-making capacity of international organizations in its Article 6 ('Capacity of international organizations to conclude treaties') in the following manner: the capacity of an international organization to conclude treaties is governed by the rules of that organization. And, 'the rules of the organization' means, in particular, the constituent instruments, decisions and resolutions adopted in accordance with them, and established practice of the organization. It thus includes both the acts of a very different legal force (if any) and 'established practice'.

The theoretical difficulties to be addressed largely arise from those faced by international law itself. Many authors departed from the old definitions of the state's national legal systems and did not succeed in incorporating a new branch – international law – in these definitions; many therefore thought it necessary to deny the legal nature of international law. The situation was quite similar with respect to the international legal personality of international organizations. Many of those departing from the subjects of international law known for centuries – the states – had difficulty recognizing the personality of the new entities which, of course, have different features. If all subjects of international law were required to possess a territory, a population and sovereign power subsuming international organizations under that definition would be impossible. On the other hand, theory also encountered difficulties of a political character due to this identification of a state with an international legal personality: a number of authors were of the view that the recognition of the international legal personality of international organizations would simultaneously mean the recognition of their statehood and, moreover, their supra-statehood, which is why they a priori denied all personality to international organizations. Hence the controversies about the treaty-making capacities of international organizations.

The result is visible in two opposing phenomena: on the one hand, the practice of concluding international agreements is developing unstoppably. The fact that these agreements are going beyond the provisions of the constituent treaties of international organizations cannot be qualified as a sporadic occurrence; far from it. Furthermore, some inter-state conventions uphold the current practice and authorize the United Nations to conclude agreements with states not envisaged by the UN Charter (safety of international personnel) and, albeit indirectly, expand the rights and obligations of the UN and the specialized institutions in proceedings before the International Court of Justice (conventions on privileges and immunities).

And, which is very important, the ICJ's jurisprudence unreservedly recognizes the treaty-making capacity of international organizations and solves disputes on it by issuing advisory opinions which the parties to the proceedings are obligated to enforce.

On the other hand, the two conventions of relevance to the issues discussed here (albeit still not in effect) have avoided resolving the issue of the definition of international organizations and their treaty-making capacity. This further puts off the resolution of the issue of both their international legal personality and their treaty-making capacity. Notwithstanding, as noted above, many states have avoided ratifying them, and even some important international organizations have failed to deposit their acts of formal confirmation.

Belgrade, March 2013

CHAPTER 7

Suspension of a Member State in an International Integration Organization: Mercosur

*Ernesto J. Rey Caro**

Suspension of a member State from an international integration organization is not common. Moreover, there are few precedents and each of them has its own peculiarities. This is the reason why such events capture the attention of scholars and deserve some particular consideration. We will focus attention on the suspension of Paraguay as a full Member of Mercosur.

On 21st July, 2012, the Permanent Review Court (PRC) of Mercosur delivered judgment in the emergency proceedings requested by the Republic of Paraguay in relation to the suspension of its participation in the organs of the Southern Common Market and the admissibility of Venezuela as a full Member.[1]

The situation which gave rise to Paraguay's request began with Fernando Lugo's removal from office by the Senate of the Republic of Paraguay with the previous participation of the House of Representatives, and with Federico Franco assuming power in his place. This took place on 22nd June of the same year.

Certainly, in the summit that took place in the city of Mendoza, at the end of June 2012, the Presidents of the Member States of Mercosur adopted a Decision on 29th June. It was decided:

> 1. To suspend the Republic of Paraguay from the right to participate in the Mercosur organs and from the deliberations, under the terms of article 5 of the Ushuaia Protocol.[2]

The grounds state that, in compliance with this Protocol, on Democratic Commitment, the full life of the democratic institutions is an essential condition for the development of the integration process and that any breach of the democratic order constitutes "an unacceptable obstacle for the continuity of the integration process". In like manner, it points out that in compliance with

---

* Professor of Public International Law; Professor Emeritus of the National University of Córdoba, Argentina.
1   *Cf.* Mercosur, Permanent Review Court, Arbitration Award No. 1/2012.
2   *Cf.* 'Decision on the Suspension of Paraguay from the Mercosur in compliance with the Ushuaia Protocol on Democratic Commitment'.

the foundation treaties of Mercosur, the suspension resulted in Paraguay being limited in its participation in the organs, "as well as the loss of the rights of vote and veto". The 'Declaration of the Member States of Mercosur and Associated States on the breach of the democratic order in Paraguay' was also mentioned. The declaration was issued on 24th June of the same year.[3]

The above-mentioned decision also states that:

> 2. As long as the suspension lasts, whatever stated in subsection (iii), article 40 of the Protocol of Ouro Preto will take effect with the incorporation (of the norms approved by the organs of Mercosur) provided by Argentina, Brazil and Uruguay, in compliance with subsection (ii), of said article.

The suspension will cease (paragraph 3) when, in compliance with the provisions of Article 7 of the Ushuaia Protocol, full re-establishment of the democratic order in the party affected has been verified. The Foreign Ministers will maintain regular contact in this respect. It is also agreed to communicate the present decision to the Mercosur Parliament.

It is important to note that the Declaration of 24th June, signed by the Republic of Argentina, the Federative Republic of Brazil, the Republic of Uruguay, the Bolivarian Republic of Venezuela, the Plurinational State of Bolivia, the Republic of Chile, the Republic of Colombia, the Republic of Ecuador and the Republic of Peru, pointed out that according to the Ushuaia Protocol of 1998 the life of the democratic institutions was an essential condition for the development of the integration process, and the decision expressed, in the first place, "the most energetic condemn[nation of] the breach of the democratic order in the Republic of Paraguay because it did not apply due process" and that it would "immediately suspend Paraguay and thereupon, ... suspend it from the right to participate in the XLIII Meeting of the Common Market Council and in the Summit of Mercosur Presidents, as well as from the preparatory meetings that will be held in the city of Mendoza, between 25th and 29th June, 2012." Paragraph 3 states that other measures would later be adopted at the Summit of Mercosur Heads of State.

Together with the abovementioned Decision, of 29th June, the Presidents of Argentina, Brazil and Uruguay signed a 'Declaration' that ruled, in its first paragraph, on "the admissibility of the Bolivarian Republic of Venezuela in Mercosur" and it summoned a special meeting on 31st July, 2012, for the "official

---

3   *Cf.* 'Declaration of the States Parties of Mercosur and the Associate States on the breach of the democratic order in Paraguay'.

admissibility of this country in Mercosur." In the third paragraph, it called for all the South American countries

> to stay together in the present complex international scenery so that they deepen the growth and inclusion process that has taken place in our region in the last decade and to act as an economic and social stability factor in an environment where democracy in the continent is in full force.

Therefore, it is observed that the events that took place in Paraguay gave rise to two decisions in Mercosur: on the one hand, the suspension of Paraguay under the said terms and on the other, the admissibility of Venezuela as a Full Member. On 24th June, a first suspension had been applied, by virtue of which, Paraguay's participation in the Mendoza Summit was denied.

From the facts we can see that the main instrument used to support the decision to suspend Paraguay was the Ushuaia Protocol on Democratic Commitment in Mercosur, July 1998, signed by the four Member States, the Republic of Bolivia and the Republic of Chile.

This instrument states (Article 2), that "it will apply to relations deriving from the respective integration Agreements in force among States Parties to the present Protocol, in case of the breach of democratic order in any of them", and if such an event takes place (Article 3) it will "produce the application of the procedures envisaged in the following articles". These procedures and the way the corresponding measures will be adopted are regulated in Articles 4, 5 and 6.

In the first place (Article 4), in the case of a 'breach' of the democratic order in a State Party, "the other States Parties shall promote the relevant consultations among themselves and with the State concerned". If such consultations (Article 5) are not successful, the other States Parties to the Protocol, under the integration Agreements in force among them, "will consider the nature and the scope of the measures to be applied, considering the seriousness of the existing situation". Such measures in compliance with this same instrument "may range from suspension of the right to participate in the organs of the respective integration processes to the suspension of the rights and obligations deriving from such processes". The measures referred to in Article 5 are taken by common consensus and are notified to the State 'concerned', which will not participate in the corresponding decision-making process. These measures will enter into force on the date of notification. The measures will cease to be applicable (Article7) on the date the State concerned is notified that the States which took such measures, have agreed "that it has been verified that the democratic order has been fully restored", and this will take place as soon as restoration takes place.

From the analysis of the situation and the instrument invoked for the suspension, there are some issues which have to be especially considered.

In the first place, in the decisions taken on 24th June and 29th June, there is no express reference to the concrete events underlying these decisions. Only the "breach of democratic order" and "the fact that due process has not been respected" are mentioned broadly. We could infer that the interruption of the democratic order was the result of not having respected due process in Lugo's overthrow, but there is no reference to this. Such measures, which imply the suspension of a State Party under the Ushuaia Protocol, in our opinion, should have been adequately supported and the facts expressly mentioned, notwithstanding the assessment that each State Party that took part in the decision could make.

However, what is most worrying is that the procedure set out in the Protocol has not been respected. The Protocol calls for consultation with 'the concerned State'. Paradoxically, the resolution that suspends Paraguay "because due process was not respected" violates the 'due process' that the conventional instrument applied prescribes.

Another consequence derived from the suspension applied to Paraguay is the admissibility of Venezuela. Indeed, the terms under the Protocol of Asuncion are clear on this point, since in the case of adherence to the treaty (Article 20, last part) they state that approbation of a request will be subject to "the unanimous decision of the States Parties". The legal force of this instrument is expressly reiterated in the Framework Agreement for the Adhesion of the Bolivarian Republic of Venezuela to Mercosur, 8th December, 2005.

The fact that Paraguay had still not given the necessary consent required under the Treaty of Asuncion is well known. The suspension has not deprived it of its position of State Party and Member of Mercosur. Therefore, the Resolution of June 29th, adopted by the other three States of the Mercosur, to include Venezuela is a clear violation of the Treaty of 1991.

It is noteworthy to mention that the Protocol of Montevideo, also known as Ushuaia II, signed in December 2011, and which has not entered into force yet, apart from having a wider range of application seems to be a more complete instrument. This Protocol will apply (Article 1) in the event of "breach or threat of breach against the institutional order, of violation of constitutional order or any other situation that risks the legitimate exercise of power and the legal force of democratic values and principles." It lists the authorities or organs competent to intervene, and their place of meeting (Article 2); the procedure to follow (Articles 3, 4, and 5); and something important to point out: there is also a catalogue of measures that can be adopted. These measures are: to suspend the right to participate in the different organs of the institutional structure of Mercosur; to close land borders totally or partially; to suspend or limit trade, air and maritime traffic, communications and energy supply, services and supplies; to suspend the Party concerned from enjoying the rights and benefits emerging from the Treaty of Asuncion and its Protocols and from the integration treaties adhered to among the Parties; to promote the suspension of the Party concerned in the scope of other regional and international organizations; to promote before third countries or groups of countries the suspension of the Party concerned from the rights and/or benefits deriving from cooperation agreements to which it may be a party; to support regional and international efforts, especially in the United Nations framework, aimed at solving and finding a pacific and democratic solution to a situation occurring in the Party concerned; and to adopt additional political and diplomatic sanctions. It states that such measures

> shall be proportionally adequate for the seriousness of the existing situation, they shall not risk the peoples' welfare and their effective enjoyment of human rights and fundamental freedoms in the Party concerned; to respect the sovereignty and territorial integrity of the Party concerned, the situation of the countries with no maritime boundaries and the treaties in force.

Other norms set out how the decisions adopted are to be applied, their legal force, the end of their application, *etc*. It is not the aim of this work to analyse this instrument which, by itself, deserves a detailed study of its virtues and also of the numerous doubts that arise from a deep reading of it. It has only been mentioned to emphasize the silence and absence of prevention in the Protocol of Ushuaia.

Another issue which gives rise to a lot of questioning deriving from the regulations of the Heads of States' Decision, of 29th June, is the norm in paragraph 2 that refers to subsections ii and iii, Article 40 of the Ouro Preto Protocol, to be applied during the period of suspension, applied to Paraguay. Indeed, in compliance with such terms, it will be possible to incorporate norms without Paraguay's participation. If they are norms that have been approved with the participation of that country – which has not ceased to be a State Party in the Treaty of Asuncion, the Ouro Preto Protocol and in all the other Agreements – but which have not yet been incorporated, that determination clearly violates Article 40, since it rules that "when *all* the States have informed of the incorporation to their respective internal legal systems, the Secretariat of Mercosur will notify this to each State Party". Was this the aim of the States that applied the sanction? Moreover, there is another question in relation to whether that norm, which was incorporated only with the participation of the three States that applied the sanction, could produce effects in relation to Paraguay. In like manner, if that determination included in the Decision referred to norms that could be approved during the suspension, that is to say, approved without the participation of Paraguay, because its participation in the organs of Mercosur was suspended, we would find ourselves looking at a 'right' applicable to only one part of the State Members of Mercosur. We also wonder if it would be legally binding for Paraguay once the suspension had come to an end. We understand that the modification of the conventional instruments cannot be done without Paraguay's consent, as long as it remains a State Party, since this would constitute a clear violation of the principles governing the Law of Treaties and the Vienna Convention of 1969 on that matter, in force for the four States. In like manner, we repeat, the Decision of 29th June does not have the required basis that the adoption of such serious measures as applied to Paraguay would demand. We believe that there has been great improvisation, which does not contribute to strengthening this integration process, without judging the events that took place in Paraguay and their relation with the sanction imposed. As stated before, this issue by itself would deserve detailed study. We also wonder if the equal treatment that the Ushuaia Protocol gives to the Member States of Mercosur and the Associate States is adequate, since it allows the latter to apply certain sanctions to the former. We also have doubts about the effects that could derive from the suspension in relation to the representation of Paraguay and its rights in the Mercosur Parliament. In our opinion, this would not affect it.

Going back to the remarks about the PRC's Arbitration Award of 21st July, it is necessary to point out that Paraguay's appearance in Court was aimed at applying for an exceptional emergency measure in compliance with Article 24 of the Olivos Protocol,[4] so that, according to the application: (1) the decision to suspend Paraguay from participating in the organs of Mercosur should be declared inapplicable and, (2) that the declaration that incorporated the Bolivarian Republic of Venezuela as a full Member of Mercosur should be declared inapplicable. The Court's competence was based on

---

4 *Cf.* this mechanism of States: "The Common Market Council may establish special procedures to have jurisdiction over exceptional urgent cases that could cause irreparable damage to the Parties."

Article 2, subsection b of the 23/04 Decision[5] and collaterally, on Article 1 and Article 23 of the Olivos Protocol, referring to the direct recourse in a unique instance to the PRC.[6]

In the action Paraguay argues that on 22nd June, 2012 the Paraguayan Senate removed president Fernando Lugo Méndez from office after impeachment under Article 225 of the Paraguayan constitution, adding that on the night of that same day, the removed president accepted Congress' decision. The file also lists the events that took place within Mercosur as a consequence of that event and complains about the seriousness of the measures taken in the Presidents' Summit. The measures caused irreparable damage because they denied Paraguay the exercise of its vested and sovereign rights as a Mercosur founding State.

It also argues that the suspension is not supported by a norm emanating from the organs mentioned in the Ouro Preto Protocol, nor by the application of the legal sources set out in Article 41 of that Protocol, and it questions the legality of the Heads of State taking binding decisions since the Presidents' Summits neither constitute nor form part of the organs of Mercosur and that the decisions do not comply with their regulations.

Paraguay considers that it had not caused a breach of the democratic order and that the prior consultations prescribed in Article 4 of the Ushuaia Protocol did not take place.

As regards the incorporation of Venezuela as a full member, Paraguay essentially claims that its participation as a Full Member of Mercosur had not been considered, and there was a lack of unanimous consensus necessary for taking decisions under Article 20 of the Treaty of Asuncion, and the non-compliance with what Article 40 of the Ouro Preto Protocol states about the simultaneous legal force of the norms emanating from the organs of Mercosur. To support its position, Paraguay invokes norms and principles of international law which were violated by the Presidents' decision, as well as the 1969 Vienna Convention on the Law of Treaties. Paraguay believes that the decisions, which are the

---

5 Article 2, subsection (b):"That the situation originates from actions or measures adopted by a State Party, violating or not complying with the Mercosur regulations in force."

6 Article 23: "1. After the proceeding established in Articles 4 and 5 of this Protocol has ended, the parties in conflict may expressly agree to abide by directly and in unique instance to the Permanent Review Court. In this case, this Court shall have the same competences as an *Ad Hoc* Arbitration Court and the Articles applicable in this matter will be Articles 9, 12, 13, 14, 15 and 16 of the present Protocol. 2. After the respective notification, the awards of the Permanent Review Court will be binding for the State parties of the conflict; they will not be subject to appeal for revision and they will have effect of *res judicata*."

object of the action lack reasoning and they imply international legal liability because there is non-compliance with the regulatory system of Mercosur and with other norms and principles of international law.

Paraguay argued that it had resorted directly to the Court because of the reasons already mentioned, since all the other instances it could resort to under the system for the settlement of disputes in Mercosur would be ruled out as a result of its suspension and it was impossible for its representatives to participate in the organs that should intervene to comply with the proceeding.

The three defendant countries answered together. In the first place, they filed the preliminary argument of the incompetence *ratione materiae* of the Court, on the basis that the decision questioned in the framework of the Ushuaia Protocol and in the system for the settlement of disputes "was not of a commercial nature". In the same way the defendant States argued that democracy was the *sine qua non* for the development of the integration process and that the Ushuaia Protocol was outside the scope of the system for the settlement of disputes of Mercosur. Therefore the decision to suspend Paraguay under Article 5 of the Ushuaia Protocol could not be examined by the Permanent Review Court.

The second question set out was based on the inappropriateness of the mechanism chosen since the urgent cases prescribed in Article 24 of the Olivos Protocol did not apply to the object of Paraguay's petition, because this provision referred to specific cases of a commercial nature.

The third preliminary question stated that Paraguay had not started the prior direct negotiations and that it did not have the consent of the defendant States for the exercise of the original competence under Article 23 of the Olivos Protocol.

As regards the merits of the case, the defendant countries argued that the procedure for applying Article 5 of the Ushuaia Protocol did not prescribe any 'solemn rite' or any 'formalities', and that the measures taken had been of a 'strict political nature'. In like manner, they argued the legality of the suspension of Paraguay because they stated that "they had made previous consultations to various Paraguayan political actors and that they had asked them to respect the right to defence and the procedural safeguards: due process". They claimed that the Heads of State had competence to adopt such decision since the Ushuaia Protocol does not prescribe anything about this issue, and they claimed that the breach of the democratic order was due to the removal of that country's president by means of a summary procedure which did not respect due process.

While the Court was in session, Paraguay submitted a writ 'Applying for Provisional Measures', under Article 15 of the Olivos Protocol[7] and Articles 29[8] and 39[9] of the Olivos Protocol's Regulations.

In its arbitral award, the Court examined the allegations produced by the parties involved. As regards the Court's competence *ratione materiae*, the Court pointed out that in spite of the fact that in the Protocol of Ushuaia there is no express mention of a forum for the settlement of disputes or for its application and interpretation, the Preamble to that conventional instrument expresses that it is connected with the "legal framework of Mercosur".[10] Moreover, it points out that Article 8 expressly states that the Protocol is part of the Treaty of Asuncion and of the respective integration Agreements adhered to by Mercosur and the Republics of Bolivia and Chile.

---

7   Article 15, about provisional measures, prescribes: "1. The *Ad Hoc* Arbitration Court, after request by the party concerned, may order the provisional measures it considers appropriate in order to avoid damage, as long as there exists reasonable presumption that the situation may cause serious and irreparable damage to one of the parties in the conflict. 2. The Court may, at any moment, deprive such measures of any legal effect.3. In case the award was subject to revision, the provisional measures that were still in force before the award will continue to be in force until the Permanent Review Court addresses them in the first meeting. The Court shall decide about their continuance or termination."

8   Article 29 ('Provisional Measures') reads: "1.The request to the AHC, to order provisional measures can be submitted at any moment after the third arbitrator has accepted the appointment. In its request, the party concerned, shall specify the serious and irreparable damage intended to avoid with the application of the provisional measures, the elements that will allow the Court to assess such possible damage and the provisional measures it considers appropriate. 2. The party that requests the provisional measures shall notify the other party of its request simultaneously. The latter may submit to the AHC any considerations it finds relevant, no more than five (5) days after the day of notification. 3. The provisional measures ordered by the AHC shall be complied with within the time prescribed by the AHC. The liable party shall inform about the compliance with such measures. 4. After pronouncing on the continuance or termination of the provisional measures ordered by the AHC, the PRC shall immediately notify its decision to the parties."

9   Article 39 ('Direct Access to the Permanent Review Court (Art. 23 Olivos Protocol)'): "1. The State Parties, which in conflict, agree to abide by the PRC directly and in unique instance, shall notify such Court in written form, through the MS. 2. The said Court will take action with the totality of its members when acting in unique instance. 3. In this case, the PRC's functioning will be regulated, in the pertinent issues, by Articles 18, 25, 26, 27, 28, 29, 30, 34, 40 and 41 of this Regulation. The functions vested to the MS in such norms, will be complied with by the MS. The notifications among parties and the PRC shall go with true copy to the MS."

10 See para. 40.

The Court held that, as a consequence, the system for the settlement of disputes established by Mercosur includes the norms of the Protocol of Ushuaia "as long as they affect or may affect the rights and obligations of any of the Sates Parties".[11] Therefore, it continued, the right of the State Party to resort to this system, when it considers that its rights, in compliance with the Protocol of Ushuaia, have been violated, is not a matter of discussion. To finish this analysis, the Court concluded "that observance of the legality of the proceedings prescribed in the Protocol of Ushaia is susceptible of revision under the framework of the system for the settlement of disputes of Mercosur". The same applies to the questions related to the application and interpretation of the Protocol, as long as the concrete facts deserve an analysis of its legality because of its nature.

After the Court had accepted that it had the competence to adjudicate on the issue concerning Paraguay, it turned its attention to the consideration of the extraordinary urgent measures invoked by that country. After the Parties had presented their opposing views as regards the requirements that must be present for the appropriateness of such measures, the Court mentioned that in the Olivos Protocol the Parties had agreed (Article 24) that the Council of the Common Market (CCM) could set special proceedings for exceptional urgent cases that could cause irreparable damage to the Parties, and that this possibility was provided for by Decision 23/04, of that organ, which stated that the system of proceedings was applicable to such cases.[12] The Court pointed out that when the Decision of the CCM set out the admissibility requirements, it did not make it clear whether these requirements were independent or cumulative, so for a correct interpretation it was necessary to read the rest of the text of the Decision. Thereafter – it stated – there were two things that helped the interpretation: (a) Art. 6 of Decision 23/04 mentions "all the established requirements2; (b) Article 52 indicates that non-observance of some of the

---

11 See para. 43.
12 The Decision states in Art. 2: "Any State Party may resort to the Permanent Review Court (PRC) under the proceeding established in the present Decision, as long as the following requirements are present: a. that they are perishable goods, seasonal goods or that by their nature and particular characteristics they are goods that could lose properties, utility and/or commercial value, in a short period of time, if they were unfairly delayed in the territory of the defendant country; or if they were goods destined to satisfy needs originating from a crisis in the importing State; b. that the situation was originated due to actions or measures adopted by the State Party under violation or non-compliance with the Mercosur ruling in force; c. that the continuance of those measures or actions could cause irreparable damage; d. that actions or measures under question were not the object of a conflict occurring among the Parties involved."

requirements does not imply that the defendant brings a new action". The Court held that it could not substitute the States' will shown in the necessary requirements of Decision 23/04 which limit the jurisdiction of the PRC in relation to exceptionally urgent proceedings. According to the views of the defendant countries, it reaffirmed that it did not have jurisdiction over the matter by means of the system of urgent proceedings.[13]

After working on this aspect of the conflict, the Court continued to examine the contrary positions of the parties about direct access to the Court. Paraguay had resorted to the Court to exercise jurisdiction through this mechanism in compliance with Articles 1 and 23 of the Olivos Protocol, and that due to the facts that formed the basis of the presentation, the requirements of this last mechanism were considered as met. The defendant countries denied that the requirements had been met, and, particularly, that Paraguay had demonstrated that it had the intention to have direct negotiations with the defendant countries.

The Court mentioned that the Olivos Protocol allows direct access without compliance with the prior stage of the *Ad Hoc* Arbitration Court, when the parties in conflict had agreed to abide by the PRC directly in a unique instance. According to the Court, there had been no such consent. As emphasized by the Court:

> The parties' consent is a fundamental condition to exercise the jurisdictional legality of the PRC. This is different from an ordinary process, where this consent has already been given at the moment of signing the incorporation to the Olivos Protocol. We can understand Paraguay's argument that access to direct jurisdiction is the necessary mechanism to suspend an arbitrary measure, about which it was not even asked to make a statement. However, without express consent, the PRC cannot precede the Olivos Protocol, in spite of the damages that the delay in the ordinary decision making process could cause to Paraguay or to the judicial-institutional stability of the region.[14]

Later, the Court addressed the question of direct negotiations as a necessary stage in the process for the settlement of disputes in Mercosur, in compliance with Article 4 of the Olivos Protocol. Paraguay had contended that it was a requirement incapable of enforcement since it had been suspended from Mercosur, without right of defence. The Court reiterated the necessity to

---

13   See para. 52.
14   See para. 58.

respect this procedural stage, and it held —and this is very important — that if Paraguay had applied for direct negotiations and these negotiations had been denied "we would have a different situation."[15]

It is important to stress that in this issue there was a minority opinion in the Court. Far from providing a different interpretation about the extraordinary urgent measures, this position pointed out that if the defendant States Parties, through their Heads of State, had adopted a decision that suspended Paraguay from participating in the organs of the Mercosur, and if the State concerned could not take the case to another court before resorting to the PRC, it was admissible to consider that it would be allowed to bring the case to the Court in a direct way and not necessarily respecting the mechanisms of Decision 23/04, in extraordinary urgent situations, and that if the suspension did not exclude Paraguay as a Member State, it was inadmissible to accept its *de facto* rejection as a Member State of Mercosur, or prevent the access of Paraguay to the judicial system.[16]

Thereupon, the decision states (item 3) that by a majority

> the PRC decides that, according to the conditions of the present file, the direct intervention of the PRC without the express consent of the other State Parties is considered inadmissible. For this same reason, the PRC considers that, in this instance, the provisional measure applied in the framework of the file is inadmissible.

In the next item, unanimously and without considering the merits of the file, the PRC does not pronounce "on the compliance or violation of the Mercosur's regulations in relation to the file in this proceeding" and affirms that the Court's decision did not restrain other mechanisms to which the State Members could resort in the framework of the system for the settlement of disputes.

Without intending to analyse exhaustively the arbitral award of the Permanent Review Court and in spite of the discrepancy about direct access to the Permanent Review Court, which is questionable, we believe that it sets a precedent and that it contributes to strengthening the legal framework which must support the integration process that began in 1991. It would have been worrying to admit the position of the defendant countries which pleaded that the application of the Ushuaia Protocol and the interpretation of its norms were excluded from the jurisdictional control of the PRC, and, moreover, denial of jurisdiction on the basis that it was 'of a political nature'. It is also interesting

---

15 See para. 60.
16 See paragraphs 62, 63 and 64.

for the Court to have admitted that there were other mechanisms to which the States Parties could have resorted to in the framework of the system for the settlement of disputes of the Mercosur, and that it had mentioned that the judgement could have been different if some of the stages prior to the petition to the Court had been observed or complied with.

The Permanent Review Court did not decide on the action brought concerning the admission of Venezuela as Full Member of Mercosur.

Also, an analysis of the conflict begun by Paraguay's suspension and by the circumstances that led to this decision has evidenced the faults of the Ushuaia Protocol, which is open to arbitrariness, apart from the decisions that could be taken without compliance with the proceedings set out in the Protocol itself.

Briefly, we believe that the situation caused by the suspension of Paraguay, by the circumstances that led to the decision taken by the other three State Members of Mercosur and by the decision to make Venezuela's admissibility effective without its having complied with the proceedings prescribed in the conventional regulations applicable to the case, are facts that did not contribute at all to the consolidation of this integration process which, by itself, is facing difficulties that raise doubts about the possibility of reaching the foundational objectives.

CHAPTER 8

Due Diligence: Fault-Based Responsibility or Autonomous Standard?

Maja Seršić*

I   Introductory Remarks

The problem of fault in connection with international responsibility has fascinated scholars for centuries. The reasons are twofold. Firstly, responsibility is a fundamental principle the roots of which spread deeply beneath the entire field of international law. In addition, the difficulty in employing private law concepts such as fault to the responsibility of States necessarily produces a lot of controversies.

This question has been studied so much and by such distinguished scholars that it may seem redundant to undertake a further study of the problem. However, in our opinion, new research should be done periodically to see how the new developments in different areas of international law and practice influence this classic question.

Special emphasis in this study is placed on the notion of due diligence, which, as will be shown in the analysis of the doctrinal views regarding the basis of the international responsibility of States, is invoked by both the supporters of fault as a prerequisite for State responsibility and partisans of the objective approach. The notion invoked by the supporters of different doctrinal views relating to responsibility for internationally wrongful acts deserves even more attention if we recall that due diligence was one of the main concepts in the work of the International Law Commission (ILC) on the topic of international liability for injurious consequences arising out of acts not prohibited by international law (prevention of transboundary harm from hazardous activities) *viz.*, liability without wrongfulness.

This paper tries to comprise all the above-mentioned aspects of the notion of due diligence.

---

*   Professor of Public International Law at the University of Zagreb, Faculty of Law.

11 Position of the Element of Fault in the Internationally Wrongful Act: Historical Overview

Fault (in the broad sense of *dolus* and *culpa*) is an essential element of the traditional concept of the wrongful act: the person responsible for the illicit act must have acted intentionally or negligently, in violation of an obligation. The Roman law notion of *culpa* was introduced into international law by Grotius and remained the dominant basis of responsibility of States until the beginning of the twentieth century. It posed no difficulty since the king personalized territorial collectivity. The actions of a modern State, though, are often the result of acts of many people, and it is difficult and sometimes even impossible to say which organ or agent of the State committed the illicit act. Therefore, at the beginning of the twentieth century the tendency towards 'objective' responsibility arose, *i.e.*, responsibility which results merely from the failure of a State to comply with the international obligation. In spite of such tendencies, fault-based responsibility was still largely supported in the doctrine.[1]

Doctrinal consensus on fault as the necessary element of the internationally wrongful act was broken by Dionisio Anzilotti[2] who, in his famous book *Teoria*

---

1 For more on the historical development of the concept of fault as the element of the international wrongful act of State until the twentieth century see R. Ago, "La colpa nell'illecito internazionale", in: *Scritti giuridici in onore di Santi Romano*, Vol. 3, Padova, 1939 (offprint), pp. 1–6; *id.*, "Le délit international", *Recueil des cours de l'Académie de droit international de La Haye* (hereinafter: RC), 1939-II, Vol. 68, pp. 477 *et seq.*; G. Arrangio-Ruiz, "State Fault and the Forms and Degrees of International Responsibility: Questions of Attribution and Relevance", in: *Le droit international au service de la paix, de la justice et du développement, Mélanges Michel Virally*, Paris, 1991, pp. 25–27 *et seq.*; B. Cheng, *General Principles of Law as Applied by International Courts and Tribunals*, London, 1953, pp. 218–219; C. Eagleton, *The Responsibility of States in International Law*, New York, 1928, pp. 3–25, 208–211; J. Garde Castillo, "El acto ilícito internacional", *Revista española de derecho internacional*, 1950, Vol. 3, No. 1, pp. 131–132; C. Rousseau, *Cours de droit international public*, Paris, 1959–1960, pp. 21–23. See also "'Force majeure' and 'fortuitous event' as circumstances precluding wrongfulness: survey of State practice, international judicial decisions and doctrine", Study prepared by the Secretariat, Doc. A/CN.4/315, *Yearbook of the International Law Commission* (hereinafter: YBILC), 1978, Vol. II, Part 1, pp. 189–190.

2 In fact, the first author who abandoned the traditional fault theory was Triepel. He considered that two kinds of international responsibility had to be distinguished: the obligation of States to grant satisfaction, which arises from the mere breach of the international obligation, and, the obligation to make reparation, which arises only if there is fault on the part of the State, see H. Triepel, *Völkerrecht und Landesrecht*, Leipzig, 1899, pp. 334 *et seq.* His rather complicated theory was severely criticized because of its inconsistency; for more see Ago, "La colpa...", *op. cit.*, p. 5.

generale della responsabilità dello Stato nel diritto internazionale, published in 1902,[3] held that the State was responsible for the violation of its international duty. Fault, *i.e. dolus* or *culpa*, as a psychological category relates only to individuals and it is not applicable to international responsibility, explained Anzilotti.[4] Thus, the responsibility arises from the sole breach of an international obligation, and the *animus* of the individual organ of the State is not the cause or condition of responsibility, he wrote.[5]

In spite of the influence of Anzilotti's theory, most authors,[6] as well as international jurisprudence[7] continued to follow the traditional concept of fault as the necessary condition for the international responsibility of States. The Institute of International Law, at its session at Lausanne in 1927, adopted the resolution according to which the responsibility of a State arose in principle as a consequence of the fault of its agents, unless the specific treaty provision or customary rule provided for responsibility without fault.[8]

Despite the prevailing fault-based approach, many authors between the two world wars began to support Anzilotti's views and affirmed the objective notion of State responsibility, holding that no inquiry into whether the wrongful act was committed in a manner which involved fault was required.[9]

---

3   The book was reprinted in *Corso di diritto internazionale*, Vol. 1, Padova, 1955, and in *Scritti di diritto internazionale publico*, Vol. 1, Padova, 1956.
4   See Anzilotti, *Corso..., op. cit.*, p. 407.
5   *Ibid.*, p. 410.
6   See *e.g.* H. Lauterpacht, "Les règles générales du droit de la paix", RC, 1937-IV, Vol. 62, pp. 359–363; L. Oppenheim, *International Law, A Treatise*, Vol. 1, Peace, 2nd edn., London, 1912, p. 212; F. von Liszt, *Das Völkerrecht*, Berlin, 1918, p. 177.
7   See *e.g.* arbitral awards in the *Home Frontier and Foreign Missionary Society Case* between USA and UK in 1920 (United Nations, *Reports of International Arbitral Awards* (hereinafter: UNRIAA), Vol. 6, p. 44), and *G.L. Solis* between USA and Mexico in 1928 (*ibid.*, Vol. 4, p. 361).
8   Resolution I, Art. 1, para. 4, see *Annuaire de l'Institut de Droit international*, 1927, Vol. 3, p. 330. In fact, in his first draft M.L. Strisower, who was the *rapporteur*, conditioned State responsibility by the presence of *dolus* or *culpa* on the part of its organs without any additional text (*ibid.*, Vol. 1, p. 471). After the interventions of Anzilotti and Bourquin (*ibid.*, pp. 499–502), Strisower's final proposal was revised: he repeats that a State is responsible for violation of an international obligation if it is the consequense of *dolus* or *culpa* of its organs or culpa on the part of its organs, but adds that it is an open question whether and in what cases a State may be responsible without fault on the part of its organs (*ibid.*, p. 536). After the discussion in the committee (*ibid.*, pp. 103–107), Art. 1, para. 4 of the Resolution I was drafted as stated *supra*.
9   See *e.g.* E.M. Borchard, "Theoretical Aspects of the International Responsibility of States", *Zeitschrift für ausländisches öffentliches Recht und Völkerrecht*, 1929, Vol. 1, Part 1, pp. 225–226. Cavaglieri endorsed the theory of Anzilotti, but only *de lege ferenda*, considering that

The objective theory was accepted in some arbitral awards, too.[10] It is not without significance that only three years after the Institute of International Law's Resolution in 1927, the League of Nations Codification Conference, convened at The Hague in 1930, and in particular its Committee on the Responsibility of States for Damage Caused in Their Territory to the Person or Property of Foreigners,[11] endorsed the objective approach. Although no final report was provided by the Committee, the proposal relating to State responsibility in the event of the failure of a State to carry out its international obligation was supported by the necessary majority of votes.[12]

In addition to the prevalent theory based on fault and the 'objective theories' which were gaining ground between the two world wars, wide variations of their interpretations as well as many conciliatory solutions existed.[13]

---

the – then – positive international rules were fault-oriented, see A. Cavaglieri, *Corso di diritto internazionale*, 2nd edn., Naples, 1932, pp. 425–427. Similarly Eagleton, *op. cit.*, pp. 213–214 *et seq.*

10 See *e.g.* the 1926 decision in the *Harry Roberts* case between USA and Mexico (*UNRIAA*, Vol. 4, p. 80).

11 See *Official Document, Conference for the Codification of International Law, The Hague, March 13, 1930, First Report Submitted to the Council by the Preparatory Committee for the Codification Conference*, in: *American Journal of International Law* (hereinafter: *AJIL*), 1930, Vol. 24, No. 3, p.75 (also available at <http://www.uniset.ca/naty/maternity/24AmJIntLSpSup1.pdf>).

12 It is well known that the (Third) Committee on Responsibility of States (the Rapporteur of the Committee was Charles de Visscher) unanimously agreed that it could provide no report to the Conference and that the Chairman simply announced at the plenary session that the Third Committee had been unable to complete its work. However, it should be stressed that a few proposals, including the one relating to the basis of State responsibility, got the necessary majority of votes at the Third Committee. See more E.M. Borchard, "'Responsibility of States' at the Hague Codification Conference", *AJIL*, 1930, Vol. 24, No. 3, pp. 522–525; J.G. Guerrero, *La Codification de Droit International*, La Première Conférence (La Haye, 13 mars-12 avril 1930), pp. 143–144. Although the divergence of views made it impossible to get approval by the requisite two-thirds majority at the Conference, due to, according to some authors, the "chaotic organisation of the Conference" (see C. Bories, "The Hague Conference of 1930", in: *The Law of International Responsibility*, ed. by J. Crawford, A. Pellet, S. Olleson, K. Perlett, Oxford, 2010, p. 63), its importance for the future codification of the topic of State responsibility must not be underestimated.

13 Mention should be made of Schoen, who supported the 'objective' theory in cases of responsibility for acts of State organs, and accepted the fault theory in cases of State responsibility for acts of individuals, see P. Schoen, "Die völkerrechtliche Haftung der Staaten aus unerlaubten Handlungen", *Zeitschrift für Völkerrecht*, 1917–1918, Vol. 10, App., pp. 50 *et seq.* Similarly de Visscher, see C. de Visscher, "La Responsabilité des Etats", in: *Bibliotheca Visseriana*, Leyden, 1924, Vol. 2, pp. 91–93 *et seq.* Strupp also held that two

Doctrinal disagreements and divisions concerning the basis of international responsibility continued after the Second World War and continue, although at lower intensity, to the present day.

State responsibility for internationally wrongful acts based on fault continued to be endorsed by some authors, for all[14] or some[15] wrongful acts.

It should be stressed, however, that the writers who consider fault to be the requirement for the establishment of international responsibility do not attach the same meaning to the term *fault*. While some authors stick to the traditional psychological content of the notion of fault, referring to the state of mind of the organ or agent of the State, thinking thus in classical terms of *dolus* or *culpa*,[16] others tend to equate fault with violation of an obligation, considering that the fault of the State is established if its organ or agent failed to observe an international obligation. Thus, the conduct of the organ or the agent of the State should be compared to the conduct required by the

---

bases of State responsibility existed: responsibility based on fault (Schuldhaftung) for offences of omission, and 'objective' criteria (Erfolgshaftung) for offences of comission attributable to State organs, see K. Strupp, "Das völkerrechtliche Delikt", in: *Handbuch des Völkerrechts*, 1920, Vol. 3, ed. by F. Stier-Somlo, pp. 45 *et seq.* See *id.*, "Les règles générales du droit de la paix", RC, 1934-I, Vol. 47, pp. 564 *et seq.*

14   *E.g.* Ago, "La colpa...", *op. cit.*, p. 32; J.L. Brierly, *The Law of Nations: An Introduction to the International Law of Peace*, 6th edn. (ed. by H. Waldock), Oxford, 1963, p. 289; A. Favre, "Fault as an Element of the Illicit Act", *The Georgetown Law Journal*, 1963–1964, Vol. 52, pp. 560–561, 570; Garde Castillo, *op. cit.*, p.130; R. Luzzato, "Responsabilità e colpa in diritto internazionale", *Rivista di diritto internazionale*, 1968, pp. 65 *et seq.*; L. Oppenheim, *International Law: A Treatise*, Vol. 1., 8th edn. (ed. by H. Lauterpacht), London, 1955, p. 343; A. Verdross, *Völkerrecht*, 5th edn., Vienna, 1964, p. 379. See also F. Orrego Vicuña, Final Report, Commission on Responsibility and the Environment, *Annuaire de l'Institut de Droit international*, 1997, Vol. 67-I, pp. 318–319.

15   For Zemanek, who continued and expanded Strupp's theory, fault is a condition of State resonsibility for offences of omission, see K. Zemanek, "Schuld und Erfolgshaftung im Entwurf der Völkerrechtskommission über Staatenverantwortlichkeit", in: *Festschrift für R. Bindschedler*, Bern, 1980, pp. 323 *et seq.*; *id.*, "La responsabilité des Etats pour faits internationalement illicites, ainsi que pour faits intenationalement licites", in: *Responsabilité internationale*, ed. by. P. Weil, Paris, 1987, p. 36. Andrassy's views are similar, see J. Andrassy, *Medunarodno pravo*, 6th edn., Zagreb, 1987, p. 361. García-Amador is of the opinion that fault is required not for all offences of omission, but only for those relating to acts of private individuals, see F.V. García Amador, "State Responsibility – Some New Problems", RC, 1958-II, Vol. 94, pp. 382 *et seq.* See also C. Rousseau, *Droit international public*, Vol. 5, *Les rapports conflictuels*, Paris, 1983, pp. 19 *et seq.* See also arbitral award of 1955 in the case between Italy and France relating to the interpretation of Art. 79, para. 6 of the Peace Treaty, UNRIAA, Vol. 13, pp. 431–433.

16   *E.g.* Ago, "La colpa...", *op. cit.*, pp. 16–17; Verdross, *op. cit.*, pp. 376–379.

international obligation, and there is no need for an examination of their psychological status.[17] Some authors combined both elements, requiring examination of psychological elements (state of mind) and conduct of the organ or agent.[18]

In the last few decades most of the authors who dealt with the topic of State responsibility abandoned fault as a basis of State responsibility and those who favour the 'objective' approach have prevailed. The majority of the 'objectivists' took the rigid position, completely excluding fault from the internationally wrongful act. According to them the notion of fault is entirely inappropriate due to the practical impossibility of establishing fault of the State. The only thing that matters is the 'outer' conduct of the State organs and agents which is to be compared with the content of the international obligation in question.[19] Thus, State responsibility arises merely from a breach of an international obligation attributable to the State.

Some of the 'objectivists' allowed fault to be exceptionally a condition for State responsibility if the primary rule that was breached required fault to be the element of the wrongful act.[20]

---

17 *E.g.* Orrego Vicuña, *op. cit.*, p. 318; Visscher, *op. cit.*, p. 93. See also Rousseau, *Cours...*, *op. cit.*, p. 25, but compare with *id.*, *Droit...*, *op. cit.*, p. 21. See also Cheng, *op. cit.*, pp. 225–226; H. Accioly, "Principes généraux de la responsabilité internationale d'après la doctrine et la jurisprudence", RC, 1959-I, Vol. 96, pp. 369–370. See also G. Perrin, "L'aggression contre la légation de Roumanie à Berne et le fondement de la responsabilité internationale dans les délits d'omission", *Revue générale de droit international public* (hereinafter: RGDIP), 1957, Vol. 61, p. 424.

18 *E.g.* Favre, *op. cit.*, pp. 560–562. Similarly Luzzato, *op. cit.*, pp. 65–66 and G. Sperduti, "Sulla colpa in diritto internazionale", *Comunicazioni e studi*, 1950, Vol. 3, p. 93.

19 See *e.g.* J. Combacau, S. Sur, *Droit international public*, 2nd edn., Paris, 1996, pp. 554–555; V. Coussirat-Coustère, P.M. Eisemann, "L'enlèvement de personnes privées et le droit international", RGDIP, 1972, Vol. 76, No. 2, pp. 370–371; T. Meron, "International Responsibility of States for Unauthorized Acts of Their Officials", *The British Yearbook of International Law* (hereinafter: BYBIL), 1957, Vol. 33, p. 96. See also Schwarzenberger who holds that general international law does not contain a rule which would oblige the international judge to use a subjective criterion of fault or objective test while establishing international responsibility of States, see G. Schwarzenberger, *International Law*, Vol. 1, *International Law as Applied by International Courts and Tribunals*, 3rd edn., London, 1957, p. 649.

20 *E.g.* P.W. Birnie, A.E. Boyle, *International Law and the Environment*, Oxford, 1992, pp. 141–142; Brownlie, *op. cit.*, pp. 436, 441 *et seq.*; Jiménez de Aréchaga, *op. cit.*, p. 535. See also P.M. Dupuy, "Le fait générateur de la responsabilité internationale des Etats", RC, 1984-V, Vol. 188, pp. 21 *et seq.*; *id.*, *Droit international public*, 3rd edn., Paris, 1995, p. 361; D. Ruzié, *Droit international public*, 13th edn., Paris, 1997, p. 96.

The International Law Commission, which in 2001 adopted the Draft articles on responsibility of States for internationally wrongful acts,[21] did not specify fault among the constituent elements of the internationally wrongful act. It does not, however, exclude fault from State responsibility: *culpa* or *dolus* may be a condition for the State responsibility if the content of the primary rule involves some degree of fault. The example of a primary rule providing for fault as a condition for State responsibility is the 1971 Convention on International Liability for Damage Caused by Space Objects. Article 3 of the Convention sets out fault-based responsibility in respect of injuries caused by space objects of the launching State to other States' objects operating in outer space.[22]

It seems that the Commission's draft reflects the now prevailing view in the doctrine, which appears to be logical. The insistence on fault as the prerequisite to State responsibility even in cases when the primary rule does not provide for the existence of fault as a condition for State responsibility is redundant, and may lead to unnecessary complications, requiring in every case an analysis of the psychological attitude of the State's organs or agents in respect of the breach of the international rule. Besides being practically impossible in some cases (*e.g.* how can one establish *dolus* of a State parliament that passed an Act which is in contravention of an international rule?), it may have other unacceptable consequences. Suffice it to mention the *ultra vires* conduct of State organs, which would – if the condition of fault were required in all cases – not necessarily lead to State responsibility. In such cases officials act contrary to the instructions of their superior officials or the State's laws and, thus, contrary to the will of the State, which matters in the case of fault-based responsibility. Lack of fault of a State would mean the absence of the necessary element of wrongful act and no responsibility could arise.[23] The same would be true in the case of a breach of international obligation caused by conduct of State organs which does not have elements of fault. Mention could be made of the 1921 case of *The Jessie, the Thomas F. Bayard and the Pescawha* between Great Britain and the United States of America. The British sealing schooners were boarded on the high seas by the US naval authorities who sealed the firearms found on board the British ship. Although it was established that the US

---

21 See Draft articles on responsibility of States for internationally wrongful acts, *YBILC*, 2001, Vol. II, Part 2, p. 20.

22 See text in: *International Legal Materials*, Vol. 10, No. 6, p. 965. As to the damage on the surface of the Earth or to aircraft in flight Article 2 of the Convention provides for strict liability, being the only convention providing for that basis of State responsibility.

23 See B.D. Smith, *State Responsibility and the Marine Environment, The Rules of Decision*, Oxford, 1988, p. 19.

authorities acted *bona fide*, believing they had authority to act, the arbitral tribunal stated that "...any Government is responsible to other Governments for errors in judgment of its officials purporting to act within the scope of their duties and vested with power to enforce their demands."[24]

On the other hand, insistence on strict objectivity and the complete abandonment of fault would not respond to real needs. As mentioned, there are primary rules which require fault as a prerequisite for responsibility.

III   Due Diligence

Although the notion of due diligence in civil law – at least in the States belonging to the 'continental' legal system – will automatically be connected with fault, it is not the case in international law. The preceding analysis of the doctrinal views regarding the basis of the international responsibility of States showed that both partisans of fault as a prerequisite for State responsibility and partisans of the objective approach invoke the same notion, that of due diligence (*l'obligation de vigilance*), to justify their views.

The authors who strongly support fault-based State responsibility try to justify their views by invoking judicial decisions that base State responsibility on the non-observance of due diligence. Likewise, the supporters of the objective approach call upon the same decisions, arguing that they based State responsibility merely on violation of an obligation to act in accordance with due diligence.

The notion invoked by the supporters of different doctrinal views deserves closer analysis.

The notion of due diligence was introduced into international law by the arbitral award in the 1872 *Alabama* case between Great Britain and the USA. The dispute arose out of the different understandings of the parties of the scope of duties of neutral States in sea warfare. The key difference concerned the content of due diligence. According to the view of the USA a neutral State must use 'active diligence', proportional to risk and possible consequences of negligent conduct.[25] Great Britain's interpretation was more restrictive: due diligence means "such care as governments ordinarily employ in their domestic concerns and may reasonably be expected to exert in matters of international

---

24   See *UNRIAA*, Vol. 6, p. 59.
25   See *History and Digest of the International Arbitrations to which the United States has been a Party*, ed. by J.B. Moore, Vol.1, Washington, 1898, pp. 495 *et seq.*

interest and obligation."[26] The arbitral award accepted the definition of due diligence given by the USA.[27]

Ever since the award in the *Alabama* case, the principle of *due diligence* has been considered to be well-accepted in international legal theory and practice. This acceptance comes inextricably linked to two questions: about the degree of due diligence required by international law and about the character of due diligence as either a standard by which to 'measure' fault or as a self-standing and objective standard, independent of fault, which allows for a comparison of a State's conduct in a given situation with behaviour required by international law. Deviation from the required behaviour in such a case is itself a breach of a State's international obligations and as an autonomous delict triggers the international legal responsibility of States, notwithstanding the motives and cause of deviations.

The theory and practice of international law have long tried to find a universally applicable criterion to determine the degree of due diligence required by international law. In doing so, not many followed the award in the *Alabama* case which linked the degree of due diligence with potential damage caused.[28] On the contrary, the jurisprudence has for a long time resorted to the *diligentia quam in suis*[29] criterion which was built upon the British understanding of the principle of due diligence in the *Alabama* case. This was especially the case with regard to the protection of foreigners and their property, where the term due diligence was most often used. It soon became obvious, however, that this criterion does not always suffice and that significant shortcomings in national

26   *Ibid.*, p. 610.
27   *Ibid.*, p. 654.
28   For criticism of the award in the *Alabama* case see Report III of 1924 in the *British Claims in the Spanish Zone of Morocco 1923–1925* case, in which arbitrator M. Huber said that linking the degree of due diligence with the importance of interests at stake as well as potential consequences of omissions is unrealistic and confronts States with obligations which they will often not be able to meet. Huber thinks that under international law States are required to exercise the degree of due diligence which corresponds to the means that are at their disposal, see UNRIAA, Vol. 2, p. 644. Cheng, on the other hand, believes that a careful analysis of the entire *Alabama* case shows that the final award should not be understood as a request for a degree of due diligence that would not take into account the capabilities of a State, see Cheng, *op. cit.*, pp. 221–222.
29   This criterion was introduced into international jurisprudence by M. Huber as an arbitrator in the *British Claims in the Spanish Zone of Morocco 1923–1925* case, see previous footnote, p. 644. He emphasized that a State needs to ensure the same level of protection to foreigners as it does to its own citizens. Notwithstanding the *diligentia quam in suis* principle, Huber held that the level of protection cannot sink below the level of an objective, minimal international standard, *ibid.*

legislation and practice cannot justify departures from certain internationally accepted standards of behaviour.[30] It is for this reason that the jurisprudence took the view that there needs to be an international minimum standard. As examples of international minimum standards of protection of foreigners and their property arbitral awards list "ordinary standards of civilization",[31] "practices of civilized nations",[32] "international law standards",[33] "insufficiency...so far short of international standards that every reasonable and impartial man would readily recognize its insufficiency."[34]

Similarly, one of the resolutions adopted by the Institute of International Law in Lausanne in 1927 talked about measures to which, under the circumstances, it was proper normally to resort to prevent or eliminate injury,[35] and the text adopted by the Third Committee of the 1930 Codification Conference referred to "...measures as in the circumstances should normally have been taken..." by the State.[36]

Efforts to find a universally applicable standard of due diligence showed, however, that it was impossible to determine clearly and with precision a level of due diligence which would apply to all situations. This is to say that, although due diligence represents an objective standard, it remains flexible; the level of diligence which a State needs to employ by and large depends on the special circumstances of each situation. Circumstances which can influence the required level of due diligence are, for example, the level of control which a State has over parts of its territory,[37] the importance of the interests which

---

30 See H. Blomeyer-Bartenstein, "Due Diligence", in: *Encyclopedia of Public International Law*, ed. by R. Bernhardt, Vol. 1, 1992, p. 140. Huber opined in the same way; that there needs to be a certain objective international minimum standard, see previous footnote.

31 See, *e.g.*, the award in the *Harry Roberts* case, *op. cit.*, p. 80.

32 See, *e.g.*, the award in the *John. D. Chase* case between the United States and Mexico from 1928, UNRIAA, Vol. 4, p. 339.

33 See, *e.g.*, the award in the *Dickson Car Wheel Company* case between the United States and Mexico from 1931, *ibid.*, p. 678.

34 See awards in cases *L.F.H. Neer and Pauline Neer* between the United States and Mexico from 1926, *ibid.*, p. 62, and *H.G. Venable* between the same parties from 1927, *ibid.*, p. 229.

35 See Resolution I, Article III, *Annuaire...*, Vol. 3, *op. cit.*, p. 330.

36 See Art. 10 adopted by the Third Committee, see Borchard, "Responsibility...", *op. cit.*, pp. 535 *et seq.* "Bases of Discussion Drawn up by the Preparatory Committee" referred to diligence which, in the given circumstances, could have been expected by a civilized State, see the bases of discussion nos. 10, 17 and 18, *ibid.*, p. 536.

37 See, *e.g.*, the award in the *Buckingham* case between Mexico and Great Britain from 1933, *Digest of International Law*, ed. by G.H. Hackworth, Vol. 5, Washington, 1943, p. 480.

need to be protected[38] and the level of foreseeability of injurious consequences.[39] International legal rules will sometimes explicitly define situations in which an increased level of diligence is required. For example, the level of due diligence in the protection of diplomatic agents and consular officers of foreign States must be higher than in the protection of 'ordinary' foreign nationals. Also, when it comes to ultrahazardous activities which can cause significant transboundary harm, a State must employ a very high level of diligence, significantly higher than that required in other activities that can cause environmental harm.

Therefore, even if 'the behaviour of a well organized State' or another similar standard were used as a general criterion for the scope of due diligence, as is often suggested in the doctrine, it would not be of much practical help in concrete situations. Having in mind special circumstances, international legal rules will not ask States to act just as 'ordinarily organized States', but rather as 'very well organized States' or, for example in the case of ultrahazardous activities as 'excellently organized States'. One has to keep in mind that in some areas of international law, especially in the field of conservation and the protection of the environment, the scope of due diligence is increasingly becoming a technical criterion expressed in quantifiable technical and scientific terms. As the level of detail and precision with which international legal rules prescribe certain behaviour increases, the required scope of due diligence is ever more exact and precise, thus losing the character of a general and flexible standard of behaviour.[40]

The preceding paragraphs have shown that there is overwhelming consensus in international legal theory that the scope of due diligence depends on the circumstances of the actual situation. However, there is little doctrinal consensus about the second issue that has attracted attention for nearly a century – the one about the meaning of the principle of due diligence itself. While due diligence is seen by some as a measure of fault and deviations from the standard of due diligence as a type of fault, others see due diligence as an autonomous and objective standard, independent of fault, which States need to observe in their actions. In that sense, deviations from due diligence *per se*,

---

38 See, *e.g.*, the award in the *Francisco Mallén* case between the United States and Mexico from 1927, UNRIAA, Vol. 4, pp. 175–176.

39 See, *e.g.*, case *De Brissot*, in: *History and Digest...*(Moore), *op. cit.*, Vol. 3, Washington, 1898–1906, p. 2969. See also the Judgment of the ICJ in the case of hostages in Iran, *ICJ Reports 1980*, p. 33.

40 See R. Pisillo-Mazzeschi, "The Due Diligence Rule and the Nature of the International Responsibility of States", *German Yearbook of International Law*, 1992, Vol. 35, p. 45.

notwithstanding the motives, constitute a breach of international obligations and trigger international legal responsibility.

Proponents of the idea that fault is a general basis of international responsibility of States are primarily those who consider the breach of an obligation of due diligence as a type of fault.[41]

On the other hand, proponents of the idea of objective responsibility, *i.e.* of State responsibility without fault, say that due diligence is not a subjective element of responsibility, but rather the very content of a specific international obligation which consists of employing the degree of diligence required by international law in a given situation. This would mean that State responsibility arose if the State breached its obligation to act in accordance with due diligence. Anzilotti, the first 'objectivist', admitted that the analogy with the traditional concept of fault was obvious.[42] Additionally, as Anzilotti noted, if one also considers the fact that the due diligence can be measured by, for example, diligence which the State employs in its own affairs or diligence which a well organized State would employ, the analogy seems complete. Yet, Anzilotti said that this "simple and comfortable analogy" does not stand the test. It suffices to test it by giving an example of a State organ which did not take certain measures because doing so would constitute a violation of a domestic law. In such a situation, as Anzilotti concluded, if State responsibility were based on fault, there would be no responsibility of the State because there would be no fault on the part of the State organ.[43] Later on, 'objectivists' expanded on Anzilotti's work and said that due diligence is not a subjective-psychological element, but that it is 'materialized' in objective standards of

---

41   See, *e.g.*, Ago, "La colpa...", *op. cit.*, pp. 24–27; Orrego Vicuña, *op. cit.*, p. 318. See also Andrassy who proposes a criterion of fault for wrongful acts done by omission, Andrassy, *op. cit.*, p. 361. However, these views are also expressed by authors who do not belong to the circle of proponents of the fault-based responsibility of States. See *e.g. Oppenheim's International Law* (eds. Jennings, Watts), *op. cit.*, p. 509. See also Rousseau, *Cours...*, *op. cit.*, p. 24, but see *id.*, *Droit...*, *op. cit.*, p. 21. Perrin thinks that deviations from due diligence are a type of objective fault which, like subjective fault, represents the will of the wrongdoer who chose behaviour which deviates from due diligence, while they could have chosen the course of action which would have met their obligation of due diligence. However, unlike subjective fault which requires an analysis of the state of mind of the wrongdoer to assess the motives for their behaviour, objective fault is, as Perrin states, measured abstractly, and acts of organs of a well organized State in similar circumstances are used as the criterion, see Perrin, *op. cit.*, pp. 423–425.

42   Anzilotti, *Corso...*, *op. cit.*, p. 412.

43   *Ibid.*

behaviour.[44] This makes deviations from due diligence a breach of an international obligation, *i.e.* a breach of a standard of behaviour prescribed in a given situation by international law. The breach is assessed by comparing the State's actions in question with the standard of behaviour required by international law in such situations.[45] Some authors say that the breach of an obligation of due diligence which in international law *per se* triggers the international legal responsibility of States resembles the principle of *negligence* in the common law system. According to those authors, provided certain preconditions have been met, negligence as a deviation from due diligence can be a special and autonomous delict.[46]

IV Scope of Application of the Due Diligence Rule

Before discussing the legal nature of the notion of due diligence, it is important to stress that in certain fields of international law the standard of due diligence has been widely accepted in international jurisprudence and treaty practice. However, it is not a universally applicable standard. For example, the standard will never be applied in respect of obligations requiring the State to refrain from certain conduct. The due diligence standard is applied only to obligations requiring a particular course of conduct, but not to obligations requiring the achievement of a specified result. If we look at international jurisprudence and treaty practice, such an application of the due diligence standard is particularly relevant when it comes to the protection of foreigners and representatives of foreign States, as well as the protection of the environment.[47]

The distinction between obligation of conduct and obligation of result, widely accepted in the doctrine and jurisprudence of international law, depends on whether the obligation focuses on the conduct (procedure) or on the achievement of the required result. The obligation of conduct, which is of

---

44 See Pisillo-Mazzeschi, "Forms of International Responsibility for Environmental Harm", in: *International Responsibility for Environmental Harm*, ed. by F. Francioni, T. Scovazzi, London/Dordrecht/Boston, 1991, p. 17.

45 P. Guggenheim, *Traité de Droit international public*, Vol. 2, Geneva, 1954, p. 54; *id.*, "Les principes de droit international public", RC, 1952-I, Vol. 80, p. 149; Jiménez de Aréchaga, *op. cit.*, p. 536; Pisillo-Mazzeschi, "The Due Diligence...", *op. cit.*, p. 42 *et seq.*; P. Reuter, "Principes de droit international public", RC, 1961-II, Vol. 103, p. 598. See also Rousseau, *Droit...*, *op. cit.*, p. 21.

46 See P.A. Zannas, *La responsabilité internationale des Etats pour les actes de négligence*, Montreux, 1952, pp. 67 and 131.

47 See Pisillo-Mazzeschi, "Forms...", *op. cit.*, pp. 22 *et seq.*

interest to us in the present context, must be implemented through the performance of particular acts. In this regard obligations to prevent should be mentioned, since they are the most typical obligations of conduct, fully conditioned by the due diligence rule. If all necessary measures have been taken, a State has fulfilled its obligation and no responsibility can be invoked if the measures taken have not achieved the desired result. The important obligations to cooperate and protect also fall within the category of obligations of conduct.

Despite their importance, many authors stressed the relativity of this and other classifications of international obligations, pointing out that the existing categorizations do not include all international obligations. The lack of precise criteria for distinguishing between the different categories of obligations often leads to their different interpretation in jurisprudence.[48] That was the reason why the obligation of conduct and obligation of result, traditional concepts which Rapporteur Ago attempted to develop further and systematize,[49] did not appear in the final 2001 Draft articles of the International Law Commission.[50] In addition, the view was expressed in the ILC that the distinction "clearly related to primary rules" and the Commission decided to focus on its primary task of working on the secondary rules on State responsibility.[51]

It is beyond doubt, though, that the proper classification of a particular international obligation has an impact on responsibility, especially as far as the obligation of conduct and the obligation of result are concerned. Suffice it to mention the obligation to take all necessary measures. If a State has taken all necessary measures and in spite of that damage occurs (*e.g.* pollution of the environment), the key question would be which category of obligation was at stake. If an obligation of conduct is in question, no violation of an international obligation occurs in the case of pollution. On the other hand, in the case of an obligation of result, the occurrence of pollution triggers responsibility and the measures taken are

---

[48] See *e.g.* C.P. Economides, "Content of the Obligation: Obligations of Means and Obligations of Result", in: *The Law of International Responsibility* (Crawford *et al.*), *op. cit.*, pp. 375 *et seq.*;

R. Wolfrum, "Obligation of Result Versus Obligation of Conduct: Some Thoughts About the Implementation of International Obligations", in: *Looking to the Future: Essays on International Law in Honor of W. Michael Reisman*, ed. by M.H. Arsanjani, J. Katz Cogan, R.D. Sloane, S. Wiessner, Leiden, 2011, pp. 363 *et seq.*

[49] For the ILC's analysis of obligation of conduct and obligation of result see *YBILC*, 1977, Vol. II, Part 2, pp. 11–30 *et seq.*

[50] J. Crawford, Second Report on State Responsibility, 1999, A/CN.4/498, paras. 60 *et seq.*; Report of the ILC on the Work of Its Fifty-first Session, A/CN.4/10, pp. 59 *et seq.*; Draft articles..., 2001, *op. cit.*, p. 20.

[51] Report of the ILC on the Work of Its Fifty-first Session, A/CN.4/10, para.163, pp. 60–61.

not relevant. Thus, it would be very useful if the 2001 Draft articles contained provisions on these categories of obligation since that would facilitate the application of the secondary rules, enabling the determination if and at what moment the primary rules were violated. However no lamentation is needed in this respect – although the distinction between the obligation of conduct and obligation of result was not included in the final 2001 Draft articles, the traditional concepts of these obligations remained the important part of customary international law. Their further development in international jurisprudence and doctrine will eventually bring more precise and unified criteria for distinguishing between the different categories of obligation.

v   Due Diligence within International Liability for Injurious Consequences Arising out of Acts not Prohibited by International Law

Before assessing whether due diligence in the context of State responsibility is to be viewed as a form of fault or as an independent standard, mention should be made of another topic in which due diligence plays a very important role, namely, the topic of international liability for injurious consequences arising out of acts not prohibited by international law (prevention of transboundary damage from hazardous activities). The obligation of prevention, which is mostly a due diligence obligation, was also addressed by the ILC under the above-mentioned topic, although in a different context.

The concept of the duty of due diligence contained in the Schematic Outline[52] elaborated by the special rapporteur Quentin-Baxter in 1982 was based on the possibility of avoiding the injury (appropriate technology) and the proportionality between the precautions required and the danger created by the activity. If the potential injury actually occurred, the Outline provided that reparation had to be made.

Contrary to the regime of State responsibility, in a regime of liability without wrongfulness or liability for risk, even if all the required procedures have been followed, when injury occurs reparation must still be made. This satisfies the basic prerequisite for conducting ultrahazardous activities, which must go on because they are indispensable for the public good, but a need to compensate innocent victims of such activities – which cannot be entirely controlled – must be taken into account.

---

52   See *YBILC*, 1982, Vol. II, Part 1, pp. 62 *et seq.*, see sections 2 and 3.

The duty of due diligence, comprising different obligations, appears to be in a different context here: it depends on the occurrence of injury. Only if injury occurs do the consequences of the breach come into play within the regime of liability for risk, becoming a new obligation of reparation. Thus, it is not an autonomous obligation, such as that of conduct, where mere non-compliance is already a source of unlawfulness. It is an obligation within the regime of liability for risk which depends on the occurrence of injury. The State which is obliged to make reparation must adopt all the appropriate precautions, and only if the event which had to be prevented occurs does the comparison begin between the preventive methods followed and those which should have been followed (*viz.* those which are considered reasonable and appropriate in relation to that particular activity). At this stage, due diligence is defined in the same way as in all fields of international law where the concept is of importance. Although the definition is analogous, the due diligence concept within the topic of liability, however, acquires a completely new dimension. The nature of the ultra-hazardous activities requires compensation to be paid in the event of injury even if all merited diligence had been taken. The obligation to pay compensation for injurious consequences arising out of acts not prohibited by international law represents a 'primary' obligation. The liability here does not arise out of wrongfulness, but out of the 'primary' obligation. Failure of a State to pay compensation would constitute a breach of an international obligation of that State, thereby entailing its international responsibility.

It is beyond any doubt that the specific nature of ultrahazardous activities requires specific legal solutions, such as obligation to pay compensation even in the event of injury arising out of acts not prohibited by international law, *viz.* when no internationally wrongful act exists. Instead of following legal solutions from internal law, the ILC, aware of the probable resistance of States to liability without wrongfulness, tried to 'soften' the concept of such liability in order to make it more acceptable to them. That is a reason why the work on the topic of liability for acts not prohibited by international law, which started in 1980, was controversial from the very beginning and met with strong scepticism and opposition in the legal doctrine.

In dealing with this topic, the Commission has gone beyond the study of reparation of significant transboundary harm to the management of a transboundary risk, with a strong emphasis on the prevention of transboundary losses. The integration of preventive and reparative elements in a single instrument led to the weakening of obligations that are twin pillars of the topic, *viz.*, the obligation of prevention and the obligation of compensation. According to the 1996 Draft articles,[53] violation of the obligation of prevention entailed no responsibility, and the obligation to compensate became a negotiation duty.

The 1997 session of the Commission opened the possibility for modifying these problematical solutions. The Working Group, established by the Commission to make recommendations on further work on the topic, noted that the scope and content of the topic remained unclear due to, *inter alia*, some conceptual and theoretical difficulties. One of the basic recommendations of the Working Group was to treat separately the issues of prevention and international liability.

The Commission accepted the suggested approach, and in 2001 completed the first part of the task, *i.e.*, the articles on the topic of prevention,[54] and in 2006 the second, *i.e.*, the principles on liability. The new drafts did not fulfill the primary task assigned to the ILC within the topic of liability, *viz.*, to ensure compensation even in cases when no wrongfulness exists. The draft articles on prevention, though, elaborate in more detail the duty of prevention, bringing some useful clarifications of the scope and nature of prevention of transboudary harm from hazardous activities.[55] On the other hand, the 2006 Draft principles on the allocation of loss in the case of transboundary harm arising out of hazardous activities[56] not only did not bring any added value to the topic of liability for acts not prohibited by international law, but formed the basis for a regressive development of international law, having recommended lower standards than those contained in the existing conventions dealing with civil liability for environmental damage.

Given a context in which due diligence is used in the framework of the, unfortunately abortive, attempt of the ILC to develop rules applicable to the important topic of liability for ultrahazardous activities, this aspect of due diligence cannot be taken into account in the assessment of the legal nature of due diligence within State responsibility.

---

53   See draft with commentary in: Report of the ILC on the Work of Its Forty-eighth Session, 6 May-26 July 1996, *General Assembly, Official Records, Fifty-first Session, Supplement No.10* (A/51/10), Annex 1, p. 101.

54   See Articles on Prevention of Transboundary Harm from Hazardous Activities (Articles on Prevention of Transboundary Harm), in: *Official Records of the General Assembly, Fifty-sixth Session, Supplement No. 10* (A/56/10), p. 366.

55   Some authors, such as *e.g.* Barnidge, find many positive aspects of the draft articles on prevention, see R. Barnidge, "The Due Diligence Principle under International Law", *Academia Edu., Shared Research*, <http://www.academia.edu/430200/The_Due_Diligence_Principle_Under_International_Law>, pp. 57–60.

56   See *YBILC*, 2006, Vol. II, Part 2.

VI Due Diligence – A Form of Fault or Independent Standard?

Having before him a case where the due diligence standard is applicable, the international judge has to assess whether, in the particular case at hand, the conduct which is attributable to the State meets the degree of diligence required by international law. If he finds that the State has deviated from the due diligence standard and if there are no circumstances precluding wrongfulness, the responsibility of the State will be engaged since both elements required for State responsibility in international law have been fulfilled: the objective element (breach of an international obligation) as well as the subjective element (attributability of the breach to the State). Thus, while proceeding in the described manner, there is no need for the international judge to decide whether in the particular case State responsibility is based on an existing degree of fault or on the deviation from the particular content of the international obligation. In other words, the question about the legal nature of due diligence has in fact no practical import; it is solely of theoretical interest. Neither is there a practical difference in the way a wrongdoing State may avoid responsibility. If we assume a case of presumed fault, then the State may exculpate itself by proving that due diligence has been exercised. If, on the other hand, we assume that due diligence figures as the particular content of an international obligation, then a wrongdoing State may exonerate itself from responsibility by proving that it has acted in accordance with the international obligation, *i.e.* that the State's organs have acted in accordance with the standard of conduct required by international law.

Advocates of an objective approach might point to the fact that in most judicial decisions and arbitral awards which based the responsibility of States on a deviation from due diligence the international judges did not characterise such a deviation as fault *i.e. culpa*, and this might be used in favour of the argument that due diligence is embedded in the objective content of the international obligation requiring a certain conduct, *i.e.* that the deviation from due diligence is an autonomous delict. Although this argument – as well as all the other arguments put forward by authors who recognize due diligence as a separate standard contained in the very international obligation, and not as a degree of fault – is not unconvincing, to us it does not seem convincing enough to dissuade us from taking into consideration classic civil law categories. Furthermore, no practical reason exists that would make it necessary to deviate from the 'convenient analogy' with the traditional notion of fault (as Anzilotti would put it). The comparison of particular conduct with the objective standard contained in an international obligation actually constitutes a means of determining fault (*culpa*).

Objections that the psychological category of fault cannot be applied to States might be plausible in respect of *dolus*.[57] However, such objections cannot be sustained in respect of *culpa*, since here objective criteria are applied, *i.e.* particular conduct is measured against the conduct required by a certain legal rule. Thus, although the specifics of international law call for the bases of State responsibility to be objectified, there is no reason for the international lawyer not to regard the deviation from due diligence as it is viewed in classic civil law, namely as negligence, *i.e.* a form of fault.

Although in our opinion the cases where the lack of due diligence entails the responsibility of States are to be viewed as cases of responsibility based on (presumed) fault, in some fields of international law, admittedly, recent developments show a trend towards a complete objectification of the due diligence standard. Such a development may especially be observed in the field of international environmental law. Here the due diligence standard is turned from a flexible standard requiring States to take 'all necessary measures' into a detailed elaboration of obligations falling into the category of 'necessary measures', which are often expressed in numerical terms. Thus, the rules are formulated in such a way that they contain a detailed elaboration of due diligence obligations in the cases they refer to, which makes it impossible to assess the lack of due diligence separately from the breach of the international obligation.

The need for a further objectification of the due diligence standard and its separation from subjective elements is also stressed by the *Institut de Droit international* in its 1997 Resolution on the responsibility for damage to the environment.[58]

VII   Concluding Remarks

At the end of our discussion on the place and role of fault (and due diligence) in State responsibility we may, it seems, conclude that in last decade a certain rapprochement has occurred between the heretofore irreconcilable positions of the advocates of fault as a necessary element of wrongfulness, on the one hand, and the advocates of a complete rejection of fault as a condition for State responsibility, on the other hand. This was facilitated primarily by the work of the International Law Commission on the codification of the rules on State responsibility. Although the International Law Commission in its Draft articles

---

57   See, however, G. Arangio-Ruiz, Second Report on State Responsibility, *YBILC*, 1989, Vol. II, Part 1, pp. 48 *et seq.*
58   See Art. 3, para. 2 of the Resolution, *Annuaire...*, Vol. 67-II, *op. cit.*, p. 491.

on State responsibility does not mention fault as an essential element of wrongfulness, it is not impossible that in certain cases fault will constitute a condition for the responsibility of States. This may happen owing to the categories of 'primary' and 'secondary' rules. Indeed, although fault has not been provided for as an element of wrongfulness by the 'secondary' rules on State responsibility, fault may become a condition for the responsibility of States if provided for in a particular 'primary' rule. That way the work of the International Law Commission has served as the basis for the compromise position which has recently, so it seems, prevailed in international legal doctrine: the responsibility of a State is in principle engaged by the mere breach of an international obligation attributable to the State, but, exceptionally, fault (*dolus* or *culpa*) may be a condition for the responsibility of States, if the very rule of international law which has been violated stipulates fault as a condition of wrongfulness. By 'objectifying' State responsibility as a matter of principle, the application of the rules on State responsibility is made easier, and an assessment of the subjective elements in a State's conduct can be avoided in those cases where this is not necessary. At the same time fault can still play a certain role, if provided for as a condition for responsibility in certain special international legal rules (these will be mostly treaty rules).

Regarding the legal nature of due diligence, so far also no consensus has been reached in international legal doctrine. However, there are a growing number of contemporaneous authors who do not regard due diligence as a degree of fault, but rather view it as directly forming part of the international obligation's content, whereby the breach of the obligation *per se* engages the responsibility of the State.

Nevertheless, none of the arguments put forward by the advocates of due diligence as a separate content of an international obligation seems to us convincing enough to persuade us to abandon the traditional teaching of due diligence as a degree of fault (*culpa*), at least in the cases where it is still formulated as a general standard to be measured against a State's conduct in a particular case (*e.g.* the conduct of a well-organized State, taking all necessary measures).

PART 2

Law of the Sea

∴

CHAPTER 9

A Succinct Historical Overview of the Status of Straits in International Law

*Hugo Caminos**

I   Preliminary Remarks

The term international straits usually refers to straits which are within the territorial sea of the bordering State or States but which, because of their use for international navigation, are subject to special norms of international law designed to secure the right of passage for all ships and aircraft. A strait which is part of the high seas is not an international strait in the legal sense of the term, because ships and aircraft in transit through them do so in the exercise of the freedom of the high seas and, therefore, do not require any special treatment as far as the needs of international navigation are concerned.[1]

Issues related to passage through international straits are perhaps more sensitive than those related to passage through other parts of the territorial sea, in that the former could pose a greater threat of international conflict. Any discrimination amongst users of these straits, any imposition of conditions upon passage, or any attempt by the coastal State to close these straits to international navigation would, undoubtedly, have a negative impact on the peaceful relations between the countries involved and would probably provoke a reaction by the naval powers. Uncertainty of transit rights through international straits would not only jeopardize international trade and threaten the global strategic balance, but would, in all likelihood, increase political tension and conflict worldwide as coastal States barter passage in return for political or economic gain. Given these serious consequences, the leading naval powers have naturally responded to the general acceptance of the extended territorial sea up to 12 nautical miles by advocating the adoption of a special legal régime that would ensure the maintenance of free and open passage through the world's international straits.

Contrary to the interest of naval powers, States bordering straits have identified equally valid interests in the promotion of safe navigation and in the protection of the marine environment of international straits. As a result, States

---

*   Former Judge, International Tribunal for the Law of the Sea; Member of the *Institut de Droit International*.
1   Fleischer, C.A. "International Straits: A Key Issue at the Law of the Sea Conference", 1 *Environmental Policy and Law*, 120 (1975).

bordering straits have supported a legal régime that affords stricter regulation of maritime traffic and pollution controls. The failure of any international legal régime to take account of these concerns would also have worldwide negative effects. Coastal States could react by advancing unilateral claims over international straits, hindering international communications. Likewise, the existence of differing environmental protection regulations from country to country, or the prescription of standards for vessel construction and/or operation, could also affect international navigation. Additionally, the absence of pollution-prevention regulations could result in permanent damage to the marine environment as a whole.

This scenario of competing interests in formulating a special legal régime for straits is similar to that existing 370 years ago as Grotius and Selden contested the pros and cons of wide coastal State jurisdiction. Drawing a parallel from this historical controversy, the noted Danish scholar Erik Brüel,[2] in his classic work on the topic, placed the question of straits in the context of conflicting interests between strait States and the international community:

> The struggle between the demands of the international community on the one hand and the interests of the individual state on the other hand seems now to have ended, as far as the open sea is concerned, in a legal settlement that may at least in principle be called a victory of the international community. As to that part of the ocean which is nearest to the coast, the struggle has resulted in the victory of the individual state, complete in respect of the national waters, and in all essentials in respect of territorial waters. At present, therefore, the conflict only concerns the international straits. An analysis of the legal position of the latter seems, therefore – in addition to the particular interest it has to examine the position of these straits owing to their general importance – to present a more general interest by way of illustrating the dynamic and static forces struggling against each other during the crisis in the process of adjustment, the solution of which is perhaps the foremost problem of the international community at the present time.[3]

---

2   Brüel, E., *International Straits*, Vols. I–II, Sweet and Maxwell, London (1947). This book is a doctoral thesis presented in June 1940 at the Faculty of Law and Political Science of the University of Copenhagen. Publication of its English translation was delayed until after the Second World War. In Volume I, Brüel sets out three main questions as the basis for his work: (1) the right of passage through international straits as a distinct legal régime; (2) the extent of territorial waters; and (3) limitations upon the right of belligerents to use straits as theatres of war. Volume II, the "Special Part", discusses régimes established by treaty concerning specific straits.
3   *Ibid.*, at 11.

According to Brüel, resolution of this conflict must recognize the vital and legitimate interests of both sides. He adds: "[T]he principle of the freedom of the seas, if extended to straits, would have to be submitted to considerable modification and elucidation."[4] Assuming that a legal régime *sui juris* for passage through straits could be agreed upon, Brüel recognizes that not all straits within a strict geographical sense should be subject to a special régime. The difficulty, therefore, was two-fold: (1) to agree on a legal régime that accommodated all interests, and (2) to identify the type of straits that would be subject to these special norms of international law. As we shall see, it has taken a good part of the 20th century to achieve the compromise which the Danish author suggested 50 years ago.[5]

Only two years after the publication of the English translation of Brüel's treatise, the International Court of Justice, in an oft-quoted passage from the *Corfu Channel* case, indelibly marked the evolution of the legal status of international straits:

> It is in the opinion of the Court, generally recognized and in accordance with international custom that States in time of peace have a right to send their warships through straits used for international navigation between two parts of the high seas without the previous authorization of a coastal State, provided that the passage is *innocent*. Unless otherwise prescribed in an international convention, there is no right for a coastal State to prohibit such passage through straits in time of peace.[6]

---

4 *Ibid.*, at 38.
5 Brüel considered one of the most significant developments in the evolution of the legal régime of straits to be Article 23 (*e*) of the Covenant of the League of Nations, which imposed upon Members the obligation to "make provisions to secure and maintain freedoms of communications and of transit". According to him, this was the first time that the legal status of straits, as far as the right of passage was concerned, was consciously recognized "as a principle". Admittedly, a survey of the application of this principle "showed 'a curious forward and backwards', proving that conflicting, almost equally strong interests make themselves felt in this respect". *Ibid.*, at 202. Kelsen points out, however, that the introductory clause of Article 23 of the Covenant specifically limits the application of Article 23 (*a*) to (*f*). He states:
"[these provisions] are laid down under one condition, namely, that the questions referred to shall be the object of treaties concluded by the Members of the League, between themselves or between third States. In so far as the tasks assigned in paragraphs (*a*) through (*f*) fall within the general competence of the League, as formulated in the Preamble, the introductory clause of Article 23 signifies a limitation of this general competence".
See Kelsen, H., *Legal Technique in International Law. A Textual Critique of the League Covenant*, 165, Vol. x, No. 6, Geneva Studies (1939).
6 *Corfu Channel* case (United Kingdom v. Albania), ICJ Reports 1949, 4 (Judgment of 9 April) (hereinafter: *Corfu Channel* case).

The *Corfu Channel* case was the first international judicial case pronouncement on the issues related to the passage of ships through straits used for international navigation.

The *Corfu Channel* case, however, did not settle the many questions concerning the formulation of a legal régime for straits that could equitably balance competing State interests. In 1949, the same year the case was decided, the International Law Commission (ILC) met for the first time to consider the codification and progressive development of various outstanding issues of the law of the sea, including territorial waters. In 1958, using the draft articles prepared by the ILC as a basis for its work, the First United Nations Conference on the Law of the Sea (UNCLOS I) adopted the Convention on the Territorial Sea and the Contiguous Zone (1958 Convention), codifying a somewhat broader version of the *Corfu Channel* case rule within the context of innocent passage in the territorial sea. However, the inability of the international community to agree upon the breadth of the territorial sea, both in 1958 and in 1960 during the Second United Nations Conference on the Law of the Sea, precipitated the erosion of the régime of non-suspendable innocent passage through straits used for international navigation embodied in the 1958 Convention.

Even before the 1958 Convention entered into force, signs of its inadequacy were beginning to surface. The technological revolution, the new uses of the sea and its resources, and the substantial increase in the membership of the international community in the 1960s brought about by the decolonization process precipitated the collapse of the traditional regime for the oceans. The exploitation of the resources of the sea, both living and non-living, acquired a new dimension. The threat of the exhaustion of some species of fish stocks in the areas adjacent to their coasts, as well as the need to protect those areas from the threat of pollution, prompted a number of States, particularly in Africa and Latin America, to proclaim territorial seas or other maritime zones up to 200 miles from the coast. Moreover, the continued uncertainty over the maximum breadth of the territorial sea was particularly troublesome to the legal régime of international straits.

If one were to think of the factor in recent history which most affected the régime of straits codified in the 1958 Convention, it would have to be the extension of the breadth of the territorial sea up to 12 nautical miles. As an increasing number of developing coastal States claimed a 12-mile territorial sea in the early 1960s, the need for a new legal régime of passage through straits used for international navigation became apparent. Under the traditional three-mile rule, adopted by most leading naval powers at the time, ships and aircraft enjoyed unrestricted freedom of navigation and overflight through the high seas corridors which existed in over 100 of the world's most important straits.

As extended territorial waters overlapped these straits, the United States and the Soviet Union, unwilling to accept the navigational limitations imposed by the régime of innocent passage in the territorial sea, lobbied for a new round of international negotiations under the auspices of the United Nations that would accommodate the 12-mile territorial sea together with the right of unimpeded passage through and over straits used for international navigation.

The Third United Nations Conference on the Law of the Sea (UNCLOS III) convened in late 1973. Throughout its preparatory work and during the first years of negotiation, the positions of States bordering straits and those of the leading naval powers were clearly defined along a historical theme reflective of national interests: developing coastal States sought control over the seas closest to their shores, including international straits, and the naval powers insisted on the maintenance of unrestricted navigation and overflight through those straits. States bordering straits thus supported a unitary régime of innocent passage in the territorial sea, including straits used for international navigation, in order to restrict freedom of navigation and aircraft passage, safeguard their national sovereignty and protect their marine environment. The naval powers, on the other hand, because of their need to preserve unimpeded navigation and overflight through straits, guaranteeing international trade and strategic mobility, were natural allies of a régime analogous to the freedom of the high seas.

UNCLOS III was an unprecedented accomplishment in international co-operation and in the treaty-making process. The multi-faceted instrument which resulted, the United Nations Convention on the Law of the Sea 1982,[7] not only represents an attempt to establish true universality in the legal order for the oceans, but also marks the first time that a distinct legal régime for international straits was adopted. This régime was designed to overcome the legal implications of the generally accepted 12-mile territorial sea and to accommodate the valid concerns of States bordering straits.

II   Opinion of the Most Important Authors up to the Twentieth Century

The seventeenth-century father of international law, Grotius, was the first to study the question of rights of passage through territorial waters and straits in

---

[7] United Nations Convention on the Law of the Sea, opened for signature 10 December 1982, reprinted in *United Nations, The Law of the Sea: United Nations Convention on the Law of the Sea* (UN Pub. Sales No. E.83.V.5) (hereinafter: 1982 Convention).

his work *De Jure Belli ac Pacis*.⁸ Notwithstanding his earlier proclamation that the ocean was *res communis*, the common property of all, Grotius maintained that although rivers and other parts of the ocean may be subject to appropriation, innocent passage may not be forbidden even through those parts of the sea which fall under a sovereign State's jurisdiction.⁹ He further proclaimed the coastal State's right to protect and promote navigation through straits by keeping the thoroughfares lighted and marked off, and by conditioning such passage upon payment of a moderate toll.¹⁰

In reaction to Grotius' freedom of the seas doctrine, and its implications for Western-European plans to expand trade routes and monopolize the New World, Selden's *Mare Clausum* maintains that the sea was decreed to be controlled by man. Unlike Grotius, who actually used custom to disprove the appropriation theory, Selden believed that customary usage and control of the sea justified such acquisition. Although a coastal State could rightfully refuse passage to a foreign vessel, in Selden's opinion, humane considerations should normally lead to innocent passage not being denied.¹¹

To Grotius and Selden, however, the question of straits formed a small part of a larger and more important issue, freedom of the seas. Following their historical controversy, the practical problems of actually claiming and controlling large parts of the ocean resulted in a temporary lull to the polemic. The first writer to take a direct interest in the question of straits, Pufendorf, was greatly influenced by the growing tide of nationalist sentiment towards the end of the seventeenth century. In reference to Grotius' proclamation advocating the freedom of the seas, Pufendorf stressed the need to secure the harbours of the coastal State, as well as the need to control that part of the strait nearest to the coast.¹²

During the eighteenth century, when the question of the breadth of the territorial sea was first being discussed, none of the authors of the time

---

8   Grotius, H., *De Jure Belli Ac Pacis*, Libri tres, Amstld. Lib. II Cap. III, Sec. VIII (1646), see Brüel, *supra*, note 2, at 49–50.

9   Grotius wrote: "It has, however, been a fairly easy matter to extend sovereignty over a part of the sea without involving the right of ownership; and I do not think that any hindrance is put in the way of this by the universal customary law of which I have spoken...", quoted in MacRae, L.M., "Customary International Law and the United Nations' Law of the Sea Treaty", 13 *California Western International Law Journal*, 181, 191 (1983).

10 Brüel, *supra*, note 2, at 50.

11 Selden, J., *Mare Clausum Seu De Dominio Maris*, Libri duo, London (1636), in Brüel, *supra*, note 2, at 49.

12 Pufendorf, S., *De Jure Naturae et Gentium*, Libri octo. Lundini Scanorum, (1672), in Brüel, *supra*, note 2, at 50.

considered the effect that such claims over territorial waters would have upon straits. Not even Vattel, perhaps that century's most influential writer, made any exception for straits when he calculated the breadth of the territorial sea.[13] Vattel, however, was first to draw the distinction between straits that "servent à la communication des deux mers, dont la navigation est commune à toutes les Nations, ou à plusieurs", and straits which do not serve such a function. In straits which connect two seas passage cannot be refused, "pourvu que ce passage soit innocent et sans danger" for the littoral State. Like Grotius, Vattel conditioned such passage upon payment of a moderate toll. He also emphasized coastal State interests with regards to safety and the right to "user de certaines précautions, à exiger des formalités, établies d'ordinaire par la coutume des nations".[14]

Throughout the nineteenth century, as the political and economic climate of the world settled and steam-powered transportation became a way of life, the coastal State interests promoted by Vattel became secondary to more liberal notions of the right of passage through straits. The right of passage is thus conceived as a natural complement to the freedom of the seas.[15]

Gerard Reyneval, one of the first authors of the nineteenth century to study the question of straits as a distinct legal concept, said:

> Les détroits sont des passages pour communiquer d'une mer à l'autre; si l'usage des mers, domaine commun de l'humanité, est libre, la communication entre elles doit l'être également, ou autrement la liberté de ces mêmes mers ne serait qu'une chimère.[16]

Hautefeuille, also in the nineteenth century, commented that "le passage est libre sans aucune exception", even if the strait is so narrow as to be considered territorial waters in its entirety.[17]

---

13   Vattel, E., *Le droit des gens*, Libre I, chap. 23, sec. 292 (1758). See also *The Classics of International Law* (Scott, ed.), Washington, D.C. (1916), in Brüel, *supra*, note 2, at 53–54. It was Vattel who pronounced the formula that would determine the breadth of the territorial sea by saying: "L'espace de mer qui est à la portée du canon le long des côtes est regardé comme faisant partie du territoire."
14   Brüel, *supra*, note 2, at 54.
15   Brüel, *supra*, note 2, at 54.
16   Rayneval, J.M.G. de, *Institutions du droit de la nature et des gens* (2e éd., Paris), liv. 2, chap. 9, sec. 7 (1803), in Brüel, *supra*, note 2, at 55.
17   Hautefeuille, L.B., *Des droits et des devoirs des nations neutres en temps de guerre maritime*, I-III (3e éd., Paris, 1868), in Brüel, *supra*, note 2, at 55–56.

Probably the first author to recognize that straits ought to be subject to "un régime tout special" was Godey, who insisted that even though their waters might be territorial for some purposes, straits were equivalent to the high seas for the purposes of transit. Within a strait he limits the breadth of the territorial waters to three miles, but forbids hostilities "dans tout l'espace inférieur à 12 milles au minimum."[18]

Holland goes on to distinguish between conditions in time of peace, when the passage of all ships, including warships, through straits may be considered 'innocent' and cannot be hampered, and passage in time of war, when the belligerent littoral State may "deal with the ships of the enemy as it pleases".[19]

The twentieth century saw a growing tendency towards an even more liberal interpretation of the right of passage. Amongst the writers of that time, Schücking presented the most comprehensive study of the problems related to international straits. He stresses that not all straits which connect two high seas are necessarily of interest to international law; only those straits that are of practical value to international shipping should be subject to a special set of rules. Moreover, even in those straits which contain high seas corridors through their middle, the general rules of the high seas should be modified to limit any warlike manœuvre in that area.[20]

III   The *Institut de Droit International*, 1894 to 1912

A decisive step towards the formulation of an autonomous legal régime to govern passage through straits was taken in 1894 by the *Institut de Droit International*. The underlying notion in formulating a definition of an international strait was the recognition that the waters of a strait which did not exceed double the territorial sea in width would be territorial waters. Coastal State jurisdiction over such waters, however, did not include a right to interrupt passage; transit would be free. The definition found in the *Institut's* Report of 1894, therefore, covers straits which serve as "un passage habituel d'une mer libre à une autre". Such straits, while territorial waters, "ne peuvent jamais être fermés".[21]

---

18   Godey, P., *La mer calière*, Paris (1896), in Brüel, *supra*, note 2, at 59. See also O'Connell, D.P., *International Law of the Sea*, 300, Vol. I, Clarendon Press, Oxford (1982).

19   Holland, T.E., *Studies in International Law*, 288, Oxford (1898), in Brüel, *supra*, note 2, at 60.

20   Schücking, W., *Die Verwendung von Minen im Seekrieg*, 121 (NZIR, 1906), in Brüel, *supra*, note 2, at 65.

21   O'Connell, *supra*, note 18, at 301. For a full discussion of the debates and proposals of the *Institut de Droit International* from 1894 to 1912, see Brüel, *supra*, note 2, at 70–80.

In 1910, at the *Institut*'s Paris Session, it was agreed that a coastal State would not be in breach of the law of neutrality if it failed to prevent the passage of belligerent warships through a strait. The right to prevent such passage only applied "en dehors des routes maritimes nécessaires à la navigation". In other words, a neutral State 'ought' to allow the passage of warships of belligerent powers "dans le détroit qui constitue le seul moyen de passage d'une mer libre à une autre mer libre".[22]

IV   The Hague Peace Conference of 1907

The question of the legal status of international straits was again discussed during the Second International Peace Conference at The Hague in 1907. While considering whether the right to lay mines in the territorial sea extended to straits, the Conference stated, without opposition, that "personne ne contestait l'obligation de laisser un passage dans les détroits qui unissent deux mers libres".[23] Although this proposal was later amended to become less categorical and was eventually omitted from the draft convention, one commentator has observed that "the impression left is unmistakably in favour of the view that international straits were in an exceptional position which would require separate codification".[24]

V   The Hague Codification Conference of 1930

The First World War interrupted the work of the *Institut de Droit International*, as well as the work of other non-governmental organizations, on the issue of the legal status of straits.[25] Up to that time, the writings of the most important

---

22   Brüel, *supra*, note 2, at 74.
23   *Ibid.*, at 89.
24   O'Connell, *supra*, note 18, at 303. The proposal was made less categorical with the addition of the following: "dans aucun cas la communication entre deux mers ne peut être barré entièrement, mais le passage ne sera permis qu'aux conditions qui seraient indiquées par les autorités compétentes". A reservation was also inserted with regard to existing treaties and the sovereign rights of a State. See Brüel, *supra*, note 2, at 89.
25   Other international bodies working on the issue of straits were the International Law Association and the Interparliamentary Union. See Brüel, *supra*, note 2, 78–88, for a summary of the work of these two organizations from 1895 to 1914. In its 1910 Conference at Brussels, the Interparliamentary Union appointed a Commission for the purpose of examining the possibility of extending the régimes of the Straits of Magellan, the Suez Canal, and the Panama Canal to all straits and canals connecting two oceans. The debate

authors of international law had reflected the liberal tendencies that had become dominant by the end of the nineteenth century. After the War, the debate on the legal status of straits seemed to focus not so much on the fact that international straits should enjoy a special legal status, but on the criterion that should be used to qualify which straits would be subject to the special legal régime.[26]

---

concluded in a statement to the effect that, for the time being, it would only be possible to apply some of the principles contained in those special regulatory régimes to all straits. See Brüel, *supra*, note 2, at 81–88.

26 Of the many international legal scholars of the post-First World War period, a number of the most important authors addressed the question of the legal status of international straits. Marcel Moye, for example, places international straits on an equal footing with the open seas and criticizes coastal States that attempt "à faire acte de maître". Moye, M., *Les droits des gens modernes*, 278, Paris (1920); Pitt Cobbett maintains that the decisive factor in determining the legal status of a strait is the extent to which the strait is formed by territorial waters. Even if the strait is territorial waters from coast to coast, if it "is a natural waterway, or a necessary and convenient channel of communication between two parts of the high seas", a right of innocent passage must be accorded to all vessels, public as well as private, in time of peace as in time of war, except of course to enemy vessels. Cobbett, P., *Leading Cases in International Law*, I, 153, 4th edn. (Bellot, ed.), London (1922–1924); Charles De Visscher, placing the question of the legal status of straits in its broadest context, said: "la théorie générale de la liberté de transit s'applique de nos jours à tous les modes des transport." All straits joining two open seas hold "un intérêt primordial" to international shipping. Warships, "en principe", shall enjoy the right of innocent passage, subject to the right of the littoral State to limit the number of warships passing through the strait. Even in time of war, when the littoral State is neutral, this right is generally recognized through those straits that form the only passage between two parts of the high seas; it is "cet aspect naval et militaire de la question qui fait la difficulté du problème des détroits". Visscher, C. De, *Le droit international des communications*, 98–99, Gand, Paris (1924). Franz Münch adopts one of the most liberal views amongst post-First World War writers and contributes greatly to the understanding of the issues, as well as to the solution of the problems inherent to the legal status of straits. He abandons the traditional distinction between straits bordered by one or more littoral States and emphasizes that those straits characterized as international, that is, those that are important to international commerce, can never be considered internal waters in their entirety. He questions whether a State can "round off" its territorial waters, to extend State jurisdiction over enclaves within the strait and over the narrow strip of open sea through the middle of the strait. Münch, F., *Die Technischen Fragen des Küstenmeers*, Aus dem Institut für internationales Recht an der Universität Kiel (1934). For a summary of the post-war work of the above-mentioned authors, as well as the work of the other writers and scientific associations, see Brüel, *supra*, note 2, at 123–153.

In September 1924, the Assembly of the League of Nations requested the Council to convene a committee of experts to prepare a memorandum of those questions in international law which they considered to be ripe for codification. Various subcommittees were subsequently formed, one of them, with Walther Schücking serving as *rapporteur*, to consider and report upon the relationship of the rules of the territorial waters to straits. A series of questionnaires were then circulated amongst the governments soliciting comments on the various issues and topics.

In 1927, the Assembly, after receiving the Committee's Report to the Council, decided that a conference should be held at The Hague for the purpose of codifying three subjects. These topics, better known as the 'Bases de discussion', included: (i) Nationality; (ii) Territorial Waters; and (iii) Responsibility of States for Damage Done in Their Territory to the Person or Property of Foreigners.[27] The Council then appointed a Preparatory Committee to prepare a Report to serve as the basis for the work of the upcoming conference, based upon the strength of the replies to the questionnaires from governments and on the subcommittee reports previously submitted.

The subcommittee report prepared by Schücking had made it clear from the outset that straits regulated by special treaty régimes would be excluded from consideration.[28] A rather confusing distinction is made, however, between those straits whose entrances are less than 12 miles wide (given a 6-mile territorial sea), and whose shores belong to one State, and those straits with the same characteristics whose shores belong to two States. In the case of the former, the principle of internal bays, with no right of passage, is said to

---

27   The Report of the Committee of Experts initially recommended seven topics for codification: (i) Nationality; (ii) Territorial Waters; (iii) Responsibility of States for Damage Done to the Person or Property of Foreigners; (iv) Diplomatic Privileges and Immunities; (v) Procedure of International Conferences and Procedure for the Conclusion and Drafting of Treaties; (vi) Piracy; and (vii) Exploitation of the Products of the Sea. For an account of the preparatory work of the Conference up to 1930 see Hudson, M.O., "The Progressive Codification of International Law", 20 *American Journal of International Law* (hereinafter: *AJIL*), 655 (1926); Reeves, J.S., "Progress of the Work of the League of Nations Codification Committee", 21 *AJIL*, 659 (1927); Reeves, J.S., "The Hague Conference Codification of International Law", 24 *AJIL*, 52 (1930); Hale, R.W., "Territorial Waters as a Test for Codification", 24 *AJIL*, 65 (1930); Hudson, M.O., "First Conference for Codification of International Law", 24 *AJIL*, 447 (1930).

28   Apparently due to a misprint on page 16 of the Report, the Sub-Committee states that it shall disregard straits "which are *not* subject to conventional regulations." League of Nations Doc. C.196.M.70.1927, V.1. (hereinafter: Report of the Subcommittee). See also Brüel, *supra*, note 2, at 176, note 1.

apply. In the case of the latter, the strait would be divided down the middle and the principle of innocent passage through territorial waters would apply.[29]

The subcommittee limited itself to the question of passage through straits in relation to the rights of belligerents. This was done because of the presumption at the time that because the question of passage for merchant vessels in time of peace was covered by the general rules of the territorial sea, it did not need to be discussed independently. The subcommittee report, therefore, stipulates that "straits serving as a passage to open seas, ...should never be closed"; this rule being in "accordance with the idea that a riparian State is not entitled in time of war completely to close its territorial sea".[30]

Of the responses to the questionnaires submitted to governments, Germany's seemed most cogent. Germany proposed that straits which connect two open seas should never be regarded as national waters. Even in cases where a strait consists of national waters[31] the right of innocent passage for either merchant ships or warships should not be affected. Germany further emphasizes the importance and the need to establish a right of overflight in the airspace above a strait connecting two seas.

When the First Conference on the Progressive Codification of International Law (the 1930 Hague Codification Conference) met to examine the Preparatory Committee's final report and the replies of the governments, three committees were formed to consider each of the three topics presented to the Conference in the 'Bases de discussion'. The question of the breadth of territorial waters was referred to the Second Committee. That Committee, in effect, adopted the same approach with regard to the passage of merchant ships as had the Preparatory Committee before it. Thus, passage through straits was considered to be on the same footing as passage through the territorial sea generally; the passage of warships through straits was emphasized and examined at length.

On the subject of overflight through straits, Schücking, the German delegate, demanded that the right to overfly straits be recognized. In his own words: "This is clearly the present tendency of the juridical outlook...irrespective of the wishes of the coastal State."[32] Schücking then proposed that the Lausanne

---

29 Brüel, *supra*, note 2, at 176.
30 Report of the Subcommittee, *supra*, note 29, at 17. See also Brüel, *supra*, note 2, at 176.
31 As an example of straits which may be considered to be national waters Germany cited two cases: (1) when the width of the strait is narrower than the combined territorial waters of the riparian States, and (2) when a strait is formed by an island and a greater area of land. See Brüel, *supra*, note 2, at 178.
32 According to Germany the right to overfly straits attached regardless of the fact that a strait may not be sufficiently wide to allow a strip of open seas through its middle. *Ibid.*, at 179.

Convention of 24 July 1923, which recognized the right to fly over the Turkish straits, be accepted as the general rule.[33]

After the Second Committee debated and amended the 'Bases de discussion', two subcommissions were appointed to continue discussions. Subcommission 1[34] was to deal with the juridical nature of territorial waters altogether, and Subcommission 2[35] was assigned to the technical aspect of calculating the breadth of territorial waters.[36]

During the long discussions that followed, Subcommission 2, unable to reach agreement on the main issue – a uniform limit for the breadth of the territorial sea – decided not to attach its report to the Report of the Second Committee, but rather to include it only as an appendix. As a result, the draft convention presented by the Second Committee reflected the work of Subcommission 1, but not that of Subcommission 2.

Subcommission 2's Report had examined most of the issues associated with straits. In it, the distinction between straits belonging to one State and straits belonging to two or more States was abandoned, and substituted by the distinction between those straits which serve as a thoroughfare between two parts of the high seas and straits which give access only to internal waters. As to the passage of warships, the report of Subcommission 2 was much more comprehensive than that of Subcommission 1. The latter, in the part of the draft convention dealing with the passage of warships through the territorial sea, did not venture further than to say that the littoral State "en règle générale

---

33 In response to Schücking's proposal, the Italian delegation countered that the question of overflight was distinct from freedom of navigation and should not be dealt with in the Conference. Sweden, Great Britain and Denmark concurred, and the Second Committee, by a vote of 16 to 8, decided not to consider the question of overflight in straits. *Ibid.*, at 188.
34 In Arts. 1–13 of the draft convention.
35 In Arts. 14–20 of the draft convention.
36 Articles 18 and 19 of the Subcommission 2 Report address the question of straits. Article 18 speaks of passage through straits "qui servent de passage entre deux parties de la haute mer." Article 19 proclaims freedom of passage for warships "entre deux parties de la haute mer qui forment les routes ordinaires pour la navigation internationale." Attached to Article 19 was an 'Observation' whose aim was to "assurer en temps de paix, dans toutes les circonstances, le passage de navires de commerce et des bâtiments de guerre dans les détroits entre deux parties de la haute mer qui forment des routes ordinaires pour la navigation internationale." Although this 'Observation' belonged in Subcommission 2 Report, it was added to Article 12, in the part of the draft convention prepared by Subcommission 1, with the right of passage for warships generally. Thus, this important phrase, which embodied a special rule concerning the passage of warships through straits, appeared only as an observation and not as part of the draft convention. Brüel, *supra*, note 2, at 191.

... n'empêchera pas le passage inoffensif des bâtiments de guerre étrangers."[37] Subcommission 2, on the other.hand, had explicitly recognized that straits were part of territorial waters, but had found it doubtful that the right of passage for warships existed in the territorial sea. In order to clarify the status of warships passing through straits, Article 19 of Subcommission 2's report had added a provision prohibiting the coastal State, "sous aucun prétexte", from preventing the passage of warships through straits serving international navigation between two parts of the high seas.[38] Thus, even though Subcommission 2 guaranteed the right of innocent passage for warships through straits, the provisions that appeared in the draft articles of the convention made only a vague reference to the passage of warships in the territorial sea generally.

In sum, the Hague Codification Conference proved a limited success. Although the work of the First Committee resulted in the adoption of several conventions,[39] the objectives of the Second and Third Committees were not fulfilled. With regard to territorial waters, the Conference was unable to adopt a convention as no agreement could be reached on the breadth of the territorial sea and a 'contiguous zone'. As for State responsibility, the Conference revealed complete disagreement on the issue.[40]

Despite the inability to agree on a convention on the territorial waters, there was some measure of progress on the question of straits. The debates of the Second Committee served to shed light on the many difficult legal questions relating to straits and on the differing State positions. The value of this contribution was clear to all concerned, including the President of the Second Committee who referred to the work of Subcommission 2 as "un matériel précieux pour la continuation des études en cette matière".[41] Surely this material would not go to waste. In it, various tests were offered as to what constituted an international strait, all of them based upon two criteria: a geographical and

---

37   *Ibid.*, at 186.
38   *Ibid.*, at 191.
39   Gidel, G., *Le Droit International Public de la mer*, III, 152, Sirey, Paris. (1934). As a result of the work of the First Committee, the Conference adopted the following international instruments: (*a*) a Convention concerning Certain Questions Relating to the Conflict of Nationality Laws; (*b*) a Protocol Relating to Military Obligations in Certain Cases of Double Nationality; (*c*) a Protocol Relating to Certain Cases of Statelessness; and (*d*) a Special Protocol concerning Statelessness.
40   On the various aspects of the 1930 Hague Codification Conference see generally Alvarez, A., *Les résultats de la Ire Conférence de codification de droit international* (1931). The views of the Conference were embodied in a Report submitted by the Second Committee to the Conference, see 24 *AJIL*, 234, Suppl. (1930).
41   Brüel, *supra*, note 2, at 193–194.

a functional one. The extent to which the strait was to be used by shipping, however, received little attention.[42] Also vague was the question of whether innocent passage through straits was an exceptional right or simply an application of the rule relating to territorial waters. As for the passage of warships, it was generally agreed that the right of innocent passage through straits applied in time both of war and peace. This right, however, would only be exceptional if the coastal State could exclude warships from its territorial waters; the latter was not clearly established. Brüel summarizes the legal status of warships at the time:

> [T]he right of passage of *merchant vessels* in international straits was certain, and *warships* were supposed to have the same rights – although not with the same degree of certainty, so that warships at any rate on principle have the right to pass through territorial waters *in straits* in time of peace, regardless of whether they may be taken to have the same right in the other parts of the territorial waters.[43]

Following the 1930 Hague Codification Conference the work of the Second Committee became the subject of many exhaustive scholarly studies. So contentious were the issues related to international straits that many of the problems that prevented the total success of the Hague Codification Conference in 1930 were to go unresolved for 50 years.

---

42 The draftsmanship ranged from mere 'use' of the strait to the strait being 'indispensable' for international communication. Between these extremes, however, no one test gained pre-eminence. See O'Connell, *supra*, note 18, at 305. See also Münch's work, *supra*, note 27; Brüel, *supra*, note 2, at 137.

43 Brüel, *supra*, note 2, at 202. See also O'Connell, *supra*, note 18, at 305.

CHAPTER 10

Modern Piracy off the Coast of Somalia: A Test-Bed for Old and New International Prevention and Repression Instruments

Maria Clelia Ciciriello* and Federica Mucci**,***

I   Foreword

In recent years, the traditional crime of piracy under customary international law has once again attracted the attention of the International Community with renewed emphasis, as a result of the events that have occurred in the Gulf of Aden and off the Somali coast. The situation is rather complex and transcends the aspects related to the prevention and repression of acts of piracy, which are, at one and the same time, the consequence and an aggravating circumstance of the internal instability of the Somali State, to the point of convincing the UN Security Council to tackle the matter in its resolutions adopted in accordance with Chapter VII of the UN Charter.

The legal praxis that is developing with regard to this issue tends to classify piracy, within the international legal system, as a 'simple' *delictum juris gentium*, while emphasizing the need to strengthen international cooperation for more effective prevention and repression of the phenomenon, considered by the domestic legal systems of States to be a predominantly economic crime.

II   Piracy as an Offence under the Law of Nations (*Juris Gentium*) and the Interest Protected by International Law

Piracy is included among those crimes which, due to their seriousness, disgust the civil conscience of all peoples, being an offence that is prejudicial to the internal public order of all States. Consequently, the international legal system

---

*   Former Professor of International Law at the Faculty of Law of Tor Vergata University in Rome. Professor Ciciriello passed away before this volume went into production.
**   Researcher and Aggregate Professor at the Faculty of Law of Tor Vergata University in Rome.
*** Maria Clelia Ciciriello is the author of sections I, II and III of this paper, while Federica Mucci is the author of Sections IV, V and VI.

authorizes all States to punish any individual who commits that crime by means of their judicial and administrative bodies, on the basis of universal jurisdiction.

The legal framework for the repression of piracy began to take shape in an historical period in which the protection of maritime trade and the safety of navigation represented a fundamental interest, such as to justify the extension of the authority recognized to States in the high seas for the purpose of legitimating any interference with maritime navigation. The exceptional degree of freedom recognized, in this case, to the domestic legal system of all the members of the International Community, considered *uti singuli*, in derogation from the general principle of abstaining from the exercise of material coercive power in free spaces, on foreign individuals and goods, can nevertheless be viewed as part of the power of the State, and of the coercive power of the State, and not as the exercise of a power delegated by the International Community.

When, therefore, the State intervenes to punish an individual guilty of acts of piracy, it is not acting as a body of the International Community but is simply exercising the freedom that the international system recognizes to all its subjects, in the presence of acts which, because of their cruelty, are liable to arouse the conscience of its members and are, therefore, such as to interfere with the undisturbed life of each territorial community. The harm caused by piracy, with respect to the security of maritime trade, is primarily to property; piracy, in fact, consists of any illegitimate acts of violence, detention or any acts of depredation, committed for private ends by the crew or the passengers of a private ship and directed, on the high seas, against another ship, or against persons or property on board such ship; of any act of voluntary participation in the operation of a ship with knowledge of facts making it a pirate ship; and, lastly, of any act of inciting or of intentionally facilitating any of the acts described above. An act of piracy is such, within the traditional meaning of the term, if committed *animo furandi, i.e.* with the intention to steal.[1]

When, after the abolition of privateering, under the Paris Declaration of 1856,[2] the crime of piracy, in its modern meaning, started to coalesce, to be

---

[1] On the notion of piracy and the related international regime see Articles 14–21 of the 1958 Geneva Convention on the High Seas, and Articles 100–107 of the 1982 Montego Bay Convention on the Law of the Sea; see on the subject, *inter alia*, the entry on piracy by M.C. Ciciriello, in *Enciclopedia giuridica Treccani* (*international law*), 1991.

[2] The practice of issuing letters of marque and reprisal to private citizens – whereby a government would authorize private individuals to perform violent acts at sea – was prohibited first by the Treaty of Utrecht of 1713, and then finally stopped by the Paris Declaration of 1856. The United States, however, were not among the signatories of the Paris Declaration, as a result of which they are not formally bound by its provisions, and Article 1, Section 8, of the

subsequently 'encoded' firstly by the 1958 Geneva Convention on the High Seas, followed, in 1982, by the Montego Bay Convention, the international legal system had not yet evolved enough to protect superior collective interests, such as, in particular, human rights, which characterize it so strongly today. The system put into place to oppose piracy could not at the time, nor can it today, draw from legal solutions that developed only at a later date for the protection of different interests, and which are characterized by their tendency to assert the obligation – and not the simple option – for States to ensure some form of reaction to the violation of the law.³

United States Constitution still lists issuing letters of marque and reprisal as among the powers of Congress, theoretically at least. However, it should be remembered that the USA issued declarations, after the Civil War and during the war against Spain (1898), undertaking to abide consistently by the terms of the 1856 Paris Declaration for the entire length of the hostilities, and the same Section 8 of Article 1 of the US Constitution empowers Congress to define and punish acts of piracy committed on the high seas and offences against the 'Law of the Nations'. The issue of marque and reprisal, unenforced for many years, was raised before the Congress in 2001 by Texas Congressman Ron Paul – also in connection with its hypothetical application outside maritime spaces – with the introduction of the 'Marque and Reprisal Act' and the 'Air Piracy Reprisal and Capture Act' (*cf. Air Piracy Reprisal and Capture Act of 2001 – Hon. Ron Paul, Extensions of Remarks – October 10, 2001*).

3   On the distinction between pirates as 'enemies of humanity', because they obstruct freedom on the seas and threaten private property, and any forbidden conduct criminally sanctionable under international law, more recently introduced and defined as true *crimina juris gentium*, see A. Cassese-P. Gaeta, *Le sfide attuali del diritto internazionale*, Bologna, 2008, at p. 174. The International Community has shown its desire to exclude impunity effectively only by reference to the latter, also by establishing international courts of law. On the definition of piracy as an offence under the law of nations (*delictum juris gentium*) which, although it does not give rise to international criminal liability for the perpetrator, nevertheless determines an important extension of the criminal jurisdiction of the State see, *inter alia*, G. Carella, "Il Tribunale penale per la ex Jugoslavia: bilancio di due anni di attività", in F. Lattanzi-E. Sciso (eds.), *Dai tribunali penali ad hoc ad una corte permanente, Atti del Convegno, Roma, 15–16 dicembre 1995*, Napoli, 1996, at pp. 479–480 and I. Caracciolo, *Dal diritto penale internazionale al diritto internazionale penale*, Napoli, 2000, pp. 164 ss. The obligation of reaction, in the case of serious violations of imperative provisions – which, at the current state of development of international law, all impose *erga omnes* obligations – is laid down in Article 41 of the Draft Articles of the International Law Commission on the responsibility of States of 2001, which, although it is not a treaty, has nevertheless also been confirmed by the rulings of the International Court of Justice (*cf.* the opinion on the legal consequences of the construction of a wall in the occupied Palestinian territories, in part., § 159). In consequence of the violation, in fact, the article provides for the 'obligation of non recognition' of the legitimacy of the situations created as a result of such serious violations. 'Non recognition', in this case – as clarified in the comment on the Draft – should not be understood just formally, but

The effectiveness of international actions of prevention and repression of piracy, therefore, continues to depend on individual and voluntary actions by States, based on a system whereby they have the power to intervene, but are not obliged to do so. In time, however, conventional international law has attempted to develop mechanisms of cooperation suited to translating the simple power of intervention granted to them into concrete commitments, although much remains to be done.[4] As a consequence of the evolution of international law, today, unlike in the past, States, when exercising their punitive functions on individuals guilty of piracy, must also take into account the international principles protecting human rights, which, in some cases, further condition the effective exercise of their repressive function.[5]

---

substantially as well, and therefore effectively, entailing the prohibition of any acts "which would imply such recognition" (see, on the matter, M.C. Ciciriello-F. Mucci, "L'effettività quale principio informatore del diritto internazionale", in *La Comunità internazionale*, 2009, pp. 571–588). Regarding the possible establishment of an International Court for judging individuals guilty of committing acts of piracy, despite the difficulties encountered by the national jurisdictions, such a proposal has not received significant support (see, on the matter, Chatham House, *Africa Program and International Law Conference Report, Piracy and Legal Issues: Reconciling Public and Private Interests*, 1 October 2009, available at <http://www.chathamhouse.org.uk/publications/papers/view/-/id/799/>, p. 10).

[4] The principal conventional instrument in this respect is the Convention for the Suppression of Unlawful Acts Against the Safety of Maritime Navigation, concluded in Rome on 10 March 1988 (the 'SUA Convention'), whose scope of application does not fully coincide with the definition of piracy as a *delictum juris gentium*. For example, acts of robbery that do not threaten the safety of a ship, and are committed by one ship against another ship, although qualifying as acts of piracy, do not fall within the scope of the SUA Convention, which, on the contrary, applies to cases of hijacking of a ship by persons already on board the ship, which, however, does not constitute an act of piracy [the negotiation initiative was taken by Italy, Austria and Egypt precisely after a case of 'internal' hijacking, the *Achille Lauro* case (*cf.* IMO Doc. PCUA 13/3, 3 February 1987, *Annex*, para. 2)]. However, the most common acts of piracy committed off the coast of Somalia generally entail both an attack by one ship against another and acts of violence aimed at gaining control of the ship. These acts fall within the scope of the SUA Convention. Recently, and with specific reference to the events occurring in the Gulf of Aden and, generally speaking, off the coast of Somalia, on 29 January 2009, the *Code of Conduct concerning the Repression of Piracy and Armed Robbery against Ships in the Western Indian Ocean and the Gulf of Aden* was adopted, on the initiative of the International Maritime Organisation ('IMO'), which, however, is not binding (see, on the matter, Chatham House, *Africa Program and International Law Conference Report, Piracy and Legal Issues*, cit., § 50 ss.; for more in-depth information on these conventional instruments see *infra*, Section V; for a recent comprehensive study on maritime piracy in international law see F. Graziani, *Il contrasto alla pirateria marrittima nel diritto internazionale*, Naples, 2009).

[5] On the matter see M.H. Passman, "Protections Afforded to Captured Pirates under the Law of War and International Law", in *Tulane Maritime Law Journal*, 2008, pp. 1 ss.; see also

III The Only Apparent Bending of Customary International Law of the Sea in the Somali Case

Piracy off the coast of the Horn of Africa has reached such serious levels in recent years as to drive the International Community to undertake concerted action aimed at re-establishing the security of navigation. The phenomenon exploded against the backdrop of the absolute instability in the effective government of Somalia, in the wake of the breakdown of the State and the difficult creation of new authorities. A crisis broke out in 1991, throwing the country into a state of profound turmoil and chaos, which then worsened over the following years, and the identification of the transitional government as a valid interlocutor for the International Community has sparked considerable controversy, to say the least, in consideration of its only partial control over the country.[6]

Against this backdrop, piracy, which had already appeared in the 1980s and increased in the following years, escalated to unprecedented levels in 2008.

M.C. Noto, "La repressione della piracy in Somalia: le misure coercitive del Consiglio di sicurezza e la competenza giurisdizionale degli Stati", in *La Comunità internazionale*, 2009, pp. 439 ss., at pp. 453 s.

[6] The admission by the transitional federal government that it had limited control of Somali territory is already implicit in the letter of 9 November 2007, addressed to the President of the UN Security Council, in which the government acknowledged its need for international assistance in tackling the problem of piracy (the letter is mentioned in resolution 1816 (2008)). Somalia has been without an effective central government since President Siad Barre was overthrown in 1991. The transitional federal government (TFG), established in 2004 and supported by the United Nations, effectively controlled only a limited part of the country. Originally based in Nairobi, Kenya, in 2005 it moved to the Somali town of Baidoa, but not to Mogadishu, the capital city, which was controlled by the Islamist insurgents. When the Union of Islamic Courts took power in 2006, piracy in Somalia all but disappeared, because the Union announced that it would punish those found guilty of piracy according to Sharia law. In December 2006, Ethiopian troops drove the Islamic forces out of Mogadishu and re-established the TFG, but the fighting and instability continued, even after the withdrawal of the Ethiopian troops from Somalia on 13 January 2009. The weak transitional government had to face the anti-Islamist warlords, the anti-government militias and the Islamist groups, several of which have ties to al-Qaeda. Moreover, the TFG had no control over the region of Puntland, which declared itself semi-autonomous in 1998 and served as the base for the acts of piracy, and Somaliland, which declared itself independent in 1991 (see, on the matter, J. Ho, "Piracy around the Horn of Africa", in *EchoGéo*, no. 10, 2009, available at <http://echogeo.revues.org/index11370.html>; about political developments in Somalia see the report by the Secretary-General of the United Nations of 8 January 2010, *UN Doc. S/2009/684*, published on the official UN website).

The phenomenon no longer involves simple individuals driven by the desire for making money, but includes Somali warlords, clan chiefs and corrupt officials, assuming such dimensions that the Security Council of the United Nations felt itself duty-bound to find a solution to the problem, although the intervention of the Security Council against piracy, as part of a broader set of measures adopted to tackle the situation in Somalia, viewed as a threat to peace, had already been called for in 2005 by the International Maritime Organisation (IMO).[7]

By the terms of resolution 1816, adopted on 2 June 2008, for the first time the Council authorized the States cooperating with the transitional Government of Somalia, for a period of six months, to enter the country's territorial waters and use 'all necessary means' to repress acts of piracy and armed robbery at sea. Despite the existence of a conceptual distinction

---

7 The IMO initiative on the Somali question dates back to 2005, when a resolution adopted by the IMO Assembly was transmitted to the Security Council, through the UN Secretary-General, voicing concern about the situation and calling on the Parties to take the necessary action to end the acts of piracy. This led, in March 2006, to a declaration by the Chairman of the SC which acknowledged, for the first time within the institutional context of the United Nations, the problems caused by piracy and the depredation of ships off the coast of Somalia, and encouraged the "Member States of the United Nations, whose naval vessels and military aircraft operate in international waters and airspace adjacent to the coast of Somalia, to be vigilant to any incident of piracy therein and to take appropriate action to protect merchant shipping, in particular the transportation of humanitarian aid, against any such act, in line with relevant international law". Later on, in 2007, the Secretaries-General of the IMO and of the World Food Program (WFP) wrote a letter to the Secretary-General of NATO proposing the formalization of a coordination mechanism between the three Organizations, to supply the naval operation centres of the region with prompt and systematic information on the details of the merchant ships that would be used to deliver humanitarian aid to Somalia, on behalf of the UN system, to facilitate the task of the naval forces operating in the region and responsible for providing assistance to the convoys. In June 2007, the IMO Council adopted a proposal by its Secretary-General Mitropoulos, requesting the Secretary-General of the United Nations, Ban Ki-moon, to bring to the attention of the SC the situation of piracy off the coast of Somalia, specifically calling on the Council to request the Somali TFG to authorize the entry into the country's territorial sea of the foreign ships and aircraft engaged in providing assistance to the merchant ships attacked by the pirates. In November 2007, the IMO Assembly adopted a resolution (A.1002(25)) requesting the TFG to transmit to the SC its authorization to the foreign ships and aircraft in government service to enter its territorial sea, in order to oppose the commission of acts of piracy and to notify its willingness to conclude the necessary agreements adequately to escort the ships employed by the WFP for the delivery of the humanitarian aid (*cf. High-level meeting in Djibouti adopts a Code of Conduct to repress acts of piracy and armed robbery against ships*, available at <http://www.imo.org/newsroom/mainframe.asp?topic_id=1773&doc_id=10933>).

between piracy as an offence under the law of nations (*juris gentium*), on the high seas, and so-called piracy 'by analogy', meaning a crime committed in the territorial waters of a State and, therefore, sanctioned not by the general international rules against piracy, but only by domestic law,[8] the intervention in the territorial waters of Somalia was made necessary in the light of the manner in which the pirates organized their attacks, using sophisticated instruments and high-seas ships capable of transporting small fast craft, which were then used to board ships on the high seas and hijack them into the territorial waters of Somalia.

Now, the ability to enter and intervene in territorial waters is only apparently a bending of the international law of the sea, which restricts universal jurisdiction over piracy to the high seas, in that the control and repression activities are exercised in the territorial waters on the basis of an agreement with the transitional Government, and the exceptional nature of the coercive measures adopted is clearly stated, being justified in the case in question, but without constituting a precedent for the evolution of customary international law.[9]

The following resolutions passed by the Security Council, which extended the timeframe of the intervention requested under Chapter VII of the UN Charter, demonstrate that the Council's intention was not to derogate from the principles of the law of the sea, but to ensure that the solution of the Somali problem be pursued through an overall approach. Resolution 1851 of 16 December 2008, which extended the scope of the previous mandate, also legitimizing military actions on the ground to free any hostages captured by the pirates and to destroy their logistical bases, is illuminating in this respect.

Moreover, a sort of 'safeguard clause' with respect to the traditional provisions of the law of the sea is contained in all the resolutions adopted by the Security Council on this matter and reiterated in resolution 1897 of 30 November 2009, through a general reference to the respect for international law, a clear declaration that the measures put into place should not

---

8   For the definition of piracy see Article 101 of the Montego Bay Convention of 1982 on the law of the sea; the SUA Convention of 1988 and the Code of Conduct adopted by the IMO Assembly in 2001 (*Code of Practice for the Investigation of the Crimes of Piracy and Armed Robbery Against Ships, Resolution A.922(22)*) are aimed at opposing all acts of violence at sea, including but not limited to piracy.

9   This is the meaning of the declarations of vote of several States, such as China, Indonesia and Vietnam (*cf.* UN Doc S/PV.5902, of 2 June 2008). The same concept is explicitly affirmed in para. 13 of Security Council Resolution 2077(2012).

be considered a relevant practice for the purpose of amending the existing customary law, being justified solely in the light of the agreement of the transitional Government, and, lastly, the confirmation of the necessary respect of the right of innocent passage for merchant ships through territorial waters.[10]

Finally, the situation of piracy off the Somali coast features the intervention of the Security Council, being viewed within the broader context of the threat to peace in the area, but as regards the application of the rules of the international law of the sea it is more of a confirmation of, rather than a derogation from, the traditional understanding of the applicable regime, even though at first it engendered doubts as to the full legitimacy of the transitional Government to give its agreement, on the basis of which the intervention by third parties in Somali territorial waters was justified.

The transitional period ended, as planned, on 20 August 2012, the election of the President on 10 September 2012 and the subsequent appointment of a Prime Minister and a Cabinet being formally considered as the completion of the transition in Somalia.[11] The Somali situation, though, is far from being fully stabilized; the Security Council in February 2012 expressed its concern that many of the deadlines for the completion of the task in the 'Roadmap to End the Transition' had been missed, thus delaying the full implementation of the Roadmap, and in March 2013 authorized the member States of the African Union to maintain the deployment of AMISOM until 28 February 2014, to carry out a series of tasks in coordination with the Federal Government of Somalia.[12] As regards the Somali authorization of third States' activities to prevent piracy in the Somali territorial waters specifically the Security Council "notes that the new Somali authorities assume the previous role of the Transitional Federal Government".[13]

---

10   The IMO had brought the matter to the attention of the Security Council as early as in 2005 (*cf. supra*, note 7). The first Security Council resolutions tackling the issue of piracy off the coast of Somalia are: 1816 of 2 June 2008, 1838 of 7 October 2008, 1846 of 2 December 2008, 1851 of 16 December 2008 and the above mentioned 1897 of 30 November 2009. Since the situation continued to escalate, with new incidents occurring almost every day during 2008, the IMO attempted to develop a joint effort with various organizations, with a view to achieving substantially three objectives: ensuring the protection of innocent ship crews, fishermen and passengers; ensuring the continuous flow of humanitarian aid to Somalia; and enabling international maritime traffic to continue passing through the Gulf of Aden.

11   See Security Council Resolution 2077(2012).

12   See respectively Security Council Resolutions 2036(2012) and 2093(2013).

13   See Security Council Resolution 2067(2012), para. 14.

IV Possible Solutions to the Complex Issues Relating to the Exercise of Jurisdiction: The 'Shiprider Agreements', Inspired by the Drug Trafficking Repression, and Other Conventional Law Instruments

In practical terms, one of the most obvious limits to the adequate repression of piracy was the difficulty States had in exercising their criminal jurisdiction against the pirates for a number of reasons. First of all, only a few domestic systems have actually passed legislation enabling the State to exercise universal jurisdiction, based on certain procedures, in particular with regard to acts of piracy. In fact, although the principle of universal jurisdiction is a provision of customary international law, the lack of specific provisions in this respect in the domestic legal systems of States prevents judges from effectively pursuing crime in the light of the principle of legality.[14]

Secondly, we must take into account the difficulties encountered by States required to act far away from their territorial sovereignty, relating, *inter alia*, to the temporary detention and transportation of persons suspected of acts of piracy. In fact, if the State with the closest legal links fails to take any steps, in several cases the exercise of the powers recognized to the other international subjects is unsuccessful; as shown in practice, there have been cases where persons suspected of acts of piracy have been first captured then released without being prosecuted.[15]

---

14 It is, in fact, the responsibility of the States – and, indeed, their duty, when necessary – to adopt suitable legislation enabling the exercise of universal jurisdiction (see, on the matter, I. Caracciolo, *supra*, note 3, at p. 82 and related references). This apparent contradiction between the provision of universal jurisdiction for serious offences, such as piracy, slave trafficking, war crimes, crimes against peace, crimes against humanity, genocide and torture, according to general international law, and the need for national legislation to enforce it is reflected in practice and also expressed in the 'Princeton Principles on Universal Jurisdiction', published in 2001, which refer, respectively, to "reliance on universal jurisdiction in the absence of national legislation" and to "the adoption of national legislation" (*cf. The Princeton Principles on Universal Jurisdiction*, Princeton, 2001, in particular, Principles 3 and 11, available at: <http://www.law.depaul.edu/centers_institutes/ihrli/downloads/Princeton%20Principles.pdf>).

15 Lacking any legal connections, it can be complex for a State to prosecute any piracy suspects for economic reasons but also, and above all, for issues related to the respect of human rights and the necessary prolonged detention on board its ships. There has been a case, in fact, of pirates captured by a Danish ship on 17 September 2008, which ended with the pirates being set free on a Somali beach without being prosecuted (because Somalia does not have an effective legal system). In other cases of capture by French ships, regular trials were held before the French courts because the victims were French citizens (see, on the matter, M.C. Noto, *supra*, note 5, at pp. 453 s.).

Faced with such situations, the Security Council has identified a possible solution based on the so-called 'shiprider agreements'. Referring to its previous resolution 1816, relating to actions by States in Somali territorial waters, in resolution 1851 the Council invites all States and regional organizations engaged in fighting piracy off the coast of Somalia to conclude special agreements or arrangements with countries willing to take custody of individuals suspected of piracy, allowing them to embark law enforcement officials, known as 'shipriders', from the latter countries to facilitate the investigation and prosecution of persons detained as a result of operations conducted under the resolutions of the Council on piracy and armed robbery at sea in the area.[16]

The non-binding Code of Conduct adopted on the initiative of the IMO on 29 January 2009 by the States of the region (Djibouti, Ethiopia, Kenya, Madagascar, Maldives, Seychelles, Somalia, Tanzania and Yemen), too, refers to so-called 'embarked officers'.[17] The instrument in question effectively coincides with the suggestion made in resolution 1851, and has already been successfully employed in the fight against drug trafficking (there are, in fact, agreements in this direction concluded by the United States and certain Caribbean countries[18]). Despite the differences in the specific solutions agreed

---

16   *Cf.*, to this effect, para. 3 of resolution 1851.
17   See Art. 7 of the Code of Conduct, annexed to IMO Doc. C 102/14, of 3 April 2009, available at <http://www.imo.org/OurWork/Security/PIU/Documents/DCoC%20English.pdf>.
18   The United States of America have concluded agreements to this effect with various Caribbean States, such as Jamaica, Suriname, Trinidad & Tobago, Barbados, St. Vincent and Grenadines, for illegal drug trafficking repression purposes (see, on the matter, M. Williams, "Caribbean Shiprider Agreements: Sunk by Banana Trade War?", in *The University of Miami Inter-American Law Review*, 2000, pp. 163–195.) Outside the Caribbean as well, based on a 'shiprider' agreement, which has recently been made permanent and not limited to the fight against drug trafficking, the United States and Canada have strengthened controls in the common maritime, river and lake border areas (*cf. US Department of Homeland Security Press Release* of 26 May 2009, available at: <http://www.dhs.gov/ynews/releases/pr_1243354565323.shtm>; the text of the *Framework Agreement on Integrated Cross-Border Maritime Law Enforcement Operations between the Government of the United States of America and the Government of Canada* is available at <http://www.dhs.gov/xlibrary/assets/shiprider_agreement.pdf>). Agreements such as the ones mentioned above, which are aimed at transcending the control limitations dictated by the general rules on jurisdiction in maritime areas and internal waters, represent a more effective and evolved form of cooperation compared to the previous arrangements, such as the agreement concluded in 1981 between the US and the UK, to be applied to the actions for fighting illegal drug trafficking in the Gulf of Mexico and the Caribbean Sea, and in other high-seas areas off the US Atlantic coast. This agreement, in fact, limited its scope to the high seas and assigned to the US authorities the power to hold private UK

to in each case, it nevertheless represents an operational means of overcoming the above-mentioned difficulties in exercising jurisdiction at sea, especially in the Somali situation, which also features uncertainties relating to the extension of its territorial waters.[19]

The presence on board of the law enforcement officers of one State embarked on the military ships of another contracting State legitimates the access to the territorial sea of the 'shiprider' regardless of any *ad hoc* authorizations, but it may also, depending on the model of the agreement, entail the absence of responsibility by the flag State of the ship that captured the pirates, should the latter be subjected to ill-treatment or serious violations of their fundamental rights in the State to which they are delivered, entailing the responsibility solely of the State to which the 'shipriders' belong. In the light of the Draft Articles on Responsibility of States for Internationally Wrongful Acts, the behaviour of an organ placed at the disposal of one State by another is considered to be the act of the former State if the organ acts exclusively in the exercise of elements of the governmental authority of the State at whose disposal it is placed.[20]

---

vessels, based on a model of cooperation which, although representing a significant derogation of customary international law, according to which jurisdiction on the high seas follows the ship's flag, is nevertheless less effective in incentivizing the development of synergies. A similar agreement, also against drug trafficking, was concluded between Italy and Spain in 1990 (on the matter of the above mentioned agreements, see U. Leanza, *Il diritto degli spazi internazionali. Parte prima, La tradizione*, Torino, 1999, pp. 176 ss.).

19 The uncertainty concerning the current extension of the territorial sea of Somalia is due to the fact that it has never repealed Law 37 of 10 September 1972, which sets the extension at 200 miles, despite having ratified the Montego Bay Convention of 1982, which sets at 12 miles the maximum extension of the territorial sea (*cf.*, on this matter, T. Treves, "Piracy, Law of the Sea and Use of Force: Developments off the Coast of Somalia", in *European Journal of International Law*, 2009, pp. 399–414 and M.C. Noto, *supra*, note 5).

20 In fact, in the case in question, the intervening military ship can be considered, if the agreement so provides, as an organ of the flag State, placed at the service of the State to which the shiprider belongs (M.C. Noto refers to this possible 'discharging' of responsibility by the flag State of the ship, see *ibid.*, at p. 455). However, it should be noted and, indeed, pointed out, that the exclusive responsibility of the State of the 'embarked officer' would, in this case, descend from a precise conventional choice, which would entail the full 'making available' of the ship, without this constituting an operation carried out under the direction of the 'embarked officer' as a joint operation. In this case, in fact, the international responsibility for any illegal actions would be joint, as illustrated by the practice mentioned by the International Law Commission, with respect to Article 6 of the Draft Articles on Responsibility of States for Internationally Wrongful Acts, where mention is made, *inter alia*, of a case of exercise in Liechtenstein by the Swiss police of

The 'special' conventional framework, aimed at overcoming the difficulties related to the exercise of jurisdiction, to which reference is made by the Security Council in its resolution 1851 also includes the agreement concluded, in the form of an exchange of notes, between the European Union and the Government of Kenya on 6 March 2009, relating to the conditions and procedures for transferring individuals suspected of acts of piracy, who are detained on board any European Union ships participating in the military operation in support of the Security Council resolutions; the European Union, in fact, is actively participating in the international effort aimed at fighting piracy off Somalia's coast, through EU NAVFOR Operation Atalanta.[21] Due to Kenya's

'delegated powers' which, in actual fact, consisted of the acceptance by Liechtenstein, on the basis of a convention, of the exercise of Swiss jurisdiction within its own territory and, therefore, entailed the responsibility of Switzerland for the acts carried out in the territory of Liechtenstein (cf. p. 44 of the Draft, which is published, complete with the relevant comments, on the official website of the Commission, <http://www.un.org/law/ilc/>). The shiprider agreements will hardly allow 'full availability'; the one recently confirmed between the United States and Canada for control of shared – marine and internal – waters, for example, despite the fact that, in principle, it sets out that the designated officials for cross-border maritime control should apply exclusively to the domestic laws of the host country in which they operate (Art. 3) is less univocal in identifying the State that is responsible for any damage caused by the operations regulated by the Agreement. It is provided, in fact, that any claims for damages will be handled according to the legislation in force in the State in which the claim is made, consistently with international law, and that, on request, the Parties will consult each other to solve any issues relating to reimbursement (Art. 11.2). Concerning the Agreement, see *supra*, note 18.

21 The EU adopted a common action on 10 November 2008 relating to the *Atalanta* military operation, for the purpose of contributing to the protection of the World Food Program ships, which were engaged in providing humanitarian relief to the displaced people of Somalia consistently with the mandate granted under resolution 1814 (2008) of the UN Security Council, and protecting vulnerable ships navigating off the coast of Somalia, besides dissuading, preventing and repressing acts of piracy and of armed robbery off the Somali coast, in accordance with the mandate set out in resolution 1816 (2008). Among other things, the mandate of the *Atalanta* mission, with regard to any judicial actions by the competent States, includes the authority to arrest, detain and transfer any persons who have committed, or are suspected of having committed, acts of piracy or armed robbery in the areas covered by the mission, and seizing the ships of any pirates or robbers, or the ships captured in connection with an act of piracy or armed robbery and which are under the control of the pirates, along with the goods found on board (Article 2, letter (e) of the Joint Action 2008/851/CFSP of the Council, published in the *Official Journal of the European Union L 301*, of 12 November 2008, pp. 33 ss.). The decision to carry out the *Atalanta* operation is a step forward, compared to the previous decision aimed at establishing, in Brussels, a coordination unit for supporting the surveillance and protection

willingness to prosecute any individuals suspected of acts of piracy,[22] the EU, in fact, thus intends to guarantee respect for the fundamental human rights of the individuals it delivers over to the Kenya authorities by setting out the conditions and procedures for their transfer and subsequent treatment after delivery.

The general principles and manner of treatment of the transferred persons are set out in detail in the appendix to the Agreement; besides their fundamental rights, such as not to be subjected to torture or other inhumane or degrading treatment, and the right to receive adequate accommodation and nutrition, as well as access to medical care, it also provides for the application of what can be called the general principles of law recognized by the civil Nations and applicable to the trial. Moreover, Article 3, letter h, of the agreement provides that Kenya shall not transfer the persons delivered into its custody to another State for the purpose of the investigations or prosecution without the prior consent in writing of EU NAVFOR. This provision tackles the issue of responsibility recognized, by the European Court of Human Rights at least to the States that deliver or extradite individuals to countries where respect for the fundamental rights and freedoms are not guaranteed.[23]

---

activities by several member States off the coast of Somalia (EU NAVCO, set up under Joint Action 2008/749/CFSP, published in the *Official Journal L 252*, of 20 September 2008). The acronym EU NAVFOR is used for the first time in the agreement between the European Union and the Republic of Djibouti, aimed at determining the charter of the 'forces under the command of the European Union', 'EU NAVFOR' (agreement published in the *Official Journal L 33*, of 3 February 2009).

[22] Kenya has concluded similar agreements with the US and UK (*cf.*, on this matter, T. Treves, *op. cit.*), the text of the agreement concluded with the European Union is published in the *Official Journal of the European Union L 79*, of 25 March 2009. In consideration of the exchange of letters between the EU and the Kenyan Government for perfecting the agreement on the transfer of persons suspected of piracy, the Italian Decree Law of 15 June 2009, no. 61 (published in the *Official Journal of the Italian Republic* no. 137 of 16 June 2009 and then converted into Law 100/2009, published in the *Official Journal* no. 177 of 1 August 2009), amended paragraph 4 of Article 5 of the previous Decree Law no. 209 of 2008 (converted into Law 12/2009) to restrict Italian jurisdiction to the offences of piracy committed against the State or Italian citizens and property in the area of the Atalanta mission.

[23] As already known, in the *Soering* case the Strasbourg Court ruled that the decision by a contracting State to extradite a prisoner can entail the responsibility of that State, based on the European Convention on Human Rights, if there is good reason to believe that the person, if extradited, would be exposed to the real risk of torture or otherwise suffer torture or other inhuman or degrading treatment in the State requesting the extradition. In the case in question, the inhuman treatment that the person might be subjected to, if extradited to the US, would consist in his or her detention on 'death row'. This does not entail

The two types of agreements mentioned above are obviously complementary, and the Security Council itself has shown appreciation for Kenya's commitment to prosecuting in its courts of law individuals suspected of piracy, with a view to further developing cooperation in the matter.[24] The Seychelles, Mauritius and Tanzania have also engaged in such cooperation and been commended by the Security Council for their efforts to prosecute suspected pirates in their national courts; assistance is being provided by the United Nations Office of Drugs and Crime (UNODC) and other international organizations and donors to support Somalia and other States in the region to take steps to prosecute, or incarcerate in a third State after prosecution elsewhere, pirates, including facilitators and financiers ashore, consistently with applicable international human rights law.[25]

v A Large-Scale International Action for Fighting Piracy, within a Regulatory Framework That Requires the Proper Application of the Instruments Already in Force

The deployment of forces by a number of States, followed by the establishment of the EU NAVFOR, emphasize the high level of attention and commitment by the International Community, at both global and regional levels. The international legal framework within which intervention by the States is taking place is very vast, because, as we have seen above, it draws from both the system of law enforcement and judicial cooperation in criminal matters, and international conventional instruments not specifically targeting piracy, concluded for the repression of violent acts at sea. Moreover, in the Somali situation, the instruments relating to the prevention and repression of international terrorism may also be used, if they apply.[26]

---

any judgment of responsibility by the Court against the third-party State requesting the extradition, but only a judgment as to the behaviour of the State granting the extradition, which can be considered responsible if the exposure of the individual to the forbidden treatment is the direct consequence of its action. In short, the Court disallowed the claim by the United Kingdom, according to which the Convention should not be interpreted so as to recognize the responsibility of a contracting State for any actions taking place outside its jurisdiction (*cf.* the decision of 7 July 1989 in case 14038/88, *Soering v. United Kingdom*).

24 *Cf.* Security Council Resolution 1897(2009).
25 *Cf.* Security Council Resolution 2077(2012).
26 On the connections between several of the Islamic groups fighting in Somalia and members of al-Qaeda see J. Ho, *op. cit.* and R. Bongiorni, "Somalia, il nuovo paradiso di al-Qaeda", in *IlSole24ore.com* of 18 June 2009.

In this vast legal framework, in the light of the obligation to cooperate in the repression of piracy, set out in Article 100 of the Montego Bay Convention on the law of the sea, several international conventional instruments play a key role, such as the above mentioned SUA Convention of 1988 and the 1979 Convention against the Taking of Hostages, which, by establishing the obligation to either prosecute or extradite, are aimed at ensuring the exercise of jurisdiction and, therefore, avoiding impunity. Fundamentally, attempts are under way, today, through the conclusion of implementation agreements, to improve the effectiveness of these conventional instruments, as also highlighted by the Security Council which, in its resolution 1897 (2009), calls upon the signatory States to the Convention of Rome of 1988 fully to implement their obligations thereunder, by means of effective enforcement measures.

In parallel to the considerations formulated in the Security Council resolutions relating to the effective implementation of the existing conventional instruments on the matter and the identification of new operational instruments, such as the shiprider agreements, the International Maritime Organisation (IMO) too has confirmed the importance of ensuring the increasingly effective implementation of the obligations under the conventions concluded in the past, in a resolution passed in December 2009.[27] Of course, while the interest of the Security Council is limited exclusively to the protection of certain public law interests, endangered by the situation of instability in Somalia, cause and consequence together of the piracy phenomenon, the IMO also takes into account the behaviour of the private parties that should be encouraged by the States, in view of both the effective prevention of and opposition to the phenomenon, and the protection of the private-sector interests harmed by the acts of piracy.[28]

---

27 The IMO has adopted resolutions aimed at improving the prevention and repression of piracy in general, wherever it occurs, since 1983 (*cf.* Resolutions A.545(13) of 17 November 1983, A.683(17) of 6 November 1991 and A.738(18) of 4 November 1993); it then adopted Resolutions A.1002(25), specifically aimed at tackling the situation of piracy off the coast of Somalia, and A.1025(26), adopting the *Code of Practice for the Investigation of the Crimes of Piracy and Armed Robbery against Ships*. Resolution A.1026(26), to which reference is made in the text, adopted on 2 December 2009, repeals – in that it replaces – the previous A.1002(25).

28 The Resolution was adopted also due to the awareness "of the serious safety and security concerns that the shipping industry and the seafaring community continue to have as a result of the attacks against ships sailing in waters off the coast of Somalia"; it expressed huge appreciation also for the efforts made by the industry organizations to raise awareness of the problem among its members, provide instructions and encourage them to report to the Organization (point 3(d)); lastly, it calls on the States also to introduce

The importance of these interests, which singles piracy out compared to other criminal activities directly considered as such internationally,[29] reveals the primarily 'patrimonial' nature, even today, of the interest harmed by the offence of piracy, which, in itself, is prejudicial to the domestic public order of States. The extraordinary international mobilization in the case of piracy off the coast of Somalia is not, in fact, motivated solely by the intention to repress piracy itself but, as declared by the Security Council, is related to the need to ensure the protection of more general rights which are threatened in this specific case.[30] Suffice it to mention, for example, the depredation of a cargo of humanitarian aid, destined to alleviate the sufferings of a population affected by a serious humanitarian emergency, or the depredation of any other maritime cargo – or the ransom money requested for the release of a ship and its cargo – which is then used to finance organized crime or even international terrorism.

The Somali case, therefore, highlights not just the obsolescence of the traditional legal definition of the crime of piracy, but also the connections this crime may have with the repression of more serious actions capable of harming the general interests recently protected by the international legal system. In view of the need to perfect the existing conventional instruments and enhance their effectiveness, it has become necessary to pursue a suitable balance between the protection of both public and private interests endangered by piracy.

---

       directives or prepare instructions, if necessary, for ships flying their flag attacked, or threatened with attack, taking into account, for this purpose, the recommendations and instructions already developed by the IMO and the industry (point 5(c)). Although no specific reference is made to the SUA Convention and to other conventional instruments, such as the Convention Against the Taking of Hostages, the actions required from the States by the Resolution reiterate – and in some cases circumstantiate – the principal obligations set out in such conventional instruments, such as the previously mentioned commitment to prosecute or extradite (point 5(l)) and the information and coordination obligations aimed at enhancing the effectiveness of the prevention actions.

29   Regarding the difference between the interests protected by the international rule authorizing any State to intervene on the high seas to oppose acts of piracy and any other *crimina juris gentium*, *cf. supra*, note 3.

30   On the assessment of piracy as an element that aggravates instability in Somalia, considered as a "threat to peace", see *supra*, Section III. For a global assessment of piracy today see R. Cazzola Hofmann, *I nuovi pirati. La pirateria del terzo millennio in Africa, Asia e America Latina*, Milano, 2009.

Such a balance of the endangered interests is at the base of the development of mixed public-private measures countering Somali-based piracy. In September 2011 the IMO adopted some circulars envisaging and regulating the possible use of privately contracted armed security personnel onboard ships in high risk areas – thus changing its previous policy, which was to recommend non-violent protection measures – recently complemented by a new set of circulars adopted in May 2012.[31] In line with this new policy, which has also been endorsed by the UN Security Council,[32] a number of States have adopted domestic laws regulating the presence and operation of armed groups on private ships – either military teams or private contractors – for purposes of defence in the event of pirate attacks. Actions of an Italian military team on board the private cargo ship *Enrica Lexie* and subsequent reactions by India are the object of the dispute between Italy and India relating to the exercise of Indian criminal jurisdiction over organs of a foreign State for facts occurring outside the territorial sea.[33]

---

31 See IMO Docs. MSC.1/Circ.1405/Rev.1, MSC.1/Circ.1406/Rev.1 and MSC.1/Circ.1408, adopted on 16 September 2012; MSC.1/Circ. 1443 and MSC.1/Circ.1405/Rev.2, adopted on 25 May 2012.

32 *Cf.* Security Council Resolution 2077(2012), "commending the effort of flag States for taking appropriate measures to permit vessels sailing under their flag transiting the High Risk Area to embark vessel protection detachments and privately contracted armed security personnel" and encouraging flag States and port States further to consider the development of safety and security measures onboard vessels "including, where applicable, developing regulations for the deployment of privately contracted armed security personnel onboard ships through a consultative process, including through the IMO" (see preamble and para. 30).

33 On the *Enrica Lexie* case see N. Ronzitti, "Gli sviluppi delle missioni antipirateria: il caso della Enrica Lexie", *addendum* to F. Caffio-N. Ronzitti, "La pirateria: che fare per sconfiggerla?", in *IAI Osservatorio di politica internazionale-Approfondimenti*, no. 44 – April 2012. Prof. Ronzitti thinks that two lessons are to be learned from the *Enrica Lexie* case. The first is that it is necessary to define precisely the command and control roles on board and that, in the case of a military team onboard, all measures to be adopted must be taken in common agreement by the master of the ship and the commanding officer of the military team, who will be in contact with the Ministry of Defence and have the overriding authority on board in the event of disagreement with the master (in the different circumstance of the presence on board of privately contracted armed security personnel, the aforementioned IMO circular MSC1/Circ.1405/Rev.2 chooses the opposite solution, requiring the provision of "a clear statement recognizing that at all times the Master remains in command and retains the overriding authority on board"). The second is that it is necessary to make sure that all other 'incidents at sea', and not just collision, are included in the scope of Art. 97 of the United Nations Convention on the Law of the Sea – to the effect that they are under the exclusive jurisdiction of the flag State – perhaps through a 'legislative' resolution of the UN Security Council.

VI   Closing Observations

The attitude of the International Community against the recurring episodes of piracy at sea in the last few years off the coast of Somalia is proof of a strongly felt intention to combat the phenomenon. States have reacted consistently and are actively engaged in encouraging and coordinating their efforts at international level, with a view to ensuring the increased effectiveness of preventive and repressive actions.

Results have been achieved, but experience has also clearly highlighted the weaknesses of the system. These largely depend on the difficulties encountered by States in ensuring the completion of repression operations conducted far from home and with virtually no real connection with it, in the exercise of a potentially universal jurisdiction, but effectively conditioned by domestic legislative and political decisions, despite the commitments already undertaken under the conventions. Regarding the full implementation of such conventional instruments, and the remedying of the shortcomings and failures they feature, there is a focus by the international organizations directly concerned, which address States and provide organizational support, directives, and proposals for operational solutions.

Overall, the regulatory framework that is being perfected to tackle this emergency does not stray from the initial definition of the offence of piracy as a crime deemed odious by all and which, therefore, can be prosecuted by all States in the common spaces, but which, however, is not seriously damaging of and prejudicial to a fundamental interest shared by the International Community. Ultimately, the Somali case has emphasized the need more effectively to repress piracy, being associated with the threat to peace, but at the same time it has highlighted how, to date, the International Community has believed in the adequacy and, indeed, the sufficiency of instruments focusing on the optional nature of the fight against piracy, which can facilitate, but which should not oblige, States to pursue such actions, accepting, as a rule, that failed international cooperation can effectively result in impunity, an effect that is considered and viewed as unacceptable for another set of international crimes committed by individuals, for which the International Criminal Court has been set up, with complementary powers to those of the States.

CHAPTER 11

Le régime des baies et des golfes dans la Mer Méditerranée

*Umberto Leanza**

1   Le régime des baies et des golfes : les baies au sens juridique

Dans le cadre des dispositions relatives à la détermination des lignes de base de la mer territoriale, celles qui concernent la fermeture des baies sont particulièrement importantes. Comme on le sait, la condition juridique des baies a toujours présenté un intérêt spécial, car les Etats côtiers ont toujours utilisé comme ligne de base de leur mer territoriale dans les baies, non pas un tracé qui suit toutes les sinuosités de la côte à marée basse, mais une ligne fictive tracée à l'entrée ou à l'intérieur de la baie, reliant entre eux les points qui se font face sur chacun des rives et considérant comme eaux intérieures, et non comme mer territoriale, toutes les eaux qui se trouvent en deçà de cette ligne.

La détermination de la ligne de base à l'intérieur des baies a toujours été très controversée. Les principaux problèmes concernent tout d'abord la disposition et l'étendue maximale de la ligne qui ferme la baie, et en second lieu, les droits que l'Etat côtier peut exercer à l'intérieur de cette ligne artificielle. La ligne de fermeture peut être utilisée dans le cas d'une baie, qui est définie comme une échancrure bien marquée dont la pénétration est telle, proportionnellement à la largeur de son ouverture qu'elle contient des eaux renfermées qui constituent plus qu'une simple inflexion de la côte. La ligne de fermeture, qui ne peut excéder vingt-quatre milles marins, peut être utilisée seulement si la superficie de la baie est égale ou supérieure à celle d'un demi-cercle ayant pour diamètre la ligne tirée à son ouverture.[1]

---

*   Professeur émérite de droit international à l'Université de Rome « Tor Vergata » ; Ancien chef du Service juridique du Ministère des affaires étrangères de l'Italie.

1   La littérature en matière de tracé des lignes de fermeture des baies est désormais très vaste. Parmi les auteurs qui se sont occupés spécifiquement du problème, voir : Mitchell P. Strohl, *The International Law of Bays* (The Hague : Nijhoff, 1963) ; Leo J. Bouchez, *The Regime of Bays in International Law* (Leyden : Sythoff, 1964) ; Torsten Gihl, « The Baseline of the Territorial Sea », *Scandinavian Studies in Law* (1967) : 119–133 ; Felicetta Lauria, *Il regime giuridico delle baie e dei golfi* (Napoli : Jovene, 1970) ; Andrea Gioia, « Tunisia's Claim over Adjacent Seas and the Doctrine of Historic Rights », *Syracuse Journal of International and Comparative Law* (1984) : 327–350 ; L.F.E. Goldie, « Historic Bays in International Law – An Impressionistic

L'exception prévue à propos de ces baies est la plus importante dérogation à la règle de la laisse de basse mer. La notion juridique de baie ne coïncide pas totalement avec la notion géographique, car, pour parler de baie selon le droit international, l'échancrure doit remplir certaines conditions ; appartenance à un seul Etat ; pénétration très accentuée à l'intérieur des terres ; et superficie égale ou supérieure à celle d'un demi-cercle ayant pour diamètre la ligne tracée entre les deux points extrêmes de l'entrée ; la distance entre les deux points extrêmes de basse mer, situés à l'entrée de la baie, n'excédant pas vingt-quatre milles. Quand toutes ces conditions se trouvent réunies, la ligne de délimitation intérieure de la mer territoriale est précisément celle qui relie les deux points extrêmes de basse mer, situés à l'entrée de la baie. Il faut observer en outre que l'absence de la dernière condition détermine le déplacement de la ligne de délimitation intérieure de la mer territoriale vers l'intérieur de la baie, jusqu'au point où la distance entre les deux côtes qui se font face ne dépasse plus la mesure indiquée.

En négligeant la pratique des Etats d'avant 1958, il faut rappeler qu'à cet égard la Convention de Genève constitue un important point de référence pour ce problème. Ce n'est pas par hasard que la Convention de Montego Bay de 1982 reprend sans le modifier le texte de la Convention de Genève. Ce dernier donne une définition des baies, fixe les critères de leur fermeture et précise que les dispositions qu'il contient ne s'appliquent pas aux baies dites historiques, ni dans le cas où le système des lignes de base droites est appliqué.[2]

Lorsque la distance entre les points d'entrée naturels de la baie n'excède pas vingt-quatre milles marins, la mer territoriale est mesurée à partir de la ligne qui relie ces points, et toutes les eaux de la baie sont considérées comme des eaux intérieures. Si au contraire la distance excède vingt-quatre milles marins, on peut tracer à l'intérieur de la baie une ligne droite de vingt-quatre milles toujours, de manière à conserver en tant qu'eaux intérieures la plus grande superficie de mer possible. Ce qui signifie avoir adopté comme longueur

---

Overview », *Syracuse Journal of International and Comparative Law* (1984) : 211–234 ; Dermott J. Devine, « Bays, Baselines, Passage and Pollution in South African Waters », *Comparative International Law Journal of Southern Africa* (1986) : 85–121 ; Robert D. Hodgson, *Towards an Objective Analysis of Special Circumstances : Bays, Rivers, Coastal and Ocean Archipelagos and Atolls* (Kingston : Law of the Sea Institute, 1972), Occasional Paper, n° 13 ; Gayl S. Westerman, *The Juridical Bay* (Oxford : Oxford University Press, 1987) ; Andrea Gioia, *Titoli storici e linee di base del mare territoriale* (Padova : Cedam, 1990) ; Merrill C. Clark, *Historic Bays and Waters* (New York : Oceana Pub., 1994).

2   Voir l'article 10 de la Convention de Montego Bay sur le droit de la mer de 1982.

maximum de la ligne droite de fermeture de la baie une mesure égale au double de l'étendue de la mer territoriale qui, comme on le sait a été fixée à douze milles par la Convention de Montego Bay.

Cette réglementation soulève de délicats problèmes. En faisant abstraction de celui de la définition des baies historiques, le problème le plus complexe semble être celui de la détermination des rapports existant entre le système des lignes de base droites, pour la longueur desquelles aucune limite n'est prévue, et les lignes de fermeture des baies, dont la longueur maximale ne devrait pas excéder vingt-quatre milles marins. En conséquence, en présence de toutes les conditions requises par la Convention de Montego Bay, l'Etat côtier pourra tracer ou une ligne de fermeture ou une ligne de base droite. Naturellement, les conséquences du choix de l'une ou l'autre des solutions seront différentes. Il faut rappeler que le régime des eaux à l'intérieur de la ligne de base présente de substantielles différences selon que la ligne a été tracée comme ligne de base droite ou comme ligne de fermeture d'une baie : dans le premier cas, un droit de passage inoffensif continuera à s'appliquer dans ces eaux ; alors que dans les baies juridiques et dans les baies historiques il n'existe pas un tel droit pour les navires des Etats étrangers.[3]

La différence entre une baie juridique et une simple inflexion de la côte dépend de la règle du demi-cercle. S'agissant d'une inflexion bien marquée, une baie doit avoir une superficie au moins égale à celle d'un demi-cercle ayant pour diamètre la ligne tirée en travers de l'entrée de l'inflexion. La baie juridique ne doit pas seulement satisfaire à la règle du demi-cercle mais doit de plus être fermée par une ligne n'excédant pas vingt-quatre milles marins. Les conditions pour pouvoir entrer dans la catégorie des baies juridiques peuvent donc être établies pratiquement dans chaque cas avec une précision mathématique. Le seul élément qui peut parfois rester incertain, c'est-à-dire la détermination précise des points d'entrée naturels de la baie, ne semble pas d'habitude avoir une importance essentielle aux fins de l'étendue de la limite des eaux intérieures. Les dispositions relatives aux profondes échancrures et autres situations géographiques comparables concernent, au contraire, des endroits où la côte est profondément échancrée et présente des indentations, ou il existe un chapelet d'îles le long de la côte à proximité immédiate de celle-ci. Dans ces circonstances, l'Etat côtier peut tracer des lignes de base droites qui relient des points appropriés. Même s'il est prévu que la trace d'un système de lignes de base droites ne peut s'écarter de manière appréciable de

---

3 Voir à ce propos l'article 8, par. 2 de la Convention de Montego Bay de 1982 sur le droit de la mer.

la direction générale de la côte, il n'y a aucune indication sur la longueur maximale des segments de la ligne de base droite.[4]

En présence de deux normes différentes qui devraient s'appliquer à deux situations différentes, il faut se demander quelle est la différence entre une baie et une profonde échancrure. Une profonde échancrure a *ipso facto* la forme d'une baie, étant donné qu'il est difficile d'imaginer de quelle façon elle pourrait ne pas satisfaire à la règle du demi-cercle et être en même temps profonde. Mais, alors qu'une profonde échancrure est donc toujours une baie, toutes les baies ne peuvent pas rentrer parmi les profondes échancrures, car en principe, une profonde échancrure devrait être constituée par une situation géographique où la dimension de la profondeur prime sur celle de la largeur. Cette distinction n'est pas dénuée de sens au niveau juridique. La ligne de fermeture des profondes échancrures peut excéder la longueur de vingt-quatre milles marins. Alors que l'on ne peut pas tracer de lignes de base droites le long d'une côte qui ne présente que quelques petites indentations, une ligne de fermeture peut être établie dans une petite indentation exceptionnellement présente à l'intérieur d'une côte profondément découpée dans son ensemble.

La Convention de Montego Bay ne considère cependant comme baies au sens juridique que les échancrures qui pénètrent profondément dans la côte, et plus précisément les échancrures dont la superficie, comme nous l'avons déjà dit, est au moins égale ou supérieure à celle d'un demi-cercle ayant pour diamètre la ligne d'entrée. On ne peut appliquer qu'à ce type de baies la règle des vingt-quatre milles. Il en ressort que les golfes, les baies et les autres échancrures qui présentent, par exemple, une longue ligne d'entrée mais ne présentent pas une aussi profonde pénétration dans la côte, ne sont pas soumis au régime spécial des baies et ne peuvent être fermés en vertu du régime général des lignes de base droites de la mer territoriale, que si les conditions requises pour l'application de la méthode des lignes de base droites sont réunies.

---

4 Comme l'on sait, le problème de la détermination de la longueur maximum des lignes de base droites a été évoqué par la Cour internationale de Justice dans l'arrêt de 1951 laquelle a abouti à la conclusion de l'inexistence d'une norme coutumière fixant cette limite à 10 milles marins, comme le prétendait le Royaume Uni (*Cour internationale de Justice Recueil* (1951) : 131). A cet égard, il est utile de rappeler que la proposition du Comité d'experts, interrogé à l'époque par François, de fixer la longueur maximum des lignes de base droites à 10 milles marins (*cf. International Law Commission Yearbook*, II (1953) : 78) fut par la suite critiquée tant par Garcia Amador (*International Law Commission Yearbook*, I (1955) : 197), que par Sandström (*International Law Commission Yearbook*, I (1954) : 66 et 68) ; alors que Fitzmaurice et Edmonds (*International Law Commission Yearbook*, I (1995) : 198 et 203) se déclarèrent favorables à l'opportunité de déterminer avec précision la longueur de chaque ligne de base droite.

En ce qui concerne les golfes, en particulier, jusqu'à une époque récente, on considérait que s'agissant d'échancrures très larges et peu profondes ils ne pouvaient pas poser de tels problèmes.

11   À suivre : les baies historiques et les baies vitales

Il faut noter au contraire une tendance récente, commune également à certains Etats riverains de la Méditerranée, à renfermer les eaux de certains golfes et à les considérer à tous les effets comme des eaux intérieures, malgré leur large ouverture et leur faible profondeur. Cette pratique nous amène à parler des baies dites historiques, qui méritent en effet une place à part. Il s'agit de baies souvent très larges reconnues comme faisant partie des eaux intérieures des Etats côtiers, en raison d'un usage établi depuis une époque reculée. Les espaces marins qui entrent dans cette catégorie étaient, en effet, contrôlés par les Etats côtiers déjà pendant une période précédant celle où naquit le principe de la liberté des mers. La territorialité au sens strict des baies historiques se pose donc actuellement comme une exception au principe de la liberté des mers, ce principe leur étant resté inapplicable.[5]

Les premières revendications officielles de souveraineté exclusive sur certaines baies ont été avancées au cours du siècle dernier, mais il s'agissait en vérité d'extensions concernant exclusivement la réserve de pêche en faveur des ressortissants de l'Etat côtier. C'est à cette fin particulière que ces prétentions furent introduites, et on comprend qu'elles furent motivées par référence à la pratique coutumière et au comportement historique. A ce propos il faut rappeler que le terme « baie historique » fut utilisé pour la première fois au cours d'une réunion de l'Institut de Droit international, en 1894, pour faire référence aux revendications avancées par les Etats à propos de certaines baies, qui trouvaient leur fondement dans un usage continu et séculaire du droit de pêche dans les eaux de la baie, usage qui justifiait, de manière exceptionnelle, la soustraction de cette zone de mer au libre usage de tous les Etats et sa soumission à la souveraineté de l'Etat côtier. La légitimité de ces comportements était conditionnée par l'existence de certains éléments de fait, tels que, outre l'usage

---

5   Pour la doctrine sur les baies historiques, se reporter entre autres à : Lauria, *Il regime giuridico delle baie e dei golfi* ; Donat Pharand, « Historic Waters in International Law, with Special Reference to the Arctic », *University of Toronto Law Journal* (1971) : 1–32 ; George N. Barrie, « Historical Bays », *Comparative and International Law Journal of Southern Africa* (1973) : 39–53 ; Giorgio Gaja, « Incoerenze sui golfi », *Rivista di diritto internazionale* (1986) : 68–86 ; Gioia, *Titoli storici e linee di base del mare territoriale* : 787.

dont nous avons parlé, l'exercice effectif de l'autorité et du contrôle par l'Etat côtier et le consentement des autres Etats.[6]

Certaines fermetures ont été justifiées par la qualification d'historique de la baie, mais sans apporter de preuves sérieuses à ce sujet. Les prétentions des Etats, visant à affirmer la territorialité de certaines baies, ont parfois donné lieu à des contestations des autres puissances maritimes et de leurs ressortissants. Dans le passé, quand des contestations de ce genre étaient soumises au jugement des tribunaux internationaux ou nationaux, elles étaient presque toujours rejetées, justement en raison de la position particulière et des intérêts particuliers qui étaient attribués à un Etat côtier à regard de certaines espaces maritimes. On reconnaissait que ces positions et intérêts devaient amener à considérer ces espaces comme étrangères et à part par rapport à la sphère d'irradiation habituelle de la souveraineté étatique sur les eaux côtières.[7]

Par la suite, la théorie élaborée pour les baies historiques a subi une certaine évolution,[8] à tel point qu'aujourd'hui une partie de la doctrine soutient que les prétentions avancées par un Etat à propos d'une baie peuvent se fonder sur certains éléments particuliers, comme les intérêts vitaux de cet Etat, sans qu'il soit nécessaire de prouver l'usage immémorial par l'Etat concerné. En effet, on parle toujours plus souvent, dans la pratique, et toujours en vue d'en justifier la fermeture, de baies vitales, en entendant souligner par cette notion les

---

6   Voir, *Annuaire de l'Institut de Droit international*, 12 (1892–1894) : 119–123. Les fermetures de baies les plus célèbres sont celles de la Baie de Pierre le Grand par l'Union Soviétique ; de différentes baies de très large ouverture dans la zone du Rio de la Plata par l'Argentine et l'Uruguay ; de toutes les baies gabonaises et guinéennes ; de la Baie d'Ungwana par le Kenya, déclarée baie historique par la proclamation présidentielle du 6 juin 1969 ; du Golfe de Panama par le Panama, déclaré baie historique par la loi du 30 janvier 1956, n° 9. En revanche, le Golfe de Californie n'a pas été revendiqué par le Mexique. En Méditerranée, les cas les plus célèbres sont ceux de la fermeture du Golfe de Syrte et du Golfe de Gabès, respectivement par la Libye et la Tunisie, ainsi que du Golfe de Tarente par l'Italie. La prétention de l'Egypte concernant la Baie d'El Arab, qui constitue un peu plus qu'une indentation de sa côte, est très contestée (*cf. Revista española de derecho internacional*, 7 (1951) : 91, ainsi que la carte publiée en *Revista española de derecho internacional*, 8 (1952) : 127 ; et l'est plus encore la prétention libyenne relative au Golfe de Syrte, dont l'ouverture est de 296 milles marins et la profondeur de 96 milles marins, qui a provoqué les incidents de 1981 et la crise de 1986, avec l'intervention militaire américaine.

7   *Cf. Second Court of Commissioners*, 1885, affaire *The Alabama c. Etats-Unis* : Baie de Chesapeake ; *Cour permanente d'arbitrage*, 1910, différend entre les *Etats-Unis* et la *Grande Bretagne* : zones de pêche de la côte de l'Atlantique Nord ; *Cour internationale de Justice*, 1951, différend entre la *Grande Bretagne* et la *Norvège* : zones de pêche.

8   L'origine de cette évolution remonte à l'opinion dissidente du juge Drago dans l'arbitrage sur les pêcheries de l'Atlantique Nord, du 7 septembre 1910.

exigences économiques et de défense qui sont à la base de cette fermeture. Mais il ne semble pas qu'actuellement cette notion de baie vitale soit reconnue par le droit international positif.

Il faut discerner parmi les innombrables revendications historiques, les prétentions limitées au problème de la pêche et celles que l'on ne peut réellement considérer comme s'y référant quand il s'agit de baies sur lesquelles donnent de nombreux Etats[9] et les discussions concernant les mers qui peuvent certainement être considérées comme intérieures, aux termes des normes générales du droit international.[10] Des véritables revendications du caractère historique de l'appartenance des golfes et des baies ont souvent été provoquées par des différends ou incidents en matière de pêche.[11]

La Convention de Montego Bay fait également référence au régime particulier des baies historiques lorsqu'elle affirme que les dispositions prescrites pour les baies ne s'appliquent pas aux baies dites historiques. Elle sauve de la sorte le régime des baies sur lesquelles l'Etat côtier peut revendiquer des droits exclusifs consolidés dans le temps grâce au consentement des autres Etats et, qu'en conséquence, il faut considérer comme eaux intérieures, quelles que soient leur superficie, leur ouverture et leur profondeur. Mais cela ne signifie cependant pas que l'on peut déterminer quelles sont et combien sont ces baies historiques et quelles caractéristiques elles doivent présenter. Donc, le problème désormais séculaire de la détermination des eaux, des baies historiques et de leurs caractéristiques reste ouvert.[12]

---

9   Il faut rappeler à ce propos le différend sur le Golfe de Fonseca, résolu par la Cour de justice d'Amérique centrale par les arrêts du 7 octobre 1916 et du 9 mars 1917 (*International Legal Reports*, 11 (1917) : 181 et 674). À la suite de ces arrêts, certains auteurs ont soutenu le caractère historique du Golfe de Fonseca. Dans ce sens, entre autres, voir : Carlos López Contreras, « El régimen internacional de la Bahía de Fonseca », en *Pacis artes – obra homenaje al profesor Julio D. González Campos* (Madrid : Universidad Autónoma de Madrid, Eurolex, 2005) : 361–390.

10 Ainsi ont été considéré par exemple la Mer d'Azov, le Zuiderzee, et par certains même le Golfe de Tunis. Sur le problème des mers soi-disant intérieures, voir Gioia, *Titoli storici e linee di base del mare territoriale*, 520.

11 On peut considérer à ce propos les revendications relatives au Varangerfjord, large de 30 milles, et au Vestfjord, large de 60 milles, pour la Norvège ; au Golfe de Gabès, large de 55 milles, pour la Tunisie ; au Beloe More et Karskoe More pour l'ex-Union Soviétique et à la Baie d'Hudson pour le Canada. Parmi les principales baies historiques, on peut rappeler celles de Chaleur, de Chesapeake, de Delaware, de Conception, de Miramichi, de Fonseca et de Cancale. Pour la pratique en la matière, *cf.* Gioia, *Titoli storici e linee di base del mare territoriale*, 521.

12 *Cf.* à ce propos l'article 10, par. 6 de la Convention de Montego Bay sur le droit de la mer. Il faut rappeler d'autre part que, intervenant devant la Commission du droit international des Nations Unies, Ago affirma que : « seule la prétention d'un Etat qui a reçu une certaine

Le régime juridique incertain des eaux historiques apparait donc, après la Troisième Conférence de Codification du droit de la mer, encore plus incertain, car la Convention de Montego Bay confirme l'existence des baies historiques, tout en évitant cependant d'en préciser le régime ; mais la Convention de Montego Bay ne dit rien à propos de l'existence et du régime des eaux historiques en général, pour lesquelles les Etats participants à la Troisième Conférence ont évité de prescrire toute résolution.[13]

Bien qu'il ne faille pas sous-évaluer les tentatives d'expliquer au niveau théorique le régime des eaux historiques, les prétentions relatives aux eaux historiques semblent toujours fondées sur des bases obscures et controversées. Il en ressort que ces prétentions doivent être appréciées individuellement, sans accorder trop d'importance aux raisons qui sont avancées pour les expliquer. Les Etats qui désirent déplacer vers le large la limite intérieure de leurs zones côtières sont certainement enclins à avancer des justifications plausibles, comme l'usage immémorial et les intérêts vitaux. Ces justifications, qui le plus souvent sont extra-juridiques, sont apportées pour persuader les autres Etats du caractère raisonnable des prétentions. Quelles que soient les justifications, la prétention doit être appréciée sur la base de l'attitude successive des autres Etats, qui peuvent l'accepter ou bien la contester. Toute prétention relative aux eaux historiques est étroitement liée à une situation particulière qui doit être analysée en fonction de ses caractéristiques spécifiques.[14]

---

reconnaissance des autres Etats pourra contribuer à la formation d'une règle du droit international. À cet égard il ne serait pas sage de demander aux Gouvernements de préciser leurs prétentions sur les eaux historiques et sur les baies historiques. Les Gouvernements pourraient être tentés, par prudence, de protéger leurs positions en avançant toutes leurs prétentions, y compris également certaines prétentions complètement nouvelles, de façon à ne pas compromettre leur position dans une future conférence. Des réponses de cette nature auraient peu de sens du point de vue du travail de la Commission. Il serait par conséquent opportun que le Secrétariat continuât son travail sur une base strictement scientifique, sans demander aucune donnée aux Gouvernements » (*cf. International Law Commission Yearbook*, I (1960) : 113).

13 Une vaste étude d'un intérêt doctrinal essentiel fut rédigée par le Secrétariat des Nations Unies (*cf. International Law Commission Yearbook, Juridical Regime of Historic Waters Including Historic Bays*, II (1962) : 1–54) et se conclut par la détermination de trois éléments déterminants, aux fins de l'existence d'un titre sur des eaux historiques, constitués par : l'exercice d'une autorité, la continuité de cet exercice et l'attitude des Etats tiers. Mais l'étude admet que l'affirmation d'un tel titre comportait inévitablement une importante marge d'appréciation subjective et qu'il serait par conséquent opportun d'instituer une procédure pour la solution obligatoire des différends.

14 On peut ajouter que les eaux et les baies historiques ne peuvent pas se déterminer *ipso jure*. Même si le facteur temps doit être considéré comme un élément important, une

La doctrine la plus récente trouve le vrai fondement de cette institution exceptionnelle, non seulement dans les titres historiques en général, mais également dans l'existence de caractéristiques physiques et géographiques particulières : la baie doit toujours être une échancrure et non pas une simple inflexion de la côte, et doit par conséquent être renfermée sur les côtes par deux *fauces terrae* bien déterminées ; auxquelles s'ajoute l'élément, que l'on peut considérer comme historique du point de vue chronologique, de l'exercice effectif dans le temps d'une exclusive souveraineté fonctionnelle et territoriale par un seul Etat, permettant de constater l'existence de liens d'intimité stables et continus entre les eaux de la baie et le territoire de l'Etat riverain, de façon à ce que la souveraineté de ce même Etat s'irradie sur ces eaux, avec la même intensité que dans les eaux intérieures. Le jugement dans cette matière exceptionnelle ne peut donc être exprimé qu'au cas par cas, après un examen profond et complet de ces éléments. Ces mêmes observations conduisent à apprécier avec une certaine perplexité les mesures unilatérales de fermeture de baies et de golfes qui ne semblent pas encore fondées sur des liens intimes consolidés dans le temps entre certains espaces marins et les terres émergées environnantes, surtout quand les eaux revendiquées comme eaux intérieures ont une largeur et une configuration difficilement assimilables à celles d'une baie, ce qui est probablement le cas, pour nous borner à la Méditerranée, des revendications de la Libye sur le Golfe de Syrte.

Il y a d'autre part des éléments de la pratique internationale dont il semble légitime de déduire que les eaux d'une baie, dont deux ou plusieurs Etats sont

---

prétention de nature historique pour produire des effets sur les Etats tiers doit être fondée sur une déclaration ou une manifestation de volonté officielle de l'Etat côtier, suivie par une publicité appropriée. Ce n'est qu'à partir du moment où est manifestée la volonté de l'Etat côtier d'exclure les autres Etats des activités qui s'exercent dans une zone marine donnée, que l'on peut apprécier l'issue d'une revendication historique. Il faut établir une sorte de date critique, étant donné que les Etats tiers ne peuvent pas être contraints d'accepter ou de contester une prétention qui reste secrète. L'exercice continu de certaines activités par l'Etat côtier peut aussi s'expliquer très simplement par sa proximité des eaux en question et non pas par sa volonté d'en exclure les autres Etats. En outre, les limites attribuées aux prétendus titres historiques doivent être exprimées en des termes clairs et explicites, afin de pouvoir déterminer dans quelle mesure elles repoussent vers le large l'extension des zones côtières, c'est-à-dire dans quelle mesure elles réduisent la haute mer. Pour un commentaire de la doctrine sur ce point, voir : Paolo Mengozzi, « La funzione ed i caratteri dell'acquiescenza e del riconoscimento nella pronuncia che ha reso la Camera speciale della Corte internazionale di giustizia nel Caso del Golfo del Maine », en Budislav Vukas, éd., *The Legal Regime of Enclosed and Semi-Enclosed Seas : The Particular Case of the Mediterranean* (Zagreb : Birotehnika, 1988) : 461–479.

riverains, pourraient être revendiquées par ces Etats comme eaux intérieures, lorsqu'ils sont d'accord en ce sens et lorsque des conditions déterminées existent. Les baies dont les côtes appartiennent à plusieurs Etats peuvent être aussi bien juridiques qu'historiques. Leur régime est compliqué par le fait que les eaux et les bénéfices qui en sont tirés sont partagés entre deux ou plusieurs Etats. Elles ne sont pas réglementées par la Convention de Montego Bay, sans doute parce que le meilleur moyen pour régler ces situations est constitué par des accords *ad hoc* entre tous les Etats côtiers. En l'absence d'accords, il semble qu'il faille nier un droit de tracer une ligne de fermeture à l'embouchure de la baie, surtout dans les cas où un ou plusieurs Etats riverains ne sont pas située à l'entrée de celle-ci.[15]

III   Les baies et les golfes de la Méditerranée : les baies européennes

De nombreux Etats, dont certains Etats de la Méditerranée, ont au cours de ces dernières années fermé des baies et des golfes, même de grande superficie et de médiocre profondeur, en déplaçant en conséquence vers le large la ligne de

---

15   La position prise par trois Etats riverains du Golfe de Fonseca est significative à cet égard : le Nicaragua, le Honduras et le Salvador, à l'occasion du différend provoqué par le Traité Bryan-Chamorro, entre le Nicaragua et les Etats-Unis d'Amérique et jugée par la Cour de justice d'Amérique centrale en 1916 et en 1917, dont nous avons déjà parlé. Une autre affaire célèbre, outre celle du Golfe de Fonseca, est constituée par l'affaire du Rio de la Plata revendiqué par l'Argentine et l'Uruguay (*cf. Declaración conjunta del Uruguay y la Republica Argentina sobre limite exterior del Rio de la Plata*, Montevideo, enero 30 de 1961, dans *Anuario uruguayo de derecho internacional* (1962) : 325). Pour la doctrine en la matière, voir : Lauria, *Il regime giuridico delle baie e dei golfi*, 109. En ce qui concerne tout particulièrement le Golfe de Fonseca, il faut rappeler que ce dernier fait actuellement l'objet d'un différend entre trois Etats riverains – El Salvador, Honduras et Nicaragua – devant la Cour internationale de Justice, pour la délimitation de la frontière terrestre et des espaces marins dans le golfe et pour la détermination du statut juridique des îles s'y trouvant (*cf. Affaire du différend frontalier terrestre, insulaire et maritime (El Salvador/ Honduras)*, ordonnances du 27 et du 29 mai 1987, *Cour internationale de Justice Recueil* (1987) : 15 et 176 ; requête d'intervention du Gouvernement du Nicaragua du 17 novembre 1989 ; ordonnance du 13 décembre 1989, *Cour internationale de Justice Recueil* (1989) : 129 ; ordonnance du 28 février 1990, *Cour internationale de Justice Recueil* (1990) : 3 ; *Application by Nicaragua for Permission to Intervene*, Judgement of 13 September 1990, *International Legal Materials*, 3 (1990) : 637). Pour la doctrine sur le différend en question, *cf.* Jamal Seifi, « Nicaragua Granted Permission to Intervene in the (El Salvador/Honduras) Land, Island and Maritime Frontier Case », *International Journal of Estuarine and Coastal Law*, 3 (1991) : 253–270.

base de la mer territoriale et en augmentant ainsi leurs possibilités de s'accaparer des ressources marines. Des fois, certaines de ces fermetures ont été justifiées par référence à la qualification de baies historiques, même sans fournir la preuve d'un usage continu et séculaire de l'exercice de l'autorité dans le cadre de la zone réclamée ni de la reconnaissance des Etats tiers. D'autres fois, pour en justifier la fermeture, la baie a été qualifiée de vitale pour l'Etat côtier, en mettant ainsi en évidence les exigences économiques ou de défense pour fonder cette fermeture, même si la notion de baie vitale ne semble pas encore être admise par le droit international.

Si l'érosion des zones de haute mer en faveur des zones soumises à des titres différents au contrôle et à la juridiction de l'Etat côtier peut ne pas avoir des graves effets dans des zones géographiques de type océanique, l'appréciation à donner semble différente, au moins sous certains aspects, quand le discours se déplace sur la Mer Méditerranée. Il est évident que toute limitation à la navigation est susceptible d'avoir des répercussions sur le trafic maritime qui s'y déroule.

Dans cette zone, donc, l'influence des décisions unilatérales sur les intérêts opposés de l'ensemble des autres Etats de la région est plus directe. Il convient de se demander si, dans la Méditerranée toute entière, quand on compare les intérêts de l'Etat côtier et les exigences de la situation globale de la région, il ne faut pas attribuer une plus grande importance à ces dernières. Nous ne voulons pas par la prétendre que dans tous les cas celles-ci devront primer sur les exigences de l'Etat côtier. Il ne faut pas négliger non plus les intérêts économiques impliqués et en particulier les intérêts stratégiques, en cas de présence de bases militaires. Cependant, il faudrait d'une part les considérer avec plus de pondération pour en éviter la surestimation; de l'autre, il serait souhaitable d'avoir moins souvent recours aux mesures unilatérales aux fins de l'appropriation d'autres zones marines.

Dans la Méditerranée, les configurations côtières sont diversifiées comme cela arrive pour les îles. Les côtes de la Croatie, de la Grèce continentale et de la Turquie continentale ne sont pas très différentes du *skjærgaard* norvégien, avec leurs nombreuses échancrures qui ont un lien étroit avec les îles côtières. Des baies de dimensions diverses constituent la caractéristique normale des côtes des Etats intéressés. Mais la majeure partie des baies significatives en termes de dimensions sont: le Golfe français du Lion, les Golfes italiens de Gènes, Tarente et Venise, les Golfes turcs d'Antalya et Iskenderun, le Golfe égyptien d'El-Arab, le Golfe de Syrte sur la côte libyenne et les Golfes tunisiens de Tunis et de Gabès. La largeur de ces baies à l'ouverture varie de vingt-cinq milles environ pour le Golfe d'Iskenderun à trois cent milles environ pour le Golfe de Syrte. Il convient d'examiner la façon dont les Etats de la Méditerranée, qui ont adopté le système des lignes de base droites, ont réglementé la fermeture des baies. Dans ce cas, les problèmes que nous venons de mettre en évidence apparaissent dans toute leur complexité. À cet égard, les législations de l'Espagne, de la France, de l'Italie, de l'ex-Yougoslavie et de l'Albanie sont emblématiques.

Pour commencer l'examen de la fermeture des baies par l'Espagne, il faut dire que la législation espagnole définit les lignes de base droites, qui sont utilisées également comme lignes de fermeture des baies dont l'ouverture n'excède pas vingt-quatre milles.[16] En fait, le long des côtes espagnoles de la Méditerranée, il existe de nombreux golfes, tels que Almería, Cartagena, San Jorge qui, bien que ne correspondant pas à la description des baies juridiques fournie par la Convention de Montego Bay, ont été fermés par de telles lignes de base.[17]

Le long des côtes françaises de la Méditerranée, il existe de nombreux golfes et baies, mais seuls certains d'entre eux semblent correspondre aux conditions requises par la Convention de Montego Bay.[18] À l'ouest et à l'est des segments principaux des lignes droites tracées par la législation française, on trouve respectivement deux ou trois segments qui ferment les baies. Dans ces cas, la règle conventionnelle selon laquelle la fermeture des baies et des golfes a été réalisée n'est cependant pas précisée. Et, par conséquent, le régime de la navigation dans les eaux de ces golfes est incertain, même s'il semble qu'un droit de passage inoffensif devrait être garanti à tous les navires étrangers. Le Golfe du Lion, qui est le plus étendu sur la côte continentale de la France, n'a pas été fermé. Une ligne de base droite a également été tracée autour des côtes à l'ouest et au sud-est de la Corse, où il existe une série de profondes échancrures. On a remarqué qu'alors que certains golfes sont des baies juridiques, comme par exemple les Golfes de Saint Florent et de Calvi en Corse, d'autres ne le sont pas, comme par exemple les Golfes d'Aigues Mortes et de Beauduc. Il y a des doutes

16   *Cf.* le décret royal espagnol du 5 août 1977, n° 2510/77 (*Boletin Official de l'Estado*, 30 september 1977, n° 234, 2108). Aux termes de l'article 2 est abrogé le décret du 5 mars 1976, n° 627, qui étendait la juridiction de l'Espagne, aux fins de la pêche, à 12 milles de la côte.

17   *Cf.* l'article 10 de la Convention de Montego Bay de 1982 sur le droit de la mer. Voir Victor L. Gutiérrez Castillo, « Le système espagnol de lignes de base », *Annuaire du droit de la mer*, 13 (2008) : 23–40.

18   Les lignes de fermeture des baies françaises furent établies pour la première fois par un décret du 9 juillet 1888. Par le décret du 19 octobre 1967 (*Journal Officiel*, 1 novembre 1967, n° 255, 10755), les lignes de base droites et les lignes de fermeture des baies ont été tracées simultanément. Voir aussi l'article 2 du décret du 18 octobre 1912, « Dispositions sur l'extension de la mer territoriale à des fins de neutralité et normes de neutralité de la République française », dans Ministero della Difesa Marina, SG 14, *Norme e disposizioni sul regime del mare, Francia* (Rome : 1989) : 8.

en particulier sur la qualification du Golfe d'Aigues Mortes comme baie juridique, mais sa ligne de fermeture n'augmente pas de manière significative les prétentions de la France relatives aux eaux intérieures et donc à la mer territoriale.[19]

La législation italienne de 1974, qui fixe à douze milles la largeur de la mer territoriale, soumit à la souveraineté de l'Etat des golfes, des anses et des baies, dont les côtes font partie du territoire de la République, quand la distance entre les points extrêmes de l'ouverture du golfe, de l'anse ou de la baie n'excède pas vingt-quatre milles marins. Si cette distance est supérieure, n'est soumise à la souveraineté de l'Etat que la portion du golfe, de l'anse ou de la baie, située en deçà de la ligne droite, tirée entre les deux points les plus forains distants l'un de l'autre par vingt-quatre milles marins.[20] Par la suite, de nombreux golfes et baies, qui ne peuvent être définis comme des baies juridiques, ont été fermées sur la base de la nouvelle réglementation adoptée en 1977 pour tracer les lignes de base droites. La nouvelle discipline italienne ne précise pas plus que la réglementation française sur la base de quelles dispositions de la Convention de Genève de 1958 sur la mer territoriale ont été tracés les différents segments de la ligne de base.[21] Certains ont cependant émis l'avis selon lequel toute la côte italienne du Cap Santa Maria de Leuca au Cap Spartivento pourrait être considérée comme une côte profondément découpée, à la lumière de la disposition de la Convention de Genève sur les lignes de base droites.[22] Parmi les grands golfes italiens celui de Gênes n'a pas été fermé ; tandis que la lagune de Venise a été fermée par une ligne de base droite. La seule baie historique expressément mentionnée dans la législation de 1977 est le Golfe de Tarente, dont nous traiterons un peu plus loin. La frontière maritime entre l'Italie et la Slovénie, dans le Golfe de Trieste, une baie dont les côtes appartiennent aux

---

19 Conformément au décret de 1967 cité à la note précédente, des lignes ont été tracées pour fermer les golfes d'Aigues-Mortes, Sainte Marie, Fos, Saint-Tropez, Fréjus, Juan et les baies de Sanary, Cavalaire, Pampelonne, Anges, Beaulieu et Roquebrune.

20 *Cf.* article 2 du code de la navigation, approuvé par le décret royal du 30 mars 1942, n° 327 (*Gazzetta Ufficiale della Repubblica Italiana*, 18 avril 1942, n° 93, 1), modifié par la loi du 14 aout 1974, n° 359 (*Gazzetta Ufficiale della Repubblica Italiana*, 2 aout 1974, n° 218, 5542).

21 *Cf.* le décret du Président de la République du 26 avril 1977, n° 816 (*Gazzetta Ufficiale della Repubblica Italiana*, 9 novembre 1977, n° 305, 8124). Le Golfe de Gioia Tauro et le Golfe de Sant'Eufemia ont été fermés respectivement par les segments : de Scilla Faro à Scoglio Foraneo à Capo Vaticano, et de Capo Cozzo à Foce Fiume Savuto (rive nord). En Sicile, le Golfe de Castellammare a été fermé par le segment qui va de Punta di Solanto à Punta Raisi ; alors qu'en Sardaigne, le Golfe de Cagliari a été fermée par le segment qui va d'Isolotti au sud à Isolotto San Macario.

22 *Cf.* l'article 7 de la Convention de Montego Bay de 1982 sur le droit de la mer.

deux Etats, a été établie par le Traité d'Osimo de 1975. Par une note annexée au Traité, l'Italie informa la Yougoslavie de son intention de tracer des lignes de base droites dans l'Adriatique. En effet, une ligne de base droite a été également établie autour de la partie italienne du Golfe de Trieste.[23]

Le cas du Golfe de Tarente, qui présente une ouverture de soixante milles marins, entre Punta Alice et Santa Maria di Leuca et au centre duquel l'ouverture est éloignée d'environ soixante trois milles du point le plus intérieur de la côte, est tout à fait différent. L'Italie a actuellement fermée le Golfe de Tarente par une ligne de base droite en le déclarant baie historique et en considérant ses eaux comme des eaux intérieures, assimilées en tout au territoire national au sens propre. Jusqu'à présent la prétention italienne n'a pas été sérieusement contestée. D'après ce que l'on sait, la fermeture du Golfe de Tarente par l'Italie n'a été contestée que par Malte qui continue à considérer comme lignes de base celles qui étaient reconnues avant 1977.[24] Le comportement des deux grandes puissances à cet égard est significatif. En 1982, l'Union Soviétique, à l'occasion d'une protestation italienne à la suite d'une double intrusion de sous-marins inconnus, mais probablement soviétiques, immergés dans le Golfe de Tarente, se contenta d'affirmer qu'aucun de ses sous-marins ne se trouvait dans cette zone, en se gardant bien de revendiquer la légitimité d'une éventuelle présence.[25] En 1986, les Etats-Unis se limitèrent à manifester une divergence d'opinions avec le Gouvernement italien, à propos de la conformité

---

23 Voir à cet égard les Annexes III et V au Traité d'Osimo du 10 novembre 1975 (mis en application en Italie par la loi du 14 mars 1977, dans *Gazzetta Ufficiale della Repubblica Italiana*, 21 mars 1977, n° 77), ainsi que le décret présidentiel n° 816/1977 déjà cité. Une carte officielle du Golfe de Trieste, où sont également tracées les lignes de base italiennes, est jointe à l'Échange de notes entre l'Italie et la Yougoslavie du 18 février 1983, relatif à une zone de pêche à l'intérieur du golfe (mis en application en Italie par la loi du 2 mai 1987, n° 107, *Gazzetta Ufficiale della Repubblica Italiana*, 25 mars 1987, n° 70). Cet accord, ainsi que les autres accords stipulés avec l'ex-Yougoslavie, concernent aujourd'hui les pays issus de la désagrégation de l'Etat yougoslave, en particulier la Slovénie et la Croatie.

24 Dans la note verbale du 24 juin 1981, le Gouvernement maltais déclarait « ne pas pouvoir reconnaître la prétention selon laquelle certaines zones situées au sud de la Sicile, que nous avons décrites en annexe, font partie du territoire italien et relèvent de la souveraineté italienne » (*cf.* Umberto Leanza et Luigi Sico, éds., *Mediterranean Continental Shelf* (Dobbs-Ferry (NY) : Oceana Pub., 1988) I, 520).

25 Le premier accident eut lieu le 24 janvier 1982, par l'intrusion d'un sous-marin à propulsion nucléaire de la catégorie Victor : les autorités militaires italiennes, âpres avoir découvert le sous-marin, se bornèrent à maintenir le contact avec lui jusqu'à sa sortie du golfe. Une seconde intrusion dans le golfe eut lieu le 30 août 1982, par un autre sous-marin non identifié, repère au cours d'un exercice OTAN, qui s'éloigna rapidement du golfe à la suite de la demande d'identification. Sur ce point, *cf.* Natalino Ronzitti, « Sommergibili non

au droit international des modalités par lesquelles avait été réalisée la fermeture du Golfe de Tarente, divergence d'opinion qui fut éliminée à la suite de colloques bilatéraux entre les parties. La doctrine la plus récente n'a pas seulement mis en évidence le rôle historique que le Golfe de Tarente a joué et joue toujours en tant que base pour les unités de la marine militaire italienne et donc, pour la défense du Pays, depuis son unification, mais s'est également chargée de démontrer la validité des titres historiques relatifs dans l'exclusivité en matière de navigation, de pêche, de droits douaniers, de cabotage et de servitudes militaires, qui remontent non seulement au Royaume d'Italie mais aussi au Royaume des Deux Siciles et à la Vice Royauté espagnole de Naples. Le caractère historique des titres revendiqués par l'Italie pour légitimer la fermeture du Golfe de Tarente semble être suffisamment démontré par la doctrine qui, pour soutenir l'exercice effectif du contrôle et de la juridiction, depuis des temps immémoriaux, par Tarente sur cette zone de mer, cite le Traité conclu entre Rome et Tarente en 302 avant Jésus-Christ, ainsi que les règlements et les statuts pour la pêche dans les mers de Tarente, dont la portée est synthétisée dans un avis du Conseil royal de Naples de 1857, selon lequel la pêche dans les mers de Tarente constitue un monopole dont l'origine remonte à 1463.[26]

En Croatie et en Monténégro, le système des lignes droites détermine la plupart des lignes de base des eaux territoriales. Pour le régime des baies qui se

---

identificati, pretese baie storiche e contromisure dello Stato costiero », *Rivista di diritto internazionale* (1983) : 44.

26   Il existe donc une grande différence entre le Golfe de Tarente et le Golfe de Syrte, qui bien souvent sont comparés à tort. Avant tout, les dimensions du Golfe de Tarente sont complètement différentes de celles de Syrte ; l'entrée de Syrte est large de 296 milles nautiques et sa profondeur maximum est de 96 milles nautiques, alors que l'entrée de Tarente est large de 60 milles et sa profondeur maximum est de 63 milles seulement. Il est licite de soutenir que Tarente rentre dans la catégorie des baies historiques car il existe des actes du Royaume d'Italie, du Royaume des deux Siciles et de la Vice Royauté espagnole affirmant l'exclusivité du pouvoir national dans le cadre du Golfe de Tarente à diverses fins : militaires, douanières, de pêche etc. ; alors qu'au contraire, dans le cas de la Syrte, comme nous l'avons également observé, on ne trouve aucun acte du Royaume libyen d'Idris ni des précédents souverains italiens et ottomans permettant de qualifier d'historique le Golfe de Syrte. *Cf.* à cet égard, l'avis du Conseil royal de Naples du 1er septembre 1857. Dans un sens favorable à la qualification du Golfe de Tarente comme baie historique, se reporter à Fabio Caffio, « Il Golfo di Taranto come baia storica », *Rivista marittima* (1986) : 73–80. Semblent en revanche d'un avis différent : Natalino Ronzitti, « New Criticism on the Gulf of Taranto Closing Line : A Restatement of a Different View », *Syracuse Journal of International and Comparative Law* (1986): 465–480 ; Gioia, *Titoli storici e linee di base del mare territoriale*, 676.

trouvent à l'intérieur de ces lignes de base droites, aucune règle spéciale n'est prévue. La définition des baies donnée par la législation yougoslave de 1965, plusieurs fois modifiée, rappelle la règle du demi-cercle, bien qu'aucune longueur maximale des lignes de fermeture ne soit déterminée. La même législation dispose que la ligne de base de la mer territoriale est donnée non seulement par la laisse de basse mer et par les lignes droites, mais également par les lignes qui ferment les entrées des baies.[27] Bien qu'une limite à l'étendue de ces lignes de fermeture ne soit pas fixée, on peut considérer qu'elles ne jouent un rôle autonome que dans la partie sud de la Croatie, après Zarubača, c'est-à-dire dans la partie où des lignes droites n'ont pas été établies. Dans cette zone il existe au moins une baie, celle qui se trouve à côté des Bouches de Kotor en Monténégro, à laquelle on pourrait appliquer la disposition de la loi qui prévoit les lignes de fermetures des baies.[28] On a successivement tracé un nouveau segment, qui est séparé des autres et qui relie les Caps de Platamoni et de Mendra ; mais la zone ainsi renfermée dans les eaux intérieures ne peut être considérée comme une baie juridique.[29]

L'Albanie a prévu un système de lignes de base droites qui couvre la majeure partie de ses côtes. Bien qu'il n'y ait pas de portions supérieures à vingt-quatre milles, certains des segments qui ferment des golfes ne sont pas conformes à la règle du demi-cercle ; alors que d'autres segments relient les embouchures de baies juridiques. On trouve en effet de basses éminences de roches calcaires qui forment des promontoires, qui alternent avec des baies peu profondes, remplies de matières alluviales, apportées par les fleuves Drin et Shkumbin. À l'exception d'une courte déviation vers l'Île de Sazan, la ligne de base passe d'un promontoire à un autre, en fermant deux baies juridiques et cinq baies qui ne satisfont pas aux conditions requises du demi-cercle. Cependant, en raison du fait que les baies ne pénètrent pas profondément dans la terre, les lignes de base n'ont qu'un faible effet sur la limite extérieure des eaux intérieures et donc également sur celui de la mer territoriale de l'Albanie. Le Golfe de Vlorë semble correspondre à la définition de baie donnée par la Convention de Montego Bay. Les points d'entrée naturelle de ce golfe restent d'autre part à

---

27   *Cf.* à cet égard les articles 3 et 11 de la loi yougoslave du 12 mai 1965 (*Journal officiel de la* RFSY, 12 mai 1965, n° 22, 1), plusieurs fois modifiée par la loi du 27 mars 1979 (*Journal officiel de la* RFSY, 30 mars 1979, n° 13, 409) et par la loi du 23 juillet 1987, n° 726 (*Journal officiel de la* RFSY, 25 juillet 1987, n° 49).

28   Stojan Novaković, « Boka Kotorska », *Jugoslovenska revija za međunarodno pravo*, 43 (1996) : 547–560.

29   Voir à ce sujet l'article 11, n° 3, (a) de la loi de 1965 telle que modifiée par la loi du 30 mars 1979 citée à la note précédente.

l'intérieur des lignes de base droites. Il faudrait en conclure que le régime de ses eaux correspond à celui qui est visé par la Convention de Montego Bay et que par conséquent, au moins théoriquement, le droit de passage inoffensif pour les navires des Etats tiers continue à s'appliquer.[30]

La législation grecque de 1936 dispose que l'étendue de la mer territoriale grecque doit être mesurée à partir de la côte et rien d'autre. Une disposition spécifique sur les baies est cependant contenue dans la loi précédente de 1913, qui toutefois n'est applicable qu'au passage et au séjour des navires marchands le long du littoral grec. Cette législation prévoit une bande côtière de dix milles qui, dans le cas des baies et des golfes dont l'ouverture n'excède pas la distance de vingt milles, est mesurée à partir d'une ligne de base droite tracée à travers la limite foraine du golfe ou de la baie. La limite maximale de la ligne de fermeture prévue par cette dernière législation, qui n'est pourtant applicable qu'en temps de guerre, est donc inférieure à celle qui est établie par les conventions de codification pour les baies juridiques.[31]

IV À suivre : les baies asiatiques et africaines

A la différence de la plupart des législations nationales des autres Etats de la Méditerranée, la législation turque sur la mer territoriale ne prévoit aucune règle spécifique pour la réglementation de la fermeture des baies ; alors que, comme on le sait, les côtes turques de la Méditerranée présentent de profondes échancrures et indentations, et seulement quelques îles au nord. Le long de la côte turque, on trouve quatre segments : trois de ceux-ci consistent en une ligne unique de fermeture de deux baies plus petites en Méditerranée, qui satisfont toutes deux à la condition requise du demi-cercle ; le quatrième, qui est le plus long et mesure environ vingt-trois milles marins ferme la Baie d'Iskenderun, qui est une baie juridique ; en revanche, la grande Baie d'Antalya n'a pas été fermée.[32]

---

30 Voir à cet égard l'article 8, par. 2 de la Convention de Montego Bay de 1982 sur le droit de la mer.

31 *Cf.* à ce sujet la loi du 17 septembre 1936, n° 230 (*Journal officiel grec*, 13 octobre 1936, n° 450, 2387) et l'article 1 de la loi précédente du 26 mars 1913 (*Journal officiel grec*, 11 avril 1913, n° 68, 203).

32 *Cf.* à cet égard la loi turque du 20 mai 1982, n° 2674 sur la mer territoriale (*Journal officiel turc*, 29 mai 1982, n° 17703, 1) ; ainsi que le décret du Conseil des Ministres n° 8/4742 (*Journal officiel turc*, 29 mai 1982, n° 17708, 1).

En ce qui concerne la Syrie, la définition de baie se trouve dans la législation de 1963, relative à la mer territoriale. Selon cette réglementation, le terme golfe doit être entendu comme une déviation visible dont la profondeur rejoint la largeur de son ouverture de façon à englober des eaux entourées par des terres. La déviation n'est pas considérée comme constituant un golfe, à moins que sa surface ne soit égale ou supérieure à la moitié d'un demi-cercle tracé à son ouverture. Selon cette législation, les lignes de base droites peuvent être tirées dans quatre cas différents. Dans les baies la ligne de base pour la mesure de la mer territoriale est donnée par des lignes qui doivent être tracées à l'embouchure du golfe de l'une à l'autre des deux extrémités. Bien que la règle du demi-cercle soit mentionnée, on ne trouve aucune indication sur la longueur maximale de la ligne de fermeture de la baie. Malgré cela, de graves problèmes ne se posent pas dans ce cas, car il semble que le long des côtes syriennes aucune baie ne corresponde à la définition donnée par la législation en question.[33]

En ce qui concerne l'Égypte, dans le cas des baies, la mer territoriale est mesurée par des lignes tirées d'une extrémité à l'autre le long de l'entrée de la baie, sans aucune restriction liée à la longueur de la ligne de fermeture ou à la règle du demi-cercle. Selon la législation égyptienne, le terme de baie comprend toute anse, échancrure, incurvation ou autre bras de mer ; tandis que les lignes de base sont tracées entre les extrémités de la terre situées à l'entrée de la baie. Cette définition de baie est très vague et n'exige pas que celle-ci ait une pénétration raisonnable dans la terre par rapport à sa largeur ; de plus, rien n'est dit sur l'étendue maximale de l'ouverture des baies.[34] Cette législation a été officiellement critiquée aussi bien par le Royaume-Uni que par les Etats-Unis, parce que, sur sa base, de nombreuses baies égyptiennes dans la Méditerranée pourraient être fermées.[35] Une question qui demeure non résolue concerne le Golfe d'El Arab dont l'embouchure est large d'environ quatre vingt quatorze milles et que l'Égypte avait déjà considéré comme étant totalement compris dans sa mer territoriale dans une réponse donnée en 1927 au

---

33   Cf. à ce sujet les articles 1 et 5 du décret législatif du 28 décembre 1963, n° 304 (*Journal officiel syrien*, 9 janvier 1964, n° 2, 383).

34   Cf. à cet égard les articles 1 et 6 du décret royal du 15 janvier 1951, modifié par la suite par le décret présidentiel du 17 février 1958, n° 180 (*Journal officiel égyptien*, 17 février 1958, n° 15/bis).

35   Cf. les notes diplomatiques du Royaume-Uni et des Etats-Unis émises respectivement le 23 mai et le 6 juin 1951 (*Revista española de derecho internacional* (1951) : 91 et 94). Une carte non officielle égyptienne publiée en 1955 trace cinq lignes droites qui ferment les golfes de Salun, Abu Hashaifa, El Arab, Pelusium et El Arish, ayant une longueur respective de 45, 31, 94, 49 et 65 milles.

Comité pour la codification de droit international. Mais on ne trouve pas de textes législatifs spécifiques à ce sujet et l'Egypte jusqu'à maintenant n'a pas officiellement revendiqué ce golfe comme zone d'eaux historiques. En faisant abstraction du problème du Golfe d'El Arab, aucune des baies égyptiennes ne répond à la condition du demi-cercle prévue par la Convention de Montego Bay. D'autre part, déjà en 1951, le Royaume-Uni avait émis l'avis selon lequel aucune baie historique ne serait située en Egypte.

En Libye, la législation qui concerne la délimitation des eaux territoriales, ne fournit aucune indication à propos des lignes de base.[36] En réalité, les côtes libyennes ne présentent pas d'échancrures appréciables, si l'on exclut le Golfe de Bumbah, près de Tobrouk, qui ne constitue certainement pas une baie juridique. Pourtant, en 1973, la Jamahiriya arabe libyenne a procédé à la fermeture du Golfe de la Grande Syrte, en englobant dans les eaux intérieures libyennes des espaces marins de vastes dimensions qui, selon le droit international en vigueur, relèvent de la mer libre.[37] De tels espaces soustraits à la mer internationale ont été ainsi soumis au régime de l'autorisation d'accès. Le Golfe de Syrte qui, de cette façon, depuis quelques années est au centre de nombreux et graves incidents internationaux, présente une ouverture d'environ trois-cent-sept milles marins, entre Bengazi et Misurata et, à partir du centre de cette ouverture, le golfe s'avance à l'intérieur jusqu'à environ cent trente-sept milles, en englobant ainsi une zone marine de vingt-deux mille milles carrées. La Libye déclara qu'elle considérait le Golfe de Syrte comme vital pour sa sécurité nationale, et qu'elle exerçait depuis plusieurs siècles des droits de souveraineté et de possession sur celui-ci. En conséquence, elle traça au niveau du parallèle 32°30' nord une ligne droite de base pour fermer ce golfe et les eaux en deçà de la ligne de fermeture furent considérées comme eaux intérieures, avec un régime juridique assimilé au territoire national. L'entrée des navires étrangers dans le golfe fut soumise à une autorisation administrative préalable. La doctrine ne s'est pas limitée à contester le titre sur la base duquel le Golfe de Syrte a été fermé, ce golfe n'étant ni une baie historique ni une baie vitale, en l'absence de prétentions précédentes allant dans ce sens, mais a également mis en

---

36   Cf. la loi libyenne du 18 février 1959, n° 2 sur l'étendue de la mer territoriale (*Journal officiel libyen*, 31 mars 1959, n° 7).

37   Cf. la note verbale libyenne du 10 octobre 1973, selon laquelle : « Le Golfe de Syrte, qui est situé dans le territoire de la République arabe de Libye, qui est entouré à l'est, au sud et à l'ouest par des frontières terrestres, et qui s'étend au large vers le nord, jusqu'à la latitude de 32° et 30', fait partie intégrante du territoire de la République arabe de Libye et se trouve soumis à sa complète souveraineté (...) » (Leanza et Sico, éds., *Mediterranean Continental Shelf*, 575).

évidence le fait que cette fermeture ne pourrait pas non plus être fondée sur l'application de la méthode des lignes de base droites qui n'est applicable que lorsque la côte est profondément découpée, alors que le Golfe de Syrte est situé sur une côte plate.[38] À la lumière de ce qui précède, on peut donc affirmer que la configuration géographique de Syrte ne rentre pas dans la définition de baie juridique donnée par les conventions de codification et qu'il n'aurait donc pas été possible non plus d'appliquer à ce golfe l'hypothèse d'une ligne de fermeture reculée de vingt-quatre milles.[39] De plus, comme on le sait, les raisons historiques invoquées par le Gouvernement libyen au moment de la fermeture de la baie en question ne semblaient pas résister à la lumière de la pratique internationale constante en la matière. D'autre part, les intérêts vitaux invoqués ne sont pas fondamentaux pour le droit international en vigueur, afin de rendre légitime ce comportement.

De nombreux Etats, tels que la France, la Grèce, l'Italie, Malte, le Royaume-Uni et même l'Union Soviétique, ont protesté contre la fermeture du Golfe de Syrte, en avançant des réserves de caractère juridique et politique. Dans le but déclaré de contester une telle prétention, les Etats-Unis, à leur tour, ont opposé à la Libye la prétention à la liberté de navigation et, à partir de 1981, ont exercé des manœuvrés navales dans le golfe et à proximité, provoquant divers incidents internationaux, avec un échange de feu entre les deux parties, au moins en deux occasions. Bien que les Etats Unis aient mis en doute la question d'un exercice long, pacifique et continu de la juridiction de la Libye sur le golfe, leur protestation matérielle vigoureuse pourrait avoir pour effet de renforcer les intérêts de sécurité de la prétention libyenne. Plus récemment, en 2005, l'Union européenne a présenté une démarche à la Lybie, en contestant la décision n° 37 qui établie la zone de protection de pêche de la Lybie.

En d'autres termes, la prétention avancée par la Libye semblerait analogue aux prétentions de zones de sécurité et aux restrictions imposées au passage des navires de guerre étranger à travers la mer territoriale par de nombreux autres Etats de Méditerranée. Comme nous l'avons déjà dit, la fermeture du

---

38   Pour la doctrine sur la fermeture du Golfe de Syrte et ses implications pour le droit international, se reporter à : Francesco Francioni, « The Gulf of Sirte Incident (United States v. Libya) and International Law », *Italian Yearbook of International Law* (1980/81) : 95–105 ; Gaja, « Incoerenze sui Golfi » ; John M. Spinnato, « Historic and Vital Bays : an Analysis of Libya's Claim to the Gulf of Sidra », *Ocean Development and International Law*, 13 (1983) : 65–80 ; Robert C. Haer, « The Gulf of Sidra », *San Diego Law Review* (1987) : 751 ; Gioia, *Titoli storici e linee di base del mare territoriale*, 646 ; Fabio Caffio, « Baie storiche a confronto », *Rivista marittima* (1991) : 79–90.

39   *Cf.* à ce sujet l'article 10 de la Convention de Montego Bay sur le droit de la mer, et notamment le paragraphe 5.

Golfe de Syrte constitue donc un fait illicite international, car le golfe, par les dimensions de son ouverture et par le rapport avec sa profondeur, ne rentre pas dans la réglementation générale des baies et des golfes. En outre, par l'absence de titres historiques, il ne rentre pas non plus dans l'exception constituée par les baies historiques : dans le cas de la Syrte, en effet, il n'existe aucun acte du Royaume libyen d'Idris ni des précédents souverains italiens et ottomans permettant de qualifier cette baie d'historique. On peut encore fortement douter qu'il puisse rentrer dans la catégorie des baies vitales ; et mis à part cela, il faut ajouter la constatation que cette catégorie n'est pas reconnue par le droit international général, ni par le droit conventionnel, comme l'une des exceptions à la réglementation des baies, qui permettrait une fermeture supérieure aux vingt-quatre milles, considérée comme licite au niveau international.[40] Donc, les prétentions avancées par le Gouvernement libyen, même le nouveau gouvernement après la chute de Gaddafi, à l'égard de l'entrée dans le Golfe de Syrte et de la soumission à un régime d'admission des navires étrangers qui se dirigent vers la côte, à partir de la ligne d'ouverture de la baie, ne peuvent pas non plus être considérées comme admissibles car, indépendamment du fait qu'aucune restriction n'est en vigueur dans le cadre du droit international à propos de l'entrée des navires étrangers en passage inoffensif dans les eaux territoriales des Etats côtiers, la ligne en question ne détermine pas la délimitation entre la mer territoriale et les eaux intérieures libyennes. Le régime de l'accès ainsi institué est la conséquence directe de la violation que la Libye a perpétrée en procédant à la fermeture de la baie par le tracé d'une ligne droite

---

40   Pour conclure sur ce point, il faut mettre en lumière le fait que les problèmes soulevés au niveau international par la fermeture de la Syrte par la Libye ont été ignorés par la Cour internationale de Justice dans sa décision de 1985 sur le cas Libye/Malte, non pas parce que cette fermeture pouvait être considérée comme licite par le droit international, mais plutôt en raison du manque d'influence que la ligne de fermeture exerçait sur la délimitation du plateau continental entre les deux Pays, que la Cour était chargée de définir. Cela s'explique facilement par la position géographique que l'île de Malte présente par rapport au Golfe de Syrte. Malte ne donne pas sur le Golfe de Syrte, mais sur la Tripolitaine, c'est-à-dire sur la portion de la côte libyenne qui précède, en allant de l'ouest vers l'est, le Golfe de Syrte. D'autre part, même si en aucun cas la Cour internationale de Justice n'aurait pu reconnaître la fermeture du golfe en question, il n'en reste pas moins que la déclaration d'un tribunal international désavouant la légitimité d'une telle fermeture aurait été extrêmement opportun. C'est probablement pour ne pas devoir prendre une position ouverte sur le problème que la Cour a très soigneusement évité de l'aborder (cf. *Plateau continental (Jamahiriya arabe libyenne/Malte), Arrêt, Cour internationale de Justice Recueil* (1985) : 13).

de base environ de trois cent milles nautiques et en déplaçant donc arbitrairement la limite intérieure de sa mer territoriale vers le large.[41]

Les côtes de la Tunisie sont généralement régulières si l'on excepte les Golfes de Tunis et de Gabès. Les lignes de fermeture de ces deux golfes ont été expressément déterminées par la législation tunisienne de 1973 sur la délimitation des eaux territoriales.[42] La ligne de fermeture du Golfe de Tunis, qui remplit la condition du demi-cercle, est constituée par trois segments qui relient les deux points d'entrée de Cap Sidi Ali Mekki à Cap Bon et deux petites îles situées à l'embouchure du golfe. Bien que la distance entre les deux caps entre lesquels est tirée la ligne de fermeture soit environ de trente-huit milles, on pourrait selon certains considérer comme ligne de fermeture celle qui part des deux îles, Plane et Zembra, situées à l'embouchure de la baie, et de la sorte la ligne ne mesurerait que vingt-trois milles. Le discours est différent pour le Golfe de Gabès qui présente une ligne de fermeture de quarante-six milles, tirée de la bouée de Samoun au Cap de Turgueness, et qui ne remplit pas la condition requise du demi-cercle, ne pouvant donc être qualifié comme une baie juridique. Aucune revendication officielle du Golfe de Gabès en tant que baie historique n'a été avancée par la Tunisie, si l'on excepte la carte présentée à la Cour internationale de Justice au cours du différend qui l'a opposée à la Libye pour la délimitation du plateau continental, dans laquelle le Golfe de Gabès était compris dans une vaste portion d'eaux appelée « zone des droits historiques de la Tunisie ». Il faut, par conséquent, considérer que la législation de 1973 n'a pas été abrogée par une carte produite au cours d'un différend international et que, donc, le Golfe de Gabès doit toujours être considéré comme

---

41 Par une note verbale suivante du 23 mai 1985, la Jamahiriya a étendu le régime de l'autorisation d'accès également à la mer territoriale libyenne pour les navires étrangers, en prévoyant simultanément une série de sanctions en cas de non respect de la réglementation établie, et violant de cette manière la règle du passage inoffensif que le droit international reconnaît même aux navires de guerre. Cette dernière limitation semble cependant avoir été révoquée par la suite, après avoir suscité de nombreuses protestations. Voir sur ce sujet, Umberto Leanza, « Ingresso e navigazione nel mare territoriale secondo una recente normativa libica », en *Nuovi Saggi di diritto del mare* (Torino : Giappichelli, 1988) : 27–40. Voir en outre la note de protestation présentée au Conseil de sécurité des Nations Unies par le Président de garde de la Communauté européenne au nom de ses Etats membres, le 27 mars 1986, dans UN Doc. S/PV. 2669, 32 et *British Yearbook of International Law* (1986) : 580.

42 *Cf.* à ce sujet l'article 2 de la loi du 2 août 1973, n° 49 (*Journal Officiel de la République tunisienne*, 31 juillet/3-7 août 1973, n° 29, 1189) et le décret d'application suivant du 3 novembre de la même année, n° 527 (*Journal Officiel de la République tunisienne*, 2–6 novembre 1973, n° 41, 1697).

compris dans un système de lignes de base droites, dont la légitimité internationale semble douteuse.[43]

L'Algérie a procédé à l'institution de son propre système de lignes de base en 1984, aux termes duquel six échancrures sont appelées baies : Oran, Arzew, Alger, Bejaïa, Skikda et Annaba, qui ne semblent pas toutes remplir les conditions requises par la Convention de Montego Bay pour être qualifiées de juridiques. D'autre part, le littoral algérien ne semble pas présenter une côte avec de profondes échancrures et le recours aux lignes de fermeture par l'Algérie a été réalisé avec beaucoup de modération, en se déplaçant même souvent à l'intérieur de la baie à fermer, au point que la ligne de fermeture la plus longue ne mesure que dix milles marins.[44]

En ce qui concerne enfin le Maroc, la législation de 1975 par laquelle ont été établies les lignes de fermeture des baies sur les côtes marocaines fixe le tracé des lignes droites sans définir la notion de baie. À cet égard, il faut pourtant rappeler que des dispositions précédentes prévoyaient déjà, bien que toujours sans définir la notion de baie, que dans celles-ci la ligne de base est donnée par une ligne droite, tracée à travers la baie dans la partie la plus proche de l'embouchure, au premier point où l'ouverture n'excède pas douze milles marins.[45]

v Conclusions

Il ressort d'une analyse de la pratique que les Etats riverains de la Méditerranée n'ont pas toujours tenu en juste considération la distinction entre les lignes droites de base et les lignes de fermeture des baies. En effet, il est rarement précisé sur lequel des deux critères a été fixée la ligne de base pour la mesure des eaux territoriales. Cela rend particulièrement lourd le rôle de l'interprète, avec pour conséquence que le régime de la navigation dans certaines zones

---

43 *Cf.* Cour internationale de Justice, *Mémoires, Plateau continental (Tunisie/Jamahiriya arabe libyenne)*, I, 122. Voir aussi les conclusions du juge Evensen dans son opinion dissidente (*Cour internationale de Justice Recueil* (1982) : 9). Pour la doctrine, *cf.* Gioia, « Tunisia's Claims over Adjacent Waters », 350.

44 On peut faire remonter le tracé des lignes de base dans les baies de l'Algérie au décret français du 9 juillet 1888. Pour le tracé des lignes de base actuellement en vigueur, *cf.* le décret du 4 août 1984, n° 84–181 (*Journal Officiel de la République algérienne*, 7 août 1984, 813).

45 *Cf.* à ce sujet le décret du 21 juillet 1975, n° 2-75-311 (*Bulletin Officiel*, 13 août 1975, n° 3276, 996), ainsi que le décret précédent du 30 juin 1962. Voir Said Ihraï, « Les lignes de base marocaines », *Annuaire du droit de la mer*, 13 (2008) : 111–120.

données de la Mer Méditerranée est incertain, ce qui est à l'origine de dangereuses situations de tension internationale. Parfois, l'utilisation de la ligne de fermeture des baies s'est aussi révélée problématique. Des lignes de fermeture qui ne remplissent pas les conditions du critère du demi-cercle ont été utilisées pour certaines baies par quelques Etats de la Méditerranée. Et en dépit de la condition posée de donner la publicité nécessaire aux cartes et aux listes des coordonnées des lignes de base et de déposer ces informations auprès du Secrétariat général des Nations Unies, peu d'Etats se sont acquittés de cette condition. En traçant les lignes droites, certains Etats méditerranéens ont prétendu considérer de larges baies le long de leurs côtes comme des baies historiques avec pour conséquence que les eaux renfermées par ces lignes sont considérées comme des eaux intérieures. Le fait que de telles prétentions doivent être considérées comme exceptionnelles, de façon à exclure l'application des principes généraux et conventionnels ainsi que des normes et règles sur le tracé des lignes droites, constitue un point controversé. La justification alléguée pour ces prétentions n'est pas seulement celle de l'historicité ; des considérations d'ordre historique, socio-économique, de sécurité, ou bien concernant le caractère vital de la baie sont également invoquées.[46] Le plus souvent, ces comportements ne semblent conciliables ni avec le droit conventionnel, ni avec le droit coutumier, en dépit de l'évolution continue de la pratique en la matière.

---

46   Le problème de savoir si les critères relatifs à la fermeture des baies doivent ou non être tirés des principes rappelés dans le texte pour l'appréciation des prétentions de l'Egypte, de l'Italie, de la Tunisie et de la Libye, dépend au moins en partie des préférences doctrinales. S'agissant essentiellement de principes classiques (typiquement européens) du droit international, qui sont similaires à des principes que l'on trouve dans la doctrine de l'occupation et dans la formation du droit coutumier, ils peuvent donner lieu à de grandes difficultés d'application dans le droit de la mer moderne, qui tend à l'équité et au développement, et tente de freiner la juridiction rampante.

CHAPTER 12

ITLOS's Approach to the Delimitation of the Continental Shelf beyond 200 Nautical Miles in the *Bangladesh/Myanmar* Case: Theoretical and Practical Difficulties

*Alex G. Oude Elferink**

1   Introduction

When I was asked to contribute to the *Liber Amicorum* for Budislav Vukas it took me little time to decide on a subject. Closely following the jurisprudence of the International Tribunal for the Law of the Sea (ITLOS), I always read his individual opinions with interest for the originality of their views and because of the insights they provided on the orders and judgments of the Tribunal. Just prior to my being invited to contribute, the Tribunal had rendered its judgment in the *Dispute concerning delimitation of the maritime boundary between Bangladesh and Myanmar in the Bay of Bengal (Bangladesh/Myanmar)*.[1] The judgment was a first in a number of respects. It was the first maritime delimitation case decided by the ITLOS, it was the first instance in which a court or tribunal had to deal with the relationship between the procedure for the establishment of the outer limits of the continental shelf beyond 200 nautical miles and its delimitation between neighboring states, and it was the first international case pronouncing on the principles and rules applicable to this delimitation. In the light of the judgment's breaking new ground, I regretted that Judge Vukas was no longer on the Tribunal to shed his light on it.[2]

---

*   Director of the Netherlands Institute for the Law of the Sea, School of Law, Utrecht University; Professor at the K.G. Jebsen Centre for the Law of the Sea, University of Tromsø.
1   Hereinafter *Bangladesh/Myanmar* case. Judgment of 14 March 2012 (available at <www.itlos.org/fileadmin/itlos/documents/cases/case_no_16/C16_Judgment_14_03_2012_rev.pdf>).
2   As his writings indicate, Budislav Vukas has critically assessed the delimitation provisions of the United Nations Convention on the law of the sea (1833 UNTS 396; hereinafter UNCLOS) and in this connection among others considered the relationship between the delimitation of the exclusive economic zone and the continental shelf (B. Vukas "The LOS Convention and Sea Boundary Delimitation" in B. Vukas *The Law of the Sea; Selected Writings* (Martinus Nijhoff Publishers, Leiden: 2004), pp. 83–109 at pp. 101–102). This was one of the matters at issue in the *Bangladesh/Myanmar* case (see judgment of 14 March 2012, paras. 463–476). UNCLOS provided the applicable law between Bangladesh and Myanmar.

As the title of my contribution indicates, I feel that there is room to question the approach of the Tribunal to the delimitation of the continental shelf beyond 200 nautical miles, but other parts of this fascinating judgment also deserve scholarly attention. To give one example, the Tribunal in delimiting the exclusive economic zone and continental shelf up to the 200-nautical-mile limit of Myanmar first determined that Bangladesh's St. Martin's Island should not be taken into account in establishing a provisional equidistance line.[3] In the second stage of determining this part of the maritime boundary the Court then adjusted this provisional equidistance line to account for the circumstance that the concavity of Bangladesh's coast made that the provisional equidistance line led to "a cut-off effect on that coast requiring an adjustment of that line".[4] The Tribunal in the second stage also revisited St. Martin's Island, posing the question whether the island should be considered a relevant circumstance requiring an adjustment of the provisional equidistance line.[5] Considering the Tribunal's treatment of St. Martin's Island at the first stage of the delimitation, which was concerned with the selection of basepoints for the provisional equidistance line and rejected using the island in this connection, it should not come as a surprise that St. Martin's Island was not considered a relevant circumstance requiring an adjustment of the provisional equidistance line.[6] The Tribunal's rejection of St. Martin's island as a basepoint for the provisional equidistance line was couched in language that rather was reminiscent of the jurisprudence in relation to the assessment of relevant circumstances than that concerning the selection of basepoints.[7]

To arrive at a boundary in the second stage of the delimitation process, the Tribunal adjusted its provisional equidistance line giving no weight to St. Martin's Island to a considerable extent, and to this effect used an azimuth of 215°. The Tribunal justified this approach by observing that:

> the direction of any plausible adjustment of the provisional equidistance line would not differ substantially from a geodetic line starting at an azimuth of 215°. A significant shift in the angle of that azimuth would

---

3 Judgment of 14 March 2012, para. 265.
4 *Ibid.*, para. 297.
5 *Ibid.*, para. 316.
6 For the conclusion of the Tribunal in this respect see *ibid.*, para. 319.
7 See *ibid.*, para. 265. To illustrate my point I refer the reader to the International Court of Justice's approach to the selection of basepoints and the assessment of islands as relevant circumstances in its judgment of 19 November 2012 in *Territorial and Maritime Dispute (Nicaragua v. Colombia)*, paras. 202–204 and 215–216.

result in cut-off effects on the projections from the coast of one Party or the other.[8]

This approach was criticized by a number of judges for the tenuous link between the provisional equidistance line and the azimuth of 215°.[9] Such criticism would have been avoided if the Tribunal had taken basepoints on St. Martin's Island into account in determining the provisional equidistance line and considered whether the island constituted a relevant circumstance requiring an adjustment of the provisional equidistance line at the second stage of the delimitation process. It can be noted that the provisional equidistance line giving full effect to St. Martin's Island is much closer to the maritime boundary established by the Tribunal than its provisional equidistance line.[10] A limited shift of the equidistance line giving full weight to St. Martin's Island at the second stage of the delimitation process, taking into account as relevant circumstances St. Martin's Island and the concavity of Bangladesh's coast, would have resulted in a boundary that would have been quite similar to the boundary established by the Tribunal. Such an approach would also seem to reflect better the requirement of balancing all relevant circumstances "rather than reliance on one to the exclusion of all others".[11]

The remainder of this contribution is concerned with the delimitation of the continental shelf beyond 200 nautical miles effected by the ITLOS in the *Bangladesh/Myanmar* case. The first section will set out the background to this part of the case. The next section will set out how the Tribunal dealt with the delimitation of the continental shelf beyond 200 nautical miles. The third section will evaluate the Tribunal's approach in the light of the existing case law on maritime delimitation. This, among others, concerns the link between the provisional delimitation method and the basis of entitlement to maritime

---

8 Judgment of 14 March 2012, para. 334.
9 See declaration of judge Wolfrum, pp. 3–5 and separate opinion of judge Cot, Section 5; see also joint declaration of judges Nelson, Chandrasekhara Rao and Cot.
10 For a comparison of these two equidistance lines and the maritime boundary along the azimuth of 215° see illustration map 2 appended to the separate opinion of judge Gao and sketch-map no. 9 included in the judgment of the Tribunal.
11 *North Sea continental shelf* cases (Federal Republic of Germany/Denmark; Federal Republic of Germany/Netherlands), judgment of 20 February 1969 [1969] *ICJ Reports*, para. 93; see also *Continental Shelf (Tunisia/Libyan Arab Jamahiriya)* (hereinafter *Tunisia/Libya*), judgment of 24 February 1982 [1982] *ICJ Reports*, paras. 107 and 133; *Continental Shelf (Libya/Malta)* (hereinafter *Libya/Malta*), judgment of 3 June 1985 [1985] *ICJ Reports*, paras. 73 and 79; *Maritime delimitation in the area between Greenland and Jan Mayen*, judgment of 14 June 1993 [1993] *ICJ Reports*, para. 92.

zones. The next section looks at an example from practice to illustrate the kind of difficulties the approach of the Tribunal might run into and explains how the states concerned in that case have addressed the delimitation. A final section before the conclusions will briefly discuss the literature on the delimitation of the continental shelf beyond 200 nautical miles and suggests possible alternatives to the Tribunal's approach.

11 Background to the Delimitation of the Continental Shelf beyond 200 Nautical Miles

Bangladesh and Myanmar are neighboring states in South East Asia and both are coastal states of the Bay of Bengal. Bangladesh and Myanmar, like Bangladesh's other neighbor, India, are parties to UNCLOS. Bangladesh's position in the north of the Bay of Bengal in between India and Myanmar might potentially considerably limit the extent of its maritime zones. Due to the configuration of the Bay of Bengal, the 200-nautical-mile limit of Bangladesh is located in its entirety within 200 nautical miles of the coasts of India and Myanmar. This situation acquires particular significance because the continental shelf of the coastal states in the Bay of Bengal extends beyond 200 nautical miles. Myanmar contended that Bangladesh was not entitled to a continental shelf beyond 200 nautical miles because recognizing such an entitlement would be against the rights Myanmar enjoyed automatically to a continental shelf within 200 nautical miles and Myanmar's right to extend its exclusive economic zone to the outer limit of 200 nautical miles under UNCLOS.[12] This position is based on the view that the continental shelf beyond 200 nautical mile of one coastal state cannot extend into the 200-nautical-mile zone of another coastal state. In the case of Bangladesh, this view would imply that it would be 'shelf locked' within the 200-nautical-mile zones of Myanmar and India. Myanmar during the proceedings before the ITLOS had also submitted that the delimitation of the exclusive economic zone and continental shelf within 200 nautical miles should lead to an outcome that would even preclude Bangladesh from extending its continental shelf to Bangladesh's 200-nautical-mile limit.[13]

---

12 See Judgment of 14 March 2012, para. 468; see also *ibid.*, para. 469.
13 *Ibid.*, para. 470; see also Note of the Permanent Mission of the Republic of the Union of Myanmar to the United Nations No. 146/032017 of 31 March 2011 (available at <www.un.org/Depts/los/clcs_new/submissions_files/bgd55_11/mmr_nv_un_001_08_04_2011.pdf>), p. 1.

Being parties to UNCLOS, Bangladesh and Myanmar had to comply with the obligations in relation to the establishment of the outer limit of the continental shelf beyond 200 nautical miles contained in the Convention's article 76. The Convention requires a coastal state to submit information on such outer limits within 10 years of the entry into force of the Convention for the state concerned to the Commission on the Limits of the Continental Shelf (CLCS).[14] The CLCS is charged with considering this information and issuing recommendations on the outer limits to the coastal state. Outer limits established by the coastal state on the basis of the recommendations of the Commission shall be final and binding.[15] Myanmar complied with its obligation to submit information to the CLCS on 16 December 2008.[16] The outer limits of Myanmar's continental shelf contained in the submission extend as far south as approximately 12.86° N and are between 240 and 400 nautical miles from the coast of Myanmar.[17] Bangladesh, in a reaction to Myanmar's submission, indicated that it did not give its consent to the consideration of the submission by the CLCS. Bangladesh among others indicated that it considered that Myanmar did not have a natural prolongation in the area concerned and that it had objected to the baselines Myanmar had employed in its submission.[18] In view of the Rules of Procedure of the CLCS, this reaction implied that the Commission would not be in a position to consider Myanmar's submission or to make recommendations on the establishment of outer limits by Myanmar.[19]

Bangladesh made a submission to the Commission in February 2011.[20] The outer limits of Bangladesh's continental shelf contained in the submission extend between approximately 380 and 390 nautical miles from Bangladesh's

---

14   LOS Convention, Annex II, article 4.
15   *Ibid.*, article 76(8).
16   The Executive summary of Myanmar's submission and other information related to the submission are available at <www.un.org/Depts/los/clcs_new/submissions_files/submission_mmr.htm>.
17   See Continental Shelf submission of Union of Myanmar; Executive Summary, pp. 6–7 for the coordinates of the points defining Myanmar's outer limit and their location.
18   Note verbale No. PMBNY-UNCLOS/2009 of the Permanent Mission of Bangladesh to the United Nations to the Secretary General of the United Nations of 23 July 2009.
19   *Rules of Procedure of the Commission on the Limits of the Continental Shelf* (CLCS/40/Rev.1 of 17 April 2008), Annex I, para. 5(a).
20   The Executive summary of Bangladesh's submission and other information related to the submission are available at <www.un.org/Depts/los/clcs_new/submissions_files/submission_bgd_55_2011.htm>.

coast.[21] The entire continental shelf of Bangladesh as defined in its submission overlapped with the continental shelf of Myanmar's submission.[22] Myanmar's continental shelf as defined in its submission extends some 130 nautical miles south beyond the outer limit submitted by Bangladesh. Myanmar reacted in a similar fashion to its neighbor's submission as Bangladesh had done previously in relation to Myanmar's submission. Myanmar observed that it considered that Bangladesh's continental shelf did not extend beyond the 200-nautical-mile limit and "*a fortiori*, [not] beyond this limit",[23] and also protested the straight baselines established by Bangladesh.[24] Like Bangladesh, Myanmar invoked the Rules of Procedure of the CLCS to block the consideration of the submission of its neighbor.[25]

Bangladesh had brought the case against Myanmar in respect of the delimitation of their maritime zones in October 2009. Originally this concerned arbitration in accordance with Annex VII of UNCLOS, but in December 2009 the case was transferred to the ITLOS. In order to arrive at the last part of its judgment concerned with the delimitation of the continental shelf beyond 200 nautical miles, the Tribunal had to address a number of other issues. First, the delimitation method it would adopt within 200 nautical miles might result in a boundary that would exclude a delimitation beyond that distance. As was observed above, this was the position of Myanmar. The Tribunal held otherwise. The boundary it determined within 200 nautical miles made a boundary beyond that distance a possibility. Next, the Tribunal had to consider Myanmar's argument that Bangladesh was 'shelf locked'. The Tribunal rejected Myanmar's arguments in this respect, and thus opened the way for the delimitation of the continental shelf beyond 200 nautical miles. However, before addressing this matter it still had to consider Bangladesh's contention that the natural prolongation of Myanmar did not extend beyond 200 nautical miles. The Tribunal found that this primarily concerned an issue of interpretation of the

---

21 See Submission by the People's Republic of Bangladesh; Executive Summary, p. 11 and Annex for the coordinates of the points defining Bangladesh's outer limit and their location.

22 Most of the continental shelf as defined in Bangladesh's submission moreover overlaps with India's continental shelf. The delimitation of this continental shelf between Bangladesh and India currently is the subject of an arbitration under Annex VII of UNCLOS.

23 Note verbale No. 146/03 20 17 of the Permanent Mission of the Republic of the Union of Myanmar to the United Nations, New York to the Secretary General of the United Nations of 31 March 2011, p. 1.

24 *Ibid.*, p. 2.

25 *Ibid.*

Convention, and that it could deal with this matter. The Tribunal concluded that Myanmar, like Bangladesh, had entitlements to the continental shelf that, as their submissions to the CLCS indicated, "overlap in the area in dispute in this case".[26]

The Tribunal also had to consider the implications of the absence of recommendations of the CLCS on the outer limits of the continental shelf of Bangladesh and Myanmar. In this connection, two aspects need to be distinguished. On the one hand, the question was whether the Tribunal could proceed with a delimitation in the absence of recommendations of the Commission. For a number of reasons, the Tribunal concluded that it could exercise its jurisdiction in this case.[27] On the other hand, the absence of certainty concerning the location of the outer limits of the continental shelf might impact on the delimitation process itself. This uncertainty would not allow the precise determination of the extent of the entitlement of each party. This determination might be relevant in assessing the equitableness of the outcome of the delimitation process. This issue is further considered below.

III   The Tribunal's Approach to the Delimitation of the Continental Shelf beyond 200 Nautical Miles

The case between Bangladesh and Myanmar constituted the first instance in which an international court or tribunal had to determine the boundary of the continental shelf beyond 200 nautical miles. However, this matter had been previously considered in an arbitration between two of Canada's provinces, Nova Scotia and Newfoundland and Labrador.[28] The arbitral tribunal first concluded that article 6 of the Convention on the continental shelf,[29] to which Canada was a party, remained part of the applicable law. It observed that the

---

26   Judgment of 14 March 2012, para. 449. The discussion on this point is contained in *ibid.*, paras. 395–449.

27   See *ibid.*, paras. 360–394.

28   The arbitral tribunal had been instructed to "apply the principles of international law governing maritime boundary delimitation, with such modifications as the circumstances require" (Arbitration between Newfoundland and Labrador and Nova Scotia concerning portions of the limits of their offshore areas as defined in the *Canada-Nova Scotia Offshore Petroleum Resources Accord Implementation Act* and the *Canada-Newfoundland Atlantic Accord Implementation Act* (hereinafter *Newfoundland and Labrador and Nova Scotia* arbitration); Award of the tribunal in the second phase of 26 March 2002 (available at <www.cnsopb.ns.ca/sites/default/files/pdfs/phaseii_award_english.pdf>), para. 2.1).

29   Adopted on 29 April 1958 (499 *UNTS* 311).

case law of the International Court of Justice (ICJ) did not suggest that parties to the Convention were no longer bound by it due to developments in the law relating to the continental shelf or its delimitation. Article 6 also applied to the area extending to the outer edge of the continental margin beyond 200 nautical miles.[30] Article 6 provides that the boundary of the continental shelf is the equidistance line unless another boundary is justified by special circumstances. The tribunal subsequently considered the relationship between article 6 and article 83 of UNCLOS.[31] The tribunal observed that the "apparent contrast between these two articles has been attenuated by subsequent practice and the case law".[32] In the case law, it generally had "become normal to begin by considering the equidistance line and possible adjustments, and to adopt some other method of delimitation only if the circumstances justify it".[33] The applicability of the Convention on the continental shelf in the case before the arbitral tribunal reinforced the case for beginning with an equidistance line, but that in any case provided the starting point in most cases, including under article 83 of UNCLOS.[34]

The ITLOS in the *Bangladesh/Myanmar* case took a similar approach to the tribunal in the *Newfoundland and Labrador and Nova Scotia* arbitration. It first of all noted that article 83 of UNCLOS does not contain any limitation as to the area to which it is applicable: "Article 83 applies equally to the delimitation of the continental shelf both within and beyond 200 [nautical miles]".[35] The Tribunal then immediately turned to the delimitation method to be employed. At the outset the Tribunal seems to suggest that its selection of this specific method was based on the case before it, observing that:

> the delimitation method to be employed in *the present case* for the continental shelf beyond 200 nautical miles should not differ from that within 200 [nautical miles].[36]

This implied that the equidistance/relevant circumstances method, which had been applied by the Tribunal to the delimitation within 200 nautical miles and which is the standard approach within that distance, continued to be

---

30   *Newfoundland and Labrador and Nova Scotia* arbitration; Award of the tribunal in the second phase of 26 March 2002, para. 2.25.
31   Ibid., paras. 2.26 and following.
32   Ibid., para. 2.27.
33   Ibid., para. 2.28
34   Ibid.
35   Judgment of 14 March 2012, para. 454.
36   Ibid., para. 455; emphasis provided.

applicable.[37] This focus on the specific case is also present in the Tribunal's explanation of the effects of the equidistance/relevant circumstances method. The Tribunal noted that:

> this method can, *and does in this case*, permit resolution also beyond 200 nm of the problem of the cut-off effect that can be created by an equidistance line where the coast of one party is markedly concave...[38]

Thus, the Tribunal might seem to be suggesting that in other cases the equidistance/relevant circumstances method might not be able to achieve an equitable solution.

The Tribunal, however, also posited that the equidistance/relevant circumstances rule had general application because of its relationship to the basis of entitlement to maritime zones:

> This method is rooted in the recognition that sovereignty over the land territory is the basis for the sovereign rights and jurisdiction of the coastal State with respect to both the exclusive economic zone and the continental shelf. This should be distinguished from the question of the object and extent of those rights, be it the nature of the areas to which those rights apply or the maximum seaward limits specified in articles 57 and 76 of the Convention.[39]

After its pronouncement on the applicable method, the Tribunal proceeded with a reexamination of the relevant circumstances.[40] Interestingly, the Tribunal refrained from describing the provisional equidistance line, which would normally be the first step in the application of the equidistance/relevant circumstances method. Presumably, this may be explained by the fact that the provisional equidistance line beyond 200 nautical miles is governed by the same basepoints as the Tribunal had selected for drawing a provisional equidistance line within that distance.[41]

In the area beyond 200 nautical miles, the Tribunal had to consider only two relevant circumstances that had been presented by Bangladesh. Myanmar,

---

37 *Ibid.*
38 *Ibid.*; emphasis provided.
39 *Ibid.*
40 *Ibid.*, para. 456.
41 As a matter of fact one of these basepoints, μ4 on the coast of Myanmar, seems to become relevant only beyond 200 nautical miles (see *ibid.*, sketch-maps nos. 4 and 5).

which considered that Bangladesh's continental shelf did not extend beyond 200 nautical miles, had refrained from presenting any argument in this respect.[42] Bangladesh had argued that the concavity of its coast constituted a relevant circumstance within 200 nautical miles and submitted that this continued to be the case beyond that distance. It submitted that the cut-off effect caused by applying an equidistance line became even more pronounced further off shore.[43] The second relevant circumstance Bangladesh invoked in the area beyond 200 nautical miles was based on the different basis of entitlement of the shelf within and beyond the 200-nautical-mile limit. Beyond that limit distance did not have a role to play in determining entitlement, which instead was only based on geological and geomorphological continuity with the land territory. As Myanmar at best only had a geomorphological continuity, Bangladesh considered that it had "the most natural prolongation into the Bay of Bengal".[44]

Bangladesh's 'most natural' prolongation theory was summarily dismissed by the Tribunal. The Tribunal had already determined that the natural prolongation of both parties extended beyond 200 nautical miles and that they had overlapping entitlement. There thus could be no question of Bangladesh getting a larger part of the disputed area for having "the most natural prolongation".[45] The Tribunal agreed with Bangladesh that the concavity of Bangladesh's coast had a continued effect beyond the 200-nautical-mile limit. As a consequence, it held that the equidistance line could be adjusted by the same method that had been used to delimit the exclusive economic zone and the continental shelf within 200 nautical miles.[46]

Having determined the extent of the adjustment of the provisional equidistance line on the basis of an assessment of the relevant circumstances, the Tribunal applied the disproportionality test to check whether the line it had arrived at within and beyond 200 nautical miles led to an equitable result. This required the Tribunal to determine the relevant maritime area and the lengths of the relevant coasts of the parties. The Tribunal held that the relevant maritime area "is that resulting from the projections of the relevant coasts of the Parties".[47] The relevant area established by the Tribunal is bounded by a number of straight lines along the coasts of the parties, a

---

42   Ibid., para. 459.
43   Ibid., para. 458.
44   Ibid., para. 457.
45   Ibid., para. 460.
46   Ibid., paras. 461–462.
47   Ibid., para. 489.

meridian running from the land boundary between Bangladesh and India and a parallel running west from Cape Negrais on the coast of Myanmar.[48] This relevant area includes most of the continental shelf area that is beyond an equidistance line with India but does not include those parts of the continental shelf of Bangladesh and Myanmar that are beyond that equidistance line. Thus most of the overlapping continental shelf entitlements beyond 200 nautical miles are excluded from the relevant area.[49] The Tribunal represented the relevant coasts of Bangladesh and Myanmar by a number of straight lines.[50] The ratio between the relevant coasts was approximately 1:1.42 in favor of Myanmar, and the relevant area was divided in a ratio of 1:1.54 in favor of Myanmar. The Tribunal found that this did not lead to "any significant disproportion in the allocation of maritime areas...relative to the respective coastal lengths" and that there was no need for shifting of the Tribunal's provisional line to arrive at an equitable result.[51]

IV The Tribunal's Approach Evaluated

The Tribunal's starting point to the delimitation of the continental shelf beyond 200 nautical miles – that article 83 of UNCLOS does not make a distinction between areas within and beyond that distance – might at first sight seem to be beyond reproach. The wording of the article indeed seems neutral in this respect. However, article 83 is silent on the content of the substantive rules to be applied, but only refers to the result that is to be achieved. The attainment of this result may require applying different principles and rules within and beyond 200 nautical miles. Article 83 in itself thus does not provide support for applying the same delimitation methodology within and beyond 200 nautical miles.

As was set out above, the Tribunal's reasoning for choosing to apply the same delimitation methodology within and beyond 200 nautical miles is based on two strands: it hints at its appropriateness in the case at hand and this method being grounded in the basis of coastal state rights over maritime zones. As to the first strand, it is of course required that the method found to be applicable, can actually be applied to the case at hand, but this does little to substantiate its appropriateness in general. In view of the criticisms that the

---

48   For the Tribunal's definition of the area and its depiction see *ibid.*, paras. 489–496 and sketch-map no. 8.
49   See also below text after note 69.
50   See *ibid.*, paras. 202, 204 and 498.
51   *Ibid.*, paras. 498–499.

case law in the past has placed too much emphasis on the individual case and too little on the predictability and general applicability of the law,[52] this argument rather might have received less emphasis. It could be argued that this could have been especially so in view of the Tribunal's conviction that the equidistance/relevant circumstances method was grounded in the basis of coastal state rights over maritime zones.

The fundamental question is whether the Tribunal was right in concluding that the equidistance/relevant circumstances method:

> is rooted in the recognition that sovereignty over the land territory is the basis for the sovereign rights and jurisdiction of the coastal State with respect to both the exclusive economic zone and the continental shelf.[53]

First, it can be noted that the reference is to the combined rule of equidistance and relevant circumstances. This contrasts with the International Court of Justice's justification for applying the equidistance line as a provisional line in *Libya/Malta*:

> As the Court has found above, the law applicable to the present dispute, that is, to claims relating to continental shelves located less than 200 miles from the coasts of the States in question, is based not on geological or geomorphological criteria, but on a criterion of distance from the coast or, to use the traditional term, on the principle of adjacency as measured by distance. It therefore seems logical to the Court that the choice of the criterion and the method which it is to employ in the first place to arrive at a provisional result should be made in a manner consistent with the concepts underlying the attribution of legal title.[54]

It will be obvious that the Tribunal could not have based itself on this reasoning of the Court to justify the equidistance line as a provisional line for the delimitation of the continental shelf beyond 200 nautical miles. Entitlement in this case is not based on distance from the coast, but mainly on geomorphological criteria. In the specific case of Myanmar and Bangladesh, a strict equidistance line would have no relation to the area of overlapping entitlements beyond 200 nautical miles, and the Tribunal's provisional equidistance line

---

52 The most prominent publication in this respect is probably P. Weil *The Law of Maritime Delimitation – Reflections* (Grotius Publications, Cambridge: 1989), which at one point talks about the "crusade against equidistance" (*ibid.*, p. 203).
53 Judgment of 14 March 2012, para. 455.
54 *Libya/Malta*, judgment of 3 June 1985 [1985] *ICJ Reports*, p. 13 at pp. 46–47, para. 61.

was located in the northwestern corner of the part of the relevant area beyond 200 nautical miles defined by the Tribunal.

How should the Tribunal's innovative approach of linking the equidistance/relevant circumstances method, instead of the equidistance method, to the basis for entitlement be judged? First, it can be noted that the Tribunal employs a more general notion of basis of entitlement than the Court in *Libya/Malta*. The basis is the sovereignty of the coastal state over the coast. That notion is also at the basis of the above finding of the International Court of Justice in *Libya/Malta*. However, instead of linking this basic notion to the more specific basis for entitlement of the continental shelf, as the Court did in *Libya/Malta*, the Tribunal explicitly severs this link, observing that a distinction has to be made between the basis of entitlement rooted in sovereignty over the coast and the object and extent of the rights of the coastal state, "be it the nature of the areas to which those rights apply or the maximum seaward limits specified in articles 57 and 76 of the Convention".[55]

The Tribunal fails to explain what distinguishes the relationship of the equidistance/relevant circumstances method to its very general definition of the basis for entitlement from the relationship of other possible methods to that basis for entitlement. As was already argued above, a provisional equidistance line may be located beyond the area of overlapping continental shelf entitlements beyond 200 nautical miles. This would seem to make a method that results in a provisional line in the area of overlapping claims more appropriate. In the past, the jurisprudence has in fact applied such an approach, which implies immediately balancing all relevant circumstances to arrive at a boundary line without first establishing a provisional equidistance line. Without submitting that this is the right approach to the delimitation of the continental shelf beyond 200 nautical miles, it should be clear that this method is just as much rooted in the Tribunal's basis of entitlement as the equidistance/relevant circumstances method, or even more so, as it does not entail using a provisional line that may be outside the area of overlapping entitlements.

The Tribunal considered two relevant circumstances advanced by Bangladesh. The rejection of Bangladesh's argument that its natural prolongation was 'most natural' can only be welcomed. Entitlement to an area of continental shelf either exists or does not exist. There are no different classes of entitlement that deserve different treatment in delimitation between neighboring states.[56] The Tribunal's finding that the concavity of Bangladesh's coast remained a relevant circumstance beyond 200 nautical miles is not surprising

---

55   Judgment of 14 March 2012, para. 455.
56   See also *ibid.*, joint declaration of judges *ad hoc* Mensah and Oxman, para. 11.

in the light of the fact that the same coastal geography is relevant for areas within and beyond 200 nautical miles.

The Tribunal's approach to the proportionality test is in line with the earlier jurisprudence, and the conclusion that there is no disproportion is unexceptional. The exact definition of the relevant area would seem to raise a question. As was noted above, the Tribunal defined this area as that resulting from the projections of the relevant coasts. The Tribunal does not explain how the projections of the relevant coasts are related to those coasts. A comparison of the straight line the Tribunal used to represent Bangladesh's south-facing coast shows that the western limit of the relevant area is not a perpendicular to the straight line representing coast, but has an angle to that coast of 95°. A similar issue exists in relation to the southern limit of the relevant area. However, it does not seem that a definition of the relevant area based on frontal projection would have led to radically different outcomes of the proportionality test.

A final assessment of the boundary established by the Tribunal will only be possible once the boundaries of Myanmar and Bangladesh with India beyond 200 nautical miles will have been established. A preliminary assessment might suggest that the Tribunal has gone quite far in adjusting the provisional equidistance line to address the concavity of Bangladesh's coast as a relevant circumstance. If the tribunal in the arbitration between Bangladesh and India were to apply a similar approach to the delimitation as the Tribunal, and Myanmar and India were to extend their existing boundary beyond the 200-nautical-mile limit using the same method as within that limit, Bangladesh's continental shelf would extent further from its coast than Myanmar's continental shelf would from Myanmar's coast. This again points to the need for a further consideration between the nature and extent of continental shelf entitlements and their delimitation. Within 200 nautical miles an equidistance line between Myanmar and India no doubt leads to an equitable result, and this method was agreed between the two states. Beyond that distance, application of this same method would give Myanmar only a small part of the area of overlapping continental shelf entitlements.

v   An Example Illustrating the Difficulties Involved in Applying the Equidistance/Relevant Circumstances Method

An example may illustrate the difficulties one may run into in applying the equidistance/relevant circumstances rule advocated by the Tribunal in *Bangladesh/Myanmar*. This concerns the delimitation of the continental shelf between Denmark/Greenland and Iceland in the Irminger Sea.

Iceland made a submission to the CLCS in respect of the western part of the Reykjanes Ridge in April 2009.[57] The area enclosed in the outer limit submitted by Iceland starts from the point of intersection of Iceland's 200-nautical-mile limit with that of Greenland to the south west of Iceland. From that point Iceland's continental shelf beyond 200 nautical miles extends south for hundreds of nautical miles along the outer limit of Greenland's 200-nautical-mile zone and beyond. Denmark/Greenland made a submission to the CLCS in relation to two areas of continental shelf to the south of Greenland in June 2012.[58] One of these areas in the Irminger Sea overlaps in its entirety with the continental shelf included in the outer limits submitted by Iceland. The Danish/Greenlandic limit in this area also starts at the intersection of the 200-nautical-mile limits and then continues south at a distance of between a couple and some tens of nautical miles from the 200-nautical-mile limit of Greenland. This overlap means that there is a need for the delimitation of the continental shelf beyond 200 nautical miles between Denmark/Greenland and Iceland.

A provisional equidistance line between Denmark/Greenland and Iceland would only be located in the area of overlapping continental shelf entitlement in a small section close to the intersection of the 200-nautical-mile limits. In the most southerly part of the area of overlapping claims an equidistance line between Greenland and Iceland would be some 100 nautical miles distant from the area of overlapping entitlements. This clearly makes the equidistance line inappropriate as a provisional line.

Iceland and Denmark/Greenland have agreed upon a provisional delimitation for their continental shelf beyond 200 nautical miles in the Irminger Sea.[59] The Agreed Minutes indicate that the area of overlapping continental shelf beyond 200 nautical miles is divided giving 53% of the area to Greenland/Denmark and 47% to Iceland. The provisional delimitation line is determined

---

57   The Executive summary of Iceland's submission is available at <www.un.org/Depts/los/clcs_new/submissions_files/submission_isl_27_2009.htm>.

58   The Executive summary of Denmark/Greenland's submission is available at <www.un.org/Depts/los/clcs_new/submissions_files/submission_dnk_61_2012.htm>.

59   Agreed Minutes on the delimitation of the continental shelf beyond 200 nautical miles between Greenland and Iceland in the Irminger Sea of 16 January 2013 (on file with the author). The same approach had been followed previously between Denmark the Faroe Islands, Iceland and Norway in relation to the continental shelf beyond 200 nautical miles in the North East Atlantic (Agreed Minutes on the Delimitation of the Continental Shelf beyond 200 Nautical Miles between the Faroe Islands, Iceland and Norway in the Southern Part of the Banana Hole of the Northeast Atlantic of 20 September 2006 (available at <www.regjeringen.no/en/dep/ud/documents/Laws-and-rules/retningslinjer/2006/Agreed-Minutes.html?id=446839>)).

taking this ratio into account for all turning points of the line. The Agreed Minutes do not specify the reasons for this division. A number of factors might have played a role in this respect: the lengths of the relevant coasts of the parties facing the area; the distance of the area to the coasts of the parties; and the extent of the continental shelf of both parties beyond the area of overlapping entitlements beyond 200 nautical miles.

VI   Is There an Alternative to the Equidistance/Relevant Circumstances Method?

The delimitation of the continental shelf beyond 200 nautical miles has received limited attention in the legal literature. The existing literature does not suggest that there is one readily available generally applicable method.[60] Colson has cautiously suggested that the equidistance line would be a useful tool as a starting point in the delimitation of the continental shelf beyond 200 nautical miles.[61] Marques Antunes and Lilje-Jensen and Thamsborg instead have suggested that the extent of the 200-nautical miles limit of a coastal state linking up with its continental shelf beyond 200 nautical miles could be the basic parameter for the delimitation of the continental shelf beyond the 200-nautical-mile limit.[62] However, Marques Antunes adds that this notion should not be seen as "an absolutely overriding fact. Its weight is to be determined in the delimitation process through an approach that integrates all relevant facts."[63] Lilje-Jensen and Thamsborg submit that equidistance also can be expected to play an important role in the delimitation of the continental shelf beyond 200 nautical miles.[64] This conclusion should not come as a complete surprise. In cases in which the continental shelf within 200 nautical miles has

---

60   See D.A. Colson "The Delimitation of the Outer Continental Shelf between Neighboring States" 97 (2003) *The American Journal of International Law*, pp. 91–107; J. Lilje-Jensen and M. Thamsborg "The Role of Natural Prolongation in relation to Shelf Delimitation beyond 200 Nautical Miles" 64 (1995) *Nordic Journal of International Law*, pp. 619–645; N.S. Marques Antunes *Towards the Conceptualisation of Maritime Delimitation* (Martinus Nijhoff publishers, Leiden: 2003), pp. 330–333; R. Meese "La Délimitation du Plateau Continental au-delà des 200 Milles" in Académie de la Mer *Le Plateau Continental Étendu aux Termes de la Convention des Nations Unies sur le Droit de la Mer du 10 Décembre 1982; Optimisation de la Demande* (Pedone, Paris: 2004), pp. 181–229.
61   Colson, *op. cit.*, p. 107.
62   Lilje-Jensen and Thamsborg, *op. cit.*, p. 643; Marques Antunes, *op. cit.*, pp. 330–331.
63   *Ibid.*
64   Lilje-Jensen and Thamsborg, *op. cit.*, p. 644.

already been defined by lines in which the equidistance method played a major role, the "basic parameter" of the 200-nautical-mile opening would be no more than a thinly disguised variation of the equidistance method. Meese at first sight fully supports using the equidistance-relevant circumstances method to delimit the continental shelf beyond 200 nautical miles.[65] However, he then points to the crucial problem of the equidistance method:

> Pourquoi appliquer la méthode d'équidistance – qui s'apparente à une division égale d'un surface – applicable à un critère de distance dégagé pour le plateau continental dans les 200 M dans un espace à identité de formes à un plateau continental basé sur un critère de fonds sous-marins à diversité de formes et qui ne pourra pas aboutir à une division égale identique de cette surface additionnelle?[66]

Although this short review shows considerable support for the equidistance method, as Meese's observation indicates, it is not linked to entitlement like it is within 200 nautical miles. As was set out above, this link provided the justification for the International Court of Justice for selecting the equidistance line as a provisional delimitation line for delimitations within that distance. In view of the fact that there is no other single method of delimitation that could occupy this place in the case of the delimitation of the continental shelf beyond 200 nautical miles, it is submitted that one should rather look for generally formulated principles that allow one to identify the appropriate methods in the light of the parameters defining entitlement in the individual case. A starting point for this search could be the judgment of the ICJ in the *North Sea continental shelf* cases. The Court in that instance was faced with a similar situation to the one we are at present studying for the continental shelf beyond 200 nautical miles. Denmark and the Netherlands had persistently argued that continental entitlement was based on absolute proximity (*i.e.* distance) from the coast. The Court refuted this contention and instead held that entitlement was based on natural prolongation.[67] In the light of that conclusion, the Court had to determine the applicable rules of delimitation. According to the Court in the cases before it:

---

65   Meese, *op. cit.*, p. 228.
66   *Ibid.*, p. 229; see also *ibid.* p. 213.
67   *North Sea continental shelf* cases (Federal Republic of Germany/Denmark; Federal Republic of Germany/Netherlands), judgment of 20 February 1969 [1969] *ICJ Reports*, paras. 43–46.

delimitation is to be effected by agreement in accordance with equitable principles, and taking account of all the relevant circumstances, in such a way as to leave as much as possible to each Party all those parts of the continental shelf that constitute a natural prolongation of its land territory into and under the sea, without encroachment on the natural prolongation of the land territory of the other[.][68]

Let me first of all stress that I am not suggesting giving primacy to geomorphology or geology. No such primacy as a matter of fact was given to these factors by the Court.[69] Rather, the first step in a delimitation should be to determine the extent of overlap of continental shelf entitlements. In addition, it should be established to what extent the natural prolongation of one of the parties extends beyond that of the other party. If this area also overlaps with that of a third state, it should be considered how the delimitation of the continental shelf between the parties would affect the delimitation in the area beyond.

If the equidistance line were to result in a broadly equal division of the area of overlap and did not cut a party off from areas beyond the area of overlapping claims that is also subject to delimitation with a third state, it could be taken as the point of departure for the further delimitation process. However, if that is not the case, a different method should be chosen that achieves a similar result. Alternatively, in this latter case it could be considered to refrain from defining a provisional delimitation line, but instead to move directly to the stage of balancing all relevant circumstances, the approach that was also found to be applicable by the Court in its 1969 judgment.

The above approach would require a closer consideration of the location of the outer limits of the continental shelf than was the case in *Bangladesh/Myanmar*. This would seem to make this approach difficult to implement in the absence of certainty about these outer limits because the CLCS has not yet issued recommendations to all of the coastal states concerned or is blocked from considering the submissions because the consent of one or more if the states is lacking. A number of options would seem to be available in this case. One would be for a court or tribunal to consider whether it would be justified to block the consideration of a submission in the light of the relevant

---

68   *Ibid.*, para. 101(C)(1).
69   See A.G. Oude Elferink *The delimitation of the continental shelf between Denmark, Germany and the Netherlands: Arguing law, practicing politics?* (Cambridge University Press, 2013), Chapter 9.3.

provisions of UNCLOS.[70] Secondly, a court or tribunal could limit itself to stating the consequences of the applicable law for the specific case without defining a specific line. Finally, it could be considered to apply the approach that has been taken by Iceland and Denmark/Greenland[71] of provisionally delimiting the areas of overlapping continental shelf agreements and providing at the same time that this delimitation will be adjusted in a specific way if one or more of the parties concerned will receive recommendations from the CLCS indicating that its limits fall short of those contained in the submission.

VII Concluding Remarks

The judgment in *Bangladesh/Myanmar* was the first instance in which an international court or tribunal considered the rules applicable to the delimitation of the continental shelf beyond 200 nautical miles in detail. In the light of the circumstances of the case, the Tribunal's choice to apply the equidistance/relevant circumstances method is understandable. The provisional equidistance line established by the Tribunal was located in the area of overlapping continental shelf entitlements beyond 200 nautical miles and the boundary resulting from the adjustment to take into account the relevant circumstances can be said to lead to an equitable outcome. Moreover, when asked by the Tribunal, the parties had not argued that the Tribunal should apply a different methodology. Bangladesh explicitly supported the equidistance/relevant circumstances method, while Myanmar did not address the delimitation beyond 200 nautical miles because it considered that the boundary did not extend to this area.[72] Nonetheless, the Tribunal's finding that this method is generally applicable to the delimitation of the continental shelf beyond 200 nautical miles is problematic. In certain cases, the equidistance method will have no relation to the area of overlapping entitlements, making it inappropriate as a provisional starting line. As was argued above, there does not seem to be one other method that can take the place of the equidistance method. It is suggested that it could be worthwhile to return to the International Court of Justice's finding on the applicable law in the *North Sea continental shelf* cases.

---

70 See further A.G. Oude Elferink "Causes, consequences and solutions relating to the absence of final and binding outer limits of the continental shelf" (in: C.R. Symmons (ed.) *Selected Contemporary Issues in the Law of the Sea* (Martinus Nijhoff Publishers, Leiden)) pp. 253–272 at pp. 264–271.

71 See further above.

72 See judgment of 14 March 2012, paras. 451–453.

The equidistance line could still provide a provisional starting point where it results in a broadly equal division of overlapping entitlements and does not cut a party off from areas beyond the area of overlapping claims that are the subject of delimitation with a third state. However, if that is not the case, a different method that does achieve such a result should be chosen as a starting point. Alternatively, it could be considered to refrain from defining a provisional delimitation line in that case, but instead move directly to the stage of balancing all relevant circumstances, the approach that was also found to be applicable by the Court in its 1969 judgment.

CHAPTER 13

The Status of Islands in the International Law of the Sea: Megisti Island

*Nicholas M. Poulantzas**

I   Introduction

According to Article 121, para. 1 of the UN Convention on the Law of the Sea (1982):[1] "An island is a naturally formed area of land, surrounded by water, which is above water at high tide." In para. 2, the Article provides that islands have a territorial sea, contiguous zone, exclusive economic zone and continental shelf of their own, "in accordance with the provisions of this Convention". However, in para. 3, the Article provides that "rocks which cannot sustain human habitation or economic life of their own shall have no exclusive economic zone or continental shelf".

A contrario, one may conclude that rocks have a territorial sea and contiguous zone of their own. Yet, any artificial creation of the conditions of 'human habitation' or 'economic life' does not elevate rocks to the status of islands. In fact, this is what 'of their own' denotes.

The Convention does not make any distinction between small islands (islets) and medium or large islands, all of which have the same rights on claiming maritime zones in the international law of the sea. Nevertheless, in order to define the baseline for measuring the breadth of the territorial sea of states, the Convention, in Articles 6 and 13, determines what are 'reefs' and 'low-tide elevations', which have no territorial sea of their own.

Likewise, artificial islands and installations beyond the territorial sea of states do not possess the status of islands in international law.[2]

---

*   Prof. Dr.; Professor Emeritus of the Law of the Sea and of Maritime Law of the University of Piraeus (Greece); Hon. Barrister at the Supreme Court of Greece.
1   Hereinafter it will be referred to as 'LOSC (1982)'. See also *The Law of the Sea: Régime of Islands*, New York, 1988.
2   See Article 60, para. 8, LOSC (1982), which reads as follows: "Artificial islands, installations and structures do not possess the status of islands. They have no territorial sea of their own, and their presence does not affect the delimitation of the territorial sea, the exclusive economic zone or the continental shelf." For an extensive discussion of the status of artificial islands and installations in the international law of the sea, see N.M. Poulantzas, *The Right of*

One may notice that in the interpretation of the above Articles of the Convention, states try to protect their own particular interests. Thus, upon signature of the LOSC (1982), the Islamic Republic of Iran, according to Article 310 of the Convention, made the following declaration:

> 5. Islets situated in enclosed or semi-enclosed seas which potentially can sustain human habitation or economic life of their own, but owing to climatic conditions, resource restriction or other limitations, have not yet been put to development, fall within the provisions of paragraph 2 of article 121 concerning 'Regime of Islands', and have therefore full effect in boundary delimitation of various maritime zones of the interested Coastal States.[3]

In state practice, there has been little hesitation by coastal states in asserting extensive EEZ and continental shelf limits for their islands irrespective of size. Extreme examples of EEZ claims for minute islands is the United Kingdom's claim for a fisheries zone of 200 nautical miles and a continental shelf around Rockall islet, which raised strong protests on the part of Iceland, Denmark and Ireland,[4] and Aves Islet,[5] which, besides its very small size, had no habitation.

However, several other claims for an EEZ for uninhabited islands exist on the part of developed states, such as New Zealand – which calculates uninhabited islands, such as Auckland and Bounty Island, in order to define the baseline which serves for the measurement of its EEZ – Australia[6] and Canada.[7]

Hot Pursuit in International Law, 2nd edn., The Hague, London, New York, 2002, pp. 174–177; idem, *The Law of the Sea* [in Greek], 2nd edn., Athens, 2007, pp. 72–75.

3 See *The Law of the Sea: Declarations and Statements with respect to the United Nations Convention on the Law of the Sea and to the Agreement Relating to the Implementation of Part 11 of the United Nations Convention on the Law of the Sea of 10 December 1982*, New York, 1997, pp. 89 and 91.

4 D.W. Bowett, *The Legal Regime of Islands in International Law*, Dobbs Ferry, 1979; R.R. Churchill, A.V. Lowe, *The Law of the Sea*, 2nd edn., Manchester, 1988, pp. 41–42, 135–136.

5 See *United States-Venezuela Maritime Boundary Agreement*, 1978.

6 For Australia's claims to an EEZ around the uninhabited rocky islands of Heard and McDonald, see N.M. Poulantzas, "Certain Oversights of the International Tribunal for the Law of the Sea (ITLOS) and Other Interesting Cases Where Recourse to ITLOS Has Not Taken Place", in B. Vukas, T.M. Šošić, eds., *International Law: New Actors, New Concepts – Continuing Dilemmas*, Leiden, Boston, 2010, pp. 281–285.

7 See *Fishing Zones Order*, 1976. Yet, Canada's Sable Island, off Halifax, N.S., although seemingly a sandbar, breeds wild horses, as the present writer, as a visiting Professor to Dalhousie Law School and a member of Dalhousie's University Ocean Studies Program (DOSP), witnessed in

Moreover, uninhabited rocks have been counted as basepoints for the delimitation of the EEZ and continental shelf.[8]

In the last twenty years the number of states that have claimed an EEZ has grown immensely. Several of these claims are no longer made for exclusive fishing rights but for the exploitation of gas and oil in the depth of the oceans.[9] In the southeast Mediterranean several new EEZ claims to 200 nautical miles were made after the discovery of large amounts of gas and oil deposits.[10]

11 Megisti Island: Some Coordinates

Megisti Island or Castellorizo belongs to the Greek islands of the Dodecanese in the southeastern Aegean Sea. It forms into a cluster with the small islands of Ro (Saint George) and Strongyli (Ypsili).[11]

Megisti is situated 72 nautical miles south east of Rhodes Island and two nautical miles off the coast of Turkey. It has an area of 9 sq. kilometres and the extension of its coastline is 17 kilometres. Its purely Greek population in 1821, when it took part in the uprising for the liberation of Greece from the Ottoman Empire, was nearly 17,000. Today, following years of emigration to Australia, Egypt and mainland Greece, the population has decreased to approx. 500 inhabitants.

Megisti Island sits on the tip of the 'Levantine Basin', which extends further to the south of Crete Island and to the west of Cyprus and still further to Barqah (in Libya) and Egypt. The 'Levantine Basin' is separated by a submarine ridge, in the south of Crete, by the other major basin of eastern Mediterranean Sea, the 'Ionian Basin', which lies south of Italy, the Ionian Sea of Greece, west of Crete and further to Cyrenaica to the west of Libya.[12] Older and recent

---

1974–1975. See also N.M. Poulantzas, "Marine Land-Based Pollution in International Law and the Mediterranean", *Shipping, International Monthly Review*, December 1989, pp. 21–24, 44.

8   See D. Attard, *The Exclusive Economic Zone in International Law*, Oxford, 1987, pp. 259–264.

9   See Joan Goldstein, ed., *The Politics of Offshore Oil*, New York, 1982, "Foreword" by Senator Bill Bradley, pp. vii–viii.

10 See N.M. Poulantzas, "The Exclusive Economic Zone (EEZ) of Greece and the *Casus Belli* of Turkey" [in Greek], *Shipping, International Monthly Review*, October 2011, pp. 55–57, and November 2011, pp. 50–51.

11 For the history and maps of Megisti Island see *Archaeological Atlas of the Aegean*, Athens, 1998, pp. 97, 384. *Cf.* also Otto Maull, *Griechisches Mittelmeergebiet*, Breslau, 1922, pp. 2, 4, 7, 8, 100.

12 See *The New Encyclopaedia Britannica, Macropaedia*, Vol. 11, New York, 1973, pp. 854–55.

oceanographic research in both these basins has revealed immense deposits of hydrocarbons.[13]

We have chosen to deal with Megisti Island because of its proximity to Asia Minor and of the fact that it sits on the tip of the 'Levantine Basin'. More important, however, is the fact that Turkey disputes its status as a small island to have an EEZ and a continental shelf of its own.

Recently, Turkey granted research and exploration permits to the French company *CGG Veritas* over the continental shelf and EEZ of Megisti Island and intended using to this effect the Norwegian flagged oil-exploration vessel *The Bergen Surveyor*. Moreover, the Turkish oil-exploration vessel *Piri Reis*, accompanied by Turkish naval units, started exploration on the 'Levantine Basin' and on the Cypriot EEZ.[14]

III   The Continental Shelf and the EEZ of Megisti Island

The legal status of the Dodecanese islands has been governed by the Italian Peace Treaty of Paris of February 10, 1947.[15] Thus, Article 14 of this Peace Treaty included the cession of sovereignty to Greece by Italy of the Dodecanese islands and explicitly of Castellorizo.

It is interesting to note here that for the delimitation of the territorial waters between the island of Castellorizo and the coasts of Anatolia both Italy and Turkey had agreed to have recourse to the Permanent Court of International Justice, the predecessor of the International Court of Justice.[16]

However, the proceedings in this case before the PCIJ were discontinued on January 3, 1933,[17] after notification to the Registrar of the Court on November 18,

---

13   See N.M. Poulantzas, "Greece as an Oil and Gas Transporting and Producing Country" [in Greek], *Shipping, International Monthly Review*, April 2012, pp. 54–55.

14   See N.M. Poulantzas, "Proposals for the Establishment and Delimitation of an EEZ of Greece and the *Casus Belli* of Turkey" [in Greek], *Legal Tribune*, No. 10, 2011, pp. 2434–2440.

15   For the historical conditions prevailing before the ceding of the Dodecanese islands to Greece see N.M. Poulantzas, "Some Interesting Points regarding the Second World War and Some Relevant Thoughts", *Revue hellénique de droit international*, Vol. 63, No. 2, 2010, pp. 1003–1010.

16   See *Case concerning the Delimitation of the Territorial Waters between the Island of Castellorizo and the Coasts of Anatolia*, Order of 26 January 1933, Series A/B, No. 51, discussed by J.H.W. Verzijl, *The Jurisprudence of the World Court*, Vol. I (The Permanent Court of International Justice, 1922–1940), Leyden, 1965, at p. 316.

17   For several cases where the proceedings were discontinued by the International Court of Justice, resulting from aerial incidents mainly between the USA and the USSR during the

1931, of the Italo-Turkish Special Agreement of May 30, 1929, concerning the delimitation of the territorial waters between the island of Castellorizo and the coast of Anatolia,[18] and finally caused by the conclusion by the two states concerned of the 'Maritime Boundary Convention of Ankara' of January 4, 1932.[19]

This is a good example of the influence which the submission of a dispute to the World Court may have on the willingness of the parties to reach an agreed solution before the hatchet of International Justice falls. As the late Professor J.H.W. Verzijl wrote: "this is an aspect of international litigation which is not without importance."[20]

The Italo-Turkish Agreement of 1932 on "the sovereignty over the islets situated between the Anatolian coast and the island of Castellorizo and on the delimitation of the territorial sea of the said islets" accepted the median line principle.[21] The Italo-Turkish Agreement of 1932 is still in force today for the delimitation of the territorial sea between Greece and Turkey in the Dodecanese, and more particularly between the Anatolian coast of Turkey and the Greek island of Castellorizo and the islets in the area, which form the

---

'cold war' years, when these cases were brought unilaterally before the ICJ by virtue of the institution of the *forum prorogatum* (namely, when one state applies unilaterally to the ICJ and invites the other state to do the same, in case the second state does not comply), see N.M. Poulantzas, *The Right of Hot Pursuit in International Law*, op. cit., at pp. 314 et seq.

18   See the 'Special Agreement for Arbitration' between the Government of the Turkish Republic and the Royal Italian Government of May 30, 1929. In Article 1 this Agreement read as follows: "The Permanent Court of International Justice at The Hague shall be requested to give its decision on the following points: 1. A – Whether, according to the Treaty of Lausanne, the following islands should be assigned, purely and simply and in their entirety, to Turkey, or whether they should be assigned, in their entirety to Italy: Volo (Catal Ada), Ochendra (Uvendire), Furnachia (Furnakya), Cato Volo (Katovolo), Prasoudi (Prasudi), Rho (San Giorgio), Maradi, Tchatulata (Catulata), Pighi (Pigi), Dassia (Dasya), Macri (Makri), Psomi, San Giorgio (Aya Yorgi), Polifados (Psoradya), Ipsili, Alimentaria (Alimentarya), Caravola (Karavola), Roccie Vutzachi (Roksi Vucaki), Mavro Poini, Mavro Poinachi (Mavro Poinaki)." For the text of this 'Special Agreement', see *Revue hellénique de droit international*, Vol. 51, No. 2, 1998, pp. 558–568.

19   See J.H.W. Verzijl, *The Jurisprudence of the World Court*, Vol. II (The International Court of Justice, 1947–1965), Leyden, 1966, pp. 533–537.

20   *Ibid.*, at p. 534.

21   See N.M. Poulantzas, "The New International Law of the Sea and the Legal Status of the Aegean Sea", *Revue hellénique de droit international*, Vol. 44, 1991, pp. 251–272, especially at p. 254.

Megisti group of islands, since Greece has succeeded Italy in sovereignty over these islands.[22]

So far as the principle of equidistance is concerned, the Greek position over the years has been that this principle offers an equitable solution. It has also been adopted in the great majority of cases, where the delimitation of the continental shelf was agreed between coastal states with opposite or adjacent coasts. Greece has also repeatedly invited Turkey to submit the dispute regarding the delimitation of the continental shelf between the Greek islands of the Aegean Sea and mainland Turkey, which has been the only legal dispute between the two states, to the International Court of Justice. It should also be noted here that the continental shelf between Greece and Italy was delimited by agreement between the two states – on the basis of the median line principle – a few years ago.[23]

Turkey systematically refuses to accept the jurisdiction of the International Court of Justice to pronounce on the question of the delimitation of the continental shelf.[24] The Turkish Government contends that because it did not sign or ratify the Geneva Convention on the Continental Shelf (1958) or the Law of the Sea Convention (1982), it is not bound by their provisions. This contention is not correct, because both these Conventions represent today the general consensus of world states and the codification and progressive development of the international law of the sea. Besides, Turkey follows the provisions of the LOSC (1982) so far as the extension of its territorial sea to 12 nautical miles is concerned, in the Black Sea and in the Mediterranean. Moreover, Turkey proceeded to the extension of its EEZ to 200 nautical miles in the Black Sea and its delimitation – using the equidistance principle – with riparian states of the Black Sea, like Russia, Romania and Bulgaria.[25]

---

22 See Article 11 of the 1978 Vienna Convention on Succession of States in respect of Treaties, which is worded as follows: "A succession of States does not as such affect: (a) a boundary established by a treaty; or (b) obligations and rights established by a treaty and relating to the regime of boundary."

23 See 'Agreement between the Hellenic Republic and the Italian Republic on the delimitation of the boundary of the continental shelf which belongs to each of these two states', signed in Athens on May 4, 1977. This Agreement came into force on December 12, 1980. See also the Greek Law 786 of June 21, 1978, in *Government Gazette*, No. 101.

24 See *Aegean Sea Continental Shelf Case (Jurisdiction of the Court)*, ICJ Decision of September 19, 1978. For a discussion of this case, see N.M. Poulantzas, *The Law of the Sea*, *op. cit.*, pp. 113–122.

25 See N.M. Poulantzas, "The EEZ of Greece and the *Casus Belli* of Turkey" [in Greek], *Energy and Law*, No. 16, 2011, pp. 40–46.

Turkey also alleges incorrectly that the dispute regarding the continental shelf (and now the EEZ) with Greece is a *political* and not a *legal* dispute, according to international law. In addition, Turkey ignores the existence of the Greek islands in the Aegean Sea and their inherent right to a continental shelf and an EEZ of their own. It also claims incorrectly that, because of special circumstances, the dispute with Greece concerns the delimitation of the continental shelf of the whole of the Aegean Sea between the mainland of Greece and Turkey. According to the Greek position, which is correct by international law, the only special circumstances is the existence of the eastern Aegean islands, and therefore the object of the delimitation dispute is the continental shelf and the EEZ between the Greek islands of the eastern Aegean and the Dodecanese and the mainland of Turkey.[26]

In the case of the delimitation of the continental shelf and the EEZ between Megisti Island, the Greek islets in the same area, and mainland Turkey, because of the proximity of these Greek islands to the coast of mainland Turkey, one may profitably draw an analogy with the dispute regarding fishing quotas and maritime boundaries between Canada and France. France claimed for the French islands of St. Pierre and Miquelon, which lie a few miles off the Canadian coast of Newfoundland, a territorial sea of 12 nautical miles, a contiguous zone of 24 nautical miles and an EEZ of 200 nautical miles. Canada contended that because of the circumstances prevailing in the area and the proximity of the islands to the Canadian coast, they were entitled only to a 12-mile territorial sea. The parties referred the dispute to a five-member Arbitration Tribunal which, by its decision or award of June 10, 1992, recognized for the two French islands a territorial sea of 12 nautical miles, a contiguous zone of 24 nautical miles and a narrow strip of 200-mile EEZ running out to the Atlantic Ocean.[27]

Thus, Greece should claim for the group of Megisti Island and the islets in the area a territorial sea which, by applying the equidistance principle, would be the median line between those islands and mainland Turkey and the delimitation of the continental shelf and the EEZ between those islands and mainland Turkey on the basis of the 'equidistance' principle. To the south-west, in the open Mediterranean Sea, Greece should claim an EEZ of 200 nautical miles, which will bring the EEZ of these islands and of Greece to the limits of the EEZ of Cyprus.[28]

---

26   See *supra*, note 21.
27   See Nicholas M. Poulantzas, *The Right of Hot Pursuit in International Law, op. cit.*, pp. XXIII and XLIII.
28   See *supra*, note 14, p. 2437.

IV Delimitation of the Continental Shelf and the EEZ of Islands: Equidistance v. Special Circumstances/Equitable Solution

The Geneva Convention on the Continental Shelf (1958), which was the only one of the four Geneva Conventions ratified by Greece, entered into force on June 10, 1984. By 1971 the Convention had been ratified by 44 states.

So far as the delimitation of the continental shelf between states with opposite or adjacent coasts is concerned, Article 6 of this Convention provided that the boundary shall be determined by agreement between the states concerned. If such an agreement does not exist and another boundary is not justified by special circumstances, the boundary shall be the median line, every point of which is equidistant from the nearest points of the baselines from which the breadth of the territorial sea of each state is measured. This is the 'equidistance principle'.

Articles 74 and 83 of the LOSC (1982) on the delimitation of the EEZ and the continental shelf between states with opposite or adjacent coasts, which have a similar wording, provide that the delimitation of the EEZ and the continental shelf between states with opposite or adjacent coasts shall be effected by agreement on the basis of international law, as referred to in Article 38 of the Statute of the International Court of Justice, in order to achieve an 'equitable solution'.

However, the Geneva Convention on the Continental Shelf (1958) did not set down a criterion for defining 'special circumstances'. Likewise, the LOSC (1982) did not designate the limits of an 'equitable solution'.

The International Court of Justice, in a series of decisions starting with the North Sea Continental Shelf Cases (1969) which were pronounced by the full Court[29] or by a five-member Chamber of the Court,[30] did not succeed in establishing a uniform criterion, or test, regarding 'special circumstances', which call for an 'equitable solution'.[31]

What we are witnessing now is a recurrence of the 'equidistance principle', which is gaining momentum in delimitation agreements in the eastern

---

29   See *North Sea Continental Shelf Cases*, ICJ Reports, 1969; *Tunisia v. Libya*, ICJ Reports, 1982; *Continental Shelf Case (Libyan Arab Jamahiriya v. Malta)*, ICJ Reports, 1985; *Maritime Delimitation and Territorial Questions between Qatar and Bahrain*, ICJ Reports, 2001.; *Land and Maritime Boundary between Cameroon and Nigeria*, ICJ Reports, 2002; etc.

30   See *Delimitation of the Maritime Boundary in the Gulf of Maine (Canada v. United States of America)*, ICJ Reports, 1997.

31   See also in this sense, Budislav Vukas, "The Vagueness of the International Rules on the Continental Shelf", in B. Vukas, T.M. Šošić, eds., *op. cit.*, pp. 351–358.

Mediterranean and the Black Sea. Thus, the Agreement of May 4, 1977, on the delimitation of the continental shelf between Italy and Greece, which entered into force on December 15, 1980, is based on the 'principle of equidistance'.[32]

The same is also true of the EEZ delimitation agreements of 200 nautical miles signed by Cyprus with Egypt in February 2003, with Lebanon in January 2007, and with Israel in December 2010, which were based on the 'equidistance principle'.[33]

Likewise, in the Black Sea, several delimitation agreements for an EEZ of 200 nautical miles were concluded in 1986 by Turkey with Russia, Romania and Bulgaria. All these agreements were also based on the 'equidistance principle'.[34] We hope that this preference for the 'equidistance principle' over the 'equitable solution' will continue in future in EEZ delimitation Agreements.

V Some Recent Case Law Regarding the Delimitation of the Territorial Sea, the Continental Shelf and the EEZ of Islands

1 *Territorial and Maritime Dispute between Nicaragua and Honduras in the Caribbean Sea*

This case concerned a mixed dispute of the law of the sea and territorial questions. The case was brought before the International Court of Justice on December 8, 1999, by an application filed by Nicaragua. The proceedings lasted for many years and the ICJ delivered its Judgment on October 6, 2007.[35]

It is to be noted that both Nicaragua and Honduras asked the Court to draw 'a single maritime boundary' delimiting their respective territorial seas, exclusive economic zones and continental shelves in the disputed area. So far as the delimitation of the territorial seas of the two states is concerned, the Court, after mentioning the text of Article 15 of the LOSC (1982), which is binding on both those two states, observed:

> The most logical and widely practised approach is first to draw provisionally an equidistance line and then to consider whether that line must be adjusted in the light of the existence of special circumstances.[36]

---

32 See the Greek Law 786 of June 21, 1978, in *Government Gazette*, No. 101.
33 See *supra*, note 14.
34 *Ibid.*
35 See *ICJ Reports*, 2007, p. 659.
36 *Ibid.*, p. 740, para. 268. See also *Maritime Delimitation and Territorial Questions between Qatar and Bahrain (Qatar v. Bahrain), Merits, Judgment, ICJ Reports,* 2001, p. 94, para. 176.

THE STATUS OF ISLANDS IN THE INTERNATIONAL LAW OF THE SEA   259

The ICJ further, after considering the special circumstances in the case at hand, concluded that it could not apply the equidistance principle while, at the same time, equidistance remained the general rule.[37]

Then, among the geometrical methods of delimitation proposed, such as perpendiculars and bisectors, "which may produce equitable delimitations in some circumstances", the Court selected a bisector method "faithful to the actual geographical situation",[38] and drew a bisector line of delimitation.

With regard to the delimitation by a single maritime boundary for the four disputed islands, namely, the Bobel Cay, Sabanna Cay, Port Royal Cay and South Cay, which the Court found belonged to Honduras, the ICJ drew a provisional equidistance line, using co-ordinates for these islands as the base points for their territorial seas of 12 nautical miles.

The ICJ applied the 'equidistance principle', as it did not find any legally relevant 'special circumstances' in this case. The Court also drew a median line of the territorial seas of these Honduran islands in the areas where there was an overlap with the territorial waters of the Nicaraguan island of Edinburgh Cay.

So far as the outer limit of the single maritime boundary was concerned, the Court noted that in no case might the boundary line be interpreted as extending more than 200 nautical miles from the baselines from which the breadth of the territorial sea was measured. It further added that any claim of continental shelf rights beyond 200 nautical miles had to be in accordance with Article 76 of the LOSC (1982) and reviewed by the Commission on the Limits of the Continental Shelf, which was established by this Article.[39]

2   *Maritime Delimitation in the Black Sea (Romania v. Ukraine)*

On September 16, 2004, Romania filed an application instituting proceedings against Ukraine in respect of a dispute concerning "the establishment of a single maritime boundary between the two States in the Black Sea, thereby delimiting the continental shelf and the exclusive economic zone appertaining to them".[40]

As it turned out, during the proceedings the main point of difference was the status under the LOSC (1982) of Serpents' Island in the Black Sea. Indeed, the presence of this tiny island could have an effect on the delimitation of adjacent maritime zones.

---

37   See *supra*, note 14, p. 2436.
38   See also *Continental Shelf (Libyan Arab Jamahiriya/Malta), Judgment, ICJ Reports*, 1985, p. 45, para. 57.
39   See *supra*, note 14.
40   See International Court of Justice, *Yearbook 2007–2008*, The Hague, 2008, pp. 297–298.

Romania, through the whole procedure before the ICJ, held the view that Serpents' Island was a rock, and by virtue of Article 121, para. 3, of the LOSC (1982) could only have a territorial sea and a contiguous zone. This was a view on islands in general held by Romania during the whole period of codification of the Law of the Sea (1973–1982).[41]

At the signing and ratification of the Convention on the Law of the Sea, Romania appended a statement to the effect "that according to the requirements of equity, as it results from articles 74 and 83 of the Convention on the Law of the Sea, the uninhabited islands and without economic life can in no way affect the delimitation of the maritime spaces belonging to the main land coasts of the coastal states".[42]

On the other hand, Ukraine defended the status of Serpents' Island as an island under Article 121, para. 1, of the LOSC (1982), and its entitlement to a territorial sea, a contiguous zone, an exclusive economic zone and a continental shelf, by virtue of Article 121, para. 2, of the LOSC (1982).

Oddly enough, the International Court of Justice, by its decision of February 2009, without pronouncing on the question whether Serpents' Island was an 'island' or a 'rock', granted Ukraine a 12 nautical mile territorial sea around it.[43]

Thus, the ICJ unanimously decided that

> starting from Point 1, as agreed by the Parties in Article 1 of the 2003 State Border Regime Treaty, the line of the single maritime boundary delimiting the continental shelf and the exclusive economic zones of Romania and Ukraine in the Black Sea shall follow the 12-nautical mile arc of the territorial sea of Ukraine around Serpents' Island until Point 2 (with co-ordinates 45°03'18.5" N and 30°09'24.6" E) where the arc intersects with the line equidistant from Romania's and Ukraine's adjacent coasts. From Point 2 the boundary line shall follow the equidistance line through Point 3 (with co-ordinates 44°46'38.7" N and 30°58'37.3" E) and Point 4 (with co-ordinates 44°44'13.4" N and 31°24'35.0" E). From Point 5 the maritime boundary line shall continue along the line equidistant from the opposite coasts of Romania and Ukraine in southerly direction starting at a

---

41   See *The Law of the Sea: Declarations and Statements with Respect to the United Nations Convention on the Law of the Sea and to the Agreement Relating to Implementation of Part XI of the United States Convention on the Law of the Sea of 10 December 1982*, United Nations, New York, 1997, p. 90.

42   *Ibid.*, p. 91.

43   This is one of the recent 'bizarre' decisions of the International Court of Justice.

geodetic azimuth of 185°23′54.4″ until it reaches the area where the rights of third States may be affected.⁴⁴

However, the case of Serpents' Island – which has only a military garrison and no other inhabitants – has no bearing on the delimitation of the maritime boundary of Megisti Island, which is a fully-fledged island inhabited since time immemorial and having, as part also of the Dodecanese islands, its own history, customs, economic life and cultural traditions.

3   Dispute concerning Delimitation of the Maritime Boundary between Bangladesh and Myanmar in the Bay of Bengal

This dispute between Bangladesh and Myanmar concerned the delimitation of the maritime boundary between Bangladesh and Myanmar, and more particularly around the Bangladeshi island of Saint Martin in the Bay of Bengal. The dispute arose following the discovery of deposits of natural gas by Indian and Myanmar companies in the Bay of Bengal. The two States in the dispute agreed to have recourse to the International Tribunal for the Law of the Sea (ITLOS) for the resolution of their dispute.⁴⁵

On March 14, 2012, the ITLOS delivered its judgment. The Court, influenced by the decision of the International Court of Justice in the Serpents' Island case, granted the Bangladeshi island of Saint Martin only a territorial sea of 12 nautical miles.⁴⁶

However, it is difficult to draw an analogy between this case, which concerns adjacent and not opposite zones, with the case of Megisti Island which, as we noted above,⁴⁷ can find a legal basis for the delimitation of its maritime boundary with Turkey in the decision of the ICJ regarding the delimitation of the maritime zones between the French islands of St. Pierre and Miquelon and the Canadian coast of Newfoundland. After all every case of delimitation of boundaries of islands has its own particular characteristics.⁴⁸

---

44   See *Maritime Delimitation in the Black Sea (Romania v. Ukraine), Judgment, ICJ Reports*, 2009, p. 131, para. 219.
45   See *ITLOS/Press Release 174* of March 8, 2012.
46   ITLOS, Year 2012, 14 March 2012, List of Cases, *No. 16*: Dispute Concerning Delimitation of the Maritime Boundary between Bangladesh and Myanmar in the Bay of Bengal (Bangladesh/Myanmar), *Judgment*.
47   See *supra*, Section III, at note 27.
48   See also D. Attard, *The Exclusive Economic Zone in International Law, op. cit.*, note 8.

VI Concluding Remarks and Some Proposals

Greece should try to further strengthen her relations and co-operation with other States in the Mediterranean, like *e.g.*, Israel, Egypt and Libya, in the field of exploration and exploitation of gas and oil resources in the Mediterranean.

The present Greek Government should in no way proceed to a proclamation of an exclusive economic zone in the area of Megisti Island following the acquiescence of Turkey, as is rumoured nowadays. Such acquiescence by Turkey would mean reduced sovereign rights on Greece's EEZ in this area, and probably a concealed distribution of profits with Turkey out of the exploitation of the EEZ.

The Greek Government should also not try to enter into definitive territorial agreements with Turkey, like the delimitation of the territorial waters, the continental shelf and the EEZ in this area, while Greece is still in the middle of an economic recession or crisis.

It is far better for Greece to proceed to the proclamation of an EEZ in the area of Megisti Island, and then invite Turkey to discussions for an agreement on the delimitation of the EEZ. If no agreement is reached within a reasonable time-limit, then, according to Article 74, para. 2, of the LOSC (1982), Part XV of this Convention, which concerns 'resolution of differences', will be applicable.[49]

Pending such an agreement, provisional arrangements of a practical nature could be entered with Turkey, without prejudice to the final delimitation.[50]

Before proclaiming an EEZ in the area of Megisti Island, Greece should draw the outer limit lines of the exclusive economic zone in this area and the proposed lines of delimitation, according to Article 74 of the LOSC (1982). These lines must be shown on "charts of a scale or scales adequate for ascertaining their position."[51]

Where appropriate, lists of geographical co-ordinates of points specifying the geodetic datum may be substituted for such outer limit lines or lines of delimitation.

Finally, Greece should give due publicity to such charts or lists of geographical co-ordinates, and must deposit a copy of each such chart or list with the Secretary-General of the United Nations, pending a final delimitation agreement with Turkey.[52]

---

49 See N.M. Poulantzas, *Law of the Sea, op.cit.*, pp. 107–112.
50 See Article 74, para. 3, LOSC (1982).
51 See Article 75, para. 1, LOSC (1982).
52 See Article 75, para. 2, LOSC (1982).

CHAPTER 14

Theorizing about Conventional Environmental Sea Regimes as International Trusts: The Case of the Barcelona Convention System

*Evangelos Raftopoulos**

I   An Overview

The Barcelona Convention for the Protection of the Marine Environment and the Coastal Region of the Mediterranean and its seven performative Protocols, the so-called Barcelona Convention System (BCS),[1] constitutes a conventional

---

* LLB (Athens), LLM (Cantab.), PhD (Cantab.); Professor of International Law at the Panteion University of Athens; Founding Director of MEPIELAN Centre; Former UNEP/MAP Legal Advisor.
1   *The Barcelona Convention for the Protection of the Marine Environment and the Coastal Region of the Mediterranean* (1976, as amended on 10 June 1995, amendment entered into force 9 July 2004) is a framework convention being specifically implemented by the following seven Protocols: *The Protocol for the Prevention of Pollution of the Mediterranean Sea by Dumping from Ships and Aircraft or Incineration at Sea* (1976, as amended on 10 June 1995, amendment not yet in force) ('Dumping Protocol'); *The Protocol concerning Cooperation in Preventing Pollution from Ships and, in Cases of Emergency, Combating Pollution of the Mediterranean Sea* (2002, entered into force 17 March 2004) ('Prevention and Emergency Protocol'), replacing the Emergency Protocol, 1976; *The Protocol for the Protection of the Mediterranean Sea against Pollution from Land-based Sources and Activities* (1980, as amended on 7 March 1996, amendment entered into force 11 May 2008) ('LBS Protocol'); *The Protocol concerning Specially Protected Areas and Biological Diversity in the Mediterranean* (1995, entered into force 12 December 1999) ('SPA and Biodiversity Protocol'), replacing the SPA Protocol, 1982; *The Protocol for the Protection of the Mediterranean Sea against Pollution Resulting from Exploration and Exploitation of the Continental Shelf and the Seabed and its Subsoil* (1994, entered into force 24 March 2011) ('Offshore Protocol'); *The Protocol on the Prevention of Pollution of the Mediterranean Sea by Transboundary Movements of Hazardous Wastes and their Disposal* (1996, entered into force 19 January 2008) ('Hazardous Wastes Protocol'); and *The Protocol on Integrated Coastal Zone Management* (2008, entered into force 24 March 2011) ('ICZM Protocol'). On the initiation of the term 'Barcelona Convention System' see Raftopoulos, E., *The Barcelona Convention and Protocols – The Mediterranean Action Plan Regime*, Simmonds & Hill Publishing Ltd., London, 1993. Also, Scovazzi, T., "The Recent Developments in the 'Barcelona System' for the Protection of the Mediterranean Sea against Pollution", *International Journal of Marine and Coastal Law*, Vol. 11, 1996, 95; Juste Ruiz, J., "Regional Approaches to the Protection of the Marine Environment", in: *Thesaurus*

sea regime of international common interest (ICI) *in processu*. It governs the protection of the marine environment and the resources of the Mediterranean in a sustainable manner so that the needs of present and future generations will be met equitably. Such sustainability governance should be understood to operate from two interrelated pragmatic – but often neglected – perspectives: in conditions of uncertainty and in context, responding progressively, feasibly and effectively to the exigencies of an evolving conventional environmental regime (CER) perpetually serving ICI; purposively and as a special, undivided responsibility to the future, as a fiduciary concept, as an international trust relationship. Theorizing about the international trust nature of the BCS – and of any other conventional environmental regime in its context – is inherently dynamic, open-ended and operates on two interrelated levels.

First, it conceptualizes treaties as conventional regimes of international common interest *in processu*: they constitute relational regime patterns and process patterns of ICI in pairs, in a complementary relationship, *sufficiently contextualized*. Treaties punctuate regime relations between States and other international legal entities through conventional patterns of ICI which are produced, implemented and revised by constant and continuous reference to their external and internal context, and through a structured negotiating process of conferential governance.

Second, it conceptualizes the governance of a conventional environmental regime and its sustainability objective as a relationship of public trust, thus bringing out the overlooked fiduciary aspect of the relational base of a conventional environmental regime associated with the special position and role of its Parties. The employment of the paradigm of public trust may, thus, come to fill out the sustainability function of governance of such regimes.

II Some Theoretical and Philosophical Considerations

The international trust approach to the BCS basically defies the prevailing but misleading legal positivist view of constructing and objectifying fundamental legal concepts of international law on the basis of 'Private Law Analogies'. It manifests the inadequacy of transposing into treaty relations the logic of two fundamental interweaving Private Law Analogies, the private law contract analogy for treaties and ownership for sovereignty, both of which crudely

---

Acroasium, 2002, 402; Scovazzi, T., "The Mediterranean Sea", in: *Environmental Governance of the Great Seas – Law and Effect* (ed. by J.F.C. Dimento and A.J. Hickman), Edward Elgar, 2012, Ch. 5B, 96 *et seq.*

underlie the discussion on the nature and governance of the inappropriately named *Multilateral Environmental Agreements* (MEAs).[2] Such a positivist theoretical construct ignores the real world of MEAs[3] and their ICI-creative effect on international relations.

1 Defying the Private Law Contract Analogy to Treaties

Treaties are not analogous to private law contracts.[4] They constitute conventional regimes of governance for constituting, protecting and promoting international common interest (ICI) which are sufficiently and operatively contextualized.[5] Their purpose is legislative, serving ICI, rather than contractual. They are constituted, implemented and developed, through a continuous and structured negotiating process and in a creative consistency with their context (coherence with a plurality of interrelated contexts), particular patterns of *relations* between States (relational foundations) panctuating the ever-expanding realm of governance consensus. As Clive Parry insightfully

---

2   The term MEAS was consistently promoted by UNEP as a working definition for certain projects (policy papers, handbooks and other projects). Being a recent development, this abstraction was not used in UNEP's earlier projects (*e.g.* UNEP: *Selected Multilateral Treaties in the Field of the Environment* (ed. by A.C. Kiss), UNEP: Reference Series 3, UNEP-Nairobi, 1983). Despite its generic construction as a subset of the universe of international agreements focusing on environmental issues (UNEP: *Guide for Negotiators of International Environmental Agreements*, 2007, Introduction, 7), this definition has not even achieved a generally agreed definition, see UNEP: *Trade-related Measures and Multilateral Environmental Agreements*, 2007, 5 *et seq.*, available at: <http://www.unep.ch/etb/areas/pdf/MEA%20Papers/TradeRelated_MeasuresPaper.pdf>. Also, UNEP: *Multilateral Environmental Agreements: A Handbook for Afghan Officials*, 2008, UNEP, 8 *et seq.*, available at: <http://postconflict.unep.ch/publications/afg_tech/theme_02/afg_mea_handbook.pdf>.
3   A special – and overlooked – feature of MEAs is that they establish a self-governing, treaty-based autonomous institutional arrangement which may be considered to be intergovernmental organizations (IGOs) "albeit of a less formal, more ad hoc nature than traditional IGOs", Churchill, R.R., Ufstein, G., "Autonomous Institutional Arrangements in Multilateral Environmental Agreements: A Little-Noticed Phenomenon in International Law", *American Journal of International Law*, Vol. 94, 2000, 623–659.
4   Raftopoulos, E., *The Inadequacy of the Contractual Analogy in the Law of Treaties*, Publications of the Hellenic Institute of International & Foreign Law, Vol. 14, Alkyon Publishers, Athens, 1990; Parry, C., *The Sources and Evidences of International Law*, Manchester University Press, 1965, 48–55.
5   There is nothing that can have existence outside of context but context is never absolutely determinable, see Critchley, S., *The Ethics of Deconstruction – Derrida and Levinas*, Edinburgh University Press, 1999, 32 *et seq.*; Levinson, S.C., *Pragmatics*, Cambridge University Press, 1983, 35 *et seq.*

remarked, an essential characteristic of a treaty is "that it is negotiable as that it is binding".[6] Treaties form aspects of the canvass of international order that evolves horizontally and continuously and contextually.[7]

Relatedly, the BCS – like all conventional environmental regimes of ICI – is built up and governed by States, with the contributing participation of relevant Non-State Actors, *in relation to the internal context* (domestic orders of the State Parties, particular socio-economic, political, technological, geographical and cultural conditions featuring the Mediterranean Region, or the developing internal order – established practice and decisions – of the conventional regime) as well as *to the external context* (the existing and developing related international order – conventional or declarative, which forms a horizontal order in process). It is constituted and implemented as *an aspect* of the process of polycentric international environmental governance. It is constructively related to the multiplicity of conventional regimes managing the protection of the environment and sustainable development at interacting regional and global levels, and it presupposes, for its operation, national, vertical orders. In fact, *the States Parties are in a particular, sufficiently contextualized, treaty relationship of international common interest governing the protection of the marine environment and the natural resources of the Mediterranean towards sustainability*. They form, in brief, a conventional regime of ICI for environmental sustainability governance.

2 *Sovereignty over Natural Resources as Relational Fiduciary Governance*

Sovereignty with respect to the sustainable governance of States' marine environment and their natural resources should not be viewed as analogous to ownership. Its character is, in fact, not proprietary but fiduciary. It should, in other words, be explained as *a relationship of confidence* in which the 'fiduciary' (the State or the States) is vested with the role of exercising a governance for public benefit, 'for the commonwealth',[8] for international common interest, protect-

---

6 Parry, C., *supra* note 4, 50–52.

7 As Judge Huber, the sole arbitrator in the *Island of Palmas Case, 1928*, most perceptively declared, long ago, "International law, the structure of which is not based on any super-State organization, cannot be presumed to reduce a right such as territorial sovereignty...to the category of an abstract right, without concrete manifestations... Manifestations of territorial sovereignty assume, it is true, different forms, according to conditions of time and place", Permanent Court of Arbitration (1928): No. XIX, *Island of Palmas case (Netherlands, USA), 4 April 1928*, in: *Reports of International Arbitral Awards*, Vol. II, 829, 839, 840.

8 *Salus populi suprema lex est* found in Cicero's *De Legibus* (book III, part 3, sub. VIII). According to Locke, this is "certainly so just and fundamental a rule, that he who sincerely

ing and promoting the interests of present and future generations ('the principal') on equitable bases. In effect, States' role within the framework of conventional environmental regimes of ICI is akin to a kind of international public trusteeship (Sovereign Trusteeship).

All current or second generation conventional environmental regimes (CERS) of ICI display a strong relational turn denoting *a continuously progressing institutionalization of relationships with Non-State Actors for better sustainability governance*. This relational turn does not, in actuality, bring about any transformation of the legal nature of these conventional regimes. States continue to be the central actors, the 'Parties',[9] retaining their determining position and role by virtue of which their fiduciary duties (and powers) arise. A clear manifestation of this point is the 'conventionality element' of the environmental regime of ICI. States, playing a pivotal role in the governance of these regimes, negotiate their constitution[10] and their consensus-establishment, the required level of their specific implementation, their progressive advancement and the scope of their revision *in context*. Relevant Non-State Actors, including competent intergovernmental organizations and a variety of 'stakeholders' (non-governmental organizations, professional groups, local governments, private

---

follows it cannot dangerously err." Locke, J., *Two Treatises of Government*, 1690, Bk. II "An Essay concerning the True Original, Extent and End of Civil Government", Everyman's Library (Introduction by W.S. Carpenter), 1978, Ch. XIII, para. 158.

9 The term may also include this type of intergovernmental organization (the European Union or any similar regional economic integration organization) having a special functional and legal link to the Conventional Environmental regime (competence in respect of matters governed by the Conventional Environmental regime); and, if regional, having 'at least one member' belonging to the region (*e.g.* Barcelona Convention, Art. 30) or even affecting it (*e.g.* OSPAR Convention, 1992, Art. 25). Some recent Conventional Environmental regimes provide the standard clause that these regional economic integration organizations may become a Party "without any of its member States being a Party" and if one or more of its member States is a Party to the Convention "the organization and its member States shall decide on their respective responsibilities for the performance of their obligations under the Convention" but they are not entitled to "to exercise rights under the Convention concurrently" (*e.g.* Convention on Climate Change, 1992, Art. 22(2); Convention on Biodiversity, 1992, Art. 34(2); Basel Convention, 1989, Art. 22(2); Aarhus Convention, 1998, Art. 19(3)).

10 For the constitutive phase of negotiating a conventional environmental regime referring to the process of its establishment or enhancement (negotiation as constitutive governance) see Raftopoulos, E., "International Environmental Negotiation as a Governance Technique", in: *Contributions to International Environmental Negotiation in the Mediterranean Context* (ed. by E. Raftopoulos and M.L. McConnell), MEPIELAN Studies in International Environmental Law and Negotiation – 2, Ant. N. Sakkoulas-Bruylant, 2004, 28 *et seq*.

sector, indigenous peoples, the public and other interest groups) contribute to this unceasing process as 'related actors' for the better and, potentially,[11] more democratic, more socially acceptable and harmonized ICI governance of the conventional environment regime.

In this framework, the governance of CERs of ICI is relational because the regime is authoritatively constructed and developed *in relation to its context* (*international context*: compatible with, and expansive of, the field of international order – *internal context*: compatible with political, legal, socio-economic, geographical or cultural conditions determining the scale of application and advancement of the conventional regime at the collective and individual/ national level). Its constitution, implementation, progressive specification and revision are generated through a structured (institutionally and procedurally) negotiating process, *authoritatively* punctuating the continuous course of the ICI CER relationship of States in context – *a process of horizontal governance*. In fact, a "generative, continuous governance of ICI serving its legislative purpose" is required instead of "exact contractual-type performance".

At the same time, the very 'occurrence' of CERs' constitution, implementative specification and revision requires a *vertical governance/government, it presupposes* the authority structure of a State (ratification, effective legal implementation by a hierarchically structured administration including compatible adaptations, revision). Vertical governance/government is also associated with the legally recognized instances of individual/sovereign action in the framework of the conventional regime (reservations, interpretative declarations, withdrawal, or interpretation/settlements of disputes). In brief, at the interstate level, *relational governance of CERs of ICI advances as an interaction between horizontal and vertical governance/ between governance and government* where 'subjective normativity' unfolds from the fiduciary aspect of such governance and the specific conception of States as international trustees.

At the level of State – Non-State Actors, the relational character of CERs' governance is institutionalized as a vertical top-to-bottom (down-scaling) governance relationship: States, exercising sovereign trusteeship governance of the CERs of ICI, are vested with *the relational duty to ensure public participation* in the governance of the regime by appropriately and effectively orientating their domestic orders. Such participation refers to the granting of specified procedural rights to the public regarding access to information, participation

---

11 For an interesting analysis of this potentiality and the tensions and contradictions of the 'governance-beyond-the-state' see Swyngedouw, E., "Governance Innovation and the Citizen: The Janus Face of Governance-beyond-the-State", *Urban Studies*, Vol. 42, No. 11, 2005, 1991–2006.

in the decision-making process, and access to justice. Their scope and scale of specification are context-dependent.

Moreover, it is institutionalized as a horizontal relational governance: States Parties grant to Non-State Actors *the status of observer*, thus forging their contributing function to the relational governance of CERs in accordance with their relevance and competence, while final decisions rest with State Parties – and Intergovernmental Organizations when, exercising competence in fields covered by CERs, may also be Parties.[12] Non-State Actors may provide an important input in the Pre-Negotiation and Constitutive Negotiation of CERs, in the formulation of the various forms of implementative specification instruments, as well as in the Renegotiation for their revision, opening the door to the integration of social, scientific, technological and economic perspectives, concepts and principles.[13] States Parties may also proceed to set up *subsidiary relational organs* within the framework of CERs comprising States Parties and representatives of Non-State Actors on an equal footing, vesting them with significant competence.[14] They may also establish *partnerships implementing CERs with relevant Non-State Actors.* These forms of relational governance are conditional upon the contextual requirements of CERs and they are scaled accordingly.

3 On the Paradigmatic Relationship between Public Trust and Sustainability Governance

In essence, the international trust approach to the BCS and other CERs relates to the contemporary approach to the public trusteeship which has mainly been developed in the framework of domestic orders. In fact, public trusteeship is well established in the US, emanating from the English Common Law of Charitable Trust, and is widely internationalized, in an express or implied

---

12 For instance the EU is a Party to many CERs, taking an active part in their constitutive negotiation, their ratification and their implementation. For a detailed table see <http://ec.europa.eu/environment/international_issues/pdf/agreements_en.pdf>.

13 For the three phases of the negotiation process as a governance process see Raftopoulos, E., "International Environmental Negotiation as a Governance Technique", *supra* note 10, 3–64.

14 For instance, in the framework of the BCS, the CPs have established such an organ, the *Mediterranean Commission on Sustainable Development (MCSD)*, see MAP: *Report of Ninth Ordinary Meeting of the Contracting Parties to the Convention for the Protection of the Marine Environment and the Coastal Region of the Mediterranean and its Protocols*, Barcelona 5–8 June 1995, UNEP(OCA)/MED IG.5/16, 8 June 1995, UNEP/MAP, Annex XIII, 1(A)(iv)a.1.

form, in the Constitutions and Statutes of many States all over the world.¹⁵ However, approaching the BCS and other CERs as an international trust regime for the purpose of adequately explaining the element of its sustainability governance, we should not be caught up in the legal verbiage and logical problems of *measuring* the application of the domestic law analogy of the well-known Public Trust Doctrine (PTD): the traditional narrowness of the PTD (its application only to water resources),¹⁶ or whether the PTD is not simply a common law doctrine but a doctrine incorporated into the Constitution or legislation of States and having a general scope including all natural resources.¹⁷ Further, despite its wider evolution into a 'doctrine of ecological protection' in many domestic orders – incorporating the precautionary principle, sustainable development and intergeneration equity as a result of the courts' interpretation of the doctrine or as a part of constitutional and statutory pronouncements of the public's right to a healthy environment or the right to life¹⁸ – thus

---

15 See Blumm, M.C., Guthrie, R.D., "Internationalizing the Public Trust Doctrine", *UC Davis Law Review*, Vol. 44, 2012, available at: <http://ssrn.com/abstract=1816628>.

16 Recognizing that the waters of the State are a public resource owned by and available to all citizens equally for the purposes of navigation, conducting commerce, fishing, recreation, and similar uses, which is not invalidated by private ownership of the underlying land, and that the public trustee – usually the State – must act to maintain and enhance the trust's resources for the benefit of future generations. The PTD has historically been applied by American courts primarily to submerged lands on the shores of the ocean, lakes, rivers and streams, to the waters above them, to groundwater, and to parklands, while some decisions extended its application to protection to wildlife found in public areas or to migratory fowl – others refused to expand it beyond its traditional scope. A pioneering theoretical vision of the PTD going beyond the doctrine's traditional scope was developed by Joseph L. Sax, "The Public Trust Doctrine in Natural Resource Law and Management", *Michigan Law Review*, Vol. 68, 1970, 471.

17 In a very recent decision by a Texas District Court, *Bonser-Lain v. Texas Commission on Environmental Quality*, Case No. D-1-GN-11-002194 (201st Dist. Ct., Travis County, Texas), the Court stated that "the doctrine includes all natural resources of the State", and that the PTD "is not simply a common law doctrine" but "is incorporated into the Texas Constitution". And relying also upon the Texas Clean Air Act authorizing the Texas Commission on Environmental Quality to act "to protect against adverse effects, including global warming", the Court recognized the possibility that the PTD may justify the creation of an "atmospheric trust".

18 See Blumm, M.C., Guthrie, R.D., *supra* note 15. As is clearly pointed out, the development of the PTD has taken place in several diverse countries on four continents (India, Pakistan, the Philippines, Uganda, Kenya, Nigeria, South Africa, Brazil, Ecuador, Canada), being equated with environmental protection and frequently entrenched in constitutional and statutory provisions, whereas in two countries (India and the Philippines) the PTD jurisprudence has located it in *natural law*.

usefully pointing to the process of *internationalization of the* PTD, we should not attempt to construct a uniform theoretical argument justifying an extra-contextual, comparable transfer of the doctrine from national to international law. Instead, we have to grasp the paradigmatic field relationship between Public Trust and sustainability governance of the BCS whereby the former makes the latter more robustly intelligible, more comprehensible (γνωριμώτερον according to Aristotle), bringing out the fiduciary nature of this relationship.[19] In fact, the concept of public trust is the medium of 'knowability' of sustainability governance of CERs.

In light of this, the paradigmatic relationship between Public Trust and sustainability governance of CERs for ICI is to be understood as follows: Public Trust exposes, in its own knowable elements, the field in which sustainability governance of CERs becomes more equitably intelligible, pointing out beyond,[20] and generating a new dynamic context for its development and guidance in conditions of uncertainty, complementarity and paradoxes in implementative-specification.[21] *It is not the dichotomically-based logical comparability between sustainability governance of CERs and public trust that matters, but their paradigmatic field relationship making the former more robustly intelligible through the contextual knowability of the latter.* And this contextual knowability is characteristically associated not only with *the potentialities of its express aspect* (the Anglo-American PTD, its remarkable internationalization in Southeast Asia, Africa, South America and North America) or with *the potentialities of implied aspects of its domestic orders operation* (*e.g.* environmental legislation of continental European countries where the common law trust is not part of their national legal tradition). It is also, more subtly, associated with its *cross-cultural familiarity*: thus, the Islamic *waqf for charitable purposes* bears a notable resemblance to the common law charitable trust.[22] For our purposes, however, this is important for evaluating the potential paradigmatic force of this concept as providing an Islamic approach to a kind of sustainable governance for social purposes rather than searching for

---

19 For this conception of 'paradigm' see the Aristotelian treatment of paradigm in his *Rhetorics*, 1357b. Also, Agamben, G., "What is a Paradigm?", Lecture at the European Graduate School, August 2002, available at <http://www.egs.edu/faculty/giorgio-agamben/articles/what-is-a-paradigm/>.

20 Etymologically, the meaning of the Greek word 'para-digm' comes from the word παρά = 'beside' and δείκνυμι = 'to point out': it is something that 'points out beside/beyond'.

21 The paradox lies in the fact that the more the ostensible thing is specified through its implementation in context, the more it is changed.

22 See Fratcher, W.F., "Trust", *International Encyclopedia of Comparative Law*, Vol. 6:11, Mohr, Tübingen, 1973, 84–141.

comparisons.[23] All in all, the public trust paradigm embraces public trusteeship potentialities integrated in *an all-encompassing multi-dimensional context,* as a public interest normative medium encoding a socially and culturally significant meaning and function.[24]

III Sustainability Governance in the Barcelona Convention System: Evidence and Prospects of Its Public Trust Language

The force of the contemporary public trusteeship as a paradigm lies in its extension to environmental governance and its projection of conservationist principles to natural resources, both aquatic and terrestrial, thus being liberated from the confines of its static traditional notion of 'another ownership'. It functions as a 'fiduciary' institution which creates a legal status for the sovereign to hold and govern natural resources in trust for its people, protecting and preserving the environment and resources as a unit in a sustainable manner, for present and future generations. As such, it fosters democratization of decision-making and broadly reveals the qualities in the evolutionary management of public resources, while containing a legal right to the public which had to be enforceable against the government and had to advance contemporary environmental management and juridical concerns in context.[25] At the same time, trusts should be seen "as self contained, autonomous institutions, zones of self-regulation"[26] into which positive law judgments should not intrude and, as a result, they should inevitably require finesse and judgment on the part of the trustees. As the idea of any legal trust, and especially of a public trust, may well exist in some extra-legal sense, varying in accordance with the detected purpose requirements, so the BCS, as an autonomous international trust regime of ICI, serves sustainability *inter-subjectively* and *in context.*

As a creative context, the public trust approach provides the platform for the better law and policy knowability of sustainability governance exercised in the framework of the BCS – and of any CER – in its continuous finding and

---

23   See, in this respect, Stibbard, P., Russell, D., Bromley, B., "Understanding the Waqf in the World of Trust", *Trusts and Trustees,* Vol. 18, 2012, 785–810.

24   This is to paraphrase an excellent contemporary account of 'art' given by the anthropologist Richard Anderson which encompasses all cultural diversity by defining it as "culturally significant meaning, skillfully encoded in an affecting, sensuous medium", Anderson, R., *Calliope's Sisters: A Comparative Study of Philosophies of Art,* Prentice Hall, Englewood Cliffs, NJ, 1990, 238.

25   See, generally, Sax, J.L., *supra* note 16, *passim.*

26   See Gardner, S., *An Introduction to the Law of Trusts,* Clarendon Press, Oxford, 1990, 192.

building of ICJ. Unlike "the frequent invocation of trust metaphors without juridical content" and the use of the words 'stewardship' and 'trustee' or 'custodian' in the environmental field "as purely metaphorical formulations",[27] or even as metaphors for navigating negotiations and creating more options,[28] the evidence of trust language in the BCS emerges from its textual and contextual aspects.

1 *The Textual Aspect of the Trust Base*

The Preamble to the Barcelona Convention sets out a far-reaching communitarian approach: it declares that "the marine environment of the Mediterranean Sea Area" is "common heritage for the benefit and enjoyment of present and future generations" and, as a result, the CPs are responsible for its preservation and sustainable development.[29] Interestingly, the Preamble to the ICZM Protocol (2008) takes a step further: it states that the coastal zones of the Mediterranean Sea "are the common natural and cultural heritage of the peoples of the Mediterranean" and, as a result, "they *should be preserved and used judiciously* for the benefit of present and future generations".[30]

Under Art. 4 of the Barcelona Convention, the CPs are vested with the general relational obligation, jointly or individually, "to prevent, abate, combat and to the fullest possible extent eliminate pollution of the Mediterranean Sea Area and to protect and enhance the marine environment in that Area so as to contribute towards its sustainable development."[31] At the same time, they are under the duty to implement the Mediterranean Action Plan (MAP) by taking all appropriate measures, and, further, to pursue the protection of the marine environment and the natural resources of the Mediterranean as an integral part of the development process, "meeting the needs of present and future generations in an equitable manner".[32] In doing so, they are entrusted with the application of the precautionary principle, the polluter pays principle, the EIA procedures at national and transnational level, and the promotion of ICZM.[33] Further, they are required to adopt implementing programmes and measures with time limits, to utilize BAT and BET to promote environmentally sound

---

27 Sand, P., "Sovereignty Bounded: Public Trusteeship for Common Pool Resources?", *Global Environmental Politics*, Vol. 4, No. 1, 2004, 47, 54–55.
28 On this function of metaphors see Smith, T.H., "Metaphors for Navigating Negotiations", *Negotiation Journal*, Vol. 21, No. 3, 2005, 343–364.
29 See Barcelona Convention (1976), Preamble, para. 2.
30 See ICZM Protocol (2008), Preamble, para. 3 (*emphasis mine*).
31 Barcelona Convention, Art. 4(1).
32 *Ibid.*, Art. 4(2).
33 *Ibid.*, Art. 4(3).

technology in context, to cooperate in the adoption of performative Protocols and to promote the implementing measures of the BCS within the competent international bodies.[34]

2 The Contextual Aspect of the Trust Base

The Barcelona Convention and its Protocols contain general relational obligation-duties and powers *contextualizing the trust governance of the conventional regime* in terms of *regime referential linkage, normative consistency* at all levels (global, regional bilateral, national) and *added value approach*. They thus provide:

- the relational obligation-duty of the CPs to act in conformity with international law when applying the BCS (consistency with the Law of the Sea Convention (LOSC) or applicable IMO Conventions, the Basel Convention or the UN Biodiversity Convention);
- the relational power-right of the CPs further to constitute 'related' bilateral or multilateral agreements for the protection of the Mediterranean marine environment and the conservation of its natural resources consistent with BCS and in conformity with international law;
- the relational power-right of the CPs *to individuate* their participation by standard 'disclaimer or without prejudice clauses' preserving or reserving "the rights, the present and future claim or legal views of any Party relating to the Law of the Sea"[35] or the right of any Party to apply 'stricter domestic measures' under its national legislation,[36] or the sovereign immunity of warships or other ships 'in government service',[37] or the right of any Party to operate 'national security and defence activities' in its coastal zone;[38]
- the relational obligation-duty of the CPs to promote, individually or collectively and through relevant international organizations the implementation of the BCS to all the non-party States.[39]

Such a contextualization should be generally understood not only as 'a regime body' (relational duties and powers prescribed by the CER) but also as 'a regime

---

34 *Ibid.*, Art. 4(4–6).
35 SPA and Biodiversity Protocol (1995), Art. 2(2); ICZM Protocol (2008), Art. 4(1).
36 SPA and Biodiversity Protocol (1995), Art. 27; ICZM Protocol (2008), Art. 4(3). See also the more specified terms in the Hazardous Wastes Protocol (1996), Art. 4.
37 Barcelona Convention (1976), Art. 3(5).
38 ICZM Protocol (2008), Art. 4(4).
39 See *e.g.* Barcelona Convention (1976), Art. 3, Prevention and Emergency Protocol (2002), Art. 4(2), Hazardous Wastes Protocol (1996), Arts. 6 (4–5), 7(5), 9(8).

process' (continuous negotiating process of the CER). Such a fusion manifests the complementary relationship between normative content and its continuous specification process effectuated through negotiation. In fact, normative content is continuously revealed through negotiated specification required by the progressive development in the implementation of the CER.

A clear indication of this complementarity relationship is provided by the LOSC which in Art. 197 sets out the encapsulation of the three fundamental criteria of contextualization:

> States shall cooperate on a global basis and, as appropriate, *on a regional basis*, ...in formulating and elaborating international rules, standards and recommended practices and procedures *consistent with* the Convention, for the protection and preservation of the marine environment, taking into account *characteristic regional features*.

Such fusion in contextualization is even more striking in Art. 237 LOSC which sets out the requirement of consistency of special conventions on the protection and preservation of the marine environment, constituted in furtherance of the general principles set out in this Convention (added value), "with the general principles and objectives of this Convention".

Overall, the BCS provides the establishment of an international environmental trust regime of fiduciary governance, the *corpus* of which is *conventionally identified* – explicitly or impliedly – by the framework Barcelona Convention and its gradually specified performative Protocols. To attain sustainability, the trust governance of the BCS is associated with principles, relational power-rights and obligation-duties/operating in conditions of uncertainty, complementarity within the internal and external context, and in a process of negotiably agreed transformations better serving sustainability. Thus, the trust corpus of the BCS becomes progressively specified by the scaled adoption of performative Protocols, expanding the scope of conventional environmental governance of the Mediterranean Sea and its resources as a unit. In this process, the BCS manifests *two basic contextual characteristics*: first, the specifying Protocols *are not exhaustive* – further performative Protocols may also be implied by ICI purpose of the conventional environmental regime; second, the framework Convention-performative Protocols system *is evolved gradually and in a continuous progress responding to the conventional regime exigencies* – its expansion is scaled and generated through a consensus-negotiating process in a time-space context advancing sustainability. This has the implication that the conventionally identified corpus of the international trust regime in its continuous progress to sustainability should remain unaffected by general economic or social pressures to decrease environmental protection and diverge from the sustainable development objective.

3 *The Trilateral Structure*

A fundamental consequence of envisaging BCS – and any conventional environmental regime – as an international trust regime is structural. It is now pertinent to proceed to an adequate determination of the trilateral legal structure[40] entailed by the public trust paradigm.

The CPs to the BCS (the Mediterranean States and the EU) should be considered as ICI regime Trustors or Settlors in two senses: as collective founders of the BCS, who have negotiated the consensus-establishment of this conventional regime (Mediterranean Trustors or Settlors), and as collective representatives of the international community, who have negotiated the scope of the contextuality of the BCS related to conventional regimes or established international practices (International Community Trustors or Trustees). In these two combined senses, they serve ICI.

At the same time, the CPs should also be considered as ICI regime Trustees: they are vested with powers-rights and duties, as international public trustees, to govern the specified aspects of the trust regime for the benefit of the present and future generations. Likewise, they constitute Trustees in two senses: Mediterranean Trustees for the implementation or revision of the BCS in their individual-collective identity and International Community Trustees for the effective and expanding operation of the contextual inter-linkages of the BCS with related conventional regimes or established international practices, thus serving ICI.

The people concerned should be considered as Beneficiaries: the CPs as ICI regime trustees are responsible to all beneficiaries (present and future generations), whereas the current generation is both beneficiary and trustee for the future generations. Acting as Beneficiaries, the public, whatever their legal identity, are empowered to participate in, and hold the CPs accountable for, societally adequate intergenerational decision-making regarding the trust governance of the specified aspects (Protocols, decisions) of the BCS. Non-State Actors participating in a horizontal governance partnership with the CPs – the International Trustees, hold both the role of Beneficiaries towards the International Trustees and the role of Relational Trustees towards future generations. And this hybrid role of Non-State Actors as Beneficiaries and Relational Trustees is entirely consistent with the sustainable environmental governance of trust resources.

---

40 See *e.g.* Sand, P., *supra* note 27, 55–57.

IV On the Fiduciary Aspects of the Governance of the Barcelona Convention System: Mapping the Trust Language

1 *The Public Participation Pattern*

The public trust approach to the BCS requires a stronger, more meaningful participation pattern of the *public-as-beneficiaries* or *intergenerational beneficiaries* – thus introducing a temporal dimension (present and future generations) to the beneficiaries. As a result, the fiduciary aspect of environmental governance will be specifically implemented, facilitating the enforceability of the terms of the conventional trust regime, the advancement of its legislative (ICI) purpose and, relatedly, the participatory democratization of its legislative or administrative decision-making. Addressing the current deficiencies of the participatory level in relational environmental governance, it will provide the basis for the development of a coherent, compatible and complementary right to *public participation as beneficiaries* (access to information, public participation, and access to justice). Of decisive importance in this regard is the normative impact of the relational external context and its specific developments provided by the Aarhus Convention[41] or the EU's relevant legislation.

Art. 15 of the Barcelona Convention refers to the standard a-temporal conception of the public and the widely discretionary duty of the CPS 'to ensure' that their competent authorities will give the public *appropriate* access to environmental information, *without prejudice to their right to refuse in certain cases*, and the *opportunity* to participate in the decision-making process.

All in all, Art. 15 retains a state-centric backbone. It simply lays down a framework, widely discretionary duty of the CPS *to give adequate effect* to the participatory right of the public, through its national system and its competent authorities – a 'State obligation of result' as was stated by the Arbitral Tribunal in the MOX Plant Case when constructing the similar Art. 9 of the OSPAR Convention.[42] On the other hand, the Protocols approach the issue, at the level of specification, in a diverse manner, presenting a fragmented and widely

---

41 *Convention on Access to Information, Public Participation in Decision-Making and Access to Justice in Environmental Matters, 1998,* in: *International Legal Materials (ILM),* Vol. 38, 1999, 517. It entered into force on 30 October 2001.

42 Permanent Court of Arbitration: *Dispute Concerning Access to Information under Article 9 of the OSPAR Convention (Ireland v. United Kingdom)* (The MOX Plant), in: *ILM,* Vol. 42, 2003, 1118, 1143. The Tribunal took the view that Art. 9(1) of the OSPAR Convention "is advisedly pitched at a level that imposes an obligation of result rather than merely to provide access to a domestic regime which is directed at obtaining the required result" (para. 137).

discretionary picture. Thus, whereas two of the Protocols do not refer this matter (the Dumping Protocol, 1976, as amended, and the Offshore Protocol, 1994), the remaining five Protocols contain variable general references. Of these, the ICZM Protocol, 2008, as the last and most sustainability-oriented Protocol, is of particular interest: it provides a distinctly specified and progressive framework for public information and participation, incorporating even some of the fundamendal standardized language of the Aarhus Convention, thus adding to the fiduciary aspect of governance.

More specifically, the ICZM Protocol sets out the duty of the Parties to ensure "appropriate governance allowing adequate and timely participation in a transparent decision-making process by local polulations and stakeholders in civil society concerned with coastal zones".[43] It also stipulates their duty to "take the necessary measures to ensure the appropriate involvement *in the phases of the formulation and implementation of coastal marine strategies, plans and programmes or projects, as well as the issuing of the various authorizations*, of the various stakeholders" and to provide information "in an adequate, timely and effective manner", so as to ensure "efficient governance *throughout the process* of the integrated management of coastal zones".[44] The "various stakeholders" include "the territorial communities and public entities concerned, economic operators, non-governmental organizations, social actors, and the public concerned", and their participation involves, *inter alia*, "*consultative bodies, inquiries or public hearings, and may extend to partnerships.*" More importantly, the Protocol provides for *the stakeholders' right to access to justice*: the Parties have the duty to make available the right to recourse to legal or administrative justice "to any stakeholder challenging decisions, acts or omissions." In addition, this duty of the Parties is expanded to ensure *the right of the stakeholders to access to other independent means of settlement of disputes* – "other than a court of law" in the wording of the Aarhus Convention (Art. 9(1)) – of a political (mediation) or a mixed character (conciliation). Finally, the Protocol prescribes the duty of the Parties to develop a systematic, long-term strategy of information which will enable stakeholders to enjoy meaningful and knowlegable participation in the plans, programmes and projects concerning the coastal zone.[45]

The public trust approach would require an integrated pattern of the public participation in the BCS being appropriately supplemented by the 1998 UNECE

---

43   ICZM Protocol, 2008, Art. 6.
44   *Ibid.*, Art. 14 *(emphasis mine)*.
45   *Ibid.*, Art. 15.

Aarhus Convention. In fact, the Aarhus Convention *constitutes the normative supplementary context* for those CPs to the BCS which have ratified this Convention. Twelve CPs, including the EU, have done so,[46] and one has signed it (Monaco) for which the Convention has a relevant normative and evidentiary value that points to the accurate expression of its views and intention at the time of signature.[47] Moreover, the Aarhus Convention *constitutes a powerful referential context* for the rest of the CPs which are not members of the ECE. Being already obligatory for more than half of the CPs, the Aarhus Convention provides for the rest of them a frame of reference representing specific standards and procedural rights to be appropriately applied by them in context and within the objects and purposes of the BCS and its developing practice. Clear evidence of this is the reference to the Aarhus Convention in the development of guidelines concerning public participation for the preparation, adoption, implementation and follow up of National Action Plans (NAPs) in the framework of the Strategic Action Programme (SAP) for the implementation of the amended LBS Protocol, 1980,[48] or, its declared importance for the attainment of the major objectives of the Mediterranean Strategy on Sustainable Development (MSSD) where the ratification of the Aarhus Convention is stated to be *an indicator* for MSSD follow-up.[49]

Moreover, the Aarhus Convention sets out the potentiality of expanding the scope of its geographical application and, hence, of *relativizing its regionality*: Art. 19(3) states that any other State that is simply a Member of the United Nations may accede to the Convention upon approval by the Meeting of the

---

46   Albania (2001), Bosnia and Herzegovina (2008), Croatia (2007), Cyprus (2003), European Union (2005), France (2002), Greece (2006), Italy (2001), Malta (2002), Montenegro (2009), Slovenia (2004), and Spain (2004).

47   Permanent Court of Arbitration: The MOX Plant, *supra* note 42, Dissenting Opinion of Gavan Griffith, 1162–1163. See also Aust, A., *Modern Treary Law and Practice*, Cambridge University Press, 2000, 93–96.

48   MAP: GEF *Project "Determination of Priority Actions for the Further Elaboration and Implementation of the Strategic Action Programme for the Mediterranean Sea" – Common Methodology*, UNEP-Athens, 2003, 2. Also MAP: *Strategic Action Programme – Public Participation in the National Action Plan (NAPs) for the Strategic Action Programme (SAP) to Address Pollution from Land-Based Sources in the Mediterranean Region*, UNEP(DEC)/MED/GEF WG.245/7, 3 Feb. 2004, UNEP/MAP, Athens, 2004.

49   MAP: *Mediterranean Strategy for Sustainable Development – A Framework for Environmental Sustainability and Shared Prosperity*, 14th Ordinary Meeting of the Contracting Parties to the Convention for the Protection of the Marine Environment and the Coastal Region of the Mediterranean and its Protocols, UNEP(DEC)/MED IG.16/7, 27 June 2005, UNEP/MAP, Athens, 2006, 8, Annex 2, 33.

Parties, thus indicating the potentiality of the progressive *de-regionalization* of its standards and procedural rights and, in effect, for its eventual transformation into a conventional regime with more global/extra-regional characteristics.

2   *The Fiduciary Duties of the Contracting Parties to Act as Public Trustees*

A cluster of fiduciary duties of the CPs as public trustees should now be examined, making the BCS even more intelligible as an international trust relationship.

a   The Fiduciary Duty of Institutional Coordination

Building on the concept of public trusteeship, the CPs are under the fiduciary duty to establish contextually efficient and effective institutional coordination at the domestic level. While maintaining their autonomy, State authorities/agencies *should be directed to operate in an integrated manner coordinating their activities*, thus abandoning their hitherto diverse, sectoral approaches and actions. They should operate as trustees with complementary activities for the comprehensive attainment of a common interest purpose and work proactively with one another to ensure that their actions are consistent with the sustainable development of the trust resources. A public trust approach would require responsible comprehensive management of the trust resources as the basis of coordination of all related 'trustees', each from the perspective of its role and specified responsibilities but all in a common mission to protect the environment and the trust resource.

In fact, this fiduciary aspect of environmental governance at the domestic level is envisaged only in the last adopted ICZM Protocol (2008) where the challenge of institutional fragmentation within each State Party is met by a special provision. Thus, Art. 7 prescribes the duty of the States Parties to ensure *institutional coordination* through appropriate bodies or mechanisms in order to avoid sectoral approaches and facilitate the establishment of comprehensive approaches. This institutional coordination should be *horizontal* ("between the various authorities competent for both the marine and land parts of the coastal zones in the different administrative services") as well as *vertical* (operating at "the national, regional and local levels"). Moreover, *an additional layer of coordination* is stipulated: the development of coastal strategies, plans and programmes and the various authorizations for activities require close coordination between national authorities and regional and local bodies "through joint consultative bodies or joint decision-making procedures". As is specifically required, the competent national, regional and local coastal zone authorities should work together to strengthen the coherence and effectiveness of the coastal strategies, plans and programmes relying on an equitable contextual balance ("insofar as practicable").

Unlike the recently entered into force Offshore Protocol (1994), where the challenge of institutional fragmentation is inadequately treated and institutional coordination is conspicuously missing,[50] the Specially Protected Areas and Biodiversity Protocol (1995) clearly indicates this fiduciary duty in Art. 7(4) stipulating the duty of the CPs to ensure the coordination of administration and management of the established specially protected areas covering both land and marine areas as a whole. Despite its overtly open-textured language, this provision manifests the (legislative) intention of the Parties effectively to reduce administrative barriers through appropriate coordination of the administration and management of these specially protected areas.

b   The Fiduciary Duty of Compliance

The more recent structural development of the BC regime which led to the establishment of a full *compliance mechanism* goes beyond the general procedural provision on compliance of Art. 27. Set up by *the Decision IG. 17/2 on Compliance Procedure and Mechanisms at the 15th MOP*, the so-called *Compliance Committee*[51] emerged as an advanced subsidiary organ of the BCS to attain its better, more eficient implementation, taking into account the specific situation of each CP. However, its structure and its function still remain largely faithful to the positivist state-centric model with no relational concessions to the public.

Thus, the seven members of the Committee are elected "by the Meeting of the Contracting Parties from a list of candidates nominated by the Contracting Parties",[52] and there is no such right for the public that would allow *direct*

---

50   See *e.g.* contingency planning (Art. 16 and Annex VII), monitoring (Art. 19) or the removal of installations (Art. 20).

51   MAP: *Decision IG 17/2: Procedures and Mechanisms on Compliance under the Barcelona Convention and its Protocols*, Report of the 15th Ordinary Meeting of the Contracting Parties to the Convention for the Protection of the Marine Environment and the Coastal Region of the Mediterranean and its Protocols, Almeria (Spain), 15–18 January 2008, UNEP(DEC)/MED IG. 17/10, Annex V, Decisions of the 15th Meeting of the Contracting Parties, 23–27. See also, MAP: *Decision IG. 19/1: Rules of Procedure for the Compliance Committee and its Work during 2010–2011 Biennium*, Report of the 16th Ordinary Meeting of the Contracting Parties to the Convention for the Protection of the Marine Environment and the Coastal Region of the Mediterranean and its Protocols, Marrakesh (Morocco), 3–5 November 2009, UNEP(DEPI)/MED IG.19/8, Annex II, 1–23.

52   MAP: *Decision IG 17/2: Procedures and Mechanisms on Compliance under the Barcelona Convention and its Protocols, op. cit.*, Section II(3).

involvement, as the Aarhus Convention does. More importantly, the right to trigger the Committee is exclusively conferred upon the CPs and the Secretariat (Self-trigger, Party to Party trigger, Secretariat trigger).[53] No such right is conferred upon the public nor is the right to attend the Meetings of the Committee and to make interventions, as the Bern Convention on the Conservation of European Wildlife and Natural Habitats, 1979, or the Protocol on Water and Health to the UNECE Water Convention, 1999,[54] actually do. Moreover, the inclusion of the right of the public to trigger the Committee could perceptively generate developments in the related operation of the domestic order and its remedies.[55] Relatedly, the more *indirect involvement of the public* is strictly limited to access to documents and information.[56] Other aspects of indirect involvement of the public, like the right of the public to comment on nominations to the Committee or its capacity to be indirectly involved in any follow-up to implement the Committee's findings at the national level, remain out of the purview of the compliance mechanism.

In addition, the fact that the 17th MOP, in view of the total absence of referrals by the CPs and the Secretariat, was only able to deal with the Committee exclusively within the confines of the state-centric approach to compliance, thus lapsing into familiar generalities, raises a lot of questions. Using the typical hortatory language of political appeals to the CPs, the 17th MOP "encourages the CPs to bring before the Compliance Committee for its consideration any problems of interpretation concerning implementation" of the Convention and its Protocols, "urges" those – unidentified – CPs who have not yet done

---

53   *Ibid.*, Section V (18–23).

54   As is provided by Decision I/2, Section VI(16), contained in the Report of the First Meeting of the MOP to this Protocol, "communications may be brought before the Committee by one or more members of the public concerning that Party's compliance with the Protocol, unless that Party has notified the Depositary in writing by the end of the applicable period that it is unable to accept, for a period of not more than four years, the consideration of such communications by the Committee" and that "the Depositary shall without delay notify all Parties of any such notification received", ECE/MP.WH/2/Add.3, EUR/06/5069385/1/Add.3, 3 July 2007, Annex, 5–6.

55   In regard to communications from the public, Section VI (19) of Decision I/2 of the Protocol on Water and Health to the UNECE Water Convention, 1999, provides that "the Committee should, at all relevant stages, take into accountany available domestic remedy unless the application of the remedy is unreasonably prolonged or obviously does not provide an effective and sufficient means of redress." *Ibid.*

56   See Rule 15 "Public Access to Documents and Information", *Rules of Procedure for the Compliane Committee, supra* note 51, providing for the availability to the public of the provisional agenda, reports of the Committee meetings, official documents and, under the conditions stated in Rule 14, of any other non-confidential document.

so to submit their reports on implementation, and "requests" the Committee to "consider general compliance issues, such as recurrent non-compliance problems"!⁵⁷

c   The Fiduciary Duty of Care

In view of the the *autonomous nature* of the BCS – and of all CERs of ICI – and the need authoritatively to advance its public benefit (sustainability) purpose under conditions of uncertainty, complementarity and implementative openness, the required 'finesse and judgment' on the part of the CPs, acting as fiduciary trustees, are also associated with their duty of care. Thus, the CPs are vested with a fiduciary duty that State authorities/agencies act prudently: they should *specifically make use of knowledge, expertise and skills* and *apply continuous monitoring* aiming at the effective, efficient and socially acceptable sustainable governance of the Mediterranean marine and coastal environment and its natural resources. Knowledge, expertise and special skills should be *properly solicited and practised* by the CPs, acting as Trustees, so that *a comprehensive, integrated* (inter-disciplinary, inter-linked) and *contextually relevant* (social/public contribution, process-dependent knowledge) approach to the governance of public trust resources will be generated. State authorities/agencies as public trustees should adequately base their decisions on a multifaceted and evolving expertise knowledge, on established international practices as well as on related traditional and local community knowledge systems which actually reflect the interests of these communities.[58]

Closely associated with this is their procedural duty to conduct continuous monitoring of activities that may affect the marine and coastal environment, and their (unexpected) consequences.[59] Resulting from considerations of

---

57   MAP: *Decision IG 20/1: Compliance Committee: Amendment to the Compliance Procedures and Mechanisms, Programme of Work for Bienniuim 2012–2013 and Partial Renewal of Membership*, Report of the 17th Ordinary Meeting of the Contracting Parties to the Convention for the Protection of the Marine Environment and the Coastal Region of the Mediterranean and its Protocols, Paris (France), 8–10 February 2012, UNEP(DEC)/MED IG. 20/8, Annex II, 1–2.

58   This is particularly true of traditional environmental knowledge, see, generally, International Council for Science, *Science and Traditional Knowledge*, Report from the ICSU Study Group on Science and Traditional Knowledge, 2002, available at: <www.icsu.org/publications/reports-and-reviews/science-traditional-knowledge/Science-traditional-knowledge.pdf>.

59   As asserted by the International Court of Justice (ICJ) in the *Case concerning the Pulp Mills on the River Uruguay* "once operations have started and, where necessary, throughout the life of the project, continuous monitoring of its effects on the environment shall

prudence,[60] this type of fiduciary duty should not only be carried out through appropriate mechanisms but also linked to public access to information derived from continuous monitoring. Such an integrated approach is stipulated in the ICZM Protocol[61] as well as in the LBS Protocol,[62] while continuous monitoring – though less clear about public involvement – is explicitly set out in the SPA & Biodiversity Protocol.[63] Interestingly, continuous monitoring is provided for in the Guidelines on Dumping of Platforms and Other Man-Made Structures at Sea, 2003, adopted by the 13th MOP of the CPs in Catania to assist the CPs in the specific implementation of Art. 4(2)(c) of the Dumping Protocol as amended in 1995.[64]

All these have certain consequences. First, a failure to exercise such prudence may lead to poor decision-making and eventually endanger the sustainability of the public trust resources, thus giving rise to fiduciary *responsibility*. Second, the CPs, in soliciting expert advice, applying established international practices and incorporating local community knowledge, should *ensure their proper consideration in the framework of their sustainability governance*. They should regularly review their performance and safeguard their consistency with the dynamically evolved context (internal and external). As a result, they should be organized by establishing reliable and dynamically working data banks related to the corpus of international environmental trust set up by the BCS, and threats to it, providing good and accessible records with continuously updated information. Finally, the CPs, in their autonomy to act as intergenerational trustees, should *apply expertise prudently and diligently*. Thus,

---

be undertaken." ICJ: *Pulp Mills on the River Uruguay (Argentina v. Uruguay)*, Judgment, 2010, para. 205, 73–74.

60 See, ICJ: *Gabčíkovo-Nagymaros Project (Hungary/Slovakia)*, 1997, Separate Opinion of Vice-President Weeramanty, 111.

61 See ICZM Protocol, Art. 16 on Monitoring and Observation Mechanisms and Networks.

62 See LBS Protocol, Art. 8.

63 See Arts. 3(5), 7(b), Annex I (D.8) of the Protocol as well as the *Strategic Action Programme for the Conservation of Biological Diversity (SAP BIO) in the Mediterranean Region, 2003*, sec. 2.1.2., 31.

64 Monitoring is defined as "the repeated measurement of an effect, whether direct or indirect, on the marine environment and/or of interferences with other legitimate uses of the sea" and contains "predisposal investigations" and "post-disposal studies" referring to compliance monitoring and field monitoring, MAP: *Guidelines on Dumping of Platforms and Other Man-Made Structures at Sea*, 13th Ordinary Meeting of the Contracting Parties to the Convention for the Protection of the Marine Environment and the Coastal Region of the Mediterranean and its Protocols, Catania (Italy), 11–14 November 2003, UNEP(DEC)/MED IG. 15/Inf. 13, at 15.

on the one hand, they should not use scientific dissent as an excuse to avoid action when a reasonable degree of scientific consensus is established, being under the consequential duty to evaluate "the soundness of the scientific opinions proferred." On the other hand, they should apply the 'precautionary principle' – which is largely consistent with the 'prudence' required of fiduciary trustees – in the management of highly uncertain and potentially catastrophic events ("where at best only subjective probabilities can be assigned").[65]

d   The Fiduciary Duty of Liability and Compensation

An important fiduciary duty of the CPs permeates through their framework obligation to determine a liability and compensation regime for damage in the Mediterranean marine environment. As is provided in Art. 16 of the Barcelona Convention, the CPs "undertake to cooperate in the formulation and adoption of appropriate rules and procedures" for the determination of such a regime, posing from the beginning a difficult, multifaceted negotiating problem: should the CPs proceed to negotiate the construction of a generic or a thematic liability and compensation regime? Should they, instead, proceed on a step-by-step approach negotiating, first, guidelines on liability and compensation, thus preparing the ground for a future legal regime? What would be the relationship of such a regime with the existing or evolving related liability and compensation regimes or its reception by their domestic orders?

A conservative direction, called 'a prudent approach', was finally followed. The CPs decided to adopt a step-by-step approach, negotiating generic guidelines on liability and compensation for damage in the Mediterranean marine environment, with a view to forming the basis for an appropriate future binding instrument, a Protocol, and in the hope that, because of their non-binding nature, they would have "an advanced content".[66]

The *Guidelines on Liability and Compensation for Damage Resulting from Pollution of the Marine Environment in the Mediterranean Sea Area*, adopted by

---

65   As A. Scott remarks, "Both trust law and the precautionary principle are…concerned not with maximizing welfare but with protecting against bad outcomes", Scott, A., "Trust Law, Sustainability, and Responsible Action", *Ecological Economics*, Vol. 31, 1999, 139–134, 150.

66   MAP: *Report of the Open-Ended Working Group of Legal and Technical Experts to Propose Appropriate Rules and Procedures for the Determination of Liability and Compensation for Damage Resulting from Pollution of the Marine Environment in the Mediterranean Sea Area, Loutraki, Greece, 7–8 March 2006*, UNEP(DEP)/MED WG 285/4, UNEP/MAP, Athens, Greece, para. 42, 11.

Decision IG 17/4 in 2008 at the 15th MOP,[67] provide a generic model approach[68] related to existing – and listed – global and regional environmental liablity and compensation regimes by a 'without prejudice' Guideline.[69] Despite some substantive merits[70] and their inherently flexible nature, these Guidelines in fact continue to serve a state-centric positivist view, allowing for only carefully restricted participation by the public. Thus, *Guideline 30 on Access to Information* "pursuant to Art. 15 of the Convention", vaguely speaks of "wide" access to information, and it only specifies the duty of the CPs to give replies to requests for information "within specific time limits". *Guidelines 31 and 32 on Action for Compensation*, merely refer to the general duty of the CPs to "ensure" in their legislation that actions for compensation for environmental damage[71] "are as widely accessible to the public as possible", and that "natural and juridical persons that are victims of traditional damage[72] may bring actions for compensation in the widest possible manner."

The Working Group of Legal and Technical Experts for the Implementation of Guidelines,[73] in its third meeting in 2009, underlined "the fact that not all Contracting Parties give to the public access to information as regards environmental damage or the threat thereof, or ensure actions for compensation to the public, seems to suggest an important area where certain national legislations

---

67 MAP: *Report of the 15th Ordinary Meeting of the Contracting Parties*, supra note 51, Annex V, Decision IG 17/4, 133–140.

68 According to Guideline A(4), they apply "to the activities to which the Barcelona Convention and any of its Protocols apply." *Ibid*.

69 Guideline B(5) complements the 'without prejudice' relationship to these regimes with "the need to ensure their effective implementation in the Mediterranean Sea Area."

70 *E.g.* Guidelines referring to damage and the standard of liability.

71 'Environmental Damage', according to Guideline 9, means "a measurable adverse change in a natural or biological resource or measurable impairment of a natural or biological resource service which may occur directly or indirectly." *Ibid*.

72 'Traditional damage', according to Guideline 14, means "(a) loss of life or personal injury; (b) loss of or damage to property other than property held by the person liable; (c) loss of income directly deriving from an impairment of a legally protected interest in any use of the marine environment for economic purposes, incurred as a result of impairment of the environment, taking into account savings and costs; (d) any loss or damage caused by preventive measures taken to avoid damage referred to under sub-paragraphs (a), (b) and (c)." *Ibid*.

73 See MAP: *Third Meeting of the Working Group of Legal and Technical Experts for the Implementation of Guidelines for the Determination of Liability and Compensation for Damage Resulting from Pollution of the Marine Environment in the Mediterranean Sea Area, Athens, Greece, 22–23* January 2009, UNEP(DEP)/MED WG 329/3, UNEP/MAP, Athens, Greece.

could be strengthened in the near future."[74] It generally referred to "an important governance deficit...identified by the answers provided by most Contracting Parties pointing...to the inadequate participation of the civil society in the introduction of elements of the compensation for damage and damage assessment into their domestic legislation", thus concluding that one of the main directions for facilitating the implementation of these Guidelines by the CPs is "introducing appropriate measures and actions to enhance public participation and involvement."[75] So far, the legislation of very few CPs contains the elements for compensation for environmental damage provided by the Guidelines.[76] Moreover, these Guidelines continue to leave unsettled two issues of decisive importance: *the question of establishing a Mediterranean Trust Fund*, as a second tier of the liability and compensation system under certain conditions, and the question of *establishing a compulsory insurance regime for operators*; both issues are left to future – and uncertain – decisions of the Parties to the BCS.[77]

Even more subtly, these Guidelines should not be *used complacently to diverge from the process of developing an appropriate* (contextually consistent) *legal regime* specifying the framework obligation of the CPs under Art. 16 of the Barcelona Convention. The collectively agreed step-by-step approach for the more adequate development of a future Mediterranean liability and compensation regime[78] should not defy its ICI purposive character, encompassing its legal specification. After all, the Offshore Protocol (1994) has already made an important first step in this direction by setting out, in Art. 27(2), three provisional but substantive obligations: the parties to the Offshore Protocol are vested with the duty to take measures to ensure that, first, liability is channelled on the operators, second, they must pay prompt and adequate compensation and, third, they must have and maintain compulsory insurance or other financial guarantee.

---

74 *Ibid.*, para. 11, 2.
75 *Ibid.*, paras. 13, 14, 3.
76 *Ibid.*, Annex 1 , 2.
77 See Guidelines K and L, *ibid.*, 138.
78 See Raftopoulos, E., "The Mediterranean Response to Global Challenges: Environmental Governance and the Barcelona Convention System", in: *The World Ocean in Globalization – Climate Change, Sustainable Fisheries, Biodiversity, Shipping, Regional Issues* (ed. by Davor Vidas & Peter Johan Schei), Martinus Njhoff Publishers, Leiden-Boston, 2011, Chapter 27, 507, 527–532; Scovazzi, T., "The Mediterranean Guidelines for the Determination of Environmental Liability and Compensation: The Negotiations for the Instrument and the Question of Damage That Can Be Compensated", *Max Planck Yearbook of United Nations Law*, Vol. 13, 2009, 183.

e   The Fiduciary Duty of Effective Legislative Implementation
     of the BCS

Finally, the CPs are vested with a fiduciary duty to implement the Convention and its performative Protocols legislatively in an effective and efficient manner. This duty emanates from the framework formulation of Art. 14 of the Barcelona Convention which provides that the CPs "shall adopt legislation implementing the Convention and the Protocols" and that the Secretariat may assist any CP to draft "environmental legislation in compliance with the Convention and the Protocols" if requested to do so. Stimulated by Rio Declaration Principle 11, and proposed by the Secretariat during the amendment negotiating process of the Convention (1994–1995), the purpose of this Article was to respond to the observed scarce legislative implementation of the Convention and its Protocols.[79] It underlined the importance of an appropriate legislative follow-up at national level which, coupled with the creation of a compliance mechanism, was considered a key element for achieving the effectiveness of the BCS. Relatedly, the CPs are, according to Art. 26(1) of the Convention, under the duty to report on the "effectiveness" of "the legal, administrative and other measures" taken by them for, as well as on "problems encountered" in the implementation of, the Convention, its Protocols and, even, the implementative recommendations adopted by the MOPs. And these reports serve as grounds for assessing compliance with the BCS, according to Art. 27 of the Barcelona Convention.

In exercising this fiduciary duty, the CPs should secure *a certain standard of care and competence linked to the higher level of their conduct as fiduciaries*. They should specifically adopt and apply laws and regulations and take administrative measures within the framework of their legal systems implementing the Convention and its Protocols *effectively and in their specific context*. They should care for the *purposive operation* of these implementing laws, regulations and administrative measures, focusing on their *creative results in their particular context of application*,[80] rather than on their mechanical, formalistic or perfunctory act of enactment. They should secure the necessary specificity and clarity in their formulation so as to improve implementation, appropriate integration, consistency and enforcement of the BCS into their legal systems

---

79 See Raftopoulos, E., *Studies on the Implementation of the Barcelona Convention: The Development of an International Trust Regime*, Ant. Sakkoulas Publishers, Athens, 1997, Study 1, 1–116.

80 To paraphrase the eloquent remark by Lord Bingham on purposive interpretation in the Samex Case, characterizing it as "creative process of supplying flesh to a spare and loosely constructed skeleton" *Commissioners of Customs and Excise v. Samex [1983] 1 All ER 1042*.

and traditions. And they should also regularly assess them to determine how they attain their purported results and make the necessary progressive amendments or enact progressive new laws accordingly. A failure to act thus clearly undermines the fiduciary base of environmental governance of the BCS and may provide another ground for assessing the *fiduciary responsibility* of the State Party.

Relatedly, such a legal implementation process *should not, in practice, be digressed from* by retreating to national strategies, plans or other declarative kinds of instruments It should not be diverted to a collective recourse to Action Plans for the implementation of Protocols which have entered into force – which of course can be most useful if operating synergetically with, and in view of the exigencies of, legal implementation 'deepening' its technical scope.[81] It therefore raises some pertinent questions on the newly developed practice by the MOPs of the CPs to adopt Action Plans for the implementation of Protocols which have recently entered in force.

Perhaps the most striking example is the Offshore Protocol. The 17th MOP decided to adopt "the Action Plan to Implement the Protocol of the Barcelona Convention concerning the Protection of the Mediterranean Sea against Pollution Resulting from Exploration and Exploitation of the Continental Shelf and the Seabed and its Subsoil",[82] entirely overlooking the fact that the seventeen years which had elapsed between its signature (14 October 1994) and its entry into force (24 March 2011) had had far-reaching implications for its effective operation and legal implementation. In fact, the real Protocol implementation problems faced by the CPs, after its entry into force, are threefold: its adaptation to the contemporary sustainable environmental governance requirements (public participation, legal and technical updating of the regulated issues); its harmonization with the other related Protocols to the BCS rectifying the existing inconsistencies and discrepancies between them; finding out what legal form would be the most appropriate for responding to the previous two challenges in order to make sustainably effective the legal implementation of the Protocol.

---

81 For instance, the *Action Plan concerning the Species Introduction and Invasive Species in the Mediterranean Sea, 2003,* and the *Guidelines for Controlling the Vectors of Introduction into the Mediterranean of Non-Indigenous Species and Invasive Marine Species, 2008,* both progressively 'deepening' the implementation of a relevant specific obligation of the CPs to the SPA and Biodiversity Protocol, 1995, at a technical level, see Raftopoulos, E., "The Mediterranean Response to Global Challenges: Environmental Governance and the Barcelona Convention System", *supra* note 78, 508–532, 511 *et seq.*, 523 *et seq.*

82 *Ibid.*, Decision IG 20/12, 217.

Instead, the above Action Plan orientates implementation towards technical, coordinative and cooperative actions thus diverging from the urgent, multifarious legal implementation issues. On the other hand, the EU, while preparing its very recently completed accession to the Protocol,[83] elaborated carefully and through broad consultation an advanced Draft Directive on the safety of offshore exploration and exploitation activities in the Mediterranean and is still meticulously working on the complementary function between the 'proposed Directive' and the Offshore Protocol.

83 See *EU Council Decision of 17 December 2012 on the accession of the European Union to the Protocol for the Protection of the Mediterranean Sea against pollution resulting from exploration and exploitation of the continental shelf and the seabed and its subsoil, Official Journal of the European Union*, L 4, 09/01/2013, 13.

CHAPTER 15

Harlequin and the Mediterranean

*Tullio Scovazzi**

1   Introduction

The Mediterranean is a respectable sea.[1] Its cultural heritage "is unique in that it embodies the common historical and cultural roots of many civilizations".[2] Bordered today by 23 States,[3] the Mediterranean is one of the biggest among the seas which fall under the definition of 'enclosed or semi-enclosed sea' given by Art. 122 of the United Nations Convention on the Law of the Sea:[4]

> For the purposes of this Convention, 'enclosed or semi-enclosed sea' means a gulf, basin or sea surrounded by two or more States and

---

* Professor of International Law, University of Milano-Bicocca, Milan, Italy.
1 The international regime of the Mediterranean Sea is one of the preferred fields of research of the scholar and friend to whom this collection of essays is dedicated: see Vukas (ed.), *The Legal Regime of Enclosed or Semi-enclosed Seas: The Particular Case of the Mediterranean*, Zagreb, 1988.
2 As recalled in the Declaration on the Submarine Cultural Heritage of the Mediterranean Sea, adopted on 10 March 2001 in Syracuse, Italy, by the participants in an academic conference. The Mediterranean countries were consequently invited to "study the possibility of adopting a regional convention that enhances cooperation in the investigation and protection of the Mediterranean submarine cultural heritage and sets forth the relevant rights and obligations". See Beurier, "Commentaire de la Déclaration de Syracuse sur le patrimoine culturel sous-marin de la Mer Méditerranée", in Camarda & Scovazzi (eds.), *The Protection of the Underwater Cultural Heritage – Legal Aspects*, Milano, 2002, p. 279 (for the text of the Declaration see *ibid.*, p. 448).
3 The Mediterranean coastal States (without considering the States bordering only the Black Sea) are Spain, the United Kingdom (as far as Gibraltar and the sovereign base areas of Akrotiri and Dhekelia are concerned), France, Monaco, Italy, Malta, Slovenia, Croatia, Bosnia and Herzegovina, Montenegro, Albania, Greece, Cyprus, Turkey, Syria, Lebanon, Israel, Palestine, Egypt, Libya, Tunisia, Algeria, Morocco. For certain matters, the European Union should be added to the list. It is an international organization of which twenty-eight European States have so far become members, including eight Mediterranean States (France, Italy, Spain, Greece, Cyprus, Malta, Slovenia and Croatia). It has, *inter alia*, exclusive competence in the field of fisheries management and conservation and a competence shared with its member States in the field of environmental protection, including the marine environment.
4 Hereinafter: UNCLOS.

connected to another sea or the ocean by a narrow outlet or consisting entirely or primarily of the territorial seas and exclusive economic zones of two or more coastal States.[5]

The Mediterranean countries differ as far as their internal political systems and levels of economic development are concerned. The Mediterranean region is an area of major strategic importance and, in certain cases, of political tension. Highly populated cities, ports of worldwide significance, extended industrial areas and renowned holiday resorts are located along the Mediterranean shores. Important routes of international navigation pass through Mediterranean waters, which connect the Atlantic and the Indian Oceans through the Strait of Gibraltar and the Suez Canal.[6] The protection of the Mediterranean environmental balance, which is particularly fragile because of the very slow exchange of waters, is a serious concern. The parties to the Convention for the Protection of the Marine Environment and the Coastal Region of the Mediterranean (Barcelona, 1976; amended in 1995) declare themselves to be "mindful of the special hydrographic and ecological characteristics of the Mediterranean Sea Area and its particular vulnerability to pollution" (preamble).

Harlequin is a comic servant character of the Italian *Commedia dell'Arte*, well-known also in other countries. Endowed with great physical agility, Harlequin is distinguished by a motley costume made up of many patches in different colours.

The connection between the Mediterranean Sea and Harlequin is due to two factors. First, today the Mediterranean States are still far from taking a uniform attitude as regards the extent and nature of their coastal zones.[7] Looking at the map, a patchwork of differently coloured coastal zones mixed with holes of high seas is immediately visible. If all the coastal States were to establish an exclusive economic zone, the high seas would disappear, since there is no point in the Mediterranean that is further than 200 n.m. from the nearest land or island. This geographical situation would require the conclusion by the States concerned of several bilateral (or even multilateral) agreements for the delimitation of maritime boundaries. However – and this is the second relevant factor – only a limited number of such agreements have so far

---

5   On enclosed or semi-enclosed seas see Vukas, *The Law of the Sea – Selected Writings*, Leiden, 2004, p. 263.
6   Although it covers only 0.8% of the surface of oceans and seas, about 30% of world marine trade and 20% of the global volume of fuel transport passes through the Mediterranean Sea.
7   See *infra*, 11.

been concluded.[8] The presence of several grey areas where boundaries are not defined does not contribute to the clarity of the present picture of coastal States' jurisdiction over Mediterranean waters and seabed.[9]

II   The Nature and Extent of Present Coastal Zones

The general rules of international law on the regime and extent of marine spaces within and beyond national jurisdiction, as reflected in UNCLOS, apply also in semi-enclosed seas, such as the Mediterranean. There is no doubt that any coastal State is entitled to establish an exclusive economic zone, whenever it wishes to do so, even in cases where for geographical reasons it cannot claim a full 200-mile zone.[10] International law does not prevent States bordering seas of limited dimensions from establishing their own exclusive economic zones, provided that maritime boundaries are not unilaterally imposed by one State on its adjacent or opposite neighbouring States.[11]

In the case of the costal zones established in the Mediterranean Sea, a number of peculiarities must be taken into account that make the present picture particularly complex.[12] Not all the Mediterranean coastal States have so far

---

8   See *infra*, III.

9   For the situation of confusion that existed some years ago see Scovazzi, "Les zones côtières en Méditerranée: évolution et confusion", in *Annuaire du Droit de la Mer*, 2001, p. 95.

10 The only case in which a coastal State cannot establish an exclusive economic zone occurs if, for geographical reasons, its coastal waters do not extend beyond the 12-mile limit of its territorial sea (this is, for example, among the Mediterranean coastal States, the case of Bosnia and Herzegovina, whose territorial sea is enclosed within the internal maritime waters of Croatia).

11 As remarked by the International Court of Justice in the judgment of 18 December 1951 on the *Fisheries* case (United Kingdom v. Norway), "the delimitation of sea areas has always an international aspect; it cannot be dependent merely upon the will of the coastal State as expressed in its municipal law. Although it is true that the act of delimitation is necessarily a unilateral act, because only the coastal State is competent to undertake it, the validity of the delimitation with regard to other States depends upon international law" (International Court of Justice, *Reports of Judgments, Advisory Opinions and Orders*, 1951, p. 20).

12 A unique instance of coastal zone is provided for by the Agreement between Israel and the Palestine Liberation Organization on the Gaza Strip and the Jericho Area (Cairo, 4 May 1994), according to which Israel shall transfer authority, as far as specified in the agreement, to the Palestinian Authority. Under Art. V, para. *a*, the territorial jurisdiction of the Palestinian Authority "shall include land, subsoil and territorial waters, in accordance with the provisions of this Agreement". Art. XI (relating to security along the

decided to establish an exclusive economic zone. However, some coastal States have proclaimed two kinds of *sui generis* zones beyond the territorial sea, namely fishing zones and ecological protection zones. While neither of them is mentioned in UNCLOS, they are not prohibited either. They encompass only some of the rights that can be exercised within the exclusive economic zone. Such a fragmentation of rights does not seem incompatible with international law, considering that the right to do less is implied in the right to do more (*in maiore stat minus*, to say it in Latin).

The current picture of Mediterranean coastal zones (as at April 2013) seems to be the following.

1   Maritime Internal Waters

Several Mediterranean States (Albania, Algeria, Croatia, Cyprus, Egypt, France, Italy, Libya, Malta, Morocco, Montenegro, Spain, Tunisia and Turkey) apply legislation measuring the breadth of the territorial sea from straight baselines joining specific points located on the mainland or islands. Historical bays are claimed by Italy (Gulf of Taranto) and Libya (Gulf of Sidra).

2   Territorial Sea

Most Mediterranean States have established a 12-mile territorial sea. The exceptions are the United Kingdom (3 n.m. for Gibraltar[13] and the Sovereign Base Areas of Akrotiri and Dhekelia on the island of Cyprus), Greece (6 n.m.) and Turkey (6 n.m. in the Aegean Sea, but 12 n.m. elsewhere).

3   Contiguous Zone

24-mile contiguous zones have been established by Algeria, Cyprus, Egypt, France, Malta, Morocco, Spain, Syria and Tunisia for customs, fiscal, immigration or sanitary purposes.[14]

---

coastline and in the sea of Gaza) of Annex I sets out three so-called Maritime Activity Zones (K, L and M) extending 20 n.m. from the coast. Zones K and M are closed areas, in which navigation is restricted to activity of the Israeli Navy. Zone L is open for fishing, recreational and economic activities, in accordance with the rules specified in para. 2, *b*.

13 A long-lasting dispute is pending between Spain and the United Kingdom as to whether Gibraltar is entitled to a territorial sea.

14 In 2002 a contiguous zone only for immigration purposes was apparently established by Italy (Art. 9-bis of Legislative Decree 25 July 1998, No. 286, as modified by Law 30 July 2002, No. 189). The doubts arise from the fact that the Italian legislation does not specify the breadth of the contiguous zone, leaving officials responsible for its implementation without any indication as to the limit up to which they should exercise their powers. Nor does

Algeria, Cyprus, France Italy and Tunisia claim to exercise rights in the field of archaeological and historical objects found at sea within the 24-mile limit from the baselines of the territorial sea, as allowed by Art. 303, para. 2, UNCLOS (so-called archaeological contiguous zone).

4 Continental Shelf

Every coastal State is entitled *ipso iure* and without any express proclamation to a continental shelf, that is an extension of the seabed beyond the territorial sea, as defined by Art. 76 UNCLOS.[15] As soon as the Mediterranean States proclaim an exclusive economic zone, their continental shelf is to be considered as the seabed of such a zone.

5 Fishing Zone

Some Mediterranean States have declared a fishing zone beyond the limit of the territorial sea.

Tunisia has established along its southern coastline (from Ras Kapoudia to the frontier with Libya) a fishing zone delimited according to the criterion of the 50-metre isobath,[16] based on legislation dating back to 1951 (Decree of the Bey of 26 July 1951) which was confirmed by subsequent enactments (Laws No. 63–49 of 30 December 1963 and No. 73–49 of 2 August 1973).

In 1978 Malta established a 25-mile exclusive fishing zone (Territorial Waters and Contiguous Zone Amendment Act of 18 July 1978). Under Legislative Act No. X of 26 July 2005, fishing waters may be designated even beyond the limits laid down in the 1978 Act and jurisdiction in these waters may be extended also to artificial islands, marine scientific research and the protection and preservation of the marine environment.

In 1994 Algeria created a fishing zone whose extent is 32 n.m. from the maritime frontier with Morocco to Ras Ténès and 52 n.m. from Ras Ténès to the maritime frontier with Tunisia (Legislative Decree No. 94–13 of 28 May 1994).

In 1997 Spain established a fishing protection zone in the Mediterranean (Royal Decree 1315/1997 of 1 August 1997, modified by Royal Decree 431/2000 of

---

the subsequent Decree of 14 July 2003, which also mentions a 'contiguous zone', provide any indication about its breadth. Can a 'blank' contiguous zone be established?

15 The only case in which a coastal State cannot claim a continental shelf occurs if, for geographical reasons, its seabed does not extend beyond the 12-mile limit of its territorial sea.

16 The Tunisian fishing zone encompasses the bank commonly called 'the Big Breast' (*le Grand Mamelon*). This zone is considered by Italy to be a high seas zone of biological protection where fishing by Italian vessels or nationals is prohibited (Decree of 25 September 1979).

31 March 2000). The zone was delimited according to the line which is equidistant between Spain and the opposite or adjacent coasts of Algeria, Italy and France.[17] However, today the Spanish fishing zone seems to have been implicitly superseded by Royal Decree 236/2013 of 5 April 2013 which recently established an exclusive economic zone along the eastern Mediterranean Spanish coast.[18]

In 2005 Libya established a fisheries protection zone whose limits extend seaward up to a distance of 62 n.m. from the external limit of the territorial sea (General People's Committee Decision No. 37 of 24 February 2005), according to the geographical co-ordinates set out in General People's Committee Decision No. 105 of 21 June 2005.

6   *Ecological Protection Zone*

Some Mediterranean States have adopted legislation for the establishment of an ecological protection zone.

In 2003, France adopted Law No. 2003–346 of 15 April 2003 which provides that an ecological protection zone may be created.[19] A zone of this kind was established along the French Mediterranean coast by Decree No. 2004–33 of 8 January 2004 which specified the co-ordinates to define the external limit of the zone. It has however been superseded by the subsequent proclamation in 2012 of an exclusive economic zone in the Mediterranean.[20]

In 2005 Slovenia provided for the establishment of an ecological protection zone (Law of 4 October 2005).[21]

In 2006 Italy adopted framework legislation for ecological protection zones (Law No. 61 of 8 February 2006) to be established by decrees. Within the ecological zones, Italy exercises powers which are not limited to the prevention and control of pollution, but extend also to the protection of marine mammals, biodiversity and the archaeological and historical heritage. The first of the implementing enactments is Presidential Decree 27 October 2011, No. 209,

---

17   No fishing zone was established as regards the Spanish Mediterranean coast facing Morocco.
18   See *infra*, 11.8.
19   In this zone, France exercised only some of the powers granted to the coastal State under the exclusive economic zone regime, namely the powers relating to the protection and preservation of the marine environment, marine scientific research and the establishment and use of artificial islands, installations and structures.
20   See *infra*, 11.8.
21   Croatia objected to Slovenia's right to establish national coastal zones beyond the territorial sea. A dispute in this regard is pending between the two States and will be decided by arbitration.

which established an ecological protection zone in the Ligurian and Tyrrhennian Seas.

7 Zone for Fishing and Ecological Purposes

On 3 October 2003, the Croatian Parliament adopted a "decision on the extension of the jurisdiction of the Republic of Croatia in the Adriatic Sea" and proclaimed "the content of the exclusive economic zone related to the sovereign rights for the purpose of exploring and exploiting, conserving and managing the living resources beyond the outer limits of the territorial sea, as well as the jurisdiction with regard to marine scientific research and the protection and preservation of the marine environment, whereby the ecological and fisheries protection zone of the Republic of Croatia is established as of today" (Art. 1). However, on 3 June 2004, the Parliament amended the 2003 decision in order to postpone implementation of the ecological and fishing zone with regard to Member States of the European Union.[22]

8 Exclusive Economic Zone

A number of Mediterranean States have established, or officially announced the establishment of, an exclusive economic zone.

In 1981 Morocco created a 200-mile exclusive economic zone (Dahir No. 1-81-179 of 8 April 1981), without making any distinction between the Atlantic and the Mediterranean coasts.

Upon ratifying UNCLOS on 26 August 1983, Egypt declared that it "will exercise as from this day the rights attributed to it by the provisions of parts V and VI of the... Convention...in the exclusive economic zone situated beyond and adjacent to its territorial sea in the Mediterranean Sea and in the Red Sea."

By Law No. 28 of 19 November 2003 Syria established an exclusive economic zone.

Cyprus proclaimed an exclusive economic zone under the Exclusive Economic Zone Law adopted on 2 April 2004.

Tunisia established an exclusive economic zone under Law No. 2005–60 of 27 June 2005. The modalities for the implementation of the law will be determined by a decree that has not yet been adopted.

Under a declaration of 27 May 2009 and a decision of 31 May 2009, No. 260, Libya proclaimed an exclusive economic zone. The external limit of the zone will be determined by agreements with the neighbouring States concerned.

---

22 See Vidas, "The UN Convention on the Law of the Sea, the European Union and the Rule of Law: What is going on in the Adriatic Sea?", in *International Journal of Marine and Coastal Law*, 2009, p. 1.

By a framework Law adopted on 19 September 2011, Lebanon established an exclusive economic zone. Three annexes define the limits of the zone between Lebanon and, respectively, Syria, Cyprus and Palestine.

In 2011 and 2012 Israel deposited with the Secretary-General of the United Nations the list of the geographical coordinates of the limits of its territorial sea and exclusive economic zone.

Under Decree No. 2012–1148 of 12 October 2012, France established an exclusive economic zone along its Mediterranean shore, within the same limits that applied to its previous ecological protection zone.

The last relevant enactment is Royal Decree 236/2013 of 3 April 2013, by which Spain established an exclusive economic zone along its eastern Mediterranean coast. The zone is delimited according to the line which is equidistant between Spain and the opposite or adjacent coasts of Algeria, Italy and France.[23]

The French and the Spanish exclusive economic zones partially overlap.

III   Maritime Boundaries

So far only some of the required maritime delimitation treaties have been adopted, and not all of them have entered into force. Several instances of maritime boundaries are still unsettled in the Mediterranean, including some that are quite complex to handle due to the peculiar geographical configuration of the coastlines of the States concerned.[24] The present picture of Mediterranean maritime boundaries, according to the alphabetical order of the States concerned, is the following.[25]

> (1) Albania – Greece. Not delimited (delimitation of all marine boundaries: treaty signed in Tirana on 27 April 2009 and not yet entered into force).

---

23   No exclusive economic zone was established as regards the Spanish Mediterranean coast facing Morocco.

24   See Scovazzi, "Maritime Delimitations in the Mediterranean Sea", in *Cursos Euromediterraneos Bancaja de Derecho Internacional*, 2004–2005, p. 349. For the delimitation questions pending in the Adriatic see Vukas, "Maritime Delimitations in a Semi-Enclosed Sea: The Case of the Adriatic Sea", in Lagoni & Vignes (eds.), *Maritime Delimitation*, Leiden, 2006, p. 205.

25   The Mediterranean maritime boundaries may be more than those indicated in this study if the claims advanced by some States are taken into account.

(2) Albania – Italy. Delimitation of the continental shelf: treaty signed in Tirana on 18 December 1992 and entered into force on 26 February 1999.
(3) Albania – Montenegro. Not delimited.
(4) Algeria – Italy. Not delimited.
(5) Algeria – Morocco. Not delimited.
(6) Algeria – Spain. Not delimited.
(7) Algeria – Tunisia. Not delimited (provisional delimitation of all marine boundaries: treaty signed in Algiers on 11 February 2002, entered into force on 11 February 2002, and expired on 10 February 2008; delimitation of all marine boundaries: treaty signed in Algiers on 11 July 2011 and not yet entered into force).
(8) Bosnia and Herzegovina – Croatia. Not delimited (delimitation between the territorial sea of Bosnia-Herzegovina and the internal waters of Croatia: treaty signed in Sarajevo on 30 July 1999 and not yet entered into force).
– Croatia – Bosnia and Herzegovina. See No. 8.
(9) Croatia – Italy. Delimitation of the territorial sea: treaty signed in Osimo on 10 November 1975 by the predecessor State (Yugoslavia) and entered into force on 3 April 1977; delimitation of the continental shelf: agreement signed in Belgrade on 8 January 1968 by the predecessor State (Yugoslavia) and entered into force on 21 January 1970.
(10) Croatia – Montenegro. Not delimited
(11) Croatia – Slovenia. Not delimited.
(12) Cyprus – Egypt. Delimitation of the exclusive economic zone: agreement signed in Cairo on 17 February 2003 and entered into force on 7 April 2004.
(13) Cyprus – Israel. Delimitation of the exclusive economic zone: agreement signed in Nicosia on 17 December 2010 and entered into force on 25 February 2011.
(14) Cyprus – Lebanon. Not delimited (delimitation of the exclusive economic zone: agreement signed in Beirut on 17 January 2007 and not yet entered into force).
(15) Cyprus – Syria. Not delimited.
(16) Cyprus – Turkey. Not delimited.
(17) Cyprus – United Kingdom (Akrotiri, Dhekelia). Delimitation of the territorial sea: treaty concerning the establishment of the Republic of Cyprus, signed in Nicosia on 16 August 1960 and entered into force on 16 August 1960.
– Egypt – Cyprus. See No. 12.
(18) Egypt – Greece. Not delimited.

(19) Egypt – Libya. Not delimited.

(20) Egypt – Palestine. Not delimited.

(21) France – Italy. Delimitation of the territorial sea in the area of the Mouths of Bonifacio: convention signed in Paris on 28 November 1986 and entered into force on 15 May 1989.

(22) France – Monaco. Delimitation of all marine boundaries: agreement signed in Paris on 16 February 1984 and entered into force on 22 August 1985.

(23) France – Spain. Not delimited.

– Greece – Albania. See No. 1.

– Greece – Egypt. See No. 17.

(24) Greece – Italy. Delimitation of the continental shelf: agreement signed in Athens on 24 May 1977 and entered into force on 12 November 1980.

(25) Greece – Libya. Not delimited.

(26) Greece – Turkey. Not delimited.

– Israel – Cyprus. See No. 13.

(27) Israel – Lebanon. Not delimited.

(28) Israel – Palestine. Not delimited.

(29) Israel – Syria. Not delimited.

– Italy – Albania. See No. 2.

– Italy – Algeria. See No. 4.

– Italy – Croatia. See No. 9.

– Italy – France. See No. 20.

(30) Italy – Libya. Not delimited.

(31) Italy – Malta. Not delimited (provisional and partial delimitation of the continental shelf: exchange of notes concluded on 31 December 1965 / 29 April 1970 and entered into force on 29 April 1970).

(32) Italy – Montenegro. Delimitation of the continental shelf: agreement signed in Belgrade on 8 January 1968 by the predecessor State (Yugoslavia) and entered into force on 21 January 1970.

(33) Italy – Slovenia. Delimitation of the territorial sea: treaty signed in Osimo on 10 November 1975 by the predecessor State (Yugoslavia) and entered into force on 3 April 1977.

(34) Italy – Spain. Delimitation of the continental shelf: agreement signed in Madrid on 19 February 1974 and entered into force on 16 November 1978.

(35) Italy – Tunisia. Delimitation of the continental shelf: agreement signed in Tunis on 20 August 1971 and entered into force on 6 December 1978.

– Lebanon – Cyprus. See No. 14.
– Lebanon – Israel. See No. 27.
(36) Lebanon – Syria. Not delimited.
– Libya – Egypt. See No. 19.
– Libya – Greece. See No. 25.
– Libya – Italy. See No. 30.
(37) Libya – Malta. Delimitation of the continental shelf: agreement signed in Valletta on 10 November 1986 and entered into force on 11 December 1987.[26]
(38) Libya – Tunisia. Delimitation of the continental shelf: agreement signed in Benghazi on 8 August 1988 and entered into force on 11 April 1989.[27]
– Malta – Italy. See No. 31.
– Malta – Libya. See No. 37.
(39) Malta – Tunisia. Not delimited.
– Monaco – France. See No. 22.
– Montenegro – Albania. See No. 3.
– Montenegro – Croatia. See No. 10.
– Montenegro – Italy. See No. 32.
– Morocco – Algeria. See No. 5.
(40) Morocco – Spain. Not delimited.
– Palestine – Egypt. See No. 20.
– Palestine – Israel. See No. 28.
– Slovenia – Croatia. See No. 11.
– Slovenia – Italy. See No. 33.
– Spain – Algeria. See No. 6.
– Spain – France. See No. 23.
– Spain – Italy. See No. 34.
– Spain – Morocco. See No. 40.
(41) Spain – United Kingdom (Gibraltar): Not delimited.
– Syria – Cyprus. See No. 15.
– Syria – Lebanon. See No. 36.
(42) Syria – Turkey. Not delimited.
– Tunisia – Algeria. See No. 7.
– Tunisia – Italy. See No. 35.

---

26 The agreement was concluded following the judgment of the International Court of Justice on 3 June 1985.

27 The agreement was concluded following the judgment of the International Court of Justice on 24 February 1982.

- Tunisia – Libya. See No. 38.
- Tunisia – Malta. See No. 39.
- Turkey – Cyprus. See No. 16.
- Turkey – Greece. See No. 26.
- Turkey – Syria. See No. 42.
- United Kingdom (Akrotiri, Dhekelia) – Cyprus. See No. 17.
- United Kingdom (Gibraltar) – Spain. See No. 41.

As can be seen, the instances of maritime boundaries to be delimited are more numerous than those which have been settled. In some cases, the situation is further complicated by the question whether the delimitation lines of present or future exclusive economic zones should follow the lines that have been defined in previous agreements relating only to the seabed (the continental shelf) or whether they could depart from it.[28]

IV   Concluding Remarks

As a result of UNCLOS, the international law of the sea has moved from the previous system, based on the territorial sea (under the regime of State sovereignty) and the high seas (under the regime of freedom), to a more articulated system, based also on the exclusive economic zone, where the coastal State is granted rights in the field of exploitation of natural resources and the other States are granted rights in the field of maritime communication (navigation, overflight, laying of cables and pipelines and other related internationally lawful uses of the sea).

Today, the concept of the exclusive economic zone, that can roughly be considered as the sum of the fishing and the ecological zone, could receive full acceptance also in the Mediterranean region. In this sea, the transition from the previous to the new regime has not yet been completed or, to say it in another way, has taken place only in a fragmentary and inconsistent way.[29] The expression 'sea of Harlequin'[30] depicts in a perhaps too emotional, but quite evocative, manner a situation in which fishing zones, ecological zones, eco-fishing zones, exclusive economic zones, continental shelves and the high seas

---

28   See Papanicolopulu, *Il confine marino: unità o pluralità?*, Milano, 2005.
29   The predominant coastal States' practice in other semi-enclosed seas (such as the Baltic, the Caribbean, the Black Seas) is to establish exclusive economic zones.
30   A less emotional expression could be 'sea in transition'.

coexist and sometimes overlap in marine spaces that would be exclusive economic zones only if the new UNCLOS regime had been fully followed.

Art. 123 of UNCLOS[31] calls for co-operation among States bordering the same enclosed or semi-enclosed sea. As stated by a scholar:

> Art. 123 should stimulate to co-operation of States and international organizations in respect to the use and protection of enclosed and semi-enclosed seas as well as to the adoption of regional and subregional rules concerning particular seas. In fact, besides being based on existing rules every international co-operation contributes also to the development of further international rules, standards, procedures and practices.[32]

Far from being the manifestation of excessive unilateralism, the establishment in the Mediterranean of a regionally agreed and consistent jurisdictional basis in the form of exclusive economic zones could lead to the strengthening of regional co-operation to manage resources and address common environmental concerns. Future Mediterranean governance cannot be built on the vacuum determined by the high seas regime or on the confusion of different kinds of zones of national jurisdiction. The present uncertain situation of national coastal zones in the Mediterranean gives rise to a number of problems that can also affect the specific systems of regional co-operation already agreed upon in the fields of protection of the environment or of fisheries, such as the already mentioned Barcelona Convention and its seven protocols[33] or the General

---

31 "States bordering an enclosed or semi-enclosed sea should cooperate with each other in the exercise of their rights and in the performance of their duties under this Convention. To this end they shall endeavour, directly or through an appropriate regional organization: (a) to coordinate the management, conservation, exploration and exploitation of the living resources of the sea; (b) to coordinate the implementation of their rights and duties with respect to the protection and preservation of the marine environment; (c) to coordinate their scientific research policies and undertake where appropriate joint programmes of scientific research in the area; (d) to invite, as appropriate, other interested States or international organizations to cooperate with them in furtherance of the provisions of this article".

32 Vukas, "The Mediterranean: An Enclosed or Semi-Enclosed Sea?", in Vukas, *op. cit.* (*supra*, note 1), p. 64.

33 Protocol for the Prevention and Elimination of Pollution of the Mediterranean Sea by Dumping from Ships and Aircraft or Incineration at Sea (Barcelona, 1976; amended in 1995), Protocol concerning Cooperation in Preventing Pollution from Ships and, in Cases of Emergency, Combating Pollution of the Mediterranean Sea (Valletta, 2002; replacing a previous protocol of 1976); Protocol for the Protection of the Mediterranean Sea against Pollution from Land-Based Sources and Activities (Athens, 1980; amended in 1996),

Fisheries Commission (formerly Council) for the Mediterranean, established by an Agreement concluded in Rome in 1949 and subsequently amended in 1963, 1976 and 1997. Calls for extending national jurisdiction in Mediterranean waters have already been made also at the international level to ensure the strengthened protection of the marine environment[34] or the establishment of an integrated maritime policy.[35]

It is true that pending questions of maritime boundaries can be an obstacle to the effort to harmonize the jurisdictional condition of Mediterranean waters. But an advanced system of future Mediterranean co-operation could also include a mechanism for the negotiation, mediation and conciliation of questions on maritime delimitations.[36]

Protocol concerning Specially Protected Areas and Biological Diversity in the Mediterranean (Barcelona, 1995; replacing a previous protocol of 1982), Protocol concerning Pollution Resulting from Exploration and Exploitation of the Continental Shelf, the Seabed and its Subsoil (Madrid, 1994), Protocol on the Prevention of Pollution of the Mediterranean Sea by Transboundary Movements of Hazardous Wastes and their Disposal (Izmir, 1996), Protocol on Integrated Coastal Zone Management in the Mediterranean (Madrid, 2008).

34 According to a Declaration adopted in 2009 by the meeting of the Parties to the Barcelona Convention, Mediterranean States are invited to "extend, in accordance with international law, the areas under their jurisdiction recalling that the right to do so can be used to achieve the protection of the marine environment."

35 In a Communication made in 2009 to the Council and the European Parliament ('Towards an Integrated Maritime Policy for better governance in the Mediterranean'), the European Commission stated that "...a large part of the waters of the Mediterranean sea is outside the areas under the jurisdiction or sovereign rights of coastal States. Consequently these States do not have prescriptive and enforcement powers to regulate comprehensively human activities beyond such areas, including for the protection of the marine environment and how fishing and the development of energy sources is carried out. Beyond these areas, States can only adopt measures with regard to their own nationals and vessels. Certain actions can be jointly undertaken within the limited framework of regional conventions, for the protection of the marine environment and the conservation and management of living resources, although there remains the problem of enforcement of decisions adopted, including against third States non-party" (Doc. COM(2009) 466 final of 11 September 2009, para. 3.2).

36 For instance, in 2002 the Caribbean Conference on Maritime Delimitation (CCMD) was established in another semi-enclosed sea. As stated in Art. 1 of the rules of the CCMD, its mandate consists in "facilitating, mainly through technical assistance, the voluntary negotiations for the maritime delimitation among the Caribbean coast nations, under the principle that this negotiation can be carried out when and in the form freely agreed upon by the parties, under the terms accepted by them and without any external intervention."

CHAPTER 16

The 24-Mile Archaeological Zone: Abandoned or Confirmed?

*Trpimir M. Šošić**

I   Introduction

After the adoption of the United Nations Convention on the Law of the Sea (LOSC) in 1982 commentators took disparate views on the legal effects of Article 303(2) LOSC. The question arose whether that provision, which concerns archaeological and historical objects found on the seabed, had created a new jurisdictional zone distinct from the contiguous zone, well-established in the pre-existing law of the sea as a maritime zone in which the coastal State had the possibility of using a limited set of jurisdictional powers in order to protect certain interests regarding its territory, including the territorial sea.[1] In 2001 the Convention on the Protection of the Underwater Cultural Heritage (UCHC) was adopted under the auspices of the United Nations Educational, Scientific and Cultural Organization (UNESCO).[2] It entered into force in 2009 and establishes a comprehensive international mechanism for the protection of the underwater cultural heritage, thus supplementing the fragmentary provisions of the LOSC on archaeological and historical objects found at sea.

It is the aim of this essay to re-examine the issue of the so-called 'archaeological zone', taking into account new developments following the adoption and entry into force of the UCHC. However, it will first be necessary to revisit the controversy concerning the proper interpretation and application of

---

*   LLM, PhD; Assistant Professor at the University of Zagreb, Faculty of Law, Chair of International Law.
1   On the contiguous zone in general see *e.g.* V.L. Gutiérrez Castillo, "La zone contiguë dans la Convention des Nations Unies sur le droit de la mer de 1982", 7 *Annuaire du droit de la mer* (hereinafter: ADM), 2002, pp. 149–164; A.V. Lowe, "The Development of the Concept of the Contiguous Zone", 52 *British Year Book of International Law*, 1981, pp. 109–169; S. Oda, "The Concept of the Contiguous Zone", 11 *International and Comparative Law Quarterly*, 1962, pp. 131–153; H. Pazarci, "Le concept de zone contiguë dans la Convention sur le droit de la mer de 1982", 18 *Revue belge de droit international*, 1984/85, pp. 249–271.
2   *United Nations Treaty Series*, Vol. 2565 – Part 1, 2009, p. 51. To date 48 States have become bound by the UCHC; see the status of ratifications available on UNESCO's website at: <http://www.unesco.org/eri/la/convention.asp?KO=13520&language=E> (20 August 2014).

Article 303(2) LOSC. Based on that discussion, we will, thereafter, analyse the legal consequences of Article 8 UCHC which deals with the protection of submerged cultural objects on the seabed beneath the contiguous zone.

II   Law of the Sea Convention

1   *The Jurisdictional Powers of Coastal States in the Contiguous Zone According to Article 33 LOSC*

The jurisdictional powers that the coastal State may exercise in its contiguous zone are determined by Article 33(1) LOSC:

> In a zone contiguous to its territorial sea, described as the contiguous zone, the coastal State may exercise the control necessary to:
> (a)   prevent infringement of its customs, fiscal, immigration or sanitary laws and regulations within its territory or territorial sea;
> (b)   punish infringement of the above laws and regulations committed within its territory or territorial sea.[3]

First of all, as generally accepted by doctrine, it should be noted that in its contiguous zone the coastal State has enforcement jurisdiction in order to prevent and punish violations of only those laws and regulations that are exhaustively listed in Article 33(1), *i.e.* customs, fiscal, immigration or sanitary laws and regulations. In addition, from the wording of the provision it is clear that the violations must be linked to the State's territory, including the territorial sea. Thus, the coastal State may not use the afforded powers to punish acts occurring in the contiguous zone itself. In other words, on the basis of Article 33(1), States are not allowed to extend their legislative jurisdiction to the maritime zone adjacent to their territorial seas.[4]

---

3   Article 33(1) LOSC follows the wording of Article 24(1) of the 1958 Geneva Convention on the Territorial Sea and the Contiguous Zone almost *verbatim*. The only noteworthy difference is that in the LOSC the contiguous zone is no longer defined as being part of the high seas, as was the case with the 1958 Geneva Convention. This adjustment of the wording was necessary due to the creation of the exclusive economic zone. Article 33(2) LOSC sets the maximum breadth of the contiguous zone at "24 nautical miles from the baselines from which the breadth of the territorial sea is measured."

4   *Cf.* Pazarci, *op. cit.* (note 1), p. 250; L. Caflisch, "Submarine Antiquities and the International Law of the Sea", 13 *Netherlands Yearbook of International Law*, 1982, p. 12; R.R. Churchill, A.V. Lowe, *The Law of the Sea*, Manchester, 1999, p. 137; N.C. Pallas, *Maritimer Kulturgüterschutz*, Berlin, 2004, p. 245; A. Strati, *The Protection of the Underwater Cultural Heritage: an Emerging*

However, in view of the topic we are discussing it is primarily of interest to us if Article 33(1) *per se* has any implications on the protection of the underwater cultural heritage. It is immediately evident that regulations concerning immigrants or sanitary laws can hardly have anything to say about the protection of historic shipwrecks and other artefacts found at sea. On the other hand, an application of the coastal State's fiscal or customs laws and regulations might be conceivable when it comes to preventing the illegal trade in artefacts. But in order for that to be possible the cultural objects must have been lifted from the bottom of the sea and their importation into the coastal State's territory, *i.e.* its territorial sea, must at least have been attempted, since Article 33(1) LOSC *per se* cannot be applied to objects that are found beyond the outer limits of the territorial sea and do not come within the reach of the coastal State's territorial sovereignty.[5] Indeed, as already noted, in the contiguous zone the coastal State has strictly limited control powers that serve the protection of certain interests with respect to its territory. This makes it impossible to construe a situation where these control powers regarding customs, fiscal, immigration or sanitary matters might extend to the cultural heritage located on the seabed. Thus, for this reason alone, Article 33 LOSC, if considered on its own,[6] cannot be applied to the underwater cultural heritage while *in situ* on the seabed.[7]

As may be concluded, Article 33 LOSC *per se* is not of great import for the protection of the underwater cultural heritage, which is hardly surprising, bearing in mind the concept and purpose of the contiguous zone. Hence, it is all the more astonishing that in the framework of the LOSC this provision,

---

Objective of the Contemporary Law of the Sea, The Hague, 1995, p. 160; W. Vitzthum, "Maritimes Aquitorium und Anschlusszone", in: *idem* (ed.), *Handbuch des Seerechts*, München, 2006, pp. 150, 152 *et seq.*; W. Vitzthum, S. Talmon, *Alles fließt: Kulturgüterschutz und innere Gewässer im Neuen Seerecht*, Baden-Baden, 1998, p. 34. Nevertheless, a number of States have in practice extended their laws also to the contiguous zone and have claimed jurisdictional powers going beyond the *numerus clausus* set by Article 33(1) LOSC, notably regarding security matters (an example is India, on the basis of its 1976 Territorial Waters, Continental Shelf, Exclusive Economic Zone and other Maritime Zones Act). For an overview and evaluation of excessive claims in State practice see *e.g.* Churchill, Lowe, *op. cit.*, pp. 138 *et seq.*

5 Caflisch, *op. cit.* (note 4), p. 13. *Cf.* also A.C. Arend, "Archaeological and Historical Objects: the International Legal Implications of UNCLOS III", 22 *Virginia Journal of International Law* (hereinafter: VJIL), 1982, p. 783.
6 Of course, as will be discussed shortly, if Article 33(1) LOSC is linked with Article 303(2) the outcome is rather different.
7 Pallas, *op. cit.* (note 4), pp. 245 *et seq.*; Pazarci, *loc. cit.*; Vitzthum, Talmon, *loc. cit.*; R. Garabello, *La Convenzione UNESCO sulla protezione del patrimonio culturale subacqueo*, Milano, 2004, p. 153; L. van Meurs, "Legal Aspects of Marine Archaeological Research", *Acta Juridica*, 1986, p. 93.

which facilitates the more effective enforcement of the coastal State's customs, fiscal, immigration and sanitary laws, should have been coupled to the protection of the underwater cultural heritage, resulting in a somewhat bizarre and hybrid bond between the two.

2   Article 303(2) LOSC: A Legal Basis for the Establishment of an Archaeological Zone?

The most significant novelty that was added to the regime of the contiguous zone by the LOSC will in vain be looked for in Part II, Section 4 with the heading "Contiguous Zone", *i.e.* in Article 33. On the contrary, it is contained in one of the only two Convention articles dealing with archaeological and historical objects found at sea, namely in Article 303, itself placed in Part XVI among the Convention's general provisions. The pertinent Article 303(2) LOSC reads as follows:

> In order to control traffic in such [*i.e.* archaeological and historical] objects, the coastal State may, in applying article 33, presume that their removal from the seabed in the zone referred to in that article [*i.e.* the contiguous zone] without its approval would result in an infringement within its territory or territorial sea of the laws and regulations referred to in that article [*i.e.* customs, fiscal, immigration or sanitary laws and regulations].

Article 303(2) LOSC is obviously a compromise formula. The initial Greek proposal, put forward during the Third United Nations Conference on the Law of the Sea (UNCLOS III) in 1979, had aimed at extending the sovereign rights of the coastal State in both the continental shelf and the exclusive economic zone (EEZ) to cultural objects found at sea. However, this was unacceptable to the major maritime powers, with the USA, the UK and the Netherlands at the forefront. They strongly opposed the widening of the continental shelf or EEZ concepts beyond a strictly natural resource-oriented use, fearing that this might foster creeping jurisdiction and ultimately lead to an infringement of the high seas freedoms. Nevertheless, even those States acknowledged that, besides Article 149 concerning artefacts in the Area, a more far-reaching provision for the protection of the underwater cultural heritage was needed. In the end, based on a proposal by the USA, it was agreed to add Article 303 to the general provisions of Part XVI.[8] Apart from paragraph 2, which refers to

---

8   For more details on the *travaux préparatoires* leading to the adoption of Article 303 LOSC see Caflisch, *op. cit.* (note 4), pp. 16 *et seq.*; Garabello, *op. cit.* (note 7), pp. 19 *et seq.*; Pallas, *op. cit.*

archaeological and historical objects on the seabed of the contiguous zone, the remaining three paragraphs of Article 303 are not specifically linked to any maritime area and, thus, apply to the underwater cultural heritage anywhere in the sea. Most importantly, Article 303(1) provides that all States "have the duty to protect objects of an archaeological and historical nature found at sea and shall cooperate for this purpose."[9]

The compromise adopted at UNCLOS III has little in common with the original Greek proposal. Instead of a 200-mile zone as envisaged by Greece, the only somewhat specific obligation regarding underwater cultural heritage in the LOSC is limited to a maritime area up to the 24-mile limit, which is coextensive with the contiguous zone. Moreover, for fear of creeping jurisdiction the US proposal avoided express mention of the contiguous zone itself, only referring back to Article 33 LOSC and linking the coastal State's obligations *vis-à-vis* cultural objects to the control powers it has in that zone.[10] This led to the very complex and difficult to grasp wording of Article 303(2) LOSC.[11]

Most commentators rightly consider that Article 303(2) makes use of a legal fiction (*fictio iuris*),[12] which accounts for the complexity in the construction of

---

(note 4), pp. 256 *et seq.*; Strati, *op. cit.* (note 4), pp. 162 *et seq.*; S. Dromgoole, *Underwater Cultural Heritage and International Law*, Cambridge, 2013, pp. 32 *et seq.*

9   Article 303 includes two more paragraphs, as follows:

   3. Nothing in this article affects the rights of identifiable owners, the law of salvage or other rules of admiralty, or laws and practices with respect to cultural exchanges.

   4. This article is without prejudice to other international agreements and rules of international law regarding the protection of objects of an archaeological and historical nature.

10 *Cf.* M.H. Nordquist, S. Rosenne, L.B. Sohn (eds.), *United Nations Convention on the Law of the Sea 1982: a Commentary*, Vol. V, Dordrecht, 1989, para. 303.3., pp. 159 *et seq.*; para. 303.6., p. 161.

11 In that respect Scovazzi has made the following discerning observations: "All the textual complications of Art. 303, para. 2, are probably due to the obsession of the drafters to avoid any words that might give the impression of some kind of coastal State jurisdiction beyond the territorial sea (*horror jurisdictionis*, to say it in Latin). Rather than laying down a substantive regime to deal with a new concern, such as the protection of the underwater cultural heritage, the UNCLOS [United Nations Convention on the Law of the Sea] seems more interested in playing with abstractions, like the preservation of the right balance between the jurisdiction of the coastal State and the freedom of the other States."; T. Scovazzi, "A Contradictory and Counterproductive Regime", in: R. Garabello, T. Scovazzi (eds.), *The Protection of the Underwater Cultural Heritage: Before and After the 2001 UNESCO Convention*, Leiden, 2003, p. 6.

12 See Caflisch, *op. cit.* (note 4), p. 20; Churchill, Lowe, *op. cit.* (note 4), p. 137; Dromgoole, *op. cit.* (note 8), pp. 34, 250; Pallas, *op. cit.* (note 4), p. 249; Strati, *op. cit.* (note 4), p. 166; Vitzthum, *op. cit.* (note 4), pp. 154, 157; Vitzthum, Talmon, *op. cit.* (note 4), p. 36; J. Allain,

the text. Indeed, according to Article 303(2) the coastal State "may presume" that the removal of cultural objects from the seabed *beyond its territorial sea* "would result in an infringement *within its territory or territorial sea* of the laws and regulations referred to in...article [33]",[13] *i.e.* customs, fiscal, immigration or sanitary laws and regulations. In other words, the laws and regulations that a perpetrator 'infringes' are in fact not even applicable in the area where the removal of the artefacts takes place, since that area is not part of the coastal State's territory. How could the perpetrator, thus, be held responsible for the violation of inapplicable rules? In comes the legal fiction: the infringement of the laws and regulations is assumed.[14]

"Maritime Wrecks: Where the *Lex Ferenda* of Underwater Cultural Heritage Collides with the *Lex Lata* of the Law of the Sea Convention", 38 *VJIL*, 1998, p. 756; E. Boesten, *Archaeological and/or Historic Valuable Shipwrecks in International Waters: Public International Law and What It Offers*, The Hague, 2002, p. 58; E.D. Brown, *The International Law of the Sea*, Vol. I, Aldershot, 1994, p. 135; M.C. Giorgi, "Underwater Archaeological and Historical Objects", in: R.-J. Dupuy, D. Vignes (eds.), *A Handbook on the New Law of the Sea*, Vol. I, Dordrecht, 1991, pp. 568 *et seq.*; D. Momtaz, "La Convention sur la protection du patrimoine culturel subaquatique", in: T.M. Ndiaye, R. Wolfrum (eds.), *Law of the Sea, Environmental Law and Settlement of Disputes: Liber Amicorum Judge Thomas Mensah*, Leiden, 2007, p. 450. On the other hand, a number of authors consider that Article 303(2) LOSC establishes a presumption; see Arend, *op. cit.* (note 5), p. 799; Garabello, *op. cit.* (note 7), p. 155; C. Bories, *Le patrimoine culturel en droit international: les compétences des États à l'égard des éléments du patrimoine culturel*, Paris, 2011, p. 396; B.H. Oxman, "Third United Nations Conference on the Law of the Sea: the Ninth Session (1980)", 75 *American Journal of International Law*, 1981, p. 241; idem, "Marine Archaeology and the International Law of the Sea", 12 *Columbia-VLA Journal of Law & the Arts*, 1988, pp. 363 *et seq.*

13 Emphasis added. The meaning of this phrase was clarified in a report by the President of UNCLOS III: "It was agreed that the reference in paragraph 2 to 'result in an infringement' was understood to mean that it would constitute or constitutes an infringement within 'its territory or territorial sea'."; see *Report of the President on the work of the informal plenary meeting of the Conference on general provisions*, Doc. A/CONF.62/L.58, 22 August 1980, para. 14, in: Third United Nations Conference on the Law of the Sea, *Official Records*, Vol. XIV, para. 14, p. 129; see also Nordquist, Rosenne, Sohn, *op. cit.* (note 10), para. 303.4., p. 160.

14 It is true that sometimes the distinction between a legal fiction and a presumption might be difficult to make. However, Article 303(2) LOSC must at least be deemed an absolute, irrebuttable presumption (*praesumptio iuris et de iure*), because the wording of the provision clearly does not allow for a rebuttal of the assumed facts by evidence to the contrary; *cf.* Pallas, *op. cit.* (note 4), pp. 249 *et seq.* Surely, the qualification of Article 303(2) LOSC as a rebuttable presumption (*praesumptio iuris*) would render the provision meaningless, since the nature of the respective laws and regulations, *i.e.* customs, fiscal, immigration or sanitary laws and regulations, would in most cases make it easy to prove that by the

Due to the complex structure and the deliberate ambiguity of the wording, the interpretation of Article 303(2) LOSC presents a challenging task. It is, indeed, difficult to determine the exact content and scope of the jurisdictional powers that are afforded to the coastal State by the provision. Thus, it is not surprising that the approaches taken in the doctrine are quite diverse. Nonetheless, authors may essentially be divided into two groups. On the one hand, we have commentators who interpret Article 303(2) restrictively, more or less adhering to the ordinary, linguistic meaning of the words and expressions used.[15] On the other hand, there are authors who advocate a more liberal, extensive approach, which takes into account the object and purpose of the provision, since a purely linguistic interpretation would render the rule's meaning and scope rather obscure and ambiguous.[16]

The authors who take a restrictive view of Article 303(2) LOSC concede to the coastal State only control powers with respect to the 'traffic' and 'removal from the seabed' of archaeological and historical objects, treating such traffic and removal as though they constituted an infringement of the State's customs, fiscal, sanitary or immigration laws and regulations. Thus, according to this approach the coastal State has only restricted enforcement jurisdiction.

---

removal of the underwater cultural heritage no such laws and regulations had been violated; cf. Strati, op. cit. (note 4), pp. 166 et seq.

[15] See Allain, op. cit. (note 12), pp. 757 et seq.; Arend, op. cit. (note 5), p. 801; Boesten, op. cit. (note 12), p. 58; Oxman, "Marine Archaeology...", op. cit. (note 12), pp. 363 et seq.; Pallas, op. cit. (note 4), pp. 248 et seq.; Vitzthum, op. cit. (note 4), pp. 156 et seq.; Vitzthum, Talmon, op. cit. (note 4), pp. 35 et seq.; M. Rau, "The UNESCO Convention on Underwater Cultural Heritage and the International Law of the Sea", 6 Max Planck Yearbook of United Nations Law, 2002, p. 398.

[16] See Caflisch, op. cit. (note 4), pp. 20, 24; Garabello, op. cit. (note 7), pp. 156 et seq.; Giorgi, op. cit. (note 12), pp. 568 et seq., 570; Momtaz, op. cit. (note 12), pp. 450 et seq.; Pazarci, op. cit. (note 1), p. 252; Strati, op. cit. (note 4), pp. 167 et seq.; idem, "Protection of the Underwater Cultural Heritage: from the Shortcomings of the UN Convention on the Law of the Sea to the Compromises of the UNESCO Convention", in: A. Strati, M. Gavouneli, N. Skourtos (eds.), Unresolved Issues and New Challenges to the Law of the Sea: Time Before and After, Leiden, 2006, pp. 29 et seq.; R. Lagoni, "Marine Archäologie und sonstige auf dem Meeresboden gefundene Gegenstände", 44 Archiv des Völkerrechts, 2006, pp. 334 et seq.; U. Leanza, "La zona archeologica marina e la protezione dei beni culturali subacquei", in: P. Paone (ed.), La protezione internazionale e la circolazione comunitaria dei beni culturali mobili, Napoli, 1998, pp. 102 et seq.; idem, "Le patrimoine culturel sous-marin de la Méditerranée", in: G. Cataldi (ed.), La Méditerranée et le droit de la mer à l'aube du 21ème siècle, Bruxelles, 2002, pp. 145 et seq.; E. Roucounas, "Sub-marine Archaeological Research: Some Legal Aspects", in: U. Leanza (ed.), Il regime giuridico internazionale del mare Mediterraneo, Milano, 1987, pp. 324 et seq.

It may not regulate activities directed at underwater cultural heritage that do not entail the removal of artefacts. However, as *e.g.* Vitzthum and Talmon admit,[17] to effectively control the removal of cultural objects from the seabed beneath the contiguous zone the coastal State must at least have the possibility of prescribing in its legislation the procedure for issuing appropriate permits, and this undoubtedly amounts to an, albeit limited, legislative jurisdiction. Finally, most of these commentators are of the opinion that the coastal State may make use of the jurisdictional powers arising from Article 303(2) LOSC only if it has declared a contiguous zone.

A quite different result is obtained by authors who put emphasis on the object and purpose of the norm and, thus, endorse an extensive interpretation of Article 303(2) LOSC as the correct approach. Although there are dissimilarities concerning the content and scope, all of these writers agree that Article 303(2) makes it possible for the coastal State to extend its legislative jurisdiction regarding underwater cultural heritage to the seabed beneath the contiguous zone. While some of them consider it necessary that a contiguous zone has been established,[18] others do not make the coastal State's jurisdictional powers under Article 303(2) LOSC dependent on the declaration of a contiguous zone.[19] Strati, for example, convincingly argues that, since the removal of artefacts from the seabed constitutes an infringement of the coastal State's laws and regulations, then, *a contrario*, the coastal State must have the jurisdiction to regulate such removal, and in so doing it may set the conditions it deems necessary with a view to safeguarding the protection of the underwater cultural heritage. Strati's argument is reinforced if Article 303(2) is linked to the general obligation to protect the underwater cultural heritage, arising from Article 303(1) LOSC. The duty to protect cultural objects found at sea coupled with the jurisdictional powers regarding the traffic and removal of artefacts from the seabed beneath the contiguous zone enables the coastal State to extend its cultural heritage legislation up to the 24-mile limit. This leads Strati to the conclusion that on the basis of Article 303(2) LOSC an archaeological zone has been created which is different in nature from the contiguous zone, and its establishment is, thus, not dependent on the prior declaration of the

---

17 Vitzthum, Talmon, *op. cit.* (note 4), p. 38.
18 Leanza, "La zona...", *loc. cit.*; *idem*, "Le patrimoine...", *loc. cit.*; H. Pazarci, "Sur la recherche archéologique subaquatique en Méditerranée", in: Leanza, *op. cit.* (note 16), pp. 359 *et seq.*
19 Bories, *op. cit.* (note 12), p. 397; Garabello, *op. cit.* (note 7), p. 157; Lagoni, *op. cit.* (note 16), pp. 335 *et seq.*; Roucounas, *loc. cit.*; Strati, *op. cit.* (note 4), pp. 168 *et seq.*; see also Nordquist, Rosenne, Sohn, *op. cit.* (note 10), para. 303.6., p. 161.

latter.[20] In a similar vein Lagoni has observed that, according to Article 303(2) LOSC, neither a real nor a legal nexus can exist between the underwater cultural heritage and the mentioned laws and regulations of the coastal State, as long as the artefacts remain on the bottom of the sea. Since Article 303(2) does not prohibit the removal of cultural objects from the seabed beneath the contiguous zone, nor does such a prohibition otherwise exist under the LOSC or general international law, the removal is in principle permitted. Thus, if the coastal State is to have the power of consent to the removal of artefacts in the 24-mile zone, it must first prohibit such removal via its municipal laws. In that sense, Article 303(2) LOSC necessarily encompasses regulatory competences regarding the underwater cultural heritage on the seabed beneath the contiguous zone.[21]

Although the States that expressly make use of the jurisdictional rights provided in Article 303(2) LOSC are still few in number,[22] those that do so have implemented legislation endorsing the extensive rather than the restrictive interpretation. By way of illustration we will summarily present the pertinent legislations of Denmark, France and South Africa.

As early as in 1984,[23] Denmark introduced provisions into its Conservation of Nature Act that ancient monuments and shipwrecks older than 100 years located on the continental shelf within the 24-mile limit may not be damaged or removed without the consent of the competent Danish authorities.[24] These rather basic provisions were significantly substantiated in the Museums Act which was adopted that same year.[25] The 1984 Museums Act's rules concerning underwater cultural heritage were retained in the latest Museums Act which was adopted in 2001.[26] Under the pertinent provisions the applicability of the

---

20   Strati, *loc. cit.*
21   Lagoni, *op. cit.* (note 16), p. 334.
22   It would seem that there are no more than ten such States. For a more detailed account of the State practice see Garabello, *op. cit.* (note 7), pp. 158 *et seq.*; see also Dromgoole, *op. cit.* (note 8), pp. 253 *et seq.*; Strati, *op. cit.* (note 4), pp. 185 *et seq.*; idem, "From the Shortcomings...", *op. cit.* (note 16), pp. 30 *et seq.*; Vitzthum, Talmon, *op. cit.* (note 4), p. 40.
23   It seems that Denmark was the first country to act upon the new rights afforded by Article 303(2) LOSC, although it would ratify the Law of the Sea Convention only in 2004; *cf.* Dromgoole, *op. cit.* (note 8), p. 253.
24   Garabello, *op. cit.* (note 7), p. 161; Strati, *op. cit.* (note 4), p. 185; *cf.* also Dromgoole, *loc. cit.*; K. Bangert, "Denmark and the Law of the Sea", in: T. Treves (ed.), *The Law of the Sea: the European Union and Its Member States*, The Hague, 1997, pp. 108 *et seq.*
25   Garabello, *loc. cit.*
26   The 2001 Museums Act was last amended in 2006. An English translation of the *Consolidated Act on Museums, Executive Order No. 1505 of 14 December 2006*, is available on

Act is extended to ancient relics or monuments "on the continental shelf, but not beyond 24 nautical miles from the base lines from which the width of outer territorial waters is measured."[27] The Danish Museums Act stipulates, *inter alia*, that finds of underwater cultural heritage must be reported to the minister for culture,[28] and that underwater cultural heritage, as defined by the Act, *i.e.* including objects found in the 24-mile zone, "shall belong to the state, unless any person proves to be the rightful owner."[29] It is noteworthy that Denmark formally proclaimed a contiguous zone only in 2005,[30] more than 20 years after it had extended its cultural heritage legislation to objects found on the seabed within 24 nautical miles from the baselines.

France, as well, early on enacted legislation regarding the protection of cultural objects found on the seabed beneath the contiguous zone. This was done by Act No. 89–874 of 1 December 1989 concerning Maritime Cultural Assets.[31] The legislators' intention was to implement Article 303(2) LOSC, although France, at the time, had not yet become a party to the Montego Bay Convention.[32] Today

---

the website of the Danish Ministry of Culture at: <http://kum.dk/uploads/tx_templavoila/Consolidated_Act_on_Museums_Executive_Order_No.1505[1].pdf> (19 August 2014).

27 Section 28(1), Museums Act.
28 *Ibid.*
29 Section 28(2), *ibid.*
30 See *Act on the Contiguous Zone, 24 June 2005*, in: *Law of the Sea Bulletin* (hereinafter: *LOSB*), No. 58, 2005, p. 17. According to Section 3 of the Act the proclamation of the contiguous zone has no bearing on the existing legislation concerning "the monitoring of archaeological and historical objects". For the limits of the Danish contiguous zone see *Executive Order on the Demarcation of the Danish Contiguous Zone, 29 June 2005*, in: *ibid.*, p. 18.
31 *Loi N° 89–874 du 1er décembre 1989 relative aux biens culturels maritimes et modifiant la Loi du 27 septembre 1941 portant réglementation des fouilles archéologiques*; an English translation of the 1989 Act was published in: *LOSB*, No. 16, 1990, p. 12. For more details on the 1989 Act see G. Le Gurun, "France", in: S. Dromgoole (ed.), *Legal Protection of the Underwater Cultural Heritage: National and International Perspectives*, The Hague, 1999, pp. 43–63; *cf.* also *idem*, "Le droit français de l'archéologie sous-marine", in: M. Cornu, J. Fromageau (eds.), *Le patrimoine culturel et la mer: Aspects juridiques et institutionnels*, Vol. II, Paris, 2002, pp. 101–117; J.-P. Beurier, "Le statut juridique français des bien culturels sous-marins", in: T. Scovazzi (ed.), *La protezione del patrimonio culturale sottomarino nel Mare Mediterraneo*, Milano, 2004, pp. 203–210; J.-P. Quéneudec, "Chronique du droit de la mer", 36 *Annuaire français de Droit international*, 1990, pp. 753–755. Two years prior to the Act on Maritime Cultural Assets, France had proclaimed a contiguous zone by virtue of Act No. 87–1157 of 31 December 1987; see L. Lucchini, M. Voelckel, *Droit de la mer: La mer et son droit, Les espaces maritimes*, Vol. I, Paris, 1990, pp. 198 *et seq.*
32 *Cf.* G. Le Gurun, "France", in: S. Dromgoole (ed.), *The Protection of the Underwater Cultural Heritage: National Perspectives in Light of the UNESCO Convention 2001*, Leiden, 2006, p. 77.

the provisions of the 1989 Act are consolidated in the Heritage Code (*Code du patrimoine*), which was codified for the first time in 2004.[33] According to that legislation, most of the rules applicable to maritime cultural assets found within the *domaine public maritime*, *i.e.* the maritime spaces under France's sovereignty, extend also to such objects located in a contiguous zone lying between 12 and 24 nautical miles, as measured from the baselines of the territorial sea.[34] The pertinent rules concern, *e.g.*, the obligation to report finds of cultural objects to the competent French authorities within 48 hours of their discovery,[35] and also the obligation to obtain prior administrative authorization for any envisaged archaeological activity, including prospecting, excavations or drilling.[36] However, the provisions on State ownership in respect of cultural objects found in the *domaine public maritime* were not extended to artefacts in the contiguous zone.[37] Nevertheless, it is evident that France has not confined itself to simply determining the conditions for the removal of archaeological and historical objects from the seabed in the contiguous zone, but has asserted, albeit limited, regulatory competences with a view to safeguarding the protection of the cultural heritage found in the 24-mile zone.

South Africa seems to have gone farthest in implementing Article 303(2) LOSC pursuant to the extensive interpretation. Under the Maritime Zones Act, adopted in 1994,[38] South Africa not only proclaimed a classic contiguous zone, in which it exercises powers according to Article 33 LOSC,[39] but expressly provided for the establishment of a distinct 'maritime cultural zone'. The maritime cultural zone has a breadth of 24 miles measured from the baselines and is, thus, coextensive with the contiguous zone.[40] Even more striking is the provision that "the Republic shall have, in respect of objects of an archaeological or historical nature found in the maritime cultural zone, *the same rights and powers as it has in respect of its territorial waters.*"[41] In other words, the legal regime of cultural heritage protection beyond the territorial sea, but within the 24-mile limit, is entirely assimilated to the regime in force for maritime spaces

---

33   *Ibid.*, p. 64, note 21. The text of the *Code du patrimoine*, as currently in force, is available at: <http://www.legifrance.gouv.fr/affichCode.do?cidTexte=LEGITEXT000006074236> (19 August 2014).
34   Article L532–12, *Code du patrimoine*.
35   Article L532–3, *ibid.*
36   Article L532–7, *ibid.*
37   Le Gurun, "France", *op. cit.* (note 31), p. 52; *idem*, *op. cit.* (note 32), pp. 76 *et seq.*
38   *Maritime Zones Act, No. 15 of 1994*, in: *LOSB*, No. 32, 1996, p. 75.
39   Section 5, *ibid.*
40   Section 6(1), *ibid.*
41   Section 6(2), *ibid.*; emphasis added.

under the sovereignty of South Africa. Consequently, the 1999 South African Natural Heritage Resources Act, as currently in force,[42] which comprehensively regulates the protection and management of cultural heritage on land and under water,[43] is without limitation applicable to objects located in the maritime cultural zone.

Concluding this short overview of State practice regarding the protection of the underwater cultural heritage in the 24-mile zone, it is interesting to note the shift that seems to have occurred in the stance of the United States. Indeed, although the US, on the occasion of the establishment of the US contiguous zone in 1999, did not adopt substantive legal norms pertaining specifically to the protection of artefacts, the Presidential Proclamation nevertheless stated that this was "an important step in preventing the removal of cultural heritage found within 24 nautical miles of the baseline."[44]

In evaluating the legal scope and significance of Article 303(2) LOSC, it is certainly true that according to Article 31(1) of the 1969 Vienna Convention on the Law of Treaties (VCLT) a treaty must first and foremost be interpreted "in accordance with the ordinary meaning to be given to the terms of the treaty", as stressed also by adherents of the restrictive approach. However, according to that same provision of the VCLT, even when interpreting the terms of a treaty on the textual level, the context and the object and purpose of the treaty, *i.e.* the treaty clause, must be taken into account.[45] Hence, a teleological approach

---

42   *National Heritage Resources Act, No. 25 of 1999*, in: *Republic of South Africa Government Gazette*, No. 19974, 1999; available on the website of the South African Department of Arts and Culture at: <http://www.dac.gov.za/sites/default/files/Legislations%20Files/a25-99.pdf> (19 August 2014).

43   For more details on the protection of underwater cultural heritage according to the South African Natural Heritage Resources Act see C.J.S. Forrest, "South Africa", in: Dromgoole, *op. cit.* (note 32), pp. 247–270.

44   *Proclamation 7219 of August 2, 1999: Contiguous Zone of the United States*, in: *Federal Register*, Vol. 64, No. 173, 8 September 1999, p. 48701. *Cf.* Dromgoole, *op. cit.* (note 8), pp. 254 *et seq.*; O. Varmer, "United States of America", in: Dromgoole, *op. cit.* (note 32), pp. 382 *et seq.*

45   *Cf.* J.-M. Sorel, "Article 31 – Convention de Vienne de 1969", in: O. Corten, P. Klein (eds.), *Les Conventions de Vienne sur le droit des traités: Commentaire article par article*, Vol. II, Bruxelles, 2006, pp. 1309 *et seq.* On the rules of treaty interpretation, apart from *ibid.*, pp. 1209 *et seq.*, see *e.g.* M.K. Yasseen, "L'interprétation des traités d'après la Convention de Vienne sur le droit des traités", 151 *Recueil des cours de l'Académie de droit international de La Haye*, 1976–III, pp. 1–114. For an account of the International Court of Justice's jurisprudence regarding the application of the VCLT rules on treaty interpretation see S. Torres Bernárdez, "Interpretation of Treaties by the International Court of Justice following the

to the interpretation of Article 303(2) LOSC will be all the more appropriate if results obtained from a linguistic interpretation are obscure.

In that respect Lagoni's argument, explained above, on the essential real and legal nexus between the cultural objects located in the contiguous zone and the coastal State's legal order is compelling, since it shows that the coastal State, in applying Article 303(2) LOSC, necessarily must have a certain degree of legislative competence beyond its territorial sea. Furthermore, as we have seen, according to the linguistic interpretation of Article 303(2) LOSC, laws and regulations that concern customs, fiscal, immigration or sanitary matters are to serve a purpose for which they are utterly inadequate, namely the protection of the cultural heritage.[46] Consequently, the purely textual interpretation indeed does render the meaning and scope of Article 303(2) LOSC obscure and ambiguous. The restrictive approach virtually strips the norm of any legal effect, since the coastal State would not gain the competence required to effectively safeguard the protection of the cultural heritage concerned.[47]

As pointed out earlier, Article 303(2) LOSC is a compromise. As such the wording selected was deliberately ambiguous, and its complexity is mainly due to the fact that the maritime powers headed by the US wanted to prevent this new norm from being used by coastal States as a basis for creeping jurisdiction.

Adoption of the 1969 Vienna Convention on the Law of Treaties", in: G. Hafner *et al.* (eds.), *Liber Amicorum Professor Ignaz Seidl-Hohenveldern*, The Hague, 1998, pp. 721–748.

46 *Cf.* Scovazzi, *op. cit.* (note 11), p. 5.

47 Such an outcome is, of course, unacceptable, since the interpretation of a treaty clause must not render the legal norm in question without any effect or meaning; see *e.g.* J. Andrassy, *Medunarodno pravo [International Law]*, Zagreb, 1976, p. 340. As precisely and instructively formulated by the arbitral tribunal in *Eureko BV v. Republic of Poland*: "It is a cardinal rule of the interpretation of treaties that each and every operative clause of a treaty is to be interpreted as meaningful rather than meaningless."; see *Eureko BV v. Republic of Poland, Partial Award and Dissenting Opinion*, 19 August 2005, para. 248, p. 79, available at: <http://ita.law.uvic.ca/documents/Eureko-PartialAwardandDissenting Opinion.pdf> (19 August 2014). This basic rule of treaty interpretation was implicitly followed in the first contentious matter before the Permanent Court of International Justice; see *Case of the SS "Wimbledon", Judgment of 17 August 1923*, PCIJ, *Collection of Judgments, Series A, No. 1, 1923*, pp. 25 *et seq*. It is also consistently confirmed and adhered to in the jurisprudence of the International Court of Justice; see *e.g. Legal Consequences for States of the Continued Presence of South Africa in Namibia (South West Africa) notwithstanding Security Council Resolution 276 (1970), Advisory Opinion*, ICJ Reports 1971, para. 66, p. 35; *Border and Transborder Armed Actions (Nicaragua v. Honduras), Jurisdiction and Admissibility, Judgment*, ICJ Reports 1988, para. 46, p. 89; *Maritime Delimitation and Territorial Questions between Qatar and Bahrain, Jurisdiction and Admissibility, Judgment*, ICJ Reports 1995, para. 35, p. 19.

But even the United States, in proposing Article 303(1) LOSC which imposes a duty on all States to protect the underwater cultural heritage, had recognized that the need for such protection did exist.[48] Moreover, it follows from the *travaux préparatoires* that the purpose of the initial Greek proposal was exactly the achievement of a more effective protection of the cultural heritage in maritime spaces beyond the sovereignty of coastal States. Consequently, the protection of cultural heritage constitutes the object and purpose of Article 303(2) LOSC as well. In order to safeguard such protection, Article 303(2) LOSC, in accordance with the proper teleological approach, enables the coastal State to extend its cultural heritage legislation to the seabed beyond the territorial sea up to 24 miles from the baselines. It may do so at least in order to regulate the removal of cultural objects. However, while legislating on the removal of objects, the coastal State may make the issuance of an authorization dependent on various preconditions, *e.g.*, that certain archaeological standards be fulfilled, that the persons involved in the removal be archaeological experts, that in accordance with standard procedures *in situ* protection be considered as an alternative option to the removal, *etc.*[49] Hence, by exercising its powers regarding the removal of cultural objects from the seabed beneath the contiguous zone, the coastal State will, in a specific case, be in a position to regulate the broader context of the archaeological activities involved. Although the aim of the opponents was to prevent a further extension of coastal State jurisdiction, it would, thus, seem that such a development was implied in Article 303(2) LOSC and an inevitable outcome of its implementation by States. This is proven by the existing State practice, as limited in number as it may be. It is also noteworthy that such State practice does not seem to have attracted any protest from other States.[50]

Finally, we do not see any obstacle in the Law of the Sea Convention for the coastal State to proclaim a zone in which it will only exercise the jurisdictional powers stemming from Article 303(2) LOSC, without having previously established a contiguous zone according to Article 33 LOSC. This is perfectly in line with the *argumentum a maiori ad minus*, well-established in legal reasoning. Furthermore, nothing prevents the coastal State from referring to that zone as an 'archaeological zone' or to give it some other appropriate denomination. An analogous and rather widespread practice exists in respect of the EEZ, with States proclaiming derivatives of that maritime zone that encompass various

---

48   *Cf.* Oxman, "Third United Nations Conference...", *op. cit.* (note 12), pp. 240 *et seq.*
49   *Cf.* Pallas, *op. cit.* (note 4), p. 251.
50   *Cf.* Dromgoole, *op. cit.* (note 8), p. 255.

combinations of the respective jurisdictional competences and sovereign rights, and are appropriately denominated.[51] We see no reason why this should be approached differently in the case of the contiguous zone. Besides, the separation of the archaeological zone from the classic concept of the contiguous zone is accentuated by the fact that, systemically, Article 303 has been placed among the general provisions within Part XVI of the LOSC, well away from the section on the contiguous zone. What is more, in Article 303(2) LOSC there is no express mention of the term 'contiguous zone'. One final remark should be made concerning the distinct nature of the archaeological zone. Indeed, one must not lose sight of the paragraph preceding Article 303(2) LOSC. Although it is difficult to infer concrete obligations for States from the general duty to protect archaeological and historical objects found at sea, as contained in Article 303(1), a State in the position to undertake actions may hardly remain entirely passive in respect of endangered cultural heritage anywhere in the sea, including the seabed beyond the territorial sea up to the 24-mile limit. According to the Law of the Sea Convention, such a duty exists irrespective of proclaimed jurisdictional zones.

As will be shown, the view on Article 303(2) LOSC that we have presented is confirmed by Article 8 UCHC.

---

51 It suffices to point to Croatia's practice establishing an 'Ecological and Fisheries Protection Zone' (EFPZ) in 2003; an English translation of the *Decision on the Extension of the Jurisdiction of the Republic of Croatia in the Adriatic Sea* was published in: LOSB, No. 53, 2004, p. 68; and the first of the ensuing three amendments in: LOSB, No. 55, 2004, p. 31. On the reasons why Croatia opted for the EFPZ instead of a full-fledged EEZ and the repercussions of that proclamation see *e.g.* D. Vidas, "The UN Convention on the Law of the Sea, the European Union and the Rule of Law: What Is Going on in the Adriatic Sea?", 24 *International Journal of Marine and Coastal Law* (hereinafter: *IJMCL*), 2009, pp. 9 *et seq.*; B. Vukas, "Pomorski zakonik Republike Hrvatske i međunarodno pravo mora" ["The Maritime Code of the Republic of Croatia and the International Law of the Sea"], 58 *Zbornik Pravnog fakulteta u Zagrebu* [*Collected Papers of the Zagreb Faculty of Law*], 2008, p. 193. On the practice of the Mediterranean States in applying the LOSC's rules on the EEZ see A. Del Vecchio Capotosti, "*In Maiore Stat Minus*: A Note on the EEZ and the Zones of Ecological Protection in the Mediterranean Sea", 39 *Ocean Development and International Law* (hereinafter: *ODIL*), 2008, pp. 287–297; U. Leanza, "L'institution de zones de protection écologique dans la politique des Etats côtiers de la Méditerranée", in: B. Vukas, T.M. Šošić (eds.), *International Law: New Actors, New Concepts – Continuing Dilemmas. Liber Amicorum Božidar Bakotić*, Leiden, 2010, pp. 251–264; B. Vukas, "State Practice in the Aftermath of the UN Convention on the Law of the Sea: the Exclusive Economic Zone and the Mediterranean Sea", in: Strati, Gavouneli, Skourtos, *op. cit.* (note 16), pp. 251–258.

III Article 8 of the Underwater Cultural Heritage Convention

Article 8 of the 2001 UNESCO Convention on the Protection of the Underwater Cultural Heritage seems to confirm our view on Article 303(2) LOSC:

> Without prejudice to and in addition to Articles 9 and 10 [concerning the EEZ and the continental shelf], and in accordance with Article 303, paragraph 2, of the United Nations Convention on the Law of the Sea, States Parties may regulate and authorize activities directed at underwater cultural heritage within their contiguous zone. In so doing, they shall require that the [annexed] Rules [concerning activities directed at underwater cultural heritage] be applied.

During the negotiations on the UCHC within UNESCO, two issues were discussed in connection with the protection of cultural heritage in the contiguous zone. The first one was the question whether States should be required to apply the so-called 'Rules', *i.e.* the archaeological and technical standards annexed to the Convention, in respect of the contiguous zone, and the second one concerned the controversy whether and to what extent the article on the contiguous zone should contain an express reference to the LOSC. In the end, it was decided to make the application of the 'Rules' mandatory, and also to retain an express link to Article 303(2) LOSC, taking into account the general consensus in favour of adherence to the existing maritime zones as provided by the LOSC. Furthermore, an introductory reference to the UCHC provisions on the EEZ and the continental shelf was added.[52]

According to Article 8 UCHC, as finally adopted, coastal States "may *regulate and authorize* activities directed at underwater cultural heritage within their contiguous zone."[53] This would then mean that coastal States have general

---

52 For more details on the negotiating history of Article 8 UCHC see R. Garabello, "The Negotiating History of the Convention on the Protection of the Underwater Cultural Heritage", in: Garabello, Scovazzi, *op. cit.* (note 11), pp. 136 *et seq.* In a statement on vote Greece expressed its discontent with the extension to the contiguous zone of the reporting and consultation procedure, as envisaged by the UCHC in respect of the EEZ and the continental shelf. It was the view of the Greek delegation that such a solution diminished the existing rights of coastal States within their contiguous zones; see *Statements on Vote during Commission IV on Culture*, UNESCO, 31st Session of the General Conference, 29 October 2001, in: Garabello, Scovazzi, *op. cit.* (note 11), pp. 247 *et seq.*; also in: G. Camarda, T. Scovazzi (eds.), *The Protection of the Underwater Cultural Heritage: Legal Aspects*, Milano, 2002, pp. 428 *et seq.*

53 Emphasis added.

legislative competence in respect of maritime cultural heritage in the contiguous zone. *Prima facie* it might even be maintained that the coastal State is afforded the same jurisdiction it has regarding archaeological and historical objects found in the maritime spaces under its sovereignty.[54]

Yet, Article 8 UCHC contains the mentioned limitation that coastal States are to use their rights "in accordance with Article 303, paragraph 2, of the United Nations Convention on the Law of the Sea." The question arises what the legal effects of this express reference to the LOSC are. As our preceding analysis has shown, Article 303(2) LOSC can correctly be interpreted only if the norm's *telos* is appreciated, which inevitably implies that the provision grants the coastal State at least some degree of regulatory competence regarding the protection of submerged cultural objects located on the seabed beyond the territorial sea up to the 24-mile limit. In other words, the reference to Article 303(2) LOSC at the beginning of Article 8 UCHC is of a declaratory nature.[55] The UNESCO Convention's rule on the contiguous zone should, thus, be viewed as confirming the development already present in State practice, namely that the coastal State is entitled to apply, in respect of archaeological sites within the contiguous zone, all the protective measures provided by its pertinent internal legislation. Consequently, if not yet an unequivocal reflection of customary international law,[56] considering the limited State practice and the still relatively small number of States parties to the UCHC, Article 8 UCHC, indeed, significantly contributes to the crystallisation of a new customary rule.[57]

---

54 Bories rather boldly asserts that "[p]lutôt que de conforter l'existence de la zone archéologique nouvelle implicitement créée en 1982, la Convention de l'Unesco étend dans l'espace la mer territoriale..."; Bories, *op. cit.* (note 12), p. 401. However, she does not properly consider the limitation at the beginning of Article 8, according to which the UCHC's provisions on the EEZ and the continental shelf are in principle also applicable to objects found in the contiguous zone; see *infra*.

55 *Cf.* Garabello, *op. cit.* (note 7), p. 173.

56 That Article 8 UCHC represents a reflection of customary law was held by the Swedish delegation at the negotiations within UNESCO: "Sweden welcomes that the legal contents of the rules concerning the mandate of the coastal State in its declared contiguous zone is clarified in the Convention and regards this clarification as an indication of customary law."; see *Statements on Vote during Commission IV on Culture*, UNESCO, 31st Session of the General Conference, 29 October 2001, in: Garabello, Scovazzi, *op. cit.* (note 11), p. 250; also in: Camarda, Scovazzi, *op. cit.* (note 52), p. 431.

57 *Cf.* G. Carducci, "The Expanding Protection of Underwater Cultural Heritage: The New UNESCO Convention versus Existing International Law", in: Camarda, Scovazzi, *op. cit.* (note 52), pp. 192 *et seq.* Garabello seems to imply that Article 8 UCHC marks the completion of the crystallisation process; Garabello, *op. cit.* (note 7), p. 174. On the crystallisation of customary law through treaty rules, in particular codification conventions, see

It has to be noted, though, that according to Article 8 UCHC the coastal State's competences in the domain of underwater heritage protection are expressly associated with the concept of the contiguous zone. This might lead to the conclusion that the coastal State must have declared a contiguous zone prior to making use of these jurisdictional rights.[58] In our view, as explained earlier, the coastal State is, in accordance with the *argumentum a maiori ad minus*, at liberty to limit its jurisdictional powers in the contiguous zone solely to the protection of the submerged cultural heritage. The mention of the contiguous zone in Article 8 UCHC should, rather, be understood as a determination of the rule's scope of application *ratione territorii*, i.e. as setting the outer limit of the maritime space to which the State's jurisdiction regarding cultural objects extends.[59] The designation of such a zone as 'contiguous', 'archaeological' or 'maritime cultural' is not decisive.

As mentioned, apart from the reference to Article 303(2) LOSC, Article 8 further stipulates that the coastal State, in exercising its jurisdiction regarding the cultural heritage within the 24-mile zone, is to do so "[w]ithout prejudice to and in addition to Articles 9 and 10" of the UCHC,[60] which concern the protection of the underwater cultural heritage in the EEZ and on the continental shelf. This obviously means that the mechanism of reports and consultations, as established by the UCHC in respect of historic wrecks and artefacts found in the EEZ and on the continental shelf,[61] should, at least in principle, also be applied to objects located within the 24-mile zone. As a result, the legislative competences of the coastal State *vis-à-vis* the cultural heritage in its contiguous zone have

---

T. Treves, "Customary International Law", in: R. Wolfrum (ed.), *The Max Planck Encyclopedia of Public International Law*, Vol. II, Oxford, 2012, para. 71, p. 951; *cf.* also V.Đ. Degan, *Sources of International Law*, The Hague, 1997, pp. 207 *et seq.*

58 Pallas, *op. cit.* (note 4), p. 434.
59 *Cf.* Garabello, *op. cit.* (note 7), pp. 177 *et seq.*
60 The, albeit limited, application of Articles 9 and 10 UCHC in the contiguous zone is no doubt the reason why Article 8 does not specifically deal with the issue of wrecked State vessels and aircraft, as do the UCHC provisions on all other maritime zones. On the controversial legal status of sunken warships and other State vessels, as well as sunken State aircraft, see *e.g.* Dromgoole, *op. cit.* (note 8), pp. 134 *et seq.*; Garabello, *op. cit.* (note 7), pp. 301 *et seq.*; M.J. Aznar Gómez, "Legal Status of Sunken Warships 'Revisited'", 9 *Spanish Yearbook of International Law*, 2003, pp. 61–101; C.J.S. Forrest, "An International Perspective on Sunken State Vessels as Underwater Cultural Heritage", 34 *ODIL*, 2003, pp. 41–57.
61 On the UCHC reporting and consultation procedure regarding underwater cultural heritage in the EEZ and on the continental shelf see *e.g.* Dromgoole, *op. cit.* (note 8), pp. 288 *et seq.*; Garabello, *op. cit.* (note 7), pp. 239 *et seq.*; P.J. O'Keefe, *Shipwrecked Heritage: A Commentary on the UNESCO Convention on Underwater Cultural Heritage*, Leicester, 2002, pp. 80 *et seq.*

indeed been restricted, at least to a certain degree.[62] However, the reference to Articles 9 and 10 UCHC cannot mean that the coastal State is obliged to coordinate each and every action regarding cultural objects in the contiguous zone with the States that have, on the basis of a verifiable link with the artefacts concerned, expressed their interest in being consulted on effective protection measures.[63] As shown, the coastal State clearly has regulatory powers in respect of submerged objects of cultural value located on the seabed beyond the territorial sea up to the 24-mile limit, which necessarily implies the authorization and control of archaeological and preservation activities based on the coastal State's respective cultural heritage laws. Nevertheless, taking into account the principle of cooperation, which is an important pillar of the protection regime as envisaged by the UCHC,[64] it should be good practice to consult States that have a legitimate interest in the fate of a particular cultural object, not least because they may contribute to covering the invariably high financial costs that arise from the implementation of effective protection measures. In any case, it can hardly be maintained that according to the UCHC the coastal State's jurisdiction in the contiguous zone is the same as in its territorial sea.

We have already noted that, according to Article 8 UCHC, the coastal State has to ensure the application of the 'Rules', *i.e.* the archaeological and technical standards contained in the Annex to the Convention, in respect of cultural items located within the 24-mile zone.[65] This, indeed, further limits the legislative competence of the coastal State, but here the limitation serves the interests of a more effective protection of the underwater cultural heritage in line with the current practice and standards of archaeological expertise.[66]

---

62   *Cf.* Rau, *op. cit.* (note 15), p. 410; Strati, "From the Shortcomings…", *op. cit.* (note 16), p. 44.
63   *Cf.* Garabello, *op. cit.* (note 7), p. 179.
64   This follows expressly from Article 2(2) of the UCHC: "States Parties shall cooperate in the protection of underwater cultural heritage." *Cf.* O'Keefe, *op. cit.* (note 61), p. 50.
65   In accordance with Article 7(2) UCHC the same obligation exists in the maritime spaces under the sovereignty of the coastal State: "Without prejudice to other international agreements and rules of international law regarding the protection of underwater cultural heritage, *States Parties shall require that the Rules be applied to activities directed at underwater cultural heritage in their internal waters, archipelagic waters and territorial sea.*" (emphasis added).
66   On the archaeological and technical standards contained in the 'Rules' annexed to the UCHC see *e.g.* O'Keefe, *op. cit.* (note 61), pp. 152, 155 *et seq.*; T.J. Maarleveld, U. Guérin, B. Egger (eds.), *Manual for Activities Directed at Underwater Cultural Heritage: Guidelines to the Annex of the UNESCO 2001 Convention*, Paris, 2013, available on UNESCO's website at: <http://www.unesco.org/culture/en/underwater/pdf/UCH-Manual.pdf> (19 August 2014).

There is one more issue regarding the wording of Article 8 UCHC that warrants at least a short comment. Since, according to the text of the provision, "States Parties *may* regulate and authorize activities directed at underwater cultural heritage",[67] this might lead to the conclusion that it is entirely left to the discretion of the coastal State if it wishes to take action in respect of an underwater cultural heritage site located on the seabed within 24 miles from the baselines and beyond the territorial sea. However, as pointed out earlier, the LOSC already provides in Article 303(1) that all States "have the *duty* to protect objects of an archaeological and historical nature found at sea"[68] regardless of their location. It is, of course, the purpose of the UCHC as a whole to substantiate this general obligation that follows from Article 303(1) LOSC, but it is also specifically reiterated and expanded through Article 2(3)[69] and (4)[70] UCHC, *i.e.* in the context of the objectives and principles of the Convention. In other words, if Article 8 UCHC is read together with the mentioned provisions, one can only conclude that even if the coastal State did not expressly claim regulatory competences regarding the submerged heritage beyond the maritime spaces under its sovereignty, it would not be allowed to remain entirely passive when confronted with reports of an endangered underwater heritage site.[71]

The view that we have taken on Article 8 UCHC is, to a large extent, confirmed by an example from State practice after the UCHC's adoption.[72] In 2004 Italy adopted a new, comprehensive Cultural Heritage and Landscape Code (*Codice dei beni culturali e del paesaggio*), which in Article 94 provides the following:

---

67 Emphasis added.
68 Emphasis added.
69 Article 2(3), UCHC: "States Parties shall preserve underwater cultural heritage for the benefit of humanity in conformity with the provisions of this Convention."
70 Article 2(4), UCHC: "States Parties shall, individually or jointly as appropriate, take all appropriate measures in conformity with this Convention and with international law that are necessary to protect underwater cultural heritage, using for this purpose the best practicable means at their disposal and in accordance with their capabilities."
71 *Cf.* Rau, *op. cit.* (note 15), pp. 410 *et seq.* Dromgoole, on the other hand, does not seem to recognize the linkage and deplores the permissive nature of Article 8 UCHC; S. Dromgoole, "2001 UNESCO Convention on the Protection of the Underwater Cultural Heritage", 18 *IJMCL*, 2003, p. 79; see also *idem*, *op. cit.* (note 8), p. 287.
72 See also, T.M. Šošić, "Konvencija UNESCO-a o zaštiti podvodne kulturne baštine i jurisdikcija država u Jadranskome moru", ["The UNESCO Convention on the Protection of the Underwater Cultural Heritage and State Jurisdiction in the Adriatic Sea"], 49 *Poredbeno pomorsko pravo* [*Comparative Maritime Law*], 2010, pp. 133 *et seq.*

Archaeological and historical objects found on the seabed of the maritime zone extending twelve nautical miles from the outer limits of the territorial sea shall be protected in the sense of the 'rules concerning activities directed at underwater cultural heritage', as annexed to the UNESCO Convention on the Protection of the Underwater Cultural Heritage, adopted in Paris on 2 November 2001.[73]

The obvious conclusion to be drawn from this provision is that Italy claims to have jurisdiction, at least to a certain degree, regarding the protection of the underwater cultural heritage located on the seabed beyond its territorial sea and within the 24-mile limit. The legal significance and scope of the provision are, however, somewhat obscure.[74] In any case, it is a fact that Italy has not declared a contiguous zone. Hence, Italy evidently holds the view that its jurisdiction regarding the protection of the submerged heritage in the 24-mile zone is not dependent on the prior declaration of a contiguous zone according to Article 33 LOSC. Still, Article 94 of the Italian Cultural Heritage Code does not expressly extend the application of the Code itself to cultural objects found on

---

73   Translation provided by the author. The Italian original of the Code's Article 94 reads: "Gli oggetti archeologici e storici rinvenuti nei fondali della zona di mare estesa dodici miglia marine a partire dal limite esterno del mare territoriale sono tutelati ai sensi delle 'regole relative agli interventi sul patrimonio culturale subacqueo', allegate alla Convenzione UNESCO sulla protezione del patrimonio culturale subacqueo, adottata a Parigi il 2 novembre 2001." The initial text of the 2004 Code was contained in: Decreto Legislativo 22 gennaio 2004, n. 42, "Codice dei beni culturali e del paesaggio, ai sensi dell'articolo 10 Legge 6 luglio 2002, n. 137", *Gazzetta Ufficiale della Repubblica Italiana* (hereinafter: GURI), n. 45/2004 – Supplemento Ordinario n. 28. The Code was subsequently amended on numerous occasions, but Article 94 was only slightly changed to the wording cited above, by the amendment contained in: Decreto Legislativo 26 marzo 2008, n. 63, GURI, n. 84/2008 – Serie Generale. The consolidated Italian text of the 2004 Code, with cross-references to the legislation containing the amendments, is available at: <http://www.normattiva.it/uri-res/N2Ls?urn:nir:stato:decreto.legislativo:2004-01-22;42> (19 August 2014). On the Italian legislation regarding the protection of underwater cultural heritage before the enactment of the 2004 Code, see *e.g.* S. Benini, "Il patrimonio archeologico subacqueo nella legislazione nazionale", in: F. Maniscalco (ed.), *Tutela, conservazione e valorizzazione del patrimonio culturale subacqueo*, Napoli, 2004, pp. 75–89; D. Ferro, "La tutela del patrimonio culturale subacqueo nell'ordinamento italiano", in: Scovazzi, *op. cit.* (note 31), pp. 277–295.

74   *Cf.* T. Scovazzi, "La zone de protection écologique italienne dans le contexte confus de zones côtières méditerranéennes", 10 ADM, 2005, p. 212. Strati deems that based on the Italian legislation a *de facto* 24-mile archaeological zone has been established; Strati, "From the Shortcomings...", *op. cit.* (note 16), pp. 58 *et seq.*

the seabed beyond Italy's territorial sea. What it rather does is to provide for the application of the archaeological and technical standards contained in the Annex to the UCHC. Of course, since in accordance with the so-called 'Rules' various authorizations and approvals must be issued and activities directed at underwater cultural heritage must be strictly regulated and controlled, it would fall upon the competent Italian authorities to fulfil these tasks. It is also noteworthy that Italy was not yet a party to the UCHC when its Cultural Heritage and Landscape Code was adopted in 2004, although, as we have seen, the Code's Article 94 was explicitly based on that Convention.[75] It would actually take another six years for Italy to make the move towards ratification of the UCHC.[76] Finally, it should be noted that, as far as we are aware, there were no protests against the extension of Italy's jurisdiction in respect of historic wrecks and artefacts located beyond its territorial sea.

IV   Concluding Remarks

In analysing the emergence and development of international legal rules concerning the protection of the underwater cultural heritage found on the seabed beyond the territorial sea up to the 24-mile limit, we have shown that coastal States already on the basis of the cryptically formulated provision

---

75   In this context, Scovazzi wonders if a State may apply the annex to a convention without becoming bound by the convention itself, and in principle gives a negative answer; Scovazzi, *op. cit.* (note 74), p. 212, note 13. On the contrary, albeit somewhat peculiar from the point of legislative technique, we do not see why a State could not incorporate in its internal legislation a set of rules contained in the annex to a convention, which in addition represents a distinct and complete unit of itself, even if it had not (yet) become a party to the convention proper. Norway, for example, although having voted against the UCHC, mainly due to the lack of accordance with the LOSC, declared in its statement on vote that it would consider the unilateral application of the 'Rules'; see *Statements on Vote during Commission IV on Culture*, UNESCO, 31st Session of the General Conference, 29 October 2001, in: Garabello, Scovazzi, *op. cit.* (note 11), pp. 248 *et seq.*; also in: Camarda, Scovazzi, *op. cit.* (note 52), pp. 429 *et seq*. The Norwegian cultural heritage legislation seems to be in line with the archaeological and technical standards annexed to the UCHC, and the competent Norwegian authorities in the performance of their duties even expressly refer to the 'Rules'; see F. Kvalø, L. Marstrander, "Norway", in: Dromgoole, *op. cit.* (note 32), pp. 221, 223, 227.

76   Italy deposited its instrument of ratification on 8 January 2010. Thus, based on Article 27, the Convention entered into force with respect to Italy on 8 April 2010. See the chronological list of ratifications available on UNESCO's website at: <http://www.unesco.org/eri/la/convention.asp?KO=13520&language=E> (19 August 2014).

contained in Article 303(2) of the 1982 United Nations Convention on the Law of the Sea had the possibility of exercising, albeit limited, regulatory competences with a view to safeguarding the protection of historic shipwrecks and other artefacts. Moreover, following legal reasoning in accordance with the *argumentum a maiori ad minus* the coastal State's jurisdiction regarding cultural objects within the area in question is not dependent on the prior declaration of a contiguous zone pursuant to Article 33 LOSC, *i.e.* the protection of the cultural heritage on the seabed is not inextricably linked to the exercise of the coastal State's control and policing powers in preventing and punishing the infringement of its customs, fiscal, immigration or sanitary laws and regulations. Thus, if the coastal State chooses to exercise solely the competences regarding cultural heritage protection in the maritime area beyond the territorial sea up to 24 nautical miles from the baselines, there is no legal impediment for designating that maritime zone as 'archaeological', 'maritime cultural' or to give it any other name the State deems appropriate.

As we have seen, the 2001 UNESCO Convention on the Protection of the Underwater Cultural Heritage confirmed this viewpoint, since according to Article 8 UCHC the coastal State is, in unequivocal terms, vested with legislative powers in order to secure the protection of cultural objects on the seabed beneath the contiguous zone. Hence, taking also into account the State practice before and after the adoption of the UCHC, the argument that these competences of the coastal State have become customary law seems compelling.

CHAPTER 17

Fisheries Disputes: Judicial and Arbitral Practice since the Entry into Force of UNCLOS

*Tullio Treves**

I   Introduction

Fisheries are a major factor in the evolution of the international law of the sea. The nutritional needs of the growing population of the world have been at the basis of the transition from the time in which coastal States claimed exclusive powers over the narrow band of the territorial sea while the rest of the sea, the vast expanses of the high seas, remained free for the exploitation of its apparently inexhaustible biological resources, to the present time. Today sovereign rights on fisheries exploitation are recognized to coastal States over a 200-mile wide exclusive economic zone (EEZ). On the high seas, while freedom of fishing is still recognized in principle, broadly shared concerns for over-exploitation have opened the way to cooperative efforts to impose responsible fishing practices. The modern law of the sea concerning fisheries is set out in the provisions of the 1982 United Nations Convention on the Law of the Sea (UNCLOS)[1] concerning the EEZ (Part V) and the high seas (Part VII, Section 2) and in a myriad of global, multilateral, regional and bilateral agreements, among which the most important is the 1995 UN Fish Stocks Agreement.[2] Moreover, the Food and Agriculture Organization of the United Nations (FAO) produces a number of conventions and soft-law instruments, or fosters their adoption by States, and Regional Fisheries Management Organizations produce binding and non-binding measures.

The contemporary international law of fisheries is not an isolated set of rules. It is clearly connected with other fields of international law, especially with international environmental law. This has been judicially noticed. In fact,

---

*   Professor, Milan State University; Judge, International Tribunal for the Law of the Sea (1996–2011).
1   Montego Bay, Jamaica, 10 December 1982, 1833 UN *Treaty Series* 397.
2   Agreement for the Implementation of the Provisions of the United Nations Convention on the Law of the Sea of 10 December 1982 relating to the Conservation and Management of Straddling Fish Stocks and Highly Migratory Fish Stocks, of 4 August 1995, in force 11 December 2001, 2167 UN *Treaty Series* 3.

the International Tribunal for the Law of the Sea (ITLOS) in its 1999 Order on the *Southern Bluefin Tuna* cases stated that

> the conservation of the living resources of the sea is an element in the protection and preservation of the marine environment.[3]

This explains why in a case such as the *Southern Bluefin Tuna* one, concerning mostly fisheries, interesting arguments drawn from international environmental law have been developed by the Tribunal. This is also a consequence of the approach combining the protection of living resources and of the marine environment followed by the 1995 UN Fish Stocks Agreement which, while not applicable to the case, the Tribunal did not ignore.[4]

The above-mentioned connection is based on the circumstance that living resources, such as fish stocks, are part of the natural environment and deserve to be protected. Still, it is undeniable that provisions on these resources, even when aimed at securing their conservation, have as their real purpose ensuring their sustainable exploitation for human and animal nutrition. Provisions like Article 194, para 5, of UNCLOS, stating that the measures taken for the protection of the marine environment from pollution

> shall include those necessary to protect and preserve rare or fragile ecosystems as well as the habitat of depleted, threatened or endangered species and other forms of marine life

are the exception. And it seems significant that Article 294, para 5, is included in Part XII, on the preservation of the marine environment, and not in Part V or VII where fisheries are dealt with.

The contemporary law of the sea is characterized by the significant role played by judicial and arbitral settlement of disputes.[5] In the brief observations that follow I will give an overview of the mechanisms available for the settlement of disputes concerning fisheries and of the relevant judicial and arbitral practice since the entry into force of UNCLOS. In most of the cases that will be examined and which were dealt with by the International Tribunal for the Law of the Sea, I had the honour and the pleasure to cooperate as colleague

---

[3] Australia and New Zealand v. Japan, Order of 27 August 1999, ITLOS Reports 1999, p. 280, at paragraph 70.
[4] Separate opinion of Judge Treves, ITLOS Reports 1999, p. 316 at paragraph 11.
[5] T. Treves, "Law of the Sea", in *Max Planck Encyclopedia of Public International Law*, Vol. VI, Oxford University Press, Oxford, 2012, pp. 708–732, at 716–717.

in the Tribunal with Budislav Vukas. I could appreciate the highly independent and original, and always scholarly, approach to which he has always been faithful, as I could see even when he represented his country in United Nations activities.

II   The Dispute-Settlement Mechanisms Applicable to Fisheries Disputes under UNCLOS

The most significant aspect of the UNCLOS dispute-settlement system is that the principle adopted is that of compulsory settlement. This means that, by becoming a party to the Convention, a State acquires the right to set in motion judicial or arbitral proceedings against another State party as regards disputes concerning the interpretation or application of the Convention, and at the same time becomes bound to submit to such proceedings when they are set in motion by another State party.

As is well known, Articles 297 and 298 provide limitations on and optional exceptions to this principle. Limitations apply automatically to all parties to UNCLOS and exclude certain categories of disputes from compulsory settlement. Optional exceptions permit a State, by depositing a declaration, to exclude from compulsory settlement all or some of listed specific categories of disputes.

The limitations set out in Article 297 are particularly relevant as regards fisheries disputes. Paragraph 3 of that Article excludes from compulsory jurisdiction all disputes relating to the sovereign rights of the coastal State

> with respect to the living resources in the exclusive economic zone or their exercise, including its discretionary powers for determining the allowable catch, its harvesting capacity, the allocation of surpluses to other States and the terms and conditions established in its conservation and management laws and regulations.

A modest attenuation to such exclusion is that in the event that gross violations of the coastal State's obligations – indicated by expressions such as "the coastal State...has manifestly failed" or "has arbitrarily refused" – are claimed, the dispute may unilaterally be submitted to conciliation (Art. 297, paragraph 3(b)).

The optional exception to compulsory jurisdiction set out in Article 298, paragraph 1(c), for "disputes concerning law enforcement activities in regard to the exercise of sovereign rights or jurisdiction excluded from jurisdiction of a court or tribunal under article 297 paragraph 2 or 3" may, unless a declaration to the contrary is made, be read *a contrario sensu*, as meaning that disputes concerning fishery police activities are submitted to compulsory settlement.

In the light of the above it appears that in the EEZ compulsory jurisdiction is almost completely excluded as regards fisheries. As regards disputes concerning fisheries on the high seas the situation is different. Such disputes are submitted to compulsory jurisdiction without exception or limitation. Compulsory jurisdiction with respect to fishing on the high seas is broadened by the extension of the dispute-settlement system of Part XV UNCLOS to disputes concerning the interpretation or application of the UN Fish Stocks Agreement and of other fishing multilateral agreements, as provided in those agreements, as well as to disputes concerning other agreements through Art. 30, paragraph 2 of the Fish Stocks Agreement.[6]

To complete the picture, another provision of the UNCLOS dispute-settlement system is to be recalled for its relevance for fishing activities. This is Article 292, providing for a special procedure before the ITLOS for the prompt release of detained vessels and crews. This provision applies, in particular, when a violation is alleged of Article 73, paragraph 2, which states the obligation of the coastal State promptly to release detained fishing vessels upon the posting of a reasonable bond or other security. The possibility of expeditiously obtaining the release of vessels and crews may be seen as partial compensation given to the fishing interests for the almost complete lack of the ability to submit to an international court or tribunal disputes on the merits of the detention of fishing vessels for alleged violations committed in the EEZ.

III The Practice of ITLOS and Arbitral Tribunals: The Exclusive Economic Zone

In judicial practice based on UNCLOS fishing in the EEZ has been envisaged only through the lens of prompt release proceedings. These proceedings have allowed judicial attention to be called to various practices of fishermen fishing in foreign EEZs.

---

6 T. Treves, "Dispute-Settlement in the Law of the Sea: Disorder or System?", in M. Kohen (ed.), *Promoting Justice, Human Rights and Conflict Resolution through International Law/ La promotion de la justice, des droits de l'homme et du règlement des conflits par le droit international, Liber Amicorum Lucius Caflisch*, Brill, Leiden, 2007, pp. 927–949, at 936–948.

Among these, one may quote fishing without the coastal State's authorization (the *Camouco*,[7] the *Monte Confurco*,[8] *Grand Prince*,[9] and other cases); fishing of species not covered by such authorizations (the *Hoshinmaru*);[10] lack (or incorrectness) of prescribed reporting (the *Hoshinmaru*);[11] fishing with vessels which often change flags (the *Grand Prince*).[12] Moreover, judicial attention has been drawn to particular rules adopted by coastal States in order to fight against illicit foreign fishing: in particular, legislation prescribing notification to the coastal State of entry to the EEZ by fishing vessels sometimes introducing a presumption that fish found on board and whose presence was not notified when entering the EEZ is illegally captured if such vessels allege that they are just crossing through the EEZ, exercising the freedom of navigation (the *Camouco*,[13] the *Monte Confurco*[14] cases). Rules prescribing the use of a Vessel Monitoring System (VMS) and the payment of 'good behaviour bonds' have also been considered (the *Volga* case).[15]

These practices may in most cases be considered as covered by the notion of Illegal, Unreported and Unauthorized Fishing (IUU Fishing).[16] They have, however, never come as such to adjudication.[17] They have been seen as the background to proceedings for prompt release against coastal States which had detained foreign fishing vessels accused of these illegal fishing practices. As is well known, prompt release proceedings must concern only the question of release from detention and that of the reasonable bond to obtain such release, and not whether the detention was legal or illegal. For instance, as regards the

---

7 Panama v. France, Judgment of 7 February 2000, ITLOS Reports 2000, 10 at para 29.
8 Seychelles v. France, Judgment of 27 November 2000, ITLOS Reports 2000, 86 at para 30.
9 Belize v. France, Judgment of 20 April 2001, ITLOS Reports 2001, 17 at para 36.
10 Japan v. Russian Federation, Judgment of 6 August 2007, ITLOS Reports 2005–2007, p. 18, at para 30.
11 ITLOS Reports 2005–2007, p. 18 at para 31.
12 ITLOS Reports 2001, p. 17 at para 32.
13 ITLOS Reports 2000, p. 10 at paras 29 and 32.
14 ITLOS Reports 2000, p. 86 at paras 30 and 37.
15 ITLOS Reports 2002, p. 10, at paras 75–80.
16 T. Treves, "La pesca ilegal, no declarada y no reglamentada: Estado del pabellón, Estado costero y Estado del Puerto", in J. Pueyo Losa, J.G. Urbina (coords.), *La cooperación internacional en la ordenación de los mares y océanos*, Iustel, Madrid, 2009, pp. 135–158.
17 See the observations of M. Arenas Meza, "El Tribunal Internacional del derecho del mar ante la pesca ilegal, no declarada y reglamentada", in J.J. Urbina, M.T. Ponte Iglesias, *Protección de intereses colectivos en el derecho del mar y cooperación internacional*, Iustel, Madrid, 2012, pp. 213–256, in particular pp. 142–155.

obligation of using a VMS and of posting a 'good behaviour bond' prescribed by the Australian legislation the Tribunal stated:

> [I]t is not appropriate in the present proceedings to consider whether a coastal state is entitled to impose such conditions in the exercise of its sovereign rights under the Convention. In these proceedings, the question to be decided is whether the "bond or other security" mentioned in article 73, paragraph 2, of the Convention may include such conditions.[18]

The specific function of prompt release proceedings was very much in the mind of the ITLOS when it was confronted with the arguments of parties which had detained fishing vessels allegedly having in the exclusive economic zone committed violations of fisheries laws and regulations, to the effect that through the prompt release proceedings the Tribunal was in fact protecting IUU fishing and not joining the fight against it.

In the view of France, the detaining State in the *Monte Confurco* case, and of Australia, the detaining State in the *Volga* case, the need to fight against IUU fishing justified the high penalties imposed and required that the Tribunal engage in the fight against the practices in which the vessels were involved. ITLOS was not insensitive to these arguments. In the *Monte Confurco* case it "took note" of them.[19] In the *Volga* judgment it added:

> The Tribunal understands the international concerns about illegal, unregulated and unreported fishing and appreciates the objectives behind the measures taken by States, including the States Parties to CCAMLR [Commission for the Conservation of Antarctic Marine Living Resources], to deal with the problem.[20]

In the same judgment it explained why it coud not go beyond taking note and understanding:

> The Tribunal must...emphasize that, in the present proceedings, it is called upon to assess whether the bond set by the Respondent is reasonable in terms of article 292 of the Convention. The purpose of the procedure provided for in article 292 of the Convention is to secure the prompt release of the vessel and crew upon the posting of a reasonable bond,

---

18   ITLOS Reports 2002, p. 10, at para 76.
19   ITLOS Reports 2000, p. 86, at para 79.
20   ITLOS Reports 2002, p. 10, at para 68.

pending the completion of the judicial procedure before the courts of the detaining State.[21]

The constraints of the prompt release proceedings underlie this explanation.

It is further interesting to note that – in light of the limitation in Article 297, paragraph 3 – coastal State laws, regulations and practices regarding foreign research and fishing activities in the EEZ (and the same applies under paragraph 2 for scientific research activities) have never been challenged before judicial and arbitral bodies. Neither, and consequently, has the possibility of resorting to 'compulsory conciliation' if these laws, regulations and practices are particularly abusive.

There have been no cases in which police activities in the EEZ concerning fishing (or research) have been the subject matter of disputes, even though such activities are at the origin of most stopping and detention of foreign fishing vessels considered in prompt release cases.

Non-compliance by coastal States detaining a fishing vessel with UNCLOS Article 73, paras 3 and 4, which prescribe that penalties for fishery violations may not consist of imprisonment and that the detaining State must promptly notify the flag State of the arrest or detention of a vessel, has been argued in prompt release cases. ITLOS has rejected such claims as not included within the scope of its prompt release jurisdiction.[22]

The lack of prompt notification is not, however, considered irrelevant in prompt release cases. As remarked in the *Camouco* case judgment[23] and confirmed in the *Juno Trader* case judgment,[24]

> there is a connection between paragraphs 2 and 4 of article 73, since absence of prompt notification may have a bearing on the ability of the flag State to invoke article 73, paragraph 2, and article 292 in a timely and efficient manner.

So, non-compliance with the obligation of prompt notification of detention is seen as part of the factual background of prompt release cases.

---

21   ITLOS Reports 2002, p. 10 at para 69.
22   *Camouco* judgment of 7 February 2000, ITLOS Reports 2000, p. 10, para 59 at p. 29; *Monte Confurco* judgment of 18 December 2000, ITLOS Reports 2000, p. 86, para 64 at p. 106.
23   ITLOS Reports 2000, p. 10, para 59 at pp. 29–30.
24   Saint Vincent and the Grenadines v. Guinea-Bissau, Judgment of 18 December 2004, ITLOS Reports 2004, p. 17, at paras 76–77.

IV The Practice of ITLOS and Arbitral Tribunals: The High Seas

As regards fishing on the high seas two cases have been brought to adjudication, showing that the UNCLOS provisions relating to high seas fishing may be invoked under the jurisdictional provisions of the Convention. In neither case, however, was there a decision on the merits. In the *Southern Bluefin Tuna* case the Arbitral Tribunal competent under Annex VII of UNCLOS ruled that it lacked jurisdiction because the condition specified in Article 281, paragraph 1, was not fulfilled.[25] In the *Swordfish* case between Chile and the European Union, the case was discontinued because the parties had reached an agreement.[26]

In the *Southern Bluefin Tuna* case, New Zealand and Australia claimed that Japan, in undertaking unilateral experimental bluefin tuna fishing on the high seas, had breached Article 64 (obligation to cooperate as regards highly migratory species) and Articles 116 to 119 (obligations regarding fishing on the high seas).[27] Alleged non-compliance with Articles 64 and 116 to 119 was also the key issue submitted to a Chamber of the Law of the Sea Tribunal by Chile and the European Union in the *Swordfish* case, where the EU also claimed non-compliance with Article 87 (freedom of fishing on the high seas) and 89 (invalidity of claims of sovereignty over the high seas).[28]

So far, no dispute has been brought to adjudication under the compulsory jurisdiction provisions of the UN Fish Stocks Agreement of 1995. The possibility of such disputes, however, seems clear. The well-known *Estai* dispute between Spain and Canada and submitted (to no avail) to the ICJ[29] could – if it arose today – be envisaged within the framework of the 1995 Agreement. So could the *Southern Bluefin Tuna* case. The Arbitral Tribunal in the award of 2000 in the latter case, deciding, as noted above, that it lacked jurisdiction to settle this dispute, stated that under the 1995 Agreement (then not yet in force for the parties) the procedural and substantive issues of the case could be solved on the basis of rules more specific than those of UNCLOS.[30]

---

25 Australia and New Zealand v. Japan, Arbitral Award of 4 August 2000, 39 *International Legal Materials*, 2000, p. 1359.
26 Order of discontinuance of 16 December 2009, ITLOS Reports 2008–2010, p. 13.
27 Arbitral award of 4 August 2000 quoted at note 25, para 32.
28 ITLOS Order of 20 December 2000, ITLOS Reports 2000, p. 148, para 2.
29 *Fisheries Jurisdiction Case, Spain v. Canada*, Judgment of 4 December 1998, ICJ Reports 1998, p. 432.
30 39 *International Legal Materials*, 2000, p. 1359, paragraph 71 at p. 1392; see also my Separate Opinion to the provisional measures Order, in ITLOS Reports 1999, p. 316, at paras 10–11, p. 318–319.

V Conclusion

Judicial and arbitral practice concerning fisheries is rather limited. Because of the limitation on compulsory settlement set out in Article 297, paragraph 3, we do not have, and we will probably not have in the foreseeable future, a case on the merits of a fisheries dispute concerning the EEZ, even though we may have one (unless the relevant optional exception has been exercised by one of the parties involved) concerning the exercise of enforcement activities relating to fisheries in the exclusive economic zone. We have seen, on the other hand, cases on the merits of fishing activities on the high seas, even though they have not reached the merits phase. These cases show that the submission of such disputes to adjudication under UNCLOS provisions is possible. The relevant provisions in the UN Fish Stocks Agreement and in other agreements make the possibility stronger.[31]

It also seems to be important to underline that the relatively abundant jurisprudence of ITLOS concerning prompt release of vessels and crews, being focused on the detention of fishing vessels, has had the effect of extending judicial knowledge, and permitting discussion before an international tribunal, of practices that are dangerous for the conservation of living resources.

---

31 For speculation about the possibility of bringing to adjudication cases concerning non-compliance with its obligations by the flag State of a fishing vessel, or cases started by the flag State in the exercise of its responsibilities see T. Treves, "Action for International Adjudication by the Flag State of Fishing Vessels", in 116(3–4) *Hogaku Shimpo/ The Chuho Law Review (Essays for Yanai Shunji)*, 2009, pp. 55–80.

CHAPTER 18

Forgotten Rights? Landlocked States and the Law of the Sea

*Helmut Tuerk**

I   Introduction[1]

On 10 December 2012 the thirtieth anniversary of the opening for signature of the 1982 United Nations Convention on the Law of the Sea (UNCLOS)[2] was commemorated at United Nations Headquarters in New York. This occasion was a most propitious moment to look back at past achievements as well as to reflect on the future evolution of the law of the sea. In this context the rights of landlocked States recognized by the Convention, their historical development and their realization over the last three decades also merit particular consideration. In particular, the question needs to be asked whether these rights, or at least some of them, have perhaps fallen into oblivion.

UNCLOS, which entered into force on 16 November 1994, has rightly been called a 'Constitution for the Oceans',[3] as it provides a comprehensive legal framework to regulate all ocean space, its uses and resources. As of 1 February 2013, 165 States, including 28 landlocked countries and the European Union, were parties; another eight landlocked States have signed the Convention but

---

* Judge of the International Tribunal for the Law of the Sea in Hamburg, serving as Vice-President from 2008 to 2011; Member of the Austrian delegation to the Third United Nations Conference on the Law of the Sea, representing his country also at subsequent meetings and negotiations in the field.
1 This article is essentially based on H. Tuerk, *Reflections on the Contemporary Law of the Sea*, Publications on Ocean Development, Chapter IV, Vol. 71, V. Lowe, R. Churchill (gen. eds.), Martinus Nijhoff Publishers, Leiden/Boston (2012) and H. Tuerk, "The Landlocked States and the Law of the Sea", 40(1) *Revue Belge de Droit International*, pp. 91–112 (2007). Opinions expressed are strictly personal.
2 United Nations Convention on the Law of the Sea, 10 December 1982, 1833 UNTS 3 (hereinafter referred to as UNCLOS), available at: <http://www.un.org/Depts/los/convention_agreements/texts/unclos/unclos_e.pdf> (1 February 2013).
3 T.T.B. Koh, "A Constitution for the Oceans, Remarks made by the President of the Third United Nations Conference on the Law of the Sea", in: *Official Text of the United Nations Convention on the Law of the Sea with Annexes and Index*, at xxxiii (1983).

so far have not adhered to it.[4] At present, the total number of landlocked States with United Nations membership stands at 44[5] – 17 in Africa, 13 in Europe, 12 in Asia and two in South America.[6] It is to be noted that none of the Central Asian landlocked States has become a party to UNCLOS.

Although the Convention tries to strike a careful balance between the rights of coastal States and the freedoms enjoyed by all States, whether coastal or landlocked, it is quite obvious that the pendulum has clearly swung from the principle of *mare liberum* to that of *mare clausum* by the recognition of substantial sovereign rights and jurisdiction of coastal States over the most valuable areas of the seas.[7] UNCLOS in fact constitutes the greatest expansion of sovereign rights and jurisdiction in history,[8] substantially limiting the rights of landlocked States to maritime resources.

It should be recalled that the oceans and their marginal seas cover almost 71 per cent of the Earth's surface and have since earliest times played a significant role in the development of humanity, not only as a means of communication, but also as a source of living and non-living resources as well as an important object of scientific research.[9] The fact is, however, often overlooked that not just coastal but also landlocked States have maritime interests. Thus, it is by no means general knowledge that besides having pleasure craft flying their flags on the seas, quite a number of landlocked countries[10] – Azerbaijan, Bolivia, Czech Republic, Ethiopia, Kazakhstan, Laos, Luxembourg, Moldova, Mongolia, Paraguay, Slovakia, Switzerland and Turkmenistan – also have ocean-going merchant vessels under their own flags, and Bolivia furthermore has a small

---

4   See status of the Convention, available at: <http://www.un.org/Depts/los/reference_files/chronological_lists_of_ratifications.htm> (1 February 2013).
5   See landlocked States with UN membership: <http://www.un.org/en/members/> (1 February 2013).
6   See status of the Convention (note 4).
7   See S. Kaye, "Freedom of Navigation in a Post 9/11 World: Security and Creeping Jurisdiction", in: *The Law of the Sea – Progress and Prospects*, D. Freestone, R. Barnes & D.M. Ong (eds.), Oxford University Press, Oxford/New York, pp. 347–348 (2006).
8   See also J.N. Moore, "Conservatives and the Law of the Sea Time Warp", *The Wall Street Journal* (8 July 2012).
9   See R.N. Hass, "Foreword" to: S.G. Borgerson, *The National Interest and the Law of the Sea*, Council on Foreign Relations, Council Special Report No. 46, at vii (May 2009), available at: <http://www.cfr.org/content/publications/attachments/LawoftheSea_CSR46.pdf> (1 February 2013).
10 World Fleet Statistics 2011 (compiled by Lloyd's Register – IHS Fairplay), Table 1A – Merchant Fleets of the World – by Country of Registration, available at: <http://www.emsa.europa.eu> (1 February 2013).

high seas fishing fleet. Switzerland is even one of the three countries with the highest containership operating capacity.[11] Landlocked States also participate in the work of the International Maritime Organization (IMO), which at present has 18 landlocked Members,[12] and have become parties to international conventions elaborated in that framework.

Besides having ships sailing under their flags, landlocked States have developed other maritime interests as well. Several of them have for a long time been members of the Intergovernmental Oceanographic Commission (IOC).[13] Landlocked States have also been conducting marine scientific research, and petroleum companies therefrom have been engaged in offshore drilling and oil exploration activities for quite some years.[14] A number of these States have further become parties to international conventions relating to the prevention of marine pollution, be it by dumping of waste or from land-based sources.[15] Several of them have also adopted domestic legislation expressly criminalizing maritime piracy[16] – which many coastal States have not yet done.

---

11 See *Review of Maritime Transport 2011*, Report by the UNCTAD Secretariat, United Nations, New York and Geneva, p. 149 (2011). The three countries with the highest containership operating capacity are Denmark, Switzerland and France, which jointly have a market share of almost 30 per cent. This ranking of Switzerland does not mean that the containerships fly the Swiss flag.

12 See IMO Members States, available at: <http://www.imo.org/About/Membership/Pages/MemberStates.aspx> (1 February 2013).

13 These States are: Afghanistan, Austria, Azerbaijan, Ethiopia, Kazakhstan, Serbia and Switzerland. See International Oceanographic Commission (of UNESCO), Member States of the Commission as of 10 May 2012, available at: <http://www.ioc-unesco.org/index.php?option=com_oe&task=viewDocumentRecord&docID=4017> (1 February 2013).

14 G. Hafner, "Austria and the Law of the Sea", in: *The Law of the Sea: The European Union and Its Member States*, T. Treves & L. Pineschi (eds.), Martinus Nijhoff Publishers, The Hague, pp. 30–35 (1997).

15 See the 1973 International Convention for the Prevention of Pollution from Ships as Modified by the Protocol of 1978 Relating Thereto (MARPOL), 1340 UNTS 61, available at: <http://www.imo.org/about/conventions/listofconventions/pages/international-convention-for-the-prevention-of-pollution-from-ships-(marpol).aspx>, the 1972 London Convention on the Prevention of Marine Pollution by Dumping of Wasted and Other Matter and its 1996 Protocol, 1046 UNTS 138, available at: <http://treaties.un.org/Pages/showDetails.aspx?objid=0800000280ofdd18> and the 1992 Convention for the Protection of the Marine Environment of the North-East Atlantic (OSPAR Convention), 2354 UNTS 67, available at: <http://treaties.un.org/Pages/showDetails.aspx?objid=0800000280069bb5> (1 February 2013).

16 For instance Austria, Azerbaijan, Kazakhstan, Liechtenstein, Moldova, Czech Republic and Serbia (on file with author).

The geographical location of a State cannot therefore be considered a genuine impediment to maritime uses and concerns.[17] Landlocked States nevertheless differ from coastal States in one decisive respect: as they do not border the sea, they need transit across the territory of other countries. The lack of a coast of their own deprives them furthermore of exclusive rights with respect to maritime areas, rights which coastal States derive from the sovereignty they enjoy over the coast.[18] The geographical location of landlocked States with distances from the nearest seaport sometimes in excess of 2,000 kilometres places them at a severe disadvantage relative to their coastal counterparts.[19]

All the landlocked countries in Africa, Asia and South America as well as two of those in Central and Eastern Europe are developing countries, facing severe challenges to growth and development.[20] Lack of territorial access to the sea, poor physical infrastructure, remoteness and isolation from world markets and high transit costs continue to impose serious constraints on their overall socio-economic development.[21] It has been pointed out that landlocked developing countries find themselves on an inherently disadvantaged development path compared with countries with coastlines and deep-sea ports.[22] It is therefore not at all surprising that of altogether 32 landlocked developing countries 17 are classified as least developed, 12 of them situated in Africa.[23]

---

17   Tuerk, *Reflections on the Contemporary Law of the Sea* (note 1), p. 49; and Tuerk, "Landlocked States" (note 1), p. 92.
18   Ibid.
19   See M. Sinjela, "Freedom of Transit and the Right of Access for Landlocked States: The Evolution of Principle and Law", 12 *Georgia Journal of International Comparative Law*, p. 31 (1982).
20   See UNCTAD, UN Recognition of the Problems of Landlocked Developing Countries, available at: <http://www.unctad.org/Templates/Page.asp?intItemID=3619&lang=1> (1 February 2013).
21   Landlocked Developing Countries – About LLDCs, Website of the Office of the High Representative for the Least Developed Countries, Landlocked Developing Countries and Small Island Developing States (UN/OHRLLS), available at: <http://www.unohrlls.org/en/ldc/31> (1 February 2013).
22   UN-OHRLLS, Preparatory Process for the Comprehensive 10 Year Review Conference on the Almaty Programme of Action. Issues Note on the Participation of Landlocked Developing Countries in International Trade, August 2012, para. 2, available at: <http://www.unohrlls.org/UserFiles/File/LLDC%20Documents/ALMATY%20+10/Almaty%20Sept%202012/Concept%20note%20Thematic%20Meeting%20on%20Trade%20Sept2012.pdf> (1 February 2013).
23   These States are Burkina Faso, Burundi, Chad, Ethiopia, Lesotho, Afghanistan, Bhutan, Malawi, Mali, Niger, Rwanda, South Sudan, Uganda, Zambia and Nepal. The current list of LDCs includes 48 countries; 34 in Africa, 14 in Asia and 1 in Latin America and the

II The Historical Development of the Maritime Rights of Landlocked States

As early as in the 11th century, coastal territories in Europe began granting treaty rights to landlocked entities to allow them access to the sea, and certain rivers were internationalized.[24] It was, however, only in the course of the 19th century that Switzerland raised the question of the right of landlocked States to fly their own maritime flags. Such a right was considered particularly important for a neutral country in time of war. The Swiss initiative, however, met with opposition from major powers and ships belonging to Swiss nationals had to continue sailing under foreign flags.[25]

At the end of World War I new States lacking a sea coast – Austria, Hungary, Czechoslovakia – emerged with the consequence that the Peace Treaties formally recognized the right of landlocked States to fly a national flag on their seagoing vessels.[26] This was confirmed by the Declaration of Barcelona of 1921, which granted recognition to "the flag flown by the vessels of any State having no sea coast which are registered at some one specified place situated in its territory".[27] By choosing the form of a declaration rather than that of a convention, the Barcelona Conference emphasized that it was restating an existing principle of international law.[28]

An internationally recognized, though restricted right of transit was provided by the 1921 Barcelona Convention and Statute on Freedom of Transit.[29]

Caribbean; available at: <http://www.unohrlls.org/en/ldc/25> (1 February 2013). See further *Virginia Commentary*, Vol. III, S.N. Nandan & S. Rosenne (vol. eds.), N.R. Grandy (assistant ed.), p. 375 (1995).

24   L.M. Alexander, "The 'Disadvantaged' States and the Law of the Sea", 5 *Marine Policy*, p. 185 (1981); M. Glassner, "The Status of Developing Landlocked States since 1965", 5(3) *Lawyer of the Americas*, p. 480 (1973).

25   See J. Monnier, "Right of Access to the Sea and Freedom of Transit" in: *A Handbook on the New Law of the Sea*, R.-J. Dupuy & D. Vignes (eds.), Martinus Nijhoff Publishers, Dordrecht/Boston/Lancaster, pp. 502–506 (1991).

26   *Ibid.*

27   See Convention and Statute on Freedom of Transit, available at: <http://www.jurisint.org/doc/html/ins/en/2000/2000jiinsen159.html>, and Declaration recognizing the Right to a Flag of States having no Sea Coast, Barcelona, 20 April 1921, available at: <http://www.crwflags.com/fotw/flags/xf-frc21.html> (1 February 2013). See also Glassner, "The Status of Developing Landlocked States since 1965" (note 23), p. 481.

28   Monnier, "Right of Access to the Sea and Freedom of Transit" (note 25), p. 504.

29   H. Tuerk & G. Hafner, "The Landlocked Countries and the United Nations Convention on the Law of the Sea", in: *Essays on the New Law of the Sea*, B. Vukas (ed.), Sveučilišna naklada Liber, Zagreb, p. 59 (1985).

The Statute applied only to railway and waterway transport, thus excluding road transport, and did not specifically cater for the particular needs of landlocked countries. It provided that traffic in transit is not to be subject to any special dues in respect of transit, but only for defraying the costs of supervision and administration entailed by such transit.[30] The Barcelona Convention focused primarily on Europe, and in failing to address road transport excluded extensive portions of Africa and Asia, where landlocked States are largely dependent on overland routes to and from the sea.[31] It thus received only a limited number of ratifications.

The principle of freedom of transit – applicable to all States without express reference to landlocked countries – was only enshrined in Article V of the 1947 General Agreement on Tariffs and Trade (GATT).[32] That Article, in its updated version of 1994, sets out two main obligations for Members of the World Trade Organization (WTO): not to hinder traffic in transit by imposing unnecessary delays or restrictions or by imposing unreasonable charges, and to accord most-favoured nation treatment to transiting goods of all Members.[33]

The right of ships of landlocked States to have access to sea ports was laid down in the 1923 Convention and Statute of the International Regime of Maritime Ports. This Statute does not contain the principle of freedom of access to ports, but – subject to reciprocity – only one of equality of treatment with regard to such access, the use of the port and the full enjoyment of benefits as regards navigation and commercial operations afforded to vessels, their cargoes and passengers.[34] This equality is to be achieved by the granting of national and most-favoured nation treatment. It is worth noting that the condition of reciprocity does not apply to Contracting States which have no maritime ports.[35]

A further important step regarding the relationship between landlocked States and the sea was taken in 1958 by the First United Nations Conference on the Law of the Sea.[36] That Conference, in Article 4 of the Convention on the

---

30 See Art. 3 of the Barcelona Statute.
31 Tuerk, "Landlocked States" (note 1), p. 95.
32 Hafner, "Austria and the Law of the Sea" (note 14), p. 29. See also *Virginia Commentary*, Vol. III (note 23), p. 374.
33 See Preparatory Process for the Comprehensive 10 Year Review Conference on the Almaty Programme of Action (note 22). See further the Interpretation of Article V of GATT 1994 by the WTO Panel, available at: <http://www.iru.org/index/cms-filesystem-action?file =Webnews2009/Gatt-WTO-PANEL.pdf> (1 February 2013).
34 See Art. 2 of the Barcelona Statute (note 27).
35 Monnier, "Right of Access to the Sea and Freedom of Transit" (note 25), pp. 505–506.
36 See also Tuerk, *Reflections on the Contemporary Law of the Sea* (note 1). See also *Virginia Commentary*, Vol. III (note 23), p. 376.

High Seas,[37] confirmed the right of landlocked States to sail ships under their flags on the high seas. Furthermore, Article 3 of the Convention states that, "in order to enjoy the freedom of the seas on equal terms with coastal States, States having no sea-coast *should* have free access to the sea". Free transit was, however, made subject to common agreement between the States concerned on a basis of reciprocity,[38] a requirement that had met with strong objections from landlocked States. The question of equal treatment in sea ports was settled jointly with that of freedom of transit in Article 3: as such operations take place entirely in territory under the sovereignty of the transit States these were prepared to tolerate them merely within the framework of special agreements.[39]

It was only during the ensuing decades that it was generally realized that one of the most important decisions taken by the 1958 Geneva Conference on the Law of the Sea related to the Convention on the Continental Shelf,[40] which recognized sovereign rights of the coastal States over the continental shelf for the purpose of exploring it and exploiting its natural resources. As later developments would show, an irrevocable step had thus been taken to distribute most of the mineral riches of the oceans among a limited number of States – to the detriment of landlocked States as well as States with a short coastline.[41] It is, however, also a fact that the landlocked countries themselves were not yet quite aware of the future importance of the continental shelf as a repository of resources. Thus, at the Conference they primarily focused on questions of transit and the breadth of the territorial sea, failing to assert rights with respect to the continental shelf.[42]

The accelerated process of decolonization in the early 1960s brought a considerable increase in the number of landlocked States, most of them situated in Africa, which led to the elaboration within the framework of UNCTAD of the 1965 New York Convention on Transit Trade of Landlocked States.[43]

---

37 Geneva Convention on the High Seas, 29 April 1958, 450 UNTS 11, available at: <http://untreaty.un.org/ilc/texts/instruments/English/conventions/8_1_1958_high_seas.pdf> (1 February 2013).
38 Tuerk & Hafner, "The Landlocked Countries and UNCLOS" (note 29), p. 60.
39 Monnier, "Right of Access to the Sea and Freedom of Transit" (note 25), p. 506.
40 Geneva Convention on the Continental Shelf, 29 April 1958, 499 UNTS 311, available at: <http://untreaty.un.org/ilc/texts/instruments/English/conventions/8_1_1958_continental_shelf.pdf> (1 February 2013).
41 Tuerk, *Landlocked States*, (note 1) p. 97.
42 See also Tuerk & Hafner, "The Landlocked Countries and UNCLOS" (note 29), p. 60.
43 Convention on Transit Trade of Land-locked States, 8 July 1965, 597 UNTS 3, available at: <http://treaties.un.org/doc/publication/unts/volume%20597/volume-597-i-8641-english.pdf> (1 February 2013).

The principles laid down in this first multilateral treaty devoted exclusively to the special transit problems of landlocked countries include free access to the sea, identical treatment for vessels flying the flags of landlocked States to those of coastal States in territorial and internal waters and with respect to access and use of seaports, as well as free and unrestricted transit. The transit rights and facilities are excluded from the operation of the most-favoured nation clause; they are, however, based on reciprocity and require additional agreements with transit States.[44] The Convention entered into force in 1967 and has thus far been adhered to by only 41 States, among them a mere 23 coastal States, some of which do not even border a landlocked country.[45] Although the practical effects of that instrument have been quite limited, it nevertheless provided a good basis for further negotiations on the subject.[46]

III   The Emergence of a New Law of the Sea

During the second half of the twentieth century a major transformation of the law of the sea took place – in fact the most significant change to that law since the times of Hugo Grotius.[47] This change amounted to a transition from what has been called a 'law of movement' to a 'law of territory and appropriation',[48] also directly affecting landlocked States. In the course of this development the four 1958 Geneva Conventions[49] not only failed to gain the necessary widespread acceptance but were to an important extent also overtaken by

---

44   See also Glassner, "The Status of Developing Landlocked Countries since 1965" (note 24), pp. 484–485. See also *Virginia Commentary*, Vol. III (note 23), p. 377.
45   See status of the Convention, available at: <https://treaties.un.org/doc/publication/mtdsg/volume%20i/chapter%20x/x-3.en.pdf> (1 February 2013).
46   Tuerk & Hafner, "The Landlocked Countries and UNCLOS" (note 29), p. 61.
47   See S. Bateman, D.R. Rothwell & D. VanderZwaag, "Navigational Rights and Freedom in the New Millennium: Dealing with 20th Century Controversies and 21st Century Challenges", in: *Navigational Rights and Freedoms and the New Law of the Sea*, D.R. Rothwell & S. Bateman (eds.), Martinus Nijhoff Publishers, The Hague, p. 314 (2000).
48   R-J. Dupuy, "La mer sous compétence nationale", in: *Traité du nouveau droit de la mer*, R-J. Dupuy & D. Vignes (eds.), Economica, Paris/ Bruylant, Bruxelles, pp. 219–220 (1985).
49   See also Geneva Convention on the Territorial Sea and the Contiguous Zone, 29 April 1958, 516 UNTS 205, available at: <http://treaties.un.org/doc/Publication/MTDSG/Volume%20II/Chapter%20XXI/XXI-1.en.pdf>; Geneva Convention on Fishing and Conservation of the Living Resources of the High Seas, 29 April 1985, available at: <http://treaties.un.org/doc/Publication/MTDSG/Volume%20II/Chapter%20XXI/XXI-3.en.pdf> (1 February 2013).

State practice.[50] The progressive extension by coastal States of sovereign rights and jurisdiction over vast maritime areas placed the landlocked States in an increasingly disadvantageous position,[51] as they were facing the loss of rights they had hitherto at least theoretically enjoyed.

A thorough revision of the existing – and increasingly discarded – law of the sea had thus become inevitable if this body of law was once again to be based on a consensus of the international community. The initiative of Malta in 1967 to declare the seabed beyond the limits of national jurisdiction the 'common heritage of mankind'[52] provided a window of opportunity for the elaboration of a new convention on the law of the sea. The landlocked States became ardent supporters of that initiative and would also have preferred to include the living resources of the sea in the common heritage concept, as advocated by Malta, but it soon became clear that such a proposal would have no chance of being accepted by the international community at large.[53]

In the course of the negotiations leading to the Third United Nations Conference on the Law of the Sea in 1973 the landlocked States forged an alliance with the so-called 'geographically disadvantaged States', i.e. those coastal countries which would derive little or no benefit from a massive extension of coastal State sovereign rights and jurisdiction.[54] That interest group of 'Landlocked and Geographically Disadvantaged States' in the end comprised 55 States,[55] including 29 landlocked countries. Chaired by Austria and co-chaired by Singapore, that Group was marked by a true spirit of solidarity

---

50   Tuerk, *Reflections on the Contemporary Law of the Sea* (note 1), p. 11.
51   See M. Glassner, "Developing Land-locked States and the Resources of the Seabed", 11(3) *San Diego Law Review*, p. 636 (1973–1974).
52   Tuerk, "Landlocked States" (note 17), p. 99.
53   See also A. Pardo & C.Q. Christol, "The Common Interest: Tension between the Whole and the Parts", in: *The Structure and Process of International Law: Essays in Legal Philosophy, Doctrine and Theory*, R.St.J. Macdonald & D.M. Johnston (eds.), Martinus Nijhoff Publishers, The Hague/Boston/Lancaster, p. 654 (1983).
54   L.C. Caflisch, "Land-locked States and Their Access to and from the Sea", 49 *British Yearbook of International Law*, p. 71 (1978).
55   For a list of the members of the Group of Landlocked and Geographically Disadvantaged States see Alexander, "The 'Disadvantaged' States and the Law of the Sea" (note 23), p. 187 (1991). Romania is missing from that list as it joined that Group only at a very late stage of the Conference. See also G. Hafner, "Die Gruppe der Binnen- und geographisch benachteiligten Staaten auf der Dritten Seerechtskonferenz der Vereinten Nationen", 38 *Zeitschrift für ausländisches öffentlich Recht und Völkerrecht*, pp. 568–615 (1978).

between its developing and developed members,[56] which was rather a novelty in international negotiations of a universal character.

In this context, it should be pointed out that, with certain exceptions such as navigation rights, the interests pursued by the members of the Group with respect to a new law of the sea were rather divergent. For the developing landlocked States access to and from the sea and transit for that purpose was the primary concern.[57] That issue was of much less importance for developed landlocked States which were more interested in the exploitation of oceanic resources, above all mineral resources, and marine scientific research. The landlocked States as a whole also realized that their claim to participation rights regarding living oceanic resources was largely theoretical in view of the increasing overexploitation of these resources in general. The creation of high seas fishing fleets would thus not have made much sense for them. For the geographically disadvantaged States which already had fishing fleets the question of rights to the living resources of the sea was one of the very major issues at the Conference on the Law of the Sea in view of the important economic interests involved.

In spite of these different basic interests the Group of Landlocked and Geographically Disadvantaged States showed great unity at the Conference and endeavoured to forestall an exclusive partition of maritime resources which, under traditional international law, were common to all nations, among them primarily coastal States. While vigorously defending its interests,[58] that Group finally could not stand in the way of general agreement and had to accept political and economic realities. After protracted and arduous negotiations, lasting from 1974 to 1982, the new law of the sea was enshrined in UNCLOS as a 'package deal' which, by its very nature, could not wholly satisfy the divergent aspirations of all the segments of the international community.

IV   UNCLOS and the Landlocked States

UNCLOS contains quite a number of references to landlocked States which are defined as "States which have no sea-coast".[59] Already the Preamble to the

---

56   Tuerk, *Reflections on the Contemporary Law of the Sea* (note 1), p. 55.
57   See also J.L. Kateka, "Landlocked Developing Countries and the Law of the Sea", in: *International Law between Universalism and Fragmentation, Festschrift in Honour of Gerhard Hafner*, I. Buffard, J. Crawford, A. Pellet & S. Wittich (eds.), Martinus Nijhoff Publishers, Leiden/Boston, pp. 771–772 (2008).
58   See also S. Vasciannie, *Landlocked and Geographically Disadvantaged States in the International Law of the Sea*, Clarendon Press, Oxford, p. 218 (1990).
59   Art. 124(1)(a) UNCLOS, based on Art. 1(a) Convention on Transit Trade of Landlocked States (note 42).

Convention recognizes the need to take into account the interests and needs of mankind as a whole and, in particular, the special interests and needs of developing countries, whether coastal or landlocked. An entire Chapter – Part X[60] – is devoted to the right of access of landlocked States to and from the sea and freedom of transit.[61] Furthermore, various provisions enshrine specific rights of landlocked States relating to navigation, maritime resources, marine scientific research and to the international seabed 'Area'[62] – the common heritage of mankind.

The core provision of Part X is Article 125,[63] which enshrines the right of access by landlocked States to and from the sea and freedom of transit through the territory of transit States by all means of transport. These means are defined in the same manner as in the 1965 New York Convention on Transit Trade as comprising railway rolling-stock, sea, lake and river craft and road vehicles and, where local conditions so require, also porters and pack animals. Such important means as aircraft and pipelines are, however, omitted.[64] Unlike in the 1965 Convention the right of access is, made contingent upon bilateral, sub-regional or regional agreements between the landlocked States and transit States, laying down the terms and modalities for exercising freedom of transit.

The right of access is, furthermore, restricted to the purposes of exercising the rights provided for in UNCLOS, including those relating to the freedom of the high seas and the common heritage of mankind. As with the 1965 New York Convention, transit States, in the exercise of their full sovereignty over their territory have the right to take all measures necessary to ensure that the rights and facilities provided for landlocked States shall "in no way infringe their legitimate interests".[65] The non-applicability of the most-favoured nation clause regarding the exercise of the right of access to and from the sea has been maintained,[66] while the requirement of reciprocity was dropped. This undoubtedly represents an important improvement compared to the 1958 Geneva Convention on the High Seas and the 1965 New York Convention on Transit Trade.[67]

---

60   Arts. 124–132 UNCLOS.
61   Tuerk & Hafner, "The Landlocked Countries and UNCLOS" (note 29), p. 64.
62   According to Article 1(1)(1) UNCLOS 'Area' means the seabed and ocean floor and subsoil thereof, beyond the limits of national jurisdiction.
63   *Virginia Commentary*, Vol. III (note 23), p. 409.
64   See Art. 124 UNCLOS.
65   Art. 125(3) UNCLOS.
66   Art. 126 UNCLOS. See also Tuerk & Hafner, "The Landlocked Countries and UNCLOS" (note 29), p. 64.
67   See also Monnier, "Right of Access to the Sea and Freedom of Transit" (note 25), p. 519.

Further provisions of Part X[68] relate to the prohibition of the imposition of customs duties, taxes and other charges on traffic in transit, except charges levied for specific services, to the establishment of free zones in maritime ports and to the obligation of transit States to avoid or eliminate delays or other difficulties of a technical nature for traffic in transit. Cooperation between the transit and landlocked States concerned is indirectly encouraged with respect to the construction and improvement of means of transport if they are inadequate. Finally, UNCLOS as a whole does not derogate from any greater transit facilities that landlocked States may enjoy by agreement with particular transit States, nor is the grant of greater facilities in the future precluded.[69]

The provisions of Part X found their final formulation only after extremely difficult negotiations in an informal framework. The landlocked States stressed that their right of free access to and from the sea was one of the basic principles of the law of the sea and formed an integral part of the principles of international law. The transit States were concerned about limitations on their sovereignty and possible adverse economic effects which would result from granting too generous transit rights. The outcome of these negotiations, based in particular on the efforts by landlocked States like Austria which are also transit States,[70] was sharply criticized at the Conference, both by some landlocked and some transit countries. In the end, however, it proved to be the generally acceptable compromise.[71]

Comparing the provisions of Part X of UNCLOS to the respective provisions of the 1958 Geneva Convention on the High Seas, it can be seen that in general the legal situation of landlocked States with respect to access to and from the sea has been improved.[72] Furthermore, this right has been placed in a broader context by integrating it into the framework of the law of the sea.[73] A complete and unrestricted right of access by landlocked States to and from the sea was, however, not within the grasp of general agreement at the Conference.[74] In this context it should not be overlooked that many landlocked States are at the same time transit States and, thus, offered only qualified support for enshrining such an unrestricted right in the Convention. It is nevertheless fair to say

---

68   See Arts. 127–131 UNCLOS.
69   Art. 132 UNCLOS.
70   The author was the principal negotiator for the landlocked States, the representative of Peru for the transit States.
71   See also *Virginia Commentary*, Vol. III (note 23), p. 372.
72   See also Tuerk & Hafner, "The Landlocked Countries and UNCLOS" (note 29), p. 64.
73   *Ibid.*, p. 67. See further *Virginia Commentary*, Vol. III (note 23), p. 382.
74   Tuerk & Hafner, "The Landlocked Countries and UNCLOS" (note 29), p. 8.

that, on the whole, Part X by striking a certain balance between the interests of landlocked States on the one hand and those of transit States on the other,[75] constitutes a significant achievement by the landlocked countries.

UNCLOS contains a number of provisions relating to the maritime rights of landlocked States. Article 17 affirms that ships under the flag of landlocked States enjoy the right of innocent passage through the territorial sea of other States in the same manner as those of coastal States. Article 87 provides that the high seas are open to all States, whether coastal or landlocked – both kinds of States enjoying exactly the same rights regarding the freedom of the high seas. Article 90 reaffirms the right of landlocked States to sail ships flying their flags on the high seas. This equality between landlocked States and all other States was already set out in the 1958 Geneva Conventions on the Territorial Sea and the Contiguous Zone and on the High Seas respectively, and is undoubtedly also part of customary international law.[76]

Pursuant to Article 131 ships of landlocked States are accorded treatment equal to that of other foreign ships in maritime ports, whereas Article 3 of the 1958 Convention on the High Seas provided for combined most-favoured nation or national treatment, the more advantageous being applicable. Although this provision amounts to no more than a corollary of the right of landlocked States to sail ships under their own maritime flags[77] and not to be discriminated against in maritime ports, it is nevertheless more favourable than Article 3 of the 1958 Convention: it does not make access to ports and their use dependent on the prior conclusion of an agreement between the landlocked State and the port State, and furthermore covers all maritime ports and not just those of the coastal transit States.[78]

The concept of the Exclusive Economic Zone (EEZ), granting to coastal States resource-related sovereign rights as well as jurisdiction, *inter alia*, with respect to marine scientific research and the protection and preservation of the marine environment, up to a distance of 200 nautical miles from the baselines from which the breadth of the territorial sea is measured,[79] had at first altogether been rejected by the landlocked States. When it became obvious

---

75   *Ibid.*, p. 64.
76   See also S. Vasciannie, "Landlocked and Geographically Disadvantaged States", 31 *Commonwealth Law Bulletin*, p. 60 (2005). See further *Virginia Commentary*, Vol. II, S.N. Nandan & S. Rosenne (vol. eds.), N.R. Grandy (assistant ed.), p. 155 (1993), respectively, Vol. III (note 23), p. 80.
77   Art. 90 UNCLOS; Caflisch, "Land-locked States and Their Access to and from the Sea" (note 54), pp. 97–98.
78   Monnier, "Right of Access to the Sea and Freedom of Transit" (note 25), p. 507.
79   See Arts. 56 and 57 UNCLOS.

that acceptance of this concept would be unavoidable, they demanded the right to participate, on an equal and non-discriminatory basis, in the exploration and exploitation of both the living and the non-living resources of the economic zones of 'neighbouring' coastal States, respectively of the same region or sub-region.[80]

With respect to the living resources of the EEZ, after a long deadlock a compromise was achieved which is enshrined in Article 69 UNCLOS. That provision grants the landlocked States a right to participate "on an equitable basis" in the exploration and exploitation of the living resources of EEZs of coastal States of the same sub-region or region. This right is, however, limited by additional requirements and conditions. Thus, it exists only in relation to an "appropriate part" of the surplus of the living resources as determined by the coastal State, with a very narrow exception clause for developing landlocked States. In the sub-region or region concerned this right does not take precedence over other participation rights, but must compete with those, with the final decision being left to the coastal State.[81] It also cannot be enjoyed in the EEZ of coastal States which are overwhelmingly dependent on fisheries, nor by developed landlocked States in the EEZs of developing States.

Furthermore, the exercise of the right of landlocked States relating to fisheries is made contingent upon additional agreements with the coastal States concerned. The prohibition of the transfer of these participation rights to other States is accompanied by their subordination under Articles 61 and 62 UNCLOS, granting the coastal State the right to determine the allowable catch of the living resources of the EEZ, respectively to determine its capacity to harvest these resources. Coastal States are, however, not prevented from granting landlocked States of the same sub-region or region equal or preferential rights for the exploitation of the living resources in the EEZs. This provision constitutes a faint echo of the demand, particularly by some African landlocked States, to create regional economic zones.

The determined resistance by the vast majority of coastal States did not allow for the provision of a right in UNCLOS to some participation by landlocked States in the exploration and exploitation of the non-living resources of the continental shelf.[82] It was not even possible to obtain agreement on a mere recommendation in this respect. The continental shelf doctrine assuming the existence of sovereign rights of coastal States with respect to the resources of

---

80   Tuerk & Harfner, "The Landlocked Countries and UNCLOS" (note 29), p. 62.
81   *Ibid.*, p. 65.
82   See also *Virginia Commentary*, Vol. III (note 23), p. 371.

the continental shelf was already too firmly anchored in international law,[83] even beyond the scope of application of the 1958 Geneva Convention.

With respect to the rights of landlocked States beyond the limits of national jurisdiction, in the international seabed 'Area', dealt with in Part XI of UNCLOS, the basic principle is that activities are to be carried out for the benefit of mankind as a whole, irrespective of the geographical location of States, whether coastal or landlocked.[84] The same holds true of the use of the 'Area' exclusively for peaceful purposes by all States.[85]

Article 148 UNCLOS deals with the promotion of the effective participation of developing States in activities in the 'Area', with due regard, in particular, to the special need of the landlocked and geographically disadvantaged among them to overcome obstacles arising from their disadvantaged location, including remoteness from the 'Area' and difficulty of access to and from it. In addition, Article 152 excludes particular consideration for the developing landlocked and geographically disadvantaged States from the non-discrimination rule to be applied by the International Seabed Authority (ISA) in the exercise of its powers and functions.

Within the ISA, the landlocked States are also accorded some special rights which, however, fall short of their original expectations. The Assembly of the ISA is thus endowed with the competence to consider problems for States in connection with activities in the 'Area' that are due to their geographical location, particularly for landlocked and geographically disadvantaged States.[86] The 1994 Implementation Agreement relating to Part XI provides that developing landlocked and geographically disadvantaged States are to have representation on the Council of the Authority[87] – in the same manner, however, as several other groups of States. In electing the members of the Council, the Assembly of the Authority must ensure that landlocked and geographically disadvantaged States are represented to a degree which is reasonably proportionate to their representation in the Assembly.[88] In practice, that provision

---

83 See also S. Vasciannie, "Landlocked and Geographically Disadvantaged States and the Question of the Outer Limit of the Continental Shelf", 58 *British Yearbook of International Law*, p. 272 (1987).
84 Art. 140(1) UNCLOS.
85 See Arts. 140 and 141 UNCLOS.
86 Art. 160(2)(k) UNCLOS.
87 Annex, Section 3 Agreement Relating to the Implementation of Part XI of the United Nations Convention on the Law of the Sea of 10 December 1992, 1836 UNTS 3. See also *Virginia Commentary*, Vol. III (note 23), p. 383.
88 Art. 161 UNCLOS. The issue of representation of the Group of Landlocked and Geographically Disadvantaged States in the organs of the ISA was also raised by the

does not seem to have had any particular effect on the composition of the organs of the ISA. The demand of the landlocked and geographically disadvantaged States had been that at least two-fifths of the members of the Council should be representatives of that Group.

The system for the equitable sharing of financial and other economic benefits derived from activities in the 'Area'[89] has not yet been elaborated in view of the fact that – contrary to the original expectation that deep seabed mining would become an economic reality well before the end of the twentieth century – such exploitation has not so far taken place nor does it seem imminent. At the Conference on the Law of the Sea the landlocked and geographically disadvantaged States had voiced their expectation to be compensated for the extension of coastal States' sovereign rights and jurisdiction by being allotted a larger share of the benefits derived from the exploitation of the deep seabed,[90] at least for the developing countries among them. It seems, however, doubtful whether this demand will be met should the time for the distribution of revenues from deep seabed mining actually arrive.

On the whole, the provisions of Part XI of UNCLOS relating to landlocked States did not actually grant them preferential treatment over coastal States as a kind of compensation for their disadvantages with regard to maritime uses, but are designed to ensure their participation on an equal footing in the activities of the 'Area' and the benefits hopefully one day to be derived therefrom.[91] This alone can already be considered a certain success.

The rights of the landlocked as well as the geographically disadvantaged States regarding marine scientific research activities are contained in Article 254 UNCLOS. Although these States are entitled to be informed of planned marine scientific research projects and to participate in such projects, this right depends on additional conditions and requirements. It permits them merely to participate in projects carried out by third States and competent international organizations in the EEZ of neighbouring coastal States, and they must be given the "opportunity" to participate in such research activities only "whenever feasible".[92] This right is thus very limited and a far cry from the

---

Chairman of that Group – at that time the author – in a letter addressed to the Chairman of the Preparatory Commission for the International Seabed Authority and for the International Tribunal for the Law of the Sea; see Document LOS/PCN/114, 28 August 1990.

89　Article 160(2)(f)(i) UNCLOS.
90　Tuerk & Hafner, "The Landlocked Countries and UNCLOS" (note 29), p. 64.
91　*Ibid.*
92　The legislative history indicates that 'feasibility' must be determined according to the practicability of participation in light of available research facilities, and may be affected by the degree of anticipated participation by the coastal State; *Virginia Commentary*,

original demand that these States be permitted to participate in research projects carried out in the economic zones of neighbouring coastal States.[93]

The overall result of the intense negotiating effort at the Third United Nations Conference on the Law of the Sea is certainly quite a way from entirely satisfying the interests and needs of landlocked States, as their views are reflected in UNCLOS only to a rather limited degree. The Convention, however, constitutes the only basis on which agreement with the coastal States was possible and which nevertheless to a certain – albeit rather narrow – extent takes account of the legitimate demands of landlocked States.[94] Moreover, one of the major and lasting results of the Third United Nations Conference on the Law of the Sea was to heighten the awareness of the international community that the law of the sea is also of considerable importance and interest to the landlocked States.[95]

V The Realization of the Rights of Landlocked States under UNCLOS

In considering the question of the realization of the rights of landlocked States recognized by UNCLOS it should, first of all, be borne in mind that during the last few decades regional economic integration has made substantial progress in several parts of the world. This process has undoubtedly contributed to alleviating the difficulties faced by landlocked countries by also providing a new basis for access to and from the sea besides bilateral or regional agreements to this effect. This is particularly true for developed landlocked States, especially the five of them that have become Members of the European Union. In respect of these States it can rightly be said that a fundamental change has occurred and that they are landlocked in theory rather than in practice.[96]

It should be recalled that European Union law applies to the entire area under the sovereignty of the Member States, and thus the four basic freedoms – freedom

---

Vol. IV, M.H. Nordquist (editor-in-chief), S. Rosenne & A. Yankov (vol. eds.), N.R. Grandy (assistant ed.), p. 596 (1991).

93 Tuerk & Hafner, "The Landlocked Countries and UNCLOS" (note 29), p. 62.

94 *Ibid.*, p. 67; Vasciannie, "Landlocked and Geographically Disadvantaged States" (note 76), p. 60.

95 Tuerk, *Reflections on the Contemporary Law of the Sea* (note 1), p. 67.

96 W. Graf Vitzthum, "Die Europäische Gemeinschaft und das Internationale Seerecht", 111 *Archiv des Öffentlichen Rechts*, p. 62 (1986). See also Hafner, "Austria and the Law of the Sea" (note 14), p. 34. These EU Member States are: Austria, Czech Republic, Hungary, Luxembourg and Slovakia.

of movement of persons, goods, services and capital – are applicable:[97] any discrimination against nationals of Member States is prohibited. If a Member State extends its area of jurisdiction, the area of applicability of European Union law is automatically extended. Thus, this also holds true for the EEZ and the continental shelf.[98] When signing UNCLOS, the then European Community[99] indicated that its Member States had transferred to it competence with regard to the conservation and management of sea fishing resources, competences concerning rules and regulations for the protection and preservation of the marine environment as well as certain powers with regard to the provisions of Part X.[100] The Common European Fisheries Policy provides for the allotment of quotas of the total allowable catch to individual Member States.[101] Although it is true that the criteria underlying the quota allocation, namely traditional fishing patterns, do not favour fishing activities by nationals of landlocked countries,[102] there do not seem to be any fundamental obstacles regarding such activities. On the contrary, coastal Member States are prohibited from restricting the fishing activities of nationals of other Member States – thus including those of landlocked States – undertaken from the territory of the coastal States.

---

97   See Art. 299(1) consolidated version of 29 December 2006 of the Treaty Establishing the European Community, 25 March 1957, OJ C 321 E.
98   See J. Schwarze (ed.), *EU-Kommentar*, Nomos, Baden-Baden, Art. 299, Rz. 5 (2000) and C. Thun-Hohenstein *et al.* (eds.), *Europarecht*, Manz, Wien, p. 49 (2008).
99   On 1 December 2009, the Treaty of Lisbon amending the Treaty on the European Union and the Treaty Establishing the European Community entered into force. As of that date, the European Union has replaced and succeeded the European Community and is exercising all its rights and assuming all its obligations.
100   Declaration by the European Economic Community upon signature on 7 December 1984, available at: <http://www.un.org/Depts/los/convention_agreements/convention_declarations.htm> (1 February 2013). See also Graf Vitzthum, "Die Europäische Gemeinschaft und das Internationale Seerecht" (note 96), pp. 36–37, footnote 15.
101   The allocation is decided annually; see Council Regulations (EU) No. 39/2013 and No. 40/2013 of 21 January 2013 fixing for 2013 the fishing opportunities available to EU vessels, 2013 OJ L23 Vol. 56, 25 January 2013. The Member States divide their quota among the ships of their fishing fleet; the ships must be under the flag of the Member State or registered in that State. The freedom of establishment enables any citizen of the Union to register a ship in any Member State. There must not be any limitations in this respect as underlined by the European Court of Justice (ECJ); see Case C-221/89, R *vs.* Secretary of State for Transport, *ex parte* Factortame (No. 3), 1991 ECR I-3905.
102   G. Hafner, "The Rights of Landlocked States in the Baltic Area", in: *The Baltic Sea: New Developments in National Policies and International Cooperation*, R. Platzöder & P. Verlaan (eds.), Martinus Nijhoff Publishers, The Hague, p. 385 (1996).

Regional economic integration is also playing an increasingly important role for landlocked States in other geographical areas. In Africa the largest such organization is the Common Market for Eastern and Southern Africa (COMESA), which comprises 19 States, including eight landlocked countries.[103] The Economic Community of West African States (ECOWAS) consists of 15 States, including three landlocked ones.[104] The Southern African Development Community (SADC) has a membership of 15 States, including six landlocked countries.[105] Besides Kenya and Tanzania, the East African Community (EAC) also comprises landlocked Uganda, Rwanda and Burundi.[106]

Beyond the African continent it should be noted that Bolivia has joined the Andean Community, also comprising Colombia, Ecuador and Peru. Paraguay, together with Brazil, Argentina, Uruguay and Venezuela, has become a member of 'Mercosur' (Southern Common Market), and Bolivia an Accessing member of that organization. Both these treaties have established customs unions that are components of the continuing process of South American integration.[107] Nepal and Bhutan belong to the South Asian Free Trade Area (SAFTA)[108] and Laos has joined the Association of South-East Asian Nations (ASEAN), the aims of which include the acceleration of economic growth.[109] In Eastern Europe, Azerbaijan, Armenia, Belarus and Moldova are parties to a free-trade

---

[103] The members States are: Angola, Burundi, Comoros, D.R. Congo, Eritrea, Ethiopia, Kenya, Madagascar, Malawi, Mauritius, Namibia, Rwanda, Seychelles, Sudan, Swaziland, Tanzania, Uganda, Zambia, Zimbabwe; available at: <http://actrav.itcilo.org/actrav-english/telearn/global/ilo/blokit/comesa.htm> (1 February 2013).

[104] The members States are: Benin, Burkina Faso, Cape Verde, Cote d'Ivoire, Gambia, Ghana, Guinea, Guinea-Bissau, Liberia, Mali, Niger, Nigeria, Senegal, Sierra Leone, Togo; see ECOWAS in Brief; available at: <http://www.comm.ecowas.int/sec/index.php?id=about_a&lang=en> (1 February 2013).

[105] The members States are: Angola, Botswana, D.R. Congo, Lesotho, Madagascar, Malawi, Mauritius, Mozambique, Namibia, Seychelles, South Africa, Swaziland, United Republic of Tanzania, Zambia and Zimbabwe; available at: <http://www.sadc.int/about-sadc> (1 February 2013).

[106] See East African Community; available at: <http://www.eac.int/about-eac.hmtl> (1 February 2013).

[107] See <http://www.comunidadandina.org/ingles/who.htm> (1 February 2013). The membership of Paraguay is currently suspended for violation of the Democratic Clause of Mercosur.

[108] Agreement on South Asian Free Trade Area (SAFTA), 6 January 2004, available at: <http://www.saarc-sec.org/userfiles/saftaagreement.pdf> (1 February 2013).

[109] The other Member States are: Indonesia, Malaysia, the Philippines, Singapore, Thailand, Brunei, Myanmar, Cambodia and Vietnam, available at: <http://www.asean.org/asean/asean-member-states> (1 February 2013).

agreement with Russia as well as four landlocked central Asian States, which provides for the stage-by-stage creation of an Economic Union.[110]

The transit provisions of UNCLOS seem to have had a positive effect on bilateral and regional agreements concluded between landlocked and transit States which are nevertheless based on reciprocity. These agreements generally also provide for most-favoured nation treatment for merchant ships sailing under the flag of landlocked countries regarding navigation, entry to and use of maritime ports and harbour facilities. They often complement the provisions of treaties on regional integration.

Probably the most far-reaching agreements were concluded between Peru and Bolivia by which Bolivia was granted free use of port facilities and an industrial and special commercial free zone in the Peruvian port of Ilo, as well as the right of free transit to and from that zone.[111] (1 February 2013). Paraguay has been granted free access to and from the sea by Brazil,[112] and Argentina has accorded that country such access via the rivers Paraguay, Paraná and de la Plata.[113] Mongolia and China concluded an agreement on access to and from the sea and transit transport by Mongolia through China's territory.[114] Nepal and Bhutan are parties to new agreements with India on trade and transit partly replacing older treaties.[115] Nepal has also signed a similar agreement

---

110 Free Trade Agreement between Azerbaijan, Armenia, Belarus, Georgia, Moldova, Kazakhstan, the Russian Federation, Ukraine, Uzbekistan, Tajikistan and the Kyrgyz Republic, 15 April 1994, available at: <http://www.wipo.int/wipolex/en/other_treaties/text.jsp?file_id=228813> (1 February 2013).

111 Framework Agreement between the Government of Peru and the Government of Bolivia on the 'Grand Marshal Andrés de Santa Cruz' Binational Project for Friendship, Cooperation and Integration, 24 January 1992, Law of the Sea Bulletin, United Nations, New York, No. 21 (1992). This framework agreement provides for the conclusion of further agreements concerning free zones, transit and fishing. See also <http://www.eluniverso.com/2010/10/20/1/1361/bolivia-alcanza-un-acceso-oceano-pacifico.html>.

112 Treaty of Friendship and Co-operation between the Federative Republic of Brazil and the Republic of Paraguay, 4 December 1975, 1242 UNTS 147.

113 Treaty of Navigation, Buenos Aires, 23 January 1967, 634 UNTS 181.

114 Agreement between the Government of the Mongolian People's Republic and the Government of the People's Republic of China on the Access to and from the Sea and Transit Transport by Mongolia through China's territory, 26 August 1991 (on file with author).

115 Treaty of Trade between the Government of India and His Majesty's Government of Nepal, 6 December 1991, available at: <http://wits.worldbank.org/GPTAD/PDF/archive/India-Nepal.pdf> (1 February 2013); and Agreement on Trade, Commerce and Transit between the Government of the Republic of India and the Royal Government of Bhutan, 28 July 2006, available at: <http://www.commerce.nic.in/trade/bhutan.pdf> (1 February 2013).

with Bangladesh.[116] The Afghanistan-Pakistan Transit Trade Agreement (APTTA) recognizes the right of Afghanistan to freedom of access to the sea as an essential principle for the expansion of its international trade and economic development.[117]

Ethiopia and Djibouti have signed agreements by which Djibouti guaranteed to Ethiopia the permanent right of access to the sea and to transit goods through its territory,[118] as well as the right to use its port installations and equipment. The agreement concerning the Malawi-Tanzania corridor transport system recognizes that Malawi is a landlocked country dependent upon its neighbouring coastal States for access to the sea.[119] Uganda has concluded an agreement with Tanzania and Kenya on road transport[120] and Burkina-Faso is party to a similar agreement with Benin.[121] Burundi, Rwanda and Uganda are parties together with Kenya and the D.R. Congo to the Northern Corridor Transit Agreement, providing the most efficient route for the surface transport of goods to the sea.[122]

---

116   Trade and Payments Agreements between His Majesty's Government of Nepal and the Government of the People's Republic of Bangladesh with Protocol, 2 April 1976, available at: <http://www.tepc.gov.np/tradeagreement/treagrebang1.php?print=1> (1 February 2013).

117   Agreement between the Governments of the Islamic Republic of Afghanistan and the Islamic Republic of Pakistan, Afghanistan – Pakistan Transit Trade Agreement, 2010 (APTTA), 28 October 2010, available at: <http://www.commerce.gov.pk/APTTA/APTTA.pdf> (1 February 2013).

118   Djibouti Port Utilization Agreement between the Transitional Government of Ethiopia and the Government of the Republic of Djibouti, 12 December 1993, and the Transit and Port Services Agreement between the Transitional Government of Ethiopia and the Government of the State of Eritrea, 27 September 1993, Law of the Sea Bulletin, United Nations, New York, No. 38 (1998).

119   Agreement between the Government of the Republic of Malawi and the Government of the United Republic of Tanzania concerning the Malawi-Tanzania Transport System, 15 August 1987, 1552 UNTS 273.

120   East African Community, Tripartite Agreement on Road Transport between the Government of the United Republic of Tanzania, the Government of the Republic of Kenya and the Government of the Republic of Uganda, 29 November 2001, available at: <http://www.kituochakatiba.org/index2.php?option=com_docman&task=doc_view&gid=86&Itemid=27> (1 February 2013).

121   Accord de coopération en matière de transports et de transit entre le Burkina Faso et la République du Bénin, 13 September 1990, available at: <http://www.toefrank.net/textes/acc1990.htm> (1 February 2013).

122   Northern Corridor Transit Agreement, 8 November 1985, available at: <http://top.ttcanc.org/ncttca/page.php?id=135391578525797688> (1 February 2013).

In 2003, an international ministerial conference convened by the United Nations in Almaty, Kazakhstan, adopted a Declaration and Programme of Action to improve transit transport cooperation between landlocked and transit developing countries.[123] The so-called São Paolo Consensus adopted by the United Nations Conference on Trade and Development (UNCTAD) in 2004 also deals with the special problems of landlocked developing countries as well as the related challenges faced by transit developing countries. The document outlines the goals of UNCTAD in addressing these problems within a new global framework for transit transport cooperation between landlocked and transit developing countries.[124]

As regards the navigation rights of landlocked States enshrined in UNCLOS it can be said that they are being fully respected. The same is true concerning access to and use of ports. With respect to marine scientific research, however, coastal States in their national legislation do not seem to have taken any account of the rights of landlocked States.[125] In relation to fishing rights it appears that coastal States in their national legislation regarding the EEZ, in general, have ignored the provisions of UNCLOS in respect of the sharing of surplus living resources. In this context, the constantly diminishing yields due to overexploitation of fish stocks as well as the rising demand for fish caused by population increase and the ensuing economic difficulties for many coastal States must certainly be borne in mind. In any case, the fishing rights granted to landlocked States by UNCLOS in practice constitute a *nudum ius*.[126]

Regarding developing landlocked States there are a few exceptions in this respect, the practical effects of which may, however, mostly seem doubtful. Bolivia and Peru concluded an agreement which also contemplates the possibility that Bolivia may enter into joint ventures with Peruvian companies to engage in fishing activities in the Peruvian EEZ.[127] Brazil has granted fishing rights to Paraguayan nationals or enterprises in its maritime zones under conditions to be established under bilateral agreements.[128] Morocco and Togo, in their relevant legislation referring to African solidarity, have indicated their readiness to allow neighbouring landlocked countries access to the living

---

[123] See UNCTAD, UN Recognition of the Problems of Landlocked Developing Countries, available at: <http://www.unctad.org/Templates/Page.asp?intItemID=3619&land=1> (1 February 2013).

[124] See Report of the Secretary-General on Oceans and the Law of the Sea, UN Doc. A/59/62/Add.1 (2004), pp. 17–18.

[125] Tuerk, "Landlocked States" (note 1), p. 110.

[126] Tuerk, *Reflections on the Contemporary Law of the Sea* (note 1), p. 62.

[127] Vasciannie, *Landlocked and Geographically Disadvantaged States* (note 58), p. 65.

[128] Treaty of Friendship and Cooperation between Brazil and Paraguay (note 112).

resources of their EEZs.¹²⁹ The African States bordering the Atlantic Ocean have adopted a Regional Convention regarding fisheries cooperation, which currently has 12 States parties, in which they also "confirm their solidarity with the African landlocked and geographically disadvantaged States with whom they actively cooperate".¹³⁰

An overall assessment as to whether the rights of landlocked States recognized by UNCLOS have been realized leads to a mixed conclusion. Navigation and port access for these States do not seem to be causing any problems. In respect of transit to and from the sea, progress has undoubtedly been made since the entry into force of the Convention, also due to progressive economic cooperation and integration. The rights of landlocked States to participate in the exploitation of the living resources of the EEZ as well as their rights regarding marine scientific research seem, however, to have been largely if not totally forgotten.¹³¹ As to the rights to share in the benefits accruing from the common heritage of mankind the landlocked States – like the remainder of the international community – find themselves having to wait and see and that is most likely to continue until a point in time which cannot be predicted.

---

129   Vasciannie, *Landlocked and Geographically Disadvantaged States* (note 58), p. 65, footnote 6. See also Paper by the Commonwealth Secretariat, Landlocked and Geographically Disadvantaged States under UNCLOS, 30 *Commonwealth Law Bulletin*, p. 792 (2004).

130   Convention régionale relative à la coopération halieutique entre les Etats africains riverains de l'océan Atlantique, 5 July 1991, 1912 UNTS 53; see Article 16. The States parties are: Angola, Benin, Cape Verde, D.R. Congo, Côte d'Ivoire, Gabon, Guinea, Guinea-Bissau, Equatorial Guinea, Morocco, Nigeria, Senegal and Sierra Leone.

131   See also Y. Huang, "Land-locked and Geographically Disadvantaged States", in: *Recent Developments in the Law of the Sea*, R. Lagoni, P. Ehlers & M. Paschke (eds.), D. Damar (assistant ed.), LIT Verlag, Hamburg (2010).

CHAPTER 19

Military Vessel Protection Detachments under National and International Law

Rüdiger Wolfrum[*]

I   Introduction

The placement of military personnel or other security personnel on board merchant vessels raises several questions under general international law, as well as under the regime on the law of the sea, apart from being controversial from the point of view of constitutional law in various countries. Some States such as Italy, Cyprus and Malta have already enacted national legislation to establish the basis for the placement of security personnel on board merchant vessels; other States such as Germany and The Netherlands for example are in the process of doing so. This contribution will touch upon the international law aspects only.

The two spheres of international law referred to above interact in this area. The questions under general international law must focus on the status of these detachments, on who controls their activities, who has jurisdiction over them and who, finally, bears the ensuing responsibility. In answering these questions account has to be taken of the legal regime on the law of the sea, embracing the UN Convention on the Law of the Sea (hereafter Convention), other relevant international agreements on the law of the sea, such as the 1988 Convention for the Suppression of Unlawful Acts against the Safety of Maritime Navigation (SUA Convention) – which actually is not relevant in the context dealt with here – as well as customary international law. In referring to relevant international treaties account has to be taken of the fact that these, in particular the Convention, are living instruments open to interpretation by international courts and tribunals and modifications through the practice of States Parties as indicated in article 31, paragraph 2(b) Vienna Convention on the Law of Treaties. For that reason the existing national law concerning the suppression of piracy as well as its development should be closely monitored.

---

[*]   Professor Dr.; Judge of the International Tribunal for the Law of the Sea (President 2005–2008); Director (emeritus) of the Max Planck Institute for Comparative and International Public Law; Managing Director of the Max Planck Foundation for International Peace and the Rule of Law.

The compilation on national legislation circulated by the Secretary General is quite helpful in this respect. As far as general international law is concerned, reference is to be made to the International Law Commission's (ILC) Rules on State Responsibility, considering them to reflect customary international law, the relevant Security Council resolutions and, in particular, to the jurisdiction of States to prosecute criminal offences as developed in customary international law.

As far as the practice concerning military contingents or security forces on board merchant vessels is concerned, it is opportune to refer, amongst others, to the Autonomous Vessel Protection since 2011 undertaken by a Dutch, and successively a German, naval team on board the *Caroline Scan* under the flag of Antigua and Barbuda transporting goods to Somalia on behalf of the World Food Programme. This practice comes under a particular regime and should not be generalized without caution.

As indicated before, some States have established, or have started to establish, a national legal basis for the posting of military detachments or security units on board merchant vessels. The situation seems to differ in the various countries, mostly due to divergent constitutional constraints, in spite of international efforts for harmonization. Germany, for example, does not consider military detachments as a viable option under its constitution, whereas the Netherlands seems to take the opposite approach, without necessarily ruling out the posting of private security units.

II Status of Military Detachments

The status of military detachments on board merchant vessels can be seen from different points of view: from the point of view of the detaching State; from the point of view of the owner of the vessel or the charterer; from the point of view of the flag State (if the latter is different from the detaching State); from the point of view of the coastal States whose internal or territorial waters or exclusive economic zone the vessel in question is passing through; and from the point of view of the coastal State whose port the vessel is approaching or has entered.

Each of these situations will be dealt with in turn.

With a view to covering a preliminary issue, it is safe to say that the detachment of military personnel on board merchant vessels as such is not contrary to general international law or the legal regime governing the sea. In particular, such detachment does not transform a merchant vessel into a warship, as is clearly indicated by the wording of article 29 of the Convention. Equally, article

301 of the Convention does not prohibit such detachments. It should be noted in this context that the placing of such detachments constitutes a 'recommended option' in accordance with the 'Best Management Practices for Protection against Somalia Based Piracy (BMP4)'.

To send military units on board a merchant vessel requires a national law authorizing the attachment in general (at least that would be the situation in those European States where the employment of the military requires some parliamentary approval), as well as arrangements between the State concerned and the charterer of the vessel or its owner. It is to be assumed that such units continue to remain part of the armed forces of the State concerned, with the consequence that the national rules on military personnel remain applicable. The national law referred to, together with the arrangements between the State concerned and the charterer/owner, will have to specify who bears the costs, who decides upon taking action, *etc.* It should be borne in mind, though, that the captain of a vessel bears the ultimate responsibility for every activity undertaken on board a vessel or by that vessel. To what extend this responsibility may be split between the captain and the leader of the security team is an open question to be considered. Some information on how to structure such arrangements may be gained from Antarctic activities, where several States use military personnel for Antarctic flights. Equally some insight may be gained from the opposite situation, where private groups perform services for and within armed forces.

If a military contingent is placed on board a vessel under a different flag (probably a flag of convenience), the situation becomes more complicated. In such a situation an agreement between the flag State and the State detaching the unit is required, since the ship concerned is and remains under the jurisdiction of the flag State. Some draft agreements already seem to exist to that extent. The main issue to be dealt with in such agreements is to find a solution for the competing jurisdiction of the flag State and the State having sent the military detachment apart from distributing the responsibility between the head of the security team and the master of the vessel if the latter does not keep the ultimate responsibility. It should be borne in mind that this again has some impact upon the responsibility of the flag State and upon that of the detaching State.

From the point of international law the main question to be answered is how to qualify actions taken by military personnel and who bears the ultimate responsibility.

This question must be answered first on the basis of general public international law and may be modified from the point of view of the relevant Security Council resolutions and ultimately from the point of view of the law of the sea.

As far as State responsibility is concerned, article 2 of the ILC Articles on State Responsibility comes into play. One of the essential conditions for the international responsibility of the State is that the conduct in question (acts as well as omissions) is attributable to the State concerned under international law. It is generally agreed that the conduct attributable to a State at the international level is that conduct arising from one of its organs of government, or from others who have acted under the direction, instigation or control of those organs, *i.e.* as agents of the State. In respect of military contingents on board merchant vessels, one has to presume that these act as 'agents of the State' concerned. It would – in my view – not be sustainable to argue that such contingents act in the interest of the shipowner or the charterer. Even if it were stated in the arrangement between the shipowner and the State referred to above that only the shipowner or the charterer would bear the ultimate responsibility for acts or omissions of the military detachment that would have no bearing upon the international responsibility of that State. This would only give the latter the right of regress.

Actions of military detachments on board merchant vessels are to be considered police actions. They are legitimate from the point of view of self-defence (protection of property and lives) apart from being justified under the respective rules under the Convention and – in the case of the coast of Somalia – the Security Council resolutions adopted under Chapter VII of the UN Charter. Qualifying measures of the military detachments as police actions means that they are not governed by international humanitarian law, but by the national law of the State of the detachment. It is generally acknowledged that in the course of police actions force may be used, including lethal force. It is appropriate to refer in this context to the UN Basic Principles on the Use of Force and Firearms by Law Enforcement Officers, which permit the use of firearms in certain circumstances. However, it is equally agreed that the use of force, and in particular the use of lethal force, must be proportionate. The International Tribunal for the Law of the Sea has, in its judgment on the *M/V Saiga (No.2)*, expressed the same principle when addressing police actions undertaken by Guinea-Bissau. It stated that the use of force "must not go beyond what is reasonable and necessary in the circumstances" and "considerations of humanity must apply". This reference to 'considerations of humanity' is a clear indication that human rights place a limit on police actions at sea just as they place a limit on police actions on land. For European States, the European Convention for the Protection of Human Rights and Fundamental Freedoms is applicable, since activities of military detachments constitute the exercise of the public authority of the State concerned. For other States, the International Covenant on Civil and Political Rights is of relevance (apart from the controversy on the interpretation of its article 2), as it is for European States in addition to the European Convention. Further, the Banjul Charter and the American Convention on Human Rights are to be mentioned.

Finally, the question may arise whether members of a military detachment may invoke functional immunity. This question is answered best when considering the various scenarios for actions.

The situation in respect of private security entities raises different questions concerning the classification of actions undertaken by such entities, the governing law, their legal limits and State responsibility.

Actions undertaken by private security units do not normally qualify as police actions unless the State concerned endows them with such a function. In such a case they become agents of that State with all the consequences already set out. If that is not the case, such actions are legitimized by the principle of self-defence or self-help. However, such private security units can invoke neither the Convention nor Security Council resolutions as a legal basis since they are not their addressees. It is acknowledged at least under most national legal systems that force, even lethal force, may be used in self-defence. In this context, too, the principle of proportionality is applicable.

Even if the posting of such security teams requires the permission of the flag State concerned, or if the respective security firms require certification, they do not thereby become agents of that State under the rules of international responsibility of States. For that reason, the flag State, under normal circumstances, cannot be held responsible for their acts or omissions.

Also in respect of private security teams the question has to be considered who bears the ultimate responsibility for actions on board or from the vessel. This should be the master of the vessel.

To complete the comparison of the status of military and private security teams it is necessary to mention that according to article 105 in connection with article 107 of the Convention, only a warship or a government ship may seize pirates. It is therefore evident that vessels having a private security team on board do not qualify as such. Such vessels are restricted to self-defence. One should, though, take into account that many national legal systems provide for the citizen's right of arrest. One should consider whether under the given circumstances articles 105 and 107 of the Convention should not be considered modified in this respect.

The situation does not differ in respect of military units since, as has been indicated already, the posting of a military team on board a merchant vessel does not render the latter a warship. The minimum one should argue is that vessels with a military detachment on board have the same citizen's right of arrest, with all strings attached thereto by the relevant national law. However, one significant difference exists. Military detachments exercise public authority and therefore are limited by the human rights guarantees under their national legal systems (which also includes international human rights guarantees). In comparison thereto private security teams are not directly limited by human rights guarantees, although they may apply indirectly. That very much depends upon the national legal system concerned.

III   Taking into Account the Legal Regime Governing the Sea

It is evident that as long as a vessel with a military detachment or a security unit on board remains in the internal waters, the territorial sea or the exclusive economic zone of the flag State, it is under the sole jurisdiction of that State. The same is true according to article 92(1) of the Convention as long as the vessel is navigating the high seas. In this context it is necessary to refer to article 94(2) of the Convention. Security personnel are covered by the term 'crew', although the term may have been used more narrowly so far. The situation is more complicated where the military detachment has a nationality different from that of the flag State. In such a situation, at least according to article 92 of the Convention, the jurisdiction of the flag State would prevail. An agreement between the flag State and the State having put a military detachment on board, as referred to above, may provide for a particular attribution of jurisdictional powers between those States. However, this is only an agreement *inter partes* without effect as regards third States. The flag State remains the responsible State for outside parties.

The situation is simpler in respect of a private security team on board. It always and fully comes under the jurisdiction of the flag State.

Let us now turn to the situation where the jurisdiction of the flag State competes with the jurisdiction of a coastal State. Here a clarifying remark seems in order, considering some of the recent literature. It is generally accepted that one has to distinguish between legislative or prescriptive jurisdiction, executive jurisdiction and adjudicative jurisdiction. The potential scope of these three forms of jurisdiction differs. It is possible for a State to legislate on events beyond its territory (for example criminalizing a certain behaviour of its nationals). However, such laws can be enforced only when the national in question returns. Further, it is to be noted that a State cannot limitlessly extend its prescriptive, adjudicative or executive jurisdiction, since this would infringe upon the sovereignty of other States. Finally, it is necessary to draw attention to the fact that, as a matter of international law, the prescriptive extraterritorial jurisdiction of a State in criminal matters is not unlimited. It is, in general, necessary that there be some sort of nexus between the prescribing State and the person or event to be criminalized. The territorial principle, the nationality principle and the protective principle are generally accepted. Not all States adhere to or accept the passive nationality principle and the effects doctrine. The universal principle (applicable for example in the prosecution of piracy) constitutes another acknowledged principle for the exercise of criminal jurisdiction, although many States for different reasons refuse to implement it, or at least do not fully implement it. It is evident that there may be competing claims to jurisdiction since the flag State may invoke the territorial principle, depending upon the nationality of the crew, the national principle as well as the passive national, the protective and the universal principles. International law does not provide for a general scheme to solve conflicts on competing claims to jurisdiction. Some principles have developed, though. It is generally held that the exercise of criminal jurisdiction on the basis of the territorial principle prevails. Apart from that, the Convention contains some rules concerning a conflict on competing jurisdictional competences. These are articles 27, 28 and article 97, the last reflecting the Lotus incident.

It is widely acknowledged that vessels voluntarily located in the port of a foreign State are under the territorial jurisdiction (prescriptive, adjudicative and executive) of the port State. Criminal as well as civil law applies to foreign vessels in port, although it is in the discretion of the port State whether it exercises its jurisdictional power on incidents touching only upon the internal discipline of the ship. The basis for this statement is customary international law. The Convention does not provide for a comprehensive legal regime concerning internal waters, including ports. As stated in my Separate Opinion in the ARA *Libertad* case, the Convention does not apply to internal water at all, apart from delimiting them, but the majority of the International Tribunal for the Law of the Sea took a different position in the case.

Also a military detachment on board a vessel is covered by the territorial jurisdiction of the port State. Certainly this military detachment represents the sovereignty of a foreign power, but this does not automatically exclude the detachment from the application and enforcement of the national law of the port State. On the basis of general international law the members of such a detachment cannot claim functional immunity for activities undertaken. The fact that States conclude 'Status of Armed Forces on Foreign Territory Agreements' to achieve the immunity of their military personnel abroad at least indicates that otherwise such personnel do not enjoy immunity. The situation would be different if an agreement existed between the port State and the home State of the military detachment on the status of such military detachments while covered by the territorial jurisdiction of the coastal State concerned. Such agreements should not only define the status of military detachments on board but should also legitimize the military weapons on board as well as regulate their safe storage. As became evident in the *M/V Louisa* case coastal States may prohibit arms on board merchant vessels and may require their declaration as well as safe storage under the custody of the port authorities. Such agreements may be qualified as some kind of 'Status of Armed Forces on Foreign Territory Agreement'. One further important element deserves mentioning, namely that military attachments must not exercise their functions while being under the territorial jurisdiction of a coastal State. This would mean a violation of the sovereignty of the latter.

To conclude, in internal waters the territorial scopes of the prescriptive, the adjudicative and the executive jurisdiction of the coastal State are identical.

The territorial sea is equally covered by the territorial jurisdiction of the coastal State concerned. However, here the limitations of the Convention have to be taken into account. As can be seen from a perusal of articles 27 and 28 of the Convention, the execution of criminal as well as civil jurisdiction is limited in respect of vessels passing through the territorial sea. Also the prescriptive jurisdiction is limited in accordance with article 21 of the Convention.

From the point of view of navigation, exclusive economic zones are regarded as part of the high seas (see article 58 of the Convention). This means the prescriptive, as well as executive and adjudicative jurisdiction of the coastal States, is limited to the exercise and protection of their sovereign rights as set out in article 56 of the Convention. In particular the coastal State has, as a matter of principle, no prescriptive, executive or adjudicative jurisdiction concerning vessels exercising their right to the freedom of navigation, the most important exception being that under article 211(5) of the Convention concerning the protection of the marine environment. But, as can be seen from article 220(3) of the Convention, the coastal State has only a limited executive jurisdiction concerning a vessel having violated the coastal State's rules on the protection of the marine environment in its exclusive economic zone.

It seems appropriate also to touch upon the contiguous zones since the competences the coastal States may exercise therein occupied the International Tribunal for the Law of the Sea once. As can be taken from the wording of article 33 of the Convention, the contiguous zone extends the scope of the executive and the adjudicative jurisdiction of the coastal State for particular legal issues (customs, fiscal matters and immigration, all related to the territorial sea or the territory of the coastal State) beyond the territorial sea. The contiguous zone does not provide the coastal State with additional prescriptive jurisdiction. This means vessels only passing through a contiguous zone remain under the jurisdiction of the flag State only.

IV Conclusion

The detachment of a military contingent on board a vessel in particular raises the question how to reconcile the territorial sovereignty of a coastal State with the sovereignty of the home State of the contingent. The Convention does not offer a comprehensive solution for this new situation. It seems advisable to try to achieve a solution through bilateral agreements, but it is certainly recommendable that international fora, such as the IMO or other more informal entities, develop a blueprint for such agreements. The situation as regards private security teams is, in this respect, less problematic. However, in respect of any violation of the laws of a State other than those of the home State of the security team, there will be a competition as to who has the right to prosecute. The Convention as well as general international law only offers some guidance in this regard. Legal certainty can be achieved only through agreements between the various States concerned.

CHAPTER 20

En Route to the Final Shape of the UNCLOS Dispute Settlement System: Some Pivotal Negotiating Procedural Steps Worthy of Consideration by Future Treaty-Makers and Leaders in Treaty-Making

*Sienho Yee**

I   Introduction

1. It is a great pleasure for me to contribute this paper on the birth of the dispute settlement system under the 1982 United Nations Convention on the Law of the Sea (UNCLOS or the Convention)[1] to the collection in honor of Professor Budislav Vukas, former Judge and Vice-President at the International Tribunal for the Law of the Sea (ITLOS) at the beginning of its life.

2. Described as a "constitution for the oceans"[2] by none other than Tommy Koh (Singapore) who, as President of the Third United Nations Conference on the Law of the Sea (UNCLOS III or the Conference) after the presidency of H.S. Amerasinghe, skillfully brought the negotiations to a close, the UNCLOS contains 17 parts with 320 articles and 9 annexes, covering almost all important law of the sea issues. It is perilous for one to attempt to summarize the UNCLOS in short space. Perhaps we can say that the UNCLOS reflects (1) the reconciliation between seaward claims by the coastal States for resources and the

---

*   Changjiang Xuezhe Professor of International Law and Chief Expert, Wuhan University China Institute of Boundary and Ocean Studies and Institute of International Law, Wuhan, China (sienho@chinesejil.org). This paper (with a slightly different format in style and citations) was first published in 13 *Chinese Journal of International Law* (2014), 185–202. The preparation of this paper benefited from the support from the Fundamental Research Funds for the Central Universities in China as well as Research Project No. 08&ZD055 of the China Social Sciences Foundation, all conducted at Wuhan University. This paper was completed on 30 November 2013. The websites cited were current as of that date.

1   For text and other materials, see <http://www.un.org/Depts/los/convention_agreements/convention_overview_convention.htm>.

2   Tommy T.B. Koh, "A Constitution for the Oceans", in Myron H. Nordquist (ed.), 1 *United Nations Convention on the Law of the Sea 1982: A Commentary* (2002) (*Virginia Commentary*), 11–16.

landward claims by the international community for preserving as much as possible the international seabed for common benefit as the 'common heritage of mankind'; (2) the associated impact on or attempt at the definition and delineation as well as delimitation, if necessary, of the various maritime zones and activities within these zones, with navigational freedom considered the most important for the major maritime powers; and (3) the commitment that rights and benefits are to be enjoyed with the corresponding duties and obligations. Obviously disputes relating to all these issues are bound to arise and a system for the settlement of disputes is necessary for the UNCLOS to work and for the hard-won compromises to hold up.

3. As we know, the successful negotiation of the UNCLOS was no small feat. The successful negotiation of the UNCLOS dispute settlement system was probably a more important part of that achievement. One can imagine how difficult the negotiating process could be. That obviously cannot be treated in full here in limited space. Nor is a full treatment necessary, as there are a number of such works already published, including that by President Tommy Koh himself with his colleague Shanmugam Jayakumar.[3] What I intend to do here is to first outline the UNCLOS dispute settlement system and then summarize and comment on several of what I consider to be pivotal negotiating procedural steps en route to the final shape of the dispute settlement system.[4] These

---

3 On the UNCLOS negotiations generally, see *Third United Nations Conference on the Law of the Sea, 1973–82, Official Documents* (*UNCLOS III Official Documents*) (<http://legal.un.org/diplomaticconferences/lawofthesea-1982/lawofthesea-1982.html>); Alan Beesley, "The Negotiating Strategy of UNCLOS III: Developing and Developed Countries as Partners – A Pattern for Future Multilateral International Conferences?" 46 *Law and Contemporary Problems* (1983), 183–194; Myron H. Nordquist (ed.), 1 *Virginia Commentary*, n. 2 above; Constantin A. Stavropoulos, "Procedural Problems of the Third Conference on the Law of the Sea", *ibid.*, lvii–lxv; Bernardo Zuleta, "Introduction to the United Nations Convention on the Law of the Sea", *ibid.*, 17; Tommy T.B. Koh and Shanmugam Jayakumar, "Negotiating Process of the Third United Nations Conference on the Law of the Sea", *ibid.*, 29–134; L.D.M. Nelson, "The Work of the Drafting Committee", *ibid.*, 135–152.

4 On the negotiation of the UNCLOS dispute settlement system, see, e.g., 5 *Virginia Commentary*, n. 2 above; 2 *Virginia Commentary*, n. 2 above, 796–816; 945–985; 1000–1018; 6 *Virginia Commentary*, n. 2 above, 595–644; Eero J. Manner, "Settlement of Sea-Boundary Delimitation Disputes according to the Provisions of the 1982 Law of the Sea Convention", in Jerzy Makarczyk (ed.), *Essays in International Law in Honour of Judge Manfred Lachs* (1984), 625–643; A.O. Adede, *The System for Settlement of Disputes under the United Nations Convention on the Law of the Sea: A Drafting History and a Commentary* (1987); Shabtai Rosenne, "UNCLOS III: The Montreux (Riphagen) Compromise", in Shabtai Rosenne, *An International Law Miscellany* (1993), 495–506; Louis Sohn, "Settlement of Law of the Sea Disputes", 10 *International Journal of Marine and Coastal Law* (1995), 205.

no doubt can offer inspiration to future negotiators, but they are usually scattered in various places; as Adede pointed out, "most of the substantive negotiations of the Convention were undertaken in informal meetings of the Conference Committees and special Negotiating Groups of which no formal records were produced".[5] My limited ambition here is to sweep all these together with some comments where appropriate so as to provide convenience to future treaty makers, especially those aspiring to be leaders in treaty-making, so that they will be able to quickly get a glimpse of what may help to pave the way for success in complicated negotiations even if not as difficult as those during the monumental UNCLOS III. Of course, what I consider pivotal will inevitably show my own reflection on this matter, albeit as an outsider. In doing so, I do not hope to be comprehensive, because, not being present during the negotiations, I am handicapped to some extent.

4. These pivotal negotiating procedural steps include, for want of better phrasing, the following: (1) the package deal decision; (2) the consensus approach; (3) building consensus by privileging the best second choice; (4) building consensus by privileging the existing negotiating text through the rule of silence; and (5) failing consensus in the Negotiating Group, the Chairman presenting his own proposals as suggestions to the plenary. As we can see, the first set the overall goal of the Conference. The second specified the general method to achieve that goal. The last three were concrete steps to implement that method. I am calling these 'procedural steps' rather than 'decisions', because not all of them were formal decisions and because I am not certain about the provenance of some of them.

II   The UNCLOS Dispute Settlement System in a Nutshell

5. The UNCLOS dispute settlement system that the States parties managed to persuade themselves to accept is a comprehensive and 'non-reservable' one, embodied primarily in Part XV. It covers all disputes relating to the interpretation or application of the UNCLOS. It respects free choice of means of dispute settlement (Part XV, Section 1), but has a compulsory component in terms of binding decision-making (Part XV, Section 2), which still allows a choice of procedures under article 287 including the International Tribunal for the Law of the Sea (ITLOS or Tribunal), the International Court of Justice (ICJ), arbitration under Annex VII or special arbitration under Annex VIII. This compulsory component is subject to some automatic exceptions under article 297 (exclusive

---

5   Adede, n. 4 above, 4.

economic zone (EEZ) disputes) and optional exceptions under article 298 (delimitation and historic bays or titles, military or enforcement activities or UN Security Council action), where 'compulsory reconciliation' is used as some kind of substitute for compulsory binding decision-making in some but not all of the excepted areas. Article 299 then reminds the States parties that they can still agree afresh to submit the excepted matters to a Section 2 court or tribunal.

6. Articles 15, 74 and 83 provide for 'criteria' for delimitation of sea boundaries. Obviously these may serve as a sort of applicable law provisions, essential to the settlement of disputes and thus can be considered part of the dispute settlement system in the broad sense, but one must remember that articles 74(1) and 83(1) deal with 'delimitation by agreement', not otherwise. However, the principles employed in these provisions may have a broader application.

7. Furthermore, a special regime with very broad jurisdiction is also created under Part XI, Section 5 for settlement of disputes relating to the international seabed area (the Area), including the advisory opinion jurisdiction of the Seabed Disputes Chamber of the ITLOS, which was not envisioned for the full Tribunal.[6] This was considered necessary to meet the novel challenges coming from the exploration and exploitation of the Area.

8. Finally, the Commission on the Limits of the Continental Shelf is established under article 76(8) and Annex II to examine the claims of a State party for outer continental shelf beyond 200 nautical miles. The Commission can be considered a quasi-dispute settlement body.

III   Pivotal Negotiating Procedural Steps

9. Needless to say, many factors contributed to the emergence of the final shape of the dispute settlement system under the UNCLOS. Among these were some 'negotiating procedural steps', as explained and listed above in paragraph 4. Let us briefly examine these one by one in the order given there.

1   *The Package Deal Decision*

10. The final emergence of the dispute settlement system as an integral part of the UNCLOS as a whole, which is not reservable or optional (*i.e.*, presented as a separate system in a separate treaty or an optional protocol) owes a great deal to the common understanding very early on that "the problems of ocean space are closely interrelated"[7] and that a comprehensive regime for the law of the

---

6   See *ibid.*, 196, 275; 5 *Virginia Commentary*, n. 2 above, 416, para. A.VI.204.
7   Report of the First Committee, A/9278, as quoted in 1 *Virginia Commentary*, n. 2 above, 190 n. 1.

sea is required for building a just and equitable international economic order governing ocean space. Otherwise, raw calculation of national interest would lead to States cherry-picking the parts most favorable to them to accept, resulting in several treaties on the law of the sea with limited participation, as had happened in the past. Thus, the idea of one big package deal for all aspects of law of the sea issues was conceived. In due course, the General Assembly (GA) specified the mandate for the Conference as "to adopt a convention dealing with all matters relating to the law of the sea".[8] This decision predetermines to a great extent the final shape of the UNCLOS, including the dispute settlement system as an integral, non-reservable part.

11. The magnitude of this undertaking was of course not lost on the leaders in the negotiations. Constantin A. Stavropoulos, Under-Secretary-General and Special Representative of the Secretary-General to the Conference described this 'gigantic package deal' this way: "The 1958 Conference accepted four separate conventions and a protocol, and thus to a certain extent problems could be isolated and settled one by one. The work of the Third Conference, however, is to adopt, by consensus if possible, one gigantic 'package deal' covering the whole area under discussion, which will have sufficient support to be ratified and come into force on a substantially world-wide basis."[9]

12. Obviously, a gigantic package deal requires tough compromises and it cannot be negotiated like a big banquet with all participants making decisions all at once. The task was further complicated by the fact that there was no single negotiating text agreed upon when the Conference started. With unprecedented interest from States and an unprecedented number of participants, the Conference appreciated at the beginning that it would be impossible to conduct all the negotiations all at once in plenary. As a result, three main Committees were established, but none for dispute settlement, which was considered to be within the province of each Committee when relevant. In addition, many working groups or negotiating groups were established, formally or informally, to hammer out the decisions and then to refer them to the larger and/or formal bodies for further decision. Among the most important working/negotiating groups for the dispute settlement system was the Informal Working Group on the Settlement of Disputes, with Galindo Pohl (El Salvador), Ralph Harry (Australia) and A.O. Adede (Kenya) as co-chairmen, and Louis Sohn (USA) as the rapporteur of the Group.[10] Shabtai Rosenne, another very influential person in the negotiating process, described Sohn as also the *de facto*

---

8   A/Res/3067, para. 5.
9   Stavropoulos, in 1 *Virginia Commentary*, n. 2 above, lxv.
10   Tommy T.B. Koh and Shanmugam Jayakumar, n. 3 above, 110.

'scientific director'.[11] Subsequently, President Amerasinghe took personal interest in the topic and was authorized to produce a set of draft articles which were included in the Informal Single Negotiating Text as a basis for negotiation. But resistance remained. Subsequently Negotiating Groups 5 and 7 were formally established by the Conference[12] to wrestle with various 'hard core' issues in dispute settlement relating to EEZ disputes and delimitation. All these groups and individuals worked heroically and contributed substantially to the final agreement on the dispute settlement system.

13. Just as the big package deal could not be negotiated with all participants working together all at once, it did not arrive in one scoop. In fact, the big package deal was made up of a series of 'partial package deal',[13] or 'mini-package' deals or conditional mini-package deals, reached as the necessary compromises were struck on a particular sector, segregated from the rest. When such a mini-package solution to such sectorial issues consisting of various compromises received 'widespread and substantial support', this would be considered amounting to a 'conditional consensus': the mini-package is one conditional upon an overall package deal.[14] One can find many illustrations in the UNCLOS. A prime example in the dispute settlement system is article 297, 'Limitations on applicability of Section 2'.[15] This complicated article with about 750 words embodies a series of compromises relating to the settlement of EEZ disputes, on very tough issues relating to sovereign rights and discretion. The *Virginia Commentary* summarized them as follows:

> Disputes relating to marine scientific research and fisheries were divided into three categories: those that would remain subject to adjudication (namely all those that do not fall into the other two categories), those that would be completely excluded from adjudication (and, like all other disputes, would remain only subject to Section 1 of Part XV), and those that would be subject to compulsory resort to conciliation. To the second group belong primarily disputes relating to the exercise by a coastal State of those powers with respect to which the substantive provisions of the Convention granted such State complete discretion. The third group

---

11   Rosenne, n. 4 above, 497.
12   10 UNCLOS III *Official Documents*, 7–8 (Organization of Work: Decisions taken by the Conference at its 90th meeting on the report of the General Committee, A/CONF.62/62 (1978), para. 5); Tommy T.B. Koh and Shanmugam Jayakumar, n. 3 above, 94.
13   Stavropoulos, in 1 *Virginia Commentary*, n. 2 above, lxv.
14   Adede, n. 4 above, 174.
15   *Ibid.*, 166, 174.

includes disputes involving clear cases of abuse of discretion, where a State manifestly or arbitrarily has failed to comply with some basic obligations under the Convention. In a case relating to such an abuse of discretion, the conciliation commission shall, in accordance with Annex V, Section 2, examine the claims and obligations of the parties and make recommendations to the parties for an amicable settlement, provided that the conciliation commission shall not substitute its discretion for that of the coastal State. The report of the conciliation commission is to be communicated to the appropriate international organization.[16]

This 'mini-package deal' helped to move the negotiators closer to the big package deal. Furthermore, it apparently served as a model for the yet to be resolved dispute settlement issues, notably delimitation questions,[17] to which we will come shortly.

2   *The Consensus Approach*

14. As a most important instrument to assure the success of the big package deal, a gentlemen's agreement was reached early on to apply the 'consensus approach' to decision-making during the Conference. This was ultimately approved by the General Assembly in a decision as follows:

> Recognizing that the Third United Nations Conference on the Law of the Sea at its inaugural session will adopt its procedures, including its rules regarding methods of voting, and bearing in mind that the problems of ocean space are closely interrelated and need to be considered as a whole and the desirability of adopting a Convention on the Law of the Sea which will secure the widest possible acceptance, the General Assembly expresses the view that the Conference should make every effort to reach agreement on substantive matters by way of consensus, that there should be no voting on such matters until all efforts at consensus have been exhausted, and, further, that the Conference at its inaugural session will consider devising appropriate means to that end.[18]

15. This approach reflected the general understanding that agreements reached by a favorable vote of the majority or even a super-majority may not last, but

---

16   Rosenne and Sohn, 5 *Virginia Commentary*, n. 2 above, 105.
17   Adede, n. 4 above, 183.
18   Decision made by the GA at the 2169th meeting in 1973, 28 GAOR, 24 (Item 40), on the proposal of the First Committee, in A/9278, para. 16.

agreements reached by consensus most of the time stick. Furthermore, it was well understood that the Conference's mandate would include changing existing rules and making new ones on the law of the sea. In such a situation, it would be essential to have the widest agreement among the States since, if a significant segment of the community of States were to pursue a different path, anarchy would result. With 149 States having been invited to the Conference, in the words of Constantin A. Stavropoulos, Special Representative of the Secretary-General to the Conference,

> The two-thirds majority voting rule followed in plenary by almost every previous United Nations conference, including all the codification conferences, would obviously not be satisfactory if any alternative to it were available, since to adopt a rule over the opposition of as many as 50 States might be only a dangerous mockery.[19]

The cogency of this argument strengthens as the number of States in the international community gets bigger and bigger, now over 190.

16. Of course, the consensus approach was not a pact for the Conference participants to go to the dead end together. Thus, after "all efforts at consensus have been exhausted", recourse may be had to voting. Stavropoulos was of the view: "That moment will presumably come if a substantial majority of delegations are convinced that further efforts at reconciling viewpoints are futile."[20]

17. In due course, this was translated into detailed rules of procedure by the Conference. The effect of this approach apparently resulted in more compromises struck, and struck at the sharpest point where no further yielding by either side would be possible. Glimpses of this can be found already in article 297, as discussed above in paragraph 13. In the following discussion one will see that this effect pervaded the entire negotiation process on the dispute settlement system.

3   Building Consensus by Privileging the Best Second Choice

18. The single most distinct feature of the UNCLOS dispute settlement system is probably its assurance of maximum respect for States parties' freedom of choice of peaceful means and/or forum of settlement. Section 1 of Part XV of course can be considered as expressing only one point, and that is freedom of choice of peaceful means of settlement of disputes. Even Section 2, which

---

19   Stavropoulos, in 1 *Virginia Commentary*, n. 2 above, lxiii.
20   *Ibid.*, lxiv. For a more general treatment of the consensus approach, see Wang Chen, "Issues on Consensus and Quorum at International Conferences", 9 *Chinese Journal of International Law* (2010), 717.

provides for compulsory procedures entailing binding decisions, makes the best attempt at assuring such respect, within the framework of binding settlement. Of course, complete respect is not always possible.

19. As usual, there were a variety of existing procedures or forums for States to choose from for settling disputes relating to the interpretation and application of the Convention. At the beginning the US proposed the establishing of a new law of the sea tribunal on the ground that special expertise – rather than general expertise in international law – may be required. The US explanatory note accompanying its proposal stated that "[t]he new Law of the Sea Convention will contain many technical provisions requiring judges with a special competence in the various fields covered by this Convention".[21] With this proposed addition, the list of available means got even longer. Thus a question arose as to whether any particular means should be selected or given preference at least. The Informal Working Group on the Settlement of Disputes held an inter-sessional meeting in Montreux, Switzerland in 1975. The report of that meeting stated that:

> A participant stated that the choice of tribunals would follow the defendant. The convention would also make provision for the situation where the defendant failed to act.[22]

20. According to Rosenne, this proposal was made by Willem Riphagen, Chairman of The Netherlands delegation, and would come "to constitute the kernel of the so-called Montreux Compromise, now embodied in article 287"[23] of the Convention. Probably Rosenne's assessment goes to the general framework providing for a list of choices and a default forum in that article. Perhaps it was in this sense that Tommy Koh and Shanmugam Jayakumar stated that "Willem Riphagen of the Netherlands outlined an approach to dispute settlement which found general favor in the group and which later was embodied in the Convention".[24] Adede was of the view that the Montreux formula "became an important aspect of the acceptance of multiplicity of jurisdictions as a

---

21 As quoted in Adede, n. 4 above, 15.
22 Meeting of the Members of the Working Group Considering the Question of the Settlement of Disputes – Montreaux [sic] – 22–23 March 1975, as quoted in Rosenne, n. 4 above (1993), 500.
23 Rosenne, *ibid.*
24 Koh and Jayakumar, n. 3 above, 110.

permanent feature of the disputes settlement system being established under the Convention".[25]

21. One supposes that the normal consent principle would require the choice to follow not only the defendant but also the plaintiff, as common choice is required. So the first part of Riphagen's proposal could be only accepted on the condition that the defendant's choice is also that of the plaintiff. It was apparently not too difficult to accept this point. Greater difficulty remained in (1) implementing the second part of Riphagen's statement, because apparently no particular forum should be privileged, as article 33 of the UN Charter does not do so, and (2) settling on a forum when the defendant's choice is not that of the plaintiff, a possibility not mentioned in the summary just quoted above. On this matter, it seemed that Riphagen himself had no key to offer.

22. This issue did not get settled until later. The solution that solved the problem is what I would like to call "building consensus by privileging the best second choice". According to Louis Sohn:

> When an informal working group, on which all regional and functional groups of states were represented, discussed this issue during the Conference, the informal rapporteur of the working group suggested a non-binding secret ballot, on which each participant would list both a first choice and a second one. The result was that while the first choice listed all four dispute settlement methods, almost all of those who did not list arbitration as their first choice selected it as their second choice. It was agreed, therefore, that where the parties do not agree on a first choice, the parties would have to resort to arbitration. A complex issue was solved by a simple procedural devise, and the full meeting accepted it by consensus.[26]

This idea would ultimately find expression in article 287(3) and (4), essentially stating that if the choices of the parties in a case made in advance by declaration do not overlap or, if one of the parties did not make any choice at all, arbitration under Annex VII would be the residual forum. The beauty of this approach is that each party is given the chance to name its best choice and thus can have no complaint, or is less likely to have any, when it has to take the best second choice selected in advance by consensus at the Conference because the best choices of the parties are not the same.

---

25   Adede, n. 4 above, 54.
26   Sohn, n. 4 above, 212.

23. There was another issue relating to whether preference should be given to some form of an expert body to decide matters of a special technical nature such as those relating to seabed mining. Indeed, at the beginning it was envisioned that a seabed tribunal would be established separately as an organ of the Seabed Authority. The general idea on the need for special expertise in dispute settlement was well received and did not appear to encounter a great deal of resistance. Ultimately this idea culminated in the establishment of a Seabed Disputes Chamber as part of the ITLOS with its jurisdiction provided for under Part XI, Section 5, the availability of special arbitration under article 287(1)(d) and Annex VIII, and, I should like to add, the establishment of the Commission on the Limits of the Continental Shelf, as mentioned above in paragraph 8.

4 Building Consensus by Privileging the Existing Negotiating Text through the Rule of Silence

24. In a massive conference such as the UNCLOS III, it is usually a herculean task to move the negotiation forward, with many proposals at the table and many delegates raising their hands (or their name plaques) to speak. After a single negotiating text was presented, one device adopted at the Second Committee to carry out that task was the 'rule of silence'. According to the Chairman of that Committee:

> Early in its work the Committee agreed to follow "a rule of silence", whereby delegations would refrain from speaking on an article if they were essentially in agreement with the single text. Silence on amendments would be interpreted as lack of support for such amendments. The rule was to be applied flexibly and was not intended to result in any arithmetic calculations or be taken as a form of indicative vote. In my interpretation of the effect of this rule, I took into account the fact that with regard to certain issues, only those delegations most directly involved would normally participate in the discussion. Nevertheless, the rule allowed a general classification of the issues before the Committee.[27]

The rule obviously gives preference to the negotiating text before the Conference, for good or ill.

---

27 5 UNCLOS III *Official Documents*, 151, 153, para. 6. The "single text" refers to the 'Informal Single Negotiating Text'.

25. This tool apparently was put to wider use subsequently at the Conference.[28] Thus, a decision was adopted so that:

> Any modifications or revisions to be made in the Informal Composite Negotiating Text should emerge from the negotiations themselves and should not be introduced on the initiative of any single person, whether it be the President or a Chairman of a Committee, unless presented to the Plenary and found, from the widespread and substantial support prevailing in Plenary, to offer a substantially improved prospect of a consensus.[29]

26. The President's Collegium adopted something similar, too, in its concrete operation. Bernardo Zuleta, Special Representative of the Secretary-General to the Conference, wrote that after hard-core issues were identified, the formal institution of the President's Collegium was formed as a practice to promote agreement. This body consisted of the

> principal officers of the Conference which acted in an advisory capacity to the President. It had been the principal officers who had informally prepared and revised the negotiating texts upon which the work of the Conference had been focused all along. However, the programme of work now established stringent standards to direct the Collegium in its work: it mandated that no revision could be made without prior presentation of the proposed change to the Plenary, wherein it must have received "widespread and substantial support," indicating that it offered a "substantially improved prospect of consensus." By [this device] the Conference was able to ensure that the package remained cohesive until such time as all of the pieces fell into place.[30]

Obviously this device has the same effect as the rule of silence in moving the negotiations forward and in doing so by privileging the existing negotiating text.

27. Although this rule originated not specifically in the context of dealing with dispute settlement but in the Second Committee, it must still have had an

---

28 See *UNCLOS III Official Documents*, vol. 5, 81, *passim*; vol. 9, 80, para. 55 (Iceland), 138–140, *passim*; vol. 13, 27, para. 40; vol. 14, 144, para. 3; and vol. 16, 277.

29 10 *UNCLOS III Official Documents*, 8 (Organization of Work: Decisions taken by the Conference at its 90th meeting on the report of the General Committee, A/CONF.62/62 (1978), para. 10).

30 Zuleta, n. 3 above, 21–22.

EN ROUTE TO THE FINAL SHAPE OF THE UNCLOS DISPUTE SETTLEMENT 381

impact on the final emergence of the dispute settlement system. This rule was specifically referred to in the debates on dispute settlement.[31] This was only natural, as each Committee also dealt with settlement of the disputes relating to matters within its province. Negotiating Groups 5 and 7 were formed by the Conference to deal with 'hard core' EEZ and delimitation disputes on the agenda of the Second Committee.[32] These groups worked under the framework of this rule and their reports were considered in that Committee.[33] Furthermore, the work of the Collegium would also have a bearing on the final outcome of the entire Convention including the dispute settlement system.

5   Failing Consensus in the Negotiating Group, the Chairman Presenting His Proposals as Suggestions to the Plenary

28. For many States participants in the Conference, the ideal means of dispute settlement would be third party judicial or arbitral settlement. For others, however, the preference was different. With respect to disputes directly relating to the exercise of sovereign rights and jurisdiction in the EEZ or to the integrity of the territorial status such as the delimitation of the territorial sea, EEZ and the continental shelf between States with opposite or adjacent coasts as well as to historic bays and titles, many States did not want to resort to third party binding settlement. As a result, these two matters (settlement of EEZ activity disputes and settlement of delimitation disputes) were considered among the 'hard core' issues and special Negotiating Groups 5 (with Ambassador Stavropoulos (Greece) as Chairman) and 7 (with E.J. Manner (Finland) as Chairman) were established by the Conference to deal with these issues respectively. The Chairmen were mandated to "conduct the necessary consultations within their respective spheres of competence in order, to the extent possible, to reach compromise solutions on outstanding issues" during the first three weeks of the ninth session.[34] Of course, as described above, such compromise would have to be able to garner the widespread and substantial support so as to offer a substantially improved prospect of a consensus, to paraphrase a decision of the Conference.[35]

---

31   9 UNCLOS III *Official Documents*, 80, para. 55 (Iceland).
32   Tommy T.B. Koh and Shanmugam Jayakumar, n. 3 above, 94.
33   See, *e.g.*, 11 UNCLOS III *Official Documents*, 63; 101; see also 5 *Virginia Commentary*, n. 2 above, 127, para. 298.25.
34   13 UNCLOS III *Official Documents*, 76 (Report of the Chairman of Negotiating Group 7, A/CONF.62/L.47, para 1).
35   See above para. 25, text to n. 28.

29. Negotiating Group 5 worked hard and achieved this goal. After isolating the issues, the participants managed to strike several compromises, which would ultimately become article 297. These compromises, as described above in paragraph 13, formed a mini-package deal conditional upon an overall package being accepted. This deal[36] was such that, roughly speaking, (1) disputes relating to non-resource uses of the EEZ (*e.g.*, navigational freedom) and environmental protection would be within the jurisdiction of a Section 2 court or tribunal, (2) disputes relating to resource uses of the EEZ over which the coastal States have complete discretion would be outside the jurisdiction of any Section 2 court or tribunal, and (3) disputes relating to the abuse of the discretion mentioned would be subject to compulsory conciliation. Under the UNCLOS, compulsory conciliation, which sounds awkward, is compulsory only as a process in the sense that a party has earlier accepted it (here, by ratifying UNCLOS) and must accept it when it is invoked by another party, but it does not result in a binding decision. An additional act of acceptance by the parties is necessary to make the resulting proposals from the conciliator(s) binding. Thus, this procedure offers the pomp and formality of a Section 2 proceeding but yields only a non-binding report which may contain recommendations.[37] Of course, the process itself may at least allow the parties the opportunity to appreciate, with the help of the conciliator(s), each other's positions realistically, which should be conducive to keeping the negotiations going and perhaps, with some luck, settling their disputes. Under such a framework, the coastal States would not be in fear that their newly obtained sovereign rights and jurisdiction would be discounted by baseless and vexatious litigation.

30. Negotiating Group 7 had no such luck, however. The group segregated the delimitation issues into two categories: (1) criteria for delimitation and (2) dispute settlement procedures, but on neither did it reach consensus, except that there was consensus on the criteria for the delimitation of the territorial sea, which can be summed up as 'equidistance plus special circumstances'. This would later become article 15.

31. On the criteria for delimiting the EEZ and the continental shelf between States with opposite or adjacent coasts, there had been a strong fight from the very beginning between the 'equidistance' States (those in favor of delimitation on the basis of the equidistance principle with consideration for relevant circumstances) and the 'equitable principles' States (those in favor of delimitation on the basis of 'equitable principles' with consideration for relevant

---

36   See *Virginia Commentary*, as quoted in paragraph 13 above; Adede, n. 4 above, 166–174.
37   On this topic, see Sienho Yee, "Conciliation and the 1982 U.N. Convention on the Law of the Sea", 44 *Ocean Development and International Law* (2013), 315–334.

circumstances). Even after years of negotiation and the hard work of Negotiating Group 7, there was no prospect of either side yielding to the other. One solution thus might be that all the criteria would be stated, alternatively and without priority for either, so as to appease both, but that would also offend both at the same time. Furthermore, during the discussions, it was suggested that, in addition to other criteria, a reference to international law would improve the chances of success.[38] The group worked heroically but could not muster sufficient support for any of the formulations that would pave the way for consensus.

32. On the method for settlement of disputes relating to delimitation, there had been also a strong fight since very early on in the Conference, between the groups for and against compulsory third party binding settlement. The division of opinion was considered by the President of the Conference as nearly equal in 1977.[39] When the text of Section 2 was taking shape, it was found necessary to craft exceptions to the general obligation stated therein of submitting disputes to third party binding settlement. The States opposing third party binding settlement considered that such settlement of delimitation disputes and the EEZ disputes would infringe upon the integrity of their territory and their sovereign rights and would not agree to a dispute settlement system that would not provide for exceptions of these two kinds of disputes (EEZ disputes would be dealt with by Negotiating Group 5, as described above). The States in favor of third party binding settlement, primarily Western States, stressed the importance and advantages of third party binding settlement, while "pointing out that the more general and indefinite the criteria of delimitation, the greater the need to submit delimitation disputes to the decision of a Court or Tribunal".[40] Negotiating Group 7 went through arduous consultations and negotiations on this point, but no agreement was on the way, as each camp seemed to be entrenching its position.

33. Then the idea of compulsory conciliation was proposed to take the place of compulsory third party binding settlement regarding excepted matters. This was already accepted within Negotiating Group 5 regarding some EEZ disputes. Probably inspired by this idea and its success in the other group, the Chairman of Negotiating Group 7 offered in 1979 as his "suggestion for a basis for further negotiations on article 298, paragraph 1(a)" a formulation that would permit States parties by optional declaration to except from the applicability of Section 2:

---

38   13 UNCLOS III *Official Documents*, 77 (A/CONF.62/L.47, para. 4 and annex).
39   Manner, n. 4 above, 636.
40   *Ibid.*

> Disputes concerning the interpretation or application of articles 15, 74 and 83 relating to sea boundary delimitations, or those involving historic bays or titles, provided that the State having made such a declaration shall, when such a dispute arises subsequent to the entry into force of this Convention and where no agreement within a reasonable period of time is reached in negotiations between the parties, at the request of any party to the dispute, and notwithstanding article 284, paragraph 3, accept submission of the matter to conciliation provided for in annex IV [V, subsequently], and provided further that there shall be excluded from such submission any dispute that necessarily involves the concurrent consideration of any unsettled dispute concerning sovereignty or other rights over continental or insular land territory...[41]

34. The Chairman further stated that the "lengthy discussions on the settlement of delimitation disputes during the eighth session have strengthened [his] understanding that only a proposal based upon the procedure of compulsory conciliation is consistent with a realistic view of the possibilities, if any, to reach a compromise on this controversial issue".[42] Further tough consultations and negotiations were had subsequently, but no consensus was in sight, still, on this article.[43]

35. At this moment, what should the Chairman do? One supposes that, to be true to his or her mandate, the Chairman *could* or even *should* simply report to the Conference the fact that no consensus had emerged in the negotiating group and gave up. However, the Chairman of Negotiating Group 7 did not take such a course of action. Here perhaps one may have glimpses of a leader in treaty-making or intellectual leader never yielding to failure. Mr. Manner decided that, in addition to reporting the lack of consensus, he would present his proposals as his own suggestions for the Conference to consider. Regarding the unsettled delimitation criteria, he further improved his proposal to read as follows:

> The delimitation of the exclusive economic zone/continental shelf between States with opposite or adjacent coasts shall be effected by agreement in conformity with international law. Such an agreement shall be in accordance with equitable principles, employing the median or

---

41   12 UNCLOS III *Official Documents*, 108 (Report of Chairman, NG 7/45).
42   *Ibid.*
43   *Ibid.*, 77 (Report of Chairman, NG7/47).

equidistance line, where appropriate, and taking account of all circumstances prevailing in the area concerned.[44]

36. Regarding settlement process and optional exceptions, the Chairman reported that no new features were added to the consideration of this item, reproduced his earlier proposal and repeated his assessment: "Albeit no consensus has as yet materialized, it is still the Chairman's understanding that only a proposal [paragraph 33 above] based upon the procedure of compulsory conciliation may prove consistent with a realistic view of the possibilities to reach a final solution on the question."[45]

37. The step taken by the Chairman was, in his *post mortem* assessment, a 'well advised'[46] one or, one may say, it was, *ex ante*, a fateful one, because the final outcome on both issues was facilitated to a great extent by his suggestions and, in any event, did not stray too far from them. Regarding delimitation criteria, there was resistance from both the equidistance group and the equitable principles group and President Tommy Koh decided to personally consult with the leaders of both camps. Soon consensus was reached on the proposal by the President that the criteria formulation should jettison all references to either the equidistance principle or the equitable principles, but should specify the goal of achieving an equitable solution or, one may say, impose an obligation of result. In addition, the reference to international law would be elaborated by reference to article 38 of the ICJ Statute. One may wonder why in article 74 or 83, paragraph 1, a provision on delimitation by agreement, it was considered necessary to specify 'applicable law' because an agreement could be based on factors other than law. One may also wonder whether it might be more appropriate to put the reference to article 38 of the ICJ Statute in a provision specifically on applicable law, such as article 293. One may further wonder how much this new formulation may have added substantively (perhaps indeed materially),[47] but the fact that it succeeded in commanding consensus shows the masterful skill of the person making the proposal. Perhaps each of the equidistance camp and the equitable principles camp seemed to be happier to see its criteria not mentioned in the text of the article than to see those of the other camp mentioned, even if together with its own, or the hatred engendered in one camp by the sight of the other camp's criteria was stronger than the pride triggered by the sight of its own. Thus the language in the drafts underwent a

---

44   Ibid., NG7/47, Annex. See also Manner, n. 4 above, 630–631.
45   12 UNCLOS III *Official Documents*, 77 (NG7/47) and Annex.
46   Manner, n. 4 above, 638.
47   For a thoughtful analysis, see *e.g.*, Manner, n. 4 above, 638–640.

sea change from mentioning both camps' criteria to mentioning neither, the effect of which remains to be appreciated in the future. So it seems that each camp was content with leaving the fight and its fate to international law, within the generally recognized framework of article 38 of the ICJ Statute, but otherwise unfixed and evolving. What the content of that law may be is a task for future decision-makers, not the drafters, which may favor one or the other camp or neither. In any event, the final criteria now embodied in articles 74/83, paragraph 1 read as follows:

> The delimitation of the exclusive economic zone/continental shelf between States with opposite or adjacent coasts shall be effected by agreement on the basis of international law, as referred to in Article 38 of the Statute of the International Court of Justice, in order to achieve an equitable solution.

Regarding the limits of the outer continental shelf beyond 200 nautical miles, a special Commission on the Limits of the Continental Shelf would be established to act on the applications of coastal States, as mentioned above in paragraph 8.

38. On his suggestion regarding settlement process and optional exceptions, that is, using compulsory conciliation to replace third party binding settlement, Manner wrote subsequently as commentator that "the States opposing compulsory third party jurisdiction finally approved the proposal, although as their utmost concession, and the Western countries, on the other hand, did not directly work against its adoption."[48] After some discussion, the Collegium decided to incorporate the suggestion of the Chairman of Negotiating Group 7 in the ICNT/Rev.2 (Informal Composite Negotiating Text, Revision 2), despite some reservations even from the Chairman of the Second Committee.[49] This suggestion would essentially become article 298(1)(a)(i) ("Optional exceptions to applicability of Section 2"), which now reads:

> 1. When signing, ratifying or acceding to this Convention or at any time thereafter, a State may, without prejudice to the obligations arising under section 1, declare in writing that it does not accept any one or more of the procedures provided for in section 2 with respect to one or more of the following categories of disputes:

---

48   Ibid., 638. See also 5 *Virginia Commentary*, n. 2 above, 129–131.
49   See 5 *Virginia Commentary*, n. 2 above, 131, end of para. 298.27.

(a) (i) disputes concerning the interpretation or application of articles 15, 74 and 83 relating to sea boundary delimitations, or those involving historic bays or titles, provided that a State having made such a declaration shall, when such a dispute arises subsequent to the entry into force of this Convention and where no agreement within a reasonable period of time is reached in negotiations between the parties, at the request of any party to the dispute, accept submission of the matter to conciliation under Annex V, section 2; and provided further that any dispute that necessarily involves the concurrent consideration of any unsettled dispute concerning sovereignty or other rights over continental or insular land territory shall be excluded from such submission;...

39. One of course cannot be sure what would have happened if the Chairman of Negotiating Group 7 did not take the initiative to make his suggestions. Reverse engineering in treaty-making is not easy business. But with what in fact has happened, we should all be grateful for his suggestions.

IV   Conclusion

40. In this paper, I have highlighted and commented on these procedural steps taken during the Conference: (1) the package deal decision; (2) the consensus approach; (3) building consensus by privileging the best second choice; (4) building consensus by privileging the existing negotiating text through the rule of silence; and (5) failing consensus in the Negotiating Group, the Chairman presenting his own proposals as suggestions to the plenary. These steps no doubt contributed to the emergence of the final shape of the dispute settlement system under the UNCLOS, and, in my view, in a pivotal way. The package deal decision and the consensus approach pervaded or even framed the entire Conference. The best second choice preference and the rule of silence helped to build consensus or hold consensus together, when preferences and opinions were numerous and divergent. The Chairman's own initiative in attempting to move things forward when no consensus was forthcoming in the Negotiating Group appears to be most innovative or at least courageous, helping to lead the negotiations out of an apparent dead end. The final shape reflects the balance struck between the wish for widest participation in the Convention regime and the need to maintain the integrity and density of the rights and obligations agreed to.

41. From another angle, one can find in these negotiating procedural steps images of leadership in treaty-making, both intellectual and organizational.

One can see how the leaders aimed for overall and long term success of the UNCLOS and settled on the goal of one big package deal and on consensus as the method to achieve that goal. One can also see how a good idea started to lead the debate about, or set the agenda for discussion on, choosing forums of dispute settlement, whether or not it survived intact ultimately; how a skillful rapporteur of a working group applied a simple procedural device to work out consensus; and how a negotiating group chairman, having failed to lead *his own group* to consensus, attempted to lead *the entire Conference* by his ideas or proposals as 'suggestions', with substantial ultimate success.

42. In the light of the contribution that these negotiating procedural steps made to the final shape of the dispute settlement system and of the leadership qualities that they may exhibit, future treaty-makers and leaders in treaty-making have much to learn from these steps and the experience of the Conference. They no doubt should have a place in the toolkit that similarly tasked persons should have on their minds.

PART 3

Protection of Human Rights

∴

CHAPTER 21

Minority Protection and the Prohibition of Discrimination

*Elena Andreevska**

I Introduction

The protection of ethnic, religious and linguistic groups is one of the oldest concerns of international law. For pragmatic as well as humanitarian reasons, international law has been a protective instrument, because the minorities question has never been entirely contained within national legislation.

A new or fairly new development was started by the peace treaties that formally ended the First World War, and a few collateral conventions and declarations, which saddled some new or enlarged States with a set of obligations favouring national minorities, and entrusted to the League of Nations the task of seeing that such obligations were carried out. First in time and typical of the documents that articulated the new institution of international protection of persons belonging to racial, religious, or linguistic minorities was the treaty concluded by Poland with the principal Allied and Associated Powers on 2 June 1919.[1]

The United Nations Charter makes no specific mention of minorities. Instead the emphasis is on individual human rights.[2] As a result of the fact that

---

* Professor at SEE University, Tetovo, Republic of Macedonia.
1 The direct purposes of the minority regime were two-fold. Firstly, to ensure that persons belonging to a State's population but distinguished from its majority on account of their group peculiarities such as ethnic traits, religious creed, language, and culture, would not be made to suffer at the hands of the majority, because they were different. A second purpose of the regime was to prevent a State affected by such 'splinter groups' from proceeding to absorb and assimilate them in the pursuit of 'national unity', by preventing them, either forcefully or deviously, from keeping their cherished natural and historical common characters. See Nova, R., "The International Protection of National Minorities and Human Rights", 11 *Howard Law Journal*, 1965, p. 276; Study of the Legal Validity of the Undertakings Concerning Minorities, UN Document E/CN.4/367; UN Doc. E/CN.4/Sub.2/214/Rev. 1; and UN Doc. E/CN.4/Sub.2/221/Rev. 1, UN Sales No. 67. XIV.3.
2 Russell, R.B., Muther, J.S., *A History of the United Nations Charter. The Rule of the United States 1940–45* (Brookings Institution, Washington, 1958).

no amendments favouring the protection of minorities were submitted to the San Francisco Conference, it is obvious that the Charter refers rather to the equal enjoyment of human rights connected with the non-discrimination principle. This means that States promoting the change from a limited minorities regime to a regime of human rights perceive qualitative differences, by implication if not expressly, between the concepts of the 'prevention of discrimination' and the 'protection of minorities'.[3]

However, until recently, the main burden of minority rights in general international law had been borne by Article 27 of the International Covenant on Civil and Political Rights (1966).[4] But, this is a cautious and tentative article which reflects the very limited space that States were prepared to allow regarding minority rights. Indeed, the text prompts the following observations:

(1) Rights of minorities may not be universal rights, since the groups may not 'exist' in all States;
(2) The text refers to the rights of persons and not of groups, thus, limiting the community or collective dimension of the rights;
(3) The members of minorities are not described as *having* the rights – rather, the rights 'shall not be denied' to them;
(4) The article does not clearly imply State action or resources to benefit minorities.[5]

In adopting Resolution 47/135 on 18 December 1992, the General Assembly of the United Nations completed an important phase of standard-setting in minority rights: the resolution contains the 'Declaration on the Rights of Persons Belonging to National or Ethnic, Religious and Linguistic Minorities'. The text can be regarded as a new 'international minimum standard' for minority rights, transcending some of the limitations of Article 27.[6]

---

3 The core of the rights of minorities in international law is their right to existence and identity. Special measures to favour the flourishing of this identity are not to be regarded as discriminatory.
4 UN General Assembly Resolution 2200 A (XXI), 16 December 1966.
5 Thornberry, P., *International Law and Rights of Minorities* (Clarendon Press, Oxford, 1992).
6 A few general points arise from the Declaration: the title of the Declaration adds 'national' to the list of minorities in Article 27 of the Covenant; there is no definition of minorities at any point in the text; suggestions for including a right to autonomy for minorities were rejected during the drafting. Even the lower-level right of 'self-management' was not accepted. Any concept of rights for minorities prefaced by 'self-' was unacceptable to States; and the rights apply to 'persons belonging to' minorities, not to minorities as such: they remain individual rights, though their collective dimension is slightly more elaborate than is the case for Article 27.

Furthermore, the Council of Europe's (CoE) activities in the standard-setting field, together with all its activities as a multilateral cooperation network at governmental, parliamentary, regional and local levels, undertaken in close collaboration with NGOs, are directed at fostering mutual understanding and reinforcing confidence in human relations. For the countries of Central and Eastern Europe, which still suffer considerable identity problems, this concept of European cooperation, in preparation for future European integration, is becoming increasingly attractive.[7]

In addition, all the work of the Organization for Security and Co-operation in Europe (OSCE) on minorities stems from the 1975 Helsinki Final Act.[8]

Motivated by Article 27 of the Covenant on Civil and Political Rights concerning the rights of persons belonging to ethnic, religious or linguistic minorities, the main goal of this Declaration is to promote the materialisation of principles contained in the Charter, the Universal Declaration of Human Rights, the Convention on the Prevention and Punishment of the Crime of Genocide, the International Convention on Elimination of All Forms of Racial Discrimination, the International Covenant on the Economic, Social and Cultural Rights, the Declaration Based on Religion or Belief, and the Convention on the Rights of the Child, as well as other relevant international instruments that have been adopted at the universal or regional level and those concluded between individual Member States of the United Nations. See Andreevska, E., *The National Minorities in the Balkans under the UN and European System of Protection of Human and Minorities Rights* (Magor, 1998), pp. 69–75; UN Doc. E/CN.4/Sub.2/384/Add.1-7, UN Sales No. E. 78. XIV.I.; and Definition and Classification of Minorities, UN Doc. E/CN. 4/Sub. 2/85, para. 24.

7 It is seen as a vital alternative to the concept of the all-sovereign nation-state which is being presented again by those who want to maintain or acquire political power by undemocratic means, as the ultimate justification for political self-determination. For the sake of pluralist democracy, individual freedom and the respect for minority rights in Europe, it therefore seems essential to maintain and to strengthen the scope for a transnational regime through the CoE and its activities. Many of the CoE's daily activities include considerable achievements in the field of confidence-building – primarily in dealing with the diversity of life in multicultural societies, including the response to the appearance of pockets of deprivation and social exclusion. The fields covered by such projects are mainly education, culture, media, youth, legal, political and social questions, local democracy and the environment.

8 At the regional level, the OSCE has enshrined minority standards in a variety of instruments, the most significant of which remains the Document of the Copenhagen Meeting of the Conference on the Human Dimension of 1990. While lacking legally binding status (like all OSCE standards), such document has proved so far the most influential elaboration of international minority rights provisions. Indeed, both the UN Declaration on Minorities and the Framework Convention for the Protection of National Minorities have benefited from the Copenhagen text as one of their main sources of inspiration. Moreover, the instrument has been incorporated as a legal obligation in recent bilateral treaties, such as the 1995 basic treaty between Hungary and Slovakia (*infra*). In terms of substantive entitlements, particular

In responding to the problems of minorities, the OSCE is trying to fill two gaps: scrutiny of the records of States in putting agreed principles into practice; and intervention in areas of tension and conflict within and between States involving minorities. Without doubt, success will depend largely on the degree of commitment by States. Commitment will show itself in willingness to adjust domestic law and administrative practice, and in readiness to commit resources in terms of people and money, to OSCE activities.

The European Union Treaty of Lisbon[9] also includes three major points that warrant consideration in the context of minorities. For one, persons of minorities are for the first time explicitly mentioned in EU primary law. For another, the Charter of Fundamental Rights (CFR) receives the status of an international legally binding document. Thirdly, it is envisaged that the European Union will accede to the European Convention on Human Rights (ECHR).[10]

Finally, the promotion and protection of the rights of minorities require that particular attention be paid to issues such as the recognition of minorities' existence; efforts to guarantee their rights to non-discrimination and equality; the promotion of multicultural and intercultural education, nationally and locally; the promotion of their participation in all aspects of public life; the inclusion of their concerns in development and poverty-reduction processes; disparities in social indicators such as employment, health and housing; the situation of women and the special concerns of children belonging to minorities.

The fundamental pillars of human rights and minority legal protection are the principles of non-discrimination and equality which constitute the basis of all core human rights treaties. They apply to everyone in relation to all

---

emphasis is laid on the implications of the right of minority members to identity, free of any attempts at assimilation against their will, such as the use of their mother tongue in private and in public, association rights, transfrontier rights, mother tongue education, *etc*. Interestingly, paragraph 35 refers to autonomy arrangements as one possible means of realizing the right of persons belonging to national minorities to effective participation in public affairs, in connection with the protection of the identity of such minorities. A report produced by an expert meeting convened in Geneva by OSCE participating states in 1991 further elaborates upon such issues by offering, *inter alia*, a 'shopping list' of advisable domestic policies.

9   See Consolidated Reader-friendly Edition of the Treaty on European Union (TEU) and the Treaty on the Functioning of the European Union (TFEU) as amended by the Treaty of Lisbon (2007), Foundation for EUDEMOCRACY (2009).

10 The European Union is home to almost five hundred million people. About forty-five million of them, or nine per cent, are considered to belong to one of the many national minorities. Some of these forty-five million may have rejoiced at the Treaty of Lisbon while some may not expect many changes.

human rights and freedoms and prohibit discrimination on the basis of a list of non-exhaustive categories, such as race, colour, religion, language, nationality and ethnicity. Through respect for these two principles, the enjoyment of many human rights can be secured, including the right to effective participation in decision-making by minorities.

II Theoretical Framework: Prohibition of Discrimination

Non-discrimination as an international law principle has been embodied in many United Nations instruments,[11] but without doubt the United Nations Charter set the pattern for the development of this principle. After the United Nations Charter, the Universal Declaration of Human Rights was a significant document on human rights.[12] Among other rights, such as civil, political, economic, social and cultural rights, it contains the principle of non-discrimination or 'non-distinction'.[13] Independently of the fact that the Declaration does not embody the provision of minority rights, without doubt it lists the rights and freedoms particularly pertinent to minority identity: the right to freedom of thought, conscience and religion,[14] the right to freedom of opinion and

---

11   United Nations Charter, Articles 1(3) and 5; International Covenant on Civil and Political Rights, Articles, 2, 14, 18, 20, 26 and 27; International Covenant on Economic, Social and Cultural Rights, Articles 2(2) and 13; International Convention on the Elimination of All Forms of Racial Discrimination, Articles, 1–7 and 14; Convention on the Rights of the Child, Articles 2, 17(d), 29(d) and 30; UNESCO Convention against Discrimination in Education, Articles 1, 3(d) and 5(a); UNESCO Declaration on the Principles of International Cultural Cooperation, Article 1; ILO Convention concerning Discrimination in Respect of Employment and Occupation; ILO Convention No. 107 and Recommendation No. 104 (1957), concerning Indigenous and Other Tribal and Semi-Tribal Populations in Independent Countries; ILO Convention No. 111 (1958), concerning Discrimination in Respect of Occupation, Article 5; ILO Convention No. 169 (1989), concerning Indigenous and Tribal Peoples of Independent Countries; Declaration on the Elimination of All Forms of Intolerance and Discrimination Based on Religion or Belief; Guiding Principles for Crime Prevention and Criminal Justice in the Context of Development and a New International Economic Order, Principles 26–28, 30, 31 and 35; Body of Principles for the Protection of All Persons Under Any Form of Detention or Imprisonment, Principles 5 and 14. See *A Compilation of International Instruments*, Vol. I (1st and 2nd part), Universal Instruments (United Nations, 1994).
12   UN General Assembly Resolution 217 A (III), 3rd Session, Part 1, Resolutions, 71.
13   Article 2.
14   Article 18.

expression,[15] the right of free assembly and association,[16] the right to education which shall "promote understanding, tolerance and friendship among all nations, racial or religious groups",[17] and the right freely to participate in the cultural life of the community[18] are incorporated in the Declaration.

The term racial discrimination is defined for the first time in Article 1(1) of the International Convention on the Elimination of All Forms of Racial Discrimination as "any distinction, exclusion, restriction or preference based on race, colour, descent, or national or ethnic origin which has the purpose or effect of nullifying or impairing the recognition, enjoyment or exercise, on an equal footing, of human rights and fundamental freedoms in the political, economic, social, cultural or any other field of public life."[19]

Unlike Article 2(1) of the International Covenant on Civil and Political Rights, which only addresses distinctions in the enjoyment of the rights recognized by the Covenant, Article 1(1) of the International Convention on the Elimination of All Forms of Racial Discrimination extends to all human rights and fundamental freedoms, whatever their source may be.

Article 1(4) of the Convention allows States parties to take "special measures...for the sole purpose of securing adequate advancement of certain racial or ethnic groups or individuals requiring such protection as may be necessary in order to ensure such groups or individuals equal enjoyment or exercise of human rights and fundamental freedoms..."[20]

In addition, Article 26 of the International Covenant on Civil and Political Rights guarantees that:

> All persons are equal before the law and are entitled without any discrimination to the equal protection of the law.

Finally, the International Covenant on Civil and Political Rights[21] contains a provision dealing with minority rights:

---

15   Article 19.
16   Article 20.
17   Article 26.
18   Article 27.
19   *A Compilation of International Instruments*, Vol. 1, Universal Instruments (United Nations, 1994), General Assembly Resolution 2106 A (XX), 1965, p. 67.
20   Article 1(4) of the Convention on the Elimination of All Forms of Racial Discrimination is an important provision on disadvantaged groups which is relevant to many minorities, especially in the context of the distinction between 'protection of minorities' and 'prevention of discrimination'.
21   Article 27.

In those States in which ethnic, religious or linguistic minorities exist, persons belonging to such minorities shall not be denied the right, in community with other members of their group, to enjoy their own culture, to profess and practice their own religion, or to use their own language.[22]

The CoE has never ceased to be interested in the minority question, though the idea of elaborating specific legal standards in this field regained momentum only following developments in Eastern Europe throughout the early 1990s. The ECHR and its Protocol No. 12 do not address minority rights. However, as increasingly suggested by the Strasbourg jurisprudence in such areas as political and religious pluralism, education as well as way of life (the last aspect, interestingly reflected in the case of *Chapman* v. *United Kingdom*),[23] such texts and further protocols might generate some form of protection for minorities and their members in relation to their general needs and interests as a result of the functioning of pertinent substantive provisions.[24]

Furthermore, the CoE's Parliamentary Assembly has long been most active in attempting to develop minority rights standards. In 1993, it adopted Recommendation 1201 on an additional protocol on the rights of national minorities to the European Convention on Human Rights.[25]

Unlike the stringent rights and duties embraced by Recommendation 1201 (1993), the treaty contains programme-type provisions setting out objectives which the parties undertake to pursue. As a result, the provisions are not directly applicable, leaving the parties a measure of discretion in the implementation of

---

22 The adoption of Article 27 on the rights of minorities reflected an intention to go beyond non-discrimination. As several delegations explained in the UN General Assembly's Third Committee, the objective was combating involuntary assimilation, as opposed to promoting equal treatment, or permitting preferential treatment.
23 Chapman v. The United Kingdom, Application No. 27238/95, Judgment of 18 January 2001.
24 Most notably Articles 8 to 11 of the ECHR and Articles 2 and 3 of Protocol No. 1, and/or their respective anti-discrimination clauses (notably Article 14 of the ECHR, and Article 1 of Protocol No. 12). Various proposals have been put forward by either political or specialised bodies or individual countries.
25 The text further develops previous Assembly proposals, particularly by focusing on individual rights, and complementing the rights framework with a definition of 'national minority' (Article 1), a clause regarding restrictions on the rights recognized (Article 14), as well as a far reaching right to autonomy regimes (Article 11). Its provisions on language and education rights are also noteworthy (Articles 7 and 8). In the same year in which it was adopted, this Assembly proposal failed to be endorsed by the CoE Member States. However, in its reply of 13 June 2002, the Committee of Ministers considered it 'premature' to reopen the debate on this project. See Doc. CM/Del/Dec(2002)799, 17 June 2002.

the instrument, in view of particular local factors. The Framework Convention for the Protection of National Minorities (FCNM) builds upon previous texts.[26] The FCNM came into force on 1 March 1998.[27]

There is no doubt that two essential goals and themes of minority protection are substantive, real or full equality (as opposed to more formal equality) and the right to identity. Several distinctive conceptions of equality can be distinguished. An important distinction needs to be made between formal equality (or equality as consistency), which sets out to treat everybody in exactly the same way on the one hand, and substantive, or real or full equality on the other hand. Full equality acknowledges differences in starting positions which might necessitate differential treatment in order to reach real, effective equality. The latter, namely the need to treat persons formally differently in order to obtain substantive equal treatment is coined 'the paradox of the equality principle'. Nevertheless, the goal of substantive equality does not allow just any kind or degree of differential treatment. In this regard real or substantive equality can also be seen as a limit to 'special' rights. At the same time, the vulnerable position of persons belonging to minorities also necessitates heightened attention being paid to equal access to employment, public services and effective participation in economic, social and cultural life as well as in public affairs.

It is widely accepted that an adequate system of minority protection is constructed on two pillars, the first of which concerns non-discrimination in combination with individual human rights of special relevance for minorities, the second minority specific standards aimed at protecting and promoting the right to identity of minorities. Nevertheless, it needs to be acknowledged that this position is not universally accepted. There are indeed still academics and States that argue that effective protection of the first pillar would suffice (hence, discarding the need for the second pillar with 'specific' minority rights).[28]

In view of the fact that to some extent this rejection on the second pillar is related to concerns about these 'special rights', it should be emphasized that minority rights are not situated outside the human rights framework but are considered to be part and parcel of it. This is recognized explicitly (*inter alia*) in Article 1 of the FCNM which reads: "The protection of national minorities

---

26 As indicated earlier, the OSCE Copenhagen Document inspired it to a large extent. In fact, the treaty was generated by an attempt to translate the political commitments endorsed by that document into legal obligations.

27 Framework Convention for the Protection of National Minorities, Council of Europe Treaty Series No. 157.

28 See O'Brien, C.C., "What Rights Should Minorities Have?", in Whitaker, B. (ed.), *Minorities: A Question of Human Rights?* (Pergamon Press, Oxford, 1984), p. 21.

and of the rights and freedoms of persons belonging to those minorities forms an integral part of the international protection of human rights, …" This statement is important as it denies that 'minority rights' are 'foreign' to that framework and belong to a totally different universe.[29]

Nevertheless, the fact that minority rights are a component part of the broader human rights framework does not imply that minority rights are necessarily the same as general human rights. Still, the fact that it was felt necessary to add Article 27 to the International Covenant on Civil and Political Rights arguably means that the rights for persons belonging to minorities were considered to go beyond the other, general human rights in the sense that otherwise Article 27 would be redundant. In addition to this redundancy argument, it can also be pointed out that minority rights should be considered as one of several sets of category specific human rights for persons belonging to especially vulnerable groups. Other well-known examples of this type of 'specific' rights can be found in the Convention on the Rights of the Child,[30] the various instruments on rights of migrant workers, of incarcerated persons, and the disabled. Because of their vulnerable position, these persons need 'special' rights in order to obtain substantively equal levels of protection of their human dignity (the founding principle of human rights).

III   Special Rights for Minorities

Nowadays there is no doubt that the need for protection of minorities under internal and international law has perhaps never been as urgent as in our time. At the same time, these problems are highly complex and affect almost all spheres of the economy and society. Moreover, their explanation and solution are tasks for several branches of science, with an essential yet by no means exclusive role reserved for law and jurisprudence.[31]

It is a fact that law takes a two-way approach to addressing the minority question. First, regulation of minority status by internal laws of the States, as a

---

29   Weller, M., *The Rights of Minorities: A Commentary on the European Framework Convention for the Protection of National Minorities* (Oxford University Press, New York, 2005), pp. 86–87.

30   The Convention on the Rights of the Child (CRC) was adopted and opened for signature, ratification and accession by General Assembly Resolution 44/25 of 20 November 1989, and entered into force 2 September 1990.

31   CSCE Human Rights Seminar on Case Studies on National Minorities Issues: Positive Result, Warsaw, 1993.

whole; the second is regulation by public international law. This duality stems from the wide variety of circumstances that can arise, since minority status is apt to present problems not only within the State, but also between States. Internal law governs relations between the State and its citizens, between the State and individuals, or, under a more recent concept, between the State and not only individuals but also minority groups within the State by regulating the legal relationship of individuals belonging to a given minority, or a given minority group, to the majority of society. By contrast, international law has traditionally laid down, in various legal forms, legal norms for the conduct of States *inter se* in relation to their respective minorities.[32]

The protection of minorities under international law is a relatively new domain, and its origins, particularly certain mutual relations of the legal status of persons temporarily staying in other countries (that is aliens), can be traced back to agreements between ancient States. The treaties which were concluded to protect religious minorities and which produced such effect are of a later date and can be seen as direct antecedents of modern international minority law.[33]

However, special rights are not privileges but they are granted to make it possible for minorities to preserve their identity, characteristics and traditions. Special rights are just as important in achieving equality of treatment as non-discrimination. Only when minorities are able to use their own languages, benefit from services they have themselves organized, as well as take part in the political and economic life of States can they begin to achieve the status which majorities take for granted. Differences in the treatment of such groups, or individuals belonging to them, are justified if they promote effective equality and the welfare of the community as a whole.[34] This form of affirmative action may have to be sustained over a prolonged period in order to enable minority groups to benefit from society on an equal footing with the majority.

Finally, without doubt allowing for minority rights within the domain of human rights and comparing them, mainly, as we can see, is that minority

---

32   Glazer, N., *Ethnic Dilemmas 1964–1982: The Universalization of Ethnicity* (Harvard University Press, Cambridge, Mass., 1983), p. 249; Baka, A.B., "The Convention and the Protection of Minorities under International Law", in MacDonald, R.St.J. *et al.* (eds.), *The European System for the Protection of Human Rights* (Martinus Nijhoff Publishers, Dordrecht, 1993), pp. 875–876.

33   Rules of similar content are to be found mainly in the provisions of the 1555 Augsburg Peace of Religion, the Peace of Westphalia at the end of the Thirty Years' War, the Congress of Vienna and the 1878 Congress of Berlin. See *ibid.*, p. 877; Gotlieb, A., *Human Rights, Federalism and Minorities* (Canadian Institute of International Affairs, 1970), pp. 180–185.

34   United Nations Document E/CN.4/52, Section v.

rights have some specific characteristics. First, these rights are characterized by a much closer relationship to politics within as well as between States. The existence of notable minority groups, their relationship to political power, and their legal status and frame of mind are essential factors of stability and a well-settled pattern of relations and legal certainty within States. Obviously, this is the case generally in Central and Eastern Europe today and a fact which all pluralistic democracies should keep in mind.[35] Furthermore, the political sensitivity and motivation of minority rights and the political consequences of their violation call for delimitation, to the extent possible, of the legal and political aspects in this field.[36] Secondly, the specificity of minority rights imposes the considerable difficulty of defining the subjects protected by the laws involved.[37] Thus the questions to be solved concern the applicability of the law to a more or less vague range of subjects by law and the extent of minority rights, particularly when the goal is to reduce the disadvantages facing minorities.[38] At last, another fundamental specificity of minority rights concerns individual and collective rights, the question which was largely neglected by previous arrangements for protection of minorities under international law. Despite the fact that there is a plethora of literature on the collective rights of minorities and the rights of groups, this field of regulation is almost completely absent from international legislation. Likewise, the internal positive law of individual countries has produced little that is worth mentioning in this respect, which means that the nature of these rights is still largely unclarified.[39] Thus, it is obvious that the right of a minority group to preserve its language, religion and other essential characteristics of its minority status cannot be conceived except when, and only when, this group right has consequences closely related to the individual sphere and to individual rights.

---

35 Beer, W.R., *The Unexpected Rebellion: Ethnic Activism in Contemporary France* (New York University Press, 1980), p. xxvii.

36 Obviously enough, the constant monitoring of the actual situation of minorities, political coordination between States and quest for political solutions for disputed minority issues should be assigned, so far as possible, to organs other than those deciding concrete legal disputes on the basis of future international legislation.

37 The lack of minority definition entails unprecedented legal consequences because, while in other provinces it is possible to determine clearly the range of persons to whom the legal norms are applicable, in the case of minorities the minority group, and hence the membership of a minority, cannot be defined in exact terms.

38 Laponce, J.A., *The Protection of Minorities* (University of California Press, Berkeley, 1960), pp. 3–15.

39 Duke, V., "Human Rights and the Rights of Groups", 18 *American Journal of Political Science*, 1974, pp. 725–741.

Indeed, a group right can only be enjoyed if an individual belonging to the given minority may exercise, among other things, the individual right to acquire knowledge in his native language and to use it in different forms. Due to their direct relationship to individual rights, this group of collective rights can ultimately be guaranteed even by court action.[40]

IV   Conclusion

The right not to be discriminated against is paramount in protecting the rights of persons belonging to minorities in all regions of the world. Minorities everywhere experience direct and indirect, *de jure* and *de facto* discrimination in their daily lives.

Non-discrimination and equality before the law are two of the basic principles of international human rights law. The principle of non-discrimination prohibits any distinction, exclusion, restriction or preference which has the purpose or effect of impairing or nullifying the recognition, enjoyment or exercise by all persons, on an equal footing, of all rights and freedoms.[41] There is no requirement to demonstrate discriminatory intent. The phrase 'purpose or effect' refers to legislation and/or policies which may be textually neutral but are interpreted in a manner that results in discrimination. International human rights law prohibits both direct and indirect discrimination.[42]

In its General Recommendation No. 32 (2009), the Committee on the Elimination of Racial Discrimination provided further guidance on the scope of the principle of non-discrimination under Article 1(1) of the Convention

---

40 Today, therefore, effective international protection of collective minority rights by traditional means can in practice be imagined in the same sphere which is also capable of being influenced by means of protection of individual human rights. *Ibid.*, pp. 879–882.

41 See International Convention on the Elimination of All Forms of Racial Discrimination, Article 1(1).

42 Indirect discrimination is more subtle and, therefore, harder to recognize and eliminate. It occurs when a practice, rule or requirement is neutral on its face but has a disproportionate impact on particular groups, unless the practice, rule or requirement is necessary and appropriate to achieve a legitimate objective. Focusing on the unequal impact of a measure on an individual as a member of a group helps better to identify the root causes of discrimination and inequality. Differential treatment may be permissible if its objective is to overcome past discrimination or address persisting inequalities. In fact, international human rights law provides for the adoption of special measures in favour of certain persons or groups for the purpose of eliminating discrimination and achieving full equality, not only in law but also in practice. See *ibid.*, Article 1(4), and also Article 2(2).

and, more importantly, on the meaning of 'special measures'. The Committee specified that "the list of human rights to which the principle applies under the Convention is not closed and extends to any field of human rights regulated by the public authorities in the State party...to address racial discrimination 'by any persons, group or organization'."[43]

It is important to note that the Committee, in its general recommendation, also specified that

> special measures should not be confused with specific rights pertaining to certain categories of person or community, such as, for example the rights of persons belonging to minorities to enjoy their own culture, profess and practice their own religion and use their own language... Such rights are permanent rights, recognized as such in human rights instruments, including those adopted in the context of the United Nations and its agencies. States parties should carefully observe distinctions between special measures and permanent human rights in their law and practice. The distinction between special measures and permanent rights implies that those entitled to permanent rights may also enjoy the benefits of special measures.[44]

Moreover, the Committee on Economic, Social and Cultural Rights adopted General Comment No. 21 (2009) on the right of everyone to take part in cultural life, which entails an obligation on States parties to recognize, respect and protect minority cultures as an essential component of the identity of the States themselves.[45]

---

43   See *ibid.*, Article 2(1)(d) and (b). Regarding 'special measures' to advance equality, the Committee asserted that the term also includes measures that in some countries may be described as 'affirmative measures', 'affirmative action' or 'positive action', whereas the term 'positive discrimination' is, in the context of international human rights standards, a *contradictio in terminis* and should be avoided.

44   See also Committee on the Elimination of Discrimination against Women, General Recommendation No. 25 (2004), para. 19, and Recommendations of the Forum on Minority Issues (UN Doc. A/HRC/10/11/Add. 1, para. 12).

45   See E/CN.4/Sub.2/AC.5/2005/2, para. 53. Also, more recently, the Committee on Economic, Social and Cultural Rights adopted General Comment No. 20 (2009), which provides guidance on the obligation of States parties to guarantee non-discrimination in the exercise of each of the economic, social and cultural rights enshrined in the Covenant. It spells out various distinctions in the manifestation of discrimination. It clarifies how formal and substantive discrimination, direct and indirect forms of differential treatment, and discrimination in the private and public spheres can amount to a violation of Article 2(2) of the Covenant.

The need to ensure that minorities are treated equally and enjoy human rights and fundamental freedoms without discrimination of any kind was reiterated by the Durban Review Conference, which in its Outcome Document "urges States to bolster measures to eliminate the barriers and to broaden access to opportunities for greater and more meaningful participation by...persons belonging to national or ethnic, religious and linguistic minorities in the political, economic, social and cultural spheres of society."[46]

There is also evidence that much remains to be done. Many minorities are subject to serious and persistent violations of their basic rights. Long experience has shown that neither oppression – applied in defiance of international law – nor neglect of minority problems provides a sound basis for relations between groups. Enforced or involuntary assimilation has sometimes been attempted, but it has often failed. Although minority problems may change over time, there is no reason to believe that the groups concerned, or their claims, will disappear unless positive action is taken. Unresolved situations and conflicts involving minorities indicate that further measures to address minority issues need to be adopted and new avenues of conflict resolution need to be sought. The effective implementation of the non-discrimination provisions and special rights, as well as of the resolutions and recommendations of the various organs and bodies of the United Nations can contribute to meeting the aspirations of minorities and to the peaceful accommodation of different groups within a State. Tolerance, mutual understanding and pluralism should be nurtured and fostered through human rights education, confidence-building measures and dialogue. Persons belonging to minorities, rather than being considered adversaries, should be allowed to contribute to the multi-cultural enrichment of our societies and be involved as partners in development. This is an essential condition for greater stability and peace within and across State borders.

---

46 Geneva, 20–24 April, 2009. The following United Nations Resolutions were instrumental in establishing the Durban Review Conference and its preparatory process: General Assembly Resolutions relevant to the Durban Review Process: A/RES/61/149, A/RES/62/220, A/RES/62/143; and Human Rights Council Resolutions: Resolution 3/2, and Resolution 6/23.

CHAPTER 22

Precarious Times, Precarious Work: Lessons from Flexicurity

Nada Bodiroga-Vukobrat*, Ana Pošćić** and Adrijana Martinović***

...flexibility for outsiders, security for insiders...
OLAF VAN VLIET and HENK NIJBOER

***

I   Introduction

The EU stands at the crossroads as the prospects for the economic future of Eurozone shift from euphoric to depressing, literally by the hour. The decisions made with the aim of economic and financial stabilization will certainly influence national labour and social law regimes, particularly in the Eurozone. The question is: how dramatically will the national labour laws and market have to change, in order to adapt to the unstable circumstances? Does this imply a reinvigorated expansion of flexible, atypical labour relations which could ultimately result in precariousness?

The intention of this paper is to re-think the concept of the precariousness of labour relations, which is rising in times of uncertainty, and to examine whether a potential answer to this challenge lies in flexicurity or, on the other hand, whether flexicurity creates an even bigger gap between insiders and outsiders in the labour market.

Do new, atypical forms of employment relationships lead to precarious work? This question is not new, but it becomes current in times of crisis and recession. As the boundaries between 'atypical' and 'standard' become more and more blurred, this question deserves an interdisciplinary approach and out-of-the-box thinking. The 'Golden Age' of what the sociologists refer to as

---

*   PhD; Professor of European Public Law, Jean Monnet Chair of European Public Law, Faculty of Law, University of Rijeka, Croatia.
**   PhD; Assistant Professor, Jean Monnet Chair of European Public Law, Faculty of Law, University of Rijeka, Croatia.
***   PhD; Research Assistant, Jean Monnet Chair of European Public Law, Faculty of Law, University of Rijeka, Croatia.

'Fordist' employment[1] has long been replaced by liberalization and flexibility of 'unleashed' capitalism.[2] Standard employment in the sense of regular, steady, protected jobs is losing ground to atypical working arrangements, either by choice or by necessity. We may even speak of the 'erosion' of the employment relationship. If 'atypical' is understood as flexible or, in other words, adaptable to the changing circumstances in the labour market, can we also make security more flexible and adaptable without endangering its very essence? The idea behind flexicurity is to protect employment, not job security. In its purest theoretical meaning, there should be no 'trade-off' between flexibility and security. Implementation of this concept in practice, especially in countries with weak economies and fragile labour markets, seems, however, far from its theoretical foundations and tends to favour flexibility. This paper argues that taking the security part out of the equation leaves us only with precariousness.

II   Precarious Times, Precarious Work

There are numerous definitions of precarious work. Contingent, atypical and non-standard work[3] are sometimes used as synonyms. Nevertheless, atypical does not automatically mean precarious. Atypical is more easily defined by what it is not than by what it is.[4] It may include various forms, such as temporary or part-time employment, agency work, casual work, moonlighting, disguised self-employment, illegal work, homeworking, *etc.* Part-time employment, for example, may be a deliberate choice of the worker in order to preserve her/his work-life balance. Precariousness, on the other hand, is multidimensional and heterogeneous, as it involves a mixture of instability, lack of protection, insecurity and social and economic vulnerability.[5] The term that best describes precarious employment is insecurity, both objective and subjective.

---

1   On the period of steady economic growth between WWII and the mid-1970s see further, *e.g.* Streeck, Wolfgang (2009): "Flexible Employment, Flexible Families and the Socialization of Reproduction", *MPIfG Working Paper* 09/13, 16.
2   Glyn, Andrew (2006): *Capitalism Unleashed: Finance Globalization and Welfare*, Oxford University Press.
3   International Labour Organisation, Bureau for Workers' Activities (ACTRAV) (2011): *Policies and Regulations to Combat Precarious Employment*, 5.
4   Rodgers, Gerry; Rodgers, Janine (eds.) (1989): *Precarious jobs in labour market regulation. The growth of atypical employment in Western Europe*, International Labour Organisation, 3.
5   *Ibid.*, 3.

Although there is no agreed definition of precarious work, it is usually associated with temporary employment, fixed-term contracts and agency work. However, there are no clearly developed indicators of precariousness and the majority of definitions tend to be 'one-sided', constructed in terms of 'blaming' the employers for precariousness.[6] It is not surprising, then, that the International Labour Organization's (ILO) intention to adopt a Convention and a Recommendation on dependent workers in the second half of the 1990s ended even before any serious work started, because of employers' disapproval.[7] It seems as though precariousness exists only in the language of trade unions and other workers' interest groups, not employers.[8] In any case, we agree that a simple dichotomy between secure, regular jobs and precarious, atypical jobs may be misleading.[9]

To claim that precariousness is a logical consequence of flexible labour markets is only partially correct. Elements of precarious working conditions, such as no control over working conditions, existed even in the most rigid labour markets in the former socialist countries *i.e.* centrally planned economies. However it is true that a combination of previously mentioned elements which identify certain work as precarious are usually associated with atypical employment which, by its very nature, makes the labour markets more flexible and adaptable to changing socio-economic circumstances. Precarious employment, thus, may be viewed "as much a consequence of increased competition as it is a powerful driver of increased competition".[10] It is claimed

---

6   ACTRAV (2011), *op. cit.*, 7.
7   *Ibid.*, 1.
8   There are numerous definitions of precarious work developed by trade unions or their associations, which describe precarious work in a narrower or broader sense. For example, the International Metalworkers' Federation (IMF) proposes the following definition: "precarious work is the result of employment practices by employers designed to limit or reduce their permanent workforce to a minimum, to maximize their flexibility and to shift risks onto workers. The resulting jobs typically are non-permanent, temporary, casual, insecure and contingent. Workers in such jobs often are not covered by labour law and social security protections". The European Metalworkers' Federation (EMF) uses the term in a broader sense: "Precarious work is a term used to describe non-standard employment which is poorly paid, insecure, unprotected, and cannot support a household". Public Services International (PSI) holds that "precarious work is characterized by uncertainty and insecurity through the use of stand-by, temporary, employment-agency, casual, part-time, and seasonal contracts, pseudo self-employment, and no direct or an unclear employer/employee relationship". See further in ACTRAV (2011), *op. cit.*, 6.
9   Rodgers/Rodgers (1989), *op. cit.*, 5.
10 ACTRAV (2011), *op. cit.*, 18. "The making of the 'precariat' is a multilevel process. It is an interaction between abuse of economic power, economic liberalization, global capital

that deregulation and flexibilization of the labour market in the neo-liberal fashion leads to 'precariat' as the inevitable consequence of globalization.[11] The state, however, still retains a crucial role in making political and legislative choices: it is not only about deregulation in the sense of making job termination easier, it is about deciding about the level of protection accorded to 'precarious' and 'standard' workers.

1 Is Flexicurity a 'Cure' for Precariousness?

Every so often, the flexicurity topic comes back on the EU agenda. Despite the indolence of the Member States in conceptualizing it as such at the national level, it stubbornly keeps 'popping up' in various strategic and policy documents and publications at EU level.[12] It seems as though the Commission's eagerness to promote it competes with the Member States' tendency to, more or less, ignore it.

Is the fascination with flexicurity justified? Ever since the term was coined in the mid-1990s,[13] it has captured wide public interest, especially after the EU turned it from 2000 onwards into one of the key elements underpinning the strategy and perspective of the development of European labour law. The success of various models based on the idea of flexicurity in Denmark and the Netherlands turned it into a 'political celebrity'.[14] But what is its real impact and why is it still controversial?

Let us not forget that, as Streeck rightly observed, the reform which captured many national labour markets in the 1990s was generally not intended

---

mobility, fierce lobbying against protective labour laws, and a whole range of state policies guided by economic thinking that believes in the efficiency of free markets. It is this interconnectedness that creates the impression of inevitability, where each single measure looks like an adaptation and reaction to forces deemed beyond control of any actor."

11   ACTRAV (2011), *op. cit.*, 20.

12   Most recently, Eurofound has issued the publication "The second phase of flexicurity: an analysis of practices and policies in the Member States" (March 2012) as part of the resource pack on *Flexicurity – It takes three to tango*, available online at: <www.eurofound.europa.eu/resourcepacks/flexicurity.htm>.

13   Its proliferation is usually ascribed to Ad Melkert, the Dutch Minister of Social Affairs. See further in Bodiroga-Vukobrat, Nada; Barić, Sanja; Martinović, Adrijana (2010): "Reflexive Deliberative Polyarchy, Soft Law and OMC – Do All Pathways Lead to Flexicurity?", in Bodiroga-Vukobrat, Nada; Sander, Gerald G.; Barić, Sanja (eds.), *Die Offene Methode der Koordinierung in der Europäischen Union/Open Methods of Coordination in the European Union*, Verlag Dr. Kovač, 174.

14   Jørgensen, Henning; Madsen, Per Kongshøj (eds.) (2007): *Flexicurity and Beyond. Finding a New Agenda for the European Social Model*, Djøf Publishing Copenhagen.

to increase public spending on social security as it did not imply a general shift from old to new forms of employment security, but rather an "expansion of 'precarious', 'atypical', non-standard employment on the fringes of national labour market regimes".[15] According to Deakin and Rogowski, technological and organizational advances meant that the "paradigmatic institutions of the welfare state" (such as collective bargaining, social insurance *etc.*), which presuppose stable or permanent employment, covered and protected only a minority of workers,[16] *i.e.* 'insiders'.

It is then no surprise that flexicurity coincides with the shift of paradigms and normative reforms. Theoretically, flexicurity is a balancing exercise: it involves a combination of the employers' need for flexibility and the employees' need for security. It is about transition from job to employment security. It is usually defined as an integrated strategy consisting of four equally important components: flexible and reliable contractual arrangements, comprehensive lifelong learning strategies, effective labour market policies and modern, adequate and sustainable social protection systems.[17]

At the EU level, it is supposed to come to life through the open method of coordination (OMC), again, another concept which might seem cryptic to anyone outside limited academic and professional circles. It is (mostly) a cognitive and a mutual learning process, part of a wider 'reflexive' approach to law and governance, which some authors claim has contributed to re-legitimation of European and national labour law.[18]

When a legal scholar ventures into these subjects, he/she risks being criticized by both his/her colleagues and other scholars, who might consider them as their 'domain'. Legal scholars' first reaction might be; what is legal about it or where is 'law' in all of that? Sociologists or political scientists might claim that this is a question of policy- and decision-making, and as such better suited to methodologies devised in these particular fields of study. Indeed, a simple search reveals that the majority of scientific papers on this issue are written by non-legal scholars.[19] The intention of this paper is not to add fuel to the fire,

---

15   Streeck, "Flexible Employment, Flexible Families, and the Socialization of Reproduction", *MPIfG Working Paper* 09/13, 11.
16   Deakin, Simon; Rogowski, Ralf (2011): "Reflexive Labour Law, Capabilities and the Future of Social Europe", *University of Warwick School of Law, Legal Studies Research Paper No. 2011-04*, <http://ssrn.com/abstract=1780922>, 18.
17   See Council conclusions (2007): Toward common principles of flexicurity, Doc 16201/07, SOC 523 of 6 December 2007.
18   See further on this issue Deakin/Rogowski (2011), *op. cit.*
19   The majority of papers retrieved under the search term 'flexicurity' in the SSRN (Social Science Research Network) eLibrary Database are written by economists (37 authors),

but to transcend disciplinary boundaries in order to gain a wider and clearer picture and understanding of the manifold and complex issues surrounding these topics.

This contribution will attempt to reveal the current trends in Croatian labour regulations in the face of flexibilization pressures and rising precariousness. How will the experiences of other EU Member States shape the process of modernization of Croatian labour laws? There is a discrepancy between theoretical models and Croatian normative solutions.

III A Brief Overview of the Croatian Labour Laws and Policy

1 *The Early Days: Transformation, Globalization, Flexibilization Combined*

Croatia is no stranger to having its national policies and institutional choices shaped by external actors, through conditional financial assistance and/or more or less sophisticated means of convergence with the views of the 'helper' (technical assistance, advisory role, *etc.*).

The influence of international organizations in the reorganization of the social security systems in Croatia in the early years of its independence was implemented through various loan facilities and technical assistance. These conditional loans (dependent on the reform of social policies in the case of the World Bank or economic policy with political and social implications in the case of the International Monetary Fund) largely set the pace and direction of the reforms.[20] The involvement of these agents of neo-liberal economic globalization was practically inevitable, given the fact that the high indebtedness, rising costs and needs of the population left no other alternative but to turn to international funding and support in the transformation process.

Croatia shares the same legacy of socialist labour relations with its neighbouring and other countries of the former Socialist Federal Republic of Yugoslavia (SFRY): Slovenia, Bosnia and Herzegovina, Serbia, Montenegro, and

---

followed by sociologists and political scientists (28 authors). Only 8 authors are legal scholars. The search results for 'open method of coordination' reveal that it has attracted the attention of legal scholars to a somewhat greater extent, with 25 authors having legal background as opposed to 41 authors from non-legal (*i.e.* economic, sociologic, political) disciplines. Data retrieved on 18 June 2012.

20 Bodiroga-Vukobrat, Nada (2002): "Herausforderungen der Globalisierung für die soziale Sicherheit der kleineren Transformationsstaaten", in: 16(1) *Zeitschrift für ausländisches und internationales Arbeits- und Sozialrecht (ZIAS)*, 82–93, 91.

Macedonia. Adaptation to a market economy entailed the flexibilization of the labour market and the reform of social security systems. However, this process ran parallel with the most difficult times in Croatian contemporary history: the Homeland War for independence from 1991 to 1995.

Notwithstanding the socialist inheritance and war sufferings, coupled with privatization which turned out in many cases to be synonymous with blatant plunder, the real challenge was the financing of social security reform. The social security systems exhibited numerous structural weaknesses even prior to the 1990s and were unsustainable. Due to the state's inability to finance reform in those difficult times, the prominent role in the creation of new social security systems was given to the World Bank. For example, the creation and financing of the three-pillar pension system reform, as well as the financing (and the underlying idea behind it) of healthcare reform, is accredited to the World Bank.

All of these tendencies in the early days brought not only requests for the globalization of social security systems or, more accurately, 'adaptation' to the market oriented, privatized social security systems, but also the trend towards flexibilization and softening of the existing regulations.

The underlying question behind these initial reforms was what kind of system should replace the old socialist model: the American paradigm of individual social policy or the European-style social market economy-based social policy?[21] The resulting reforms and structural adjustments produced a peculiar combination of various elements in the European tradition of welfare states. However, financing of the social security systems remained inefficient and dependent on budgetary allocations to cover the shortages. The paradox lies in the fact that at 37.2% of gross salary, social security contributions are among the highest in Europe.[22]

2   Labour Law Transformation: A Tough(er) Nut to Crack

While the social protection systems were shaped in accordance with international influences, the field of labour law, on the other hand, proved more resistant to external influence. Until the amendments to the Labour Act which entered into force in 2004, Croatia had one of the most rigid employment protection legislation schemes, especially regarding notice periods, severance pay

---

21   Bodiroga-Vukobrat, Nada (2000): "Landesbericht Republik Kroatien", in: *Schriftenreihe für Internationales und Vergleichendes Sozialrecht*, Band 16, 177–192, 177.

22   Nestić, Danijel (ed.) (2011): *Izazovi i mogućnosti za ostvarenje primjerenih starosnih mirovina u Hrvatskoj*, Ekonomski institut Zagreb, <http://www.eizg.hr/Download.ashx?FileID=7d4509d2-866d-47b7-8214-a2cbf38ff8b9>, 22.

and the protection of employees in the civil sector.[23] The legislative reform in 2009 brought further changes regarding working time and flexible working arrangements, with limited deregulatory impact. The problem is, though, that the rigid employment protection legislation (EPL) did not translate into the employees' sense of security. The transition process included the shift from the socialist comprehension of the labour relationship as a legal status, to a market-based understanding of employment as a contractual relationship. This has also meant that the individual perception of job security had to be adapted to the changed circumstances.

However, the notion of employment security, which should theoretically imply regular and (if need be) assisted transition from one job to another, has never really achieved its potential in Croatia. Instead, it seems that insecurity (of jobs, employment, wages, *etc.*) is the only constant feature of the Croatian labour market. In that sense, even 'standard' jobs appear precarious, as employees work without being paid for months or lose their jobs practically overnight due to the employer's insolvency.[24] Job destruction was not compensated for by job creation, even in times of relative prosperity. Following a sharp contraction of the Gross Domestic Product (GDP) in the early period of transition to a market economy, steady growth was recorded in the pre-crisis period of 2000–07.[25] Despite the modest employment growth in that period, Croatia's employment level remained among the lowest of the EU-27 countries (it dropped from around 63% in the period from 2006–2010 to 55.4% in 2012).[26] The reasons for insufficient job creation lie partly in the skills mismatch in labour supply and demand.[27] Low activity rates are particularly pronounced for vulnerable groups: women, youths and older workers (50–64). Since 2008, the unemployment rate has almost doubled.[28]

---

23 Bilić, Andrijana (2011): *Fleksibilnost i deregulacija u radnim odnosima*, doctoral dissertation, Pravni fakultet Sveučilišta u Splitu, 263.

24 There are no official records, but it is estimated that approximately 80,000 employees are not receiving a regular salary (delayed or only partial payments). See, *e.g.* <http://www.vecernji.hr/vijesti/sto-tisuca-hrvata-radi-bez-place-clanak-393539>.

25 Gotovac, Viktor (2011): *Supporting Strategies to Recover from the Crisis in South Eastern Europe, Country Assessment Report: Republic of Croatia*, International Labour Organisation, Global Jobs Pact, 13.

26 European Commission (2013): Commission Staff Working Document. Assessment of the 2013 Economic Programme for Croatia, Brussels, SWD(2013) 361.

27 Bejaković, Predrag; Gotovac, Viktor (2011): "Aktivnosti na gospodarskom oporavku u Republici Hrvatskoj s naglaskom na tržište rada", in: 18(3) *Revija za socijalnu politiku (RSP)*, 331–355, 340.

28 From 8.6% in 2008 to 15.9% in 2012. See European Commission Staff Working Document (2013): Assessment of the 2013 Economic Programme for Croatia, Brussels, SWD(2013) 361.

Thus, the Croatian labour market is highly segmented, relatively underdeveloped and characterized by low mobility of the workforce.[29] The relatively inflexible formal component includes stable labour relations (mainly in the public sector), while the informal but flexible component combines both legal and illegal (shadow or grey economy), but unregistered forms of work.[30] The first reform of 2004 produced a hybrid situation,[31] with numerous inconsistencies between the normative intention and practical impact of legislative solutions. For instance, not all forms of work could be considered as employment (*e.g.* civil law contracts) and therefore awarded protection under the Labour Act. The definition of unemployed person in the Act on Employment Mediation and Unemployment Rights[32] is much wider, in that it covers practically all situations when a person is without work. The Labour Act, on the other hand, does not treat persons working under a works contract, a student's work contract or copyright agreement (*i.e.* civil law contract arrangements) as employed persons within the meaning of that Act, even though mandatory contributions are paid on those types of work as well. Relaxation of the rules concerning part-time work, dismissals and severance pay was limited by other legislative acts. For example, the amount of severance pay was nominally reduced from one-half to one-third of the average monthly salary received in the three months prior to the termination of the labour contract. The aggregate amount of severance pay was limited to six average monthly salary instalments (there was no limit prior to the amendments). However, as opposed to the previous calculation on the basis of net salary, under the amendments of 2004 salary was defined as gross salary, meaning that the actual costs of contract termination were not really relaxed (if at all). The qualification period for severance pay is two years of continuous employment by the same employer, which is relatively short, considering that the length of tenure in Croatia is traditionally over 10 years.[33]

The second reform in 2009 entailed the adoption of the completely new Labour Act,[34] which entered into force on 1 January 2010. It brings the labour

---

29 Bilić (2011), *op. cit.*, 256.
30 *Loc. cit.*
31 Crnković-Pozaić, Sanja (2007) in: Cazes, Sandrine; Nesporova, Alena (eds.) (2007): *Fleksigurnost, relevantan pristup za srednju i istočnu Europu*, TIM Press, 120.
32 Official Gazette of the Republic of Croatia *Narodne novine* 32/02, 80/08.
33 Compared to other transition countries and developed economies, the length of tenure in Croatia is high: more than a quarter of all workers in Croatia have held the same jobs for more than 20 years and another fifth between 10 and 20 years. See Gotovac (2011), *op. cit.*, 28.
34 Official Gazette of the Republic of Croatia *Narodne novine* 149/09. The new Labour Act was amended in 2011. Official Gazette of the Republic of Croatia *Narodne novine* 61/11.

legislation in line with the EU *acquis* regarding working time, rescheduling of working hours, temporary work, part-time work, night work, paid annual leave, parental leave, collective dismissals *etc*. The duration of a temporary, fixed-term employment contract is limited to three years, regardless of whether it is concluded for identical or similar work (by linking this limitation only to the same employee, *i.e.* omitting the previous express reference to identical work). The latest amendments, proposed in May 2013 (at the moment of submission of this paper in the process of adoption), attempt to bring further flexibilization of fixed-term contracts and agency work.[35] On the other hand, even with the flexibilization of the working time arrangements, the share of persons working part-time has only slightly increased: from 9.0% in 2009 to 9.7% in 2010.[36]

From this brief overview of labour legislation it is apparent that Croatia is still searching for a workable solution, one which would ensure competitiveness but also guarantee appropriate protection and dignity of employees. The economic reality and external and internal economic actors are putting more and more pressure on additional flexibilization of working arrangements. However, 20 years after the transition to a market-based economy, there is no strategy which could take advantage of previous experiences and combine them with the contemporary challenges. In a rush to run as far as possible from the socialist heritage and into the 'free world' of entrepreneurship and undistorted competition, it seems that we have gambled away all values and lessons learned in the era of collective self-management (*i.e.* solidarity, partnership, co-decision, *etc.*), which are indispensable for the creation of individual security and protection. Can the reconciliation between the requirement of work productivity and competitiveness, on the one hand, and social cohesion and existential security, on the other, in the times of globalization, technical progress and individualization be found in flexicurity?[37]

---

35   Draft Act on Amendments to the Labour Act, P.Z.E. 375, <http://www.sabor.hr/Default.aspx?art=54721>.

36   This is mostly due to underdeveloped labour market. See Republic of Croatia (2011): Report on the Implementation of the Joint Assessment of the Employment Policy Priorities of the Republic of Croatia for 2010, 12–13. In his analysis of flexicurity of labour relations in Croatia, Potočnjak is rather critical of the existing normative framework regarding working time arrangements and agency work as still too rigid and inflexible, and only formally aligned with the policies and legislation of the EU. Potočnjak, Željko (2013): "Fleksigurnost radnih odnosa u Hrvatskoj i pravna stečevina Europske unije", in: *Zbornik Susreta pravnika Opatija 2013*, 283–326.

37   Puljiz, Vlado (2008): "Prikaz knjige: Cazes, Sandrine; Nesporova, Alena (eds.) (2007): Fleksigurnost, relevantan pristup za srednju i istočnu Europu", in: 15(1) *RSP*, 101–111, 109.

IV   What Can We Learn from the EU?

If we turn to the EU experiences, it is evident that in defining and implementing its labour policy, Croatia shares the same problems with many of the EU Member States: ageing population, increased unemployment, a fall in employment levels, high youth unemployment, skills mismatch, segmentation of labour market, a high tax wedge on labour *etc.*[38] However, the risk of one-size-fits-all and silver bullet solutions should be avoided.

What is the impact of EU policies on the flexibility-security discourse in the Croatian labour market? At the EU level, flexicurity figures as the basis for EU employment policy,[39] pursued through the open method of coordination process which was initiated with the European Employment Strategy.[40] Essentially, it entails horizontal adaptation: not just in the meaning of output or performance, but also the *process* of convergence of national policies *itself*. It is directed towards improving the functioning of labour markets. The definition of flexicurity as a *"deliberate combination of flexible and reliable contractual arrangements, comprehensive lifelong learning strategies, effective labour market policies, and modern, adequate and sustainable social protection systems"*[41] highlights the importance of all of its components.

However, the concept of flexicurity is so fluid that it cannot be moulded, wrapped and sold as a finished product. The key lies in the combination of ingredients, which have to be finely tuned to the specific circumstances of each individual national labour market. Researching and 'measuring' of the impact

---

38   European Commission (2013): Communication from the Commission to the European Parliament, the Council, the European Economic and Social Committee and the Committee of the Regions, 2013 European Semester: Country-specific recommendations. Moving Europe beyond the crisis, COM(2013) 350 final; Communication from the Commission (2011): Concluding the first European semester of economic policy coordination: Guidance for national policies in 2011–2012, COM(2011) 400 final, 6–7.

39   See, *e.g.*, European Commission (2006): Green Paper Modernising Labour Law to Meet Challenges of the 21st Century, COM(2006) 708 final; Communication from the Commission (2007): Towards Common Principles of Flexicurity: More and better jobs through flexibility and security, COM(2007) 359 final; Council conclusions (2007): Toward common principles of flexicurity, Doc 16201/07, SOC 523 of 6 December 2007; Council conclusions on flexicurity in times of crisis (2009) of 8 June 2009; Communication from the Commission (2011): An Agenda for new skills and jobs: A European contribution towards full employment, COM(2010) 682 final.

40   The European Employment Strategy (EES) was launched at the Luxembourg European Council of 20–21 November 1997, also known as the 'Jobs Summit' against a background of high levels of unemployment.

41   Council conclusions (2007)..., Doc 16201/07.

of flexicurity is extremely difficult, partly because the methodology and indicators are still underdeveloped,[42] partly because of the low visibility of flexicurity measures and policies: there are no 'flexicurity' strategies; measures and policies are almost never labelled as such; and cross-comparison is virtually impossible.[43] Moreover, flexicurity, at best, is designed for times of relative economic stability and prosperity. It is about transition from job to employment security and more concentrated on the supply side of the labour market. When jobs are abundant, the spans of unemployment are relatively short and the policies designed to ease the transition from job to job can be effective. In times of economic crisis, the concept of flexicurity and its contribution towards the achievement of a freshly coined notion of 'job-rich recovery' is currently under review.[44] Thus, flexicurity expands into economic policy. For example, the key action priorities for 2011 and 2012 were making work more attractive, getting the unemployed back to work and balancing security and flexibility.[45] However, in view of persistently growing unemployment, the 2013 Annual Growth Survey admits that there is no prospect of immediate or automatic improvement in the employment situation and puts emphasis again on flexible work arrangements, simplified dismissal procedures, flexible wage setting with a view to job rich recovery.[46] The 2012 Employment Package,[47] accompanied by 9 staff

---

42   The project carried out by the Joint Research Centre (Unit G09 – Econometrics and Applied Statistics) and DG Employment (Unit D1 – Employment Analysis) of the European Commission claims to be "the richest and most comprehensive attempt to measure flexicurity in Europe available in the literature". A set of composite indicators, corresponding to the four dimensions of flexicurity, was constructed to measure flexicurity achievements of EU Member States. The results are published in Manca/Governatori/Mascherini (2010): *Towards a Set of Composite Indicators on Flexicurity: A Comprehensive Approach*, European Commission, Joint Research Centre and Institute for the Protection and Security of the Citizen.

43   In an attempt to provide qualitative approach to flexicurity research, the recent EUROFOUND study lists more than 230 public and social partner-based instruments as tangible flexicurity examples in Member States, noting that the list is not comprehensive. EUROFOUND (2012), The second phase of flexicurity: An analysis of practices and policies in the Member States.

44   Stakeholder Conference on Flexicurity (2011), retrieved on 4 April 2012 at <http://ec.europa.eu/social/main.jsp?langId=en&catId=88&eventsId=356&furtherEvents=yes>.

45   Communication from the Commission (2011): Concluding the first European semester of economic policy coordination: Guidance for national policies in 2011–2012, COM(2011) 400 final.

46   European Commission (2013): Communication from the Commission. Annual Growth Survey 2013, COM(2012) 750 final.

47   European Commission (2012): Towards a job-rich recovery, COM(2012) 173 final.

working documents, already evidently shows that the accent is shifting towards the demand side of the labour market, *i.e.* the creation of jobs and reallocation of labour. In other words, flexicurity is just one piece in the puzzle of employment-intensive growth. The most recent Communication from the Commission on the 2013 European Semester implicitly takes a step away from flexicurity, in that it requires "introducing more internal and external flexibility" in the labour market.[48]

We could agree with Chalmers and Lodge that the Lisbon process, which is the platform for pursuing the flexicurity agenda, *"leads to a transformation of the politics of the Welfare State, whereby it becomes less centred around a discourse of social citizenship and more around economic growth and competitiveness"*.[49] Nevertheless, this is just one more reason why, in the process of mutual learning from others, convergence should not be understood as unconditional compliance with the *instruments* for achieving shared objectives. There is still room for discretion in designing the labour and social security policies and strategies, which will not entail a *"trade-off between competitiveness and social protection"*.[50] The challenge for the government is to devise appropriate procedures for horizontal coordination at the national level.[51]

Evidence from other EU Member States shows that flexicurity policies are hard to implement in times of crisis. Recent Italian labour market reform ("Riforma Fornero", 2012) attempts to implement flexicurity as an answer to economic crisis and the rise of atypical forms of employment (fixed-term and part-time employment).[52] It is widely criticized because it is primarily aimed at the reduction of employment protection at the exit ('easy firing') and fails to devise a satisfactory regulatory model of flexibility within the employment

---

48   European Commission (2013): Communication from the Commission to the European Parliament, the Council, the European Economic and Social Committee and the Committee of the Regions, 2013 European Semester: Country-specific recommendations. Moving Europe beyond the crisis, COM(2013) 350 final.

49   Chalmers, Damian; Lodge, Martin (2003): "The Open Method of Co-ordination and the European Welfare State", *Discussion Paper No. 11*, ESRC Centre for Analysis of Risk and Regulation, 10.

50   Huiskamp, Rien; Vos, Kees J. (2007): "Flexibilization, Modernization and the Lisbon Strategy", in: 23(4) *International Journal of Comparative Labour Law and Industrial Relations*, 587–599, 597.

51   Borrás, Susana; Peters, Guy B. (2011): "The Lisbon Strategy's empowerment of core executives: centralizing and politicizing EU national co-ordination", in: 18(4) *Journal of European Public Policy (JEPP)*, 525–545, 528.

52   Legge n. 92 of 28.6.2012. Disposizioni in materia di riforma del mercato del lavoro in una prospettiva di crescita.

relationship.[53] Slovenia undertook a labour reform in March 2013 to reduce labour market segmentation and increase flexibility by simplifying dismissal procedures and reducing dismissal costs. On the other hand, it brought further restriction of fixed-term contracts and agency work. The reform is a result of a compromise between social partners, but the European Commission already doubts whether it is ambitious enough to address labour market segmentation and flexibility and attract foreign direct investments.[54]

This shows that a specific challenge of implementing flexicurity has to do with the function of labour law in national legal systems.[55] The reform pathways have to resemble national traditions and constitutional values if they are to strengthen the internal coherence of national legal systems.[56] However, flexicurity takes (un)expected turns when it hits volatile labour markets and, as previously stated, tends to be interpreted to fit the needs of the current political decision-makers.

V   The Translation of the Flexicurity Concept to the Particular Croatian Context

1   *Joint Assessment of the Employment Policy Priorities*

The preparation for participation in the process of the open method of coordination started within the Accession Partnership and was developed in two directions: the first concerns employment policy and is based on the Joint Assessment of the Employment Policy Priorities (JAP; the agreement between the Commission and RC was signed in 2008) and the second concerns the field of social inclusion, based on the Joint Memorandum on Social Inclusion (JIM; 2007). Implementation of the priorities agreed in the JAP is monitored on the basis of regular annual reports on the progress achieved by Croatia, and at JAP follow-up conferences including all the relevant stakeholders. Monitoring of

---

53   Carinci, Maria Teresa (2012): "Il rapporto di lavoro al tempo dall crisi: modelli europei e flexicurity 'all'Italiana' a confronto", in: *Giornale di diritto del lavoro e di relazioni industriali* n. 136(4), 527–573. See more on the Italian reform Casale, Giuseppe; Fasani, Mario (2012): "Labour Reform in Italy and its Implications for Labour Administration", *Working Document No. 23*, International Labour Organisation.

54   European Commission (2013): Recommendation for a Council Recommendation on Slovenia's 2013 national reform programme and delivering a Council opinion on Slovenia's stability programme for 2012–2016 (SWD(2013) 374 final), COM(2013) 374 final.

55   Sciarra, Silvana (2008): "Is Flexicurity a European Policy?", *URGE Working Paper 4/2008*, 6.

56   *Loc. cit.* See also Flexicurity Pathways. Turning hurdles into stepping stones, Report by the European Expert Group on Flexicurity (2007) Bruxelles.

the application of both processes was amalgamated in 2010 with a view to streamlining both of these parallel processes.

The main challenges facing the Croatian labour market have been identified and defined in the JAP as follows: low employment rate, long-term unemployment, unemployment of young people, skills mismatch, low employability of vulnerable groups, and regional disparities. These challenges still persist.

The JAP expressly refers to flexicurity as a tool for improving the adaptability of workers and enterprises (a key employment policy priority identified in the revised Lisbon agenda for growth and jobs) and sets the following priorities:

– Define a policy strategy aimed at improving the existing combination of flexibility and security in Croatia's labour market, taking into account the principles and pathways laid down for flexicurity (EC Communication "Towards Common Principles of Flexicurity: More and Better Jobs Through Flexibility and Security" (27.06.2007 Brussels, COM(2007) 359 final)) adopted by the European Council on 5 December 2007.
– Implement particular incentives and measures to increase the participation of adults in training under two components of the flexicurity concept: comprehensive Lifelong Learning strategy and effective active labour market policies.
– Develop and implement policies aimed at improving the chances of workers in temporary jobs of progressing towards obtaining regular contracts.
– Actively involve the social partners in discussions and development of the above policy solutions.[57]

Basically, Croatia is well aware of the stages and requirements of horizontal coordination processes and will be fully prepared to participate in the coordination of policies once it becomes an EU Member State. However, whether it will be able to meet the ambitious objectives with the current employment strategies and policies is a wholly different issue. The question is whether deregulation and yet another amendment of the Labour Act or a coherent flexicurity strategy with the already existing instruments is needed.

2 *Implementation of the JAP Priorities*

It is interesting to observe how the process of implementation of the JAP priorities has evolved. 'Bureaucratization' of the process is evident.[58] In many

---

57 Joint Assessment of the Employment Policy Priorities of the Republic of Croatia (JAP) (2008), 54.
58 As with National Strategy Reports (NSR) on Social Protection and Social Inclusion, which state the developments in each country in relation to the OMC indicators, the

cases, only nominal, sporadic and incidental activities can be reported, which, by themselves, do not actually address the core of the issue, but look nice on paper. For example, the Report on the implementation of JAP for 2010[59] reveals no substantial improvements in achieving either of the above mentioned aims. Only one measure (co-financing employment in shared jobs, particularly for the most vulnerable groups of the unemployed) is reported within the aim of defining a policy strategy for improving the combination of security and flexibility in the labour market. It is obvious that one measure of active labour market policy cannot make a coherent policy strategy. It is admitted that, in view of the growth in unemployment and economic crisis, there is *"no room for any significant changes to the labour and social legislation that would enhance job and employment security"*.[60]

Flexicurity is not about implementing individual measures. Since it implies only a combination of both flexibility and security components, this incidental, but express statement in the report can mean only one thing. The flexicurity agenda, as far as the government is concerned, is on hold.

VI Flexicurity Debate: Is It All about Employment Protection Legislation?

Despite the fact that several studies on flexicurity have appeared in recent years in Croatia,[61] most of them follow the (more or less evident) neo-liberal concept. None of the studies so far has shown how more or less rigid employment protection legislation would contribute (or not) to higher employability prospects or job-rich recovery from the crisis in the particular Croatian circumstances. The 2011 and 2012 World Bank policy documents,[62] unsurprisingly,

---

implementation of JIM/JAP priorities is monitored through regular annual reports. The drafting of the reports is the task of the competent ministries, which means that bureaucratization and technocratization of the process (which is criticized also for the 'real' OMC process) is inevitable. See further, Deakin/Rogowski (2011), *op. cit.*, 13; Zeitlin, Jonathan (2005): "The Open Method of Coordination in Action. Theoretical Promise, Empirical Realities, Reform Strategy" in: Zeitlin, Jonathan; Pochet, Philippe; Magnusson, Lars (eds.), *The Open Method of Coordination in Action: The European Employment and Employment and Social Inclusion Strategies*, P.I.E.-Peter Lang.

59   Republic of Croatia (2011), *op. cit.*
60   *Ibid.*, 78.
61   *Cf.* Cazes; Nesporova (2007), *op. cit.*; Kulušić, Jasminka (2009): *Isplati li se fleksibilnost? Hrvatsko tržište rada*, TIM press, Zagreb; Bilić (2011), *op. cit.*
62   See The World Bank (2012): Croatia Policy Notes. A Strategy for Smart, Sustainable and Inclusive Growth, Report No. 66673; The World Bank (2011): Employment Protection

identify strict employment protection legislation which translates into high labour costs as a major obstacle to job creation and employment growth in comparison to regional competitors.[63] Even though the EPL summary index for all countries of the former SFRY has been dropping since the late 1990s,[64] it is still above the EU average.

However, even in countries where the employment protection legislation is less rigid (*e.g.* Serbia), all former countries of the SFRY (except Slovenia) have much higher unemployment rates (by 10% or even more).[65]

The World Bank's principal 'lesson' for Croatia is to reduce the cost of firing and hiring. This is a blatant example of how the flexicurity idea becomes distorted under the neo-liberal view: the rhetoric describing the proposed actions is that of flexicurity or "moving from protecting jobs to protecting workers",[66] but the actual agenda behind it is the relaxation of legislation or deregulation. Strict employment protection legislation and high labour costs are pinpointed as major obstacles to job creation and employment growth.[67] Although a relaxation of strict employment protection legislation does bring more dynamism to the labour market, it is certainly not a *job creation* measure. Nevertheless, this (mis)perception is quite commonly exploited in Croatia as an argument for deregulation.[68] According to Rutkowski, poor labour market performance in Croatia is due to the slow pace of job creation, which in turn is caused by barriers to entry by new firms and barriers to expansion by existing

---

Legislation and Labour Market Outcomes: Theory, Evidence and Lessons for Croatia. The World Bank's recommendations for Croatia were intended to contribute to the possible labour legislation reform and implementation of the Economic Recovery Programme from 2010. They were prepared at the request of the Croatian Government in May 2011.

63   The World Bank (2012), *op. cit.*, 31–31; The World Bank (2011), *op. cit.*, 12.
64   For a detailed comparison between Croatia, FYR of Macedonia and Serbia see Corbanese, Valli (2011): "Supporting Strategies to Recover from the Crisis in Croatia, the former Yugoslav Republic of Macedonia and Serbia, Cross-Country Report", *ILO Working Paper*, 84.
65   *E.g.* in 2011, registered unemployment in Bosnia and Herzegovina was 25%, in Serbia 22.9%, in Macedonia 31.4%. Available empirical evidence reveals that EPL has no or very limited impact on unemployment. See Bilić (2011), *op. cit.*, 199.
66   The World Bank (2011), *op. cit.*, 4.
67   *Ibid.*, 12.
68   We agree with Vinković that extreme advocacy of very flexible dismissal of workers is not possible in a country with an insufficiently developed system of social protection offered to the unemployed, while at the same time it records a high unemployment rate. See further in: Vinković, Mario (2010): "European Employment Strategy and OMC", in: Bodiroga-Vukobrat, Nada, Sander, Gerald G., Barić, Sanja (eds.): *Open Methods of Coordination in the European Union*, Verlag Dr.Kovač, Hamburg.

firms.[69] Focusing on the latter issue, he finds that strict employment protection legislation and high unit labour costs combined constrain job creation and hiring.[70] Not least caused by the abovementioned, rather euphemistically called 'recommendations' from the World Bank, but also the EU,[71] the Croatian public and political discourse is directed towards achieving external numerical flexibility (mobility through easy firing and hiring), while the security and other aspects are either neglected or viewed as a completely separate issue. In this perspective, the social protection system is seen as the source of low employment, and its further 'relaxation' is demanded.[72] A recent study by Bejaković et al., aptly entitled "Does it pay to work in Croatia?",[73] shows that almost all people (even beneficiaries of welfare services) would benefit from work. However, there are significant negative incentives to work for people on low wages, families receiving a combination of several social benefits and assistance, families with only one employed adult and families with more than one child. This is mostly due to a low income threshold, which offsets the benefits. The security component of flexicurity should be designed to facilitate smooth transitions in the labour market. However, the policies that should accompany more relaxed employment protection legislation were for a long time ineffective and incoherent (i.e. active labour market policies, lifelong learning strategies). The 'nexus' between flexibility and security is thus missing.

VII   Flexicurity: How to Tackle the Challenge?

Simply put, too rigid employment protection legislation is identified as a barrier to increased labour market participation. The overall message coming from the EU is to find a more balanced approach to the protection of those with permanent contracts and those on temporary contracts. However, this

---

69 Rutkowski, Jan (2003): "Does Strict Employment Protection Discourage Job Creation? Evidence from Croatia", *World Bank Policy Research Working Paper 3104*, 56.
70 *Loc. cit.*
71 European Commission (2013): Commission Staff Working Document. Assessment of the 2013 Economic Programme for Croatia, Brussels, SWD(2013) 361.
72 See *e.g.* World Bank (2013): Knowledge Brief Croatia: a Strategy for Smart, Sustainable and Inclusive Growth, February 2013; European Commission (2013): Commission Staff Working Document. Assessment of the 2013 Economic Programme for Croatia, Brussels, SWD(2013) 361.
73 Bejaković, Predrag *et al.* (2012): "Isplati li se raditi u Hrvatskoj?", 19(1) *RSP*, 83–92, 90; doi: 10.3935/rsp.v19i1.1054.

does not mean using more temporary than open-ended contracts, since it entails a division between insiders and outsiders in the labour market.[74] Quite the contrary, this trend should be reversed. One of the key employment-related country-specific recommendations in 2011 was to reduce segmentation in the labour market by rebalancing flexibility and security through changes in employment protection legislation.[75] The accent was placed on a more effective and fair *combination* of flexibility and security in working arrangements, not on a simple reduction of the employment protection legislation.[76] This was repeated by Mr. László Andor, EU Commissioner responsible for Employment, Social Affairs and Inclusion at the 2011 Stakeholders' conference on flexicurity: *"By flexicurity measures, I do not mean relaxation of – in quotation marks – 'firing and hiring' rules. And I do not mean either a simple extension of unemployment benefits in time. It is important not to mistake flexicurity for piecemeal or disjointed practices which did not seek to address the four components* [of flexicurity] *simultaneously."*[77] The rhetoric has somewhat changed in view of the persistent growth in unemployment throughout the EU. Simplification of employment legislation is a leading thought and one of the key messages to Member States in the 2013 Annual Growth Survey.[78]

This is precisely the risk faced by Croatia. As already mentioned, job and employment security will seem to be on hold, at least for the duration of the crisis. The 2009 reform of the labour legislation is, once again, a hybrid which neither follows Danish, Austrian or Dutch models of flexicurity, nor develops an independent and effective Croatian model. The empirical evidence shows an increase in flexibility in the labour market after it entered into force. The flexible working arrangements intensified in 2010: the share of people with temporary fixed-term contracts in the total number of employed increased from 11.6% in 2009 to 12.3% in 2010. Actually, the share of temporary contracts has been on the rise for more than a decade: In 1997, it was 6.7%, in 2002 9.7% and in 2004 10.3%.[79] However, the share of involuntary temporary work is

---

74 Van Vliet, Olaf; Nijboer, Henk (2012): "Flexicurity in the European Union: flexibility for outsiders, security for insiders", MPRA *Paper No. 37012*, <http://mpra.ub.uni-muenchen.de/37012>.

75 Communication from the Commission (2011): Concluding the first European semester..., COM(2011) 400 final, 7.

76 *Loc. cit.*

77 László Andor, Flexicurity Conference 2011, retrieved on 04.04.2012 at <http://ec.europa.eu/social/main.jsp?langId=en&catId=88&eventsId=356&furtherEvents=yes>.

78 European Commission (2013): Communication from the Commission. Annual Growth Survey 2013, COM(2012) 750 final, 10–11.

79 Cazes; Nesporova (2007), *op. cit.*, 113.

high: In 2010, one in every two workers accepted work on temporary contracts because they could not find a permanent job.[80] The proportion of those newly employed under temporary contracts is high and keeps rising in times of crisis: from 73.2% in 2010 to over 90% in 2012.[81] Vulnerable groups, such as women and young workers, in particular do not have a practical chance of being employed other than for a fixed-term. The preference of employers for this type of contract is accentuated in times of crisis, as a means to circumvent rigid EPL and high firing costs. The latest proposed amendments of the Labour Act bring further flexibilization in this area.[82]

However, even in times of austerity and scarce finance, there is no reason why work on devising a coherent flexicurity strategy should be stopped. Before any further deregulation, why not reconsider using the existing tools more efficiently? By that, I mean focusing attention on other components of flexicurity, apart from the flexible working arrangements, notably through active labour market and lifelong learning measures. In addition to that, the role of social partners is of the utmost importance for the creation of trust and readiness for change in work-related attitudes. Employers' associations and trade unions should play a more pro-active and productive role in the development and implementation of socio-economic policy. This does not necessarily imply normative intervention.

1   *Social Dialogue and Social Partnership*

Without the intention of venturing into the complexities of social partnership and dialogue in Croatia, this paper will only concentrate on the impact the EU policies have or should have on the development of the culture of the Croatian social dialogue. Even though it is not a direct component of the flexicurity definition, we argue that social dialogue is essential for the development of a flexicurity strategy.

Social dialogue and social partnership in Croatia are weak. Social dialogue is (over)institutionalized, politicized and marked by communication problems.[83] In the communist era, social dialogue and partnership were practically non-existent and had to be built from scratch. The problem is that the

---

80   Gotovac (2011), *op. cit.*, 24.
81   European Commission (2013): Commission Staff Working Document. Assessment of the 2013 Economic Programme for Croatia, Brussels, SWD(2013) 361.
82   Draft Act on Amendments to the Labour Act, P.Z.E. 375, <http://www.sabor.hr/Default.aspx?art=54721>.
83   Zrinšćak, Siniša (2005): "Teškoće socijalnog partnerstva: europska i hrvatska iskustva", in: 12(2) *RSP*, 175–188, 184–185.

post-communist development stripped many social values of their legitimacy, even those with universal meaning, such as solidarity, justice, partnership, workers' co-decision.[84] The consequence is that the perception of the importance of social dialogue for overall social development is very low. The institutional framework for social dialogue was initiated in 1994 with the establishment of the Economic and Social Council, based on the concept of tripartite co-operation among the Government, trade unions and employers' associations, aimed at solving economic and social issues and problems.[85] On the employers' side, the Croatian Association of Employers is the most visible, if not the most representative, partner.

However, formal and declaratory commitments were never fully realized in practice. There is almost no social dialogue at company or branches of industry level.

Activation of the social partners figures high among the priorities of the JAP process and includes the following activities:

- Closely involve the social partners in the implementation of the JAP.
- Develop a strategy for bipartite dialogue and social dialogue at sectoral level.
- Establish clear criteria for the representativeness of the social partners in the various economic and social councils.
- Establish a programme to enforce the capacities of the social partners' organizations.[86]

It is submitted that the Report on implementation of JAP, even though it accurately describes the developments in the social dialogue, might convey a distorted picture of the real situation. Despite the intensity of trade union activity, the productivity and outcome of social dialogue do not match the activity level, nor contribute to the creation of effective solutions to existing problems.

The relatively high union density of 45%[87] and coverage of collective agreements of 50–60% do not adequately depict reality, in which over 600 registered unions are acting incoherently and are highly segmented, with sometimes conflicting and competing interests. The biggest divide is among the trade unions representing employees in the public sector and those representing the

---

84   Ibid., 176.
85   Now Art. 285, Labour Act.
86   Joint Assessment of the Employment Policy Priorities of the Republic of Croatia (JAP), 55.
87   The World Bank (2011): Employment Protection..., 22.

employees of private employers. The public sector unions managed to negotiate high standards and benefits in collective agreements for public sector employees in times of relative economic prosperity. Those benefits have always, and particularly in times of the persistent economic crisis, been disproportionate to the position of employees and the strength of unions in the private sector. In addition, most collective agreements in the public sector are concluded for a fixed period, which means that they cannot be terminated without an explicit clause to that effect or re-negotiated without the agreement of the trade unions. This so-called 'after-effect' or extended application is effectively used by the trade unions as a means to avoid re-negotiation of the extended benefits. Actually, the only time that the public sector trade unions acted in concert was in 2010, when the Government tried to amend the Labour Act to exclude 'after-effect' clauses: they mobilized all their capacities and gathered almost 800,000 citizens' signatures requesting a referendum on the issue of Labour Act amendments. Faced with the pressure of potential loss of a term of office over this issue, the Government withdrew such proposal. In addition, the unions boycotted any dialogue in the Economic and Social Council for the better part of 2009 and 2010.

Although the industrial relations systems in the EU are as diverse as can be, there is still room for convergence in the sense of the promotion of decentralization of collective bargaining, greater employee participation and dialogue at the company level and the overall culture of social dialogue. Social partners in Croatia, especially the trade unions, should be more active in fostering awareness of the open method of coordination and the concept of flexicurity, as well as the modalities of its adaptation to the Croatian circumstances. Currently, they do not seem capable of assuming such responsibility and the role in achieving and preserving the flexibility – security balance.

2   *Active Labour Market Policies*

Active labour market measures are financed out of the State Budget. The majority of funding (80%) is used for unemployment benefits, whereas the remaining funds are earmarked for programmes for activation of the labour market. The effect of the active labour market measures in Croatia is still negligible. Until a few years ago, as observed by Gotovac, they were mostly oriented to subsidies that did not improve the skills of the unemployed and had high deadweight, substitution and displacement costs.[88] However, the situation changed with the impact of EU accession partnership and the JAP, which entailed better targeting of the measures and introduced mechanisms for the

---

88   Gotovac (2011), *op. cit.*, 38, Bejaković; Gotovac (2011), *op. cit.*, 347.

evaluation of implementation. The key priorities were identified in the JAP as a result of an analysis of the labour market in Croatia, and they are:

- Increasing the employability and participation rate of prime-age women (especially those with low or inadequate skills);
- Increasing the employability and participation rate of older people;
- Increasing the employability and participation rate of young people;
- Addressing the long-term unemployment problem;
- Reducing the skills mismatch (mismatch between labour force knowledge and skills and labour market needs) and increasing investment in human capital through better education and skills;
- Improving the adaptability of workers and enterprises;
- Good governance;
- Administrative capacity-building.[89]

In 2012, 41,555 people were included in the active labour market measures (roughly 11% of the unemployed), the majority in educational and public work programmes. The reach of these measures is still very limited, since at the end of December 2012 only one quarter or 10,829 beneficiaries remained active.[90] The crisis mostly affected the subsidies programmes for the employment of workers aged 50+. In 2008, the rate of coverage *i.e.* the percentage of unemployed that benefited from this subsidy, was 9.4, whereas in 2009 and 2010 that ratio dropped significantly, to 1.8% and 2.3% respectively.[91]

In the beginning of 2012, the Ministry of Labour and Pension System identified key challenges for the activation and strengthening of competitiveness in the labour market. The main measures were aimed at the activation of the long-term unemployed, the legalization of informal work, the lowering of the tax burden for low-skilled workers, the strengthening of employability, the developing accessible information systems for professional career development, the developing of the system for tracking labour market needs and linking them to the professional education system, the lowering of labour costs, the flexibilization of employment. Special measures were designed for young people with no work experience, older workers, people with multiple barriers to entry into the labour market, people with obsolete skills and education and long-term unemployed women. These measures were to be implemented in close cooperation

---

89 Joint Assessment of the Employment Policy Priorities of the Republic of Croatia (JAP).
90 Croatian Employment Service (2013), Registered unemployed and employment in December 2012, Zagreb, <http://www.hzz.hr/docslike/PR_Nezaposlenost-Zaposljavanje_12_2012.pdf>.
91 Bejaković; Gotovac (2011), *op. cit.*, 347.

with local authorities, and the importance of decentralized decision-making on active labour market programmes and policies according to local needs was emphasized.[92] The new and adapted programmes in 2012 were meant to be better targeted at the most vulnerable unemployed (youth, older workers, prime-aged women, the long-term unemployed) and were based on the National Employment Promotion Plan 2011–2012. Apart from the subsidies for employment and self-employment, training and education for known and unknown employers, they also include subsidies for first work experience and public work. However, active labour market policies are still little used in Croatia.[93]

Even with the (still) limited reach of the active labour market measures, it would be incorrect to assume that the unemployment benefits are fostering inactivity. Only a fifth or 20.2% of the total registered unemployed are entitled to unemployment benefit.[94]

3 Lifelong Learning Strategies

Even though, at least at a rhetorical level, the importance of lifelong education is recognized in Croatia,[95] it is still at a low level of development.

The most progress in this area is directly attributed to EU influence and funding. However, it is currently mainly oriented towards strengthening capacities for "educating the educators" and experimental (pilot) programmes with limited reach. Therefore, the wider impact and further improvements are yet to be seen. Although an integral Lifelong Learning Strategy as such does not exist, many strategic documents in the field of education and science in the past several years have included lifelong learning as one of their principles and goals.

Still, one dimension of lifelong learning is systematically neglected: incentives for employers to invest in the continuous education of their

---

[92] Press conference at the Croatian Employment Service (HZZ), 13 January 2012, materials available at: <http://www.hzz.hr/>.

[93] Spending on ALMPs amounts to 0.14% of GDP, whereas only around 13% of the unemployed were covered in 2012. See European Commission (2013): Commission Staff Working Document. Assessment of the 2013 Economic Programme for Croatia, SWD(2013) 361, 19.

[94] In May 2013. This is a drop of 3.4% in comparison with the same month in 2012 (a drop of 8.1% was registered in May 2012 in comparison with May 2013). At the same time, the number of unemployed has kept rising for several years in a row. HZZ, <http://www.hzz.hr/DocSlike/PR_Nezaposlenost-Zaposljavanje_05_2013.pdf>.

[95] "*It is precisely at a time of crisis that the need for additional education is more important than ever, because once the economy recovers persons who received additional education will be more employable and competitive.*" Republic of Croatia (2011), *op. cit.*, 2.

employees. The idea is that, by putting the accent on functional flexibility, *i.e.* mobility within the enterprise and implementation of lifelong learning programmes (for both employed and unemployed), the pressure on attaining numerical flexibility may be relieved.

VIII   Conclusion

The shift of paradigms from job security to employment security implies periodic voluntary or involuntary transitions in the labour market, which means that labour is characterized as "yet another mobile factor of production, to be reallocated as and when the market so determines".[96]

Even though the reform of labour and social law started in Croatia in 2003, with the aim of implementing more flexible policies in the labour market, the appropriate model is still not in sight. Through the accession partnership and with impending EU membership, new challenges lie ahead. Flexicurity-related requirements enter our national system from the EU level, through a deliberative process of the open method of coordination in the European Employment Strategy. Thus, it becomes the obligatory reference for measurement of performance at the national level. The danger is that the Croatian comprehension (and implementation) of this concept may get caught in the trap of ambiguities associated with this term at the EU level. There is no one-size-fits-all model of flexicurity, its content is still imprecise and its methodological foundations far from complete. Its promotion as the crucial element of the EES and the open method of coordination framework may convey the wrong idea about the availability of arbitrary choices or the free 'pick and choose' approach to its flexibility and security components.

The connection between political leadership in Croatia and flexibilization or deregulation of labour legislation is quite peculiar. The first deregulation attempts took place in 2000 and are associated with the first left-centre coalition government (although the final legislative package was adopted in 2003, after the resignation of the coalition government). The second left-centre coalition government took office at the end of 2011 and so far seems to incline towards the neo-liberal concepts of deregulation. Meanwhile, all governments of the right-centre fostered a more populist approach, preferring to keep the *status quo* when it comes to social spending and relations with the trade

---

96   Bell, Mark (2012): "Between Flexicurity and Fundamental Social Rights: The EU Directives on Atypical Work", 37(1) *European Law Review*, 31–48, 34–35.

unions.[97] The result is that in the years of relative prosperity and growth with favourable economic indicators, the window of opportunity for creating consistent and applicable flexicurity strategy was not utilized. We are thus left not only with limited financial means to boost the security component (not by increasing social benefits, but by stimulating lifelong learning and active labour market policies which could improve the employability and adaptability of the labour force), but also with wasted time in which the formation, integration and streamlining of policies could have taken place. At the present time, with growing unemployment, resistance to any forms of change which would entail further flexibilization of working arrangements is particularly strong. The latest amendments to the Labour Act, proposed in May 2013, are currently going through parliament. It is interesting to note that the amendment concerning the limitation of duration of fixed-term labour contracts (currently three years), as one of the atypical forms of employment, will apply only to consecutive fixed-term contracts and not to the first one (Article 2 of the Draft Act on Amendments to the Labour Act). This means that there will be no limit for the first fixed-term labour contract, with the resulting (lower) protection regarding dismissals (notice periods), severance payments, *etc.* Reversal of the negative trends in the labour market depends on the success of the announced investment cycle which is due to take place in the next few months. Only if (and when) the favourable job creation climate is created will the comprehension of *employability* rather than job security be able to gain a foothold in the attitudes of the Croatian workforce. If not, employability in a jobless market will remain an empty and lifeless concept.

However, alongside political actors, social partners share the responsibility for adapting to challenges in the globalized world. This process will be successful when and if all of the stakeholders at the national level show readiness fully to comprehend and listen to the other side. Otherwise, those whose interests should be protected are devalued and boiled down to a number in the register of the unemployment service.

---

97 The evidence from Poland and Italy shows that flexicurity pathways are comparable to Croatian experiences, in that individual measures rather than overall strategies are applied, depending on the governing party. However, the conclusion of that paper that party politics matter when it comes to Europeanization of the domestic policies (the extent of the measures depends whether a pro-European and integrationist or eurosceptic government is in office) is not applicable to Croatian circumstances, given the pro-European orientation of both left and right-centre governing parties. See Gwiazda, Anna (2011): "The Europeanization of flexicurity: the Lisbon Strategy's impact on employment policies in Italy and Poland", 18(4) *JEPP*, 546–565.

CHAPTER 23

The Iraqi Cases: Further Elements and Thoughts concerning 'Jurisdiction' under Article 1 of the European Convention on Human Rights

*Lucius Caflisch**

I   Introduction

Article 1 of the European Convention on Human Rights (ECHR) of 4 November 1950[1] provides as follows:

> The High Contracting Parties shall secure to everyone within their jurisdiction the rights and freedoms defined in Section 1 [Articles 2 to 17] of this Convention.

According to the decision in *Banković and Others* v. *Belgium and Others*, to be discussed later,[2] Article 1 was intended to protect "all persons in the territories of the signatory States, even those who could not be considered as residing there in the legal sense of the word." An observation was made by the representative of Belgium on 25 August 1950, in a plenary meeting of the Assembly of the Council of Europe, to the effect that

> the right of protection by our States, by virtue of a formal clause of the Convention, may be exercised with full force, and without any differentiation or distinction, in favour of individuals of whatever nationality, who on the territory of any one of our States, may have had reason to complain that [their] rights have been violated.[3]

---

*   Professor (em.), The Graduate Institute of International and Development Studies, Geneva; Former Judge of the European Court of Human Rights; Member of the International Law Commission of the United Nations; Member of the Institute of International Law.
1   European Treaty Series, No. 5.
2   *Banković and Others* v. *Belgium and Others*, No. 52207/99, GC, decision of 12 December 2001, paras. 19 and 20; see below, II.2.c.
3   To be found in Collected Edition of the *Travaux préparatoires* of the European Convention on Human Rights, Vol. III, p. 260.

Article 1 does not, as has been pointed out, define the jurisdiction of the European Court of Human Rights (ECtHR) but the scope of States Parties' obligation to secure the Convention rights to individuals:

> [h]owever badly State agents may have treated the applicant, if he or she was not within the State's jurisdiction, then there was no obligation on the State to apply the Convention, and there is no case for the Court to examine.[4]

'Jurisdiction' is an element used to determine whether States, on account of the conduct of their agents, can be held responsible for violations of the ECHR and its Protocols. For present purposes, jurisdiction designates the powers to legislate, to judge and to enforce, which, under international law, are generally limited to the State's territory, although there are exceptions. The present contribution deals in particular with three relatively recent cases – *Al-Saadoon and Mufdhi*, *Al-Skeini* and *Al-Jeddah* v. *United Kingdom*[5] – where those exceptions were discussed.

II   Jurisdiction in the Case-Law of the Court

1   *Jurisdiction over State Territory*

This subdivision of the paper will succinctly recall two cases where the jurisdiction of a State Party to the Convention *over its own territory* was debated before the Strasbourg Court. In *Ilaşcu and Others* v. *Moldova and Russia*,[6] the Court stated that, despite the fact that Moldova lacked control over Transnistria, where the applicants were being detained, it did have jurisdiction under Article 1 of the Convention, but the duty to secure the rights protected by the latter was limited by a factual obstacle, *i.e.* the difficulty to obtain the release of the individuals detained. A similar situation prevailed in *Assanidze* v. *Georgia*,[7]

---

4   C. Ovey, "Extra-territorial Jurisdiction under Article 1 of the Convention", unpublished paper of 14 May 2012, cited with the kind permission of the author. For other studies of the subject, see J.-P. Costa, "Qui relève de la juridiction de quel(s) Etat(s) au sens de l'article 1er de la Convention européenne des droits de l'homme?", in *Libertés, justice, tolérance. Mélanges en hommage au Doyen Gérard Cohen-Jonathan*, Vol. I, Brussels, Bruylant, 2004, pp. 484–500; L. Caflisch, "'Jurisdiction' under Article 1 of the European Convention on Human Rights", in *International Law of [the] 21st Century. For the 80th Anniversary of Professor Igor I. Lukashuk*, Kiev, Promeni, 2006, pp. 560–583.
5   See below, III.
6   No. 48787/99, GC, judgment of 8 July 2004.
7   No. 71503/01, GC, judgment of 8 April 2004.

where the respondent State was held to have jurisdiction over an area – the Autonomous Republic of Adjaria – which was in fact in a situation of apostasy from the central State. In that case, Georgia had not availed itself of the possibility, offered by Article 56 of the Convention,[8] to exclude Adjaria from the scope of that instrument. The Court found that Georgia had ratified the Convention for its entire territory without making any reservation regarding Adjaria, despite the difficulty of exercising jurisdiction over the latter. Indeed, Adjaria was and is an integral part of Georgia and is not animated by secessionist ambitions or subjected to the control of a third State. The facts of the case were therefore under Georgia's jurisdiction as referred to by Article 1 of the ECHR. True, the central authorities had done everything in their power to obtain the execution of the Georgian Supreme Court's order to release the applicant, but in vain. However, even if a State may find it difficult to ensure the respect of Convention rights on its *entire* territory, it remains responsible for whatever occurs on it. Thus, said the Court, the situation complained of fell under the central State's jurisdiction even though, on the internal level, the facts may have been directly attributable to Adjaria's local authorities.

2 *Extraterritorial Jurisdiction*
a   Early Commission Cases

The European Commission of Human Rights, in close to forty years of activity, took a series of decisions which made States responsible for the conduct of their agents not only on their own territory but on foreign territory as well; thus, according to a decision of 10 July 1978 in *Cyprus* v. *Turkey*,[9] actions of Turkish soldiers in Cyprus brought their authors under Turkish jurisdiction.

This also happened in other situations. Some of them related to the acts of consular officials which, though accomplished abroad, were attributed to the sending State.[10] In *X. and Y.* v. *Switzerland*,[11] the Commission found that the

---

8   Article 56.1 and 2 of the Convention provide: "1. Any State may at the time of its ratification or at any time thereafter declare by notification addressed to the Secretary General of the Council of Europe that the present Convention shall, subject to paragraph 4 of this Article, extend to all or any of the territories for whose international relations it is responsible. 2. The Convention shall extend the territory or territories named in the notification as from the 30th day after the receipt of this notification by the Secretary General of the Council of Europe."

9   Decision of 10 July 1977, Yearbook of the European Convention on Human Rights, 1978, p. 100 (230–234).

10   *X.* v. *Germany*, No. 1611/62, decision of 25 September 1965, Yearbook of the European Convention on Human Rights, Vol. 8, 1965, p. 158 (163); *W.M.* v. *Denmark*, No. 17392/90, decision of 14 October 1992, DR 73, p. 193.

11   No. 7289/75, decision of 14 July 1977, DR 9, p. 76.

applicants, who had been expelled from Liechtenstein, were under Swiss jurisdiction because immigration control in the Principality was exercised by the Swiss authorities under the Treaty of 6 November 1963 on the Rules Applicable to Immigration from Third States.[12] The case of *Drozd and Janousek v. France*,[13] though decided by the Court rather than the Commission, fell into the same category: it pertained to the activity of judges deputised to Andorra by Spain and by France. The applicants argued that their conviction by these judges seconded to Andorra by France sufficed to place the issue under French jurisdiction. The ECtHR disagreed: the courts concerned were autonomous judicial entities not subject to French or Spanish authority. Another Commission case, *Freda v. Italy*,[14] concerned an individual accused of having participated in several outrages, in particular murders. That person was convicted by the Catanzaro Assises and sentenced to life imprisonment. Before his trial, he had been released from prison, as the maximum period for detention on remand had expired, and had been assigned to compulsory residence on an island as a security measure. Subsequently he was allowed to return to Catanzaro to stand trial, but he left that city before the latter and took refuge abroad. Almost two years later, he was arrested in Costa Rica, brought to the local airport and handed over to the Italian police which took him to Rome. The applicant was then served an arrest warrant for having absconded from his compulsory residence. Later on, an investigation was opened against him for having left his country without a passport and for carrying a forged one.

Freda's application was declared inadmissible by the Commission as the deprivation of freedom complained of was not in breach of Article 5 of the ECHR (right to liberty and security). Regarding his having been taken into custody by Italian police officers in Costa Rica, the Commission observed:

> The applicant was accordingly from the time of being handed over in fact under the authority of the Italian State and thus within the 'jurisdiction' of that country, even if this authority was in the circumstances exercised abroad.

This case, which recalls that of *Öcalan*,[15] was clearly one of State agents acting abroad with the consent (and participation) of the local authorities.

---

12   [Swiss] Recueil systématique (RS) 0.142.115.142.
13   No. 12747/87, judgment of 26 June 1992, ECtHR, Series A, No. 240.
14   No. 8916/80, decision of 7 October 1980, DR 21, p. 250.
15   Below, II.2.d., at note 23.

b   The Northern Cyprus Cases
In a study on "Extra-territorial Jurisdiction under Article 1 of the Convention", Clare Ovey mentions the Turkish assertion that the acts complained of by the plaintiff State were not directly imputable to the Turkish army but to an autonomous local administration.[16] Similar arguments had been examined by the International Court of Justice (ICJ) in the *Nicaragua* case,[17] in which the Nicaraguan Government unsuccessfully contended that the United States was internationally responsible for the acts performed by the *Contras* against the *Sandinistas*, i.e. the Government of Nicaragua. The Court held that the United States had aided and abetted the *Contras*, and shared intelligence and planning with them. This did not mean, however, that the relations between the *Contras* and the United States Government were equivalent to those between a State and its organs.

The ECtHR's reasoning followed a different path. In *Loizidou v. Turkey* (preliminary objections),[18] it considered that Northern Cyprus was militarily occupied by Turkey. There was, for the Court, sufficient Turkish control over the area to suggest that the local administration was, in fact, a tool of Turkey, duty-bound to secure the rights guaranteed by the Convention. The inter-State case between *Cyprus* and *Turkey*[19] yielded a similar result, the Court's Grand Chamber explaining that

> Turkey's 'jurisdiction' must be considered to extend to securing the entire range of substantive rights set out in the Convention and those Additional Protocols which she has ratified, and that violations of those rights are imputable to Turkey (para. 77).

As the Government of Cyprus was unable to meet obligations under the Convention, any other decision would have resulted "in a regrettable vacuum in the system of human-rights protection in the territory in question" (para. 78).

c   The *Banković* Decision
The case of *Banković and Others v. Belgium and Others*[20] arose in the context of the Kosovo conflict. It concerned the bombing of the Serbian Radio/TV station

---

16   *Op. cit.*, p. 4, note 4.
17   *Military and Paramilitary Activities in and against Nicaragua* (Nicaragua v. United States), merits, judgment of 27 June 1986, ICJ Reports 1986, p. 14.
18   Decision of 23 March 1995, ECtHR, Series A, No. 310.
19   No. 25781/94, judgment of 10 May 2001.
20   Decision cited above, note 2.

in Belgrade by NATO forces, which resulted in the killing or wounding of some of its personnel. The victims' relatives turned to Strasbourg, accusing 17 NATO member States of having breached the Convention's Articles 2 (right to life) and 10 (freedom of expression). They contended that the Court had jurisdiction even though NATO did not occupy Belgrade or have over the area anything similar to the control exercised by Turkey exercised over Northern Cyprus. But – so ran their argument – they were able to conduct their air strike and therefore exercised over the lives of the victims a degree of control sufficient to bring the case under the defendant States' jurisdiction.

Rejecting this line of argument, the Strasbourg Court found that the defendant States' jurisdiction under Article 1 of the Convention was, as a matter of principle, limited to the territory of those States. But the Court was willing to recognise the following exceptions: (i) the 'State agent authority' exception, applicable in situations where the agents of one State perform official functions on the territory of another State with the latter's consent or toleration (*Drozd and Janousek*); (ii) the 'effective control' exception where, as is the case in Northern Cyprus, a foreign occupant exercises such control; and (iii) situations where the exercise of extraterritorial jurisdiction is permitted by customary international law or by treaty: activities of diplomatic agents and consular officers; events on board vessels and aircraft flying the flag of, or registered in, the State concerned (paras. 67–73).

None of these exceptions could apply in the present instance, which was one of the reasons for rejecting the applicants' plea. The Court cited two further reasons: the fact that while the respondent States may have had a (temporary) power over life and death in the area concerned, they had no possibility of securing each and every human right of the people of Belgrade under the Convention; and the fact that the Convention "is a multi-lateral treaty operating...*in an essentially regional context* and notably in *the legal space (espace juridique) of the Contracting States*",[21] which was not the case for Belgrade at the time since the Federal Republic of Yugoslavia was not a Party to the ECHR. This is a somewhat enigmatic statement the justification of which will have to be verified when dealing with the Iraqi cases (paras. 74–80).

d   Post-*Banković* Cases

In 2004, the Court's Grand Chamber was faced with the previously-mentioned case of *Ilaşcu and Others* v. *Moldova and Russia*,[22] where it concluded that Russia, on account of its military presence, had jurisdiction over separatist

---

21   For full text, see paragraph 80 of the decision, cited below, II.2.d. Emphasis by the author.
22   Above, note 6.

Transnistria. Indeed the separatists in that area could not have overcome the Moldovan army without the help of the Russian Federation; their success was contingent on Russia's military, economic and political support. Transnistria therefore came under the effective authority and influence of Russia.

The next case falling under this sub-heading is *Öcalan v. Turkey*,[23] where the Strasbourg Court ruled that the irregular extradition to Turkish agents that had occurred on Kenyan territory was based on 'State agent authority' exercised by Turkey on Kenyan soil (with the connivance of the local authorities): Turkish officials arrested the applicant who was subsequently transferred to Turkey, tried and punished.

Another arrest made on foreign territory was that of *Sánchez Ramirez* ('*Carlos*'),[24] who was picked up by French agents in Sudan. There is also the case of *Medvedyev and Others v. France*,[25] where drug smugglers were arrested on the high seas, off the coast of Cape Verde, on a vessel flying the Cambodian flag. This was accomplished with the permission of the Government of Cambodia. The Grand Chamber of the ECtHR pointed out, in this connexion, that,

> as this was a case of France having exercised full and exclusive control over the [vessel] and its crew, at least *de facto*, from the time of the interception, in a continuous and uninterrupted manner until they were tried in France, the applicants were effectively within France's jurisdiction for the purposes of Article 1 of the Convention (para. 67).

France's jurisdiction in this instance could hardly be doubted since, upon a French request, jurisdiction had been transferred from Cambodia to France. As in *Öcalan*, the only sticking point was the fact that France acted outside the 'legal space' (*espace juridique*) of the Convention. In other words, the limitation to the Convention's 'legal space' suggested in *Banković* was not applied in *Medvedyev*.

The case of *Issa and Others v. Turkey*[26] concerned the relatives of Iraqi Kurdish shepherds allegedly killed by Turkish forces in the border area of

---

23 No. 46221/99, judgment of 12 May 2005.
24 No. 28780/95, decision of the Commission of 24 June 1996.
25 No. 3394/03, GC, judgment of 29 March 2010. See, on this case, by the present author, "Human Rights Law and the Law of the Sea – A Disastrous Encounter", in M. Pogačnik (ed.), *Challenges of Contemporary International Law and International Relations. Liber Amicorum in Honour of Ernest Petrič*, Nova Gorica, The European Faculty of Law, 2011, pp. 113–130.
26 No. 31821/96, judgment of 16 November 2004.

Northern Iraq. Citing decisions by the UN Human Rights Committee and the Inter-American Commission of Human Rights, the Court pointed out that

> "a State may...be held accountable for violation of the Convention rights and freedoms of persons who are in the territory of another State but who are found to be under the former State's authority and control through its agents operating – *whether lawfully or unlawfully* – in the latter State" (see: *mutatis mutandis, M.* v. *Denmark,* application No. 17392/90, Commission decision of 14 October 1992, DR 73, p. 193; *Illich Sanchez Ramirez* v. *France,* application No. 28780/95, Commission decision of 24 June 1996, DR 86, p. 155; *Coard et al.* v. *United States,* the Inter-American Commission of Human Rights decision of 29 September 1999, Report No. 109/99, case No. 10.951, §§ 37, 39, 41 and 43; and the views adopted by the Human Rights Committee on 29 July 1981 in the cases of *Lopez Burgos* v. *Uruguay* and *Celiberti de Casariego* v. *Uruguay,* Nos. 52/1979 and 56/1979, at 12.3 and 10.3 respectively). *Accountability in such situations stems from the fact that Article 1 of the Convention cannot be interpreted so as to allow a State party to perpetrate violations of the Convention on the territory of another State, which it could not perpetrate on its own territory.* (Para. 71; emphasis added.)

It found, however, that Turkey did not exercise effective control over the relevant area in Northern Iraq and, therefore, thought that

> [t]he essential question to be examined in the instant case is whether at the relevant time Turkish troops conducted operations in the area where the killings took place. The fate of the applicants' complaints in respect of the killing of their relatives depends on the prior establishment of that premise. (Para. 76.)

In the end, the Court found that Turkey could not be considered as having jurisdiction, as there was not sufficient evidence that the Turkish forces had been conducting operations in the area.

The Court's decision in *Quark Fishing Ltd.* v. *United Kingdom,*[27] which will be discussed next, related to the refusal of a fishing license for 2001 to a company registered in the Falkland islands by the authorities of South Georgia and the South Sandwich Islands (the SGSSI), a British Overseas Territory. This refusal was based on advice given by the British Foreign Office. The applicant

---

27   No. 15305/06, decision of 19 September 2006.

challenged the decision – it had so far obtained a licence every year –, complaining of a violation of Article 1.1 of the First Additional Protocol to the ECHR (protection of property).[28] In *Banković*, the Court had had this to say:

> [T]he Convention is a multi-lateral treaty operating, subject to Article 56.2 of the Convention,[29] in an essentially regional context and notably in the legal space (*contexte juridique*) of the Contracting States. The FRY [Federal Republic of Yugoslavia] clearly does not fall within this legal space. The Convention was not designed to be applied throughout the world, even in respect of the conduct of Contracting States. Accordingly, the desirability of avoiding a gap or vacuum in human rights' protection has so far been relied on by the Court in favour of establishing jurisdiction only when the territory in question was one that, but for the specific circumstances, would normally be covered by the Convention. (Para. 80.)

The principal issue here was whether Protocol No. 1 was applicable to the Territory in question. The domestic courts had agreed that SGSSI was an area for which the United Kingdom was responsible but that, in the absence of a declaration under Article 56 of the Convention, the Protocol did not apply to SGSSI. The applicant argued, however, that in certain situations the responsibility of a Contracting State could be engaged in places outside its national territory where it exercised 'effective control'. But the control principle, already highlighted in *Banković*, did not, according to the Court, override the need for declarations by which Contracting States could, pursuant to Article 56.1 of the Convention, decide to extend the scope of the Convention and its Protocols to their territories. This is undoubtedly correct: the possibility of excluding applicability and responsibility exists even where territorial sovereignty and jurisdiction under Article 1 are present. The Court further rejected the applicant's argument that Article 56 was outdated, which would have suggested that jurisdiction under Article 1 could override the absence of declarations under Article 56.1. The Court

> cannot unwrite provisions contained in the Convention; this can only be possible through an amendment to the Convention to which [the] States [concerned] agree and give evidence of their agreement through signature and ratification (p. 3 of the decision).

Accordingly, the Court declared the application inadmissible.

---

28   Additional Protocol No. 1 to the ECHR, of 20 March 1952, European Treaty Series, No. 9.
29   For text, see note 8.

The case of *Isaak* v. *Turkey*[30] pertained to complaints arising out of the killing of a Greek Cypriot who had participated in a demonstration within the UN-controlled buffer zone. There was, according to the Court, evidence that Mr. Isaak had been killed, in that zone, by Turkish and Northern Cypriot soldiers and that, consequently, he fell under Turkish jurisdiction.

Another case, *Pad and Others* v. *Turkey*,[31] was brought about by the killing of seven Iranians by Turkish soldiers in a helicopter. Turkey admitted to the shooting, so that the Court found it unnecessary to determine where the deed was committed on Turkish or Iranian territory: Turkey admitted to having had jurisdiction.

Solomou and Others v. *Turkey*[32] concerned a Greek Cypriot who, during a demonstration in the UN buffer zone separating the Southern (Greek) from the Northern (Turkish) part of the island, entered that zone despite the efforts of the United Nations Forces in Cyprus (UNFCYP) to keep him out. Solomou attempted to climb a pole behind the Turkish sentry guarding the zone, presumably to pull down the Turkish flag. He was hit by fire from the Turkish side and was fatally injured. In the application subsequently brought before the ECtHR by Solomou's family on the basis of Article 2 of the Convention (right to life), the question arose whether the respondent State had jurisdiction under Article 1 of the Convention and, therefore, could be held responsible for Solomou's death. The Court thought that it could: the deadly shots had been fired by the Turkish forces and the victim was under the authority and/or effective control of Turkey which was, therefore, responsible for his death (paras. 48–52).

The case of *Andreou* v. *Turkey*[33] related to the same demonstration. The applicant was attending the funeral of the above-named Solomou, a friend of her son. After the funeral, she observed events from outside the buffer zone, on Greek-Cypriot territory. At a certain moment, soldiers on Turkish-controlled territory started firing, wounding several people, including the applicant, who subsequently brought a case against Turkey before the ECtHR on the basis of Articles 2 (right to life), 3 (prohibition of torture) and 8 (right to respect for private and family life) of the Convention. A preliminary issue raised by the respondent State was whether there was evidence that the applicant found herself on territory of the 'TRNC' (Turkish Republic of Northern Cyprus) at the time of the incident and, therefore, under Turkish jurisdiction.

---

30   No. 44587/98, decision of 24 June 2008.
31   No. 60167/00, decision of 28 June 2007.
32   No. 36832/97, judgment of 24 June 2008.
33   No. 45653/99, decision of 3 June 2008.

The Court recalled that, in exceptional circumstances, conduct of Contracting States which produces effects outside their territory and over which they have no control or authority may amount to an exercise of jurisdiction by them under Article 1 of the Convention. When the applicant was hit, she found herself outside the buffer zone and on Greek-Cypriot soil. Unlike the applicants in *Banković*, the complainant in the present case was, therefore, in territory covered by the Convention. The Court commented:

> In these circumstances, even though the applicant sustained her injuries in territory over which Turkey exercised no control, the opening of fire on the crowd from close range, which was the direct and immediate cause of those injuries, was such that the applicant must be regarded as "within [the] jurisdiction of Turkey" within the meaning of Article 1 and that the responsibility of the respondent State under the Convention is in consequence engaged.

3   *Conclusion*

A first conclusion to be drawn from the above practice is that, as long as a Contracting State has not made a declaration removing part of its territory from the scope of the Convention, it is responsible for whatever may have happened in it, regardless of the respective attributions of the central and local authorities on the domestic level. That State may retain jurisdiction and, therefore, responsibility even if it has lost control over the area where the acts complained of occurred.

A second conclusion is that jurisdiction under Article 1 can flow from territorial sovereignty but also, as explained, from lesser degrees of control ('effective overall control', 'global control', occupation) as they have appeared in Northern Cyprus. The *Banković* case shows that a simple drone bombing, though spelling death and destruction, does not achieve the degree of control required. In the post-*Banković* cases, that notion seems to have been reduced to control: the simple shooting from helicopters hovering in foreign territory appears sufficient to generate jurisdiction under Article 1 of the ECHR.

There are, finally, types of jurisdiction entirely detached from territoriality in its traditional sense. They arise from special rules of international law on jurisdiction: jurisdiction of the flag State or State of registry, or from activities of diplomatic agents and consular offices; and jurisdiction resulting from the consent of the territorial sovereign.

All in all, the case-law, especially after *Banković*, has tended to distinguish between jurisdiction in general international law and jurisdiction in human rights matters. This may ensure a better protection of human rights but also result in a situation where every State has jurisdiction over everything. Finally, the argument limiting the exercise of extraterritorial jurisdiction to the 'legal space' of the Convention, made in *Banković*, was contradicted in *Issa*. And even if it were to continue to prevail, it would not (yet) go so far as to undo Article 56 of the Convention which, it will be recalled, turns jurisdiction and responsibility for events in outside territories into a matter of option for Contracting States.

III The Iraqi Cases

1 *Al-Saadoon and Mufdhi* v. *United Kingdom*[34]

The first instance under this heading, *Al-Saadoon and Mufdhi* v. *United Kingdom*, is important in that it forms part of a series of cases pertaining to the consequences of the Anglo-American armed action in Iraq. The factual background of this case may be summarised as follows: The invasion of Iraq by the Multi-National Force (MNF) (United States and United Kingdom, with a smaller participation by Australia, Denmark and Poland) occurred in March 2003 and was completed in May of the same year. The American and British Governments then established the Coalition Provisional Authority (CPA) to govern Iraq temporarily and accordingly informed the UN Security Council. In doing so, the two Governments drew up a list of the executive and legislative tasks they intended to carry out through the Authority. In the course of the year 2003, the CPA issued various pieces of legislation. CPA Regulation No. 1 gave that organ the power to issue binding regulations and orders. CPA Order No. 7 modified the Iraqi Penal Code by, *inter alia*, suspending the death penalty.

The occupied territory was divided into a number of regions, one of which, that of Bassorah in the South-East of the country, was placed under British authority. While the United Kingdom was not given legislative powers there – they were in the hands of the United States –, it was responsible for security. The occupation ended on 28 June 2004, when all powers were transferred to the Iraqi Interim Government. Although both the American and British forces remained in the country, this was supposed to be at the Interim Government's behest.

In August 2004, the Iraqi National Assembly re-introduced the death penalty for certain violent crimes and on 8 November of that year a Memorandum of Understanding (MoU) regarding criminal suspects was drawn up by the

---

34 No. 61498/08, decision of 30 June 2009.

United Kingdom contingent of the Multi-National Force and the Iraqi Ministries of Justice and the Interior. According to that Memorandum, the British contingent was to apprehend and detain persons suspected of having committed crimes and to transfer them to the Iraqi authorities.

The applicants, two Iraqi Ba'athists, were charged with having ambushed and killed two British soldiers in March 2003. They were arrested in the same year by United Kingdom forces and sent to British detention camps, where they remained until 2008. During that time, their cases were being investigated by British authorities and, in 2006, the applicants were handed over to the Bassorah Criminal Court. The latter requested their deferral to the Iraqi High Tribunal because the alleged offences constituted war crimes. This was not done, however; instead, judicial review proceedings were opened in the United Kingdom. These proceedings ended with a finding of the Court of Appeal that there were serious grounds for believing that the applicants would face a real risk of execution if they were deferred to the Iraqi High Tribunal. The Court of Appeal also concluded that the applicants were no longer placed under British jurisdiction in the sense of Article 1 of the ECHR and that the United Kingdom was under an international obligation to transfer them to the Iraqi authorities (MoU of August 2004).

In December 2008 the applicants, having been informed of the Court of Appeal's ruling, asked the ECtHR to indicate an interim measure under Rule 39.1 of the Rules of Court,[35] namely, a prohibition to transfer the applicants. Although this request was granted (paras. 55–58), the United Kingdom transferred them on 31 December 2008. At the time of the ECtHR's decision, the domestic trial was in progress.

Were the applicants, during the relevant period, under British jurisdiction pursuant to Article 1 of the Convention? After recalling that jurisdiction under Article 1 is essentially territorial, that that Article does not apply to States not Parties to the Convention, and that it cannot serve to impose Convention standards on third States, the Court recalls the exceptions to the territoriality principles described in the preceding heading (para. 85).

It then turns to the circumstances of the present case and notes that the applicants were, in one way or another, detained since 2003 by the British authorities. Initially, they stayed at a detention facility run by the United

---

35   Article 39.1 of the Rules of Court of 1 July 2014 provides: "The Chamber or, where appropriate, its President may, at the request of a party or of any other person concerned, or of its own motion, indicate to the parties any interim measure which it considers should be adopted in the interests of the parties or of the proper conduct of the proceedings before it."

Kingdom as an occupant power. Later on, however, this *de facto* control became one reflected in law. Thus, a CPA order of 2004 provided that all the premises currently used by the MNF should become inviolable and subject to the Force's exclusive authority and control. This rule remained in force until 31 December 2008 (see paras. 20–21 and 87).

Given the total *de facto* and, subsequently, *de jure* control exercised by the United Kingdom over the detention facility, says the Court, the applicants were under British jurisdiction. This situation lasted until 31 December 2008. The questions of whether the respondent State was under an obligation to transfer the applicants to Iraq and whether, if such an obligation existed, it displaced any human-rights duties owed to the applicants was not considered relevant for the issue of jurisdiction and was to be examined in connexion with the merits (paras. 87–88).

This case linked to the invasion of Iraq, the first in a series of three, was somewhat special regarding the facts, and a dispute which finally consisted in a tug-of-war over the transfer of two suspects belonging to the old regime to the new Government, which had re-introduced the death penalty. In its judgment on the merits,[36] the Court found violations of Articles 3 (prohibition of torture), 13 (right to an effective remedy) and 34 (individual applications) of the Convention.

Al-Saadoon and Mufdhi thus shows that there is extraterritorial jurisdiction in situations of armed conflict followed by occupation, at least in relation to persons held in detention facilities operated by the occupant power.

2 *Al-Skeini and Others* v. *United Kingdom*[37]

a The Facts

For the general background of *Al-Skeini*, the reader may consult the factual introduction to *Al-Saadoon and Mufdhi* v. *United Kingdom*.[38] The *Al-Skeini* case was brought to the Strasbourg Court by relatives of individuals allegedly killed by British soldiers during the occupation of Iraq in the region of Bassorah. According to the applicants, the United Kingdom was responsible for security in the area, and the investigations carried out by the British army and other authorities under Article 2 of the Convention were insufficient.

The House of Lords conducted an extensive review of ECtHR case-law on jurisdiction under Article 1 of the Convention. There was agreement that jurisdiction was mainly exercised by States over their own territory but that there

---

36 No. 61498/08, judgment of 4 October 2010.
37 No. 55721/07, GC, judgment of 7 July 2011.
38 Above, III.1.

were exceptions, *e.g.*, when a Contracting State militarily occupied the territory of another Contracting State – this being, apparently, how the House interpreted the 'legal space' limitation.[39] Another exception to the rule of territorial jurisdiction was that of the jurisdiction exercised by or over 'embassies, aircraft and ships'. Regarding cases of irregular extradition (as in *Öcalan* and '*Carlos*'), the House rejected the idea that the United Kingdom was exercising 'effective control' over legislation and found that control was in the hands of the United States. Moreover, the situation in the region was one of near-anarchy. In any event, extraterritorial jurisdiction could not be exercised in Iraq, outside the Convention's 'legal space', except regarding the applicants' relatives shot in the streets of Bassorah during security operations. Therefore, the only person under United Kingdom jurisdiction was a hotel receptionist who was tortured and beaten to death in a British detention centre in Bassorah, the judges considering that such centres could be compared to an embassy, a ship or aircraft flying the United Kingdom flag: according to the House of Lords, if the victim had been beaten to death *on the way* to the Centre, he would not have been within British jurisdiction, and the Convention would not have been applicable.

b   Arguments of the Parties

The *United Kingdom* accepted the *Banković* precedent, that is, the rule of territoriality and exceptional departures therefrom. These departures cannot be 'divided and tailored', that is, applied in some issues but not in others (see paras. 109 and 110 of the *Al-Skeini* judgment). The ECHR was an 'instrument for maintaining public order' in Europe. It was, therefore, confined to its 'legal space', *i.e.* the territory of the Contracting States. The argument based on the Convention's 'legal space' made it impossible to assert control over areas outside of the latter unless those areas had been incorporated into that space by declarations under Article 56 of the Convention. The fact that such a declaration was necessary to extend the Convention's 'legal space' showed that exceptions to the principle of territoriality were not readily admitted. The idea of effective control could not as such justify an exception. Moreover, it was not the United Kingdom which exercised control over the space concerned but the CPA and, subsequently, the Iraqi Interim Government, both bodies having, incidentally, been widely recognised, contrary to the 'TRNC' (Turkish Republic of Northern Cyprus) or the 'RMT' (Moldovan Republic of Transnistria); in addition, the occupation regime in Iraq was transitory in character. In any event,

---

39   On this limitation, see the *Banković* decision, above, II.2.c.

occupation regimes do not wield complete authority in all areas of occupied territory and over all persons on it (paras. 109–114).

The *exceptional* situations in which there is extraterritorial jurisdiction are those related to the activities of diplomatic agents and consular officers or of other agents authorised by the local authorities, and the activities of foreign ships and aircraft; but this was not the case here, at least for the first four applicants (para. 115).

The exercise of legal power by United Kingdom troops is based on the 1907 Hague Rules on Land Warfare,[40] Article 43 of which provides that the occupant is bound to ensure "public order and safety". This is a *sui generis* concept unsuitable in the area of jurisdiction (para. 117).

'Effective control' of the United Kingdom was exercised only over the sixth applicant, who was held in a British detention centre. This situation was compared by the respondent State to that of persons localised on extraterritorial embassy premises (para. 118).

The *applicants* agreed that jurisdiction, as understood in Article 1 of the Convention, was essentially territorial in character, but that it could also result from other factors: from the conduct of agents of foreign States, and effective control over foreign territory. This occurred where representatives of a foreign State exercised authority over given persons or objects, as in Northern Cyprus. But in the present circumstances, though there was jurisdiction, that concept – and the theory of State agent authority – could not apply because Turkey had not (yet) accepted the jurisdiction of the ECtHR. In the present case, the situation was different: the United Kingdom acted through State agents whose task it was to maintain public order and security. Thus the element of control established a link between the applicants and the United Kingdom (paras. 121–124).

There was another link between the applicants and the United Kingdom which was constitutive of jurisdiction at the relevant time: the respondent State exercised effective general control over South-Western Iraq on the basis of its authority as occupant power pursuant to Article 42 of the 1907 Hague Regulations on Land Warfare.[41] This authority, deriving from belligerent occupation, was in harmony with the ideas of extraterritorial jurisdiction and of extraterritorial application of human rights rules (para. 126).

The applicants disagreed with the idea that jurisdiction, "based on effective control over a territory", could be exercised only within the Convention's 'legal

---

40   C. Parry, *Consolidated Treaty Series*, Vol. 205 (1907), p. 289.
41   Article 42 establishes when a territory may be considered as 'occupied' and clarifies that occupation only extends to territory over which the authority of the occupation's army is effectively exercised.

space', *i.e.* the territories of the States Parties to the Convention. They also rejected the view that 'effective control' must have a quality approaching that of territorial sovereignty because that would mean that a number of individuals go unprotected and that foreign States claiming 'effective control' act with lesser determination to uphold human rights (para. 126).[42]

The duty under international humanitarian law to apply local law in occupied territories instead of the occupant's own law cannot, according to the applicants, be used to challenge the coming of such territory under the jurisdiction of the occupant State. In support the applicants cite the judgment of the ICJ on *Armed Activities on the Territory of the Congo*[43] and its advisory opinion on the *Wall*,[44] where the Court said that occupant States shall apply international human rights law to occupied territory (para. 122).

In some situations – such as that of the sixth applicant – even the respondent State would concede that it exercised control. However, the concept of jurisdiction under Article 1 of the Convention does not favour the idea that extraterritorial powers are limited to quasi-territorial enclaves such as detention centres directly run by the occupant power. The respondent State's jurisdiction – and responsibility – would exist even if the sixth applicant had been tortured at his workplace or in a van (para. 123).

It was the authority and control exercised over the victims that accounted for Britain's jurisdiction. The mandate of its armed forces and other personnel was a vast one: maintain public order, ensure the safety of civilians, support the civil administration. Moreover, authority and control were also exercised through the CPA. Such control equally results from the United Kingdom's 'effective control' over the South-East of Iraq, and this makes it possible to recognise the extraterritorial jurisdiction (and responsibility) of that State in matters of internationally protected human rights (para. 124).

A certain number of *non-governmental organisations* in the field of human rights also participated in the proceedings and contributed an interesting argument: In view of the guiding principles relating to human rights, as applied by the UN Human Rights Committee and the ICJ, wherever the conduct of a State outside its territory was at stake, it would be necessary to avoid double

---

42 The argument that 'effective control' must practically be the equivalent of territorial sovereignty also runs counter to the idea that the occupant does not acquire sovereignty over the occupied territory and may not annex it.

43 *Armed Activities on the Territory of the Congo*, Congo v. Uganda, judgment of 19 December 2005, ICJ Reports 2005, p. 168, paras. 172–180, 205–212, 216–219.

44 *Legal Consequences of the Construction of a Wall in the Occupied Palestinian Territory*, advisory opinion of 9 July 2004, ICJ Reports 2004, p. 136, paras. 102, 106, 108–111, 136.

standards and to make it impossible, for a State, to commit breaches of human rights law which, had they occurred on that State's own territory, could not have gone unpunished (para. 128).

c   The Judgment of the Court

Following established practice, the Court first sets out the *general principles* governing the matter under consideration and then applies them to the case at hand.

Mentioning *Ilaşcu* and *Banković*, the Court begins by putting forward, for the purposes of interpreting the expression 'jurisdiction' used in Article 1 of the ECHR, the principle of territoriality which, however, suffers exceptions in cases in which States exercise jurisdiction beyond their territories (paras. 131 and 132).

One of the reasons for allowing such exceptions is the authority and control exercised by a State's agents beyond its boundaries (*Drozd and Janousek*; *Loizidou*, merits;[45] *Banković*). This first exception to the principle of territoriality has been formulated by the Court in general terms and requires elaboration (para. 133).

First, jurisdiction beyond State boundaries may be exercised by a State's diplomatic agents and consular officers, in conformity with international law, if their activities denote authority and control over persons (*Banković*, among other cases) (para. 134).

Second, extraterritorial jurisdiction may result from the local government's consent, invitation or tolerance (*Banković*, para. 71). Thus, if the organs of a State wield executive or judicial power abroad, that State is deemed responsible, under the Convention, if such exercise results in violations of that instrument, provided that the conduct in question is imputable to these organs rather than to the territorial sovereign (reference to *Drozd and Janousek* and several other cases) (para. 135).

Third, the Court's case-law shows that, in some situations, the use of force by State agents abroad may place individuals under that State's jurisdiction. This is what happened in *Öcalan* (para. 91), where the Court found that, with his transfer by Kenya to Turkish agents, Öcalan passed under Turkish jurisdiction, even though Turkey's authority was exercised abroad. Similarly, in *Issa*, if it had been established that the relatives of the applicants had indeed been arrested and executed in Northern Iraq by Turkish forces, Turkey would have exercised (extraterritorial) jurisdiction under Article 1 of the Convention and, therefore, been responsible for the killings. In *Al-Saadoon* (paras. 86–89), the Court had found that the control exercised by the United Kingdom over its

---

45   No. 15318/89, GC, judgment of 18 December 1996.

military prisons and their inmates was absolute, and that this brought them under British jurisdiction. In *Medvedyev* v. *France*, those who were on board ship from its interception by French agents on the high seas to the ship's arrival in France were under continuous French control and, thus, French jurisdiction (para. 136).

Fourth, said the Court, the State may exercise effective control over foreign territory, directly or *via* a subordinate local administration, following lawful or unlawful military action. This entails jurisdiction under Article 1 of the Convention and, hence, responsibility of that State (*Loizidou*, preliminary objections, para. 62; *Cyprus* v. *Turkey*, para. 76; *Banković*, para. 70; *Ilaşcu*, paras. 314–316; and *Loizidou*, merits, para. 52[46]). If such control exists, it matters not whether the foreign State does or does not exercise *detailed* control over the administration's policies and activities. As it ensures the survival of that administration by its presence and its military and other support, the foreign State engages its responsibility for it. Article 1 of the ECHR obliges that State to secure on the territory in question the rights recognised by the Convention and its Protocols (*Cyprus* v. *Turkey*, para. 76–77). (Para. 138.)

The question of whether a Contracting State does indeed have authority and effective control over territory beyond its boundaries is one of fact. To answer it, the Court uses elements such as the number of troops on that territory (*Loizidou*, merits, paras. 16 and 56; *Ilaşcu*, para. 387), as well as factors such as the extent to which the military, economic and political support extended to subordinate local authorities confers on the latter influence and control within the region (*Ilaşcu*, paras. 388–394) (paras. 139–140).

Jurisdiction based on 'effective control', as described above, cannot, on the one hand, prevail over or replace the declaration system under Article 56 of the Convention for extending the Contracting State's jurisdiction to overseas territories.[47] That system cannot, on the other hand, be used to limit jurisdiction under Article 1. Instances where a State exercises 'effective control' must be distinguished from those where a State has failed to declare, under Article 56, the extension of 'jurisdiction' to its overseas possessions (*Loizidou*, preliminary objections, paras. 86–89; *Quark Fishing Ltd.* v. *United Kingdom*).

Finally, the Court emphasises that if a Contracting State militarily occupies the territory of another Contracting State, it will in principle be responsible for

---

46 No. 15318/89, GC, judgment of 18 December 1996.
47 Here the Court may have reached the right conclusion for the wrong reason: the real reason was the permission asked for and obtained from the Cambodian authorities. See the present author's "Human Rights and the Law of the Sea – A Disastrous Encounter", *op. cit.*, pp. 121–123.

the respect of human rights in that territory, for otherwise there would be discontinuity of protection (*Loizidou*, merits, para. 78; *Banković*, para. 80). This does not mean, *a contrario*, that there can be no jurisdiction under Article 1 outside the territories of the Contracting Parties. The Court has never sanctioned such a restriction in its case-law (see *Öcalan, Issa, Al-Saadoon* and *Medvedyev* cases).[48]

Turning to the *application* of the above general considerations to *Al-Skeini*, the Court begins with the fact that forces of the United States and the United Kingdom, together with those of their coalition partners, entered Iraq on 20 March 2003 with the aim of removing the Ba'ath regime. This was achieved by 1 May 2003. The two powers set up the CPA, one of whose attributions it was, according to a common letter sent to the President of the United Nations Security Council on 8 May 2003, to assure security in Iraq, including the respect of civil law and order. The contents of this letter were noted by the Council in its Resolution 1483 of 22 May 2003 which, *inter alia*, asked the Occupying Powers "to promote the welfare of the Iraqi people through the effective administration of the territory, in particular by restoring security and stability" (paras. 143–146).

During that period, the United Kingdom exercised military control over an area which included the province of Bassorah where the applicants' relatives had died. From 1 May 2003 onward, British forces were responsible for maintaining security there and supported the civil administration (para. 147).

July 2003 saw the establishment of the Governing Council of Iraq. The CPA remained in power but now had a duty to consult that Council. In Resolution 1511 of 16 October 2003, the United Nations Security Council stressed the temporary character of the CPA and of its powers, and authorised the creation of a multi-national force (MNF) under unified command to take the necessary measures for maintaining security and stability. Resolution 1546 of 8 June 2004, finally, endorsed the constitution of a sovereign interim government to take over full responsibility for administering Iraq; this happened at the end of June 2004, when the occupation came to an end (para. 148).

The Court's views on jurisdiction can be summarised as follows: from the removal of the Ba'ath regime to the emergence of the Iraqi Interim Government, the United Kingdom exercised, with the United States, some powers normally reserved to the territorial government, in particular authority and responsibility for the maintenance of security in South-Eastern Iraq. Considering this circumstance, the Court holds that at the relevant time the United Kingdom, through the forces engaged in security operations in and around Bassorah, exercised authority and control over individuals killed in the course of such

---

48   But see the decision in *Banković*, above, II.2.c.

operations. A jurisdictional link was thereby established, for the purposes of Article 1 of the ECHR, between the United Kingdom and these individuals (para. 149).

The Court thus concludes that the United Kingdom had jurisdiction under Article 1 (para. 150). It then proceeds to examine whether, as alleged by the applicants, the respondent State had failed in its procedural duty under Article 2 of the Convention (right to life) to conduct an effective investigation into the killings (paras. 151–177), finding that, for all but the sixth applicant, there had been a violation of that duty. Under Article 41 of the Convention, it allocated damages and costs to the five first applicants.

d   The Concurring Opinions

Though generally agreeing with the judgment, *Judge Rozakis* takes issue with the Court for having relied on the fact that, to reach its conclusions on extraterritorial jurisdiction, it relied on both 'State agent authority' and 'effective control' of foreign territory as a consequence of – lawful or unlawful – military action by the United Kingdom.

Judge Bonello agrees that the CPA vested in the members of that Authority "all executive, legislative and judicial authority necessary to achieve its objectives". While conceding that the present judgment puts the doctrine of extraterritorial jurisdiction "on a sounder footing than ever before" (para. 31), Judge Bonello still thinks it unsatisfactory in that it rests on a series of 'patchwork' decisions.

Instead he proposes a 'functional' test. Under Article 1 of the ECHR, the States Parties undertake to secure to everyone within their jurisdiction the rights and freedoms protected by the Convention, the aim being, as stated in the preamble, to ensure "the *universal* and effective recognition and observance of the rights…declared in the Convention" by: (i) not violating these rights; (ii) establishing mechanisms to prevent violations; (iii) investigating complaints for abuses of human rights; (iv) punishing agents who have committed such abuses; and (v) compensating the victims (para. 10). A State would be considered as effectively exercising jurisdiction in the sense of the Convention "*wherever the observance or the breach of any of these functions is within its authority and control*" (author's emphasis). According to Judge Bonello, this means that jurisdiction in the sense of Article 1 is no longer 'territorial' or 'extraterritorial' and simply denotes the ability of and, indeed, the obligation for a State to perform the functions listed above; "the one honest test, in *all* circumstances (including extra-territoriality) is: it depends on the agents of the [foreign] State whether the alleged violation would be committed or would not be committed" (para. 16).

If it does, the facts fall under the jurisdiction of the State concerned. In the situations addressed here, the application of the functional test advocated by Judge Bonello would lead to the conclusion that all the alleged killings "fall squarely within the jurisdiction of the United Kingdom" (para. 22). In the context of military occupation, there should, in addition, be a rebuttable presumption that the occupying power has authority and control (para. 24). It is up to that power to prove that it has not.

In a parting shot, Judge Bonello asks who would have 'jurisdiction' if the United Kingdom had not. Despite the volatile situation, there still was, in the region of Bassorah, an authority laying down the law, running the correctional facilities, maintaining communications, providing health services, food and water, controlling contraband, terrorism and crime as best it could. That authority was the United Kingdom.

3 Al-Jedda v. United Kingdom[49]

From the angle of jurisdiction under Article 1 of the ECHR, the case of *Al-Jeddah* was far simpler. It involved an Iraqi/British dual national who, in 2004, returned to Iraq with his family. There he was arrested and interned in a British detention centre until 2007, when he was set free but stripped of his British nationality. The reason for his internment was that he presented a high security risk, having personally recruited terrorists to operate in Iraq, conspired with a terrorist to build a bomb to be used against the Coalition, and contributed to introducing explosives for use against Coalition forces. The central issue of the case was not so much the applicability of Article 1 of the Convention *per se* – the applicant had spent three years in a British detention centre – as the question who, of the United Kingdom or the United Nations, had jurisdiction over, *i.e.* responsibility for, the applicant's fate.

In the course of the internal proceedings in the United Kingdom, the Government had admitted that his detention drew the applicant under British jurisdiction (para. 69). And the applicant's argument was not the absence of jurisdiction *per se* but a lack of imputability due to the fact that 'authority and control' lay with the United Nations rather than the United Kingdom (para. 64).

Accordingly, the Strasbourg Court wasted little time over the jurisdictional issue as such, having found that even the British courts had conceded that the applicant was under British jurisdiction pursuant to Article 1 of the Convention. Instead it concentrated on the question of whether responsibility rested with the United Nations or with the State (paras. 76–85). It determined that authority

---

49   No. 27021/08, GC, judgment of 7 July 2011.

and control lay with the latter and found that there had been a breach of Article 5.1 (right to liberty and security) (paras. 87–110).

IV   Recent Cases

1   *Hirsi Jamaa and Others* v. *Italy*[50]

The case of *Hirsi Jamaa and Others* v. *Italy* concerned 24 Somali and Eritrean nationals in three boats coming from Libya and attempting to reach the Italian coasts. When they were at a distance of 35 nautical miles from the Italian island of Lampedusa, they were intercepted by three Italian coast guard vessels. They were then transferred to Italian naval vessels and returned to Tripoli (Libya), their personal effects having been confiscated under a convention against clandestine immigration between Italy and Libya.

An issue arose over Article 1 of the ECHR. The applicants argued that Italy unquestionably had jurisdiction and responsibility under that provision. As soon as their boats had been boarded, they had passed under Italian control (para. 67). The Government, though admitting that the events involved Italian naval vessels, contended that they had not exercised 'absolute and exclusive control'. The interception on the high seas, in the course of a rescue operation based on a rule of international law, could not be viewed as a maritime police operation. The Italian vessels assisted the fugitives and then, in conformity with bilateral agreements, returned them to the point of departure of their journey. There was no violence, no boarding, and no weapons were used.

The Court recalls its position according to which jurisdiction under Article 1 of the Convention is essentially territorial, although in exceptional circumstances acts of the Contracting Parties can produce effects outside the Parties' territories. Such situations arose as a consequence of military action which led to the establishment of authority and effective control outside national territory (see *Loizidou*, preliminary objections); but this was not so when, as in *Banković*, only an instantaneous extraterritorial act was at stake. There are, adds the Court, other instances of extraterritorial exercise of jurisdiction in cases involving activities of diplomatic and consular personnel, and vessels on the high seas. In the present case, under the rules of the Law of the Sea, the jurisdiction is that of the flag State.[51] Italy cannot disclaim jurisdiction and, hence, jurisdiction and responsibility could not be denied by arguing that a

---

50   No. 27765/09, GC, judgment of 23 February 2012.
51   Article 92 of the United Nations Convention on the Law of the Sea, of 10 December 1982, United Nations Treaty Series, Vol. 1833, p. 397.

rescue operation was involved, even if Italy exercised but minimal control. But control there was; Italy had jurisdiction and, hence, was responsible (paras. 76–82).

2 Catan and Others v. Moldova and Russia

The case of *Catan and Others* v. *Moldova and Russia*[52] bore on the relations between the Republic of Moldova, the (unrecognised) rebel movement MRT and Russia. The relations between these three entities are described in the Court's judgment and also in the *Ilaşcu* judgment mentioned earlier. Their essential features are the domination of Transnistria by Russia, resulting from the permanent presence of Russian armed forces and an arms depot as well as from the presence of a large number of Russian-speaking (and -writing) inhabitants, and from resentment on the part of Moldova for being deprived of part of its territory and population. Attempts were undertaken to calm the situation and to obtain the departure of the Russian troops and arms, but in vain.

The present case, involving a large number of students and parents in the MRT, concerned measures directed at certain schools which had refused to teach the writing of the Moldavian language in Cyrillic letters and to follow MRT school plans. Students were harassed or evicted, and schools closed – a bundle of measures intended to achieve the russification of the MRT's population. The applicants alleged violations of Article 2 of Additional Protocol No. 1 to the Convention (right to education).

The judgment of the Court begins – as did that in the *Ilaşcu case* – by examining jurisdiction under Article 1 of the Convention. It first points out that the presence of jurisdiction is a necessary condition for holding a Contracting State responsible (para. 103). Jurisdiction is mainly territorial and "presumed to be exercised normally throughout a State's territory" (*Ilaşcu; Assanidze*). Its extraterritorial exercise is only permitted exceptionally (*Banković*, para. 67; *Al-Skeini*, para. 131) (paras. 103–104). To this day, the Court's case-law has admitted exceptions such as the effective exercise of control over an area outside the national territory, be it directly through the action of the armed forces or indirectly through a subordinate local administration (*Al-Skeini*, para. 138). Where the existence of such domination is established, it is not necessary to prove that the Contracting State concerned had 'detailed control' over the acts and policies of the local administration. The fact that the latter survives thanks to the support provided by the controlling State entails the latter's responsibility for

---

52 No. 43370/04, 8252/05 and 18454/06, judgment of 19 October 2012. See also *Ivantoc and Others* v. *Moldova and Russia*, No. 23687/05, GC, judgment of 15 November 2011.

the policies and acts in the area controlled and for the full range of substantive rights secured by the Convention and the applicable protocols (*Al-Skeini*, para. 138) (para. 106).

Whether a State exercises effective control outside its territory is a question of fact. To answer it, the Court will primarily evaluate the strength of the State's military presence in the area (*Loizidou*, merits, paras. 16 and 56; *Ilaşcu*, para. 387; *Al-Skeini*, para. 139) (para. 107).

The Court then turns to the *application* of the above principles to the case at hand. Regarding the *Republic of Moldova*, it finds that while Moldova exercises no control over the territory concerned, the latter remains State territory and that Moldova continues to be under an obligation to use all legal and diplomatic means to continue to secure the rights and freedoms in the Convention for those living in that territory (*Ilaşcu*, para. 333) (paras. 109–110).

Concerning the *Russian Federation*, the Court states that the essential part of the facts fall into the same period as those of the *Ilaşcu* case, where it had found that the MRT survived thanks to the military, economic and financial support of Russia and thus remained under Russian domination, even though the Russian Federation had no direct influence over what happened. It then seeks to establish whether Russia, in the relevant period, exercised effective control over the MRT. While the presence of Russian troops was relatively modest, considering the surface of the MRT, the importance of the Russian arms store on MRT territory was considerable; there was, moreover, the fact that the rebellion had been made possible by Russian support, as well as the fact that one-fifth of the MRT's population was granted Russian nationality (paras. 111–121). The Court thus concludes that the events of the period from 2002 to 2004 occurred under Russian jurisdiction.

The Court then finds that there *was* a breach of Article 2 of Additional Protocol No. 1 (paras. 136–144) and proceeds to examine who is responsible for it. It holds (paras. 145–148) that Moldova has done everything in its power to end the situation complained of. As far as Russia is concerned, there is no proof of direct involvement of its agents, but there is evidence that that State gave military, economic and financial support to the MRT, which could not have survived otherwise. Therefore, Russia is responsible for the violation of Article 2 of Additional Protocol No. 1 (paras. 149–150).

v Conclusion

In principle, Article 1 of the ECHR is based on territoriality, as is the notion of jurisdiction in international law generally; but there are exceptions to territoriality which bear the general label 'authority and effective control'. Article 1 is intended to uphold human rights within the territories of the Contracting States, including areas identified by declarations made under Article 56 of the Convention. This means, on the one hand, that Contracting States are responsible for activities on their territory, regardless of whether and to what extent they effectively control the latter, unless they have expressly declared their inability to do so (*Ilaşcu*; *Assanidze*; *Catan*). On the other hand, they are responsible for human rights violations in areas outside their territory over which they exercise authority and effective control.

According to the ECtHR's case-law, States Parties to the Convention may claim extraterritorial jurisdiction – and be answerable for its actions from the human rights angle – in the following situations: (i) when diplomatic representatives, consular officers or other agents are authorised to act, under customary international law, in foreign lands; (ii) when a State exercises jurisdiction over its ships, aircraft and spacecraft abroad in accordance with the rules of international law (*Medvedyev*; *Hirsi Jamaa*); (iii) where a State, on the basis of international law or of its own will, allows foreign States' agents, including judges (*Drozd and Janousek*), to operate on its territory, within the limits of that permission; and (iv) if, as a consequence of the use of force, a Contracting State extends its authority and control over territory belonging to another State for a short (*Issa*) or a longer (*Ilaşcu*; *Northern Cyprus*) period, provided that such authority and control include the power to deal with human rights situations. This was certainly not the case in *Banković*. Authority and control in the sense used here also exist where local and subordinate administrations act under the supervision of the occupying State's authority. All these elements are confirmed by the Iraqi cases examined in the present paper.

In addition, these cases improved over the situation that existed previously. First, it will be remembered that prior to that moment the United Kingdom, as respondent State, had contended that, even in the hypothesis of occupation, extraterritorial jurisdiction existed only when the complainant was kept in detention centres run by the occupant. This is not, or no longer, the case: if the occupant State holds general control over foreign territory – even such control may not be 'detailed' – under Article 1 of the Convention, it will be exercising extraterritorial jurisdiction under that Article and, accordingly, be accountable for violations of the latter (*Al-Saadoon and Mufdhi*; *Al-Skeini*). One of the follow-up cases (*Hirsi Jamaa*) further shows that salvage operations at sea conducted by naval forces entail extraterritorial jurisdiction, *i.e.* authority and effective control, and, therefore, responsibility for extraterritorially committed violations of human rights.

Second, the idea of limiting extraterritoriality and the ensuing responsibility to the 'legal space' of the Convention, expounded by the Court in *Banković*, and meaning that the Convention cannot be applied beyond the territory of the Contracting States, had already been contradicted in the cases of *Issa* and *Medvedyev*. Now, after the Iraqi cases, it has been definitively laid to rest.

There remains the problem of weapons directed by agents of one Contracting State at persons on the territory of other States (see *Isaak, Solomou, Pad, Andreou, Issa*). According to the Court, extraterritorial jurisdiction may exist even there, in the absence of authority and 'effective' control.

That leaves the proposals made by Judge Bonello in his separate opinion appended to *Al-Skeini*. In its judgment, the Court relies on concepts and ideas based on earlier case-law. Judge Bonello proposes to do away with these elements and to adopt a 'functional' approach under which States would be duty-bound to respect the Convention: (i) by not breaching Convention standards; (ii) by establishing systems to prevent breaches; (iii) by investigating complaints for abuses of human rights; (iv) by sanctioning agents guilty of such abuses; and (v) by compensating the victims. According to Judge Bonello, a State should be considered as effectively exercising jurisdiction in the sense of the Convention "wherever the observance or the breach of any of these functions is within its authority and control". This approach would have the merit of simplifying a relatively complex issue (as is the definition of territorial and extraterritorial jurisdiction in international law generally).

Judge Bonello's proposal is tempting but deviates from the case-law built up by the Court over a long period of time. It could also be viewed as over-extending the concept of extraterritoriality. Consider, for instance, the effect this approach could have had on the *Banković* case where, indeed, one could have argued that the NATO States had been in a position to avoid the human rights violations complained of by the applicants – simply by not undertaking the raid. Moreover, as Judge Bonello himself recognises, the situation has significantly improved with the *Al-Skeini* judgment. Another improvement could be made by accepting Judge Bonello's less far-reaching proposal to create a – rebuttable – presumption that, in the event of occupation, the occupying power *does* have jurisdiction as well as authority and effective control.

CHAPTER 24

Some Reflections on the Right of Access to Justice in Its Wide Dimension

Antônio Augusto Cançado Trindade [*]

I   Introduction

It is with special satisfaction that I associate myself with this just and timely tribute to Professor Budislav Vukas, with whom I have shared some memorable moments of fruitful academic work at the *Institut de Droit International*. I take the occasion to address briefly a topic which is of great significance to me, namely, that of the right of access to justice in its wide dimension. The right of access to justice (comprising the right to an effective domestic remedy and to its exercise with full judicial guarantees of the due process of law, and the faithful execution of the judgment), at national and international levels, is, in effect, a fundamental cornerstone of the protection of human rights. It is provided for, *e.g.*, under the human rights treaties endowed nowadays with international human rights tribunals, namely, the European Convention on Human Rights, the American Convention on Human Rights, and the African Charter on Human and Peoples' Rights. The right of access to justice conforms a true *right to the Law*, disclosing a conception of access to justice *lato sensu*.

II   The Normative Dimension

In so far as access to international justice is concerned, the right of individual petition has proven to be an effective means of resolving not only cases pertaining to individuals, but also cases of massive and systematic violations of human rights. At normative level, the fundamental importance of the provision on the

---

[*]   Former President of the Inter-American Court of Human Rights; Judge of the International Court of Justice; Emeritus Professor of International Law of the University of Brasília, Brazil; Honorary Professor of the University of Utrecht; Honorary Fellow of the University of Cambridge; Member of the *Curatorium* of the Hague Academy of International Law, and of the *Institut de Droit International*; President of the Latin American Society of International Law.

right of individual petition was reckoned in the corresponding *travaux préparatoires* of the three aforementioned regional Conventions on Human Rights. Under each of them the right of individual petition has, in practice, and not surprisingly, had a distinct historical development. Under the three Conventions, however, the pursuance of a wide conception *ratione personae* of the right of individual petition – a wide conception of the *legitimatio ad causam* – has had the immediate effect of enlarging the scope of protection, mainly in cases where the alleged victims (*e.g.*, *incommunicado* detainees, disappeared persons, among other situations) find themselves in the impossibility to act on their own, and stand in need of the initiative of a third party as petitioner on their behalf.

III The Procedural Dimension

Of all the mechanisms of international protection of human rights, the right of individual petition is in effect the most dynamic, in attributing the initiative of action to the individual petitioner himself (the ostensibly weaker party *vis-à-vis* the public power), distinctly from the exercise *ex officio* of other methods (such as those of reports and investigations) on the part of the organs of international supervision. The granting of *locus standi in judicio* to individuals before international human rights tribunals, in all stages of the procedure before them, has contributed to render the protected rights truly effective.

The human person has thus been erected as subject of the International Law of Human Rights, endowed with juridico-procedural capacity in the proceedings before the Inter-American Court. This has undoubtedly been a development of much significance; as I saw it fit to ponder in my intervention of 10.06.2003 at the plenary of the General Assembly of the OAS in Santiago of Chile, as then President of the Inter-American Court of Human Rights, this latter, in the evolution of its procedures and of its case-law, has given a relevant contribution to

> the consolidation of the new paradigm of International Law, the new *jus gentium* of the XXIst century, which recognizes the human being as subject of rights.[1]

---

1 OAS, *Asamblea General, XXXIII Período Ordinario de Sesiones (Santiago de Chile, Junio de 2003)* – *Actas y Documentos*, vol. II, Washington D.C., OAS General Secretariat, pp. 168–171.

The consolidation of the *locus standi in judicio* of individuals before the Court is an appropriate and logical development, as it does not seem reasonable to conceive rights at international level without the corresponding capacity to vindicate them. Upon the right of individual petition is erected the legal mechanism of emancipation of the human being *vis-à-vis* the State itself for the protection of his rights in the domain of the International Law of Human Rights, – an emancipation which comes at last to confer an ethical content to the norms of both domestic public law and international law.

The necessary recognition of the *locus standi in judicio* of the alleged victims (or their legal representatives) before international human rights tribunals constitutes a most significant advance, but not necessarily the final stage of the improvement of the mechanism of protection under the American Convention: from the *locus standi*, the evolution points towards the future recognition of the right of *direct access* of individuals before them (*jus standi*), so as to lodge a complaint directly with it. This is already the case, for the last decade, in the experience of the European Court of Human Rights in particular.

In effect, to recognize the *locus standi in judicio* of the victims (or their relatives or representantives) before the Court (in cases already submitted to it by the Commission) contributes to the 'jurisdictionalization' of the mechanism of protection, putting an end to the ambiguity of the role of the Commission, which rigorously is not a 'party' in the process, but rather the guardian of the correct application of the Convention. The free and full exercise of the right of individual petition has also contributed to secure respect for the obligations of objective character binding States Parties.[2]

IV   The Hermeneutic Dimension

The compulsory jurisdiction of international human rights tribunals (as in the case of the European Court) is the indispensable complement of the right of individual petition under the American Convention: both constitute the basic pillars of the international protection, of the mechanism of emancipation of the human being *vis-à-vis* his own State.[3] Furthermore, both the European and

---

2   In several cases, such exercise of the right of petition has gone further, having brought about changes in the domestic legal order and in the practice of the public organs of States Parties concerned.

3   As foreseen by the so-called 'founding fathers' of the law of nations; cf. A.A. Cançado Trindade, "The Emancipation of the Individual from His Own State – The Historical Recovery

Inter-American Courts have rightly set limits to State voluntarism, have safeguarded the integrity of the respective human rights Conventions and the primacy of considerations of *ordre public* over the will of individual States, have set higher standards of State behaviour and established some degree of control over the interposition of undue restrictions by States, and have reassuringly enhanced the position of individuals as subjects of the International Law of Human Rights, with full procedural capacity.

In so far as the basis of their jurisdiction in contentious matters is concerned, eloquent illustrations of their firm stand in support of the integrity of the mechanisms of protection of the two Conventions are afforded, for example, by the decisions of the European Court in the *Belilos* versus *Switzerland* case (1988), in the *Loizidou* versus *Turkey* case (Preliminary Objections, 1995), and in the *I. Ilascu, A. Lesco, A. Ivantoc and T. Petrov-Popa* versus *Moldovia and the Russian Federation* case (2001), as well as by the decisions of the Inter-American Court in the *Constitutional Tribunal* and *Ivtcher Bronstein* versus *Peru* cases, Jurisdiction (1999), and in the *Hilaire, Constantine and Benjamin and Others* versus *Trinidad and Tobago* (Preliminary Objection, 2001).

The two aforementioned international human rights tribunals, by correctly resolving basic procedural issues raised in the aforementioned cases, have aptly made use of the techniques of public international law in order to strengthen their respective jurisdictions of protection of the human person. They have decisively safeguarded the integrity of the mechanisms of protection of the American and European Conventions on Human Rights, whereby the juridical emancipation of the human person *vis-à-vis* her own State is achieved.

v The Jurisprudential Dimension

Such jurisprudential dimension (added to the aforementioned previous dimensions) is of the utmost importance, as it discloses the endeavours of international human rights tribunals to secure the effective protection (*effet utile*) of the rights provided for in the respective regional Human Rights Conventions. In this respect, in the Judgment (on preliminary objections) of the Inter-American Court of Human Rights in the case of *Castillo Petruzzi and Others* versus *Peru* (of 04.09.1998), I saw it fit, in a lengthy Concurring Opinion,

---

of the Human Person as Subject of the Law of Nations", in: *Human Rights, Democracy and the Rule of Law – Liber Amicorum L. Wildhaber* (eds. S. Breitenmoser *et al.*), Zürich/Baden-Baden, Dike/Nomos, 2007, pp. 151–171.

to single out the *fundamental* character of the right of individual petition (Article 44 of the American Convention) as the "cornerstone of the access of the individuals to the whole mechanism of protection of the American Convention" (paras. 3 and 36–38).[4] After reviewing the *historia juris* of that right of petition (paras. 9–15), and the expansion of the notion of 'victim' in the international case-law under human rights treaties (paras. 16–19), I referred to the *autonomy* of the right of individual petition *vis-à-vis* the domestic law of the States (paras. 21, 27 and 29), and added:

> With the access of individuals to justice at international level, by means of the exercise of the right of individual petition, concrete expression was at last given to the recognition that the human rights to be protected are inherent to the human person and do not derive from the State. Accordingly, the action in their protection does not exhaust – cannot exhaust – itself in the action of the State. ...Had it not been for the access to the international instance, justice would never have been done in their concrete cases. ...It is by the free and full exercise of the right of individual petition that the rights set forth in the Convention become *effective*. (paras. 33 and 35)

The *contentieux* of the leading case of the *Street Children* (case *Villagrán Morales and Others* versus *Guatemala*, 1999–2001) disclosed the importance of the direct access of individuals to the international jurisdiction, enabling them to vindicate their rights against the manifestations of the arbitrary power, and giving an ethical content to the norms of both domestic public law and international law.[5] Its relevance was clearly demonstrated before the Court in the proceedings of that historical case, in which the mothers (and one grandmother) of the murdered children, as poor and abandoned as their sons (and one grandson), had access to the international jurisdiction, appeared before the Court,[6] and, due to the Judgments as to the merits and reparations of the

---

4 By means of such right of petition – a "definitive conquest of the International Law of Human Rights" – the "*historical rescue* of the position of the human being as subject of the International Law of Human Rights, endowed with full international procedural capacity" took place (paras. 5 and 12).

5 In my Separate Opinion in the case of the *Street Children* (reparations, 2001), I saw it fit to warn that the suffering of the most humble and vulnerable projects itself into the community or social *milieu* as a whole, and their close relatives are forced to live with the silence, the indifference and the oblivion of the others, permeating the whole community with suffering (para. 22).

6 Public hearings of 28–29.01.1999 and 12.03.2001 before the Court.

Inter-American Court,[7] which found in their support, they could at least recover the faith in human justice.

Four years later, the case of the *Institute of Reeducation of Minors* versus *Paraguay* (Judgment of 02.09.2004) came once again to demonstrate, as I pointed out in my Separate Opinion (paras. 3–4), that the human being, even in the most adverse conditions, has emerged as subject of the International Law of Human Rights, endowed with full international juridico-procedural capacity. The Court's Judgment in this last case duly recognized the high relevance of the historical reforms introduced in the fourth and current Rules of Court (paras. 107, 120–121 and 126), in force as from 2001,[8] in favour of the individuals' *titularity* of the protected rights. The aforementioned cases of the *Street Children* and of the *Institute of Reeducation of Minors* bear eloquent witness of such titularity, asserted and exercised before the Court, even in situations of the most extreme adversity.[9] To them, other cases can be added, with numerous other victims – *e.g.*, in infra-human conditions of detention, in forced displacement from their homes, in the condition of undocumented migrants, in situation of complete defencelessness, and even victims of massacres and their relatives – which, despite so much adversity, have had access to international justice.

It is significant that cases of massacres, which some decades ago fell into oblivion, are nowadays brought before an international human rights tribunal, as exemplified by the Judgments of the Inter-American Court in the cases of the massacres of *Barrios Altos* versus *Peru* (of 14.03.2001), of *Plan de Sánchez* versus *Guatemala* (of 29.04.2004), of the *19 Tradesmen* versus *Colombia* (of 05.07.2004), of *Mapiripán* versus *Colombia* (of 17.09.2005), of the *Community Moiwana* versus *Suriname* (of 15.06.2005), of *Pueblo Bello* versus *Colombia* (of 31.01.2006), of *Ituango* versus *Colombia* (of 01.07.2006), of *Montero Aranguren and Others* (*Retén de Catia*) versus *Venezuela* (of 05.07.2006), of the *Prison of Castro Castro* versus *Peru* (of 25.11.2006), of *La Cantuta* versus *Peru* (of 29.11.2006).

---

7 Of 19.11.1999 and of 26.05.2001, respectively.
8 *Cf.*, in this respect, A.A. Cançado Trindade, "Le nouveau Règlement de la Cour Interaméricaine des Droits de l'Homme: quelques réflexions sur la condition de l'individu comme sujet du Droit international", in: *Libertés, justice, tolérance – Mélanges en hommage au Doyen G. Cohen-Jonathan*, vol. I, Bruxelles, Bruylant, 2004, pp. 351–365.
9 In the case of the *Institute of Reeducation of Minors*, some of the interns were hurt or died burnt amidst three fires; yet, their cause, despite the limitations of their juridical capacity given their existential condition of minors of age, reached an international tribunal of human rights, thus asserting their *titularity* of rights emanated directly from International Law.

VI   The Epistemological Dimension

The International Law of Human Rights is ineluctably *victim-oriented*, and it could not be otherwise. The centrality of the victim in the international *contentieux* of human rights is unquestionable.[10] The right of access to justice, in its wide scope, is an imperative at both national and international levels. On this particular issue, there is a convergence between domestic public law and international law. From the perspective of the protected persons, effective domestic remedies integrate the international protection of human rights.[11]

1   *The Right of Access to Justice* Lato Sensu

The understanding of the matter at issue advanced by the Inter-American Court in its evolving case-law in recent years has been to the effect that the right of access to justice (*lato sensu*) at national and international levels amounts to the right to the *realization of material justice*. As such, it comprises not only the formal access to a tribunal or judge, but also respect for the guarantees of due process of law, the right to a fair trial, and to reparations (whenever they are due), and the faithful execution of judgments.[12]

---

10   To this effect, in my Separate Opinion in the case of the *Street Children* (*Villagrán Morales and Others* versus *Guatemala*, Judgment on Reparations, of 26.05.2001), I drew attention to this, concentrating attention on the triad conformed by victimization, human suffering, and rehabilitation of the victims (paras. 1–43). Moreover, in my Separate Opinions in the Judgments of the Court on the cases *Bulacio* versus *Argentina* (of 18.09.2003) and *Tibi* versus *Ecuador* (of 07.09.2004), I sought to identify the sense of the *reparatio* as from the centrality of the suffering of the victims, which I duly emphasized also in my Separate Opinions in the Judgments in the cases of *Brothers Gómez Paquiyauri* versus *Peru* (of 08.07.2004) and *Ximenes Lopes* versus *Brazil* (of 04.07.2006). And, in my Separate Opinion in the Judgment in the case of the *Community Moiwana* versus *Suriname* (of 15.06.2005), I sought to demonstrate the projection of human suffering in time, with direct implications for measures of reparation to the victims and their relatives. *Cf.* texts of the aforementioned Separate Opinions in: A.A. Cançado Trindade, *Derecho Internacional de los Derechos Humanos – Esencia y Trascendencia* (*Votos en la Corte Interamericana de Derechos Humanos, 1991–2006*), México, Ed. Porrúa/Univ. Iberoamericana, 2007, pp. 251–267, 363–374, 444–456, 417–432, 748–765, 980–983, and 539–567, respectively.
11   A.A. Cançado Trindade, *The Application of the Rule of Exhaustion of Local Remedies in International Law*, Cambridge, Cambridge University Press, 1983, pp. 1–445.
12   In fact, States Parties assume, each one individually, the duty to comply fully with the judgments and decisions of the Inter-American Court, as established in Article 68 of the American Convention itself, in application of the principle *pacta sunt servanda* (this being also an obligation of their own domestic law).

2   Access to Justice as an Imperative of Jus Cogens

Ever since the Inter-American Court, in its pioneering Advisory Opinion n. 18 (of 17.09.2003), on the *Juridical Condition and the Rights of Undocumented Migrants*, rightly enlarged the material content of *jus cogens* so as to comprise also the fundamental principle of equality and non-discrimination (including equality before the law), I began insisting on the need of widening further that material content so as to encompass likewise the right of access to justice.[13] I did so, *inter alia*, in my Separate Opinion (devoted to the right of access to justice *lato sensu*) in the Court's Judgment (of 31.01.2006) in the case of the *Massacre of Pueblo Bello* versus *Colombia*, drawing attention to the fundamental importance precisely of that right of access to justice (para. 65).

It was in the case of *Goiburú and Others* versus *Paraguay* (Judgment of 22.09.2006), concerning the sinister 'Operation Cóndor' of the so-called 'intelligence services' of the countries of the Southern Cone of South America (at the time of the dictatorships of three decades ago) that the Inter-American Court at last endorsed my thesis,[14] further enlarging the material content of *jus cogens*, so as to comprise the right of access to justice. In my Separate Opinions in the case *Goiburú and Others*,[15] as well as in the subsequent cases of *Almonacid Arellano* versus *Chile* (Judgment of 26.09.2006, paras. 58–60 of the Opinion), and of *La Cantuta* versus *Peru* (Judgment of 29.11.2006, paras. 49–62 of the Opinion), I stressed the considerable importance of such expansion of the material content of *jus cogens*.[16]

---

13   *Cf.*, to this effect, my Separate Opinions in the Court's Judgments in the cases of the *Massacre of Plan de Sánchez* versus *Guatemala* (merits, of 29.04.2004), paras. 22, 29–33 and 35 of the Opinion; and (reparations, of 19.11.2004), paras. 4–7 and 20–27 of the Opinion; of the *Brothers Gómez Paquiyauri* versus *Peru* (of 08.07.2004), paras. 37–44 of the Opinion; of *Tibi* versus *Ecuador* (of 07.09.2004), paras. 30–32 of the Opinion; of *Caesar* versus *Trinidad and Tobago* (of 11.03.2005), paras. 85–92 of the Opinion; of *Yatama* versus *Nicaragua* (of 23.06.2005), paras. 6–9 of the Opinion; of *Acosta Calderón* versus *Ecuador* (of 14.06.2005), paras. 4 and 7 of the Opinion; of the *Massacres of Ituango* versus *Colombia* (of 01.07.2006), para. 47 of the Opinion; of *Baldeón García* versus *Peru* (of 06.04.2006), paras. 9–10 of the Opinion; of *López Álvarez* versus *Honduras* (of 01.02.2006), paras. 53–55 of the Opinion.

14   *Cf.* the text of my Separate Opinion therein, reproduced in: A.A. Cançado Trindade, *Derecho Internacional de los Derechos Humanos – Esencia y Trascendencia* (*Votos en la Corte Interamericana de Derechos Humanos, 1991–2006*), Mexico, Edit. Porrúa/Universidad Iberoamericana, 2007, pp. 779–804.

15   Paras. 62–68 of the Opinion, text in *ibid.*, pp. 801–804.

16   *Cf.*, on the matter, recently, A.A. Cançado Trindade, "The Expansion of the Material Content of *Jus Cogens*: The Contribution of the Inter-American Court of Human Rights", in: *La Convention Européenne des Droits de l'Homme, un instrument vivant – Mélanges en l'honneur de Chr.L. Rozakis* (eds. D. Spielmann *et al.*), Bruxelles, Bruylant, 2011, pp. 27–46.

VII Conclusion

As I had the occasion to point out, as guest speaker, in my inaugural address at the opening of the judicial year of 2004 of the European Court of Human Rights in Strasbourg, the two international human rights tribunals (the European and Inter-American Courts) have achieved remarkable advances in the realization of justice, in the correct perspective, namely, that of *the justiciable*.[17] Both have contributed decisively to the emancipation of the human being *vis-à-vis* his own State, to the establishment of a new paradigm in the present domain of international protection, and to what I coined, in my Concurring Opinion (paras. 34–35) in the Court's Advisory Opinion n. 16 (of 01.10.1999) on *The Right to Information on Consular Assistance*, as the historical process of *humanization of International Law*.[18]

The theme of the right of access to justice *lato sensu* (encompassing the access to a competent court or a judge, the judicial guarantees of the due process of law, and the faithful execution of the judgment) has lately been object of close attention in the debates among members and former members of the three international human rights tribunals – the European, Inter-American and African Courts – held in the *Palais des Droits de l'Homme* in Strasbourg, on 8–9 December 2008, of which I keep the best memory. One is to expect convergence on the approach to the matter to be pursued in their respective case-law in the future.

Accordingly, and last but not least, the human person has come to occupy, in our days, the central position which corresponds to her, as *subject of both domestic and international law*, with international procedural capacity, amidst that process of *humanization of International Law*, more directly attentive to the identification and realization of common superior values and goals. She has exercised her capacity, in the vindicating of her rights, in situations of extreme vulnerability and under circumstances of the utmost adversity.[19] This evolution, in turn, paves the way for the new primacy of the *raison d'humanité* over the old *raison d'État*. The proper interpretation and application of Human Rights Conventions has contributed decisively to that effect.

---

17 A.A. Cançado Trindade, "Le développement du Droit international des droits de l'homme à travers l'activité et la jurisprudence des Cours européenne et interaméricaine des droits de l'homme", 16 *Revue universelle des droits de l'homme* (2004) n. 5–8, pp. 177–180.

18 A.A. Cançado Trindade, *A Humanização do Direito Internacional*, Belo Horizonte/Brazil, Edit. Del Rey, 2006, pp. 3–409.

19 *Cf.*, recently: A.A. Cançado Trindade, *The Access of Individuals to International Justice*, Oxford, Oxford University Press, 2011, pp. 1–236; A.A. Cançado Trindade, *State Responsibility in Cases of Massacres: Contemporary Advances in International Justice* (Inaugural Address, 10.11.2011), Utrecht, Universiteit Utrecht, 2011, pp. 1–71.

CHAPTER 25

Nation et minorités en Europe

*Giorgio Conetti**

I   Le principe de nationalité et ses correctifs

La question des minorités nationales s'est posée en Europe, en termes généraux et parfois dramatiques, notamment dans la partie centre-orientale du continent, en deux situations historiques qui présentent des analogies considérables. Bien que les causes aient étés différentes, une vaste réorganisation géopolitique a intéressé ces régions à la suite de la Première Guerre mondiale en 1918–1919 ou, à partir de l'année 1990, avec la fin de la division du continent entre deux blocs politiques idéologiquement opposés. Dans les deux cas, cette réorganisation a été marquée par la formation ou la restauration des Etats avec un fondement politique et constitutionnel basé sur le principe de nationalité, c'est-à-dire sur une homogénéité historique, de langue, culture, tradition et, parfois, religion. La formation ou l'extension spatiale de l'Etat s'assumait légitime en tant qu'exercice d'un droit d'autodétermination d'un peuple qui s'identifiait avec une nation, historiquement stabilisée sur un territoire qui, de ce fait, recevait le caractère presque sacral de patrie, mais, au même temps, exprimait une tendance à ignorer ou sous-estimer la présence de disparités en son intérieur. À leur tour, des groupes différenciés au sein d'un autre majoritaire, mais ayant pareillement les caractéristiques d'homogénéité et de stabilisation historiques, étaient amenés à revendiquer le même droit.

La réorganisation de vastes régions de l'Europe en raison du principe de nationalité, déjà affirmé au cours du XIXe siècle pour justifier l'indépendance de la Grèce, de la Belgique, des Etats balkaniques et de l'unité de l'Italie et de l'Allemagne, mais pas appliqué à la Pologne, se faisait, en 1919–20, à la suite de la dissolution des Empires multinationaux de l'Autriche-Hongrie, de la Russie tzariste et, en mesure plus réduite, de l'Allemagne. L'unité de ce dernier pays reposait jadis sur un facteur dynastique et une organisation institutionnelle détruits par la guerre et les mouvements révolutionnaires intérieures ; en 1990–91, la réorganisation sur base nationale se faisait à cause de l'effondrement des fédérations, dont la cohésion était obtenue par une idéologie politique jadis dominante mais qui venait de perdre toute effectivity.

---

*   Professeur émérite de Droit international, Université de l'Insubrie, Italie.

Largement spontané, bien que favorisé par les circonstances politiques de la guerre et de l'échec des partis communistes, le processus de formation des Etats en application du principe de nationalité avait été reconnu, aux époques considérées, comme bien fondé par la communauté internationale mais soumis chaque fois à des conditions à satisfaire, entre lesquelles se situe l'adoption de régimes de non-discrimination et de protection des minorités ayant, à leur tour, un caractère national. Cette exigence prenait origine dans l'impossibilité pratique d'une application intégrale et parfaite du dit principe et d'obtenir une complète homogénéité de la composition des peuples pour la formation d'Etats qui, néanmoins, revendiquaient leur légitimation sur ce fondement.

La réalisation approximative de l'uniformité nationale s'est donnée, par un ensemble des circonstances, aussi bien à la suite de la Première Guerre mondiale avec les traités de paix qui, en application du programme de paix du président Wilson, dessinaient pour la formation de nouveaux Etats ou l'agrandissement de quelques déjà existants des frontières correspondantes à la composition nationale de leurs populations, qu'à la suite de la situation issue de la dissolution des fédérations soviétique, yougoslave et tchécoslovaque.

Au cours de la Conférence de la paix de Paris en 1919, l'imparfaite application pratique du principe de nationalité a dû se faire pour des considérations d'ordre politique, de sécurité militaire, économiques, de voies de communication, aussi bien que, en plus d'un cas, à cause de l'inextricable situation d'enchevêtrement des populations intéressées, toutes raisons auxquelles même le président Wilson se plia. Il est bien vrai que, conscient des solutions inadéquates mais imposées par les circonstances, par la nécessité de conclure les traités et d'accepter des compromis, Wilson, accueillant une suggestion déjà avancée par Thomas Masaryk dans son essai *The New Europe. The Slav standpoint*, publié à Washington en octobre 1918, avait inséré, à l'article 3 de son premier projet du Pacte de la Société des Nations, la prévision d'une procédure de révision des traités. Celle-ci visait à corriger les situations inadéquates et disposer, avec le consentement de la majorité des Etats membres de la Société, des rectifications territoriales en raison des aspirations nationales et en conformité du principe de l'autodétermination. Dans la rédaction finale du Pacte, cette prévision spécifique devait venir substituée par une clause plus générale, à l'article 19, attribuant à l'Assemblée le droit de promouvoir un nouvel examen des traités devenus inapplicables, dont le maintien aurait mis en danger la paix.

Pour ces raisons, dans l'organisation des travaux de la Conférence de Paris, une de ses commissions fut destinée aux questions relatives aux nouveaux Etats et aux minorités, de cette façon liant les deux matières et envisageant la prévision de régimes de protection parallèlement à la naissance ou à l'agrandissement de ces Etats à l'œuvre des traités. Cette liaison devait rencontrer la méfiance et la résistance des Etats concernés, qui, tout de même, n'étaient pas en condition pour s'opposer valablement en vue du résultat de la reconnaissance internationale de leur indépendance et de leur admission à la Société des Nations. Aux observations critiques de la Pologne au moment de la rédaction du traité qu'on lui imposait, le Président de la Conférence, Clemenceau, répliquait, le 24 juin 1919, par une lettre soulignant la conformité à une pratique internationale établie de la subordination de la reconnaissance de nouveaux Etats à l'acceptation de principes communs aux Etats européens, avec référence, en particulier, à la condition du respect de la liberté religieuse requise aux Etats balkaniques par la Conférence de Berlin de 1878. Dans le cas du traité envisagé, puisque la garantie de son respect devait être attribuée à la Société des Nations et, en présence d'un différend, à la juridiction de la nouvelle Cour permanente de Justice internationale, il n'y aurait plus eu de danger que le traité puisse servir comme motif d'interférence ou pression des puissances dans les affaires intérieures des pays concernés.

La réorganisation de l'Europe suivie à la dissolution des fédérations, bien que faite en obsèques des principes de nationalité et d'autodétermination, à son tour s'est produite d'une façon insatisfaisante sous les deux profils, dès que les nouveaux Etats, issus ou rétablis par ce processus, maintenaient les mêmes frontières, en origines intérieures ou administratives, des unités déjà composant la fédération, sans corrections justifiées par une plus appropriée correspondance à la composition nationale de la population. Cette solution, comportant l'application, tout à fait nouvelle pour l'Europe, de la règle de l'*uti possidetis*, avait été reconnue comme nécessaire pour éviter des conflits, qui cependant se sont également produits, sans que les revendications nationales difformes aient obtenu soutien par la communauté internationale.

La conservation des frontières internes en qualité de nouvelles frontières internationales a été établie d'un consentement commun par les Etats successeurs de l'Union Soviétique avec la déclaration de Minsk (8 décembre 1991) et le Protocole de Alma-Ata (21 décembre 1991), par les Républiques Tchèque et Slovaque par l'Accord du 23 novembre 1992 ; dans la plus complexe et troublée situation yougoslave, le maintien des frontières établies entre les républiques fédérées, acquis par la Commission Badinter dans son avis n° 3 du 11 janvier 1992 et par le plan Vance-Owen de la Conférence pour la Yougoslavie du 26 mars 1993, fut retenu dans les accords serbo-croate pour la Slavonie du 12 décembre 1995 et les accords de Dayton-Paris du 21 novembre-14 décembre 1995 pour la Bosnie.

À la différence du système suivi à la première guerre mondiale, cette conservation n'a pas été corrigée, au moins partiellement pour les situations plus problématiques, par le recours aux plébiscites, par lesquels on avait cherché auparavant une solution dans les controverses concernant le Schleswig, la Haute Silésie, la Carinthie et, plus tard, la Saar. Heureusement, au moins, on n'a plus retenu praticables les accords entre les Etats intéressés pour effectuer mouvements ou échanges de populations, forcés ou optionnels, tout à fait contraires aux droits fondamentaux – pratique suivie pour la correction de la composition ethnique des populations dans quelque cas dans la période entre deux guerres avec le traité gréco-bulgare du 1919, gréco-turc du 1923 et, encore, italo-allemand du 1939 pour les options des résidants au Tyrol du Sud, bien que des expulsions de masse aient néanmoins eu lieu, en fait ou par des actes unilatéraux, en conséquence de la Seconde Guerre mondiale ou du conflit yougoslave.

II Conceptions diverses de la protection des minorités nationales

Dans les deux situations, se révélant impossible une révision consensuelle des frontières, le remède envisagé pour donner quelque satisfaction aux aspirations nationales de quelque façon frustrées et garantir la paix et la sécurité intérieure aussi bien que les bonnes relations entre les Etats concernés, a été donnée avec la substitution de l'autodétermination extérieure et potentiellement sécessionniste au moyen de l'attribution aux groupes minoritaires de la jouissance d'un ensemble de droits linguistiques, culturels, éducatifs, d'autogestion et participation aux affaires publics, ceux qui constituent l'essence d'une vie de relation nationale.

La voie suivie pour la mise en œuvre du remède a, toutefois, été très différente dans la situation après la Première Guerre mondiale et de la nouvelle Europe issue des grands changements à partir de l'année 1990.

La proposition, toujours soutenue par le président Wilson, d'insérer dans le Pacte une clause générale, bien que générique, destinée à soumettre la reconnaissance des nouveaux Etats ou, dans une deuxième version, l'admission à la Société des Nations à l'engagement d'accorder aux minorités ethniques ou nationales égalité de traitement et sécurité, en droit et en fait, fut rejetée par la Conférence en faveur d'un système de traités particuliers, à conclure séparément entre les Puissances alliées et associées et les Etats intéressés, bien qu'avec des contenus largement correspondant sauf pour la considération de quelque situation spéciale, et à placer sous la garantie de la Société. En conséquence, cinq traités sur la condition à faire aux minorités ont été signés, en concomitance avec la conclusion des traités de paix, avec la Pologne (Versailles, 28 juin 1919), qui a servi de modèle pour les autres, la Tchécoslovaquie (Saint Germain, 10 septembre 1919), l'Etat serbe, croate et slovène en même date, la

Roumanie (Trianon, 9 décembre 1919), la Grèce (Sèvres, 10 août 1920). Les obligations correspondantes furent formulées par des déclarations unilatérales, reçues par le Conseil de la Société, émises par l'Albanie, la Lettonie, la Lituanie et l'Estonie à l'occasion de leur admission à la Société des Nations. Encore des accords bilatéraux, conclus pour des situations particulières entre la Suède et la Finlande pour les îles Åland ou entre l'Allemagne et la Pologne pour la Haute Silésie, furent soumis à la garantie de la Société.

Toute autre la conception de la protection internationale des minorités dans l'Europe actuelle qui, non conditionnée par les résultats d'un conflit, est considérée constituer une responsabilité et un intérêt commun à tous les Etats du continent en parité de condition, et faire partie d'une conscience juridique et politique conforme. De cette raison, à partir de l'affirmation de la protection et de la promotion de l'identité des minorités par la Charte de Paris pour une nouvelle Europe, du 21 novembre 1990, comme condition pour obtenir relations amicales entre les peuples, la paix, la justice, la stabilité et la démocratie, la matière a fait objet des instruments juridiques multilatéraux, adoptés au sein des institutions de coopération régionale : d'une part, la CSCE (ensuite OSCE) avec le Chapitre IV du Document sur la Dimension Humaine du 29 juin 1990, le Rapport de la Réunion de Genève des experts CSCE sur les minorités nationales, et le Document de la Réunion de Helsinki sur les défis du changement du 10 juillet 1992, entre autres instituant l'office de l'Haut Commissaire pour les minorités nationales et la procédure pour le respect des engagements et la promotion de la dimension humaine ; d'autre part, le Conseil de l'Europe par l'adoption de la Convention-cadre pour les minorités nationales du 1er février 1995 et de la Charte européenne des langues régionales et minoritaires du 2 octobre 1992. La dimension multilatérale n'empêche et, au contraire, consent et favorise son complètement avec l'adoption des traités bilatéraux pour correspondre aux situations spécifiquement intéressant des Etats déterminés.

Nonobstant la différence de conceptions et solutions, les mesures considérées nécessaires pour donner satisfaction aux aspirations des minorités se présentent avec des remarquables correspondances dans les deux catégories d'instruments. L'obligation fondamentale d'appliquer égalité de traitement, parité de condition et non-discrimination se complète toujours avec la prévision d'une série des mesures spéciales, destinées à obtenir une égalité de fait pour la jouissance des droits civils, culturels et politiques pour les membres des minorités, dans les matières de l'emploi de la langue nationale, de l'instruction, de la vie culturelle, de la participation à la vie sociale et de relation.

Cueillant les aspects plus significatifs du régime de protection, en matière d'emploi de la langue minoritaire, le traité avec la Pologne, qui sert de modèle aux autres, prévoit l'exclusion de toute restriction dans les relations personnelles, de commerce, de religion, pour la presse et les publications, ou dans les réunions publiques. Des facilités sont prévues pour l'usage de la langue, soit verbalement que par écrit, dans les tribunaux. En matière d'instruction, l'enseignement est donné dans la langue minoritaire dans les villes et districts de présence d'une portion considérable de personnes appartenant à la minorité. En tout cas à ces sujets est accordé le droit de créer, diriger et contrôler des institutions charitables, religieuses et sociales, écoles et établissements d'instruction et, dans les régions de présence considérable de la minorité, celle-ci devait être admise à obtenir une partie équitable de fonds publics affectés à l'éducation, la religion ou à la charité.

Le document sur la dimension humaine de la CSCE prévoit que les personnes appartenant à des minorités nationales aient la possibilité d'apprendre leur langue maternelle et de recevoir un enseignement en cette langue et, si possible et nécessaire, utiliser cette langue dans les rapports avec les pouvoirs publics, conformément à la législation nationale en vigueur. Dans la Convention-cadre, les Parties s'engagent à reconnaître le droit d'utiliser librement et sans entrave la langue minoritaire en privé et en public, et s'efforceront d'assurer, dans les aires d'implantation substantielle ou traditionnelle de la minorité, l'utilisation de cette langue dans les rapports avec les administrations. En matière de justice il est consenti aux personnes appartenant à la minorité de se défendre dans leur langue, si nécessaire avec l'assistance gratuite des interprètes. Des mesures devront être prises pour promouvoir la connaissance de la langue, culture, histoire et religion minoritaire et, dans les régions d'implantation substantielle ou traditionnelle de la minorité, peut être donnée la possibilité d'apprendre la langue minoritaire ou de recevoir un enseignement en cette langue, demeurant, en tout cas, acquis le droit de créer et gérer des établissements privés d'enseignement et formation.

Il n'y avait, dans le modèle général des traités, une prévision pour la concession des institutions d'autonomie aux régions de présence substantielle de la minorité ce qui était, toutefois, prévu pour des situations particulières, par le traité avec la Tchécoslovaquie avec la disposition d'une administration autonome pour la région de la Ruthénie sub-carpatique, avec larges pouvoirs législatifs en matière de langue, instruction, gouvernement local et religion, et dans le traité avec la Roumanie par la concession d'autonomie en matière religieuse et scolaire aux communautés des Saxons et des Szeckler en Transylvanie. Cette possibilité est considérée comme praticable par le Document sur la dimension humaine, où la mise en place des administrations locales et autonomes appropriées est appréciée comme un des moyens pour réaliser la promotion de l'identité de certaines minorités nationales, pourvu que cela soit en correspondance avec la situation historique et territoriale spécifique et en conformité à la politique de l'Etat concerné. La concession des autonomies n'est pas envisagée par la Convention-cadre qui se limite à prévoir la création des conditions nécessaires à la participation effective des personnes appartenant aux minorités nationales à la vie culturelle, sociale et économique, aussi bien qu'aux affaires publiques, en particulier pour celles qui les concernent.

III   Variété des instruments de protection

Bien qu'il y ait des analogies quant au contenu des mesures de protection entre les traités successifs à la Première Guerre mondiale et les instruments issus de la nouvelle Europe, leur portée est très largement différente. Dans les premiers, les Etats destinataires acceptaient des obligations juridiques précises, rigides et contraignantes, qui devaient être reconnues comme constituant des lois internes fondamentales, supérieures à toute autre loi, règlement ou action officielle, de cette façon imposant une limitation substantielle à la souveraineté nationale. Les seconds se différencient entre les actes de la CSCE, à caractère éminemment politique et programmatique, posant des paramètres, des principes, des modèles, des objectifs pour constituer une guide à l'activité des Etats, et les conventions promues par le Conseil de l'Europe, qui, bien que constituant des sources des obligations internationales, ne contiennent pas des règles complètes et d'application directe mais, envisageant des résultats, donnent aux Etats signataires une large discrétion quant aux moyens à utiliser en raison de l'appréciation des diverses situations.

Le langage de la Convention-cadre est celui propre aux dispositions programmatiques avec un large, réitéré usage des locutions comme : « s'il y a lieu », « besoin réel », « dans la mesure du possible », « si nécessaire », « s'il existe une demande suffisante », etc., et les obligations acceptées par les Etats signataires souvent consistent seulement en « s'efforcer », « promouvoir », « offrir des possibilités » ; dans d'autres cas, il s'agit de s'engager ou de s'abstenir, ce qui postule une œuvre ultérieure d'action ou d'omission à tenir dans le cadre des systèmes législatifs nationaux. À son tour, la Charte européenne des langues régionales et minoritaires laisse aux Etats signataires une choix entre les possibles mesures en faveur de l'emploi des langues, avec un niveau minimum d'application, mais en tout cas comportant une activité législative et administrative largement discrétionnaire.

Correspondant à la différente portée des règles, les systèmes de contrôle et garantie prévus pour leur application présentent une radicale difformité. En présence des engagements précis à application directe, les traités sur les minorités attribuaient au Conseil de la Société des Nations un vaste pouvoir de contrôle par lequel toute modification aux articles affectant les conditions des personnes appartenant aux minorités aurait dû préalablement obtenir l'assentiment de la majorité des membres de cet organe. À chaque membre était attribué le droit de signaler une infraction ou un danger d'infraction et le Conseil aurait pu procéder donnant à l'Etat concerné les instructions appropriées, telles que retenues efficaces dans les circonstances. Au cas où la question de l'application du traité aurait assumé le caractère d'un différend international entre l'Etat obligé et un membre du Conseil, à la demande de celui-ci la question devait être déférée à la juridiction obligatoire de la Cour permanente de Justice internationale.

Adoptant des règles pour l'exercice de ses pouvoirs de contrôle, le Conseil allait jusqu'à prévoir la possibilité de signalisation des possibles infractions aussi par des personnes ou des organisations privées au moyen de pétitions lui adressées qui, soumises à un examen préalable de recevabilité par le Secrétariat, et, ensuite, d'un Comité de trois Etats membres, pouvaient donner lieu à la constatation de l'infraction et à la conséquente saisie du Conseil pour l'examen de la question.

Bien plus souple la nature des procédures de garantie envisagées par les instruments de la nouvelle Europe. En raison du caractère politique des actes adoptés au sein de la CSCE, celle-ci a institué des organes, procédures et compétences correspondants donnant vie, à la réunion de Helsinki de 1992, à l'Haut Commissaire pour les minorités nationales, qui, sur la base d'informations et rapports transmis par des parties intéressées, et, si nécessaire, des visites dans les Etats concernés, agit pour la prévention des conflits, promouvant dialogue, confiance et coopération et, au cas des tensions, s'engage en requérant l'activité du Conseil de la CSCE ou du Comité des Hauts Fonctionnaires.

De son côté, la Convention-cadre attribue au Comité des Ministres du Conseil de l'Europe, en correspondance avec la nature très articulée et ouverte de ses règles et au caractère médiat et indirecte des obligations qui en découlent, une fonction plus de guide pour l'application que de strict contrôle, veillant à la mise en œuvre de la Convention sur la base des rapports et informations transmis, aussi à sa demande, par les Etats signataires sur les mesures assumées par eux pour donner effet aux principes énoncés par le texte conventionnel. Dans son œuvre d'évaluation, le Comité est assisté par un organe consultatif, composé des individus experts dans le domaine de la protection des minorités, dont la fonction se limite à l'expression d'avis. Il n'y a pas mention, dans la Convention, des pouvoirs que le Conseil pourrait exercer à la suite de la procédure d'examen des rapports, bien que la pratique ait développé l'expression de recommandations tout à fait plus faibles que la compétence de donner des instructions, jadis attribué au Conseil de la Société des Nations.

IV Droits des nations et droits de l'homme

Des conceptions très différentes du problème des minorités sont à la base de solutions différentes quant à la nature des sources des régimes de protection, à la détermination de ses contenus, à l'efficacité obligatoire des règles et des contrôles. C'est bien la logique de l'application générale du principe de nationalité qui a guidé la rédaction des traités sur les minorités conclus après la Première Guerre mondiale, en lui donnant le caractère de remède aux imperfections de sa mise en œuvre par l'introduction d'une sorte de parallélisme en garantissant l'existence de nations minoritaires au-dedans de nations majoritaires.

Cette solution contenait en soi-même les germes de sa criticité, contestation et faillite finale, étant politiquement irréaliste et abstraite et source de conflits, revendications, révisionnisme et, en dernière instance, revanchisme. Hannah Arendt, dans son œuvre classique *The Origins of Tolitarianism*, publiée premièrement en 1948, a vu clairement les défauts et les illusions artificieuses contenues dans le système des traités. La question minoritaire, caractérisée par une sorte d'antagonisme généralisé entre les groupes nationaux, était devenue un élément de désagrégation politique, en présence de l'incapacité des nouveaux Etats de garantir effectivement et de bonne foi les droits humains fondamentaux, les traités ayant au contraire accentué les raisons de l'antagonisme.

La création des Etats nationaux se liait, par les traités leur imposés, à la création contemporaine des nations minoritaires, donnant vie à une difficile situation de dichotomie législative et institutionnelle, avec pour conséquence que les premiers considéraient ces traités comme des prévarications, les secondes comme une situation de servitude et de spoliation de leurs droits naturels. La garantie internationale offerte par la Société des Nations, bien que progressivement toujours moins effective, finissait par favoriser les minorités plus fortes et mieux soutenues, en les constituant comme des Etats ou portions d'Etats diminués.

La riposte à la question minoritaire dans le cadre des institutions communes de la nouvelle Europe, a pu se faire après l'acquisition de la doctrine et de la pratique de l'affirmation générale des droits de l'homme, à respecter, en condition paritaire, par tous les Etats et dans le cadre de l'acceptation de quelques principes d'organisation politique et civile acceptés par les Etats de la région européenne. Données ces présuppositions, dans les documents de la CSCE et du Conseil de l'Europe la condition à faire aux membres des minorités devient un chapitre de la reconnaissance et application des droits de l'homme, objet de protection internationale mais réalisable, concrètement, seulement avec l'effectivité de la jouissance des droits au sein des ordres juridiques inspirés aux principes de la primauté du droit, garantis par l'indépendance de la juridiction et issus de la démocratie représentative et pluraliste.

Il ne s'agit plus de bâtir des nations à l'intérieur d'autres nations, mais, utilisant les mots du Document CSCE sur la condition humaine, de réaliser sociétés où l'égalité des droits et conditions se lie avec la libre expression de tous les intérêts et aspirations légitimes.

CHAPTER 26

Protection of Croatian as a Minority Language in Europe

*Vesna Crnić-Grotić**

Protection of minorities has been one of the main focuses of Professor Vukas's professional work, especially regarding treatment of the Croatian minority living in other European countries.[1] I will always be grateful to him for introducing me to this fascinating field of international law.

Croats have been present in a number of mostly Eastern and Central European countries for centuries. They were driven from their old country by a range of reasons, be it economic, political or, on many occasions, by wars and violent changes of rulers and borders. In their new countries, nevertheless, they have managed to preserve their national and cultural identity despite sometimes hostile environments. Since the dissolution of former Yugoslavia this issue has received a new momentum – once members of one of the majority nations, Croats, just like other nations in former Yugoslavia (Serbs, Slovenes, Macedonians, Muslims), became members of minorities in all the new republics except Bosnia and Herzegovina.[2]

One of the main tokens of identity of national minorities in Europe is their proper language. Croatian, besides being the official language in Croatia, is also spoken in other European countries: Austria, Bosnia, the Czech Republic, Slovakia, Hungary, Italy, FYR Macedonia, Montenegro, Romania, Serbia and Slovenia. In most of them Croatian is spoken as a minority language, whereas in some of the former Yugoslav republics it is one of the co-official languages. In Bosnia and Herzegovina Croatian is one of the official languages. In practice,

---

* Professor of Public International Law at the University of Rijeka, Faculty of Law.
1 "The Rights of the Slovene and Croatian minorities in Austria in the light of international law", in: *Actual questions*, Ljubljana, 1976, pp. 17–21; *Le problème des minorités dans les rapports yougoslavo-autrichiens: recueil d'articles et de documents* (with J. Matjaž), Beograd, 1977; "Pravila međunarodnog prava o pravnom položaju gradišćanskih Hrvata u Austriji", in: *Razprave in gradivo*, Nos. 7–8, Ljubljana, 1976, pp. 49–68.
2 According to the Constitution of Bosnia and Herzegovina three nations – Croats, Serbs and Bosniacs – are considered 'constituent' peoples and their languages are equal. The Constitution is an annex to the General Framework Agreement for Peace in Bosnia and Herzegovina ('the Dayton Peace Agreement'), signed in Paris on 14 December 1995.

however, the closeness to and similarity of Croatian with Serbian, Montenegrin and Bosnian may blur the distinction between the different language usages. In Slovenia Croatian is not recognized as a minority language, nor are Croatians recognized as a national minority.

It is the purpose of this article to give an overview of the status of the Croatian language as a minority language under the respective national legislations as well as under international law. In particular, we shall look into the implementation of the Council of Europe Charter for Regional or Minority Languages (hereafter: the Charter) and the Framework Convention for the Protection of National Minorities (hereafter: FCNM). All but two of the above listed states are parties to both of these treaties and are subject to their respective monitoring mechanisms. Accordingly, they are obliged to submit periodical reports about their implementation which are examined by independent expert bodies and evaluated by the Committee of Ministers of the Council of Europe. In this way, it is possible to acquire an objective picture of the state of the Croatian language as a minority language in other European countries. Italy and FYR Macedonia are parties only to the FCNM. Although not language-specific, this treaty also imposes certain language-related obligations with regard to minority languages.

In addition, Croatia has concluded several bilateral treaties with the objective of granting reciprocal protection to languages spoken in both kin-states. This is the case with Hungary, Italy, Serbia, Montenegro and the FYR Macedonia, so Croatian receives specific protection in these countries as a minority language.

1   The European Charter for Regional and Minority Languages

The Charter was signed in 1992 but it came into force in 1998 for the first five states parties. As of September 2014 it has 25 states parties and 8 signatories.[3] It was conceived within the Council of Europe in an effort to preserve the multilingual profile of Europe, and after the attempts to integrate linguistic rights

---

3   European Charter for Regional or Minority Languages, ETS No. 148, adopted on 5 November 1992, entered into force on 1 March 1998. The Parliamentary Assembly obliged a group of east European countries, upon their accession to the Council of Europe, to sign and ratify the Charter within a certain time-limit. However, out of eleven designated states, Albania, Azerbaijan, Georgia, Moldova, the Russian Federation and 'the former Yugoslav Republic of Macedonia' have still not ratified the Charter.

into human rights protection had failed.[4] The protected languages are those that have been:

i. traditionally used within a given territory of a State by nationals of that State who form a group numerically smaller than the rest of the State's population; and
ii. different from the official language(s) of that State. (Article 1)

According to its drafters, it is not a human rights treaty, but it has a cultural purpose – to preserve regional or minority languages as a cultural wealth of Europe.[5] However, as a consequence of the protection of languages their speakers necessarily also enjoy certain rights that can be qualified as human rights (*e.g.* education in one's own language).

The Charter is divided into five parts, two of which contain substantial provisions. Part II of the Charter lists the objectives and principles that states parties should pursue with respect to all regional or minority languages spoken on their territory and which comply with the definition given in its Article 1. The Charter specifically excludes languages of migrants or dialects of the official language of the state.

Part III of the Charter is based on the so-called menu system: parties are free to choose a certain number of obligations (min. 35) among those offered by articles 8 to 14 for any or all of the regional or minority languages spoken on their territory. The level of commitment is different in all provisions – various levels of stringency of undertakings allow states parties to choose the appropriate level adapted to a concrete situation of each language. However, not all states used this opportunity, but chose the same level of commitment for all languages.

At the time of ratification states can also define the territory in which a particular language is spoken and where Part III will be applied. It will be a traditional territory where the number of speakers justifies these particular measures. However, states are not at liberty to decide arbitrarily that they would not apply the Charter in a certain language area.

---

4 J.M. Woehrling, "Introduction", in: *Shaping language rights – Commentary on the European Charter for Regional or Minority Languages in light of the Committee of Experts' evaluation*, Regional or Minority Languages, No. 9, 2012, pp. 11–31. The European Convention on Human Rights was not adequate for minority or linguistic rights protection, but the attempts to create a specific protocol to it were not successful.
5 The Charter's Explanatory Report, § 11: "The Charter sets out to protect and promote regional or minority languages, not linguistic minorities."

The monitoring of implementation is given to the Committee of Experts.[6] It receives periodical state reports, examines them, asks for additional information, if necessary, and makes its own report to the Committee of Ministers with a proposal for recommendations. This committee adopts the report and the recommendations, sometimes with minor amendments, and the report then becomes public.[7]

11 The Framework Convention for the Protection of National Minorities

The Framework Convention for the Protection of National Minorities[8] is the most comprehensive of the Council of Europe instruments on minority rights.[9] It was opened for signature in 1995 and came into force in 1998, some months after the Charter. Today it has 39 states parties. Unlike the Charter, this treaty deals with human rights protection and it has clear links to the European Convention for the Protection of Human Rights and Fundamental Freedoms.[10] This is the first multilateral international agreement on the protection of national minorities. It makes the protection of national minorities and of the rights and freedoms of persons belonging to those minorities an integral part of the international protection of human rights.[11] It has several articles dealing with the rights of members of national minorities to use their respective languages in private and public in general (Article 5),[12] but also in some specific

---

6   Articles 15 to 17 of the Charter. Reports are submitted to the Secretary General of the Council of Europe within one year of the entry into force of the Charter for the respective party and then every three years. An extensive commentary on the Charter and the work of the Committee of Experts is found in the publication *Shaping Language Rights*, edited by A.N. López, E.J. Ruiz Vieytez and I.U. Libarona, Strasbourg, 2012.

7   All state reports, evaluation reports and Committee of Ministers' (CM) recommendations are available at the website of the Charter: <http://www.coe.int/t/dg4/education/minlang/Default_en.asp>.

8   Framework Convention for the Protection of National Minorities, ETS No. 157, signed on 1 February 1995, came into force since 1 February 1998 for the first 12 states parties.

9   P. Thornberry and M.A.M. Estébanez, *Minority Rights in Europe*, Strasbourg, 2004, p. 89. A comprehensive commentary on the FCNM was published in the Oxford Commentaries on International Law series: *The Rights of Minorities in Europe*, ed. M. Weller, Oxford, 2005.

10 FCNM, Article 23.

11 FCNM, Article 1.

12 FCNM, Article 5: "The Parties undertake to promote the conditions necessary for persons belonging to national minorities to maintain and develop their culture, and to preserve

fields such as in freedom of expression, public administration and criminal justice and education.

This convention also provides for monitoring by the Committee of Ministers through the Advisory Committee of independent experts. The Advisory Committee examines periodical state reports and adopts its opinion on the implementation of the convention. If necessary, it may also propose recommendations to the Committee of Ministers. All reports are public.[13]

III Croatian in Austria

Austria is one of the countries that have ratified both the Charter and the FCNM.[14] According to the respective ratification instruments, Croats living in Burgenland and their language, Burgenland Croatian, are covered by the treaties.[15] Croats inhabited that area as early as in the 16th century. They have managed to preserve their sense of national identity despite strong assimilating tendencies. Language remains the most important distinguishing feature of their identity, although the distinction between Burgenland Croatian and Croatian is of a more recent origin.[16]

According to the 2001 census around 20,000 people use Burgenland Croatian as their 'everyday language' (*Umgangssprache*) in Burgenland and about another 2,500 live in Vienna. The estimations by the group itself, however, are much higher. According to it, there are about 50,000 Croats in Austria. Most of them live in Burgenland, but up to 15,000 Burgenland Croatian speakers live in

---

the essential elements of their identity, namely their religion, language, traditions and cultural heritage."

13 The official website of the FCNM where all the state reports, Advisory Committee's (AC) opinions and Committee of Ministers' recommendations are found: <http://www.coe.int/t/dghl/monitoring/minorities/default_en.asp>.

14 Austria ratified the FCNM on 31 March 1998 and the Charter on 28 June 2001.

15 The protection of regional or minority languages in Austria is closely linked to the notion of *Volksgruppe* ('ethnic group' or 'national minority') in the Ethnic Groups Act. It defines ethnic groups as "groups of Austrian nationals living and residing in parts of the federal territory whose mother tongue is not German and who have their own traditions and folklore".

16 The instrument of ratification of the Charter appears to be the first significant official document where this distinction is made on the basis of the specific features of the language due to its more or less independent and isolated development distinct from 'proper' Croatian. The 2001 census confirmed this distinction. Application of the Charter in Austria, 1st Evaluation Report, ECRML(2005)1, § 15.

Vienna. Austria ratified the Charter's Part III in favour of Burgenland Croatian with a selection of undertakings. Viennese Croatian is covered only by Part II and Austria still has to develop adequate protection for that group of speakers.

The legal framework for the protection of minorities and their languages in Austria is rather extensive. An international obligation to protect minorities was established in the State Treaty of Saint-Germain-en-Laye of 1919 after World War I and in Article 7 of the State Treaty for the Re-establishment of an Independent and Democratic Austria of 1955 after World War II. The Basic Law of Austria as well as the Federal Constitution Act further confirmed this obligation.[17] The main federal legal act remains the Ethnic Groups Act (Volksgruppengesetz). It was amended in July 2011, in order to respond to the Committee of Ministers' recommendations and improve the topography in minority languages as well as the use of minority languages as official languages.[18] Burgenland Croatian benefits also from the Minority Schools Act for Burgenland and the Ordinance of the Federal Government of 24 April 1990 defining the courts, administrative authorities and other official bodies where Croatian is allowed as an official language in addition to German.

Nevertheless, in practice, there are certain discrepancies between the legal texts and their application, so the minority language speakers have to struggle to preserve and implement their legal rights.[19] Regarding education, the situation is rather favourable in Burgenland, less so in Vienna, as the Croats in Burgenland have a constitutional right to have Croatian as a language of instruction or to learn it as a compulsory subject in schools. Burgenland

---

17 According to Professor Vukas, the provisions of the State Treaty are both *lex posterior* and *lex specialis* with respect to the Treaty of Saint-Germain. Vukas, "The Rights...", op. cit. n. 1, p. 17.

18 Application of the Charter in Austria, 3rd State Report, 2011, p. 13. The main novelty is the list of municipalities in the Federal *Länder* of Burgenland and Carinthia where bilingual topographical signs and inscriptions must be put up. The sections of regions in Burgenland which are included in the annex correspond to the territorial sections that were already laid down in the Ordinance on Topographical Signs in Burgenland, Federal Law Gazette II No. 170/2000.

19 In 1987 Burgenland Croats brought a successful court case against the non-implementation of the rights guaranteed by the 1955 State Treaty by the Burgenland provincial government. Their language rights were confirmed in the subsequent Federal Ordinance. Furthermore, based on the 1977 legislation providing for Advisory Councils for minorities, that for Croatians was established only in 1993! Practice of Minority Protection in Central Europe, Legal-theoretical part, Legal Country Study: Austria, available at: <http://www.eurac.edu/en/research/institutes/imr/Documents/LCS_Austria_1.pdf> (visited: 14.02.2013).

Croatian is taught at different levels of education. At the lower level it is taught as the local variant, but gradually students are introduced to standard Croatian.[20] Bilingual schools are open to all children so it is not unusual for monolingual German-speaking children to attend these schools and learn Croatian. Regardless of the positive social effect, their lack of any knowledge of Croatian tends to weaken the quality of teaching for Burgenland Croatian children who already have basic or even advanced knowledge. The language can be studied in a number of universities in Austria as there are no universities in Burgenland.[21]

The real challenges for the use of language are in the courts and administration. Despite the legal entitlement, Burgenland Croatian is rarely used in practice.[22] Practical difficulties, such as the lack of Burgenland Croatian-speaking judges[23] or any relevant measure of encouragement as well as psychological barriers (fear of being seen as trouble-makers), impede the practical use of Burgenland Croatian in court proceedings. On the other hand, Article 22 of the Ethnic Groups Act provides, *inter alia*, that the costs and fees arising from translations due to the use of a language admitted as an official language have to be borne *ex officio*. Similar difficulties exist in the administration. The Ordinance of the Federal Government regarding the use of Croatian as an official language defines the municipalities (*Gemeinde*) of Burgenland where the use of Croatian is allowed before local administrative authorities (Article 2, paragraph 1).[24] However, the use of Burgenland Croatian before administrative authorities is very rare in practice, except at the local administration, since very few civil servants have sufficient written command of Burgenland Croatian and as there is a lack of Burgenland Croatian or bilingual forms.[25] It is interesting that Austria did not choose the obligation relating to the use of

---

20 Application of the Charter in Austria, 1st Evaluation Report, § 111.
21 The Institute of Slavic Studies in Vienna has a section dealing specifically with Burgenland Croatian. In addition, Croatian can be studied at the universities of Vienna, Graz, Innsbruck, Salzburg and Klagenfurt.
22 Legally Croatian is admitted as an official language in addition to German before several district courts (*Bezirksgericht*) of Eisenstadt/Željezno, Güssing/Novigrad, Mattersburg/Materštof, Neusiedl am See/Niuzalj, Oberpullendorf/Gornja Pulja and Oberwart/Gornja Borta as well as before the Eisenstadt/Željezno Regional Court.
23 According to the second periodical report (page 67), the local court in Oberwart/Gornja Borta as well as the regional court in Eisenstadt/Željezno employs staff, including judges, who speak Croatian. Application of the Charter in Austria, 2nd Evaluation Report, § 131.
24 These municipalities are in the districts (*Bezirke*) of Eisenstadt Umgebung (9 municipalities), Güssing (3), Mattersburg (3), Neusiedl (3), Oberpullendorf (5), and Oberwart (3).
25 Application of the Charter in Austria, 1st Evaluation Report, § 167.

"traditional and correct forms of place-names in regional or minority languages" (Article 10.2.g) despite the similar obligation stemming from the State Treaty of 1955. The problem of bilingual signs was dealt with by the Constitutional Court of Austria. In its decision of 13 December 2001 the Constitutional Court ruled that the threshold of 25% for entitlement to the display of topographical indications in minority languages contained in the Ethnic Groups Act of 1976 runs counter to Article 7, paragraph 3 of the State Treaty and is therefore unconstitutional.[26] The Constitutional Court further ruled that if a national minority formed more than 10% of the total population in an area over a long period, this was sufficient to entitle its inhabitants to the display of bilingual topographical signs.

However, Austria's obligation exists also under the FCNM (Article 11). The Advisory Committee expressed its disappointment that the relevant decisions by the Austrian Constitutional Court had not been implemented.[27] It also agreed with the representatives of the Croat minority in Burgenland that this issue should not be limited to the issue of bilingual signposts but encompass other indications in minority languages such as street names or traditional local names on maps.[28] It will be interesting to see whether the Advisory Committee will accept new legislation amendments as satisfying its concerns.

The situation in the media in 2001 was not in accordance with the undertakings chosen under the Charter, since the language was available in a rather limited way on public radio and TV and it was not available on private radio or TV. However, according to the latest report by Austria, the situation has improved. In addition to a short daily news bulletin (2 min), public radio offers diverse daily programmes (30 min magazines) that cover interests of many social groups. The TV offering on the national broadcasting company ORF is limited to a weekly programme in Burgenland Croatian and a quadrilingual magazine in German, Croatian, Hungarian and Romani.[29] There are, however, still no private radio or TV stations broadcasting in Burgenland Croatian despite the financial support available for private media. The authorities also support the publication and distribution of a weekly *Hrvatske novine* and the

---

26   It took a proactive stand arguing that "depending on the relevant object of the regulations that are dealing with the protection of members of minorities *vis-à-vis* members of other groups of society, it may justify or even make it necessary in certain matters to give preferential treatment to the minority…" Austrian Constitutional Court: *Cf.* VfSlg 9224/1981. See J. Marko, "Minority Protection through Jurisprudence in Comparative Perspective: An Introduction", 25(3) *Journal of European Integration*, 2003, pp. 175–188.
27   Advisory Committee (AC FCNM), 3rd Opinion on Austria, 2011, § 88.
28   *Ibid.*, § 92.
29   Application of the Charter in Austria, 3rd State Report, p. 85.

Eisenstadt/Željezno diocese weekly *Glasnik – Crikvene novine Zeljezanske biskupije Eisenstadt*.

Burgenland Croatian is recognized as a traditional minority language in Austria. However, its practical position still lags behind its legal status and Austria should probably do more to promote its use in public in order to combat assimilation and its demise.

IV Croatian in the Czech Republic

The Czech Republic ratified the FCNM in 1997 and the Charter only in 2006. When ratifying the Charter the Czech Republic did not include Croatian among the protected minority languages.[30] In the first evaluation round the Committee of Experts of the Charter asked the authorities to clarify the status of the Croatian language spoken in Southern Moravia. According to the available information, 1,585 people had declared Croat nationality at the 2001 census.[31] Furthermore, according to the Advisory Committee, the FCNM is applied to all groups represented on the Council for National Minorities, a government advisory body. These are Bulgarians, Croats, Hungarians, Germans, Poles, Roma, Ruthenians, Russians, Greeks, Slovaks, Serbs and Ukrainians.[32]

During the second monitoring round, the Committee of Experts established that in fact Croats had had a centuries-old traditional presence in Southern Moravia. They came to the area in the same migrant wave as the Burgenland Croats in the 16th century and settled along the present-day border with Austria mostly in the three villages of Jevišovka, Nový Přerov and Dobré Pole. The Moravian Croats have traditionally spoken Croatian, Czech and German. After World War II, regarded as a hostile minority which had collaborated with

---

30 According to the declaration contained in the instrument of ratification the Czech Republic considers the Slovak, Polish, German and Roma languages as minority languages which are spoken in its territory and in respect of which it will apply the provisions of Part II of the Charter. Polish and Slovak are further covered by Part III of the Charter. List of declarations made with respect to the Charter is also available at the official web-site of the Charter, see above n. 7.

31 Some of them are Croats who arrived in the Czech Republic after World War II. The authorities make no distinction between the traditional and newly arrived members of minorities.

32 The Czech Republic recognizes all national groups meeting the criteria established in the definition of the concept 'national minority' contained in Article 2 of the Act on the Rights of Members of National Minorities of 10 July 2001. AC FCNM, 3rd Opinion on the Czech Republic, 2011, § 28.

the Germans during the war, most Moravian Croats (about 1,500) were displaced by the authorities in more than 100 villages throughout Moravia. Only a small number of people from the traditional Moravian Croat minority remained in their traditional villages.

As far as the language is concerned, today there is a very small number of speakers of Croatian.[33] They refer to the local variety as Moravian Croatian, different from modern Croatian as it has kept its basic structure since the 16th century and it has many loan words from Czech and German. It has been used orally and has never been taught in schools. There is no public use of the language. According to the Czech authorities the small number of speakers and their dispersal makes the promotion of the language difficult. Nevertheless, according to the standard approach taken by the Committee of Experts, the authorities should treat the language as a Part II minority language and take appropriate measures to address its precarious situation.[34]

v Croatian in Slovakia

The FCNM came into force for Slovakia in February 1998. It signed and ratified the Charter in 2001 and it entered into force on 1 January 2002. Croatian was one of the languages specifically recognized in the instrument of ratification as a Part III language covered by a specified selection of undertakings.[35]

The wave of migrations that took Croatians to Austria and the Czech Republic took them also to present-day Slovakia in the 16th century. They settled in western Slovakia. Today, the Croatian population is concentrated mainly in four villages, or rather boroughs of Bratislava: Čuňovo, Devínska Nová Ves, Chorvátsky Grob and Jarovce (*Hrvatski Jandrof*).[36] According to the results of

---

33 According to the estimates given by the speakers, there are 15–20 people in Jevišovka who speak Moravian Croatian while 50–60 understand it. Throughout Moravia, there are about 100 people speaking and about 500 understanding Moravian Croatian. There is an initiative to create a museum in Jevišovka to document 300 years of the presence of Croats in southern Moravia.

34 Application of the Charter in the Czech Republic, 2nd Evaluation Report, § 10–14.

35 The same set of undertakings was selected for the Bulgarian, Croatian, Czech, German, Polish and Romani languages except Article 14.b (transfrontier co-operation) that was ratified only in favour of the Czech, German and Polish languages. List of declarations made with respect to treaty No. 148.

36 The speakers use different Croatian dialects, depending on the part of the country from where they originally came. Croats in Devínska Nova Ves (Cr. Devinsko Novo Selo) are Čakavian speakers, and in Chorvátsky Grob (Cr. Hrvatski Grob) are *Kajkavian-Ikavian*

the 2011 census the number of Croatian speakers rose to 1,234 as compared to 988 speakers in 2001 census.[37] At the same time 1,022 people declared themselves to belong to the Croatian minority as compared to 890 people in 2001.[38]

The third evaluation report on the application of the Charter by the Slovak Republic was adopted in January 2013.[39] According to the findings of the Committee of Experts the situation of Croatian is not meeting the requirements of the undertakings chosen by Slovakia. First of all, Croatian is not taught in Slovak public schools at any level, from kindergarten to secondary education, but Croatian can be studied as a foreign language at the Universities of Bratislava and Banská Bystrica. There is some teaching of the language organized by Croatian minority associations with little or no support from the authorities. However, as of 2011, Croatian may be chosen as a subject for the school-leaving examination (*matura*). It is standard Croatian and it may not correspond to the objective of the Charter, *i.e.* to preserve local varieties as minority languages with all their peculiarities.

There is no use of Croatian before courts in criminal cases since Slovakia failed to guarantee the accused the right to use his/her minority language regardless of his/her understanding of the Slovak language. The obligation under Article 9.1.1 of the Charter, however, is different from the right guaranteed by Article 6 of the European Convention for the Protection of Human Rights and Fundamental Freedoms. On the other hand, pursuant to a 2008 amendment of the Civil Procedure Code parties "have the right to use their mother tongue or the language they understand". This applies to civil and administrative proceedings, although, in practice, there does not seem to be any practical implementation due to the 'usual' reasons: lack of staff and interpreters, no encouragement measures, *etc.*

Slovakia is one of the European states that adopted the 20% threshold as a precondition for allowing the co-official use of minority languages in administration. The Committee of Experts expressed its concern that this threshold is arbitrary and that it does not allow the full implementation of the Charter's

---

speakers. For the first group it is believed that they came from the Croatian coastal regions and the others from the Kostajnica region. J. Kovacevic-Cavlovic, "The Croatian Minority in Slovakia", available at: <http://www.croatianhistory.net/etf/croslov.html> (21.02.2013).

37 Statistical Office of the Slovak Republic, <http://portal.statistics.sk/files/table-11.pdf> (visited: 18.02.2013).

38 *Ibid.* As a curiosity, the current president of the Slovak Republic Mr. Ivan Gašparovic is of a Croat descent.

39 Available at: <https://wcd.coe.int/ViewDoc.jsp?Ref=CM(2012)144&Language=lanEnglish&Site=CM&BackColorInternet=DBDCF2&BackColorIntranet=FDC864&BackColorLogged=FDC864#P78_7727> (visited: 21.02.2013).

undertakings under Article 10.[40] So, for example, Bulgarian and Polish minorities do not attain the threshold in any municipality according to the 2001 census. Croatians represent 20.4% of the population in Jarovce, but not in any of the other boroughs of Bratislava.[41] Nevertheless, Croatian is in practice not being used in contacts with state or local administration other than some sporadic use orally. The same threshold appears as an obstacle where bilingual signs and place names are concerned. According to the law in force, there is no legal duty to put up bilingual signs in municipalities with less than 20% of the population belonging to a minority. In practice, there are no bilingual signs in Croatian in Jarovce. The authorities thus failed to fulfil the obligation under Article 10 of the Charter and Article 11 of the FCNM.[42]

The presence of Croatian in the media is very poor. There are no broadcasts on radio in Croatian and very little on public TV. In addition, there is no private radio or TV station broadcasting in Croatian.[43] *Hrvatska rosa* is published in Croatian four times a year, helping to preserve and present the written language. Nevertheless, what seems to have helped most was a rich cultural life of Croatians in Slovakia. Since 1989 the Croatian associations have organized cultural festivals in Devínska Nová Ves alongside local festivals. In 2005 the Croatian centre and the museum were opened with the support of Slovakia and Croatia as a focal point for Croatian cultural life.[44] In Jarovce and Čuňovo the tradition of Croatian theatre was renewed in 2013. Nevertheless, the enthusiastic members of the Croatian minority need adequate support from the authorities if they want to preserve Croatian in Slovakia as a living minority language.

---

40   The Committee of Experts has expressed the same opinion on the thresholds in every similar case, starting from Croatia and its one-third threshold. See Application of the Charter in Croatia, 3rd Evaluation Report, 2008, § 23–26.

41   After two rounds of recommendations by the Committee of Ministers, the relevant legislation was changed and the threshold was lowered to 15%. In order to be applied, it has to be confirmed in two subsequent censuses. In practice, it means that this new threshold will be applicable in 2021 at the earliest, but it will not be applicable to the boroughs of Bratislava, only to municipalities.

42   Both the Committee of Experts and the Advisory Committee invited the Slovak authorities to be more flexible in deciding where to use the bilingual topographical signs regardless of the 20% threshold if the number of people using the minority language in question justifies such a measure.

43   In 2011 Slovakia removed from the State Language Act the obligation of private radio broadcasters to provide a Slovak language version of the radio programme broadcast in a minority language.

44   Ministry of Foreign Affairs, Croatia, <http://www.mvep.hr/hmiu/tekst.asp?q=01hmi-hmi010> (visited: 10.03.2013).

VI Croatian in Hungary

Hungary was among the original states parties to the Charter and the FCNM. When ratifying the Charter Hungary presented a declaration stating that it would apply Part III of the Charter to all six recognized minority languages: Croatian, German, Romanian, Serbian, Slovak and Slovene.[45] These languages were recognized in the 1993 Minorities Act as the languages of the autochthonous minorities protected by Hungarian legislation. According to the 2001 census there were 25,730 Croats living in Hungary and 14,345 people declared Croatian to be their mother tongue.[46] They are mostly concentrated in Baranya County, but there are Croatian settlements also in Győr-Moson-Sopron, Bács-Kiskun, Vas and the Zala County. They are, however, very diverse with respect to the time of their arrival to Hungary and their specific features.[47]

They are included in the system of minority self-governments. In the course of the 2010 minority self-government elections, Croatian minority self-governments were elected in 127 localities in total.[48] The system of minority self-governments created by Hungarian legislation secures participation of the minorities in the formulation of minority-related policies, so they can take responsibilities in education and culture over from the local and central governments. Education in Croatian is by and large available at all levels of education although the number of children being taught in Croatian and those in bilingual education has not been steady. In culture Croatian is used in many activities. There are numerous culture and folk clubs and associations that nurture Croatian culture and language. In Pécs (*Pečuh*) there is the only professional theatre in Croatian outside Croatia. There is also the Scientific Institute of Croats in Hungary. In the town of Peresznye (*Prisika*) the Museum of Croatian Church Art was established. The publishing house *Croatica* publishes textbooks for education in Croatian as well as cultural magazines and other publications. It also runs a radio station broadcasting in the language. In addition, the state-run *Magyar Rádió* and

---

45   In a subsequent note in 2008 Hungary adopted a different set of obligations for Romani and Beás. The Committee of Experts of the Charter concluded that Armenian, Bulgarian, Greek, Polish, Ruthenian and Ukrainian should also be considered traditional languages of Hungary.
46   Application of the Charter in Hungary, 5th State Report, 2012, p. 10.
47   Bunjevci, Šokci, Raci, Dalmatians, Burgenland Croats, Croats from the Mura and Podravina area as well as Croats from Bosnia came to Hungary between the 15th and 18th century, although there is evidence that Croats from the Podravina area came in the early Middle Ages.
48   Regional Croatian minority self-governments were also established in the capital and in six counties. Application of the Charter in Hungary, 5th State Report, 2012.

Televízió are responsible for programmes in minority languages, including Croatian. However, the presence of Croatian on TV is still not satisfactory. The same can be said about the use of Croatian in courts and partly in administration. Hungary has failed to ensure the right of Croatian speakers to use their language regardless of their knowledge of Hungarian. Since basically all citizens of Hungary speak the official language it makes this right practically obsolete.

Hungary and Croatia concluded a bilateral treaty on the protection of minorities in 1995.[49] The two states undertook to protect the Croatian and Hungarian minorities on their respective territories. The agreement established a joint committee as a working body. In accordance with the agreement a number of educational and cultural institutions were established in both countries with the objective of preserving minorities, their languages and cultures, including the creation of educational centres in Pécs and Osijek. This agreement can be taken as an example of good practice in Europe.

VII Croatian in Italy

Italy was among the original states parties to the FCNM. It signed the Charter in 2000, but has never ratified it. Therefore, Italy's international obligations with respect to Croatian are limited to the FCNM and the bilateral agreement with Croatia signed in 1996.[50]

Croats settled in the Italian region of Molise as early as the 15th century, fleeing from the Turkish invasion. Today there may be up to 2,600 people belonging to this minority, but their number has been declining. They mostly live in the province of Campobasso: in Acquaviva Collecroce (*Kruč*), Montemitro (*Mundimitar*) and in San Felice (*Filič*).

In 1997 the Region of Molise adopted Law No. 15 on the "Protection and development of the cultural heritage of the linguistic minorities of Molise". This Law provides for the protection of the Croatian and Albanian minorities established in Molise by financing programmes for the study of both languages, including in school curricula. The same law also asserts that the Region of Molise encourages and supports, by means of specific programmes, the "organisation of information and in-service courses for teachers, competitions for pupils and other extra-curricular activities aimed at improving knowledge

---

49   The agreement was published in the *Official Gazette, Treaties* (*Narodne novine, Medunarodni ugovori*, hereafter: NN-MU), No. 8/1995.
50   The treaty between Croatia and Italy concerning minority rights was published in NN-MU, No. 15/1997.

of the history, culture, language and traditions of Croatia and Albania".[51] The law was reinforced by the 1999 national Law on the Protection of Historic Linguistic Minorities adopted by the Italian Parliament.[52] It specifically recognized Croatian as one of the historic minority languages in Italy.

Nevertheless, more than ten years after the adoption of the law and Italy's international obligations, there is still a lot to do for Croatian and its speakers. At present, there are two primary schools but no secondary school teaching the language due to the low number of speakers and their territorial dispersal.[53] Nevertheless, the Advisory Committee noticed commendable examples of educational projects – bilingual publications and books for children, the acquisition of materials and development of specialised libraries devoted to the minority's linguistic and cultural identity that included the Croatian minority. In administration there have been efforts to preserve traditional Croatian place-names and to set up the so-called *sportelli linguistici* – administrative services for users of Croatian. Despite these efforts, the Advisory Committee was informed that the desks are in some cases understaffed and they are not able to guarantee sufficient opening hours.[54] As with many other cases, the biggest burden of preservation and promotion of the language still lies with the enthusiastic minority associations, who organize cultural events, theatres and exhibitions and more recently web-pages on the internet *Na-našu*: Foundation *Agostina Piccoli* of Montemitro, the Association *Naš Zivod, Naš Grad* in Acquaviva Collecroce and the *Naš Jezik* Association in San Felice del Molise. The bilingual periodical magazine *Kamasutra*, published in the Municipality of Montecilfone, contains information on the Croatian and Albanian minority.[55]

As far as the bilateral treaty with Croatia is concerned, out of nine articles only one refers to Italy's obligations towards the Croatian minority. Article 8 reads as follows:

> Without prejudice to the implementation by the Parties of all the provisions included in the present Treaty, and taking into account the provisions contained in the "Statuto" of the Molise Region, the Italian Republic undertakes to grant the Croatian autochthonous minority in the territory of traditional settlement where its presence has been ascertained, to

---

51 FCNM, 1st Report by Italy, 1999, p. 76.
52 Norme in materia di tutela delle minoranze linguistiche storiche, Legge No. 482/99.
53 Lingue di minoranza e scuola a dieci anni dalla Legge 482/99, Quaderni della Direzione Generale per gli Ordinamenti Scolastici e per l'Autonomia Scolastica, N. 1–11 marzo 2010, available at: <http://jemi.myblog.it/files/lingue_minoranza_scuola.pdf> (visited: 12.03.2013).
54 AC FCNM, 3rd Opinion on Italy, 2010, § 164.
55 FCNM, 3rd Report by Italy, 2009, p. 42.

preserve and freely express its cultural identity and heritage, to use its mother tongue in private and in public and to establish and maintain its cultural institutions and associations.

VIII   Croatian in Macedonia

The Former Yugoslav Republic of Macedonia ratified the FCNM in 1997 but has so far not ratified the Charter despite the recommendation by the Parliamentary Assembly to do so.[56]

Croatians in the FYR of Macedonia do not enjoy the status of national minority, nor is their language protected as a minority language, although 2,686 people in the 2002 census declared themselves as Croats. On the other hand, in 2007 Macedonia and Croatia concluded a bilateral treaty on the preservation and promotion of the national identity of the respective ethnic communities living in both countries.[57] The Advisory Committee considered that it was an important step towards formal recognition of the status of persons of Croat ethnicity as a national minority.[58] It encouraged the authorities to consider introducing measures leading to the recognition of the status of persons of Croat ethnicity, as a national minority. It also encouraged the authorities to "draw on the provisions of the 2007 Agreement…and consider introducing measures for the preservation, protection and promotion of national identity of persons belonging to the Croat community".[59]

In practice, Croatian speakers rely on their NGOs and assistance and support from Croatia. The biggest NGO is the Association of Croats in Macedonia. It publishes *Hrvatska riječ* in Croatian, books in Croatian written by its members and it fosters Croatian classes with assistance from the *Matica Hrvatska* and teachers from Croatia. However, without official recognition they are not entitled to measures existing in Macedonia for the activities of national minorities.

IX   Croatian in Romania

Romania became a state party to the Charter in May 2008, making a rather elaborate declaration covering 20 minority languages spoken on its territory. Croatian is one of the ten languages covered by specific undertakings under

---

56   See above, n. 3.
57   The agreement was published in NN-MU, No. 3/2008.
58   AC FCNM, 3rd Opinion on FYR Macedonia, 2011, § 36.
59   *Ibid.*, § 180.

Part III of the Charter.[60] According to the 2002 census, 6,807 persons belonged to the Croat minority and 6,304 declared the Croatian language to be their mother tongue. The Croatian minority is concentrated in the Caraş-Severin and Timiş counties. They arrived in Romania in several waves from the 14th century. Today they still use an old and archaic form of Croatian due to living in isolation from the kin-state for centuries. The best preserved variety is that spoken near the town of Reşiţa in Caraş-Severin County, the so-called Caraşova/*Karaševo* Croatian.

Romania provides pre-school and primary education in Croatian in accordance with its obligations under the Charter in the traditional areas. There is only teaching of the language in secondary schools although Romania undertook to offer "a substantial part of secondary education in Croatian". The Committee of Experts concluded that it was insufficient. In judicial matters minority languages may legally be used, but, as in some other countries, there is no practical use of it in court proceedings. Regarding the administration, Romania uses the 20% threshold as the precondition for using minority languages in administration. This, however, is not considered to be in accordance with the Charter obligations.[61] Nevertheless, there is some use of Croatian in state and local administration, especially in their strongholds. In some municipalities bilingual place-names are used so the traditional Croatian names of settlements appear on road-signs and institutions, but only in those municipalities where the minority reaches the threshold.

There is a limited presence of Croatian on public radio and TV. Several cultural organisations are active in promoting the Croatian identity and language, the Union of Croats of Romania being the most prominent.[62] Its activities include the publication of a bilingual magazine (Croatian-Romanian) *Hrvatska Grancica*.[63]

Romania relies on co-operation with Croatia in catering for the needs of the Croatian minority. Together they have launched a 'Dialogue on National Minorities' which aims at promoting minority languages *inter alia* in education and media as well as exchanging experience on good practice in the field of minority protection. Furthermore, they co-operate in the field of education so that Croatia provides textbooks for Croatian-language education, there is an on-going exchange of professors and students between the universities of Bucharest, Timişoara and Zagreb as well as the provision by the Croatian authorities of scholarships for study visits to Croatia.

---

60   List of declarations made with respect to treaty No. 148.
61   See above n. 40.
62   The Union has a well maintained web-site: <http://www.zhr-ucr.ro/index.php?lang=hr> (visited: 10.03.2013).
63   Application of the Charter in Romania, 1st Evaluation Report, 2012, § 265.

x   Croatian in Serbia

Serbia ratified the FCNM in 2001 and the Charter in 2005 when it was still a member of the State Union of Serbia and Montenegro. After the dissolution of the Union Serbia became the successor to the State Union and the Charter came into force for Serbia on 1 June 2006.[64] In its declaration Serbia included Croatian among the protected minority languages. In addition to these multilateral treaties, Serbia also concluded a bilateral treaty with Croatia on the protection of the Croatian, Montenegrin and Serbian minority in 2004.[65] The treaty has a joint committee in place as a working body.

Croatian has traditionally been used on the territory of the Autonomous Province of Vojvodina. According to the 2002 census, 70,602 people belonged to the Croatian national minority and 34% of them declared Croatian as their mother tongue, but the number of Croatians significantly declined in the 1990s. They mostly live in the municipalities of Apatin and Subotica (Bačka). In the first evaluation round the Committee of Experts established that around 20,000 people declared that they belonged to the Bunjevac minority with their own language. While most speakers consider Bunjevac a language in its own right, some regard it as a variety of Croatian. The dominant view in Croatia, however, is that the Bunjevac minority is an integral part of the Croatian people in Vojvodina.[66] The Committee of Experts concluded that the status of Bunjevac is unclear and asked for more information.[67] The position of Croats and their number have been affected by the recent war in former Yugoslavia.

As far as education is concerned, it is available in Croatian at various levels. However, the number of children included is very low considering the number of speakers. It may be due to the proximity between Croatian and Serbian but also to the lack of information about the ability to receive education in Croatian. For example, only 10 children were included in pre-school groups

---

64   The two states agreed that Serbia would succeed to the membership of the Council of Europe while Montenegro had to re-apply. Montenegro was admitted on 11 May 2007 but it is considered the state party to the Charter since 6 June 2006.
65   The treaty was concluded with the common state of Serbia and Montenegro and published in NN-MU, No. 3/2005. In particular, it covers education, culture and information.
66   *Cf.* Foreign Ministry of Croatia, <http://www.mvep.hr/hmiu/tekst.asp?q=01hmi-hmi012> (visited: 12.03.2013).
67   Application of the Charter in Serbia, 1st Evaluation Report, 2008, § 12, 35–36. In its following state report Serbia provided additional information on Bunjevac. Serbia, 2nd Periodical Report (MIN-LANG/PR) (2010) 7. The Committee of Experts evaluated this report in November 2011 but it has not been adopted by the Committee of Ministers by March 2013.

and 197 pupils in Subotica attended primary-school classes teaching in Croatian.[68] Furthermore, 362 children in 3 municipalities attended classes teaching Croatian with elements of national culture. There did not seem to be any classes in secondary schools although Serbia undertook to provide at least for the teaching of the language.

Croatian has been used in court proceedings in courts in Subotica. In administration, persons belonging to a national minority whose population makes up, according to the latest census, at least 2% of the total population of Serbia may communicate with the public authorities in their language and are entitled to a reply in that language.[69] However, since the Hungarian minority is the only minority reaching the 2% threshold, this applies only to them. The use of Croatian is, therefore, limited to local and regional authorities where the language is in co-official use: the municipality of Subotica and localities in Apatin, Sombor and Sremska Mitrovica. Serbia uses the 15% threshold, so the Committee of Experts warned the authorities that such thresholds, whatever the percentage, may be contrary to the Charter if the number of speakers may nevertheless be considered sufficient.[70] The language is also used in the Provincial Assembly of Vojvodina.

In the media, the language is used on public radio and TV and also on one private television channel (2 hours per week). There are many publications covering a wide range of topics and groups. Croatian is also used in numerous cultural activities, from literary works to amateur theatre, although the speakers wish to have a professional theatre, as well.

XI Croatian in Montenegro

As stated above, Montenegro became an independent state after the dissolution of the Union with Serbia on 3 June 2006. It declared that it would assume the Union's treaty obligations within the Council of Europe including the Charter and the FCNM. Montenegro thus acceded to both treaties on 6 June 2006. The instrument of ratification of the Charter was updated by a letter

---

68 In its 2nd Periodical Report Serbia states that in primary schools more than 3,000 Croatian children attended classes in Serbian as compared to 311 attending Croatian classes.
69 Law on the Protection of the Rights and Freedoms of National Minorities, Article 11.7.
70 Application of the Charter in Serbia, 1st Evaluation Report, 2008, § 29. The possible negative effects of the thresholds have frequently been counterbalanced by the statutory competence of municipalities to introduce traditional languages in official use regardless of the number of their speakers. Croatian has not benefited from that possibility.

from the Ministry of Foreign Affairs of Montenegro on 13 October 2006. In the appended declaration it was stated that the Charter applied to Albanian and Romani as the minority languages in Montenegro.

The ratification instrument made no mention of Croatian although Croatians are recognized as a national minority in Montenegro. According to the data of the 2003 census 6,811 people declared themselves to be Croats but only 2,791 declared that they had Croatian as their mother tongue.[71] The numbers have been influenced by the demographic changes during the war in Croatia because many Croatians moved to Croatia. In the 2011 census there were 6,021 Croats and 2,791(!) spoke Croatian as their mother tongue. So, while the number of Croats diminished the number of speakers remained the same.[72] They live mostly on the coast around the bay of Boka Kotorska where they have kept their traditional presence for centuries. In 2007 the Croatian National Council was established under the Minority Act for the protection and improvement of their rights. In 2009 Croatia and Montenegro concluded a bilateral agreement on the protection of their respective minorities, replacing the previous treaty with Serbia and Montenegro.[73] A joint committee was provided for as a working body.

The initial periodical report under the Charter made it clear that the authorities did not deny the existence of Croatian or other similar languages (Serbian and Bosnian) in Montenegro. However, the issue of Croatian was dealt with in the subsequently adopted Constitution of Montenegro in 2007 according to which:

> The official language in Montenegro shall be Montenegrin. Cyrillic and Latin alphabet shall be equal. Serbian, Bosnian, Albanian and Croatian shall also be in the official use.

It was not clear to the Committee of Experts what was meant by the phrase "in the official use" since the Charter recognizes either the minority or the "less widely used official" languages.[74] In the second monitoring round and after

---

71 FCNM, 1st Report by Montenegro, 2007, p. 10.
72 In addition, 224 declared Croatian-Serbian as their mother tongue. Statistical Office of Montenegro: <http://www.monstat.org/userfiles/file/popis2011/Tabela%20CG1.xls> (visited: 20.03.2013).
73 Agreement between Croatia and Montenegro on the protection of the Croatian minority in Montenegro and the Montenegrin minority in Croatia was published in NN-MU, No. 9/2009.
74 Application of the Charter in Montenegro, 1st Evaluation Report, 2009, p. 5.

consultations with the speakers it was agreed that Croatian should be treated as a traditional minority language covered by, at least, Part II of the Charter.[75]

The situation of the language is best described as that of transition from being considered part of the 'Serbo-Croatian' variety to a 'proper' Croatian with some local peculiarities but distinct from Montenegrin. In the field of education Croatian speakers are entitled to have up to 20% of the curriculum freely designed related to the regional or minority language, including teaching of regional or minority languages or about their history, culture, music, *etc.* in accordance with the Law on General Education. However, there are apparently only five teachers who make use of that possibility for Croatian. That is clearly insufficient for the number of speakers and their needs. The language is under-represented in the media. In culture, although there are many NGOs promoting Croatian culture and language, their work is hampered by insufficient funding and the lack of a satisfactory mechanism for the promotion, preservation and development of minority cultures.[76] The authorities have yet to develop an appropriate policy regarding the protection and promotion of Croatian in Montenegro.

XII   Croatian in Slovenia

Slovenia is a state party to both the FCNM and the Charter. The former entered into force for Slovenia on 1 February 1998 and the latter on 1 January 2001. When ratifying the Charter Slovenia declared that Hungarian and Italian were the minority languages in Slovenia. Although there were 35,642 Croats in Slovenia according to the 2002 census (1.81% of the total population) and around 54,000 people declared Croatian to be their mother tongue they do not enjoy the status of a national minority, nor was their language included in the instrument of ratification of the Charter.[77] The Slovenian authorities claimed that Croats, Bosniaks and Serbs were migrants from former Yugoslavia and not national minorities.[78] Accordingly, migrant languages do not enjoy protection

---

75   Application of the Charter in Montenegro, 2nd Evaluation Report, 2011, p. 6. The same was agreed with respect to Bosnian. The status of Serbian, the most widely used language in Montenegro, remained unclear.

76   The AC called on the authorities to review the situation. AC FCNM, 1st Opinion on Montenegro, 2008, p. 17.

77   However, according to the same source, only 2,700 people use Croatian as the primary language at home.

78   See the 3rd Opinion on Slovenia, AC FCNM, 2011. Slovenia also excluded German from the scope of protection of these two instruments although there has been a traditional presence of Germans in Kočevje.

under the Charter.[79] However, neither the Advisory Committee nor the Committee of Experts was prepared to accept such a view. As for the latter, it established that Croatian in fact had had a traditional presence on Slovenian territory for centuries in the area known as Bela Krajina.[80] The Committee of Experts therefore concluded that Croatian should be protected under, at least, Part II of the Charter. It is regrettable that after the third round of monitoring and recommendation made by the Committee of Ministers Slovenia still refuses to change its legislation and practice and recognize Croatian as a traditional minority language.[81]

XIII Conclusion

Croatians have preserved their language and culture in many European countries. The language of Croats spoken as a minority language, however, has in many cases been 'freeze-framed' in time, preserving the language spoken at the time of migration, with many dialectical and archaic features. Croatian has been developing over centuries surrounded by other, in most cases, dominant languages, so a number of loan words from them entered the local variety. At the same time, the Croatian spoken in Croatia has developed and built a standard form in different circumstances.[82] This process has led to a diversification of Croatian. It is not surprising that today some varieties of Croatian want to be recognized as separate languages, but most want to be connected to Croatian, even though the possibility of using standard Croatian as part of the local variety is limited.

Today Croatians enjoy national minority status in most of the countries where they have traditionally lived, except Slovenia and Macedonia. Their home countries pledged to protect their language internationally by accepting

---

79 Article 1 of the Charter excludes migrant languages from the definition of 'minority or regional languages'.

80 Application of the Charter in Slovenia, 1st Evaluation Report, 2004, p. 7, 9. Today Croats mostly live in Ljubljana, Maribor and Novo Mesto.

81 Application of the Charter in Slovenia, 3rd Evaluation Report, 2010, p. 9. It is interesting that during the same period the Committee of Experts had been looking into the position of the Slovene language in Croatia and came to the same conclusion that it is a traditional language in Croatia. Croatia finally conceded and admitted Slovene under the protection of the Charter. Application of the Charter in Croatia, 4th Evaluation Report, 2010, § 7.

82 Standard Croatian is based on one of the Croatian dialects – the *Štokavian* dialect, but some of the local varieties are based on two other Croatian dialects (*Čakavian* or *Kajkavian* dialect).

the Council of Europe treaties on the protection of minorities and their languages: the European Charter for Regional or Minority Languages and/or the Framework Convention for the Protection of National Minorities. By subjecting themselves to the respective monitoring mechanisms, they also expressed their commitment to align the protection they provide with the European standards.

CHAPTER 27

Some Considerations on the Legal Role of the Sentences and Recommendations of International Bodies Created for the Protection of Human Rights

*Zlata Drnas de Clément**

The International Court of Justice in the case of *Ahmadou Sadio Diallo* (*Republic of Guinea* v. *Democratic Republic of the Congo*) – judgment of 30 November 2010 – referred to the 'jurisprudence' ('case law') of the Human Rights Committee and ruled that "[a]lthough the Court is in no way obliged, in the exercise of its judicial functions, to model its own interpretation of the Covenant [International Covenant on Civil and Political Rights] on that of the Committee, it believes that it should ascribe great weight to the interpretation adopted by this independent body that was established specifically to supervise the application of that treaty."[1]

---

*   Professor Emeritus of the National University of Cordoba-Argentina, and Professor Emeritus of the Catholic University of Cordoba-Argentina; Member of the National Academy of Law and Social Sciences of Cordoba-Argentina.

1   "66. *L'interprétation qui précède est pleinement corroborée par la jurisprudence du Comité des droits de l'homme institué par le Pacte en vue de veiller au respect de cet instrument par les Etats parties (voir, par exemple, en ce sens:* Maroufidou c. Suède, no 58/1979, par. 9.3; Comité des droits de l'homme, observation générale no 15: situation des étrangers au regard du Pacte).

   Le Comité des droits de l'homme a, depuis sa création, développé une jurisprudence interprétative considérable, notamment à l'occasion des constatations auxquelles il procède en réponse aux communications individuelles qui peuvent lui être adressées à l'égard des Etats parties au premier Protocole facultatif, ainsi que dans le cadre de ses "Observations générales".

   Bien que la Cour ne soit aucunement tenue, dans l'exercice de ses fonctions judiciaires, de conformer sa propre interprétation du Pacte à celle du Comité, elle estime devoir accorder une grande considération à l'interprétation adoptée par cet organe indépendant, spécialement établi en vue de superviser l'application de ce traité. Il en va de la nécessaire clarté et de l'indispensable cohérence du droit international; il en va aussi de la sécurité juridique, qui est un droit pour les personnes privées bénéficiaires des droits garantis comme pour les Etats tenus au respect des obligations conventionnelles.

   67. De même, lorsque la Cour est appelée, comme en l'espèce, à faire application d'un instrument régional de protection des droits de l'homme, elle doit tenir dûment compte de l'interprétation dudit instrument adopté par les organes indépendants qui ont été spécialement créés, si tel a été le cas, en vue de contrôler la bonne application du traité en cause..." (*CIJ Recueil 2010*, paras. 66–67). The French is the authoritative text.

This leads us to reflect on the role of the pronouncements of the various specialized bodies for the protection of human rights and the legal meaning and scope of the 'weight' assigned by the Court to the interpretations of human rights instruments by expert entities.

I   Some International Bodies Created for the Protection of Human Rights

1   *Universal Level*[2]

The *United Nations Human Rights Council* (subsidiary body of the United Nations General Assembly established in 2006, successor to the United Nations Commission on Human Rights) is an inter-governmental body of 47 States responsible for strengthening the promotion and protection of human rights around the globe and for addressing situations of human rights violations and making recommendations on them (specific country situations or thematic issues). The format of the outcome of the review will be a *report* consisting of a summary of the proceedings of the review process, *conclusions and/or recommendations*, and the *voluntary commitments* of the State concerned. Special procedures may be individual ('Special Rapporteur' or 'Independent Expert') or carried out by a working group usually composed of five members (one from each region). In 2007, the Human Rights Council decided to create an Advisory Committee of eighteen members to provide expert advice and adopted a new Complaints Procedure, established to address consistent patterns of gross and reliably attested violations of all human rights and all fundamental freedoms occurring in any part of the world.

The *Human Rights Committee*[3] – the principal quasi-judicial human rights body within the UN human rights system – has 18 independent experts who are persons of high moral character and recognized competence in the field of human rights. The committee monitors the implementation by its States Parties of the International Covenant on Civil and Political Rights (adopted by General Assembly Resolution 2200 A (XXI) of 16 December 1966, in force from 23 March 1976).[4] States must report initially one year after acceding to the Covenant and then whenever the Committee requests (usually every four years). The Committee

---

2   See <http://www.ohchr.org>.
3   Office of the United Nations High Commissioner for Human Rights, "Civil and Political Rights: The Human Rights Committee", *Fact Sheet No. 15* (Rev.1).
4   The Committee meets in Geneva or New York and normally holds three sessions per year. We specially remember the outstanding participation of Professor Budislav Vukas as a Member

examines each report and addresses its *concerns* and *recommendations* to the State Party in the form of *concluding observations*, generally divided into the following sections: Introduction, Positive factors, and Principal subjects of concern and recommendations. In addition to the reporting procedure, Article 41 of the Covenant provides for the Committee to consider inter-state complaints[5] and, under the First Optional Protocol, individual complaints.[6] The Committee also publishes its interpretation of the content of human rights provisions, known as *general comments*.

The *Committee on Economic, Social and Cultural Rights* (CESCR) is the body of 18 independent experts that monitors the implementation of the International Covenant on Economic, Social and Cultural Rights by its States Parties. All States Parties submit regular reports to the Committee on how the rights are being implemented. States must report initially within two years of accepting the Covenant and thereafter every five years. The Committee examines each report and addresses its *concerns* and *recommendations* to the State Party in the form of *concluding observations*. With regard to individual complaints, in 2008, the General Assembly adopted an Optional Protocol (GA Resolution A/RES/63/117) to the International Covenant on Economic, Social and Cultural Rights which gives the Committee competence to receive and consider communications from individuals. The Committee transmits its findings, together with *comments* and *recommendations*, to the State Party concerned. The Committee publishes its interpretation of the provisions of the Covenant, known as *general comments*.

The *Committee on the Elimination of Racial Discrimination* (CERD) is the oldest body created for the protection of human rights. It has 18 independent experts that monitor the implementation of the Convention on the Elimination of All Forms of Racial Discrimination by its States Parties. States Parties are obliged to submit regular reports to the Committee on how the rights are being implemented. States must report initially one year after acceding to the Convention and then every two years. The Committee examines each report and addresses its concerns and recommendations to the State Party in the

---

of the Croat Delegation before the Human Rights Committee in matters relating to the protection of human rights in the Croatian territory as a result of war in the former Yugoslavia.

5 If a matter referred to the Committee (Article 41) is not resolved, the Committee may, with the prior consent of the States Parties concerned, appoint an *ad hoc* Conciliation Commission with instructions to complete its business and submit a *report* to the Chairperson of the Committee and, through that person, to the parties in dispute.

6 Boerefijn, Ineke, "Towards a Strong System of Supervision: The Human Rights Committee's Role in Reforming the Reporting Procedure under Article 40 of the Covenant on Civil and Political Rights", 17 *Human Rights Quarterly*, 1995, p. 767.

form of *concluding observations*. The Convention establishes three other mechanisms through which the Committee performs its monitoring functions: the early-warning procedure, the examination of inter-state complaints and the examination of individual complaints. The Committee includes in its annual *report* a summary of the communications and, where appropriate, a summary of the explanations and statements of the States Parties concerned and of its own *suggestions* and *recommendations*. The Committee also publishes its interpretation of the content of human rights provisions (*general recommendations* or *general comments*).

The *Committee on the Elimination of Discrimination against Women* (CEDAW) is the body of 23 independent experts that monitors implementation of the Convention on the Elimination of All Forms of Discrimination against Women. States Parties are obliged to submit regular reports to the Committee on how the rights of the Convention are implemented. During its sessions the Committee considers each State Party's report and addresses its *concerns* and *recommendations* to the State Party in the form of *concluding observations*. In accordance with the Optional Protocol to the Convention, the CEDAW receives communications from individuals or groups of individuals. These procedures are optional and are only available where the State concerned has accepted them. The Committee also formulates general *recommendations* and *suggestions*.

The *Committee against Torture* (CAT) is the body of 10 independent experts that monitors implementation of the Convention against Torture and Other Cruel, Inhuman or Degrading Treatment or Punishment by its States Parties. States Parties submit regular reports to the Committee on how the rights are being implemented. States must report initially one year after acceding to the Convention and then every four years. The Committee examines each report and addresses its *concerns* and *recommendations* to the State Party in the form of *concluding observations*. The *Subcommittee on Prevention of Torture and other Cruel, Inhuman or Degrading Treatment or Punishment* (SPT), composed of 25 independent and impartial experts, began its work in 2007 pursuant to the Optional Protocol to the Convention against Torture. It is a new kind of treaty body with purely *preventive mandate* (visits, assessment, advice). It produces *recommendations* and *observations* to States.

The *Committee on the Rights of the Child* (CRC) is the body of 18 independent experts that monitors the implementation of the Convention on the Rights of the Child by its States Parties. It also monitors the implementation of two optional protocols to the Convention, on the involvement of children in armed conflict and on child trafficking, child prostitution and child pornography. On 19 December 2011, the UN General Assembly approved a third optional protocol on a Communications Procedure, which will allow individual children to submit complaints regarding specific violations of their rights under the Convention and its first two optional protocols. The Protocol opened for signature in 2012 and will enter into force upon ratification by 10 UN Member States. States Parties submit regular reports to the Committee initially two years after acceding to the Convention and then every five years. The Committee examines each report and addresses its *concerns* and *recommendations* to the State Party in the form of *concluding observations*.

The *Committee on the Protection of the Rights of All Migrant Workers and Members of Their Families* (CMW) is the body of 14 independent experts that monitors implementation of the International Convention on the Protection of the Rights of All Migrant Workers and Members of Their Families by its State Parties. States Parties submit regular reports to the Committee initially one year after acceding to the Convention and then every five years. The Committee examines each report and addresses its *concerns* and *recommendations* to the State Party in the form of *concluding observations*. Under certain circumstances, the Committee is also able to consider individual complaints or communications from individuals claiming that their rights under the Convention have been violated once 10 States Parties have accepted this procedure in accordance with Article 77 of the Convention. At the moment, two States have accepted this procedure.

The *Committee on the Rights of Persons with Disabilities* (CRPD) is the body of 12 (later 18) independent experts which monitors the implementation of the Convention by the States Parties. States Parties submit regular reports to the Committee on how the rights are being implemented. States must report initially within two years of accepting the Convention and thereafter every four years. The Committee shall examine each report and shall make *suggestions* and *general recommendations* on the report. The Optional Protocol to the Convention gives the Committee competence to examine individual complaints with regard to alleged violations of the Convention by States Parties to the Protocol. After examining a communication, the Committee shall forward its *suggestions* and *recommendations*, if any, to the State Party concerned and to the petitioner.

The *Committee on Enforced Disappearances* (CED) is the body of 10 independent experts which monitors implementation of the Convention by the States Parties. States must report initially within two years of accepting the Convention. The Committee examines each report and shall make such *suggestions* and *general recommendations* on the report. A State Party may, at the time of ratification of the Convention or at any later time, declare that it recognizes the competence of the Committee to receive and consider communications from or on behalf of individuals subject to its jurisdiction claiming to be victims of a violation by that State Party of provisions of this Convention. The Committee produces *comments*, *observations* or *recommendations*.

2 Regional Level
a Europe[7]

The *European Court of Human Rights* (ECtHR) is a court established in 1959 by the European Convention for the Protection of Human Rights and Fundamental Freedoms (1950) which hears complaints about a contracting party having violated the human rights enshrined in the Convention and its 14 protocols.

It consists of a number of judges equal to the number of Member States of the Council of Europe. The Court's judges sit in their individual capacity and do not represent any State. In dealing with applications, the Court is assisted by a Registry consisting mainly of lawyers from all the Member States (who are also known as legal secretaries). They are entirely independent of their country of origin and do not represent either applicants or States.[8]

The Court receives complaints by individuals or other contracting States. The Convention was adopted under the auspices of the Council of Europe and all of its 47 Member States are parties to the Convention.[9] In final *judgments* the Court declares that a contracting State has violated (or not) the Convention, and may order the State to pay material and/or moral damages and the legal costs of the case. Under the Convention the contracting parties undertake to abide by the final judgment of the Court in any case to which they are parties. *Advisory opinions* are not binding, regardless of the legal weight they have in the system.

b America[10]

The legal regime to which the organs of the inter-American system of protection of human rights must adhere is based on the declaration of the fundamental human rights contained in the Organization of American States (OAS) Charter and the American Declaration of the Rights and Duties of Man, and – as a result of progressive efforts during the twentieth century – a *sui generis* system has been completed by: the American Convention on Human Rights; the Additional Protocol to the American Convention on Human Rights in the Area of Economic, Social and Cultural Rights; the Protocol to the American

---

7   See <http://www.echr.coe.int> (accessed February 2, 2013).
8   European Court of Human Rights – Registry, "Questions and Answers", available at: <http://www.echr.coe.int> (accessed August 24, 2012).
9   Under Protocol No.11 of the Convention, the Court became full-time and the European Commission of Human Rights was abolished.
10 See <http://www.corteidh.or.cr> and <http://www.oas.org/es/cidh> (accessed February 2, 2013).

Convention on Human Rights to Abolish the Death Penalty; the Inter-American Convention to Prevent and Punish Torture; the Inter-American Convention on Forced Disappearance of Persons; the Inter-American Convention on the Prevention, Punishment and Eradication of Violence Against Women, and the Inter-American Convention on the Elimination of All Forms of Discrimination Against Persons with Disabilities. However, the Charter and the Convention are the only instruments that establish rules of due process for the proceedings of the system's organs (Inter-American Commission and Inter-American Court). The other instruments refer to the Convention with regard to everything that concerns proceedings. The OAS Charter establishes the powers and competence of the Commission. So, in the case of the OAS Member States not parties to the Convention, the due process regime refers the administration of requests and communications to Articles I, II, III, IV, XVIII, XXV and XXVI of the American Declaration, based on the provisions of Article 24 of the Statute of the Commission which, in turn, refers to its Rules of Procedure. In the case of the parties to the Convention, the competent organs are the Inter-American Commission of Human Rights and the Inter-American Court of Human Rights.[11] Both the Commission and the Court – in different ways – are empowered to interpret the Convention. The Commission is an organ of the OAS; but, it is also an organ of the American Convention, and its powers are established in Article 41 of that instrument. As an organ of the Convention, the Commission is linked to the Court, because both have the authority to examine individual and State communications in accordance with Articles 44, 45, 51, 61 and *ff.* of the Convention, though in different ways. Only in the mentioned area has the Court the power to review whether the Commission has complied with the provisions of the American Convention and the different inter-American human rights instruments. The Inter-American Court controls due process of law in the proceedings before the Inter-American Commission of Human Rights in relation to the processing of matters that have been submitted for the Court's consideration, in accordance with the competence granted to it by the American Convention and other inter-American instruments for the protection of human rights. In the other areas the Commission and the Court have autonomy and functional independence.[12]

The *Inter-American Commission of Human Rights* (IACHR) is a principal and autonomous organ of the OAS, created in 1959, composed of seven independent

---

[11] See Inter-American Court of Human Rights (IACtHR), *Advisory Opinion OC-19/05* of November 28, 2005 (requested by the Bolivarian Republic of Venezuela), *Control of due process in the exercise of the powers of the Inter-American Commission on Human Rights (Articles 41 and 44 to 51 of the American Convention on Human Rights)*, para. 13.

[12] *Ibid.*, paras. 24, 25, 31.

members. Together with the Inter-American Court of Human Rights, the Commission is one of the institutions of the American Convention on Human Rights (ACHR, Pact of 'San José-Costa Rica'). The Commission exercises three types of functions with the basic purpose of the promotion, observance and protection of human rights: (i) administrative; (ii) advisory and promotional, and (iii) quasi-jurisdictional, as set forth in Articles 44 to 51 of the Convention.[13] The Commission makes *requests* or *recommendations* to the governments of the Member States, prepares *studies* or *reports*, and issues *conclusions*.

The *Inter-American Court of Human Rights* (seven judges, nationals of the Member States of the OAS) is the judicial organ of the American Convention on Human Rights, established in San José-Costa Rica, in 1979.

The Court enforces and interprets the provisions of the ACHR through its *adjudicatory and advisory functions*. Only the States Parties and the Commission have the right to submit a contentious case to the Court.

The jurisdiction of the Court shall comprise all cases concerning the interpretation and application of the provisions of the ACHR that are submitted to it, provided that the States Parties to the case recognize or have recognized such jurisdiction, whether by special declaration, or by a special agreement.

If the Court finds that there has been a violation of a right or freedom protected by the ACHR, the Court shall rule that the injured party be ensured the enjoyment of the right or freedom that was violated. It shall also rule, if appropriate, that the consequences of the measure or situation that constituted the breach of such right or freedom be remedied and that fair compensation be paid to the injured party.

The States Parties to the Convention undertake to comply with the judgment of the Court in any case to which they are parties. The *judgment* of the Court is final and not subject to appeal (at request, only interpretation is admitted). The advisory function of the IACtHR enables it to respond to consultations submitted by agencies and Member States of the OAS (*advisory opinions* on domestic laws and proposed legislation, and whether or not they are compatible with the Convention's provisions).

c   Africa[14]

The African Charter on Human and Peoples' Rights established the *African Commission on Human and Peoples' Rights* (eleven members) to promote, protect

---

13   Ibid., para. 13.
14   African Commission on Human and Peoples' Rights, Centre for Human Rights of the University of Pretoria, *Celebrating the African Charter at 30: A Guide to the African Human Rights System*, Pretoria University Law Press, 2011, available at: <http://www.achpr.org> and <http://african-court.org> (accessed February 2, 2013).

and interpret the rights enshrined under the Charter, and to ensure that Member States comply with their obligations undertaken under the Charter. The Commission was inaugurated on 2 November, 1987. It produces *reports* and *recommendations*.

The *African Court on Human and Peoples' Rights* (eleven judges) was established by virtue of Article 1 of the Protocol to the African Charter on Human and Peoples' Rights on the Establishment of an African Court on Human and Peoples' Rights, which was adopted by Member States of the then Organization of African Unity (OAU) in Ouagadougou, Burkina Faso, in June 1998. It has jurisdiction over all cases and disputes submitted to it concerning the interpretation and application of the African Charter on Human and Peoples' Rights, the Protocol and any other relevant human rights instrument ratified by the States concerned.

The Court complements the protective mandate of the African Commission on Human and Peoples' Rights conferred upon it by the African Charter on Human and Peoples' Rights.

The Court's jurisdiction applies only to States that have ratified the Court's Protocol.

The Court may receive complaints and/or applications submitted to it either by the African Commission of Human and Peoples' Rights or States Parties to the Protocol or African Intergovernmental Organizations. Non-Governmental Organizations with observer status before the African Commission on Human and Peoples' Rights and individuals from States which have made a Declaration accepting the jurisdiction of the Court can also institute cases directly before the Court. The *judgment* of the Court shall be final and not subject to appeal. At the request of a Member State of the OAU, the OAU, any of its organs, or any African organization recognized by the OAU, the Court may provide an *opinion* on any legal matter relating to the Charter or any other relevant human rights instruments, provided that the subject matter of the opinion is not related to a matter being examined by the Commission.

The African Court on Human and Peoples' Rights is seized of matters of interpretation arising from the application or implementation of the Protocol to the African Charter on Human and Peoples' Rights on the Rights of Women in Africa.

The African Charter on the Rights and Welfare of the Child (ACRWC) adopted in 1990, established the *African Committee of Experts on the Rights and Welfare of the Child* (eleven members), *inter alia* to promote and protect the rights enshrined in the ACRWC; to monitor the implementation and ensure protection of the rights enshrined in the Charter; to interpret the provisions of the Charter at the request of a State Party, an Institution of the Organization of

African Unity or any other person or Institution recognized by the Organization of African Unity, or any State Party. The Committee monitors the implementation of the Charter and may receive communications, from any person, group or non-governmental organization recognized by the OAU, from a Member State, or the United Nations, relating to any matter covered by the Charter. As final outcome, it produces *reports*.

3 Some Partial Reflections

As we can see, the different bodies, with the exception of the courts, have a merely *recommendatory or informative role* and are not able to produce genuine jurisprudence.

Some domestic tribunals have recognized the binding value of the pronouncements of quasi-judicial bodies, and have referred to such decisions as 'jurisprudence'.[15]

José Ovalle Favela points to Norberto Bobbio who stated that the activities of international organizations for the protection of human rights could be considered under three aspects: promotion (a set of actions aimed at inducing States to introduce or improve internal regulation), control (a set of international measures implemented to check whether the recommendations have been accepted and to what extent), and safeguard (real organization of jurisdictional international protection).[16] Some quasi-judicial bodies interpret the law with guarantees similar to those of the courts.

As Thomas Buergenthal noted, the system has its built-in limitations: the initial step rests with the States, which must first ratify or accede to a legally

---

15 For example, the Supreme Court of Argentina, in the *Bramajo, Hernán Javier s/ incidente de excarcelación* (12/09/1996) case stated: "The opinion of the Inter-American Commission on Human Rights should serve as a guide for the interpretation of the provisions of the American Convention on Human Rights" (para. 4); "[T]he contested decision should be reversed because the interpretation adopted by the lower court of Art. 1 of Law 24,390 has been inconsistent with the case law developed by the Inter-American Commission on Human Rights..." (para. 15). In the case *Simón, Julio Héctor y otros* (14/06/2005) the same Court pronounced: "[A]s has been recognized by this Court on several occasions, the jurisprudence of the Inter-American Court of Human Rights and the Inter-American Commission directives, are an indispensable guide for interpreting the duties and obligations of the American Convention on Human Rights" (para. 17).

16 Ovalle Favela, José, "La Influencia de la Corte Interamericana de Derechos Humanos en el Derecho interno de los Estados Latinoamericanos", 45(134) *Boletín Mexicano de Derecho Comparado, nueva serie*, 2012, pp. 595 *et sq*. (available at: <http://www.biblio.juridicas.unam.mx>; accessed November 18, 2012.). See also Garcia-Sayán, Diego, "The Inter-American Court and Constitutionalism in Latin America", 89 *Texas Law Review*, 2011, pp. 1835 *et sq*.

binding instrument; the system continually requires at least some level of voluntary cooperation by States; and there are no effective sanctions for non-compliance with the obligations States Parties have accepted.[17]

In regard to the courts, the American Court has been more expansive and progressive than the European and African courts. This may find its basis in the wide powers assigned by the Convention to the American tribunal, which exceed those provided by the European and African conventions. The American Court is mandated *inter alia* to assure the injured party the enjoyment of his right or freedom that was violated.[18]

II Legal Meaning and Scope of the Pronouncements of the Different Human Rights Bodies

Only at the regional level (European, American and African) are there human rights courts able to deliver judgments which are binding for the States Parties involved in a case, and – according to the broad interpretations of those courts – also binding *erga omnes*.[19]

There are human rights bodies at all levels capable of producing quasi-judicial pronouncements. The International Court of Justice has described these pronouncements as 'jurisprudence', and regional and domestic courts have

---

17 Buergenthal, Thomas, "The U.N. Human Rights Committee", 5 *Max Planck Yearbook of United Nations Law*, 2001,pp. 341–398, at 391 *et sq*. Although the author only referred to the Human Rights Committee, the statement is valid for the entire system.

18 American Convention on Human Rights, Article 63(1): "If the Court finds that there has been a violation of a right or freedom protected by this Convention, the Court shall rule that the injured party *be ensured the enjoyment of his right or freedom that was violated*. It shall also rule, if appropriate, that the consequences of the measure or situation that constituted the breach of such right or freedom be remedied and that fair compensation be paid to the injured party." (Emphasis added.) – Convention for the Protection of Human Rights and Fundamental Freedoms, Article 41 ('Just satisfaction'): "If the Court finds that there has been a violation of the Convention or the Protocols thereto, and if the internal law of the High Contracting Party concerned allows only partial reparation to be made, the Court shall, if necessary, afford just satisfaction to the injured party." – Protocol to the African Charter on Human and Peoples' Rights on the Establishment of an African Court on Human and Peoples' Rights, Article 27 ('Findings'): "1. If the Court finds that there has been violation of a human or peoples' right, it shall make appropriate orders to remedy the violation, including the payment of fair compensation or reparation."

19 See *infra*.

considered such documents to be valid interpretations of the general application of a treaty as living instrument.[20]

However, many scholars and domestic tribunals understand that the statements of quasi-jurisdictional bodies are mandatory for the States involved in a case, as there is a real process with all guarantees. Furthermore, their decisions have the same formalities as judgments.[21] Nevertheless they have only indirect binding effects.

The principal arguments to support the jurisdictional role of the non-judicial bodies are: the protection system "is endowed with a series of guarantees that ensure the principle of the supremacy of the Convention"; "some of the guarantees, such as the principles of good faith and *pro homine*, guide the proceedings"; "there are some specific guarantees related to the individual petition proceedings, namely: conditions for the admissibility of petitions, and the principles of adversarial proceedings, procedural balance, and legal certainty"; "the proceedings before the quasi-jurisdictional bodies contain guarantees for adversarial

---

[20] Hellen Keller and Geir Ulfstein consider the common view that international human rights treaties should be interpreted as 'living instruments'. They assert: "As a result of this constant progress, comparisons with the law as laid down at the time of ratification become difficult. In addition, even new rules of interpretation may develop over time, if there is state consensus and corresponding practice in this regard." – "Then, a new customary rule of treaty interpretation has developed." – "There appear to be two possible ways in which consensus may legitimise a certain human rights interpretation and connected to both is the object and purpose of the human rights treaty. ...The first refers to the object and purpose of the treaty as a whole, and the second to the object and purpose of the individual treaty provision. Regarding the whole treaty, its object and purpose is possibly expressed in its preamble, which informs us about the general scope of state consensus. As every human rights treaty is limited to a particular set of rights, any interpretation which goes beyond that scope is questionable, and likely to be illegitimate. Concerning individual treaty provisions, it is the consensus and practice of the states members to the treaty, which may legitimise a subsequent interpretation. If the majority of states parties to the treaty consent to and practice a certain interpretation of a particular human rights provision, also at the national level, there is a strong indication that this interpretation will be legitimate." Keller, Helen and Ulfstein, Geir (eds.), *UN Human Rights Treaty Bodies: Law and Legitimacy* ("Aspects of Human Rights Interpretation by the UN Treaty Bodies"), Cambridge University Press, 2012.

[21] See Hitters, Juan Carlos. "¿Son vinculantes los pronunciamientos de la Comisión y de la Corte Interamericana de Derechos Humanos? (control de constitucionalidad y convencionalidad)", 10 *Revista Iberoamericana de Derecho Procesal Constitucional*, 2008, pp. 131–156; See also Sagües, Néstor P, "Nuevamente sobre el valor para jueces argentinos de los pronunciamientos de la Corte Interamericana y de la Comisión Interamericana de Derechos Humanos", *Jurisprudencia Argentina*, 1999-II, p. 364.

proceedings similar to those that exist in litigation proceedings before the Courts"; "one of the functions of the quasi-jurisdictional bodies...is to monitor the adherence of its *quasi*-jurisdictional proceedings to these principles."[22]

In relation to what we have said in the preceding paragraphs, given the limited extent of the present paper, we will only cite as examples some of the pronouncements that reflect such situations.

The Inter-American Court, in expansive perception, has said:

> 44. Owing to the manifest incompatibility of *self-amnesty laws* and the American Convention on Human Rights, *the said laws lack legal effect* and may not continue to obstruct the investigation of the grounds on which this case is based or the identification and punishment of those responsible, nor can *they have the same or a similar impact with regard to other cases* that have occurred in Peru, where the rights established in the American Convention have been violated.[23] (Emphasis added.)

> 14. In its request for interpretation, the Commission asked the Court to determine the following: "Is the Judgment in the Barrios Altos Case, concerning the incompatibility of laws Nos.26479 and 26492 with the American Convention, general in scope or confined to that specific case only?" The Commission's contention is that *"the effects of the Court's judgment are not confined exclusively to the Barrios Altos Case, but rather to all those in which those amnesty laws were applied."* It points out that paragraph 44 of the Court's judgment of March 14, 2001 "can hardly be interpreted any other way."[24] (Emphasis added.)

> 18. The Court decides...2. That given the nature of the violation that amnesty laws No. 26479 and No. 26492 constitute, *the decision in the judgment on the merits in the Barrios Altos Case has generic effects.*[25] (Emphasis added.)

> 115. *The* corpus juris *of international human rights law comprises a set of international instruments of varied content and juridical effects (treaties, conventions, resolutions and declarations).* Its dynamic evolution has had

---

22   Inter-American Court of Human Rights (IACtHR), *Advisory Opinion OC-19/05* of November 28, 2005 (requested by the Bolivarian Republic of Venezuela), *Control of due process in the exercise of the powers of the Inter-American Commission on Human Rights (Articles 41 and 44 to 51 of the American Convention on Human Rights)*, para. 13.

23   IACtHR, *Case of Barrios Altos v. Peru*, Judgment of March 14, 2001 (Merits).

24   IACtHR, *Case of Barrios Altos et al. v. Peru*, Judgment of September 3, 2001 (Interpretation of the Judgment on the Merits).

25   *Ibid.*

a positive impact on international law in affirming and building up the latter's faculty for regulating relations between States and the human beings within their respective jurisdictions. *This Court, therefore, must adopt the proper approach to consider this question in the context of the evolution of the fundamental rights of the human person in contemporary international law.*[26] (Emphasis added.)

101. Accordingly, this Court considers that the *principle of equality before the law, equal protection before the law and non-discrimination belongs to jus cogens,* because the whole legal structure of national and international public order rests on it and it is a fundamental principle that permeates all laws. Nowadays, no legal act that is in conflict with this fundamental principle is acceptable...[27] (Emphasis added.)

34. ...[I]t is necessary to emphasize *that the system of international protection must be understood as an integral whole*...*[T]he adoption of a restrictive interpretation as to the scope of the Tribunal's jurisdiction would not only be contrary to the purpose and end of the Convention,* but it would also affect the effective application of the treaty and of the guarantee of protection that it provides, with negative consequences for the alleged victim in the exercise of his right to access to justice.[28] (Emphasis added.)

99. *Pursuant to the principle of effectiveness and the need of protection in those cases of people or groups in situation of vulnerability, ...this Tribunal shall interpret and give essence to the rights enshrined in the Convention, according to the evolution of the international corpus juris existing in relation to the human rights of migrants, taking into account that the international community has recognized the need to adopt special measures to ensure the protection of the human rights of this group*...[29] (Emphasis added.)

225. This Court has held in its case law that it is aware that domestic authorities are bound to respect the rule of law, and therefore, they are bound to apply the provisions in force within the legal system. ... But

---

26 IACtHR, *Advisory Opinion OC-16/99* of October 1, 1999, *The Right to Information on Consular Assistance in the Framework of the Guarantees of the Due Process of Law.*

27 IACtHR, *Advisory Opinion OC-18/03* of September 17, 2003, *Juridical Condition and Rights of Undocumented Migrants.*

28 IACtHR, *Case of Vélez Loor v. Panama,* Judgment of November 23, 2010 (Preliminary Objections, Merits, Reparations, and Costs).

29 *Ibid.*

> when a State has ratified an international treaty such as the American Convention, all its bodies, including its judges, are also bound by such Convention, which forces them to see that all the effects of the provisions embodied in the Convention are not adversely affected by the enforcement of laws which are contrary to its purpose and end. ...To perform this task, *the Judiciary has to take into account not only the treaty, but also the interpretation thereof made by the Inter-American Court, which is the ultimate interpreter of the American Convention*...[30] (Emphasis added.)

In his separate opinion in the *Case of the 'Street Children' (Villagrán-Morales et al.) v. Guatemala*, Judge Cançado Trindade said:

> 9. In my view, the absence of an objective criterion of assessment of human suffering should not be invoked as a justification for a 'technical' – or rather mechanical – application of the relevant juridical norms. To the contrary, the lesson which appears to me necessary to extract from the present case of the *'Street Children'* (and also from the case *Paniagua Morales and Others*) is in the sense that one ought to be guided by the victimization and the human suffering, as well as the rehabilitation of the surviving victims ..., also in order *to fill gaps in the applicable juridical norms and, furthermore, on the basis of considerations of equity, to reach a solution* ex aequo et bono *for the concrete case in conformity with Law*. Ultimately, *the jurisdiction* (jus dicere, jurisdictio) *of the Tribunal is summed up in its power to declare the Law, and the sentence (from the* Latin *sententia, etymologically derived from 'sentimiento', feeling) is something more than a logical operation in the framework of predetermined juridical limits*.[31] (Emphasis added.)

Ashley Mason deems that the Court's expansion of the American Convention was supported by the Inter-American Court's previous case law and advisory opinions interpreting the American Convention, the European Court of Human Rights' case law, and global soft law of human rights.[32] We can add that

---

30 IACtHR, *Case of Cabrera-García and Montiel-Flores* v. *Mexico* (Preliminary Objection, Merits, Reparations, and Costs), Judgment of November 26, 2010.

31 IACtHR, *Case of the 'Street Children' (Villagrán-Morales* et al.) v. *Guatemala* (Reparations and Costs), Judgment of May 26, 2001.

32 Mason, Ashley, "Interpretation of the American Convention in Latin America: The impact of the Inter-American Court of Human Rights' decision in *Vélez Loor* v. *Panama* on irregular migrant rights", 18 *Law and Business Review of the Americas*, 2012, pp. 71 et sq.

the expansion was also founded on considerations of equity, judges' feelings and a transitional-ideological perception of justice.[33]

The ECtHR, for example, expands the applicable law. The Grand Chamber in *Demir and Baykara* v. *Turkey* (Application No. 34503/97), Judgment of 12 November 2008, concludes:

> 85. The Court, *in defining the meaning of terms and notions in the text of the Convention, can and must take into account elements of international law other than the Convention*, the interpretation of such elements by competent organs, and the practice of European States reflecting their common values. The consensus emerging from specialized international instruments and from the practice of Contracting States may constitute a relevant consideration for the Court when it interprets the provisions of the Convention in specific cases. (Emphasis added.)

> 86. In this context, *it is not necessary for the respondent State to have ratified the entire collection of instruments that are applicable in respect of the precise subject matter of the case concerned. It will be sufficient for the Court that the relevant international instruments denote a continuous evolution in the norms and principles applied in international law or in the domestic law of the majority of member States of the Council of Europe and show*, in a precise area, that there is common ground in modern societies (see, *mutatis mutandis*, Marckx, cited above, § 41). (Emphasis added.)

Some experts criticize such kind of *constructivism*, which creates new rights and obligations, in regard to substantive and procedural aspects.

Julian Arato considers that, unlike formal amendment (through the express decision of the Member States according to a certain procedure), informal

---

[33] See Abramovich, Victor, "From massive violations to structural patterns: New approaches and classic tensions in the Inter-American Human Rights System", 6(11) *SUR – International Journal on Human Rights*, 2009, pp. 7–11 (available at: <http://www.surjournal.org/eng/conteudos/getArtigo11.php?artigo=11,artigo_01.htm>, accessed August 28, 2011). The author states the cascading effect of the pronouncements of the Court and the Commission and their influence in the domestic tribunals, *e.g.*the Argentine courts (*inter alia*, *Simón, Julio Hector* et al., 2005), Chilean courts (*inter alia*, *Pinochet, Augusto*, 2001) and issues of transitional justice in Guatemala, El Salvador, Honduras, Paraguay and Uruguay, as well as in the cases alleging crimes against humanity that were committed during the 'Cold War' brought before the Court of Brazil (IACtHR, *Julio Gomez Lund* et al. vs. *Brazil*, 2009c), Bolivia (IACtHR, *Renato Ticona Estrada* et al. vs. *Bolivia*, 2007b), Mexico (IACtHR, *Rosendo Radilla Pacheco* vs. *Mexico*, 2008b).

transformation occurs more subtly, through the practice of the specialized bodies. He thinks that the question is not whether the court's interpretation does or does not expand a convention right, but rather whether its approach to interpretation entails a novel assertion of authority over the States Parties. So, from the political perspective it represents a critical shift in the powers of the court to hold the States Parties to legal instruments beyond their control and will. "By pushing the limits of the technique a court can dramatically expand its competence to consider legal materials beyond the treaties to which it has supposedly been confined."[34] The court asserts competence over and above the States Parties in clear manifestation of judicial activism. The same author, in a different article, mentions Rietiker, who argues that "the mere label of 'human rights' instrument is, as such, not relevant to justify special treatment" with regard to interpreting a treaty as evolutive. Rietiker does not object to the evolutive interpretation as such, but rather the reasoning that such an interpretation is warranted for the interpretation of human rights treaties *per se*.[35]

John Tobin notes that monitoring bodies and advocates can be quick to offer interpretations that reflect personal and political preferences. He says that "such 'result driven jurisprudence' may well persuade those who focus on what the law should be (*lex ferenda*) but its impact is limited to those who focus on what they perceive the law is (*lex lata*). Moreover, this *lex ferenda* approach encourages criticisms like David Kennedy's, that 'the human rights movement degrades the legal profession by encouraging a combination of overly-formal reliance on textual articulations that are anything but clear or binding and sloppy humanitarian argument.' Simply clothing an assertion about the content of an internationally recognized human right with the apparel of humanity may satisfy a moral or political urge, but it does not necessarily accord with the nature of the *legal* obligations actually assumed by a state under a human rights treaty."[36]

---

34 Arato, Julián, "Constitutional Transformation in the ECtHR: Strasbourg's Expansive Recourse to External Rules of International Law", 37 *Brooklyn Journal of International Law*, 2012, pp. 349 *et sq*. See also Lixinski, Lucas, "Treaty Interpretation by the Inter-American Court of Human Rights: Expansionism at the Service of the Unity of International Law", 21 *European Journal of International Law (EJIL)*, 2010, pp. 585 *et sq*.

35 Arato, Julián, "Subsequent Practice and Evolutive Interpretation: Techniques of Treaty Interpretation over Time and Their Diverse Consequences", 9 *The Law and Practice of International Courts and Tribunals*, 2010, pp. 443 *et sq*. See also *supra*, note 20.

36 Tobin, John, "Seeking to Persuade: A Constructive Approach to Human Rights Treaty Interpretation", 23 *Harvard Human Rights Journal*, 2010, pp. 1–2. See Kennedy, David, "The International Human Rights Movement: Part of the Problem?" 15 *Harvard Human Rights Journal*, 2002, pp. 101 *et sq*.

Although the International Court of Justice in the *Ahmadou Sadio Diallo* case explicitly referred to the Human Rights Committee in relation to the International Covenant on Civil and Political Rights, the concept of 'external system coherence' seeks to accommodate and exceeds the requirements under Article 31(3)(c) of the Vienna Convention on the Law of the Treaties, that the application of the general rule under Article 31(1) takes into account any relevant rules of international law applicable in the relations between the parties. The requisite of external system coherence requires a consideration of the entire system of international law, especially the provisions of other human rights treaties (in this case, also its bodies), but also other multilateral treaties and regimes within international law.[37]

At the time of their adoption, the conventions on human rights aimed at laying down minimum standards. This approach is generally based on the argument that courts and tribunals respect the sovereignty of the States and the necessity of the cooperation of the States Parties. The human rights' tribunals (following conventions) have adopted the position that their role is subsidiary to that of the contracting States. The principle of 'subsidiarity' refers to the subsidiary role of the respective convention machinery and entails, first of all, what may be termed a 'procedural relationship' between the national authorities responsible for implementing the convention and deciding human rights issues on the one hand and the convention institutions on the other.[38] Nevertheless, the judges and their literal interpretation of law face obstacles imposed by reality. In addressing the issues raised by parties in litigation, judges exercise choices because the parties argue that the same laws apply in different ways in regard to the underlying case. The task of the person who decides is not to satisfy logical precepts, but the objectives of law,[39] which entail various theories of justice, based on philosophical doctrines and ideological positions. A purposive approach to judicial interpretation involves teasing out the meanings behind the words of the law, based on the intended purpose behind the law. George Letsas, the author of the definition *of autonomous concepts* ("technical terms that are employed in legal sources and are invested with special, non-ordinary meaning"), considers that, by invoking a 'non-ordinary meaning', judges determine freely the scope and significance of

---

37 Tobin, "Seeking to Persuade (...)", *op. cit.*, p. 34.
38 Ambrus, Mónika, "Comparative Law Method in the Jurisprudence of the European Court of Human Rights in the Light of the Rule of Law", 2(3) *Erasmus Law Review*, 2009, pp. 353 *et sq.*
39 Popovic, Dragoljub, "Prevailing of Judicial Activism over Self-restraint in the Jurisprudence of the European Court of Human Rights", 42 *Creighton Law Review*, 2009, pp. 361 *et sq.*

the law, 'making' new law.⁴⁰ Major alteration occurs in cases of evolutionary, progressive or innovative interpretation. It is observable that the specialized bodies often produce interpretations contrary to the drafters' intentions, giving precedence to the convention's purpose or to the feeling of the judges over the international instrument. Giuseppe Martinico, in relation to the European system of human rights protection, wonders if the European Convention is going to be 'supreme'.⁴¹

III   Some Final Considerations

In a great number of cases, jurisprudence and quasi-jurisprudence of tribunals and other specialized bodies have changed the real substance of the human rights conventions and have entered the legal bloodstream of the States at a supreme level. At this time, the International Court of Justice has allowed human rights case law to enter into international law as a 'body' of great weight, incorporating and legitimizing thereby not only the achievements but also the excesses of those agencies.

However, in subsequent cases, such as *Georgia* v. *Russian Federation* (Judgment of 1 April 2011),⁴² the ICJ has not kept that 'humanized' position. The Court declared itself not competent based on a formalistic interpretation of Article 22 of the CERD, and ignored the value (declared 'great weight') of the Concluding Observations of the Committee on the Elimination of All Forms of Racial Discrimination.⁴³ It also ignored the *pro homine* principle maintained

---

40   Letsas, George, "The Truth in Autonomous Concepts: How to Interpret the ECHR", 15 *EJIL*, 2004, pp. 285 *et sq.*

41   Martinico, Giuseppe, "Is the European Convention Going to Be 'Supreme'? A Comparative-Constitutional Overview of ECHR and EU Law before National Courts", 23 *EJIL*, 2012, pp. 401 *et sq.*

42   ICJ, *Case concerning application of the international Convention on the Elimination of all Forms of Racial Discrimination* (Georgia v. Russian Federation), Preliminary objections, Judgment of 1 April 2011.

43   Committee on the Elimination of All Forms of Racial Discrimination, Concluding Observations: Georgia, para. 4 (April 27, 2001), UN Doc. CERD/C/304/Add.120. The document states the following: "[T]he situations in South Ossetia and Abkhazia have resulted in discrimination against people of different ethnic origins, including a large number of internally displaced persons and refugees. On repeated occasions, attention has been drawn to the obstruction by the Abkhaz authorities of the voluntary return of displaced populations, and several recommendations have been issued by the Security Council to facilitate the free movement of refugees and internally displaced persons." In their joint

by all specialized bodies of human rights. Perhaps the fact that Russia was the respondent may have influenced the decision of the Court, given the inconvenience of taking a position in relation to a sensitive political situation.

Despite the above, one wonders if the 'great weight' that the Court gives to the 'jurisprudence' of specialized human rights bodies does not imply a new parameter for the interpretation of treaties and general international law, and constitutes the basis of a new human rights constitutional and moral superiority in the international legal system.

This means that decisions and recommendations of the judicial and quasi-judicial bodies specializing in human rights – and their evolutionary standards – can enter the bloodstream of the international law, and create a new 'law *ad gentes*', a sacred right to expand and impose.[44]

---

dissenting opinion to the ICJ's judgment of 1 April 2011, Owada, Simma, Abraham, Donoghue and Gaja found that the Court's interpretation of Article 22 was questionable and that the Court's analysis on this point ignored or gave short shrift to arguments which might have led to a different conclusion (para. 3). Meanwhile, Judge Cançado Trindade, in his dissenting opinion, stressed that the CERD was a *living* instrument, but that the Court had interpreted it in a formalist-static way, although a dynamic-evolutive interpretation was present in the international case-law of the ICJ and of the other bodies of human rights (paras. 169 *et sq.*).

44 See Prieto Sanchís, Luis, *Ideología e Interpretación Jurídica*, Madrid: Tecnos, 1993, pp. 13 *et sq.* See also Orozco Henríquez, José de Jesús, "Human Rights and the New Amendment to Article 1 of the Constitution", 5(28) *Revista IUS*, 2011.

CHAPTER 28

Doctrinal Views *versus* State Views on Humanitarian Assistance in the Event of Disasters: Comparing the Work of the *Institut De Droit International* with That of the International Law Commission

Gerhard Hafner [*]

1   Introduction

It is a pleasure to contribute to a *liber amicorum* for Professor Budislav Vukas. We cooperated in international negotiations on a number of occasions. I also had the opportunity to participate in the most recent discussion concerning the question of humanitarian assistance which took place under his guidance within the *Institut de Droit International*.

Undoubtedly, an urgent need to address humanitarian assistance in the event of disasters exists: The gap between the need to provide more and effective humanitarian assistance in the event of disasters and the legal regime governing humanitarian assistance is, in many cases, large.[1] According to the so-called Failed State Index,[2] more than half the world's population lives in States which in one way or another fail to guarantee their inhabitants' safety and welfare to an alarmingly large extent. Consequently, cross-border assistance in the case of

---

[*] Professor of International Law, University of Vienna, Comenius University and Paneurópska Vysoká Škola, Fakulta Práva, Bratislava; Member of the *Institut de Droit International*; Member of the Permanent Court of Arbitration; Former Member of the International Law Commission. The author is very grateful to Mr. Gregor Novak, research assistant, for his valuable assistance in the elaboration of this contribution.

[1] See for a comprehensive overview UN Secretariat, "Protection of persons in the event of disasters", Memorandum by the UN Secretariat and Annexes (11 December 2007) UN Doc. A/CN.4/590, see also Add. 1, Add. 2, and Add. 3; see also H.-J. Heintze, A. Zwitter (eds.), *International Law and Humanitarian Assistance: A Crosscut through Legal Issues Pertaining to Humanitarianism* (Springer 2011).

[2] Produced by the Washington, DC based Foreign Policy Magazine and the Fund for Peace, Failed State Index 2011 (available at <http://www.fundforpeace.org/global/?q=fsi-grid2011>, retrieved in January 2012).

disasters is frequently called for on humanitarian grounds. While even highly industrialized societies, such as Japan, can face difficulties in providing and organizing assistance in the event of disasters,[3] individuals living under the least favourable material conditions are especially affected by a lack of effective provision or organization of assistance by their governments or other domestic actors in the event of disasters.

While numerous soft law instruments concerning humanitarian assistance exist, and many States and international organizations have concluded bi- or multilateral treaties concerning humanitarian assistance,[4] certain basic questions are still disputed. Even the solidarity clause in Article 222 of the Treaty on the Functioning of the European Union,[5] whose purpose is to provide a legal

---

3   See *e.g.* Hiroko Tabuchi, "Japan Panel Cites Failure in Tsunami" (New York Times, 26 December 2011).
4   The list of the relevant treaties is provided in UN Secretariat, "Protection of persons in the event of disasters", Addendum 2 to the Memorandum by the UN Secretariat and Annexes (11 December 2007) UN Doc. A/CN.4/590.Add. 2.
5   Article 222 of the Treaty on the Functioning of the European Union provides as follows:
    1. The Union and its Member States shall act jointly in a spirit of solidarity if a Member State is the object of a terrorist attack or the victim of a natural or man-made disaster. The Union shall mobilise all the instruments at its disposal, including the military resources made available by the Member States, to:
    (a) - prevent the terrorist threat in the territory of the Member States;
        - protect democratic institutions and the civilian population from any terrorist attack;
        - assist a Member State in its territory, at the request of its political authorities, in the event of a terrorist attack;
    (b) assist a Member State in its territory, at the request of its political authorities, in the event of a natural or man-made disaster.
    2. Should a Member State be the object of a terrorist attack or the victim of a natural or man-made disaster, the other Member States shall assist it at the request of its political authorities. To that end, the Member States shall coordinate between themselves in the Council.
    3. The arrangements for the implementation by the Union of the solidarity clause shall be defined by a decision adopted by the Council acting on a joint proposal by the Commission and the High Representative of the Union for Foreign Affairs and Security Policy. The Council shall act in accordance with Article 31(1) of the Treaty on European Union where this decision has defence implications. The European Parliament shall be informed.
        For the purposes of this paragraph and without prejudice to Article 240, the Council shall be assisted by the Political and Security Committee with the support of the structures developed in the context of the common security and defence policy and by the Committee referred to in Article 71; the two committees shall, if necessary, submit joint opinions.
    4. The European Council shall regularly assess the threats facing the Union in order to enable the Union and its Member States to take effective action.

basis for mutual assistance in the case of disasters, raises a number of questions that the wording of this provision cannot answer.[6] The lack of clarity and predictability in the legal regime governing humanitarian assistance, while giving governments a large amount of leeway in their foreign policies, places the costs that can result from a lack of appropriate and responsive assistance disproportionately on the least privileged members of society. Some of the legal questions concerning humanitarian assistance that are still disputed include the following, among others:

i. Under what circumstances, if any, do States, groups of States or international organizations have an obligation to give assistance and what does this obligation entail?
ii. In what circumstances, if any, does a State have an obligation to accept, not hinder or facilitate assistance and what does this obligation entail?
iii. What is the law applicable to States or non-state actors when providing or organizing assistance?
iv. Do States have a good faith obligation to facilitate assistance by negotiating and concluding bi- or multilateral agreements or by implementing appropriate domestic regulation?

Two reasons in particular serve to explain the increased focus of international bodies, policy-makers, and lawyers on the problem of the regulation of disaster relief and management. On the one hand, we can identify the growing clamour for increased accountability of governments, also in view of the emerging concept of a 'responsibility to protect'.[7] On the other hand, in particular in the period following World War II, international law has become much more focused than it used to on the protection of individuals. Both factors explain why the call for a better regulation for the provision of humanitarian assistance has gained in importance. It can be said that the former, overwhelmingly State-oriented approach of international law became replaced or, at least, supplemented by the individual-oriented approach. Whereas formerly international law was understood as being

---

6 See *e.g.* S. Myrdal, M. Rhinard, "The European Union's Solidarity Clause: Empty Letter or Effective Tool? An Analysis of Article 222 of the Treaty on the Functioning of the European Union", 2 *Occasional Papers of the Swedish Institute of International Affairs* (2010).
7 J.M. Welsh, "The Responsibility to Protect: Securing the Individual in International Society", in B.J. Goold, L. Lazarus (eds.), *Security and Human Rights* (Hart 2007) 363–383.

focused on the interests of States, it is presently increasingly understood as being oriented towards the protection of the individual's interests. While this understanding has certainly not fully prevailed in practice, its influence is felt in many areas of international law and it certainly frames the discussion on international law in important ways.[8] The described tendency was explicitly acknowledged by international judicial bodies, such as the International Tribunal for Former Yugoslavia (ICTY), which stated in the *Tadić Case (Appeals Chamber)* that:

> The State-sovereignty approach has been gradually supplanted by a human-being-oriented approach. Gradually the maxim of Roman law *hominum causa ius constitutum est* (all law is created for the benefit of human beings) has gained a firm foothold in the international community as well.[9]

Two important international bodies which serve as *loci* of legal thinking and for the codification of international law have addressed the issue of disaster relief and management as well as humanitarian assistance: the *Institut de Droit International* (IDI) and the UN International Law Commission (ILC).

1   *The Work within the* Institut de Droit International

The *Institut de Droit International* is an institution independent of any governmental influence whose work is designed to contribute to the development of

---

[8] See *e.g.*, on the position of the individual in international law, a topic which a number of general and specialized works discuss, K. Parlett, *The Individual in the International Legal System: Continuity and Change in International Law* (CUP 2011); J.E. Nijman, *The Concept of International Legal Personality: An Inquiry into the History and Theory of International Law* (T.M.C. Asser 2004); M.S. Korowicz, "The Problem of the International Personality of Individuals", 50 *American Journal of International Law* (1956) 533; R. Portmann, *Legal Personality in International Law* (CUP 2010); P.P. Remec, *The Position of the Individual in International Law according to Grotius and Vattel* (Martinus Nijhoff 1960); R. Bruno, "Access of Private Parties to International Dispute Settlement: A Comparative Analysis", 13 *Jean Monnet Center for International and Regional Economic Law and Justice Paper* (1997) (available at <http://centers.law.nyu.edu/jeanmonnet/archive/papers/97/97-13.html>, retrieved in June 2012); M. Shaw, *International Law* (CUP 2008) 258; I. Brownlie, *Principles of Public International Law* (7th edn. OUP 2008) 65; P. Daillier, M. Forteau, A. Pellet, *Droit International Public* (8th edn. LGDJ 2009) 709 *et seq.*

[9] *Prosecutor* v. *Tadić* (Decision on the Defence Motion for Interlocutory Appeal on Jurisdiction) ICTY-94-1 (2 October 1995), at para. 97.

international law.[10] It consists of not more than 132 members (members and associate members), international lawyers elected by the Institute itself.[11]

The main work of the institution results in reports, declarations and resolutions on particular issues of public or private international law. Resolutions usually make proposals or try to codify existing law in the form of articles or principles. In this manner, the IDI contributes to the codification and development of international law.

The working method of the IDI is organized in committees created for each individual topic. Committees are led by a rapporteur who elaborates reports and, eventually, a draft declaration or resolution on the basis of a permanent exchange of views among the Committee members formalized mainly through written responses to questionnaires. The plenary discusses the work of the relevant committee, sometimes even in a working group, if necessary amends it and, finally, may adopt a resolution by vote. This working method ensures that governments do not – at least not directly – influence the work of the IDI, which remains entirely in the hands of internationally renowned scholars. Although it cannot be ruled out that one or the other of the members who are closely connected with their respective governments represent governmental views, the views are only attributable to the relevant member in their private capacity.

In 1993, the IDI decided to create a committee regarding the issue 'Humanitarian Assistance' and appointed Juan Antonio Carillo-Salcedo as rapporteur.[12] He delivered a provisional *rapport* in 1997.[13] However, he was unable to continue his work and Professor Budislav Vukas was designated as a new rapporteur. Professor Vukas delivered his final report in 2003 at the session of the IDI in Bruges where his draft resolution was discussed in a working group. Accordingly, Professor Vukas as Rapporteur was finally responsible for the elaboration of the draft resolution regarding the issue of humanitarian assistance

---

10   See on the origin and the first session of the Institut, Albéric de Rolin, *Les origines de l'Institut de droit international, 1873–1923: Souvenirs d'un témoin* (Vromant 1923). A list of the IDI's members and its resolutions are available on the website of the IDI, <http://www.idi-iil.org/> (retrieved in March 2013); see also W. Wengler (ed.), *Justitia et Pace: Festschrift zum 100jährigen Bestehen des Institut de Droit International* (Duncker & Humblot 1974).

11   See Article 3 of the Statute of the IDI (adopted on 10 September 1873, amended subsequently) (available at: <http://www.idi-iil.org/idiE/navig_statutes.html>, retrieved in March 2013).

12   IDI, *Annuaire de l'institut de droit international*, Vol. 70-I (2002–2003) 399–576, 400.

13   *Ibid.*

which formed the basis of the resolution finally adopted by the IDI.[14] Through his work, he made a very significant contribution to clarifying some of the legal principles relevant for an issue which continues to attract significant attention from legal scholars, States and international organizations.[15]

2   The Work within the International Law Commission

Besides the IDI, the ILC[16] also commenced work on this issue, however at a later point in time. In 2007, it included the topic 'Protection of persons in the event of disasters' in its program of work and appointed Mr. Eduardo Valencia-Ospina as Special Rapporteur.[17] At the moment in 2013, the ILC has already proceeded very far in the elaboration of the first reading draft under the guidance of Mr. Valencia Ospina.

Although the Statute of the ILC spells out different procedures, on the one hand regarding the progressive development of international law and, on the other, regarding its codification,[18] there are no real differences in the actual

---

14   At its 70th session, held in Bruges in September 2003, the *Institut de Droit International* adopted a resolution on humanitarian assistance; see the Provisional Report (June 2002) and the Final Report (February 2003) on that subject, by Budislav Vukas, in IDI, *Annuaire de l'Institut de Droit International*, Vol. 70-1, 457–490 and 541–569. The text of the resolution is reproduced in B. Vukas, "Sixteenth Commission: Humanitarian Assistance", 42 *Archiv des Völkerrechts* (September 2004) 347–352 (also available on the IDI website at: <http://www.idi-iil.org/idiE/resolutionsE/2003_bru_03_en.PDF>, retrieved in March 2013).

15   See especially the three addenda of the Secretariat, collecting the practice of States and international organizations as well as legal scholarship on the topic (UN Doc. A/CN.4/590/Add.1 (26 February 2008); UN Doc. A/CN.4/590/Add.2 (31 March 2008); UN Doc. A/CN.4/590/Add.3 (19 June 2008)).

16   The ILC's website offers a complete collection of the documents relating to the ILC's work on the topic 'protection of persons in the event of disasters' (available at: <http://untreaty.un.org/ilc/guide/6_3.htm>, retrieved in March 2013).

17   ILC, "Report on the work of its sixtieth session (2008)" UN Doc A/63/10, Chapter IX, paras. 217–264, para. 217 and note 677; for a recent discussion of the ILC's work on the topic, see F. Zorzi Giustiniani, "The Works of the International Law Commission on 'Protection of Persons in the Event of Disasters': a Critical Appraisal", in A. De Guttry, M. Gestri, G. Venturini (eds.), *International Disaster Response Law* (TMC Asser Press 2012); J.B. Heath, "Disasters, Relief, and Neglect: the Duty to Accept Humanitarian Assistance and the Work of the International Law Commission", 43 *New York University Journal of International Law and Politics* (2011) 419–477; A. Pronto, "Consideration of the Protection of Persons in the Event of Disasters by the International Law Commission", 15 *ILSA Journal of International and Comparative Law* (2009) 449–457.

18   Statute of the International Law Commission, UNGA Res 174 (II) (21 November 1947) GAOR 2nd Session Part XVI Resolutions 105 (Article 15 of the ILC Statute defines the two

process of carving out the texts, not least because of the difficult distinction between progressive development and codification.

The text of the ILC is mostly based on preparatory work by the Secretariat[19] and the subsequent work is mainly done by the Special Rapporteur appointed by the ILC, who submits reports which, sometimes, after being discussed in working groups, are submitted to the plenary of the ILC (after passing a drafting committee of the ILC), voted upon and presented annually to the 6th Committee of the General Assembly.[20] In this body, State representatives take stances on the drafts; the Special Rapporteur takes these opinions into account in his or her further work in order not to risk a failure of the draft. The text, consisting of draft articles and commentaries, is submitted as the first reading text to the States for their written comments. In light of these and other comments, the ILC, mainly the Special Rapporteur, reviews the drafts and draws up the second and final report (second reading) in the form of draft articles and commentaries,[21] which are thereupon submitted to the GA for adoption. This second (and final) reading text is supplemented by a resolution on the appropriateness of a codification conference or some other procedure, and is submitted to the General Assembly (GA) for its decision. Since the ILC is interested

---

concepts as follows: "In the following articles the expression 'progressive development of international law' is used for convenience as meaning the preparation of draft conventions on subjects which have not yet been regulated by international law or in regard to which the law has not yet been sufficiently developed in the practice of States. Similarly, the expression 'codification of international law' is used for convenience as meaning the more precise formulation and systematization of rules of international law in fields where there already has been extensive State practice, precedent and doctrine.").

19   See on the relationship between the ILC and the UN Secretariat e.g. B.G. Ramcharan, *The International Law Commission: Its Approach to the Codification and Progressive Development of International Law* (Martinus Nijhoff 1977) 46 *et seq.*; A. Pronto, M. Wood, *The International Law Commission 1999–2009, Volume IV: Treaties, Final Draft Articles, and Other Materials* (OUP 2010) 6 *et seq.*; UN, *The Work of the International Law Commission*, Vol. I (7th edn. 2007) UN Sales No. E.07.V.9, 80–82.

20   See generally on the organization, program and methods of work of the ILC and its relationship with the Sixth Committee of the GA, the GA and the Secretariat, among others, UN, *The Work of the International Law Commission*, Vol. I (7th edn. 2007) UN Sales No. E.07.V.9, 7–82 (Part II).

21   Under Article 20 of its Statute, the ILC is called upon to prepare draft articles and corresponding commentaries. A 'commentary', according to Article 20, contains an "[a]dequate presentation of precedents and other relevant data, including treaties, judicial decisions and doctrine" and "[c]onclusions defining ... (i) [t]he extent of agreement on each point in the practice of States and in doctrine ... (ii) [d]ivergencies and disagreements which exist, as well as arguments invoked in favour of one or another solution."

in the adoption of the text by States, their views are, if not totally, at least considerably reflected in the final ILC draft. The first draft drawn up by the ILC (first reading) is sent to States with a request for written comments. Its acceptability to the community of States can be assessed on the basis of their replies to the ILC's questionnaires or comments made by States in the 6th Committee of the General Assembly during discussions of the ILC's report to the GA. The advantage of this method derives from the availability of direct feedback from States, allowing the ILC to take into account their views when completing its work, thus contributing to the acceptability or legitimacy of its final product.

Upon a recommendation from the ILC, the GA can decide whether the ILC's report should only be taken note of, whether a conference of plenipotentiaries should be convened for the purpose of elaborating and adopting the final text of a convention, or on some other measure.[22]

3 The Difference between These Two Approaches

Given that a very similar topic has been dealt with by these two institutions, it accordingly seems useful to juxtapose their respective work, keeping in mind that the ILC's work is still preliminary: on the one hand, the resolution adopted by an NGO, namely the IDI, gathering eminent international lawyers acting in a private capacity, without any State influence and, on the other, the ILC draft, although elaborated by independent international lawyers, is nevertheless influenced by States through the institutional environment in which the ILC operates, in particular the annual debate within the 6th Committee of the General Assembly and replies to the ILC's questionnaires.

Accordingly, the instruments elaborated by the IDI represent what are essentially the views of private persons, whereas the ILC results are essentially influenced by States, or at the very least arise from strongly State-centric process.

It thus seems that to juxtapose and compare these two drafts would help reveal not only the possibly different approaches to the same problem by two institutions, one essentially private, the other essentially public, but also throw light on the differences between the common position of States from that of the independent lawyers acting within the IDI. It is also interesting to note that Professor Vukas still conceded that "in the majority of its aspects and problems" the issue of "humanitarian assistance" is "less controversial than humanitarian intervention" (a topic currently dealt with by the IDI separately),[23]

---

22   UN, *The Work of the International Law Commission*, Vol. I (7th edn. 2007) UN Sales No. E.07.V.9, 70–75.

23   Budislav Vukas, "Humanitarian Intervention and International Responsibility", in Maurizio Ragazzi (ed.), *International Responsibility Today* (Brill 2005) 235–240.

whereas the ongoing discussions within the ILC and the sheer complexity of the relevant legal issues make it a very challenging and controversial topic.

II   Selection of the Topics Compared in This Contribution

Since a comparison of the full texts elaborated by the ILC and the IDI would go far beyond the scope of this contribution, it should be confined to the issues of the definition of disasters, the problem of the duty to request assistance and the duty to offer assistance, respectively the duty to comply with the requests for assistance. These are the core issues of such assistance since they define the extent to which the State affected by a disaster, on the one hand, and the other States and international organizations are under obligation to provide assistance to the victims.

1   *The Definition of Disasters*
The two instruments under scrutiny substantially differ regarding the definition of 'disasters', the triggering fact of the assistance. The IDI resolution defines 'disasters' in Point 2 of Article 1 as

> calamitous events which endanger life, health, physical integrity, or the right not to be subjected to cruel, inhuman or degrading treatment, or other fundamental human rights, or the essential needs of the population, whether
> – of natural origin (such as earthquakes, volcanic eruptions, windstorms, torrential rains, floods, landslides, droughts, fires, famine, epidemics), or
> – man-made disasters of technological origin (such as chemical disasters or nuclear explosions), or
> – caused by armed conflicts or violence (such as international or internal armed conflicts, internal disturbances or violence, terrorist activities).

This definition goes far beyond the definition offered by the ILC, according to which a disaster is meant to constitute

> a serious disruption of the functioning of society, posing a significant, widespread threat to human life, health, property or the environment, whether caused by accident, nature or human activity, and whether developing suddenly or as the result of complex, long-term processes.[24]

---

24 See Draft Article 3 (ILC, "Protection of Persons in the Event of Disasters: Texts of draft articles 1, 2, 3, 4 and 5 as provisionally adopted by the Drafting Committee" (24 July 2009) UN Doc. A/CN.4/L.758, 1).

In addition, draft article 4 of the ILC's draft text establishes that the articles "do not apply to situations to which the rules of international humanitarian law are applicable" so that both international armed conflicts and non-international armed conflicts in the sense of the two Additional Protocols of 1977[25] to the Geneva Conventions[26] are excluded from their scope of application. This definition provides a threshold insofar as it only applies to emergency situations of a relatively significant dimension. This obviously excludes those situations that fall below the threshold of non-international conflicts such as riots and other cases of situations of internal disturbances and tensions, such isolated and sporadic acts of violence or other acts of a similar nature (ICC Statute).[27] It can be expected that these situations would not meet the criteria listed in the ILC's definition.

In contrast, the IDI's resolution applies to situations of armed conflict, according to Professor Vukas including "[i]nternational and non-international armed conflicts, terrorist acts and dictatorial régimes, cause and/or incite genocide, crimes against humanity and other acts endangering life, freedom and dignity of human beings"[28] in order to encompass "toutes les situations d'urgence et de détresse".[29] Nevertheless, the report admits that humanitarian assistance in times of war "will be restricted in comparison with the assistance in peacetime".[30] The relation between these rules and international humanitarian law is settled in a manner that gives priority to "principles and rules of

---

25 Protocol Additional to the Geneva Conventions of 12 August 1949, and relating to the Protection of Victims of International Armed Conflicts (Protocol I) (adopted 8 June 1977, entered into force 7 December 1978) 1125 UNTS 3; Protocol Additional to the Geneva Conventions of 12 August 1949, and relating to the Protection of Victims of Non-International Armed Conflicts (Protocol II) (adopted 8 June 1977, entered into force 7 December 1978) 1125 UNTS 609.

26 Geneva Convention for the Amelioration of the Condition of the Wounded and Sick in Armed Forces in the Field (adopted 12 August 1949, entered into force 21 October 1950) 75 UNTS 31 (Geneva Convention I); Geneva Convention for the Amelioration of the Condition of Wounded, Sick and Shipwrecked Members of Armed Forces at Sea (adopted 12 August 1949, entered into force 21 October 1950) 75 UNTS 85 (Geneva Convention II); Geneva Convention relative to the Treatment of Prisoners of War (adopted 12 August 1949, entered into force 21 October 1950) 75 UNTS 135 (Geneva Convention III); Geneva Convention relative to the Protection of Civilian Persons in Time of War (adopted 12 August 1949, entered into force 21 October 1950) 75 UNTS 287 (Geneva Convention IV).

27 Rome Statute of the International Criminal Court (adopted 17 July 1998, entered into force 1 July 2002) 2187 UNTS 90.

28 IDI, *Annuaire de l'Institut de Droit International*, Vol. 70-I (2002–2003) 399–576, 460.

29 *Ibid.*

30 *Ibid.*, 461.

international humanitarian law applicable in armed conflict, in particular the 1949 Geneva Conventions for the Protection of War Victims and the 1977 Additional Protocols" (Art X of the IDI Resolution; see *e.g.* Article 70 Additional Protocol I). This rule was proposed by Professor Vukas[31] and retained in the finally adopted text.

However, this expansion raises certain difficulties as it entails the right of any person on the territory where the armed conflict occurs to ask for humanitarian assistance. Even the definition of the victim does not rule out this possibility since it encompasses "groups of human beings whose fundamental human rights or whose essential needs are endangered". Accordingly, not only the civilian population of occupied territories, but even enemy soldiers or prisoners of war would fall under this definition. As the Geneva Conventions or Additional Protocols do not fully regulate the situation of such persons the rules regarding disaster relief would apply unless they contradict the Geneva rules. The problems likely to be caused by the application of both regimes can easily be identified.

A further, but nevertheless similar difference consists in the reference in the IDI resolution to events endangering "the right not to be subjected to cruel, inhuman or degrading treatment, or other fundamental human rights" as a possible detrimental consequence of certain events. It is very likely that such situations would occur only in man-made disasters such as armed conflicts that are not encompassed by the ILC definition. This extension in the IDI resolution, compared to that of the ILC, again poses a number of problems that can hardly be adequately resolved by the regime of the IDI's resolution.

A major distinction between the two definitions results from the criterion of the "serious disruption of the functioning of society", which is used by the ILC and taken from the 'Tampere Convention on the Provision of Telecommunication Resources for Disaster Mitigation and Relief Operations'[32]; it restricts the situations addressed by the ILC definition. This criterion has already been used in the 'Internationally agreed glossary of basic terms related to Disaster Management', elaborated by the UN Department of Humanitarian Affairs in 1992.[33] The IDI resolution does not contain such a criterion; it is questionable

---

31 See IDI, *Annuaire de l'Institut de Droit International*, Vol. 70-I (2002–2003) 570 and Vol. 71-II (2004) 134.

32 Tampere Convention on the Provision of Telecommunication Resources for Disaster Mitigation and Relief Operations (adopted 18 June 1998, entered into force 8 January 2005) 2296 UNTS 5.

33 UN Department of Humanitarian Affairs, "Internationally agreed glossary of basic terms related to Disaster Management" (1992, revised in 2000) UN Doc. DHA/93/36.

whether it is appropriate in these circumstances to make the assistance dependent on the disruption of the State organization since this would require a total breakdown of the State system before assistance could be provided under this regime. However, it is imaginable that, in remote areas of a State's territory, access to provide assistance is easier for other States than for the affected State itself so that the breakdown of the affected State's system is not a generally adequate criterion for opening the way for the assistance from other States. It must also be asked whether total disruption of the State organization is necessary or only the local or regional one as it is imaginable that disasters such as earthquakes or inundations could affect only part of the State territory, but nevertheless require assistance from other States. In this point the IDI definition of disasters is preferable to that of the ILC although the otherwise broad definition of the IDI does not seem useful. In particular the latter's reference to armed conflicts creates more problems than it can solve.

2   *The Duty to Request Assistance*

A major problem of disaster relief is the question whether the affected State is under an international obligation to seek assistance from other States and under what circumstances. The ILC's Special Rapporteur on the topic acknowledged a tendency towards the recognition of such a duty once the response capacity of the affected State could not suffice to cope with the emergency situation.[34] Such a tendency was said to ensue from the development of international human rights law under which individuals were seen as entitled to receive assistance. The Special Rapporteur also chose this approach. In accordance with the duty of the affected State, "by virtue of its sovereignty, ... to ensure the protection of persons and provision of disaster relief and assistance on its territory" (draft article 9), draft article 10 establishes the duty of that State "to seek assistance from among other States, the United Nations, other competent intergovernmental organizations and relevant nongovernmental organizations, as appropriate". Accordingly, it is the decision of that State whether it is appropriate and, in the affirmative case, to select among the other States actors, States, international organizations or NGOs, which of them should be requested for assistance.

---

34   See ILC, "Protection of Persons in the Event of Disasters: Texts of draft articles 10 and 11 provisionally adopted by the Drafting Committee" (20 July 2011) UN Doc. A/CN.4/L.794, 1; ILC, "Protection of Persons in the Event of Disasters: Statement of the Chairman of the Drafting Committee" (2 August 2011) 2; ILC, "Fifth report on the protect ion of persons in the event of disasters by Eduardo Valencia-Ospina, Special Rapporteur" (9 April 2012) UN Doc. A/CN.4/652, 8–10.

The IDI resolution shares this approach insofar as it likewise provides for a primary responsibility of the affected State to take care of the victims of a disaster. Is the affected State

> unable to provide sufficient humanitarian assistance to the victims placed under its jurisdiction or de facto control, it shall seek assistance from competent international organizations and/or from third States.[35]

Professor Vukas, whose draft contained a similar provision,[36] based the right to humanitarian assistance and the corresponding duty of the affected State to provide it on a wide range of international instruments, such as the 'Guiding Principles on the Right to Humanitarian Assistance' of the San Remo Institute[37] as well as resolutions of the General Assembly.[38] However, Professor Vukas' draft went even further insofar as it extended this duty so as to encompass also the duty to "accept aid from competent international organizations and/or from third States"[39] – an addition that does not figure in the final text.

The concordance of views of the ILC concerning the duty to seek assistance as generated by the position of the States and that of the IDI indicates that a general conviction of the existence of such a duty under international law emerges. It is only interesting to note that such a duty cannot be based on the 'Responsibility to Protect' concept although it is characterized by a similar structure of duties and rights relations; in both systems a duty is placed on the

---

35 Article III (3) of the IDI Resolution.
36 See IDI, *Annuaire de l'Institut de Droit International*, Vol. 70-I (2002–2003) 570 and Vol. 71–II (2004) 134.
37 "Guiding Principles on the Right to Humanitarian Assistance", 33 *International Review of the Red Cross* (December 1993) 519525.
38 UNGA, "Strengthening the Co-ordination of Emergency Humanitarian Assistance of the United Nations: Report of the Secretary-General" (14 May 2002) UN Doc A/57/77–E/2002/63; UNGA Res 64/250 "Humanitarian Assistance, Emergency Relief and Rehabilitation in Response to the Devastating Effects of the Earthquake in Haiti" (22 January 2010) GAOR 64th Session Supp 49 vol 3, 2; UNGA Res 43/131 "Humanitarian Assistance to Victims of Natural Disasters and Similar Emergency Situations" (8 December 1988) GAOR 43rd Session Supp 49 vol 1, 207; UNGA Res 60/125 "International Co-operation on Humanitarian Assistance in the Field of Natural Disasters, from Relief to Development" (15 December 2005) GAOR 60th Session Supp 49 vol 1, 92; UNGA Res 46/182 "Strengthening of the Co-ordination of Humanitarian Emergency Assistance of the United Nations" (19 December 1991) GAOR 46th Session Supp 49 vol 1, 49.
39 IDI, *Annuaire de l'Institut de Droit International*, Vol. 70-I (2002–2003) 399–576, 574; see also *infra*.

affected State and on the other States or international organizations to prevent and react to a calamity and assist the population affected by the calamities.

However, the UN excluded the applicability of the 'Responsibility to Protect' concept to the case of these disasters and emphasized that any attempt to cover calamities other than four specified crimes and violations,

> such as HIV/AIDS, climate change or the response to natural disasters, would undermine the 2005 consensus and stretch the concept beyond recognition or operational utility.[40]

Nevertheless, the 'Responsibility to Protect' concept can be applied to situations of man-made disasters as understood by the IDI insofar as it applies "to the four specified crimes and violations: genocide, war crimes, ethnic cleansing and crimes against humanity", hence to situations that exist in cases of military conflicts and accordingly are covered by the wider definition of disasters in the IDI resolution that is likely to encompass also emergency situations caused by the four specified crimes.

Accordingly, the IDI resolution is still closer to the 'Responsibility to Protect' concept than the ILC draft articles. Like this concept, the IDI resolution establishes a right of individuals to receive such assistance. Thus, it clearly stipulates that "[t]he victims of disaster are entitled to request and receive humanitarian assistance" as had been proposed by Professor Vukas. The Report of the International Commission on Intervention and State Sovereignty, which first dealt with the concept, also declared that "[e]veryone is entitled to basic protection for their lives and property".[41]

In contrast to the IDI Resolution, the ILC draft articles do not couch this duty in the form of a right of the individuals being victims of disasters but as a duty of the affected State. This duty is certainly conditioned by the inability to manage the crisis, as defined by the affected State. Nevertheless, both instruments do not clearly establish to whom this duty is owed and who would be entitled to invoke it, not to mention indicate ways of operationalizing a 'Responsibility to Protect'.[42]

---

40 UN SG, "Implementing the Responsibility to Protect: Report of the Secretary-General" (12 January 2009) UN Doc. A/63/677, 8.

41 ICISS, "The Responsibility to Protect: Report of the International Commission on Intervention and State Sovereignty" (December 2001), para. 5.8, page 41 (available at <http://responsibilitytoprotect.org/ICISS%20Report.pdf>, retrieved in March 2013).

42 The work by scholars, NGOs, and public bodies concerning the 'Responsibility to Protect' is abundant. Some of the most relevant documents are made available on the following website: <http://www.responsibilitytoprotect.org/index.php/publications> (retrieved in March 2013).

It could certainly be asked whether and before which administrative or judicial institutions individuals suffering from the effects of such a disaster and the inability or unwillingness of the affected State to cope with the situation would be able to invoke the responsibility of the respective State. The ILC draft articles obviously leave it to the further development of international law as to whether it would grant individuals a right to invoke a corresponding right against the State engaged by this duty. One possibility for individuals to claim such rights already presently could be derived from human rights as positive duties incumbent upon the State[43] such as Article 11 CESCR,[44] which obliges the State to care for adequate food *etc*. The difficulty of invoking such a right consists in the fact that there hardly exists any mechanism enabling an individual to take legal action against a State in order to enforce this right.[45]

3 The Offer by Other States or International Organizations to Provide Assistance

Under the rights approach which proceeds from a right of individuals to such assistance the question arises, provided this right has an *erga omnes* effect, whether not just the affected State, but also other States are under a duty in the case of disasters to offer assistance addressed either to the individuals affected by such disasters or the States concerned. The *erga omnes* effect would certainly coincide with the duty to formulate such a right as a human right such as proposed by Pogge.[46]

---

43 See *e.g.* "Report of the Representative of the Secretary-General on the human rights of internally displaced persons, Walter Kälin – Addendum – Operational Guidelines on the protection of persons in situations of Natural Disasters" (31 January 2011) UN Doc. A/HRC/16/43/Add.5; Brookings-Bern Project on Internal Displacement, "Human Rights and Natural Disasters: Operational Guidelines and Field Manual on Human Rights Protection in Situations of Natural Disaster" (2008).

44 International Covenant on Economic, Social and Cultural Rights (adopted 16 December 1966, entered into force 3 January 1976) 993 UNTS 3.

45 With regard to individual complaints, on 10 December 2008, the General Assembly unanimously adopted an Optional Protocol (GA Resolution A/RES/63/117) to the International Covenant on Economic, Social and Cultural Rights, which provides the Committee competence to receive and consider communications. The General Assembly took note of the adoption by the Human Rights Council by its Resolution 8/2 of 18 June 2008, of the Optional Protocol. The Optional Protocol was opened for signature at a signing ceremony in 2009. In addition to the Committee on Economic, Social and Cultural Rights, other committees with competence can consider individual communications involving issues related to economic, social and cultural rights in the context of its treaty.

46 T. Pogge, "Comment: Are We Violating the Human Rights of the World's Poor?", 14(2) *Yale Human Rights & Development Law Journal* (2011) 1–33, 11–12 (arguing that "[d]uties to

The IDI resolution does not provide for a direct obligation as according to it

> [a]ll States should to the maximum extent possible offer humanitarian assistance to the victims in States affected by disasters, except when such assistance would result in seriously jeopardizing their own economic, social or political conditions. Special attention should be paid to disasters affecting neighbouring States.[47]

Accordingly, irrespective of the right of victims of disaster to request and receive humanitarian assistance, all States are only requested, but not required, to offer assistance whereas, in contrast, relevant international organizations are put under an obligation to do so. However, the inconsistency between the right of the victims, which normally entails a respective obligation, and the absence of an obligation on the part of other States can hardly be overcome.

The draft presented by Professor Vukas still established a duty of assistance incumbent on particular States, namely "States and/or international organizations having caused emergency situations".[48] Such a duty is obviously derived from the idea that such actors have to assume responsibility for disasters, but this idea was not maintained in the final draft.

The ILC's draft articles do not go even that far and do not foresee such a duty, neither of States nor even of international organizations; they only provide, in Article 12 (on 'Offers of assistance') for a right to offer assistance:

> In responding to disasters, States, the United Nations, and other competent intergovernmental organizations have the right to offer assistance to the affected State. Relevant non-governmental organizations may also offer assistance to the affected State.

---

respond to natural disasters that threaten the fulfillment of human rights are generally classified as duties to provide. Exemplified in human rights documents (including General Comment 12), this is an unfortunate practice because it obscures the fact that, as in the case of social threats, the task can be discharged in two fundamentally different ways: by preventing the harm from reaching people or by assisting people in coping with it. The common label tends to draw attention to the latter approach; and nearly all international efforts to cope with natural disasters are indeed focused on assistance *ex post* rather than on (often more cost-effective) prevention *ex ante*. A good step toward correcting this irrational bias would be to break out duties to protect human beings from natural disasters as a separate category of human-rights-correlative duties.").

47   See Article 5 of the IDI Resolution.
48   See *supra*, note 36.

One particular question raised by the ILC was whether States are under a duty to provide assistance if so requested by the affected State. The response of the States was negative so that it remains within the discretion of the other States to offer assistance, even if so asked by the affected State.[49]

The recent reaction of the States in the 6th Committee even questions the use of the term 'right'[50] as this would imply a corresponding duty and add confusion to the pre-existing system. Instead, reference should only be made to the acceptance of offers of assistance. This concern signifies that the system of assistance provided by unaffected States is still guided by the principle of voluntariness and that there is no duty to offer assistance. In this respect, the IDI resolution, despite its very careful formulation, does not coincide with the position of the States.

Thus, although carefully formulated by the IDI, its proposed rules are not corroborated by emerging State practice, which is still tied to the principle of voluntariness, and even less do they correspond to existing customary rules of international law. In view of the fact that the IDI resolution was adopted prior to the ILC draft articles it must be admitted that as yet the approach taken by the IDI is likely not to be approved by the States.

4   The Duty to Accept Assistance

The third main pillar of this regime is the question of the duty of the affected State to accept the assistance offered by any State or organization. This duty supplements the duty to seek assistance, but with a different connotation insofar as the initiative lies with the assisting State so that the affected State is left with just the possibility to react. On the one hand, a duty of the affected State to accept would certainly be in conformity with the right of individuals to humanitarian assistance as well as with the duty of the affected State to provide assistance to the victims of disasters. On the other hand, the need of consent by the affected State is said to form a cornerstone of this legal regime.

---

49   ILC, "Fifth report on the protect ion of persons in the event of disasters by Eduardo Valencia-Ospina, Special Rapporteur" (9 April 2012) UN Doc. A/CN.4/652, 8–10.

50   *Ibid.*, 9 (reporting (in para. 28) that "[o]n the other hand, a number of States opposed the idea that the affected State was placed under a legal obligation to seek external assistance in cases where a disaster exceeded its national response capacity. In their view, the imposition of such a duty constituted infringement of the sovereignty of States as well as of international cooperation and solidarity and had no basis in existing international law, customary law or State practice. It was preferable that the provision of draft article 10 be reworded in hortatory terms, namely, to use instead of the mandatory phrase 'duty to seek assistance' the formulation 'should seek assistance'.").

The ILC derived from this set of legal duties that the affected State shall not withhold its consent arbitrarily[51] so that any denial must be justified. This solution tries to reconcile the respect of the sovereignty of the affected State, which is reflected in the requirement of consent, with its duty to protect the victims of disasters.

In this respect the ILC explicitly referred to the work of the IDI: the Resolution of 1989 'The Protection of Human Rights and the Principle of Non-intervention in the Internal Affairs of States' already provided:

> Les États sur le territoire desquels de telles situations de détresse [où la population est gravement menacée dans sa vie ou sa santé] existent ne refuseront pas arbitrairement de pareilles offres de secours humanitaires.[52]

Nevertheless, this reference is weak as far as it goes as it relates only to the duty of the affected States and not to that of third States. Moreover, the question of who is to judge whether the justification offered by the affected State is adequate is the central question that is left unanswered and thus tilts the balance in favour of the affected State.

In his reply to the former Rapporteur, Professor Vukas, seemingly inspired by Schindler's report,[53] already favoured a duty of the affected State to accept assistance offered by others.[54] Accordingly, he proposed a formulation according to which the affected State was under a duty to admit humanitarian assistance offered by other States, intergovernmental or non-governmental organizations, should it not be able to provide sufficient humanitarian assistance to the victims itself.[55]

The resolution finally adopted by the IDI, however, softened this approach, including also the issue of military conflicts according to its definition of disasters and provided that

---

51 Article 11 of the ILC's Draft ('Consent of the affected State to external assistance') reads as follows:
  1. The provision of external assistance requires the consent of the affected State.
  2. Consent to external assistance shall not be withheld arbitrarily.
  3. When an offer of assistance is extended in accordance with the present draft articles, the affected State shall, whenever possible, make its decision regarding the offer known.
52 IDI, "Resolution on the Protection of Human Rights and the Principle of Non-intervention in Internal Affairs of States" (available at: <http://www.idi-iil.org/idiE/resolutionsE/1989_comp_03_en.PDF>, retrieved in March 2013).
53 IDI, *Annuaire de l'Institut de Droit International*, Vol. 70-I (2002–2003) 407.
54 *Ibid.*, 416.
55 *Ibid.*, 574.

[a]ffected States are under the obligation not arbitrarily and unjustifiably to reject a bona fide offer exclusively intended to provide humanitarian assistance or to refuse access to the victims. In particular, they may not reject an offer nor refuse access if such refusal is likely to endanger the fundamental human rights of the victims or would amount to a violation of the ban on starvation of civilians as a method of warfare.[56]

By referring to the methods of warfare, this formulation already interferes with the concept of the 'Responsibility to Protect', and goes beyond its conceptualization by the UN[57] insofar as the latter does not relate to the assistance by other States and the problem of consent of the affected State. However, the IDI resolution still attempted to strike a balance between the sovereignty of the affected State and humanitarian intervention by other actors in addressing also the consequence of a failure of consent. Although the affected State would certainly have to assume international responsibility for the failure of consent, the situation of emergency and the problem of the invocation of such a responsibility obviously induced the IDI to provide for a different consequence. In the case of such a denial, the assisting State is entitled to bring this question to the attention of relevant international organizations "in order to induce the affected State to comply". If such a denial leads to a threat to international peace and security the Security Council may take the matter up under Chapter VII. This last part is, as was observed quite correctly,[58] redundant since it only confirms a competence of the Security Council, which is enshrined in the Charter itself.

III Conclusions

What conclusions can be drawn from this comparison of the ILC's and the IDI's work on a similar topic?

---

56 Article VIII (1) of the IDI Resolution.
57 UN SG, "Implementing the Responsibility to Protect: Report of the Secretary-General" (12 January 2009) UN Doc. A/63/677 (note that according to this first report of the SG on the topic "the responsibility to protect applies, until Member States decide otherwise, only to the four specified crimes and violations: genocide, war crimes, ethnic cleansing and crimes against humanity. To try to extend it to cover other calamities, such as HIV/AIDS, climate change or the response to natural disasters, would undermine the 2005 consensus and stretch the concept beyond recognition or operational utility").
58 IDI, *Annuaire de l'Institut de Droit International*, Vol. 70-1 (2002–2003) 567.

The comparison reveals a mixed picture: agreement on some points is accompanied by significant differences in approach and result. The main difference consists in the extension of the meaning of disaster to military conflicts by the IDI resolution whereas the ILC explicitly excludes them.

1. As far as there is a coincidence of the substance, this indicates a conviction in doctrine and practice, represented by the members of the IDI on the one hand and the representatives of States on the other, that a relevant rule does exist in international law and is even firmly rooted in international law. At least, this conviction expresses a kind of *opinio iuris* as a constitutive element of a rule of customary international law.
2. Given the composition and nature of the IDI, it would have been expected that the views expressed by the scholars as members of the IDI would have been progressive and led to the adoption of a *lege ferenda* approach. However, it is interesting to note that in substantive fields the views of State practice and doctrine coincided. Accordingly, even doctrine seems to be well aware of the limits of a progressive development and that rules could not be formulated which would go far beyond that which seems acceptable in the near future. A sense of realism also guided the work of the scholars who tried to work out formulations that States would not reject from the outset under the present political environment. It can also be concluded that the IDI is convinced that the authority of its work depends more on the high probability of acceptability by the States and application in practice than on a one-sided orientation and only on the future-oriented character of the formulation.
3. Despite this realism it can nevertheless be observed that a certain progressive nature is reflected in the work of the IDI. At least, the IDI does not abstain from formulations that deviate from existing practice in favour of human rights. The IDI approach is still more under the influence of the right-approach than the ILC, although the latter originally also emphasized this approach.

Nevertheless and despite the described divergences between the ILC's and the IDI's work certain rules such as that on the obligation incumbent on the affected State to seek assistance in the case of its inability and the duty not to deny the offer of assistance arbitrarily can be ascertained as already existing rules under international law. The work of Professor Vukas contributed substantially to this result.

CHAPTER 29

Application of Article 20 of the 1989 Convention on the Rights of the Child in the Republic of Croatia

Mira Lulić*

I   Introduction

> *1. A child temporarily or permanently deprived of his or her family environment, or in whose own best interests cannot be allowed to remain in that environment, shall be entitled to special protection and assistance provided by the State.*
> *2. States Parties shall in accordance with their national laws ensure alternative care for such a child.*
> *3. Such care could include,* inter alia, *foster placement, kafalah of Islamic law, adoption or if necessary placement in suitable institutions for the care of children. When considering solutions, due regard shall be paid to the desirability of continuity in a child's upbringing and to the child's ethnic, religious, cultural and linguistic background.* (Article 20 of the United Nations Convention on the Rights of the Child, 1989.)

The United Nations Convention on the Rights of the Child (hereinafter referred to as the UNCRC) was adopted by the UN General Assembly at its 44th session held on 20 November 1989, and it entered into force on 2 September 1990.[1] It is universally accepted and currently legally binds 193 parties.[2] The Republic of Croatia (hereinafter referred to as the RC) became a party to the Convention on the Rights of the Child on 6 October 1991,[3] as well

---

*   Professor of Public International Law at the Josip Juraj Strossmayer University of Osijek, Faculty of Law.
1   *UN Treaty Series*, Vol. 1577.
2   It is one of the few international agreements which almost all countries of the world are parties to. The UNCRC has only not been ratified by Somalia, the USA and South Sudan. For more details on the status of the UNCRC, see the official website of the United Nations at: <http://treaties.un.org/Pages/ViewDetails.aspx?src=TREATY&mtdsg_no=IV-11&chapter=4&lang=en>.
3   The official text with translation of the UNCRC was published in 1990 in the *Official Gazette of the SFRY*, No. 15, and so far the UNCRC has not been published in the Official Gazette of the Republic of Croatia.

as to the First[4] and the Second Optional Protocols[5] to the UNCRC. The RC has not signed the Third Optional Protocol to the UNCRC (2011) on a communications procedure.[6] Let us recall that pursuant to Article 141 of the Constitution of the RC "international agreements concluded and ratified in accordance with the Constitution and made public, and which are in force, shall be part of the internal legal order of the Republic of Croatia and shall be above the law in terms of legal effects."[7] It should be noted that the Constitution of the Republic of Croatia does not give priority to international law in relation to its national law, but only to international agreements explicitly accepted by the RC,[8] and that is exactly what the UNCRC is about.

The international community started to take care of children who live outside the family environment with the formulation of the principles relating to human rights, and as early as in 1924 one of the League of Nations Declarations states that "the orphan and the waif must be sheltered and succoured."[9] In 1959, some three decades before the UNCRC was adopted, the UN General Assembly adopted the Declaration on the Rights of the Child which states in Article 6, "Society and the public authorities shall have the duty to extend particular care to children without a family and to those without adequate means of support".[10] Another important document relating to children in alternative care is the 1986 UN Declaration on Social and Legal Principles relating to the Protection and Welfare of Children with special emphasis on foster care or adoption, at national or international level.[11] Some of the most important principles and conditions of this legally non-binding text later influenced the text of Article 20 of the UNCRC and therefore the text of the Declaration is looked to help us understand Article 20 of the UNCRC.[12]

Article 20 of the UNCRC (1989) is very important for the protection of children's rights, because for the first time an international agreement contains

---

4 UN Treaty Series, Vol. 2173, p. 222.
5 UN Treaty Series, Vol. 2171, p. 227.
6 General Assembly Resolution 66/138 of 19 December 2011.
7 Constitution of the Republic of Croatia, *Official Gazette of the Republic of Croatia* (hereinafter: OGRC), Nos. 56/1990, 135/1997, 113/2000, 28/2001, 76/2010.
8 Andrassy, J. et al.: Međunarodno pravo, 1. dio, 2. izmijenjeno izdanje [*International Law, Part 1, Second edition (revised)*], Školska knjiga, Zagreb, 2010, p. 7.
9 Geneva Declaration on the Rights of the Child, League of Nations, 26 September 1924, *League of Nations OJ Spec. Supp.*, p. 43, cit. according to Cantwell, N. and Holzscheiter, A.: *Children without Parental Care (Commentary on the UN Convention on the Rights of the Child)*, Martinus Nijhoff Publishers, Leiden – Boston, 2008, p. 9.
10 General Assembly Resolution 1386 (XIV) of 10 December 1959.
11 General Assembly Resolution A/RES/41/85 of 3 December 1986.
12 Cantwell and Holzscheiter, *op. cit.*, pp. 16 et seq.

a provision governing the issue of alternative care provision for children without parental care who are forced to live outside their biological family, but also outside their extended family. It is known that the very concept of family is not defined by the UNCRC, although it imposed the obligation on all States Parties to preserve the family. It is difficult to come up with a uniform definition as the concept of family differs from one country to another, or even within a State.[13] The family is the fundamental grouping of society and the natural environment for the growth, well-being and protection of children.[14] The Universal Declaration of Human Rights and the two International Covenants define *family* as "the natural and fundamental group unit of society" which is "entitled to protection by society and the State."[15] Both International Covenants state that the family is a natural environment for raising a child, without specifying what is implied by the term family ("biological parents *vs.* extended concepts of the family").[16]

Parents are still the primary caregivers for their children and, presumably, it is in the best interests of the child to live with his or her parents. Unlike a more indefinite term 'family environment' and a rather unclear definition of those considered to be part of the family environment of the child, 'parental care' is more clearly defined, although in some cultures even the term 'parent' can be questionable.[17] The Committee on the Rights of the Child also recognises "the primary position of families in child caregiving and protection strategies."[18] The Committee also believes that the family has "the greatest

---

13 In its General Comment No. 19, the Human Rights Committee recognises the existence of various forms of family (*e.g.* unmarried couples and their children or single parents and their children). But, it also warns that States Parties should indicate "whether and to what extent such types of family and their members are recognised and protected by domestic law and practice". Human Rights Committee, General Comment No. 19, Article 23 (Thirty-ninth session, 1990), *Compilation of General Comments and General Recommendations Adopted by Human Rights Treaty Bodies*, UN Doc. HRI/GEN/1/Rev.1 at 28 (1994), para. 2.

14 Guidelines for the Alternative Care of Children, General Assembly A/HRC/11/L.13, 15 June 2009, para. 3, p. 2.

15 Art. 16(3) of the Universal Declaration of Human Rights (adopted by General Assembly Resolution 217 A (III) of 10 December 1948); Art. 23(1) of the International Covenant on Civil and Political Rights (16 December 1966, UN *Treaty Series*, Vol. 999, p. 171); and Art. 10(1) of the International Covenant on Economic, Social and Cultural Rights (16 December 1966, UN *Treaty Series*, Vol. 993, p. 3).

16 Cantwell and Holzscheiter, *op. cit.*, p. 19.

17 Roby, J.L.: *Children in Informal Alternative Care* (working document), UNICEF, Child Protection Section, New York, 2011, p. 9.

18 According to the Committee on the Rights of the Child, 'families' also include "extended families and other forms of family-type care arrangements". Committee on the Rights of

potential to protect children and to prevent violence" and "to support and empower children to protect themselves."[19] It is this knowledge that makes it clear that the family and family life should be strengthened, which should be taken into account by the State. Early intervention and prevention of family breakdown, all possible assistance provided by the State for that not to happen, are crucial in this regard, as the Committee warned.[20]

Although there is no universally accepted definition of family, we can agree that the family includes not only the parents of the child, but also extended family members of the child. Thus, Art. 5 of the UNCRC specifies responsibilities, rights and duties of parents, as well as "the members of the extended family or community" in relation to the child. Unfortunately, not all children have parents as their primary caregivers who are willing and able to care for their children or family members who would help them in case of need. Not all children live in a healthy family environment; some are exposed to neglect, abuse and other forms of violence, and because of that the State is obliged to ensure appropriate alternative family care to children who do not live in an adequate family environment. Unfortunately, some children will always need institutional care.[21] Therefore, if it is not in the best interests of the child to remain with his or her parents or if the child has no parents, firstly family members should take care of the child in question (*e.g.*, grandparents, brothers, sisters, aunts, uncles, *etc.*) . In terms of 'the extended family', the Committee on the Rights of the Child noted that it is still "a main pillar of childcare in many communities and is considered one of the best alternatives for childcare."[22] It was also emphasised that this extended family "should be strengthened and empowered to support the child and his or her parents or others taking care of the child."[23]

---

the Child, General Comment No. 13 (2011), "The right of the child to freedom from all forms of violence", 18 April 2011, para. 72d.

19 On the other hand, the Committee on the Rights of the Child is also aware that "much of the violence experienced by children, including sexual abuse, takes place within a family context and stresses the necessity of intervening in families if children are exposed to violence by family members". *Ibid.*

20 *Ibid.*

21 The Parliamentary Assembly of the Council of Europe: "The rights of children in institutions, follow-up to Recommendation 1601 (2003) of the Parliamentary Assembly", Recommendation 1698 (2008), (see the official website of the Council of Europe at: <http://assembly.coe.int/Mainf.asp?link=/Documents/AdoptedText/ta05/EREC1698.htm/>).

22 Committee on the Rights of the Child, General Comment No. 9 (2006), "The rights of children with disabilities", para. 45.

23 *Ibid.*

Only if the child does not have (adequate) parental care and when there are no other family members who would take care of him or her is he or she placed in alternative care the State is responsible for. The obligation of the State regarding care of the child outside the family environment lasts until the conditions are met for return to the natural family or, if this is not possible, until another appropriate family environment is found for the child (*e.g.*, foster care or adoption), or at least until a child is placed in a family-type children's home, but not in a classical institution. The application of the principle of the best interests of the child should be taken into account at all stages of this process. The Committee on the Rights of the Child, for example, points out that in the case of children with disabilities "the placement in institution is used only as a measure of last resort, when it is absolutely necessary and in the best interests of the child."[24] For decades, the practice of placing children without parental care and children with developmental disabilities in institutions was accepted as the only and best way to care for those children. The lives of hundreds of millions of children worldwide have irrevocably and tragically been altered because of this social policy. Today this practice is clearly marked as extremely hazardous and therefore it must be urgently abandoned. Institutions should be the last resort, because the child lives there in an unnatural environment and isolated from the outside world.

Studies have shown that institutionalised children suffer from poor health, they are physically underdeveloped, have hearing and vision problems, motor development problems, reduced cognitive and social ability, and are potentially exposed to various forms of violence and abuse (psychological, physical and sexual).[25] Growing up in such an unhealthy environment without the love and support that only families can provide leaves a long-term negative impact on the life of that child, and therefore of the local community and, ultimately, of the whole society. The attitude and policy that the problem of children outside the family environment is solved in the fastest and easiest way by placing them in an institution was abandoned some 20 years ago. Under the influence of the increased interest in the concept of protection of the rights of the child, "it is only in recent years...that it has been possible to break the rigidity of those social policies that entrusted children and adolescents to the care of care institutions."[26] But the number of institutionalised children has still not been reduced. Moreover, it seems that this severe economic crisis effected an

---

24 *Ibid.*, para. 29(D).
25 Carter, R.: *Family Matters: A Study of Institutional Childcare in Central and Eastern Europe and the Former Soviet Union*, EveryChild, 2005, p. 13.
26 Ducci, V.: "Beyond the Orphanage: The Process of Deinstitutionalizing Children in Italy. Post-war Developments", in: *Children in Institutions: The Beginning of the End?*, UNICEF, 2003, p. 1.

increase in the number of children in institutional care. A dramatic number of families are sinking into (extreme) poverty and because of that fact there is an increasing number of children at risk of being placed in institutional care. Therefore, in these economically difficult times of crisis special attention must be given to the issue of children's rights protection.

The issue of combating discrimination against children in institutional care is particularly sensitive and important. Unfortunately, these children are most frequently exposed to various biases, stereotypes and discrimination during institutionalisation, but also after leaving the system. All of this leads to the cruel stigmatisation of these children. Unlike children living in a family environment, the so-called 'institutional kids' do not have equal access to, for example, educational, cultural, social and health institutions, which puts them at a substantial disadvantage in relation to children living in a family environment. Deprived of investment in their development, which can only be obtained in a family environment, they have significantly reduced opportunities for further successful life and work. Research clearly shows that "institutions are almost always harmful for children's development".[27]

If the child has already been placed in an institution as a last resort, such accommodation cannot be a permanent solution. Unfortunately, practice has shown that in a disturbingly large number of cases such accommodation is long-term or even permanent. On the other hand, the State must take into account that research has shown that family-based care (*e.g.* foster care or placement of a small number of children in the family home) is not only better for children than institutional care but it is also significantly cheaper for the State.[28] This view is also shared by the Committee on the Rights of the Child. Deprivation of a family environment and institutional placement of the child not only harm child development and education, but are much more expensive than family-based alternatives.[29]

11 The Problem with the Lack of Data and Statistics on Children Who Do Not Live in a Family Environment

Before presenting the figures and estimates referring to the number of children in alternative care, it should be noted that today there is an acute lack of data

---

27 Carter, *op. cit.*, p. 8.
28 *Ibid.*
29 Report of the Committee on the Rights of the Child, General Assembly Official Records Sixty-seventh Session, Supplement No. 41 (A/67/41) (hereinafter referred to as: 'Report of the Committee on the Rights of the Child 2012'), para. 39.

and statistics on the number of those children, but there are also great methodological differences and differences in definitions, as well as problems with data collection.[30] According to UN figures, it is estimated that today about eight million children worldwide live in residential care institutions.[31] But the actual figure is likely to be much higher, due to the aforementioned lack of research and data on the number of children, but also because of the proliferation of unregistered care institutions in a number of States.[32] UNICEF estimates that more than 17.5 million children have lost one or both parents to AIDS, over 14 million of whom live in sub-Saharan Africa.[33] In 2007, more than 82 million children in South Asia and East Asia had lost one or both parents due to all causes.[34] Furthermore, it is estimated that about 143 million children in the developing world (one in every 13) are orphans, and more than 16 million children were orphaned in 2003 alone.[35] In 2005, more than approximately one million children from Europe and Central Asia lived only in child care institutions.[36] According to UNHCR data, at the beginning of 2007 there were an estimated 24.5 million internally displaced people, mostly as a result of war or persecution.[37] The vast majority of them were women and children. Child

---

30   See "The Rights of Vulnerable Children under the Age of Three – Ending Their Placement in Institutional Care", OHCHR, Europe Regional Office, 2013 (hereinafter referred to as: 'The Rights of Vulnerable Children under the Age of Three, OHCHR'), p. 24; and "UNCRC Committee's Day of General Discussion on Children Without Parental Care", UN Doc. UNCRC/CC/153, 2006. See also UNICEF: *Children Protection Information Sheet: Children without Parental Care*, UNICEF, 2006, cit. according to Cantwell and Holzscheiter, *op. cit.*, p. 3.

31   Pinheiro, P.S.: *World Report on Violence against Children*, Published by the UN Secretary-General's Study on Violence against Children, UNICEF, New York, 2006, p. 83.

32   For example, a government study in January 2009 concluded that only eight of the 148 known orphanages in Ghana were licensed. Asamoah, H. Obeng, Assistant Director Ghana Social Welfare Department, quoted in IRIN News: <http://www.irinnews.org/Report.aspx?ReportId=84582>, cit. according to *A Last Resort: The Growing Concern about Children in Residential Care*, Save the Children UK, International Save the Children Alliance, London, 2003, p. 3.

33   For more details see the official UNICEF website at: <http://www.unicef.org/media/media_45451.html/>.

34   *Ibid.*

35   *Children on the Brink 2004: A Joint Report of New Orphan Estimates and a Framework for Action*, The Joint UN Programme on HIV/AIDS (UNAIDS), the UN Children's Fund (UNICEF), and the United States Agency for International Development (USAID), 2004, p. 7.

36   "Children in residential institutions desperately vulnerable to abuse", UNICEF, 2005. See the official UNICEF website at: <http://www.unicef.org/infobycountry/media_27185.html/>.

37   *Internally Displaced People: Questions & Answers*, UNCHR, 2006, p. 4.

victims of trafficking are "almost entirely invisible in statistics", it is estimated that about 1.2 million children are trafficked every year.[38] Children living on the streets are especially vulnerable and exposed to various forms of violence and exploitation. The exact number of street children is impossible to quantify, but it is likely to be in the tens of millions or higher. Some estimates place the figure as high as 100 million.[39] All these figures are deeply disturbing, alarming and call for urgent changes to the system of care for children in most States.

One of the biggest myths about institutional care is that orphans, *i.e.* children with no parents, end up in orphanages. Reports speak of the data that in a significant number of States more children have been placed in institutions due to the severe financial and economic conditions the family lives in than because of abuse or neglect at home.[40] Studies suggest that the proportion of orphaned children living in residential institutions is in fact between 2 and 5% and most children living in institutions have at least one living parent.[41] This means that 95% of children placed in institutions have one parent, or maybe even both parents, alive but they are not able to take care of their child. The State should react in such cases and help these parents in every possible way in order to enable the child to reunite with his or her natural family in new conditions. Because of inability, incompetence, lack of information and ignorance, many parents who cannot cope with the responsibility of having children place their child(ren) into institutional care rather than being supported and educated to care for them at home.[42]

Several surveys carried out in the last 10 years have helped us recognise the extent of institutional placement of young children and its wide diversity across Europe and within the EU.[43] Although most countries recognise

---

38 For more details see the official UNICEF website at: <http://www.unicef.org/sowc06/press/who.php/>.
39 *The State of the World's Children 2006: Excluded and Invisible*, UNICEF, 2005.
40 See *e.g.* Cantwell and Holzscheiter, *op. cit.*, p. 8.
41 See Carter, *op. cit.*, p. 19 and authors mentioned therein.
42 Lim Ah Ken, P.: *Children without Parental care in the Caribbean – Systems of protection*, UNICEF, 2007.
43 The Rights of Vulnerable Children under the Age of Three, OHCHR, *op. cit.*, p. 24. See *e.g.* the survey on the number and the situation of children in alternative care across 30 European countries conducted by a European network called Eurochild. See the official website at: <http://www.eurochild.org/>. The TransMonEE (Transformative Monitoring for Enhanced Equity) is another example of an important database in Central and Eastern Europe and the Commonwealth of Independent States (CEECIS). It contains 180 economic and social indicators related to the situation of children divided into ten topics. Unfortunately, for a number of countries data are missing or incomplete, and there is a

placement in an institution only exceptionally and over a time-limited period as the solution of last resort, "the number of children in institutions is stable or rising in several EU countries", which is worrying.⁴⁴ It can be roughly estimated that around 1% of children are taken into public care across the EU (approximately 1 million children), and this proportion of course varies between countries.⁴⁵ Other studies that were conducted across Central and Eastern Europe and the former Soviet Union show that the number of children placed in institutions in this region is significantly higher and, possibly, one of the highest in the world. Estimates suggest that in this region alone there are more than 1.3 million children in institutional care.⁴⁶ At first glance, it seems that the number of children is statistically lower in relation to some previous period, but this is in fact a general decrease in the number of children born, so that the number of institutionalised children seems to have dropped as well.⁴⁷ Alarming data show that the number of orphanages (except in the developed West) remained the same or has even increased in the meantime.⁴⁸

III Some Issues and Problems Related to the Interpretation and Application of Article 20 of the UNCRC

What groups of children are beneficiaries of Article 20 of the UNCRC and why have they found themselves, temporarily or permanently, in a situation where they are deprived of parental care and a family environment? These groups of children, as is evident from the text of the article, are not listed explicitly. It can

---

problem of different criteria and methods by which data is collected. See TransMonEE 2012 Database, UNICEF Regional Office for CEECIS, the official website at: <http://www.transmonee.org/>. It is also important to mention here The Manual for the Measurement of Indicators for Children in Formal Care that was adopted within the framework of the Better Care Network/UNICEF (2009). It is an important document because it helps governmental and non-governmental bodies and organisations in the area of alternative care data collection and reporting. For more details see *The Manual for the Measurement of Indicators for Children in Formal Care. Better Care Network*, UNICEF, 2009.

44 Children in Alternative Care – National Surveys, Eurochild, *op. cit.*, p. 7.
45 *Ibid.*
46 Carter, *op. cit.*, p. 17.
47 *Ibid.*
48 *Ibid.*, pp. 7 et seq. See also the Parliamentary Assembly of the Council of Europe: The rights of children in institutions, follow-up to Recommendation 1601 (2003), *op. cit.*, para. 7.

be assumed that they include children whose parents have died or abandoned them, the temporary inability of parents to cope with this issue and parental incapacity (*e.g.* imprisonment, illness or disability), voluntary placement by parents (for the child's medical or general care), instances of domestic violence or neglect, the child refuses to return home to his or her family, arrival in a country as an unaccompanied minor seeking asylum or arrival in a country as an immigrant or as a victim of trafficking, or loss of contact with parents and family due to an armed conflict and an administrative or judicial decision to remove a child from parental care in his or her best interests, *etc.*[49] Since the provisions specifying who exactly is encompassed by Article 20 are not accurate enough, different interpretations are possible. For example, the issue of children living in child-headed households is unclear, as well as cases where children and young people who are deprived of their liberty and placed in detention centres or prisons, or cases where the State allows children to stay in prisons with their mothers serving their prison sentences.[50] Or, for example, children living on the streets are also arguable; they need not necessarily be without a family (not obligatorily "deprived of their family environment" – they can live on the streets, and regularly or occasionally return to their parents or extended family members).[51] These different interpretations can easily cause legal uncertainty, which is not good, especially given the sensitivity of this topic.

When referring to alternative care, Article 20 of the UNCRC reads "such care could include, *inter alia*", suggesting its optional nature and the non-exclusivity of the list of types of alternative care, though due regard is paid to different legal and cultural systems in the world.[52] Furthermore, the UNCRC does not give a clear-cut definition of the term 'institution'. The text of the given article does not mention any other variants of placement of children outside the family environment that are somewhere between institutions and families, and that have developed in the meantime (*e.g.* small units to accommodate a small number of children, such as family homes).[53] In practice, the care institutions children are placed in vary from small church community-based homes and internationally funded SOS children's villages to penal institutions.[54]

---

49   Cantwell and Holzscheiter, *op. cit.*, pp. 39 *et seq.* and *Children in Institutions: the Beginning of the End?*, *loc. cit.*
50   See Cantwell and Holzscheiter, *op. cit.*, pp. 42–43.
51   *Ibid.*
52   *Ibid.*, pp. 51–53.
53   *Ibid.*, p. 53.
54   Dybsland, Na.: *Children's Institutions. A Study of Children's Homes in Addis Ababa, Ethiopia*, Norwegian University of Science and Technology, Trondheim, 2011, p. 2.

Every child has the right to "continuity in upbringing" and the right to preserve its "ethnic, religious, cultural and linguistic background" (Article 20(3)). It would be good if the child had the opportunity to maintain contact with his or her parents, families and the local community he or she originates from. Although not precisely defined, it is assumed that a child has the right to adopt the culture, tradition, language, religion and other aspects of the identity of an ethnic group he or she, and his or her biological family come from.[55] In this regard, attention should be paid to the application of Article 27 of the International Covenant on Civil and Political Rights, if the child in question is a member of a national minority in the culture he or she originates from. 'Continuity in upbringing' would imply finding an adoptive or foster family from the same cultural milieu, or ensuring that some or all staff members of the institution belong to the same culture and, if possible, that the institution itself is located in an appropriate community.[56] Unfortunately, this is often not the case in practice and this UNCRC requirement is ignored. Finally, it is important to note that Article 20 is of course not the only article relating to children in alternative care. Other parts of the UNCRC refer to these children equally, just like to any other child. However, there are some provisions that indirectly apply only to children placed in alternative care.[57]

These are just some of the problems relating to the interpretation of Article 20 of the UNCRC, which does not speak clearly and precisely of topics important for the alternative care of children. A detailed analysis of all problems and questions that are raised by an insufficiently clear provision would exceed the scope of this paper, in which we are also limited by the number of pages. But here we must mention an important international document that helps us interpret Article 20 of the UNCRC. This text was passed under pressure of an excessive number of children in institutional care and increased public interest in this topic. Symbolically, marking the 22nd anniversary of the adoption of the UNCRC, in November 2009, the General Assembly unanimously adopted an extremely important document on the protection of children outside the family environment. It is the UN Guidelines for the Alternative Care of Children

---

55 For more details, see Cantwell and Holzscheiter, *op. cit.*, pp. 59–63.

56 Ruxton, S.: *Separated Children and EU Asylum and Immigration Policy*, Save the Children Denmark, Copenhagen, 2003; and Worrall, J.: "Kinship Care of the Abused Child: The New Zealand Experience", *Child Welfare*, Vol. 80, No. 5, 2001, pp. 497–511, both cited according to Cantwell and Holzscheiter, *op. cit.*, p. 62.

57 Cantwell and Holzscheiter systematically and carefully analyse other UNCRC provisions, except Art. 20, referring directly to children in alternative care. These are, *e.g.*, Art. 7(1), Art. 9(1), Art. 18, Art. 27(2 and 3), Art. 3(3), Art. 20, Art. 25 and Art. 2 of the UNCRC. For more details, see Cantwell and Holzscheiter, *op. cit.*, pp. 5–6.

(2009),[58] which aimed to fill the gaps in and provide the necessary additional interpretations of Article 20 of the UNCRC. The Guidelines are not a legally binding document, but they rather serve as a guide for governments, government agencies and authorities to apply the Convention on the Rights of the Child (1989) properly and more easily.[59] Although this text is not legally binding, its value is exceptional. A more detailed analysis of these Guidelines would be beyond the scope of this paper, hence we will mention only some parts of the Guidelines that are relevant to our topics.

Unlike Art. 20 of the UNCRC, UNICEF Guidelines for the Alternative Care of Children (2009) clearly define in Art. 29b forms of alternative care, and cite two, *i.e.* formal and informal. Informal alternative care implies a private arrangement for care in a family environment that has not been ordered by an administrative, judicial authority or other authority. In this case the child is looked after on an ongoing or indefinite basis by his or her relatives or friends, at the initiative of the child or his or her parents. It is widely known that in the majority of States and societies mostly grandparents look after children without parental care. The second case refers to formal care, which, pursuant to Guidelines, includes all care provided in a family environment which has been ordered by a competent administrative body or judicial authority, or all care provided in a residential environment. In para. 29, the Guidelines for the Alternative Care of Children (2009) clearly state that the scope of alternative care as foreseen in the Guidelines does not extend to: (a) children in conflict with the law and deprived of their liberty by decision of a judicial or administrative authority, (b) cases where the procedure for adoption of a child is completed, because the child is considered to be in parental care, and (c) informal arrangements (*e.g.* when a child voluntarily stays with relatives or friends for recreational purposes and reasons not connected with the parents' general inability or unwillingness to provide adequate parental care). The main principles for the placement of children in alternative care include *inter alia* an individual approach to each child, informing the child about the whole process of the placement in alternative care and the fight against discrimination on all grounds.

---

58 See *supra*, note 14.

59 The Council of Europe Recommendation on the rights of children living in residential institutions (2005) is also important in this context since it defines the main principles relating to the placement of children in institutional alternative care. For more details see Council of Europe Recommendation Rec (2005)5 of the Committee of Ministers to Member States on the rights of children living in residential institutions adopted by the Committee of Ministers on 16 March 2005 at the 919th meeting of the Ministers' Deputies.

The aim of these Guidelines is to reduce the number of children and shorten their stay in institutional care, to prevent the separation of children from their families and, if such separation is necessary, then to ensure the most appropriate forms of alternative care in the best interests of the child. Children should be firstly placed in a family environment, and then, only as an extreme last resort, should they be placed in institutions, which should last for as short a period as possible. It is emphasised that poverty should never be the sole justification for the removal of a child from parental care or for the prevention of his or her reintegration. The importance of these Guidelines is indicated by the fact that in its latest report for the year 2012 the Committee on the Rights of the Child called on all States to apply the principles contained in these detailed Guidelines.[60] These Guidelines should be taken into account as an important tool for the prevention of and fight against family disintegration, for deinstitutionalisation of children in alternative care, as well as for helping children at risk of such care.

IV Review of Relevant Legislation and National Policy on Alternative Care for Children in the Republic of Croatia

Protection of and respect for human rights as well as protection of and respect for the rights of the child are one of the foundations of the Croatian legal system and society in general. These rights are listed and elaborated in the Constitution of the Republic of Croatia as well as in a number of acts and national plans and strategies of the Government of the RC. The Republic of Croatia is proclaimed as a social State (Article 1 of the Constitution), and one of its main goals is the fight against poverty. The RC is a party to almost all major international treaties that protect human rights at the International and European level. In order to join the EU, the RC has undertaken a series of activities the aim of which was to harmonise its legislation with the EU acquis, but also with the principles and provisions of the UNCRC and other international documents.[61]

Protection of children's rights is first and foremost found in the provisions of the following legislation: the Constitution of the Republic of Croatia, the

---

60 Report of the Committee on the Rights of the Child 2012, *op. cit.*, para. 6.
61 For more details see the third and fourth periodic reports under Art. 44(1b) of the Convention on the Rights of the Child to the UN Committee on the Rights of the Child, Republic of Croatia, December 2010 (reporting period June 2004 to December 2010), on the official website of the Government of the Republic of Croatia: <http://www.vlada.hr/hr/content/download/152607/2222968/file/101.%20-%204.pdf/>, p. 4.

Social Welfare Act (2012),[62] the Foster Care Act (2011),[63] the Anti-Discrimination Act (2008)[64] and the Domestic Violence Protection Act (2009).[65] Pursuant to the Constitution of the RC (Article 57), the State is obliged to help "the poor, the weak and the neglected", and this category includes children deprived of their own family. Protection of the rights of children in the RC is the responsibility of the Ministry of Social Policy and Youth, the Ministry of the Interior, the Ministry of Foreign Affairs and European Integration, the Ministry of Justice, the Ministry of Science, Education and Sports, social welfare centres, judicial bodies (*e.g.* youth courts for juvenile offenders), the Office of the Ombudsperson for Children, as well as a number of other State authorities and bodies responsible for the education of children, their health, social welfare, religious rights, and the like. Care and protection for persons with disabilities, and especially care and protection for children with disabilities, is one of the important parts of the human rights protection programme of the Government of the RC. Thus, in addition to the UNCRC (1989), the RC also ratified the Convention on the Rights of Persons with Disabilities (2006) and the Protocol thereto (2007).[66]

A very serious and systematic process of changing the entire social welfare system is currently ongoing in the RC, a process which was expected to culminate in 2012 when the previously mentioned new Social Welfare Act was adopted. New rules should be harmonised and networked in the existing legal system, which is a demanding and unfinished task. The reform of the social welfare system in the RC is also visible from a number of new legal documents. The following two documents were enacted: (a) the Strategy of Development of the Social Welfare System in the Republic of Croatia (2011–2016),[67] and (b) the decision on the Plan for deinstitutionalisation and transformation of

---

62 *OGRC*, No. 33/2012.
63 *OGRC*, No. 90/2011.
64 *OGRC*, Nos. 85/2008 and 112/2012.
65 *OGRC*, Nos. 137/2009, 14/2010 and 60/2010.
66 Both the Convention on the Rights of Persons with Disabilities and the Optional Protocol were adopted on 13 December 2006 during the sixty-first session of the General Assembly by Resolution A/RES/61/106. The Act on the Ratification of the Convention on the Rights of Persons with Disabilities and the Optional Protocol thereto was passed by the Croatian Parliament at its session held on 1 June 2007 (*OGRC, Treaties*, Nos. 6/07 and 5/08). The Ombudsperson for Persons with Disabilities was also appointed and the Office of the Ombudsperson for Persons with Disabilities was established (in 2008), (*OGRC*, No. 107/07).
67 Strategy of Development of the Social Welfare System in the Republic of Croatia (2011–2016), Zagreb, April 2011, see the official website of the Ministry of Social Policy and Youth: <http://www.mspm.hr/content/download/6031/47076/file/Strategija_kona%C4%8Dno-travnja.pdf/>.

social welfare institutions and other legal entities providing social welfare activities in the RC 2011–2016, adopted in 2010 by the former Ministry of Health and Social Welfare, a predecessor of today's Ministry of Social Policy and Youth. The decision on the Plan for deinstitutionalisation was made to intensify the reform process, transform the existing system and deinstitutionalise social service providers. The aim of the Plan was to reduce the placement of children in institutions and increase their transfer from institutions into new forms of care, particularly by stimulating family reintegration.[68] However, the Social Welfare Act has encountered a lot of criticism, for example, that the system has been further centralised, that the bureaucracy has been further strengthened and that no essential steps have been taken as to the proclaimed deinstitutionalisation of children in the social welfare system.

In accordance with the Constitution of the RC (Article 61), "the family shall enjoy special protection of the state" and it is considered the main social unit. In the RC, a child can be placed in alternative care pursuant to Article 103 of the Family Act (2003),[69] *i.e.* the Social Welfare Act (2012).[70] In accordance with the Family Act (Article 152) and the Social Welfare Act (Article 95), children without adequate parental care are persons under 18 years of age with no parents, who were abandoned by parents, neglected and/or abused by parents, children whose parents have been pronounced legally incompetent or deprived of the right to exercise parental care. Furthermore, in accordance with Article 95 of the Social Welfare Act, alternative care in the RC includes care for children "with behavioural problems", children with developmental disabilities (mental, physical or sensory impairments), children who are victims of domestic violence or human trafficking victims and, exceptionally, if it is in the interests of the child, also children whose parents "due to illness, lack of housing or other adverse life events are unable to care for the child."

Although foster care in the RC has a long tradition and practice, the Foster Care Act was passed in 2007 as the first of this kind in the RC, and it was significantly altered in 2011.[71] The Foster Care Act was passed in order to promote non-institutional forms of child care and prevent the institutionalisation of

---

68   *Ibid.*, p. 3.
69   OGRC, Nos. 116/2003, 17/2004, 136/2004, 107/2007, 57/2011 and 61/2011.
70   OGRC, No. 33/2012.
71   The first Foster Care Act of 2007 was published in the OGRC, No. 79/07, while the new Foster Care Act of 2011 was published in the OGRC, Nos. 90/2011 and 78/2012. Pursuant to Article 1 (1), this Act governs "conditions to be met by the foster family, provision and termination of foster care and other issues related to foster care". In addition to this Act, a series of regulations and decisions was adopted that governs keeping of the records referring to foster families, their training and, conditions for foster care and foster care

children.[72] It is important to note that, in addition to foster care in the RC, 'family-like homes' also exist as forms of alternative care in which children are treated in individual family homes integrated into the local community.[73] In accordance with Article 167 of the Social Welfare Act, four to ten children may be placed in a family-like home. It is important at this point to mention two special homes for children without parental care where the RC is not the founder. These are the SOS Children's Village Lekenik and the SOS Children's Village Ladimirevci.[74] This concept of placing children in alternative care in the RC entered into force in 1993 and is in line with the recommendations of the Committee on the Rights of the Child.[75] Adoption is a special form of family law care and protection of children that is regulated by the Family Act (Articles 123–148). The aforementioned provisions of the Family Act set out the conditions for adoption, the adoption process and the rights and responsibilities arising from adoption. Children living in institutions in the RC stay in three types of homes: homes for children deprived of adequate parental care, homes for children with behavioural disorders and homes for children (and adults) with developmental problems and disabilities.

v   Number of Children Placed in Alternative Care in the Republic of Croatia and the Problems They Face

According to the last 2011 census performed by the Central Bureau of Statistics, there are 4,284,889 people in the RC, 847,770 of whom are children and adolescents (aged 0–18 years), which totals 19.8% of the total population.[76] Half a

---

licenses are prescribed, as well as the amount of compensation for placement with a foster family, *etc.*

72   Strategy of Development of the Social Welfare System in the Republic of Croatia (2011–2016), *op. cit.*, p. 5.
73   Ajduković, M.: "Pristupi zbrinjavanju djece bez odgovarajuće roditeljske skrbi u Europi" ["Approaches to the care for children without adequate parental care in Europe"], *Revija za socijalnu politiku* [*Croatian Journal of Social Policy*], Vol. 11, No. 3–4, p. 313.
74   Association of SOS Children's Village Croatia has operated since 25 February 1992 as an equal member of SOS Kinderdorf International, the world's largest non-governmental organisation for children and youth, with headquarters in Innsbruck, Austria. For more details see the official website: <http://www.sos-dsh.hr/>.
75   Report of the Committee on the Rights of the Child 2012, *op. cit.*, paras. 35 and 39.
76   The 2011 Census of Population, Households and Dwellings in the Republic of Croatia, from the official website of the Croatian Bureau of Statistics: <http://www.dzs.hr/Hrv/censuses/census2011/results/censustabshtm.htm/>.

century ago (1961), children represented 27.2% of the total population, while in 2001 the proportion of children in the population was 20.72%.[77] This makes Croatia a State with a relatively low proportion of children in the general population and below the average of EU countries.[78] According to the Plan on Deinstitutionalisation and Transformation of Social Welfare Homes and Other Types of Legal Entities Providing Social Welfare Services in the RC (2011–2016), in 2011 there were 114 state-owned and non-state-owned homes and other entities engaged in social welfare activities for children and adolescents without adequate parental care, children and adolescents with behavioural disorders, children with developmental disabilities, mentally disabled adults, and persons with disabilities.[79] Out of that number, there were 71 state-owned social welfare homes (*i.e.* 14 for children and adolescents without adequate parental care with 782 users, 11 for children and adolescents with behavioural disorders with 1,477 users, 28 for children with developmental disabilities and adults with disabilities with 4,207 users and 18 for mentally disabled adults with 3,205 users), and 24 non-state-owned homes (2 for children and adolescents without adequate parental care with 188 users, 12 for children with developmental disabilities and adults with disabilities with 1,259 customers and 10 for mentally disabled adults with 901 users).[80] Out of 19 other legal entities, 6 are for children and adolescents without adequate parental care with 164 users, 11 are for children with developmental disabilities and adults with disabilities with 600 users and 2 for mentally disabled adults with 30 users.[81]

The Plan for deinstitutionalisation states that the total number of foster families for children and adolescents amounts to only 1,332 providing homes for 1,955 children (*i.e.* 1,675 children and adolescents without adequate parental care, 250 children with developmental disabilities and 30 children and adolescents with behavioural disorders).[82] There are 27 family homes in the RC, 2 of which are for children and adolescents without adequate parental care and

---

77 Ibid.
78 Cf. Brajša-Žganec, A. et al.: *Situation Analysis of Children's and Women's Rights in Croatia, Report for UNICEF Office for Croatia*, Zagreb, 2011, pp. 17–18.
79 Plan deinstitucionalizacije i transformacije domova socijalne skrbi i drugih pravnih osoba koje obavljaju djelatnost socijalne skrbi u Republici Hrvatskoj 2011.–2016. [National Plan on Deinstitutionalisation and Transformation of Social Welfare Homes and Other Types of Legal Entities Providing Social Welfare Services in the Republic of Croatia 2011–2016], see the official website of the Ministry of Social Policy and Youth: <http://www.mspm.hr/content/download/6087/47360/file/plan_DEINSTITUCIJALIZACIJE.pdf/>, p. 6.
80 Ibid.
81 Ibid.
82 Ibid.

4 for children with developmental disabilities and adults with disabilities. *Inter alia*, 20 children and adolescents without adequate parental care, and 24 children with developmental disabilities and adults with disabilities are placed in these institutions.[83] Approximately 240 children and adolescents are placed in SOS Children's Villages (preschoolers and primary school children) and youth communities (after the completion of primary school education) in the RC.[84] On 31 December 2012, there were 76 children in institutions that were eligible for adoption (33 girls and 43 boys), of whom 11 were under the age of three.[85] The Ombudsperson for Children warns that a significant number of parents are abusing current legislation since one telephone call by parents to the authorities in the home every three months is sufficient to extend the measure of delegation, custody and care of their child in the home, despite the opinion of competent authorities in the home that parents have systematically neglected their child and that all they have done for their child is make one telephone call.[86] This slows down or prevents the authorities from making a decision on deprivation of parental care, placing the child in the adoption process and releasing the child from the institution.

Despite the proclaimed deinstitutionalisation, there are still a disturbing number of children who remain in institutions too long. Even when it is estimated that return to the biological family is not in the best interests of the child or not possible at all, it is impermissible to continue keeping these children in institutions or in foster care rather than starting the adoption process in order to provide permanent care for the child in question.[87] Older children are particularly vulnerable, since there is little interest by potential adoptive and foster parents who are, as a rule, interested in adopting younger children with no developmental disabilities. In practice, the following problems have been noticed in relation to the institutionalisation of children without adequate parental care in the RC: obvious regional disparities with respect to the institutional care of children (*e.g.* in Lika and Dalmatia there are almost no

---

83   *Ibid.*
84   Data on the number of children from the official website of SOS Children's Village Croatia, *loc. cit.*, note 74.
85   Izvješće o radu pravobraniteljice za djecu za 2012. [Report about the Work of the Ombudsperson for Children for 2012], Zagreb, March 2013 (hereinafter referred to as: 'Report about the Work of the Ombudsperson for Children for 2012') on the official website of the Office of the Ombudsperson for Children: <http://www.dijete.hr/hr/izvjemainmenu-93/izvjeo-radu-pravobranitelja-za-djecu-mainmenu-94/doc_download/365-izvjee-o-radu-pravobraniteljice-za-djecu-za-2012-godinu.html/>, p. 34.
86   *Ibid.*
87   *Ibid.*, p. 35.

foster families), long-term stays of children in institutional care (average length of stay is 10.5 years), the number of adoption requests exceeding the number of approved adoptions, court delays relating to deprivation of parental care for children who have long been in homes or in foster families and social workers' reluctance to apply more stringent criteria to this issue, a lack of effective communication between social workers and children and social workers and homes, too few professional staff in alternative care, the disadvantages of different services and programmes on a local level, lack of support for biological parents, lack of help and support for children leaving public care at age 18 (potentially becoming homeless), *etc.*[88]

As already pointed out, pursuant to Article 20 of the UNCRC, the child must be placed not only in a stable care setting, but in the same socio-cultural environment, even in the same educational institution he or she is attending.[89] Unfortunately, to date we have witnessed systematic violations of these provisions in a number of countries. Even in the RC it is often the practice of centres for social work that a child is deliberately given for adoption to a family that is far away from the child's place of residence. The reason for this is that the child's parents or extended family and friends would not interfere with the 'new life' and the 'new family' of the child. This clearly violates Article 20(3) of the UNCRC and other international standards and guidelines relating to alternative care.

According to data provided by the Ombudsperson for Children, on 31 December 2012 there were 1,046 children and young people accommodated in children's homes in Croatia, 522 and 524 of whom were girls and boys, respectively (mostly (292) children aged 11–14).[90] Out of those 1,046 children in institutions for children without adequate parental care, 845 (or 80.78%) are placed there permanently.[91] 284 children and young people were placed in

---

[88] For more details see: Plan deinstitucionalizacije i transformacije domova socijalne skrbi i drugih pravnih osoba koje obavljaju djelatnost socijalne skrbi u Republici Hrvatskoj 2011.–2016. [National Plan on Deinstitutionalisation and Transformation of Social Welfare Homes and Other Types of Legal Entities Providing Social Welfare Services in the Republic of Croatia 2011–2016], *op. cit.*, pp. 16–18; SOS Analiza prava i skrbi za djecu bez roditeljske skrbi i pod rizikom gubitka roditeljske skrbi [SOS Analysis of the Rights and Care of Children without Parental Care and under the Risk of Losing Parental Care], SOS Dječje selo, Zagreb, 2010; Izvješće o radu pravobraniteljice za djecu za 2009. [Report about the Work of the Ombudsperson for Children for 2009], Zagreb, pp. 107, 130–131; Report about the Work of the Ombudsperson for Children for 2012, *op. cit.*, pp. 28–36.; Brajša-Žganec *et al.*, *op. cit.*, pp. 84–85.

[89] Cantwell and Holzscheiter, *op. cit.*, pp. 61–62.

[90] Report about the Work of the Ombudsperson for Children for 2012, *op. cit.*, p. 31.

[91] *Ibid.*

institutions for children without adequate parental care in 2012 on the basis of the Family Act and 385 children on the basis of the Social Welfare Act.[92] What is disturbing is the fact that when it comes to the placement of 284 children in institutions under the Social Welfare Act, these are children whose status in alternative care is reviewed irregularly or not at all.[93] Out of 385 children and young people placed in alternative care in 2012, 247 were removed from the parental home, 32 from hospital or maternity hospital, 28 from some other home for children without adequate parental care, 29 from their relatives, 8 from the shelter for women and children who are victims of violence, while no prior accommodation was given for 31 children.[94] The Ombudsperson for Children has particularly expressed her concern that 167 children up to 7 years old were placed in institutions in 2012.[95] This is contrary to the principles of deinstitutionalisation and the prohibition of institutionalisation of children up to 7 years old, but also to Article 96 of the Social Welfare Act, under which a child under the age of seven has the right to be placed in a foster family (paragraph 1). In 2012, 24 children under the age of three were placed in institutions for children without adequate parental care on the basis of the Family Act and 83 children under the age of three were placed in these institutions on the basis of the Social Welfare Act.

In relation to the total number of children and young people in institutions in the Republic of Croatia (1,046), 272 (or 29.3%), according to the Ombudsperson for Children, have mental health problems.[96] Furthermore, out of the total number of children in institutions, 343 are undergoing psychological or psychiatric treatment (32.8%), while as many as 153 children are being treated with psychoactive drugs (14.6%).[97] The RC has no unregistered children's homes, although it was established that there are unregistered and illegal homes for elderly and disabled persons. What are the reasons for terminating the placement of 447 children in child care institutions in 2012 in the RC? Return to the biological family (168), foster family placement (74), staying with relatives (14), placement in a family home (1), adoption (38), placement in another children's home or institution (66), the age of majority (27), finishing education (35), and other (24).[98]

---

92 *Ibid.*
93 *Ibid.*
94 *Ibid.*, p. 32.
95 *Ibid.*
96 *Ibid.*
97 *Ibid.*
98 *Ibid.*

Experts in the social welfare system in the RC work, as a rule, with too many demanding children, which puts additional pressure on the efficiency of the social welfare system. Children in alternative care lack the chance of having decisions of competent authorities on alternative care reviewed regularly and more frequently, especially those referring to children who are institutionalised and older. Some sort of old and nowadays abandoned models of treating children are still applied where they have no opportunity to express their position regarding their stay in the institution, or their views are ignored. The key point is that generally an insufficient number of professionals and experts who do not practise (enough) the concept of lifelong learning, constant learning and informing are engaged in the alternative care of children. Hence children are potentially exposed to institutionalisation and long-term stay in institutions, inadequate accommodation in a family environment, neglect, abuse and other forms of violence and discrimination. All this puts them in a difficult position, significantly worse than that of their peers who grow up in a family environment.

VI Concluding Remarks

The Republic of Croatia is well on track when it comes to a comprehensive change in the legal system of social welfare and care of children. Like many other modern countries, the RC has adopted a number of modern legal solutions, plans and measures to help and support children in alternative care and their families, but their implementation in practice is questionable. Some new problems have occurred that the experts in the alternative care system have difficulty coping with. The process of harmonising Croatian legislation with the provisions and principles of the UNCRC, and the international and regional standards, is an extremely complex and demanding job that is still going on. In the first place, far more effective monitoring and sanctions are necessary in the event of non-compliance with the provisions. In order to make it all happen it is important to establish clear, objective and firm control of high quality over that system, the so-called 'competent monitoring institution' (*e.g.* such as a commissioner or inspectorate, to monitor compliance with the rules and regulations governing the provision of care, protection or treatment of children).[99] Networking of new regulations with other acts of the RC is also one of the problems. Generally, we can say that important steps forward have been made,

---

99 See Committee on the Rights of the Child, General Comment No. 12 (2009), "The right of the child to be heard", para. 97.

there was a positive change in the existing legislation, a number of actions were carried out to protect the rights of children, but they are still far from the given ones. Based on the analysis, we can recommend a number of proposals to the legislator, policy makers and professionals in practice who work in children's social care aimed at improving that part of the welfare system.

The State should support family preservation and prioritise it, except in cases where the child is exposed to violence, neglect, abuse and other forms of damage in his or her nuclear/biological family. The first step in reducing the number of children placed in alternative care should be prevention by the State which should take all measures to prevent family breakdown because of poverty or other adverse circumstances (*e.g.* neglect or abuse of the child). A family, if in need, should get professional, educational, financial, material and any other assistance and support from the State. Parents should be prepared, educated and supported for the reintegration of a child in alternative care, if possible. However, if the child is placed in any form of alternative care, reintegration of the child with his or her parents and other family members should be made possible. In this respect, help should be provided to both sides. When deciding on the placement of children in alternative care it should be taken into account that children should not be separated from the local communities of their origin, in order to be able to maintain contacts with their (extended) family and other previously established contacts. Always and at all times, the principle of the best interests of the child should be applied. Deinstitutionalisation, (extended) family support, favouritism and return to the family environment, non-discrimination and social inclusion, are becoming the main objectives in terms of children and all other persons placed in institutions.

In this difficult time of recession we should be particularly careful when separating children from their families and placing them in institutional care because of their poverty-stricken parents. The foster care system must be in accordance with current international standards and guidelines, and specialised foster care (*e.g.* for children under 3 years of age and for children with disabilities) should be strengthened in particular. We should continue to work on expanding the range of other forms of care provided for children outside the family, especially 'small family-type homes'.[100] The adoption system should be accelerated, especially to prevent abuse and obstructions to adoption by uninterested parents who are detrimental to the best interests of the child. With regard to this, the termination of parental rights proceedings in the RC should be accelerated, especially for children who stay too long in homes or in

---

100 Ajduković, *op. cit.*, p. 318.

foster families and whose parents abuse legislation and their rights, thereby causing irreparable damage to their child.

The State should specifically take into account the systematic collection, monitoring, coordination, analysis and standardisation of data on the number of children in alternative care. All components of social welfare in the RC should be networked and better communication should be achieved between centres for social work, the family and the child. In general, national legislation, practices and experiences of other countries in the region in terms of alternative care models should be followed, and a network and regional standards in this regard should be established. Furthermore, a national, but also regional database should be established on children in formal care, but it would also be important to know about informal alternative care arrangements, as well as a database of abused and neglected children, taking strictly into account the privacy of children and their families. We should undertake research into what happens to young people who have just reached the age of majority and have to leave social welfare institutions as well as the problems they face. Their experiences, criticisms and suggestions are valuable and essential in improving the social welfare system for children in alternative care.

According to the UN Guidelines for the Alternative Care of Children (2009), all children in institutions in the Republic of Croatia should be deinstitutionalised. The principle of systematic deinstitutionalisation of children requires a revolutionary change in thinking and decision-making of all those involved in alternative care in the Republic of Croatia. The first step is to reduce the large number of children staying too long in institutions. Children younger than seven years of age (preschoolers) must under no circumstances be placed in institutions, but a surrogate family should be provided, either temporarily or permanently. Further institutionalisation of children under the age of three should be completely stopped and in this regard pressure should be put on the authorities to stop this practice immediately. As highlighted by the Committee on the Rights of the Child, in addition to very young children (under the age of three), children with disabilities and children belonging to minorities are especially vulnerable groups.[101] Also, we should strengthen the system of specialised foster care for children younger than three years and, in general, work on the professionalization of foster care. The ratio of the number of children placed in non-institutional care in relation to the number of children placed in homes must be 80:20.

Education and informing of professionals in the practice should be continued, in line with the latest scientific and technical knowledge on alternative

---

101   Report of the Committee on the Rights of the Child 2012, *op. cit.*, para. 39.

care for children. Collaboration between the government (competent ministries) and the NGO for the protection of human rights and the protection of children's rights should be fostered, and these bodies should be connected not only with the academic community, but also with other countries in the region and international/regional organisations dealing with this issue. The State shall provide all assistance and support organisations fighting for the protection of children's rights. Finally, it is particularly important to use the media, by organising workshops, panel discussions, lectures and other means, to educate and inform but also to sensitise the public on the issues of placement of children in alternative care and to ensure a sufficient number of high quality prospective foster and adoptive parents.

CHAPTER 30

Social Rights and International Law

*Bernd v. Maydell**

I   **Introductory Remarks**

Professor Budislav Vukas, to whom this article is dedicated, has been a collegial friend to me for many years as we got to know each other and worked together on the International Labour Organization's (ILO) Committee of Experts on the Application of Conventions and Recommendations in Geneva. The question of international protection of social rights, the topic of the present article, was discussed on a regular basis by the Committee of Experts. Budislav Vukas went further and devoted much of his scientific work to this problematic area.[1]

The present article therefore seemed to be a good opportunity for a return to the subject matter of social rights. Quite frequently in this context, the terms social human rights,[2] basic social rights, or social standards[3] are also used, but we will not examine this diverse terminology here.

II   **Social Rights in National and International Law**

Social rights can be anchored in national and international law. Even though only the latter will be studied in this article, it needs to remain clear that various interconnections exist between the different levels. The international social human rights may be reflected in national law, but national law can also be far more detailed. Finally, the national law may omit any formulation of basic social rights, as is the case in the German Basic Law. It appears doubtful whether this deficit, as Eichenhofer argues,[4] was based on the thinking that the Basic Law was just meant to create a temporary constitutional system for the period until the reunification of Germany. There is every reason to believe

---

*   Professor Emeritus for Civil Law, Labour Law, and Social Law; formerly Director of the Max-Planck-Institute for Social Law and Social Policy (Munich).
1   For example, see Vukas, "The Diverse Supervisory Procedures in a Comparison", in: v. Maydell, Nußberger (eds.), *Social Protection by Way of International Law*, 1996, pp. 105–132.
2   Such as, finally, Eichenhofer, *Soziale Menschenrechte im Völker-, europäischen und deutschen Recht*, 2012.
3   See in particular Nußberger, *Sozialstandards im Völkerrecht*, 2005.
4   Eichenhofer (see note 2), p. 3.

that the writers of the constitution were, among others, well aware of the fact that the broad judicial protection which in consideration of the historical experiences was very consciously accorded to the liberal rights of freedom, could not be granted in the same way to social rights.[5] The lack of expressed basic social rights, by the way, does not mean that the domestic law of social security receives less attention. As shown by the German example, the social law regulated by statutory law can be highly developed and very complex.[6] This indirectly proves just how positive the effects of the flexible principle of the social state laid down in the Basic Law can be.[7]

The question whether the restraint of the Basic Law with regard to the social human rights is enough to corroborate the conclusion reached by Eichenhofer,[8] namely that the scientific and political debate in Germany would suggest that social human rights do not even exist, is debatable, since the conclusion in this absolute form appears to be overstated. Indeed, German scholarly discussions do include serious deliberation of social human rights.[9] On the levels of national as well as of international law, this is certainly a much-discussed topic among German scholars of jurisprudence. In particular, this debate often raises the question of the manner in which the national social human rights affect German law and German politics and policies.[10]

III   International Social Norms – Attempt to Take Stock

Social rights are regulated in very different international sources of law; the content and purpose of regulation varies, while the effect for the citizens, the

---

[5]   Thereto Herzog, in: Maunz-Dürig-Herzog, *Grundgesetz, Kommentar* (loose-leaf), Art. 20 Rz. 28, who sees a "rejection of unfulfillable promises" in the omission of social rights.

[6]   Insofar also in agreement, Eichenhofer (see note 2), p. 2.

[7]   Thereto Herzog (see note 5), Art. 20 Rz. 6 *ff.*

[8]   Eichenhofer (see note 2), p. 1.

[9]   This is already corroborated by numerous studies cited by Eichenhofer (see note 2), as for example Nußberger, *Sozialstandards im Völkerrecht*, 2005, beyond which the picture gets even more multifaceted. There are additional studies – which are not referenced by Eichenhofer – as for example that by Köhler, *Sozialpolitische und sozialrechtliche Aktivitäten in den Vereinten Nationen*, 1987; Becker, v. Maydell, Nußberger (eds.), *Die Implementierung internationaler Sozialstandards*, 2006; Bundesministerium für Arbeit und Sozialordnung, Max-Planck-Institut für ausländisches und internationales Sozialrecht, Akademie der Diozöse Rottenburg Stuttgart, *Soziale Grundrechte in der Europäischen Union*, 2000/2001.

[10] See, among others, Becker, v. Maydell, Nußberger (see note 9).

states and the international community also differs; and this compels us to begin by presenting an overview.

1   Differing Contents

International social standards differ in various respects:

- The intent of the regulations may be that they are aimed at a coordination of the various national social security systems, that is to say they function as conflict-of-laws rules.[11] As examples we could name numerous bilateral and multilateral social security agreements,[12] as well as the migrant worker regulations of the European Union.[13] The intent of the regulations may however also be aimed at the establishment of a uniform international social standard by enacting minimum standards and implementing them as comprehensively as possible.[14] These social standards formulate social human rights or at the very least are inspired by such basic rights.
- The social standards may be focused on the various social human rights,[15] as for example the right to work, to health, to education, to social security, *etc.*
- The international social standards come with different degrees of concretization. They may be formulated as general legal principles, such as the right to social security in Article 22 of the UN Declaration of Human Rights.[16] On the other hand, numerous ILO conventions, as for example the ILO Convention No. 102 dealing with the minimum social standards, include very complex social rights positions. This concretization however has the consequence that the number of countries assuming these obligations by ratifying the ILO Convention is relatively small.[17]

2   Legal Sources

International Law (and thus also the social human rights) is based on international treaty law and international customary law. To a very large extent, social

---

[11]   Thereto v. Maydell, *Sach- und Kollisionsnormen im Internationalen Sozialversicherungsrecht*, 1967.
[12]   *Cf.* Petersen, "Sozialversicherungsabkommen", in: Sozialrechts-Handbuch, 5th edn., 2012, Part 5, § 35.
[13]   Thereto Schulte, "Supranationales Recht", in: Sozialrechts-Handbuch, 5th edn., 2012, Part 5, § 33.
[14]   *Cf.* Nußberger, "Das Sozialrecht der Internationalen Organisation", in: Sozialrechts-Handbuch, 5th edn., 2012, Part 5, § 34.
[15]   For the individual social human rights see Eichenhofer (see note 2), pp. 95 *ff.*
[16]   Thereto *cf.* Nußberger (see note 3), pp. 64 *ff.*
[17]   With regard to Convention No. 102 of the ILO, see Nußberger (see note 14), Rz. 13 *ff.*

human rights have not (yet) been recognized as customary law.[18] This means that social standards derive their legally binding character from international treaty law.[19] International treaty law comprises not only the bilateral and multilateral treaties between states, but also and – with regard to the social standards – above all, the conventions and agreements developed and negotiated by international organizations and then ratified by the states. Organizations of this type, such as the UN or the ILO, can be active globally as well; they may also, however, be restricted to a regional area, such as the Council of Europe.[20]

One peculiarity of the global and regional social standards is the fact that social human rights are regulated in parallel by quite similar formulations and more than once, while the legal implications of such side-by-side regulations most often are ignored.[21]

3   Enforcement of the International Social Human Rights[22]

The international social standards obligate the ratifying states to adapt their legal systems to these standards. Generally an internal act of legislation is required, unless the standards are self-executing, which does occur in exceptional cases.

It is necessary to review the compliance of the states with the obligations they assumed with reference to the ratification.[23] After ratification, the adaptation of the domestic law to the standards of international law by the states needs to be verified. For this purpose, international organizations, such as the ILO or the Council of Europe, have developed monitoring procedures to verify, on the basis of state reports, the consistency of the national law with the international conventions.[24] Insofar, the individual citizen has no legal remedy available for forcing compliance with the granted social human rights.[25]

---

18   See Nußberger (see note 3), p. 436, with additional references.

19   The particular characteristics of the so-called soft law cannot be discussed in detail in this context, cf. thereto the discussion in Pennings (ed.), *International Social Security Standards*, 2007, pp. 139 ff.

20   See for example Öhlinger, "Standard-Setting Activities by Regional Institutions. Taking the Council of Europe as an Example: The European Social Charter", in: v. Maydell, Nußberger (see note 1), pp. 43 ff.

21   Insofar, however, the study by Nußberger represents an exception (see note 3), pp. 377 ff.

22   Thereto Becker, v. Maydell, Nußberger (see note 9).

23   With respect to the ILO, for example, these obligations relate to the submission of the convention to the legislative bodies.

24   For the ILO procedures cf. Wagner, *Internationaler Schutz sozialer Rechte*, 2002.

25   For the special possibilities of a complaint to be filed at the European Court of Human Rights in cases where the European Human Rights Convention is violated due to national

An evaluation of international social standards should not just concentrate on the juridical analysis of the effectiveness, but also on the effects produced by the very process of creating, implementing, and monitoring such standards on political discourse and public opinion. The status of social issues thus assumes a higher standing in the longer term on the international level as well.

IV Effect, Relevance, and Future Prospects of International Social Standards

1 Point of Departure

The controversial international and national discussion[26] about social human rights demonstrates the multilayered complexity of this subject matter. It is therefore pertinent to analyse the relevance of social human rights on their different impact levels, in particular where they are based on international norms.

2 International Social Rights as Basis for Claims by Individual Citizens

On the international level, social law is governed by norms and standards of widely differing content. There are on the one hand coordination norms determining which national legal system should be applied to issues involving contact with foreign countries; these norms are then called collision-of-laws rules.[27] Of special practical importance for the European Community are the coordination norms under social law,[28] because they facilitate the free movement of labour. The coordination provisions in European law, but also those in international law (particularly in international treaty law) directly impact on the legal position of the individual; the rights bestowed under these norms can be claimed by the individual and asserted in a court of law.

The situation is different for the social human rights in international law. They are predominantly formulated in very general terms as principles and are intended for the states that have committed to align their internal legal systems

---

regulations in the area of social security *cf.* Schmidt, *Europäische Menschenrechtskonvention und Sozialrecht*, 2003.

26 This discussion was somewhat escalated by Eichenhofer in his recently published monograph (see note 2) about the social human rights where he puts forward the theory that the existence of social human rights is largely denied in the German discussion (see *supra*, II).

27 Thus v. Maydell (see note 11); *cf.* also Eichenhofer, *Internationales Sozialrecht und Internationales Privatrecht*, 1987.

28 *Cf.* Schulte (see note 13).

with these principles. This obligation ensues from membership of the international community, *i.e.* the UN, or from a special ratification of the respective convention, such as the ILO conventions. The adherence to these obligations by the states is verified by special monitoring procedures, where committees of experts usually play a decisive role.[29]

The potential of these social human rights to allow concrete claims to be asserted in national courts is very questionable, though in the final analysis this may not be of importance, since the national constitutional and social law will in most instances offer a corresponding legal basis. Insofar as this is not the case, one can determine whether a state obligation of protection with respect to the implementation of social human rights can be derived from the constitution, thus for example from the German Basic Law. Insofar as the state does not create protective provisions in the national social law, this omission could be subject to a plea in the Federal Constitutional Court.[30,31]

International social protection standards are usually not actionable by the individual in international courts. The European Court of Human Rights, which adjudicates upon individual complaints, only has jurisdiction over violations of the European Convention of Human Rights, and not in cases of an infringement of the European Social Charter or other social standards of the Council of Europe. Nevertheless, the European Court of Human Rights has ascertained numerous violations of the Convention of Human Rights which affect the social status of the individual.[32] Thus for example, the protection of property and the prohibition of discrimination have prompted rulings with relevance for social law.[33]

3   *International Social Law Protection and the National Legal System*

International social standards raise a variety of questions concerning their effect on national legal systems. To begin with, there is the question of how the

---

[29]   Thus for example the ILO Committee of Experts on the Application of Conventions and Recommendations, *cf.* Wagner (see note 24).

[30]   The Federal Constitutional Court has recognized, for example, the duty to protect in cases of the termination of pregnancy (BVerfGE 39, 1 [42]).

[31]   With respect to the possibility of complaints of unconstitutionality filed by persons in need of care on the grounds of poor care *cf.* the not yet published Regensburg dissertation by Susanne Moritz, *Staatliche Schutzpflichten gegenüber pflegebedürftigen Menschen*, 2013.

[32]   With respect to this administration of justice *cf.* Schmidt (note 25).

[33]   *Cf.* finally v. Maydell, "Soziale Grundrechte unter den Bedingungen wirtschaftlicher und finanzieller Krisen", 19 *Juridica International, Law Review, University of Tartu*, 2012, pp. 5 *ff.*

international norms influence national law (thereto see under a.).[34] This is related to the question of which obligations to act arise for the legislator based on the existence of the international standards (*cf.* under b.).

a. International law can be directly applicable in a state. This may be stipulated by the national constitution, as is the case in Germany for the general rules of international law in accordance with Article 25 of the Basic Law. However, the social standards are not regarded as general rules of international law.[35] They therefore are applicable in Germany with the legal effect of national law only when they have been ratified.[36] The ratification then leads to the obligation of incorporating the norm of international law into national law, unless the particular norm is self-executing, which is rarely the case with social standards.[37]

Effectiveness within the state, for its part, does not imply transformation if the states surrender the power to create law to a special organization, such as for example the European Union. Nevertheless, the social realm has in a very large part remained within the sphere of the member states; in this context, considerable coordination problems arise between certain supranational rules and the national social law.[38]

b. When analysing the effect of international social standards on national law,[39] the interactions between international and national levels are rather significant, and already begin with the formulation and adoption of the international standards. This is an area where the representatives of the states play a decisive role, while a special feature applies for the ILO[40] in

---

34 Thereto *cf.* Pennings (ed.), *Between Soft and Hard Law. The Impact of International Social Security Standards on National Social Security Law*, 2006; for the protection of social rights in the constitutions of European states, *cf.* Iliopoulos-Strangas (ed.), *La protection des droits sociaux fondamentaux dans les Etats membres de l'Union européenne*, 2000.

35 *Cf.* Nußberger (see note 3), p. 436.

36 See however Eichenhofer (see note 2), who views the international human rights in Germany according to Art. 1, par. 2 of the Basic Law, as directly applicable (p. 196), because, he says, Germany had committed to the inviolate and unalienable human rights in this constitutional provision.

37 For the exceptions for which a direct national application is possible *cf.* Nußberger (see note 3), pp. 223, 226, 241.

38 Thereto Schulte, Zacher, *Wechselwirkungen zwischen dem Europäischen Sozialrecht und dem Sozialrecht der Bundesrepublik Deutschland*, 1991.

39 Thereto Pennings (see note 34).

40 *Cf.* v. Maydell, "Das Sozialrecht in der Normensetzung der ILO", in: *Weltfriede durch soziale Gerechtigkeit. 75 Jahre Internationale Arbeitsorganisation*, 1994, pp. 47–54.

that not only the International Labour Office and the representatives of the states, but also the agents of employers and trade unions, participate in the creation of the ILO norms.[41]

In the remaining aspects as well, the ILO provides an example of a particularly structured and intensive cooperation by the international organization with national states. Once the conventions have been adopted by the Labour Conference, the states are committed to transmitting the conventions to the national legislative institutions having to decide about the ratification (Art. 19 V of the ILO Constitution).[42] If ratification occurs, the ratifying state assumes the obligation to comply with the respective social standards. Insofar as the norms are self-executing, they become part of the national law without the need for further action. Moreover, and that is the normal case, the ratifying state is obligated to adapt domestic law to the social standards. Whether this actually occurs is verified at regular intervals by a special monitoring procedure based on the national reports of the states.[43] This procedure, where the social partners are involved, could also exert still more intensive influence on the domestic socio-political reform debates than has so far been mostly the case. All this could help the international developments, as reflected in the statements of the ILO, to enrich the national discussion.

4   *The International Social Standards and Their Significance on the Global Level*

According to the traditional concept, international law regulates the relationship between the states, but not the legal relationship among individuals, nor that between the individual and the state. The social human rights originating from international law represent a further development insofar as they refer to the individual as a legal entity. This however does not extend so far that concrete legal claims for the individual can be derived from these social standards

---

41   Thereto Wagner (see note 24).

42   Even when ratification is withheld, the international law may provide obligations for the member states. Thus the members of the Council of Europe, who also has developed social standards such as the European Code of Social Security, have, according to Art. 76 of the Code, the obligation to regularly file reports concerning the question whether the national law is in agreement with the rules of the Code, thereby making a ratification possible. This report procedure (*cf.* Nußberger, see note 3, pp. 132 *ff.*) facilitates a discussion about the further development of the national law and the incorporation of the international standards, which could be exploited far more than has been done up to now for the national discussion of social reform.

43   For this procedure *cf.* Pennings (see note 19), pp. 33 *ff.*

against his or her state. Insofar, the practice continues that the social standards are concretized by the national legislator and incorporated into the national law. A different situation arises only when the states surrender the power to create law to an association under international law, as is the case with the European Union. Within the framework of this surrender, the EU holds the power to create its own – supranational – law. However, powers of this kind in the social sector exist only in certain selected cases.

Globalization, as it impacts more and more on areas of life, leads to the ever more prevalent view that the lack of worldwide content rules for social issues is a deficit, even though the trend toward internationalization has not yet acquired the intensity present in other areas (commercial law, in particular antitrust law and law on competition, environmental law, revenue law *etc.*). The increase in cross-border economic activities, above all by multinational corporations, and the mobility of the workforce lead to the growing urgency for cross-border regulations – and not merely coordination – in the social area as well, because the national states with their commercial, revenue-related, and social law-related legislation are no longer able to react adequately to the new globalized conditions.[44] Against this background, the idea of a worldwide social code of law is being discussed. Even though a number of approaches to creating international laws have emerged,[45] it is still questionable whether this idea can be realized in the foreseeable future. The experiences gained with the European Union, in particular, show that the deterrents are to be seen not only in the lack of suitable international tools for action. The differences in mentality, in the economic and social conditions as well as in the perception of the state that prevail in the different countries represent substantial barriers for a uniform social code of law.

V Conclusions

Social human rights which are also anchored in international law have significance in various aspects, as this analysis illustrates. This significance results less from a direct improvement of the situation of the citizens with respect to their social rights than from the influence exerted on the states that align their legal systems with the international standards. This already starts with the exertion of influence on the socio-political discussion, as it is affected by international standards. Furthermore however, there are a multitude of procedures

---

44 *Cf.* v. Maydell, "Einführung", in: Becker, v. Maydell, Nußberger (see note 9), pp. 11–20.
45 *Ibid.*

which can be used to work towards the incorporation of social human rights into the national law. Insofar as the coordination of the national systems of social law is concerned, the international and above all the supranational law have moved beyond this rather indirect mechanism of action, and have proceeded to norm directly applicable conflict-of-laws rules.

It is questionable whether the future will bring a comprehensive worldwide social code of law, because the deterrents to a system of this type will probably be impossible to overcome in the foreseeable future, in spite of continuing globalization. Nevertheless, this does not mean that social human rights could not or should not be expanded and strengthened in certain areas on the international level as well.

CHAPTER 31

Les droits de l'homme aujourd'hui

*Tafsir Malick Ndiaye**

Les droits de l'homme[1] apparaissent comme une pièce de musée à restaurer, exigeant du juriste qu'il joue le rôle de l'archéologue et parfois même celui de l'architecte car la matière est demanderesse en règles. L'on peut observer deux

---

* Juge au Tribunal International du Droit de la Mer. – C'est avec un plaisir tout particulier que nous rendons hommage à notre cher collègue et ami Budislav VUKAS que j'ai appris à connaître après neuf années passées au Tribunal International du Droit de la Mer : un homme à la courtoisie exquise et à l'humour incomparable.

1 Les études relatives aux droits de l'homme ne se comptent plus. L'on retiendra : F. Ermacora, « Human Rights and Domestic Jurisdiction », *Recueil des Cours de l'Académie de Droit international de La Haye* (RCADI), 1968-I, Vol. 124, pp. 371–452 ; K. Vasak, « Le droit international des droits de l'homme », RCADI, 1974-IV, Vol. 140, pp. 333–416 ; P. Sieghart, *The International Law of Human Rights*, Clarendon Press, Oxford, 1983, 569 p. ; N. Valticos, « La notion de droits de l'homme en droit international », *Mélanges Virally*, 1991, pp. 483–491 ; Ph. Alston (ed.), *The United Nations and Human Rights. A Critical Appraisal*, OUP, Oxford, 1992, 748 p. ; SFDI, *Colloque de Strasbourg, La protection des droits de l'homme et l'évolution du droit international*, Pédone, Paris, 1998, 344 p. ; T.M. Ndiaye, « Introduction aux droits de l'homme », *Revue Pax Africa*, Dakar, n° 1, juin-août 1989, p. 8 et s. ; J.S. Watson, *Theory and Reality in the International Protection of Human Rights*, Transnational Publishers, New-York, 1999, 325 p. ; Ch. Tomuschat, *Human Rights : Between Realism and Idealisation*, OUP, Oxford, 2003, 333 p. ; O. De Frouville, *L'intangibilité des droits de l'homme en droit international*, Pédone, Paris, 2004, 561 p. ; E. Decaux (dir.), *Les Nations Unies et les droits de l'homme*, Pédone, Paris, 2006, 348 p. ; SFDI, *Colloque de Nanterre, La responsabilité de protéger*, Pédone, Paris, 2008, 358 p. ; R. Cassin, « La Déclaration Universelle et la mise en œuvre des droits de l'homme », RCADI, 1991-II, Vol. 79, pp. 237–367 ; P.R. Ghandhi, « The Universal Declaration of Human Rights at fifty years », *German Yearbook of International Law*, 1998, pp. 206–251 ; M. Nowak, UN *Covenant on Civil and Political Rights*, CCPR Commentary, Engel, Kehl, 1974, 936 p. ; M. Sepulveda, *The Nature of the Obligations under the International Covenant on Economic, Social and Cultural Rights*, Intersentia, Antwerp, 2003, 446 p. ; J. Dhommeaux, « Les méthodes du Comité des droits de l'homme dans l'examen des rapports soumis par les Etats parties au Pacte sur les droits civils et politiques », *Annuaire français de Droit international*, 1988, pp. 331–364 ; R. Sodini, *Le Comité des droits économiques, sociaux et culturels*, Montchrestien, Paris, 2000, 220 p. ; K. Vasak, *La Convention européenne des droits de l'homme*, LGDJ, Paris, 1964, 327 p. ; H. Gros-Espiell, « La Convention américaine et la Convention européenne des droits de l'homme : Analyse comparative », RCADI, 1989-VII, Vol. 218, pp. 167–412 ; F. Ouguergouz, *La Charte africaine des droits de l'homme et des peuples*, PUF, Paris, 1993, 477 p. ; K. Mbaye, *Les droits de l'homme en Afrique*, Pédone, Paris, 1992, 312 p.

tendances dans l'ordre international des droits de l'homme ; des principes universalistes et l'existence de particularismes nationaux. Cette situation engendre la dialectique de la solidarité et de l'identité qui fait que, dans cette matière, les ordres interne et international sont synchrones.

Il faut cependant remarquer que le caractère universel est aujourd'hui consacré. Un rapide coup d'œil sur les chartes fondamentales des Etats suffit à le prouver, sans parler de la consécration par les instruments juridiques de nature conventionnelle ou autre.

L'appareil instrumentaire est en effet impressionnant puisque l'on note plusieurs dizaines de textes.[2] Le fondement à cet édifice normatif est la dignité de l'homme.

La première affirmation universelle de l'ensemble des droits de l'homme est la Charte de l'Organisation des Nations Unies. C'est que, jusque-là, les droits de l'homme avaient un caractère purement national et les tentatives internationales étaient pour le moins partielles et obéissaient à une logique de subsidiation dans un monde relationnel marqué par des souverainetés omniprésentes et rebelles à toute immixtion extérieure.

Il faudra attendre la deuxième guerre dite mondiale avec les atrocités commises par le régime hitlérien pour voir une communauté internationale meurtrie[3] se décider à régenter la matière des droits de l'homme. Et dès le départ, la Charte des Nations Unies établit un lien intime entre les droits de l'homme et la paix.

Les articles 1er paragraphes 3, 55 et 68 de la Charte sont ceux qui ont trait aux droits de l'homme.[4] La Charte des Nations Unies apparaît ainsi comme un

---

2 Voir I. Brownlie, *Basic Documents on Human Rights*, Clarendon Press, Oxford, 1992, 603 p. ; Haut-Commissariat des Nations Unies aux Droits de l'Homme, *Droits de l'Homme : recueil d'instruments internationaux*, Vol. I : Instruments Universels, 2 tomes, New-York/Genève, 2002, 1090 p. ; Vol. II : Regional instruments, 1997, 484 p. ; P.R. Ghandhi, *Blackstone's International Human Rights Documents*, OUP, Oxford, 2004, 507 p. ; O. de Schutter *et al.*, *Code de droit international des droits de l'homme*, Bruylant, Bruxelles, 2005, 851 p. ; P. Rolland et P. Tavernier, *La protection internationale des droits de l'homme*, « Que sais-je ? », n° 2461, PUF, Paris, 1994, 128 p.

3 L'on peut lire dans le Préambule de la Charte des Nations Unies : « Nous, Peuples des Nations Unies, Résolus : à préserver les générations futures du fléau de la guerre qui, deux fois en l'espace d'une vie humaine, a infligé à l'humanité d'indicibles souffrances, à proclamer à nouveau notre foi dans les droits fondamentaux de l'homme, dans la dignité et la valeur de la personne humaine, dans l'égalité des droits des hommes et des femmes, ainsi que des nations, grandes et petites ».

4 L'article premier paragraphe 3 dispose : « Réaliser la coopération internationale en résolvant les problèmes internationaux d'ordre économique, social, intellectuel ou humanitaire, en

élément considérable dans l'ordre des droits de l'homme. Cependant, ces dispositions y relatives comportent une part d'incertitude conceptuelle.

En effet, la notion de coopération[5] est moins restrictive de la souveraineté des Etats que celle d'action[6] qui infère des initiatives internationales destinées à protéger les droits de l'homme. Ces initiatives peuvent émaner de chancelleries d'Etat ou être le fait d'organisations non gouvernementales.

Seulement, la sensibilité croissante de l'opinion publique dans le monde due au développement prodigieux des moyens de l'information est apparue comme un facteur facilitant l'épanouissement de la cause des droits de l'homme. Il suffit de penser à *l'internet* et à ses réseaux sociaux [*Facebook*; *Twitter, etc.*] ainsi qu'aux applications qu'ils sont susceptibles de générer dans l'ordre des droits de l'homme.

Nous vivons en effet à une époque où les hommes sont contemporains de l'événement; c'est-à-dire que ce qui se passe dans un pays est connu et révélé ailleurs, de sorte qu'il s'est vite constitué ce que l'on pourrait qualifier de réseau international des droits de l'homme.

Pour autant, ce mouvement n'a pas la faveur des Etats qui y voient une atteinte à leur souveraineté. Ils savent qu'ils disposent du pouvoir exclusif d'action à l'égard de leurs administrés de par leur compétence personnelle et territoriale, et sont souvent les premiers à vanter les mérites de leur droit interne relatif aux droits de l'homme. C'est pourquoi, les Etats sont réticents – qu'ils l'avouent ou pas – face aux interventions extérieures dans le domaine des droits de l'homme, que celles-ci proviennent de « gestes significatifs » de chancelleries, de la communauté internationale ou encore d'Organisations non gouvernementales. En particulier, les Etats sont souvent rebelles au système de protection internationale indifférenciée ou tolèrent plus facilement les mécanismes distinguant les nationaux et les résidents étrangers.

---

développant et en encourageant le respect des droits de l'homme et des libertés fondamentales pour tous sans distinction de race, de sexe, de langue ou de religion ». Pour ce qui est de la coopération économique et sociale internationale, l'article 55 (c) énonce « le respect universel et effectif des droits de l'homme et des libertés fondamentales pour tous, sans distinction de race, de sexe, de langue ou de religion ». L'article 56 se lit : « Les Membres s'engagent en vue d'atteindre les buts énoncés à l'article 55, à agir, tant conjointement que séparément, en coopération avec l'organisation ». En ce qui concerne la Procédure, l'article 68 dispose : « Le Conseil Economique et Social institue des commissions pour les questions économiques et sociales et le progrès des droits de l'homme ainsi que toutes autres commissions nécessaires à l'exercice de ses fonctions ».

5 Article 1er paragraphe 3, *op. cit.* (note 4).
6 Article 56, *op. cit.* (note 4).

Toujours est-il que le jeu des Conventions internationales a fini par asseoir un véritable système international des droits de l'homme même si les Etats le contrôlent. Paul Valéry ne nous avertissait-il pas à la fin de la deuxième guerre mondiale : « le temps du monde fini commence » ?[7]

Cependant, les équivoques du langage politique et constitutionnel ont fait que des Etats à régime très différent entretiennent suivant leur option des conceptions particulières des droits de l'homme : d'où la liste des principes.

On a ainsi un ordre de l'équivalence dans lequel le droit des gens a évolué et la Déclaration universelle des droits de l'homme du 10 décembre 1948 restait à faire puisque la Charte des Nations Unies ne définit pas les droits de l'homme.

La Déclaration universelle[8] est sans conteste le plus connu des textes issus des Nations Unies et relatifs aux droits de l'homme. Le projet a trois illustres parrains : le Français René Cassin, l'Américaine Eléonore Roosevelt et le Libanais Charles Malek.

Quels sont les droits que l'on trouve énoncés dans ce texte fondamental ? L'on peut dire que quatre colonnes soutiennent le portique. D'abord, les droits personnels ; ensuite les droits qui régissent les rapports de l'homme avec les autres hommes et qui renvoient à un critère de latéralité ; après les facultés d'ordre spirituel et enfin les droits d'ordre matériel.

L'on peut les ramener, pour l'essentiel, à deux types de droits : les droits civils et politiques et les droits économiques, sociaux et culturels. Les droits de l'homme se présentent d'abord et avant tout comme des droits, c'est-à-dire un intérêt juridiquement protégé, pour parodier Ihering, inhérent à l'homme et destiné à lui assurer sa dignité d'homme face à l'Etat et aux autres hommes.

Quels sont les caractères des différents droits de l'homme ?

Les droits civils et politiques s'analysent en droit, comme opposables à l'Etat. Ils supposent pour être mis en œuvre une abstention de l'Etat. Ces droits ont connu leur consécration avec la Révolution française de 1789. On les qualifie parfois de droits-attributs ou de droits de la liberté ou encore de droits de l'homme de la première génération.[9] Ces droits apparaissent le plus souvent comme des droits individuels : droit d'aller et venir, liberté d'expression, *etc.*

En ce qui concerne les droits économiques, sociaux et culturels aussi appelés droits de la deuxième génération, ils naissent avec les révolutions mexicaine (1910) et bolchévique (1917) et peuvent s'apprécier comme des

---

7 P. Valéry, *Regards sur le monde actuel*, Collection Idées, Gallimard, Paris, 1979, 376 p., voir p. 19.
8 Déclaration universelle des droits de l'homme du 10 décembre 1948, A/RES.217 (III) de l'Assemblée générale des Nations Unies.
9 Suivant la terminologie utilisée par le Pr. K. Vasak dans son Cours à l'Académie de droit international de La Haye en 1974, voir note 1, *supra*.

droits de l'homme non pas opposables à l'Etat mais exigibles de lui. Ils s'analysent ainsi en créances à la charge de l'Etat. Ce sont les droits de l'égalité dont la mise en œuvre suppose une prestation de l'Etat. Ces droits sont le plus souvent des droits collectifs : droit au travail, doit à la santé, à l'éducation, à l'information, *etc.*

Mais les droits de l'homme ne sont pas des concepts statiques. Chaque jour peut apporter son nouveau droit de l'homme.

Claude Bernard ne disait-il pas que « la fonction crée l'organe » ? Aussi, parle-t-on de droits de la troisième génération ou encore de solidarité. Ce sont des droits à la fois opposables à l'Etat et exigibles de lui et qui supposent la conjonction des acteurs du jeu social. Il s'agit, par exemple, du droit au développement ;[10] du droit à la paix ; du droit à l'environnement sain qui trouve une assise constitutionnelle dans la Déclaration de Stockholm de 1972 ;[11] du droit au patrimoine commun de l'humanité tel que dégagé par l'Assemblée générale des Nations Unies ;[12] cette dernière catégorie de droits a trait au fond des mers et à l'espace interstellaire.

Les droits de la troisième génération ont fait l'objet de vives critiques dans la doctrine.[13] On leur reproche d'être moins des droits que des aspirations et de

---

10 Voir K. Mbaye, « Le droit au développement », *Revue des droits de l'homme*, Strasbourg, 1971, pp. 5–34.

11 Voir T.M. Ndiaye, « La responsabilité internationale des Etats pour dommages au milieu marin », in *International Law : New Actors, New Concepts Continuing Dilemmas, Liber Amicorum B. Bakotic*, Martinus Nijhoff Publishers, Leiden, Boston, 2010, pp. 265–279. En effet, la Conférence des Nations Unies sur l'environnement, tenue en 1972 à Stockholm devait réitérer la règle. Le Principe 21 de la Déclaration de Stockholm se lit « Conformément à la Charte des Nations Unies et aux principes du droit international, les Etats ont le droit souverain d'exploiter leurs propres ressources selon leurs politiques d'environnement, et ils ont le devoir de s'assurer que les activités exercées dans les limites de leur juridiction ou sous leur contrôle ne causent pas de dommage à l'environnement dans d'autres Etats ou dans des régions ne relevant d'aucune juridiction nationale ». Le même principe sera proclamé par la Déclaration de Rio sur l'environnement et le développement, adoptée le 13 juin 1992 [A/CONF/51/26.Rev. 1 du 14 juin 1992]. Dans son avis consultatif du 8 juillet 1996 relatif à la licéité de la menace ou de l'emploi d'armes nucléaires, la Cour internationale de justice confirme la force obligatoire du principe : CIJ, Recueil 1996, p. 226, spéc. pp. 241–242, paragraphe29. Voir en outre, l'affaire relative au Projet Gabcikovo-Nagymaros (Hongrie/Slovaquie), arrêt du 25 septembre 1997, CIJ, Recueil 1997, p. 7, spéc. P. 41, paragraphe 53.

12 Résolution 2749 (XXIV) de 1969 de l'Assemblée générale des Nations Unies.

13 Voir R. Pelloux, « Vrais et faux droits de l'homme : Problèmes de définition et de classification », *Revue du droit public et de la science politique en France et à l'étranger*, 1981, p. 53.

manquer d'objet précis. Ces droits seraient insusceptibles de mise en œuvre juridictionnelle et risqueraient même d'affaiblir les droits de l'homme.

Ces critiques nous paraissent peu fondées. Les droits de l'homme doivent constituer un espace de plus en plus ductile. Autrement dit, la mutabilité des droits de l'homme doit aller dans le sens de leur amplification.

De plus, tout droit a d'abord été aspiration avant de devenir droit. Quant à l'impossibilité de mise en œuvre juridictionnelle, elle procède d'une erreur théorique consistant à fonder l'existence de la norme sur la sanction. C'est ce mouvement conceptuel qui a été jusqu'à nier l'existence du droit constitutionnel et du droit international.

La vérité est que la sanction ne conditionne nullement l'existence de la norme. Elle conditionne seulement son exécution. Ce n'est pas parce que le dakarois n'emprunte pas le passage clouté que celui-ci n'existe pas.

Un autre argument soulevé contre les droits dits de solidarité a trait à la hiérarchisation. A ce propos, il convient de souligner l'indivisibilité des droits de l'homme et l'absence de priorité en droit. C'est seulement au plan logique que l'on peut concevoir une certaine préséance car certains droits de l'homme – le droit à la vie par exemple – sont des droits sans lesquels le titre à la plainte devient soluble.

Nous avons de nos jours la catégorie des droits de l'homme que l'on pourrait appeler les droits de l'humanité, symbolisés par l'institution de la Cour pénale internationale que crée le Statut de Rome. En effet, la Conférence de Rome a débouché, le 17 juillet 1998, sur l'adoption de la Convention portant Statut de la Cour pénale internationale. Cette nouvelle juridiction permanente est compétente pour réprimer des individus accusés de crimes internationalement qualifiés et imprescriptibles : crime de génocide ; crimes contre l'humanité ; crimes de guerre et crime d'agression.[14] La juridiction a eu des devancières qui avaient plutôt un caractère ponctuel puisqu'il s'agit de tribunaux *ad hoc*. Qu'il s'agisse des tribunaux de Nuremberg et de Tokyo établis par les puissances victorieuses de la seconde guerre mondiale ou des Tribunaux spéciaux créés par le Conseil de Sécurité pour les crimes commis en ex-Yougoslavie, au Rwanda, au Cambodge, en Sierra Leone ou encore au Liban.

---

14   L'article 5 du Statut de Rome dispose en son paragraphe premier : « La compétence de la Cour est limitée aux crimes les plus graves qui touchent l'ensemble de la communauté internationale. En vertu du présent Statut, la Cour a compétence à l'égard des crimes suivants : (a) Le crime de génocide ; (b) Les crimes contre l'humanité ; (c) Les crimes de guerre ; le crime d'agression ». Voir le document A/CONF.183/9 du 17 juillet 1998 et amendé par les procès-verbaux en date des 10 novembre 1998, 12 juillet 1999, 30 novembre 1999, 8 mai 2000, 17 janvier 2001 et 16 janvier 2002. Le Statut est entré en vigueur le 1er juillet 2002.

Les Etats-Parties au Statut de Rome se disent conscients que tous les peuples sont unis par des liens étroits et que leurs cultures forment un patrimoine commun, et soucieux du fait que cette mosaïque délicate puisse être brisée à tout moment. Ils ont à l'esprit qu'« au cours de ce siècle, des milliers d'enfants, de femmes et d'hommes ont été victimes d'atrocités qui défient l'imagination et heurtent profondément la conscience humaine ».[15] Les Etats se sont déterminés à mettre un terme à l'impunité des auteurs de ces crimes et à concourir ainsi à la prévention de nouveaux crimes. Pour ce faire, ils ont institué la Cour pénale internationale qu'ils reconnaissent « complémentaire des juridictions pénales nationales ».[16]

Comme le remarque un auteur,[17] des individus deviennent les objets directs des obligations posées, en ce sens qu'ils peuvent être directement attraits devant une juridiction internationale, à la suite d'une action internationalement diligentée et qui peut intégralement échapper à leur Etat national. C'est là une différence sensible par rapport à des développements institutionnels antérieurs, qui avaient vu par exemple le Conseil de Sécurité demander à un Etat, la Libye, la remise de certains de ses nationaux à d'autres Etats pour qu'ils puissent y être jugés, obligation imposée qui allait au-delà de la coopération établie par les conventions relatives à la répression de la piraterie aérienne.[18]

Les individus sont cependant objets plus que sujets des normes ainsi posées, puisqu'ils ne peuvent eux-mêmes déclencher l'action pénale, déclenchement qui reste l'apanage des Etats parties, du Conseil de Sécurité ou du Procureur sous le contrôle d'une Chambre préliminaire.

**

Quelles sont les normes relatives aux droits de l'homme ?

La valeur universelle des droits de l'homme justifie l'adoption d'instruments juridiques destinés à définir les différents droits et à permettre aux Etats de prendre des engagements à leur sujet. En revanche, les spécificités telles qu'elles résultent du partage Est-Ouest et des indépendances conduisent à une régionalisation de la promotion et de la protection des droits de l'homme. C'est pourquoi, il faut distinguer les instruments à vocation régionale.

---

15   Préambule du Statut de Rome.
16   *Ibid.*
17   Pr. S. Sur, « Vers une Cour pénale internationale : la Convention de Rome entre les ONG et le Conseil de Sécurité », *Revue générale de droit international public*, 1999, n° 1, pp. 29–45.
18   Res. 731 du 21 janvier 1992 ; Res. 748 du 31 mars 1992.

Au plan universel, on peut relever ce que l'on appelle la Charte internationale des droits de l'homme composée de la Déclaration universelle des droits de l'homme de 1948[19] et des deux Pactes de 1966 adoptés au sein des Nations Unies et qui regardent les droits civils et politiques d'une part et les droits économiques, sociaux et culturels de l'autre.

Au plan régional, il convient de mentionner la Convention européenne de sauvegarde des droits de l'homme signée à Rome le 4 novembre 1950 et complétée par cinq Protocoles additionnels ; la Convention américaine des droits de l'homme signée à San José de Costa Rica le 22 novembre 1959 et enfin la Charte africaine des droits de l'homme et des peuples qui a été élaborée sous les auspices de l'OUA et qui fut adoptée par acclamation le 28 juin 1981 par la Conférence au Sommet des Chefs d'Etat et de Gouvernement réunis à Nairobi (Kenya). La Charte africaine est entrée en vigueur le 21 octobre 1986.

A côté des normes écrites en matière de droits de l'homme qui proviennent de sources prolifiques (résolutions, déclarations et conventions) n'ayant pas toutes la même portée juridique, il convient de relever la consécration de l'implantation coutumière des différents instruments relatifs aux droits de l'homme qui est un point fondamental du droit des gens.

La jurisprudence de la Cour internationale de justice et celle du Tribunal international du droit de la mer le montrent assez.[20] Comme on le voit, les règles relatives aux droits de l'homme sont d'origines diverses. Elles sont d'inégale force juridique et diffèrent quant à leurs domaines d'application et leur portée. Elles sont également différentes quant à leurs bénéficiaires et à leurs destinataires.

Mais si on passe du plan de la pensée juridique à celui de la réalisation, celui de la mise en œuvre, on s'aperçoit que les aspérités sont tenaces. Les droits de l'homme sont en effet l'objet de « travaux pratiques » pour ne pas dire plus. C'est qu'il existe un certain nombre de facteurs limitant l'épanouissement des droits de l'homme.

D'abord, le caractère totalitaire de nombre de régimes politiques. Ces dictatures honteuses qui se nourrissent de sang et de silence et dont notre continent fournit des exemples sinistres.

---

19   *Op. cit.* (note 8).

20   Voir Affaire du Détroit de Corfou (1949) ; Affaire du crime de génocide (1950) ; Affaire de la Barcelona Traction (1970, § 33 et 34) ; Affaire de la Namibie (1971, § 131) ; Affaire des otages américains à Téhéran (1980, § 91) ; Affaire Lagrand (1999) ; Affaire Avena et autres ressortissants mexicains (2004). En ce qui concerne le Tribunal International du Droit de la Mer, voir les 9 Affaires de prompte mainlevée et l'Affaire Louisa (2013). Voir B. Vukas, « Droit de la mer et droits de l'homme », in *The Law of the Sea, Selected Writings*, Martinus Nijhoff Publishers, 2004, pp. 71–79.

Ensuite, le sous-développement économique et les dirigeants corrompus qui limitent certains droits de la deuxième génération : droit au travail, à la santé, à l'éducation.

Après, la diversité des civilisations et des contextes culturels qui a tendance à remettre en cause le caractère universel des droits de l'homme dans un « monde fini » (Valéry), en suscitant des modes d'allégeance soustraite au contrôle étatique.

Enfin, il y a la structure internationale avec « sa pierre d'angle qui semble résister au temps »[21] et qui se nomme souveraineté avec son corollaire : le principe de non-ingérence dans les affaires intérieures d'un Etat.[22] C'est que depuis qu'il existe cet « artifice de menuiserie » que l'on appelle trône et des hommes pour s'y installer, l'homme lui-même n'a plus où se mettre. Autrement dit, l'homme est en exil dans la société des Etats.

Ces facteurs rendent impossible le contrôle de l'exécution des obligations des Etats. C'est pourquoi la lutte pour la protection des droits de l'homme enregistre de nouvelles pratiques. Et les violations des droits de l'homme suscitent la réaction d'Etats – démarches individuelles ou collectives ; expression de la désapprobation ; gestes significatifs ; suspension de l'aide – *etc.*, d'organisations internationales : commissions d'enquête, rapports, *etc.*, et/ou des organisations non gouvernementales.

Ces dernières apparaissent comme les plus efficaces dans l'ordre des droits de l'homme dans la mesure où leurs actions sont multiples et multiformes et elles peuvent dissuader l'Etat le plus puissant.[23]

Cette mobilisation de la honte apparaît souvent salutaire en cas de violation des droits de l'homme. Il faut souhaiter que les citoyens dans les différents pays au monde prennent l'habitude d'exercer leur titre juridique à la plainte – rompant ainsi le mur du silence – en cas de violation de leurs droits pour faire progresser la quête perpétuelle de dignité pour les hommes qu'est le mouvement *inter*, *trans* et *intra* national pour les droits de l'homme. Alors les droits de l'homme pourront passer du stade de « machin » à celui de « machine ».

Dakar, le 7 février 2013

---

21 M. Virally, « Une pierre d'angle qui résiste au temps : avatars et pérennité de l'idée de souveraineté », in *Les relations internationales dans un monde en mutation*, HEI 50, Sijthoff, Leiden, 1977, pp. 179–196.
22 Article 2 paragraphe 7 de la Charte des Nations Unies.
23 Il suffit de penser à *Amnesty International* ou *Human Rights Watch*.

CHAPTER 32

Sovereignty of State *v.* Protection of Persons in the Case of Disasters

*Ernest Petrič**

I   Introduction[1]

It is an honour to contribute to the *Liber Amicorum* in honour of Professor Budislav Vukas, an outstanding international lawyer who is respected not only in the area of the former Federal Socialist Republic of Yugoslavia but around the world. The friendly and fruitful academic cooperation on the inter-university level and within the then Yugoslav Association for International Law is one of my pleasant and encouraging memories.

In choosing the topic of my short contribution I decided to touch upon a topic – protection of persons in the event of disasters – also close to Professor Vukas. As a member of the most respected International Law Institute (*Institut de Droit International*; IDI) he contributed decisively, as Special Rapporteur, to this very topic. The Institute's Report[2] has been considered and used with great interest and attention in the work of the International Law Commission (ILC), the United Nations body of experts in international law, a member of which I

---

*   Professor of International Law and International Relations; Member and former Chairman of the International Law Commission; Member of the Advisory Committee on Nominations of Judges of the International Criminal Court; Member and Former President of the Constitutional Court of the Republic of Slovenia; Former Ambassador.
1   This essay was, as requested, finalized by March 2013. The International Law Commission (ILC), at its 66th session in 2013 and at its 67th session in 2014, concluded the drafting and first reading of all the articles of the draft convention on 'Protection of Persons in Event of Disaster' and presented it for comments to the 6th Committee of the UN General Assembly. The articles added at the 66th and 67th session of the International Law Commission are not relevant concerning the topic of this essay. However, there have been changes in the numeration of the draft articles. Thus, the draft articles dealt with in the essay (Articles 1, 2, 5, 9, 10, 11 and 12) are now Articles 1, 2, 8, 12, 13, 14 and 16 of the draft convention, adopted at the 3238th and 3239th meetings of the ILC in 2014; the new numbers of the articles are indicated in square brackets.
2   See "Humanitarian Assistance", Resolution, Institut de Droit International, 16th Commission (Bruges, 2 November 2003), *Annuaire de'l Institut de Droit International*, 71 (2004).

have been since 2007. Within the ILC's mandate to "progressively develop and codify"³ international law, the topic 'Protection of Persons in the Event of Disasters'⁴ has been on its agenda since 2007.

II   Disasters – Concern to International Community

The topic 'Protection of Persons in the Event of Disasters' has enjoyed generally widespread support in the 6th Committee of the UN General Assembly (GA) since it was introduced into the programme of the ILC.⁵ Disasters have been and still are frequent in all parts of the world, taking human lives, causing human suffering and huge damage to property, infrastructure and also environment. Disasters often lead to suffering and destruction across several States and may have an impact on international relations as well as on national and international security.

Without diving into substantial humanitarian and material aspects of problems associated with disasters, let me only as illustrations mention some catastrophic disasters in recent decades which have harmed millions of people and caused widespread suffering and destruction: the Chernobyl nuclear disaster in 1986, catastrophic earthquakes in Iran, China, Peru, Japan, Haiti, costing tens of thousands of lives, floods in Myanmar, hurricane 'Katrina' in the Gulf coast of the USA, and hundreds of other disasters every year causing death and destruction. The *tsunami* of 26 December 2004 alone killed approximately 226,000 people in 12 States, and left close to 2 million people affected in one single day. According to the Memorandum by the ILC Secretariat, in a single year, 2006, "there were 427 natural disasters affecting approximately 143 million people and resulting in over 23,000 deaths worldwide".⁶ According to the Centre for Research on the Epidemiology of Disasters (CRED)⁷ data, the earthquake in

---

3   Charter of the UN, Article 13, and the Statute, Article 1, para. 1: "The International Law Commission shall have for its object the promotion of the progressive development of international law and its codification."; see also E. Petrič, "Komisija za mednarodno pravo med *de lege lata* in *de lege ferenda*" ["International Law Commission between *de lege lata* and *de lege ferenda*"], in: *Zbornik znanstvenih razprav ob 60. obletnici Komisije Združenih narodov za mednarodno pravo* (eds. S. Drenik *et al.*), Ljubljana, 2008, pp. 11–20.

4   For the adoption of this topic into the ILC's programme see: Preliminary report on the protection of persons in the event of disasters (E. Valencia-Ospina, Special Rapporteur), A/CN.4/598, paras. 1–9.

5   See summaries of UN Member States comments presented in the 6th Committee of GA; Reports of the ILC of its 60th, 61st, 62nd and 63rd session in GA Official Records, Supplements A/63/10, A/64/10, A/65/10 and A/66/10.

6   A/CN.4/590, para. 2.

7   CRED data available at: <http://www.cred.be>.

China on 12 May 2008 killed 88,000 and affected close to 50 million people, whereas, according to the data of CRED, the earthquake in China in July 1976 killed 242,000 people; the flood on 15 June 2007 in China affected 105 million people. In addition, such disasters, natural as well as man-made such as Chernobyl, cause huge economic damage at the level of an individual State. The flood in Thailand on 5 August 2011 caused 40 billion US dollars' worth of damage, the flood in the USA on 9 June 2008 10 billion US dollars, the flood in Germany on 11 August 2002 over 11 billion US dollars, *etc.* In 2010 which was 'bad' as far as natural catastrophes are concerned, 385 natural disasters killed more than 297,000 people worldwide, affected over 217 million others and caused nearly 124 billion US dollars' worth of economic damage. In this very year alone Haiti suffered 222,570 fatalities due to the 12 January earthquake. Since I was present on the site and personally involved in humanitarian efforts on the spot, let me also mention the 'great famine' in Ethiopia in the years 1984–1986, taking around one million lives, and the famine in the same country ten years earlier also costing close to a million lives. Due to their effects, disasters[8] can be compared to armed conflicts and should in principle be given the same attention by the international community and in international law.

Having in mind the catastrophic dimensions and also frequency of disasters it is no surprise that these phenomena and their effects are within the focus of the international community, international organizations, NGOs and of course individual States.

III   Need for Legal Regulation

Since disasters[9] often affect several States, it is understandable that international law may be involved. But even more so because, based on human solidarity, it is usual in the contemporary world that even in the event of a disaster affecting only a single State other States, international organizations, as well as NGOs will

---

8   On disasters see also D. Alexander, *Natural Disasters*, London, 1993; D. Caron, C. Leben (eds.), *The International Aspects of Natural and Industrial Catastrophes*, The Hague, 2001.

9   In the case of ILC project 'Protection of persons in event of disasters' it was agreed in the Commission from the start of its work, that both natural and man-made disasters should be covered within the definition of disaster, excluding only armed conflicts, since in international law they are regulated under a specific regime of international humanitarian law as *lex specialis* and by *ius in bello* generally. See the summary of the debate in the ILC in Report of the ILC, 60th session (2008), GA Official Records, Suppl. No 10 (A/63/10), paras. 232–237; so the holistic approach is adopted in the definition of disaster (in draft Article 3); see the draft Article and commentary to it in Report of the ILC, 62nd session (2010), GA Official Records, Suppl. No 10 (A/65/10), para. 331.

offer and provide assistance to the affected State. The provision of assistance by foreign providers requires legal regulation, on both the international and national levels. Both the legal framework of relations between the affected State and the providers of assistance (such as the respect for sovereignty of the affected State, basic rights and duties of both the affected and assisting States, in the process of requesting, offering and delivering assistance, the rights of persons in need, particularly the respect for their human dignity and human rights) as well as numerous practical aspects of the process of providing assistance (waiving of legal and practical obstacles so that the assistance can promptly reach the affected persons, waiving of customs and border crossing rules, *etc.*) require legal regulation[10] to enable the assistance to be effective, transparent and performed solely in the interest of the affected persons, their rights and needs. In spite of the existence of both legal and programmatic, formally non-binding rules regulating various specific and practical aspects of cooperation and assistance in case of disasters (*i.e.* assistance in telecommunications in the case of disasters; nuclear disasters, *etc.*), the ILC Secretariat in its comprehensive Memorandum properly notes, "The increasing involvement of the international community in the provision of such assistance has given rise to a need for enhanced legal regulation. Nonetheless, despite the large proportions and international nature of some disasters, the international law regulating activities in relation to them remains relatively underdeveloped. Currently no universal convention comprehensively governing all the main aspects of disaster relief – including prevention, response and protection – exists".[11] The lack of comprehensive regulation of this important topic – protection of persons in the event of disasters – in general international law appears to be the *raison d'être* for this topic to be included in the ILC programme of progressive development and codification of international law, and for the general support it enjoys among States, as is evident from their statements in the 6th Committee of the GA.

IV International Legal Roots of the Protection of Persons in the Event of Disasters

The purpose of international activities and consequently of legal instruments regulating these activities should *sine dubio* be to help, protect and rehabilitate victims of disasters, and protect their human dignity, their lives, their health, to

---

10 For the broad scope of topics which in the context of international assistance need to be legally regulated see Protection of persons in the event of disasters, Memorandum by the Secretariat, ILC 60th session (2008), A/CN.4/590.
11 *Ibid.*, para. 3.

supply them with food, medicine, shelter *etc*. Using the words of draft Article 2,[12] defining the purpose of the ILC's progressive development and codification endeavour of this topic the "purpose...is to facilitate an adequate and effective response to disasters that meets the essential needs of the persons concerned, with full respect for their rights."[13] The purpose of codification and progressive development of international law undertaken by the ILC concerning this topic is the protection of people affected by disasters, the delivery to them of adequate, effective and prompt assistance, thus meeting their urgent basic needs and respecting their basic human rights, and upholding their human dignity. The human person and her inherent dignity are, and should be, at the centre of any international legal instrument concerning protection of persons in the event of disasters.

Given the above considerations, the international legal roots of protection of persons in the event of disasters are to be found in those areas of international law, treaties and customary law, as well as in the instruments of soft international law, whose common *raison d'être*, the basic aim, is protection of the person, her human dignity, her human rights. Such entails regulation in international humanitarian law, in human rights law, in legal regulations of international cooperation and assistance in the case of specific activities, as much as they exist in regional and sub-regional arrangements regulating different aspects of cooperation and assistance in case of disasters or disaster-related activities, and in programmatic international instruments, resolutions of the UN GA and other international organizations, in sets of principles and rules established by NGOs, the International Federation of Red Cross and Red Crescent Societies (IFRC) in particular, and scientific associations like IDI, the International Law Association (ILA), *etc*. Actually, the entire vast body of principles and rules reflecting the modern development of humanity since the 19th century and correspondingly growing *opinio juris* is that in any disaster, including armed conflict, a human person should not be denied her human dignity and human rights. Respect for the dignity of the human person in all situations, respect for humanity and solidarity, can be considered as the common *telos* of the contemporary and even more so of the future world.

Similarly, the ILC and the Special Rapporteur on this topic, Mr Eduardo Valencia-Ospina, consider as sources of "present day international disaster protection and assistance law" those parts of international law whose imminent purpose and goal is to protect the human person and single out "international

---

12 See draft Article 2 (and commentary) in Report of the ILC, 62nd session (2010), GA Official Records, Suppl. No. 10 (A/65/10), para. 331, p. 325.

13 *Ibid*.

humanitarian law, international human rights law and international law on refugees and internally displaced persons."[14]

V Main Sources of Law concerning the Protection of Persons in the Event of Disasters

Without any intention of adding to the comprehensive presentation of principles of international law relevant to our topic elaborated by the ILC Secretariat[15] and sources indicated by the Special Rapporteur,[16] it is necessary to single out and pay attention to those of them which are particularly significant to the core problem of this paper dealing with the relationship between sovereignty of States and the protection of persons in the event of disasters. Consequently, we are limiting ourselves to those instruments of both international hard and soft law relevant to the very problem of this paper, the 'tension' between the sovereignty of States and the protection of persons.

Within international humanitarian law the Martens Clause should be considered of great importance also for the protection of persons in the event of disasters. It is the historic source of the contemporary generally recognized principle of humanity. According to this principle in any situation, in armed conflicts and in peace, including of course humanitarian needs in case of disasters, States should respect the principles of humanity and of the civilized treatment of human persons. Although this basic humanitarian principle was originally promulgated within the law of war (*ius in bello*), the principle of humanity is nowadays a "long-standing principle in international law"[17] and "guides the international legal system both in war and in peace."[18] The basic importance and validity of the principle of humanity also in peace was confirmed by the International Court of Justice (ICJ) as early as in 1949 in the Corfu Channel case,[19] and again in the Military and Paramilitary Activities in and against Nicaragua case.[20]

---

14   See above, note 4, para. 21.
15   See above, note 10, paras. 11–24.
16   See above, note 4, paras. 21–42.
17   See the Third report on the protection of persons in the event of disaster (Spec. Rap. E. Valencia-Ospina), A/CN.4/629, para. 37.
18   *Ibid.*, para. 41.
19   "Such obligations are based on certain general and well-recognized principles, namely: elementary considerations of humanity, even more exacting in peace than in war"; Corfu Channel case, Judgement of 9 April, *ICJ Reports 1949*, para. 22.
20   "[T]hey are rules which...reflect...elementary considerations of humanity"; Military and Paramilitary Activities in and against Nicaragua, Judgement of 26 June 1986, *ICJ Reports 1986*, para. 113.

The principle of humanity provides the "common ground shared by international humanitarian law and the law of human rights".[21] The principle of humanity is the basis for both main branches of international law protecting the human person and her inherent dignity, humanitarian law and the law of human rights. These two bodies of international law are both the result of the humanization of society in the last century and both reflect the principle of humanity.

Both, humanitarian law and human rights law, interrelated in their fundamental function of preventing and stopping human suffering, violations of human dignity and human rights in peace and in armed conflicts are the fence, the line of protection by international law of persons, their dignity and human rights. This protective line should be respected by States also in the event of disasters which expose persons to suffering, endanger their human rights and their human dignity. States and other actors should always act according to the principle of humanity. The human dignity is "the core principle that informs and underpins international human rights law... The principle of respect of human dignity undergirds international human rights instruments and has been interpreted as providing the ultimate foundation of human rights law."[22] One could not but agree with this guiding philosophy, reflecting the contemporary developments in international law,[23] to be applied also in the ILC's endeavour to codify and progressively develop in international law the protection of persons in the event of disasters.[24]

VI   Sovereignty in the Context of the Protection of Persons in the Event of Disasters

Sovereignty and its corollary principle of non-intervention are *sine dubio* valid fundamental principles of international law based on the UN Charter and

---

21   *Ibid.*, para. 43.
22   See Report of the ILC, 63rd session (2011), GA Official Records, Suppl. No. 10 (A/66/10), para. 289.
23   On human dignity as a principle of international law based on the UN Charter see R. Wolfrum, "Preamble", in: *The Charter of the United Nations. A Commentary* (eds. B. Simma et al.), Vol. I, 2nd edn., Oxford, 2002, pp. 33–37; O. Schachter, "Human Dignity as a Normative Concept", *American Journal of International Law*, 11 (1983), p. 849.
24   See the Preliminary report, note 4, para. 50: "The fundamental tenet of international humanitarian law and international human rights law applicable in the event of disasters is the principle of humanity which underpins all humanitarian action."

other universal and regional international instruments,[25] and as such of the utmost importance for conducting international relations. Since the Congress of Westphalia in the 17th century, the international community has been based on the principle of the sovereign equality of States. It is confirmed by several ICJ decisions.[26]

Like any other legal principle, the principle of sovereignty of States is also a dynamic fundamental principle of international law. As such (*per se*) it is undisputed by State practice, by the judiciary and by doctrine. However, its substance and scope are dynamic, reflecting the changes in society, changes in values and of moral and legal principles. No legal principle functions in isolation but in relationship and in balance with other legal principles. In the case of the protection of persons in the event of disasters the principle of sovereignty and its corollary, the principle of non-interference, have to be related to the principle of humanity and the protection of human rights. Through the centuries the Westphalian concept of sovereignty has changed in its substance. Sovereignty today is no longer just the legal guardian of States' supremacy in their domestic affairs and their independence (non-interference), but entails also the responsibility to ensure the security and wellbeing of their population, including the protection of their human rights. Besides, in their common interest and in the interest of their populations, States have, according to their proper will (*i.e.* according to their sovereignty), accepted limitations on their sovereignty, in particular limitations and obligations concerning the respect and protection of human rights.

Sovereignty is in contemporary international law neither absolute nor unlimited. To claim unlimited, absolute sovereignty would mean to go back in time more than a century and to ignore all changes that have taken place in the international community and in international law. In fact, the Permanent Court of International Justice (PCIJ) in S.S. Wimbledon already declined "to see in the conclusion of any Treaty by which a State undertakes to perform or refrain from performing a particular act an abandonment of its sovereignty", the right of entering into international engagements is an attribute of State sovereignty.[27]

No doubt, in recent decades the States have, according to their sovereignty, entered into international legal obligation in many spheres of life, many of those obligations reflecting the principle of humanity and the protection of

---

25 See Declaration on Principles of International Law Concerning Friendly Relations and cooperation among States in accordance with the Charter of the UN, Annex to GA Resolution 2625 (XXV).

26 See Corfu Channel case, *ICJ Reports 1949*; Military and Paramilitary Activities in and against Nicaragua case, *ICJ Reports 1986*.

27 See S.S. Wimbledon case, *PCIJ Series A*, No. 1 (1923), para. 35.

human rights. States have not waived their sovereignty but accepted profound and far reaching limitations of it. It might be said that State sovereignty is profoundly transforming and is becoming more a responsibility than just an exclusive right of the State. Nothing more than the acceptance within the UN of the concept of the principle of 'Responsibility to Protect' (R2P), though its legal character is still disputed, could be a better indication of the dynamic character of the principle of sovereignty.

The Special Rapporteur Eduardo Valencia-Ospina is right in stating that principles of sovereignty and non-intervention must be considered in the light of the responsibilities and obligations of States. States may owe obligations to other States or to individuals within their territory. Within the topic of 'Protection of persons in the event of disasters' "particular attention should be paid to the duties of States under international human rights instruments and customary international human rights law to provide protection to those persons within their territory."[28]

In many spheres of international law 'tension' may exist between the principle of sovereignty and other principles and obligations under international law. In the case of the protection of persons in the event of disaster the Special Rapporteur correctly notes that "tension is created between...the principles of sovereignty of States and of non-intervention and...international human rights law," as well as tension "between the rights and obligations of the assisting actor and those of the State affected by a disaster."[29] To codify a useful and for the majority of States acceptable international instrument (draft convention) in which these 'tensions' are to be overcome, the establishing of a proper balance reflecting the realities in contemporary human society and in the international community, reflecting the co-existence of the core principle of sovereignty on the one hand and the existence of the principle of humanity and protection of human rights on the other, is the condition *sine qua non*.

This balance is indicated *inter alia* by the ICJ in the Nicaragua *v.* US case. The Court stated explicitly that "the provision of strictly humanitarian aid to persons or forces in another country...cannot be regarded as unlawful intervention or as in any other way contrary to international law."[30]

There are several instruments establishing the balance between the principle of State sovereignty and human rights in the context of disasters: the balance

---

28 Fourth report on the protection of persons in the event of disaster (Spec. Rapporteur E. Valencia-Ospina), A/CN.4/643.
29 See above, note 4, paras. 54–55.
30 See Military and Paramilitary Activities in and against Nicaragua, Judgement of 26 June 1986, para. 242.

between a State's sovereign right (primary responsibility) to act, direct and control the activities to cope with a disaster, including its right to accept or to refuse foreign assistance – and its primary duty to protect the persons affected. Let us mention, since the Rapporteur was B. Vukas, the Resolution adopted by the IDI at its session in Bruges (2003):[31]

1. States and organizations have the right to offer humanitarian assistance to the affected State. Such an offer shall not be considered unlawful interference in the internal affairs of the affected State, to the extent that it has an exclusively humanitarian character.
2. States and organizations have the right to provide humanitarian assistance to victims in the affected States, subject to the consent of these States.

VII The Balance between Sovereignty and the Protection of Persons

Before turning to analyse the corresponding draft Articles[32] from the point of view of the relationship ('tension') between the principle of the sovereignty of States and the protection (rights) of persons affected in the event of a disaster some general remarks should be made. After extensive and often contradictory debates since 2007[33] the Special Rapporteur and the Commission have attempted to establish the necessary balance among the interests (safeguards) of States resulting from upholding their sovereignty and non-interference, and the protection of persons, *i.e.* an approach similar to many past codifications in the sphere of human rights, humanitarian law, protection of refugees, displaced persons, *etc*. This approach could be identified as a 'triangle' approach since we are dealing with a triangular relationship.[34] In the triangle the base line is the relationship between States. In our case of the protection of persons

---

31 See above, note 2, p. 262.
32 See the draft Articles and commentaries to them as provisionally adopted by the Commission and being transferred to the GA 6th Commission in Report of the ILC, 62nd session, GA Official Records, Suppl. 10, A/64/10, para. 331 (draft Articles 1–5), and in Report of the ILC, 63rd session, GA Official Records, Suppl. 10, A/66/10, para. 289 (draft Articles 6–11).
33 At its 60th (2008), 61st (2009), 62nd (2010), 63rd (2011) sessions; see the Reports of the Commission (A/63/10; A/64/10; A/65/10; A/66/10).
34 The Special Rapporteur similarly speaks of 'two different axes'. These are the rights and obligations of States in relation to one another and the rights and duties of them to protect persons affected by disaster.

in the event of disaster this is the relationship between the affected State and the assisting State (or States), or any other assisting entity, *i.e.* international organizations or NGOs. This is a horizontal relationship between affected State and assisting actors in which the respect for sovereignty and non-interference is crucial, and includes respect for the sovereignty of States on both sides, of the affected State and assisting States. This relationship, the mutual rights and obligations between the affected State and assisting States and other actors involved in assistance, this base line of the 'triangle' should be regulated strictly in accordance with the principle of sovereignty and non-interference.

Concerning disasters this relationship is, nevertheless, established and regulated by international law with a clear purpose: to protect according to the principle of humanity the persons affected by disaster; to protect their lives, human dignity, their human rights; to assure prompt and effective access to and delivery of assistance to them to alleviate their suffering. In this noble activity, based on respect of humanity and solidarity and the protection of human rights, the interests of the affected State and assisting State meet. Thus the protection of persons in the event of disasters is the top of the 'triangle'; it is the *raison d'être* also for the horizontal relationship established and regulated for the sole purpose of protecting persons affected by disaster. This international legal framework – sovereign States among themselves establish legal obligations to protect and assure the protection and rights of human persons – is common in contemporary international law. States, reflecting contemporary values of humanity, limit their sovereignty, transform it into obligations and duties for another beneficiary, for the human person. This is the case, as already mentioned, in particular in the protection of human rights and the prevention of any discrimination, in the case of humanitarian law, refugee law, *etc.*, including the courageous step made by the GA in introducing the concept of R2P.

While in the relationship between the affected State and assisting States and other assisting entities the protective dimensions of sovereignty (non-interference, supremacy, independence) are crucial, in the relationship of both the affected State and assisting States and other assisting entities to the affected persons sovereignty entails responsibility, the duty of the affected State and of the assisting States and other assisting entities based on the principle of humanity to protect the persons who are victims of disasters.

At the apex of the 'triangle' – the protection of persons – the endeavours and interests of the affected State and assisting States and other assisting entities should meet. The affected State and the assisting entities must both act in all assistance activities in *bona fides* solely in the interest of persons affected by the disaster.

If the lines of the 'triangle' – the horizontal line between the affected State and assisting entities, the side line between the affected State and its persons affected by disaster, and the side line between the assisting entity and the affected persons – function with the sole common purpose of protecting the affected persons, *i.e.* if both the affected State and assisting entities act in *bona fides*, the conflict of respect for the principle of sovereignty and non-interference, on the one side, and respect for the principle of humanity and respect for human rights law, on the other, does not occur. However, in the case of the *mala fides* attitude of either the affected State or assisting States or other assisting entities, the 'tension' between sovereignty and the protection of persons becomes acute. The assisting entities may, besides offering and providing assistance, have other vested interests by which they might infringe the sovereignty of the affected State and interfere in its internal affairs. The affected State might as well for whatever reason (by its negligence and ignorance of the disaster and its effects; to discriminate against part of its population *etc.*), by its passivity or even actively, prevent prompt and effective assistance from reaching persons affected by disaster. Both the affected State and assisting entities may act in *mala fides*, although this is exceptional and rare. Such a *mala fides* attitude is in fact a misuse of either the principle of sovereignty and non-interference or of the principle of humanity and duty to protect the affected persons, their human dignity and their human rights. The ILC should, by drafting the Articles on the protection of persons in the event of disaster, establish the proper balance between these principles to enable the affected State and assisting entities to cope effectively with disaster and its consequences – in the sole interest of protecting persons affected by a disaster.

VIII   Draft Articles between Sovereignty and Protection

Not all Articles provisionally adopted by the ILC are relevant from the point of view of the relationship between sovereignty and the protection of persons. Those draft Articles,[35] in which during the drafting process the 'tension' we spoke about did not appear, are not within the scope of our interest. In drafting those Articles, the Commission did not face the problem of balance between

---

35   These are draft Article 2 (Purpose), draft Article 3 (Definition of disaster), draft Article 4 (Relationship with international humanitarian law), draft Article 6 (Humanitarian principles in disaster response), draft Article 7 (Human dignity), draft Article 8 (Human rights); see the Articles and commentaries in Report of ILC, 62nd session, GA Official Records, Suppl. No. 10 (A/65/10), para. 331 (Articles 1–5) and in the Report of ILC, 63rd session, GA Official Records, Suppl. No. 10 (A/66/10), para. 288.

the sovereignty of the State and the protection of persons. The discussions in the Commission and their provisional drafting did not touch upon the problem of respect of sovereignty. Of course, due to their forming one part of the whole draft, they influence other draft Articles indirectly. Undoubtedly, the principles established in draft Article 6 [7] (humanity, neutrality, impartiality, and non-discrimination in accordance with which the responses to disasters shall take place) have an important impact on all Articles of the draft. Similarly, Article 7 [5] establishing the obligation of States and other entities involved in responding to disaster to respect and protect the "inherent dignity of the human person" decisively marks more or less all of the draft and is a guiding principle to all involved in the process of response to disasters. Likewise Article 8 [6], stipulating that the human rights of persons affected by disasters should be respected, reconfirms the already existing obligation of all actors in international relations to respect human rights, in particular of those most vulnerable as is the case of persons affected by disaster.

Draft Articles which are 'contaminated' by the 'tension' between the sovereignty of the State and non-intervention, and protection of persons, based on the principles of humanity and respect for human dignity are: draft Article 1 [1] (Scope), Article 5 [8] (Duty to cooperate), Article 9 [12] (Role of the affected State), Article 10 [13] (Duty of the affected State to seek assistance) and Article 11 [14] (Consent of the affected State to external assistance). These Articles have been intensely debated in the Commission, but also in the GA 6th Committee, particularly from the point of view of how far the prerogatives (rights and obligations) of the affected sovereign State, *i.e.* its sovereignty, might be limited in the event of disasters, that is how far and under what conditions the sovereign State is bound to accept the involvement of the assisting actors in response to disaster. To put it simply, how far in the event of a disaster and in response to it to protect affected persons, the sovereignty of the affected State could be subjected to obligations and duties limiting its free action.

IX   Scope (Article 1) [1] and Purpose (Article 2) [2]

Draft Article 1 [1] as provisionally adopted by the Commission after it was debated extensively in the Commission and also commented on by the States in the GA 6th Committee is short and clear.[36] In fact it reproduces the title of this topic under the ILC ('Protection of Persons in Event of Disasters'). The

---

36   Draft Article 1 (Scope): "The present draft Articles apply to the protection of persons in the event of disasters", Report of ILC 62nd session, GA Official Records, Suppl. 10, A/64/10, para. 331.

original draft Article 1 [1] (Scope) as it was originally proposed[37] to the Commission by the Special Rapporteur was more extensive and built around his 'two axes' approach. It was built on the original reasoning by the Special Rapporteur and several members of the Commission, as well as several States in the GA 6th Committee, that the most appropriate, having in mind progressive development of international law, would be the 'rights-based' approach combined with the 'needs', whereby it should be stipulated clearly enough that it is "for States to ensure the realisation of the rights of persons."[38] While proposing the original draft Article 1 [1] to the Commission, the Special Rapporteur clearly indicated, based also on the decisions of the ICJ,[39] the dual nature of the protection of persons in the event of disasters.

This dual character entails that "firstly, rights and obligations of States in relations to one another may be discussed in order to define at a later stage the *rights and obligations of States* in relation to persons in need to protection" (emphasis by E.P.).[40] As mentioned above, in the case of the protection of persons in the event of disasters, the 'triangle' approach, in fact the same as the 'two axes' approach, would mean that the 'scope' of the future international legal instrument (Convention) should be framed around the mutual rights and obligations of the States (*i.e.* affected State and assisting States and other assisting entities) and obligations of them both (the affected State and the assisting States and other assisting entities) regarding the rights of the persons in need of protection. This approach should put the persons and their protection, including protection of their human rights, at the centre of the whole codification enterprise and should oblige the affected State, but also the assisting States and other assisting entities, to act solely for the benefit of persons in need and to protect their human rights.

The original 'rights-based' approach was exposed to criticism and reservations by several members of the Commission in its drafting committee. It was agreed that in Article 1 [1] (Scope) the reference to "rights" was to be deleted. The "needs" aspect, which was in the originally proposed Article 1 [1] combined with "rights" in an obligatory manner ("realisation of the right of persons...

---

37 See Second report on the protection of persons in the event of disasters (Spec. Rap. E. Valencia-Ospina), A/CN. 4/615, para. 30: "The present draft Articles apply to the protection of persons in the event of disasters, in order for States to ensure the realisation of the rights of persons in such an event, by providing an adequate and effective response to their needs in all phases of a disaster."
38 See the text of the original draft Article, note 37.
39 Second report, *ibid.*, paras. 19–30.
40 Second report, *ibid.*, para. 27.

providing an adequate and effective response to their needs") is now dealt with separately (Article 2) [2],[41] but in a less binding manner ("facilitate" instead of "providing"; "facilitate...with full respect" instead of "ensure the realisation of the rights of persons"). Evidently, the Commission hesitated to make a bolder step in the progressive development of international law, which would nevertheless be sufficiently based on the ICJ decisions as explained by the Special Rapporteur in his Preliminary and Second reports.[42] However, even in the adopted Articles 1 [1] (Scope) and 2 [2] (Purpose) it is stipulated clearly enough that both the "scope" and "purpose" of this codification (and progressive development) are devoted to "protection of persons in the event of disasters" as also confirmed by its title. This attempt at codification by the ILC is meant to guarantee that the persons affected by disaster will be assured prompt, adequate and effective assistance. This should be the primary goal of the codification and progressive development of 'Protection of persons in event of disaster', and not a reconfirmation or repetition of the nevertheless undisputed right of States to sovereignty and its corollary principle of non-intervention. In this particular codification and progressive development of international law the sovereignty of States should not be primarily involved as a right but as a responsibility of the sovereign States, of both the affected ones and those ready to assist, to protect persons in the event of disasters.

x Duty to Cooperate (Article 5) [8]

The draft Article 5 [8],[43] as provisionally adopted by the Commission, is close in its substance and its wording to the original draft proposed by the Special Rapporteur in his Second report.[44]

Prima facie, there does not appear to be any significant substantive difference between the two drafts. It seems, however, that the final draft provisionally

---

41   See the draft Article 2, Report of the ILC, 62nd session, GA Official Records, Suppl. No. 10 (A/65/10), para. 331.
42   A/CN.4/598 and A/CN.4/615.
43   Draft Article 5 (Duty to cooperate): "In accordance with the present draft articles States shall, as appropriate, cooperate among themselves, and with the United Nations and other competent intergovernmental organizations, the International Federation of the Red Cross and Red Crescent Societies and the International Committee of the Red Cross and with relevant non-governmental organizations," Report of the ILC, 62nd session, GA Official Records, Suppl. 10, A/64/10, para. 331.
44   The original draft Article 3 (Duty to cooperate), proposed by the Special Rapporteur, see Second report, cited above in note 37, para. 70.

adopted as draft Article 5 [8] is a step backwards rather than forwards, reflecting the comments made by the delegates in the GA 6th Committee and by some members of the Commission.

Worries were expressed regarding the relationship between the duty to cooperate and the obligation of the affected State to accept the disaster relief. This is a rather odd worry since it is very clear that the 'duty to cooperate' cannot entail the duty to accept anything which is not part of cooperation. In any case, the duty to cooperate is a well-established principle of international law, based primarily on the Charter (Articles 1(3), 55, and 56), and confirmed in a set of international instruments, including the Declaration on Principles of International Law concerning Friendly Relations and Cooperation among States in accordance with the Charter of the United Nations.[45]

The duty to cooperate is closely related to the principle of solidarity; it is actually an expression of the latter. In particularly in the topic at hand – protection of persons in the event of disasters – cooperation is a means to enable solidarity to be achieved. It would be useful if in this particular codification and progressive development of international law cooperation were explicitly bound to the principle of solidarity, either in one of the Articles or at least in the commentaries. The duty to cooperate in this particular topic should be understood and consequently stipulated in the draft as an obligation to cooperate to achieve the aim of the cooperation – the protection of persons in the event of disasters. The general international law principle of the duty to cooperate does not need to be reconfirmed unless it is put in the direct context of the specific topic. Thus, "cooperation" in the draft Article 5 [8] means cooperation with the purpose of achieving the protection of persons in the event of disasters.

Cooperation is an expression of the free will of those who cooperate. Duty to cooperate can by no legal logic be understood as interfering with the sovereignty of the affected as well as of the assisting States. They both are to cooperate based on their free will, within the framework of international law and with the aim of achieving the purpose of the cooperation. Cooperation can also not be understood as an interference in the domestic affairs of either the affected or assisting State since 'cooperation' presupposes that the cooperative activities are agreed and performed according to the agreement achieved to enable the solidarity to be realized. The duty to cooperate in our case entails that neither the affected State nor other States can ignore the disaster and its consequences and turn their back on solidarity and on their duty to

---

45   GA Res. 2625 (XXV).

cooperate in providing prompt, effective and adequate assistance to the victims of a disaster.

If we compare the two draft Articles, it cannot be overlooked that the former draft Article 3 as originally proposed by the Special Rapporteur puts 'duty to cooperate' into a direct relationship with the purpose of this codification enterprise ("for the purposes"), which is more appropriate. The draft Article 5 [8] as provisionally adopted by the Commission misses this important and logical link with the 'purpose' of cooperation. It seems that worries that the 'duty to cooperate' may infringe upon the sovereignty of the affected State and harm its primary responsibility to protect persons on its territory, its own people, from the effects of a disaster, has had a negative effect on the final draft. Finally, the affected State is the one basically interested and often also dependent on the solidarity and cooperation.

The assisting States and other assisting entities, could be expected to have reservations and objections to the 'duty to cooperate'. For them, the 'duty to cooperate' entails that they are to be involved in assistance via cooperation. Since their involvement in cooperation is the expression of their solidarity according to the humane principle of solidarity, it would be useful if in this particular draft Article stipulating the duty to cooperate to protect persons in the event of disasters, or in the commentary to this Article, the explicit connection between the solidarity and duty to cooperate were to be established.

XI Role of the Affected State (Article 9) [12]

Article 9 [12] as provisionally adopted[46] by the Commission and as generally approved in the GA 6th Committee is the crucial stipulation concerning the relationship ('tension') between the principle of sovereignty and non-interference *vis-à-vis* the protection of persons in the event of disasters and their human rights. This draft Article as provisionally adopted provides a general orientation to the interpretation of other Articles in which the 'tension' between 'sovereignty' and 'protection' occurs. The basic stipulation that the affected State has "by virtue of its sovereignty the duty to ensure the protection

---

46 Draft Article 9 (Role of the affected State):
   1. The affected State, by virtue of its sovereignty, has the duty to ensure the protection of persons and provision of disaster relief and assistance on its territory.
   2. The affected State has the primary role in the direction, control, coordination and supervision of such relief and assistance.
   See Report of the ILC, 63rd session (2011), GA Official Records, Suppl. 10 (A/66/10), para. 289.

of persons" should be understood as the guiding principle in interpreting all the other Articles of the draft.

In the 'sovereignty' of the affected State its 'duty' to protect its population is also enshrined. In the words of Judge Alvarez, "sovereignty confers rights upon States and imposes obligations on them".[47] The sovereign State affected by disaster has by virtue of its sovereignty the primary role in the activities for coping with the effects of a disaster: direction, control, coordination and supervision. It has the right – as a sovereign State – to give or not to give consent to any activities of the assisting entities on its territory. It should, however, in using its sovereign prerogatives and rights act according to its duty to ensure the protection. Simply put: it should act in *bona fides*, respecting the principle of humanity, with the sole purpose of protecting persons affected by disaster. In this Article the proper balance is established, which should be kept in mind while interpreting other draft Articles of this codification and progressive development and while drafting additional Articles. In this draft Article the "two desiderata of preserving State sovereignty and protecting the affected population"[48] are properly reconciled.

The affected State's primary role in disaster response is not based only on its sovereignty, but also on the fact that it is best positioned to direct, control, coordinate and supervise activities regarding disaster response. The affected State is normally in the best position to estimate the effects of a disaster, to prioritize needs, direct the distribution of resources, *etc*. This is well reflected in para. 2 of draft Article 9 [12]. However, the primary position of the affected State by virtue of its sovereignty also entails that it bears "the ultimate responsibility of protecting disaster victims on its territory."[49]

Comparing the provisionally adopted draft Article 9 [12] to the draft Article originally proposed by the Special Rapporteur,[50] it is interesting to note that the expression "has the primary responsibility" has been redrafted into "has the duty". This is a welcome modification, since such entails a clearer and an unconditional obligation.

Let us mention that the drafting of this crucial Article was clearly influenced by the wording used in the resolution on humanitarian assistance adopted by the IDI in Bruges in 2003. According to this resolution, where B. Vukas was the Rapporteur, the affected State is also under duty "to prevent misappropriation

---

47 See Corfu Channel case, *ICJ Reports 1949*, Separate Opinion by Judge Alvarez, p. 43.
48 See Fifth report on the protection of persons in the event of disasters, (Spec. Rap. E. Valencia-Ospina), A/CN.4/652, para. 23.
49 See Third report, cited above in note 17, para. 78.
50 The original draft Article 8, see *ibid.*, para. 96.

of humanitarian assistance and other abuses".[51] This important aspect of the primary role of the affected State is unfortunately missing both in the draft Article 9 provisionally adopted by the Commission and in the commentary to it.

XII   Duty of the Affected State to Seek Assistance (Article 10) [13]

Article 10 [13] as provisionally adopted by the Commission[52] defines the duty of the affected State to "seek" assistance to the extent that a disaster "exceeds its national response capacity." Though there have been several comments insisting that 'the duty to seek assistance' runs against State sovereignty[53] and proposals were made that instead the formulation "that States should seek assistance" should be used, the original approach as proposed by the Special Rapporteur has been kept. Therefore, the provisionally adopted draft Article 10 [13] does not substantially differ from the draft Article as originally proposed by the Special Rapporteur.[54] The 'duty to seek assistance' clearly flows from the affected State's primary 'duty' to provide protection to affected persons within its territory. The affected State is by virtue of its sovereignty under the obligation to protect its population in the case of disasters. This duty reflects the protective part of the sovereignty of States and its obligations particularly in international humanitarian and human rights law. To 'seek' means that the affected State is not under an obligation either to 'request' or to 'accept' assistance. To 'seek' does not mean that an agreement shall be reached, but marks only the beginning of a process to assure the protection of persons also in situations when the affected State is not able or not willing to cope with the effects of a disaster.

The affected State is under a duty to seek assistance only to the extent to which a disaster "exceeds its national response capacity". With regard to these clear limitations, it is difficult to assert there is any contradiction ('tension') with the principle of sovereignty and non-interference. It is for the affected

---

51   Resolution adopted by the IDI on 2 Sept. 2003, Bruges, Article III, para. 1.
52   Draft Article 10 (Duty of the affected State to seek assistance): "To the extent that a disaster exceeds its national response capacity, the affected State has the duty to seek assistance from among other States, the United Nations, other competent intergovernmental organizations and relevant nongovernmental organizations, as appropriate." See Report of the ILC, 63rd session (2011), GA Official Records, Suppl. 10 (A/66/10), para. 289.
53   See the Comments provided by several countries at the 6th Committee at the 66th session of GA, 2011, e.g. Austria (A/C.6/66/SR.23, para. 23), France (A/C.6/66/SR.23, para. 38), China (A/C.6/66/SR.23, para. 42), UK (A/C.6/66/SR.23, para. 45), Russian Federation (A/C.6/66/SR.24, para. 37), etc.
54   For the original text see the Fourth report, cited above in note 28, para. 45.

State to establish whether the disaster exceeds its national response capacity or not. As a sovereign State it may at any time seek the assistance of other States, international organizations, NGOs or even of private entities. This is its sovereign prerogative. It is however by virtue of its sovereignty also under the obligation to ensure the protection of persons on its territory, their human dignity and human rights in the event of disasters. It is to be expected that the affected State will be acting in the interest of the affected population in *bona fides* and will, according to its obligations, seek assistance from abroad if necessary. A State is obliged to 'seek assistance' only when its national response capacities do not suffice to cope with the effects of a disaster. When the national response capacities are insufficient or exhausted, not to seek assistance would practically amount to abandoning the affected persons to their fate, that is to suffering, misery and eventually death.

The affected State is, naturally, the best qualified – if not in fact the only capable one – to estimate whether a disaster exceeds its national response capacities. It should do so in *bona fides* with regard primarily to the interests of the affected persons. States are by international law obliged always to act in *bona fides*. This fundamental principle common to all national legal systems as well as to international law is as crucial as the *pacta sunt servanda* principle. If an affected State which is not capable by itself of coping with a disaster does not seek assistance, it in fact abandons the affected persons. It should be recalled in this context that the UN GA acknowledged that "the abandonment of the victims of natural disasters and similar emergency situations without humanitarian assistance constitutes a threat to human life and an offence to human dignity."[55] By virtue of the provisionally adopted draft Article 10 (Duty of the affected State to seek assistance) the Commission has established the appropriate balance between the principle of State sovereignty and non-interference on the one hand and the obligation of protection of persons on the other, both concepts being *sine dubio* part of contemporary international law, both in fact based on the sovereignty of States.

XIII   Consent of the Affected State to External Assistance (Article 11) [14]

Draft Article 11 [14] as provisionally adopted by the Commission[56] is crucial for the balance of the whole project. It confirms that the consent of the affected State

---

55   GA Resolution No. 45/100 (14 December 1990), sixth preambular paragraph.
56   Article 11 (Consent of the affected State to external assistance):
   1. The provision of external assistance requires the consent of the affected State.

is the precondition for any assistance to take place, while at the same time limiting the right of the affected State "arbitrarily" to withhold consent to external assistance. This Article is particularly interesting in the context of the 'tension' between the principles of sovereignty and non-intervention and the obligation of the affected State to protect persons, their lives and their human rights in the event of disasters. Achieving the internal balance of this Article required a lot of discussion within the Commission and was subject to several comments of the 6th Committee of the UN GA. It should also be mentioned that the original draft of this Article as proposed by the Special Rapporteur[57] stipulated clearly an obligation of the affected State not to withhold its consent to external assistance arbitrarily. The final version of the draft as provisionally adopted by the Commission, however, emphasizes the consent of the affected State, which has to be acquired as a precondition for the provision of external assistance. This shift in emphasis is also reflected in the title of the draft Article 11 [14].

Undoubtedly, by virtue of its sovereignty the affected State has the right to accept or to refuse an offer of assistance. It may or may not give consent to such an offer. The consent should be the precondition for the beginning of the process of cooperation in providing assistance or the activities of the assisting entities. Given the dual nature of sovereignty in contemporary international law – as both a right and an obligation – and taking into account the consequences which could be caused to the affected persons by withholding consent, it is understandable that in giving or withholding consent the affected State should not be entirely free and should face limitations. In particular, the affected State should not withhold its consent arbitrarily whenever it was itself "unable or unwilling to provide the assistance required."[58] This logical limitation of the absolute right to give or to withhold consent was deleted in the provisionally adopted draft Article 11 [14] and is being replaced by the more general stipulation that "consent to external assistance shall not be withheld arbitrarily".[59] It should be noted that the wording as provisionally adopted by the Commission was objected to by several of the members of the Commission, suggesting that

---

2. Consent to external assistance shall not be withheld arbitrarily.
3. When an offer of assistance is extended in accordance with the present draft articles, the affected State shall, whenever possible, make its decision regarding the offer known.

See Report of the ILC, 63rd session (2011), GA Official Records, Suppl. 10 (A/66/10), para. 289.

57   See the text of the original draft Article in the Fourth report, cited above in note 28, para. 72.
58   *Ibid.*
59   See draft Article 11, cited above in note 56.

due to respect of the sovereignty of the affected State the "shall" should be replaced by the less obliging "should". The opposition arose from the argument that a State, while coping with the effects of a disaster, may by itself successfully cope with it, provide assistance, protect the affected persons, and assure the protection of their lives, their dignity and human rights. The affected State is by virtue of its sovereignty in a position to give consent to those offers of assistance it considers appropriate, useful and adequate according to the needs arising from coping with the disaster and its consequences. It may choose among offers given by assisting entities, *i.e.* States, international organizations, NGOS.

It has already been sufficiently elaborated while discussing other provisionally adopted Articles that sovereignty includes the obligation of the affected State to protect persons, their lives, human dignity, and human rights. The State shall act in *bona fides* according to its obligations also when providing or withholding its consent to offers of assistance. The right of the affected State is not unlimited; it is limited by its obligation to protect persons in the event of disasters. The stipulation in draft Article 11 [14] that "consent to external assistance shall not be withheld arbitrarily" is an appropriate confirmation of the obligation of the affected State to protect persons, their human dignity and human rights and to act in *bona fides*.

'Arbitrarily' is a vague concept. Deciding whether the consent was withheld arbitrarily is a case-by-case matter. Some features of 'arbitrariness' are elaborated in the commentary to Article 11 [14]. It is clear that one cannot claim 'arbitrariness' whenever the affected State can by itself protect the persons or has accepted or is going to accept another, probably more appropriate, offer of assistance. The affected State does not act arbitrarily when it expresses any reasonable reason to prove that by withholding the consent it has acted in *bona fides* and according to its duty to protect the persons affected by the disaster, or when it exposes as reasons to withhold consent dubious or *mala fides* intentions of the assisting entity.

Arbitrariness could however be claimed whenever it was evident from the circumstances of the disaster situation that the affected State either did not have sufficient means of its own to cope with the disaster, was not prepared or was unwilling to use its own resources or in the evident of any other indication that the affected State was ignoring, for whatever reason the suffering and precarious situation of the victims of the disaster. The affected State would also act arbitrarily if it acted contrary to basic principles of disaster response: humanity, neutrality, impartiality and non-discrimination.

The withholding of consent to foreign offers of assistance could consequently cause the non-delivery of assistance needed and the reduction of the scope of relief activities. The non-delivery of assistance would leave the affected persons without help and without means needed for their survival.

This could result in several cases of disasters, such as earthquakes, famines, floods *etc.*, in a threat to human lives and violation of human dignity and basic human rights of the affected persons. However State sovereignty, in our case the sovereignty of the affected State, "should be exercised in the way that best contributes to the protection and assistance of those in need".[60] As H. Lauterpacht also states, "the protection of human personality and of its fundamental rights is the ultimate purpose of all law, national and international."[61]

The affected State which, by arbitrarily withholding its consent to foreign assistance, would endanger the lives of affected persons would in fact violate their right to life. In a case where, due to its arbitrarily withholding consent, a certain group or a large number of population would be left due to absence of relief activities and assistance in life-threatening conditions, the *mala fides* attitude of the affected State would not be far from committing the crime of genocide.[62]

To leave huge numbers of persons, belonging to a group, or those in opposition or even rebellion against the government of the affected State, in the case of an earthquake, flood or famine without food, water, medicine, shelter, exposed to starvation, disease, suffering, without help and protection, and without law and order by arbitrarily, without any persuasive reason, withholding consent to an offer of foreign assistance and thus in fact preventing it – the question could be asked is it indeed far from committing the crime of genocide?

It cannot be claimed that 'neglect' is also included in Article 2 (c) of the Genocide Convection since the Soviet proposal to include negligent acts was explicitly rejected. However, since 1949 time has passed and the principle of humanity has acquired its additional confirmation also outside humanitarian law. Respect for human dignity and the protection of human rights have become the established concepts in international law, so that it is possible, at least in the context of the progressive development of international law, to claim that the affected State's neglect of its duty to protect the affected persons in the event of disasters is not far from genocide.[63]

---

60 See Fourth report, cited above in note 28, para. 56.
61 E. Lauterpacht (ed.), *International Law: Collected Papers of H. Lauterpacht*, Vol. II, Part 1, Cambridge, 1975, p. 47.
62 Article 2 (c) of the Convention on the Prevention and Punishment of the Crime of Genocide (GA Res. 260(III)/1948) stipulates that "genocide means any of the following acts committed with intent to destroy, in whole or in part, a national, ethnical, racial or religious group, as such: ...(c) Deliberately inflicting on the group conditions of life calculated to bring about its physical destruction in whole or in part."
63 See F. Jessberger, "The Definition and the Elements of the Crime of Genocide", in: *The UN Genocide Convention – A Commentary* (ed. P. Gaeta), Oxford, 2009; see also W.A. Schabas, *Genocide in International Law*, Cambridge, 2000.

The IDI in its Resolution of 2003[64] is clear in declaring that affected States are under the obligation not arbitrarily to reject a *bona fide* offer of assistance or to refuse access to the victims. Special Rapporteur Valencia-Ospina in his Fourth report clearly established not only that consent is required before assistance can be provided, but also that such consent of the affected State shall not be arbitrarily withheld. Thus in this context the sovereign right to give consent has been recognized, but with the clear qualification that consent shall not be withheld arbitrarily.[65] The balance between the right to sovereignty and the obligation to protect the victims of a disaster has thus been appropriately resolved in the provisionally adopted draft Article 11 [14].

XIV Right to Offer Assistance (Article 12) [16]

In his Forth Report,[66] the Special Rapporteur also proposed draft Article 12 [16] concerning the right of States and other assisting entities "to offer assistance".[67] This Article was considered by the Commission at its plenary session and was referred to the Drafting Committee. Due to the lack of time, the Drafting Committee did not at the 63rd session (2011) provisionally adopt this Article. Nevertheless, the Article as proposed by the Special Rapporteur was commented on by the States in the 6th Committee at the 66th session of the GA.

According to the wording of draft Article 12 [16] as originally proposed by the Special Rapporteur, it is clear that its substance was no more and no less than the 'right to offer assistance'. In humanitarian activities in the case of disasters it is a well-established practice that offers of assistance are welcome. They are an expression of solidarity and a reflection of the principles of humanity and cooperation.

To 'offer' assistance can by no means mean to 'provide' assistance. The affected State has a free choice either to accept the offer of assistance or to decline it. It is free to accept or not to accept the whole or any part of the offer of assistance whether it is an offer by a State or by any other entity, international organization, NGO or private entity, and without regard to the manner in

---

64 See above, note 51.
65 See Fourth report, cited above in note 28, para. 62.
66 At the 63rd session of the Commission (2011), A/CN.4/643, para. 109.
67 The text of the proposed draft Article 12 (Right to offer assistance) was as follows: "In responding to disasters, States, the United Nations, other competent Inter-Governmental Organizations and relevant Non-Governmental Organizations shall have the right to offer assistance to the affected State."

which the offer of assistance was made. The affected State is 'sovereign' to decide either to accept or to decline any offer of assistance. Actually, the question could be raised whether it is at all necessary and useful to draft such a provision since it only confirms the usual reality in the event of disasters: States and other entities offer assistance as an expression of solidarity and according to the principle of humanity. They are sovereign and independent entities in offering the assistance – with the sole exception of special arrangements (*i.e.* specific multilateral and bilateral treaties), by which they might have already in advance accepted the obligations of mutual assistance.[68]

Offers of assistance cannot be considered as an interference in the internal affairs of the affected State or as in any way harmful to its sovereignty. The affected State has the primary responsibility to protect persons in the event of disasters on its territory and can accept or not the offers of assistance by virtue of its sovereignty. It is free to choose and to act. There is, however, only one limitation stipulated in provisionally adopted draft Article 11 [14]: a State should not arbitrarily withhold consent to external assistance when it would be unable or unwilling by itself to provide the necessary assistance. The offering of assistance in the case of disasters is a well-established and welcome practice in the contemporary world. It can in no way be considered an unlawful intervention in the internal affairs of the affected State. Such an understanding has been confirmed also by the IDI in its 2003 resolution on humanitarian assistance. It clearly stated that "States and organizations have the right to offer humanitarian assistance to the affected State".[69]

Keeping in mind that the protection of persons in the event of disasters is the ultimate purpose of this endeavour of the ILC to codify and progressively develop international law, the provision on the 'right to offer assistance' might have a stimulating effect on those who are in a position to offer such assistance. The 'right to offer assistance' is neither in collision with the sovereignty of the assisting State nor an act of interference.

Like the affected State, which can accept or refuse any offer of assistance, the assisting State can also, according to its capabilities and its feeling of solidarity, offer assistance or not. However, according to the principles of humanity and solidarity the successful protection of persons in the event of disasters

---

68   Such as Convention on Assistance in Case of a Nuclear Accident or Radiological Emergency, *UN Treaty Series*, Vol. 1457, No. 24643; Tampere Convention on the Provision of Telecommunication Resources for Disaster Mitigation and Relief Operations, *UN Treaty Series*, Vol. 2296, No. 40906; ASEAN Agreement on Disaster Management and Emergency Response, *ASEAN Documents Series*, 2005, p. 157; and several others.

69   See above, note 2, p. 262.

is in the common interest of the international community and should be considered a common responsibility. The right to offer assistance should also be understood in this broader context and should be stimulated also by the codification and progressive development of international law.

At its 64th session (2012) the Commission re-discussed Article 12 [16] (Offers of assistance) and the Drafting Committee provisionally adopted its new text.[70] The change to the original draft Article 12 is minimal. The basic concept of the right of States and competent intergovernmental organizations to offer assistance has been kept in the new provisionally adopted Article 12 [16], although several members of the Commission have expressed their reservations as they had already done at the 63rd session. The improvement from Article 12 as originally proposed by the Special Rapporteur[71] to the draft Article 12 [16] as provisionally adopted at the 64th session concerns the title of the Article. Instead of 'Right to offer assistance' the title of the provisionally adopted Article is 'Offers of assistance'. This change in the title has been introduced and agreed in the Commission to reflect the next change in the Article 12 [16], *i.e.* the limitation of the 'right to offer assistance' to States and the United Nations (including of course the UN special agencies) and "other competent intergovernmental organizations" but not to "relevant non-governmental organizations", which "may" also offer assistance. This change reflects the acceptable view that non-governmental organizations, though relevant in providing assistance in the event of disasters, are from the point of view of international law not equal either to sovereign States or to intergovernmental organizations whose members are sovereign States.

xv   Duty to Offer Assistance

At the 63rd session of the Commission in 2011, it was suggested[72] that the Commission should also consider the 'duty to offer assistance'. This idea was met by general disapproval in the GA 6th Committee. A 'duty to offer assistance' would be a negation of the noble and growing principle of solidarity; it would cause unsurpassable practical and conceptual problems, *e.g.* what the

---

70   Draft Article 12 (Offers off assistance): "In responding to disasters, States, the United Nations, and other competent intergovernmental organizations have the right to offer assistance to the affected State. Relevant non-governmental organizations may also offer assistance to the affected State," see A/CN.4/L.812.

71   Text see note 67.

72   See Fifth report, cited above in note 48.

extent of such a duty should be, what assistance should be offered *etc*. It is true, however, that in the contemporary world by relying on the principles of humanity and solidarity the offering of assistance could be considered a moral duty. The attempt to codify such a duty as a legal obligation of all States would indeed encroach on sovereignty, in this case on the sovereignty of assisting States. The imposing of a 'duty to offer assistance' on States as a general legal obligation would probably destroy any chance such a draft had of being adopted by States in a foreseeable time and would thus harm the noble endeavour to help by the codification and progressive development of international law to protect persons affected by disaster.

Concerning other assisting entities, international organizations and NGOs in particular, it remains unclear how their 'duty to offer assistance' could be stipulated by international law.

Considering the expressed disapproval of States and the functional and practical inconsistencies of the concept of the 'duty to offer assistance' it has not been included among the draft Articles and was dropped from the Commission's further considerations.

XVI Conditions on the Provision of Assistance and Its Facilitation

In the Fifth report presented by the Special Rapporteur to the 64th session of the Commission (2012)[73] he proposed three new Articles.[74] The Drafting Committee, besides provisionally adopting Article 12 [16], provisionally also adopted four additional Articles (Articles 5 [9] *bis*, 13 [15], 14 [17], and 15 [19]).[75] Apart from Article 12 [16],[76] among the other articles provisionally adopted by the Drafting Committee at the 64th session of the Commission, only Article 13 [15] is relevant from the point of view of our discussion, *i.e.* the 'tension' between the 'sovereignty' of the affected State and 'protection' of persons affected by disasters.

Article 13 [15][77] authorizes the affected State to place conditions on the provision of external assistance. The text of this Article is clear and a logical reflection

---

73 See Fifth report, cited above in note 48.
74 *Ibid.*, paras. 116, 181, and 187.
75 See texts of the Articles in A/CN.4/L.812.
76 Discussed above under 'Duty to offer assistance'.
77 Text of the Article 13 [15] (Conditions on the provision of external assistance): "The affected State may place conditions on the provision of external assistance. Such conditions shall be in accordance with the present draft articles, applicable rules of international

of the primary duty and responsibility of the affected State – and its sovereignty – to protect persons affected by disaster on its territory. The establishing of conditions is in fact part of affected States' consent to the external assistance. The affected State may, as stipulated in provisionally adopted Article 13 [15], withhold its consent to external assistance and can thus also place conditions to it. As in the case of its 'consent' in the case of 'conditions' the affected State is also not entirely free. It shall not withhold its consent 'arbitrarily'[78] and it can also not place conditions on external assistance arbitrarily, *i.e.* in *mala fides*.

As stipulated in provisionally adopted Article 13, conditions "shall be in accordance with the present draft Articles, applicable rules of international law, and the national law of the affected State". It is thus clear that, in placing conditions, the affected State shall act in accordance *inter alia*, with Article 11 [14] of the draft, with principles and rules of international law, including humanitarian law and human rights law, its national law, including its constitutional guarantees, and other laws concerning the protection of the dignity of the human person and his or hers human rights. In addition, the provisionally adopted draft Article 13 [15] clearly stipulates that conditions "shall take into account the identified needs of the persons affected", thus reconfirming the basic purpose of the Commission's endeavour to codify and progressively develop principles and rules of international law concerning protection of persons in the event of disasters.

In provisionally adopted draft Article 14 [17] it is stipulated that the affected State "shall take the necessary measures, within its national law to facilitate the prompt and effective provision of external assistance".[79] Thus, the primary responsibility of the affected State is confirmed as its obligation to act in *bona fides*, in the sole interest of the protection of persons affected by the disaster.

While terminating assistance, both the affected State and assisting States and other assisting actors shall act in the interest of the protection of affected persons. They should not terminate the process of assistance without previous consultation, as stipulated in the provisionally adopted draft Article 15 [19],[80] and without considering the needs of affected persons. Duty to cooperate

---

law, and the national law of the affected State. Conditions shall take into account the identified needs of the persons affected by disasters and the quality of the assistance. When formulating conditions, the affected State shall indicate the scope and type of assistance thought."

[78] See above our discussion on the provisionally adopted Art. 11 [14]; see also Fifth report, cited above in note 48, paras. 33–43.

[79] See text of Art. 14 in A/CN.4/L.812 and also in A/CN.4/L.803.

[80] See text of Art. 15, *ibid.*

(draft Art. 5 [8]) is the obligation of both the affected State and the assisting States and other assisting actors through all phases of disaster, including the termination of assistance.

These draft Articles (Articles 12 [16], 5a *bis* [9], 13 [15], 14 [17], and 15 [19]) provisionally adopted by the Drafting Committee at the 64th session of the Commission will be commented on at the 67th GA session (6th Committee) and rediscussed at the next, 65th session of the Commission either in May or July 2013.

XVII Conclusion

It may take some more time for the ILC to prepare a comprehensive set of draft Articles on the protection of persons in the event of disasters. The first reading of the draft Articles may at best be completed at the 65th session of the Commission in 2013 or even in 2014. Although up to now only 16 Articles have been provisionally approved, among them are those in which the 'tension' between 'sovereignty' on the one hand and 'protection' of persons on the other had to be resolved.

The next Articles may be of a more technical character. Nevertheless, it should be kept in mind that practical and technical aspects of humanitarian assistance are well elaborated in particular by the International Federation of Red Cross and Red Crescent Societies.[81] The first reading of draft Articles may be followed by the second reading in the Commission in 2015 or in 2016. From the diverse and often contradictory comments of States in the GA 6th Committee and considering also different views present in the Commission itself it might be expected that at the second reading the problems and disagreements connected to the 'tension' between 'sovereignty' and 'protection of persons' will recur. The final draft of the Commission thus may be delivered to UN GA at best in 2016, at the end of this quinquennium of the work of the ILC.

The Commission and the Special Rapporteur have in the provisionally adopted Articles established an appropriate balance between the rights of States based on the principle of sovereignty and non-interference on the one hand

---

81   See IFRC Guidelines for The Domestic Facilitation and Regulation of International Disaster Relief and Initial Recovery Assistance, adopted at 30th International Conference of the Red Cross and Red Crescent (2007), Geneva, 26–30 November, Doc. 301C/07/R4; Annex: 'Measures to expedite international relief', Res. 6 adopted at the 23rd International Conference of the Red Cross and Red Crescent Movement (1994) in: *Handbook of International Red Cross and Red Crescent Movement*, 3rd edn., 1994, pp. 811–815.

and, on the other hand, other principles of international law, humanitarian law and the law of human rights in particular, which are the main legal sources of the international legal protection of persons in the event of disasters.

The purpose of codification and progressive development in this case is 'protection' of persons, not 'protection' of States and their sovereignty. Thus the principle of sovereignty and non-intervention, which *sine dubio* remains to be the cornerstone of international law, has been dealt with in the provisionally adopted Articles only as much as it is relevant in the context of the protection of persons in the event of disasters.

The 'balance' established in the provisionally adopted draft Articles which partly codify and partly progressively develop international law could be summarized as follows: the affected State, by virtue of its sovereignty, has the *primary duty* to act and protect its population in the event of disasters. Based on the principle of humanity other States, the United Nations and competent intergovernmental organizations have the *right to offer* assistance as an expression of the principle of solidarity. The affected State *shall seek* assistance from abroad in cases when it is by itself unable or unwilling effectively to protect persons affected by disaster. It is *not bound* to accept assistance offered; it may decline it *unless it does so arbitrarily*, acting *in mala fides* by ignoring or misusing its primary duty to protect the affected persons. The assisting entities have *no right* – due to the sovereignty of the affected State – *to provide assistance without the consent* of the affected State. They can provide it only if there is *consent of the affected State* concerning all aspects and all phases of the assistance. The affected State can by virtue of its sovereignty withhold its consent to assistance or to any particular aspect of it. It is bound only *not to withhold its consent arbitrarily* in *mala fides*. It may place conditions on the provision of external assistance in accordance with the present draft Articles, international law and its national law. Conditions imposed by the affected State shall *take into account the needs of the persons* affected by disasters, and not create, in *mala fides*, obstacles to the assistance. The affected State shall undertake necessary means, to *facilitate* the prompt and effective assistance. The assisting entities have to *respect the sovereignty* of the affected State. Both the affected State and the assisting entities *have the duty to cooperate* in protection of persons in event of disasters in all phases of assistance including the termination of assistance. They have to act, both in accepting and providing assistance, *in bona fides* and *solely in the interest of protection of person affected by the disaster*.

By this well-balanced approach introduced in the provisionally adopted draft Articles, the basic framework in international law of rights and obligations of those involved in assistance, in the event of disasters, *i.e.* the affected

State and the assisting States, international organizations and NGOs, would be established – in the ultimate interest of persons affected by a disaster. By this codification and progressive development of international law an important step would be made to protect persons, human beings, from suffering, and to protect their human dignity and their human rights in the most dramatic circumstances caused by disasters. This codification and progressive development of international law would thus immensely contribute to ensuring solidarity in international community in the very circumstances in which the solidarity is most needed.

Ljubljana, 1 March 2013

CHAPTER 33

Avoiding Plurality of International Proceedings in the European Court of Human Rights

Nina Vajić* and Vadim Pak**

1. A preliminary issue to be decided by the European Court of Human Rights (ECtHR) when examining the admissibility of a case is set in Article 35 § 2(b)[1] of the Convention for the Protection of Human Rights and Fundamental Freedoms (Convention). In order to prevent duplication of international procedures related to applications that are substantially the same (principle of *lis alibi pendens*) the Court can decide to examine the matter of compliance with Article 35 § 2(b) of the Convention *motu proprio*.

Although the question whether a matter had already been submitted to another procedure of international investigation or settlement has in fact been addressed in the context of individual applications on a number of occasions in the past by the former European Commission of Human Rights, the Court itself has not been called on to examine questions under Article 35 § 2(b) in a great number of cases.

However, in a world where proliferation and overlapping of international jurisdictional institutions has in recent years considerably increased it is worthwhile to see how this issue has been dealt with in the ECtHR. In particular, we sought to reflect on this topic as a contribution to the essays in honour of Budislav Vukas, a dear friend and colleague, having in mind his own participation in various international judicial fora – as a Judge at the International Tribunal for the Law of the Sea, Arbitrator, and not least *Ad Hoc* Judge at the International Court of Justice.

I

2. Article 35 § 2(b) of the Convention, in its relevant parts, provides:

> 2. The Court shall not deal with any application submitted under Article 34 that… (b) is substantially the same as a matter that has already been

---

* Former Judge and Section President, European Court of Human Rights. Any views expressed are personal.
** Legal Secretary, Registry of the European Court of Human Rights. Any views expressed are personal.
1 Former Article 27 § 1(b).

examined by the Court or has already been submitted to another procedure of international investigation or settlement and contains no relevant new information...

Accordingly, if some of the complaints are substantially the same as those already examined by the ECtHR in another case, they must be rejected pursuant to Article 35 §§ 2(b) and 4 of the Convention.[2]

3. In addition, as the Court noted in its decision *Smirnova and Smirnova v. Russia*:[3]

> [T]his provision is intended to avoid the situation where several international bodies would be simultaneously dealing with applications which are substantially the same. A situation of this type would be incompatible with the spirit and the letter of the Convention, which seeks to avoid a plurality of international proceedings relating to the same cases...

The purpose of the research presented in this brief paper is to outline the principles that have emerged and to present the practice of the Convention organs in this respect.

4. In determining whether its jurisdiction is excluded by virtue of Article 35 § 2(b) the Court has to examine whether the case before it is substantially the same as a matter that has already been submitted to a parallel set of international proceedings and, if that is so, whether the simultaneous proceedings may be seen as "another procedure of international investigation or settlement" within the meaning of Article 35 § 2(b) of the Convention.[4]

5. General principles relevant to the application of Article 35 § 2(b) have been summarized by the Court in its Decision on the competence of the Court to give an advisory opinion[5] in the following way:

> 29. The Court observes that the question whether a matter raised in an individual application had already been submitted to another procedure of international investigation or settlement has in fact been addressed in the context of individual applications on a number of occasions in the

---

2   *Dinc v. Turkey* (dec), no. 42437/98, 22 November 2001.
3   *Smirnova and Smirnova v. Russia* (dec.), nos. 46133/99 and 48183/99, 3 October 2002.
4   *OAO Neftyanaya Kompaniya Yukos v. Russia*, no. 14902/04, § 520, 20 September 2011.
5   *Decision on the competence of the Court to give an advisory opinion* [GC], §§ 29–31, ECHR 2004-VI.

past by the Commission in relation to the similar provision which was contained in former Article 27 § 1(b) of the Convention. In several decisions the Commission concluded that the matter was not "substantially the same" and consequently did not find it necessary to examine whether the other procedure in issue fell within the terms of former Article 27 § 1(b) (see *Council of Civil Service Unions and Others* v. *the United Kingdom*, no. 11603/85, Commission decision of 20 January 1987, Decisions and Reports (DR) 50, p. 228, concerning the Committee on Freedom of Association of the International Labour Organisation (applicants not identical); and *Pauger* v. *Austria*, no. 16717/90, Commission decision of 9 January 1995, DR 80-A, p. 24 (issue not the same), and *Peltonen* v. *Finland*, no. 19583/92, Commission decision of 20 February 1995, DR 80-A, p. 38 (applicant not the same), both concerning the United Nations Human Rights Committee). In other cases, however, it accepted, albeit implicitly, that the other procedure to which the same matter had been submitted was indeed "another procedure of international investigation or settlement" (see *Calcerrada Fornieles and Cabeza Mato* v. *Spain*, no. 17512/90, Commission decision of 6 July 1992, DR 73, p. 214, *Pauger* v. *Austria*, no. 24872/94, Commission decision of 9 January 1995, DR 80-A, p. 170, and *cw* v. *Finland*, no. 17230/90, Commission decision of 9 October 1991, unreported, all concerning the United Nations Human Rights Committee; and *Cereceda Martin and Others* v. *Spain*, no. 16358/90, Commission decision of 12 October 1992, DR 73, p. 120, concerning the Committee on Freedom of Association of the International Labour Organisation, all of which were declared inadmissible pursuant to Article 27 § 1(b)).

30. More significantly, in two other cases the Commission made it clear that the mere fact that the matter had been submitted to another procedure of international investigation or settlement did not suffice in itself to exclude the Commission's competence and that a qualitative assessment was also necessary in order to ensure that the procedure fulfilled certain criteria. Thus, in *Lukanov* v. *Bulgaria* (no. 21915/93, Commission decision of 12 January 1995, DR 80-A, p. 108), the Commission had to consider whether the procedure for examination of the applicant's situation by the Human Rights Committee of the Inter-Parliamentary Union could be regarded as "another procedure of international investigation or settlement". In reaching the conclusion that it could not, the Commission expressed the view that the term "another procedure" referred to "judicial or quasi-judicial proceedings similar to those set up by the Convention" and that the term "international investigation or settlement" referred to institutions and procedures set up by States, thus excluding non-governmental

bodies, which it considered the Inter-Parliamentary Union to be. Similarly, in *Varnava and Others* v. *Turkey* (nos. 16064-66/90 and 16068-73/90, Commission decision of 14 April 1998, DR 93-A, p. 5), which concerned the United Nations Committee on Missing Persons in Cyprus, the Commission not only asserted that the procedures envisaged referred to those instituted by way of a "petition" lodged formally or substantively by the applicant but also took into account the limited nature of the committee's investigative capacity and the fact that the committee could not attribute responsibility for the deaths of any missing persons. In these cases, therefore, the Commission adopted the approach of ascertaining, in the context of its examination of admissibility, whether a particular procedure fell within the scope of former Article 27 § 1(b) of the Convention.

31. The Court itself has been called on to examine questions under Article 35 § 2(b) in only a handful of cases (see *Yağmurdereli* v. *Turkey* (dec.), no. 29590/96, 13 February 2001, in which the Court noted that since Turkey had not ratified the Optional Protocol to the International Covenant on Civil and Political Rights, the same matter could not have been submitted to the United Nations Human Rights Committee, and *Smirnova* v. *Russia* (dec.), nos. 46133/99 and 48183/99, 3 October 2002, in which the Court found that the matter referred to the United Nations Human Rights Committee was not "substantially the same"; see also *Hartman* v. *the Czech Republic* (dec.), no. 53341/99, 17 December 2002, in which the matter was not addressed, as the complaint was declared inadmissible on another ground, and *Folgerø and Others* v. *Norway*, no. 15472/02, communicated to the respondent Government on 4 December 2003, both concerning the United Nations Human Rights Committee). Nevertheless, the Court endorses the approach of the Commission and considers that its decisions – in particular, those in *Lukanov* and *Varnava*, cited above – amply demonstrate that, in the context of proceedings instituted under Article 34 of the Convention, an examination of the question whether the same matter has already been submitted to another procedure of international investigation or settlement may be required and that this examination is not limited to a formal verification but extends, where appropriate, to ascertaining whether the nature of the supervisory body, the procedure it follows and the effect of its decisions are such that the Court's jurisdiction is excluded by Article 35 § 2(b). Consequently, the question whether a particular procedure comes within the scope of Article 35 § 2(b) is a question which the Court might have to consider in consequence of proceedings instituted in accordance with the Convention, and its advisory jurisdiction is in principle excluded.

II

6. In view of these principles the questions the Court has to consider when examining parallel international proceedings are the following:

(1) whether the parties in the proceedings are the same;
(2) whether the subject matter is the same;
(3) whether the proceedings can be seen as judicial or quasi-judicial similar to those set up by the Convention;
(4) whether the introduction dates of the two respective proceedings are of any relevance.

1   *Whether the Parties in the Proceedings are the Same*
a   Cases Where the Parties Were the Same

7. In *Cereceda Martin and Others* v. *Spain*,[6] the applicants, who were activists in a trade union movement, complained about their dismissal. They applied directly to Strasbourg and indirectly, through their trade union, to the ILO Committee on Freedom of Association. Since their application through the trade union to the Committee concerned their individual situations and, even though the parties were formally different, the Commission decided that the matter was essentially the same and rejected the case:

> While it is true that formally the 23 individual applicants before the Commission are not the complainants who appealed before the ILO organs, access to those bodies being reserved for trade union organisations it is no less true that in the present case, unlike the case mentioned above the complaint was, in substance, submitted by the same complainants. On that basis the Commission concludes that in this case the parties were substantially the same.

In *Peraldi* v. *France*,[7] the applicant complained to the Court about the irregularity of his detention. The complaint about the applicant's detention was also made by the applicant's brother to the UN Working Group on Arbitrary Detention. Since, among other things, the brother complained about the violations of the applicant's rights and not his own, the Court decided that the parties in the two parallel sets of proceedings were the same:

---

6   *Cereceda Martin and Others* v. *Spain*, no. 16358/90, Commission decision of 12 October 1992.
7   *Peraldi* v. *France* (dec.), no. 2096/05, 7 April 2009.

La Cour observe tout d'abord que ce n'est pas le requérant lui-même qui a saisi l'organe des Nations Unies mais son frère. Certes, selon sa jurisprudence, si les personnes qui se plaignent devant les deux institutions ne sont pas les mêmes, la "requête" reçue à la Cour ne peut passer pour être "essentiellement la même qu'une requête...déjà soumise" à une autre instance internationale (voir notamment *Calcerrada Fornieles et Cabeza Mato c. Espagne*, n° 17512/90, décision du 6 juillet 1992, Décisions et rapports 73, p. 214, et *Folgero et autres c. Norvège* (déc.), n° 15472/02, 14 février 2006).

Toutefois, en l'espèce, et bien que formellement les auteurs des deux requêtes soient différents, la Cour estime qu'il ressort des éléments soumis à son appréciation que le frère du requérant a saisi le Groupe de travail d'une requête afin de faire examiner la situation du requérant et non pas sa situation personnelle.

b   Cases Where the Parties Were Different

8. In *Ivo KOVAČIĆ, Marjan MRKONJIĆ and Dolores GOLUBOVIĆ v. Slovenia*,[8] the Court found that the parties in the Strasbourg proceedings and in the International Monetary Fund (IMF) and the Banko for International Settlement (BIS) were totally unrelated:

> Even assuming that arbitration proceedings before the International Monetary Fund and mediation proceedings under the auspices of the Bank for International Settlement in the framework of succession negotiations are pending and that their subject-matter were the same as that in the present cases, the Court notes that the parties to the IMF and BIS procedures are not the same as those to the proceedings before the Court.
>
> It follows that it has not been shown that an application identical to, or substantially the same, as those before the Court in the present cases has already been submitted to another procedure of international investigation or settlement. This objection is accordingly rejected.

In *Folgerø and Others v. Norway*,[9] a number of parental couples were unhappy with a provision of domestic law in the sphere of religious education. All of

---

[8] *Ivo KOVAČIĆ, Marjan MRKONJIĆ and Dolores GOLUBOVIĆ v. Slovenia* (dec.), nos. 44574/98, 45133/98 and 48316/99, 9 October 2003 and 1 April 2004.

[9] *Folgerø and Others v. Norway* (dec.), no. 15472/02, 4 February 2006.

these parents took part in the same proceedings at domestic level. Later, however, some couples complained to Strasbourg, whilst others applied to the United Nations Human Rights Committee. The Court decided that the claimants were different and continued with the case:

> The Court observes that the applicants before the Court and the "authors" before the UN Committee all complained, at the outcome of the same national proceedings to which they had all been parties, about the absence of a possibility under Norwegian law to obtain a full exemption for their children from the KRL subject. However, according to principles established in the Convention case-law, if the complainants before the two institutions are not identical (see *Council of Civil Service Unions v. the United Kingdom*, no. 11603/85, Commission decision of 29 January 1987, *Decisions and Reports* 50, pp. 236–37; *Peltonen v. Finland*, no. 19583/92, DR 80-A, p. 43; cf. *Calcerrada Fornieles and Cabeza Mato v. Spain*, no. 17512/90, decision of 6 July 1992, DR 73, p. 214, and *Miguel Cereceda Martin and 22 Others against Spain* (dec.), no. 16358/90, 12 October 1992; see also *Smirnova v. Russia* (dec.), nos. 46133/99 and 48183/99, 3 October 2002), the "application" to the Court cannot be considered as being "substantially the same as a matter that has...been submitted" for instance to the UN Committee (see also the somewhat stricter wording of the French version of this provision: "elle [la requête] est essentiellement la même qu'une *requête*...soumise à" *etc.* – emphasis added). Notwithstanding the common features between the application lodged under the Convention in Strasbourg and the communication filed under the UN Covenant in Geneva, the Court does not find that making an exception from this principle would be justified in the instant case.
>
> It follows that the Government's request to the Court to declare the application inadmissible under Article 35 § 2(b) of the Convention must be rejected.

In *Yukos v. Russia*,[10] the applicant company's former majority shareholders Hulley Enterprises Ltd, Yukos Universal Ltd and Veteran Petroleum Ltd, brought arbitration proceedings against the Russian Federation for the alleged breaches of the Energy Charter Treaty in the Permanent Court of Arbitration in The Hague. The Court decided that the parties in the two sets of proceedings were different as all of the shareholders of OAO Neftyanaya kompaniya Yukos

---

10   *OAO Neftyanaya Kompaniya Yukos v. Russia*, no. 14902/04, §§ 523–526, 20 September 2011.

were parties to the proceedings before the ECtHR, whilst only its majority shareholders were parties to the proceedings in The Hague. It thus continued with the examination of the case:

> Turning to the case at hand, the Court finds that there is no need for it to examine whether the proceedings in the Hague brought by the company's majority shareholders or the proceedings brought under the bilateral investment treaties brought by various groups of the company's minority shareholders may be seen as "another procedure of international investigation of settlement" as it is clear that the cases are not "substantially the same" within the meaning of Article 35 § 2(b) of the Convention for the following reasons.
>
> The Court observes that it was Hulley Enterprises Ltd and Veteran Petroleum Ltd (both registered in Cyprus) and Yukos Universal Ltd (registered in the Isle of Man), which in February 2005 initiated arbitration proceedings against the Russian Federation before the Permanent Court of Arbitration in the Hague, referring, among other things, to the same events and proceedings as those complained of by the applicant company in the present application before the Court and alleging numerous violations of their rights as investors under the Energy Charter Treaty. Some of the company's foreign minority shareholders also initiated similar proceedings under bilateral investment treaties. The Court notes, however, that despite certain similarities in the subject-matters of the present case and of the arbitration proceedings, the claimants in those arbitration proceedings are the applicant company's shareholders acting as investors, and not the applicant company itself, which at that moment in time was still an independent legal entity.
>
> The Court further notes that the present case has been introduced and maintained by the applicant company in its own name. Although the above-mentioned entities could arguably be seen as having been affected by the events leading to the applicant company's liquidation, they have never taken part, either directly or indirectly, in the Strasbourg proceedings. The Court reiterates that in November 2007 the applicant company was liquidated and that despite this fact in its admissibility decision of 29 January 2009 it nevertheless accepted the application "because the issues raised by the case transcend[ed] the person and the interests of the applicant [company]" and "...striking the application out of the list under such circumstances would undermine the very essence of the right of individual applications by legal persons, as it would encourage governments to deprive such entities of the possibility to pursue an application

lodged at a time when they enjoyed legal personality...", which shows that the Court has throughout placed emphasis on the applicant company in its own right.

In these circumstances, the Court finds that the parties in the above-mentioned arbitration proceedings and in the present case are different and therefore the two matters are not "substantially the same" within the meaning of Article 35 § 2(b) of the Convention. It follows that the Court is not barred, pursuant to this provision, from examining the merits of this case.

c   Cases Where the Subject Matter and the Parties Were Different

9. In *Evaldsson and Others* v. *Sweden*,[11] both the parties and the subject matter were different:

> The Court notes that the freedom enshrined in Article 5 of the European Social Charter resembles the rights guaranteed by Article 11 of the Convention. However, the Court finds that the present applicants are not identical with the complainant before the European Committee of Social Rights. It notes that the five individual applicants in the present case could not have been represented before the Committee by the Confederation, as the Confederation protects employers' interests and not those of individual workers, and that they would not have been able to bring proceedings before the Committee themselves, as that organ may only receive complaints from employers' organisations and trade unions. As regards the sixth applicant, the Industries, the Court takes into account that it is a legal entity separate from the Confederation and that it did not participate in the proceedings before the Committee as a party. Moreover, with respect to the subject-matter of the two proceedings, the Court further finds that it is of importance under Article 35 § 2(b) that the Confederation's complaint before the Committee was of a general character whereas the present application concerns the Labour Court's judgment of 7 March 2001 which addressed the specific situation of the five individual applicants. Accordingly, the present application cannot be regarded as being substantially the same as the complaint brought before the European Committee of Social Rights. The Government's objection in this regard must therefore be rejected.

---

11   *Evaldsson and Others* v. *Sweden* (dec.), no. 75252/01, 28 March 2006.

In *Celniku v. Greece*[12] the Court found that the parties to the two proceedings were not the same and that the nature and the purpose of the applications were clearly different:

> En l'occurrence, la Cour note, en premier lieu, que la communication en vertu de la "procédure 1503" a été présentée non pas par les requérantes mais par l'Organisation mondiale contre la torture. Partant, il n'y a pas d'identité des auteurs des deux requêtes. En second lieu, la nature et l'objectif des deux requêtes se distinguent de manière claire.
>
> Il s'ensuit que la présente requête n'est pas substantiellement la même que la communication présentée auprès du Haut Commissaire aux Droits de l'Homme des Nations unies. Il y a dès lors lieu de rejeter l'exception formulée par le Gouvernement au titre de l'article 35 § 2 b) de la Convention.

In *Council of Civil Service Unions and Others v. the United Kingdom*,[13] the Commission rejected the case because the subject matter and parties were different.

10. To sum up, it transpires from the Court's case law that the question whether the parties are identical may not be resolved formalistically. The assessment will often involve at least some measure of the substantive assessment of all relevant circumstances, including the subject matter of the complaints and the nature of relations between various claimants.

2   *Whether the Subject Matter is the Same*

11. Under this head three different aspects may be distinguished, namely, whether the provisions relied on by the claimants are similar or identical, whether the scope of the respective claims is the same and whether the redress sought is similar.

a   Whether the Provisions Relied on by the Claimants Are Similar

12. The Convention case law shows that on a number of occasions the Commission and the Court were faced with this question and they usually applied a functional approach without insisting on full textual similarity of two legal instruments.

---

12   *Celniku v. Greece*, no. 21449/04, §§ 39–41, 5 July 2007.
13   *Council of Civil Service Unions and Others v. the United Kingdom*, no. 11603/85, Commission decision of 7 January 1987.

In *Cereceda Martin and Others*[14] the Commission found Article 2 of the 1948 ILO Convention No 87 concerning freedom of association and protection of the right to organize sufficiently similar to Article 11 of the Convention not to deal with the case:

> The Commission notes in the first place that the rights set forth in Article 2 taken together with Article 10 of Convention No 87 of 1948 include the right to freedom of association which is also guaranteed by Article 11 para. 1 of the Convention. The Commission accordingly notes that the complaint submitted to the ILO and the complaint submitted to the European Commission of Human Rights are identical.

In *Pauger v. Austria*,[15] the Commission found Article 26 of the ICCPR[16] sufficiently similar to Article 14 of the Convention to reject the case:

> The Commission observes that while the applicant's communication to the Human Rights Committee related to discrimination with regard to his entitlement to a widower's pension, his present application to the Commission concerns discrimination regarding a one-off payment replacing this widower's pension, calculated in accordance with the transitory provisions of the 8th Amendment to the Pensions Act.
>
> Nevertheless, the Commission finds that the applicant's communication to the Human Rights Committee and his present application concern essentially the same issue, namely discrimination, both as regards his claim to a widower's pension and as regards the application of transitory provisions to his pension right.
>
> It follows that the Commission is prevented from dealing with the present application by virtue of Article 27 para. 1 (b) (Art. 27-1-b) of the Convention.

b   Whether the Scope of Claims Is the Same

13. The Convention case law takes account of the cause of action by making a detailed comparison of the facts referred to by the parties. In some cases, the

---

14 *Supra*, note 6.
15 *Pauger v. Austria* (dec.), no. 24872/94, Commission decision of 9 January 1995.
16 Article 26 of the ICCPR reads: "All persons are equal before the law and are entitled without any discrimination to the equal protection of the law. In this respect, the law shall prohibit any discrimination and guarantee to all persons equal and effective protection against discrimination on any ground such as race, colour, sex, language, religion, political or other opinion, national or social origin, property, birth or other status."

similarity of the cause of action was decisive, whilst in others this factor only played a secondary role.

In *Smirnova and Smirnova*,[17] the Court compared the contents of the application in Strasbourg to that before the UN Human Rights Committee and, having established that the scope of the application to the Court was wider than the complaint to the Committee, rejected the Article 35 § 2(b) argument:

> [T]he first applicant's complaints in that case were directed against her arrest on 26 August 1995 and, in particular, the question whether this arrest was justified, the impossibility to challenge it in the courts, and the alleged inadequate conditions of detention. The scope of the factual basis for the first applicant's application to the Court, although going back to the arrest of 26 August 1995, is significantly wider. It extends to the whole of the proceedings which terminated in 2002, and includes the first applicant's arrest on three more occasions since 26 August 1995.
>
> It follows that the first applicant's application is not substantially the same as the petition pending before the Human Rights Committee, and that being so, it falls outside the scope of Article 35 § 2(b) of the Convention and cannot be rejected pursuant to that provision.

In *Malsagova and Others* v. *Russia*,[18] and *Evaldsson and Others*,[19] the Court applied essentially the same comparative approach. In those cases, however, the difference in the underlying factual circumstances played a role in conjunction with other relevant factors:

> [T]he Court reiterates that in deciding whether the complaints raised before it have already been submitted for examination before another international body, it is necessary to verify whether the applications to the different institutions concern substantially the same persons, facts and complaints (see *Calcerrada Fornieles and Cabeza Mato* v. *Spain*, no. 17512/90, Commission decision of 6 July 1992, Decisions and Reports (DR) 73, p. 214, and *Pauger* v. *Austria*, no. 24872/94, Commission decision of 9 January 1995, DR 80-A, p. 170). The Court notes in this respect that the report submitted by Human Rights Watch concerned only the fact of Saydi Malsagov's disappearance, while the scope of the complaints that the applicants raised before the Court is significantly wider...

---

17   *Supra*, note 3.
18   *Malsagova and Others* v. *Russia* (dec.), no. 27244/03, 6 March 2008.
19   *Supra*, note 12.

> ... Moreover, with respect to the subject-matter of the two proceedings, the Court further finds that it is of importance under Article 35 § 2(b) that the Confederation's complaint before the Committee was of a general character whereas the present application concerns the Labour Court's judgment of 7 March 2001 which addressed the specific situation of the five individual applicants...

In the *Peraldi* decision[20] the Court came to the opposite conclusion, having found that the applicant's claims in Strasbourg had been identical to those in the proceedings before the UN Working Group on Arbitrary Detention:

> La Cour observe ensuite que les deux requêtes concernent la détention provisoire du requérant, et notamment la question de savoir si la durée de cette détention provisoire a été excessive...

14. It is clear that Article 35 § 2(b) of the Convention disallows parallel proceedings where the scope of claims overlaps.

c   Whether the Effect Sought is Similar

15. This factor has so far not played a decisive role in the Court's case law although, as already previously mentioned, in its Decision on the competence of the Court to give an advisory opinion, the Court noted that examination extends, where appropriate, to ascertaining whether the effect of its decisions is such that the Court's jurisdiction is excluded by Article 35 § 2(b).[21]

16. In this context, the question might be asked whether the *Yukos* v. *Russia* judgment could be interpreted as analysing in fact also the different effects of the parallel proceedings.

The redress sought by the applicant company in The Hague and in Strasbourg was essentially very similar: in both cases the claimants sought declaratory relief (breaches of Articles 10 and 13 of the Energy Charter Treaty and various Convention Articles) and pecuniary compensation and the Court did not analyse this issue.

The Court held that the two parallel proceedings (before the ECtHR and the Permanent Court of Arbitration) were not "substantially the same" because the parties were different.[22] In doing so it, however, referred back to

---

20   *Supra*, note 7.
21   See *supra*, note 5, § 31.
22   See *supra*, § 7 and note 10, §§ 525 and 526.

its admissibility decision[23] to reason as it did "because the issues raised by the case transcend[ed] the person and the interests of the applicant [company]" and "...striking the application out of the list under such circumstances would undermine the very essence of the right of individual applications by legal persons, as it would encourage governments to deprive such entities of the possibility to pursue an application lodged at a time when they enjoyed legal personality...", which shows that the Court may have indeed proceeded to an examination that was not limited to a formal verification of the various factors but extended to possible broader effects of its decision.

3 Whether the Proceedings Can be Seen as Judicial or Quasi-Judicial Similar to Those Set Up by the Convention

17. In this respect the Convention case law has evolved over time to include a number of criteria, such as the legal nature of the parallel proceedings, composition of the body, its competence and procedural rules. In addition, due regard has to be had to the text of the provision which speaks of "another procedure of international investigation or settlement".

18. In the *Peraldi*[24] decision, after a thorough analysis the Court ruled that the UN Working Group on Arbitrary Detention satisfied the criteria set out in Articles 34 and 35 of the Convention:

> [L]e Groupe de travail sur la détention arbitraire...est un mécanisme extra-conventionnel composé d'experts indépendants...
> La procédure des communications au Groupe de travail se distingue clairement des plaintes déposées en vertu de la "procédure 1503" de l'ONU ..., laquelle a été considérée par la Cour comme n'étant pas une procédure internationale d'enquête ou de règlement (*Mikolenko c. Estonie* (déc.), n° 16944/03, CEDH 2006-..., et *Celniku*, précité). ... [L]e Groupe de travail peut être saisi de requêtes individuelles et les auteurs de ces requêtes bénéficient d'un droit de participer à la procédure et d'un droit à être informés des avis rendus par le Groupe. Ces avis, assortis de recommandations au gouvernement concerné si le Groupe estime que la détention est arbitraire, sont annexés au rapport annuel transmis à la Commission des droits de l'homme, laquelle peut à son tour prendre des résolutions et adresser des recommandations à l'Assemblée générale des Nations Unies par l'intermédiaire du Conseil économique et social. Il

---

23   *OAO Neftyanaya Kompaniya Yukos v. Russia* (dec.), no. 14902/04, § 443, 29 January 2009.
24   *Supra*, note 7.

s'ensuit que la procédure devant le Groupe de travail s'apparente, tant sous l'angle procédural que sous l'angle de ses effets potentiels, à la requête individuelle prévue par l'article 34 de la Convention (voir *a contrario Celniku*, précité, § 40).

Le Groupe de travail peut en outre formuler des délibérations...fixant sa position sur une question d'intérêt général aux fins de "jeter les bases de sa propre jurisprudence". Ces délibérations ne sont pas adoptées "dans l'abstrait mais en liaison avec l'examen de cas individuels qui lui sont soumis". Elles constituent des principes généraux à caractère essentiellement juridique auxquels le Groupe se réfère lorsqu'il rend un avis sur un cas particulier.

Dès lors, si le Groupe de travail n'a pas été institué par un traité mais par une résolution de la Commission des droits de l'homme, il n'en demeure pas moins qu'il s'agit d'une instance dont la procédure est contradictoire et dont les décisions sont motivées, notifiées aux parties et publiées en annexe de son rapport. En outre, les recommandations du Groupe permettent de déterminer les responsabilités étatiques quant aux cas de détention arbitraire constatés, voire de mettre fin aux situations litigieuses (voir *a contrario Malsagova et autres* c. *Russie* (déc.), n° 27244/03, CEDH 2008-...). Les avis du Groupe font également l'objet d'une procédure de suivi visant à assurer la mise en œuvre des recommandations formulées. La procédure devant le Groupe de travail présente de nombreuses similitudes avec celle devant le Comité des droits de l'homme des Nations Unies qui constitue, selon une jurisprudence constante de la Cour, une "instance internationale d'enquête ou de règlement" (voir notamment *Calcerrada Fornieles et Cabeza Mato*, précité)...

Partant, la Cour estime que le Groupe de travail sur la détention arbitraire est une "instance internationale d'enquête ou de règlement" au sens de l'article 35 § 2 b) de la Convention...

19. However, in the following cases it was found that the parallel proceedings did not meet the requirements of Article 35 § 2(b) of the Convention.

In *De Pace* v. *Italy*[25] the applicant lodged his complaint also before the European Committee for the Prevention of Torture and Inhuman or Degrading Treatment or Punishment (CPT). The Court held that the CPT is not a judicial or quasi-judicial procedure similar to the procedures set up by the Convention, either as to its procedure or as to its potential effects.[26]

---

25   *De Pace* v. *Italy*, no. 22728/03, 17 June 2008.
26   *Ibid.*, §§ 26 and 27.

La Cour relève que le CPT n'est pas une instance judiciaire ou quasi judiciaire et que son rôle, tel que défini par la Convention qui l'a institué, est de nature préventive. En outre, les informations recueillies par le CPT ont un caractère confidentiel et les particuliers ne disposent ni d'un droit de participation à la procédure, ni d'un droit à être informés des recommandations qui peuvent être formulées par le CPT, à moins qu'elles ne soient rendues publiques.

Partant, la procédure devant le CPT ne saurait être assimilée ni sous l'angle procédural ni sous l'angle des effets potentiels à la requête individuelle prévue par l'article 34 de la Convention.

As regards the "1503 procedure" before the UN Commission on Human Rights, in *Nikolai, Ljubov and Oleg Mikolenko* v. *Estonia*,[27] the Court decided that that procedure was not to be seen as judicial or quasi-judicial similar to those set up by the Convention:

[U]nder the "1503 procedure" (United Nations Economic and Social Council resolution 1503 (XLVIII) of 27 May 1970) the United Nations Human Rights Commission examines situations involving "a consistent pattern of gross and reliably attested violations of human rights". The Court is of the opinion that the Human Rights Commission is essentially an inter-governmental organ composed of State representatives, which deals with situations rather than individual complaints and which offers no redress to individual victims. Therefore, it finds that the "1503 procedure" cannot be considered as "another procedure of international investigation or settlement" within the meaning of Article 35 § 2.

In *Celniku* v. *Greece*[28] it confirmed that ruling:

En effet, à la différence de la procédure devant la Cour, la "procédure 1503" vise à identifier l'existence d'un ensemble de violations flagrantes et systématiques des droits de l'homme et des libertés fondamentales. En outre, il s'agit d'une procédure confidentielle et, par conséquent, les auteurs des communications faites en vertu de la procédure 1503 n'ont de droit de participation à aucun stade de cette procédure; ils ne sont pas informés des mesures qui peuvent être prises par les Nations unies, à moins qu'elles ne soient rendues publiques (paragraphes 33 et 34 ci-dessus). Partant, la

---

27   *Nikolai, Ljubov and Oleg Mikolenko* v. *Estonia* (dec.), no. 16944/03, 5 January 2006.
28   *Supra*, note 11.

"procédure 1503" ne saurait être assimilée ni sous l'angle procédural ni sous l'angle des effets potentiels à la requête individuelle prévue par l'article 34 de la Convention.

In *Jeličić* v. *Bosnia and Herzegovina*,[29] the Court found that the Human Rights Chamber was not an international body in the sense of Article 35 § 2(b), but a domestic one. The relevant part of the ruling read as follows:

> The Court is required, therefore, to determine whether the Chamber was or was not an "international" body within the meaning of Article 35 § 2 (b). In this connection, the Court considers the legal character of the instrument founding the body to be a logical starting-point for its assessment. However, it considers the following factors, concerning as they do the essential nature of the body, to be determinative of the issue: the body's composition, its competence, its place (if any) in an existing legal system and its funding.

The Court then proceeded to examine each of these factors before concluding:

> Moreover, and importantly, the Chamber's mandate did not concern obligations between States but strictly those undertaken by Bosnia and Herzegovina and its constituent entities. Pursuant to Article 11 § 1 of the Agreement on Human Rights, the Chamber was designed to assist Bosnia and Herzegovina and the entities in honouring their obligations under the Convention and various other human-rights treaties. As pointed out by the Venice Commission, the Chamber's competence was that of a "domestic" body.

In *Varnava and Others* v. *Turkey*,[30] the Commission decided that the Committee on Missing Persons did not meet the criteria:

> As regards the Government's arguments concerning the Committee on Missing Persons, the Commission has always considered that the procedures envisaged by the second limb of Article 27 para. 1(b) (Art. 27-1-b) of the Convention are procedures in which a matter is submitted by way of

---

29 *Jeličić* v. *Bosnia and Herzegovina* (dec.), no. 41183/02, 15 November 2005.
30 *Varnava and Others* v. *Turkey* (dec.), no. 16064-66/90 and 16068-73/90, Commission decision of 14 April 1998.

"a petition" lodged formally or substantively by the applicant... This is not, however, the case with the Committee on Missing Persons... Moreover, the Commission notes that Turkey is not a party to the procedure before that Committee and that the Committee cannot attribute responsibility for the deaths of any missing persons or make findings as to their cause. Finally, the Commission notes that the Committee's investigating capacity is limited. In these circumstances, the Commission considers that the Committee is not "a procedure of international investigation or settlement" of the "matter" which is pending before the Commission in the present applications...

In *Malsagova and Others*,[31] the Court ruled as follows:

The Court observes in this respect that the Working Group does not investigate disappearances. Nor does it provide the relatives of those missing with legal means of redress. It is not capable of attributing responsibility for the deaths of any missing persons or making findings as to their cause. Therefore, the Court considers that the Working Group is not "a procedure of international investigation or settlement" of the "matter" which is pending before the Court in the present application...

In *Lukanov v. Bulgaria*,[32] the Commission reasoned that only institutions and procedures set up by States are to be seen as procedures within the meaning of Article 35 § 2(b):

[It] observes that the Inter-Parliamentary Union...is a non-governmental organisation. The organs of the Union may adopt resolutions which are communicated by the parliamentarians concerned to the national parliaments and to international organisations...

The Commission considers that the Inter-Parliamentary Union constitutes a non-governmental organisation, whereas Article 27 para. 1(b) (Art. 27-1-b) refers to inter-governmental institutions and procedures. It follows that the procedures of the Inter-Parliamentary Union do not constitute "another procedure of international investigation or settlement" within the meaning of Article 27 para. 1(b) (Art. 27-1-b) of the Convention...

---

31 *Supra*, note 18.
32 *Lukanov v. Bulgaria* (dec.), no. 21915/93, Commission decision of 12 January 1995.

In *Karoussiotis* v. *Portugal*[33] the applicant had submitted the same application to the European Commission. The Court had to determine whether the procedure before the executive organ of the European Union is similar in its procedural aspects and potential effects, to the individual application before the Court. After a lengthy analysis of the procedure of complaints lodged by an individual with the European Commission, the Court decided to reject the Article 35 § 2(b) argument as follows:[34]

> Having regard to the foregoing, the Court takes the view that the procedure in question is not similar, in its procedural aspects or its potential effects, to the individual application provided for in Article 34 of the European Convention on Human Rights.
>
> The Court thus concludes that where the European Commission decides, as in the present case, on a complaint by a private individual, this does not constitute a "procedure of international investigation or settlement", within the meaning of Article 35 § 2(b) of the Convention. The objection raised by the Government must therefore be dismissed.

20. As can be seen from the above examples, to satisfy the criteria of Article 35 § 2(b) of the Convention as to the character of the proceedings, the body in question should:

- be international in nature[35] (although not necessarily based on an international treaty);[36]
- its members individually, or the body's composition in general,[37] should satisfy the requirement of impartiality;
- have powers to investigate and examine individual cases, not just general situations,[38] to establish responsibility[39] and, where appropriate, to provide adequate redress;[40]

---

33   *Karoussiotis* v. *Portugal*, no. 23205/08, 1 February 2011.
34   *Ibid.*, §§ 75 and 76.
35   *Jeličić* v. *Bosnia and Herzegovina*, *supra*, note 29.
36   *Peraldi* v. *France* (dec.), *supra*, note 7.
37   *Varnava and Others* v. *Turkey* (dec.), *supra*, note 30; *Nikolai, Ljubov and Oleg Mikolenko* v. *Estonia*, *supra*, note 27; *Peraldi* v. *France* (dec.), *supra*, note 7.
38   *Yagmurdereli* v. *Turkey* (dec.), no. 29590/96, 13 February 2001.
39   *Peraldi* v. *France* (dec.), *supra*, note 7; *Varnava and Others* v.*Turkey* (dec.), no. 16064-66/90 and 16068-73/90, Commission decision of 14 April 1998 and *Malsagova and Others* v. *Russia* (dec.), no. 27244/03, 6 March 2008.
40   *Ljubov and Oleg Mikolenko* v. *Estonia*, *supra*, note 27.

– from the point of view of procedure, it should ensure adequate participation by victims in adversarial proceedings,[41] and should issue motivated decisions.

4 Whether the Introduction Dates of the Two Respective Proceedings Are of Any Relevance

21. The Convention case law contains no authority which would support the view that in cases where two sets of parallel proceedings are pending simultaneously, the introduction dates of the proceedings may be of relevance. Neither the Court nor the Commission ever considered the above-mentioned dates of any importance – both the Commission and the Court rejected the cases as substantially the same as "a matter submitted to another procedure of international investigation or settlement" in all four hypothetical situations, *i.e.*, when:

- the applicant applied to the Convention organs first (*Calcerrada and Others* v. *Spain*; *Peraldi* v. *France*; *Yukos* v. *Russia*);
- at the time of the Court's or Commission's decision parallel proceedings were pending (*Calcerrada and Others* v. *Spain*; *Yukos* v. *Russia*);
- at the time of the Court's or Commission's decision parallel proceedings had already finished (*Cereceda Martin* v. *Spain*; *Peraldi* v. *France*);
- the applicant applied to other international bodies first (*Calcerrada and Others* v. *Spain*; *Cereceda Martin* v. *Spain*).

22. In *Calcerrada and Others*[42] the Commission noted specifically that mere suspension of parallel proceedings has no incidence on the question of compliance with Article 35 § 2(b) of the Convention – the parallel proceedings should be discontinued before the final decision has been taken.

It also held, in line with the existing rules of international law, that:

> ...it is consistent with national and international practice for a court's power to extend to consideration of facts which occur during the course of the proceedings before it... On many occasions moreover, the Commission has taken into consideration events subsequent to the introduction of an application but directly related to the facts adverted to therein...

---

41 *De Pace c. Italie*, supra, note 25; *Nikolai, Ljubov and Oleg Mikolenko* v. *Estonia*, supra, note 27.

42 *Calcerrada Fornieles and Cabeza Mato* v. *Spain*, no. 17512/90, Commission decision of 6 July 1992.

III

23. To summarize, it is possible to say that when it comes to individual applications the European Court in order to avoid plurality of international proceedings concerning the same case has a settled jurisprudence, based to a large extent on the Commission's experience and performed strictly on a case-by-case basis. The analysis of the Court's case law on Article 35 § 2(b) suggests that the Court was careful to avoid abstract rulings on the principle *lis alibi pendens*, limiting its analysis each time to questions that are necessary to resolve the case at hand.

24. In considering the issue, the Court needs to verify whether the applications to the different institutions concern "substantially the same" persons, facts and complaints.

As to the term "another procedure" it refers to proceedings that can be seen as judicial or quasi-judicial similar to those under the Convention, while "international investigation or settlement" refers to institutions and procedures set up by States, excluding non-governmental bodies.

25. The mere fact that the same matter has already been investigated or is being investigated by an international body will not suffice in itself to exclude the Court's competence. As the Court repeated on several occasions, a qualitative assessment is needed in order to ensure that the established criteria are met in the concrete case.

If, however, during such assessment the Court finds that one of the elements relating to another international procedure shows that the cases are different, it will not proceed with the examination of all the other factors. In other words, if it considers that the parties to a case before it and before another international institution are not the same, or that the subject matter is different, it will conclude that the two matters are not "substantially the same" within the meaning of Article 35 § 2(b). Consequently, the Court will not be barred from examining the merits of the case before it.[43]

26. Insofar as the Court is called upon to examine new facts that are posterior to the decision taken by the other international institution in question, it is not prevented by virtue of Article 35 § 2(b) of the Convention from dealing with such application.[44]

---

43   *Cf. OAO Neftyanaya Kompaniya Yukos* v. *Russia*, no. 14902/04, § 526, 20 September 2011.
44   *Patera* v. *Tcheque Republic* (dec.), no. 25326/03, 10 January 2006.

27. With a multitude of international bodies whose competences might be seen as overlapping to a certain extent at least, individual applicants may not always be aware of the consequences their multiple actions may have for the outcome of their case before the ECtHR. Therefore, and in particular if they are not represented by specialized lawyers, they may wish to double-check the admissibility criteria before bringing an application before the Strasbourg Court and, not least, also those of Article 35 § 2(b) of the Convention.

CHAPTER 34

The Role of Provisions on Human Rights Protection in Constructing Croatian-Italian (Formerly Yugoslav-Italian) Relations

Budislav Vukas Jr. *

I   **Introductory Remarks**

Professor Budislav Vukas is my dear uncle and highly admired scientific role model; it is thus an exceptional pleasure as well as an honour to be invited to be a contributor to his *Liber Amicorum*. On many occasions in his several-decades-long scientific and professional work, Professor Vukas dealt with various international legal aspects of Italian-Yugoslav (today the Italian-Croatian) relations. He was a participant in many intergovernmental forums and committees concerned with the legal regulation of these relations, hence the topics of his papers, books and other publications in general frequently touched upon different features of these relations. Being an expert in human rights, especially minority rights, he also contributed to the abundant international legal scholarship in this field. Therefore, I hope to pay tribute to his work by addressing the issue of human rights protection in the context of international relations between Italy and Croatia (formerly Yugoslavia).

Subsequent to forming their respective national identities and state entities in the second half of the 19th century, Croatian (Slovenian)-Italian relations were particularly replete with unacceptable standards and conduct by the state authorities towards the members of the other ethnic groups, especially Croats and Slovenians in Istria. Some of the identical political features may be recognized in certain activities and legal norms implemented by Austrian state politics and Austrian authorities starting from the second half of the 19th century, and even more radically in the politics of the Italian Fascist regime in Istria and Rijeka during the 1920s and 1930s. Such circumstances were bound to result in significant disruptions in Croatian (Slovenian)-Italian relations, while the conflicts and major confrontations escalated in the course of the Second World War. In this short period of time, the Italian Fascist regime accumulated additional militant and imperialistic attributes, partially inspired by the Nazi German model, whereas, subsequent to its breakdown in 1943, the justifiable

* Associate Professor, University of Rijeka, Faculty of Law.

Croatian and Slovenian liberation movement underwent some tendencies towards revenge and provocation. These are only a few of the historical trends which point to the reasons making the standards in protection of human rights extremely important in the context of creating Yugoslav-Italian relations, but also those in more recent times upon the dissolution of the former Yugoslavia.

11 The 1947 Italian Peace Treaty and the Annex 11 (Special Statute) to the 1954 Memorandum of Understanding regarding the Free Territory of Trieste

In the period of the post-war diplomatic crisis between Yugoslavia and Italy, which was only partially resolved when the Peace Treaty was signed in 1947, international standards for the protection of human rights were one of the focal points.

Already the 1947 Italian Peace Treaty, in Article 15, imposed the obligation on Italy to respect fundamental human rights, *i.e.* to take all measures necessary to secure to all persons the enjoyment of human rights and of the fundamental freedoms, without distinction as to physical, national, social, economic or religious criteria. Given their prominent struggle against Fascism, Croatians and Slovenians considered the provisions of Articles 16 and 17 of the Italian Peace Treaty particularly important because they obliged Italy to abolish the Fascist legislation and dissolve the Fascist regime organizations in Italy.[1]

In addition to these general clauses on protection of human rights, specific supplementary guarantees for such protection were incorporated in Annex VI to the Italian Peace Treaty (Permanent Statute of the Free Territory of Trieste).[2]

---

1 The cited provisions of the Italian Peace Treaty contain: a general clause prohibiting discrimination of any person under Italian jurisdiction on any basis (Article 15); a special clause prohibiting discrimination of persons who during the period from 10 June 1940 to the entry into force of the Peace Treaty, in some way participated in, expressed sympathy with or took action in support of the cause of the Allied and Associated Powers (Article 16.); and a clause related to the dissolution of the Fascist organizations in Italy pursuant to Article 30 of the Peace Treaty. The text of the Italian Peace Treaty was published in *Časopis za suvremenu povijest*, Vol. 7, No.1, 1975.

2 Annex IV to the Italian Peace Treaty defines the general processes in constructing the government in the Free Territory of Trieste, the general principles for its operation as well as the constitutional procedure. In this context, the Permanent Statute, in its Article 4 entitled 'Human rights and fundamental freedoms', states that the future constitution of the Free Territory of Trieste should contain also the provisions on basic human rights and fundamental freedoms. This provision reads as follows: "The constitution of the Free Territory shall

National equality proclaimed in the Permanent Statute opens up further considerations on the subject of the protection of ethnic minorities. However, the starting point in the new Italian Constitution, enacted on 27 December 1947, was merely a general principle of protection of human rights, phrased in the sense of equality of all citizens before the law (Article 3). Only in Article 6 of the Italian Constitution is it explicitly stated that "the Republic safeguards linguistic minorities by means of special provisions", envisaging the establishment of five autonomous regions which were supposed to guarantee special minority rights, given their special constitutional status.[3]

Nonetheless, the very complex circumstances surrounding political relations in the course of the Trieste Crisis (1947–1954) strongly affected the already tense interethnic relations, resulting in frequent violations of these modest safeguards guaranteed by the cited legal instruments. The complexity of interethnic relations in the Free Territory of Trieste was not at all an unexpected outcome of the then intensely traumatic experiences related to their genesis, since the end of the 19th century and particularly the period characterized by the national monolithic approach of the Italian state between the two World Wars, until the explosion of the national liberation endeavours of the Croatian and Slovenian peoples in 1943–1945 coupled with the new challenges of the socialist revolution and revanchism. Against this background, there could hardly be any guarantees for rapid acceptance and implementation of democratic standards, which the United Nations attempted to promote among the members of the international community as part of international law.

> ensure to all persons under the jurisdiction of the Free Territory, without distinction as to ethnic origin, sex, language or religion, the enjoyment of human rights and of the fundamental freedoms, including freedom of religious worship, language, speech and publication, education, assembly and association. Citizens of the Free Territory shall be assured of equality of eligibility for public office." This general provision creates a basis for other provisions related to human rights: civil and political rights (Article 5), citizenship (Article 6), official languages (Article 7) etc. Cited according to M. Udina, *Scritti sulla questione di Trieste: sorta in seguito al secondo conflitto mondiale ed i principi atti internazionali ed interni ad essa relativi*, Milano: Dr. Giuffré Editore, 1969, pp. 357–371. The full text of the Permanent Statute of the Free Territory of Trieste is available at the official United Nations website at <http://unispal.un.org/UNISPAL.NSF/0/973F5ACC5148F42B85257506007BDAC2> and at <http://domino.un.org/pdfs/AAC25ComJerW4.pdf>.

3 B. Vukas, *Etničke manjine i međunarodni odnosi*, Zagreb: Školska knjiga, 1978, pp. 141–142. On the Italian constitutional legislation concerned with the protection of the Slovenian national minority see also J. Jeri, G. Kušej, S. Polič, *The Special Statute and Some Elements of the Legal Situation of the Slovenian Ethnic Group in Italy and of the Italian in Yugoslavia*, Ljubljana, 1970, pp. 7 et seq. See also: G. Bevilacqua, *La minoranza Slovena a Trieste e il raporto Italia – Slavia – Cenni di diritto e di storia*, Trieste: LINT, 1984.

The implementation of the said mechanisms as well as the implementation of the then created standards within the United Nations was not at all a straightforward process in the territorially, diplomatically and ideologically divided area of the Free Territory of Trieste. Although, in the juridical sense, the Free Territory of Trieste was certainly in existence, its practical functioning was severely inhibited by the complexity of the diplomatic surroundings, the Cold War and the specific variable interests of the Eastern and the Western forces. Until the time of its dissolution (in 1954, and according to some authors in 1975), the Free Territory of Trieste remained divided into two occupation zones: Zone A was occupied by the Anglo-American joint forces (it generally included the area of the City of Trieste with surrounding villages), and Zone B which, according to the military arrangements, was occupied by the Yugoslav Army and generally consisted of part of Slovenian Istria as well as the northwestern part of Croatian Istria.[4] In the area of Zone A, the status of the Slovenian national community was only moderately improved. The main objections by the Slovenian minority were concerned with the Italian legislation intended to discriminate against Slovenian ethnic rights, which was adopted during the Fascist era and still in force at the time. The other main objection related to the politics exercised by the joint British and American administration there, which supported Italianization and processes of Italian national homogenization, thus failing to safeguard the national interests of the Slovenian community and to create the climate needed for the rehabilitation of the Slovenian ethnic institutions with a view to preserving Slovenian ethnic diversity and integrating them into the newly-founded social structures.[5]

---

4   On the legal and historical aspects of the Trieste Crisis see B. Vukas, Jr., "The Free Territory of Trieste as a Subject of International Law", in: B. Vukas, T.M. Šošić (eds.), *International Law: New Actors, New Concepts – Continuing Dilemmas. Liber Amicorum Božidar Bakotić*, Leiden: Martinus Nijhoff Publishers, 2010, pp. 149–156. On the diplomatic relations see *e.g. idem*, "Tršćanska kriza u prijelomnim vremenima prve polovice 50-tih godina XX. stoljeća – diplomatsko-političko i državnopravno razmatranje", *Zbornik Pravnog fakulteta Sveučilišta u Rijeci*, Vol. 28, No. 2, 2007, pp. 1017–1065.

5   The Slovenian ethnic community was complaining about discrimination by the Anglo-American administration in providing opportunities to exercise civil and political rights. The rights to employment and return for Slovenians born and living in Trieste prior to being relegated by the Fascist authorities were not upheld by the Anglo-American authorities there, whereas the requests of the members of the Italian people, who fled the territory which was allocated to Yugoslavia pursuant to the Italian Peace Treaty, were accepted. These Italians were equal in rights with the domestic Trieste population. This was the method which the Anglo-American authorities used to facilitate the national homogenization of Italians, supporting the Italian supremacy over the Slovenian minority based on their

On the other hand, the objections raised by the Italian ethnic community in Zone B were likewise numerous and substantiated. Although the newly-formed Yugoslav occupation authority, functioning within the military administration of the Yugoslav Army, continuously attempted to prove that elements of social ideology entirely negate ethnic differences among the Slovenian, Croatian and Italian peoples, these Italian objections were rather reasonable and justified. According to Bogdan Novak, they basically consisted of accusations that Yugoslav authorities took repressive measures and used police terror against their political opponents, and that the Yugoslav military administration thus violated fundamental human rights, civil and political rights, which was evident from the undemocratic institutions and activities of the Yugoslav Army authorities. In addition to the fundamental human rights, civil political and social rights were also violated, such as freedom of press, freedom of religion, freedom of conscience, freedom of speech, freedom of movement, voting rights and similar. The third objection was directed to the denationalization of the property of Italian citizens, which was not limited to the territory of Zone B. This problem continued to burden, for a very long time, not only interethnic relations in the area of Trieste, but also the relations between Italy and Yugoslavia, and more recently Italy and Croatia/Slovenia.[6]

All the mentioned difficulties created a necessity rapidly to seek solutions. A huge step in the improvement of Yugoslav-Italian relations was the adoption

---

relative population. The rights of the Slovenian community were violated especially in the suburban municipalities where they made up the majority of the population (Duino-Aurisina). This was an attempt to make Slovenians less nationally homogenous in the western suburbs of Trieste, in order to prevent national alienation of Trieste from the Italian state. The Anglo-American authorities also tolerated the expropriation of Slovenian property (land), it often ending up in the hands of the Italian newcomers so that virtually new villages were created in this area. Discrimination policy was also evident in the field of education. The number of Slovenian schools was considerably reduced as opposed to the increasing number of Italian schools. The Anglo-American occupation administration ignored the calls from the Slovenian ethnic societies and authorities in the Slovenian municipalities for the protection of the use of the Slovenian language, which was guaranteed under the Annex VI of the Italian Peace Treaty. Particularly unacceptable to the Slovenian community was the fact that the Fascist legislation with discriminatory traits, such as the Law No. 800 of 1923, which violated the personal rights of Slovenian people to the integrity of their names and similar, was still in force. All these trends were intensified following the adoption of the First London Memorandum of Understanding in October 1953. Detailed facts are available in B.C. Novak, *Trieste 1941–1954: The Ethnic, Political, and Ideological Struggle*, Chicago: University of Chicago Press, 1970, pp. 404–411, and in the sources cited therein.

6   See the facts related to this in B.C. Novak, *op. cit.*

of the Memorandum of Understanding regarding the Free Territory of Trieste in 1954, which fundamentally changed the direction of solutions to the Trieste Crisis, while its Annex II – the Special Statute – put together a thorough and detailed system for the protection of human rights and minority rights, thus advancing the basic objectives of the 1954 Memorandum of Understanding.[7] At the outset, it is important to emphasize the position in the legal scholarship that the Special Statute was actually a precondition for the implementation of the provisions of the 1954 Memorandum of Understanding, and that the entire new system for establishing the civil governments by extending the Yugoslav and Italian administration over the territories of the former Zones A and B, and the legal regimes instituted by the Memorandum were in fact conditioned by the implementation of the Statute. The other general remark is related to the manner of implementation of this regional Yugoslav-Italian instrument: while the Memorandum was only initialled, the Statute was signed, which eliminates any discussion about the significance of the latter from the perspective of international law, which was in fact the issue in relation to the Memorandum. Soon after its adoption, the Yugoslav Federal Assembly ratified the Statute.[8] The third determinant adding to the weight of the Statute is related to the mechanisms for its implementation. The Statute establishes a special Mixed Yugoslav-Italian Committee, institutionalizing the minority protection, which was then an absolute innovation within the international law. This body functioned on the principle of parity. In contrast to similar attempts at institutionalization of the minority protection process in the period of the League of Nations, the Mixed Italian-Yugoslav Committee was characterized by significant novelties and a new role of a national state, which may now carry out the international control over another national state when it comes to the

---

[7] The Memorandum of Understanding regarding the Free Territory of Trieste between United States of America, United Kingdom of Great Britain and Northern Ireland, France and Yugoslavia of 5 October 1954, with annexes and exchange of notes, was a first step towards the final resolution of the issue of Trieste in Yugoslav-Italian relations. The Memorandum dissolved the occupation system in the Free Territory of Trieste, in both Zones A and B, so that the Free Territory of Trieste ceased to exist. It also defined the border between the 'civil administrations' which were then established by Italy in the former Zone A, and Yugoslavia in the former Zone B. Finally, the system for the protection of the human rights was defined in the Memorandum. For more details on the Memorandum see B. Vukas, Jr., "The Free Territorry...", *op. cit.*; *idem, Osimski sporazumi i hrvatsko-talijanski odnosi – pravnopovijesni pogled*, Rijeka-Mošćenice: Pravni fakultet, 2007.

[8] The Federal Assembly of Yugoslavia ratified the Statute at its meeting of 25 October 1954. See J. Jeri, G. Kušelj, "Slovenska narodnostna skupnost v Italiji (II.)", *Teorija in praksa*, Nos. 5–6, 1973.

protection of its ethnic group, citizens of the other state. The novelty was also the introduction of the right of individual complaints and questions that could have been addressed to the Committee by members of the respective minorities. Such bilateral and subject-specific mechanism for intergovernmental control, and the right of direct international protection for individuals, was entirely unknown in the then international law.

The Special Statute contains the general provisions on protection of human rights prohibiting any discrimination on the basis of sex, language, religion or other criteria. The model for this provision can be found in the United Nations Universal Declaration of Human Rights (UDHR) of 1948, which laid the basis for the international legal protection of individuals in the post-war period. The Special Statute provides for the equality of citizens of the respective ethnic groups in the Free Territory of Trieste, not allowing any discrimination. Different aspects of this concept of equality are listed in Article 2(a)-(f) of the Special Statute, which encompasses the following: equality in civil, political and other human rights and fundamental freedoms guaranteed by the UDHR; equality in acquiring and performing any public service, functions, professions and honours; equality in accessing public and administrative office; equality in following a trade and profession in agriculture, commerce, industry and other fields, and in organizing and operating economic organizations for this purpose; equality in taxation; equality in the use of languages; and equality in social security and pension schemes. Traumatic experiences in interethnic relations have emphasized the need to provide particular solutions in the Special Statute, hence the provisions obliging the Italian and Yugoslav governments to assure fair representation of the respective ethnic groups in administrative positions, along with the general provision prohibiting any discrimination with regard to the criteria for admission to the public service.

In addition to the general provisions on protection of human and minority rights, the Special Statute also contains special provisions guaranteeing exclusive rights to the members of the ethnic minority groups, for instance, the right to their own press in their mother tongue, and educational, cultural, social and sports associations. In organizing these activities the minorities have to abide by the laws of the state where they act, respecting the interests of the majority population in using public buildings, radio and television, as well as assistance from public financial means (Article 4 of the Special Statute). Minorities are also guaranteed the right to teaching in their mother tongue in kindergartens, primary, secondary and professional schools. Given the then predominant trends of abolishing minority schools (Slovenian in Zone A, and Italian in Zone B), the Statute was detailed about these aspects of minority rights protection. Thus, the list of Italian schools in Zone B and Slovenian schools in Zone A, which were active in those areas at the moment the Memorandum of Understanding was initialled, is attached to the Statute. Detailed provisions are devoted to the manner in which a certain minority school or other minority institution may be closed down, which prescribe compulsory consultations before the Mixed Committee. Furthermore, the equality of minority schools is guaranteed in the sense of all organizational and financial issues relevant to other schools which are active in this area. Due to the regular practice of inappropriate treatment of teachers in the minority schools in the areas of the two Zones (primarily in Zone B), the Statute provides for special protection for minority school teachers, prescribing that authorities shall make an effort to ensure that teaching in such schools is entrusted to teachers whose mother tongue is that of the minority group.

The Special Statute guarantees also the personal use of the mother tongue in personal and official relations with the administrative and judicial authorities, providing for the option to communicate with those authorities in their mother tongue. Members of the minority groups were also vested with the right to request administrative documents and judicial decisions to be issued in their mother tongue. Likewise, the use of inscriptions on public institutions and the names of localities and streets in the area where the ethnic minority group made up not less than one quarter of the population had to be in the mother tongue of that minority (Article 5 of the Special Statute).

As opposed to the majority of international treaties of that era, the Special Statute also provides for the special economic protection of members of the ethnic minority group, guaranteeing its economic prosperity without any discriminatory measures (Article 6 of the Special Statute). There are also other principles incorporated in the Special Statute, such as the principle prohibiting change in the administrative boundaries within the area of the Free Territory of Trieste, so that the national homogeneity and minority interests remain preserved (Article 7 of the Special Statute), and the principle prohibiting and punishing the criminal acts of incitement to national and racial hatred (Article 3 of the Special Statute).

The Mixed Italian-Yugoslav Committee established under Article 8 of the Special Statute was already mentioned above. In this context, it is important to note that among the *ratione materiae* competences of the Mixed Committee were the following: monitoring and deciding on the implementation of the Special Statute, especially the problems that may occur in relation to its interpretation and understanding. However, the special task of the Mixed Committee was to examine complaints and questions raised by individuals who were members of the ethnic minorities in the Free Territory of Trieste. The Rules of Procedure of the Mixed Italian-Yugoslav Committee established under Article 8 of the Special Statute (Annex II of the Memorandum of Understanding of 5 October 1954)[9] laid down the provisions concerning the Committee's structure, competences and activities in accordance with the principles of parity and reciprocity, and bilateral and subject-specific nature of this extraordinary and very progressive system for the protection of human and minority rights.

III The 1975 Treaty of Osimo

Some twenty years after the specific international arrangement, the above-mentioned Memorandum of Understanding, was reached between Italy and Yugoslavia, discussion intensified regarding certain aspects of its legal nature. In several diplomatic notes in 1974, Italy tried to obstruct some of the solutions incorporated in the international bilateral arrangements, thus hindering the opportunities for improvement in Yugoslav-Italian relations. Instead of discussing the ecological protection of the Adriatic Sea, the standards applicable to Adriatic cooperation and the improvement of economic relations, the Italian diplomacy questioned some of the issues which seemed to have been resolved already in the 1947 Italian Peace Treaty. For instance, the Italian side refused to accept that, by the entry into force of the 1947 Italian Peace Treaty, Italian sovereignty over the Free Territory of Trieste had ceased. These were some of the reasons that led these states towards the process of negotiation of a new bilateral treaty. The result of this process was the Treaty of Osimo signed on 10 November 1975.

And while the Treaty of Osimo was exceptionally important in the context of defining the final territorial delimitation between Italy and Yugoslavia (removing the disagreements about its legal nature, defining the boundary on the sea and similar), in respect of protection of human rights and minority rights it builds upon the improvement achieved by the Special Statute. According to the provision of Article 7 of the Treaty of Osimo, the Memorandum of Understanding signed at London on 5 October 1954 (along with both of its Annexes, of course) ceased to have effect on the date of entry into force of the Treaty of Osimo.[10] Article 8 of the Treaty of Osimo, however, neither leaves the Special Statute in force nor transfers it into an annex to the Treaty of Osimo, yet it provides that the parties "shall maintain in force the internal measures already taken in application of the aforesaid Statute and shall ensure under its

---

9 The text of the Rules of procedure was published in *Službeni list FNRJ*, No. 1/1956.
10 The Treaty of Osimo entered into force on 11 October 1977.

domestic law that the level of protection stipulated for members of the respective ethnic groups (of the respective minorities) in the expired Special Statute is maintained". This phrasing helped to avoid the objection by the Italian government raised due to lack of ratification of the Special Statute, at the same time leaving Italy's obligation to guarantee special status to the Slovenian ethnic minority in its laws, which were already supposed to have been aligned with the Special Statute, and Yugoslavia's obligation to do the same for the Italian ethnic minority in the former Zone B.

As a result, the main centre of gravity relating to ethnic minority rights protection shifted to the level of national legislation. Considering the contents of the Italian national laws and regulations, it may be concluded that its constitutional provisions as well as regional provisions prescribe only the general framework for this issue. This is well illustrated by the already cited Articles 3 and 6 of the Constitution of the Italian Republic, while Article 3 of the Special Statute of the Autonomous Region of Friuli-Venezia Giulia states: "In the Region equality in rights is granted to all citizens, regardless of the linguistic group they belong to, with special safeguards for the respective ethnic and cultural characteristics."[11] Although the scholarship calls attention to the perfect protection of the Slovenian national community,[12] neither national nor regional laws in Italy contain anything concerning its special protection.

In contrast to abstract and general provisions on ethnic minority protection, the Constitution of the Socialist Federal Republic of Yugoslavia (SFRY) of 1974, as well as the constitutions of both federal republics, the Socialist Republic of Croatia and the Socialist Republic of Slovenia of the same year, uses wording that lists the minorities to which special rights are guaranteed, given the large number of their members in relation to the majority population, and specifying special measures for their protection. The Slovenian constitutional provisions, today as well as in 1974, provide for the protection of the rights of the autochthonous Italian and Hungarian national communities (not mentioning any other). From 1974 until the present day, the Croatian constitutional provisions, as amended over time and modifying the statutes of different ethnic communities, has recognized special status to the Italian minority (and other ethnic minorities using the combined method of a non-exhaustive list in the preamble and a general clause in the respective provision) not limited to

---

11   The text of this Statute is printed in L. Paladin, *Commento allo Statuto della Regione Friuli-Venezia Giulia*, Udine: Del Bianco Editore, 1969.
12   On the status of the Slovenian ethnic minority under the Italian laws see S. Bartole, "Tutela della minoranza linguistica Slovena ed esecuzione del Trattato di Osimo", *Rivista di diritto internazionale*, Vol. 15, Nos. 3–4, 1977, pp. 519–525.

the former Zone B; such special status is further developed in the Croatian laws, by-laws and other legal instruments. The Italian minority enjoys special protection also in the areas which, pursuant to the provision of Article 11 of the Italian Peace Treaty, passed into the sovereignty of Croatia, then a federal republic, and today an independent and sovereign state.[13]

IV International Legal Issues Related to the Status of Ethnic Minorities in the Context of Croatian-Italian Relations

The processes leading to the independence of the former federal socialist republics of Croatia and Slovenia in 1991 in no way impaired the then international standards for protection of human and minority rights. Succession to treaties obliged the newly-founded states to respect the standards for human rights protection created on the bilateral or multilateral level by the former Yugoslavia. It appears that from the time when the two states' independence was declared those standards have only been upgraded and improved.

This is proved by the notes sent by both the Croatian and Italian ministries of foreign affairs in March 1992. In its diplomatic note of 25 March 1992, on the basis of paragraph III of the Constitutional Decision on Sovereignty and Independence of the Republic of Croatia, the Ministry of Foreign Affairs of the Republic of Croatia acting on behalf of the Croatian Government stated that "it has an honour to propose that the treaties concluded between the Republic of Italy and the former Yugoslavia continue to be applied in the relations between the Republic of Italy and the Republic of Croatia, until both parties agree otherwise".[14] In its response through the Italian Embassy in Zagreb, the Italian Government "declares that the act on recognition of the Republic of Croatia of 15 January 1992, the Italian Government acknowledges that the Republic of Croatia is one of the successors to the former SFRY".[15] The Italian Government expressed its willingness to commence negotiations with Croatia and other successor states to the former SFRY for the purpose of reviewing and

13 See the Constitution of the Socialist Federal Republic of Yugoslavia, *Službeni list*, 21 February 1974, Articles 1, 3, 4, 154, 170, 171, 214, 243, 245–248, 251, 269 and 271; the Constitution of the Socialist Republic of Croatia, *Narodne novine*, 22 February 1974; the Constitution of the Socialist Republic of Slovenia, *Uradni list*, 28 February 1974.

14 Diplomatic Note by the Ministry of Foreign Affairs of the Republic of Croatia No. 1506-18/92 of 25 March 1992, obtained from the Ministry of Foreign Affairs and European Integration of the Republic of Croatia.

15 Diplomatic Note by the Embassy of the Italian Republic addressed to the Ministry of Foreign Affairs of the Republic of Croatia (No. 233, Pos A/14), obtained from the Ministry of Foreign Affairs and European Integration of the Republic of Croatia.

updating certain agreements, and especially the Osimo Treaty. The Italian Ministry of Foreign Affairs appointed a committee, chaired by the Italian Ambassador to the Republic of Croatia Sergio Berlinguera, to carry out the mentioned diplomatic negotiations. In this manner the Italian Government undoubtedly recognized the Republic of Croatia as a successor state to the former Yugoslavia respecting all international legal provisions regulating such situations. This has laid the basis for the future negotiations and treaties defining the relations between the two states.

Besides the issue of succession regarding the boundary between the states, another important public law problem regulated under the Osimo Treaty and linked to the present day legal structure in the Republic of Croatia is certainly the minority rights protection system. The problem of implementation of the Osimo Treaty in the Croatian laws derives from Article 8 of the Osimo Treaty, which *inter alia* states that, despite the provision that the London Memorandum of Understanding of 1954, including the Special Statute annexed to it, had ceased to have effect, each party declared "it shall maintain in force the internal measures already taken in application of the aforesaid Statute and shall ensure under its domestic law that the level of protection stipulated for members of the respective ethnic groups (of the respective minorities) in the expired Special Statute is maintained." As a consequence of the constitution of Croatia and Slovenia as independent states, Italy became concerned about the destiny of the mentioned minority protection measures in the respective laws of the two new states. Given that the former Constitution of the SFRY, which in a number of its provisions guaranteed the rights of the Italian minority, was no longer in force in Slovenia and Croatia (as of 8 October 1991 in Croatia) and the new Slovenian and Croatian constitutions and accompanying laws were not sufficiently structured or reliable, the Italian Government insisted on comprehensive negotiations to assure new provisions regarding the status of the Italian minority in the new states. On the other hand, the disadvantage was in the fact that the Italian minority was now split between the two newly-founded states. All this brought about efforts to provide legal reassurance to the Italian minority, in accordance with the Osimo Treaty, at both the internal and international (bilateral and multilateral) levels.

The issue of human and minority rights protection was specifically emphasized in the period of international recognition of the Republic of Croatia. Thus, the opinions adopted at the Conference on Yugoslavia, in accordance with the Guidelines on the Recognition of New States in Eastern Europe and in the Soviet Union (European Council, 16 December 1991)[16] and the Declaration on Yugoslavia adopted by the European Community and its Member States

---

16 *International Legal Materials*, Vol. 31, 1992, pp. 1486–1487.

(Extraordinary EPC Ministerial Meeting, Brussels, 16 December 1991),[17] highlight that the prerequisite for recognition of the new states is the states' guarantees of the human rights and rights of national or ethnic groups. For Croatia, international recognition was further conditioned upon the amendments to its Human Rights and Minority Rights Constitutional Act of 4 December 1991.[18] Against this background, the Memorandum of Understanding – *Memorandum d'intesa* – was signed in Rome on 15 January 1992 by the representatives of the Italian and Croatian Governments, but without a Slovenian signature. The Memorandum consists of two documents, the first concerning the status of the Italian minority in Croatia and Slovenia, and the other concerning the status of the Slovenian minority in Italy. These documents put in place the basic principles defining the status of the Italian minority in Croatia and Slovenia, and the Slovenian minority in Italy. The 1992 Memorandum of Understanding recognized the intention of the newly-founded states to recognize the authenticity, unity (*unicità*) and specificity of the Italian minority in these states. The Italian Union (*Unione Italiana*) was recognized as the only representative of the Italian minority in Croatia and Slovenia. Additional rights recognized in the 1992 Memorandum of Understanding were the right to free movement and the right to employment of members of the Italian community who are citizens of the other states, in the relations between those states.[19]

As already mentioned, Slovenia eventually did not sign the 1992 Memorandum of Understanding. Thus, further negotiations on the status of the Italian minority were held bilaterally. The experiences in Slovenian-Italian relations in this field are substantially different from those in Croatian-Italian relations, and this is undoubtedly due to, *inter alia*, the relatively large Slovenian minority in Italy. Slovenian laws and regulations follow the constitutional principles set in the 1974 Constitution of the Socialist Republic of Slovenia as well as the new Constitution of the Republic of Slovenia dated 28 December 1991. The latter Constitution, in its Article 5, contains the general clause on human rights and national minority rights protection which obliges Slovenia to "protect and guarantee the rights of the autochthonous Italian and Hungarian

---

17 *European Journal of International Law*, Vol. 4, No. 1, 1993, pp. 73.
18 For details on these conditions and the process of international recognition of the Republic of Croatia see B. Vukas, Jr., "Državnopravni aspekti konstituiranja hrvatske države 1989.-1992.", *Zbornik Pravnog fakulteta Sveučilišta u Rijeci*, Vol. 23, No. 2, 2002, pp. 668 *et seq.*
19 The text of the Treaty printed in E. Giuricin, L. Giuricin, *La comunità nacionale italiana II. – Documenti 1944–2006*, Fiume: Unione italiana, Trieste: Università popolare, Rovigno: Centro di ricerche storiche, 2008, pp. 294–295.

national communities", and in its Article 11 provides for special minority rights in those municipalities where Italian or Hungarian national communities reside and where "Italian or Hungarian shall also be official languages" in addition to Slovenian.[20] Further comments on the relations between Slovenia and Italy are beyond the scope of this paper.

A huge step forward in Croatian-Italian relations, which brought about the closure of the one hot issue in their several decades or even centuries long genesis, is most certainly the signing of the Treaty between the Republic of Croatia and the Italian Republic concerning Minority Rights on 5 November 1996.[21] This Treaty is mindful of the international treaties as well as other international instruments on the protection of human and minority rights, including the universal international legal instruments adopted under the auspices of the United Nations and an increasingly abundant catalogue of regional, particularly European legal instruments in the field. The 1996 Treaty is also founded on national standards for minority protection in Croatian and Italian laws and regulations. The basic principle of the 1996 Treaty is codified in its Article 1 where the Republic of Croatia confirms "the recognition of the autochthonous character and the unity of the Italian Minority and its specific characteristics".

With the aim of ensuring protection to the Italian minority in accordance with the abovementioned sources of international law (Article 2), the 1996 Treaty establishes the treatment granted to the Italian minority in the former Zone B as the basic level of protection granted to the Italian minority in the Republic of Croatia in general (Article 3), by gradually extending such treatment across the areas of the Republic of Croatia traditionally inhabited by the Italian minority. This has enabled *via facti* the entry into force of the 1954 Special Statute, which set the criteria and the content to the Italian minority rights, not only in the former Zone B, but also in the entire area of the autochthonous habitation of the Italian minority. Today, the Italian minority mostly inhabits the areas of the Istrian Peninsula, Rijeka, the

---

20   The entire provision of Article 5 of the 1991 Constitution of the Republic of Slovenia, *Uradni list*, No. 33/9, 28 December 1991, states: "In its own territory, the state shall protect human rights and fundamental freedoms. It shall protect and guarantee the rights of the autochthonous Italian and Hungarian national communities. It shall maintain concern for autochthonous Slovene national minorities in the neighbouring countries and for Slovene emigrants and workers abroad and shall foster their contacts with the homeland. It shall provide for the preservation of the natural wealth and cultural heritage and create opportunities for the harmonious development of society and culture in Slovenia."

21   *Narodne novine, Medunarodni ugovori*, No. 15/1997. The Treaty entered into force on 8 July 1998, see *Narodne novine, Medunarodni ugovori*, No. 10/1998.

Island of Cres, the Island of Lošinj and several villages in Western Slavonia (Pakrac). These high standards for the protection of the Italian minority reveal both the huge importance and legal quality of the 1954 Special Statute, certain elements of which bind *via facti* the Republic of Croatia on the basis of the 1996 Treaty. Moreover, these high protection standards also demonstrate superior democratic criteria which the Republic of Croatia adopts when it comes to the protection of the rights of its citizens, specifically the members of ethnic minority groups. In accordance with earlier declarations, the 1996 Treaty recognizes the Italian Union (*Unione Italiana*) as the organization representing the Italian minority, and assures unity to the Italian minority in Croatia and Slovenia by providing the members of the Italian minority who have Slovenian citizenship with freedom of movement and employment in Croatia, if they are engaged in minority-related activities, such as within the Italian Union, other institutions, schools, media, *etc.* (Articles 5 and 6). The said protection is aligned with the International Labour Organization standards (Article 7).

The reciprocal character of this Treaty becomes apparent in its Article 8, where the Italian Republic guarantees protection to the autochthonous Croatian minority in the Region of Molise (also pursuant to the provisions of the Statute of this Region – *Statuto della Regione Molise*), as well as "in the territory of traditional settlement where its presence has been ascertained". This extends the protection of the Croatian minority to the entire north of Italy which the Croatian minority has traditionally populated. The guarantees to the Croatian minority include the right of preserving and freely expressing its own cultural identity and heritage, using its mother tongue in private and public schools, and establishing and maintaining its cultural institutions and associations, *etc*. The main difficulty in the protection of the Croatian minority in Italy is that its members are generally failing to declare their Croatian ethnic affiliation, and hence they do not use the rights granted under this Treaty. The only organized activity of Croatian cultural and educational institutions is traditionally anchored in the Region of Molise. This said, the number of Croats in northern Italy is certainly significant. Since the notion of ethnic minority is hard to define, it is common that the ethnic minority rights are afforded to those members who declare their respective ethnic affiliation. It is therefore not possible to request the guaranteeing of rights to the minority which does not declare itself as such, as is the case with Croats in northern Italy, where their presence is the consequence of various motives or historical reasons and the awareness of their Croatian origin is insufficiently preserved.

v   Concluding Remarks

The complexity in the relations between Italy, Croatia and Slovenia, throughout the history they have shared, confirms the impact that the provisions on human rights protection have on its genesis. The implementation of international standards, along with the bilateral treaties between the former Yugoslavia and Italy, have considerably improved mutual relations among the neighbouring nations in the North Adriatic area. Among a number of factors, it is the international law that significantly affected the transformation of these relations from exceptionally conflictual opposites to internationally stable and structured cooperation. This has been the tendency after the cataclysm that characterized the period of the Second World War.

It is interesting to note that some bilateral treaties, such as the Special Statute – Annex II to the 1954 Memorandum of Understanding regarding the Free Territory of Trieste – have innovatively introduced new standards into international law, principally in order to strengthen the imperative of the human rights protection. Implementation laws and regulations (such as the right of individual complaints and questions that could have been addressed to the bilateral committee by members of the respective minorities), and other instruments aligned with the international law, have *per se* enriched the international law in this field.

Contemporary tendencies in international relations put fundamentally changed interests and challenges before the North Adriatic neighbours. These challenges are now related to the cooperation between states within the stability endeavours guaranteed within the Euro-Atlantic integration. This system, put into action primarily through the mechanisms of the Council of Europe and its persuasive legal infrastructure and authority, achieved accentuated human rights guarantees, generally adding new dimensions to the so-called 'Adriatic Peace' – to employ the terminology used by Lujo Tončić Sorinj, a renowned Austrian diplomat and politician of Croatian ethnic origin, to denote these relations.

CHAPTER 35

The Role of the Committee of Experts in the ILO's Supervisory Mechanism: Reflections on Ten Years' Experience as a Member

*Yozo Yokota**

I   Introduction

Strictly speaking, this is not an academic paper analysing in detail the structure and functions of the Committee of Experts on the Application of Conventions and Recommendations ('Committee of Experts' or CEACR) of the International Labour Organization (ILO).[1] Rather, it represents some reflections on the author's ten years' experience, from 2003 up to now, as a member, and between 2010 and 2013 as its Chairperson.

However, such characterization of this paper by no means implies that it has no academic value. The intention of this contribution is to share with the readers, who, it is assumed, are largely international law specialists, some aspects of the organization and activities of the Committee of Experts that the author has found extremely interesting and insightful from the viewpoint of the study of international law in which the author has been engaged over the past forty-plus years. The author believes that a paper of this nature is perhaps most appropriate for the *Liber Amicorum* for Professor Budislav Vukas who has established the highest international reputation as a distinguished professor of international law and who also served on the Committee of Experts as a prominent member for twenty-one years up to 2007.

In 1987, the author published a paper regarding "the impact of international organizations on international law".[2] In that paper, the author concluded in

---

*   President, Center for Human Rights Education and Training, Tokyo.
1   The acronym 'ILO' is sometimes used to mean the 'International Labour Office' which is the secretariat headed by the Director-General. In this paper, the author follows the usual usage of this expression representing the 'International Labour Organization'. When the author needs to refer specifically to the secretariat of the ILO, he uses 'the Office' to avoid confusion.
2   Yozo Yokota, "The Impact of International Organizations on International Law", in: Yasuaki Onuma, ed., *International Law, United Nations and Japan* (in Japanese), Kobundo, 1987, pp. 123–116.

summary that international organizations, particularly the United Nations and its specialized agencies including the ILO, are today providing an institutional framework, while still rudimentary, for the legislation, execution and application of international law which had long been regarded as 'weak law', or even just 'positive morality'. This finding is a partial, but fairly convincing, answer to a doubt expressed by some lawyers and political scientists about the legal quality of international law by reason of the lack of legislature, courts and government.[3]

For an international law student who had reached a conclusion that international law today is constantly and progressively under the influence of the existence and activities of various international organizations, experience as a member of the Committee of Experts has been most inspiring and stimulating. Through this paper, the author wishes to share with the readers some insights gained during his service on the Committee.

II   The Place of the Committee of Experts in the ILO's Supervisory Mechanism

Before coming to the main part of this paper, it is useful to review briefly the place and role of the Committee of Experts in the whole structure and functions of the ILO generally, and its supervisory mechanism specifically.

The ILO was established in 1919 under Part XIII of the Treaty of Versailles, which later became the Constitution of the International Labour Organization, in order to improve conditions of labour such as hours of work, wages and health and safety at work.[4] Over the years, it has undergone a number of amendments, the most significant of which is the Declaration of Philadelphia of 1944 which solemnly affirmed the principle that the promotion of material and spiritual wellbeing must constitute the central aim of ILO policy "in conditions of freedom and dignity, of economic security and equal opportunity".

Since its creation, the ILO has set up and developed an innovative method of achieving its aim through: (a) setting international labour standards; and (b) supervising their application and implementation by the Member States.

---

[3] Malcolm N. Shaw, *International Law*, Grotius Publications, Cambridge University Press, 1991, p. 3.

[4] For more details about the establishment and activities of the ILO in general see Klaus Theodor Samson, "International Labour Organisation", *Encyclopedia of Public International Law*, Vol. 5 (International Organizations in General: Universal International Organizations and Cooperation), North-Holland, 1983, pp. 87–94 and the publications listed in the bibliography at the end of the article.

International labour standards take the form of either (a) Conventions which are legally binding on the ratifying States, or (b) Recommendations which are non-binding guidance. From its establishment in 1919 up to 2013, the ILO has adopted 189 Conventions and 201 Recommendations covering a broad range of subjects including, for instance, hours of work, minimum wages, health and safety at work, freedom of association, right to collective bargaining, discrimination in the employment, forced labour and child labour.

The unique aspect of the ILO's activities in the areas of the promotion and protection of rights, safety and health at work is that it not only sets international labour standards through the adoption of Conventions and Recommendations but it also supervises the application and implementation of such standards within the Member States.[5] In fact, the ILO has quite complex and sophisticated mechanisms and procedures to supervise the application and implementation of the international labour standards, some of which are based on the provisions of the ILO Constitution but others have also been formulated and developed through practice.

1 *Constitution-Based Supervision Procedures*
a In the Case of a Recommendation

Submission to Competent Authorities: Under Article 19, paragraph 6 (b), of the Constitution, all Member States must, within one year in principle[6] after the closing of the Conference which has adopted it, bring the Recommendation before the competent authority or authorities for legislation or other action to give effect to it. If any Member fails to fulfill this obligation, the matter will be reported to the Conference.[7]

---

[5] Since the ILO deals with the rights, health, safety and interest of individual workers, the international labour standards stipulated in Conventions and Recommendations need to be applied and implemented by the Member States through domestic laws, regulations and policies.

[6] More precisely, "within the period of one year at most from the closing of the session of the Conference, or if it is impossible owing to exceptional circumstances to do so within the period of one year, then at the earliest practicable moment and in no case later than 18 months after the closing of the Conference."

[7] Reporting to the Conference, or Governing Body, for deliberation is generally considered by the Member States as a kind of sanction in the form of psychological pressure because it is an embarrassment to the States concerned. It also involves additional work for the governments to explain the reasons for the failure to comply. On the power of discussion and deliberation in international fora in general see Ian Johnstone, *The Power of Deliberation: International Law, Politics and Organizations*, Oxford University Press, 2011.

Periodic Report: Under Article 19, paragraph 6 (d), the Member States are required to report to the Director-General (DG) of the ILO, at appropriate intervals decided by the Governing Body, the position of law and practice regarding matters dealt with in the Recommendation.

b   In the Case of a Convention

Submission for Ratification: Under Article 19, paragraph 5 (b), of the Constitution, all Member States must, within one year in principle[8] from the closing of the session of the Conference, bring the Convention before the competent authority or authorities for ratification. If any Member fails to fulfill this obligation, the matter will be reported to the Conference. Once ratified, the Member must communicate this fact to the DG.

Periodic Report: Under Article 22 of the Constitution, each party to a ratified Convention will have to report, at an appropriate interval,[9] to the ILO on the measures taken to give effect to it. Such report should also be communicated to the representative organizations of employers and workers of that country (Art. 23, para. 2).[10] A summary of information and reports communicated to the ILO will be laid before the next meeting of the Conference (Art. 23, para. 1).

---

8   See note 5 above.

9   The Constitution provides that such reports should be submitted annually. However, over the years, the numbers of Conventions and ratifying Members have increased dramatically. It has become impracticable to maintain the policy of annual reports. Currently, ILO Members are required to report every three years for the eight fundamental Conventions and every five years for all the other Conventions. The eight fundamental Conventions, which require a three-year reporting cycle, are: (1) Freedom of Association and Protection of the Right to Organize Convention, 1948 (No. 87); (2) Right to Organize and Collective Bargaining Convention, 1949 (No. 98); (3) Forced Labour Convention, 1930 (No. 29); (4) Abolition of Forced Labour Convention, 1957 (No. 105); (5) Minimum Age Convention, 1973 (No. 138); (6) Worst Forms of Child Labour Convention, 1999 (No. 182); (7) Equal Remuneration Convention, 1951 (No. 100); and (8) Equality of Opportunity and Treatment in Employment and Occupation Convention, 1958 (No. 111).

10 It should be noted that the ILO from its establishment in 1919 has had a unique system of 'tripartite representation'. Unlike almost all delegations to international conferences and meetings of international organizations, which are composed of the representatives of the governments of the participating States, the representatives of the Member States to the ILO Conference are composed of two government representatives and one representative each of the workers' and employers' organizations who act (including voting) not as a group but individually. The tripartite representation is present not only at the Conference but also at the Governing Body and other important organs of the ILO including some supervisory bodies.

Representation: Under Article 24 of the Constitution, any industrial association of employers or of workers may make representations in the case of failure to observe a provision of a ratified Convention. When such representation is made, the Governing Body may communicate it to the government concerned for a statement. If, within a reasonable time, no statement is received, or if the statement received appears to be unsatisfactory, the Governing Body may publish the representation and the statement, if any (Art. 25).[11]

Complaint Procedure: Under Article 26, paragraph 1, any party to a Convention may file a complaint with the ILO regarding non-compliance by another party. The Governing Body may communicate on such complaint with the government in question (para. 2) or appoint a Commission of Inquiry (COI) to consider the complaint (para. 3). The COI will adopt, after consideration, a report containing its findings and recommendations for steps to be taken with a timeframe (Art. 28). The parties will be requested either to accept such recommendations or to refer the complaint to the International Court of Justice (ICJ) (Art. 29, para. 2). Any failure to carry out the recommendations of the COI report or ICJ decision, as the case may be, may result in the Governing Body's recommendation to the Conference for action to secure compliance (Art. 33).[12]

2   Practice-Based Supervision Procedures

In addition to the Constitution-based supervision procedures described above, the ILO has created practice-based supervision bodies. They are: (a) the Committee of Experts; (b) the Conference Committee on the Application of Standards ('Conference Committee'); and (c) the Committee on Freedom of Association.

a   The Committee of Experts

The Committee of Experts is composed of a maximum of twenty members[13] who are independent and qualified experts in the fields of labour law,

---

11   Publication of these documents can also serve as a kind of sanction because their contents may have some information that can be an embarrassment to, or damage the reputation of, the countries involved.

12   When the defaulting government takes the steps necessary to comply with the COI recommendation or ICJ decision, as the case may be, it may request the Governing Body to constitute a COI to verify the matter. If the COI finds that the recommendation or decision is faithfully carried out, it will recommend the discontinuance of any action taken under Article 33.

13   The number of the Committee's membership is set at twenty but there are usually some vacancies because it takes time to fill the vacancies. At the 83rd Session of the Committee in November-December 2012, there were eighteen members and two vacancies.

international law, human rights law and social security law appointed by the Governing Body for a term of three years, which is renewable up to a maximum of fifteen years.

As explained above, Article 22 of the Constitution requires the ratifying Members to send periodic reports to the ILO at intervals of three or five years. The States also send such reports to the workers' and employers' organizations for comments. It is the role of the Committee of Experts to examine these reports and comments.[14] The results of the examination will be put together in the form of either (a) 'direct requests' or (b) 'observations'. Direct requests are not published. They are only sent to the governments concerned for response to the requests or queries by the Committee. They deal with relatively less serious points such as queries for clarification of law and practice, requests for further information and explanation of issues that the ILO is concerned about. Observations, on the other hand, deal with more serious matters including comments on non-application, or violation, of a provision of a ratified Convention, or on the discrepancy found between domestic law, regulations or policies and the Convention. The observations are published in the form of the report of the Committee of Experts to the Conference annually.[15]

The observations of the Committee of Experts are not legally binding but are generally given great weight because they are regarded as the work of internationally reputed legal experts who carry out their mandate observing faithfully the principles of independence, impartiality and objectivity. For this reason, a well-informed former high-ranking ILO legal officer stated, "The Report of the Committee of Experts is already a powerful tool for those who want to compare their country's performance with its international obligations".[16] The author intends to come back to this important point later.

b   The Conference Committee

The Conference Committee was created in 1926 to assist the Conference to consider selected, most serious cases of deviation by national legislation and practice from the international labour standards. The report of the Committee

---

14   The Committee of Experts also examines Article 19 reports (regarding Recommendations) and Article 35 reports (regarding non-metropolitan territories). But, the main part of the Committee's work is focused on Article 22 reports (regarding ratified Conventions for the metropolitan territories of the Member States).
15   It is marked as Report III (IA) for each year.
16   Lee Swepston, "The International Labour Organization's System of Human Rights Protection", in: Janusz Symonides, ed., *Human Rights: International Protection, Monitoring, Enforcement*, UNESCO, 2003, p. 96.

of Experts is submitted to the Conference Committee which is, unlike the Committee of Experts, tripartite in its composition, *i.e.*, comprising representatives of governments, employers and workers. Again unlike the Committee of Experts whose meetings are private, the Conference Committee usually meets in public during the session of the Conference which is held in June every year.

The Conference Committee selects, with the agreement of employers' and workers' groups, twenty-five more serious cases out of hundreds of observations included in the report of the Committee of Experts. The Committee invites the representatives of the governments concerned to appear before it and explain the reasons for the difficulties addressed. The Committee then asks to clarify the situation, indicates a timetable for the implementation of measures requested by the Committee of Experts, or commits to inviting the ILO to carry out 'direct contacts' or technical assistance to resolve the problems. As pointed out by Swepston, "[T]hese sessions can be very difficult for government representatives"[17] and therefore could be a sanction against serious deviation from the international labour standards. For this reason, most governments try hard to exclude their country situation from the list of twenty-five, by, for instance, trying to improve the situation to the satisfaction of the ILO.

c   The Committee on Freedom of Association

In 1951, the ILO entered into an agreement with the Economic and Social Council (ECOSOC) of the United Nations (UN) to create a Committee on Freedom of Association. Initially, its objective was to screen for the fact-finding and conciliation commission on freedom of association. It later became the body to receive complaints of violations of freedom of association filed by employers' or workers' organizations. The unique feature of this Committee is that it may receive complaints not only against the ratifying Member States of relevant Conventions[18] but also against non-ratifying States.

Like the Conference Committee, the Committee on Freedom of Association is tripartite, comprising three members each from the employer, worker and government members of the Governing Body. Its decisions and recommendations are usually well respected by the governments concerned. For instance, as a result of the interventions by the Committee on Freedom of Association,

---

17 Swepston, *op. cit.*, p. 96.
18 The most relevant Conventions are the Freedom of Association and Protection of the Right to Organize Convention, 1948 (No. 87) and the Right to Organize and Collective Bargaining Convention, 1949 (No. 98).

the governments in question in the past have freed many imprisoned union leaders and introduced changes in labour law and industrial relations.

III The Work of the Committee of Experts

As seen above, the role of the Committee of Experts is unique in the supervisory mechanisms of the ILO. First, its composition is not tripartite. It is an expert body similar to the treaty bodies of the major universal human rights treaties such as the Human Rights Committee of the International Covenant on Civil and Political Rights.[19] Second, its reports, which are submitted to the Conference as well as the Conference Committee, containing observations on the situations of application of ratified Conventions in the Member States, are published and stand alone. Although the observations of the Committee of Experts are not legally binding, they are nevertheless often referred to or quoted with some weight. Third, the recommendations and views included in the observations of the Committee of Experts are backed by the follow-up mechanisms at the level of the Conference Committee, Governing Body and Conference, which are all tripartite in composition.

The Committee of Experts meets once a year from the last week of November to the middle of December, for about three weeks. The first week is mostly assigned to 'individual examinations', which means that each expert examines the reports submitted under the Convention(s) he or she is responsible for, together with any comments by the workers' or employers' organizations and any other documents including national legislation and practice (such as court cases, if any), statistics, exchanges of letters and notes between the Office and the government concerned and previous observations and direct requests regarding the same Convention.[20] During the first week, the expert usually prepares, with the useful assistance of capable and experienced staff of the Office, particularly the Department of International Labour Standards (often abbreviated to 'Normes'), draft comments in the form of observations or direct requests on the cases under examination.

---

[19] Torkel Opsahl, "The Human Rights Committee", in: Philip Alston, ed., *The United Nations and Human Rights: a Critical Appraisal*, Oxford University Press, 1995, pp. 369–443.

[20] In preparing a draft observation, the expert also looks at the reports of the field staff, special missions, 'direct contact missions', and the Committee on Freedom of Association. In addition, account is also taken of the reports of the UN and other related organizations such as international financial institutions, the Council of Europe and the European Union.

Starting with the second week, the Committee meets in full plenary meeting and deliberates the draft observations and direct requests prepared by the responsible expert. Some drafts are easy to reach consensus on, but in other cases the Committee spends a considerable amount of time in agreeing on the adequate wording of the observations and direct requests. But after careful and serious discussion, the Committee almost always comes to a consensus. The main thrust of the Committee's observation is to "indicate the extent to which each member State's legislation and practice are in conformity with ratified Conventions and extent to which each member States have fulfilled their obligations under the ILO Constitution in relation to standards."[21] The Committee of Experts carries out this task fully respecting the principles of independence, impartiality and objectivity. In this connection, it is useful to refer to a statement in its 1987 report which reads:

> [I]ts [the Committee of Experts'] function is to determine whether the requirements of a given Convention are being met, whatever the economic and social conditions existing in a given country. Subject only to any derogations, which are expressly permitted by the Convention itself, these requirements remain constant and uniform for all countries. In carrying out this work, the Committee is guided by the standards laid down in the Convention alone, mindful, however, of the fact that the modes of their implementation may be different in different States.[22]

Apart from the observation on a ratified Convention, the Committee of Experts prepares and adopts a 'comparative analysis' for a particular country under the Convention. It is a detailed analysis comparing law and practice in a particular country and the provisions of a ratified Convention to determine the extent to which the Convention is applied. It is usually prepared when the first report is received after the entry into force of the Convention or when important legislation on the subject is adopted or has been formally submitted as a draft text.

A direct request rather than an observation is considered appropriate when a minor discrepancy is found, or additional information is required on points

---

21 Report of the Committee of Experts on the Application of Conventions and Recommendations, Report III (Part 1A), International Labour Conference, 102nd Session, 2013, p. 2.

22 Report of the Committee of Experts on the Application of Conventions and Recommendations, Report III (Part 4A), International Labour Conference, 73rd Session, 1987, para. 24.

of doubt, or a complicated technical point needs to be clarified. However, an observation is preferred when one or more of the following points needs to be raised:

(a) A fundamental discrepancy is found;
(b) There is an absence of measures to give effect to the Convention under consideration;
(c) No effective action has been taken on previous comments;
(d) Information supplied indicates no clear improvement in the situation; and
(e) Important points are raised by the workers' or employers' organization to which the government has not responded adequately or has not taken any measures.

In the observation, when the Committee of Experts recognizes a clear case of progress, it notes it with "satisfaction" or "interest". "Satisfaction" is used when a government has taken appropriate measures, either through an amendment of the legislation or a significant change in the national policy or practice, achieving fuller compliance with the Convention. "Interest" is used when the measures taken by the government are sufficiently advanced to justify the expectation that further progress will be achieved. The list of cases noted by the Committee of Experts with "satisfaction" or "interest" is published in its report.[23]

When the Committee finds a serious case of discrepancy or violation, it expresses its "regret" or "concern", the former being used in a more serious case and the latter in a less serious one. The Committee sometimes strengthens its observation by adding the word "deeply" before "regret" or the word "gravely" before "concern".

In more serious cases or cases that require the Committee to obtain more information outside the normal reporting cycle, the Committee of Experts puts a footnote to the observation under consideration to call for a reply to the comments of the Committee in the following year.[24]

In certain, more serious cases, the Committee puts a double footnote to the observation, which means that the government concerned is requested to

---

[23] When the Committee of Experts expresses "satisfaction" or "interest", it does not reflect the overall compliance with the Convention by the country in question. The expression relates only to the specific issue under consideration.

[24] The footnote reads: "The Government is asked to reply in detail to the present comments in 20xx."

supply detailed information to the Conference.[25] In deciding to put a double footnote to a particular observation, the Committee takes into account the following criteria:

(a) The seriousness of the problem particularly involving fundamental rights, safety, health and well-being of the workers and matters adversely affecting workers internationally or workers belonging to the categories of protected persons;
(b) The persistence of the problem for which the government does not seem to be willing to take effective measures for improvement;
(c) The urgency of the situation such as life-threatening situations or a problem which is likely to cause irreversible harm; and
(d) The quality and scope of the government's response which is unsatisfactory, such as the cases of clear and repeated refusal to comply with its obligation under the ratified Convention under consideration.

IV   A Recent Challenge Faced by the Committee of Experts

In this Chapter, the author wishes to deal with a serious problem recently raised in the Conference Committee by its employers' group, concerning the role of the Committee of Experts in the ILO's supervisory mechanism.

But, before getting into the substance of the problem, the author would like to underline the good working relationship between the two committees developed over decades of working in tandem with a spirit of mutual respect, cooperation and responsibility for the promotion and protection of the rights of workers. The relationship is not at all competitive or redundant. Rather, it is complementary in view of their composition and roles. With regard to the composition, the Committee of Experts comprises about twenty independent legal experts, while the Conference Committee is tripartite. On the roles, the Committee of Experts provides independent, impartial and objective analyses on the application of Conventions and Recommendations while the Conference Committee plays a much broader role of searching solutions through dialogue among the tripartite constituents. Thus, the two Committees are complementary and mutually supportive. With this understanding in mind, the author tries to describe the problem posed by one constituent of the Conference Committee.

---

25   In the double footnote case, the sentence reads: "The Government is asked to supply full particulars to the Conference at its xth Session and to report in detail in 20xx."

In the last several years, the employers' representatives have raised issues related to the interpretation of Convention No. 87 and the mandate of the Committee of Experts. during the sessions of the Conference Committee where the Chairperson of the Committee of Experts is invited to appear to give an oral presentation of the report of the Committee of Experts and the general survey. The two issues are inter-related, but for the sake of analysis it is useful to deal with them separately.

1 *Interpretation of Convention No. 87*

The employers' group's view on the interpretation of ILO Convention No. 87 of 1948 on 'Freedom of Association and Protection on the Right to Organize' is perhaps best summarized in the following statement:

> The Employers' group in the Conference Committee considers that neither the preparatory work for Convention No. 87, nor an interpretation based on the Vienna Convention on the Law of Treaties, offers a basis for developing, starting from the Convention, principle regulating in detail the right to strike.
>
> According to the Employer members, the right to strike has no legal basis in the freedom of association Conventions. In their view, Convention No. 87 at most contains a general right to strike, which nonetheless cannot be regulated in detail under the Convention. They consider that when the Committee of Experts expresses its views in detail on strike policies, especially on essential services, it applies a 'one-size-fits-all' approach that fails to recognize differences in economic or industrial development and current economic circumstances. They add that the approach of the Committee of Experts undermines tripartism and ask it to reconsider its interpretation of the matter.[26]

The workers' group, another constituent of the tripartite structure of the Conference Committee, takes an almost opposite view from the employers' in the following words:

> The Worker members of the Conference Committee contest the position of the Employer members and consider that, although the right to strike is not explicitly mentioned in the Convention, that does not prevent its

---

26 Report of the Committee of Experts on the Application of Conventions and Recommendations, Report III (1B), International Labour Conference, 101st Session, 2012, p. 47.

existence being recognized particularly on the basis of several international instruments.

In the discussion of the 1994 General Survey, they stated that the right to strike is an indispensable corollary of the right to organize protected by Convention No. 87 and by the principles enunciated in the ILO Constitution. In their view, without the right to strike, freedom of association would be deprived of its substance.[27]

On this issue, the Committee of Experts explains its position as follows:

> Strikes are essential means available to workers and their organizations to protect their interests, but there is a variety of opinions in relation to the right to strike. While it is true that strike action is a basic right, it is not an end in itself, but the last resort for workers' organizations, as its consequences are serious, not only for employers, but also for workers, their families and organizations and in some circumstances for third parties. In the absence of an express provision in Convention No. 87, it was mainly on the basis of *Article 3* of the Convention, which sets out the right of workers' organizations to organize their activities and to formulate their programmes, and *Article 10*, under which the objective of these organizations is to further and defend the interests of workers, that a number of principles relating to the right to strike were progressively developed (as was the case for other provisions of the Convention) by the Committee on Freedom of Association as a specialized tripartite body (as of 1952), and by the Committee of Experts (as of 1959, and essentially taking into consideration the principles established by the Committee on Freedom of Association).[28]

The Committee of Experts further elaborates on another point raised by the employers' group in the following words:

> With regard to the views put forward that the preparatory work would not support the inclusion of the right to strike, the Committee would first observe that the absence of a concrete provision is not dispositive, as the terms of the Convention must be interpreted in the light of its objective and purpose. While the Committee considers that the preparatory work is an important supplementary interpretative source when reviewing the

---

27 *Ibid.*, p. 48.
28 *Ibid.*, p. 46, para. 117.

application of a particular Convention in a given country, it may yield to the other interpretative factors, in particular, in this specific case, to the subsequent practice over a period of 52 years (see Articles 31 and 32 of the Vienna Convention on the Law of Treaties).[29]

The author is a current member of the Committee of Experts and had taken a full part in the discussion on the above quoted statement wherein his views were adequately reflected. Accordingly, the author agrees with the above statement of the Committee of Experts. He would wish to add, however, that when the Committee states that "a number of principles relating to the right to strike were progressively developed...by the Committee on Freedom of Association as a specialized tripartite body", the Committee of Experts is well aware of the importance of tripartism in the whole ILO's supervisory mechanism. In other words, the Committee of Experts had no intention to, and in fact did not, "undermine tripartism". Rather, it fully respects it. It is precisely by reason of respect for 'tripartism' that, while the Committee of Experts always welcomes the opportunity to exchange views with employers' and workers' representatives to further understanding of the respective positions, it is awaiting the consensus position of the tripartite Conference Committee on this issue.

Given the seriousness and gravity of the problem, the issue will continue to exist unresolved for some time. However, the author believes that, through the process of constructive dialogue in the spirit of mutual respect, cooperation and responsibility, the solution can be found in due course. If, however, the presence of an unresolved problem of this nature is felt to be a nuisance, the issue might be brought to the International Court of Justice in accordance with the provision of Article 37 (1) of the ILO Constitution which stipulates:

> Any question or dispute relating to the interpretation of this Constitution or of any subsequent Convention concluded by the Members in pursuance of the provisions of this Constitution shall be referred for decision to the International Court of Justice.

There is only one case that has made use of this provision in the whole history of the ILO. It is an Advisory Opinion of the Permanent Court of International Justice (PCIJ) regarding the interpretation of the Night Work (Women) Convention of 1919 (No. 4).[30]

---

29   *Ibid.*, p. 48, para. 118.
30   PCIJ Advisory Opinion No. 15, 15 November 1932.

In this connection, the author considers it useful to note that, recently, the ICJ delivered a judgment which contains its views on a similar case involving the interpretation of a human rights treaty by a treaty body as follows:[31]

> 66. The interpretation above is fully corroborated by the jurisprudence of the Human Rights Committee established by the Covenant (on Civil and Political Rights) to ensure compliance with that instrument by the States parties...
>
> Since it was created, the Human Rights Committee has built up a considerable body of interpretative case law, in particular through its findings in response to the individual communications which may be submitted to it in respect of States parties to the first Optional Protocol, and in the form of its 'General Comments'.
>
> Although the Court is in no way obliged, in the exercise of its judicial functions, to model its own interpretation of the Covenant on that of the Committee, it believes that it should ascribe great weight to the interpretation adopted by this independent body that was established specifically to supervise the application of that treaty. The point here is to achieve the necessary clarity and the essential consistency of international law, as well as legal security, to which both the individuals with guaranteed rights and the State obliged to comply with treaty obligations are entitled.

2   Mandate of the Committee of Experts

In disagreeing with the position of the Committee of Experts on the interpretation of Convention No. 87 in relation to the right to strike, the employers' group of the Conference Committee criticized the exercise of the power of the Committee of Experts beyond its mandate. The position of the employers' group on this point is summarized as follows:

> 14. The Employer Vice-Chairperson recalled that the role of the Committee of Experts was first mandated at the ILC (International Labour Conference) in 1926 and that it had been explicitly stated at the time that the functions of this new committee would be entirely technical and that the Committee of Experts would have no judicial capacity, nor would it be competent to give interpretations of the provisions of Conventions or to decide in favour of one interpretation rather than

---

[31] 'Case concerning Ahmadou Sadio Diallo (Republic of Guinea v. Domocratic Republic of the Congo)', ICJ Judgment, 30 November 2010, para. 66.

another. Further explanation was provided on the role of the Committee of Experts at the ILC in 1947 when it was stated that the supervisory machinery in question consisted of a Committee of Experts appointed by the Governing Body for the purpose of carrying out a preliminary examination of the annual reports of governments.[32]

The above statement was made during the special sitting of the 83rd Session of the Committee of Experts (November-December 2012) to which the two Vice-Chairpersons of the Conference Committee were invited to exchange views with the members of the Committee. During the sitting, the Employer Vice-Chairperson further stated that the unclear and imprecise nature of the Committee's mandate "could lead to misunderstandings outside the ILO that they [interpretations given by the Committee] were approved by the ILO's tripartite constituents or were legally binding...since the ILO Constitution provided that the authority to interpret ILO Conventions was vested with the International Court of Justice."[33] However, he acknowledged that "a certain degree of interpretation by the Experts was inevitable when the provisions of a Convention were not clear, but insisted that the main issue was when this rule of interpretation was extended into the development of policy considerations which were the sole domain of the ILO tripartite constituents."[34]

In the same meeting, the Worker Vice-Chairperson stated in summary as follows:

> 20. With regard to the question of the mandate of the Committee of Experts, the Worker Vice-Chairperson recalled that as early as 1928 the Conference Committee on the Application of Standards had considered, after noting that the Committee of Experts was confining itself to examine the compliance of national laws and regulations with international Conventions, that its analysis of the subject should not be limited to assessing the concordance of the provisions of national laws and regulations with those of Conventions, but should also go more deeply into the issue of the effective application of the Conventions. He emphasized that the role of the Committee of Experts was fundamental and that its work was an essential and permanent instrument in improving the application of standards. That role consisted of preparing, under unimpeachable conditions of scientific rigour, independence and objectivity, the work

---

32   Report III (1A), International Labour Conference, 102nd Session, 2013, p. 8, para. 14.
33   *Ibid.*, p. 9, para. 16.
34   *Ibid.*, p. 9, para. 17.

that would be taken up by the Conference Committee on the Application of Standards with a view to ensuring that effect was given to standards in law and practice.[35]

The views of the Committee of Experts on the issue of its mandate are summarized below:

> 26. The Committee (of Experts) very much welcomed the frank and constructive interventions of both Employer and Worker Vice-Chairpersons. Concerning its mandate, the Committee recalled that, since 1947, and during the past 50-plus years, it had regularly expressed its views on its mandate and methods of work. Since 2001, it had done so even more thoroughly through the efforts of its subcommittee on working methods. The Committee recalled three elements of particular relevance in this regard: (i) it had repeatedly stressed its status as an impartial, objective, and independent body, with members appointed by the tripartite Governing Body in their personal capacity precisely because of that impartial and independent status; (ii) it had regularly clarified that, while its terms of reference did not authorize it to give definitive interpretations of Conventions (competence to do so being vested in the International Court of Justice (ICJ)), in order to carry out its mandate of evaluating and assessing the application and implementation of Conventions, it had to consider and express its views on the legal scope and meaning of the provisions of these Conventions; and (iii) as from at least the 1950s, it had expressed its views on the meaning of specific ILO instruments in terms that inevitably reflected an interpretive vocabulary.[36]

For the same reasons stated earlier, the author is in agreement with the above described position of the Committee of Experts on the issue of the mandate of the Committee. As the Committee of Experts states, "in order to carry out its mandate", "it had to consider and express its views on the legal scope and meaning of the provisions of these Conventions". This position is more or less acknowledged by the Employer Vice-Chairperson himself who stated that "a certain degree of interpretation by the Committee of Experts is inevitable". The employers' representative stresses, however, that the interpretation given by the Committee of Experts is "non-binding" and "not definitive". As is clear

---

35 *Ibid.*, p. 10, para. 20.
36 *Ibid.*, pp. 10–11, para. 26.

from the foregoing, the Committee of Experts does not challenge this characterization of the interpretation by the Committee; on the contrary, it basically agrees with it. Consequently, in the view of the author, there is no fundamental difference between the position of the Committee of Experts and the views of the employers' group on the issue of the mandate of the Committee.

v   Lessons for International Law

In ten years of service as a member of the ILO's Committee of Experts, the author has observed how international law, such as the ILO Constitution and labour Conventions, is applied in reality. He is deeply inspired by the actual working of the ILO which requires revisiting the well-established general theories and principles of international law. For instance, the tripartite representation of the ILO is unique and we can draw many interesting lessons therefrom that would raise interesting questions related to the whole system of international law, such as the relationship between the sovereignty of the Member States and the role and status of non-governmental representatives, the relationship between the principle of sovereign equality (Art. 2 (1) of the UN Charter) and the ILO's tripartite representation, and the basis of privileges and immunities enjoyed by the non-governmental representatives.

The author, however, does not intend to deal with all these fascinating points but would wish to focus on three questions that are derived from his experience on the Committee of Experts, that are related to what has been explained in this paper: (1) institutional framework for international law affecting the theory of legal quality of international law; (2) the ILO's supervisory mechanism and the theory of the relationship between international law and national law; and (3) the ILO's internal legal system and the definition of international law. These topics are chosen because they all affect the general theory of international law and, at the same time, the author has already done some initial work.

1   *Institutional Support*

In a paper entitled "Institutionalization of International Law",[37] the author argued that, as a consequence of the birth and subsequent development of various international organizations in the past decades, international law, which has long been regarded as law among equal, sovereign States without a

---

37   Yozo Yokota, "Institutionalization of International Law" (in Japanese), *Shosai-no Mado* [*Windows of the Library*], January/February 2013, pp. 28–32.

central government, has reached the stage where the law is created, implemented and applied in a more structured manner through various mechanisms and procedures. The author vividly observed, and experienced, this phenomenon through his membership of the Committee of Experts.

With regard to international legislation, the ILO has the most advanced and well-structured system of law creation. After negotiation among the tripartite constituents, the Conference adopts a Convention (which is a treaty) by a majority of two-thirds of the votes cast (Art. 19 (2)). Two copies of the adopted Convention will be authenticated by the signatures of the President of the Conference and of the Director-General (Art. 19 (4)). This procedure is quite unique in the sense that: (i) non-governmental representatives (representatives of workers' and employers' organizations) participate in the negotiation and deliberation of the draft Convention and cast votes separately; and (ii) unlike the provision of Article 10 (b) of the Vienna Convention on the Law of Treaties which in principle requires, for authentication of the adopted treaty, the signature of the representatives of all the participating States, the ILO requires only the signature of the President of the Conference and the DG, a much simpler procedure. After authentication, a copy of the Convention is sent to each Member State for submission to the competent authority or authorities for ratification.

With regard to the application and implementation of the ratified Convention, the ILO has a sophisticated procedure of supervision described in detail in this paper, namely, (i) periodic reports by the governments, examination of the reports by the Committee of Experts, (iii) deliberation of serious cases of discrepancy by the Conference Committee, and (iv) discussion in the Conference on the most serious violation cases. All of this procedure is not through orders or directives from the superior bodies but takes the form of consultation, dialogue, persuasion and provision of technical assistance, as if between equal partners. It is interesting to note from the traditional theory of international law that places importance on forceful sanction as a means to pressure States to comply with international obligations, that even such mild approach can be a pressure on the government to try to do something to avoid the situation of being singled out. This kind of structured pressure on the Member States to comply with the rules of international law practised in the ILO supervisory mechanism is innovative and indicates the future goal of the institutionalized system of application of international law.

With respect to resolving issues, the ILO Constitution has provisions for settlement of disputes through: (i) representation by "industrial association of employers or of workers" for failure to secure compliance (Art. 24); (ii) complaint filed by a ratifying Member against another ratifying Member (Art. 26) which may be referred to the COI or even to the ICJ as a last resort. This whole process of dispute settlement is still rudimentary but approaching closer to the resolution of disputes by a court of law in national legal system.

As seen, the ILO is providing certain institutional mechanism to legislation, implementation and adjudication of ratified Conventions which strengthens the legal quality of international law.

2 The ILO's Supervisory Mechanism and the Theory of the Relationship between International Law and National Law

It is well-known that there are three schools of thought on the relationship between international law and national law (sometimes called 'municipal law' or 'domestic law'), *i.e.*, 'dualist', 'monist with supremacy of international law' and 'monist with supremacy of national law'. For many years, these three schools of thought existed in parallel without coming to any compromise. In recent years, however, the fourth school, which may be called 'neo-dualist' has emerged and seems to gain strong support. This fourth theory looks at the relationship between international law and national law on two different levels. On the international law plane, international law is supreme. On the national law plane, national law, particularly the Constitution, prevails over international law. When one looks at the whole picture this theory is essentially dualist because it looks at the international law plane and national law plane separately. The reason it is called 'neo-dualist' is because, unlike the classical dualist, it recognizes the possibility of dealing with the same subjects and the same matters for both international law and national law.

The way the ILO's supervisory mechanism functions supports this fourth, new theory. The ILO always takes the position of supremacy of Conventions over national law when it examines whether the national law and practice are in conformity with the international obligations at the international law plane such as at the Conference, Governing Body, Conference Committee or Committee of Experts. However, when it engages in a dialogue with government officials or national employers' or workers' representatives, it pays due regard to the national legal system. When a discrepancy is found, it tries to invite or urge the government to take the necessary measures to bring national law and practice into conformity with the provisions of the Convention in question. This approach is totally in line with the description of the neo-dualist theory by Malcolm Shaw:

> A third [in the context of this paper, fourth] approach, being somewhat a modification of the dualist position and formulated by Fitzmaurice and Rousseau amongst others, attempts to establish a recognized theoretical

framework tied to reality. This approach begins by denying that any common field of operation exists as between international law and municipal law by which one system is superior or inferior to the other. Each order is supreme in its own sphere, much as French law and English law are in France and England.[38]

The author has held the neo-dualist view since 1986,[39] but in Japan this theory was not widely supported. It has not been popular in Japan because Japanese international law scholars are mostly theorists in nature and generally not exposed to the practical world. As Shaw correctly states, "[t]his method of solving the problem does not delve deeply into theoretical considerations, but aims at being practical and in accord with the majority of state practice and international judicial decisions."[40] The author is encouraged to find that the practice of the ILO supervisory procedure supports this new theory he adheres to.

3   The ILO's Internal Legal System

One benefit the author has enjoyed through his experience on the Committee of Experts is the constant exposure to the internal legal framework of the ILO. As an expert for the ILO, he travels to Geneva to attend the sessions of the Committee of Experts. His travel expenses are paid in accordance with the internal regulations of the ILO. The meetings of the Committee are regulated by internal procedural rules.

As the discussion on the mandate of the Committee of Experts covered in this paper clearly indicates, the establishment of the Committee and its functions and mandate are regulated by the rules of the Conference and the Governing Body. From the experience of being a member of the Committee of Experts, the author has to recognize the important role of the internal law of the ILO. No one can deny the existence and daily work of the internal rules and regulations.

The question is the characterization of such internal law of the ILO or, more generally, of international organizations. Rudolf Bernhardt recognizes the existence of an internal law of internal organizations in the following words:

> It [the Constitution] also often provides for the enacting of rules by the different organs: if there is no provision in this regard in the treaty,

---

38   Shaw, *op. cit.*, pp. 103–104.
39   Yozo Yokota, *International Society and Law: Conditions for Peace and Development* (in Japanese), University of the Air Press, 1986, pp. 58–63.
40   *Ibid.*, p. 104.

the organs can nevertheless be considered to have implicit rights to adopt rules for their effective functioning...

The norms for the internal order of the organization contained in the basic treaty as well as the 'secondary' rules enacted by the organization constitute the internal law of the organization.[41]

Bernhardt then introduces three different theories on the legal nature of the internal law of international organizations. One theory denies the legal quality of internal law of international organizations. The second school regards the internal law of international organizations as a legal system *sui generis*, which means it is not a part of international law or national law of a country but a legal system of its own. The third theory, which Bernhardt supports, considers that the internal law of international organizations forms a part of international law.

From the experience of the author as a member of the Committee of Experts, the first theory which rejects the legal character of the internal law of international organizations does not reflect the reality. At the same time, in spite of the Bernhardt' position in favour of the third theory, the author tends to agree with the second school which regards internal law as a system of law *sui generis*. The reason is that most writers of international law textbooks do not list the internal law of international organizations as a source of international law.[42] Furthermore, Article 38 of the Statute of the ICJ does not list the internal law of international organizations among the sources of international law.[43]

When we dealt with the issue of the mandate of the Committee of Experts, it was pointed out that the mandate of the Committee was regulated by a resolution of the Governing Body. The whole discussion of the mandate is in fact based on legal analyses of internal rules because the Committee was established by such rules, not by the Constitution, or a treaty, or more generally international law. Thus, if the issue of the mandate of the Committee of Experts is ever to be referred to the ICJ, it is only possible through a request

---

41 Rudolf Bernhardt, "International Organizations, Internal Law and Rules", *Encyclopedia of Public International Law*, Vol. 5 (International Organizations in General: Universal International Organizations and Cooperation), North-Holland, 1983, p. 143.

42 See, for instance, Shaw, *op. cit.*, pp. 58–60.

43 Article 38 of the ICJ Statute lists (i) customary international law, (ii) treaties, and (iii) general principles of law, as the formal sources of international law, and judicial decisions and teachings of the most highly qualified publicists of the various nations as subsidiary sources, but no mention of internal law of international organizations.

for an advisory opinion rather than a decision or judgment because the latter can only be made on the basis of international law under Article 38 of the Statute, which does not list such internal rules as a source of international law to be applied by the ICJ, but the former can be given "on any legal question" (Art. 65 (1)).

The author appreciates the opportunity to experience the functioning of the internal law of the ILO as an example of the internal law of international organizations, and to verify that such internal law is a legal system *sui generis*, but is under the authority of international law, in particular, the Constitution.

VI   Conclusions

As already mentioned earlier in this paper, the ILO is unique in many ways as an international organization. Its tripartite system is unparalleled. Its law-creating procedure is most efficient and effective as well as democratic in the sense of involving non-governmental stakeholders in the process. It deals with the issue of the protection and promotion of rights and interests of individual workers. Its supervisory mechanism involving two distinct bodies, one with the membership of independent legal experts and the other with tripartite composition, which places importance on consultation, dialogue, persuasion and technical assistance, is innovative and generally works well. Such unique aspects of the structure and functions of the ILO raise many interesting points which call for revisiting the theories and principles of traditional international law.

However, most international law scholars have so far paid little attention to these phenomena and therefore lessons that can be learnt from the ILO's work are rarely taken up in international legal discourse. It is the author's hope that this paper will serve as an initiator of further studies on the structure and functions of the ILO from the viewpoint of international law and reflection on the traditional international law theories and principles on the basis of the actual working of the ILO's law-making process as well as the application and supervision of international labour standards by the ILO.

PART 4

Settlement of Disputes

∴

CHAPTER 36

International Arbitration: A Judicial Function?

*Chittharanjan F. Amerasinghe**

I   Introduction

The thesis of this brief essay is that modern international arbitration has come to involve a judicial function rather than being a method of conciliatory or other settlement of international disputes. The essay seeks to be exploratory rather than definitive.

The kind of arbitration being discussed is that between states or between international organizations and states or between international organizations. In addition, what is said would cover arbitrations between states or international organizations and individuals where the arbitrations arise as a result of and under an agreement between states or an agreement between international organizations and states or between international organizations.

II   Development of International Arbitration

As long as there have been identifiable separate groups in the world, there have been methods of peacefully settling disputes between them. Clearly some form of negotiation or consultation between the parties to the dispute was the most elementary form of dispute settlement. The use of these methods can be found in the pre-Christian era, whether in the west or in the east.

There is also evidence that settlement of disputes akin to the modern international dispute with intervention of a third party, whether by mediation, conciliation or arbitration, was also known in early times. More particularly there were systems of arbitration which have been documented going back to the Greek city states and even early civilizations in other parts of the world. The history of the development of arbitration as a method of peaceful settlement of disputes between groups and later between nation-states demonstrates how

---

*   BA, LLB, PhD, LLD (Cambridge, UK); LLM (Harvard, USA); PhD (Ceylon). Member, *Institut de Droit International*. Former Judge, UN Administrative Tribunal; Judge, Commonwealth Secretariat Tribunal; Registrar, World Bank Tribunal. Full Professor and Honorary Professor of Law, University of Ceylon, Colombo; Fellow, Trinity Hall, Cambridge; Adjunct Professor of International Law, American University Law School, USA.

third party intervention became accepted as a legitimate means of settling disputes. However, arbitration in its modern form does not bear a resemblance to these early forms of arbitration. In the early days there is no indication that settlement of disputes by arbitration involved the strict application of law and judicial methods. There was instead, perhaps an element of compromise which entered into the process. Now international arbitration in reality tends to be more of a judicial function.

History shows that third party settlement is not a modern phenomenon, although it never existed in its modern forms until recently, and its development into the current systems of arbitrations and institutionalized adjudication took a long time.[1] Much of the evidence available concerns dispute settlement in the western world. Whatever may have been the position in other parts of the world, that did not influence modern developments. The settlement of disputes by arbitrators in its pre-modern form between groups such as city-states and later other polities occurred from pre-classical antiquity in the west down to the late Middle Ages. The importance of this kind of arbitration varied at different times. It was very different from modern international arbitration, and did not influence significantly the structure of international arbitration as prevails today. The Hellenic system of arbitration is know from inscriptions, from a number of actual decisions, *e.g.*, the arbitration between Athens and Mytilene by Periander of Corinth concerning the possession of the strategically important fortress of Sigeion on the Hellespont and that between Athens and Megara by a tribunal of Salamis (both around 600 BC) and from events within the Hellenic Amphiktyony. The mechanism was through regional religious organizations exercising a limited jurisdiction under sacral law.[2] The arbitrations among the non-hegemonial confederacies, however, were closer to arbitration in the modern sense. In the second half of the fifth century BC Athens and Sparta concluded treaties with some provision for the settlement of disputes by arbitration but they were never applied, since no arbitrator was prepared to make a decision between the two powers, and the hegemony of one subsequently prevented the use of these provisions. Arbitrations are also to be found in the period from the battle of Chaironeia (338 BC), which put an end to the independence of the Greek communities in

---

1 See on the development of arbitration Schlochauer, "Abritration" in Bernhardt (ed.), 1 *Encyclopedia of Public International Law* (1981) at pp. 15 *ff.* See also C.F. Amerasinghe, *Jurisdiction of International Tribunals* (2003) at pp. 12 *ff.* The material in this section is dependent on the latter source.

2 Lammasch, *Die Lehre von der Schiedsgerichtsbarkeit in ihrem ganzen Umfange* (1914) p. 24.

foreign relations, to the beginning of Roman rule (168 BC).[3] These arbitrations were, however, clearly based on the dominance of Macedonian and, later, Roman tribunals. Similarly, in Roman times arbitral awards were, as a general rule, made either in the exercise of the sovereignty of Rome over other political bodies or as imperial measures to maintain the *Pax Romana*; Rome itself was never party to arbitration.

A thousand years later in the Middle Ages there arose a form of arbitration which became widespread in the later Middle Ages. Again this was nothing like modern international arbitration. It occurred first between the city-states of Italy, between Italian princes and communities and between Swiss cantons, and was later used between smaller political communities. On rare occasions it was to be found between other states. Medieval arbitration was generally characterized by the fact that it was either a substitute for decision by the courts, similar to trial by ordeal, or in the nature of a feudal court to decide between parties of equal status, or jurisdiction claimed by the Emperor or by the Pope in virtue of his spiritual authority for himself or for his representative which can be traced to the idea of a *Res publica Christiana*. It was only in a formal sense an arbitration. Popes Innocent III and Boniface VII sought unsuccessfully to introduce a system of compulsory arbitration with the Pope as an independent arbitrator. In the kind of disputes which are typical of modern arbitration, such as frontier disputes, the exchange of prisoners of war and compensation for breaches of the peace by illegal acts of war, there was no clear dividing line between arbitration and diplomatic methods of settling the disputes. The position of the arbitrator was frequently that of a conciliator or *amiable compositeur*. Awards were generally based on rules borrowed from canon law, modified in part by legal scholars, or on principles taken from Roman private law and applied to questions of public and international law. In the course of the 15th century, as a result the political changes principally, there was an increase in the nonobservance of arbitral awards and this led to the decline of the medieval system of arbitration and its ultimate demise in the 16th century.

As early as 1306[4] scholars and statesmen began to consider plans for an international peace organization, in which the establishment of arbitral tribunals would play a decisive part. Later Georg von Podebrad, for example, in his plan for a perpetual peace alliance (1492) recommended the creation of a Court for the Maintenance of Peace and Duke of Sully suggested the settlement of

---

3 Some of these concerned territorial disputes on the borders of the Hellenic empire, *e.g.*, the disputes between Crete and Aegean island states: see Lammasch, *ibid.*

4 See *e.g.*, Pierre Dubois, *De recuperatione terrae sanctae* (1306).

disputes by arbitration within the framework of a world organization.[5] There were also similar suggestions by Eméric Crucé[6] and, at the time of the Peace of Utrecht by Abbé Saint Pierre.[7] Hugo Grotius and later Jeremy Bentham[8] considered arbitration and judicial settlement to be the most effective means for maintaining the peace. The same idea inspired the Quakers[9] in the new world.

The conditions for the use of international arbitration in its modern form were only created with the gradual breaking up of the medieval world from the 17th century onwards and the rise of *nation-states* in a society of independent, sovereign states. The idea of arbitration was promoted by the existence side by side of equal powers maintaining legal relations with one another, and also by the gradual recognition of their interdependence. It was not till the 18th century that disputes between states were submitted to impartial bodies deciding according to objective rules. The development of modern international arbitration began in Anglo-American international legal relations and on the American continent. Its origin can be traced to the conclusion of the Jay Treaty of 1794 between Great Britain and the USA. Numerous other similar treaties followed.[10] After that arbitration was referred to in numerous treaties and it became a common feature of international relations in the west, principally. In 1899 and 1907 the Hague Peace Conferences produced a codification of the existing international law on arbitration and attempted to develop them further. These conferences produced the Conventions for the Pacific Settlement of International Disputes of 1899 and 1907. In the 20th century international arbitration developed further and has been frequently used.

III   Modern Arbitration as a Dispute Settlement Mechanism

There are two kinds of settlement methods consisting of adjudication. The first and earlier of the two is arbitration, characterized by choice of adjudicators (arbitrators) by the parties and the absence of a permanent bench of

---

5   See de Bethune, *Memories* (between 1617 and 1635).
6   *Le nouveau Cynée* (1623).
7   *Projet pour rendre la paix perpétuelle en Europe* (1713).
8   "Plan for an Universal and Perpetual Peace" in *Principles of International Law* (1787).
9   See Penn, *Essay towards the Present and Future Peace of Europe* (1693).
10 See La Fontaine, "Histoire sommaire et chronologiques des arbitrages internationaux (1794–1900)", 34 *Revue de droit international et de législation comparée* (1902) pp. 349–80, 558–582, 623–648. For a short but very perceptive description of the evolution of international tribunals, including permanent courts, from 1794 to 1944 see Hudson, *International Tribunals* (1944) pp. 3–14.

arbitrators. The second is judicial settlement by an international court which enjoys a permanent status, or may even be *ad hoc*, the judges not being chosen by the parties. In both cases now the common characteristic is that settlement is according to law, *i.e.*, by the application of legal rules, although in both it is possible that settlement may occur on the basis of extra-legal considerations, as where settlement is *ex aequo et bono*. But the latter happens only by specific agreement between parties, the basic principle being that settlement is, unless otherwise agreed, according to law. In both cases also, unlike the other methods of settlement, decisions given by the judicial or arbitral bodies are binding as such on the parties. Settlement is by a third party and is dispositive, in that sense. While, as has been seen earlier, arbitration has a long history, in its modern form it dates back to the late 18th century – to the Jay Treaty, between the UK and the USA. But, the commissions set up under the Jay Treaty, as also some other commissions established subsequently,[11] were supposed to blend juridical with diplomatic considerations to produce what was in effect a negotiated settlement. It is only from the beginning of the twentieth century that the juridical element not only predominated but became potent.

The 1899 and 1907 Hague Conventions for the Pacific Settlement of International Disputes described the object of international arbitration as the settlement of disputes between states by judges chosen by the parties themselves and on the basis of law.[12] They further provided that recourse to the procedure implied submission in good faith to the award of the tribunal. These treaties established two basic characteristics of arbitration – decisions binding upon the parties and on the basis of law. That the organs of decision are referred to as 'tribunals' does not as such differentiate them from the permanent courts of the international system in regard to these two aspects.

While both arbitration and settlement by a court are similar in these respects, they are structurally different from each other. In arbitration the parties to the dispute retain considerable control over the process, particularly through the power of appointing arbitrators of their own choice.[13] By contrast, settlement by courts relies upon pre-constituted international courts or tribunals, the composition of which is not in principle subject to control by the parties to the dispute.

---

11   See, *e.g.*, the commissions established under the Treaty of Ghent (USA and UK) of 1814. On this section of the essay see also C.F. Amerasinghe, *op. cit.* note 1, pp. 19 *ff.*
12   See Article 15 of the 1899 Hague Convention and Article 37 of the 1907 Hague Convention.
13   Sometimes the parties may be bound by advance agreement to appoint arbitrators from a pre-existing list: see the 1907 Hague Convention and the 1982 UN Convention on the Law of the Sea (UNCLOS) in Article 2 of Annex VII and Article 2 of Annex VIII.

Arbitration generally or basically has as parties, states or international organizations or such international entities. But sometimes arbitration in the international sphere pertaining to international disputes may be between states, international organizations or such entities, and individuals or juridical persons, provided these arbitrations are constituted under international treaties or agreements to which the above entities are parties. Strictly, arbitrations between states, international organizations or such entities and individuals as are not under the aegis of an international treaty or agreement as far as their sponsorship goes are not international arbitrations but are really in the realm of national legal systems. While these[14] are important in across-the-border relations they are not international arbitrations of the international legal system as such.

Apart from the 1899 and 1907 Hague Conventions, arbitration, as a means of peaceful settlement of disputes between states, is provided for in a number of multilateral treaties of global or regional character and also in several bilateral treaties.[15] Arbitration, thus, emerged as one of the third-party procedures most frequently chosen for settling, for example, territorial and boundary disputes,[16] disputes concerning interpretation of conventions or treaties,[17] and those relating to any violation of international law.[18] The 1899 and 1907 Hague Conventions established the Permanent Court of Arbitration (PCA) to facilitate the settlement of disputes which diplomacy has failed to settle.

In practice there are many types of disputes which states have excluded from arbitration made available under a particular treaty, such as disputes

---

14   See, *e.g.*, the *Texaco* v. *Libya* arbitration (1977), 53 *International Law Reports* (hereinafter: *ILR*), p. 389; the *Saudi Arabia* v. *Aramco* arbitration (1958), 27 *ILR*, p. 117.

15   See, *e.g.*, arbitration under the auspices of the ICSID established under the Convention for the Settlement of Investment Disputes between States and Nationals of Other States (1965): 4 *International Legal Materials* (hereinafter: *ILM*) (1965) p. 532, and the Iran-US Claims Tribunal established under the Algiers Accords: 20 *ILM* (1981) p. 224.

16   See, *e.g.*, the *Rann of Kutch* arbitration (India v. Pakistan) (1968), 7 *ILM*, p. 633; *Argentina – Chile Frontier Case* (1966), 16 *United Nations Reports of International Arbitral Awards* (hereinafter: *UNRIAA*), pp. 109–181; the *Beagle Channel* arbitration (Chile v. Argentina) (1978), 52 *ILR*, p. 93; the *Walfish Bay Boundary Case* (Germany v. GB) (1911), 11 *UNRIAA*, pp. 253–308.

17   See, *e.g.*, the *Air Transport Agreement Case* (USA v. France) (1963), 16 *UNRIAA*, pp. 5–71; *Air Service Case* (USA v. France) (1978), 18 *UNRIAA*, pp. 417–453.

18   See, *e.g.*, the *Alabama Claims* (USA v. UK), Moore, 1 *History and Digest of the International Arbitration to which the United States has been a Party* (1898) p. 653; the *Trail Smelter Arbitration* (USA v. Canada), 3 *UNRIAA*, pp. 1907–1982; *Lake Lanoux Arbitration* (France v. Spain), 12 *UNRIAA*, pp. 281–317, and generally cases reported in 1–9 *UNRIAA*.

arising from facts or events which occurred prior to the treaty establishing the arbitral procedure in question, disputes relating to questions which are within the exclusive jurisdiction of a state, disputes which concern the territorial integrity of a state, disputes concerning military activities, including military activities by government vessels and aircraft engaged in non-commercial service, and disputes in respect of which the Security Council of the United Nations is exercising the functions assigned to it in the Charter of the United Nations, unless the Security Council decides to remove the matter from its agenda or calls upon the parties to settle it by another peaceful procedure.

Consent of the parties to arbitration may be expressed prior to or after the occurrence of a dispute. Parties may agree to submit all or special categories of future disputes to arbitration. This may be done through multilateral or bilateral treaties of a general nature or by the inclusion of a compromissory clause in a treaty which covers disputes in general arising from the treaty or by special agreement or a *compromis* subsequent to the occurrence of the dispute. Compromissory clauses, which are generally drafted in general terms, while expressing the consent of the parties to submit all or certain types of disputes to arbitration, often lack specificity as to the rules of establishment and operation of the tribunal. In addition the compromissory clause the parties concerned must usually enter into a special *compromis* which deals with the constitutional aspects of the arbitral tribunal to be established. Thus, in such a *compromis* the parties to the dispute may deal with such issues as the composition of the tribunal, including the size and the manner of appointments and the filling of vacancies; the appointment of agents of the parties to the dispute; the questions to be decided by the tribunal; the rules of procedure and method of work of the tribunal including, where applicable, the languages used; the applicable law; the seat and administrative aspects of the tribunal, the financial arrangements for the expenses of the tribunal and the binding nature of the award of the tribunal and obligations and rights of the parties relating thereto. Not all these matters are always dealt with in *compromis* and sometimes other issues are addressed.

Arbitration as a third-party procedure may be performed by one individual appointed by the parties to the dispute, as a sole arbitrator or umpire,[19] or by a group of individuals appointed to form an arbitral tribunal. In most cases an odd number of arbitrators is usually provided for: some require five

---

19 See, *e.g.*, the appointment of the King of Italy as the sole arbitrator under the treaty of 6 November 1901 between the United Kingdom and Brazil regarding the boundary dispute between British Guyana and Brazil, 12 UNRIAA, p. 17; and the *Island of Palmas Case*, 2 UNRIAA, p. 830.

arbitrators,[20] while the most common practice has been arbitral tribunals of three members.[21] Each party to the dispute has then the right to appoint either one of three arbitrators, or two of the five arbitrators as the case may be. The third or the fifth arbitrator, who is also often designated chairman, is normally appointed by a joint decision of parties to the dispute and, in some cases, by a joint decision of the respective arbitrators already appointed by the parties. Where difficulties arise in the appointment of either the third or the fifth member, preventing the completion of the composition of the tribunal, the parties to the dispute may assign the right of making the necessary appointment in such a case to a third state, or a prominent individual.[22]

Some *compromis*, after specifying certain rules of procedure, leave the determination of the remaining procedural questions entirely to the arbitration tribunal. For example, one *compromis* provided that "the Tribunal shall subject to the provisions of this *compromis*, determine its own procedure and all questions affecting the conduct of the arbitration."[23] Some *compromis*, on the other hand, have used a more restrictive language in granting full competence to the tribunal to set rules of procedure. For example, one *compromis*, after specifying rules of procedure for the arbitration tribunal, provided that: "In determining upon such further procedure and arranging subsequent meetings, the tribunal will consider the individual or joint requests of the agents of

---

20 See, *e.g.*, Geneva General Act for the Pacific Settlement of International Disputes, Article 22, 93 *United Nations Treaty Series* (hereinafter: *UNTS*), p. 345. The *Compromis* of 11 September 1986 between Egypt and Israel regarding their boundary dispute in the Taba beachfront established a five-member tribunal. Each party appointed one member and the three other members, one of whom was the president, were appointed by the parties jointly: Article 1 of the *Compromis*, 26 *ILM*, p. 1.

21 See, *e.g.*, International Convention for the Protection of New Varieties of Plants of 2 December 1961, Article 36, 815 *UNTS*, p. 80; Protocol on Privileges and Immunities of the European Space Research Organization of 31 October 1963, Article 27, 805 *UNTS*, p. 279.

22 See, *e.g.*, Article 45 of the 1907 Hague Convention for the Pacific Settlement of International Disputes, in which the task is assigned to a third state, and Article 23 of the 1949 Revised General Act for the Pacific Settlement of International Disputes, in which that appointment task is first assigned to a third state and then to the President of the International Court of Justice.

23 Article V of the *Compromis* of 22 January 1963 between France and the US regarding the interpretation of the Air Transport Services Agreement, 16 *UNRIAA*, p. 9. Similarly, a broad competence was provided for another tribunal. The *Compromis* of that tribunal stated that "the Court shall, subject to the provisions of this Agreement, determine its own rules of procedure and all questions affecting the conduct of the arbitration."; Article 3 of the *Compromis* of 19 July 1975 (France and UK), 18 *UNRIAA*, p. 5.

the two governments."[24] Another agreement instructs the tribunal to ascertain the views of the parties before determining a particular rule of procedure.[25]

Parties to an arbitration may agree on the law that the tribunal should apply to their disputes. Some arbitration agreements require that specific rules be applied,[26] and some only make a general reference to the applicable law. Many arbitration agreements in some way specifically stipulate international law as the applicable law.[27] Some arbitration agreements have remained silent on this issue, in which case the assumption is that international law in general shall be applicable. Other arbitration agreements have chosen principles of equity, justice, equitable solution, *etc.*, as applicable to the dispute.[28]

Parties to a dispute submitted to an arbitral tribunal are represented by agents whose appointment and powers may be stipulated in the *compromis* indicating the time-period within which they are to be appointed.[29] Such agents are usually entitled to nominate an assistant agent as occasion may require, and may be further assisted by such advisers, counsel and staff as the agent deems necessary. The agents of the parties to the dispute file written pleadings which may be limited to memorials and counter-memorials[30] and which may be submitted in the order and within the time-limits determined by the tribunal. Such determination may also be made by the tribunal with respect to the oral proceedings and relevant documentary evidence. As appropriate, arbitral tribunals have also heard witnesses on behalf of parties to the dispute and have also made use of expert witnesses providing expert opinion

---

24   The Convention of 3 August 1935 between the United States and Canada concerning the Settlement of Difficulties Arising from Operation of a Smelter at Trail, 3 UNRIAA, p. 1907.

25   The Treaty for Conciliation, Judicial Settlement and Arbitration (with annexes) of 7 July 1965 between the United Kingdom of Great Britain and Northern Ireland and Switzerland, 605 UNTS, p. 205.

26   See the Treaty of Washington of 6 May 1871, which constituted the basis for establishing the *Alabama Claims* tribunal between the United States and the United Kingdom, in Moore, 1 *International Arbitrations*, p. 547.

27   See, *e.g.*, those mentioned in *Systemic Survey of Treaties for the Pacific Settlement of International Disputes, 1928–1948* (UN Publication).

28   See, *e.g.*, the 'equitable solution' principle applied by the 1872 arbitral tribunal in the *Delagoa Bay Case* (GB v. Portugal), Moore 5 *International Arbitrations*, p. 4954; the 1893 *Bering Sea Case* (GB v. US), 6 *American Journal of International Law* (1912) p. 233. See also the 1949 Revised General Act, Article 28 (71 UNTS, p. 101), which recommends the application of these principles.

29   Some *compromis* do not do either.

30   See, *e.g.*, Article 5 in the *Ambatielos Arbitration*, 12 UNRIAA, p. 8.

to the tribunal on a given issue, as may be explicitly stated in a *compromis*.[31] The arbitrators as well as the parties to the dispute have the right to cross-examine such witnesses in the manner stipulated in a *compromis*.[32]

The seat of the arbitral tribunal is usually specified in the *compromis*. Where there is no such specification, the tribunal itself may, as recommended by its president,[33] determine where to conduct its business. Arbitral tribunals are usually assisted by a secretariat or a registry to be responsible for the administrative arrangements for the arbitration.

Two kinds of expenses are involved in an arbitration proceeding. One relates to the preparation of each party's case and its presentation to the arbitral tribunal. These expenses are borne by the parties themselves. Other expenses include the common expense of the arbitral tribunal, such as the arbitrators' fees, the salary of the registrar and the staff of the arbitral tribunal, interpreters, clerical facilities and such like. Parties to the dispute share the administrative costs of the tribunal. Generally the arbitrators' fees are borne equally by both parties. Occasionally, however, some *compromis* provide that each party pay the fees of their appointed arbitrator.[34]

Awards of arbitral tribunals are binding upon the parties to the dispute. Invariably, in all the *compromis*, parties to the dispute also stipulate that they undertake to abide by the decision of the arbitral tribunal. However, after an award has been rendered, it may be subject to correction or revision in connection with obvious errors such as clerical, typographical or arithmetical errors.[35] An award may also be subject to interpretation. Article 82 of the 1907 Hague Convention provides for a general competence for the arbitral tribunal which rendered the award to interpret it. There are also circumstances in which an award may be annulled, *e.g.*, for fraud, or reviewed but there is generally no appeal from an award.

---

31 See, *e.g.*, Articles 9 and 10 of the 20 July 1954 *Compromis* between the UK and Saudi Arabia, 201 UNTS, p. 317.

32 See, *e.g.*, the 30 June 1965 *Compromis* between India and Pakistan regarding boundary arbitration, 17 UNRIAA, p. 9, and the 16 July 1930 *Compromis* between Guatemala and Honduras, 2 UNRIAA, p. 1312.

33 See, *e.g.*, Article 5 of the 10 July 1975 *Compromis* between France the UK in the case concerning the delimitation of the continental shelf, 18 UNRIAA, pp. 5 and 6.

34 See, *e.g.*, Article 12 of the Convention for Arbitration of Questions regarding the Jurisdictional Rights in the Bering Sea of 29 February 1892, in Moore, 5 *International Arbitrations*, p. 4762.

35 See Article 31 of the ILC Model Rules, in the *Work of the International Law Commission*, 4th ed. (UN Publication) p. 154.

Arbitration in its modern form began as an attempt to bring into the international system the rule of law and to replace with a technique of litigation resort to the use of armed force in the settlement of disputes. Since the establishment of the Permanent Court of International Justice and International Court of Justice (ICJ) resort to arbitration in strictly inter-state disputes has been less frequent. However, there are examples of significant inter-state arbitrations, especially in territorial disputes, such as the *Rann of Kutch* arbitration (*India v. Pakistan*) in 1968,[36] the *Beagle Channel* arbitration (*Chile v. Argentina*) of 1978[37] and the *Taba* arbitration (*Egypt v. Israel*)[38] of 1988, but also in other kinds of disputes, such as those involving the interpretation of treaties. What is to be noted, though, is that the number of arbitrations involving a state as only one party, the other being an individual or juristic person, which have taken place under some kind of treaty between states, has increased.

Arbitration may also now be institutionalized. The first attempt to do this was in the Hague Conventions of 1899 and 1907 pursuant to which the PCA was created. But the PCA was not a court nor did the institutionalization associated with it have any compelling nature. Much later, pursuant to the ICSID Convention of 1965, the International Centre for Settlement of Investment Disputes (ICSID) was created with a true institutionalized and cogent structure for a particular kind of dispute.

IV The Judicial Nature of the Functions of International Arbitral Tribunals

The question to be answered is whether basically international arbitral tribunals perform judicial functions. It is clear that, because international arbitration is based on the consent of the parties, the parties may bestow any kind of power, including non-judicial powers, on the tribunal. But barring that and in the usual case it is possible to come to the conclusion that international arbitral tribunals perform judicial functions as reasonably defined.

In relation to common law jurisdictions and for the purpose of considering the separation of the judicial power from legislative and executive powers, efforts have been made to define the judicial power.[39] It must be conceded that

---

36   (1968), 7 *ILM*, p. 633.
37   (1978), 52 *ILR*, p. 39.
38   (1988), 80 *ILR*, p. 224.
39   See the discussion in C.F. Amerasinghe, *The Doctrines of Sovereignty and Separation of Powers in the Law of Ceylon* (1970) pp. 190 *ff*.

such a definition has not been easily forthcoming. But for the purpose of this essay what was stated by W. Blackstone in the late 18th century may be taken as a starting point:

> In every Court there must be at least three constituent parts, the *actor*, *reus*, and *judex*: the *actor*, or plaintiff, who complains of an injury done; the *reus*, or defendant who is called upon to make satisfaction for it, and the *judex*, or *judicial power*, which is to examine the truth of the fact, to determine the law arising upon that fact, and, if any injury appears to have been done, to ascertain, and by its officers apply the remedy.[40]

The last requirement in the citation, namely application by the court's officers of the remedy, does not necessarily inhere in the judicial function. In the international legal system there is no automatic enforcement mechanism for decisions of courts and tribunals as there is in national systems of law and yet there are courts such as the ICJ and International Tribunal for the Law of the Sea which perform judicial functions. What is critical is that the finding of facts and the application of law to settle a dispute given the reservation in Blackstone's description is adequate.

International arbitral tribunals basically do perform judicial functions according to the definition given above. But beyond this truth there are two observations to be made.

The first is that as a result of consent between the parties to the arbitration the arbitral tribunal may be required in settling the dispute to apply specific rules which are different from the prevailing rules of law. This is not a serious difference which detracts from the judicial nature of international arbitral tribunals, as even in this case the application of the rules is nevertheless in the hands of the tribunals. In like manner the facts may be agreed upon by the parties, as, indeed, they may be before standing international courts. This feature again, does not detract from the basically judicial nature of international arbitral tribunals.

The second point is that the tribunal may be required by the agreement between the parties to settle the dispute without the sole application of rules of law, as where a resolution is required *ex aequo et bono*. In this case, too, the international legal system recognizes that such settlement is compatible with the judicial function. Even the ICJ is endowed with powers to settle disputes *ex aequo et bono*, where the parties agree upon this mode of settlement.

---

40   3 *Commentaries on the Laws of England* (1768) p. 15.

What is equally important is the answer to the question whether the arbitrators of international arbitral tribunals have sufficient independence in order to be characterized as judicial tribunals. What is characteristic of arbitral tribunals is the existence of party appointed arbitrators. While arbitration tribunals are different from established or standing courts in this respect, the difference does not in practice have much effect. Once the arbitrators are appointed, they are not subject *ipso facto* to the control of the respective party nor do they owe a party their allegiance. In short, they can act independently. Party selection of arbitrators has not in practice been a problem in regard to their independence.[41]

The fact that in regard to the expenses of the tribunal as pointed out in the previous section, a party may have undertaken to pay the fees of the arbitrator it appoints has not in reality affected the independence of the tribunal. This practice is not regarded as the payment of a 'retainer'. It is an administrative practice which is common and should not impinge on what arbitrators do. However, in accordance with the maxim 'justice must not be done but also seen to be done,' it is better that all arbitrators be paid from a common pool funded by the parties to the arbitration.

All in all the practices in relation to arbitration outlined in the previous section do not as such create problems impacting on the independence of arbitrators. This is so, considering particularly that the features of arbitration in the international legal system are based on the agreement and active participation of the parties in setting up the tribunals.

Further, international arbitral tribunals now give, and for a long time have given, *reasoned* awards or decisions. This is a characteristic of the judicial function. For example, all the decisions and awards of the Iran-US Claims Tribunal and of ICSID are of this nature.[42]

---

41 In the case of the ICJ, it is to be noted, where a party is not represented by a judge of its nationality, an *ad hoc* judge may be appointed by that party.

42 See the cases reported in the *Iran – USCTR* and the *ICSID Reports*.

CHAPTER 37

Flexibility in the Award of Reparation: The Role of the Parties and the Tribunal

*James Crawford**

1   Introduction[1]

It is axiomatic that jurisdiction to determine breach of an obligation implies jurisdiction to award reparation for any breach found. This principle was articulated in general terms by the Permanent Court of International Justice (PCIJ) in the *Chorzów Factory* case:

> The decision whether there has been a breach of an engagement involves no doubt a more important jurisdiction than a decision as to the nature or extent of reparation due for a breach of an international engagement the existence of which is already established.[2]

As elaborated by the PCIJ in its subsequent decision on the merits, "jurisdiction as to the reparation due for the violation of an international convention involves jurisdiction as to the forms and methods of reparation".[3] This principle has been affirmed by the International Court of Justice (ICJ) in clear terms,[4] and is firmly established.[5]

---

*   Whewell Professor of International Law, University of Cambridge.
1   This article expands on two ramifications of the *Chorzów Factory* principle discussed in J Crawford, "Jurisdiction of International Tribunals: Some Ramifications of the *Chorzów Factory* Principle", in B Krzan (ed), *Jurisdictional Competition of International Courts and Tribunals* (2012) 11, and J Crawford, *State Responsibility: The General Part* (2013), ch 19. It also expands on issues of reparation discussed in *ibid*, chs 14–16.
2   *Factory at Chorzów*, Jurisdiction, (1927) PCIJ Ser A No 9, 23.
3   *Factory at Chorzów*, Merits, (1928) PCIJ Ser A No 17, 61.
4   In 1987 Gray stated in respect of the *Chorzów Factory* principle that "the Court has consistently maintained this approach in all its later decisions": C Gray, *Judicial Remedies in International Law* (1987), 60. As one example, in *LaGrand* the ICJ stated "[w]here jurisdiction exists over a dispute on a particular matter, no separate basis for jurisdiction is required by the Court to consider the remedies a party has requested for the breach of the obligation": *LaGrand (Germany v. United States of America)*, Judgment, ICJ Reports 2001 pp. 466, 485.
5   Commentary to the ILC Articles on the Responsibility of States for Internationally Wrongful Acts, Art 36, para 2, printed in *Yearbook of the International Law Commission*

Less well explored are the ramifications of the *Chorzów Factory* principle, two of which will be considered in this chapter. The first is the extent of judicial discretion to determine the appropriate form of reparation. The second is the exercise of an injured state's right to elect between available forms of reparation and the effect on that right of any action taken by an injured state in connection with judicial proceedings.

II Judicial Discretion in Awarding Remedies

An injured state's entitlement to reparation for breach is affirmed in the International Law Commission (ILC) Articles on the Responsibility of States for Internationally Wrongful Acts (ARSIWA).[6] Article 31(1) of the ARSIWA provides that:

> The responsible State is under an obligation to make full reparation for the injury caused by the internationally wrongful act.

As is clear from the wording of the Article, reparation is an 'obligation' of a responsible state. That is, an obligation to provide reparation arises automatically on the commission of an internationally wrongful act. It is not contingent upon, for example, a demand or protest by the injured state.[7]

Article 34 goes on to identify the three forms which reparation may take:

> Full reparation for the injury caused by the internationally wrongful act shall take the form of restitution, compensation and satisfaction, either singly or in combination...

The ARSIWA contain separate articles on restitution, compensation and satisfaction. While each of those Articles refers to an 'obligation' to provide restitution,

---

2001, vol II(2), 31 (ARSIWA *Commentary*); C Brown, *A Common Law of International Adjudication* (2007), 66.

6 The ARSIWA are annexed to GA Res 56/83, 28 January 2002, and are also printed in *Yearbook of the International Law Commission 2001*, vol II(2), 26 (ARSIWA).

7 J Crawford, "Third Report on State Responsibility", *Yearbook of the International Law Commission 2000*, vol II(1), 3, at 18; ARSIWA *Commentary*, *supra* n 5, Art 31, para 4. This is one of the reasons why the Article was changed after the first reading from a provision which expressed reparation to be an *entitlement* of an injured state: Draft Articles on the Responsibility of States for Internationally Wrongful Acts, Art 42(1), printed in *Yearbook of the International Law Commission 1996*, vol II(2), 58.

compensation or satisfaction,[8] the "forms of reparation...represent ways of giving effect to the underlying obligation of reparation. There are not, as it were, separate obligations of restitution, compensation and satisfaction".[9] An injured state has no entitlement to a particular remedy and thus international courts and tribunals retain some measure of discretion.

Nonetheless, there are principles to guide international courts and tribunals in the exercise of their discretion. The ICJ's practice regarding the award of compensation provides an illustrative case study in that regard. It has also been queried whether international courts and tribunals are competent to make orders which equate to injunctions or orders of specific performance (to use common law terminology) in the exercise of discretion.

1   The Reluctance of the ICJ to Award Compensation

A responsible state is obliged to provide reparation for any damage, both material and moral.[10] The three forms of reparation (restitution, compensation and satisfaction) address different subsets of damage. Satisfaction remedies moral damage to the state, damage which is not financially assessable but which amounts to an affront to the state (for example, a violation of sovereignty). Many internationally wrongful acts result in damage which goes beyond this, however. There is often material damage (damage to property or other substantive interests of a state and its nationals which is assessable in financial terms) or moral damage to nationals of the state (including, for example, individual pain and suffering). To the extent that an internationally wrongful act results in material damage or moral damage to nationals, more than satisfaction will be required.

In the vast majority of its decisions involving a claim for reparation, the ICJ has awarded declarations of wrongfulness (a form of satisfaction), often as the sole remedy.[11] In 1985, Gray observed that declaratory judgments were "the norm in the practice of the ICJ".[12] This is still true today,[13] despite the fact that

---

8   ARSIWA, *supra* n 6, Arts 35(1), 36(1) & 37(1), referring respectively to the 'obligation to make restitution', the 'obligation to compensate' and the 'obligation to give satisfaction'.
9   ARSIWA Commentary, *supra* n 5, Art 34, para 6.
10 ARSIWA, *supra* n 6, Art 31(2). On material and moral damage see Crawford (2013), *supra* n 1, 486–487.
11 On declaratory judgments as a form of satisfaction see Crawford (2013), *supra* n 1, 529–530.
12 C Gray, "Is there an International Law of Remedies?", (1985) 56 *British Year Book of International Law* 25, 39. See also Gray (1987), *supra* n 4, 96.
13 For example, Brown states that declaratory judgments are "the most common form of remedy in litigation before the PCIJ and ICJ": Brown, *supra* n 5, 208–209. A striking

PCA tribunals, *ad hoc* tribunals, ITLOS, ICSID tribunals and increasingly human rights courts accompany such declarations with an award of sometimes substantial compensation.[14] The ICJ has rarely awarded compensation, despite its affirmation that:

> It is a well-established rule of international law that an injured State is entitled to obtain compensation from the State which has committed an internationally wrongful act for the damage caused by it.[15]

The PCIJ awarded compensation on one occasion, in the first case it heard, the *Wimbledon*.[16] The ICJ similarly awarded compensation in the first case it heard, the *Corfu Channel* case,[17] but it was not until *Diallo* that the ICJ awarded compensation for a second time, in 2012.[18] While these decisions indicate that the ICJ is open to awarding compensation, more instructive as to the ICJ's approach to compensation are the decisions in which the court has declined to award compensation.

A number of techniques employed by the ICJ have enabled it to avoid awarding compensation or at least to avoid determining the quantum of compensation due. In at least two cases in which compensation was sought (the *Nicaragua* case and the *Armed Activities* case), the ICJ held that the issue of reparation would only be determined by the Court if the parties failed to reach an agreement on the issue. In the *Nicaragua* case, the ICJ ordered that "the form and amount of...reparation, failing agreement between the Parties, will be settled by the Court, and [the Court] reserves for this purpose the subsequent

---

example of a case in which the ICJ awarded a declaration of wrongfulness as the sole remedy was the *Bosnian Genocide* case: *Application of the Convention on the Prevention and Punishment of the Crime of Genocide (Bosnia and Herzegovina v. Serbia and Montenegro)*, Judgment, ICJ Reports 2007 pp. 43, 234–235. The ICJ held that restitution was not possible (*ibid*, 233) and compensation not appropriate (*ibid*, 234).

14   Brown (2007), *supra* n 5, 209.
15   *Gabčíkovo-Nagymaros Project (Hungary/Slovakia)*, Judgment, ICJ Reports 1997 pp. 7, 81.
16   *S.S. "Wimbledon"*, (1923) PCIJ Ser A No 1, 33. In the *Chorzów Factory* case, the PCIJ held that Poland was required to pay compensation to Germany: *Factory at Chorzów*, Merits, (1928) PCIJ Ser A No 17, 63. It reserved the fixing of the amount of compensation pending an expert report (*ibid*, 64), but the parties reached a settlement in the interim: *Factory at Chorzów*, Order, (1929) PCIJ Ser A No 19, 12.
17   *Corfu Channel*, Judgment on Compensation, ICJ Reports 1949 pp. 244, 250.
18   *Ahmadou Sadio Diallo (Republic of Guinea v. Democratic Republic of the Congo)*, Compensation owed by the Democratic Republic of the Congo to the Republic of Guinea, Judgment of 19 June 2012, para 61.

procedure in the case".[19] Nicaragua took some steps to initiate a subsequent phase of the case,[20] but the matter was ultimately settled between the parties following a change of leadership in Nicaragua.[21] In the *Diallo* case, although the ICJ ultimately determined the quantum of compensation due, it initially left the matter to be resolved between the parties (admittedly, at the claimant's request).[22] It was only when the parties failed to reach an agreement within the six month time limit specified by the ICJ that it was required to determine the quantum of compensation due.[23]

Another example of an avoidance technique is found in the *Gabčíkovo-Nagymaros* case. In that case, the ICJ observed that "Hungary and Slovakia are both under an obligation to pay compensation and are both entitled to obtain compensation",[24] but reasoned that "[g]iven...that there have been intersecting wrongs by both Parties, the Court wishes to observe that the issue of compensation could satisfactorily be resolved in the framework of an overall settlement if each of the Parties were to renounce or cancel all financial claims and counter-claims".[25] It seems very unlikely that the quantum of compensation due to Hungary and that due to Slovakia would have been the same.[26]

---

19 *Military and Paramilitary Activities in and against Nicaragua (Nicaragua v. United States of America)*, ICJ Reports 1986 pp. 14, 149. See also *Armed Activities on the Territory of the Congo (Democratic Republic of the Congo v. Uganda)*, Judgment, ICJ Reports 2005 pp. 168, 281.

20 For example, Nicaragua filed a Memorial: Memorial of Nicaragua (Compensation), 29 March 1988, Pleadings, 244.

21 *Military and Paramilitary Activities in and against Nicaragua (Nicaragua v. United States of America)*, Order of 26 September 1991, ICJ Reports 1991 pp. 47. See C Schulte, *Compliance with Decisions of the International Court of Justice* (2004), 205–207.

22 *Ahmadou Sadio Diallo (Republic of Guinea v. Democratic Republic of the Congo)*, Merits, Judgment, ICJ Reports 2010 pp. 639, 691 & 693.

23 *Ahmadou Sadio Diallo (Republic of Guinea v. Democratic Republic of the Congo)*, Compensation owed by the Democratic Republic of the Congo to the Republic of Guinea, Judgment of 19 June 2012, para 61.

24 *Gabčíkovo-Nagymaros Project (Hungary/Slovakia)*, Judgment, ICJ Reports 1997 pp. 7, 81.

25 *Ibid*. The Court had been asked to indicate on what basis compensation should be paid: *ibid*.

26 The parties were entitled to compensation in relation to wrongful acts of different characters. Slovakia was entitled to compensation in relation to damage suffered "as a result of Hungary's decision to suspend and subsequently abandon the works at Nagymaros and Dunakiliti, as those actions caused the postponement of the putting into operation of the Gabčíkovo power plant, and changes in its mode of operation once in service": *ibid*. Hungary was "entitled to compensation for the damage sustained as a result of the diversion of the Danube, since Czechoslovakia...deprived Hungary of its rightful part in the shared water resources, and exploited those resources essentially for their own benefit": *ibid*.

Furthermore, the solution proposed by the ICJ did not account for the fact that in their ongoing relations, Hungary would be required to make payments to Slovakia in relation to the use of the Čunovo complex, although those contributions were technically not damages.[27]

It is difficult to explain the small number of decisions in which the ICJ has awarded compensation (and the larger number in which it has not done so) on any basis other than reluctance on the part of the Court to make such awards. It is not the case that compensation is not sought by parties. For example, out of the thirty-eight contentious cases brought before the PCIJ, approximately one third involved a claim for compensation.[28] It has been suggested that the few awards of compensation made by the ICJ are explicable on the basis that "[m]any sovereign interests do not lend themselves to quantification".[29] But this is neither here nor there. To the extent to that the infringement of a sovereign interest gives rise to financially assessable damage, a declaration of wrongfulness is not the appropriate remedy.

The ICJ's decision in *Cameroon v Nigeria* is illustrative. In connection with a boundary dispute, Cameroon alleged that part of its territory had been occupied by Nigeria and that it had suffered material damage as a result.[30] The ICJ side-stepped this claim, stating that "by the very fact of the present Judgment and of the evacuation of the Cameroonian territory occupied by Nigeria, the injury suffered by Cameroon by reason of the occupation of its territory will in all events have been sufficiently addressed".[31] It is plainly not the case that any material damage would be made good by this remedy. Other international courts and tribunals are much more willing to engage with these issues. One example which is a stark contrast is the awards delivered by the Eritrea-Ethiopia Claims Commission, which awarded damages, *inter alia*, in relation to Ethiopia's occupation of parts of Eritrea.[32]

---

27   *Ibid*, where the ICJ stated that "[i]f Hungary is to share in the operation and benefits of the Čunovo complex, it must pay a proportionate share of the building and running costs". For a further example see *Fisheries Jurisdiction (Federal Republic of Germany v. Iceland)*, Merits, Judgment, ICJ Reports 1974 pp. 175, 203–205.

28   Gray (1987), *supra* n 4, 77.

29   J Barker, "Compensation", in J Crawford, A Pellet & S Olleson (eds), *The Law of International Responsibility* (2010) 599, 603.

30   *Land and Maritime Boundary between Cameroon and Nigeria (Cameroon v. Nigeria: Equatorial Guinea intervening)*, Judgment, ICJ Reports 2002 p 303, 317.

31   *Ibid*, 452.

32   In the final award relating on Eritrea's damages claims, the Commission awarded compensation under 17 different heads of damages (totalling US$163,520,865): *Eritrea's Damages Claims*, Final Award, (2009) 140 ILR 235, 373–375. In the final award relating to Ethiopia's

2   Orders of 'Specific Performance'

The competence of international courts and tribunals to make orders which equate to injunctions or orders of specific performance has at times been questioned. In 1987, Gray stated that "the jurisdiction of the International Court of Justice to give remedies such as specific performance or injunctions where there is no express provision for this in the agreement from which the Court derives its jurisdiction is not clear".[33] More recently in 2007, Brown observed that:

> [T]here is uncertainty concerning the power of international courts to issue judgments and awards in mandatory terms… While orders for specific performance and injunctive relief are commonly available in domestic legal systems, the power of international courts to make such orders is less clear.[34]

Some suggest that orders having mandatory effect are not appropriate judicial remedies in international law, seemingly on the basis of limitations inherent in the judicial function.[35] One decision used to support that view is the *Haya de la Torre* case,[36] which concerned Colombia's and Peru's implementation of the ICJ's earlier judgment in the *Asylum* case.[37] In the *Haya de la Torre* case, both states requested the ICJ to "state in what manner the Judgment [in the *Asylum* case] shall be executed",[38] a formulation which the ICJ considered showed that the parties "desire[d] that the Court should make a choice amongst the various courses by which the asylum may be terminated".[39] The ICJ declined to make any choice, explaining that:

> [T]hese courses are conditioned by facts and by possibilities which, to a very large extent, the Parties are alone in a position to appreciate. A choice amongst them could not be based on legal considerations, but

---

claims, it awarded compensation under 37 different heads (totalling US$174,036,520): *Ethiopia's Damages Claims*, Final Award, (2009) 140 ILR 376, 373–375.

33   Gray (1987), *supra* n 4, 95.
34   Brown (2007), *supra* n 5, 209–210.
35   See *ibid*, 210–211.
36   *Haya de la Torre Case*, Judgment, 13 June 1951, ICJ Reports 1951 p 71.
37   *Colombian-Peruvian asylum case*, Judgment, 20 November 1950, ICJ Reports 1950 p 266.
38   *Haya de la Torre Case*, Judgment, 13 June 1951, ICJ Reports 1951 p 71, 78.
39   *Ibid*, 79.

only on considerations of practicability or of political expediency; it is not part of the Court's judicial function to make such a choice.⁴⁰

Notwithstanding such limitations on the judicial function, it is clear that in principle international courts and tribunals can make orders having mandatory effect, whether by way of declaration or otherwise,⁴¹ and the ICJ does in fact make such orders. The ICJ makes orders having mandatory effect in at least two contexts: first, relating to the cessation of wrongful conduct,⁴² and, second, relating to restitution.⁴³ As to the former, the *Tehran Hostages* case can be cited as an example. In the *Tehran Hostages* case, the ICJ ordered that Iran terminate the detention of the US diplomatic and consular staff.⁴⁴ It stated in the *dispositif* that Iran, for example,

> must immediately terminate the unlawful detention of the United States Chargé d'affaires and other diplomatic and consular staff and other United States nationals now held hostage in Iran, and must immediately release each and every one and entrust them to the protecting Power...⁴⁵

---

40 *Ibid*. It later stated again that it was "unable to give any practical advice as to the various courses which might be followed with a view to terminating the asylum, since, by doing so, it would depart from its judicial function": *ibid*, 83.

41 Gray states that "[i]n those cases such as the *Serbian Loans*, *Lighthouses*, and *Socobelge* cases where the Court declares that a contract has been duly entered into and is binding on the parties or that an arbitral award is binding, although this is not formally an order for specific performance it is clear what the parties ought to do: Gray, *supra* n 4, 98.

42 As affirmed in Article 30 of the ARSIWA (*supra* n 6): "The State responsible for the internationally wrongful act is under an obligation: (a) to cease that act, if it is continuing; ..." Generally on the issue of cessation see Crawford (2013), *supra* n 1, 461–469.

43 The result of cessation may be indistinguishable from that of restitution, but the two are distinct. On the distinction between cessation and restitution see Crawford (2013), *supra* n 1, 465–469 & 512.

44 This order is better seen as one of cessation. The ICJ held separately that Iran was under an obligation to make reparation to the US, the form and amount of which could not be determined at the date of judgment: *United States Diplomatic and Consular Staff in Tehran*, Judgment, ICJ Reports 1980 p 3, 41–42 & 45.

45 *Ibid*, 44. More recently, in *Belgium v. Senegal* the ICJ ordered that "Senegal must, without further delay, submit the case of Mr. Hissène Habré to its competent authorities for the purpose of prosecution, if it does not extradite him": *Questions relating to the Obligation to Prosecute or Extradite (Belgium v. Senegal)*, Judgment, 20 July 2012, para 122(6).

An example of the latter includes the ICJ's order in the *Arrest Warrant* case:

> [T]he Kingdom of Belgium must, by means of its own choosing, cancel the arrest warrant of 11 April 2000 and so inform the authorities to whom that warrant was circulated.[46]

The ICJ has only made orders having mandatory effect in the remedial context, with a view to stopping internationally wrongful conduct or to repairing its consequences. It has not issued orders directed towards parties' prospective observance of their international obligations.[47] This is evident, for example, from the ICJ's repeated refusals to make orders mandating that assurances and guarantees of non-repetition be provided.[48]

In the *Armed Activities* case, for example, the Democratic Republic of the Congo (DRC) requested that Uganda provide assurances and guarantees of non-repetition of the wrongful acts complained of, which included violations of the principle of non-use of force and the principle of non-intervention.[49] The ICJ declined the request, stating:

---

46   *Arrest Warrant of 11 April 2000 (Democratic Republic of the Congo v. Belgium)*, Judgment, ICJ Reports 2002 p 3, 33. This order is better seen as one relating to restitution. The ICJ reasoned that "[i]n the present case, 'the situation which would, in all probability, have existed if [the illegal act] had not been committed' cannot be re-established merely by a finding by the Court that the arrest warrant was unlawful under international law": *ibid*, 32.

47   This of course excludes orders made in provisional measures phases of cases: see Brown (2007), *supra* n 5, 210.

48   As affirmed in Article 30 of the ARSIWA (*supra* n 6): "The State responsible for the internationally wrongful act is under an obligation: ... (b) to offer appropriate assurances and guarantees of non-repetition, if circumstances so require". Article 29 also affirms that the "legal consequences of an internationally wrongful act...do not affect the continued duty of the responsible State to perform the obligation breached". On the continued duty of performance and assurances and guarantees of non-repetition see Crawford (2013), *supra* n 1, 461 & 469–479.

49   The DRC requested "a solemn declaration that [Uganda] will in future refrain from pursuing a policy that violates the sovereignty of the Democratic Republic of the Congo and the rights of its population" and "demands that specific instructions to that effect be given by the Ugandan authorities to their agents": *Armed Activities on the Territory of the Congo (Democratic Republic of the Congo v. Uganda)*, Judgment, ICJ Reports 2005 p 168, 255. The DRC alleged that assurances and guarantees of non-repetition were justified on the basis of threats made, including an alleged statement by the then Minister of Foreign Affairs that "the withdrawal of our troops from the Democratic Republic of the Congo does not mean that we will not return there to defend our security!": *ibid*, 255.

> [I]f a State assumes an obligation in an international agreement to respect the sovereignty and territorial integrity of the other States parties to that agreement...and a commitment to cooperate with them in order to fulfil such obligation, this expresses a clear legally binding undertaking that it will not repeat any wrongful acts. In the Court's view, the commitments assumed by Uganda under the Tripartite Agreement must be regarded as meeting the DRC's request for specific guarantees and assurances of non-repetition. The Court expects and demands that the Parties will respect and adhere to their obligations under that Agreement and under general international law.[50]

This is reflective of the tendency on the part of the ICJ to consider that the continued existence of an international obligation breached, combined with the Court's declaration that a state's previous conduct was a breach of the obligation, is sufficient protection against repetition.[51] In *Germany v Italy*, for example, the ICJ stated that:

> [A]s a general rule, there is no reason to suppose that a State whose act or conduct has been declared wrongful by the Court will repeat that act or conduct in the future, since its good faith must be presumed.[52]

From the above survey of the ICJ's practice, it is evident that international courts and tribunals can and do make orders having mandatory effect. This is not to say that the limitations inherent in the judicial function identified above have no role to play, however. Even when the ICJ makes orders having mandatory effect, these limitations influence the content of the orders made. Thus, while the ICJ requires a certain outcome in mandatory terms, it leaves the parties some freedom to determine the specific modality for achieving that outcome.[53] For example, the ICJ required Belgium to cancel the arrest warrant,

---

50   *Ibid*, 256.
51   As noted by Higgins, there are also evidentiary challenges in making such orders: R Higgins, "Overview of Part Two of the Articles on State Responsibility", in J Crawford, A Pellet & S Olleson, *The Law of International Responsibility* (2010) 537, 543.
52   *Jurisdictional Immunities of the State (Germany v. Italy: Greece Intervening)*, Judgment, 3 February 2012, para 138. See also *Land and Maritime Boundary between Cameroon and Nigeria (Cameroon v. Nigeria: Equatorial Guinea intervening)*, Judgment, ICJ Reports 2002 p 303, 452; *Application of the Interim Accord of 13 September 1995 (the former Yugoslav Republic of Macedonia v. Greece)*, Judgment, 5 December 2011, para 168.
53   Apart from considerations of judicial function, it has also been suggested that the discretion left to states might also be partly influenced by difficulties regarding enforcement:

but "by means of its own choosing",[54] as the choice of means was a matter within the inherent competence of Belgium.

III The Right of Election

An injured state is normally entitled to elect between available forms of reparation. As Article 43(2)(b) of the ARSIWA provides, an "injured State may specify…what form reparation should take".

This right is not absolute, however. It is qualified in several respects and can be limited by virtue of conduct taken by an injured stated in connection with judicial proceedings.[55] The right will be qualified where proceedings are brought by multiple injured states. Additionally, conduct taken by an injured state both prior to commencing proceedings and during the course of proceedings can affect the availability of certain remedies.

1 *Multiple Injured States*

Evidently, more than one state may be injured by an internationally wrongful act. This possibility is recognised in Article 46 of the ARSIWA, which provides that "[w]here several States are injured by the same internationally wrongful act, each injured State may separately invoke the responsibility of the State which has committed the internationally wrongful act". One example of a situation in which multiple states invoked responsibility is the *Nuclear Test* cases,

---

Brown (2007), *supra* n 5, 215–216. In situations where the subject-matter of the obligation breached falls within the inherent competence of the state (for example, in the case of the termination of a concession concerning natural resources), a mandatory order to restore the *status quo ante* may be inappropriate or even futile and compensation the only effective remedy. The appropriateness of the mandatory order, equivalent to specific performance, in *Texaco* v. *Libya*, (1977) 53 ILR 389, 511, has been questioned on this ground: *cf LIAMCO* v. *Libya*, (1977) 62 ILR 140, 197–199. The ultimate effect of the *Texaco* order was, it appears, a higher settlement.

54 *Arrest Warrant of 11 April 2000 (Democratic Republic of the Congo* v. *Belgium)*, Judgment, ICJ Reports 2002 p 3, 33. See also *Jurisdictional Immunities of the State (Germany* v. *Italy: Greece Intervening)*, Judgment, 3 February 2012, para 137. After determining that the "decisions and measures infringing Germany's jurisdictional immunities which are still in force must cease to have effect, and the effects which have already been produced by those decisions and measures must be reversed", the ICJ stated that Italy "has the right to choose the means it considers best suited to achieve the required result".

55 For further qualifications not discussed in this chapter see ARSIWA Commentary, *supra* n 5, Art 43, para 6. There are also requirements relating to notification and non-waiver: ARSIWA, *supra* n 6, Arts 43(1) & 45.

in which Australia and New Zealand alleged that France, *inter alia*, had violated the right of all states to be free from atmospheric nuclear weapons testing.[56]

There is the potential for states in such a situation to make inconsistent elections. This possibility is noted in the ARSIWA Commentary, which observes that "one State may claim restitution whereas the other may prefer compensation".[57] It does not appear that such a situation has arisen in practice and it is unclear how it would be resolved. The ARSIWA Commentary states that "[i]f restitution is indivisible in such a case and the election of the second State is valid, it may be that compensation is appropriate in respect of both claims".[58] It is too simplistic to say that here is recognised a hard and fast rule that "where one injured State seeks restitution and the other seeks compensation, then compensation is to prevail".[59] This is clear from the following statement made by the ILC Drafting Committee:

> [Article 46] did not deal with the case where injured States took different attitudes to the forms of reparation... Such cases, if they arose, were likely to present special features and to be significantly affected by the content of the obligation breached.[60]

But it is clear that, if such a situation arose, the injured states would need to coordinate their claims so as to avoid double recovery.[61] It does not seem that this would be unrealistic in practice, as seen from, for example, the *Aerial Incident of 27 July 1955* cases brought by Israel, the United Kingdom and the United States against Bulgaria.[62] Although the ICJ ultimately held that it did

---

56 *Nuclear Tests (New Zealand v. France)*, Judgment, ICJ Reports 1974 p 457; *Nuclear Tests (Australia v. France)*, Judgment, ICJ Reports 1974 p 253.
57 ARSIWA Commentary, *supra* n 5, Art 46, para 4.
58 *Ibid.*
59 C Gray, "The Different Forms of Reparation: Restitution", in J Crawford, A Pellet and S Olleson (eds), *The Law of International Responsibility* (2010) 589, 593.
60 *Yearbook of the International Law Commission 2000*, vol I, 395 (Chairman of the Drafting Committee).
61 ARSIWA Commentary, *supra* n 5, Art 46, para 4. On the rule against double recovery see Crawford (2013), *supra* n 1, 673–674.
62 *Case concerning the Aerial Incident of 27 July 1955 (Israel v. Bulgaria)*, Preliminary Objections, ICJ Reports 1959 p. 127; *Case concerning the Aerial Incident of 27 July 1955 (United Kingdom v. Bulgaria)*, Order, ICJ Reports 1959 p. 264; *Case concerning the Aerial Incident of 27 July 1955 (United States of America v. Bulgaria)*, Order, ICJ Reports 1960 p. 146.

not have jurisdiction over Israel's claim,[63] in its Memorial Israel acknowledged that:

> One of the primary reasons for establishing co-ordination [with the United Kingdom and the United States] from the earliest stages was to prevent, so far as possible, the Bulgarian Government being faced with double claims leading to the possibility of double damages. It is a well-known rule of law that the defendant State cannot be asked or compelled to pay reparation due in respect of damage twice over.[64]

2 Choices Made Prior to Commencing Proceedings

An injured party's ability to pursue certain avenues of international dispute settlement, and their associated remedies, can be affected by action taken prior to the commencement of international proceedings. One well known context in which this issue arises is in relation to fork-in-the-road clauses found in many investment treaties. Such clauses have the effect that where an international tribunal would otherwise have jurisdiction pursuant to a bilateral investment treaty, a party may lose the ability to avail itself of that jurisdiction by choosing another forum for the resolution of its dispute. A choice under a fork-in-the-road clause is made, and access to international arbitration lost, only if the *same* dispute is submitted by the same party to the other forum, usually domestic courts. This is well established. The degree of identity required between the dispute submitted to the domestic courts and that submitted to international arbitration is what is contested.

The tribunal in *Vivendi*, for example, considered a clause which provided that "[o]nce an investor has submitted the dispute to the courts of the Contracting Party concerned or to international arbitration, the choice of one or the other of those procedures is final".[65] It was observed by the tribunal that the same type of claims must be in existence in both the domestic and international proceedings for the clause to be activated. That is, the provision would only apply if claims were brought before the domestic courts explicitly alleging a cause of action under the bilateral investment treaty or charging Argentina

---

63   *Case concerning the Aerial Incident of 27 July 1955 (Israel v. Bulgaria)*, Preliminary Objections, ICJ Reports 1959 p 127.

64   *Ibid*, Memorial of the Government of Israel, 2 June 1958, Pleadings, 45, at 106.

65   Agreement between the Government of the Argentine Republic and the Government of the Republic of France for Reciprocal Protection and Promotion of Investments, 3 July 1991, 1728 UNTS 282, Art 8(2), reproduced in *Compañía de Aguas del Aconquija SA & Vivendi Universal v. Argentina*, Decision on Annulment, (2002) 6 ICSID Reports 340, 355.

with a violation of the bilateral investment treaty. It would not capture claims brought on the basis of the concession contract between Argentina and the claimant.[66]

This view, suggesting that a fork-in-the-road clause does not spring into action when an investor brings a local claim for breach of contract and an international claim based on breach of a bilateral investment treaty, also has support in the literature. For example, Schreuer has argued that the relevant national and international disputes would have to be identical in order for a fork-in-the-road clause to apply so that, if the international claim is based on a breach of a treaty, "the dispute before the domestic courts or administrative tribunals would also have to concern an alleged breach of a right conferred or created by the BIT".[67]

This interpretation has been refuted, including by McLachlan, Shore and Weiniger who argue that the approach is excessively restrictive and that "the fork in the road clause ought to operate should the investor choose to pursue *a claim equivalent in substance* to that created by the BIT against the host State".[68] An example of such equivalent claims could be a claim of expropriation under a bilateral investment treaty and a claim of unjustified taking of property under national law.[69] There is also support for this view in the case law. In *Pantechniki*, for example, the sole arbitrator Paulsson stated that "there comes a time when it is no longer sufficient merely to assert that a claim is founded on the Treaty".[70] The Albanian court case in question concerned a Minister's refusal to pay the amount of contractual compensation set by a commission. Paulsson stated that this conduct "might be challenged as an arbitrary act by a senior official which falls to be examined for compliance with the substantive

---

66 *Compañía de Aguas del Aconquija, SA & Compagnie Générale des Eaux* v. *Argentine Republic*, Award, (2000) 5 ICSID Reports 296, 316; *Compañía de Aguas del Aconquija SA & Vivendi Universal* v. *Argentine Republic*, Decision on Annulment, (2002) 6 ICSID Reports 340, 352–353. See also for example *CMS Gas Transmission Co* v. *Argentine Republic*, Decision on Objections to Jurisdiction, (2003) 7 ICSID Reports 492, 511.
67 C Schreuer, "Travelling the BIT Route: Of Waiting Periods, Umbrella Clauses and Forks in the Road", (2004) 5 *Journal of World Investment and Trade* 231, 248.
68 C McLachlan, L Shore & M Weiniger, *International Investment Law: Substantive Principles* (2007), 107 (emphasis in original).
69 See further *ibid*, 104 & 107.
70 *Pantechniki SA Contractors and Engineers (Greece)* v. *Republic of Albania*, Award, ICSID Case No ARB/07/21, 30 July 2009, para 64, available from <www.italaw.com/cases/810>. See also *Compañía de Aguas del Aconquija SA & Vivendi Universal* v. *Argentine Republic*, Decision on Annulment, (2002) 6 ICSID Reports 340, 356.

standards of the Treaty".[71] He reasoned that if the Albanian courts accepted that the claimant was entitled to payment, "it would grant the Claimant exactly what it is seeking before ICSID – and on the same 'fundamental basis'. The Claimant's grievance thus arises out of the same purported entitlement".[72]

This broader view of the scope of fork-in-the-road clauses is to be preferred. Under the alternative view, fork-in-the-road clauses in some treaties would have no effective scope of operation; for example, where the clause is included in a treaty between two states which have a dualist approach to the reception of treaties.[73]

Whether access to international arbitration has been lost by virtue of a fork-in-the-road clause is generally considered in the context of earlier domestic proceedings. However, it would seem equally possible for the issue to arise in relation to parallel international proceedings.[74] Fork-in-the-road clauses are one manifestation of the more general principle of *electa una via*. Another such manifestation is found in Article IV of the Pact of Bogotá,[75] which states:

> Once any pacific procedure has been initiated, whether by agreement between the parties or in fulfillment of the present Treaty or a previous pact, no other procedure may be commenced until that procedure is concluded.

This provision was considered by the ICJ in the *Border and Transborder Armed Actions* case.[76] To determine whether Nicaragua's claim before the ICJ was

---

71 *Pantechniki SA Contractors and Engineers (Greece) v. Republic of Albania*, Award, ICSID Case No ARB/07/21, 30 July 2009, para 65.
72 *Ibid*, para 67.
73 See also McLachlan, Shore & Weiniger (2007), *supra* n 68, 106–107.
74 For example, the fork-in-the-road clause in the Argentina-United States bilateral investment treaty precludes recourse to, *inter alia*, ICSID arbitration where a dispute has been previously submitted "in accordance with any applicable, previously agreed dispute-settlement procedures", an expression broad enough to include other international dispute settlement procedures: Treaty between United States of America and the Argentine Republic concerning the Reciprocal Encouragement and Protection of Investment, 14 November 1991, Art VII, available at <http://unctad.org/sections/dite/iia/docs/bits/argentina_us.pdf>.
75 American Treaty on Pacific Settlement, 30 April 1948, 30 UNTS 83. See also E Valencia-Ospina, "Bogota Pact (1948)", *Max Planck Encyclopedia of Public International Law* (2011), para 10.
76 *Border and Transborder Armed Actions (Nicaragua v. Honduras)*, Jurisdiction and Admissibility, Judgment, ICJ Reports 1988 p. 69.

admissible, it was necessary for the court to first consider whether the Contadora process, which had commenced before Nicaragua filed its claim, was a "pacific procedure" which had not yet been "concluded".[77] The ICJ held that the Contadora process had been concluded (without ruling on whether the process was a "pacific procedure") and that thus Nicaragua's claim was admissible.[78]

Article IV arose again in the *Certain Activities* case brought by Costa Rica against Nicaragua. In that case, Nicaragua sought to bring as a counter-claim a claim it had already brought in substance in separate proceedings (the *Construction of a Road* case).[79] Costa Rica argued, as recounted by the ICJ, "that, consistent with a basic principle (*electa una via*), under which two legal actions cannot be pursued simultaneously by the same applicant against the same party for the same cause of action, it cannot be open to a party to request the Court to condemn the same State twice".[80] Prior to its decision on the issue of counter-claims, the ICJ determined that the two cases should be joined.[81] The ICJ thus did not need to rule on the admissibility of the counter-claim and the issue of *electa una via*: as a result of the joinder, the substance of the counter-claim was "to be examined as a principal claim, within the context of the joined proceedings, thereby eliminating the need to examine it as a counter-claim".[82]

While not ruling on the issue, the order appears to recognise the "basic principle" of *electa una via*, and the fact that it would apply in relation to two claims brought before the same body. Principle, in particular considerations of the integrity of the judicial process, would also suggest that that should be the case.

3 Choices Made in the Course of Proceedings

It is open to a state to ask for a variety of remedies at the start of proceedings and to narrow this range as the case progresses or to change the preferred

---

77   *Ibid*, 100.
78   *Ibid*, 105.
79   *Certain Activities Carried Out by Nicaragua in the Border Area (Costa Rica v. Nicaragua); Construction of a Road in Costa Rica Along the San Juan River (Nicaragua v. Costa Rica),* Counter-Claims, Order, 18 April 2013, para 24.
80   *Ibid*, para 23.
81   *Construction of a Road in Costa Rica Along the San Juan River (Nicaragua v. Costa Rica),* Joinder of Proceedings, Order, 17 April 2013.
82   *Certain Activities Carried Out by Nicaragua in the Border Area (Costa Rica v. Nicaragua); Construction of a Road in Costa Rica Along the San Juan River (Nicaragua v. Costa Rica),* Counter-Claims, Order, 18 April 2013, para 24.

remedy in the course of proceedings. In the *Chorzów Factory* case, for example, Germany decided to accept compensation after initially insisting on restitution of the factory.[83] In the *Passage through the Great Belt* case, Finland eventually accepted compensation in a negotiated settlement after initially appearing to insist on the deconstruction of the disputed bridge.[84] At common law, parties are entitled to change the remedies they seek up to the date of judgment. No general limit on the period during which parties may seek such a change has been established in international law, but presumably it extends at least to the making of formal submissions at the end of the oral phase.

When the international court or tribunal comes to determine any reparation due, it will be limited by the claims which have been advanced by the parties. This is known as the *non ultra petita* rule,[85] which prevents a court or tribunal from going beyond the request put to it. Courts and tribunals have held the rule to restrict both the forms of reparation, including the quantum of compensation, it can award.[86]

An example of the former situation is the decision of the tribunal in the *Rainbow Warrior* arbitration.[87] The arbitration concerned claims made by New Zealand in relation to two French agents responsible for the sinking of the *Rainbow Warrior*, who had initially been detained on the island of Hao but were released for medical reasons. New Zealand sought the return of the French agents to the island and specifically rejected any other remedy.[88] The tribunal determined that the return of the agents to the island was not an available remedy,[89] and it appears to have been of the view that, in light of New

---

83 For example, in the *Chorzow Factory* case, Germany sought compensation rather than the return of the factory in question. The PCIJ referred to Germany having "abandoned its original claim for the restitution of the factory": *Factory at Chorzów*, Jurisdiction, (1927) PCIJ Ser A No 9, 17.

84 See M Koskenniemi, "Case Concerning Passage Through the Great Belt", (1996) 27 *Ocean Development & International Law* 255. In its Provisional Measures order, the ICJ observed that "if it is established that the construction of works involves an infringement of a legal right, the possibility cannot and should not be excluded *a priori* of a judicial finding that such works must not be continued or must be modified or dismantled": *Passage through the Great Belt (Finland v. Denmark)*, Provisional Measures, Order, ICJ Reports 1991 pp. 12, 19.

85 See S Rosenne, *The Law and Practice of the International Court, 1920–2005* (2006), vol II, 576–577.

86 On the application of the principle in relation to interest rates see Crawford (2013), *supra* n 1, 627, discussing the *Spanish Zone of Morocco Claims* arbitration (*Affaire des biens britanniques au Maroc espagnol (Espagne contre Royaume-Uni)*, (1925) 2 RIAA 615).

87 *Rainbow Warrior (New Zealand v. France)*, (1990) 82 ILR 499.

88 *Ibid*, 570–571.

89 *Ibid*, 573. See further Crawford (2013), *supra* n 1, 465–467.

Zealand's pleadings, there was a limitation on its discretion to award other forms of reparation:

> New Zealand has not however requested the award of monetary compensation – even as a last resort should the Tribunal not make the declarations and orders for the return of the agents. The Tribunal can understand that position in terms of an assessment made by a State of its dignity and its sovereign rights. The fact that New Zealand has not sought an order for compensation also means that France has not addressed this quite distinct remedy in its written pleadings and oral arguments, or even had the opportunity to do so. Further, the Tribunal itself has not had the advantage of the argument of the two Parties…on…relevant matters, such as the amount of damages.[90]

The tribunal thus decided not to award compensation.[91]

As to the latter situation, in the *Corfu Channel* case the ICJ held that the *non ultra petita* rule prevented it from awarding more compensation than requested by the United Kingdom. That case concerned damage suffered by ships due to mines in Albanian territorial waters. After finding that compensation was due, the ICJ entrusted the evaluation of the quantum of compensation to appointed experts.[92] In relation to the first head of damages claimed by the United Kingdom, £700,087 was claimed for the destruction of the *Saumarez*.[93] The court-appointed experts determined that the replacement value of the vessel was greater (£716,780),[94] but the ICJ held that it could not "award more than the amount claimed in the submissions of the United Kingdom".[95]

While the *non ultra petita* rule is explicitly mentioned only occasionally, it is likely implicitly in play in other decisions. For example, there are cases where a form of reparation which would seem appropriate (or at least open) has not

---

90 *Rainbow Warrior (New Zealand v. France)*, (1990) 82 ILR 499, 575.
91 *Ibid*.
92 *Corfu Channel case (United Kingdom v. Albania)*, Order, ICJ Reports 1949 p. 237.
93 *Ibid*, Judgment, ICJ Reports 1949 pp. 244, 248–249.
94 *Ibid*, 249.
95 *Ibid*. This approach was criticized by Judge ad hoc Ečer, who argued that "the Court, without any reference to [the *non ultra petita*] rule, must decide, in the first place and on grounds of law, and not of mathematics, what basis [for the calculation of compensation] is juridically to be adopted. And if the figure estimated on this basis is higher than the sum claimed, the Court must limit its award in accordance with the rule *non ultra petita*": *Corfu Channel case (United Kingdom v. Albania)*, Judgment, ICJ Reports 1949 p 244, 253 (Judge ad hoc Ečer, dissenting).

been considered by the ICJ, presumably because it was not sought by the claimant. A case in point is the *LaGrand* case. In that case, Germany sought no compensation in relation to the execution of the LaGrand brothers and the issue was not discussed by the court.[96] Despite limited references to the rule, it is not open to doubt.

IV   Conclusion

While the proposition that jurisdiction to determine breach implies jurisdiction to award reparation appears straight forward, there are complexities regarding its implementation. The entitlement to reparation underlying the *Chorzów Factory* principle is one which is affected in practice by choices made by an injured state and by the discretion of courts and tribunals. This suggests a more flexible situation than orthodox statements of the *Chorzów Factory* principle would suggest.

---

96   Germany's Application had sought compensation: *LaGrand* (*Germany* v. *United States of America*), Judgment, ICJ Reports 2001 pp. 466, 472. But this claim was apparently dropped: *ibid*, 473–474.

CHAPTER 38

The International Court of Justice and Diplomatic Settlement of Disputes: Could ICJ Judgments Play an Effective Role in the Negotiation of Interstate Disputes?

Sašo Georgievski*

The relationship between the International Court of Justice (ICJ)'s adjudication of and diplomatic settlement of disputes may take different forms. In most cases submitted to the ICJ, the Court proceedings have usually been initiated after negotiation or some other diplomatic dispute settlement has failed or has not been possible, so the Court's judgment has been *ipso facto* intended to bring about a final settlement of the dispute, without, in principle, any further substantive negotiations between the disputing parties being needed.[1] But in many other cases ICJ adjudication and diplomatic means have been used cumulatively or simultaneously by the disputing parties, with the Court exercising its jurisdiction within the limits of its primary law-based dispute settlement function.[2] Yet, referring to some of this type of cases, John Collier long ago questioned the assumption that the ICJ *always* acted within its basic operational limits, submitting that, in the Court's practice, there were indeed judgments where the Court had exceeded the bounds of its primary function,

---

* PhD; Full Professor at the Department of International Law and International Relations at the Ss. Cyril and Methodius University, 'Iustinianus Primus' Faculty of Law, Skopje, Republic of Macedonia. During his professional career, he occasionally served as legal adviser to the relevant ministries regarding disputes involving the Republic of Macedonia. The views expressed in this essay are his personal views and cannot be ascribed to any official policy, institution, or representative of the Republic of Macedonia.
1 Even with these types of ICJ cases, however, it is possible for additional negotiations by the parties to take place, for example, when the implementation of the Court's judgment requires further detailing by the parties (usually) through a technical agreement, or when new or resumed negotiations are prompted by a denial of and non-compliance by one (often more powerful) party with parts of the Court's judgment (total denial and non-compliance are not contemplated herewith).
2 Collier, G.J., "The International Court of Justice and the Peaceful Settlement of Disputes," in Lowe, V., Fitzmaurice, M., eds., *Fifty Years of the International Court of Justice, Essays in honor of Sir Robert Jennings*. Cambridge: Cambridge University Press, 1996: 364–372, 366.

and where it had even "almost abdicated its special function of judicial settlement in substance, though not in form, in favor of one or more of the other methods of settlement."[3] Such occasional shifts by the ICJ towards performing functions of other dispute settlement methods, according to Collier, relate to those of an arbitration (in view of the Court's practice of sitting in Chambers), but also to those of "less formal methods of settlement, especially mediation and conciliation."[4]

Indeed, the Court has often resorted to exercising elements of mediation or conciliatory functions in its practice, especially, in cases concerned with maritime delimitation,[5] but also in other types of cases.[6] In these, instead of finally settling the dispute at hand, it has proceeded to "giv[e] the parties guidance as to the principles and rules *they*, not the Court, should apply, in settling their dispute by negotiation leading to an agreement."[7] And, in many of these and other cases, the Court often had to decide on the conduct of the disputing parties in active negotiations going on between them based on the principle of acting in 'good faith',[8] or sometimes to determine the subject and the scope of negotiations.[9]

---

3   *Ibid.*, 368.
4   *Ibid.*, 369.
5   In these cases, the Court merely restated the international law principles and rules applicable for the delimitation of the whole or part of the disputed maritime territorial issue, leaving the parties to reach an agreement on the basis of the judgment. Examples include *North Sea Continental Shelf*, Judgment, ICJ Reports (1969) 3; *Continental Shelf (Tunisia/Libyan Arab Jamahiriya)*, Judgment, ICJ Reports (1982) 18; *Continental Shelf (Libyan Arab Jamahiriya/Malta)*, Judgment, ICJ Reports (1985) 13; *etc*. Among the more recent cases see, for instance, *Territorial and Maritime Dispute between Nicaragua and Honduras in the Caribbean Sea (Nicaragua* v. *Honduras)*, Judgment, ICJ Reports (2007) 659; with respect to the delimitation of a certain portion of the territorial sea, see point 4 at p. 763 of the Judgment.
6   *E.g. Gabčíkovo-Nagymaros Project*, Judgment, ICJ Reports (1997) 5; *Pulp Mills on the River Uruguay*, Judgment, ICJ Reports (2010) 13, especially 95, para. 281; *Maritime Delimitation and Territorial Questions between Qatar (Qatar* v. *Bahrain)*, Jurisdiction and Admissibility, Judgment, ICJ Reports (1994); *Fisheries Jurisdiction (United Kingdom* v. *Iceland)*, Merits, Judgment, ICJ Reports (1974), 3; *etc.*
7   Collier, "International Court of Justice", 370; emphasis added.
8   *E.g. Application of the Interim Accord of 13 September 1995 (the former Yugoslav Republic of Macedonia* v. *Greece)*, Judgment (December 5, 2011) 4, available at <http://www.icj-cij.org/docket/files/142/16827.pdf>, 41–42, paras. 133–138; *Pulp Mills on the River Uruguay*, *supra* note 6, 132–150; *Fisheries Jurisdiction*, *supra* note 6, 33, para. 78; *North Sea Continental Shelf*, *supra* note 5, 47, para. 85; *etc.*
9   See, for instance, *Application of the Interim Accord*, *supra* note 8, discussed *infra* under III.

In these types of cases, in fact, the ICJ's dispute-settlement function and that of diplomatic settlement interact, or occasionally even converge, based on the will of the disputing parties expressed when presenting their case to the ICJ, or on the Court's own will. To these, one may also add another group of cases of more direct interaction between the two different methods of dispute settlement, cases in which the Court was invited to decide only parts of a broader political issue that was subject to pending diplomatic settlement, and where the Court's judgment, even if not intended, directed itself towards upholding or assisting an ongoing diplomatic settlement process by virtue of its subject-matter.[10]

Having these points of convergence between ICJ adjudication and diplomatic dispute settlement in mind, in the remainder of this essay we will try to explore the potential effectiveness of ICJ judgments in a negotiation process through which the settlement of the same or wider disputes addressed by these judgments is being tried. Of particular interest to us are the ICJ's judgments in which the Court has decided on the merits of a case, and not those judgments where it has declined to exercise its jurisdiction.

The topic of this short essay seems quite suitable for this occasion of honoring Professor Budislav Vukas, since, within his extremely rich professional biography, apart from being a former judge and vice-president of the International Tribunal for the Law of the Sea, Professor Vukas also served as judge *ad hoc* in ICJ cases. Of course, given the shortage of space, the purpose of the essay is to offer only a sketchy outline of some preliminary thoughts on the issues relating to the complex relationship between ICJ judgments and negotiation that would normally require far more interdisciplinary in-depth analysis than that offered here. Hence, it necessarily suffers from selectiveness and oversimplifications that follow such a straightforward presentational approach.

I   The International Court of Justice, Dispute and Conflict Resolution and Negotiation: What Role for the ICJ?

As is often submitted, negotiation and related bargaining, including interstate bargaining, are typically conducted "in the shadow of the law".[11] In a broader

---

10   See *e.g. Application of the Interim Accord*, *supra* note 8, and *infra* under III.
11   Howse, R., Teitel, R., "Beyond Compliance: Rethinking Why International Law Really Matters", *Global Policy (Online)*. Vol. 1, No. 2, 2010, NYU *School of Law, Public Law and Legal Theory Research Paper Series*. Paper No. 10–08 (February 2010), available at SSRN: <http://ssrn.com/abstract=1551923>: 1–29, 19.

perspective, resorting to law and legal language may change the context of the dispute or conflict, especially in the early stages, when the parties find themselves in a constant 'battle for control of the language', and hence of the context of the dispute and conflict.[12]

But how would the ICJ, given the stricter nature of its law-based dispute settlement function, affect the often more complicated political relationships between the parties (including interested third parties) involved in conflict and negotiation?

In his analysis of state compliance with ICJ decisions, Aloysius Llamzon concluded that the Court has been largely successful at "striking the right tone between expositor of international law and political actor, between arbitral body encouraging negotiated settlement and impartial adjudicator of rights."[13] In order to understand the reality of these varying functions exercised by ICJ and, more specifically, its potential to have an effective role in a political negotiation context, one has to consult the extremely rich more general theoretical discussion on international politics and law and on state compliance with international law and courts' (ICJ) judgments.[14]

The proponents of 'legalization' of international relations and 'judicialization' of dispute settlement,[15] for instance, seem to give out an implicit message that the ICJ (together with other international courts and tribunals) should stick to its rule-of-law-ensuring mission in a political settlement context,[16] basing the latter on a general presumption that the decisions of international courts and tribunals are themselves capable of having a causal impact on state (*i.e.* conflicting parties') behaviour.[17] Their particular findings on the ICJ, however, reveal only a moderate potential of the Court to act according to that strict rule-of-law-securing assignment, since, under the rigid criteria for

---

12   Collier, J., Lowe, V., *The Settlement of Disputes in International* Law. Oxford: Oxford University Press, 1999, 4–5.

13   Llamzon, A.P., "Jurisdiction and Compliance in Recent Decisions of the International Court of Justice", *European Journal of International* Law. Vol. 18, No. 5, 2008: 815–852, 852.

14   Given the abundance of valuable literature on state compliance, we will refer here to only one often cited book written by Schulte, C., *Compliance with Decisions of the International Court of Justice*. Oxford: Oxford University Press, 2004.

15   In particular, see the articles published in "Legalization of World Politics", in the special issue of *International Organization*. Vol. 54, No. 3, 2000.

16   See for instance Helfer, L.R., Slaughter, A.-M., "Towards a Theory of Effective Supranational Adjudication", *Yale Law Journal*. Vol. 107, 1997: 273–397, 387, suggesting that international courts (ICJ) should be modelled on the ECJ and ECtHR.

17   Keohane, R.O., Moravcsik, A., Slaughter, A.-M., "Legalized Dispute Resolution: International and Transnational", *International Organization*. Vol. 54, No. 3, 2000: 457–488, 488.

measuring the degree of legalization of international courts and tribunals offered by 'legalization' scholars (the degree of their independence, their access and embeddedness), the ICJ is still ranked as falling within the 'modest' group when compared with the highest ranked transnational courts, largely because of the more heavily exercised political control ('gate-keeping') by states when it comes to its composition, access to it by private parties and the enforcement of its judgments.[18]

Other authors, however, express their reservation as to the overly emphasized rule-of-law-promoting function of courts inherent in the concept of 'legalization' of international relations, and point to the serious drawbacks of the removal of conflicts from the diplomatic to the judicial realm implied by it.[19] In line with their basic understanding that states always act in their self-interest, on their part, rational choice theorists defy the basic claim of 'legalization' promoters about the causal role of international courts and tribunals on state behaviour, granting these courts and the ICJ a much more 'symbolic value' in the political dispute settlement process,[20] that is, a mere informative, conciliatory or mediating role. International tribunals and the ICJ could (and should) merely serve as 'problem-solving devices' in dispute settlement and conflict resolution processes, provided that they are neutral and reflect the '*ex ante* interests' of the parties, and act as a "neutral arbiter that can help overcome prisoners' dilemma problems."[21] As states enter into bilateral and multilateral treaties "without having a clear view of their obligations and needs decades later", these can be clarified by courts; however, enforcing these treaties by courts "is not simply a matter of enforcing them impartially, but of enforcing them in a way that reflects the interests of states as they have developed over time."[22]

Indeed, in their empirical study on the role of international organizations (including adjudication) in settling territorial, river and maritime contentious

---

18   Ibid., 457–458, 469.
19   Shany, Y., "No Longer a Weak Department of Power? Reflections on the Emergence of a New International Judiciary", *European Journal of International Law*. Vol. 20, No. 1, 2009: 73–91, 88. See also Finnemore, M., Toope, S., "Alternatives to 'Legalization': Richer Views of Law and Politics", *International Organization*. Vol. 55, No. 3, 2001: 743–758.
20   Posner, E.A., "The Decline of the International Court of Justice", *Chicago, John M. Olin Law & Economics Working Paper No. 233* (2nd series) (December 2004): 1–38, 1; Posner, E.A., Yoo, J.C., "A Theory of International Adjudication", *Chicago, John M. Olin Law & Economics Working Paper No. 206* (2nd series) (February 2004); both papers are available at: <http://www.law.uchicago.edu/Lawecon/index.html>.
21   Ibid., 5, 14.
22   Posner, "The Decline of the International Court of Justice", 24.

cases in the Americas (equally applicable more globally, and to the ICJ), Mitchel and Hensel concluded that "institutions are more effective conflict managers when they choose binding settlement techniques."[23] Grounding their theoretical research model on Fearon's bargaining model and his rationalist explanations for war, and Boehmer, Gartzke and Nordstrom's theory linking international institutions and rationalist bargaining models, they arrived at the later conclusion basing their research on the theoretical presumption that *inter alia*: (a) active involvement of binding forms of settlement (including by the ICJ) may better help to mitigate the uncertainties caused by the parties' incentives to misinterpret their true interest in the bargaining process, as these are more suitable to collecting detailed information for the parties; (b) their engagement may better help decrease commitment problems in the conflict resolution process by offering greater legitimacy in reaching an agreement, allowing leaders to save face, and helping to mitigate the security dilemma that arises in contentious dyads; and that (c) binding forms of settlement may increase the prospect for parties' compliance by raising their reputation costs for reneging from their obligations.[24]

On the other hand, many useful suggestions for understanding the complex relationship between the ICJ and diplomatic dispute settlement are implied in the works of scholars that prefer a norm-oriented theoretical approach when explaining the relationship between politics and international law. In their own response to pro-legalization arguments, among others, Finnemore and Toope presented a 'richer view on law and politics', reminding one that *inter alia* conceptualization of law and obligation should take into account alternative features of law *i.e.* 'legitimacy' as a source of obligation and 'compliance pull' in law.[25] Legitimate law generates obligations not just in the formal sense but "also in a felt sense", and it also includes "adherence to legal process values, the ability of actors to participate and feel their influence, and the use of legal forms of reasoning",[26] which also applies to ICJ judgments.

---

23   Mitchell, S.M., Hensel, P.R., "International Institutions and Compliance with Agreements", *American Journal of Political Science*. Vol. 51, No. 4, 2007: 721–737, especially 721–724 and 734–735, and the references at these pages.

24   *Ibid.*, 725.

25   Finnemore, Toope, "Alternatives to 'Legalization'", 743–746, especially 746. The authors refer to the well-known 'legitimacy' theory of Thomas Franck, see Franck, T.M., *The Power of Legitimacy among Nations*. New York: Oxford University Press, 1990; and to Byers, M., *Custom, Power, and the Power of Rules: International Relations and Customary International Law*. Cambridge: Cambridge University Press, 1999.

26   Finnemore, Toope, "Alternatives to 'Legalization'", 749–750, 755.

From a similar 'richer' perceptive of understanding law and politics, Howse and Teitel went even a step further, defying the prevalent reliance by scholars (especially by positivist rational choice scholars) on explaining international law's (the ICJ's) performance only in terms of compliance. As opposed to the latter approach, they strongly advised that, when conceiving the real effectiveness of law (and ICJ judgments), one has to proceed by "much more reflection on those properties of 'law' that it possesses which make international law distinctive as a mode of discourse in international order, and *then* to see the effects of international law [and ICJ judgments] through such an understanding."[27] Using that broader theoretical approach, these authors identified various 'real world effects' that may be produced by international law and adjudication which offer valuable insights for research into the ICJ's potential to impact on an ongoing diplomatic dispute settlement process, in particular, as to its judgments' ability to influence "the way policy makers view international problems and conflicts", to bring about a total or partial "shift in the actors' decision-making and/or the interpretative or legitimating power from one set of elite actors to another", and to affect state bargaining, as "rather obviously, legal agents bargain in the shadow of the law", and "instead of simply 'complying' with international rules [they] may bargain in light of them".[28]

In general, what we can learn from the norm-oriented, and from the constructivists', theoretical explanations of the relationship between politics and law and of state compliance is that there is a need to focus more on the ideational and normative aspects of the behaviour of actors involved in a diplomatic interstate dispute settlement exercise prompted by a related ICJ judgment, rather than exclusively on instrumental or material aspects of their conduct. Under the constructivists' theoretical accounts, apart from complying instrumentally, state actors also operate in part "by figuring out, or being socialized towards, the 'right thing' in a particular general context" (*i.e.* negotiation context), that is, following the 'logic of appropriateness' instead of one of consequences.[29] Hence, according to Ruggie "[n]orms [including ICJ judgments] may 'guide' behavior, they may 'inspire' behavior, they may 'rationalize'

---

27 Howse, Teitel, "Beyond Compliance", 4, 10 and 25–28, especially 26 and 28.
28 *Ibid.*, 11–13, 19–20.
29 Raustiala, K., Slaughter, A.-M., "International Law, International Relations and Compliance," in Carlsnaes, W., Risse, T., Simmons, B.A., eds., *Handbook of International Relations*. London: SAGE Publications Inc., 2002: 537–558, 538, referring to Finnemore, M., Sikkink, K., "International Norm Dynamics and Political Change", *International Organization*. Vol. 52, No. 4, 1998: 887–917, 1, and March, J.G., Olsen, J.P., "The Institutional Dynamics of International Political Orders", *International Organization*. Vol. 52, No. 4, 1998: 943–969.

or 'justify' behavior, they may express 'mutual expectations' about behavior, or they may be ignored by state actors."[30] In order to understand properly the effectiveness of ICJ judgments in a diplomatic context, one has to take into account both the communicative dynamics going on between them, that is, how a state's behaviour "is interpreted by other states, the rationales and justifications for behavior that are proffered, together with pleas for understanding or admission of guilt, as well as the responsiveness of such reasoning on the part of other states", as "absolutely critical component parts of any explanation involving efficacy of norms."[31]

II Factors Determining the Potential Effectiveness of ICJ Judgments in a Negotiation Context

Theories on politics and international law and on state compliance, when combined with conflict resolution and negotiation theories,[32] may also help us to identify factors that could influence the potential impact of ICJ judgments on the behaviour of the conflicting parties and of the other actors involved in an open diplomatic dispute settlement process.

One such major factor certainly consist of the parties' interests affected by an ICJ judgment, as parties constantly engage with interest-based calculations when forming their positions and strategies during conflict dynamics and negotiation. The more an ICJ judgment is 'high-cost' and touches upon the parties' vital interests as perceived by them with respect to the issues involved, the less is the possibility that the judgment will influence the respective party's conduct in negotiations.[33]

To that add the character of the underlying conflict that may considerably affect the ICJ judgment's potential role and effectiveness in a particular

---

30 Ruggie, J.G., "Epistemology, Ontology and the Study of International Regimes", in Ruggie, J.G., ed., *Constructing the World Polity*. London, New York: Routledge, 1998: 97–98.
31 *Ibid.*
32 For a comprehensive presentation of conflict resolution theories and methods, including in their foundational and historic development context, see Miall, H., Ramsbotham, O., Woodhouse, T., *Contemporary Conflict Resolution*. Polity Press and Blackwell Publishing Ltd, 2003.
33 Shany, Y., "Compliance with Decisions of International Courts as Indicative of their Effectiveness: A Goal-Based Analysis", *Hebrew University of Jerusalem Faculty of Law Research Paper No. 04–10* (October 24, 2010), available at SSRN: <http://ssrn.com/abstract=1697488> or <http://dx.doi.org/10.2139/ssrn.1697488>: 1–17, 4–5.

diplomatic dispute settlement context.[34] Thus, in conflicts involving a relationship characterized by conflicts of interests that are "typically resolved through a bargained compromise",[35] a Court's judgment may aid in reaching such compromise by authoritatively providing information, legally clarifying the framework for possible compromises, and setting the limits for the respective parties' legitimate claims in the state bargaining process,[36] whereas, in conflicts characterized by conflict of values, these are more difficult to negotiate "as the parties attach their identities to the values in dispute".[37] Hence an ICJ judgment would presumably have less chance of producing the desired transformative effect.

The ICJ judgment's effectiveness in negotiations is equally dependant on the willingness of the disputing parties to compromise in the related negotiations, and on existing opportunity costs associated with the negotiated settlement of the dispute, for instance, with respect to the parties' interest in maintaining good trade relations, political or other forms of cooperation *etc.*, that may provide incentives for reaching agreement according to the ICJ judgment.[38] Whereas, some researchers into state compliance with ICJ judgments concluded that they have had more chances to be respected in cases where the Court's proceedings were instituted under special agreement by the disputing parties,[39] often in circumstances of otherwise good relations between them, than when filed unilaterally, others disproved such conclusion asserting that the way the Court is seized does not have much bearing on parties' compliance with its judgments.[40]

---

34   For the types of conflict and their relationship to negotiation see Druckman, D., "Conflict Escalation and Negotiation: A Turning Points Analysis", in Zartman, W., Faure, G.O., eds., *Escalation and Negotiation in International Conflicts*. Cambridge: Cambridge University Press, 2005: 185–212, 188–194.

35   *Ibid.*, 188–189, and the authors quoted at that place.

36   *E.g.* with respect to the dispute between Libya and Chad, where the acceptance by the parties of the ICJ judgment (*Territorial Dispute (Libyan Arab Jamahiriya/Chad)*, Judgment, *ICJ Reports* (1994) 6) meant that Libya could no longer claim sovereignty over the region during negotiations. See Llamzon, "Jurisdiction and Compliance in Recent Decisions", 831.

37   Druckman, "Conflict Escalation and Negotiation", 188–189. See also Miall *et al.*, *Contemporary Conflict Resolution*, 9.

38   See, for instance, the post judgment developments related to: *Maritime Delimitation and Territorial Questions (Qatar v. Bahrain)*, Judgment, *ICJ Reports* (2001) 40; *Maritime Delimitation in the Area between Greenland and Jan Mayen (Denmark v. Norway)*, Judgment, *ICJ Reports* (1993) 38; *etc.* See Schulte, *Compliance with Decisions of the International Court of Justice*.

39   Posner, Yoo, "A Theory of International Adjudication", 33, referring to statistics presented by Ginsburg and McAdams.

40   See Llamzon, "Jurisdiction and Compliance in Recent Decisions", 845, in response to Posner and Yoo.

Of course, power relations between the conflicting parties and their assessment of their own ability to rely on coercion during negotiation and conflict despite an issued ICJ judgment have a large role to play. A shift to a legal context incited by a judgment, however, may help to increase the power of the one party at the expense of the other,[41] which could sometimes bring about a change in existing power asymmetries between the conflicting parties as a prerequisite for the beginning and further pursuit of constructive negotiations. An ICJ judgment, in turn, may potentially contribute to the occurrence of a 'ripe moment' for negotiation during conflict escalating dynamics.[42] Since, this is "a perceptual event based on the values and preferences of the political leaders making the assessments",[43] an ICJ judgment (together with other factors) may occasionally cause a positive perceptional change in the respective actors' leadership (and that of the intermediaries) for the 'ripeness' for negotiation, enabling them to reach a positive decision to start or resume negotiations. A Court's judgment may produce such effect, especially, by facilitating the respective governments' gaining of domestic legitimacy for the decision, and through inserting an objective and credible element in the domestic political process, it may help the creation of domestic public consensus and building up of 'coalitions for peace', which are often necessary for the party leadership's turn to constructive negotiation "without taking the risk of being called a traitor who is selling out national interests".[44]

Domestic linkages may have a considerable impact on the ICJ judgment's effectiveness in negotiations, as shifts in the preferences of domestic societal actors around an issued ICJ judgment may result with "shifts of compliance preferences of governments"[45] of the respective parties. Equally significant, however, are external factors. Both lawyers and political scientists have long ago recognized the importance, internationally, to a party of reputation costs

---

41 Collier, Lowe, *Settlement of Disputes in International Law*, 4–5.

42 The so-called 'ripeness theory' has been advanced by Zartman. See Zartman, W.I., *Ripe for Resolution*. New York: Oxford University Press, 1989. See also Aggestam, K., "Enhancing Ripeness: Transition from Conflict to Negotiation", in Zartman, Faure, eds., *Escalation and Negotiation*: 271–292, and the authors referred to at these pages.

43 *Ibid.*, 273–274, and the authors quoted at that place.

44 *Ibid.*, 275–276. The above effect of the ICJ's judgments, however, may be less likely in circumstances of sharply politically divided societies, where it is particularly difficult to gain unequivocal legitimacy and public support for a turn to constructive negotiation.

45 Raustiala, Slaughter, "International Law, International Relations and Compliance", 545. See also Simmons, B.A., "Capacity, Commitment and Compliance. International Institutions and Territorial Disputes", *Journal of Conflict Resolution*. Vol. 46, No. 6, 2002: 829–856.

that it may incur for reneging on its obligations imposed by an ICJ judgment.⁴⁶ "States normally want to look good in the community of nations", they want "to be seen as law abiding"⁴⁷ including during active negotiations.

The chances that an ICJ judgment would effectively affect the conflicting parties' conduct during negotiations increase considerably in the presence of third parties interested in the dispute or conflict settlement, in particular when more powerful third states and international organizations are involved.⁴⁸ An ICJ judgment may *inter alia* provide additional leverage for "mediators with muscle" when they try "to influence the parties' preferences and perceptions of de-escalation [of conflict] and negotiation" by exercising power and, hence, to alter the structure and distribution of power through coercive bargaining.⁴⁹

With respect to the particular involvement of international organizations, as noted earlier, Mitchell and Hensel demonstrated in their study the importance of both the active and the passive presence of international organizations for the settlement of territorial, river and maritime contentious cases,⁵⁰ equally applicable to the settlement of other types of contentious issues. Disputes like the one between Cameroon and Nigeria, for instance, would probably not have been successfully resolved diplomatically following the issued ICJ judgment without the active assistance of an international organization (IO), in that case, the UN.⁵¹ IOs can produce positive effects on dispute settlement both by their passive involvement, since the disputing parties' joint membership of an

---

46   Mitchell, Hensel, "International Institutions and Compliance", 725, 734.
47   Warioba, S.J., "Monitoring Compliance with and Enforcement of Binding Decisions of International Courts", *Max Plank Yearbook of United Nations Law*. Vol. 5, 2001: 41–52, 51. See, for instance, post-judgment developments on: *Land, Island and Maritime Frontier Dispute (El Salvador/Honduras, Nicaragua intervening)*, Judgment, *ICJ Reports* (1992) 351; *Territorial Dispute*, supra note 36. See Schulte, *Compliance with Decisions*, 215–220 and 229–234; Llamzon, "Jurisdiction and Compliance in Recent Decisions", 825–829 and 829–832; Paulson, C., "Compliance with Final Judgments of the International Court of Justice since 1987", *American Journal of International Law*. Vol. 98, No. 3, 2004: 434–461, 437–439 and 439–443.
48   See, for instance, the post-judgment developments with respect to: *Land and Maritime Boundary between Cameroon and Nigeria (ICJ Reports* (2002) 303), and Llamzon, "Jurisdiction and Compliance in Recent Decisions", 836–838, especially 838.
49   Aggestam, "Enhancing Ripeness", 280. On the role and forms of third party intervention in conflict and achieving conflict structural transformation, see Miall *et al.*, *Contemporary Conflict Resolution*, 9–10, 156–162.
50   Mitchell, Hensel, "International Institutions and Compliance", 723–727, 734–735.
51   See *Land and Maritime Boundary between Cameroon and* Nigeria, *supra* note 48.

10 (*e.g.* the UN, OAS or the EU) often exerts additional pressure on them to settle their disagreements peacefully.⁵²

To all the above factors, many (especially norm-oriented) scholars add the possibility that the quality of an ICJ judgment may be a major determinant for its potential effectiveness (including) in a negotiation context, in particular with respect to the level of determinacy of the judgment.⁵³ The choices made in the remedial part of a judgment may also have an impact on the effectiveness of the judgment. Since the ICJ exercises considerable discretion as to how to formulate its judgments and what remedies to impose in a particular negotiation context, it "may arguably impact through aiming 'high' or 'low' (by facilitating different levels of state resistance), the degree of compliance pull that [its] decisions would generate".⁵⁴ Furthermore, the ICJ could equally adjust to the political realities of particular cases by including 'legitimate statements' in the judgment,⁵⁵ suitable for meeting the particular parties' interests in pending negotiations in a more balanced way.

III Testing the Factors for ICJ Judgments' Effectiveness: A Brief Glance at the Ongoing Negotiation of the 'Difference over the Name' between the Republic of Macedonia and Greece

The interplay between different factors for ICJ judgments' effectiveness in a diplomatic dispute settlement context identified in the previous section may be demonstrated by the ongoing process of negotiation of the 'difference' between Greece and the Republic of Macedonia (RM) over its name. In brief, that 'difference' results from Greek objections to the RM's use of the term 'Macedonia' in its official name (and to the use by it of the 'derivatives' of that name *i.e.* 'Macedonian' nation, language, culture *etc.*), that allegedly imply territorial aspirations towards the Greek northern provinces bearing the same name. Negotiations between the parties have been ongoing for twenty years

---

52 Mitchell, Hensel, "International Institutions and Compliance", 723, 734.
53 See Franck, T.M., *Fairness in International Law and Institutions*. Oxford: Clarendon Press, 1995. The Court's judgment in *Gabčíkovo-Nagymaros Project*, *supra* note 6, for instance, has often been pointed to as a perfect example of how an ambiguous ICJ judgment may not serve the purpose of leading the parties towards a successful negotiated outcome. See Llamzon, "Jurisdiction and Compliance in Recent Decisions", 835–836.
54 Shany, "Compliance with Decisions of International Courts", 4–5.
55 See Treves, T., "Aspects of Legitimacy of Decisions of International Courts and Tribunals", in Wolfrum, R., Röben, V., eds., *Legitimacy in International Law*. Berlin: Springer, 2008: 169–188.

under the 'good offices' (in fact mediation) of the UN General Secretary's envoy established pursuant to Security Council Resolution 817 of 1993, assisted by various interested third parties, especially by the US.

Unsatisfied with the way negotiations had been progressing, especially at the beginning of 2007, Greece resorted to a conflict escalating strategy by using coercive tactics of blocking the entry of the Republic of Macedonia into the international organizations of which it had been a member (NATO and the EU). As part of that strategy, Greece prevented the RM from being invited to join the Alliance at the NATO Bucharest Summit of the Alliance of 3 April 2008. This caused ICJ proceedings to be filed by the Republic of Macedonia on 17 November 2008 in an obvious effort to restore the relative balance between the parties in the negotiations, which had been disrupted by the Greek acts of blocking its accession to NATO.

The ICJ's judgment in *Application of the Interim Accord of 13 September 1995*[56] dealt with only one aspect relating to the overall diplomatic process of settlement of the name difference between the Republic of Macedonia and Greece, most notably with upholding the parties' obligations deriving from the 1995 Interim Accord. The Interim Accord had been concluded by the parties for the important purpose of providing a legal framework for conducting regular negotiations on the name issue.[57] Hence, that ICJ judgment qualifies to be regarded as a judgment aimed at facilitating an ongoing diplomatic dispute settlement process.

In the remedial part of its judgment, the ICJ warranted to the Applicant (RM) "a declaration that the Respondent [Greece] violated its obligation not to object to the Applicant's admission to or membership in NATO deriving from Article 11, paragraph 1, of the 1995 Interim Accord."[58] In its deliberative part, however, the Court provided various important clarifications over substantive points of disagreement between the parties relevant for the ongoing negotiations, in particular with respect to some key positions and arguments advanced by Greece in the diplomatic discourse as part of its 'blaming' strategy ever since the occurrence of the name dispute and, especially, before and during the Bucharest NATO Summit. These clarifications essentially include:

(a) confirmation by the Court that the RM has the right to use its constitutional name (the 'Republic of Macedonia') under SC Resolution 817 of 1993, contrary to the Greek opposite claim that it had been obliged to call

---

56 *Application of the Interim Accord*, supra note 8.
57 Ibid., 31, para. 97.
58 Ibid., 47, para. 168.

itself by the provisional reference 'the former Yugoslav Republic of Macedonia' provided by that resolution, as, in the Greek view, once Resolution 817 had been issued, it had already 'changed' its name into a new 'provisional name';[59] the Court's finding is particularly significant in the negotiation context since it implicitly defies the Greek steady 'red line' position maintained in the negotiations hitherto, that the object and purpose (hence the solution) of the negotiations is to find a 'single' final name 'for all purposes' (*erga omnes*), which should replace the 'provisional' name already established by Resolution 817;[60]

(b) confirmation by the Court that the RM (together with Greece) had been negotiating in good faith, despite constant Greek allegations that it had been 'intransigent' in the negotiations;[61] and

(c) the ICJ's rejection of the Greek manifold allegations that the RM had not been maintaining 'good neighbourliness' in its policy towards Greece by *inter alia* publishing 'hostile propaganda' against it, using antique symbols belonging exclusively to the Greek heritage, interfering in Greek internal affairs *etc.*, in breach of the respective provisions of the 1995 Interim Accord.[62]

As could have been expected, the parties reacted differently to the issue of the ICJ judgment. Whereas the RM's representatives welcomed the judgment and called the other party to comply in the hope that the country's unimpeded access to NATO would thus be ensured, they unequivocally supported the continuation of the negotiation process under the auspices of the UN.[63] As for Greece, while it did not reject the ICJ judgment outright because of reputational costs that it might have incurred by an opposite move, it tried to downplay its importance (and that of the 1995 Interim Accord)[64] in the

---

59 *Ibid.*, 30, 32, 32–33, paras. 93, 98, 101 and 103; see also the Counter-Memorial, available at <http://www.icj-cij.org/docket/files/142/16356.pdf>, paras. 2.26, 4.9 and 8.39, and Rejoinder, available at <http://www.icj-cij.org/docket/files/142/16360.pdf>, paras. 7.56, 7.53–7.54.

60 See Rejoinder, para. 7.56.

61 *Application of the Interim Accord, supra* note 8, 41, para. 138.

62 *Ibid.*, 42–46, paras. 142, 147, 153, 159–160, and 163, where the Court established a single incident of violation by RM of Article 7(2) of the Interim Accord, that "ended in 2004" and that "could not be regarded as a material breach within the meaning of the 1969 Vienna Convention."

63 Macedonia wins major ruling against Greece at the Hague Court, 05.12.2012, <http://vlada.mk/node/991?language=en-gb> (accessed on 28 March 2013).

64 Witness to these tactics, among others, is the Greek proposal to the RM of a draft of a non-binding Memorandum of understanding of 3 October 2012, available at:

name-negotiation process.⁶⁵ In general, despite the judgment, sticking steadily to its self-perceived interests and values, Greece has not given up on its coercive tactics of preventing the RM from progressing towards entering NATO (and the EU) and on its 'red line' insistence on a single (*erga omnes*) negotiated name, or on its rhetoric of constant accusations directed toward the other side.⁶⁶ Such Greek coercive tactics eventually materialized at the NATO Summit in Chicago of 20–21 May 2012, where the RM was not extended an invitation to join the Alliance once again, and later at the Brussels meeting of the European Council of 13–14 December 2012, where, despite many intensive efforts by third parties to ensure the start of the RM's accession negotiations with the EU, the Council's decision had to be once more postponed.

The reactions of the interested third parties engaged in the process in turn have been mixed and varying over time. While the mediator Mr. Mathew Nimetz welcomed the judgment and proceeded immediately to intensify the negotiations, initially the representatives of NATO, including those of the US, forwarded rather discouraging messages as regards the possibility of the RM's accession to the Alliance without a final negotiated solution of the name issue,⁶⁷

<http://balkanstory.wordpress.com/2012/11/09/2012-10-05-greece-draft-memorandum-of-understanding/> (accessed on 30 March 2013). Though merely restating the well-known Greek negotiating positions without any mention of the ICJ judgment and the 1995 Interim Accord (except for the obligation to negotiate in good faith of IA Article 5), the Greek side tried to present it as an instrument aimed at speeding-up the name negotiations. Its obvious aim was, however, to set aside the binding 1995 Accord as clarified by the ICJ's judgment. See the reply of the RM's Minister for Foreign Affairs Mr. Nikola Popovski in a letter addressed to the Foreign Minister of Greece Mr. Dimitris Avramopoulos of 5 November 2012, available at: <http://www.mfa.gov.mk/sites/default/files/Dokumenti/Letter-Grcija-en.pdf> (accessed on 30 March 2013).

65 See Statement by Foreign Minister Dimas regarding the recent developments following the ICJ judgment of 7 December 2011, <http://www.mfa.gr/en/current-affairs/statements-speeches/statement-by-foreign-minister-dimas-regarding-the-recent-developments-following-the-icj-judgement.html> (accessed on 28 March 2013).

66 See for example the briefings of diplomatic correspondents by the Greek Foreign Ministry spokesman Gregory Delavekouras of 19 January 2012, available at: <http://www.mfa.gr/en/current-affairs/press-briefings/briefing-of-diplomatic-correspondents-by-foreign-ministry-spokesman-gregory-delavekouras-18.html>, and of 23 February 2012, available at: <http://www.mfa.gr/en/current-affairs/press-briefings/briefing-of-diplomatic-correspondents-by-foreign-ministry-spokesman-gregory-delavekouras-1250.html> (both accessed on 30 March 2013), where *inter alia* he said that the ICJ ruling "has nothing whatsoever to do with the negotiating process."

67 See, for example, Statement by the NATO Secretary General on ICJ Ruling of 5 December 2012, available at: <http://www.nato.int/cps/en/natolive/news_81678.htm>, and the interview

stressing the importance of the consensus-driven decision-making process in NATO that also included Greece. Such initial warning by representatives of NATO and the US and of some of its other member states that effectively materialized at its 2012 Chicago Summit could probably be partly explained by their uncomfortable feeling about the fact that the Court's judgment implicitly (though not formally) encroached upon the internal affairs of that organization, but also by their awareness of its inner decision-making limitations to ensure full respect for the ICJ judgment. In particular, such reactions may have been motivated by their possible concern that adverse conflict-escalating responses from Greece might have been triggered (and presumably the RM's reduced motivation to proceed constructively in the negotiations) with detrimental consequences on the name-issue diplomatic settlement process. In a press conference statement made at the close of the NATO Chicago Summit, however, the (then) US Secretary of State Mrs. Hillary Clinton stressed that that Summit "should be the last summit that is not an enlargement summit", and that, while urging both parties to reach an agreement on the name dispute, "Macedonia should join the Alliance as soon as possible."[68]

On the other hand, more positive responses following the ICJ's judgment came from the EU and from many of its member states, and especially from some of its non-governmental institutions (the European Commission and the European Parliament).[69] Though unable to agree to the beginning of accession negotiations at the time of the issue of the judgment, shortly thereafter the EU (through its Commission) opened a 'High-Level Accession Dialogue' with the RM, as an interim substitute for accession negotiations.[70] The European

---

with the US Ambassador Paul Wohlers in the weekly magazine Kapital of 21 December 2011, available at: <http://macedonia.usembassy.gov/interviews2/interviews-2012/int12212011.html> (both accessed on 30 March 2013).

68 "Hillary Clinton Says NATO Membership Should Grow at the Next Summit", available at: <http://wn.com/hillary_clinton_on_macedonia_in_nato_summit_2012> (accessed on 28 March 2013).

69 See, for example, European Parliament Resolution of 14 March 2012 on the 2011 progress report on the former Yugoslav Republic of Macedonia (2011/2887 (RSP)), <http://www.europarl.europa.eu/sides/getDoc.do?pubRef=-//EP//TEXT+TA+P7-TA-2012-0083+0+DOC+XML+V0//EN&language=EN>, paras. 12 and 14, and the Commission's *The Former Yugoslav Republic of Macedonia 2012 Progress Report*, Commission Staff Working Document (COM (2012) 600 final), <http://www.consilium.europa.eu/uedocs/cms_data/docs/pressdata/EN/genaff/134234.pdf>, 19.

70 See "Start of the High Level Accession Dialogue with the Government of the former Yugoslav Republic of Macedonia", <http://ec.europa.eu/commission_2010-2014/fule/headlines/news/2012/03/20120315_en.htm>.

Commission further on recommended the start of accession negotiations with the RM "for a fourth time", expressing its readiness "to present without delay a proposal for a negotiating framework, which also takes into account the need to solve the name issue at an early stage of accession negotiations".[71] But the General Affairs Council of the EU, and the European Council (EC) that endorsed its conclusions, unable to reach a decision on the start of accession negotiations with the RM at their 2012 December meetings due to expressed disagreement by Greece and some other EU members that had allied with it (Bulgaria), chose to postpone their decision on the beginning of accession negotiations with the RM until the next EC meeting scheduled for June 2013.

This time, however, the Council and the EC framed the deliverance of their delayed decision with a timely and more structured procedure. Under that procedure, the General Affairs Council and the European Council will decide on the matter "on the basis of a report to be presented by the Commission in spring 2013", in view *inter alia* of the "*steps taken* [by both parties *sic!*] to promote good neighbourly relations and to reach a negotiated and mutually accepted solution to the name issue under the auspices of the UN".[72] At the time of the writing of this essay, that report of the Commission (together with a new resolution of the European Parliament on Macedonia) was expected to come out in about a month, with promising signals on its recommendations regarding the opening of the RM's accession negotiations.

IV   Conclusion

This essay was written in order to contribute to the analysis of the potential role and effectiveness of ICJ judgments in an interstate dispute settlement negotiation process. It was not meant to develop any comprehensive theoretical model for the purpose of such analysis. Rather, it has a more modest aim of merely restating the necessity of developing a combined methodology specifically suited to analysing the effectiveness of the Court's judgments in a

---

71   *Enlargement Strategy and Main Challenges 2012–2013*, Communication from the Commission to the European Parliament and the Council (COM (2012) 600 final), <http://ec.europa.eu/enlargement/pdf/key_documents/2012/package/strategy_paper_2012_en.pdf>, 25, para. 19.

72   Council Conclusions on Enlargement and Stabilisation and Association Process, 22th General Affairs Council meeting, Brussels, 11 December 2012, <http://www.consilium.europa.eu/uedocs/cms_data/docs/pressdata/EN/genaff/134234.pdf>, 10, para. 42; and European Council Conclusions of 13/14 December 2012 (EUCO 205/12), <http://www.consilium.europa.eu/uedocs/cms_data/docs/pressdata/en/ec/134353.pdf>, 11, para. 27. Emphasis added.

particular negotiation context, that would have to unite valuable insights offered by various relevant theories and related empirical research, including those on politics and law, state compliance with international rules and judgments, and conflict and negotiation. The use of such an interdisciplinary methodological analytical approach seems indispensable in order to be able to capture multiple aspects of extremely complex relationships involved when an ICJ judgment adds to the political dispute settlement process.

Each of the above theories, from its particular (often conflicting) perspective, provides useful suggestions for conceiving how an ICJ judgment could potentially affect a negotiation process. In sum, when taken together, they imply multiple ways for how an ICJ judgment may influence the course of negotiations. ICJ judgments may *inter alia* supply valuable information for the negotiating parties (and intermediaries) that could help mitigate the uncertainties in the related state bargaining, and stabilize parties' expectations during conflict and negotiation. They may cause shifts in their leaders' perceptions as regards the dispute and conflict that could lead to a positive shift in their decision-making towards negotiation. Related to that, the Court's judgments could also help to increase governments' legitimacy, and facilitate the creation of domestic consensus and the mobilization of public support. ICJ judgments often create pressure on the negotiating parties to conform to the judgment in view of their reputation concerns internationally, especially in the presence of third parties interested in the negotiations. Depending on other factors, they could sometimes contribute to overcoming existing power asymmetries between the conflicting parties as a prerequisite for the beginning and further pursuit of constructive negotiations, as they may provide additional leverage for the weaker party in the dispute and conflict.

But the above and other possible effects of ICJ judgments in a negotiation process are subject to some rather obvious limitations. The chances that a Court's judgment would impact on the conflicting parties' conduct in negotiations would largely depend on their own calculation of the costs of conforming to the judgment against their self-perceived interests and values, and on their related ability to persist in exercising coercion during conflict and negotiation. The type of the underlying conflict could also have a bearing on that, in particular, when relationships of conflict of values between the parties are involved.

On the other hand, the parties' willingness for a compromise and the existence of shared interests going beyond their mere interest in resolving the dispute and conflict could add considerably to ICJ judgments' chances of achieving effectiveness in the overall diplomatic dispute settlement effort. The engagement of third parties in the negotiation process could increase the likelihood of ensuring these judgments' effectiveness, including that of IOs, as a result of both their active and passive presence in the process. The still pending inability of the Republic of Macedonia to join NATO and the EU due to the obstructive actions of Greece despite an ICJ judgment, however, reveals that internal constraints related to decision-making may severely reduce that IO's role in promoting ICJ judgments' effectiveness when one of the parties uses its membership as a leverage for influencing the course of pending negotiations.

The quality of the Court's judgment, with respect to its precision and its ability to respond to the parties' concerns in a balanced way through a particular remedy design and legitimate statements included in it, could be a further significant factor determining the potential effectiveness of ICJ judgments in negotiations. As to the latter, however, the Court would often find itself between that concern and the imperative of keeping itself within the limits of its primary 'law-based' dispute settlement function, and with the need to avoid 'shallowness' in its judgments.

Developments in the negotiation process regarding the settlement of the 'difference over the name' between the Republic of Macedonia and Greece following the issue of the ICJ's judgment of 5 December 2011, chosen as a test case in this essay, demonstrate the interplay among different factors determining ICJ judgments' effectiveness in a diplomatic dispute settlement context. On the one hand, that case reveals how a Court's judgment, aimed at supporting an ongoing negotiation process (through restating the contracted obligation of Greece not to impede the RM's access to IOs), could not effect change in the losing party's conduct in that process due to the importance it attaches to its self-perceived interests and values, its perceived ability to continue exercising coercive negotiation tactics (of utilizing the leverage of being a member of NATO and the EU to which the other party tries desperately to accede), and to the lack of any domestic pressure for compliance. On the other hand, the Greek-Macedonian case highlights the subtle way in which various third parties involved in the process gradually increase pressure on the parties to engage in constructive negotiation in the post-judgment phase. After the initially reserved responses by some of these actors to the ICJ judgment, probably due to their worries that its explicit endorsement by them might excite reactions from the parties detrimental to the negotiation process, in the year following the issue of the Court's judgment, obvious pressure was exerted by different actors to ensure the RM's start of accession negotiations with the EU that culminated at the EC's 2012 December Summit. While the beginning of the RM's accession negotiations at the later EC Summit did not take place, the pressure on both parties to proceed with constructive negotiations on the name issue is still there, since the decision of the European Council on the start of accession negotiations was timed and conditioned by positive steps taken by both parties in the name-negotiation process.

Not surprisingly, the most positive responses to the ICJ's judgment came from the EU and from many of its member states, and in particular from its non-governmental institutions, the European Parliament and the European Commission. It seems that the constructivists are right when they point to the need to take into account both actors' normative sensitivities when assessing the effectiveness of international rules and court judgments, given the importance that the EU and, especially, the European Parliament and the Commission attach to the foreign policy identity of the Union as a 'normative power'.

CHAPTER 39

Wrong Address? Advisory Opinion of the ICJ on the Judgment No. 2867 of the ILOAT upon a Complaint Filed against the International Fund for Agricultural Development

Dražen Petrović*

The International Court of Justice (ICJ) does not often have the opportunity to deal with cases directly involving individuals, even referring specifically to their names.[1] This unusual situation occurred recently when the International Fund for Agricultural Development (IFAD) requested an advisory opinion regarding a judgment rendered by the Administrative Tribunal of the International Labour Organization (ILOAT). The advisory opinion resulting from this request is one of the rare situations in which the ICJ arrived at its opinion by unanimity. As is usually the case, the ICJ's advisory opinion delivered on 1 February 2012[2] (the 'IFAD Advisory Opinion') represents a complex and interesting piece of legal writing, which gives rise to a number of questions. As regards those questions, one has to be selective. The present paper deals

---

* Registrar, Administrative Tribunal of the International Labour Organization. Former Principal Legal Officer of the International Labour Office, Geneva. The views expressed herein are those of the author and do not necessarily reflect the views of the International Labour Organization.

1 Although, as Judge Cançado Trindade recalled in Section XI of his Separate Opinion, the ICJ has dealt with many cases in which "one of...their predominant elements was precisely the concrete situation of the individuals directly affected", available at <http://www.icj-cij.org/docket/index.php?p1=3&p2=4&k=ad&case=146&code=fida&p3=4> (accessed 17 February 2013), p. 23, para. 79. – It is also important to recall that the ICJ dealt with several cases involving the UN Administrative Tribunal. Some of these cases are referred to in the present paper and their summary is also provided in the Separate Opinion of Judge Cançado Trindade. On those cases see also T.O. Elias, "The International Court of Justice in Relation to the Administrative Tribunals of the United Nations and the International Labour Organisation", in: *International Administration, Law and Management Practices in International Organisations*, Chris de Cooker (ed.), Martinus Nijhoff Publishers, 2009, p. 727.

2 International Court of Justice, *Judgment No. 2867 of the Administrative Tribunal of the International Labour Organization upon a Complaint Filed against the International Fund for Agricultural Development*, Advisory Opinion, 1 February 2012, available at <http://www.icj-cij.org/docket/index.php?p1=3&p2=4> (accessed 17 February 2013).

with only three aspects of this Advisory Opinion, namely the question of the legal basis for the ICJ's jurisdiction, the question of the binding effect of the Advisory Opinion given in this context and the question of due process. It should be noted that the ICJ itself devoted much more space to these questions than to the concrete answers to the questions put forward by IFAD. These three topics help one to understand whether or not the ICJ is the appropriate forum for dealing with issues involving the rights of individuals.

1   Background and Context of the IFAD Advisory Opinion

Unlike advisory opinions arising out of publically-known situations, such as the question of Kosovo,[3] the construction of a wall in the Occupied Palestinian Territory[4] or the legality of the threat or use of nuclear weapons,[5] the factual background of advisory opinions dealing with judgments of administrative tribunals are well-known to only a few specialists. It may therefore be worth recalling briefly the main facts.

On 8 July 2008, Ms Ana Teresa Saez García, a national of the Bolivarian Republic of Venezuela, filed a complaint with the ILOAT against IFAD regarding its decision not to renew her fixed-term contract as Programme Manager for Latin America and the Caribbean within the Global Mechanism. The Global Mechanism was established by the United Nations Convention to Combat Desertification in Countries Experiencing Serious Drought and/or Desertification, Particularly in Africa (UNCCD). Based on a Memorandum of Understanding with the Conference of the Parties of the UNCCD, IFAD was supposed "to house the Global Mechanism for the administrative operations of such Mechanism". While the final decision not to renew the contract, which was challenged before the ILOAT, was taken by the President of IFAD, the initial decision was notified to Ms Saez García by the Managing Director of the Global Mechanism and was based on the abolition of Ms Saez García's post for reasons of budgetary constraint.

During the proceedings before the ILOAT, IFAD challenged the Tribunal's competence to hear the complaint. This competence is established by Article II, paragraph 5, of the ILOAT Statute, which reads as follows:

---

3   *Accordance with International Law of the Unilateral Declaration of Independence in Respect of Kosovo*, Advisory Opinion, ICJ Reports 2010, p. 403.
4   *Legal Consequences of the Construction of a Wall in the Occupied Palestinian Territory*, Advisory Opinion, ICJ Reports 2004, p. 136.
5   *Legality of the Threat or Use of Nuclear Weapons*, Advisory Opinion, ICJ Reports 1996, p. 226.

The Tribunal shall also be competent to hear complaints alleging nonobservance, in substance or in form, of the terms of appointment of officials and of provisions of the Staff Regulations of any other international organization meeting the standards set out in the Annex hereto which has addressed to the Director-General a declaration recognizing, in accordance with its Constitution or internal administrative rules, the jurisdiction of the Tribunal for this purpose, as well as its Rules of Procedure, and which is approved by the Governing Body.[6]

As the ILOAT understood it, the "argument with respect to the Tribunal's jurisdiction [was] based, in the main, on the proposition that '[t]he Fund and the Global Mechanism are separate legal identities'."[7] As a consequence, IFAD argued, the staff members of the Global Mechanism were not staff of IFAD and the ILOAT did not have the competence to receive the complaint against IFAD. The ILOAT eventually affirmed its competence to consider the complaint having concluded that "the personnel of the Global Mechanism are staff members of the Fund"[8] and that "decisions of the Managing Director relating to staff in the Global Mechanism are, in law, decisions of the Fund."[9]

The ILOAT concluded in its Judgment No. 2867 that the Managing Director had no authority to abolish Ms Saez García's post and that, as a result, his decision not to renew her contract on the ground of this abolition constituted an error of law. Accordingly, the President of IFAD had also erred in law by rejecting her internal appeal. Consequently, the ILOAT decided to set aside the President's decision dismissing Ms Saez García's internal appeal and ordered IFAD to pay material damages equivalent to the two years' salary and other allowances she would have received if her contract had been extended, together with interest at the rate of 8% *per annum* from the due dates until the date of payment, with the possibility of deducting wages or salary earned by Ms Saez García within that period. The ILOAT also awarded 10,000 Euros in moral damages and 5,000 Euros for costs.

IFAD failed to execute the judgment within the standard 30 day period[10] as of 3 February 2010. Instead, its Executive Board decided at its 99th session held

---

6   Adopted by the International Labour Conference on 9 October 1946. The full text of the Statute can be found at <http://www.ilo.org/public/english/tribunal/about/statute.htm>.
7   Para. 5 of Judgment No. 2867.
8   *Ibid.*, para. 11.
9   *Ibid.*, para. 8.
10 ILOAT Judgment No. 3152, para. 20, pp. 7–8.

on 21–22 April 2010 to request an advisory opinion of the ICJ on the validity of the judgment.[11]

In the meantime, on 4 May 2010, IFAD also filed an application for the suspension of the execution of Judgment No. 2867 with the ILOAT pending the advisory opinion of the ICJ. The ILOAT dismissed this application by its Judgment No. 3003 of 6 July 2011, which was later communicated to the ICJ by IFAD.[12] The ILOAT invoked several arguments in its reasoning leading to the dismissal of IFAD's request. Firstly, it noted that neither its Statute nor its Rules contained any provision by which the submission of a request for an advisory opinion under Article XII of its Statute would result in a stay of execution of the contested judgment pending the ICJ's opinion. It also noted that there was no precedent, since the previous applicant for an advisory opinion, UNESCO,[13] did not make a similar request. The ILOAT further considered that it would be a "legal anomaly" if the ILOAT were to rule on such a request, as this is normally done by a court handling the appeal and not a court whose judgment is contested. In fact, the ILOAT could not give any appraisal of the correctness or soundness of its own judgments to determine whether a challenge raised by the organization against the judgment in question had at least some chance of succeeding.[14] The ILOAT also found that a stay of execution granted by the Tribunal could harm equality between the parties as it could run counter to the interests of the staff member who does not have the possibility to request an advisory opinion of the ICJ, and would not therefore have the opportunity to request a stay of execution.[15] The ILOAT also made several interesting comments about the nature of the procedure instituted by Article XII of its Statute that will be referred to in the particular context below. Judgment No. 3003 continued by requesting IFAD to proceed "without delay" to execute Judgment No. 2867, by deducting from the material damages the defendant's total earnings for the period concerned amounting to 6,487.55 Euros.[16]

---

11   EB 2010/99/R.43/Rev.1.
12   While the ICJ itself did not give too much importance to it in the Advisory Opinion, Judge Cançado Trindade devoted some space to it in paragraphs 13–16 of his Separate Opinion appended to the Advisory Opinion.
13   *Judgments of the ILOAT upon Complaints Made by UNESCO*, Advisory Opinion of 23 October 1956, ICJ Reports 1956, p. 77.
14   Judgment No. 3003, para. 35.
15   *Ibid.*, paras. 40–44.
16   IFAD failed to comply with this judgment. Consequently, the ILOAT found IFAD's "unlawful conduct" to be "extremely serious" in its Judgment No. 3152. The ILOAT concluded that "by acting in disregard of *res judicata*, IFAD not only ignored its duty, flowing from its recognition of the Tribunal's jurisdiction, to comply with the judgments delivered by it,

II   The Advisory Opinion

The Executive Board of IFAD formulated the following questions:

I   Was the ILOAT competent, under Article II of its Statute, to hear the complaint introduced against the International Fund for Agricultural Development (hereby the Fund) on 8 July 2008 by Ms S-G., an individual who was a member of the staff of the Global Mechanism of the United Nations Convention to Combat Desertification in Those Countries Experiencing Serious Drought and/or Desertification, Particularly in Africa (hereby the Convention) for which the Fund acts merely as housing organization?

II   Given that the record shows that the parties to the dispute underlying the ILOAT's Judgment No. 2867 were in agreement that the Fund and the Global Mechanism are separate legal entities and that the complainant was a member of the staff of the Global Mechanism, and considering all the relevant documents, rules and principles, was the ILOAT's statement, made in support of its decision confirming its jurisdiction, that "the Global Mechanism is to be assimilated to the various administrative units of the Fund for all administrative purposes" and that the "effect of this is that administrative decisions taken by the Managing Director in relation to staff in the Global Mechanism are, in law, decisions of the Fund" outside its jurisdiction and/or did it constitute a fundamental fault in the procedure followed by the ILOAT?

III   Was the ILOAT's general statement, made in support of its decision confirming its jurisdiction, that "the personnel of the Global Mechanism are staff members of the Fund" outside its jurisdiction and/or did it constitute a fundamental fault in the procedure followed by the ILOAT?

IV   Was the ILOAT's decision confirming its jurisdiction to entertain the Complainant's plea alleging an abuse of authority by the Global Mechanism's Managing Director outside its jurisdiction and/or did it constitute a fundamental fault in the procedure followed by the ILOAT?

V   Was the Administrative Tribunal's decision confirming its jurisdiction to entertain the Complainant's plea that the Managing Director's decision

---

but also behaved towards the complainant with a bad faith ill-befitting an international organisation." Therefore, the ILOAT added to amounts already awarded under Judgment No. 2867 (which according to IFAD totals 438,055 USD, see the letter of the IFAD President to the Executive Secretary of the UNCCD of 8 February 2012), the additional amount of 72,000 Euros for interest, costs and moral damages.

not to renew the Complainant's contract constituted an error of law outside its jurisdiction and/or did it constitute a fundamental fault in the procedure followed by the ILOAT?

VI Was the ILOAT's decision confirming its jurisdiction to interpret the Memorandum of Understanding between the Conference of the Parties to the United Nations Convention to Combat Desertification in Those Countries Experiencing Serious Drought and/or Desertification, Particularly in Africa and IFAD (hereby the MoU), the Convention, and the Agreement Establishing IFAD beyond its jurisdiction and/or did it constitute a fundamental fault in the procedure followed by the ILOAT?

VII Was the ILOAT's decision confirming its jurisdiction to determine that by discharging an intermediary and supporting role under the MoU, the President was acting on behalf of IFAD outside its jurisdiction and/or did it constitute a fundamental fault in the procedure followed by the ILOAT?

VIII Was the ILOAT's decision confirming its jurisdiction to substitute the discretionary decision of the Managing Director of the Global Mechanism with its own outside its jurisdiction and/or did it constitute a fundamental fault in the procedure followed by the ILOAT?

IX What is the validity of the decision given by the ILOAT in its Judgment No. 2867?

It is important to note that this was not the first opportunity for the ICJ to deal with a challenge to an ILOAT judgment. It had already done so in 1956, when UNESCO requested an advisory opinion of the ICJ regarding four judgments of the ILOAT (hereinafter 'UNESCO Advisory Opinion').[17] While the substance of the ILOAT's judgments which were challenged differed in the two requests, many of the general issues involved were the same.

As in 1956, the ICJ started by inviting third parties to intervene in accordance with Article 66, paragraph 2, of its Statute. The ICJ decided to invite Member States of IFAD, the States parties to the UNCCD[18] and UN specialized

---

17 *Judgments of the ILOAT upon Complaints Made by UNESCO, op. cit.*
18 But not the Conference of Parties of the UNCCD itself. See an interesting point raised by Marie-Clotilde Runavot, "L'oxymore, nouvel exercice de style pour la CIJ: un avis inattendu pour une solution sans surprise", *Journal du droit international*, Vol. 139, No. 3, 2012, p. 860, in paras. 41–42, pp. 876–877. It should be noted that UNCCD considered intervening in the proceedings but this would require a request for extending the deadlines set forth by the ICJ. The decision was made not to do this. See the series of documents available at <http://webcache.googleusercontent.com/search?q=cache:Ow-w_L8VqRgJ:www.unccd.int/Lists/OfficialDocuments/cop10/INF3ENG.pdf+ifad+advisory+opinion&cd=70&hl=fr&ct=clnk&gl=ch> (accessed 16 March 2013).

agencies recognizing the jurisdiction of the ILOAT to make written statements relating to the question. The choice of international organizations so invited, *i.e.*, only UN specialized agencies and no other international organizations that recognized the ILOAT's jurisdiction Statute, was rather curious. Out of the 59 international organizations that currently recognize the ILOAT's jurisdiction, only 12 are UN specialized agencies.[19] As the ICJ has an important margin of discretion in inviting international organizations to make their comments, Article 66 of the ICJ Statute referring to those "considered by the Court"[20] and not only to those who have the right to request an advisory opinion, there must be a policy reasoning behind such limited application of Article 66. In fact, the previous ICJ practice was different. In 1956, the ICJ invited all international organizations which had recognized the jurisdiction of the ILOAT to provide written comments. These included not only the ILO, WHO, ITU, WMO and FAO, all of them being UN specialized agencies, but also the European Organization for Nuclear Research (CERN). There is no explanation for this restrictive approach in the IFAD Advisory Opinion itself, and indeed, in the absence of any legal restrictions, one is to hope that such restrictive approach will not be applied in the future, as it may deprive the ICJ of a valuable source of information and views. It is obvious that the ICJ's debate about the applicability of Article XII of the ILOAT Statute would have benefited from views of the international organizations that do not have the authorization of the UN General Assembly to request an advisory opinion from the ICJ.

Only the Plurinational State of Bolivia responded positively to the invitation and filed a written submission. None of the specialized agencies invited decided to intervene. While the reasons for their absence from these proceedings are not known, it may be important to note that the practice of some of them to accept responsibility for entities they hosted would not be in favour of the main arguments raised by IFAD.[21]

---

19 See the list available at <www.ilo.org/public/english/tribunal/membership/index.htm> (accessed 16 March 2013).

20 If the English version may appear ambiguous, the French text is very clear: "toute organisation internationale jugés, par la Cour ou par le Président si elle ne siège pas, susceptible de fournir des renseignements sur la question".

21 In paragraph 66 of the IFAD Advisory Opinion, the ICJ refers to the situation of WIPO 'hosting' the International Union for the Protection of New Varieties of Plants. However, one has to emphasize that International Union for the Protection of New Varieties of Plants itself recognized the competence of the ILOAT and acts on its own behalf without WIPO's intermediary role. It is also not unusual that the 'main' organization provides defence for an organization being part of it, although the latter may have an independent structure and rules. This is the case of the ILO in relation to the International Training

Having confirmed its jurisdiction and willingness to give an advisory opinion,[22] which will be discussed in more detail below, the ICJ proceeded to answer the questions put forward by IFAD.[23] The main issue was whether or not Ms Saez García was deemed to be a staff member of IFAD. After an analysis of evidence before it, the ICJ concluded that "an employment relationship, based on the...contractual and statutory elements, was established between Ms Saez García and the Fund."[24] Furthermore, the ICJ determined that her complaint "falls within the scope of allegations of non-observance of her terms of appointment and of the provisions of the staff regulations and rules of the Fund".[25]

Having thereby examined competence *ratione personae* and *ratione materiae*, the ICJ expressed its opinion that the ILOAT was competent, under Article 11 of its Statute, to hear the complaint introduced against IFAD by Ms Saez García, and consequently that the decision given in Judgment No. 2867 was valid.[26]

Centre of the ILO in Turin (see, for example, ILOAT Judgment No. 1200), the WHO acting on behalf of PAHO (see, for example, ILOAT Judgment No. 1308), or the FAO acting on behalf of the World Food Programme (WFP), an autonomous joint subsidiary programme of the United Nations and the FAO (see for example, ILOAT Judgment No. 2384). Furthermore, the practice of international organizations providing the secretariat for another organization, and therefore accepting responsibility for staff-related issues, is also not so rare. For example, the WHO provided the secretariat for the United Nations System Standing Committee on Nutrition and defended a case before the ILOAT for this Committee (see, ILOAT Judgment No. 2497). It also, until 31 December 2008, provided the secretariat for the Global Fund to Fight AIDS, Tuberculosis and Malaria (see, ILO Governing Body document GB.303/PFA/15/2). The ILO has been providing the secretariat for the International Social Security Association (ISSA) and even defended cases before the ILOAT in that respect (See ILOAT Judgments No. 2406 and No. 3008). Another possible example outside the scope of the ILOAT may be the World Bank's relations with the Global Partnership for Education.

22   The ICJ did not fail to recall that Article 65 of its Statute made it clear that it had a discretion whether to reply to a request for an advisory opinion ("The Court may give an advisory opinion on any legal question...", IFAD Advisory Opinion, *op. cit.*, p. 14, para. 33).

23   In passing, the ICJ noted that "such questions should be asked in neutral terms rather than assuming conclusions of law that are in dispute. They should not include reasoning or argument. The questions asked in this case depart from that standard as reflected in normal practice", IFAD Advisory Opinion, *op. cit.*, p. 24, para. 62.

24   *Ibid.*, para. 76, p. 28.

25   *Ibid.*, para. 91, p. 33.

26   Judge Greenwood went even further by making the following remark: "I find it more than a little surprising that IFAD has tried to argue that she was not its employee. Such an argument is plainly unsustainable. It also seems to me to be beyond serious argument that

III Legal Basis for the Request and for the ICJ's Jurisdiction

The ICJ unanimously found a legal basis for accepting the request for an advisory opinion, although this legal basis was not specifically invoked in the request. While the solution found by the ICJ resolves the practical problem of avoiding declaring the request non-receivable, it is not without ambiguity.

IFAD made the request for the advisory opinion on the basis of Article XII of the ILOAT Statute. Its paragraph 1 has two versions. For the ILO, it reads as follows:

> In any case in which the Governing Body of the International Labour Office or the Administrative Board of the Pensions Fund challenges a decision of the Tribunal confirming its jurisdiction, or considers that a decision of the Tribunal is vitiated by a fundamental fault in the procedure followed, the question of the validity of the decision given by the Tribunal shall be submitted by the Governing Body, for an advisory opinion, to the International Court of Justice.

For all other organizations that recognized the ILOAT's jurisdiction, it reads as follows:

> In any case in which the Executive Board of an international organization which has made the declaration specified in article II, paragraph 5, of the Statute of the Tribunal challenges a decision of the Tribunal confirming its jurisdiction, or considers that a decision of the Tribunal is vitiated by a fundamental fault in the procedure followed, the question of the validity of the decision given by the Tribunal shall be submitted by the Executive Board concerned, for an advisory opinion, to the International Court of Justice.

Paragraph 2 of Article XII is the same in both instances and provides that "the Opinion given by the Court shall be binding."

This was the only legal basis invoked by IFAD and not contested by Ms Saez García. However, the ICJ, *proprio motu*,[27] decided to deal with this question

---

Ms Saez García's complaint concerned matters falling within the jurisdiction of ILOAT." (Declaration of Judge Greenwood appended to the IFAD Advisory Opinion, available at <http://www.icj-cij.org/docket/index.php?p1=3&p2=4&k=ad&case=146&code=fida&p3=4>, accessed 20 February 2013).

[27] The ICJ itself notes that "its jurisdiction was not challenged", IFAD Advisory Opinion, *op. cit.*, p. 10, para. 21.

and concluded without ambiguity that this Article cannot create a legal basis for requesting an advisory opinion. The ICJ took "the opportunity to emphasize that the ILO could not, when it adopted the Tribunal's Statute, give its organs, or other institutions, the authority to challenge decisions of the Tribunal by way of a request for an advisory opinion." This affirmation goes well beyond the position of the ICJ in the UNESCO Advisory Opinion.[28]

It may be interesting at this stage to recall why and when this clause was included in the ILOAT Statute. In fact, the ILOAT was originally created on 26 September 1926, as the Administrative Tribunal of the League of Nations. Upon the dissolution of the League of Nations on 18 April 1946, the ILOAT became the direct successor[29] to this Tribunal by a resolution adopted by the Assembly of the League and a corresponding resolution adopted by the International Labour Conference.

In 1946, the Assembly of the League decided not to implement judgments delivered by the Administrative Tribunal of the League of Nations in 1939 on acquired rights of certain officials.[30] To avoid future episodes of this type, Article XII was introduced in the ILOAT Statute,[31] when the only 'client' of the ILOAT was the ILO itself. As the ILO had an authorization of the UN General Assembly, given through the approval of the text of the ILO-UN Relationship Agreement, to "request advisory opinions of the International Court of Justice on legal questions arising within the scope of its activities",[32] it was not

---

28 In the UNESCO Advisory Opinion the ICJ simply ignored this legal basis and concluded that "in formulating the Request for an Advisory Opinion, the Executive Board exercised a power conferred upon Unesco by Article XI of the Agreement between that Organization and the United Nations, approved by the General Assembly on December 14th, 1946", *op. cit.*, pp. 83–84.

29 For more on this situation see Frank Gutteridge, "The ILO Administrative Tribunal", in: *International Administration, Law and Management Practices in International Organisations, op. cit.*, p. 655, at pp. 657–659.

30 *Ibid.*, p. 655.

31 See the Memorandum of the International Labour Office submitted within the proceedings leading to the Advisory Opinion, *Effect of Awards of Compensation made by the UN Administrative Tribunal*, Advisory Opinion of 13 July 1954, ICJ Reports 1954, p. 47.

32 On 30 May 1946 the ILO signed an agreement which entered into force on 14 December 1946 by its approval by the UN General Assembly. Paragraph 2 of Article IX of this Agreement provides that "the General Assembly authorises the International Labour Organisation to request advisory opinions of the International Court of Justice on legal questions arising within the scope of its activities other than questions concerning the mutual relationships of the Organisation and the United Nations or other specialised agencies."

surprising that the ILO could request an advisory opinion on its activities[33] performed through the judicial body it established, *i.e.*, the ILOAT, as no mechanism existed for resolving potential differences of opinion between the ILOAT and the International Labour Conference or the ILO Governing Body.[34] The ICJ's statement that "the ILO could not, when it adopted the Tribunal's Statute, give *its organs*...the authority to challenge decisions of the Tribunal by way of a request for an advisory opinion" (emphasis added), does not therefore seem to be legally correct when considered in the light of the authorization given to the ILO by the UN General Assembly in full conformity with the ICJ Statute.[35] Article XII of the ILOAT does not seem to be *a priori* in contradiction to the UN Charter and the ICJ Statute.

Indeed, when the UN General Assembly approved the first agreement with an international organization outside the newly-created United Nations, the representatives of Member States should have been aware of the problems that most of them had simultaneously had as members of the League of Nations in relation to the Administrative Tribunal. It seems strange that a limited number of State representatives acting in a limited number of international fora at that time would have made a major oversight in amending a Statute to make it not conform to the UN Charter.

What about the ILO giving such authority to 'other institutions'? When the ILOAT Statute was amended in 1949 to provide for the possibility of other organizations recognizing the jurisdiction of the ILOAT, WHO, the first applicant, already had the opportunity to request an advisory opinion of the ICJ based on an agreement with the United Nations.[36] The same was true for UNESCO, ITU, FAO and WMO when they made the application to recognize the jurisdiction of the ILOAT. However, when approving in 1955 the request of CERN, an

---

33   There is no doubt that functioning of the Administrative Tribunal comes within the scope of the activities of the ILO. To be able to effectively defend the immunity of jurisdiction before national courts in relation to labour disputes with its staff, the ILO had to establish a settlement mechanism. Instead of relying on an *ad hoc* arbitration, which does not necessarily provide guarantees of due process, the ILO (or rather the League of Nations) opted for a more suitable mechanism of an administrative tribunal. It is therefore an integral part of its activities. Other organizations, such as the United Nations, the World Bank, the International Monetary Fund or the Council of Europe, followed the same approach.

34   ILO has never used the possibility to request such an advisory opinion regarding a judgment of the ILOAT.

35   However, it is true that the authorization to the Governing Body does not flow from the ILOAT Statute, but from the UN General Assembly's approval of the agreement between the UN and the ILO.

36   See, WHO Basic Documents, 47th edn., 2009, p. 41.

organization which does not have the status of a specialized agency of the UN, the ILO did not deal with this issue and the applicability of Article XII was not mentioned in relevant documents.[37]

In the process of subsequent applications of other organizations, this issue has not been raised and the requests of other non-UN specialized agencies to recognize the jurisdiction of the ILOAT have been approved by the ILO Governing Body. They therefore became bound by the ILOAT Statute. One can only assume that the reasoning may have been that any such requests for an advisory opinion should have been construed as being made by the ILO or through the transferred authority of either the International Labour Conference, which adopted the ILOAT Statute, or the ILO Governing Body, which approved the applications of other international organizations and was authorized to make requests for the ICJ Advisory Opinion based on the agreement between the ILO and the UN. The ICJ did not want to go that far. As seen above, the ICJ considers that the ILO did not have the authority to give other international organizations the capacity to challenge ILOAT decisions by way of a request for an advisory opinion, although such an affirmation may have benefitted from some elaboration.

The IFAD Advisory Opinion puts the ILO and all other international organizations that recognized the jurisdiction of the ILOAT in a strange situation. By force of precedent, it would lead to the potential refusal of a request for an advisory opinion in relation to an ILOAT judgment made by an international organization that does not have the authorization of the 'gatekeeper', i.e., the UN General Assembly, in accordance with Article 96, paragraph 2 of the ICJ Statute. This would make Article XII of the ILOAT Statute meaningless for such an organization. As a consequence, it would appear that some organizations that obtained from the General Assembly the general authorization to request an advisory opinion on an alternative basis could challenge the ILOAT's decisions while the others could not. Such an interpretation of the agreement between the ILO and the UN, without analysing the scope of the authorization that the UN General Assembly gave to the ILO, may lead to an "unreasonable" result,[38] to which the ICJ may come back in the future, if the procedure is not modified in the meantime.[39]

---

37   See Minutes of the 120th (May–June 1955) session of the Governing Body, pp. 43–44.
38   As the Permanent Court of International Justice (PCIJ) stated in the case concerning the *Polish Postal Service in Danzig*, PCIJ, Series B, No. 11, p. 39.
39   The ICJ seems to have put the ball now in the ILO's court. Should the version of Article XII applicable to other international organizations simply be deleted? Maybe the ILO should request authorization from the UN General Assembly for challenging decisions of one its organs by international organizations that have recognized the competence of this organ.

Practically, the position of the ICJ means that any non-UN system organization wishing to accept the Statute of the ILOAT should beforehand request an authorization of the UN General Assembly to challenge a judgment of the Tribunal though an advisory opinion of the ICJ. While this may be logically coherent with the opinion of the ICJ, we will see below that the standard wording underlying such authorizations could, in fact, deprive the organization concerned of such possibility.

Indeed, when it declared that Article XII of the ILOAT does not give the right to request an advisory opinion, the ICJ could have stopped its consideration of the IFAD's request. Surprisingly, the ICJ did not do that. Following the precedent of the UNESCO Advisory Opinion, it simply found *proprio motu* an alternative legal basis for the request.[40] The ICJ found that the UN General Assembly Resolution 32/107 of 15 December 1977, which approved the Relationship Agreement between the UN and IFAD, represented a sufficient legal basis for authorizing a request for an advisory opinion.[41] While very appealing, such a conclusion does not seem so obvious.

The Relationship Agreement authorized IFAD to request an advisory opinion "on legal questions arising within the scope of the Fund's activities" except on "questions concerning the mutual relationships of the Fund and the United Nations or other specialized agencies."[42]

Even if one can argue that the judgments of the ILOAT may deal with issues "arising within the scope of the Fund's activities", it seems difficult to overcome the exception made in the Relationship Agreement. While ICJ analysed this limitation in relation to the Global Mechanism, its relevance for the relationship between IFAD and the ILO was not given full consideration.

Given that the ILOAT is a very particular judicial body of the ILO,[43] IFAD, by challenging a judgment, challenged a decision made by one of the ILO

Or all requests for an advisory opinion should go through the ILO. It seems that the ILO will have to consult the organizations concerned and propose some options.

40 "While the resolution does not also refer to the authorization granted by the General Assembly under Article 96, paragraph 2, of the Charter, that authorization, as the Court has already stated, is a necessary condition to the making of such a request." However, IFAD did make this argument in paragraph 19 of its written statement.

41 As in 1956, "après avoir torturé les règles", as René de Lacharrière described it. See, René de Lacharrière, "Avis consultatif sur les jugements du Tribunal administratif de l'OIT sur requête contre l'UNESCO", *Annuaire français de droit international*, Vol. 2, 1956, p. 396.

42 Article XIII, paragraph 2, of the Relationship Agreement.

43 Besides giving it its name, the ILO adopts the Statute and amendments to it, appoints judges and regulates budgetary questions. However, the ILO does not have any influence on the way the ILOAT's judges preform their judicial function and in that respect they have been given total independence from the ILO to be able to perform their function properly.

bodies.[44] In fact, IFAD even specifically made this point,[45] as noted in paragraph 41 of the Advisory Opinion, by arguing that the questions submitted to the ICJ "deal exclusively with the application and the interpretation of the agreement between the ILO and IFAD in the context of Article XII" and that its request for an advisory opinion pertains "not to any dispute between the Fund and Ms Saez García, but to the relationship between the Fund and the ILO…" In other words the request clearly related, in the view of IFAD, to the mutual relationship between IFAD and the ILO which, as we have seen above, is excluded from the scope of the Relationship Agreement. This is the conclusion of the ICJ when it stated that IFAD "in any event would not be able to bring a matter about its relationship with the ILO before the Court," given the exclusion in the Relationship Agreement. But even after such an affirmation and despite IFAD's insistence on this point, the ICJ went on to give an advisory opinion. The ICJ did not elaborate beyond the conclusion that "the Court cannot see that a question arises between the Fund and the ILO."[46] However, IFAD's request for any advisory opinion would be obviously contrary to the UN General Assembly authorization forming the basis of the Relationship Agreement to the extent that IFAD, in effect, challenged a decision of the ILO. However, IFAD did not have the intention of relying on this legal basis. If it did, it would have informed the Economic and Social Council of any such request, as required by Article XIII, paragraph 2, of the Relationship Agreement. While the ICJ noted this requirement in the Advisory Opinion,[47] it failed to attach any importance to it.

If, as the ICJ concluded, Article XII of the ILOAT Statute does not create a satisfactory legal basis for challenging a judgment by requesting an advisory

---

44   In paragraph 3 of its written statement, IFAD argued that the ILOAT "acting through its judges whom are appointed for a period of three years by the Conference of the International Labour Organization", "caused the terms of the aforementioned agreement [*i.e.*, the agreement allegedly entered to in 1988 between the ILO and IFAD] to be violated." This was duly noted by the ICJ in paragraph 41 of the Advisory Opinion, *op. cit.*, p. 17.
45   The opening argument of IFAD was that there was an agreement between the ILO and IFAD concluded in 1988, when the ILO Governing Body approved IFAD's request to recognize jurisdiction of the ILOAT. Even if this were true, which is debatable, ILO, by opening its own administrative tribunal to others has undertaken responsibility for its functioning as a judicial body. In this case, it has made available judges that properly exercised their function by determining the competence of the ILOAT to hear the complaint lodged by Ms. García. The ICJ confirmed the opinion that the ILOAT acted within its powers and correctly determined its jurisdiction.
46   IFAD Advisory Opinion, *op. cit.*, para. 42, p. 17.
47   *Ibid.*, paras. 23 and 26, pp. 11–12.

opinion of the ICJ, the traditional wording of a relationship agreement with the United Nations[48] does not seem to represent more solid ground for such a challenge.

There may be another contradiction in the reasoning of the ICJ. If the Relationship Agreement was "a necessary condition" for making IFAD's request for an advisory opinion, there would seem to be no further need to refer to Article XII of the ILOAT Statute. The Article XII limitation to the scope of review of the ILOAT's judgment would not be applicable and IFAD could ask any question "arising within the scope of the Fund's activities", provided such a question did not concern "the mutual relationships of the Fund and the United Nations or other specialized agencies". Indeed, in paragraph 27 of the IFAD Advisory Opinion the ICJ refers only to the UN Charter, the ICJ Statute and the Relationship Agreement to establish its jurisdiction to consider IFAD's request. In other words, IFAD would be able to request an advisory opinion on a judgment of the ILOAT regardless of whether there was a provision in the ILOAT Statute to this effect.

However, the ICJ still relies on Article XII in determining the scope of its jurisdiction. It states that "the scope of that jurisdiction is however subject to the effect in the present case of Article XII of the Annex to the Statute of the ILOAT". So, after having confirmed that the provisions of the ILOAT Statute are irrelevant for establishing its jurisdiction, the ICJ in both the UNESCO and IFAD Advisory Opinions continued to refer to Article XII of the ILOAT Statute to determine the scope of its review. In both situations it even refused to give an advisory opinion on issues it found to fall outside the scope of Article XII.[49]

If the ICJ established its jurisdiction on the basis of the General Assembly authorization of IFAD and UNESCO, to what extent should the scope of the

---

48   The wording of the ILO-UN Relationship Agreement was later applied to other specialized agencies, as for IFAD and UNESCO.

49   See para. 97 of IFAD Advisory Opinion, *op. cit.*, p. 35. This simply follows the position in UNESCO Advisory Opinion expressed in the following terms: "Undoubtedly, Unesco has the general power to ask for an Advisory Opinion of the Court on questions within the scope of its activity. But the question put to the Court has not been put in reliance upon the general power of Unesco to ask for an Advisory Opinion. It has been expressly linked with Article XII. In its terms and by virtue of the place which it occupies in the Resolution requesting the Advisory Opinion, Question II as put to the Court refers to the judgments which the Executive Board has challenged in relation to the jurisdiction of the Tribunal which rendered these judgments. It is on that basis that the question must be considered by the Court", *op. cit.*, p. 99. It has to be noted, however, that the UNESCO Advisory Opinion did not go so far as to deny the legal value of Article XII of the ILOAT, as did the IFAD Advisory Opinion.

ICJ's consideration of the questions put to it be affected by an external instrument? In an earlier advisory opinion the ICJ stated that "under Article 65 of the Court's Statute, its competence to give advisory opinions extends only to legal questions on which its opinion has been requested. The Court may interpret the terms of the request and determine the scope of the questions set out in it."[50] In a few advisory proceedings, the ICJ even reformulated the question put before it.[51] In such a case, the scope should have been found in the questions asked by UNESCO and IFAD and not in Article XII of the ILOAT.[52]

What would be the practical value of aspects of the advisory opinion that go beyond the scope of Article XII and are therefore not 'binding'[53] should not be the concern of the ICJ when providing the advisory opinion in response to a legal question on which its opinion is requested. If the ICJ were to follow its practice of ignoring the use that the organ which asked the opinion would make out of it,[54] it should not really worry whether or not IFAD and UNESCO would consider its advisory opinion as binding, and should have given an opinion on all legal questions raised by the two organizations.

IV Binding or Not Binding?

Nowhere in the UN Charter or the Statute of the ICJ can one find the legal effect of 'advisory opinions' that the ICJ may give. It simply flows from the

---

50 *Application for Review of Judgment No. 158 of the United Nations Administrative Tribunal*, Advisory Opinion, ICJ Reports 1973, p. 166, at p. 184, para. 41.

51 See examples quoted by the ICJ in paragraph 50 of the Advisory Opinion *Accordance with International Law of the Unilateral Declaration of Independence in Respect of Kosovo*, op. cit., p. 423.

52 See, for example, *Interpretation of the Greco-Turkish Agreement of 1 December 1926 (Final Protocol, Article IV)*, Advisory Opinion, 1928, PCIJ, Series B, No. 16, at p. 16.

53 The binding nature of the advisory opinion according to the ILOAT Statute is discussed below.

54 As the ICJ stated in an earlier advisory opinion, "the purpose of the advisory jurisdiction is to enable organs of the United Nations and other authorized bodies to obtain opinions from the Court which will assist them in the future exercise of their functions. The Court cannot determine what steps the General Assembly may wish to take after receiving the Court's opinion or what effect that opinion may have in relation to those steps.", *Accordance with International Law of the Unilateral Declaration of Independence in Respect of Kosovo*, op. cit., p. 421, para. 44. Similarly, the ICJ also stated that "it is not for the Court itself to purport to decide whether or not an advisory opinion is needed by the Assembly for the performance of its functions. The General Assembly has the right to decide for itself on the usefulness of an opinion in the light of its own needs.", *Legality of the Threat or Use of Nuclear Weapons, Advisory Opinion*, op. cit., p. 237, para. 16.

understanding of the words 'advisory' and 'opinion'.[55] However, nothing prevents those requesting the advisory opinion to consider it 'binding' for their further actions. So, the fact that the ILOAT Statute declares the opinion as 'binding' did not prevent the ICJ from answering positively a request for an advisory opinion. In other words, the ICJ considered that it would give its advisory opinion and that all interested parties might rely on it to the extent they chose. Article XII's designation of the binding effect of advisory opinions is not therefore contrary to the UN Charter and the ICJ Statute.

Article XII of the ILOAT Statute does not, however, clarify for whom the advisory opinion would be binding. An obvious answer is that it is binding for those who requested it, in this case, IFAD.[56] But beyond this point, things become complicated.

Is it binding for the individual complainants who were parties to the underlying dispute before the ILOAT? To the extent that individuals do not even have standing before the ICJ, it would be contrary to fundamental notions of legal process that they suffered adverse effects of a legal procedure to which they were not parties. But what if the ICJ says that the ILOAT went beyond its competence in issuing a judgment? The individual's interests would be directly affected and there would be no further recourse. So, the advisory opinion should be binding on the complainant also. A legal justification may be that by submitting his or her complaint under the ILOAT Statute, the complainant accepts that a binding advisory opinion of the ICJ may find incorrect an ILOAT judgment which was favourable to the complainant.

However, even this is not without problems. By the time the ICJ gives its advisory opinion, the ILOAT judgment should normally have been executed. As the ILOAT said in Judgments No. 3003 and No. 3152, IFAD was ordered to pay compensation to the complainant. If the ICJ had found that the ILOAT judgment was vitiated, IFAD would have had to try to recover the money paid in

---

55   The web site of the ICJ has the following explanation: "Contrary to judgments, and except in rare cases where it is stipulated beforehand that they shall have binding effect (for example, as in the Convention on the Privileges and Immunities of the United Nations, in the Convention on the Privileges and Immunities of the specialized agencies of the United Nations, and the Headquarters Agreement between the United Nations and the United States of America), the Court's advisory opinions have no binding effect. The requesting organ, agency or organization remains free to decide, by any means open to it, what effect to give to these opinions.", <http://www.icj-cij.org/jurisdiction/index.php?p1=5&p2=2> (accessed 17 March 2013).

56   In the UNESCO Advisory Opinion, the ICJ was very explicit: "the provision in question is nothing but a rule of conduct for the Executive Board, a rule determining the action to be taken by it on the Opinion of the Court.", *op. cit.*, p. 84.

national legal proceedings, as it did not have any authority over the complainant.⁵⁷ The situation would be even more serious if the person concerned was reinstated in his or her post and the ICJ found that this resulted from a vitiated judgment.

Is it binding on the ILOAT? This obvious question is not easy to answer. Article VI of the ILOAT Statute affirms that the Tribunal's judgments are final and without appeal. While the perception of its binding effect on the finding that the ILOAT incorrectly asserted its competence seems obvious, as the judgment would be invalid, the question is more complicated in situations in which the ICJ finds that there was a fundamental flaw in the procedure followed by the ILOAT. In other words, the question is what impact would such a binding opinion have on the original procedure? Should the ILOAT repeat the procedure? Would the advisory opinion be binding in the new and any future proceedings? One could argue in favour of positive answers and the notion of 'binding' is in the Statute of the ILOAT itself.

Whatever the status of the advisory opinion in the UN Charter, it is generally understood to be an appeal against the ILOAT judgments. As a French author defined it, it is "une sorte de recours en cassation".⁵⁸ It goes beyond simple advice and many legal practitioners would agree with such a conclusion.

The reason is that the authority of the ICJ – the highest judicial body of the newly-created United Nations – was considered necessary, especially in 1946 and 1949, to guarantee that a potential conflict between a judicial body and the highest representative and legislative body of an international organization would be treated with the necessary seriousness. Given the limits of the UN Charter opening the contentious procedure to States only, the only solution available was a binding advisory opinion. The fact that in San Francisco⁵⁹ a proposal to have the ICJ acting on appeals against decisions of the administrative tribunals was not adopted⁶⁰ should not be overestimated, because the practical case arose only in 1946, at the last session of the League of Nations' Assembly. If an assembly could simply declare that it disagreed with the

---

57 IFAD raised this argument before the ILOAT. Although the Tribunal found it "more substantial", it did not find it "sufficient to justify suspending the effects of a judgment without having regard to the interests of the staff member concerned", see paras. 18 and 19 of Judgment No. 3003, pp. 7–8.
58 De Lacharrière, *op. cit.*, p. 385.
59 At the United Nations Conference on International Organization at San Francisco. See details in the Dissenting Opinion of Judge Cordova to the UNESCO Advisory Opinion, *op. cit.*, p. 160.
60 See Separate Opinion of Judge Winiarski to the UNESCO Advisory Opinion, ICJ Reports 1956, p. 77, at 107.

administrative tribunal and refuse to execute the judgment, as was the case with 13 individual judgments in 1946,[61] the whole system of internal justice would lack credibility. That is why a judicial review appeared necessary. Although the advisory opinion is the only solution compatible with the UN Charter, it is still given by a court. As the ICJ said, "the Court and its predecessor have emphasized that, in their advisory jurisdiction, they must maintain their integrity as judicial bodies."[62]

The ILOAT itself does not feel comfortable with this process. As it stated in Judgment No. 3003,

> Article XII of the Statute of the Tribunal, cited above, which at present is the only provision specifically indicating that the International Court of Justice may be called upon to examine a judgment handed down by an international administrative tribunal, establishes a procedure which is highly original in several respects. Indeed, although it provides in paragraph 1 for the possibility of requesting the Court to render an "advisory opinion" on the validity of a judgment of the Tribunal, it adds in paragraph 2 that the opinion given shall be "binding", without however defining how consequences should be drawn from the opinion if it undermines the validity of the impugned judgment. In view of the scope thus attributed to the Court's opinion, it is hard to reconcile this procedure with the principle laid down in Article VI of the Statute whereby the Tribunal's judgments are final and without appeal. From this there undoubtedly arises a degree of ambiguity as to the nature and the legal effects of the mechanism prescribed. Moreover, whereas a request to the Court for an opinion could be regarded, in this context, as a form of appeal against a judgment of the Tribunal, it appears – although the matter is wholly for the Court to decide – that the submission of such a request is not subject to any time limit. Lastly, by virtue of the wording of Article XII, the option of resorting to this procedure is confined to international organisations, to the exclusion of staff members of such organisations who are parties to proceedings before the Tribunal.

A little later, the ILOAT concluded that "regardless of any ambiguity which, as mentioned earlier, may arise from the nicety of combining the applicable

---

61 Eleven former staff members of the League of Nations and two former staff members of the International Labour Office.
62 IFAD Advisory Opinion, *op. cit.*, para. 34, p. 14.

provisions, this procedure must in fact be regarded as tantamount to an appeal."[63]

The next question that comes naturally is what could be subject to such an appeal? The ICJ found limits in Article XII of the ILOAT Statute. The challenge to the judgment may be made with respect to the ILOAT's jurisdiction, or on the process followed by the ILOAT, if an organization considers that a decision of the ILOAT is vitiated by a fundamental fault in procedure. Both the question submitted to the ICJ and the answer must therefore be very specific. As the ICJ already stated in the UNESCO Advisory Opinion, "errors of fact or of law on the part of the Administrative Tribunal in its Judgments on the merits cannot give rise to that procedure."[64] On those issues, as the ICJ confirmed, judgments of the ILOAT are "final and without appeal", as provided by Article VI of the ILOAT Statute. This means that the ILOAT's excess of powers cannot be challenged if its jurisdiction is properly determined.[65]

V   Due Process

What was supposed to be a preliminary question to justify the ICJ's decision to agree to give an advisory opinion became the *raison d'être* of the IFAD Advisory Opinion.[66] In both the UNESCO and IFAD Advisory Opinions the ICJ struggled with the very fundamental elements of due process: inequality of access to it and inequalities in the proceedings before it. The ICJ clearly states that "in the case of the ILOAT, the Court is unable to see any such justification for the provision for review of the Tribunal's decisions which favours the employer to the disadvantage of the staff member." The ICJ also declared that the "principle [of equality] must now be understood as including access on an equal basis to available appellate or similar remedies unless an exception can be justified on objective and reasonable grounds".[67] There are strong voices considering that

---

63   Judgment No. 3003, para 22. This conclusion is supported by quotations of the ICJ in the UNESCO Advisory Opinion in para. 23 of the same judgment.
64   UNESCO Advisory Opinion, *op. cit.*, p. 87.
65   De Lacharrière, *op. cit.*, p. 389.
66   Runavot, *op. cit.*, para. 22, p. 868.
67   To determine the general concept of equality, the ICJ turns in paragraph 39 of its IFAD Advisory Opinion to comments made by the Human Rights Committee. As Marie-Clotilde Runavot observes, this is strange in the context of 'appeals' against the ILO Administrative Tribunal judgments as Article 14, paragraph 1, of the International Covenant on Civil and Political Rights of 1966, which the comments are about, refer to, as the ICJ notes itself, to "domestic courts and tribunals", Runavot, *op. cit.*, para. 28, p. 870.

the ICJ should have refused to exercise its advisory function.[68] However, the ICJ simply followed its previous jurisprudence which found that there were no "compelling reasons" to refuse to reply to the request.[69]

It is definitely not the ILOAT that would argue for justification of the system, although it clearly stated limits in its ability to criticize its own Statute. In paragraph 46 of its Judgment No. 3003, the ILOAT stated that:

> Clearly, it is not for the Tribunal to express a critical opinion on a provision of its own Statute. However, it does have to take care, given that this particular provision creates an objective inequality between the parties, to ensure that its own case law does not in any way amplify the consequences of this inequality...

Both distinguished judicial bodies, based on the two precedents, consider that the ILOAT's judgments would be challenged only in circumstances in which the organization 'lost' the case. Judge Cançado Trindade speaks about advisory procedures disguising a contentious case of international administrative law.[70] This seems also to be the prism though which the ILOAT sees Article XII of its Statute, considering that the challenges relate to judgments "unfavourable"[71] to the organization concerned. In other words, an employer could challenge a judgment while the employee could not.

While in most of the potential cases this is surely true, this is not an absolute rule. One can imagine that an organization, dissatisfied with the way the ILOAT

---

68 Within the context of the IFAD Advisory Opinion see the position of Ms Saez García referred to in para. 40 of the IFAD Advisory Opinion, *op. cit.*, p. 16. Judge Greenwood seemed to be of the same opinion but considered, however, that he "believed that the Court should not, without warning, withdraw its participation in a procedure for challenging Tribunal decisions which has been in place for many years and has therefore formed part of the assumptions made by all concerned – employees as well as employers – in proceedings before the Tribunal.", see Declaration of Judge Greenwood appended to the IFAD Advisory Opinion, para. 3, at p. 1.

69 Eric De Brabandere, "Individuals in Advisory Proceedings before the International Court of Justice: Equality of the Parties and the Court's Discretionary Authority", *The Law and Practice of International Courts and Tribunals*, Vol. 11, 2012, pp. 253–279, available at SSRN: <http://ssrn.com/abstract=2175429>, p. 17.

70 Separate Opinion of Judge Cançado Trindade, *op. cit.*, para. 102, p. 29. Some scholars see it from the same angle. For example Eric De Brabandere considers that the ICJ was "in fact confronted with the existence of an actual dispute between two parties – one or more officials and an international organization", De Brabandere, *op. cit.*, p. 2.

71 Judgment No. 3003, para. 43, p. 17.

asserted its jurisdiction in a particular case, which may have ended in the dismissal of the complaint on merits or due to a lack of evidence so that the organization concerned did not 'lose' the case, may still want to challenge the judgment to avoid the force of precedent for other similar cases or for the future.

Furthermore, the 'employer' organization which is the defendant in the ILOAT proceedings is not the only one that can challenge a judgment. The text of Article XII of the ILOAT Statute[72] does not exclude the possibility of another organization recognizing the ILOAT's jurisdiction to challenge a judgment if it considers that the jurisdiction is incorrectly confirmed or considers there to have been "a fundamental fault in the procedure followed".[73] This is not only a theoretical possibility since the Rules of the ILOAT, in Article 13, paragraph 2, provide specifically that "an organization which has recognized the Tribunal's jurisdiction may intervene in a complaint on the grounds that the ruling which the Tribunal is to make may affect it." If the resulting judgment continues to affect an organization which is not the employer in a specific case, the possibility that it may challenge the judgment for the reasons mentioned in Article XII of the ILOAT Statute cannot be excluded.

Yet it is true that even in those cases, as the ILOAT put it, "a judgment whose validity is challenged through this procedure can be affected by the opinion rendered by the Court."[74] However, it is not only the ILOAT Statute that prevents an individual challenging a judgment before the ICJ. It is also the Statute of the ICJ that does not provide for *ius standi* of individuals before the ICJ. So, individuals cannot request an advisory opinion of the ICJ. Even if the ILO were to modify the Statute of its Administrative Tribunal, the practical effect of the modification would not be such as to establish the equality of the parties to the original dispute as regards the access of individuals to the ICJ advisory procedure.

What seems more striking is the second aspect of inequality, *i.e.*, the procedural inequality of the parties originally involved in the case submitted to the

---

[72] The English text of the ILOAT Statute refers to a decision and the French to "une decision", without qualifying it further as a decision concerning a specific organization.

[73] Although the ICJ explained this concept in its Advisory Opinion of 1973 on the *Application for Review of Judgment No. 158 of the United Nations Administrative Tribunal* (*op. cit.*, p. 209, para. 92) and referred to it in paras. 30–31 and 98 of its IFAD Advisory Opinion, the concept seems rather dynamic and may be subject to further refinements. Besides the fact that the wording of the UN Administrative Tribunal Statute and the ILOAT Statute did not correspond entirely, one has to note that the ICJ gives only "criteria helpful in identifying fundamental errors in procedure" which may be revisited in future.

[74] Judgment No. 3003, para. 22, p. 8.

ILOAT. The complainant before the ILOAT, who is an individual, does not have even *locus standi in judicio* in advisory proceedings before the ICJ. The reason is in Article 66 of the ICJ Statute, which opens the procedure only to States and international organizations. While this would be sufficient to respond to a request formulated by an international organization, in such cases the ICJ always has in mind that an underlying dispute between an employee and an employer led to the judgment challenged before it.[75]

For this purpose, the ICJ considers that "while the Court is not in a position to reform this system, it can attempt to ensure, so far as possible, that there is equality in the proceedings before it." As in 1956, the result was that ICJ had to do "une adaptation assez acrobatique pour laquelle la Cour n'est pas faite."[76] The arguments in favour of searching for a solution are best summarized by Judge Cançado Trindade when he says that

> one can surely argue that the participation of the individuals concerned in legal proceedings contributes to a better instruction of the process, by giving the Court the opportunity to have a better knowledge of the parties' perception of the facts and their arguments as to the law. Furthermore, it preserves the *principe du contradictoire*, essential in the search for truth and the realization of justice, guaranteeing the equality of arms (*égalité des armes*) in the whole procedure before the Court, essential to *la bonne administration de la justice*.[77]

To remedy the lacunae of its Statute, the ICJ firstly ordered the President of IFAD to transmit to it any written statement setting forth the views of Ms Saez García.[78] Secondly, the ICJ decided not to hold oral proceedings because the ICJ Statute does not allow individuals to appear in such proceedings.

Despite expressing its concerns "about the length of time it took the Fund to comply with the procedures aimed at ensuring equality in the present proceedings", the ICJ nevertheless concluded "that, by the end of the process, it does have the information it requires to decide on the questions submitted; that both the Fund and Ms Saez García have had adequate and in large measure

---

75   Marie-Clotilde Runavot makes distinction between participants in the proceedings, who cannot be designated as parties, and the parties to the original dispute, which may be underlying the request for the advisory opinion, Runavot, *op. cit.*, p. 861.
76   De Lacharrière, *op. cit.*, p. 387.
77   Separate Opinion of Judge Cançado Trindade, *op. cit.*, para. 116, p. 33.
78   This process was not without difficulties, as the ICJ noted in paragraph 46 of its Advisory Opinion, *op. cit.*, pp. 18–19.

equal opportunities to present their case and to answer that made by the other; and that, in essence, the principle of equality in the proceedings before the Court, required by its inherent judicial character and by the good administration of justice, has been met."[79]

In this way, the ICJ attempted to remedy the issue of equality in the proceedings, but the question is whether by doing so it had given up searching for full information to be able to make a fully-informed advisory opinion. This question concerns in particular one of the means at the disposal of the ICJ in gathering information, namely its right to organize an oral hearing. The decision on whether or not this should be done is "a matter within the discretion of the Court."[80] The fact that in relation to other 'normal' requests, the ICJ has systematically organized oral proceedings indicates the value of such proceedings for bringing to light the proper information on which the ICJ is to formulate its opinion. This important element is missing in the two Advisory Opinions regarding the ILOAT. Judge Cançado Trindade, who qualifies this as an "abnormal procedure"[81] warns that "the procedural *acrobatie* is not to hold oral hearings: this is not a solution either, as the Court thereby ends up depriving itself to instruct better the *dossier* of the case, by imposing such limit to the freedom of expression of the 'parties' concerned."[82] He concludes that "by deciding not to have oral hearings in the course of the proceedings, – has been and is, in my understanding, most unsatisfactory: rather than a solution, it is the capitulation in face of a persisting problem."[83]

Given the place that the arguments of Ms Saez García found in the Separate Opinion of Judge Cançado Trindade and in the Advisory Opinion of the ICJ, it seems clear that the ICJ would have difficulties arriving at the advisory opinion only on the basis of arguments presented by IFAD.

VI Concluding Remarks

What seems obvious from the IFAD Advisory Opinion and arguments presented above is that the ICJ is the wrong address for this type of request. Neither the ICJ nor the individual claimants feel comfortable with this type of

---

[79] Ibid., para. 47, p. 19.
[80] *Application for Review of Judgment No. 158 of the United Nations Administrative Tribunal*, op. cit., p. 181.
[81] Separate Opinion of Judge Cançado Trindade, op. cit., para. 48, p. 14.
[82] Ibid., para. 104, p. 30
[83] Ibid., para. 52, p. 15.

binding advisory opinion disguising an appeal. UNESCO and IFAD would surely not argue in its favour. The ILOAT sees its judgments challenged and the authority of *res judicata* affected.

The ICJ itself, in spite of all its efforts, cannot satisfactorily remedy the procedural obstacles to ensure due process. The indirect manner of ensuring the participation of an individual, as the ICJ did in the IFAD Advisory Opinion, cannot but emphasize this problem. As an author put it, the ICJ responded positively to the request for an advisory opinion, "mais à l'évidence pour ne plus avoir à le faire".[84]

It seems that the existence of Article XII of the ILOAT Statute does not respond to the need originally envisaged by the International Labour Conference in 1946 and 1949. The possibility of challenging the judgments of the ILOAT before the ICJ is now an exception in international administrative law as there is no such possibility for administrative tribunals created by other international organizations. The ICJ's second warning should not be ignored and a change seems indeed necessary.[85] The question is in what direction? Even if some improvements may be envisaged within the framework of the ILOAT Statute, namely the ILO could request a general authorization from the UN General Assembly for all organizations that recognized the ILOAT jurisdiction, the ICJ still appears to be the wrong address for these types of legal questions. To the extent that the review by the ICJ is seen as an appeal from the ILOAT judgment, the inequality of parties to the original dispute cannot be remedied satisfactorily both with respect to the *jus standi* and the *locus standi in judicio*. This simply flows from the limits of the Statute of the ICJ. The ICJ does not (yet?) have a place for individuals in its rules, in spite of serious arguments in favour of it presented by Judge Cançado Trindade in his Separate Opinion to the IFAD Advisory Opinion.[86]

This is what Judge Tomka, President of the ICJ, may have hinted at in his address to the 67th session of the UN General Assembly on 1 November 2012, when he said that "the question arises whether the time has not come for the International Labour Organization to also consider initiating a reform of the current system, such as the one already carried out by the UN."[87] Indeed, Judge

---

84   Runavot, *op. cit.*, p. 860.
85   To avoid another "56 years the force of inertia and mental lethargy", to use an expression often repeated in Judge Cançado Trindade's Separate Opinion.
86   See Separate Opinion of Judge Cançado Trindade, *op. cit.*
87   Available at <http://www.icj-cij.org/court/index.php?p1=1&p2=3&p3=1> (accessed 24 March 2013).

Tomka may have been inspired by the fact that a previous criticism by the ICJ[88] of the ability to challenge judgments of the UN Administrative Tribunal before the ICJ resulted in a substantive change in the UN system. The UN General Assembly simply suppressed the review procedure of the ICJ in respect of the UN Administrative Tribunal by its Resolution 50/54 of 29 January 1996.[89] The ICJ recalled this with some insistence in the IFAD Advisory Opinion.[90]

While Judge Greenwood argues that "the need for reform of Article XII of the ILOAT Statute is urgent and it is very much to be hoped that a new procedure for challenging judgments of the Tribunal can be put in place within a short period of time",[91] one can question whether a procedure for challenging judgments of the ILOAT is indeed necessary. Recourse to the ICJ has been used only twice since 1946 and in both cases the ICJ confirmed the validity of the ILOAT's judgments. The system of the ILOAT is rather different from the one within the United Nations. Although the UN system of justice recently became open to other organizations, none of those who recognized the jurisdiction of the ILOAT decided to change and join the new UN system and recognize the jurisdiction of the United Nations Appeals Tribunal. On the contrary, many international organizations keep showing interest in recognizing the jurisdiction of the ILOAT.

The justification for keeping Article XII in the ILOAT Statute is not evident. In any legal system there is always a final judgment. When dealing with administrative law, as is the case before the ILOAT, a one-tier system may be quite sufficient and satisfactory. The advantage for the parties of having an efficient and reliable system on which they can count when they define their dispute may be more advantageous than relying on a review mechanism that is inadequate for their needs and, perhaps, raises more problems than it resolves.

---

88   See *Application for Review of Judgment No. 158 of the United Nations Administrative Tribunal, op. cit.*, p. 209, para. 92.
89   In that sense, see Runavot, *op. cit.*, para. 32, p. 872.
90   IFAD Advisory Opinion, *op. cit.*, paras. 36 and 38, pp. 15–16.
91   Declaration of Judge Greenwood, *op. cit.*, para. 3, p. 1.

CHAPTER 40

Asia and Dispute Settlement: The Law of the Sea

M.C.W. Pinto*

Teacher, jurist, publicist, judge – Budislav Vukas has made an outstanding contribution to our understanding and appreciation of the 1982 UN Convention on the Law of the Sea and its 1994 Implementing Agreement.

1   Introduction: Asian States and International Dispute Settlement

It is often suggested that a distinctive attitude to international dispute settlement prevails among Asian States, an attitude characterized by reluctance to submit such disputes to decision by a third party or, to use the title of Section 2 of Part XV of the United Nations Convention on the Law of the Sea (UNCLOS), to 'Compulsory Procedures Entailing Binding Decisions'. To assess the validity of such a proposition is not easy, given the number of States included in the geographic entity 'Asia' (comprising over 50 Member States of the United Nations) and the cultural diversity of populations within their borders; as well as the difficulty of distinguishing any such suggested 'reluctance' from that manifest in States from other regions when asked to choose whether or not to relinquish their freedom of action to an external entity, however 'independent' and 'impartial', empowered to restrict that freedom by its decision.

Assessment of 'Asian' attitudes to dispute resolution has been hindered by a lack of relevant data from the region as a whole. However, we do have today authoritative assessments of evolving attitudes to international adjudication among a group of South East Asian States as reflected in their declared aim of creating "a sense that each…belongs to a family of countries…interlinked economically, politically and culturally", and seeking to establish a formal dispute settlement mechanism offering "a way of resolving disagreements without being disagreeable".[1]

---

*   Attorney of the Supreme Court of Sri Lanka, and of the Inner Temple, Barrister; Member of the *Institut de Droit International*.
1   An address by Professor Walter Woon, Attorney-General of Singapore to the 10th General Assembly of the ASEAN Law Association.

Thus, Professor Walter Woon, the Attorney-General of Singapore, recounts how the Member States of ASEAN have moved from rudimentary references to dispute settlement in the Declaration on the Zone of Peace, Freedom and Neutrality (1971), the Declaration of ASEAN Concord (1976), and the Treaty of Amity and Concord (1976). In the last Treaty, Member States committed themselves to the settlement of differences or disputes by 'peaceful means' through agreements which, while focussing on the improvement of economic relations re-affirmed, in addition, the commitment to 'amicable settlement' and required that "whenever necessary an appropriate body shall be designated for the settlement of disputes" (1992). The Vientiane Protocol for Enhanced Dispute Settlement Mechanism (2004) and Chapter VIII of the ASEAN Charter (2007) provided mechanisms for the settlement of disputes in all areas of ASEAN cooperation, while the Protocol to the ASEAN Charter on Dispute Settlement Mechanisms (2010) provides for consultations within a fixed time frame, and the ability to convene an arbitral tribunal. Unresolved disputes and non-compliance with the findings of dispute settlement mechanisms are to be referred to the ASEAN Summit, while the ASEAN Charter maintains Member States' right of recourse to the modes of dispute settlement listed in Article 33 of the Charter of the United Nations.[2]

Although ASEAN countries[3] appear to move ever closer to a complete mandatory system of dispute resolution, it is evident that some of ASEAN's members still prefer to resolve disputes by less formal means, and non-legal avenues to dispute settlement such as consultation and negotiation rather than a formal process. In any event, the better view appears to be that, for the time being, ASEAN is "not ready for a court".[4]

Another authoritative source suggests a similar evolution in the attitudes of Asian States toward international adjudication. In a wide-ranging article, Hisashi Owada, a judge of the International Court of Justice and, until recently its President, recalls that only five Asian States (Afghanistan, China, India, Japan and Siam) were signatories to the Statute of the Permanent Court of

---

2 Walter Woon, "Dispute Settlement in ASEAN", 1 *Korean Journal of International and Comparative Law*, 2013, pp. 92–104; *Dispute Settlement in ASEAN*, National University of Singapore, <http://cil.nus.edu.sg/dispute-settlement-in-asean>.
3 Indonesia, Malaysia, Philippines, Singapore, Thailand, Brunei Darussalam, Viet Nam, Laos, Myanmar, Cambodia.
4 As Professor Walter Woon observes, although the ASEAN Charter creates 'a new paradigm' in regard to international dispute settlement mechanisms, progress along that path will take time. *Ibid.* at p. 104.

International Justice in the inter-war period of 1922–1945.[5] He recounts how, in Japan, appreciation of an international law developed in the West changed from early confidence based on positive experience with international arbitration, through difficult decades-long negotiations aimed at revising unfair and unequal treaties, to the bitter disappointment that arose from the award against Japan by the Permanent Court of Arbitration in the *Yokohama House Tax* case. The resulting disillusionment with the system lasted for a century, until Japan became a party to the *Southern Bluefin Tuna* case before the International Tribunal for the Law of the Sea (ITLOS).[6] Observing that a sceptical perception of international adjudication as a mechanism developed by the West and likely to ensnare the unwary is one that prevails among many Asian States, Judge Owada suggests that such attitudes were the result of the experiences of those States during a shared history of colonial exploitation, their resentment being brought into sharp focus by the decision of the International Court of Justice in the *South West Africa (Second Phase) cases (1966)*. However, writing in 2005 he remarks the emergence among Asian States of a new trust in international law as a guiding principle, as well as confidence in the International Court of Justice, perhaps born of a new self-confidence with roots in the phenomenal economic growth achieved by many of those States. Judge Owada does concede, however, that another element continues to affect negatively the attitude of Asian States to international adjudication:

> It is the cultural heritage of this region that tends to tilt towards the direction of reconciling differences – whether they be between States or individuals – through negotiation and accommodation, rather than through adjudication on the basis of a clear-cut application of the law. In fact, one reason why East Asia remains to this day the only region of the world where no multilateral framework exists for the pacific settlement of disputes, such as arbitration and judicial settlement, on a regional or sub-regional basis may well be linked with this cultural trait of the region.[7]

---

5 Hisashi Owada, "The Experience of Asia with International Adjudication", 9 *Singapore Year Book of International Law*, 2005, pp. 9–18, at 10.

6 *Ibid.* at p. 14.

7 *Ibid.* at p. 15. See also Walter Woon, *op. cit.*, note 4 above, commenting on the judgments of the International Court of Justice cited therein: "The three ICJ cases highlight the weakness of the adjudication process: it is a zero-sum game. There is always a loser, and the loss may rankle a generation after the court decision... The ASEAN way is to seek compromise using the [ASEAN] Charter and peer pressure as levers.", p. 104. See also Michael Pryles, *Dispute Resolution in Asia*, The Hague, 2002, pp. 1–20, and the present author's modest essay "Some thoughts on 'Asian' approaches to international dispute resolution" in S. Charnovitz,

11   Asian States and Dispute Settlement under the UN Convention on the Law of the Sea

Several Asian States have made declarations on signing UNCLOS or upon ratification or thereafter dealing essentially with assertion of sovereignty or jurisdiction over marine areas and islands, but very few have, in their initial declarations, made the explicit choice among dispute settlement mechanisms contemplated in Section 2 of Part XV of UNCLOS,[8] although some foresee making that choice at a later time.[9] This means that most Asian States, absent that choice, would, by paragraph 3 of Article 287 "be deemed to have accepted arbitration in accordance with Annex VII" of the Convention. Some States have preferred to avail themselves of a different aspect of the flexibility of the Convention's dispute settlement provisions by exercising the option offered by Article 298 to declare their non-acceptance of the 'binding decisions' procedures in Section 2 of Part XV in relation to one or more of the categories of dispute listed in paragraph 1 of that Article.[10]

D.P. Steger and P. van den Bossche, eds., *Law in the Service of Human Dignity, Essays in Honour of Florentino Feliciano*, Cambridge, 2005, pp. 350–377.

8   *Bangladesh*, by separate declarations dated 14 December 2009 relating to Article 287 of UNCLOS, accepted the jurisdiction of ITLOS for settlement of a dispute with India and a dispute with Myanmar relating to the delimitation of their respective maritime boundaries in the Bay of Bengal. *China*, by its declaration dated 7 June 1996 upon ratification of the Convention while not making the choice, (1) states that it will effect delimitation of the boundary of maritime jurisdiction with States with opposite or adjacent coasts through consultations and "on the basis of international law and in accordance with the principle of equitability"; (2) reaffirms its sovereignty over all its archipelagos and islands as listed in Article 2 of the Law of the People's Republic of China on the territorial sea and the contiguous zone, which was promulgated on 25 February 1992; and (3) by a declaration dated 25 August 2006 made pursuant to Article 298 of UNCLOS, affirms that "China does not accept any of the procedures provided for in Section 2 of Part XV of the Convention with respect to all the categories of disputes referred to in paragraph 1(a)(b) and (c) of Article 298 of the Convention"; *Fiji*, by its declaration upon ratification dated 10 December 1982 made under Article 287 of UNCLOS, "chooses the International Tribunal for the Law of the Sea...for the settlement of disputes concerning the interpretation or application of the Convention"; *Oman*, by its declaration No. 7 upon ratification dated 17 August 1998 accepts "the jurisdiction of the International Tribunal for the Law of the Sea and of the International Court of Justice with a view to the settlement of any dispute that may arise between it and another State concerning the interpretation or application of the Convention."

9   Bangladesh (with regard to disputes other than those specified in its declaration dated 14 December 2009); India; Iran; Pakistan; Thailand; Timor-Leste.

10 China; Korea; Republic of Thailand; Palau.

Whether the result of a burgeoning confidence in the international legal system with its roots in spectacular economic and social progress, or driven by the realization that to promote commercial relations with countries from which they invite investment, Asian States do appear to be more willing than in the past to accept dispute settlement mechanisms that provide for binding decisions, at least where time bound efforts through consultation and negotiation have failed to resolve pending issues that have become too burdensome. The dispute settlement system provided by UNCLOS, designed to offer a broad range of settlement methods and to be 'user-friendly',[11] does seem able to attract at least some Asian States.

Since the entry into force on 16 November 1994 of the 1982 UN Convention on the Law of the Sea, together with the Agreement relating to the Implementation of Part XI of the Convention, several Asian States have sought to apply the provisions of the Convention's Part XV and Annexes thereto in resolving disputes to which they are parties, or to obtain clarification of the Convention's provisions through a request for an Advisory Opinion from the Seabed Disputes Chamber of the Tribunal.

Thus, Japan was respondent in cases instituted before the International Tribunal for the Law of the Sea by New Zealand (Case No. 3 on the docket of ITLOS) and Australia (Case No. 4) for provisional measures aimed at preventing alleged excessive fishing for Southern Bluefin Tuna by Japan; Yemen was respondent in a case instituted before the Tribunal by Panama for the prompt release of a seized vessel[12] (Case No. 9); Malaysia instituted proceedings against Singapore before the Tribunal seeking provisional measures (Case concerning Land Reclamation by Singapore in and around the Straits of Johor, Case No. 12), later submitting the dispute to an arbitral tribunal constituted pursuant to Annex VII of the Convention, and accepting settlement on the basis of an Award on Agreed Terms issued by that tribunal; Japan instituted proceedings against the Russian Federation in Cases No. 14 (*Hoshinmaru*) and No. 15 (*Tomimaru*) for prompt release of seized vessels.

---

11   A descriptive term used by the principal architect of the Convention's dispute settlement system, the late Professor Louis B. Sohn, "Settlement of Law of the Sea Disputes", 10(2) *International Journal of Marine and Coastal Law*, 1995, p. 206. For an overview see Tullio Treves, "The Law of the Sea Tribunal: Its Status and Scope of Jurisdiction after November 16, 1994", 55(2) *Zeitschrift für ausländisches öffentliches Recht und Völkerrecht*, 1995, pp. 421–451; Budislav Vukas, *The Law of the Sea: Selected Writings*, Leiden, 2004, Chapter X; Natalie Klein, *Dispute Settlement in the UN Convention on the Law of the Sea*, Cambridge, 2005.

12   Vessels seized pursuant to Articles 73, paragraph (1), 220 paragraphs (6) and (7), or Article 226 of the Convention.

Bangladesh instituted proceedings against Myanmar in *Dispute concerning delimitation of the maritime boundary between Bangladesh and Myanmar in the Bay of Bengal* (Case No. 16 on the docket of ITLOS), while applications made by the Republic of Nauru and the Kingdom of Tonga to the Legal and Technical Commission of the International Seabed Authority were events that led to the Request to the Seabed Disputes Chamber by the Council of the Authority for an Advisory Opinion on 'Responsibilities and Obligations of States sponsoring persons and entities with respect to activities in the Area' (Case No. 17 on the docket of ITLOS). Both the decision by the Tribunal in *Bangladesh v. Myanmar*, and the Advisory Opinion by the Seabed Disputes Chamber have contributed substantially to the practitioner's understanding of the provisions of the Convention dealt with, as briefly noted below.

Arbitral proceedings instituted by Bangladesh against India and by the Philippines against China under Annex VII to the Convention are in progress. The Sea-Bed Disputes Chamber is currently dealing with a Request for an Advisory Opinion from the Sub-Regional Fisheries Commission (Dakar, Senegal) (Case No. 21 on the docket of ITLOS).

III Determination of a Maritime Boundary between Adjacent States in the Bay of Bengal

Of particular interest to States in Asia and elsewhere concerned with the making of boundaries between territorial seas, exclusive economic zones, and continental shelves of States that are opposite or adjacent to one another (Articles 15, 74 and 83 of the Convention) or between a State and the Area that is the Common Heritage of Mankind (Article 76 of the Convention) is the judgment of the International Tribunal for the Law of the Sea in the case brought before it by special agreement between Bangladesh and Myanmar relating to delimitation in an area in the northern part of the Bay of Bengal.

While the Statute of the Tribunal makes it clear that the decision of the Tribunal "shall have no binding force except between the parties in respect of that particular dispute" (Article 33, paragraph 2 of the Statute of the Tribunal), many of the Tribunal's pronouncements in the judgment provide authoritative clarification of the provisions of the 1982 Convention dealing with delimitation of maritime areas. They do so, of course, with particular reference to the geomorphology of the Bay of Bengal which contains the world's largest submarine sedimentary feature, the Bengal Fan. Those pronouncements are carefully constructed and anchored firmly in State practice as well as the reasoned decisions of the International Court of Justice and other international tribunals, demonstrating that the early apprehension of some commentators that creation of the Tribunal could contribute to a 'fragmentation' of international law may not have been justified.[13]

In this case the Tribunal was called upon to determine the maritime boundary between Bangladesh and Myanmar in the Bay of Bengal with respect to their territorial seas, exclusive economic zones and continental shelves. The Tribunal concluded that it had jurisdiction to determine the boundary with respect to the continental shelf even beyond 200 M from the baselines, and did so in areas where the entitlements of the two States overlapped, but only up to where the rights of third States in the area, or those of the international community in the Area declared to be the 'common heritage of mankind', could be engaged.[14]

1 Boundary between the Territorial Seas of the Parties

Having considered the terms of Article 15 of the Convention, which would permit the territorial seas of the Parties as a rule to extend up to the 'median line' as defined therein, absent agreement with them or the existence of 'historic title or other special circumstances' that might make it necessary to vary that rule, the Tribunal noted that neither Party had invoked the existence of historic title. It did however discuss at some length an argument that an island lying parallel to the coast of one Party constituted a 'special circumstance', concluded that it did not and gave the island full effect in establishing the equidistance line between the territorial seas of the Parties.[15]

2 Boundary between the Exclusive Economic Zones and Continental Shelves of the Parties

As to the method of apportionment to be used in determining the boundary between exclusive economic zones and continental shelves the Tribunal based its reasoning on a statement of the International Court of Justice in its judgment in the *North Sea Continental Shelf Case* that "land is the legal source of the power which a State may exercise over territorial extensions seaward",[16]

---

[13] See generally Shigeru Oda, "Dispute Settlement Prospects in the Law of the Sea", 44 *International and Comparative Law Quarterly* (hereafter *ICLQ*), 1995, p. 863; Gilbert Guillaume, "The Future of International Judicial Institutions", 44 *ICLQ*, 1995, p. 848.

[14] *Dispute concerning delimitation of the maritime boundary between Bangladesh and Myanmar in the Bay of Bengal*, Judgment dated 14 March 2012 (hereafter 'Judgment'), para. 462.

[15] Judgment, paras. 146–152.

[16] *ICJ Reports 1969*, p. 3, at 51.

and having examined a number of decisions by international courts and tribunals, concurs with the conclusion of the arbitral tribunal in the *Case between Guyana and Suriname* that

> The case law of the International Court of Justice and arbitral jurisprudence as well as State practice are at one in holding that the delimitation process should, in appropriate cases, begin by positing a provisional equidistance line which may be adjusted in the light of relevant circumstances in order to achieve an equitable solution.[17]

Thereafter, having again carefully reviewed the jurisprudence of international courts and tribunals,[18] the Tribunal decided to follow a three-stage approach: (i) first, to construct a provisional equidistance line, based on the geography of the Parties' relevant coasts and mathematical calculations; (ii) second, to determine whether there are any relevant circumstances requiring adjustment that produces an equitable result; and finally, (iii) to check whether the line, as adjusted, results in any significant disproportion between the ratio of the respective coastal lengths and the ratio of the relevant maritime areas allocated by the process to each Party. In applying this approach the Tribunal, as a preliminary step, reviewed the base points proposed by each Party for construction of a provisional equidistance line, and having identified those base points that it found to be appropriate applied them in constructing its provisional equidistance line.[19]

Proceeding to the second stage, the Tribunal considered three circumstances that the Parties argued were relevant to the issue whether, and if so to what extent, the provisional equidistance line should be adjusted so as to produce an

---

17 Award of 17 September 2007, 47 *International Legal Materials*, 2008, p. 116, at 213.
18 *E.g. Maritime Delimitation in the Black Sea (Romania v. Ukraine)*, Judgment, ICJ Reports 2009, p. 61, at 89; *Arbitration between Barbados and the Republic of Trinidad and Tobago*, Decision of 11 April 2006, *Reports of International Arbitral Awards*, Vol. XXVII, p. 147, at 210–211.
19 Judgment, paras. 177–271. The Tribunal did consider a proposal by one Party to apply a different method of apportionment, the "angle-bisector method" that had been used in the *Territorial and Maritime Dispute between Nicaragua and Honduras in the Caribbean Sea (ICJ Reports 2007*, p. 659, at 746). Observing that the angle-bisector method was "in effect an approximation of the equidistance method", the Tribunal concluded that the jurisprudence had developed in favour of the equidistance/relevant circumstances method, having been adopted by international courts and tribunals in the majority of delimitation cases before them, and decided that under the geographic realities and particular circumstances prevailing in the present case, the equidistance/relevant circumstances method could lead to an equitable result.

equitable result: the concave nature of one Party's coastline; the position of an island territory of a Party lying parallel and near to the coastline of the other Party; and the depositional origins of the physical, geological, and geomorphological connection of the exclusive economic zone and continental shelf of each Party.

The Tribunal considered that while the concavity of a coast *per se* was not necessarily a relevant circumstance, if the equidistance line between the Parties were to produce a cut-off effect on the maritime entitlement of one of them, as in the present case, adjustment of that line would be necessary in order to reach an equitable result.[20] As to the island feature considered, the Tribunal found that giving it effect in the delimitation of the exclusive economic zone and the continental shelf would result in a line blocking the seaward projection of one Party's coast, and an unwarranted distortion of the delimitation line, and accordingly that it should not be treated as a relevant circumstance in the present case.[21] The Tribunal decided that the maritime boundary applicable would be determined on the basis of the geography of the coasts of the Parties, and did not consider the Bengal depositional system relevant to delimitation of the exclusive economic zone and the continental shelf of the Parties within 200 M.[22]

The Tribunal thus decided that the provisional equidistance line was to be deflected at the point where it began to cut off the seaward projection of one Party as the result of the concavity of its coast, emphasizing that the adjustment was to be determined in the light of relevant geographic circumstances in a balanced way and so as to produce an equitable solution.

Having determined the maritime boundary between the Parties on their adjacent territorial seas, exclusive economic zones and continental shelves, the Tribunal dealt with the question whether, as argued by one Party, it should project that boundary beyond that point on the basis of their respective entitlements to maritime areas; or, as argued by the other Party, it should refrain in the present case from exercising jurisdiction to delimit their continental shelves beyond 200 M until such time as the outer limits of the continental shelf had been established by each Party pursuant to Article 76, paragraph 8 of the Convention, or at least until such time as the Commission on the Limits of the Continental Shelf had made recommendations to each Party, and each Party had had the opportunity to consider its reaction to those recommendations.

---

20 Judgment, paras. 290–297.
21 Judgment, paras. 316–319.
22 Judgment, paras. 320–322.

The Tribunal first clarified and distinguished its functions under the Convention from those of the Commission on the Limits of the Continental Shelf. The latter, composed of experts in the fields of geology, geophysics and hydrography, is assigned the function of considering data and other material submitted by coastal States and making recommendations to them on establishment of the outer limits of their continental shelves in any areas lying beyond 200 M from their baselines in accordance with Article 76 of the Convention. By contrast, interpreting the provisions of the Convention and settling disputes with respect to delimitation of maritime boundaries are functions entrusted to dispute settlement procedures under Article 83 and Part xv of the Convention which include international courts and tribunals. Noting that the Commission had earlier decided to defer consideration of the submission of a Party pending action to be taken in the interim, the Tribunal concluded:

> 392. In the view of the Tribunal it would be contrary to the object and purpose of the Convention not to resolve the existing impasse. Inaction in the present case, by the Commission and the Tribunal, two organs created by the Convention to ensure the effective implementation of its provisions, would leave the Parties in a position where they may be unable to benefit fully from their rights over the continental shelf;

and that

> 393. ...the exercise of its jurisdiction in the present case cannot be seen as an encroachment on the functions of the Commission, in as much as the settlement, through negotiations, of disputes between States regarding delimitation of the continental shelf beyond 200 nm is not seen as precluding examination by the Commission of the submissions made to it or hindering it from issuing appropriate recommendations.

Proceeding to determine the maritime boundary between the two adjacent Parties beyond 200 M from the baselines, the Tribunal based the entitlement of each on the provisions of paragraph 1 of Article 76. Observing that the term 'natural prolongation' had been a notion employed to support the trend towards expanding national jurisdiction over the continental margin and had never been defined as an independent concept, the Tribunal held that

> Entitlement to a continental shelf beyond 200 nm should thus be determined by reference to the outer edge of the continental margin, to be

ascertained in accordance with Article 76, paragraph 4. To interpret otherwise is warranted neither by the text of Article 76 nor by its object and purpose.[23]

The Tribunal then proceeded to determine the maritime boundary delimiting the entitlements of the Parties beyond 200 M[24] by applying the equidistance/relevant circumstances method, noting that the cut-off effect of the concavity of the coast of one Party remained a relevant circumstance that had to be taken into account. The Tribunal observed that the method is rooted in the recognition that sovereignty over the land territory is the basis for the sovereign rights and jurisdiction of the coastal State with respect to both the exclusive economic zone and the continental shelf. Taking into account that a thick layer of sedimentary rocks covers practically the entire floor of the Bay of Bengal including areas appertaining to both Parties, the continuous and substantial layer extending from the coast of each Party supported its claim to a 'natural prolongation' beyond 200 M. The Tribunal (i) did not accept that "a significant geological discontinuity" alleged by one Party had affected the other Party's entitlement beyond 200 M; and (ii) observed that

> the text of article 76 of the Convention does not support the view that the geographic origin of the sedimentary rocks of the continental margin is of relevance to the question of entitlement to the continental shelf or constitutes a controlling criterion for determining whether a State is entitled to a continental shelf.[25]

Having determined the direction and course of the boundary delimiting the exclusive economic zones and the continental shelves of the Parties within 200 M as well as beyond, up to where the rights of third parties could be affected or to where a boundary could be established with the Area declared to be the "common heritage of mankind" by Article 136 of the Convention, the Tribunal proceeded to the final phase of the equidistance/relevant circumstances method applied by it, *viz.* to determine whether the adjusted equidistance line had caused a significant disproportion by reference to the ratio of the length of the coastlines of the Parties and the ratio of the relevant maritime area allocated to each Party. Upon scrutiny, the Tribunal found that the ratios of allocated maritime areas did not lead to any significant disproportion

---

23 Judgment, para. 437.
24 Judgment, paras. 461–462.
25 Judgment, paras. 437–447.

relative to the respective lengths of their coasts that would require the shifting of the adjusted equidistance line in order to ensure an equitable solution in the circumstances of this case, and accordingly decided, by a substantial majority, to incorporate that line in its judgment.[26]

In this, its first decision determining the maritime boundary between adjacent States, the Tribunal was called upon to interpret the provisions of Articles 15, 74, 76 and 83 of UNCLOS, as well as those of Annex II to the Convention when applied in relation to the complex geology and geomorphology of the Bay of Bengal. The care and sensitivity with which the Tribunal analysed each Party's claims, evaluating them in the light of the wealth of decisions by international courts and tribunals on similar issues, seems to have garnered the satisfaction of both Parties. This fact, and the Tribunal's clear interpretative statements on the meaning of terms that are of critical practical importance such as 'natural prolongation' and 'continental shelf', as well as on other matters not strictly related to the reasons for the judgment, such as the notion of estoppel,[27] the legal status of undertakings in early negotiations between the Parties;[28] and the emphasis given to the formal representation by one Party in the course of the arbitration relating to the other Party's rights regarding navigation and access,[29] could well encourage other States to seek resolution of their disputes before the Tribunal.

IV Request to the Sea-Bed Disputes Chamber of the International Tribunal for the Law of the Sea for an Advisory Opinion[30]

Two Asian States, the Republic of Nauru and the Kingdom of Tonga, were the first to initiate a procedure which culminated in a request by the Council of the International Sea-Bed Authority addressed to the Sea-Bed Disputes Chamber of the International Tribunal for the Law of the Sea in accordance with Article 191 of the Convention and Article 131 of the Rules of the Tribunal, for an Advisory Opinion on a legal question arising within the scope of its activities. In 2008, Nauru sponsored an application by Nauru Ocean Resources Inc. for a plan of work to explore for polymetallic nodules in the Area. Noting that, as a developing State, it did not yet possess the technical and financial capacity to

---

26 Judgment, paras. 461–462.
27 Judgment, paras. 119–129.
28 Judgment, paras. 88–117.
29 Judgment, paras. 170–176.
30 Case No. 17 on the docket of the Tribunal. Advisory Opinion dated 1 February 2011.

undertake seafloor mining but would, if it wished to do so, have to engage entities for the purpose in the 'global private sector'; and recalling that the Convention called for promotion of the effective participation of developing States in activities in the Area, Nauru proposed that it obtain guidance by way of an Advisory Opinion from the Sea-Bed Disputes Chamber to enable it to decide whether it would be in a position to mitigate effectively the potential liabilities and costs it might be required to undertake as sponsor of such entities under the provisions of the Convention.[31]

Having adopted Nauru's proposal, the Council decided by consensus to request an Advisory Opinion and formulated the questions to be submitted to the Sea-Bed Disputes Chamber as follows:

1. What are the legal responsibilities and obligations of States Parties to the Convention with respect to the sponsorship of activities in the Area in accordance with the Convention, in particular Part 11 and the 1994 Agreement relating to the Implementation of Part 11 of the United Nations Convention on the Law of the Sea of 10 December 1982?
2. What is the extent of liability of a State Party for any failure to comply with the provisions of the Convention, in particular Part 11, and the 1994 Agreement, by an entity whom it has sponsored under Article 153, paragraph 2(b) of the Convention?
3. What are the necessary and appropriate measures that a sponsoring State must take in order to fulfil its responsibility under the Convention, in particular Article 139 and Annex III, and the 1994 Agreement?[32]

Having heard statements from Member States[33] and from invited intergovernmental and non-governmental organizations[34] the Chamber delivered its opinion as required by Article 191 of the Convention "as a matter of urgency". The Chamber analysed key provisions of the Convention including Article 139, paragraph 1, Article 153, paragraph 4 and Annex III, Article 4, paragraph 4, and enumerated a sponsoring State's direct responsibilities which, if not carried out in accordance with a standard of due diligence, could entail that State's

---

31   For a description of the events leading up to the Request, see Advisory Opinion (hereafter AO), para. 4.
32   Decision of the Council at AO, para. 1.
33   Germany, Netherlands, Argentine Republic, Fiji, Mexico, Nauru, United Kingdom, Russian Federation.
34   International Sea-Bed Authority, Intergovernmental Oceanographic Commission of UNESCO, International Union for the Conservation of Nature and Natural Resources.

liability. It distinguished those responsibilities from the obligations of the State-sponsored private entity which, when breached, would engage that entity's liability, but not that of the sponsoring State, absent a causal link with the latter. The Chamber's wide-ranging Opinion contributes substantially to an appreciation of the responsibilities of States planning to invest in sea-bed activities, in particular the developing countries among them which are likely to engage contractors from the technologically advanced countries.[35] The Chamber is careful to emphasize, however, that preferential treatment provided by the 1982 Convention for developing countries engaging in sea-bed activities through sponsored contractors does not operate to reduce the stringency of provisions concerning their responsibilities and liability when they act as sponsoring States. Those provisions apply equally to all sponsoring States, developing or developed. In that connection the Chamber observes:

> Equality of treatment between developing and developed sponsoring States is consistent with the need to prevent commercial enterprises based in the developed States from setting up companies in developing countries, acquiring their nationality and obtaining their sponsorship in the hope of being subjected to less burdensome regulations and controls. The spread of sponsoring States "of convenience" would jeopardize uniform application of the highest standards of protection of the marine environment, the safe development of activities in the Area and protection of the Common Heritage of Mankind.[36]

***

The Third United Nations Conference on the Law of the Sea that commenced in New York in 1973 and concluded at Montego Bay on 10 December 1982 may have been the last of the great treaty-making conferences. Over a decade, more than 150 States negotiated and adopted by agreed procedures rules to govern the uses of the oceans, including the exploitation of their living and non-living resources, navigation and overflight, protection, and preservation of the marine environment and the resolution of disputes concerning the interpretation or application of the Convention. Whether because of confidence in the Convention's rules that had been adopted in the course of a genuinely cooperative enterprise, taking into account the aspirations of a number of States which had but recently regained their independence; because of emphasis on

---

35   AO, paras. 151–163.
36   AO, para. 159.

policies that sought to attract foreign direct investment; or because of a perceived flexibility and range of choice offered by the Convention's dispute settlement provisions, it seems that Asian States have shown a certain willingness to submit disputes to the procedures offered by the Convention. The capacity shown by the International Tribunal for the Law of the Sea to deal expeditiously and with expert attention to the concerns of the Asian States before it so as to foster recognition of fairness in the outcome may well encourage others to approach the Tribunal in the future.

CHAPTER 41

The State as a Party in Arbitral Proceedings on Settlement of Private Law Disputes – Miscellaneous

Krešimir Sajko*

I   **Introduction**

The jurisdiction of institutions for settlement of private law disputes is bifurcated. Depending on the fulfilment of the prescribed legal requirements, jurisdiction is exercised either by state courts or by arbitration. However, some of these disputes could be solved by other methods of alternative dispute resolution, *i.e.*, by conciliation (mediation) which is provided for by several national laws. At the level of the European Union, such a method is stimulated, *inter alia*, by Directive 2008/52/EC of the European Parliament and of the Council of 21 May 2008 on certain aspects of mediation in civil and commercial matters.[1]

In this paper are analysed some aspects of situations in which a state is a party to arbitral proceedings on settlement of private law disputes. The provisions on these matters are set out in national arbitration laws and in several international conventions.

First we will focus on situations where a state is a party to arbitral proceedings on settlement of investment disputes provided by international conventions whose scope is the protection of investments. That discussion will especially concentrate on some issues regarding bilateral treaties on investment protection (hereinafter: BIT) concluded by Croatia taking into account the consequences of Croatia's accession to the EU on 1 July 2013. Thereafter our analysis will turn to issues dealing with the state's capacity to be a party to arbitral proceedings on the resolution of private law disputes.

I dedicate this paper to my old friend and colleague Professor Budislav Vukas, one of the greatest scholars in the field of international law. In his scientific research and his activities not only as a law professor and former judge at the International Tribunal for the Law of the Sea in Hamburg, but also as a renowned international arbitrator, he displays a great ability to analyse,

---

*   Professor Emeritus of the University of Zagreb; Former Member of the International Court of Arbitration, International Chamber of Commerce; Member of the European Academy of Sciences and Arts (Austria).

1   *Official Journal of the European Union* (hereinafter: *OJ*), L 136, 24 May 2008.

evaluate and judge the most complicated legal matters and provide very strongly argued solutions for them. Therefore I have with great pleasure prepared this paper as I would like it to express my appreciation both for his scientific contributions and for his long friendship.

II   Croatia as a Party to Bilateral Investment Treaties – An Overview

1   *General Remarks*

The settlement of investment disputes between states and nationals of other states is regulated by several multilateral and by many bilateral treaties.

As to the former, the most important is the Washington Convention on the Settlement of Investment Disputes between States and Nationals of other States of 1965 (hereinafter: ICSID Convention) by which the International Centre for Settlement of Investment Disputes (hereinafter: ICSID) was established. There are currently (as of 20 May 2013) 158 signatory states to the ICSID Convention – 149 states have deposited their instruments of ratification, acceptance or approval of the Convention. In Croatia the ICSID Convention entered into force on 22 October 1998.[2] In the Preamble to this Convention it is clearly stated that no contracting state shall by the mere fact of its ratification, acceptance or approval without its consent be deemed to be under any obligation to submit any particular dispute to conciliation or arbitration.[3] The main purpose of the ICSID Convention is to promote increased flows of international investment by facilitating the settlement of investment disputes. Besides, several other multilateral treaties covering specific subject matters also provide dispute resolution by arbitration, such as the Energy Charter Treaty of 1994,[4] the North American Free Trade Agreement of 1992 (hereinafter: NAFTA) and the Central American Free Trade Agreement of 2004.

In addition to the mentioned multilateral conventions, there are a great number of bilateral treaties on settlement of disputes between states and nationals of other states (BITs). The first BIT was concluded between Germany

---

2   See *Croatian Official Gazette, International Treaties*, (hereinafter: *Off. Gaz. IT*), No 13/1998.
3   For the time being there are two pending ICSID arbitration proceedings connected with Croatia. In one, a Croatian company is the claimant – HRVATSKA ELEKTROPRIVREDA d.d. *v.* REPUBLIC OF SLOVENIA, ICSID Case No. ARB/05/24; in the other case Croatia is the respondent – GAVRILOVIĆ & GAVRINOVIĆ d.o.o. *v.* REPUBLIC OF CROATIA, ICSID Case No. ARB/12/39.
4   Croatia ratified the Treaty in 1997; the Treaty entered into force for Croatia on 16 April 1998. For data on other member states, see: <www.encharter.org/index.php>.

and Pakistan in 1959. Since then, more than 2900 have been concluded, some 1700 of which are in force. Since gaining independence in 1991 Croatia has to date concluded 56 such BITS with countries from all continents, except Australia.[5] In doing so, Croatia joined the large family of countries which, through such bilateral treaties, are furthering international acceptance of common standards for the treatment and protection of foreign investment.[6] There is an abounding literature both about the ICSID Convention and the BITS, both in Croatia and abroad.[7]

According to the qualified source, the great majority of arbitration cases were initiated on grounds of violation of BITs, followed by the NAFTA and the Energy Charter Treaty.

It is worth mentioning that in 2012 the number of known treaty-based investor-state dispute cases filed under international investment agreements grew by at least 62. Of that number, 39 were filed with the ICSID, of which 7 cases are under the ICSID Additional Facilities Rules,[8] 5 under the arbitration

---

5 Croatia concluded BITs with the following states: Albania (1993), Argentina (1994), Azerbaijan (2007), Belarus (2001), Belgium-Luxembourg (2001), Bosnia and Herzegovina (1997), Bulgaria (1996), Cambodia (2001), Canada (1997), Chile (1994), China (1993), Cuba (2001), Czech Republic (2008), Denmark (2000), Egypt (1997), Finland (1999), France (1996), Germany (1997), Greece (1996), Hungary (1996), India (2001), Indonesia (2002), Iran (2000), Israel (2000), Italy (1996), Jordan (1999), Republic of Korea (2005), Kuwait (1997), Latvia (2002), Libya (2002), Lithuania (2008), Macedonia (1996), Malaysia (1994), Malta (2001), Moldova (2001), Mongolia (2006), Morocco (2004), Netherlands (1998), Oman (2004), Poland (1995), Portugal (1995), Qatar (2001), Romania (1994), Russian Federation (1996), San Marino (2004), Serbia (1998), Slovak Republic (1998), Slovenia (1997), Spain (1997), Sweden (2000), Switzerland (1996), Thailand (2000), Turkey (2009), Ukraine (1997), United Kingdom of Great Britain and Northern Ireland (1997), USA (1996) and Zimbabwe (2000). The mentioned BITS are published in the *Off. Gaz. IT*. For a complete list of BITs, see the web site of ICSID at: <https://icsid.wordbank.org/ICSID/FrontServlet>; see also the web site of UNCTAD: <unctad.org/en>.

6 Some countries have an official Model BIT, such as United Kingdom, USA and Germany – see more about it, at: <www.unctad.org/en/docs/dtci3ovol3_en.pdf>.

7 As to Croatian works see, *e.g.*, Sajko, "Washington Convention on Settlement of Investment Disputes between States and Nationals of Other States", *Croatian Arbitration Yearbook*, 1999, Vol. 6, 129 *et seq.*; Sajko, "The Settlement of Disputes by Bilateral Investment Treaty: the Croatian Experience", *Uniform Law Review*, 1998, Vol. 3, Nos. 2–3, 657 *et seq.* – As to the comparative law literature see, instead of other works, the excellent commentary on the ICSID Convention published very recently by Schreuer (with Malintoppi, Reinisch and Sinclair), *The ICSID Convention, A Commentary*, 2nd edn., 2009.

8 These Rules have been adopted by the Administrative Council of the ICSID which authorized the Secretariat of the ICSID to administer certain categories of proceedings between states and nationals of other states that fall outside the scope of the ICSID Convention. These Rules – Schedule C) – open ICSID arbitration to disputes (1) where only one side is either the party

rules of UNCITRAL, another 5 under the Stockholm Chamber of Commerce. Of all mentioned cases, 39 were filed by investors from developed countries.[9]

Both, the BITs and other mentioned investments treaties are international instruments between states and are governed by the international law of treaties. The standards of protection are fixed by the respective convention, but liability for their breach gives rise to private law awards rendered by the competent arbitral tribunal.[10] There are, however, problems of enforcement of awards against states in third states. Although this issue is beyond the scope of this paper, it is necessary to make a few general comments. The general solution on enforcement of foreign arbitral awards is provided in the New York Convention on Recognition and Enforcement of Foreign Arbitral Awards of 1958 (hereinafter: New York Convention). This Convention, which is in force in 146 states (as of April 2013), imposes obligations on the party to honour any arbitral award made; however, an implied waiver of immunity from execution of the award could hardly be argued.[11]

The ICSID Convention reiterates this principle as it states that its member states are obliged to recognize and enforce ICSID awards on its territory (Article 54); such an award does not require a special recognition and enforcement procedure like that of the New York Convention, but is instead directly enforceable in any contracting state like a final judgment delivered in that state. However, these general obligations of states shall not be construed as derogation from the law in force in any contracting state relating to the immunity of that state or any foreign state from execution (Article 55). Put differently, a state retains the right to plead that certain sovereign assets remain immune

---

to the ICSID Convention or a national of a party to the ICSID Convention, and (2) which do not arise directly out of any investment, provided that at least one side is either a party to the ICSID Convention or a national of a party to the ICSID Convention. The Rules' latest amendments came into force on 10 April 2006.

9 In addition, concerning arbitrations initiated in 2012, the ICC International Court of Arbitration and the Cairo Regional Centre for International Commercial Arbitration received one case each. For more on these and other data see the website of UNCTAD at: <www.unctad.org/diae>. – On similarities and differences between ICSID and non-ICSID arbitration see Bernardini, "ICSID Versus Non-ICSID Investment Treaty Arbitration", in: *Liber Amicorum Cremades*, 2010, 158 *et seq.*

10 For more about it see, among others, Douglas, "The Hybrid Foundations of Investment Treaty Arbitration", *British Year Book International Law*, 2003, Vol. 74, 152 *et seq.*

11 See, *e.g.*, Fox, *The Law of State Immunity*, 2nd edn., 2008, 496. It has to be pointed out that the application of the New York Convention to ICSID awards is debatable, but the legal doctrine seems to admit it; see Poudret, Besson, *Comparative Law on International Arbitration*, 2nd edn., 2007, 815 *et seq.*

from execution under the law of the enforcing state, even if the state has waived its immunity as to jurisdiction.[12]

It has to be noted that the scope of immunity is governed by public international law, established in treaty law as well as customary law. Over the centuries foreign states were considered to enjoy absolute immunity from jurisdiction and measures of execution in courts other than their own, but at present most countries follow a restrictive immunity doctrine;[13] the first multilateral treaty which reflected such a shift was the European Convention on State Immunity of 1972, which came into force on 11 June 1976. Pursuant to Article 12 of this Convention, a contracting state, if it has agreed to submit in writing to arbitration a dispute which has arisen or may arise out of a civil or commercial matter, may not claim immunity from the jurisdiction of a court of another contracting state on the territory or according to the law of which the arbitration has taken or will take place in respect of any proceedings relating to: (a) the validity or interpretation of the arbitration agreement, (b) the arbitration procedure, (c) the setting aside of the award, unless the arbitration agreement otherwise provides.

Further, without entering into detail on sources of law regarding exception to state immunity from jurisdiction and post-judgment measures of constraint, the UN Convention on Jurisdictional Immunities of States and Their Property of 2004, which is not yet in force, has to be mentioned. Article 17 of the mentioned Convention refers to effects of an arbitration agreement and Article 19 lists exceptions to state immunity from post-judgment measures of constraint.[14] Next, it has to be pointed out that some national laws, such as the US

---

12 Compare, *e.g.*, Miles, "Sovereign Immunity", in: *Enforcement of Arbitral Awards against Sovereigns* (Doak Bishop, ed.), 2009, 42 *et passim*. – In conjunction with these issues, it is worth mentioning the position of the French *Cour de cassation* expressed in its judgment on enforcement of the ICSID award *SOABI* v. *Senegal* (ARB/82/1 of 25 February 1988). According to the *Cour de cassation*, for the purpose of state immunity, a distinction is to be made between *exequatur*, *i.e.*, the procedure on the basis of which judgments are recognized and declared enforceable in the state addressed, and *enforcement* in the strict sense, *i.e.*, effective enforcement measures against property belonging to it, but situated in a foreign territory; see, *Cour de cassation*, Judgment of 11 June 1991, *Revue de l'arbitrage*, 1991, 657.

13 See more about it in Lew, Mistelis, Kroell, *Comparative International Commercial Arbitration*, 2003, 274 *et seq.*; see also Andrassy, Bakotić, Seršić, Vukas, *Međunarodno pravo* [*International Law*], Part 1, 2nd edn., 2010, 118.

14 According to, *e.g.*, the Swiss case law and doctrine, this Convention, based on the theory of restrictive immunity, has the status of trade usage – see *e.g.* Swiss Federal Tribunal decision of 19 June 1980; *Socialist People's Libyan Arab Republic Jamahiriya* v. *Libyan*

Foreign Sovereign Immunities Act 1976 (Title 28, US Code, section 1605 (a) (1)) amended in 1988 by subsection 6 to permit an action to enforce an arbitration agreement to which a foreign state was a party, the UK's State Immunity Act 1978 (section 9) and the Canadian State Immunity Act 1985, lay down that a state is sovereign, but that it may waive its sovereign immunity explicitly or implicitly by entering into certain agreements, such as to arbitrate disputes with private parties.[15]

American Oil Company (*LIAMCO*), ATF 106 Ia 142; *Moscow Center for Automated Air Traffic Control* contre *Commission de surveillance des offices des poursuites et des faillites du canton de Genève* – Judgment of 15 August 2007, *ASA Bulletin*, 2008, Vol. 26, No. 1, 141 *et seq.*; see also the decision of 12 July 2010 – ATF 136 III 575, 5 A. That Tribunal views immunity as a single concept and makes little distinction between immunity from jurisdiction and immunity from execution – ATS 124 III 322; it distinguishes between matters involving foreign states acting in their sovereign capacity – *de iure imperii* – and those involving foreign states acting in their private capacity – *de iure gestionis* (*activité économique privé*); in the latter cases, sovereign immunity from jurisdiction may be lifted, provided that the matter has an *appropriate* connection with Switzerland (*rattachement suffisant*; *Binnenbeziehung*), and further, as regards immunity from execution – *les biens saisis en Suisse ne doivent pas être affectés à des tâches incombant à l'Etat comme détenteur de la puissance publique*. For more about it see, *e.g.*, Giroud, "Enforcement against States Assets and Execution of ICSID Awards in Switzerland: How Swiss Courts Deal with Immunity Defences", *ASA Bulletin*, 2012, Vol. 30, No. 4, 758 *et seq.* – As regards immunity from execution let us mention the decision of the French *Cour de cassation* of 6 July 2000 in *Creighton v. Qatar*, ICC arbitration award of October 1993 (*Yearbook Commercial Arbitration*, 2000, Vol. 25, 458); relying on Article 24 of the then applicable ICC Rules, which since 1 January 2012 have been laid down in Article 36(6), – by which the parties have undertaken to carry out any award without delay and to have waived their right to any form of recourse insofar as such waiver can validly be made – the Court found that in agreeing to ICC arbitration, a state waives not only its immunity from jurisdiction but also its immunity from execution. – See also Swedish Supreme Court decision of 1 July 2011, *Sedelmayer v. Russian Federation*, Case OE 170–10, according to which "enforcement measures are permitted with respect to (state) property that is used or intended to be used for commercial purposes, even if the state has not rescinded its immunity" (point 9 of the grounds – unofficial translation). – But see *DR Congo v. FG Hemisphere Associates* – 2011 HKEC 747 – an overruled judgment of the Hong Kong's Court of Final Appeal of 8. June 2011 which held that no state may be sued in Hong Kong's courts unless the state waives its immunity and that submission to arbitration does not constitute a waiver, <http://asia.legalbusinessonline.com/news/analysis/106870/details.aspx> (last visit, May 2013).

15   For details on these national laws see Oparil, "Waiver of Sovereign Immunity in the US and Great Britain by an Arbitration Agreement", *Journal of International Arbitration*, 1986, Vol. 3, No. 4, 61 *et passim*.

The mentioned shift to the restrictive immunity doctrine is accepted in several national laws dealing with international arbitration; thus the state's capacity to conclude an arbitration agreement is explicitly provided, *inter alia*, in the 1987 Swiss Law on Private International Law (Article 177(2)) and in the 2001 Croatian Law on Arbitration (Article 7(2)) involving disputes on property, *i.e.*, regarding rights the parties may freely dispose of (for details about it see the analysis below in section III. of this paper).

Let us turn now again to BITs.

Generally, the contracting parties of BITs determine the manner, the scope and the methods of mutual promotion and protection of investment. They regulate the legal status and manner of protecting investments that natural and legal persons from one contracting state make in the other contracting state and, *inter alia*, the mechanisms of resolution of dispute settlements between both the contracting states and the investors and their host contracting state.

To date in Croatia there are 50 BITs in force, of which 21 are with EU countries and the rest with other states.[16]

Croatia became a member of the European Union on 1 July 2013. Since that date the law of the EU has been a part of the Croatian legal system. Further on we will analyse the consequences of this accession to the BITs which are in force in Croatia, upon which we are going to examine some issues regarding the scope of application and jurisdiction for settlement of disputes according to the BITs between Croatia and extra-EU states.

2 Consequences of the Accession of Croatia to the EU on Its BITs

With the entry into force of the Lisbon Treaty on the Functioning of the European Union on 1 December 2009 (hereinafter: TFEU),[17] the Union has exclusive competence with respect to the common commercial policy (Articles 3(1)(e) and 207(1)). According to its Article 207, foreign direct investments have been added to the exclusive external trade competence of the Union. Despite the fact that foreign direct investments are not defined in the EU Treaties, it seems that the European Commission assumes that all issues which are regulated in BITs – such as MFN, national treatment, fair and equitable treatment and dispute settlement procedure – fall under the new exclusive competence of the EU.

---

16 See ICSID database of all BITs concluded by Croatia, available at: <https://icsid.worldbank.org/ICSID>; and *supra*, note 5.

17 See the consolidated version of this Treaty, *OJ*, C 115, 9 May 2008.

Pursuant to Article 2(1) of the TFEU, in matters within such exclusive competences of the Union only the Union may legislate and adopt legally binding acts, whereas the member states can do so themselves only if empowered by the Union or for implementation of Union acts. In line with such division of legislative competences is Regulation (EU) No. 1219/2012 of the European Parliament and of the Council of 12 December 2012 establishing transitional arrangement for bilateral investment agreements between member states and third countries which came into force on 9 January 2013 (hereinafter: Regulation).[18] The Regulation addresses the status of the bilateral investment agreements of the member states under Union law and establishes the terms and conditions and the procedure under which the member states are authorized to amend or conclude bilateral investment agreements (Article 1(1));[19] the mentioned competence is extended to bilateral investment treaties concluded between EU member states and third countries; it is not applicable to so-called intra-EU BITs, *i.e.*, to BITs concluded between two EU member states.

At the time of writing, there were altogether over 1,000 such extra-EU BITs in existence.

The Regulation provides how member states and the EU will enforce existing extra-EU BITs and negotiate new such treaties; in addition it envisages that in future the Commission itself is going to prepare bilateral investment treaties that will replace existing BITs entered into by member states.

According to Article 2 of the Regulation, by 8 February 2013 or within 30 days of the date of its accession to the Union, the member state shall notify the Commission of all bilateral investment agreements with third countries signed before 1 December 2009 or before the date of its accession, whichever is later, that it either wishes to maintain in force or permit to enter into force. However, without prejudice to other obligations of the member states under Union law, such notified bilateral investments agreements may be maintained in force or enter into force in accordance with the TFEU and this Regulation until a bilateral investment agreement between the Union and the same third country enters into force.

Furthermore, the Commission shall authorize the member states to open formal negotiations with a third country to amend or conclude a bilateral investment agreement, unless it concludes that the opening of such negotiation would be contrary to requirements very precisely set up in the Regulation (Article 9).

---

18   *OJ*, L 351, 20 December 2012.
19   According to the Regulation, bilateral investment agreement means any agreement with a third country that contains provisions on investment protection, and it covers only those provisions of such agreements dealing with investment protection (Article 1(2)).

In the event that a dispute arises from existing, amended or newly executed extra-EU BITs, the Commission will have the right to participate in the proceedings in order to ensure the best defence against any claim (Article 13).

It is quite obvious that the existing extra-EU BITs would be substantially changed in the near future which would include their provisions on dispute settlements.

At present, there are 29 such BITs which are in force in Croatia;[20] it is difficult to predict whether Croatia, now upon accession to the EU would wish to maintain in force all or only some of such BITs, which would be its option according to the already mentioned Article 2 of the Regulation.

Be that as it may, further on we are going to concentrate our discussion on some very important matters covered by such BITs, *i.e.*, on their rules determining the scope of their application *ratione personae* and competent organs for dispute settlement.[21]

3 BITs between Croatia and Extra-EU States – An Overview on BITs' Application Ratione Personae and on Their Dispute Settlement Provisions

BITs make uniform the legal regime of promotion and protection of investments of natural and legal persons of one contracting state in the other contracting state. The determination of such persons is regulated by the definition of the term *investor*.

The nationality of a natural person is assessed under municipal law to the extent that that law is in compliance with international conventions, international custom and principles of law generally recognized with regard to nationality, such as the European Convention on Nationality of 1997[22] and conventions on human rights.[23]

For natural persons the term *investor* means nationals of a contracting state. Sometimes, domestic nationals are equated with natural persons having

---

20   See complete list of all BITs concluded by Croatia – *supra*, note 5.
21   Let us repeat: a typical BIT is essentially designed to cover, *inter alia*, the following procedural and substantial subject matters: definition of investment and investor, admission of foreign investors, standards of treatment of foreign investments and investors, compensation in the event of expropriation, damage or loss, methods of dispute resolution; the latter refers both to state-state and investor-state dispute resolutions.
22   This Convention is not yet in force in Croatia.
23   For more about it see Sasson, *Substantive Law in Investment Treaty Arbitration, Unsettled Relationship between International Law and Municipal Law*, 2010, 63.

permanent residence on the territory of that state.[24] The conventions do not resolve the issues of their application to natural persons having the nationality of both contracting states – thus dual nationals are not prevented from bringing a claim against the host state[25] – nor the question of the BIT application to the investors, *i.e.*, natural persons that had become *beneficiaries* of the BIT as nationals of a contracting state but have lost that nationality over time.[26]

Under the ICSID Convention, a natural person must satisfy two conditions before being entitled to participate in the arbitration proceedings – he must be a national of a state which is a party to the Convention and must *not* be a national of the host state.[27] The critical date for the determination of such nationality is the date on which the parties consented to submit the dispute to arbitration as well the date on which the request was registered.[28]

As to the BIT's application to legal persons, it is simply required that the entity is incorporated or constituted under the law of one of the contracting parties. The definitions of investors are often broad enough to include juridical persons, companies and economic subjects. Some BITs require in addition that entities have their seat in the relevant state.[29]

---

24 See BIT with Malaysia (Article 1(2)(c)(1)); BIT with Canada (Article 1(e)).

25 Such approach is taken, *e.g.*, by Switzerland – see Burger, "Swiss Bilateral Investment Treaties: A Survey", *Journal of International Arbitration*, 2010, Vol. 27, No. 5, 475. This possibility is however excluded by the ICSID Convention, as it provides that a person may not bring a claim against the state of which he is a national (Article 25(2)(a)). – In BITs concluded between other contracting states, the issue of dual nationals is rarely regulated expressly. One exception is the Protocol to the Agreement between Israel and Romania of 2 September 1991, expressly regulating that if a person being a national of both contracting states invests in Israel, such person shall not be considered a Romanian national according to Israeli law. Therefore, the Agreement adopts a general legal principle with respect to multi-nationality; if one of the nationalities is domestic, only the domestic nationality shall be taken into account. Such an approach is generally adopted in several national laws on citizenship and on Private International Law, *e.g.*, in the Croatian Law on Citizenship of 1991 (Art. 2) and in the Croatian Law on Private International Law of 1991 (Art. 11(1)). On issues of multi-nationality in private international law in general *cf.* Sajko, *Međunarodno privatno pravo* [*Private International Law*], 5th edn., 2009, 121 *et seq.*

26 In the ICSID arbitration award entitled *Hussein Nuaman Soufraki* v. *United Arab Emirates*, the Tribunal declined jurisdiction under the Italy-UAE BIT because the claimant had lost his Italian nationality upon acquiring the Canadian one – he was therefore no longer a protected *investor* under the mentioned BIT (ICSID Case No ARB/02/7, IIC 131 (2004)).

27 See Article 25(2)(a) in reference to Article 25(1) of the ICSID Convention.

28 Article 25(2)(a) of the ICSID Convention.

29 See BIT with Switzerland (Article 1(1)(b)), Albania (Article 1(3)(b)) and Argentina (Article 1(2)(b)).

The nationality requirement for juridical persons has to be fulfilled only on the date of the consent to arbitration, if the ICSID Convention is applicable[30] – any change in the juridical person's nationality after that date is irrelevant.

In addition, according to some BITs, corporations incorporated in the host state may be protected if they are controlled by entities incorporated in the other contracting state,[31] which solution is in line with Article 25(1)(b) of the ICSID Convention; according to this provision, if a juridical person has the nationality of the host state, the parties are allowed to agree to treat it, on the basis of foreign control, as a national of another contracting state. Expressed differently, by BITs the protection could be extended to legal persons effectively controlled directly or indirectly by nationals of one of the contracting parties or by legal persons having their registered office in the territory of one of the contracting parties and constituted in accordance with the legislation of the latter.[32]

In BITs concluded by Croatia there is no reference to the critical dates for foreign control. It is held that such foreign control must exist, if ICSID is applicable, at the time of consent to such arbitration proceedings.[33]

Only if the parties cannot resolve the dispute amicably, by means of negotiations, is the dispute referred to the competent authority.[34] BITs often provide a period during which attempts should be made to resolve the dispute by negotiations. The commencement of that period sometimes is *the date of*

---

30 For more about the issue of the mentioned critical time see Petrochilos, Noury et al., in: *Concise International Arbitration* (Mistelis, ed.), 2010, 72 et seq. There are several ICSID arbitral decisions on investor nationality: *Tokios Tokeles* v. *Ukraine*, Decision on jurisdiction, 29 April 2004, ICSID Rev. FILJ 20 (2005), 205; dissenting opinion, 245, para. 21; *Plama Consortium* v. *Bulgaria*, Decision on jurisdiction, 8 February 2005, ICSID – FILJ 20 (2008), 13, 268; *Czechoslovenska Obchodni Banka A.S.* v. *Slovak Republic*, Decision on jurisdiction, 24 May 1999, ICSID Case No. ARB/97/4, ICSID Report 13 (2008), 178; *Hussein Nuaman Soufraki* v. *United Arab Emirates*, Award, 7 July 2004, ICSID Case No. ARB/02/7, ICSID Report 12 (2007) 156.

31 The BIT with Switzerland (Article 1(1)(c)) and with Kuwait (Articles 1, 2(2) and (3)).

32 See such BIT provisions, *ibid*. The ICSID Convention left the term control undefined. On further issues regarding control see Redfern, Hunter et al., *Redfern and Hunter on International Arbitration*, 2009, 472.

33 It is debatable whether subsequent foreign control changes have to be taken into account – see on this point the ICSID tribunal decision in *Amco* v. *Indonesia*, ICSID Case No. ARB/81/1.

34 See the details on the comparative analysis of typical dispute settlement provisons in *e.g.*, McLachlan, Shore, Weiniger, *International Investment Arbitration*, 2007, 46 et seq.

written notice submitted to the host of investment by the investor[35] or *the date on which the dispute arose.*[36]

The period for reaching an amicable settlement is usually set at six month,[37] while a few BITs give the parties only three months.[38] Without such provisions – by the mere vague determination that the dispute should be attempted to be resolved amicably before it is submitted to the competent authority – the question of the time limits of such negotiation period could arise in practice.

The BITs concluded by Croatia contain elaborate provisions on dispute resolution, offering to the investors, as a rule, more than one jurisdiction.

The BITs provide for selective jurisdiction, such as jurisdictions of competent courts of the host state accepting the investment, the ICSID[39] and the *ad hoc* arbitral tribunal in accordance with the UNCITRAL Arbitration Rules.[40]

According to some BITs, the alternative jurisdiction of the ICC International Arbitration Court is also provided.[41]

---

35   BIT with Canada, Article XII(2): "A dispute is considered to be initiated...when investor has delivered notice in writing to the other Contracting Party alleging that a measure taken by the latter Contracting Party is in breach..."
36   BIT with the USA (Article 10(3)(a)). See for more about these issues Sajko, "Arbitration under BITs concluded between Croatia and other states", *Croatian Arbitration Yearbook*, 1998, Vol. 5, 131 *et seq.*
37   BIT with China (Article 8(2)).
38   BIT with Chile (Article 8(2)).
39   See, *e.g.*, BITs with Chile (Article 8(2)), Italy (Art. 9(3)(a)) and BIT with Albania: "...competent court of the Contracting Party, an arbitral tribunal applying UNCITRAL Arbitration Rules, but after the Contracting Parties would become members of the ICSID, this institution..." (Art. 10).
40   BIT with Argentina (Article 9(2) and (3)); also BIT with Macedonia, but without reference to the jurisdiction of the ICSID (Article 7(3)). The Russian Federation is not yet a member state of the ICSID Convention. The BIT between Croatia and that state of 1996, which is however not yet in force, alternatively provides for the jurisdiction of a court or an arbitration of the contracting state accepting the investment, the arbitration court at the Stockholm Chamber of Commerce or an *ad hoc* arbitral tribunal set up according to the UNCITRAL Arbitration Rules (Article 8); these Rules of 1976 were revised in 2010. The BIT with Canada provides alternatively for the jurisdiction of the ICSID, its Additional Facilities Rules and UNCITRAL Rules (Article XII). The ICSID Convention is not yet in force in Canada (as of November 2012); the choice of the ICSID rules is available only when both contracting parties are bound by the ICSID Convention, and the choice of the rules of the ICSID Additional Facility is available provided that one or the other contracting party, but not both, is a party to the ICSID Convention.
41   Pursuant to the 2009 Protocol concluded with Turkey which amended the 1996 BIT, upon negotiations and consultation in good faith the investor has a choice among the national courts of the host state, ICSID, *ad hoc* Arbitral Tribunal under UNCITRAL Arbitration Rules, and ICC Arbitration Court (Article 7).

These clauses contain the states' advance consent to all of them at the parties' choice – a reference to the ICSID jurisdiction is one of several possibilities.[42] The BITs contain the host state's offer which may be taken up by a national of the other state party to the treaty. It is accepted that the fact that the state's written consent in a BIT and the investor's written consent in the request for arbitration – although such consents are not contained in the same document – could not be an obstacle for the qualification of such consent either under the requirement of Article 25 of the ICSID Convention for *consent in writing* or the requirement in Article II of the New York Convention for an *agreement in writing*;[43] upon such consent, no party may withdraw its consent unilaterally. It is worth noting that some national investment laws also provide unequivocally for dispute settlement by ICSID.

Consent of the parties to the jurisdiction of the ICSID shall, unless otherwise stated, be deemed consent to such arbitration to the exclusion of any other remedy, but a contracting state may require the exhaustion of local administrative remedies as a condition of its consent to arbitration under that Convention[44]; in line with this approach, some BITs try to limit the occurrence of parallel proceedings through fork-in-the-road clauses which state that a choice of a particular dispute procedure once taken forecloses the possibility of electing any other available dispute procedure.[45]

Generally, for establishing jurisdiction of the ICSID, pursuant to Article 25(1) of the Washington Convention the following requirements have to be

---

42   The BIT with the USA (Art. 10) offers several methods of settlement but specifies that choice among them is with the investor – the courts of the party that is a party to the dispute, ICSID, or in accordance with the UNCITRAL Arbitration Rules. Compare similar clause of the BIT between Switzerland and Paraguay of 1993 (Art. 9).

43   Such position has been taken also in a case when the parties had elected within the US-Ecuador BIT *ad hoc* arbitration under UNCITRAL Rules; thus even in such a case, although an investment treaty award is not made under the ICSID Convention, it will be enforceable under the New York Convention as having been made pursuant to a written agreement; see *Republic of Ecuador v. Occidental Exploration and Production Co*, (2005) EWHC 774 (Comm); 2005 2 Lloyd's Rep 240, 249.

44   Pursuant to Article 25(3) of the ICSID Convention, consent by a constituent subdivision or agency of a contracting state shall require the approval of that state unless that state notifies the Centre that no such approval is required.

45   See, *e.g.*, the BIT with Turkey (Article 7(3)), and Article 9(2) of the BIT with Argentina which reads: "Once an investor has submitted the dispute to the courts of the Contracting Party concerned or to international arbitration, the choice of one or the other of these proceedings is final [...*la elección de uno u otro de esos procedimientos será definitiva*]"; for more about such provisions see, among others, McLachlan, Shore, Weiniger, *op. cit.*, *supra*, note 34, 103 *et seq.*

fulfilled: the dispute must be a legal dispute arising directly out of an investment between a contracting state or one of its constituent subdivisions or agencies designated to the ICSID by that state, and a national of another contracting state.[46]

If a request for arbitration is submitted to the ICSID, the proceedings should be according to the ICSID Convention and its Arbitration Rules. However, if BITs provide for the jurisdiction of a court of the state accepting the investment or of an arbitral tribunal in accordance with UNCITRAL Arbitration Rules, the applicable procedural rules would in the first case be those of the *lex arbitri*, *i.e.*, by the law of the state of the place of arbitration, and in the latter case, by the mentioned Rules which provide a comprehensive set of procedural rules covering all aspects of arbitral proceedings; these Rules govern the arbitration except that where any of these Rules are in conflict with provisions of the law applicable to the arbitration from which the parties cannot derogate (Article 1(3) of the Rules as revised in 2010).

Taking into account international practice, disputes in the framework of BITs are mostly settled before the ICSID.[47]

III   A State as a Party to an Arbitration Agreement

1   *Introductory Remarks*

Upon the foregoing analysis of the chosen issues on settlement of disputes according to BITs, we turn now to the examination of some questions on the state's capacity to be a party to an arbitration agreement according to national arbitration laws and some international conventions.

It has to be recalled that both *subjective* arbitrability, the capacity of a party to conclude an arbitration agreement, and *objective* arbitrability are conditions of the validity of the arbitration agreement.

The state's capacity, as mentioned, will be discussed after a comparative law overview of the mentioned objective arbitrability, *i.e.*, arbitrability *ratione materiae*.

---

46   In the case of arbitration before the ICSID, the parties may use the ICSID Model clauses; see these clauses on the website at: <https://icsid.worldbank.org/ICSID/FrontServlet?actionVal=Model>.

47   As regards, *e.g.*, the German BITs, most of them provide for arbitration under ICSID Rules – see for more about it Escher, Nacimiento, Weissenborn, in: *Arbitration in Germany* (Böckstiegel, Kröll, Nacimiento, eds.), 2007, 1034 *et seq.* For details on arbitral decisions made in 2012 see *supra*, *ad* II.1.

The UNCITRAL Model Law permits each implementing state to exclude from its scope of application all disputes which are not, in that state, capable of being submitted to arbitration, or are arbitrable only according to provisions other than those of the Model Law (Article 1(5)).

According to some modern laws, arbitrability *ratione materiae* is extended to all pecuniary claims (*cause de nature patrimoniale*; *vermögensrechtlicher Anspruch*) – e.g., Article 177(1) of the Swiss Statute on Private International Law, Article 1030(1) of the German ZPO and Article 582(1) of the Austrian Code on Civil Procedure. According to the mentioned laws, non-pecuniary claims are arbitrable as well, if the parties are capable of concluding a settlement upon the matter of the dispute. These laws are an example of a general tendency in both statutory and case law to enlarge the range of arbitrable disputes in such a manner.

Other national laws, case law and commentary provide variations on the criteria for such arbitrability. Matters considered arbitrable include, under Chinese law, contractual disputes and other disputes over rights and interests in property (Article 2 of the Arbitration Law), under Bulgarian law, civil property disputes (Article 1(2) of the Law on International Commercial Arbitration), under Russian law, disputes arising from contractual and other civil-law relations in foreign trade and other types of international economic relationship (Article 1(2) of the Arbitration Act), and under Spanish law, disputes relating to matters within the disposition (*libre disposition*) of the parties (Article 2(1) of the Arbitration Law).

According to Croatian law, matters regarding rights of which parties may freely dispose are arbitrable (Article 3(1) of the Arbitration Law); arbitrable disputes include not only disputes regarding pecuniary claims, but also those regarding non-pecuniary claims in respect of which parties may reach a settlement (*Vergleich*), i.e., conclude such private law contract defined by the law governing such a contract.

As has been mentioned already above, private law disputes could be settled by mediation/conciliation, too;[48] according to the Directive of the European Parliament and of the Council of 2008 on certain aspects of mediation in civil and commercial matters – Article 1(2) – states could be parties to the mediation proceedings excepting their liability for acts and omissions in exercise of their authority (*acta iure imperii*); expressed differently, the Directive is applicable to states' disputes on rights/obligations which are not qualified as *acta iure imperii*.

---

48 See *supra*, *ad* I. of this paper.

Let us repeat: the analysed *objective* arbitrability/arbitrability *ratione materiae*, together with the capacity of a party to enter into an arbitration agreement – *subjective* arbitrability – is a condition of the validity of the arbitration agreement.[49] A party, a physical or legal person interested in solving its legal dispute through arbitral proceedings, has to fulfil these requirements. In other words, whether a state or other legal person of public law could validly enter into an arbitration agreement depends on its fulfilment of requirements set up *in casu*, both of arbitrability *ratione materiae*, as dealt with above, and of arbitrability *ratione personae*.

2   On the Capacity of a State to Conclude a Valid Arbitration Agreement

The capacity of a person, either physical or legal, to bind itself by an arbitration agreement is generally governed by its personal law. According to certain national laws, the state cannot validly submit to arbitration. Conversely, several national arbitration laws and some international conventions provide such capacity not only to states but also to other legal persons of public law.[50]

In several national laws on arbitration it is provided that states have capacity to enter into arbitration agreements. Such rules are contained, *inter alia*, in the Swiss Private International Law Act of 1987, the Croatian Law of 2001,[51] the Portuguese Law of 2011, the Spanish Law on Arbitration of 2003, as amended in 2009 and 2011, the Serbian Law of 2006 and the Slovenian Law of 2008.

In the Austrian law, there are no provisions prohibiting the state or state agencies from resorting to arbitration. Pursuant to the German case law, states parties cannot invoke immunity from jurisdiction if they have consented to an arbitration agreement.[52]

Some of these Laws refer only to international arbitration, such as the Bulgarian Law on International Arbitration (Article 3), the Spanish Law on Arbitration (Article 2(1)) and the Swiss Private International Law Act (Article 177(2)). On the other hand, according to the Serbian (Article 5(2)), Croatian (Article 7(2)), Slovenian (Article 4(2)) and Portuguese Laws (Article 1(5)), provisions on the capacity of a state to conclude an arbitration agreement relate to both domestic and international arbitration.

---

49   See about it, among others, Sajko, "Intellectual Property Rights and Arbitration – Miscellaneous", in: *Liber Amicorum Joseph Straus*, 2009, 455.
50   See Redfern and Hunter, *op. cit.*, *supra*, note 32, 96.
51   Article 7(2) of the Croatian Law on Arbitration provides that the Republic of Croatia and its units may conclude arbitration agreements and be parties to an arbitration dispute.
52   See Escher, Nacimiento, Weissenborn, *op. cit.*, *supra*, note 47, 1046.

Further, it has to be pointed out that some of the mentioned rules refer only to a state or a state agency (Bulgarian Law), others to its own state and other persons of domestic public law (Slovenian Law), to its own state and its own units of local and regional self-government (Croatian Law) or to the state and other legal entities governed by public law (Portuguese Law). A larger scope of application is provided, *e.g.*, in the Serbian law, as it covers a state, its instrumentalities, institutions and companies in which a state has property interests.

Attention should be paid to Article 1(5) of the Portuguese Law on Voluntary Arbitration of 2011, according to which the state and other legal entities of public law may enter into an arbitration agreement if such agreement concerns private law matters; thereby, in the same provision, arbitrability *ratione personae* and *materiae* is set up for the mentioned legal entities.

It is worth noting the difference between the Swiss and Spanish provisions and all other mentioned national rules.

According to Article 177(2) of the mentioned Swiss Law, a state cannot invoke its own law in order to contest its capacity to arbitrate or the arbitrability of a dispute covered by the arbitration agreement. Similarly, Article 2(2) of the Spanish Law provides that – where the arbitration is international, and one of the parties is a state – that party shall not be able to invoke the prerogatives of its own law in order to avoid the obligations arising from the arbitration agreement. Conversely, other above-mentioned laws just contain a general rule on the capacity of the state to enter into arbitration agreements.

The analysed rules on the capacity of states validly to submit to arbitration refer to the settlement of disputes involving property or regarding rights of which they may freely dispose, *i.e.*, to the objective arbitrability. The latter concept is generally defined by national laws (see more about it *supra*, under section III.1. of this paper) and by some international conventions, as regards the confinement of its scope *ratione materiae*. Thus, *e.g.*, according to the New York Convention the contracting states are entitled to confine the Convention's scope of application "only to differences arising out of legal relationships...which are considered as commercial under the national laws of the State making such declaration" (Article 1(3)(2)). Next, the ICSID Convention provides for jurisdiction of the Centre in respect of "any legal dispute arising out of an investment" (Article 25(1)), and the European Convention on International Commercial Arbitration of 1961 (hereinafter: European Convention)[53] is applicable to arbitration agreements concluded for the purpose of settling disputes arising from "international trade" (Article 1(1)(a)).

---

53   At present (summer 2013), the European Convention is in force in almost all East European countries and in several West European states. See the list of the contracting states at: <http://treaties.un.org/pages/Show/MTDSGDetails.aspx>.

As to the interpretation of the mentioned wording of the European Convention – settlement of *international trade disputes* – according to the award in *Benteler* v. *Belgium*, this term is self-contained; it is an autonomous concept and thus could not be defined according to *lex arbitri*.[54] Within the mentioned treaty framework, legal persons considered by the law which is applicable to them as *legal persons of public law* have the right to conclude valid arbitration agreements; this substantive international treaty rule of Article 11(1) refers also to states. By this rule, national restrictions on entering into arbitration agreements of such persons, which still exist in some national laws, are of no effect; it is held that this provision, expressing the principle of a *common law of arbitration*, prevents a state from relying on its own law to contest its own consent to arbitrate.[55] However if a state wishes to limit this facility, it should act accordingly on signing, ratifying or acceding to the Convention (Article 11(2)).[56]

The lack of capacity of a party to enter into an arbitration agreement is ground for recourse to a court against a domestic arbitral award, by an application for setting aside according to several national arbitration laws and for refusing recognition and enforcement of a foreign arbitral award as laid down in the New York Convention – see *e.g.*, Articles 36 and 40 of the Croatian Arbitration Law, paras. 1059 and 1061 of the German Arbitration Law and Article V(1)(a) of the New York Convention; this ground has to be pleaded by the party opposing the setting aside, *i.e.* recognition.

Such capacity is determined by the national law of a party to the arbitration agreement and not to by the *lex arbitri* of the seat; it is held that the capacity to arbitrate for legal persons is determined, *e.g.*, according to Article 17(2) of the Croatian Law on Private International Law, by the law of the place of incorporation. However, in our opinion it is acceptable that states and state enterprises may not rely on their own law to avoid obligations freely entered into – they should be precluded from doing so under the *venire contra factum proprium* principle, especially where such party has not invoked the lack of capacity during the arbitral proceedings; this principle has been expressed, *e.g.*, in the European Convention on State Immunity of 1972 (sketchily analysed in this paper above, *ad* 11.1.).

As already pointed out above in this paper, the substantive rules contained in Article 177(2) of the Swiss Statute of Private International Law and Article 2(2) of the Spanish Law on Arbitration confirm the capacity of a state to enter

---

54   *Benteler* v. *Belgium*, Interim Award, 18 November 1983 – X, YBCA 1985, 37 *et seq.*
55   *Ibid.*; for different views see, *inter alia*, Poudret, Besson, *op. cit.*, *supra*, note 11, 192 *et seq.*
56   Some limitations have been made by Belgium, Latvia and Luxembourg (as of 1 November 2012).

into an arbitration agreement in international matters. Should it be taken into account in third states, *e.g.*, in Croatia, where the application for recognition and enforcement of such an award is made, in case the state against which the award is invoked relies on its own law on capacity?[57]

IV   Concluding Remarks

This paper has focused on different issues connected with situations where a state is a party in arbitral proceedings on private law disputes.

Whether and to what degree a state enjoys immunity from the arbitration jurisdiction and from post-judgment measures of constraint is provided by public international law, *i.e.*, international treaties as well as customary law. Over the centuries foreign states were considered to enjoy absolute immunity from jurisdiction and measures of execution in courts, but at present most countries follow a restrictive doctrine of state immunity as regards private law mattes in which states are engaged.

Croatia became a member of the EU on 1 July 2013, and thus it has to apply, *inter alia*, Regulation (EU) No. 1219/2012 of the European Parliament and of the Council of 12 December 2012 establishing transitional arrangements for bilateral investment agreements between member states and third countries – in that context the paper analyses the provisions of bilateral investment agreements (BIT) concluded between Croatia and non-EU member states on their scope *ratione materiae* and *personae* and on competent organs for the resolution of disputes between investors and host states.

In addition, special attention was paid to the examination of some international conventions and different national arbitration law provisions on the state's capacity to conclude arbitration agreements; the number of such national laws providing such capacity is increasing. The mentioned capacity is governed by the national law of the state, but in the author's opinion a state could not rely on its own law to avoid obligations, if it has freely concluded such an agreement.

Zagreb, 29 August 2013

---

57   Analysing the application of Article VII(1) of the New York Convention – most favourable laws – in such a case is not within the scope of this paper; for more about it see, *inter alia*, Mistelis, Di Pietro, in: Mistelis, ed., *op. cit.*, *supra*, note 30, 24 *et seq.*

CHAPTER 42

Of Courts and Competition: Dispute Settlement under Part XV of UNCLOS

*Philippe Sands**

I am delighted to offer a contribution to celebrate the work of Professor Budislav Vukas, whom I came to know in 1985, in the context of the Telders Moot competition. He has made a particularly significant contribution to our understanding of the law of the sea, in his writings and as one of the first judges of the International Tribunal for the Law of the Sea (ITLOS) in Hamburg. It is to the subject of dispute settlement under the 1982 UN Convention on the Law of the Sea (UNCLOS) that I turn.

The 1982 Convention was adopted shortly before I began my graduate studies in international law. As students we noted with some interest the elaborate provisions set out in Part XV of the 1982 Convention, and in particular those provisions that offer parties the possibility to resolve their disputes before the International Court of Justice (ICJ), or ITLOS, or arbitration.[1] Of the ICJ we knew a little, but of ITLOS, an entirely new entity, we knew nothing. As to inter-state arbitration, this was not too lively a subject in the early 1980s: I recall my first lecturer, Professor Jennings, in the final year of his academic life

---

* Queen's Counsel; Professor of Law, University College London. With thanks to Ruth Kennedy (LLM, UCL) for research assistance.

1 Article 287 of UNCLOS provides, in relevant part:

1. When signing, ratifying or acceding to this Convention or at any time thereafter, a State shall be free to choose, by means of a written declaration, one or more of the following means for the settlement of disputes concerning the interpretation or application of this Convention: (a) the International Tribunal for the Law of the Sea established in accordance with Annex VI; (b) the International Court of Justice; (c) an arbitral tribunal constituted in accordance with Annex VII; (d) a special arbitral tribunal constituted in accordance with Annex VIII for one or more of the categories of disputes specified therein. ...

3. A State Party, which is a party to a dispute not covered by a declaration in force, shall be deemed to have accepted arbitration in accordance with Annex VII.

4. If the parties to a dispute have accepted the same procedure for the settlement of the dispute, it may be submitted only to that procedure, unless the parties otherwise agree.

5. If the parties to a dispute have not accepted the same procedure for the settlement of the dispute, it may be submitted only to arbitration in accordance with Annex VII, unless the parties otherwise agree. ...

before being elected to serve as a Judge at the ICJ, telling us, according to my lecture notes: "Also PCA. Not much these days. Historical."

That was thirty years ago, and in the intervening period much has changed. The 1982 Convention unleashed a lively competition between the different modes of dispute settlement, since it came into force in 1994. The first dispute under Part XV was the prompt release in the *M/V Saiga case* (St. Vincent and the Grenadines *v.* Guinea), and there have been, as far as I am able to ascertain, a total of some 27 cases initiated under Part XV: 17 have gone to ITLOS (of which two are advisory opinions and nine are prompt release cases, and in addition ITLOS has heard four provisional measures applications in proceedings initiated before Annex VII arbitration tribunals) and the remainder have gone to Annex VII arbitration. In allowing the parties to opt for different types of dispute settlement, and offering arbitration under Annex VII as a default, the drafters of UNCLOS did not designate a home for the arbitration. For these and other mechanisms, the Permanent Court of Arbitration (PCA) has been available, and has been utilised in all but one of the eight cases brought to arbitration under Annex VII:[2] the first was the Southern Bluefin Tuna cases, filed in 1999, and it was followed by eight more:

- the MOX plant case (Ireland *v.* United Kingdom, 2001);[3]
- case concerning land reclamation by Singapore in and around the Straits of Johore (Malaysia *v.* Singapore, 2003);[4]
- maritime boundary (Barbados *v.* Trinidad & Tobago, 2004);[5]
- maritime boundary (Guyana *v.* Suriname, 2004);[6]
- *Chagos Marine Protected Area* (Mauritius *v.* United Kingdom, 2010);[7]
- maritime delimitation (Bangladesh *v.* India, 2010);[8]

---

2 The ICSID Secretariat acted as registrar in the *Southern Bluefin Tuna Cases* (New Zealand *v.* Japan; Australia *v.* Japan).
3 Details available at: <http://www.pca-cpa.org/showpage.asp?pag_id=1148>.
4 Details available at: <http://www.pca-cpa.org/showpage.asp?pag_id=1154>. An Award on Agreed Terms was issued by the Tribunal on 1 September 2005.
5 Award of 11 April 2006, at: <http://www.pca-cpa.org/upload/files/Final%20Award.pdf>.
6 Award of 17 September 2007, at: <http://www.pca-cpa.org/upload/files/Guyana-Suriname%20Award.pdf>.
7 *The Republic of Mauritius* v. *The United Kingdom of Great Britain and Northern Ireland*, details available at: <http://www.pca-cpa.org/showpage.asp?pag_id=1429>.
8 Details available at: http://www.pca-cpa.org/showpage.asp?pag_id=1376.

– the ARA *Libertad Arbitration* (Argentina *v.* Ghana, 2012);[9] and
– maritime claim (Philippines *v.* Peoples Republic of China, 2013).[10]

It is noteworthy that Part XV has not offered a jurisdictional basis for any case that has gone to the ICJ, although that Court has had many occasion to interpret and apply the rules of the 1982 Convention (or their customary incarnation), in cases brought on the basis of other dispute settlement clauses.[11]

I have been privileged to be involved as counsel in a number of these cases, and so have seen first-hand how the arrival of ITLOS and the re-emergence of the PCA have created a degree of competition amongst the bodies envisaged by Article 287. The experience to date gives rise to a number of questions. How has it come to pass that the PCA has been chosen on all Annex VII arbitrations so far initiated? Why is it that States would opt for one procedure rather than for another, for example arbitration or judicial settlement or, if judicial settlement is preferred, between the ICJ and ITLOS?

As to the first question, in the absence of any choice by the drafters of the 1982 Convention, the only with experience in inter-State arbitration was the Permanent Court of Arbitration, and it has emerged as a logical place to go. After the *Southern Bluefin Tuna cases*, in which the Tribunal was assisted by the ICSID Secretariat, every other case has gone to the PCA. The first was the MOX plant dispute between Ireland and the United Kingdom, in which the agreed on the choice of the PCA as a logical choice. It was not, however, the only possibility: there was some discussion about locating the arbitration at the home of ITLOS in Hamburg, and using that Tribunal's Registry as the secretariat for the arbitration. However, a majority of the ITLOS judges decided that such a course would not be appropriate, a decision that seems to have brought certain benefits for the PCA. Later on the issue was revisited in another case, including the possibility of opting for a five judge Chamber of ITLOS rather than a five member arbitration tribunal (an approach that has recently been chosen – in December 2014 – by Ghana and the Ivory Coast for the purposes of resolving their maritime boundary dispute). That too did not come to fruition, and the result is that The Hague has had ample opportunity to develop its experience in UNCLOS arbitration proceedings. The possibility of Hamburg has since been

---

9   ARA *Libertad* (*Argentina* v. *Ghana*), Agreement dismissing proceedings concluded on 27 September 2013, details available at: <http://www.pca-cpa.org/showpage.asp?pag_id=1526>.
10 Details available at: <http://www.pca-cpa.org/showpage.asp?pag_id=1529>.
11 See *Territorial and Maritime Dispute* (*Nicaragua* v. *Colombia*), Judgement of 19 November 2012, and *Maritime Delimitation in the Black Sea* (*Romania* v. *Ukraine*), Judgment of 3 February 2009.

revisited, but without a change of heart on the part of the majority of the ITLOS judges it seems that the ITLOS Registry and the ITLOS building will not have an opportunity to be used in Annex VII arbitrations. In a sense that is regrettable, given the excellence of the facilities, and it might yet be that ITLOS could create a facility that might enable Annex VII proceedings to take place in Hamburg, making use of the ITLOS Registry.

Why have so many cases gone to Annex VII arbitration, rather than to the ICJ or ITLOS? At one level the answer is simple: because the default mechanism offered by Article 287 of UNCLOS so provides. Indeed, in four Annex VII cases the parties have agreed to transfer the dispute to ITLOS.[12] Yet that is not always the case, and even when faced with the issue of costs – why go for five arbitrators at considerable expense when you could have 15 ICJ judges or 21 ITLOS judges for free? – it appears that many States remain more comfortable with arbitration.

Indeed, for many of those involved in assisting States on these matters a question that is often put concerns the merits and demerits of the International Tribunal for the Law of the Sea as compared with the International Court of Justice, or the merits or demerits of judicial settlement as opposed to arbitration. In my experience a number of factors emerge in contributing to a particular choice.

1   Authority

A first factor concerns the authoritativeness of the institution that is handing down the award or judgment. Will an arbitration award, for example, carry any less weight than the judgment of an international court or tribunal? The answer to that turns, of course, on the qualities of the institution that hosts the arbitration and the identity of the individuals who happen to sit as arbitrators. In both respects the answer will depend on the actions of the States themselves, since it is they who choose the arbitrators and have to agree on the hosting authority. The extent to which these awards are picked up and relied upon elsewhere, for example in cases before national courts or in other international cases, remains to be seen. But in the cases in which I have been

---

12   See the *M/V 'Saiga' (No. 2) Case* (St. Vincent and the Grenadines v. Guinea, 1999); the *Case concerning the Conservation and Sustainable Exploitation of Swordfish Stocks in the South-Eastern Pacific Ocean* (Chile/European Union, 2000); the *Dispute concerning delimitation of the maritime boundary between Bangladesh and Myanmar in the Bay of Bengal* (Bangladesh/Myanmar, 2010); the *M/V 'Virginia G' Case* (Panama/Guinea-Bissau, 2013).

involved, as well as in others, it is difficult to see how it might be said that the awards and decisions that have been handed down by arbitrators are treated by the parties to the dispute as having any lesser authority than a judgment handed down by another institution. That reflects positively on the quality of the individual arbitrators and on the effectiveness with which the PCA has carried out its functions. In all the cases in which the awards or decisions have been given, they have assisted the parties in definitively resolving their disputes, in some cases going back years or even decades.

A related question is whether, to the extent that a choice exists, the ICJ or ITLOS will be seen as more authoritative or attractive. The ICJ has a long and distinguished pedigree on law of the sea matters, whereas ITLOS is a more recent arrival on the scene, and for some States the degree of certainty and predictability that might be thought to come with the greater passage of time will certainly be seen as attractive. Another factor may be the composition of the bench – if less is more, the ICJ might be seen as more attractive. Equally, another factor that might cut in is the national background of the judges. It might be said that the ITLOS is more representative of the world's legal cultures today, and is not umbilically connected to the Security Council, a factor that might cut in either direction.

II   Timetables

A second factor that interests States concerns the calendar for proceedings. How long will it take for a case to proceed along the arbitral route as opposed to the route of judicial settlement, is a question that is often asked? There are bound to be some instances in which a Claimant State, where the case is initiated unilaterally, will not be concerned with the time element. But where time is an issue there is some indication that arbitration proceedings will be speedier than proceedings before other international bodies. Let me give one example. In 1999, Nicaragua filed proceedings before the International Court of Justice in a maritime boundary dispute with Honduras. The written pleadings were completed by 2003 and the hearing took place in the spring of 2007. The judgment in that case was handed down in the autumn of 2007, so it took about seven years from initiation of proceedings to judgment.[13] By contrast, the case of *Guyana* v. *Suriname* was initiated under Annex VII in February

---

13   *Territorial and Maritime Dispute between Nicaragua and Honduras in the Caribbean Sea* (*Nicaragua* v. *Honduras*), Judgment of 8 October 2007, details available: <http://www.icj-cij.org/docket/index.php?p1=3&p2=3&code=nh&case=120&k=14&p3=0>.

2004, by Guyana. The written pleadings were completed in the summer of 2006 and hearings were held in December 2006, in Washington DC, at the Organisation of American States, under the auspices of the PCA. There was also a separate hearing in July 2006 on issues of an interlocutory nature concerning admissibility and jurisdiction, and also an application for access to archival materials. The award in that case came down in September 2007, and so that case took three and a half years from initiation to completion.[14] There may be good reasons to explain the difference between the two cases, although they are rather similar in their level of complexity and the range of issues raised. The case of *Barbados* v. *Trinidad & Tobago* went even more quickly than that of *Guyana* v. *Suriname*. This suggests that if time is a factor, and that is not always the case, arbitration may prove to be an attractive option for a Claimant. That said, in its first maritime delimitation case the ITLOS has shown itself to be as speedy as arbitration: the case of *Bangladesh* v. *Myanmar* was initiated in December 2009 (by way of an application for arbitration), but then transferred to ITLOS, by agreement of the parties. The written proceedings were concluded by 1 July 2011, and the judgment was given in March 2012.[15] There is some indication too that the ICJ is now speeding up its procedures: in two recent cases – *Application of the Interim Accord of 13 September 1995* (the former Yugoslav Republic of Macedonia v. Greece), and *Whaling in the Antarctic* (Australia v. Japan), neither of which were maritime boundary disputes – the cases were completed within four years of the application having been filed.[16]

III   Cost

Closely related to the question of timing is a third issue: cost. Will arbitration be more or less expensive than judicial settlement? Unlike judicial settlement, where the judges come at no cost to the parties, like the registry, in arbitration

---

14   *Guyana* v. *Suriname*, Arbitral Award of 17 September 2007, details available at: <http://www.pca-cpa.org/showpage.asp?pag_id=1147>.

15   *Dispute concerning delimitation of the maritime boundary between Bangladesh and Myanmar in the Bay of Bengal (Bangladesh/Myanmar)*, Judgment of 14 March 2012, details available: <http://www.itlos.org/index.php?id=108>.

16   In *The Application of the Interim Accord of 13 September 1995* (details available at: <http://www.icj-cij.org/docket/index.php?p1=3&p2=3&case=142&PHPSESSID=>) the application was filed on 14 November 2008 and oral proceedings were completed on 30 March 2011. Similarly in *The Whaling case* (details available at: <http://www.icj-cij.org/docket/index.php?p1=3&p2=1&case=148>) the application was filed 31 May 2010 (without witness statements) and oral proceedings were completed by 16 July 2013.

the parties have to share the cost of the arbitrators' fees and the costs of the registry. Those can be quite significant. All other things being equal, and assuming that a case proceeds on the same time line, one would expect arbitration to be more expensive. But, where arbitration proceeds more speedily, there can be considerable cost savings. At the end of the day, I doubt that there would be much material difference in cost between a case that runs at the International Court of Justice for seven years and one that runs in arbitration for three and a half years.

IV   Procedural Matters

A fourth question concerns the working methods of the various dispute settlement mechanisms available under article 287. These can touch upon the efficiency of the proceedings, and the direction they might take. This includes a range of matters, such as the possibility of *third party intervention* (explicitly envisaged by the ICJ and ITLOS, whereas Annex VII is silent) or the possibility of *amicus curiae* filings (ITLOS appears more open to these than the ICJ); the rules governing the *independence and impartiality* of judges and arbitrators;[17] the approach to evidence, including the *examination of the parties' experts*,[18] the *retention by the court or tribunal of its own experts*,[19] and the possibility of discovery.[20]

---

[17] A recent decision of the Annex VII Tribunal in Mauritius v. United Kingdom is premised on the ICJ, ITLOS and Annex VII applying essentially the same standard, but it is far from certain whether, over the long-term, such an approach will find general favour; UK v. *Mauritius* (*Reasoned Decision on Challenge*), 2011 (details available at: <http://www.pca-cpa.org/showpage.asp?pag_id=1429>).

[18] Note the new approach of the ICJ, in *Whaling in the Antarctic*, when the ICJ provided for examination of parties' experts and detailed questions by the judges of the Court (details available at: <http://www.icj-cij.org/docket/index.php?p1=3&p2=1&case=148&code=aj&p3=2>), in particular Oral Proceedings on 27 June 2013.

[19] The practice of ITLOS and Annex VII arbitration tribunals has tended towards transparency. See for example *Southern Bluefin Tuna*, Provisional Measures, Award of 27 August 1999 and *Guyana v. Suriname*, Award of 17 September 2007 (in particular paras. 58–78, 95, 108, 376). By contrast, the ICJ has tended towards the use of *experts fantomes* (for a justifiable critique of this approach see Dissenting Opinion of Judge Al Khasawneh and Simma, *Pulp Mills case on the River Uruguay* (*Argentina v. Uruguay*), Judgment of 20 April 2010, in particular para. 14).

[20] This is a subject that remains generally undeveloped in public international law litigation.

Similar considerations apply in relation to the availability of interim relief and interlocutory decisions. In respect of the latter the case of *Guyana v. Suriname* was interesting. Apart from the maritime boundary issue it also dealt with issues of cooperation under more general international law, and even the threatened use of force under Article 2(4) of the United Nations Charter. The case may well attract attention also for one procedural aspect: one of the parties, Guyana, went to the Arbitral Tribunal to request an Order that the other party, Suriname, modify its position and drop its objection to Guyana having access to archival material held by the Kingdom of The Netherlands. This may look like a surprising application. Certainly, it is not immediately apparent that such an application would succeed if made at an interlocutory stage before the International Court of Justice, which has not had a practice, at least until the present day, of dealing with such issues in that way. The Annex VII Tribunal heard the parties in writing and orally and then issued a decision that had the effect, in essence, of opening up access to the archives of the Kingdom of The Netherlands.[21] The Annex VII Arbitral Tribunal went further. It appointed its own independent expert, Professor Hans van Houtte, to review the archival material, determine its relevance and provide an opinion where a question arose on the confidentiality of the material. This proved to be an efficient and effective procedure, which went a considerable way to resolving an incidental dispute between the parties which threatened to make the resolution to broader dispute even more difficult. At the time this struck me as a rather wise approach, and one from which other dispute settlement bodies might draw inspiration. It reflects, at the very least, a willingness of that body to get involved in the nitty-gritty issues that often accompany international disputes.

V   Applicable Law

Another point that is to be made relates to the treatment of the applicable law in UNCLOS. Article 293(1) of the Convention provides that:

> A court or tribunal having jurisdiction under this section shall apply this Convention and other rules of international law not incompatible with this Convention.

In *Guyana v. Suriname* the Annex VII Tribunal noted that ITLOS had interpreted Article 293 "as giving it competence to apply not only the Convention,

---

21   *Guyana v. Suriname*, Procedural Order No. 4, 12 October 2005.

but also the norms of customary international law (including, of course, those relating to the use of force)", ruled that this was "a reasonable interpretation of Article 293", and that it could not accept Suriname's contention that the Annex VII Tribunal had "no jurisdiction to adjudicate alleged violations of the United Nations Charter and general international law".[22] The Annex VII Tribunal proceeded to rule that the conduct of Suriname, in the disputed area, including its threatened use of force, constituted a breach of its obligations under Articles 74(3) and 83(3) of the Convention over which the Tribunal had jurisdiction by virtue of Article 293(1) of the Convention. This part of the award, which has not been free from criticism, nevertheless indicates a potentially more expansive view of the law and its application than one might expect from the ICJ. Relatedly, in the *Dispute concerning delimitation of the maritime boundary between Bangladesh and Myanmar in the Bay of Bengal* (*Bangladesh/Myanmar*), ITLOS interpreted and then applied the rules of the 1982 Convention to delimit maritime areas beyond 200 miles from the coast, becoming the first international court or tribunal to do so.[23] It is not certain that the ICJ, or perhaps even an Annex VII tribunal, might have taken that significant step, which was a factor in the choice of forum.

Nevertheless, it is plain that each of the courts and tribunals has been at pains to commit to a coherent and systemic approach to the identification of the applicable law, one that points against fragmentation. In *Guyana v. Suriname* and in *Barbados v. Trinidad & Tobago*, both Arbitral Tribunals relied heavily on the jurisprudence of the International Court of Justice on the issues of maritime delimitation.[24] In *Guyana v. Suriname*, the Tribunal concluded that there were no grounds for adopting "a methodology at variance with that which has been practiced by international courts and tribunals during the last two decades", namely the drawing of a provisional equidistance line and its possible adjustment to achieve an equitable solution.[25] The Tribunal rejected Suriname's argument in favour of the use of what has been called the 'angle bisector methodology'.[26] Curiously, just three weeks later, in its Judgment of 8 October 2007, the International Court of Justice appeared to re-embrace some use of the 'angle bisector methodology' as proposed by Nicaragua in the *Case concerning Territorial and Maritime Disputes between Nicaragua and Honduras*

---

22   *Guyana v. Suriname*, Arbitral Award of 17 September 2007, paras. 404–405 *et seq.*
23   Judgment of 14 March 2012, paras. 450–462.
24   *Barbados v. Trinidad and Tobago*, Arbitral Award of 11 April 2006, paras. 237–245; *Guyana v. Suriname*, Arbitral Award of 17 September 2007.
25   *Ibid.*, at para. 372.
26   *Ibid.*

in the Caribbean Sea, in circumstances in which it concluded that the construction of an equidistance line from the mainland was not "feasible", because it was "impossible" for the Court to identify the base points that could be used.[27] Five years later, ITLOS too invoked the case-law of the ICJ, although in so doing it rejected the use of the 'angle bisector methodology' as argued by Bangladesh, on the basis of that and other ICJ judgments.[28]

VI Conclusions

It is difficult to reach definitive or even general conclusions on the choice of forum for the resolution of a dispute under the 1982 Convention. Each case will turn on its own merits, every case has its own facts, and those advising or taking the decisions on which forum to have access to may have their own predilections. The simple point is that States now have a number of institutional options for resolving some of their disputes, so that a market of sorts has emerged, reflecting a competitive change in the nature of the international legal order. Provided that this does not lead to an undue fragmentation in the law, or additional conflict, that may not be a bad thing: competition in procedural and process options could certainly lead to positive developments in dispute settlement, in terms of procedures that are adopted, the functioning of the respective instructions, and the substantive outcomes. In this respect, it might be said that dispute settlement under the law of the sea resembles English law in the Middle Ages, when parties had a choice of different courts to which they might resort. Over time, it is to be hoped, procedures might be streamlined to the point that rationalisation might be undertaken.

---

[27] *Case concerning Territorial and Maritime Disputes between Nicaragua and Honduras in the Caribbean Sea*, Judgment of 8 October 2007, paras. 280 and 283.

[28] *Dispute concerning delimitation of the maritime boundary between Bangladesh and Myanmar in the Bay of Bengal (Bangladesh/Myanmar)*, Judgment of 14 March 2012, paras. 225–239.

PART 5

Miscellaneous

CHAPTER 43

Le prétendu caractère « primitif » du droit international public

Robert Kolb*

I   Introduction

Le caractère primitif du droit international est souvent affirmé dans la doctrine, qu'elle soit internationaliste ou qu'elle s'attache à la théorie du droit.[1] A peine moins fréquemment, ce constat est toutefois récusé, et ce parfois avec véhémence ou même avec dédain.[2] Il y a quelques années, on avait

---

*   Professeur de droit international public à l'Université de Genève.
1   *Cf.* par exemple H. Kelsen, « Théorie générale du droit international public », *Recueil des Cours de l'Académie de Droit international de La Haye* (RCADI), vol. 42, 1932-IV, p. 131. H. Kelsen, « Théorie du droit international public », RCADI, vol. 84, 1953-III, p. 32, 44, 96. H. Kelsen, *Reine Rechtslehre*, Leipzig, Vienne, 1934, p. 131ss. P. Guggenheim, *Traité de droit international public*, t. I, Genève, 1953, p. 22ss. P. Guggenheim, « Les principes du droit international public », RCADI, vol. 80, 1952-I, p. 27. R. Piedelièvre, *Précis de droit international public*, t. I, Paris, 1894, p. 7. J.B. Whitton, « La règle pacta sunt servanda », RCADI, vol. 49, 1934-III, p. 219. H. Lauterpacht, *The Function of Law in the International Community*, Oxford, 1933, p. 406. H. Lauterpacht, « Règles générales du droit de la paix », vol. 62, 1937-IV, p. 118. R. Ago, *Scienza giuridica e diritto internazionale*, Milan, 1950, p. 106, note 2. J.P. Cot, *La bonne foi en droit international public*, Cours de l'Institut de Hautes Etudes Internationales (Paris), 1968/9, p. 12, 33. J.P. Cot, « La bonne foi et la conclusion des traités », *Revue belge de droit international*, vol. 4, 1968, p. 141. J. Kunz, « The Meaning and Range of the norm pacta sunt servanda », *American Journal of International Law*, vol. 39, 1945, p. 196. P. Vellas, *Droit international public*, 2ᵉ éd., Paris, 1970, p. 16ss. J. Barberis, « La liberté de traiter des Etats et le *jus cogens* », *Zeitschrift für ausländisches öffentliches Recht und Völkerrecht*, vol. 30, 1970, p. 24. L. Cavaré, *Le droit international public positif*, 3ᵉ éd., t. II, Paris, 1969, p. 322. J.M. Mössner, *Einführung in das Völkerrecht*, Munich, 1977, p. 4–5. B. Conforti, « Cours général de droit international public », RCADI, vol. 212, 1988-V, p. 183–184. J.P.A. François, « Règles générales du droit de la paix », RCADI, vol. 66, 1938-IV, p. 256ss. W.L. Gould, *An Introduction to International Law*, New York, 1957, p. 580ss. Q. Wright, « The Strengthening of International Law », RCADI, vol. 98, 1959-III, p. 112. B. Simma, *Das Reziprozitätselement im Zustandekommen völkerrechtlicher Verträge*, Berlin, 1972, p. 17ss. H. Hart, *The Concept of Law*, Oxford, 1961, p. 226.
2   *Cf.* G. Vedel, « L'idée d'évolution, la société internationale et le droit des gens », *Revue générale de droit international public*, vol. 46, 1939, p. 15ss. A. Hold-Ferneck, *Lehrbuch des Völkerrechts*, t. I, Vienne, 1930, p. 79–80. A. Verdross, B. Simma, *Universelles Völkerrecht*, 3ᵉ éd., Berlin, 1984,

assisté sur cette question à l'efflorescence d'un vif débat, d'étendue il est vrai fort limitée.

Quand on affirme la primitivité du droit international on peut viser plusieurs choses nettement différentes entre elles. Le plus souvent, le constat du caractère primitif se rapporte à ce qui suit. Le droit international régit une société dans laquelle les fonctions constitutionnelles fondamentales (législation, exécution, contrôle judiciaire) n'ont pas été centralisées au sein d'organes préposés au bien commun de la communauté entière. Ces fonctions demeurent au niveau inférieur, éparpillées au sein de chaque Etat pris *uti singulus*. Droit horizontal entre puissances ne connaissant aucune autorité supérieure, le droit international est en toute conséquence un droit sans législateur, pouvoir exécutif ou pouvoir judiciaire institutionnalisés (c'est le sens du vieux reproche d'un droit « sans législateur, sans gendarme et sans juge »). D'où aussi une certaine faiblesse du phénomène juridique et la prééminence de la politique ainsi que de la puissance : création du droit sans législateur et sans législation, c'est-à-dire par voie d'accords et par voie coutumière ; chaque sujet du droit interprète lui-même ses obligations pour les exécuter en toute indépendance ; il ne peut être soumis au juge sans son consentement ; la sanction de la violation du droit repose sur les représailles (contre-mesures) individuelles. Ainsi le droit international ressemblerait à l'organisation juridique des sociétés avant l'émergence de l'Etat moderne. Chaque seigneur possédait dans son fief un faisceau personnalisé de pouvoirs de *jurisdictio* comprenant indistinctement le pouvoir d'établir des règles, de les faire exécuter et d'en constater l'étendue. Enfin, la réaction à l'illicite procédait par les voies de la guerre privée. Comme l'écrivait H. Kelsen dès 1932 :

> Le droit international général présente ainsi, sur tous les points essentiels les caractéristiques d'un ordre juridique primitif : 1° Formation fondamentalement coutumière des normes juridiques générales (...)

---

p. 33. F. Berber, *Lehrbuch des Völkerrechts*, 2ᵉ éd., t. I, Munich, 1975, p. 19. A.P. Sereni, *Diritto internazionale*, t. I, Milan, 1956, p. 106. A. Truyol y Serra, « Cours général de droit international public », RCADI, vol. 173, 1981-IV, p. 119. P. Weil, « Le droit international en quête de son identité, Cours général de droit international public », RCADI, vol. 237, 1992-IV, p. 203ss. G. Abi-Saab, « Cours général de droit international public », RCADI, vol. 207, 1987-VII, p. 123–125. Pour un aperçu général, *cf.* M. Virally, « De la prétendue 'primitivité' du droit international », dans : M. Virally, *Le droit international en devenir*, Paris, 1990, p. 91ss ; ainsi que M. Barkun, *Law without Sanctions : Order in primitive Societies and the World Community*, New Haven, 1968 ; et R. Prieto Bances, « Derecho internacional y derecho primitivo », *Mélanges en l'honneur de L. Sela Sampil*, vol. 1, Oviedo, 1970, p. 165–179.

2° Absence d'organes spécialisés et pour la législation et pour l'application des sanctions (...) 3° Responsabilité collective et responsabilité pour résultat.³

Une partie des difficultés issues de la thèse selon laquelle le droit international serait un droit primitif découle du terme utilisé, à savoir la « primitivité ». Ce terme est une molécule peu saturée. Il s'accommode par conséquent d'adjonctions les plus diverses et d'explications les plus variées. De plus, il véhicule confusément un jugement de valeur, allant nettement au-delà de son caractère à première vue purement descriptif. Enfin, il est relationnel, sans toutefois expliciter les points de référence de l'analogie à laquelle il invite. Par rapport à quels ordres juridiques le droit international est-il primitif ? Sur quelles bases établir la comparaison ? Est-ce une primitivité curable ou nécessaire ? De quel type de primitivité s'agit-il ? De la primitivité absolue, celle des ordres juridiques étudiés par l'ethnographie chez les peuples proprement appelés primitifs, ou d'une primitivité qui ne vise qu'un état relativement moins évolué par

---

3   Kelsen, Théorie (1932), *supra*, note 1, p. 131. Kelsen, Reine, *supra*, note 1, p. 131 : « [D]as Völkerrecht ist noch eine primitive Rechtsordnung. Es steht erst am Anfang einer Entwicklung, die die einzelstaatliche Rechtsordnung bereits zurückgelegt hat. Es zeigt zumindest im Bereich des allgemeinen Völkerrechts und sohin für die ganze Völkerrechtsgemeinschaft noch weitgehende Dezentralisation. Es gibt hier noch keine arbeitsteilig funktionierenden Organe zur Erzeugung und Vollziehung der Rechtsnormen. Die Bildung der generellen Normen erfolgt im Wege der Gewohnheit oder durch Vertrag, das bedeutet : durch die Glieder der Rechtsgemeinschaft selbst und nicht durch ein besonderes Gesetzgebungsorgan. Und ebenso auch die Anwendung der generellen Normen auf den konkreten Fall. Es ist der sich in seinen Interessen verletzt glaubende Staat, der sich selbst zu entscheiden hat, ob der Tatbestand eines Unrechts vorliegt, für den ein anderer Staat verantwortlich ist. Und wenn dieser das behauptete Unrecht leugnet, fehlt es an einer objektiven Instanz, die den Streit in einem rechtlich geregelten Verfahren zu entscheiden hat. Und so ist es auch der in seinem Recht verletzte Staat selbst, der gegen den Rechtsverletzer mit dem vom allgemeinen Völkerrecht eingesetzten Zwangsakt, mit Repressalie oder Krieg, zu reagieren befugt ist. Es ist die Technik der Selbsthilfe, von der auch die Entwicklung der einzelstaatlichen Rechtsordnung ausgegangen ist. Demgemäss herrscht das Prinzip der Kollektiv- und Erfolgs-, nicht das der Individual- oder Schuldhaftung. Die Unrechtsfolge richtet sich nicht gegen den – als Organ des Einzelstaates fungierenden – Menschen, der den Unrechtstatbestand absichtlich oder fahrlässig gesetzt hat, sondern gegen andere, die an ihm in keiner Weise beteiligt und nicht imstande waren, ihn zu verhindern. Repressalie und Krieg treffen nicht die Staatsorgane, die mit ihrer dem Staat zurechenbaren Handlung oder Unterlassung das Völkerrecht verletzt haben, sondern die Masse der das Volk bildenden Menschen… ». Voir aussi la liste de conséquences mentionnées par A. Bleckmann, *Grundprobleme und Methoden des Völkerrechts*, Fribourg en Br., Munich, 1982, p. 153–154.

rapport à l'ordre juridique choisi comme référence ? A propos de quels aspects précis cet état relativement moins évolué est-il déterminé ? La primitivité relève-t-elle d'un échantillonnage de facteurs les plus multiples, ou ne vise-t-elle que certains d'entre eux dont le poids est supérieur voire décisif ? Si c'est le cas, comment établir les poids respectifs ? Faut-il considérer que la primitivité d'un ordre juridique n'est que la somme de ses imperfections, insuffisances et lacunes à un moment donné ? Ne faut-il retenir que les données structurelles d'un ordre juridique pour établir sa primitivité (peut-être surtout la décentralisation du pouvoir) ou faut-il s'ouvrir aussi au contenu de ses normes, qui peut se révéler beaucoup plus moderne ? En d'autres termes, la primitivité est-elle un jugement sur le plan de normes secondaires ayant trait à l'organisation juridique dans une société, ou doit-on considérer aussi les normes primaires et la qualité des contenus qu'elles véhiculent ? Voici quelques interrogations, parmi d'autres, auxquelles le terme générique, ambigu, de primitivité ne peut en lui-même répondre. Comme si souvent dans les sciences, ce terme n'est qu'un raccourci commode, étant entendu qu'on ne saurait qualifier un problème que l'on vise par des périphrases trop longues et trop complexes, un terme clé devant en tenir lieu. Or, de tels termes, une fois entrés dans les mœurs et utilisées couramment par les uns et par les autres, voient leur sens s'altérer par les nuances et contextes divers dans lesquels ils se trouvent embrigadés. Il devient alors nécessaire de remettre de l'ordre dans les concepts et réalités auxquels renvoie le terme générique, la confusion guettant à chaque détour.

II La doctrine

Il peut être utile à cet égard de commencer par un échantillonnage des opinions doctrinales, le problème en cause étant intrinsèquement doctrinal. Ce n'est toutefois pas le lieu ici d'entreprendre une revue exhaustive et détaillée des opinions doctrinales, prises une par une. *Grosso modo*, celles-ci peuvent être ramenées à deux catégories, qui s'éparpillent ensuite en certaines sous-catégories.

1 *Les défenseurs de la primitivité*

En règle générale, le caractère primitif du droit international est affirmé au regard de ses données *structurelles*.[4] Le droit international aurait nombre de caractéristiques de l'ordre juridique primitif : son caractère coordinatif et

---

4 Voir par exemple Kelsen ou Guggenheim, *supra*, note 1.

décentralisé ; son caractère inorganique (carence institutionnelle) : l'indifférenciation des fonctions constitutionnelles (législatif, exécutif, judiciaire), concentrés aux mains du même sujet de droit, l'Etat ; son caractère fragmentaire et lacunaire (carence normative) ; son caractère non-écrit, c'est-à-dire la place éminente qu'y tient la coutume, identifiée à des stades plus reculés de l'évolution juridique ; la prédominance de l'auto-interprétation et de l'auto-qualification sans possibilité de contrôle par un tiers (relativisme du droit international) ; les représailles privées comme modalité traditionnelle de sanction du droit et le rôle de l'autoprotection en général ; la place de la responsabilité collective par rapport à celle plus effacée de la responsabilité individuelle (pendant longtemps, le droit international, à travers la guerre et les représailles, rattachait à une collectivité entière les torts de quelques-uns ; entre-temps, une certaine place a aussi été faite à la responsabilité individuelle, notamment en matière de droit international pénal) ; le règlement pacifique des différends basés sur les principes du consentement et du libre choix des moyens, transformant ceux-ci en simples modalités facultatives ; plus particulièrement, la justice purement facultative ; etc. Souvent ces caractéristiques sont présentées comme une donnée structurelle nécessaire du droit international. Sans elles, le droit international se transformerait en droit fédéral.[5] Tant que celui-ci reste un vrai droit international, c'est-à-dire l'ordre juridique des Etats souverains, indépendant et égaux, les traits structurels décrits plus haut sont ineffaçables. Il est donc impossible que le droit international sorte définitivement de sa « primitivité », faute de quoi il se transformerait et cesserait d'être du droit international. Dès lors, cet ordre juridique ne pourra jamais qu'évoluer à l'intérieur de son référent nécessaire, c'est-à-dire son caractère primitif. Il peut être *plus ou moins* primitif, se développer et s'améliorer sur tel ou tel point ; mais il ne pourra pas cesser d'être primitif en cela que ce qualificatif indique une donnée structurelle du droit international avec laquelle celui-ci vit ou périclite. Autrement dit, un droit international non primitif est une contradiction dans les termes et ne saurait exister. Du point politico-juridique, le droit international et son caractère primitif sont dans cette conception parfois maintenus

---

5 Voir déjà T.E. Holland, *Elements of Jurisprudence*, 6ᵉ éd., Oxford, 1893, p. 339. J. De Louter, *Le droit international public positif*, vol. I, Oxford, 1920, p. 59. Voir aussi E. Zitelmann, *Die Unvollkommenheit des Völkerrechts*, Munich, Leipzig, 1919. W. Burckhardt, *Die Organisation der Rechtsgemeinschaft*, Bâle, 1927 (le droit international est certes droit, mais droit non positif parce qu'il n'est pas soutenu par une organisation sociale intégrée). Sur ces deux derniers auteurs, *cf.* A. Truyol y Serra, *Doctrines contemporaines du droit des gens*, Paris, 1951, p. 26ss. G.A. Walz, *Wesen des Völkerrechts und Kritik der Völkerrechtsleugner*, Stuttgart, 1930, p. 88ss, 97ss.

dans une proportion congrue. Le droit international ne sera jamais qu'un sous-droit, situé à l'orée du phénomène juridique. Ses faiblesses le condamneront, sinon à choir, à rester cantonné dans une éternelle faiblesse, essuyant des violations, provoquant l'anarchie des qualifications juridiques non solubles, produisant un discours derrière lequel se masquent plus ou moins mal des intérêts subjectifs. Et cet état des choses est irrémédiable. L'ordre juridique international ne saurait se poser en belle au bois dormant, espérant un jour le baiser d'un prince. Il sera condamné éternellement à la besogne valétudinaire et à subir des coups, comme un être né sous une étoile maléfique et condamné aux travaux forcés par les Dieux. D'autres fois, cette primitivité est prise comme un simple fait, comme une caractéristique structurelle du droit international qu'on ne commente pas et qu'on ne perçoit pas nécessairement comme faiblesse. Chaque corps et comme il est. Le qualifier de bon ou de mauvais relève de points de vue subjectifs, dans lesquels ces auteurs n'entendent pas entrer.

Selon une autre opinion, le droit international est un droit primitif au regard de ses insuffisances ou *imperfections* dans son organisation positive actuelle.[6] La primitivité n'est pas une donnée structurelle et dans ce sens nécessaire, mais la somme des insuffisances actuelles de ce droit, contingentes dans l'histoire. La destinée du droit international est d'évoluer comme tout ordre juridique vers l'idéal d'un ordre juridique parfait. Ce modèle est constitué par le système juridique intégré, vertical et organique tel que le connaît l'Etat moderne. D'où cette vision eschatologique : « Le droit international ne peut faire partie du droit qu'autant que ses imperfections actuelles sont considérées comme passagères (…). Dès qu'elles sont considérées comme permanentes, le droit international disparaît complètement de l'horizon du droit ».[7] Ainsi, ou bien le droit international est nécessairement primitif et alors il faut nier son caractère juridique (c'est aboutir à l'ancienne doctrine d'Austin, selon laquelle tout droit, s'il veut exister, doit émaner du commandement d'un supérieur) ; ou bien la primitivité ne signifie qu'un ensemble d'imperfections passagères vouées à disparaître et alors le droit international existe, bien qu'il reste passagèrement grevé de leur poids ingrat. La primitivité n'est plus une donnée inamovible. Elle est le simple revers des imperfections du droit international à un moment donné de son histoire. Il y a ici un glissement sensible. Primitif ne signifie pas plus qu'« imparfait ». Et surtout, un programme optimiste d'évolution du droit est proposé à l'attention du lecteur. Le droit international est invité à se développer et à se renforcer pour se défaire des traits de caractère qui justifient passagèrement le qualificatif de primitif, connoté

---

6 Voir H. Lauterpacht, Règles, *supra*, note 1, p. 118–121.
7 *Ibid.*, p. 119.

de manière négative. Toute une vision politico-juridique se cache ainsi derrière cette vision. Elle assigne au droit international un rôle important, d'assurer l'ordre et la paix dans la société internationale. La qualification de primitivité ne traduit ici qu'une déception quant au rôle actuel du droit international. On en appelle à son développement afin qu'il finisse par tenir la place qu'il mériterait. Paradoxalement, le droit international, qualifié de primitif, est ici connoté très positivement : qu'il vive, mais que sa primitivité s'efface.

2 *Les négateurs de la primitivité*

La critique des conceptions présentées s'attaque généralement au *point de référence* choisi pour conclure que le droit international est un ordre primitif. Ce point de référence est manifestement le droit interne de l'Etat. A bien y regarder, on reproche au droit international de ne pas être comme le droit interne. Or, par définition, il ne peut pas l'être. En effet, le droit international est destiné à régir un environnement social très différent de celui que régente le droit interne. C'est en fonction de son aptitude à remplir efficacement les fonctions propres à cette société déterminée qu'est la société internationale, avec ses spécificités et ses différences irréductibles par rapport à la société interne, qu'il doit être jugé. Prendre comme base d'induction et de perfection de tout droit la définition du droit étatique occidental tel qu'il a progressivement émergé des XIXe et XXe siècles, ne peut mener selon cette manière de voir amener que des distorsions. Ces modèles juridiques ne sont en effet que des modalités historiques du droit à un moment donné de l'histoire et dans un espace géographique particulier, non pas l'essence même du droit. Celui-ci ne précède-t-il pas l'Etat moderne ? Le droit n'a-t-il pas existé des siècles avant la constitution des Etats territorialement organisés ? Et de quel droit dira-t-on que le seul droit parfait est celui que nous vivons de nos jours ? Dès lors, comme l'affirme A. Truyol y Serra : « Il ne s'agit pas tant, en l'occurrence, de faire valoir une différence de 'développement' entre le droit international et le droit interne des Etats que de se rendre compte d'une différence de structure ».[8] Ou encore : « il est un droit *différent* [du droit interne] beaucoup plus qu'un droit *primitif* ».[9] Cela signifie : la société internationale a sa propre structure, très différente de celle de la société interne ; il est naturel que le droit international doive dès lors avoir aussi une structure très différente du droit interne ; il en est ainsi, parce

---

[8] Truyol y Serra, *supra*, note 2, p. 119. *Cf.* aussi Weil, *supra*, note 2, p. 203ss. Verdross, Simma, *supra*, note 2, p. 33. Berber, *supra*, note 2, p. 19. Virally, *supra*, note 2, p. 98 : « Le droit international n'est pas un droit parvenu à un stade d'évolution moins avancé que la plupart des droits nationaux : par rapport à ces derniers il se présente (…) comme un droit différent ».

[9] Virally, *supra*, note 2, p. 92.

que le droit reflète toujours l'agencement d'une société particulière, notamment la distribution du pouvoir qui y règne. Mais alors comment pourra-t-on prendre l'ordre juridique interne comme étalon de mesure pour la qualité que le droit international devrait avoir, affirmant implicitement ou explicitement que le droit international deviendra du vrai droit parfait quand il se sera le plus largement possible transformé à l'image du droit interne ? Ce serait postuler une impossibilité et un non sens. Le droit international devrait alors cesser d'être adapté aux traits sociaux et politiques de la société qu'il régit pour adopter les traits d'une société qu'il n'a pas vocation à régir. A force d'être dans ce cas qualifié de « parfait », il cesserait d'avoir une utilité et une emprise quelconques, puisqu'il ne servirait plus aux besoins et aux buts de la société internationale pour laquelle il existe. Aussi parfait sera-t-il dans ce cas, il aura cessé d'exister comme droit positif, car les Etats n'y verraient plus « leur » ordre juridique et le laisseraient choir dans l'oubli. On aura ainsi perfectionné le droit international pour en réalité le dépecer. De là les auteurs du courant ici présenté condamnent les négateurs du droit international[10] ou ce courant important, surtout parmi les philosophes du droit, qui consiste à considérer le droit international comme étant un droit imparfait en voie de formation et de perfectionnement.[11] Ces courants méconnaîtraient les spécificités nécessairement propres au droit international. Celui-ci n'a pas à être comme le droit interne. Il doit régir aussi convenablement que possible la société internationale pour laquelle il est fait. C'est sur cette base qu'il doit être jugé. La vision de ce courant est en ce sens réaliste. Il s'attache à postuler l'adhérence de tout droit aux réalités de la société qu'il régit et à abandonner des visions purement abstraites et idéales du droit parfait, sans considération du soubassement social.

D'autres auteurs réfutent la primitivité du droit international en serrant de plus près le *caractère matériel* de cette branche du droit.[12] Selon eux, le droit international n'est primitif ni dans ses règles primaires, qui ressemblent beaucoup aux règles des droits internes les plus évolués et sont d'ailleurs très souvent destinées à y être incorporées par transformation dualiste ou

---

10 *Cf.* J. Austin, *Lectures on Jurisprudence or the Philosophy of Positive Law*, 5ᵉ éd., vol. I, Londres, 1885, p. 79ss. Sur cette doctrine, *cf.* Truyol y Serra, *supra*, note 2, p. 104ss. Truyol y Serra, *supra*, note 5, p. 4ss, 14ss. Walz, *supra*, note 5, p. 4ss, 56ss.

11 *Cf.* par exemple I. Vanni, *Filosofia del diritto*, Bologne, 1920, p. 81. G. del Vecchio, *Lezioni di filosofia del diritto*, 3ᵉ éd., Rome, 1936, p. 230–231. W. Schönfeld, *Die logische Struktur der Rechtsordnung*, Leipzig, 1927, p. 56. H. Ryffel, *Rechts- und Staatsphilosophie*, Neuwied, 1969, p. 188. N. Bobbio, *Il positivismo giuridico*, Turin, 1996, p. 156, citant Cernelutti. Voir aussi Walz, *supra*, note 5, p. 88ss. *Contra*, H. Henkel, *Einführung in die Rechtsphilosophie*, 2ᵉ éd., Munich, 1977, p. 124.

12 *Cf.* Abi-Saab, *supra*, note 2, p. 123–124.

réception moniste, ni dans ses règles secondaires (règles sur la production et l'application des règles juridiques), qui sont plus sophistiquées que celles des ordres juridiques internes afin de pouvoir régir une société plus complexe.[13] Sur ce plan secondaire, les sociétés dites primitives se distinguent par le formalisme et le caractère sacral de la formation du droit. Le droit y est fermement ancré dans une société à morale dite close, distinguant entre ses membres et les étrangers. Or, ces traits s'opposent au caractère très peu formaliste et fortement rationalisé du droit international, nécessaires à son universalité. A bien y regarder, les mécanismes du droit des sociétés primitives et ceux du droit international de ce siècle ne se ressemblent pas dans une quelconque primitivité, mais dans la configuration du pouvoir dans le corps social. Celui-ci est décentré ou décentralisé, émietté, diffus, non concentré en des organes collectifs. Dès lors, le terme primitif est impropre en cela qu'il soulève une gamme de connotations qui dépasse de loin les seuls aspects qu'il peut légitimement viser. En ce sens, ce terme est inadéquat parce que pour ainsi dire il trompe sur la marchandise. Il véhicule des images erronées et distord une réalité notablement plus complexe. Tel est le cas notamment par rapport au contenu du droit international : droit hautement évolué d'une société internationale postmoderne, négocié et adopté selon des procédures qui n'ont rien à envier à celles du droit interne, secrétant un droit très rationnel et de grande qualité technique, le terme d'ordre juridique « primitif » ne peut que laisser dans l'ombre ces aspects essentiels qui pourtant constituent l'essence du droit. Quelle que soit l'importance des aspects structurels du droit, celui-ci se confronte à nous tout d'abord comme ensemble de normes matérielles. Celles du droit international ne sont en rien primitives.

Selon une dernière opinion, le droit international n'est pas un droit primitif mais constitue plutôt l'ordre juridique le plus perfectionné qui soit. Il en serait ainsi parce qu'il réaliserait dans une forme assez achevé l'idéal démocratique, selon lequel les sujets de droit participent directement à la création du droit qu'ils s'appliquent, et qu'aucun d'entre eux n'est lié contre sa volonté. A un droit interne, qui doit souvent imposer ses normes à des sujets récalcitrants et mal informés par le truchement de l'épée, s'oppose un droit international qui élabore ses normes dans le respect de sujets paritaires et informés, acceptant librement ses normes. Le caractère coordinatif du droit international a ainsi été perçu comme la réalisation la plus avancée de

---

13   Et encore, *ibid.*, p. 124 : « En d'autres termes, il me semble absurde d'affirmer que les règles primaires du droit international répondent bien à la mentalité de l'homme du XXe siècle alors que ses règles secondaires reflètent toujours la mentalité de l'homme de l'âge de pierre ».

l'essence idéale d'un droit basé sur l'adhésion plutôt que sur la contrainte.[14] Dans cet angle de vue, le vrai droit primitif est le droit interne. Ayant à régir des sujets rustres et irresponsables, qui tentent à chaque moment à s'affranchir des règles, à contourner le droit, à en violer les prescrits, le législateur doit imposer des règles et les sanctionner par l'éternelle peur de la sanction. Le droit international, quant à lui, régissant les rapports entre sujets plus réfléchis, pourrait et devrait s'en remettre à une création volontaire du droit. Celle-ci n'est pas seulement plus recommandable du point de vue des idéaux participatifs et démocratiques. Elle a aussi un impact positif sur le respect du droit, car on respecte plus aisément ce à quoi on a librement souscrit. S'il ne faut pas exagérer les bienfaits de cette absence de sanction, la vision à peine présentée permet en tout cas de singulièrement retourner le compliment de la primitivité.

III   Les aspects structurels

Sans admettre que le droit international doive s'approcher des formes qu'a prises le droit interne, il reste possible de dire que sur beaucoup de points structurels il s'inspire d'une organisation sociale et politique proche de celle du Moyen Age européen. Cette société du Moyen Age, avec son éparpillement du pouvoir, correspond sous de nombreux aspects à la société internationale du XXe siècle (ainsi que du début du XXIe). Le terme « primitif » ne convient probablement guère pour décrire ces traits du droit international en le comparant au droit médiéval. On peut toutefois ramener ce terme à l'alternative que voici. Tout droit s'inscrit dans l'une des branches suivantes. *Primo*, il peut s'agir d'un droit reposant sur des structures publiques centralisées où les pouvoirs procèdent d'un pôle de pouvoir unique. C'est une forme de droit « étatique » qui serait (structurellement) « non-primitif ». *Secundo*, il peut s'agir d'un droit décentralisé où les pouvoirs publics restent répartis sur des sujets autonomes. C'est une forme de droit de « sociétés non-étatiques » qui serait (structurellement) « primitif ». Le terme primitif n'est ici qu'un descripteur de toutes les conséquences découlant du caractère coordinatif plutôt que subordinatif du droit international, c'est-à-dire du fait que le sujet de droit *uti singulus* et non la communauté juridiquement organisée détient les pouvoirs constitutionnels parce que la souveraineté individuelle n'a pas été expropriée.

---

14   Sur ce dernier point, *cf.* par exemple R. Marcic, *Rechtsphilosophie*, Fribourg en Br., 1969, p. 191, 209ss, 218.

Procédons dans cet esprit à un bref échantillonnage de divers aspects propres à la structure (actuelle) du droit international relevant d'une analogie avec l'organisation juridique du Moyen Age.

a. L'aspect le plus frappant est évidemment le *caractère coordinatif* du droit international : la décentralisation (ou décentration) du pouvoir ; la confusion entre sujets-créateurs et sujets-destinataires des règles du droit ; l'auto-interprétation et l'auto-qualification ; la confusion entre le juge et la partie quand il s'agit d'apprécier les situations juridiques des sujets de droit ; le règlement des différends et la justice facultative ; les sanctions par voie de représailles ; le rôle prédominant de la volonté (autonomie) et l'absence de loi s'imposant à tous (hétéronomie).

Tels sont les aspects cardinaux de toute organisation sociale répondant au modèle extra-étatique. Historiquement, la famille, le clan, les *gentes*, et en leur sein le chef de famille (d'où la *patria potestas* du droit romain), sont les unités premières du tissu social. Peu à peu – au début seulement pour les temps de conflits armés – le pouvoir est délégué à des rois, qui sont originairement chefs de guerre. Le Moyen Age était encore organisé selon ces principes. Il était fondé sur des droits publics distribués au sein d'une pyramide de vassalités. Chaque seigneur possédait une *jurisdictio*, c'est-à-dire un pouvoir spécifique d'édicter des règles, de les faire exécuter et de tenir justice. Tout le système se présentait dès lors comme une juxtaposition d'une multitude de pouvoirs autonomes.[15] La sanction du droit relevait essentiellement de la justice privée. Chaque sujet cherchait à s'assurer, par les moyens dont il disposait, la réparation des dommages subis.[16] La violation du droit était une affaire considérée relever de la sphère privée des sujets de droit. L'intérêt public ne porta initialement que sur les formes de l'exercice de la justice privée, pour essayer d'en limiter les pires excès : exclusion de certains moyens, par exemple l'incendie ; immunité de certains lieux, par exemple ceux voués au culte ; etc. Par accord entre les sujets, un arbitre pouvait être nommé par les parties en litige. Ce n'est que progressivement que l'Etat moderne émerge, en attirant vers lui le pouvoir et en effaçant ceux des divers « corps intermédiaires ». Les analogies structurelles du droit moyenâgeux avec le droit international sont patentes.

b. En matière de *sources* le droit international présente également beaucoup d'analogies avec les droits anciens. Les sources sont une rationalisation du pouvoir de créer le droit et reflètent la distribution du pouvoir au sein de la société.

---

15   *Cf.* notamment la théorisation raffinée de Bartole, F. Calasso, *Medio evo del diritto*, t. I, Milan, 1954, p. 499–501.
16   Sur la guerre privée, *cf.* E. Kaufmann, « Fehde », dans : A. Erler, E. Kaufmann (éds.), *Handwörterbuch zur deutschen Rechtsgeschichte*, t. I, Berlin, 1971, p. 1083ss.

Les sources du droit international sont fondamentalement indifférenciées et privées de dimension hiérarchique. Censées découler directement ou indirectement de la volonté des Etats, le critère de hiérarchie leur est étranger : toutes les expressions de volonté ont le même rang parce qu'elles émanent du même sujet, l'Etat. On ne verrait pas pourquoi il faudrait les distinguer en plaçant une expression de volonté (conventionnelle) au dessus d'une autre (coutumière, ou vice versa).[17] Dès lors, pour donner une solution à d'éventuels conflits de normes, on recourt principalement à des règles de collision ponctuelles comme celles de la *lex posterior* et de la *lex specialis*, au sein d'un processus d'interprétation. En droit interne, la hiérarchie des normes a son sens profond. Elle reflète l'inégalité d'éminence des organes édictant les sources en question. La constitution est la source suprême parce que le pouvoir constituant est le plus élevé au sein de l'Etat, possédant souvent la légitimité démocratique la plus accusée ; la loi est une source hiérarchiquement plus élevée que le règlement de l'exécutif parce que le législateur est un organe plus élevée dans la structure organique de l'Etat que l'exécutif, ceci étant dû une fois de plus à des considérations de légitimité démocratique ; etc. On retrouve d'ailleurs des phénomènes similaires dans des sociétés internationales partielles, comme au sein de l'Organisation internationale. Ici aussi, les sources sont groupées selon une hiérarchie bien précise : traité constitutif, résolutions des organes principaux (avec souvent la primauté reconnue à l'organe plénier), résolutions des organes subsidiaires, règlements du secrétaire général, etc. Les raisons de ce regroupement hiérarchique sont les mêmes qu'au sein du droit interne. A la hiérarchie des organes correspond naturellement une hiérarchie des sources.

D'un autre côté, le droit international connaît une pluralité de sources limitées à la fois *ratione personae* ou *ratione loci* : les traités ont un effet relatif ; la coutume peut être régionale ou locale ; la prescription et les droits historiques en modifient la portée ; le jeu des reconnaissances et de l'estoppel ou de l'acquiescement tisse autour des sources de droit une multiplicité de rapports spéciaux ; etc. D'où une multiplication du droit. Cet éparpillement du droit (*Rechtszersplitterung*) est l'un des grands traits du droit moyenâgeux.

Le droit international est ensuite tendanciellement un droit de principes. Il fixe les grandes orientations. L'absence d'organes centralisés et les carences dans l'administration régulière du droit explique qu'il manque dans certaines

---

17 Une hiérarchie des sources n'est imaginable qu'à travers la hiérarchie des organes qui édictent le droit : par exemple constituante, législateur, exécutif (règlements) dotés de légitimité (démocratique) décroissante. C'est pourquoi la hiérarchie des sources s'accuse au sein des organisations internationales où existe une hiérarchie des organes. Le traité constitutif l'emporte sur les textes internes de l'organisation.

de ses branches cette couche intermédiaire de normes plus concrètes qu'en droit interne on désigne de droit administratif. En d'autres termes, la prédominance de la souveraineté et de la création volontaire du droit criblent le droit international de nombreuses lacunes matérielles.[18] Rappelons encore l'importance du droit non-écrit ou coutumier. Il tend à une croissance lente et s'attache un peu archaïquement aux pratiques sociales de fait. Le droit ne se présente dans ce cas pas toujours comme un ordre rationnel, mais comme rationalisation d'un amas de faits dans les régularités contingentes desquels la règle essaie tant bien que mal de se frayer un chemin.

Les droits anciens, notamment au Moyen Age, connaissent une multiplicité de sources correspondant aux innombrables *jurisdictiones* possédés par des seigneurs locaux, des confréries, des villes, etc.[19] Comme en droit international, la loi uniforme y est inconnue. Ce grand nombre de sources se présente au premier stade d'évolution comme un ensemble peu articulé et quelque peu amorphe. Cependant, la rareté des échanges dépassant le cadre local rend moins fréquents les conflits de normes et réduit à la portion congrue l'insécurité juridique. La hiérarchie de ces sources reste incertaine jusqu'à l'émergence des statuts citadins et à la territorialisation croissante des rapports juridiques du XIIIe siècle.[20] Le droit des peuples germaniques qui dominèrent le Moyen Age était ainsi décentralisé. Le roi n'avait pas de pouvoir absolu (*nec regibus infinita aut libera potestas*). Le pouvoir et le droit restaient assez largement ancrés dans le corps social. Le droit était vécu comme un produit spontané secrété par ce corps. Il découlait de l'assemblée des hommes libres (*concilium civitatis*) et de

---

18 On pourrait soutenir que le droit international n'a pas de lacunes formelles, car dans tout ordre juridique on peut faire application de la règle résiduelle de liberté et repousser une demande insuffisamment fondée en droit. Mais l'utilisation trop fréquente de cette technique mettrait en évidence la faible densité normative (lacunes matérielles) d'un ordre juridique. *Cf.* Ch. De Visscher, « Contribution à l'étude des sources du droit international », *Revue de droit international et de législation comparée*, vol. 14, 1933, p. 418, note 2.

19 A. Cavanna, *Storia del diritto moderno in Europa – Le fonti e il pensiero giuridico*, vol. I, Milan, 1982, p. 200ss.

20 Sur les rapports entre les statuts citadins (*ius proprium*) et le droit romain commun (*ius commune*), selon le principe de la *lex specialis* (*ius commune viget ubi cessat statutum*), *cf.* G. Ermini, *Corso di diritto comune*, t. I, Milan, 1989, p. 17ss. Sur la territorialisation du droit dès le XIIIe siècle, *cf.* S.L. Guterman, *From Personal to Territorial Law*, Metuchen, 1972. O. Stobbe, « Personalität und Territorialität des Rechts und die Grundsätze des Mittelalters über die Collisio statutorum », *Jahrbuch des gesamten deutschen Rechts*, vol. 6, 1963, p. 21ss. Une hiérarchisation des sources existe bien plus tôt au sein de l'Empire romain de Byzance où la coutume est soumise à la volonté de l'Empereur (*quod principi placuit, legis habet vigorem*). *Cf.* Calasso, *supra*, note 15, p. 42ss, 51ss.

la tradition coutumière. Le droit était en suite basé sur des accords, sur des pactes.[21] Constitué par de multiples accidents et dépourvu de toute systématique, le droit reste très lacunaire et très incertain. D'où, dès le Moyen Age, la tendance de recourir à des actes notariés (*Urkunden*) créant ou attestant l'existence d'un droit[22] et les tentatives de recueillir les sources dans des codes passablement pléthoriques.[23] De plus, à côté d'innombrables règles de détail, le droit était dominé par quelques principes généraux, tels que le principe de personnalité (*jura ossibus inhaerent*)[24] ou le principe de l'*aequitas* dans l'application du droit, par exemple dans le droit canonique.[25] Le droit pénal connaissait lui aussi une poussière de normes prohibitives. Au-dessus de cette pluralité de normes s'élevaient quelques principes dominant toute l'administration de cette branche du droit. Par exemple : le principe de la responsabilité objective (*Erfolgshaftung*) ; le principe du flagrant délit (auquel se rattachaient des conséquences juridiques très différentes par rapport au délit non flagrant) ; le principe de différenciation selon le statut de la victime et de l'auteur ; le principe de la qualification du forfait commis en secret ; *etc.*[26] Comme en droit international, le caractère fragmentaire du droit laissait un espace béant entre les normes concrètes reflétant directement les expériences de la vie et les grands principes inspirateurs. Enfin, l'équité joue un rôle très important au Moyen Age.[27] Elle aboutit parfois à transférer des pouvoirs de législation vers les fonctionnaires du roi afin de tempérer des formalismes et de contribuer au développement d'un droit souvent ressenti comme trop fragmentaire ou trop archaïque. On peut songer à la compétence très large de statuer en équité de la

---

21 Calasso, *supra*, note 15, p. 118ss. Une exception se trouve dans l'Empire franc qui connaît une forte activité législative.
22 *Cf.* F. Kern, *Recht und Verfassung im Mittelalter*, Bâle, 1953, p. 48ss. W. Trusen, « Zur Urkundenlehre der mittelalterlichen Jurisprudenz », *Vorträge und Forschungen*, vol. 23, 1977, p. 197ss.
23 On a pu parler d'un mouvement de codification du droit (*Rechtsdokumentationswelle* : *consuetudo in scriptis redacta*) dès les XIIe et XIIIe siècles. Voir H. Schlosser, *Grundzüge der neueren Privatrechtsgeschichte*, 5e éd., Heidelberg, 1985, p. 11–12. Pour les compilations du XVIIIe siècle, *cf.* Cavanna, *supra*, note 19, p. 254ss.
24 F. Sturm, « Personalitätsprinzip », dans : A. Erler, E. Kaufmann (éds.), *Handwörterbuch zur deutschen Rechtsgeschichte*, t. III, Berlin, 1984, p. 1587ss.
25 *Cf.* P.G. Caron, *Aequitas romana, misericordia patristica ed epieichia aristotelica nella dottrina dell'aequitas canonica*, Milan, 1971. C. Lefebvre, « Equity in Canon Law », dans : R.A. Newman (éd.), *Equity in the World's Legal Systems*, Bruxelles, 1973, p. 93ss.
26 R. Schröder, *Lehrbuch der deutschen Rechtsgeschichte*, 4e éd., Leipzig, 1902, p. 73ss, 339ss, 755ss. R. His, *Geschichte des deutschen Strafrechts bis zur Carolina*, Munich, Berlin, 1928 (réimprimé en 1967).
27 Cavanna, *supra*, note 19, p. 120ss.

Cour royale des Francs (VIIIe siècle)[28] ou à l'*Equity* du Chancelier royal anglais.[29] Sur le plan des sources, il existe ainsi une série de parallélismes entre les droits anciens, notamment du Moyen Age, et le droit international.

c. On peut insister aussi sur une série d'autres aspects ponctuels, dont voici quelques exemples.

Premièrement, dans tous les droits basés sur la coordination entre souverainetés multiples, la doctrine de la primauté de l'intérêt commun, c'est-à-dire l'idée d'une *utilitas publica*, est peu développée. En droit international, ce n'est que récemment, et non sans confusion, que l'accent a été mis sur des intérêts *erga omnes* et un *jus cogens* qui en est l'expression.

Deuxièmement, tant le droit international que les droits du Moyen Age ne se présentent pas comme systèmes complets et exclusifs. Le droit moyenâgeux était perméable au concepts de morale ou de religion, comme le droit international est un droit ouvert à la politique ou à l'éthique.[30] Ce n'est qu'avec les codifications étatiques modernes qu'une branche du droit s'est présentée avec la prétention d'être complète en elle-même et de pouvoir interdire tout recours à des notions extérieures aux normes qu'elle pose (d'où l'interdiction initiale « d'interpréter » le code).[31] Ce paradigme légaliste n'a jamais existé en droit international. Celui-ci fut d'abord un droit rationnel ou naturel ; par la suite, après sa « positivisation », il est pour le moins resté un droit plus directement lié au corps social.

Troisièmement, tant le droit du Moyen Age que le droit international sont des droits difficiles à réformer ou à modifier. L'absence de mécanismes institutionnels de changement du droit, culminant dans un législateur unique et tout-puissant, tend à cimenter le *statu quo*, les droits acquis, la conservation. Le changement est lent ; souvent il demeure seulement partiel, car il ne s'appliquera qu'aux sujets qui acceptent les nouvelles normes. Les souverainetés accusent l'importance du principe de l'unanimité au détriment de celui de la majorité pour la prise de toute décision.[32] De même, au Moyen Age, chez les

---

28   E. Kaufmann, *Aequitatis iudicium, Königsgericht und Billigkeit in der Rechtsordnung des frühen Mittelalters*, Francfort-sur-le-Main, 1959, particulièrement p. 93ss.
29   J.L. Barton, « Equity in the Medevial Common Law », dans : R.A. Newman (éd.), *Equity in the World's Legal Systems*, Bruxelles, 1973, p. 139ss. F.W. Maitland, *Equity*, Cambridge, 1969.
30   *Cf.* Berber, *supra*, note 2, p. 24ss.
31   *Cf.* sur ce point G. Tarello, *Storia della cultura giuridica moderna*, Bologne, 1976, p. 15ss, 485ss.
32   Un exemple frappant en est, pour le droit international, la doctrine qui avait cours encore au début de ce XXe siècle et selon laquelle le désaccord d'un seul Etat pouvait empêcher la conclusion du traité même entre les autres Etats ayant participé à sa préparation. Ce fut

peuples germaniques, il existait le droit du *liberum veto*. Il permettait à chaque individu membre de l'assemblée des hommes libres de bloquer une décision. Voici un exemple. Un certain roi souhaita obtenir un vase précieux au-delà de sa part légitime au butin de guerre. Tous les associés sont d'accord, sauf un. Cet individu y oppose son veto. Il prend une hache et détruit le vase. Ce faisant, il est censé avoir exercé son droit.[33]

Quatrièmement, le droit international comme les droits du Moyen Age tendent à être des droits particuliers. Ils privilégient souvent des règles concrètes par rapport aux règles abstraites et générales du droit étatique moderne. Chaque transaction juridique tend en outre à être individualisée.[34] Le droit de la mer en fournit de nombreux exemples avec ses multiples statuts d'Etat sans littoral, géographiquement désavantagés, archipélagiques, exportateurs de certaines matières, etc. La systématisation du droit et les problèmes de méthode restent subordonnés dans ces sociétés à germination irrégulière du droit.[35] Les normes de tels ordres juridiques sont aussi souvent plus intenses dans leurs liens aux faits : recours aux circonstances de l'espèce, au raisonnable, à l'équité.

L'accent a ici été mis sur quelques parallélismes structurels – non matériels – entre les droits anciens et le droit international. Sur ces aspects matériels, le droit international actuel, ancré fermement dans le XXe siècle, diffère fortement des droits anciens. Ses contenus peuvent être comparés avec avantage aux ordres juridiques les plus évolués. Sur un plan plus général, il faut souligner le caractère non-formaliste du droit international, opposé au formalisme

---

le cas lors des Conférences de La Haye 1899/1907, *cf.* N. Politis, *Les nouvelles tendances du droit international*, Paris, 1927, p. 28ss. N. Politis, *La justice internationale*, Paris, 1924, p. 198ss.

33 Kern, *supra*, note 22, p. 84–85.

34 Comme le dit Ch. De Visscher, *Théories et réalités en droit international public*, 4e éd., Paris, 1970, p. 165–166 : « Ces différenciations profondes qui procèdent de l'individualité ethnique et historique propre des nations, des inégalités de leur constitution physique et de leurs ressources économiques, du nombre réduit des Etats par comparaison avec celui des individus, du caractère éminemment politique de leurs fins propres, de l'irrégularité et de la moindre fréquence de leurs rapports mutuels, conduisent ici à la prédominance des situations particulières sur les situations générales ».

35 *Cf.*, pour le droit international, A. Schüle, « Methoden der Völkerrechtswissenschaft », *Berichte der deutschen Gesellschaft für Völkerrecht*, t. III, Karlsruhe, 1959, p. 1ss. Pour la méthode du droit international en général, voir l'ouvrage plus récent de O. Corten, *Méthodologie du droit international public*, Bruxelles, 2009. Voir aussi, sur un plan très différent, Bleckmann, *supra*, note 3.

des droits anciens [36] ; les techniques de codification conventionnelle hautement rationalisées ; la conception selon laquelle le droit se « fait », opposée à celle des droits anciens selon laquelle le droit se « trouve » ou se « révèle » ; *etc.* Dans tous ces contextes, le droit international ressemble au droit étatique moderne et n'est d'aucune manière primitif.

On aboutit ainsi au constat qu'on peut appeler le droit international primitif (bien que le terme ne soit en rien heureux) du point de vue structurel, mais qu'il est impossible d'en faire autant du point de vue du contenu de ses règles et procédures.[37] Au contraire, celles-ci révèlent une densité et un état de développement remarquable, leur expansion étant presque sans frein et leur influence sur les ordres juridiques internes chaque jour croissante. Il est des forces qui s'inquiètent de nos jours de la perte d'autonomie du droit interne et du recul de la souveraineté des Etats, à cause du droit international. Il est réellement difficile de concilier cet état des choses avec une vue cantonnant le droit international à un état primitif, voire un peu fruste.

IV   La qualification de primitivité est-elle justifiée ?

S'il y donc quelque part une primitivité du droit international, c'est par rapport à l'expérience des droits étatiques à caractère centralisé. Le droit international correspond structurellement sur beaucoup de points davantage au droit des sociétés pré-étatiques. Et pour cause : il ne régit pas une société étatique, mais inter-étatique. C'est sur ce point empirique, dépourvu de tout jugement de valeur, qu'on peut éventuellement parler de « primitivité », en entendant par là la structure décentralisée de la société internationale et les conséquences que ce fait imprime au droit qui régit cette société en général (dans des systèmes particuliers, comme dans l'OMC, la structure du droit international peut

---

36   Voici un exemple. Pour obtenir réparation d'un préjudice corporel pour sectionnement d'un membre du corps, le lésé devait se présenter devant l'Assemblée. Un bouclier était placé à une certaine distance du lésé qui devait saisir le membre sectionné et, dans une procédure sacrale, le lancer sur le bouclier. Si tous les membres de l'Assemblée entendaient l'impact du membre et du bouclier, le lésé pouvait obtenir réparation. *Cf.* l'*Edictum Rothari*, art. 47 (droit lombard ; *cf.* F. Beyerle, *Edictum Rothari*, Weimar, 1947) et la *Lex Ribuaria*, art. 68 (droit franc) : « Si quis in caput vel in quacumque membro plagatus fuerit, et ossus exinde exierit, qui super viam 12 pedorum in scuto sonaverit, 36 solidos factus ei culpabilis iudicetur » (R. Sohm, *Lex Ribuaria*, Hannovre, 1883, p. 94). *Cf.* aussi dans : *Monumenta Germaniae Historica, Leges, Germanenrechte*, Weimar, à partir de 1934.

37   Pour l'évolution considérable de celles-ci dans le droit international moderne, voir par exemple G. Ziccardi Capaldo, *Diritto globale, Il nuovo diritto internazionale*, Milan, 2010.

s'éloigner plus ou moins fortement de ces traits généraux que nous mentionnons ici). D'un constat purement descriptif, on risque toutefois de glisser imperceptiblement vers un postulat et donc vers des plages axiologiques. Le droit interne moderne est issu des droits anciens après un long accouchement. Il a tenté de répondre à leurs imperfections. Ainsi, il se présente comme forme plus perfectionnée du droit, car il se plie aux exigences d'ordre et de justice les plus élémentaires, que les droits anciens, trop « anarchiques », ne pouvaient satisfaire. De là il n'y a qu'un pas à penser que le droit international devra aussi accoucher d'un nouveau droit de type « étatique ». Travailler sous cet angle au perfectionnement du droit international signifie toutefois aussi quelque part le supprimer. Un droit du modèle « étatique » n'est plus un droit « interétatique ». Il relèverait alors du droit fédéral. Ainsi peut-on dire qu'une dose d'imperfections fait partie de la structure même du droit international. L'organisation horizontale du pouvoir ne peut avoir en même temps les caractéristiques d'une organisation verticale du pouvoir. Mais ces imperfections sont relatives. Sous bénéfice d'inventaire, il n'est ni dit qu'un droit imposé par le législateur sous peine de sanction soit toujours mieux respecté par les sujets, ni encore moins qu'un tel droit convienne à tout environnement social.

Faut-il pour cela se résoudre à considérer inamovibles les défauts dans l'organisation actuelle du droit international (ou de la société internationale)? Faut-il peut-être plutôt œuvrer à surmonter cette phase de l'organisation sociale qui nécessite l'existence d'un droit international? Faut-il par conséquent souhaiter une forme d'Etat mondial, malgré l'énorme concentration de pouvoirs qu'il présenterait et son caractère utopique, du moins à l'heure actuelle?[38] Il est évident qu'il s'agit là de choix de politique juridique, et de politique tout court, qu'on ne saurait traiter scientifiquement dans une contribution vouée à l'analyse du concept de primitivité d'un ordre juridique. Il faut ici se borner à partir de cette réalité que le droit international existe tel qu'il est, indépendamment de ce qu'il pourrait être ou devenir. Du point de vue axiologique tout comme du point de vue du contenu, le droit international n'est en tout cas pas primitif. Il régit et reflète une société ayant une structure et des besoins particuliers, la société internationale, et c'est par rapport à sa capacité

---

38   I. Kant l'avait déjà vu, quand il affirmait que l'idéal pour la sanction du droit et l'égalité devant la loi serait qu'il existât un Etat mondial. Il ajoutait que les peuples n'en veulent pas et que faute de mieux il faudrait donc se borner à une Société des nations, sorte de fédération internationale plus ou moins décentralisée, capable de limiter l'anarchie des souverainetés individuelles et notamment la guerre: *Vers la paix perpétuelle* (1795), Section II, Deuxième définitif.

de satisfaire ces exigences là, comme il a déjà pu être souligné, qu'il faut le juger, le sonder et l'apprécier.[39]

A cette aune, le droit international se révèle comme étant parfaitement adapté. Créé avant tout par les Etats en fonction de leurs besoins et de leur volonté, ceux-ci le reconnaissent comme l'ordre juridique régissant toute une gamme de leurs relations réciproques. De ce point de vue, tout droit coordinatif ne peut pas être tenu *ipso facto* pour déficient, débilité ou imparfait. Dans certaines sociétés, eu égard à leur agencement propre, le droit ne peut pas être autre que paritaire et relativiste. Cela peut être perçu comme une faiblesse du point de vue de l'idéal d'un droit particulier. Ceux qui le professent doivent alors appeler à une réforme sociale allant dans le sens de la centralisation du pouvoir. Il pourra en émerger à son tour un droit subordinatif, tenu pour supérieur, si ce n'est parfait. Mais le droit coordinatif, rien d'autre que nécessaire dans un contexte donné, n'est nullement frappé de défauts et de tares en lui-même. La société qu'il régit peut être tenue pour mal organisée et pour insatisfaisante. Ce reproche ne saurait directement toucher le droit qui la régit, parce que ce dernier n'est très largement qu'une variable dépendante de cette réalité sociale première qu'il a vocation et devoir de refléter. Or, en jaugeant la capacité de cette réalité sociale de se réformer, il faut tenir compte de l'aspiration et de la volonté des peuples. Ceux-ci ne veulent pas abandonner leur indépendance et leur souveraineté, aujourd'hui peut-être encore moins qu'hier. S'il en est ainsi, la société paritaire subsistera, parce qu'elle repose sur la volonté la plus générale des peuples. En toute conséquence, le droit restera d'ici à longtemps un droit paritaire et dès lors parfois précaire. Peut-être faut-il appeler « primitif » cet attachement des peuples à leur souveraineté individuelle (rien n'est toutefois moins sûr, surtout dans le cadre d'un jugement aussi peu nuancé). En tout cas, il est inadapté d'appeler « primitif » le droit qui régit la société paritaire ainsi maintenue. Tout au plus, ce droit présente-t-il certaines limites et faiblesses inhérentes à la société paritaire. Mais il faut avouer que le droit interne présente ses propres limites et faiblesses, trop souvent sous-estimées par les juristes « internistes », qui, de manière point trop modeste, s'expriment parfois fortement sur le droit international, sans réfléchir aux multiples problèmes que rencontre le phénomène juridique interne.

---

39 Voir Virally, *supra*, note 2, p. 98. L'image des promeneurs présentée à la même page est également très instructive : « Lorsque deux promeneurs progressent sur deux voies parties de points séparés et conduisant à des destinations différentes, cela n'a pas beaucoup de sens d'affirmer que l'un est en retard sur l'autre. Tout au plus peut-on mesurer le chemin parcouru par chacun et, éventuellement, la distance qui lui reste à franchir pour parvenir à un but fixé ». Voir aussi, très clairement, Truyol y Serra, *supra*, note 2, p. 119.

Comme le dit la Bible[40] dans un de ses passages les plus remarquables, il y a des poutres et des pailles, sans qu'il soit ici nécessaire de localiser les unes et les autres.

En ce sens plus profond, donc, le jugement de sa primitivité est inadéquat, car il suggère au moins subliminalement, si ce n'est plus directement, que le droit international devrait être différent, meilleur, parfait, moins fruste (le terme primitif connote immanquablement quelque chose d'arriéré) et encore qu'il devrait nécessairement se développer dans un sens suggéré, celui de son « étatistation » progressive. L'inexactitude et l'équivoque portent ainsi sur deux plans : premièrement, que le droit international se compare le cas échéant aux ordres juridiques les plus arriérés de l'Antiquité appelée primitive, avec l'image vaguement évoquée de danseurs en plumes et en panaches (d'où aussi peut-être une suggestion d'inadéquation de ce droit aux besoins modernes ou actuels) ; deuxièmement que le droit international est en voie de formation progressive et qu'il deviendra parfait ou entrera dans l'horizon du vrai droit quand il s'approchera des structures du droit interne ou étatique. Ce sont là des jugements de valeur qui n'ont ni un fondement rationnel ni un fondement réel. Ils reposent sur une méconnaissance manifeste du droit international et de la société internationale. Reproches tournant à vide, attaques issue d'une *aberratio ictus*, il faut en corriger le tir, en premier lieu en abandonnant un terme – la primitivité – coupable de fourvoyer la pensée en suggérant des bases de comparaison erronées. Comme on a pu le dire dans un contexte différent :

> On ne saurait assez attirer l'attention sur les graves inconvénients que comporte une terminologie vicieuse. Il est impossible, dans la lutte des idées, d'arriver à un accord, d'approcher d'une solution, de réaliser un progrès, si l'on ne réussit pas à s'entendre sur le sens et la valeur des termes employés dans la discussion. Il est dangereux de se servir d'expressions inexactes, de locutions équivoques, de mots évocateurs d'idées fausses ou périmées. La pensée en est entravée et parfois elle s'arrête faute de pouvoir faire l'effort nécessaire pour percer le nuage qui la sépare de la réalité.[41]

De ce point de vue, le terme de primitivité – mais non tous les aspects qu'il recouvre quelque peu maladroitement – mériterait de choir et éventuellement même plus : de déchoir.

---

40 Evangile selon Luc, VI, nos 41–42 et Evangile selon Matthieu, VII, nos 3–5.
41 N. Politis, « Le problème des limitations de la souveraineté et la théorie de l'abus des droits dans les rapports internationaux », *RCADI*, vol. 6, 1925-I, p. 19.

CHAPTER 44

The United Nations Charter, Chapter VII, Non-Use-of-Force and Non-Intervention in Contemporary International Law: The Sisyphean Labours of the *Institut de Droit International* on Defining and Controlling 'Use of Force' Today

*Edward McWhinney**

I   Law and Power: From Cold War to Coexistence and *Détente*

In a widely quoted address to the American Society of International Law in Washington, DC, in the spring of 1963, Dean Acheson, as US Secretary of State during the Korean War crisis of the autumn of 1950, had presided over the evolution of the Uniting for Peace doctrine which confers plenary legal powers for the UN General Assembly if the Security Council should become blocked by a Permanent Member (Big Power) Veto in the exercise of its primary responsibility for the maintenance of international peace and security. Dean Acheson offered a *Staatsraison* defence for the legally novel 'quarantine' measures invoked by President Kennedy to resolve (peacefully) the October, 1962, Cuban Missile Crisis:

> I must conclude that the propriety of the Cuban quarantine is not a legal issue. The power, position and prestige of the United States had been challenged by another state; and law simply does not deal with questions of ultimate power – power that comes close to the sources of sovereignty. The survival of states is not a matter of law.[1]

The most challenging response to this thesis as to the limits of law – international law – and its relevance in international crisis management came almost

---

*   Queen's Counsel; Barrister-at-Law; Barrister and Solicitor; Professor Emeritus of Constitutional and International Law; Member and Past President, *Institut de Droit International*; Honorary Member, *Académie Internationale de Droit Comparé*; Former Chair, Executive Council, International Law Association (Canadian Branch); Former Member of Parliament, Parliament of Canada, and Parliamentary Secretary (Foreign Affairs). Professor McWhinney passed away shortly before this volume went into production.
1   Dean Acheson, *Proceedings of the American Society of International Law*, 1963, pp. 13–14.

immediately from Harvard Law School Professor Abe Chayes, the Principal Legal Advisor to the US State Department during the Cuban Missile Crisis. He had been present throughout President Kennedy's discussions and planning for a peaceful (non-nuclear conflict) conclusion to the Cuban Missile crisis and is generally accepted as the author of the elegant formulaic communication by President Kennedy to Secretary Khrushchev at the very height of the crisis and of the highly practical *quid pro quo* deal that accompanied it, that allowed both sides, and especially, perhaps, the Soviet Union, to retreat without intolerable political loss of face:

> The confrontation was not in the courtroom and in a world destructible by man, a legal frontier was obviously not the sole ingredient of effective action. We were armed, necessarily, with something more substantial than a lawyer's brief. But though it would not have been enough merely to have the law on our side, it is not irrelevant which side the law was on. The effective deployment of force, the appeal for world support, to say nothing of the ultimate judgment of history, all depend in significant degree on the reality and coherence of the case in law for our action.[2]

Immediately the Cuban Missile Crisis was over, both superpowers, the Soviet Union and the US, began work on agreement between the two bloc leaders on banning high-level nuclear test explosions – a project initiated between President Eisenhower and Secretary Khrushchev some years earlier after nuclear scientists from both countries, meeting during the International Geophysical Year in 1957 for the first time, had agreed to lobby their respective heads-of-state on the clear and present danger to human health, irrespective of national boundaries, from the lethal nuclear fall-out from test explosions. Within ten months of the successful, (non-violent) resolution of the Cuban Missile crisis, the previously neglected files had been activated so that President Kennedy and Secretary Khrushchev were able to sign, in Moscow, in August 1963, the Partial Nuclear Test Ban Treaty – one of the very first steps in what would become, throughout the balance of the 1960s and the 1970s, a succession of specific, empirically based Soviet-Western treaties on nuclear and general disarmament. As the Cold War gave way to Coexistence and then merged into *Détente*, legal advisors and consultants on both sides, Soviet and Western met and took charge of a continuing, long-range agenda for the international

---

2 Abe Chayes, "Law and the Quarantine of Cuba", *Foreign Affairs*, Vol. 41, 1963, p. 550.

law-making involved, with a momentum established thereby for peaceful settlement of international disputes in the international community at large.

The international community itself, as the process of decolonisation and sovereignty and independence began to be consummated in Africa, Asia and the Caribbean, increasingly became a pluralist, culturally and systemically inclusive, World Community, in place of the 'classical', largely Western-centred world public order system in place even in 1945 at the close of World War II when the United Nations was founded.

It is not surprising that, under this new impulse, the *Institut de Droit International*, founded in 1873 by a group of predominantly European (including Imperial Russia) jurists, should decide today to become involved in new 'leading edge' international-law making, this after having, in the immediate post-World War II years, refused to place on its agenda for research, study and debate by its own expert commissions, the large policy concept of peaceful accommodation and settlement, under law and legal processes of the then dangerous tension-issues of the early Cold War years. Peaceful Coexistence, the rubric favoured by Soviet bloc and also neutralist, emerging countries, would be firmly rejected for study in its legal aspects by the *Institut* and, at the same time also, by the UN's own International Law Commission (ILC), and even by the UN General Assembly's Sixth (Legal) Committee. It would, however, be taken up subsequently, and successfully in terms of early results, by the private, non-governmental, London-based International Law Association at the insistence of its Continental European members and also of non-aligned countries members (India and Yugoslavia in particular). Two months only after the Kennedy-Khrushchev Moscow Partial Test Ban Treaty of August 1963, the UN General Assembly finally agreed to strike a Special Committee – the Committee on Friendly Relations and Cooperation among States in accordance with the United Nations Charter, its title a polite euphemism to satisfy some still reluctant Western States who felt Peaceful Coexistence was 'too political'. Seven years later, the Special Committee's Declaration, the celebrated UN General Assembly Resolution 2625 (XXV) of 24 October 1970, became law. It is now to be found invoked, as authoritative starting point in its own right, for any major international treaty or accord on peace and security. The Declaration's primary principles are: mutual respect for territorial integrity and sovereignty; non-aggression; non-interference in internal affairs; equality and mutual advantage. These high-level general principles of international law certainly became guidelines for the Soviet-Western *Détente* process of the late 1960s and 1970s: the pragmatic, empirical, problem-oriented, step-by-step approach, and provided an operational methodology for conflict-resolution on peace and security questions.

11   Non-Intervention in Civil Wars – 1975 *Institut* Resolution (including Humanitarian Aid)

One of the early initiatives of the *Institut*, after it had become positively involved, of its own accord, in the Friendly Relations/Coexistence debate, was to essay a contemporary statement as to the positive law regarding non-intervention – something that had not been seriously studied, in depth, since the between-the-two World Wars era when, after some high-minded legal declarations, in particular the Kellogg-Briand Pact of 1928, it had essentially been brushed aside altogether as concerns respect for its largely customary law sources and rules, by the rush of events on to World War II: in particular, the very naked and un-apologetic involvement of Germany and Italy in the rapidly burgeoning Civil War in Spain (1936–1939) when the two Axis powers put their support, by way of material but also direct military action, behind the General Franco-led army revolt (with the dive-bombing of the defence-less civil population of Guernica as the most notable example). An *Institut* Commission, known as the 8th Commission (Chair/Rapporteur was the Swiss jurist Dietrich Schindler), tackled the problem boldly as the title of its topic, with the undoubted focus on German/Italian active military support of Franco's attempts to overthrow the elected Republican Government of Spain, indicated: 'The Principle of Non-Intervention in Civil Wars'.[3] The 8th Commission's Report, presented in 1975 with accompanying declaratory Resolution adopted by the *Institut* in plenary, is very clear in recognising in its Preamble that violation of the principle of non-intervention for the benefit of a party to a civil war too often led in practice to interference for the benefit of the opposition party to the existing legal government – a diplomatic understatement indeed. It also expressly prohibits "prematurely recognising a provisional government which has no effective control over a substantial part of the territories of the State in question"; and stipulates further that third States may give assistance only in compliance with the UN Charter and any other relevant rule of international law, subject to any measures prescribed or authorised by the United Nations. The 8th Commission Resolution does, however, in its Article 4 ('Humanitarian Aid') permit the forwarding of relief or other forms of purely humanitarian aid for the benefit of victims of a civil war, and concludes, further, that where the territory controlled by one party can be reached only by crossing the territory controlled by the other party or the territory of a third party, free passage over

---

3   "The Principle of Non-Intervention in Civil Wars" (8th Commission: Dietrich Schindler), *Annuaire de l'Institut de Droit International*, Vol. 56, Session de Wiesbaden, 1975, pp. 119 *et seq.*; p. 545 (Report, Debate, Resolution).

such territory should be granted to any relief consignment insofar as provided for in the Geneva Convention of 1949 on Protection of Civilians in War-Time. This particular reservation (humanitarian aid) to the 1975 *Institut* Resolution's general prohibition of gratuitous interventions in civil conflicts and interdiction of "premature" recognition of rebel forces would provide the inspiration for the *Institut*'s decision, thereafter, to create a new, special Commission (16th Commission; Rapporteur – Budislav Vukas) under a mandate to report on 'Humanitarian Assistance' (discussed hereunder).

III   2003 Bruges Declaration on the Use of Force[4]

The Bruges Declaration was adopted by a recorded vote of 90 to 15, with 12 abstentions, an unusual record for a body whose main research work has normally proceeded on a broad working consensus, followed by unanimous or near unanimous assent. But the Bruges Declaration on the Use of Force was presented only five months after the US/UK 'Coalition of the Willing' invasion of Iraq. Specifically, the US/UK recourse to force had taken place without prior legal validation by an express UN Security Council vote under the UN Charter's Chapter VII – this after a draft US/UK Resolution purporting to do that had lapsed due to failure to obtain more than three affirmative supporters in the 15-member Council, quite apart from any issue of Permanent Members veto.

The US/UK failure to obtain any sufficient support in the Security Council for the Iraq invasion in March 2003 was, one may suggest, the result of a profoundly negative reaction to a new 'unilateralisation' of US foreign policy under the George W. Bush presidency, though intellectual-legal roots of the opposition seem to be found also in an equally negative reaction to the earlier unilateral attack initiated by Western, predominantly NATO States in the 1999 Kosovo armed intervention. It was in fact suggested in the initial debate on the Bruges Declaration that the US/UK 'Coalition of the Willing' invasion of Iraq "under guise of a recall of the principles of International Law on the Recourse to Force the Bruges Declaration (on the Use-of-Force) was in truth a political condemnation of the US action in Iraq" (Prosper Weil). A more nuanced constitutional critique suggested that the *Institut*, in its capacity as "a scholarly body of indepedent experts…not a political assembly that dashes off resolutions of political or partisan interest" would have "negligible influence in the political sphere… and only prejudice its scholarly standing" (Stephen Schwebel). More striking

---

4   "Bruges Declaration on the Use of Force", *Annuaire de l'Institut de Droit International*, Vol. 71, II, Session de Bruges, 2003, pp. 279 *et seq.*, pp. 285–289 (Statements, Resolution).

perhaps in the sometimes impassioned discussion on the Bruges Declaration was the position taken by the former long-time British Foreign Office Legal Adviser, Sir Ian Sinclair who, much earlier in time when the *Institut*, and also the UN's own International Law Commission, and even the UN General Assembly's Sixth Legal Committee, were still refusing to allow the issue of Peaceful Coexistence between the two great opposing blocs, Soviet and Western, to be placed on their agenda (since deemed to be too 'political' and not 'legal' in character),[5] had come out nevertheless in support of its inclusion in the *Institut*'s working agenda. Sir Ian Sinclair indicated that he personally "did not support, and do not now support, the forcible action recently taken in Iraq by certain Governments", citing historical grounds for this position within *Institut* practice over the years apart from a sole exception the other way in 1877. Thereafter, as Sir Ian Sinclair suggested, the *Institut* had always refrained from expressing a collective view on particular instances of controversial recourse by one or more States to forcible action in, or against, the territory of other States. Here he listed, as examples, the use of force by the UK and France against Egypt in October/November 1956 (the Suez crisis); the Soviet Union against Hungary in November 1956, and then Czechoslovakia in 1968; and India during the action in Goa in the early 1960s. Characterising the Bruges Declaration as "barely disguised criticisms of individual Governments", he now resolved his own personal dilemma of choice by announcing his abstention in the *Institut*'s vote.

IV Military Interventions by International Organisations Other than the United Nations

When the *Institut* decided in late August 1999, at the same time that it adopted the Bruges Declaration on the Use of Force, to create a special Commission, with accelerated processes on the 'Authority under International Law of International Organisations other than the United Nations to Use Armed Force' (identified as the 10th Commission),[6] it was certainly reacting to the failed attempt by the US/UK 'Coalition of the Willing' in March 2003, to obtain

---

5   Sir Ian Sinclair, in: *Essays on International Law in Honour of Krishna Rao* (Nawaz, ed.), 1975, pp. 107, 108–109.
6   "The Authority under International Law of International Organisations other than the United Nations to Use Armed Force" (10th Commission: Thomas Franck), *Annuaire de l'Institut de Droit International*, Vol. 68, II, Session de Berlin, 1999, p. 469 (Creation of Commission).

advance UN Security Council legal approval by way of a prior, authorising resolution (dispensing with UN Charter, Chapter VII prohibitions on the Use-of-Force) for their armed invasion of Iraq. But the *Institut* reaction, then, was taken as scientific-legal Academy reacting to a manifest lack of substance in the factual premises put forward by the US/UK governments to justify that armed intervention – links to Taliban of the Iraq Regime; secret shipment of enriched uranium from former French African colonies; presence of Weapons of Mass Destruction in the Iraq government's hands. It was a technical judgment reinforced by the UN's own specially appointed Commissioner, Hans Blix, charged with the mandate to verify these allegations, who indicated that he could not as yet establish evidence to support the claims. The Security Council's considered non-action on the US/UK averments as to the facts did not, however, involve any necessary condemnation of the two governments bringing forward those claims. The *Institut*, in appointing a 19-member special Commission – its new 10th Commission[7] – had selected a US scholar (Thomas Franck) with an already established academic standing based on prior scientific-legal essays on Article 2(4) and Article 2(7) of the UN Charter, as chair/rapporteur. He had asked for, and received a mandate for a vastly accelerated process within the *Institut* that would dispense with the historical *Institut* practice, for its research Commissions, of a deliberately staged, step-by-step approach that would advance through a Preliminary Report identifying all relevant doctrinal writings and also the alternative or opposing positions taken by established jurists, followed by a Provisional Report incorporating Commission members' preliminary 'critiques' and comments and following up with a formal questionnaire as to members' own preferred policy choices; followed by a Final Report with analysis in depth of individual members' views, followed by a draft Resolution for vote in plenary session as expression of the *Institut*'s consensus. In opting for and receiving the *Institut*'s approval of a two-year maximum ceiling limit for the Commission's completion of its mandate and its definitive report back to the *Institut* in plenary session, there was the risk, always, of failure. A first short succinct Report from the Commission, that had emerged from exchange of written material and also a round-table informal meeting of Commission members immediately before the next, Vancouver plenary session in August 2001, brought only a handful of written responses from individual Commission members and no concrete conclusions or recommendations, other than to continue the Commission beyond its original, two years only ceiling, and maybe under a new, somewhat less precisely formulated

---

7 *Institut de Droit International*, Administrative Session, Bruges, *Annuaire de l'Institut de Droit International*, Vol. 71, II, Session de Bruges, 2003, pp. 36–45 (Interim Report).

title and mandate, and with a much looser, decentralised structure. The 10th Commission's failure to achieve more within the initial two-year mandate, at that particular time must be attributed, one may suggest, to the vagaries and varieties of juristic opinion on international law and policy in the post-Cold War era and also the return (hesitantly) to a unipolar world order system. The *Institut* executive, opting to hasten slowly, in a period of major historical transition and change, effectively put the issue on hold until its next, Krakow plenary session two years away in 2005. It changed the name of the 10th Commission and also divided its mandate and overall organisation into four separate and distinct problem-areas, each with four separate and distinct and autonomous Commission sub-groups that would operate independently of each other. Operationally, the 10th Commission, in its new, plural personality and also jurisdiction, did not really get under way until a still further plenary session in October 2007, at Santiago. By that time, while a majority consensus on a number of issues seemed still to be there, for all practical purposes the degree of intellectual-legal schism within the *Institut* was apparent and hardly capable of being bridged by legal drafting skills alone.

What had come back to the first plenary session, in Vancouver in 2001, after the high (beginning of the new century) legal optimism at Berlin in 1999, had been styled as a Draft Procedural Resolution that simply asked the *Institut* in plenary to determine "appropriate mode for continuing work pertaining to the law regarding the use of force by regional organisations." The reference to regional organisations was, certainly, a positive note. Presumably, in the absence of further qualification these would be the official, UN-recognised and UN-approved regional organisations for purposes of Chapter VIII of the UN Charter.

At the outset of the debate in plenary in Bruges[8] in 2003 on the 10th Commission's Draft Procedural Resolution, it had been pointed out cogently by Ian Brownlie that the only way of testing its content was by way of debating the factual record of the 1999 Kosovo crisis which was, of course, the topic at the origin of the Commission. In the same spirit Dr. Brownlie here cited UK Cabinet Minister Lord Robertson to the effect that NATO "had decided to project Western power further into the Balkans," and that it was only later that the UK Minister had decided to deal with "humanitarian intervention."

It was further suggested, critically, (Torres Bernárdez)[9] that following the 1999 intervention in Kosovo there would be, henceforward a *before* and an *after* Kosovo legal situation as to the application of armed force: for in Kosovo one

---

8 *Ibid.*, pp. 38–39.
9 *Ibid.*, p. 41.

THE UN CHARTER, CHAPTER VII, NON-USE-OF-FORCE AND NON-INTERVENTION 829

had opened the door with NATO so that now it is States in the singular sense and not only UN regional organisations – which arrogate to themselves the power to use force without the authorisation of the Security Council. One finds oneself in the situation *before* the United Nations Charter was adopted.

A much fuller and detailed opening up of the *rôle* of UN regional organisations under the United Nations Charter, was provided by Abulqawi Yusuf in suggesting that one should not limit oneself to the 1999 Kosovo crisis alone.[10] Here Dr. Yusuf recommended examining the empirical record of the African Union whose Charter legally enables interventions in cases of genocide and massive human rights abuses, noting that the 10th Commission Preliminary Report as submitted to the Vancouver plenary in 2001 had implied that the African Union was able to act in the same way as NATO had acted in 1999 in Kosovo (that is, asserting legal capacity to by-pass Article 53 of the UN Charter) and to undertake enforcement action without the Council's authorisation. This particular proposition Dr. Yusuf denied, stating that the African States' practice was inimical to the unilateral use of force: the OAU Summit Declaration of 2001 made after the 1999 Kosovo crisis stated that the African Union could not by-pass the Security Council.

V   Humanitarian Assistance: United Nations Regional Organisations, UN Charter Chapter VIII, Article 53

The emphasis throughout the *Institut*'s 2003 Bruges plenary on regional organisations – *bona fide* regional organisations in terms of Chapter VIII and Article 53 of the UN Charter – draws attention to the continuing timeliness of what was, perhaps, at the moment of its adoption in 1993, a still visionary projection of international law. The final Report of the 16th (Vukas) Commission[11] and its Resolution on Humanitarian Assistance take a large, inclusive view of their own mandate, and establish the problem-area as not merely covering the endangerment of fundamental human rights and the well-being of people resulting from international or internal armed conflicts, and from internal disturbances or violence and terrorist activities, but also from natural and technological disasters. Great disasters such as these, in the 16th Commission's view,

---

10   *Ibid.*, pp. 41–42.
11   "Humanitarian Assistance" (16th Commission: Budislav Vukas), *Annuaire de l'Institut de Droit International*, Vol. 71, II, Session de Bruges, 2003, pp. 133–250; pp. 262–277 (Report, Debates, Resolution); see also, Vukas, *The Humanitarian Assistance Bruges Resolution 2003* (Monograph with Foreword by Francisco Orrego Vicuña, President), 2003.

may affect not only individual States but also several States or entire regions and thus become a matter of concern for the international community as a whole. In postulating a right to humanitarian assistance, the Vukas Commission placed the primary responsibility to take care of the victims of disasters on the affected State in whose territory disasters occur; and the Commission also stipulated that if the affected State is unable to provide sufficient humanitarian assistance, it shall seek assistance from competent international organisations – the United Nations and the International Red Cross and Red Crescent in particular. Correlatively, the Commission expressly recognised that other States and international organisations have the right to offer humanitarian assistance to the affected State and that such an offer shall not be considered as unlawful interference in the internal affairs of the affected State, to the extent that it responds exclusively to a humanitarian character. In insisting, in terms, that the right to provide humanitarian assistance on the part of other States and international organisations to victims of the affected State is subject to the consent of the affected State, the Commission Report and Resolution place their emphasis throughout on cooperation. Article V (3) of the Resolution declares that an assisting State or organisation "shall not interfere, in any manner whatsoever in the internal affairs of the affected State"; but succeeding Articles VI and VII supplement this by affirming a duty to cooperate on the part of assisting States balanced by a duty of affected States not arbitrarily to reject *bona fide* humanitarian assistance. Legal teeth are provided to the latter proposition by the correlative proposition (Article VIII (3)) that "if a refusal to accept a *bona fide* offer of humanitarian assistance or to allow access to the victims leads to a threat to international peace and security," the UN Security Council may take the necessary measures under Chapter VII of the UN Charter.

The final section of the Resolution (X): "Relationship with other rules of international law" – declares that the Resolution is without prejudice to the principles and rules of international humanitarian law applicable in armed conflict, in particular the 1949 Geneva Conventions for the Protection of War Victims and the 1977 Additional Protocols. The latter express 'saving' clause is of some immediate relevance legally, and is unquestionably urgent in view of the repeated direct engagement of key international players in the major crisis situations of the early years of the 21th century: Kosovo in 1999 and Iraq in 2003 undoubtedly, but also Afghanistan 2004, Libya 2011–12, and Syria 2011–12. The International Law of Cooperation,[12] – a major aspiration of the triumphant Non-Aligned and Third World majority in the UN General Assembly, outside

---

12   *International Law. Achievements and Prospects* (Mohammed Bedjaoui, gen. ed.), UNESCO, 1991, pp. 427–435; 492–493.

the Bipolar Universe of the two superpowers, as Cold War gave way increasingly to Coexistence and then *Détente*, and finally Cooperation, in a number of new science and technology areas, provided an opportunity for transcending old barriers based on notions of colliding civilisations and competing political and social culture. In not merely identifying this new problem-area but also providing the means of resolving it on a thoroughly empirical, problem-oriented basis, the Resolution of the 16th Commission on 'Humanitarian Assistance' was, after extended debate, adopted by unanimity – by 38 votes to nil, with no abstentions.

VI Labours of Sisyphus: The *Institut's* 10th Commission (Use of Force), 1999–2013

In marked contrast to the ease of passage, and the unanimous vote for the Report and Resolution of the 16th Commission (Humanitarian Assistance), the 10th Commission, with its troubled mandate now operationally re-defined in bland, open-ended terms, as 'Present Problems of the Use of Force in International Law', was exposed thereafter to many exhausting trials and tribulations in the bid to obtain broad consensus support in an ultimate vote in plenary session. The strategy was manifest in the decision of the *Institut's* executive to split the Commission up into four separate, intendedly independent and autonomous Sub-Commissions, each with its own separate chair/rapporteur and reporting back directly to the *Institut* in plenary session. Approved at Bruges in 2003 but not fully operational until Krakow in 2005, the elaborate new process emerged as follows:

> 10th Commission: Sub-Group 'Self-Defence' (Emmanuel Roucounas);
> Sub-Group 'Humanitarian Intervention' (Michael Reisman);
> Sub-Group 'Authorisation of Recourse to Force by the United Nations' (Sreenivasa Rao);
> Sub-Group 'Intervention by Invitation' (Gerhard Hafner).

With the four autonomous Sub-Groups now at work, but this time using the classical, historical *Institut*-three-stage processes – Preliminary Report, with full exposé of doctrinal writings and opinions, as the first step – the *Institut* executive gave priority agenda status to the Sub-Group on 'Humanitarian Intervention' as the potentially most controversial and divisive question. The concept of Humanitarian Intervention as developed historically in the late 19th century in classical, Western-centred international law (and somewhat later in US doctrines in application to Latin America and the Caribbean), had, by the early 20th century, become generally derided and discarded by Western scholars and jurists as having served, historically, as a convenient cloak for imperial-style interventions by Western European colonial powers in advancement and enforcement of their own political and especially economic interests in colonial territories or cognate 'spheres of influence' overseas, with the military element in enforcement, or threat thereof, being especially notable in regard to usurious economic development or natural resources exploitation long-term contracts. The Sub-Group on Humanitarian Intervention was particularly well-served by its chair/rapporteur Michael Reisman, a US scholar and writer who had been a student and later legal co-author with Myres McDougal, co-founder with Harold Lasswell of the US Law-as-Policy-Science school. Allowing for the drawn-out process of discussion and debate within the Sub-Group itself, it was not effectively until 2007 at Santiago that plenary debate could begin on the terms of a Resolution that would state or re-state the international law.

The agenda for the concrete debate at Santiago in 2007 was effectively set by jurists such as Budislav Vukas.[13] He argued that only the United Nations and regional arrangements under Chapter VIII of the UN Charter are "permitted to intervene by using any form of force. Individual States could be entitled to intervene only with the authorisation of the UN. In permitting intervention, the United Nations must be sure that the reasons for intervention are humanitarian, and that there is no kind of political goals. Moreover, intervention should never be permitted if it is not sure that it will not cause additional suffering to the population which the intervener pretends to protect."

Rejoining the debate in Santiago at a later stage, Dr. Vukas, as jurist, provided a coolly dispassionate evaluation of the NATO powers Kosovo 1999 intervention:

> The 1999 NATO intervention probably contributed to the fall of the Milosevic regime a year later. However, the direct result of the bombardment was the death of more persons in Serbia [including Kosovo] than the total number of Milosevic's victims. Moreover, the NATO attacks caused the migration of tens of thousands of Albanians, Serbs, Roma and other minorities from Kosovo to the neighbouring countries. ...It can be concluded that the NATO intervention was undertaken for political

---

13 *Annuaire de l'Institut de Droit International*, Vol. 72, Session de Santiago, 2007, p. 274 (Vukas).

reasons in order to get rid of the Serbian maniacal leader who had terrorised a great part of former Yugoslavia in order to realise the idea of a Great Serbia. The victims of his forces in Kosovo in 1998 and 1999 were only an excuse for the NATO intervention. There were many moments in the preceding decade when the international community should have intervened in order to save hundreds of thousands of his victims in the Balkans.[14]

In similar vein, Abdulqawi Yusuf stated that "Armed Intervention, by whatever name it is called, or however it is justified, is still viewed with great suspicion and apprehension, unless it is carried out in the context of an operation duly authorised by the UN Security Council."[15] He contended that while it is largely settled today that the UN Security Council has the right to authorise intervention on humanitarian grounds by itself characterising the situation as a "threat to the peace or a breach of the peace" under Chapter VII of the Charter, this has come about more as a subsequent practice (and a very recent one as that) rather than as a Charter principle empowering it to do so. He concluded that, "whether one calls it 'duty to protect' or 'right of humanitarian intervention', there still appears to be a wide gap between what might be considered desirable and what constitutes the reality today in International Law." He recommended, once more, the study of developed practice within UN regional organisations constituted under Chapter VIII of the UN Charter – in the practical reconciliation of UN Charter Chapter VII, Imperative Principles of Non-Use-of-Force and Non-Intervention and of collective regional concerns, where what is involved are massacres and massive human rights violations. Members of the African Union (AU) have consented to limit their sovereignty by treaty and to confer upon the organs of their intergovernmental organs the authority to determine the circumstances calling for forcible interventions – war crimes, genocide, and crimes against humanity. Such armed intervention is predicated upon concrete fact-finding – by the African Union as the Regional Organisation under Chapter VIII of the UN Charter.

The discussion and debate in plenary session of the *Institut* on the Sub-Group on Humanitarian Intervention lasted the full week of the Santiago Session, October 21 to 28, the time being taken up in innumerable proposals for amendments or modification of the text of the original draft Resolutions as submitted. By the end of the week of debate, the original title, Humanitarian Intervention, had been dropped. In the interest of producing a Commission

---

14   *Ibid.*, pp. 286–287 (Vukas).
15   *Ibid.*, pp. 274–277 (Yusuf).

consensus that would have some teeth in it, the President of the *Institut*, Orrego Vicuña, very late in the day, announced an unusual procedural step of a Presidential Declaration which would be annexed to the Sub-Group draft final Resolution text as supplementary, on the record, but that would delete nothing from the draft Resolution itself. Otherwise, if the President's proposal were not to be accepted, one would then conclude the Sub-Group with nothing. The President's Declaration: "The question of the lawfulness of military actions which have not been authorised by the United Nations will be examined by the *Institut* in another session."[16] President Orrego Vicuña's proposal was then put to the vote at his request, and adopted by 18 votes in favour, 12 opposed, and 10 abstentions. The draft Resolution as amended over the course of the week's debates was then submitted to plenary vote and adopted by 31 votes to nil, with 2 abstentions. In the result, the substantive issues raised by President Orrego Vicuña with his Declaration – the lawfulness of military actions which had not been authorised by the United Nations – would be entrusted, as mandate, to a new Sub-Group headed by the Argentine jurist, Dr. Vinuesa, though the Sub-Group would not be able to have its report and Resolution presented in final plenary before September 2013.

What in the end would be the outcome of the 10th Commission's Sisyphean labours, with the delays – from September 1999, on to 2007 and then on to 2013, – in execution of the original (two-year express) mandate from Berlin – to report on 'The Authority over International Law of International Organisations other than the United Nations to Use Armed Force'? The original, comprehensive 10th Commission had been set up in the unhappy reaction of many jurists to the return to unilateralism with the 1999 Kosovo Armed Intervention, and the seeming deliberate intent of its main political players then to by-pass the United Nations Charter's restrictions on the use-of-force and on armed intervention by intervening without any prior legal authority from the UN Security Council. It was the same anguished reaction that led on, inevitably, to the Bruges Declaration on the Use of Force, adopted in the *Institut* by overwhelming majority but with significant negative votes and, even more, significant abstentions. The splitting up of the original comprehensive 10th Commission into the four autonomous Sub-Groups, and then the decision, when it became apparent that dissension over substantive legal issues still remained, to make the Sub-Group on Humanitarian Intervention the main arena for channeling the disagreement and blunting its impact, stemmed from an *Institut* executive search for consensus, even if it meant diluting the substantive content of any legal recommendations that might

---

16   *Ibid.*, p. 365 (Declaration of President Orrego Vicuña).

ultimately emerge. President Orrego Vicuña's high diplomatic intervention in the final debate at Santiago with his Presidential Declaration to be annexed to any final Resolution was an elegant and effective exercise on his part. Chair/Rapporteur Reisman's dropping of the title 'Humanitarian Intervention' was made gracefully, and realistically, in recognition that that very term itself had become a veritable *bête noire* for jurists, even before the collapse of the European colonial era with its purported justification and legitimisation of Western imperial invasions, political and economic alike in their origins. The overly extended debate of Santiago within this particular Sub-Group helped open the way to a full and complete acceptance of the Vukas 16th Commission's Report and Resolution on Humanitarian Assistance as the way to go forward, confidently, in incorporating the newer humanitarian impulses present in international law-in-action while fully respecting classical national sovereignty norms. The thrust of the unanimously adopted Vukas Commission Resolution is to apply strong enforcement sanctions against genocide, crimes against humanity, and war crimes – and this most effectively through regional action expressed through UN Charter Chapter VIII organisations like the African Union.

In a comment addressed to the Chair/Rapporteur Michael Reisman of the Sub-Group as it was then titled 'Humanitarian Intervention' (now re-named 'Humanitarian Assistance'), Dr. Vukas made the (logical enough in itself) proposition that the "supervision of humanitarian intervention should be accorded to a UN body having broad competence. The International Criminal Court should have the role already determined by its Statute".[17] One might well ask, why not? It seems obvious enough in constitutional-legal terms. It would be contested strongly by some in the extended political-legal debates, after the event, on the legality of the certain aspects of the armed interventions in Libya and in Syria in 2011–2012 and claims to a unilateral right to make pre-emptive air strikes. On this proposition, the International Criminal Court might be able to extend jurisdiction against heads-of-state and heads-of-government personally and their agents who violate the fundamental principles of international humanitarian law – genocide, war crimes, crimes against humanity, and the like. The new International Criminal Court is now composed, in significant measure, of new, younger jurists, from new, non-classical countries who might rise to a challenge like this, including extending grounds for asserting jurisdiction to cover illegal recourses to armed intervention made without the UN Security Council's prior authorisation.

---

17   *Annuaire* (Bruges), Vol. 70, II, pp. 38–39.

It is a pity to have to pass so quickly over other Sub-Groups Reports and debates and Resolutions – 'Self-Defence' (Roucounas) and 'Intervention by Invitation' (Hafner). Both Sub-Groups were fully aware of the obligation to respect the primacy of the UN Security Council in issues of the legality of armed intervention and the necessity of obtaining prior Security Council authority dispensing from the prohibitions on use-of-force and armed interventions imposed by Chapter VII of the Charter. The insistence by the 1975 Schindler Commission against any "premature" recognition of a rebel or invading power until the position of an incumbent government has become demonstrably hopeless, has come to mind most recently in the supervening historical re-examination of the actions of some of the prime intervenors in the recent Libyan and Syrian situations. The history, from the Spanish Civil War (1936–1939) of the spurious 'invitations' to intervene relied upon by Germany and Italy for their political-economic support and direct military aid (including aerial bombing) to the rebel military junta seeking to mount a *coup d'état* against the constitutionally elected Republican Government of Spain, are salutary reminders of the dangers of deceit or fraud in similar situations even today. These dangers are amply recognised in the Reports and Resolutions of these other Sub-Groups.

The crucial *rôle* of objective fact-finding in assessing crisis-situations and the justification for claims to armed interventions – *with* the prior authorisation of the Security Council by an enabling Resolution, and even more *without* any such prior Security Council Resolution – were adverted to by Professor Brownlie eloquently – within the *Institut*, but even more so in his magisterial expert deposition before the United Kingdom's House of Commons. The Brownlie deposition was taken up and adopted by the Canadian Senate's Committee on Foreign Affairs and also widely cited in the Canadian House of Commons in three separate house debates, held *before*, *during*, and *after* the 1999 Kosovo Armed Intervention. In these debates, the Canadian House of Commons (as with the Canadian Senate before it) insisted on the primacy of the United Nations Security Council (and also the UN General Assembly, on the 'Uniting for Peace' Resolution of 1950 precedent) in any decisions on the use-of-force and armed intervention. Although Canada did in fact, under pressure from (NATO) allies, go along with the by-passing of the United Nations for purposes of the armed intervention in Kosovo in March 1999, there were some obvious regrets within Canada, in Parliament and at large. Prime Minister Jean Chrétien in March 2003, notwithstanding strong US/UK diplomatic pressures to go along with the socalled 'Coalition of the Willing' in the invasion of Iraq, took over the files himself and said "No!"

While Prime Minister Chrétien's decision was based, in terms, on the failure of the arguments for armed intervention against Iraq in March 2003, to meet rigorous standards of proof in the proffered evidentiary grounds for the US/UK invasion – the fact-finding issue, on which Mr. Chrétien was subsequently proved to be right, did mark a re-affirmation once more, of traditional Canadian State practice, from the outset, of support for multilateralism, and for collective action (armed action, if demonstrably legal) under the aegis of the United Nations and within the UN Charter and general international law.[18]

VII Evolving Contemporary International Law on Use-of-Force and Military Interventions (including Civil Wars)

Has the time come to consider undertaking, through the United Nations (and also the International Criminal Court, if relevant) empirically-based individual case studies of the most recent exemplars of armed interventions in crisis situations: Kosovo (1999) as the starting point (the various national studies having, designedly no doubt, been rather narrow in their technical focus and therefore somewhat inconclusive in the result); Iraq (2003); and Libya and Syria (from their beginnings in 2011 and on to denouement in 2012). The experience of the *Institut*'s 10th Commission, from creation in 1999 over the ensuing two decades and more, suggests some differences on the facts, of a legal-systemic character, and others of a legal-cultural nature, between States in Dean Acheson's phrase "present at the creation" of the UN and UN Charter in 1945, and the emerging new major powers of the 21st century. Among the questions are:

1. The exact legal status in international law terms, of military alliances, whether treaty-based organisations like NATO, or more informal, *ad hoc* 'alliances of convenience' like the US/UK-led 'Coalition of the Willing' in the case of the March 2003, armed incursion against Iraq? Military alliances such as this are, clearly, not UN regional organisations under Chapter VIII of the UN Charter and do not have the inherent powers flowing from that status under the UN Charter.
2. The legal capacity of such military alliances, treaty-based or *ad hoc*, even when claiming to be exercising a legal authority derived from a prior

---

18 Prime Minister Chrétien's public addresses and statements on the US/UK armed intervention against Iraq in March 2003, are collected in documentary form in my *Guest Editorial*, in: *Canadian Council on International Law Bulletin*, Vol. 29, No. 1 (Winter/Spring), 2003, p. 1.

authorisation from the UN Security Council (or UN General Assembly), to be able to act counter to imperative principles of international customary law – as, for example, the prohibition on 'premature' recognition of a rebel group *before* the position of the *de jure* government has become hopeless.

3. In exercising what, at best, could be interpreted as a purely *delegated* legal authority to be derived from a prior, specific legal authorisation flowing from a UN Security Council (or General Assembly) Resolution addressed to the specified armed invasion involved, it would appear that such informal, treaty-based or *ad hoc*, military alliance could not itself further delegate any such UN-derived delegated power. Nor could it itself, without going back to the Security Council (or General Assembly), legislate itself into new, additional powers not specified, in terms, in the original claimed delegation. The issue has arisen in connection with the two most recent (Libya, 2011–2012; Syria 2011–2012) cases where all the publicly known facts attest to the intrusion of a 'régime change' agenda in which the intervening military alliance might actively take sides in a still evolving internal conflict so as to impose the military alliance's own preferred choice and designation of a postulated new coalition government of one or more among various hitherto unknown competing rebel groups.

4. Finally, in terms of decisions (resolutions) by the UN Security Council (or General Assembly) purporting to authorise armed interventions by duly adopted resolutions under the UN Charter, what constitutes a majority vote, beyond the special majority vote required, under the UN Charter, for purposes of important (non-procedural) questions? Up to the time of the celebrated 'Uniting for Peace' Resolution, adopted by the UN General Assembly in November 1950, in response to what the General Assembly conceived then to be the potentiality of a Permanent Member Veto in the Security Council, it had been generally assumed that the text of UN Charter Article 27(3) – clear and explicit as it was ("an affirmative vote of nine members, including the concurring votes of the permanent members") was governing. A new practice, however, stemming directly from the 1950 Korean crisis precedent, then emerged into subsequent general acceptance within the UN, that an *abstention* should not be counted as a negative for these purposes. One intriguing new question, emerging from the particular UN decision-making on the Libyan crisis in 2011, would be as to whether *mass abstention* (as in the Libyan situation) involving five Security Council members and including two Permanent Members of the Security Council, should not call for re-examination of the logic and

rationality of the 1950 precedent, reflecting as it did the power realities of the immediate post-World War II world public order system when the UN Charter was adopted. As one moves progressively to a new, pluralist, multi-culturally inclusive World Community, is there a case for insisting also on a 'representative' majority, reflecting all main political and social and, one might add, legal systems, as the predicate for UN-based decisions on war/peace crisis issues?[19]

---

19   For further discussion of these issues, reference may be made generally to the symposium volume, *Multiculturalism and International Law* (Sienho Yee and Jacques-Yvan Morin, eds.; *Foreword* by Boutros Boutros-Ghali; *Introduction* by Shigeru Oda), 2009. For exposition of recent opinions by the author, see my extended essay, "A New, Multicultural World Community and an Emerging New, Pluralist World Order System", as Honorary Editor of the *Chinese Journal of International Law*, Vol. 11, No. 3, 2012, pp. 469–486; and my lectures to the *United Nations Audiovisual Library of International Law* (variously on "Peaceful Coexistence", "Multiculturalism", "Judicial Activism and the ICJ", and the "New Pluralism in International Law") available on the UN Official Website at <http://untreaty.un.org/cod/avl/faculty/mcwhinney.html>.

CHAPTER 45

Some Remarks on Soft Law and Some Specific Forms of Treaty Making

*Robert Mrljić**

I   Introduction

In the last few decades the proliferation of and problems related to the 'soft law' phenomenon have become obvious in many fields of international law. Among the 'classical', formal sources of international law, the field of treaty law seems to be the most prevalent in this sense. The most important reason for this is the rapid proliferation of bilateral and multilateral treaties. In its many forms treaty-making has become more and more influenced by different forms of 'soft law'. Many of these forms have been known in treaty-making processes for decades, but their increased use in a 'soft-law' context imposes questions of the normative nature of such acts. In other words, the question is whether some of these acts any longer belong to the field of treaty law or to the still not completely legally charted area of 'soft law'. Bearing that in mind, we will try to offer some answers in relation to three kinds of such acts: gentlemen's agreements, memoranda of understanding and so-called 'political agreements'. Following this, a short analysis of the 'Brussels Agreement on normalisation of relations' signed by the prime ministers of Serbia and Kosovo will be conducted as well.

II   Gentlemen's Agreements

These kinds of acts can be traced back at least to 19th century diplomatic practice.[1] There are various explanations of their legal significance. In relation to that, many authors rely on Eisman's proposals. Indeed, Klabbers accepts Eisman's tripartite division of gentlemen's agreements into:

---

*   LLM (London), PhD candidate (Zagreb); Court of Justice of the European Union. All views and opinions expressed in this article belong solely to the author and do not represent the views of the author's employer.
1   See J. Klabbers, *The Concept of Treaty in International Law*, Kluwer Law International, The Hague, London, Boston, 1996, pp. 16–17.

a) those in which the moral characteristics and personal engagement of the persons who are concluding it are highlighted;
b) additional non-formal or interpretative agreements in relation to the main agreement;
c) non-formal normative agreements.

Klabbers accepts the validity of the first two categories, but objects to the third.[2] His objections are based on his generally very negative attitude towards any kind of 'soft law'.[3] For him, the third category is completely unacceptable and can be identified to some extent with other phenomena which cannot be considered as having legal significance, such as: non-formal agreements, *de facto* agreements, non-obligatory agreements, political texts, 'extra-legal' or non-legal texts, agreements without legal significance and 'soft law' instruments.[4] In addition, we adhere to his opinion about two specific kinds of documents belonging to the third group which are without any legal relevance, namely press *communiqués* and joint *communiqués* – actually different kinds of press statements, usually issued after various political meetings.[5]

M. Virally also agrees with Eisman's categorisation of gentlemen's agreements, but points out that gentlemen's agreements concluded within an international organisation have different characteristics when compared to those concluded among various states.[6] In his opinion, the difference lies in the 'greater' legal significance of the gentlemen's agreements concluded within an international organisation, as they are concluded by undisputed official representatives of states.[7]

---

2 *Ibid.*, p. 17.
3 See J. Klabbers, "Undesirability of Soft Law", 67(4) *Nordic Journal of International Law*, 1998; "Reflexions on Soft International Law in a Privatized World", 16 *Finnish Yearbook of International Law*, 2005.
4 J. Klabbers, *supra* 1, p. 18.
5 *Ibid.*, *supra* 1, p. 19. Although we agree with Klabbers on this point, it should be kept in mind that there are examples of historically very important acts which had a huge impact on the creation of some of the most important international legal texts in the 20th century which initially took the form of press statements. The most prominent example of this is the Atlantic Charter of 1941, signed by British Prime Minister W. Churchill and US President F.D. Roosevelt.
6 M. Virally, "La distinction entre textes internationaux de portée juridique et textes internationaux dépourvus de portée juridique (à l'exception des textes émanant des organisations internationales)", in: *Annuaire de l'Institut de Droit International*, Vol. 60, Tome I, Session de Cambridge, 1983, pp. 208–209.
7 *Ibid.*, pp. 210–211.

On the other hand, Nasser finds three possible categories of gentlemen's agreements. The first relates to the rules of courtesy, applied during negotiations on some international agreements, and it means that some question cannot be asked in a further stage of negotiations, after being successfully negotiated in some earlier phase.[8] The second category of his understanding of gentlemen's agreements indicates some of them as agreements which exist and produce legal effects firstly for the persons who have concluded them.[9] The specificity of the second category is related to the fact that this kind of gentlemen's agreement exists as much as the official status of the persons who have concluded them with the intention of solving some interstate problems.[10] It seems to us that the main characteristic of these kinds of agreements is their temporary nature, visible in the termination of their validity at the moment of the conclusion of a treaty dealing with the same problems. The second characteristic is the character of privacy these kinds of agreements have, based on the crucial role of persons who have concluded them. The last category of gentlemen's agreements in accordance with Nasser's classification is the most general one – one which defines them all as "*soft law* agreements resulted from the coordinated efforts of states." When analysing Nasser's categorisation of gentlemen's agreements we find the first two categories conceptually acceptable and relevant in state practice. However, the same cannot be said for his third category, which is actually defined too broadly and does not differentiate at all from the general understanding of 'soft law'.

Although Klabbers and Nasser have raised some important questions about the nature and sorts of gentlemen's agreements, we believe that Schachter's findings in this field are the most relevant. Indeed, Schachter finds that gentlemen's agreements are a kind of 'soft law' characterised with precise and clear stipulations, which do not have the force of a legal act, but are widely respected in state practice.[11] Schachter also reminds us that in practice heads of states and governments, as well as ministers of foreign affairs, are persons who in the majority of cases conclude gentlemen's agreements that can imply that the stipulated obligations will be respected.[12] By the same token, we agree with his attitude about the function of these agreements, which can be understood as

---

8 S.H. Nasser, *Sources and Norms of International Law: A Study on Soft Law*, Galda + Wilch Verlag, Glienicke/Berlin, Madison/Wisconsin, 2008, pp. 133–134.
9 *Ibid.*, p. 134.
10 *Ibid.*
11 O. Schachter, "The Twilight Existence of Nonbinding International Agreements", 71(2) *American Journal of International Law*, 1977, p. 299.
12 *Ibid.*

the preparation documents for the drafting of the obligatory – 'hard law' document.[13] The same can be claimed for his opinion that the eventual (non-)creation of a 'hard law' document on that ground is the best indicator of its usefulness in a particular case.

III Memoranda of Understanding

When analysing this kind of 'soft law' documents issued mostly by states, a variety of different opinions can be found as well. Nasser finds that there are basically two possible explanations with respect to their legal nature.[14] The first is based on the assumption that they can be treated as a kind of treaty without a clear mechanism for entering into force.[15] That is contrary to the second possible explanation by which memoranda of understanding are purely political instruments, devoid of any legal significance.[16] His choice in regard to this question is a moderate one and he finds that possible determinations of the legal, 'soft law', or purely political nature of such instruments can be properly established only after thorough analysis of every single document, and certainly not by trying to do the same for memoranda of understanding in general.[17]

Klabbers's position on this question is completely different. In general, he considers every agreement concluded among states which has a legal nature – meaning influence on future behaviour and not belonging to the domestic legal system – as undoubtedly being a treaty.[18] On the other hand, his conception of memoranda of understanding allows him to regard them as a kind of administrative agreement, meaning those concluded by persons, state agencies and/or departments whose capacity to conclude such kind of agreements may be put in question, and he supports that statement with some examples from state practice.[19]

---

13 *Ibid.* For other opinions on gentlemen's agreements see for example C. Chinkin, "Normative Development in the International Legal System", in: D. Shelton (ed.), *Commitment and Compliance: The Role of Non-Binding Norms in the International Legal System*, Oxford University Press, Oxford, New York, 2000, p. 25; K. Zemanek, "Is the Term 'Soft Law' Convenient?", in: *Liber Amicorum Professor Ignaz Seidl-Hohenvaldern*, Kluwer Law International, The Hague, London, Boston, 1988, p. 857.
14 Nasser, *supra* 8, p. 136.
15 *Ibid.*
16 *Ibid.*
17 *Ibid.*
18 See Klabbers, *supra* 1, especially pp. 121–156.
19 *Ibid.*, p. 22.

For Aust, there is no doubt that their main feature is actually their non-binding character, so he defines them as instruments concluded among states which are not binding under international law or law in general, and, consequently, their non-obligatory nature cannot be disputed.[20] For him, there is no doubt that there is a possibility for a conclusion of agreements between states which bear predominantly political characteristics.[21] He supports that statement with the argument that there is no single rule of international law finding every transaction between states to be obligatory, and that these inter-state transactions should even less be framed in obligatory treaty form.[22] The same author recalls the fact that most multilateral memoranda of understanding have a 'soft law' character, differing from 'standard', bilateral memoranda of understanding.[23] By trying to trace the reasons for the use of memoranda of understanding, he points out the ease of their conclusion due to a non-formal procedure and the inclusion of other entities different from states.[24] Other reasons include an easier procedure in relation to their change, termination, settlement of disputes and interpretation.[25] On the other hand, his critique of memoranda of understanding is related to the fact that they are often perceived as not as worthy as treaties, and that there are many cases of poorly drafted memoranda of understanding as well as those without a proper mechanism of implementation.[26] Aust reminds us not to forget that one of the main features of these acts – their confidential nature – is also the main reason why many of them are not made public at all.[27]

We find that the aforementioned facts support the cautious approach to the whole problem related to these acts. In general, our position on this question is similar to Nasser's and Aust's views. As it is clear that there can be very different kinds of memoranda of understanding, we find it necessary to make conclusions about their legal/non-legal nature only relevant for every single case, without trying to make too many generalisations in the field.

---

20 A. Aust, *Modern Treaty Law and Practice*, Cambridge University Press, Cambridge, New York, Melbourne, Madrid, Cape Town, Singapore, Sao Paulo, Delhi, 2007, p. 32.
21 *Ibid.*, p. 50.
22 *Ibid.*
23 *Ibid.*
24 *Ibid.*, pp. 45–47.
25 *Ibid.*
26 *Ibid.*
27 *Ibid.*, p. 49., pp. 52–53.

IV Political Agreements

The questions and doubts in relation to political agreements in general are most complex when compared with those associated with gentlemen's agreements and memoranda of understanding. The main reason for this is that, despite the fact that some authors consider gentlemen's agreements and memoranda of understanding to be a kind of political, non-obligatory agreement, the complexity related to their understanding is inherited from the complex relations between the orders of politics and international law.[28] In other words, there is no doubt that every treaty reflects a certain political value, but is it possible to construe a category of political agreements, meaning agreements whose main character is political, *i.e.* that they are not legally binding?

Schachter finds that it is possible to determine criteria for establishing political agreements in comparison with treaties. By doing this, he refers firstly to the intention of the parties, then to the analysis of the language, and finally to the circumstances in which the agreement was made.[29] Possible additional criterion in his classification can be whether these kinds of agreements have been registered or not in accordance with Article 102 of the United Nations Charter.[30] Aside from the aforementioned, Schachter proposes also some 'special criteria' relating to whether the agreement has been published or not in the national registry of treaties and whether or not national authorities referred to it as a treaty when submitting it to the national parliaments.[31] His general conclusion is in line with the opinion that the political character of an agreement can be established only by the empirical examination of the state practice.[32]

On the other hand, Müllerson finds four possible kinds of acts which can be found in international relations, on the edge between the political and the legal systems:[33]

---

28 For a very good analysis of the main problems in the troubled relations between political order and international law order see: R.B. Bilder, "Beyond Compliance, Helping Nations Cooperate", in: D. Shelton (ed.), *Commitment and Compliance: The Role of Non-Binding Norms in the International Legal System*, Oxford University Press, Oxford, New York, 2001, especially pp. 65–67.
29 Schachter, *supra* 11, p. 296.
30 *Ibid.*
31 *Ibid.*
32 *Ibid.*, p. 300.
33 R. Müllerson, "Sources of International Law: New Tendencies in Soviet Thinking", 83(3) *American Journal of International Law*, 1989, p. 510.

- legally binding norms of international law;
- recommendatory norms, found in resolutions of international organisations;
- rules relating to the system of morality;
- political obligations.[34]

The specificity of Müllerson's approach lies in his belief that international political agreements are obligatory considering their legal value.[35] He supports this view with arguments relating to the basic specificities of that kind of agreement:

- 'wide' application of the *rebus sic stantibus* clause;
- the impossibility of the application of sanctions in the event of their infringement, *i.e.* a significant difference exists related to their application.[36]

Müllerson finds this category of political agreements with obligatory legal force useful as it shows the need to consider the state as legally responsible in situations where its representatives sign agreements which have political value.[37] However, he allows, as well, for the possibility of existence of purely political, *i.e.* non-obligatory agreements, which can be concluded by political representatives of different states.[38] If that is the case, two elements should be detected which imply the existence of such kind of agreements:

- avoidance of traditional treaty stipulations (treaty, covenant, convention, agreement);
- insertion of clauses which show the non-obligatory character of the document (*e.g.* reference to the non-registration of the document at the United Nations Secretariat in accordance with the Article 102 of the United Nations Charter).[39]

We do not find Müllerson's arguments convincing enough. First of all, his systematisation of different categories of agreements is inconsistent. On the one side of his analysis are legally binding agreements, but on the other side there are both political agreements which are mostly legally binding acts and

---

34 *Ibid.*
35 *Ibid.*, pp. 510–511.
36 *Ibid.*
37 *Ibid.*
38 *Ibid.*
39 *Ibid.*, p. 511.

political agreements without legal significance.[40] His explanation of the use of the *rebus sic stantibus* clause does not seem very fruitful as this clause can be applied or not depending on the existence or non-existence of criteria which lead to its application/non-application. Indeed, by allowing some special, 'wider' understanding of that clause in political agreements, the meaning of the clause in its primary, legal meaning becomes obscured.

Nasser finds that international political agreements are often treated as actually valid and obligatory treaties which have certain specificities compared to 'classic' treaties.[41] These specificities are viewed as some degree of 'fragility' and instability of such treaties in relation to their content.[42] Nasser understands 'fragility' in this case as the expectation that states will not adhere to the obligations derived from that treaty, since those treaties often used to be so important for the state that their legal and obligatory character would not be respected if political circumstances significantly changed.[43] In general, he finds these explanations of 'specificities' to be simplified and as neglecting the fact that estimation of potential compliance/non-compliance with the treaty cannot be understood as the measure of its legal nature.[44] He reminds us also that infringement of the obligations found in some treaties can, depending on the concrete circumstances, be the reason for the termination of the treaty, but holds that this does not deprive the treaty of its legal nature.[45] We found Nasser's reasoning in this case to be balanced and acceptable, even more so when he states that the potential avoidance of some treaties does not mean that they are deprived of their legal status.[46]

V   The Legal Nature of the 'Brussels Agreement on Normalisation of Relations'

The practical problems relating to the classification of some international agreements in terms of the main categories discussed above – gentlemen's agreements, memoranda of understanding, political agreements and treaties – can be

---

40   *Ibid.*
41   Nasser, *supra* 8, p. 122.
42   *Ibid.*
43   *Ibid.* Nasser points to changed circumstances in the field of state security as most prominent in this field.
44   *Ibid.*, p. 123.
45   *Ibid.*
46   *Ibid.*, p. 124. It has to be mentioned as well that Nasser is aware of the danger which can be caused by the widespread appearance of treaties with imprecise or doubtful meaning. *Ibid.*

detected very well if we look at the 'Brussels Agreement on normalisation of relations' (further: Brussels Agreement) signed by the Serbian Prime Minister Ivica Dačić and his Kosovar counterpart Hashim Taçi after meeting on 19th April 2013. The Brussels Agreement consists of fifteen points intended to ease the normalisation of relations between Serbia and Kosovo and to solve many political and practical problems existing on the terrain.[47] As the intention of this article is only to analyse some of the most common problems relating to the understanding of the different kinds of previously analysed acts, we will highlight only some points of the Brussels Agreement we find useful in relation to the categorisation of these agreements, and not the whole plethora of international legal and political problems in relation to Serbia and Kosovo.

If we try to find elements of the gentlemen's agreement in the Brussels Agreement, we will first establish that, at least on the formal side, the Agreement has some elements of the gentlemen's agreement mentioned above, such as: highlighted personal engagement of those concluding the agreement and the high political status of the same persons, additional (partially) interpretative agreements in relation to the main agreement and high degree of the guarantee for the execution of the agreement. On the other hand, it cannot be stated that the Agreement itself exists and depends mostly on the will of Mr. Dačić and Mr. Taçi, as is often the case with gentlemen's agreements, since both governments and parliaments have formally accepted the Brussels Agreement.[48]

An analysis of the Brussels Agreement in relation to memoranda of understanding looks clearer, as it is obvious that the Agreement is not unmentioned

---

[47] For the text of the Brussels Agreement in English see pp. 23–24 of the report of the Serbian government about the negotiation process, as submitted to the Serbian parliament: <http://www.parlament.gov.rs/upload/archive/files/cir/pdf/akta_procedura/2013/1666-13.pdf> (26 July 2013). The formal name of the Agreement in accordance with the aforementioned document is 'First agreement of principles governing the normalisation of relations', but as the expression 'Brussels Agreement on Normalisation of Relations' is overwhelmingly used, we choose to use it as well. For the political context of the Agreement see:<http://www.un.org/apps/news/story.asp?NewsID=44708&Cr=kosovo&Cr1#.UkhQEazOyvg> (29 September 2013); <http://eeas.europa.eu/top_stories/2013/190413__eu-facilitated_dialogue_en.htm> (29 September 2013); <http://www.crisisgroupblogs.org/across-eurasia/2013/05/07/the-kosovo-serbia-agreement-why-less-is-more/> (29 September 2013); <http://www.iss.europa.eu/de/publikationen/detail/article/belgrade-pristina-un-accord-historique-en-perspective/> (29 September 2013).

[48] See: <http://kryeministri-ks.net/repository/docs/Decision-126.pdf> (30 September 2013); <http://www.slglasnik.info/sr/38-26.04.2013/Sl.-Glasnik/38/2013/> (29 September 2013).

in public so as to be deprived of its legal nature, and consequently it cannot be considered as a non-binding 'soft law' document. On the other hand, the consideration of this agreement as a memorandum of understanding in practice helps in avoiding problems relating to the statehood status of Kosovo, particularly in relation to Serbia, as memoranda of understanding can also be concluded by entities other than states.

In addition, the consideration of the Brussels Agreement as a political agreement gives much more elements which can be pointed to. In addition, we find that Nasser's view is applicable, namely that both the political and legal characters of the Agreement 'coexist'. It has very strong political implications, but it is not devoid of its legal character in the sense of a classical treaty. In this case this is clearly visible if we look at the definition of the term 'treaty' in the 1969 Vienna Convention on the Law of Treaties, which puts the accent on the structural characteristics of treaties and not on their designation.[49] These structural characteristics of the Brussels Agreement, including the clear stipulation of the obligations of the contracting parties (most of which are or will be more precisely determined in subsequent agreements based on this one, implying that the Brussels Agreement may be considered a kind of framework agreement), the obligatory language used, rapid adoption of the agreement by both governments and parliaments,[50] and the consistent repetition of the intention to fulfil the agreement on the part of both prime ministers and other high ranking representatives of both states, leave little room for doubt about the Agreement's primary nature as a treaty. These in our opinion crucial legal characteristics of the Brussels Agreement do not negate other, aforementioned features which can determine the same Agreement as a gentlemen's agreement, memorandum of understanding or act of highest political relevance, but do clarify its legal status as that of belonging to the most 'classic' international law act – a treaty concluded between two international legal entities.

---

49 See Article 2(1)(a) of the Vienna Convention on the Law Treaties; text available at: <http://legal.un.org/ilc/texts/instruments/english/conventions/1_1_1969.pdf> (29 September 2013).

50 Beside the documents stated *supra* 48, see also: <http://www.srbija.gov.rs/vesti/vest.php?id=188412> (29 September 2013); <http://www.srbija.gov.rs/vesti/vest.php?id=188630> (29 September 2013); <http://www.kuvendikosoves.org/common/docs/ligjet/Zakon%20o%20ratifikaciji%20sporazuma%20normalizacija%20odnosa%20Kosova%20-%20Serbije.pdf> (29 September 2013).

VI   Concluding Remarks

The intensive proliferation of different international acts in the last few decades often obscures problems of the legal nature of acts having at the same time characteristics of 'soft law' and 'hard law'. Although in relation to the legal value of the acts as gentlemen's agreements, memoranda of understanding and political agreements some common features can be discerned, it is necessary to analyse the intent and circumstances leading to any single act belonging to these groups before coming to conclusions about their legal nature. The complex questions and multitude meaning in this sense are shown in the example of the Brussels Agreement which, despite some characteristics of a gentlemen's agreement, memorandum of understanding and political agreement, belongs primarily to the field of treaty law.

CHAPTER 46

The Ancient Origins of General Principles in International Law

Marko Petrak*

I   Introduction

The intention of this contribution is to throw some light on the ancient origins of the concept of general principles of law as a source of international law. We dedicate it to our revered Professor Budislav Vukas, who from the very beginnings of his scholarly work has expressed a profound interest in the possible use of ancient legal maxims as principles of law applied in contemporary international law.[1]

One of the first traces of the concept of the general principles of law in the context of international law[2] can be found in Albericus Gentilis's (1552–1608) renowned work *De jure belli* (lib. I, cap. III):

> *Ius etiam, illis perscriptum libris Iustiniani non civitatis est tantum, sed et gentium, et naturae. Et aptatum sic est ad naturam universam, ut imperio extincto, et ipsum ius diu sepultum surrexerit tamen, et in omnes se effuderit gentes humanas. Ergo et Principibus stat, etsi est privatis conditum a Iustiniano... Quid? non apta Principibus ilia librorum Iustiniani, Honeste vivere, Alterum non laedere, Suum cuique tribuere, Liberos tueri, Iniuriam propulsare, Cum omnibus hominibus cognationem agnoscere, Commercia*

---

*   Professor of Roman Law at the University of Zagreb, Faculty of Law.
1   See *e.g.* B. Vukas, *Načelo pacta tertiis nec nocent nec prosunt u međunarodnom pravu* [*The Principle pacta tertiis nec nocent nec prosunt in International Law*], PhD thesis, Zagreb, 1973; idem, "Opća načela prava kao izvor prava Evropskih zajednica" ["General Principles of Law as a Source of Law in the European Communities"], 42 *Zbornik Pravnog fakulteta u Zagrebu* [*Collected Papers of the University of Zagreb Law School*], 1992, pp. 253–265.
2   On the general principles of law as a source of international law see *e.g.*: G. Gaja, "General Principles of Law", in: R. Wolfrum (ed.), *Max Planck Encyclopedia of Public International Law*, Vol. 4, Oxford, 2012, pp. 370 *sqq.*; Bin Cheng, *General Principles of Law as Applied by International Courts and Tribunals*, Cambridge, 2007; V.Đ. Degan, *Sources of International Law*, The Hague, 1997, pp. 14 *sqq.*

*retinere, id genus reliqua, et quae ex his quaeque in illis sunt libris fere totum? Isthaec iuris gentium sunt, et iuris bellici.*³

As we can see, Gentilis used the principles of Roman private law (*principes librorum Iustiniani*) as the founding principles of international law (*ius gentium*),⁴ a method that is still fruitfully applied in contemporary international law doctrine and practice today.⁵ All the seven *principes iuris* mentioned by Gentilis (*Honeste vivere; Alterum non laedere; Suum cuique tribuere; Liberos tueri; Iniuriam propulsare; Cum omnibus hominibus cognationem agnoscere; Commercia retinere*) can be easily identified at the very beginning of Justinian's *Digesta seu Pandectae*, the most important part of his codification of Roman Law that contains the law of classical Roman jurisprudence. But only the first three are grouped together under the concept of the *praecepta iuris*.

The concept of the *praecepta iuris* – according to *Digesta* 1.1.10.1. – is originally contained in the first book of the *Regulae*, written by the great classical Roman jurist Ulpian (170–228 AD).⁶ Ulpian determined the fundamental precepts of law (*iuris praecepta sunt haec...*) as follows: *honeste vivere, alterum non laedere, suum cuique tribuere*: "to live honestly, not to harm any other person, to render to each his own". Just before that, in strong connection with the third precept (*suum cuique tribuere*), he formulated the famous definition of justice as the only one from Roman legal sources that has come down to us *via* Justinian's *Digesta* 1.1.10. pr.: *iustitia est constans et perpetua voluntas ius suum cuique tribuendi* – "justice is a steady and enduring will to render unto everyone his right".

One should not overlook the fact that Gentilis mentioned the *principes iuris*, while Ulpian defined the *praecepta iuris*. In this context, it should be emphasised that modern Roman law scholarship is of the opinion that Ulpian's three

---

3   A. Gentilis, *De jure belli*, Oxonii, 1877, pp. 16 sq.
4   See *e.g.* P. Vinogradoff, *On the History of International Law and International Organization* (*Collected Papers of Sir Paul Vinogradoff*), New Jersey, 2009, pp. 125 sq.; G. Badiali, *Il diritto di pace di Alberico Gentili*, Fagnano Alto, 2010, p. 37; on Gentilis' use of Roman Law in creation of international law generally, see *e.g.* B. Kingsbury, B. Straumann (eds.), *The Roman Foundations of the Law of Nations: Alberico Gentili and the Justice of Empire*, Oxford, 2010.
5   See *e.g.* H. Lauterpacht, *Private Law Sources and Analogies of International Law (With Special Reference to International Arbitration)*, London, 1927; R. Lesaffer, "Argument from Roman Law in Current International Law: Occupation and Acquisitive Prescription", 16 *European Journal of International Law*, 2005, pp. 25–58, at pp. 25 sqq.; K. Tuori, "The Reception of Ancient Legal Thought in Early Modern International Law", in: B. Fassbender, A. Peters (eds.), *The Oxford Handbook of the History of International Law*, Oxford, 2012, pp. 1012–1033, at pp. 1027 sqq.
6   For Ulpian's life and work see T. Honoré, *Ulpian, Pioneer of Human Rights*, Oxford 2002.

precepts have the role of general principles *par excellence* in Roman law.[7] On the basis of this brief analysis, we can conclude that the modern concept of the general principles of law as a source of international law has some of its oldest roots in the classical Roman legal concept of the *praecepta iuris*.[8]

II   The Origins of *Praecepta Iuris*

However, one can try to venture a few steps further and attempt to identify the origins of the very definitions of the *praecepta iuris* and *iustitia*. In the Roman world before Ulpian, elements of the *praecepta iuris* can be found primarily in the writings of Cicero. For example, in *De officiis* he writes: "...*fundamenta iustitiae, primum ut ne cui noceatur*" or "...*violare alterum naturae lege prohibemur*."[9] In his *De finibus*, we can also read statements such as "...*alienumque esse a sapiente non modo iniuriam cui facere, verum etiam nocere*."[10] All these formulations undoubtedly have the same meaning as Ulpian's *alterum non laedere*. As

---

7   L.C. Winkel, "The Role of General Principles in Roman Law", 2 *Fundamina: A Journal of Legal History*, 1996, pp. 103–120.

8   On the meaning and importance of Ulpian's definition of *iustitia* and the *praecepta iuris* see e.g. F. Senn, *De la justice et du droit. Explication de la définition traditionnelle de la justice*, Paris, 1927; W. Waldstein, "Zu Ulpians Definition der Gerechtigkeit (D. 1,1,10 pr.)", in: H.H. Jakobs, B. Knobbe-Keuk, E. Picker, J. Wilhelm (eds.), *Festschrift für Werner Flume zum 70. Geburstag*, Köln, 1978, pp. 213–232; M. Diesselhorst, "Die Gerechtigkeitsdefinition Ulpians in D. 1,1,10 pr. und die *Praecepta iuris* nach D. 1,1,10,1 sowie ihre Rezeption bei Leibniz und Kant", in: O. Behrends, M. Diesselhorst, W.E. Voß (eds.), *Römisches Recht in der europäischen Tradition. Symposion aus Anlaß des 75. Geburstages von Franz Wieacker*, Ebelsbach, 1985, pp. 185–211; F. Gallo, "Diritto e giustizia nel titolo primo del Digesto", 54 *Studia et documenta historiae et iuris*, 1988, pp. 1–36; L.C. Winkel, "Die stoische οἰκείωσις-Lehre und Ulpians Definition der Gerechtigkeit", 105 *Zeitschrift der Savigny-Stiftung für Rechtsgeschichte, romanistische Abteilung*, 1988, pp. 669–679; U. Manthe, "Beiträge zur Entwicklung des antiken Gerechtigkeitsbegriffes II: Stoische Würdigkeit und die *iuris praecepta* Ulpians", 114 *Zeitschrift der Savigny-Stiftung für Rechtsgeschichte, romanistische Abteilung*, 1997, pp. 1–26, at pp. 12 sqq.; V. Scarano Ussani, *L'ars dei giuristi. Considerazioni sullo statuto epistemologico della giurisprudenza romana*, Torino, 1997, pp. 121 sqq.

9   Cicero, *De officiis*, 1,31; 3, 27; cf. E. Levy, "Natural Law in Roman Thought", in: *Gesammelte Schriften*, Vol. I, Köln-Graz, 1963, pp. 3–19, at pp. 16 sq.; Diesselhorst, op. cit., pp. 196 sq.; W. Waldstein, *Teoria generale del diritto. Dall' antichità ad oggi*, Roma 2001, p. 91.

10   Cicero, *De finibus bonorum et malorum*, 3, 71; cf. C. Wollschläger, "Das stoische Bereicherungsverbot in der römischen Rechtswissenschaft", in: O. Behrends, M. Diesselhorst, W.E. Voß (eds.), *Römisches Recht in der europäischen Tradition. Symposion aus Anlaß des 75. Geburstages von Franz Wieacker*, Ebelsbach, 1985, pp. 41–88, at p. 50.

far as the precept *honeste vivere* is concerned, it suffices to pay attention to a passage from *De finibus* where Cicero tried to define what *fines bonorum* are for various philosophers and philosophical schools. He pointed out that according to Stoic teaching *finis bonorum* is "*...consentire naturae, quod esse volunt e virtute, id est honeste vivere.*"[11] It is to conclude that Ulpian transformed the Stoic ethical concept of *honeste vivere* into the first precept of law. Beside these two *praecepta iuris*, in Cicero's writings one can also rather easily find the precept *suum cuique tribuere*, included in his various formulations of the definition of justice. It is obvious that Ulpian's definition – *iustitia est constans et perpetua voluntas ius suum cuique tribuendi* – defined justice as a virtue.[12] This formulation is evidently a 'descendant' of Cicero's formulations, which can be found especially in the passages where he elaborates on the notion of virtue and its divisions. So, for example, in his juvenile piece of writing *De Inventione*, he defined justice as follows: "*Iustitia est habitus animi communi utilitate conservata suam cuique tribuens dignitatem.*"[13] In this context, it is also very important to cast a glance at Cicero's definition of virtue in his *De legibus*: "*...constans et perpetua ratio vitae, quae virtus est.*"[14] These two Ciceronian definitions contain the elements from which Ulpian – obviously familiar with Cicero's opus – could deduce his own formulation of *iustitia* or the precept *suum cuique tribuere*.[15] Furthermore, a very similar definition of justice is also recorded in

---

11   Cicero, *De finibus bonorum et malorum*, 2, 34; *cf.* E. Levy, *op. cit.*, pp. 16 *sq.*; M. Diesselhorst, *op. cit.*, pp. 196 *sq.*; V. Scarano Ussani, *op. cit.*, p. 125, n. 53.

12   On this aspect of Ulpian's definition of justice see F. Senn, *op. cit.*, pp. 8 *sqq.*; W. Waldstein, "Zu Ulpians Definition der Gerechtigkeit (D. 1,1,10 pr.)", *op. cit.*, pp. 225 *sqq.*; idem, "Ist das *suum cuique* eine Leerformel", 61 *Studia et documenta historiae et iuris*, 1995, pp. 181–215 *sqq.*, at pp. 186 *sqq.*; S. Tzitzis, "*Dikaion Dianémetikon* et *ius suum cuique tribuens*. De la rétribution des Grecs à celle des Glossateurs", in: O. Diliberto (ed.), *Il problema della pena criminale tra filosofia greca e diritto romano*, Napoli, 1993, pp. 221–241 *sqq.*; U. Manthe, "Beiträge zur Entwicklung des antiken Gerechtigkeitsbegriffes I: Die Mathematisierung durch Pythagoras und Aristoteles", in: 110 *Zeitschrift der Savigny-Stiftung für Rechtsgeschichte, romanistische Abteilung*, 1996, pp. 1–31.

13   Cicero, *De inventione*, 2, 160.; *cf.* also *De finibus bonorum et malorum*, 5, 65: "*...animi affectio suum cuique tribuendi...iustitia dicitur*"; *De officiis*, 1, 42: "*...ut pro dignitate cuique tribuatur; id enim est iustitiae fundamentum...*"; *De natura deorum*, 3, 38: "*Nam iustitia, quae suum cuique distribuit, quid pertinet ad deos...*"; *De re publica*, 3, 24: "*Iustitia autem praecipit...suum cuique reddere...*".

14   Cicero, *Leges*, 1, 45; *cf.* F. Senn, *op. cit.*, pp. 8 *sqq.*; W. Waldstein, *op. ult. cit.*, pp. 186 *sqq.*

15   W. Waldstein, "Zur juristischen Relevanz der Gerechtigkeit bei Aristoteles, Cicero und Ulpian", in: M. Beck-Mannagetta, H. Böhm, G. Graf (eds.), *Der Gerechtigkeitsanspruch des Rechts. Festschrift für Theo Mayer-Maly zum 65. Geburstag*, Wien-New York, 1996, pp. 1–71, at pp. 44 *sq.* The evidence for the fact that Ulpian was acquainted with Cicero's work one

the anonymous work *Rhetorica ad Herrenium* from the 1st century BC: "*Iustitia est aequitas ius unicuique rei tribuens pro dignitate cuiusque.*"¹⁶

Starting from the aforementioned facts, the majority of contemporary scholars consider that the origins of these definitions of Cicero and Ulpian are to be found in the writings of the Stoics.¹⁷ There is no doubt that the Stoic philosophical tradition is present in Ulpian's folmulations of *praecepta iuris* and *iustitia*. It would suffice to compare Ulpian's definition of *iustitia* as *suum cuique tribuere* with Chrissipus' definition of δικαιοσύνη as "ἕξις ἀπονεμητικὴ τοῦ κατ' ἀξίαν ἑκάστῳ."¹⁸ Some modern scholars of Roman law are also of the opinion that the Stoic ethical principle τὸ καλῶς ζῆν in the meaning of τὸ κατὰ φύσιν ζῆν is the oldest philosophical foundation of Ulpian's *honeste vivere*.¹⁹

Conversely, we believe that the origins of Ulpian's definitions are older than the philosophy of the Stoa, for which reason we cannot quite agree with the prevailing opinion of modern Roman law scholars on the issue.

Definitions of justice as a virtue older than those of the Stoics can be found in Aristotle's *opus*. For example, in his work *On Virtues and Vices*, justice is defined as follows: "δικαιοσύνη δ' ἐστίν ἀρετὴ ψυχῆς διανεμητική τοῦ κατ' ἀξίαν". Similar formulations are also present in Aristotle's *Topica*, *Art of Rhetoric* and particularly in the fifth book of *Nicomachean Ethics*, in the passages where he elaborates on the notion of distributive justice (δίκαιον διανεμητικόν).²⁰

---

can find in *Digesta* 42,4,7,4 where Ulpian quoted a work of Cicero unknown to us. For details, see D. Nörr, "Cicero-Zitate bei den klassischen Juristen", in: *Atti del III Colloquium Tullianum*, Roma, 1978, pp. 131 sqq.

16 *Rhetorica ad Herennium*, 3,2,3.; cf. L.C. Winkel, op. cit., pp. 672 sqq.

17 Cf. e.g. F. Schulz, *History of Roman Legal Science*, Oxford, 1946, p. 136; M. Diesselhorst, op. cit., pp. 185 sqq., particularly p. 201; L.C. Winkel, op. cit., pp. 669 sqq.

18 H. von Arnim (ed.), *Stoicorum Veterum Fragmenta* (SVF), Vol. III, Stuttgart, 1979, 125; cf. SVF I 374; SVF III 262; 263 and 280; for a comprehensive discussion on these Stoic definitions and their influence on Ulpian see L.C. Winkel, op. cit., pp. 672 sqq.; cf. U. Manthe, op. cit., II, pp. 1 sqq.; on the Stoic concept of justice generally, see e.g. M. Schofield, "Two Stoic Approaches to Justice", in: A. Laks, M. Schofield (eds.), *Justice and Generosity. Studies in Hellenistic Social and Political Philosophy Proceedings of the Sixth Symposium Hellenisticum*, Cambridge, 1995, pp. 191–212; cf. also M. Pohlenz, *Die Stoa. Geschichte einer geistigen Bewegung*, Vol. I, Göttingen, 1978, p. 136, pp. 201 sqq.

19 SVF III 14 and 16; see e.g. F. Senn, op. cit., pp. 39 sqq.; U. Manthe, op. cit., II, p. 12, n. 37; on the Stoic ethical principle τὸ κατὰ φύσιν ζῆν generally, see e.g. M. Forschner, *Die Stoische Ethik*, Darmstadt 1995, pp. 183 sqq.; the philosophical roots of precept *alterum non laedere* can also be found in writings of Stoics; see e.g. SVF III 178, 309, 345, 558 and 578; cf. C. Wollschläger, op. cit., p. 50, n. 72; U. Manthe, op. cit., I, p. 31, n. 96.

20 Aristoteles, *De virtutibus et vitiis* 1250 a 12; cf. *Topica* 143 a 16 sq.; 145 b 35 sq.; *Rhetorica* 1366 b 9 sqq.; *Ethica Nicomachea* 1130 b 30 sqq.; 1131 a 25 sq.; 1134 a 1 sqq.; for a comprehensive

In our opinion, however, the oldest philosophical foundation of Ulpian's definition of justice which included the precept *suum cuique tribuere* is to be found in the Platonic *Definitions* ("Ὅροι): "δικαιοσύνη...ἕξις ἀπονεμητικὴ τοῦ κατ' ἀξίαν ἑκάστῳ."[21] Of course, the *Definitions* are not the writing of Plato himself, and at first glance it is doubtful: is it possible to ascribe this definition of justice as a virtue to Plato? In his *Untersuchungen zu den pseudoplatonischen Definitionen*, published in 1967, Heinz Gerd Ingenkamp showed that the meaning of the quoted Platonic definition of justice is clearly in accordance with a passage from the fourth book of Plato's *Politeia* where it is stressed that "... possession of one's own and the performance of one's own task could be agreed to be justice" ("...ἑαυτοῦ ἕξις τε καὶ πρᾶξις δικαιοσύνην ἂν ὁμολογοῖτο").[22] Therefore, Ingenkamp emphasized that the definition of justice could be ascribed, if not to Plato himself, then to the very early tradition of Academy.[23] In any case, it is to be concluded that the definition of δικαιοσύνη in Platonic *Definitions* is the oldest traceable foundation of Ulpian's definition of *iustitia*.

However, one must not neglect an important difference between philosophical definitions of justice as a virtue and Ulpian's one. According to Greek philosophers, the criterion of just distribution is always the notion of ἀξία. Cicero adopted this philosophical concept and translated the Greek term ἀξία by the Latin word *dignitas*. To the contrary, Ulpian established the notion of *ius* instead of *dignitas* as the criterion of just distribution. Therefore, Ulpian's definition of justice contains the formulation *ius suum cuique tribuere* instead of *suam dignitatem cuique tribuere*. In other words, it is to be concluded that in this fashion Ulpian transformed a Greek philosophical concept into a specifically legal concept.[24]

---

discussion on Aristotle's definitions of justice and their possible influence on Ulpian see *e.g.* U. Manthe, *op. cit.*, I, pp. 2 *sqq.*; W. Waldstein, *op. ult. cit.*, pp. 53 *sqq*. On Aristotle's concept of justice generally see *e.g.* M. Salomon, *Der Begriff der Gerechtigkeit bei Aristoteles*, Leiden, 1937; P. Trude, *Der Begriff der Gerechtigkeit in der aristotelischen Rechts- und Staatsphilosophie*, Berlin, 1955.

21 Plato, *Definitiones* 411 e; *cf.* W. Waldstein, *op. ult. cit.*, p. 57; V. Scarano Ussani, *op. cit.*, p. 124, n. 49.

22 Plato, *Respublica*, 433 e.; for details, see H.G. Ingenkamp, *Untersuchungen zu den pseudoplatonischen Definitionen*, Wiesbaden, 1967, pp. 28 *sq*. On Plato's concept of justice in *Politeia* generally see *e.g.* E. Wolf, *Griechisches Rechtsdenken*, Vol. IV, 1, Frankfurt am Main, 1968, pp. 295 *sqq.*; G. Vlastos, "Justice and Happiness in Plato's Republic", in: *idem* (ed.), *Plato: A Collection of Critical Essays II*, London 1971, pp. 35–51.

23 H.G. Ingenkamp, *op. cit.*, pp. 113 *sq*.

24 It is worth mentioning in this context that the classical definition of justice was sometimes directly used by Roman jurists as a crucial argument in solving legal cases; see

Further, it is necessary to corroborate the hypothesis that Ulpian's *praecepta iuris* also have their origins in Plato's concept of justice. The first vestiges of these *praecepta* can be found in the first book of Plato's *Politeia*, namely, in the pregnant dialogue on some fundamental ethical precepts in the context of the virtue of justice. In his majeutic manner, Socrates, together with Glaucon, Kephalos, Polemarchos and the sophist Trasimachos arrive at first at the opinion that it is just (δίκαιον) to give to each what is owed to them (τὰ ὀφειλόμενα ἑκάστῳ ἀποδιδόναι).[25] Furthermore, Socrates asked his collocutors "is the part of the just man to harm anyone at all" and pointed out that it is never just to harm anyone (οὐδαμοῦ γὰρ δίκαιον οὐδένα ἡμῖν ἐφάνη ὂν βλάπτειν).[26] Finally, at the end of the dialogue from the first book of *Politeia*, Socrates concluded that the just soul and just man will live well, while the unjust man will live badly (Ἡ μὲν ἄρα δικαία ψυχὴ καὶ ὁ δίκαιος ἀνὴρ εὖ βιώσεται...).[27] It is not hard to see that these three statements of Socrates on what is just have exactly the same meaning as Ulpian's three precepts of law: *suum cuique tribuere, alterum non laedere, honeste vivere*. Of course, Socrates or Plato did not 'invent' these precepts. For example, the earliest traces of the precept *suum cuique tribuere* can be ascribed – according to the first book of *Politeia* – to the lyric and elegiac poet Simonides

---

D. 16.3.31.1 (Tryph. 9 disp.): "*Incurrit hic et alia inspectio. bonam fidem inter eos tantum, quos contractum est, nullo extrinsecus adsumpto aestimare debemus an respectu etiam aliarum personarum, ad quas id quod geritur pertinet? exempli loco latro spolia quae mihi abstulit posuit apud seium inscium de malitia deponentis: utrum latroni an mihi restituere seius debeat? si per se dantem accipientemque intuemur, haec est bona fides, ut commissam rem recipiat is qui dedit: si totius rei aequitatem, quae ex omnibus personis quae negotio isto continguntur impletur, mihi reddenda sunt, quo facto scelestissimo adempta sunt. et probo hanc esse iustitiam, quae suum cuique ita tribuit, ut non distrahatur ab ullius personae iustiore repetitione. quod si ego ad petenda ea non veniam, nihilo minus ei restituenda sunt qui deposuit, quamvis male quaesita deposuit.*" As we can see, the late classical Roman jurist Tryphonin decided that there are situations when it is just – contrary to the general rule – not to return the thing deposited to the depositor. It is interesting to point out that the same ethical and legal problem in the context of deposit had already been analysed by Plato (*Respublica* 331 c – 332 b) and Cicero (*De finibus bonorum et malorum* 3, 95); on Tryphonin's quoted solution see further P. Cerami, " 'Ordo legum' e 'iustitia' in Claudio Trifonino", 40 *Annali del Seminario giuridico della Università di Palermo*, 1988, pp. 5–35; M. Kaser, *Ius gentium*, Köln-Weimar-Wien, 1993, pp. 121 *sqq.*; R. Knütel, "Zum Pflichtenkonflikt des Verwahrers", in: J.F. Gerkens, H. Peter, P. Trenk-Hinterberger, R. Vigneron (eds.), *Mélanges Fritz Sturm*, Liège 1999, pp. 239–265; M. Bretone, *Storia del diritto romano*, Roma-Bari, 1999, pp. 346 *sqq.*

25   Plato, *Respublica*, 331 e, 335 e; for details see E. Wolf, *op. cit.*, pp. 315 *sqq.*
26   Plato, *Respublica*, 335 e; for details see E. Wolf, *op. cit.*, pp. 321 *sq.*
27   Plato, *Respublica*, 353 e; for details see E. Wolf, *op. cit.*, pp. 331 *sqq.*

(557–468 BC),[28] and one possible formulation of the precept *alterum non laedere* is also traceable in the fragments of a contemporary of Socrates, the sophist Antiphon (5th century BC).[29] However, in the first book of Plato's *Politeia*, all these three precepts are for the first time placed together in the same context.

Furthermore, it seems important to point out that Plato was also the first who distinguished and at the same time made an inextricable relation between the two fundamental principles of justice – τὰ ὀφειλόμενα ἑκάστῳ ἀποδιδόναι and οὐδένα βλάπτειν – as the lapidary expressions of what shall later be called distributive justice (δίκαιον διανεμητικόν) and corrective justice (δίκαιον διορθωτικόν) by Aristotle, or concisely formulated in the legal precepts *suum cuique tribuere* and *alterum non laedere* by Ulpian.[30]

III   Concluding Remarks

Owing to Justinian's codification of Roman law, the *praecepta iuris* have retained to this day their extraordinary importance in the Western legal tradition. These precepts can still be treated as general principles of law in the context of international law. They are – especially the precept *suum cuique tribuere* as the expression of distributive justice and the precept *alterum non laedere* as the expression of corrective justice – an important foundation of contemporary doctrine and practice in the field of the international law of treaties and the law of international responsibility.

Thus, for example, Alfred Verdross (1890–1980), one of the last century's greatest scholars of international law, saw in the precept *suum cuique tribuere* the very basis of the rule *pacta sunt servanda*, which is the fundamental principle of the international law of treaties.[31]

---

28   Plato, *Respublica*, 331 e; cf. E. Wolf, *op. cit.*, pp. 315 *sq.*; W. Waldstein, *Saggi sul diritto non scritto*, Padova, 2002, p. 98, n. 30.

29   See *Oxyrh. Pap.* XV 120 (Pap. 1797).

30   The concept of two fundamental aspects of justice is developed in another manner in Plato's *Laws*, where he distinguishes two forms of equality, the arithmetical and geometrical one; cf. Plato, *Leges* 757; cf. *Gorgias* 507 e *sqq.*; see M. Salomon, *op. cit.*, pp. 27 *sq.*, who pointed out the considerable influence of these elements of Plato's concept of justice and equality on Aristotle's thought.

31   A. Verdross, "Le fondement du droit international", 16 *Recueil des Cours de l'Academie de Droit International*, 1927, pp. 285 *sq.*; cf. J. Salmon, "Article 26. Convention of 1969", in: O. Corten, P. Klein (eds.), *The Vienna Convention on the Law of Treaties. A Commentary*, Vol. I, Oxford, 2011, p. 663.

THE ANCIENT ORIGINS OF GENERAL PRINCIPLES IN INTERNATIONAL LAW 859

With respect to the law of international responsibility, we can quote the opinion of Cançado Trindade, the Brazilian who is currently a judge of the International Court of Justice and professor at the Netherlands Institute of Human Rights of Utrecht University, that "...*neminem laedere*, or *alterum non laedere*..." is a fundamental principle which "...was transposed from domestic into international law, encompassing the idea of a reaction of the international legal order to harmful acts (or omissions) to the human person (individually and collectively) and to shared social values."[32]

One can also find the *praecepta iuris* in the recent practice of the International Court of Justice. Thus in a *separate opinion* issued in 2013, analysing the interpretation of the judgment in the case in question, the relevance of sound legal reasoning and its ancient origins is emphasised with the following words:

> As from Ulpian's teaching, the *Digest* rendered certain maxims widespread, such as *"justitia est constans et perpetua voluntas suum cuique tribuere"* ("justice is the constant and perpetual will to give everyone his due"); or else, *"honeste vivere, alterum non laedere, suum cuique tribuere"* ("to live honourably, to harm no one, to give each one his due"). *Jurisprudencia* developed, elaborating on general principles; it started arousing attention, having assumed a certain creative role. Legal reasoning kept on attracting increasing attention in modern times, amidst widespread acknowledgment of its relevance.[33]

Taking into consideration all the aforementioned facts, it is therefore not inappropriate to conclude that the Socratic dialogue on the foundations of justice, through the *medium* of the classical Roman *praecepta iuris*, is still reverberating in the contemporary discussion on general principles of law in the context of international law.

---

32   A.A. Cançado Trindade, "The Right to Cultural Identity in the Evolving Jurisprudential Construction of the Inter-American Court of Human Rights", in: S. Yee, J. Morin (eds.), *Multiculturalism and International Law: Essays in Honour of Edward McWhinney*, Leiden, 2009, pp. 477–499, at p. 494.

33   International Court of Justice, Request for Interpretation of the Judgment of 15 June 1962 in the Case concerning the *Temple of Preah Vihear (Cambodia v. Thailand)* (Cambodia v. Thailand); Separate opinion of Judge Cançado Trindade to the Judgment of the Court of 11 November 2013, paragraph 53.

CHAPTER 47

Fraudulent Treaties: The Covenant with the Gibeonites in the Biblical Book of *Joshua*

Maurizio Ragazzi*

I Introduction

In his monograph on the Vienna Convention on the Law of Treaties,[1] Sir Ian Sinclair wrote that instances of fraud vitiating consent to be bound by a treaty "are rare, if non-existent, in State practice".[2] It should therefore not be surprising if the treaty discussed in this essay comes from a distant past (a past that is ever present, though, and speaks to the mind and heart of man as only the word of God can).

Nor is there any need to investigate whether the one that is being examined here is in all respects a treaty in the technical sense that the term has in modern international law. As one reads in Oppenheim's classic work, treaties from pre-modern times that may not have been based on international law "were nevertheless considered sacred and binding on account of religious and moral sentiment".[3] Moreover, the treaty in question was discussed by Grotius: certainly, a treaty that attracted Grotius's attention is worthy of study by other international lawyers too!

The treaty was concluded at the time of the Israelite conquest of Canaan, presumably around the middle of the 13th century BC.[4] It is the treaty between

---

* JD (Ferrara), LLM (Columbia) and DPhil (Oxford), with degrees also in theology and canon law; formerly an associate at White & Case and Senior Counsel, International Law, at the World Bank.

1   1155 *United Nations Treaty Series*, 331.

2   I. Sinclair, *The Vienna Convention on the Law of Treaties* (2nd edn., Manchester, 1984), 173. The International Law Commission, in its commentary on the then draft article 46, acknowledged the 'paucity of precedents' ('Draft articles on the law of treaties with commentaries, adopted by the International Law Commission at its eighteenth session', *Yearbook of the International Law Commission* (1966), ii, 187–274, at 244).

3   L. Oppenheim, *International Law, A Treatise*, i (8th edn. by H. Lauterpacht, London, 1955), 878.

4   As A. Stellini (*Giosuè* (4th edn., Cinisello Balsamo, 1995), 10–11) has summarized, to establish the date of the conquest of Canaan one can take as a starting point the date of the exodus and count the years down, or the date of the foundations of the temple in Jerusalem and count the years up. Both approaches lead to the same approximate date of the middle to the later part of the 13th century BC.

Israel and the Gibeonites, the conclusion of which is narrated in Chapter 9 of the book of *Joshua*,[5] which in the Christian canon is the first of the 'historical books' of the Old Testament, and in the Jewish canon is the first of the 'former prophets'. The significance of the episode within the Old Testament is that it explains why, despite the Deuteronomic law enjoining Israel not to come to terms with the peoples living in the land God had given them, Gibeonites (who were living in Canaan at the time of the conquest) would still be found in Israel, providing fuel and water for the rituals at the sanctuary. To save their lives, the Gibeonites misrepresented to the Israelites that they came from a distant land and succeeded in concluding a (fraudulent) treaty with the Israelites. When these discovered that they had been deceived, they did not renege on their word. While affirming the validity of the treaty, they sanctioned the Gibeonites to be hewers of wood and drawers of water.

As Chapter 9 of the book of *Joshua* is relatively short, and not every reader may be familiar with it, here is its text in full:

> (1) When all the kings who were beyond the Jordan in the hill country and in the lowland all along the coast of the Great Sea toward Lebanon, the Hittites, the Amorites, the Canaanites, the Per'izzites, the Hivites, and the Jeb'usites, heard of this, (2) they gathered together with one accord to fight Joshua and Israel. (3) But when the inhabitants of Gibeon heard what Joshua had done to Jericho and to Ai, (4) they on their part acted with cunning, and went and made ready provisions, and took worn-out sacks upon their asses, and wineskins, worn-out and torn and mended, (5) with worn-out, patched sandals on their feet, and worn-out clothes; and all their provisions were dry and moldy. (6) And they went to Joshua in the camp at Gilgal, and said to him and to the men of Israel, "We have come from a far country; so now make a covenant with us." (7) But the men of Israel said to the Hivites, "Perhaps you live among us; then how can we make a covenant with you?" (8) They said to Joshua, "We are your servants." And Joshua said to them, "Who are you? And where do you come from?" (9) They said to him, "From a very far country your servants have come, because of the name of the Lord your God; for we have heard a report of him, and all that he did in Egypt, (10) and all that he did to the two

---

[5] A handy English translation of the book of *Joshua*, with a short introduction and commentary, is in the Navarre Bible: *Joshua-Kings* (Dublin and New York, 2005). For commentary in greater detail, in addition to the works cited in this essay, see R.E. Brown *et al.* (eds.), *The New Jerome Biblical Commentary* (Englewood Cliffs, 1990), 110–131 (chapter on *Joshua* by M.D. Coogan), or its earlier version by the same editors: *The Jerome Biblical Commentary* (one volume edn., London, 1968), 123–148 (chapter on *Joshua* by P.J. Kearney).

kings of the Amorites who were beyond the Jordan, Sihon the king of Heshbon, and Og king of Bashan, who dwelt in Ash'taroth. (11) And our elders and all the inhabitants of our country said to us, 'Take provisions in your hand for the journey, and go to meet them, and say to them, "We are your servants; come now, make a covenant with us."' (12) Here is our bread; it was still warm when we took it from our houses as our food for the journey, on the day we set forth to come to you, but now, behold, it is dry and moldy; (13) these wineskins were new when we filled them, and behold, they are burst; and these garments and shoes of ours are worn out from the very long journey." (14) So the men partook of their provisions, and did not ask direction from the Lord. (15) And Joshua made peace with them, and made a covenant with them, to let them live; and the leaders of the congregation swore to them. (16) At the end of three days after they had made a covenant with them, they heard that they were their neighbors, and that they dwelt among them. (17) And the people of Israel set out and reached their cities on the third day. Now their cities were Gibeon, Chephi'rah, Be-er'oth, and Kir'iath-je'arim. (18) But the people of Israel did not kill them, because the leaders of the congregation had sworn to them by the Lord, the God of Israel. Then all the congregation murmured against the leaders. (19) But all the leaders said to all the congregation, "We have sworn to them by the Lord, the God of Israel, and now we may not touch them. (20) This we will do to them, and let them live, lest wrath be upon us, because of the oath which we swore to them." (21) And the leaders said to them, "Let them live." So they became hewers of wood and drawers of water for all the congregation, as the leaders had said of them. (22) Joshua summoned them, and he said to them, "Why did you deceive us, saying, 'We are very far from you,' when you dwell among us? (23) Now therefore you are cursed, and some of you shall always be slaves, hewers of wood and drawers of water for the house of my God." (24) They answered Joshua, "Because it was told to your servants for a certainty that the Lord your God had commanded his servant Moses to give you all the land, and to destroy all the inhabitants of the land from before you; so we feared greatly for our lives because of you, and did this thing. (25) And now, behold, we are in your hand: do as it seems good and right in your sight to do to us." (26) So he did to them, and delivered them out of the hand of the people of Israel; and they did not kill them. (27) But Joshua made them that day hewers of wood and drawers of water for the congregation and for the altar of the Lord, to continue to this day, in the place which he should choose.[6]

---

6   This is the English translation provided in the *Revised Standard Version*, which has also been used for the other Biblical passages quoted in this essay.

II The Parties to the Treaty and Their Representatives

1 *The Gibeonites*

The two parties to the treaty were the Israelites and the Gibeonites. Who were the Gibeonites? The word 'Gibeonites' is a collective noun referring to a confederation of four cities: Gibeon, Chephi'rah, Be-er'oth and Kir'iath-je'arim.[7] Most scholars identify Gibeon with the modern el-Jib,[8] which is about ten kilometers North-West of Jerusalem. The archeological excavations carried out in the area from 1956 to 1962 by Pritchard's expedition,[9] which brought to light some amphorae with the inscription 'gb'n' (presumably the name of Gibeon)[10] and two tombs dating back to the time of Joshua, have provided evidence of the continuous occupation of the area since the Early Bronze Age in the third millennium BC.

Observing the topography of the Canaanite region, one readily realizes that the Gibeonite cities occupied an important strategic position from which they could control the lines of communication from Jericho to Jerusalem in the South, and to the coast through the Biblical pass of Beth-hor'on in the West.[11] This strategic importance is confirmed by the action taken against Gibeon by the coalition of the five Amorite kings in *Joshua* 10, immediately after the conclusion of the treaty between the Israelites and the Gibeonites. Despite this strategic importance, Gibeon was not an important city at the time of Joshua,

---

[7] Historical information on the three Gibeonite cities other than Gibeon, and their topographical location, can be found in R.G. Boling, *Joshua* (New York, 1982), 266–267.

[8] J.B. Pritchard, who, as is recalled in the text linked to the next footnote, excavated the site, has written that the Gibeon/el-Jib identification is "an example of how excavation may terminate a lengthy debate over an identification" (*Archaeology and the Old Testament* (Princeton, 1958), 86). Many scholars have accepted Gibeon/el-Jib as 'conclusive' identification (see, for example, J.M. Miller and G.M. Tucker, *The Book of Joshua* (Cambridge, 1974), 78); others cautiously speak of 'almost certain' identification (see, for example, H.H. Rowley and M. Black, *Joshua, Judges and Ruth* (London, 1967), 99).

[9] See J.B. Pritchard, *Gibeon. Where the Sun Stood Still* (Princeton, 1962).

[10] K. Galling ("Kritische Bemerkungen zur Ausgrabung von eǧ-ǧib", 22 *Bibliotheca Orientalis* (1965), 242–245) has questioned the etymological relationship between Gibeon and el-Jib, arguing that some amphorae for wine could have been moved from Gibeon to the place where nowadays el-Jib is. But J.A. Soggin (*Joshua. A Commentary* (London, 1972), 110) has recalled that there is evidence of an ancient production of wine in remarkable quantity in the area (which would not justify importing more wine unless it was blending wine) and that, even assuming wine was imported, amphorae would not have been used for this purpose, as they were assigned to transport more valuable products.

[11] See A. Malamat, "Doctrines of Causality in Hittite and Biblical Historiography: A Parallel", 5 *Vetus Testamentum* (1955), 1–12, at 11.

which is why neither the Amarna tablets[12] nor the inscriptions from the second millennium mention it. Gibeon grew in importance over time and came to play a significant role in the history of Israel, being listed among the cities of the tribe of Benjamin and the Levite cities (*Joshua* 18:25 and 21:17), a theater of war at the time of David (2 *Samuel* 2:12), the seat of an important sanctuary and the place where king Solomon received the gift of wisdom (1 *Kings* 3:4–15), and the seat of the tabernacle of God (1 *Chronicles* 21:29).[13]

The ethnic origin of the Gibeonites is somewhat unclear. In two passages of the book of *Joshua*, they are called 'Hivites' (*Joshua* 9:7 and 11:19), and it is significant that Joshua established friendly relations with local people only in Sichem (or Shechem) and Gibeon, which were both Hivite places.[14] However, the problem remains of ascertaining who these Hivites were, as there are no sources outside the Bible confirming their existence. The Greek translation of the Old Testament dating back to the 2nd century BC (the 'Septuagint') renders the word 'Hivites' with 'Hurrites'.[15] Hence the word 'Hivites' may be a linguistic flaw confusing it with the term 'Hurrites'. Some scholars have indeed listed other factors (such as the Hurrite name of the kings of the Hivite cities in the Amarna period) in support of the hypothesis that the Hivites were a Hurrite group.[16] (If so, the Hivites would be part of the Hurrite migration towards the West which started in the 18th century BC.)[17] Other scholars, though,

---

12   The Amarna tablets or letters are clay tablets in cuneiform characters dating back to the 14th century BC and containing diplomatic correspondence between the Egyptian pharaohs and Canaanite cities. The political scientist Amos S. Hershey, writing almost a century ago, called the Amarna tablets the "most remarkable contribution to our knowledge of the international relations of the ancient Orient". (A.S. Hershey, *The Essentials of International Public Law and Organization* (revised edn., New York, 1927), 35.) For an English translation of the tablets see W.L. Moran (ed.), *The Amarna Letters* (Baltimore, 1992); on their significance for international relations see R. Cohen and R. Westbrook (eds.), *Amarna Diplomacy. The Beginning of International Relations* (Baltimore, 2000) (containing also an article by R. Westbrook on international law in the Amarna age).

13   A detailed review of the relevant passages is in R. Sánchez, "Gabaon", 3 *Enciclopedia della Bibbia* (Turin, 1970), 527–533.

14   J. Blenkinsopp ("Are there traces of the Gibeonite Covenant in Deuteronomy?", 28 *The Catholic Biblical Quarterly* (1966), 207–219, at 214–218) focuses on various elements proving the close parallelism between Sichem and Gibeon: among them are the ethnic-political similarities and the fact that both had been well-known cult centers.

15   *Joshua* 9:7: 'πρὸς τὸν Χορραῖον'. (A. Rahlfs (ed.), *Septuaginta* (Stuttgart, reprint 1979)).

16   See, for example, J.M. Grintz, "The treaty of Joshua with the Gibeonites", 86 *Journal of the American Oriental Society* (1966), 113–126, at 121–122, note 39.

17   See J. Blenkinsopp, "Are there traces", 215. Another open issue is the place of origin of the Hivites. R.G. Boling (*Joshua*, 264–265) connects it to the ancient Quwe in Asia Minor;

concentrating their attention on other factors, have disputed the identification of the Hivites with the Hurrites, also because the social organization of the Hivite cities (governed by the elders instead of a monarch) is different from that of all the other Canaanite cities.[18]

To sum up, the expression 'inhabitants of Gibeon' in Chapter 9 of the book of *Joshua* refers to four confederate cities which were minor centers at the time of Joshua but were strategically located. The ethnic composition of their inhabitants remains subject to speculation.

2 *The Representatives of the Parties*

Chapter 9 of the book of *Joshua* shows many individuals, or groups of individuals, acting for the Israelites: (i) Joshua, (ii) the 'man of Israel',[19] (iii) the 'men', and (iv) the 'leaders of the congregation'. Initially, the Gibeonites address Joshua and the 'man of Israel' (verse 6); but it is only the "man of Israel", not Joshua, who replies (verse 7). Then, in verses 8 to 13, the exchange of questions and answers is between the Gibeonites and Joshua. But it is the 'men', according to verse 14, who taste the Gibeonite provisions. After that, Joshua concludes the treaty of peace with the Gibeonites, and the 'leaders of the congregation' take the oath (verse 15). Finally, when the deception is discovered, it is the 'leaders of the congregation' who sentence the Gibeonites to be hewers of wood and drawers of water (verse 21). However, it is Joshua who forces them to perform their services at a sanctuary (verse 27).

What exactly is the congregation whose leaders act on behalf of Israel? Some commentators agree that the Hebrew term for congregation ('eda') refers to the primitive Israelite community in a wide sense.[20] This primitive community, however, did not recognize the right of all its components to participate in the public life of the group. Hence the congregation would be restricted

---

instead, T.C. Butler (*Joshua* (Waco, 1983), 102), identifying the Hivites with a Hurrite group, indicates Armenia as their place of origin.

18   See R. de Vaux, "Les Hurrites de l'histoire et les Horites de la Bible", 74 *Revue Biblique* (1967), 481–503.

19   This expression, which is lost in the *Revised Standard Version*, is a collective noun denoting, according to L.D. Hawk (*Joshua* (Collegeville, 2001), 139), the 'integrity of the Israelite community'; instead, according to D.M. Howard, Jr. (*Joshua* (Nashville, 1998), 224), this expression is used elsewhere (*Judges*, 1 and 2 *Samuel*) as referring to the Israelite army, "and such is possibly the case here".

20   According to J.M. Grintz ("The treaty", 118–119), the Hebrew 'eda' roughly corresponds to the Hittite 'pankus' and the Roman 'comitia centuriata'. On the Hittite 'pankus' see G. Kestemont, *Diplomatique et droit international en Asie occidentale* (*1600–1200 av. JC*) (Louvain, 1974), 269 (including note 38).

to an assembly of free men having reached the age of majority (*Numbers* 1:2–3).[21] This assembly fulfills an advisory function in public affairs (*Numbers* 10:1–7; *Exodus* 12:3 and 35:1), exceptionally exercises religious and legal power (*Numbers* 15:32–36), and occasionally judicial power (*Joshua* 20:6–9). The congregation is headed by 'leaders' (*Numbers* 16:2, 26:9 and 27:2), who are the ones binding themselves by the oath attached to the treaty with the Gibeonites.

The complex combination of actors on the Israelite side is mirrored by the uncertainty of identifying who acts on the Gibeonite side, namely whether it is a delegation composed of representatives of the four confederate cities or it is instead just the inhabitants of Gibeon representing the three other cities too.

Is this complexity in identifying the actors attributable to the vicissitude of the composition of Chapter 9? This may partly be so but is hardly the full story. In other treaties from the ancient Near East (such as the one between Abban and Yarim-lim in a West Semitic setting from around the time of Abraham),[22] the conclusion of the treaty by an organ of the community is followed by the solemn engagement with an oath by another organ. Hence it cannot be ruled out that, in the case also of the treaty between the Israelites and the Gibeonites, a plurality of actors may already have existed in the early narrative of Chapter 9, as a way of identifying the different subjects who played different roles in bringing about the treaty.

III   The Making of the Treaty and Its Contents

1   *Common Meal and Oath*

In verse 14 of *Joshua* 9, one reads that the Israelites partook of the provisions of the Gibeonites. The sharing of a common meal was at the time a characteristic

---

21 The term 'eda' occurs in the book of *Numbers* more frequently than in the other books of the Old Testament. B.G. Boschi (*Numeri* (Rome, 1983), 21, note 12) observes that this term is used in the texts belonging to the Priestly tradition (one of the Pentateuchal sources according to the documentary hypothesis). (B.G. Boschi, OP, a pupil of R. de Vaux, OP, was the present writer's teacher of Old Testament exegesis at the Theological *Studium* in Bologna (aggregated to the *Angelicum* in Rome) in the early 1980s.)

22 See B.T. Arnold and B.E. Beyer (eds.), *Readings from the Ancient Near East. Primary Sources for Old Testament Study* (Grand Rapids, 2002), 96–97. Treaties from the ancient Near East, especially Hittite treaties, are an important source of comparison in Bible studies. See D.J. McCarthy, *Treaty and Covenant. A Study in Form in the Ancient Oriental Documents and in the Old Testament* (2nd edn., Rome, 1978); see also R. Lopez, "Israelite Covenants in the Light of Ancient Near Eastern Covenants", 9 *Chafer Theological Seminary Journal* (Fall 2003), 92–111 (Part 1); and 10 *ibid.* (Spring 2004), 72–106 (Part 2).

element in the conclusion of a treaty, both in the Old Testament (such as the meal between Isaac and Abimelech in *Genesis* 26:30 or between Jacob and Laban in *Genesis* 31:46) and in extra-Biblical sources (such as the meal linked to the treaty between Abban and Yarim-lim, mentioned above).[23] While it remains debatable whether sharing a meal, independently of the ritual of the sacrifice, was a sufficient element to conclude a treaty,[24] most scholars agree that there is a connection between common meal and treaty. Etymology too seems to point in this direction: some authors have suggested that the Hebrew word 'berit' (covenant or treaty) derives from a word which originally meant 'fat', and generally denoted 'abundant portion', in connection with a sacrificial banquet that ratifies the conclusion of a treaty.[25] Regarding the partaking of the Gibeonites' provisions, was it part of the formation of the treaty?[26] Or was the Israelite tasting of the food merely intended to verify the Gibeonites' statement that they came from a distant land, which is why their bread was dry and crumbling? Which of these two explanations is accurate? This is difficult, if not impossible, to tell. One could certainly look for an answer in the composition of Chapter 9 of the book of *Joshua*. However, even if one were to discover that, in the last phase of the composition of Chapter 9, the tasting of the provisions was simply intended to verify the Gibeonite story, this would still not rule out the fact that the original narrative may have referred to a common meal sealing the covenant.

Another element that is strictly associated with the idea of a treaty (and often connected with a common meal, as in *Joshua* 9:14–15) is the taking of an oath, in the Biblical literature as in the texts from the ancient Near East,[27] not

---

23   D.J. McCarthy ("Three Covenants in Genesis", 26 *The Catholic Biblical Quarterly* (1964), 179–189, at 185) has written that "once more Israelite practice reflects its historical environment".

24   D.J. McCarthy, *ibid.*, supports the view that meal without sacrifice, as a constitutive element of the covenant, is a procedure which exclusively belongs to the Yahwist tradition (another one of the Pentateuchal sources).

25   See B.G. Boschi, "L'Esodo e l'Alleanza nell'esegesi moderna", R. Fabris (ed.), *Problemi e prospettive di scienze bibliche* (Brescia, 1982), 183–209, at 198.

26   A. Stellini (*Joshua*, 75) suggests that this is 'very probably' the explanation.

27   See G.M. Tucker, "Covenant Forms and Contract Forms", 15 *Vetus Testamentum* (1965), 487–503, at 488–489; D.L. Magnetti, "The Function of the Oath in the Ancient Near Eastern International Treaty", 72 *American Journal of International Law* (1978), 815–829. This author repeats, in the introduction and conclusion of his article, that resorting to an oath was (at least partly) due to the absence of an international legal structure providing for sanctions. Is this really the full explanation? The question seems to be more complex, having to do ultimately with the human response to the role of God in human affairs.

to mention Greek and Roman sources. Actually, a covenant is frequently called an 'oath', and 'covenant' and 'oath', and also 'to conclude a covenant' and 'to swear an oath', are synonyms. In the Yahwist tradition, there are many passages in which covenant and oath overlap,[28] and this connection occurs also in the Gibeonite story.[29] The oath is given in the name of God, which is why it cannot be revoked or changed. In the episode of the treaty with the Gibeonites, although the Israelites had not consulted God before taking the oath, God was the witness of the oath attached to the treaty. As such, while not a party to the treaty, God was its protector against the unfaithfulness of the parties (as evidenced in 2 *Samuel* 21) and against common enemies (*Joshua* 10).

2   The Obligations Deriving from the Treaty

In *Joshua* 9:15, it is written that Joshua 'made peace' with the Gibeonites, sealing with them a covenant 'to let them live'. Making peace by treaty has obviously many precedents in Biblical and extra-Biblical sources. Noth has pointed out that the Hebrew expressions for 'peace between…and' (*Judges* 4:17; 1 *Samuel* 7:14), 'covenant of peace' (*Ezekiel* 34:25 and 37:26), and 'to make peace' (*Isaiah* 27:5), are very close to Akkadic expressions.[30] It is also significant that, as in many ancient texts and in other passages of the Old Testament, in *Joshua* 9:15 too the word 'peace' is correlated to the word 'life': Joshua stipulates the covenant to preserve the life of the Gibeonites.

The Hebrew text of the verse uses the infinitive verbal form with an iterative meaning: the duty not to kill implies not only a negative obligation of not taking someone's life but also a positive obligation to defend the other party in

---

Despite the firmer international legal structure in contemporary relations, would not the stability of treaty obligations benefit from the parties' acknowledgment that man has to render an account for his thoughts, words, actions and omissions, not only to fellow men, but most importantly to God?.

28   See *Genesis* 21:31, 26:31 and 31:53.

29   R. de Vaux (*Histoire ancienne d'Israel* (Paris, 1971), 574) notes that, in *Joshua* 9, the word 'berit' has the meaning of 'promissory oath' ('serment promissoire'). On a more general point, it is also true that 'berit' has deeper connotation (to the point of presenting 'une note mystique') than the term 'treaty' in modern times (*La Sainte Bible. Texte latin et traduction française d'après les textes originaux avec un commentaire exégétique et théologique*, iii (Paris, 1949), 62).

30   M. Noth, "Old Testament Covenant-making in the Light of a Text from Mari", Id., *The Laws in the Pentateuch and Other Studies* (trans. by D.R. Ap-Thomas, Philadelphia, 1967), 108–117, at 113.

case of enemy assault.³¹ This emerges clearly from the continuation of the story in *Joshua* 10, where the Gibeonites, by now allies of the Israelites, are attacked by a coalition of kings. In other words, the treaty between Israel and the Gibeonites creates an obligation of military assistance, as was the case with other ancient peace treaties, whether they be concluded between equals or whether they be vassal treaties.

In *Joshua* 9 (verses 8–9 and 24), the Gibeonites call themselves 'servants', from which it logically follows that they had contracted an obligation to perform certain services for the benefit of the Israelites. It remains doubtful, though, what exactly these services were,³² and whether hewing wood and drawing water, to which they would later be sanctioned on account of their deception, had already existed as primary treaty obligations.

IV   The Fraud and Its Discovery

1   *Why Did the Gibeonites Resort to Fraud?*

The Israelites are encamped at Gilgal after having conquered the cities of Jericho and Ai. To come to term with the Israelites, and as their political structure excludes them from the league with the kings referred to in the first verse of *Joshua* 9, the Gibeonites have recourse to a trick, pretending to come from a distant land.³³

The premise to this deceit is that, in their conquest of Canaan, the Israelites would not conclude peaceful agreements with the peoples who lived there.

---

31 R.G. Boling (*Joshua*, 266) suggests that the obligation to guarantee the Gibeonites' lives may also have had to do "with such matters as pasturelands, water rights, trade, intermarriage", in addition to military assistance. Is this suggestion plausible, or is it perhaps put forward by analogy with other Biblical sources and other treaties from the ancient Near East? If so, how strong is such an argument?.

32 For example, according to J.M. Grintz ("The treaty", 124), an obligation binding on the Gibeonites to furnish men for the army would be the "inevitable conclusion to be reached from a comparison with the fixed provisions in Hittite treaties and with peace treaties of this kind from time immemorial". This may well be so, but (in accordance with what was remarked in the previous footnote) is it really legitimate to infer the existence of obligations from the comparison with treaties concluded in comparable yet separate contexts?.

33 The whole episode, including the Gibeonite deception, has inspired reflections dwelling with their significance for the spiritual life. See, for example, the passages by Origen and Ambrose reproduced in J.F. Franke (ed.), *Joshua, Judges, Ruth, 1–2 Samuel* (*Ancient Christian Commentary on Scripture*, iv) (Downers Grove, 2005), 52–56.

In fact, the rules on waging war spelled out in Chapter 20 of the book of *Deuteronomy* expressly distinguish two types of cities.[34] The Israelites are allowed to offer peaceful terms to "the cities which are very far from [them], which are not cities of the nations [of the promised land]" (*Deuteronomy* 20:15). On the contrary, the nations (including the Hivites, expressly listed in *Deuteronomy* 7:1) of the land that God has given to the Israelites as their inheritance must be wiped out ("you shall save alive nothing that breathes", *Deuteronomy* 20:16), lest the Israelites be tempted to fall into idolatry.[35] Faced with this prospect, the Gibeonites deceptively introduce themselves to the Israelites as inhabitants of a very distant land.

For some scholars, it is incomprehensible that people who live far away and who are not directly threatened should try to conclude a treaty.[36] This objection, though plausible, is not decisive. Both in the Old Testament and in the extra-Biblical literature, there are examples of long journeys carried out so as to meet an army that is advancing menacingly. Thus, Ashurbanipal boasts that Gyges, king of Lydia, and Rusas, king of Urartu, surrendered after having heard of his great enterprises.[37] Likewise, in 2 *Samuel* 8:9, one reads that To'i, king of Hamath, sent his son to king David as soon as he heard that David had crushed the army of Hadade'zer. These precedents give credibility to the story of the Gibeonites seeking peace while pretending to come from a distant land.

2 What Did the Israelites Do upon Discovering the Fraud?

The second part of Chapter 9 of the book of *Joshua* (verses 16–27) deals with the Israelites' reaction upon discovering, three days after concluding the treaty, that they had been deceived by the Gibeonites. In essence: (i) the Gibeonites are not killed, because the leaders of the Israelite community had given an oath in the name of God (verses 18–20); and (ii) though the Gibeonites are protected, they are condemned to be hewers of wood and drawers of water, and they are cursed (verses 21–23).[38] Therefore, though accompanied by sanction and curse, the treaty is still valid. So much so that,

---

34 This point was highlighted in T.A. Walker, *A History of the Law of Nations*, i (Cambridge, 1899), 31–32.

35 That the Canaanite religion was a threat to Israel can clearly be evinced from the episode of the struggle between Elijah and the followers of Baal (1 *Kings* 18).

36 See J. Blenkinsopp, "Are there traces", 211.

37 For reference see J.M. Grintz, "The treaty", 122, note 40.

38 On the curse-punishment theme, accompanied by God's protection see the well-known episode of Cain, in *Genesis* 4:10–16. While belonging to Yahwism in a special way (R.G. Boling, *Joshua*, 249–250), blessings and curses figured also generally in the treaties of the ancient world. See, for example, the relevant provision in the famous peace treaty between Egypt and the Hittites, an English translation of the Egyptian and Akkadian

when the Gibeonites are attacked by a coalition of Amorite kings, Joshua rushes to their help (*Joshua* 10:1–15).

As a treaty under oath also binds the successors to the one who sealed it, the violation by king Saul reverberates on the Israelites with a dreadful famine at the time of David ("There is bloodguilt on Saul and on his house, because he put the Gib'eonites to death", 2 *Samuel* 1). In this too, there is an element of analogy with the violation of treaties from the ancient Near East.[39] For example, catastrophe falls on the Hittites at the time of Mursili II, as a result of the violation of a treaty by his predecessor. Both David and Mursili apply to the divine oracle for an explanation of the calamities oppressing their peoples. In both cases, the answer is that these calamities derive from the violation committed by their predecessors.[40]

V   Historicity of the Treaty

Did the treaty between the Israelites and the Gibeonites really take place? Followers of the German scholar Julius Wellhausen support the view that, contrary to what is written in the Old Testament, the Israelite conquest of Palestine lasted for many generations. Treaties of peace with Canaanites were frequent, and the narrative in *Joshua* 9, presenting the treaty as an exceptional event, would have no historical basis.[41] This position, though, is fairly weak in many respects, starting from the fact that it provides no reasonable explanation for what one reads in 2 *Samuel* 21, namely the consequences ensuing from the violation of the treaty.

Likewise, acknowledging that beyond the narrative of the episode there is, in addition to the explanation of the Israelites' peaceful relations with a Canaanite people (the Gibeonites), an attempt to account for the service by the Gibeonites at an Israelite sanctuary, the house or altar of God (*Joshua* 9:23 and 9:27),[42] does not detract from the historical fact of the sealing of a treaty between the Israelites and the Gibeonites.

---

versions of which is in J.B. Pritchard (ed.), *Ancient Near Eastern Texts Relating to the Old Testament* (3rd edn. with suppl., Princeton, 1969), 199–203.

39   See F.C. Fensham, "The Treaty between Israel and the Gibeonites", 27 *The Biblical Archeologist* (1964), 96–100, at 100.

40   Another element of similarity with extra-Biblical sources is the exposure of the corpses to wild animals and inclement weather (2 *Samuel* 21:10).

41   This view is forcefully criticized in J.M. Grintz, "The treaty", 120.

42   The search for the meaning behind the episode is labelled in the literature as the etiological question. Regarding the episode in *Joshua* 9 see A. Ibáñez Arana, "El pacto con los gabaonitas (Jos 9) como narración etiológica", 30 *Estudios bíblicos* (1971), 161–175.

Where should one locate this sanctuary? Commentators agree that, at least in the final version of the narrative, the sanctuary is that of Jerusalem, which is the one mentioned in *Deuteronomy* 12:5. This, though, does not necessarily imply that this was also the case in earlier stages of the composition of Chapter 9. Some scholars identify the Gibeonites with the 'nethinim' (or temple oblates) and suggest that the reference is to the sanctuaries of Gilgal, Shiloh, Nob, Gibeon and Jerusalem.[43] But the connection between the Gibeonites and the 'nethinim' is not convincing, as the term 'nethinim' only appears in the post-exilic age (*Ezra* 2:58 and 8:20; *Nehemiah* 7:46–60).[44] Others have instead written that the sanctuary where the Gibeonites were condemned to perform their services was in Gibeon.[45] According to 1 *Kings* 3:4, Gibeon was the 'great high place', and it was there that the Gibeonites executed blood vengeance on Saul's descendants (2 *Samuel* 21).[46] Yet others refer to the sanctuary at Gilgal (which is where the Gibeonites met the Israelites in *Joshua* 9),[47] or Shiloh.[48]

In conclusion, there is no agreement in identifying the sanctuary referred to in *Joshua* 9, but this does not detract from the historical fact of the Gibeonites' service and, more generally, from the historicity of the events narrated in *Joshua* 9, including the conclusion of a treaty.

VI Composition of the Narrative

Joshua 9 was the result of progressive formation.[49] Some scholars have identified the combination of two independent traditions which were afterwards unified. Thus, Möhlenbrink thinks of an early composition in which Joshua

---

43 See, for example, the opinion expressed by Kimhi, reported in J.M. Grintz, "The treaty", 126.

44 On the complexity of this question see Baruch A. Levine, "Gibeonites and Nethinim", 7 *Encyclopaedia Judaica* (2nd edn., Detroit, 2006), 583–585.

45 See R. de Vaux, *Histoire*, 573.

46 J.M. Grintz ("The treaty", 126, note 53) rejects the identification of the sanctuary with the one in Gibeon on the ground that the sanctuary of the 'great high place' would have been built at the time of king Saul, when the Gibeonites had already been expelled from that place.

47 See, for example, the opinion expressed by Noth, mentioned in J. Blenkinsopp, "Are there traces", 211–212, note 15.

48 See J.M. Grintz, "The treaty", 126.

49 On the different theories regarding the origins and composition of the book see D. Baldi, *Giosuè* (Turin, 1956), 4–8.

concludes the treaty, followed by the insertion of the curses when their deception is discovered (tradition of Shiloh), coupled with a narrative where it is the 'man of Israel' who stipulates the treaty without the involvement of Joshua (tradition of Gilgal).[50] In contrast, Kaufmann distinguishes a tradition containing the stratagem of the Gibeonites, the treaty, the discovery of the trick, the conquest of the cities, and the condemnation of the Gibeonites to hewing wood and drawing water at the sanctuary, from a separate tradition according to which the protagonists are the Israelite congregation and its leaders, with the condemnation of the Gibeonites to be servants of the congregation.[51] The common element to these theories is that a primitive tradition would later have been revisited by a Deuteronomic compiler.[52]

Noth delineates a primitive tradition of Gilgal into which a compiler would have then introduced Joshua.[53] Hertzberg assumes the existence of a primitive story of the sanctuary of Gibeon (very close in time to the stipulation of the treaty), which did not present any element of hostility against the Gibeonites; to this narrative, the anti-Gibeonite story of the deception would have been added at the time of Solomon.[54] According to Rowley, there would be an original tradition of Gibeon subsequently transferred to Gilgal by a Deuteronomic compiler, who would have developed the theme of the service at the sanctuary.[55] Similarly, Butler speaks of Deuteronomic re-elaboration (centered on the figure of Joshua) of an earlier tradition.[56]

Yet others have linked the composition of *Joshua* 9 to the incorporation of the Gibeonite cities into the tribe of Benjamin. According to this hypothesis, the treaty would have provided for the sealing of the peace and some binding

---

50   K. Möhlenbrink, "Die Landnahmesagen des Buches Joshua", 15 *Zeitschrift für die Alttestamentliche Wissenschaft* (1938), 238–268, at 241–245.

51   Kaufmann's views are summarized in J.A. Soggin, *Joshua*, 110.

52   While recalling the "increasing and justified suspicion" regarding the application of Pentateuchal source-criticism (Yahwist, Elohist, Deuteronomist and Priestly traditions) to the historical books of the Old Testament, J. Blenkinsopp (*Gibeon and Israel. The Role of Gibeon and the Gibeonites in the Political and Religious History of Early Israel* (Cambridge, 1972), 33) has written that, clearly, the narrative of *Joshua* 9 "has undergone Deuteronomic editing". Likewise, according to J.F.D. Creach (*Joshua* (Louisville, 2003), 86), certain texts from Deuteronomy "loom in the background of Joshua 9 and provide a frame of reference that gives meaning to the story".

53   See M. Noth, *Das Buch Josua* (Tübingen, 1938), 31.

54   H.W. Hertzberg, *Die Bücher Josua, Richter, Ruth* (Göttingen, 1959), 66–69.

55   H.H. Rowley and M. Black, *Joshua*, 97–98.

56   T.C. Butler, *Joshua*, 99–100.

provisions on the Gibeonites,[57] presumably ending with the narration of the sharing of the meal. This first version did not present polemical tones against the Gibeonites and recorded a historical event. Later, this treaty, originally sealed by the tribe of Benjamin and not by all the Israelites, would have become binding on all the tribes of Israel.[58] At the time of the kings, Saul conducted a hostile policy against the Hivite cities, David transferred the ark from the Gibeonite territory to Jerusalem, and Solomon built the temple. All these circumstances would have given rise to an interest in the Gibeonite question. Since the prevailing concern was consecrating Jerusalem as the only cult center in Israel, and since its main rival was the sanctuary of Gibeon, it would have been necessary to re-elaborate the original story by introducing an anti-Gibeonite tone.[59] *Joshua* 9 may thus have been re-written bringing out the fraudulent origin of the treaty and justifying the imposition of the services at the sanctuary as a form of punishment for the Gibeonites' deception.

In summary, the idea of the revision of an original tradition is today widely accepted. But many questions remain unresolved, and the attempts to unravel them remain largely speculative, tending to focus, not so much on the episode in itself, but on its meaning within the larger history of Israel.

VII Why was the Treaty, though Fraudulent, Still Valid?

1 *Grotius's Explanation*

Grotius discussed the treaty between Israel and the Gibeonites within his treatment of oaths (*de jurejurando*) in the *De jure belli ac pacis*.[60] In his analysis, Grotius moved from the premise that, if someone took an oath believing certain facts to be true which were not, and if he would not have taken the oath had he not believed the facts to be so, then the oath would not be binding. However, if it is doubtful whether that person may not have sworn anyway, then the oath would be valid. The Israelite oath to the Gibeonites would,

---

57 J. Blenkinsopp ("Are there traces", 211), for example, posits an obligation to serve at the sanctuary. But this assumption remains doubtful.

58 How did this happen? By succession? By the conclusion of a new treaty? If by a new treaty, did this treaty merely replace the provisions of the earlier one or did it contain also new provisions?.

59 According to J. Blenkinsopp ("Are there traces", 212), there was an anti-Benjaminite tone in addition to an anti-Gibeonite one.

60 H. Grotius, *On the Law of War and Peace Three Books* (edn. J.B. Scott, London, 1925), bk. ii, ch. xiii, Section iv, at 366–367.

according to Grotius, fall under this latter category, and consequently was valid. How did he reach this conclusion?

For Grotius, from the Gibeonite deceit it did not follow that the Israelites would not have spared their lives had they known the Gibeonites in reality were inhabitants of Canaan. On the contrary, the Israelites' question in verse 7 ("Perhaps you live among us; then how can we make a covenant with you?") may be interpreted, in Grotius's view, in the sense that the Israelites were asking the Gibeonites what sort of a treaty they wished, and that, while not allowed to conclude certain types of treaties with certain peoples, the Israelites could still enter into a treaty with the Gibeonites and save their lives if they surrendered. This would be possible because, according to Grotius, the Deuteronomic law on waging war would not apply to those peoples who surrendered and paid a tribute to the Israelites. This interpretation would be confirmed by the story of Rahab (*Joshua* 2), by the situation of the Canaanites living in Gezer (*Joshua* 16:10), and by that of the descendants of the non-Israelites peoples paying a tribute to Solomon (1 *Kings* 9:21). From all this, Grotius concluded that, had the Gibeonites been truthful, "they would nevertheless have obtained the preservation of their lives on the condition of surrendering".[61] In other words, the oath (and therefore the treaty) was valid because, had the Gibeonites not resorted to deception, the Israelites would still have been able to accede to their request for a treaty.

Though Grotius appealed to several Scriptural episodes in support of his analysis, the fact remains that his interpretation and conclusion are perplexing. Firstly, Grotius's reading of verse 7 is question-begging. In reality, the Israelites would have been in a position of offering a treaty to the Gibeonites only on the premise, consistent with Deuteronomic law, that they came from a distant land. As is clearly stated in *Deuteronomy* 20:10–20, surrendering was an option for the peoples from afar, but not for the peoples (as the Gibeonites were) from the land God had given Israel for an inheritance. (If it were not so, why would the Gibeonites have cared to specify, in verse 6 of *Joshua* 9, "We have come from a far country; so now make a covenant with us"?)

Secondly, the episodes Grotius calls on in support of his interpretation of the rule are instead exceptions to the rule, and fairly difficult ones to explain. Without entering into detail, it has been remarked that there is a 'glaring contradiction' between the Deuteronomic laws on warfare and the exception for Rahab, which

---

61   The relevant passage, in the original, reads as follows: "Quare cum credibile esset, si rem ipsam Gabaonitæ indicassent, quod præ metu non fecerunt, tamen vitam salvam sub parendi conditione impetraturos fuisse, valuit jusjurandum".

makes her story "stick out like a sore thumb".[62] Likewise, from *Joshua* 16:10 and *Judges* 1:29, it is clear that the only reason why the Canaanites from Gezer were still in the land was because the tribe of Ephraim had failed to oust them. In the same vein, 1 *Kings* 9:21 is adamant in stressing that the descendants of the non-Israelite peoples that Solomon made a "forced levy of slaves" were in the land only because the Israelites were "unable to destroy [them] utterly".

As Grotius's explanation is not convincing, one needs to look elsewhere to account for the validity of the treaty despite its fraudulent origin.

2   Validity of Treaties Sealed by Oath

Under Article 49 of the Vienna Convention on the Law of Treaties,

> [i]f a State has been induced to conclude a treaty by the fraudulent conduct of another negotiating State, the State may invoke the fraud as invalidating its consent to be bound by the treaty.

There can hardly be any doubt that the treaty between Israel and the Gibeonites would hypothetically[63] fall under this provision. Borrowing from a commentator's list of conditions for the fraud to amount to a defect of consent,[64] the Gibeonite fraud (i) emanated from a negotiating party, (ii) was a determining factor in the Israelites' consent to conclude the treaty, and (iii) the Israelites (the defrauded party) did not in any way contribute to the Gibeonites' fraudulent conduct.

The other ground upon which the Gibeonite episode hypothetically fits with the modern concept of fraudulent treaty has to do with the consequences ensuing from the fraud. Article 49 (presumably declaratory of customary international law,[65] or at least reflecting a general principle of law)[66]

---

62 R.G. Boling, *Joshua*, 150.

63 'Hypothetically' because, as was explained above, there is no need to examine here the extent to which an ancient treaty such as the one between Israel and the Gibeonites is (or is instead merely analogous to) a treaty in the sense of the Vienna Convention, which in turn is the underlying condition for the operation of the international legal norm contained in Article 49.

64 See G. Niyungeko, "1969 Vienna Convention. Article 49. Fraud", O. Corten and P. Klein (eds.), *The Vienna Conventions on the Law of Treaties. A Commentary*, ii (Oxford, 2011), 1142–1166, at 1156-9.

65 See M.E. Villiger, *Commentary on the 1969 Vienna Convention on the Law of Treaties* (Leiden and Boston, 2009), 619–620.

66 See O. Dörr and K. Schmalenbach (eds.), *Vienna Convention on the Law of Treaties. A Commentary* (Berlin and Heidelberg, 2012), 848 (Rensmann).

merely provides for the possibility that the victim party 'may' invoke the fraud as invalidating its consent. In other words, in the dichotomy on the types of invalidity, a fraudulent treaty is not void but voidable: "the treaty is valid until a State claims that it is invalid".[67]

If the Gibeonite treaty was voidable, why did the Israelites not invoke the fraud as invalidating their consent? The fact is that the Israelites had taken an oath. "Such a solemn vow was like an arrow that, after being fired from a bow, could not be retracted".[68] This is therefore the most convincing explanation why, despite the preclusion under Deuteronomic law of entering into treaties with the Canaanites, and despite the deceit that had led the Israelites to conclude the treaty, the treaty remained valid. It was the oath that had made it impossible for the Israelites to claim the invalidity of the treaty: they had given their word, not only to the Gibeonites, but also to God, the witness and protector of the treaty, who is "not distracted by disguise".[69] Invoking the invalidity of the treaty would for the Israelites have been inconsistent with their very identity and the meaning that faithfulness to covenants made with God and men had for their taking possession of the land.

VIII   Conclusions

These are the main conclusions from what has been written above:

(1) The Gibeonite episode confirms the evident truth that the Bible (as befits God's word) is an inexhaustible source of reflection on legal questions, including questions of the international law of the time, however inchoate. The complex structure and narrative of the episode also show how the Biblical text has to be approached with that humility that allows one not to rush to hasty conclusions in interpreting both specific aspects of an episode and its overall significance.

(2) As the Israelites of the Old Testament lived within the particular context of their times, it is likewise obvious that "the discovery of the ancient Near East has shed significant light on the Bible",[70] such as the relevance

---

67   See M. Schröder, "Treaties, Validity", R. Wolfrum (ed.), *The Max Planck Encyclopedia of Public International Law*, x (Oxford, 2012), 51–56, at 52.
68   J.F.D. Creach, *Joshua*, 85.
69   D. Friedman, *To Kill and Take Possession. Law, Morality, and Society in Biblical Stories* (Peabody, 2002), 55.
70   J.B. Pritchard, *Archaeology*, v.

of Near Eastern documentary materials and diplomatic practice to the examination of Biblical treaties. One needs to be alert, though, to de Vaux's warning that the comparison between Biblical covenants and Near Eastern (notably Hittite) treaties should not be exaggerated, and that it would be 'grotesque' to assume that semi-nomadic groups imposed on the Gibeonites a treaty similar to those that Hittite kings imposed on their vassals.[71] Hence the need for caution and the avoidance of any forced comparison.

(3) Finally, the reason for examining the Gibeonite episode from the particular perspective of this essay was of course not that of flagging up the existence of a fraudulent treaty that would somehow fill the gap in an international practice that is otherwise short of relevant precedents. Rather, the intent was that of providing elements of reflection on the fact that instances of treaty and fraud have been part of the relations between groups since time immemorial, and that the grounds for observing a fraudulent (and therefore voidable) treaty, at least a treaty concluded within the context discussed in this essay, had deep roots in the moral and religious significance of an oath attached to a treaty and, ultimately, in the very attitude of a people towards God's governance of human affairs.

---

71   R. de Vaux, *Histoire*, 574.

CHAPTER 48

The Notion of Sources of International Criminal Law

*Mirjam Škrk**

I   Introduction

The notion of sources of international criminal law (ICL) is closely related to the question of how we treat this branch of law. There is a general understanding that ICL is a relatively young legal discipline that has gained immense importance in particular in the past two decades.[1] Some authors believe that ICL has evolved as a legal regime with the establishment of the *ad hoc* international criminal tribunals for the former Yugoslavia and Rwanda.[2] At present, five international criminal courts and several internationalized or so-called hybrid criminal courts are functioning worldwide. Although the International Court of Justice (ICJ) has jurisdiction to adjudicate on disputes between States and not to prosecute individuals accused of international crimes, its case law nevertheless proves that it has also dealt with cases that tackle ICL.[3] The case law of these Courts is indispensable for identification of the rules and principles of ICL and for their interpretation and development. Regarding the presentation of the sources of ICL, we remain in the field of violations of

---

*   Professor of Public International Law at the University of Ljubljana, Faculty of Law, and Former Judge of the Constitutional Court of the Republic of Slovenia.
1   "First, ICL is a relatively new branch of international law." Cassese, A., *International Criminal Law*, 2nd edition, Oxford University Press, Oxford, 2008, p. 4.
2   Cryer, R., Friman, H., Robinson D., Wilmshurst, E., *An Introduction to International Criminal Law and Procedure*, Cambridge University Press, Cambridge, 2007, p. 1. "It was not until the 1990s, with the establishment of the ad hoc Tribunals for the former Yugoslavia and for Rwanda, that it could be said that an international criminal law regime had evolved. This is a relatively new body of law which is not yet uniform, nor are its courts universal."
3   Arrest Warrant of 11 April 2000 (Democratic Republic of the Congo v. Belgium), Judgment, *ICJ Reports 2002*, p. 3; Certain Questions of Mutual Assistance in Criminal Matters (Djibouti v. France), Judgment, *ICJ Reports 2008*, p. 177; Certain Criminal Proceedings in France (Republic of the Congo v. France), Order of 16 November 2010 (the procedure was terminated and the case removed from the list on the basis of the withdrawal of the application by the Republic of the Congo); Questions relating to the Obligation to Prosecute or Extradite (Belgium v. Senegal), Judgment of 20 July 2012, General List No. 144.

international law that are attributable to an individual (*i.e.* a natural person) and for which he or she may be held criminally accountable before a national or an international criminal court. The violations of international law that are attributable to States are beyond our present domain.[4]

In legal theory the perception of ICL is not uniform. The leading Slovenian author on ICL, L. Bavcon, determines the scope of ICL on the basis of criminal law norms in international law. Accordingly, these norms are distributed in the following four groups: 1.) substantive norms of international law; 2.) procedural norms of international law; 3.) norms of international law of a criminal organizational nature; and 4.) international legal norms of an enforcement character.[5] In the author's view, the majority of international lawyers treat ICL as a part of public international law while, looking from a criminal lawyer's perspective, ICL is a special subdivision of national criminal substantive and procedural law or a special legal discipline.[6]

A. Cassese is probably the most eminent supporter of the view that ICL is a part of international law.[7] The rules forming this branch of law emanate from the sources of international law.[8] D. Akande also considers ICL a part of international law. However, when speaking of the sources of ICL, it is important also to discuss the organ whose task it is to apply this body of law.[9] The prosecution of international crimes may be entrusted to national, international,

---

[4] Military and Paramilitary Activities in and against Nicaragua, Merits, Judgment, *ICJ Reports 1986*, p. 14; Legal Consequences of the Construction of a Wall in the Occupied Palestinian Territory, Advisory Opinion, 9 July 2004, *ICJ Reports 2004*, p. 136; ICJ, Case concerning the Application of the Convention on the Prevention and Punishment of the Crime of Genocide (Bosnia and Herzegovina v. Serbia and Montenegro), Judgment (Merits) of 26 February 2007, General List No. 91; Armed Activities on the Territory of the Congo (Democratic Republic of the Congo v. Uganda), Judgment, *ICJ Reports 2005*, p. 168; Ahmadou Sadio Diallo (Republic of Guinea v. Democratic Republic of the Congo), Merits, Judgment, *ICJ Reports 2010*, p. 639; ICJ, Ahmadou Sadio Diallo (Republic of Guinea v. Democratic Republic of the Congo) (Compensation owed by the Democratic Republic of the Congo to the Republic of Guinea), Judgment of 19 June 2012, General List No. 103.

[5] Bavcon, L. *et al.*, *Mednarodno kazensko pravo* [*International Criminal Law*], ČZ Uradni list Republike Slovenije, Ljubljana, 1997, p. 15.

[6] *Ibid.*, p. 29.

[7] Cassese, A., *Int'l Criminal Law, op. cit.*, p. 4.

[8] *Ibid.* "International criminal law is but a branch of public international law, though it shows some unique features." Cassese, A., Acquaviva, Q., Fan, M., Whiting, A., *International Criminal Law: Cases and Commentary*, Oxford University Press, Oxford, 2011, p. 1.

[9] Akande, D., "Sources of International Criminal Law", in: Cassese, A. (gen. ed.), *The Oxford Companion to International Criminal Justice*, Oxford University Press, Oxford, 2009, p. 41.

and internationalized courts.¹⁰ While international (and internationalized) criminal courts may in the first place apply the rules and principles of international law, national courts are not always authorized to do so. To what extent a national court may apply international law will depend on the constitutional provisions that regulate the relationship between the national and international law of that State.¹¹ In some national legal orders treaties are applied directly, while in others they may be applied only if they are incorporated in national law.¹² Likewise, the position of customary law is not uniform, for in some cases it has the same or a superior position to national legislation (*e.g.* Germany, Italy, Slovenia), while in others national legislation will prevail over customary international law (*e.g.* the UK, the USA).¹³ The 'common law' countries may directly apply the rules and principles of ICL, while the 'civil law' countries that have national substantive and procedural criminal law codified in their respective criminal codes cannot directly apply the rules of ICL emanating from international law unless they are transformed into their national legislation. There are other authors who also treat ICL as a combination of international law and national criminal law.¹⁴ According to one view, ICL is a 'hybrid' between international human rights law, international humanitarian law and national criminal law.¹⁵ It is important to note that numerous substantive and procedural criminal standards of the same value are incorporated in the national criminal legislation of many States, and thus contribute to the formation of ICL.

C. Bassiouni, who is undoubtedly one of the leading scholars in this field, notes that ICL is a complex legal discipline formed by components, entwined in their functional relationship in order to pursue their value-oriented goals.¹⁶ These goals include the prevention and suppression of international criminality, the promotion of accountability and the reduction of impunity, as well as

---

10   *Ibid.*
11   *Ibid.*
12   *Ibid.*
13   *Ibid.*, pp. 41–42.
14   "International criminal law (ILC) constitutes the fusion of two legal disciplines: international law and domestic criminal law." Bantekas, I., Nash S., *International Criminal Law*, 3rd edition, Routledge-Cavendish, London, 2007, p. 1.
15   Grover, L., "A Call to Arms: Fundamental Dilemmas Confronting the Interpretation of Crimes in the Rome Statute of the International Criminal Court", 21(3) *European Journal of International Law*, 2010, p. 550.
16   Bassiouni, C., *International Criminal Law*, 3rd edition, Vol. I, Martinus Nijhoff Publishers, Leiden, 2008, p. 3.

the implementation of international justice.[17] The components forming ICL originate in different legal disciplines and their respective branches, including international law, national criminal law, comparative criminal law and procedure, as well as international and regional human rights law.[18]

Đ. Degan and B. Pavišić define ICL in the widest sense as a unity of criminal legal norms, linked to international relations.[19] ICL can also be defined as the compilation of national rules prescribing criminal offences with a foreign element and penalties for their violation or as rules of international origin.[20] Moreover, ICL comprises some of the most serious offences which have been recognized by the international community as international crimes, and for which suspects can be tried before national or international courts.[21]

Even if we recognize ICL in its broad sense, noting that it encompasses not only international law but also national criminal law protecting the values of the international legal order, comparative criminal law, and relations between States on the basis of international legal assistance, we cannot disregard the prevailing role of international law. The historical development of ICL also confirms the leading role of international law during the process of its creation. In addition, it cannot be disregarded that at present there are five international criminal courts functioning. These are two *ad hoc* criminal Tribunals for the former Yugoslavia (ICTY) and for Rwanda (ICTR), the International Criminal Court (ICC), the Special Court for Sierra Leone, and the Special Tribunal for Lebanon. The last two belong to the group of so-called internationalized or hybrid criminal courts, for they also possess certain elements of those courts. The Special Court for Sierra Leone was set up jointly by the Government of Sierra Leone and the United Nations (UN) and is mandated to try those who bear the greatest responsibility for serious violations of international humanitarian law and Sierra Leonean law committed in the territory of Sierra Leone since 30 November 1996.[22] The Special Tribunal for Lebanon, which is defined as a tribunal of an international character, has jurisdiction over persons responsible for the attack of 14 February 2005 resulting in the death of former Lebanese Prime Minister Rafiq Hariri and in the death or

---

17   *Ibid.*
18   *Ibid.*
19   Degan, Đ., Pavišić. B., *Međunarodno kazneno pravo* [*International Criminal Law*], Pravni fakultet Sveučilišta u Rijeci [Faculty of Law, University of Rijeka], Rijeka, 2005, p. 1.
20   *Ibid.*
21   *Ibid.*
22   Legal basis for its creation is the Agreement between the UN and the Government of Sierra Leone on the Establishment of the Special Court of Sierra Leone of 16 January 2002, available at: <http://www.sc-sl.org/>.

injury of some other persons.²³ Applicable law for their prosecution is the Lebanese Criminal Code and its provisions relating to acts of terrorism and crimes and offences against life and personal integrity.²⁴

11   The Sources of ICL in the Context of International Law

1   *The Presentation of the Sources of ICL Pursuant to Article 38(1) of the Statute of the International Court of Justice*

International law played a pivotal role in the development and consolidation of ICL, and thus the question arises whether Article 38 of the Statute of the ICJ, which represents a generally recognized rule on the sources of international law, can be applied to identify the sources of ICL. Legal scholars often regard Article 38 of the Statute of the ICJ as an instruction for identifying the sources of ICL.²⁵ Đ. Degan and B. Pavišić are of the opinion that with regard to the sources of international law, a part of ICL which stems in its entirety from international law and all parts which cannot develop or be applied outside the scope of the rules of international law must be analysed.²⁶

Article 38(1) of the Statute of the ICJ determines that the Court, whose function is to decide in accordance with international law such disputes as are submitted to it, shall apply:

a) international conventions, whether general or particular, establishing rules expressly recognized by the contesting states;
b) international custom, as evidence of a general practice accepted as law;
c) the general principles of law recognized by civilized nations;
d) subject to the provisions of Article 59,²⁷ judicial decisions and the teachings of the most highly qualified publicists of the various nations, as subsidiary means for the determination of rules of law.

---

23 It was established on the basis of the Security Council Resolution S/1757 (2007) of 30 May 2007.
24 The Statute of the Special Tribunal for Lebanon, Article 1.
25 Cryer, R., Friman, H., Robinson D., Wilmshurst, E., *op. cit.*, p. 6. "As international criminal law is a subset of international law, its sources are those of international law. These are usually considered to be those enumerated in Article 38(1)(a)–(d) of the Statute of the International Court of Justice..."
26 Degan, Đ., Pavišić, B., *op. cit.*, p. 19.
27 Article 59 determines that the decision of the Court has no binding force except between the parties and in respect of that particular case.

This rule is envisaged for deciding disputes between States as sovereign and independent subjects of international law. In ICL there is a relationship between a judge, a prosecutor, a suspect or an accused and his or her counsel, and victims of international crimes.[28] Legal relations therein are thus different, and this also has to be taken into account when discussing the sources of law. C. Bassiouni also draws attention to different legal relations and is of the opinion that the enforcement of international law relies essentially on the voluntary cooperation of States, while ICL contains certain enforcements mechanisms that aim to improve States' compliance with international legal norms by means which rely on the international interdependence of States' interests and, if necessary, by means of certain coercive measures.[29]

The first three groups of sources pursuant to Article 38(1) of the Statute of the ICJ are formally equal and there is no hierarchy between them; for resolving conflicts between them general rules on resolving conflicts between equal sources of law apply (*i.e. lex specialis derogat legi generali, lex posterior derogat legi priori, lex cogens derogat legi dispositivi*).[30] Most of all in ICL there are certain general peremptory norms of international law (*ius cogens*) that prevail over other principles and rules of international law. Among them are, *inter alia*, the prohibition of slavery, genocide, torture,[31] and serious violations of human rights and rules of international humanitarian law. These norms have effect *erga omnes*.[32] They are binding not only on the subjects of international law in their mutual relations, but also on other participants in armed conflicts regardless of the nature of the conflict (be it an international or a non-international conflict). These norms must be respected also at a national level. In ICL the sources of law are subordinate to the principle of legality (*nullum*

---

28 Degan, Đ., Pavišić. B., *op. cit.*, p. 20.

29 Bassiouni, C., *op. cit.*, p. 10.

30 Škrk, M., "Pojem virov v mednarodnem pravu" ["The Notion of the Sources in International Law"], in: *ZZR Pravne fakultete v Ljubljani* [*Collection of the Scientific Treatises of the Faculty of Law in Ljubljana*], Vol. XLV, Ljubljana, 1985, p. 149. The relationship between the three main sources listed in Article 38 is complex and the ICJ *de facto* uses them in a successive order. Zimmermann, A., Tomuschat, C., Oellers-Frahm, K. (eds.), *The Statute of the International Court of Justice, A Commentary*, Oxford University Press, Oxford, 2006, p. 773.

31 "In the Court's opinion, the prohibition of torture is part of customary international law and it has become a peremptory norm (*jus cogens*)." ICJ, Questions Relating to the Obligation to Prosecute or Extradite (Belgium v. Senegal), Judgment of 20 July 2012, General List No. 144, para. 99.

32 Barcelona Traction, Judgment of 5 February 1970, *ICJ Reports 1970*, para. 33.

crimen sine lege), which, taking into account Article 38 of the Statute of the ICJ, derives from the general principles of law.[33]

Judicial decisions together with doctrine are subsidiary means of international law and are intended for the interpretation of the main groups of the sources.

As regards the fact that the *ad hoc* Tribunal for the former Yugoslavia primarily applies international law, it refers to Article 38 of the Statute of the ICJ as an established rule on the sources of international law.[34]

Hereinafter we first discuss the sources of ICL deriving from the provision on the sources of international law pursuant to Article 38(1) of the Statute of the ICJ.

a Treaties

The most important treaties in the field of ICL are founding treaties of international criminal courts. A decision to establish an international military tribunal for the trial of Nazi war criminals, whose offences had no particular geographical location, was formally upheld by the London Agreement of 8 August 1945.[35] It was signed by the Governments of the USA, France, the United Kingdom, and the former Soviet Union. In accordance with its Article 5, 19 more governments of the United Nations adhered to this Agreement, among them the Yugoslav Government. The Rome Statute of the ICC is a treaty to which all States may accede; it has not yet, however, achieved universality.[36] Thus, in accordance with treaty law it is binding only on the States parties to it. The Statute of the Special Court for Sierra Leone has the nature of a treaty, as it is annexed to the Agreement between the UN and the Government of Sierra Leone on the establishment of the Court and is an integral part of that Agreement.[37] Both *ad hoc* Tribunals for the former Yugoslavia and for Rwanda

---

33 Bassiouni, C., *op. cit.*, p. 5.

34 Prosecutor *v.* Kupreškić *et al.*, IT-95-16-T, Judgement, 14 January 2000, para. 540. "Being international in nature and applying international law *principaliter*, the Tribunal cannot but rely upon the well-established sources of international law and, within this framework, upon judicial decisions."

35 Trial of the Major War Criminals before the International Military Tribunal, Nuremberg, 14 November 1945–1 October 1946, Vol. 1, Nuremberg, Germany, 1947, p. 8.

36 For the text see A/CONF.183/9 of 17 July 1998. Pursuant to Article 126, the Rome Statute entered into force on 1 July 2002. There are 139 States signatories and 122 States parties; amendments to Article 8 of the Rome Statute, 6 acceptances/ratifications; amendments to the Rome Statute on the crime of aggression, 5 acceptances/ratifications. Status as at 15 May 2013.

37 See Article 1(11) of the Agreement.

were established on the basis of UN Security Council resolutions.³⁸ The same applies for the Special Tribunal for Lebanon. There is a prevailing view that the Statutes of the *ad hoc* Tribunals that were adopted by the UN Security Council on the basis of Chapter VII ('Action with Respect to Threats to the Peace, Breaches of the Peace, and Acts of Aggression') of the UN Charter, which is a treaty, are binding on all Member States on the basis of Article 25 of the Charter.³⁹

The Special Tribunal for Lebanon has a different position compared to the ICTY and ICTR, regardless of the fact that the Security Council also acted on the basis of Chapter VII of the UN Charter. The Special Tribunal for Lebanon was established upon the request of the Government of Lebanon, whereas the agreement between the Government and the UN was annexed to UN Security Council resolution 1757 (2007).⁴⁰ The Statute of the Special Tribunal for Lebanon is attached to the above-mentioned Agreement and forms an integral part thereof. It is thus comparable with the Statute of the Special Court for Sierra Leone.

Conventions from the field of international humanitarian law, which encompasses the international law of armed conflict, including the protection of war victims, are also important. These primarily include the Geneva Conventions (GC) of 1949 for the protection of victims of war and both Additional Protocols of 1977 to the GC, namely Protocol I relating to international armed conflicts and Protocol II relating to non-international armed conflicts. The GC of 1949 achieved universality, while neither Additional Protocols has yet achieved this status.⁴¹

---

38   *Ad hoc* criminal tribunal for Yugoslavia (International Tribunal for the Prosecution of Persons Responsible for Serious Violations of International Criminal Law Committed in the Territory of the Former Yugoslavia since 1991) (ICTY) was established by UN Security Council resolution 827 (1993) of 25 May 1993, whereas *ad hoc* criminal tribunal for Rwanda (International Criminal Tribunal for the Prosecution of Persons Responsible for Genocide and Other Serious Violations of International Humanitarian Law in the Territory of Rwanda and Rwandan Citizens Responsible for Genocide and Other Such Violations Committed in the Territory of Neighbouring States, between 1 January 1994 and 31 December 1994) (ICTR) was established by UN Security Council Resolution 955 (1994) of 8 November 1994.

39   The Members of the United Nations agree to accept and carry out the decisions of the Security Council in accordance with the Charter. See also preambles to the Statutes of the ICTY and ICTR.

40   See Article 1(11) of the Agreement.

41   There are 195 States parties to the GC of 1949 and by two (*i.e.* Cook Islands and the Holy See) surpass the number of the members of the UN (193). There are 173 States parties to

Therefore, subject-matter jurisdiction of the ICTY includes only grave breaches of the GC of 1949 and not also breaches of Additional Protocols I and II, regardless of the fact that the former Yugoslavia was a State party to both Additional Protocols, since the drafters of the Statute were of the opinion that the Protocols do not contain international crimes under customary international law. Some legal scholars note that there is no reason why international courts may not apply treaties when deciding on international crimes, especially if the States that are parties to such treaties are involved, as was the case with the former Yugoslavia.[42] However, upon the establishment of the ICTY the adopted view was that the application of the *nullum crimen sine lege* principle requires that the international tribunal should apply rules of international humanitarian law which are beyond any doubt part of customary law, so that the problem of the acceptance of some but not all States of specific conventions does not arise.[43] Đ. Degan and B. Pavišić criticise the judgment of the Trial Chamber of the ICTY in the *Blaškić* case of 2000, as it applied the Agreement between Croatia and Bosnia-Herzegovina of 1992, signed under the auspices of the International Committee of the Red Cross (ICRC), by which both States agreed to respect certain rules of Additional Protocol I, which they ratified in 1992.[44] The ICTY dismissed the defence argument that Additional Protocol I was binding on both States as a treaty and not as customary international law. Thereby, the Tribunal allegedly broadly interpreted Article 3 of the Statute to the detriment of the accused.[45] In particular it did not take into account the scope of the *nullum crimen sine lege* principle and a requirement that all international crimes must be part of customary international law.[46] Regardless of such criticism the Appeals Chamber of the ICTY adopted a position in favour of the application of treaties that are not part of customary international law, on the condition that they are unquestionably binding on the parties at the time of the alleged offence and are not in conflict with or

---

Additional Protocol I (and 3 State signatories), among them also all permanent members of the UN Security Council, with the exception of the USA that only signed it. There are 167 State parties to Additional Protocol II and 3 State signatories. Status as at 15 May 2013; <http://www.icrc.org/eng>.

42 Akande, D., *op. cit.*, pp. 48–49.
43 Report of the Secretary General Pursuant to Paragraph 2 of Security Council resolution 808, UN Doc. S/25704, 3 May 1993, p. 9.
44 Degan, Đ., Pavišić, B., *op. cit.*, p. 37.
45 *Ibid.* Article 3 of the Statute determines violations of the laws or customs of war.
46 *Ibid.*

derogating from peremptory norms of international law (*ius cogens*), which includes most customary rules of international humanitarian law.[47]

A different, broader approach was adopted when establishing the ICTR, under the jurisdiction of which were also explicitly included violations of Additional Protocol II considering the circumstance that the armed conflict in Rwanda was qualified as predominantly a non-international armed conflict. When drafting the Statute of the ICTR, the Commission of experts considered the fact that Rwanda had acceded to Additional Protocols I and II to the GC of 1949.[48] Violations of both Additional Protocols of 1977 are contained in Article 8 of the Rome Statute under war crimes.

In addition to *Geneva law Hague law* is also important for ICL, primarily the Hague Conventions of 1899/1907 concerning the international law of armed conflict. Certain of them never entered into force. Certain are binding as treaty law, while the most important among them, the Hague Convention (IV) Respecting the Laws and Customs of War on Land of 1907, has become part of customary international law.[49] As such it was also an important source for determining the subject-matter jurisdiction of the Nuremberg Tribunal and the ICTY, in the case of the latter within the framework of the violation of the laws or customs of war (Article 3 of the Statute of the ICTY). Mention must also be made of the *Martens Clause*, which is laid down in the preamble to the Hague Convention (IV) and is *ultima ratio* regarding the protection of individuals in armed conflicts.[50] Sources of international humanitarian law are also conventions from the field of the prohibition of the use of certain means or weapons, *e.g.* the Geneva Protocol for the Prohibition of the Use in War of Asphyxiating, Poisonous or Other Gases,

---

47 Akande, D., *op. cit.*, p. 49. See Prosecutor *v.* Duško Tadić, IT-94-1-AR72, Decision on the Defence Motion for Interlocutory Appeal on Jurisdiction, 2 October 1995, paras. 14–40 and 143. See also Kordić and Čerkez, IT-95-14/2-A, Judgement, 17 December 2004, paras. 41–46.

48 See Letter dated 9 December 1994 from the Secretary-General Addressed to the President of the Security Council, S/1994/1405, December 1994, Annex, Final Report of the Commission of Experts Established Pursuant to Security Council Resolution 935 (1994), p. 22.

49 Brown Scott, J. (ed.), *The Hague Conventions and Declarations of 1899 and 1907*, Oxford University Press, Oxford, 1915.

50 "Until a more complete code of the laws of war has been issued, the High Contracting Parties deem it expedient to declare that, in cases not included in the Regulations adopted by them, the inhabitants and the belligerents remain under the protection and the rule of the principles of the law of nations, as they result from the usages established among civilized peoples, from the laws of humanity, and the dictates of public conscience." *Cf.* Article 1(2) of Additional Protocol I to the GC of 1949.

and of Bacteriological Methods of Warfare of 1925.[51] The list of Geneva and Hague conventions is not nearly exhausted. Other examples are Additional Protocol III relating to the Adoption of an Additional Distinctive Emblem of 2005[52] and the Hague Convention for the Protection of Cultural Property in the Event of Armed Conflict of 1954 and its Second Protocol of 1999.[53] In addition, there are a number of universal international instruments from the field of international humanitarian law, known as contemporary treaty law or *New York law*.[54] The New York law is the result of the common endeavours of the ICRC and the UN to carry on the development of international humanitarian law.[55] As a result, the Rome Statute encompasses breaches of Hague, Geneva and New York law.[56]

Universal human rights instruments are important in ICL in general, and especially from the perspective of proceedings against perpetrators of international crimes. In this regard, the International Covenant on Civil and Political Rights (ICCPR) of 1966 has a special role.[57] Article 14 of the ICCPR contains minimum procedural guarantees that are ensured to persons charged with international crimes before international criminal courts or internationalized courts, inasmuch as national procedural legislation does not ensure sufficient procedural guarantees. The European Convention for the Protection of Human Rights and Fundamental Freedoms (ECHR) is a regional treaty. Nevertheless, the Appeals Chamber of the ICTY in the *Tadić* case applied the ECHR regarding the interpretation of the phrase a *tribunal established by law* taking into consideration Article 6(1) of the ECHR.[58]

Treaty law also includes conventions on the prohibition of genocide (1948),[59] torture (1984),[60] and apartheid (1973),[61] including the Slavery Convention of

---

51   LNTS, Vol. 94, 1929, pp. 65–74.
52   It has 63 States parties and 31 States signatories. Status as at 15 May 2013; <http://www.icrc.org/eng>.
53   The Hague Convention for the Protection of Cultural Property of 14 May 1954 with the Protocol; the Second Hague Protocol for the Protection of Cultural Property of 26 March 1999.
54   Sancin, V., Švarc, D., Ambrož, M., *Mednarodno pravo oboroženih spopadov* [*International Law of Armed Conflict*], Poveljstvo za doktrino, razvoj, izobraževanje in usposabljanje [Doctrine, Development, Education and Training Command], Ljubljana, 2009, pp. 69–70.
55   Kalshoven, F., Zegveld, L., *Constraints on the Waging of War, An Introduction to International Humanitarian Law*, 4th edition, Cambridge University Press, Cambridge, and ICRC, Geneva, 2011, pp. 24–29.
56   Ibid., p. 28.
57   UNTS, Vol. 999, p. 171.
58   IT-94-1AR72, 2 October 1995, *op. cit.*, para. 43.
59   UNTS, Vol. 78, p. 277.
60   UNTS, Vol. 1465, p. 85.
61   UNTS, Vol. 1015, p. 243.

1926,[62] and the Supplementary Convention on the Abolition of Slavery, the Slave Trade, and Institutions and Practices Similar to Slavery of 1957.[63] The Convention on the Non-Applicability of Statutory Limitations to War Crimes and Crimes against Humanity of 1968 is also a part of treaty law.[64] Merely because this Convention had the character of treaty law, the International Law Commission (ILC) of the UN did not include a statute of limitations for international crimes in its final draft of the statute of an international criminal court, which it submitted to the General Assembly in 1994.[65] Non-applicability of a statute of limitations for crimes under its subject-matter jurisdiction is provided for in Article 29 of the Rome Statute.

If ICL is considered in a broader context, so that it also includes cooperation between States in the prosecution of perpetrators of criminal offences, attention must also be drawn to treaty law within the framework of the Council of Europe (CE). Examples in this regard are: the European Convention on the Suppression of Terrorism of 1977 and the European Convention on Extradition of 1957, the Additional Protocol of 1975 to the latter Convention, and the Second Additional Protocol to the European Convention on Extradition of 1978. ICL in such broader context also comprises bilateral agreements on legal assistance and extradition.

Treaties are interpreted in accordance with the rules of interpretation of the Vienna Convention on the Law of Treaties (VCLT) of 1969, the numerous provisions of which are considered customary international law.[66] By means of the rules of interpretation that apply for treaties, the Appeals Chambers of the ICTY in the *Tadić* case interpreted the ICTY's Statute regarding the question whether its provisions also refer to non-international armed conflicts. In doing so it applied literal, teleological, logical, and systematic forms of interpretation.[67] The ICTR and ICC also recognized the applicability of the VCLT for the interpretation of their Statutes.[68]

---

62 It was signed in Geneva on 25 September 1926 (together with the Protocol and Additional Protocol), *Human Rights, A Compilation of International Instruments*, Vol. I (First Part), Universal Instruments, UN, New York, 1993, pp. 201–207.

63 It was signed in Geneva on 7 September 1956, *ibid.*, p. 209.

64 UNTS, Vol. 754, p. 73. The Convention entered into force on 11 November 1970 (Article 8). There are 9 States signatories and 54 States parties. Status as at 15 May 2013.

65 Report of the ILC on the Work of its Forty-sixth Session, 2 May-22 July 1994, GA, Official Records, 49th Session, Supplement No. 10 (A/49/10), UN, New York, pp. 29–157.

66 See Articles 31–33.

67 Prosecutor *v.* Duško Tadić, IT-94-1-AR72, Judgement, 2 October 1995, *op. cit.*, paras. 71–94.

68 Grover. L., *op. cit.*, p. 546. *Cf.* Gardiner, R., *Treaty Interpretation*, Oxford University Press, Oxford, 2008, p. 126.

b   Customary International Law

Customary international law is in its origin the oldest source of international law. It develops continuously and in certain areas, such as international humanitarian law, importantly supplements the norms of treaty law, which makes it a contemporary source of law.[69] An international customary rule is formed through practice and *opinio iuris* of States (*opinio iuris sive necessitatis*). State practice, whereby general practice suffices, entails an objective (material) criterion, whereas *opinio iuris* entails a subjective (psychological) criterion.[70] Both criteria, through which the existence of a customary international law rule is established, must be fulfilled. Regardless of the fact that it is often claimed that customary international law can be an unwritten source of law, its existence is nevertheless most often proved by written sources of law (*e.g.* diplomatic correspondence). In ICL written sources that prove the existence of a customary international law rule are Security Council resolutions, treaties and case law of the courts (international and national). As evidence of state practice the operational practice of armed forces in armed conflicts, military manuals and official pronouncements are taken into consideration.[71] As a general rule, generally applicable rules of customary international law are binding on all States.[72]

Given that customary international law is in general an unwritten source of law derived from state practice accompanied by *opinio iuris*, the question is raised as to its suitability and sufficient predictability for determining criminal accountability in ICL. The question is connected with the content of the principle of legality in criminal substantive law and its interpretation. Also in the Slovenian legal order, where the principle of legality is determined in Article 28 of the Constitution, one of the four constitutional requirements for the use of criminal law repression is *nullum crimen, nulla poena sine lege scripta*, which entails the prohibition of determining criminal offences and penalties by executive regulations or by customary law.[73] The principle of legality in substantive criminal law furthermore sets the following requirements for the use

---

69 Türk, D., *Temelji mednarodnega prava* [*Foundations of International Law*], GV Založba, Ljubljana, 2007, p. 54.

70 For details on material and psychological elements of international custom, see *The Statute of the International Court of Justice, A Commentary, op. cit.*, pp. 750–753.

71 Akande, D., *op. cit.*, p. 51.

72 With the exception of the State which persistently objects to the formation of a new rule of customary international law (*persistent objector*). Brownlie, I., *Principles of Public International Law*, 7th edition, Oxford University Press, Oxford, 2008, p. 11.

73 Constitutional Court Decision No. U-I-335/02 dated 24 March 2005, para. 10. *Official Gazette RS*, No. 37/05, and *OdlUS*, XIV, 16.

of criminal law repression, namely: the prohibition of analogy at establishing the existence of criminal offences and at imposing penalties (*nullum crimen, nulla poena sine lege stricta*); the prohibition of determining criminal offences and penalties by means of void, undefined, or unclear concepts (*nullum crimen, nulla poena sine lege certa*); the prohibition of retroactive application of regulations which determine criminal offences and respective penalties (*nullum crimen, nulla poena sine lege praevia*).[74] The exception to the prohibition of retroactivity is a law that is more favourable to the alleged offender (*lex mitius*).[75]

Some authors claim that such a narrow interpretation of the principle of legality has not been accepted by 'common law' countries and has never found its way into international law.[76] A. Cassese is of a similar opinion and notes that on this score ICL bears a strong resemblance to the criminal law of England and other 'common law' countries, where next to statutory offences there exist many common law offences, developed through judicial precedents.[77] Đ. Degan allows for the possibility that in 'common law' countries new offences can be created by judicial precedents on the basis of the *stare decisis* doctrine; however, he notes that such a *judge-made law* has nothing in common with customary rules of whatever origin – national or international.[78] In his opinion, in criminal proceedings Anglo-American judges do not directly apply the existing rules of customary international law, nor can they create them by their own decisions. Therefore, he opposes international customary rules being a direct basis for incrimination before international criminal courts.[79] Other authors are also cautious and have reservations about the application of the rules of customary international law in ICL, especially if such concern unwritten rules that are not supported by written instruments, such as treaties or General Assembly resolutions.[80] Đ. Degan and B. Pavišić are critical of the

---

74 *Ibid.*

75 *Cf.* Article 24 ('Non-retroactivity ratione personae') of the Rome Statute, which prohibits retroactivity for conduct prior to the entry into force of the Statute. (1) In the event of a change in the law applicable to a given case prior to a final judgement, the law more favourable to the person being investigated, prosecuted or convicted shall apply. (2).

76 Akande, D., *op. cit.*, p. 51.

77 Cassese, A., *Int'l Criminal Law, op. cit.*, p. 17.

78 Degan, Đ., "On the Sources of International Criminal Law", 4(1) *Chinese Journal of International Law*, 2005, p. 67.

79 *Ibid.* "Customary rules cannot, as a matter of principle, be a direct basis of incrimination by an international criminal judge."

80 Cryer, R., Friman, H., Robinson D., Wilmshurst, E., *op. cit.*, pp. 7–8.

application of customary international law in ICL, especially in the case law of the ICTY.[81]

Regardless of the numerous reservations in doctrine, customary international law has been established as one of the sources of ICL. The statutes of international criminal courts refer to customary international law when they determine violations of the laws or customs of war.[82] In the *Furundžija* case, the Trial Chamber of the ICTY first considered the fact that rape in time of war is specifically prohibited by treaty law, namely by the GC of 1949 for the protection of victims of war and Additional Protocols I and II.[83] It furthermore established that the prohibition of rape and serious sexual assault in armed conflict has also evolved in customary international law.[84] The Appeals Chamber of the ICTY in the *Tadić* case applied the notion of *joint criminal enterprise*, as in its view "...the notion of common design as a form of accomplice liability is firmly established in customary international law".[85] With reference to such, the ICTY relied on criminal trials before military tribunals established by the Allied Powers after World War II.

Customary international law will provide a source of applicable excuses and defences even when not provided for in the Statute of the Tribunal or the Rules of Procedure and Evidence.[86] The Appeals Chamber of the ICTY in the *Erdemović* case found that *duress* does not afford a complete defence to a soldier charged with a crime against humanity and/or a war crime involving the killing of innocent human beings. It referred to the Joint Separate Opinion of two Judges, who noted that customary international law does not provide a sufficient basis to support the finding that duress affords a complete defence to the above-mentioned crimes.[87]

Identifying the existence of an international crime under customary international law is important from the perspective of the principle of legality with reference to the prohibition of retroactive effect of the Statute of any international criminal court or other treaty norm (*nullum crimen sine lege praevia*).[88]

---

81 Degan, Đ., Pavišić, B., *op. cit.*, pp. 45–48. *Cf.* Degan, Đ., *op. cit.*, pp. 69–70.
82 Akande, D., *op. cit.*, p. 49. *Cf.* Article 3 of the Statute of the ICTY and Article 8(2)(b) of the Rome Statute.
83 Prosecutor *v.* Furundzija, IT-95-17/1-T, Judgement, 10 December 1998, para. 165.
84 *Ibid.*, para. 168.
85 Akande, D., *op. cit.*, p. 50, from Tadić, IT-94-1-A, Judgement, 15 July 1999, para. 220. See also Cassese, A., *Int'l Criminal Law, op. cit.*, p. 19.
86 Akande D., *ibid.*
87 Erdemović, IT-96-22-A, Judgement, 7 October 1997, para. 19. See Joint Separate Opinion of Judges McDonald and Vohrah.
88 See above under footnotes 73–75.

In the *Norman* case, the Special Court for Sierra Leone in preliminary proceedings entertained a defence motion alleging that the Court had no jurisdiction over serious violations of international humanitarian law, namely conscripting or enlisting children (Article 4(c) of the Statute of the Special Court for Sierra Leone), because the offence did not entail the violation of customary international law at the time of the conduct in question.[89] In the case at issue, the Court found the violation under customary international law.

When discussing the rules of customary international law it must be underlined that peremptory norms of general international law (*ius cogens*) are in their essence an upgrade of the rules of customary international law. A peremptory norm of international law is a norm accepted and recognized by the international community of States as a whole as a norm from which no derogation is permitted and which can be modified only by a subsequent norm of general international law having the same character.[90] A peremptory norm of *ius cogens* is a norm that enjoys a higher rank in the international hierarchy than treaty law and even 'ordinary' customary rules.[91] These norms have a central position in ICL.[92] Furthermore, it must be underlined that the ICJ with reference to genocide, the prohibition of which also falls under *ius cogens* norms, in the Advisory Opinion of 1951 on the Reservations to the Convention on the Prevention and Punishment of the Crime of Genocide found that its definition under that Convention is a rule of customary international law.[93] In the Statutes of all international criminal courts that have jurisdiction to decide on genocide, the definition of genocide follows *verbatim* the definition provided in the above-mentioned Convention.[94]

Under the Genocide Convention the objects of protection against genocide are national, ethnical, racial, or religious groups. In the *Krstić* case, the ICTY decided strictly within this scope.[95]

---

89 Akande, D., *op. cit.*, p. 46, from the Decision on Preliminary Motion based on Lack of Jurisdiction (Child Recruitment), Norman, SCSL-04-14-AR72(E), AC, 31 May 2004.
90 *Cf.* Article 53 of the VCLT.
91 Prosecutor *v.* Furundzija, IT-95-17/1-T, Judgement, 10 December 1998, para. 153.
92 Degan, Đ., Pavišić, B., *op. cit.*, p. 41.
93 Advisory Opinion of 28 May 1951, *ICJ Reports 1951.*
94 *Cf.* Article II of the Genocide Convention, Article 4 of the Statute of the ICTY, Article 2 of the Statute of the ICTR, and Article 6 of the Rome Statute.
95 Prosecutor *v.* Radislav Krstić, IT-98-33-T, Judgement, 2 August 2001. The Trial Chamber found that such group were the military aged Bosnian Muslim men, because the killing of these men inevitably and fundamentally would result in the annihilation of the entire Bosnian Muslim community at Srebrenica (see para. 634).

c General Principles of Law

General principles of law were included in the Statute of the Permanent Court of International Justice in 1920, so that the Court could resort to them in order to fill gaps in international law. The majority of contemporary international lawyers agree that the expression *recognized by civilized nations* is obsolete, as all States, regardless of their geographical origin, are equally included in the present-day international community. The general principles of law as a source of international law have developed in national legal systems. A general principle of law is recognized as a source of international law if such principle exists in national laws of a great number of the States or was accepted by all major legal systems.[96]

The general principles of law have an important position in ICL and all international criminal courts apply them. The principle of legality (*nullum crimen nulla poena sine lege praevia*), which has been mentioned several times, is a fundamental principle of ICL and is in its nature a general principle of law.[97] F. Raimondo notes that the *nullum crimen nulla poena sine lege* principle as a general principle of law contains only two requirements, namely the prohibition of retroactive criminal laws (*lex praevia*) and the specificity of criminal laws (*lex certa*).[98] It is embodied in all fundamental instruments on the protection of human rights of a universal and regional character.[99] The general principles of law most often include principles such as the prohibition of double jeopardy (*ne bis in idem*), presumption of innocence, the principle of equality of arms, the rule of speciality, the rule of *res iudicata*. There is a prevailing view that the ICTY and ICTR resort to the general principles of law to assist them in their search for the applicable rules of international law.[100] In relation to criminal law, the general principles of law are not ideal; they are, by their nature, general, and thus tend to be a last resort.[101]

A. Cassese speaks of the general principles of ICL, which also include the general principles of law, and of the general principles of international law.[102]

---

96 Akande, D., *op. cit.*, p. 52.
97 See above under footnote 33.
98 Raimondo, F.O., *General Principles of Law in the Decisions of International Criminal Courts and Tribunals*, Martinus Nijhoff Publishers, Leiden, 2008, p. 107.
99 Article 11(2) of the Universal Declaration of Human Rights; Article 15 of the ICCPR; Article 7 of the ECHR; Article 9 of the American Convention on Human Rights, adopted in San Jose, Costa Rica, 22 November 1969; and Article 7(2) of the African Charter on Human and Peoples' Rights, adopted in Nairobi, 27 June 1981.
100 Cryer, R., Friman, H., Robinson D., Wilmshurst, E., *op. cit.*, p. 8.
101 *Ibid.*
102 Cassese, A., *Int'l Criminal Law, op. cit.*, pp. 20–21.

However, he understands the general principles of ICL to be broader than the general principles of law, as among them he mentions, *inter alia*, the principle of command responsibility, as developed in international humanitarian law. The general principles of ICL are the principles that have gradually been transposed from national legal systems to the international level.[103]

On the other hand, A. Cassese speaks of the general principles of international law that have developed in the international legal system.[104] To rely on the general principles of ICL is acceptable in cases in which treaties (or the Statutes of the ICTY or ICTR as secondary sources) or the rules of customary international law are unclear or incomplete; if also the general principles of ICL are not applicable, the courts should resort to the application of the general principles of international law (if such is possible).[105] As an example he cites the *Furundžija* case tried before the ICTY regarding the definition of one of the forms of rape, namely the act of oral rape. The Trial Chamber of the ICTY did not find a legal basis for such definition of rape in treaty law or in national laws. Therefore, the Trial Chamber tried to establish whether an appropriate solution can be reached by resorting to the general principles of ICL or, if such principles are of no avail, to the general principles of international law.[106] The Trial Chamber stated "…that a forced penetration of the mouth by the male sexual organ constitutes a most humiliating and degrading attack upon human dignity."[107] It noted that "…the essence of the whole corpus of international humanitarian law as well as human rights law lies in the protection of the human dignity of every person, whatever his or her gender. The general principle of respect for human dignity is the basic underpinning and indeed the very *raison d'être* of international humanitarian law and human rights law; indeed in modern times it has become of such paramount importance as to permeate the whole body of international law."[108] The Trial Chamber concluded that it is in conformity with this principle that such an extremely serious sexual outrage as forced oral penetration should be classified as rape.

---

103   *Ibid.* See also Degan, Đ., Pavišić, B., *op. cit.*, p. 23.
104   Cassese, A., *Int'l Criminal Law, op. cit.*, p. 24.
105   *Ibid.*
106   Prosecutor *v.* Furundzija, IT-95-17/1-T, Judgement, 10 December 1998, *op. cit.*, para. 182: "… Faced with this lack of uniformity, it falls to the Trial Chamber to establish whether an appropriate solution can be reached by resorting to the general principles of international criminal law or, if such principles are of no avail, to the general principles of international law."
107   *Ibid.*, para. 183.
108   *Ibid.*

Đ. Degan is cautious about the application of the general principles of law in ICL, although he recognizes their great significance in the evolution of human rights law.[109]

d   International Judicial Decisions and Opinions of Legal Scholars
A majority position in doctrine is that international judicial decisions, even of the same court, do not *per se* constitute a source of ICL.[110] Formally speaking they are subsidiary means as determined in Article 38(1)(d) of the Statute of the ICJ. However, the ICTY and ICTR have developed a binding precedent doctrine (*stare decisis*) to the extent that Trial Chambers are bound by decisions of Appeals Chambers and not by decisions of other Trial Chambers.[111] The Appeals Chambers may depart from the previous decisions of other Appeals Chambers if compelling reasons exist.[112]

The ICTY and ICTR refer not only to the case law of other international criminal courts but also to the case law of other international courts and to the case law of national courts. In the *Tadić* case, the Appeals Chamber of the ICTY referred to the interpretation of Article 1 of the GC for the protection of victims of war, which the ICJ provided in the *Nicaragua* case, namely that the States parties undertake to respect the GC in all circumstances, since such an obligation derives from the general principles of humanitarian law.[113] In the *Aleksovski* case, the Appeals Chamber of the ICTY referred to the case law of the European Court of Human Rights (ECtHR) in the *Cossey* case as regards the generally non-binding effect of the case law.[114] In the *Furundžija* case, the Trial Chamber of the ICTY referred to the case law of the Tokyo International Military Tribunal and the decision of the United States Military Commission in the *Yamashita* case regarding the evolution of universally accepted norms of international law prohibiting rape and serious sexual assault that are applicable in any armed conflict.[115]

---

109   Degan, Đ., *op. cit.*, pp. 53–55.
110   Cassese, A., *Int'l Criminal Law, op. cit*, p. 26.
111   Akande, D., *op. cit.*, p. 53. See also Prosecutor v. Aleksovski, IT-95-14/1-A, Judgement, 24 March 2000, para. 113.
112   Judgement, Aleksovski, *ibid.*, paras. 92–115. See also Cassese, A., *Int'l Criminal Law, op. cit.*, str. 27.
113   The reasoning referred to the scope of the application of Article 3 common to the four GC of 1949 and relating to the non-international armed conflicts. See IT-94-1-AR72, 2 October 1995, *op. cit.*, para. 93, from Case Concerning Military and Paramilitary Activities in and against Nicaragua, Nicaragua v. US, Merits, *ICJ Reports 1986*, p.14 at para. 220.
114   Aleksovski, IT-95-14/1-A, Judgement, 24 March 2000, *op. cit.*, para. 95 and footnote 234, ECtHR, *Cossey* Judgment of 27 September 1990, Series A, Vol. 184.
115   Case IT-95-17/1-T, *op. cit.*, para. 168.

Opinions of legal scholars also have the character of a subsidiary source of ICL. Furthermore, the ICTY in its judgments refers to international doctrine. In addition, reports of the experts on drafting the Statutes of the ICTY and ICTR also constitute a subsidiary means for the determination of ICL.[116] There is a view among legal scholars that the above-mentioned reports should be assigned the character of preparatory work pursuant to Article 32 ('Supplementary means of interpretation') of the VCLT in the interpretation of the Statutes of both *ad hoc* Tribunals.

2   Other Sources of ICL

Other sources of ICL include the Rules of Procedure and Evidence of international criminal courts. Some authors define them as secondary sources of law.[117] In the case of the ICTY and ICTR the *quasi*-legislative task of adopting these Rules is entrusted to both Tribunals.[118] In the case of the ICC the Rules of Procedure and Evidence are adopted by the members of the Assembly of States Parties by a two-thirds majority.[119] However, after the adoption of the Rules of Procedure and Evidence, in urgent cases where the Rules do not provide for a specific situation before the Court, the judges may, by a two-thirds majority, draw up provisional Rules to be applied until adopted, amended or rejected at the next ordinary or special session of the Assembly of States Parties (Article 51(3) of the Rome Statute). The Rules of Procedure and Evidence shall be consistent with the Rome Statute; in the event of conflict between them, the text of the latter prevails.[120]

This group of the sources of ICL also includes Elements of Crimes pursuant to Article 9 of the Rome Statute, which are also adopted by a two-thirds majority of the members of the Assembly of States Parties and must be consistent with the Rome Statute.

---

116   Report of the Secretary-General Pursuant to Paragraph 2 of Security Council Resolution 808 (1993), Doc. S/25704, *op. cit.* and Final report of the Commission of Experts established pursuant to Security Council resolution 935 (1994), together with the Statute of the ICTR annexed to the Letter from the Secretary-General addressed to the President of the Security Council, Doc. S/1994/1405, *op. cit.*

117   *E.g.* Akande, D., *op. cit.*, p. 47.

118   Article 15 of the Statute of the ICTY and Article 14 of the Statute of the ICTR. The Judges of the ICTR adopt the Rules of Procedure and Evidence of the ICTY with such changes as they deem necessary.

119   Article 51(1) of the Rome Statute determines that these Rules enter into force upon adoption by a two-thirds majority of the members of the Assembly of States Parties. The same procedure applies for the adoption of amendments to the Rules pursuant to Article 51(2).

120   *Cf.* Article 51(4–5) of the Rome Statute.

Finally, resolutions of the General Assembly and the Security Council of the UN also play a role in determining rules and principles of ICL. The resolutions of the Security Council adopted in accordance with Chapter VII of the UN Charter were discussed under Section II.1.a. *Treaties*. Major resolutions of the General Assembly may contribute to the strengthening of the rules of customary international law or serve as evidence for the existence of those rules.[121]

III   Article 21 ('Applicable Law') of the Rome Statute

The Statutes of the ICTY and ICTR do not include a provision dealing with applicable law. A fundamental substantive basis for their decisions is contained in provisions on their subject-matter jurisdiction. In addition, they ascertain minimum procedural guarantees for the accused.[122] A similar approach can be observed in the case of the Special Court for Sierra Leone. The Statute of the Special Tribunal for Lebanon in Article 2 ('Applicable criminal law') refers to the application of the national criminal code.

Article 21 ('Applicable law') of the Rome Statute determines:

1.   The Court shall apply:

(a)   In the first place, this Statute, Elements of Crimes and its Rules of Procedure and Evidence;
(b)   In the second place, where appropriate, applicable treaties and the principles and rules of international law, including the established principles of the international law of armed conflict;
(c)   Failing that, general principles of law derived by the Court from national laws of legal systems of the world including, as appropriate, the national laws of States that would normally exercise jurisdiction over the crime, provided that those principles are not inconsistent with this Statute and with international law and internationally recognized norms and standards.

---

121   See Judgment of the ICJ in *Nicaragua v. US*, *ICJ Reports 1986*, p. 14, para. 264. The Court referred to the General Assembly resolution 2625(XXV) containing declaration on 'Principles of International Law concerning Friendly Relations and Co-operation among States in accordance with the Charter of the UN'.
122   Article 21 of the Statute of the ICTY and Article 20 of the Statute of the ICTR.

2. The Court may apply principles and rules of law as interpreted in its previous decisions.
3. The application and interpretation of law pursuant to this article must be consistent with internationally recognized human rights, and be without any adverse distinction founded on grounds such as gender as defined in article 7, paragraph 3, age, race, colour, language, religion or belief, political or other opinion, national, ethnic or social origin, wealth, birth or other status.

Article 21 is in Part II ('Jurisdiction, admissibility and applicable law') of the Rome Statute. Therefore, it applies not only to the sources of substantive law in a narrow sense, *i.e.* to the definition of the international crimes falling within the jurisdiction of the ICC, but to all legal rules and principles which the ICC may encounter during proceedings.[123] Part II, *inter alia*, contains the rule on jurisdiction *ratione temporis* (Article 11) and the principle *ne bis in idem* (Article 20). Article 21 constitutes the first codification of the sources of ICL.[124]

Article 21(1) is a central provision dealing with the sources of law applied by the ICC. Apart from Article 38 of the Statute of the ICJ, when applying law the ICC is bound by the hierarchy of the sources determined in paragraphs (a), (b), and (c) of Article 21(1).[125] The Court in the first place applies the Rome Statute, Elements of Crimes, and its Rules of Procedure and Evidence (paragraph (a)). The Statute, which is a treaty, prevails over the Elements of Crimes and the Rules of Procedure and Evidence.[126]

In the second place, where appropriate, the ICC applies applicable treaties and the principles and rules of international law, including the established principles of the international law of armed conflict (Article 21(1)(b)). This second group in the applicable law provision includes two distinct sources with no suggested hierarchy between them.[127] The phrase *where appropriate* is not coincidental, and it entails the discretion of the Court in determining when

---

123 Degan, Đ., Pavišić B., *op. cit.*, p. 57.
124 Triffterer, O. (ed.), *Commentary on the Rome Statute of the International Criminal Court*, 2nd edition, C.H. Beck, Hart, Nomos, 2008, p. 703.
125 *Ibid.* See also Schabas, W., *The International Criminal Court: A Commentary on the Rome Statute*, Oxford University Press, Oxford, 2010, p. 385: "Article 21(1) clearly imposes a hierarchy of sources, with a three-tiered cascade of applicable norms." See *ibid.*, p. 389, from the Katanga *et al.* Case, ICC-01/04-01/07, Decision on the confirmation of charges, 30 September 2008, para. 508.
126 See more precisely under Section II.2. *Other Sources of ICL*.
127 Schabas, W., *op. cit.*, p. 390.

treaties or principles and rules of international law are applicable.[128] *Applicable treaties* are primarily those to which the ICC is itself a party.[129] In addition, such certainly also include human rights treaties and treaties on international humanitarian law. It is expected that the ICC will follow the case law of both *ad hoc* Tribunals, which have applied treaties that are binding on the States that would have jurisdiction over the prosecution of the committed crimes.[130]

The group of the sources pursuant to Article 21(1)(b) are 'the principles and rules of international law'. This group is somewhat more problematic. Under the *principles of international law* concept must be understood *general principles of law recognized by civilized nations*, as determined in Article 38(1)(c) of the Statute of the ICJ (*e.g.* the rule of *res iudicata*).[131] In addition, this group comprises principles of international law that have developed not in national law but in international law and represent the fundamental principles of such law and common values of the international community, such as the principle of *pacta sunt servanda* and (inherent) right to self-defence.[132] Finally, this group also includes the established principles and rules of the international law of armed conflict. This concerns first of all primary sources, such as the Hague Convention (IV) of 1907, the GC for the protection of victims of war of 1949, and Additional Protocols I and II of 1977 to the GC.[133] A study conducted by the ICRC can be helpful for establishing the existence of the rules of customary law of armed conflict.[134]

If sources determined in paragraphs (a) and (b) do not suffice, the ICC applies "general principles of law derived...from national laws of legal systems of the world including, as appropriate, the national laws of States that would normally exercise jurisdiction over..." the crime pursuant to the Rome Statute (Article 21(1)(c)). The application of the sources under paragraph (c) depends on the condition that the general principles of law derived from national laws and national laws of States that would normally exercise jurisdiction is not inconsistent with the Rome Statute, with applicable international law and internationally recognized norms and standards. This provision is the most

---

128 Triffterer, O. (ed.), *op. cit.*, p. 705.
129 Schabas, W., *op. cit.*, p. 390.
130 Triffterer, O., (ed.), *op. cit.*, p. 706.
131 Schabas, W., *op. cit.*, pp. 391–392. The Commentary among the examples of the general principles (of law) also mentions the principle of good faith and equity, and the obligation to make reparation for breach of an engagement.
132 Triffterer, O., (ed.), *op. cit.*, pp. 706–707.
133 See Hague, Geneva, and New York law, under Section II.1.a. *Treaties.*
134 Henckaerts, J.M., Doswald-Beck, L., *Customary International Humanitarian Law*, ICRC, Vol. II, Rules, Cambridge University Press, Cambridge, 2005.

problematic. The sources under paragraph (c) are a compromise between the supporters of the position that the ICC may apply national legislation and the opponents of this position. This provision differs from the general principles of law recognized by civilized nations that are contained under the general principles of international law in paragraph (b); paragraph (c) envisages that the ICC consults comparative criminal law as a subsidiary means for the determination of ICL.[135] Some authors regard Article 21(1)(c) as the ability of the Court to fill lacunae in ICL.[136] In this regard, the Court may resort to national law of the State that would have jurisdiction over criminal prosecution, this being the State on the territory of which or under the jurisdiction of which the crime was committed, or the State of which the perpetrator is a national.[137] The view of one of the Pre-Trial Chambers was that national case law can constitute a subsidiary means for the determination of law before the ICC, only insofar as it shows the existence of a general principle of law that can be derived from national laws of legal systems of the world and is not inconsistent with the Rome Statute, with international law and internationally recognized norms and standards.[138] Hitherto case law shows that the ICC is reserved towards national case law as a source of the general principles and has already stated that it is by no means bound by national law.[139]

Article 21(2) refers to the case law of the ICC. The wording that the Court *may* apply principles and rules of law as interpreted in its previous decisions leads to a conclusion that the ICC is not bound by its previous decisions.[140] They thus constitute a subsidiary source of ICL. The Rome Statute in this regard followed the practice of other international courts, first of all the ICJ. This also does not entail that the ICC cannot refer to the case law of other courts, especially the ICTY and the ICTR, both regional courts for human rights,[141] or perhaps even the ICJ.

---

135   Schabas, W., *op. cit.*, p. 393.
136   Triffterer, O., (ed.), *op. cit.*, pp. 709–710.
137   See Article 12 ('Preconditions to the exercise of jurisdiction') of the Rome Statute.
138   Schabas, W., *op. cit.*, str. 393, from Bemba, ICC–01/04–01/07, Decision revoking the prohibition of contact and communication between Germain Katanga and Mathieu Chui, 13 March 2008, p. 12.
139   *Ibid.*, p. 394, after Lubanga, ICC–01/04–01/06, Decision on the confirmation of charges, 29 January 2007, para. 69, and Katanga *et al.*, ICC–01/04–01/07, Decision on the confirmation of charges, 30 September 2008, para. 91.
140   "Article 21(2) clearly rejects a rule *stare decisis*, because it is worded as a permissive and not a mandatory provision. Nor does the provision explicitly establish any hierarchy in terms of the various Chambers of the Court." *Ibid.*, pp. 394–395.
141   *I.e.* the ECtHR, the Inter-American Court of Human Rights.

Article 21(3) refers to the entire application and interpretation of the provision on applicable law.[142] It determines that the application and interpretation of law before the ICC must be consistent with internationally recognized human rights, especially with the prohibition of discrimination on any grounds.[143] It seems that the primary intention of this paragraph is to strengthen the implementation of the fair trial rights, which are fairly comprehensively set out in various provisions of the Rome Statute, and to ensure that other substantive and procedural rights not included in the Statute are applied in all proceedings before the Court at every stage.[144] The prohibition of discrimination is also contained in all the existing universal and regional instruments relating to human rights. A peculiarity of these provisions is that with respect to the prohibition of gender discrimination they use a more contemporary term *gender* in the sense as explained in Article 7(3) under crimes against humanity, namely that it refers to the two sexes, male and female, as this term is understood within the context of society.[145]

Article 21 is a central provision of the Rome Statute regarding applicable law. It must be applied to any question encountered by the Court during proceedings. It applies not only in the case of substantive but also procedural principles and rules. Attention must be drawn to its systemic connection with Part III of the Rome Statute, which lists general principles of criminal law. For instance, Article 31(3) determines that the Court may consider a ground for excluding criminal responsibility other than those referred to in Article 31(1) where such a ground is derived from applicable law as set out in Article 21.

IV   Conclusion

The question of the sources of law is one of the key issues relating to the rule of law and the legal certainty of subjects who are exposed to a certain branch of law. The sources of law are of paramount importance for courts, both national and international. For instance, courts decide by applying law that

---

142 If this provision is compared with Article 38(1) of the Statute of the ICJ it can be noted that the ICJ is explicitly authorized only to apply the sources and not also to interpret them. On the distinction between application and interpretation of ICL see Grover, L., *op. cit.*, pp. 549–550.

143 On the question whether Article 21(3) creates *super-legality* or a normative superiority for international human rights within the framework of the sources enshrined in the Rome Statute see *ibid.*, pp. 558–559.

144 Schabas, W., *op. cit.*, p. 398.

145 See Triffterer, O., (ed.), *op. cit.*, p. 712. *Cf.* Schabas, W., *op. cit.*, p. 398.

they must know (*iura novit curia*). This is even more true in the case of criminal prosecution.

The sources of law are exceptionally important also in ICL. Within this scope, the importance of ICL as a special branch of law, which is a relatively young discipline in comparison with other branches of law, must be investigated; it was given major impetus by the first two acting international criminal tribunals, namely the Nuremberg and Tokyo Tribunals. It must be underlined that theoretical views regarding ICL are not entirely uniform. This concerns the question whether ICL is a part of international public law or an independent legal discipline connected with national criminal law. It is undisputed that in the field of international substantive criminal law, international law prevails. However, criminal proceedings against individuals that are conducted before national courts and under national procedural law must not be overlooked.

Even if a broader understanding of ICL is accepted which, in addition to international, also includes national and comparative criminal law as well as human rights law, the fact that at present there are three acting international criminal courts, *i.e.* the ICTY, the ICTR, and the ICC (along with two more which are classified as internationalized courts, *i.e.* the Court for Sierra Leone and the Tribunal for Lebanon) cannot be ignored.

In the present study the question of the sources of ICL in the context of international law is discussed, with the assistance of the rule on the sources of international law under Article 38(1) of the Statute of the ICJ. Such an approach allows the inclusion of the majority of the formal sources of ICL. As regards the substance, however, it is not the most well chosen. It derives from the fact that the ICJ decides in disputes between States that are sovereign and independent subjects of international law, which is also reflected in the formation and development of its sources and in their application and interpretation. This approach is not entirely satisfactory in the case of ICL. The leading principle of ICL is the principle of legality, regardless of the fact that some legal scholars claim that its significance is not entirely uniform in 'common law' and 'civil law' countries. Filling gaps by means of legal analogy or resorting to general principles of law is problematic in ICL from the perspective of the principle of legality and the requirements of minimum procedural guarantees that must be applied in proceedings against individuals tried for international crimes.

Thus, in the field of ICL the most reliable source of law remains treaties. Customary international law is not a disputable source of ICL, inasmuch as it concerns a codification of rules that are included in treaty law. Its application, however, requires of judges caution and a high level of legal expertise. The same holds true for the application of general principles of law and general principles of international law. Legal scholars point to all the above-mentioned problems regarding the functioning of the ICTY and ICTR, which are also being criticized for performing the function of the legislature (*judge-made law*). Their Statutes were written in a hurry, and perhaps one of their greatest deficiencies is that they do not contain provisions on applicable law, but regarding the application of law the Tribunals apply and interpret provisions on their subject-matter jurisdiction.

The drafters of the Rome Statute wished to remedy the above-mentioned deficiency of both *ad hoc* Tribunals by including a provision on applicable law in Article 21. It is an important innovation in the field of international criminal adjudication. Nevertheless, the rule is not flawless; certain provisions are difficult to understand and only the future case law of the ICC will give them substance.

The sources of ICL as well as their application and interpretation thus open a number of theoretical questions. An undeniably important achievement in the field of international criminal adjudication that is closely connected to the problem of the sources of ICL is the development of human rights law, which is reflected in all Statutes of international courts, especially in the Rome Statute.

CHAPTER 49

Passage from Natural Resources Law to Environmental Law to Sustainable Development Law

Amado S. Tolentino Jr.*

I   Introduction

The main concern of environmental law is to govern the relationship of man with his natural surroundings. In the past, man viewed nature and her resources as available for virtually unlimited exploitation. He had become a god in his capacity to destroy. He had little thought for the future or for the harms he may have done. Fortunately, that view of nature has been modified by the concept of man's new role of 'stewardship', *i.e.* man is the custodian rather than the conqueror of nature.

As custodian, man must not merely exploit resources; he must also conserve them. Considering the trend towards industrial development, this task extends to planning and creating an environment of his choice. He should strive to strike a harmonious balance between development and environmental protection for his survival and well-being. More so because of the recognized unity of nature and humanity and the finitude of the earth's resources. The guiding principle should therefore be: what naturally is should be respected and preserved in its present condition, or in its prior condition if restoration of the prior condition is possible and beneficial.

Law is an essential tool for the sound management of the environment and its resources, and its development and application are of vital importance to all societies. In this regard, legally trained persons have multiple tasks to perform. The range of tasks include developing new constitutional theory, drafting implementing policies, new legislation and administrative regulations as well

---

*   A member of the Philippine Bar and the New York (USA) State Bar, the author received his law education from the University of the Philippines, the Universidad de Madrid (Spain) and the Academy of International Law at the Southern Methodist University in Dallas, Texas (USA). He pioneered in the field of environmental law and served as environmental law consultant to UNEP; elected Delegate to the 3rd Philippine Constitutional Convention and Philippine Ambassador to Papua New Guinea and Qatar. He lectures at the San Beda Alabang Law School.

as the formulation of guidelines to ensure compliance with legal requirements, opportunities for litigation to halt environmentally degrading activities and reshaping the legal and administrative systems of governmental agencies so that environmental implications are properly taken into account in agency decisions. In connection therewith, the effectiveness of government implementation of development-oriented public policies involves the use of law as an instrument of social change and control and that inefficiencies in the legal system have been a contributing factor to ineffective development policies related to the environment.

Environmental law has been defined as that set of legal rules addressed specifically to activities which potentially affect the quality of the environment, whether natural or man-made. It consists of international and national laws relating to the protection and enhancement of the environment and encompasses both 'hard law' (*i.e.* international treaties and national legislations) and 'soft law' (*i.e.* guidelines, standards, *etc.*). Its elements are derived from sectoral areas (*e.g.* air, marine and inland water, soil, energy, biological diversity) and functional tasks (*e.g.* environmental impact assessment, natural resources accounting, environmental auditing, *etc.*) (Craig, 2002).

It should be noted that environmental law is only one component of environmental protection techniques and should be complemented by other functional tasks such as development plans, conservation strategies and institutional support. Consequently, technical understanding, economic analyses, public participation, access to information and access to justice, political will and a number of socio-cultural factors are required in order to establish a comprehensive approach to the protection of the environment.

II The Environment as a Field of Law

Environmental law emerged as a branch or new field of law. Other branches of law have historically been used to remedy environmental problems. In the common law system, tort law which provides remedies for harm caused by an individual to another provided the necessary legal foundation in early cases. Nuisance actions were the most popular because they allow a successful plaintiff/litigant to receive not only compensation but also an order from the court abating the nuisance.

The inadequacies and sometimes inefficiency of tort and property law convinced governments to adopt measures to tackle the most pressing environmental problems. Environmental laws were traditionally formulated around important themes such as nature conservation and protection of the principal areas of environmental concern: air, water and land. This allows the elaboration of rules with limited application which are easier to manage and enforce but may fail to acknowledge the importance of a holistic approach and to deal with important natural relationships such as the effect of pollution not only on the air but on water quality and land use as well.

Fortunately, the UN Stockholm Declaration on the Human Environment (1972) centred on man as both the creator and moulder of the environment. It recognized that both aspects of man's environment, natural and man-made, are essential to his well-being and to the enjoyment of basic human rights including the right to life itself. While man has the fundamental right to freedom, equality and adequate conditions of life in an environment of a quality that permits a life of dignity and well-being, he bears a solemn responsibility to protect and improve the environment for the present and future generations.

Environmental law is, therefore, an important tool of environmental management. It establishes the rights and duties of individuals, communities and industries in the use of environmental resources including sets of mandatory quality standards and assigns powers, responsibilities and liabilities with respect to environmental management. Its main concern is to govern the relationship of man and his environment. What was originally labelled environmental legislation is actually natural resources laws that are 'use-oriented', designed for the maximum exploitation and development of natural resources as compared to environmental legislation that is 'resource-oriented', or designed for the rational management and conservation of natural resources in order to prevent their depletion or degradation.

Law responds to a need and generally follows through such need. In the case of environmental law, however, specific environment-related legislation preceded the adoption of general or organic laws. There were instances when legislation dealing with specific issues developed gradually or when laws were amended to include the environmental dimensions. This was the situation in many developing countries during the early 1970s when virtually all countries had laws prohibiting pollution, protecting forests, regulating the exploitation of mineral resources (UNESCAP, 2005). However, such legislation has been proved an inadequate response to the environmental challenges confronting the countries in their efforts at development.

III Understanding Sustainable Development

Ten years after the UN Stockholm Conference on the Human Environment, the Earth Summit in Rio de Janeiro introduced the concept of sustainable development. What distinguished this particular Summit was that it was driven as much by people outside government and international public institutions (*i.e.* civil society) as it was by heads of governments and high officials from all UN member countries who came. The Summit ushered in a new era of multi-stakeholder partnership in pursuit of sustainable development.

The international community adopted Agenda 21, a global plan of action to implement the goals they were aiming for. At the 2002 World Summit on Sustainable Development held in Johannesburg, the challenges surrounding sustainable development became an even more important part of the world political agenda. There is much more at stake at an ecological, economic and social level. It emphasized the need to see the economic, social and environmental dimensions of human welfare as integrated and mutually supporting goals of development. On this, community-based approaches involving active stakeholder participation in resource management have been demonstrated to be most effective (Craig, 2002).

The concept is not new. Before the 1980s, conservationists alluded to the sustainable use of natural resources as the true meaning of conservation. Some countries have even done research and have implemented regimes of sustainable yield in renewable resources such as forests and fisheries. The better known initiative to popularize the concept was the publication by IUCN (International Union for the Conservation of Nature, now known as the World Conservation Union) of the 'World Conservation Strategy' in 1980.

Sustainable development is often equated with 'development without destruction'. It is optimal development with minimal destruction. In short, 'wise use' of the environment. By wise use is meant sustainable utilization for the benefit of mankind in a way compatible with the maintenance of the natural elements of the ecosystem. It is, in other words, a forward-looking development.

Actually, the World Commission on Environment and Development (WCED) was responsible for making the concept fashionable in development circles (WCED, 1987). Its report stated that "[i]n essence, sustainable development is a process in which the exploitation of natural resources, the direction of investments, the orientation of technological development, and institutional change are all in harmony and enhance both current and future potential to meet the human needs and aspirations," and goes on to say that

> ...the pursuit of sustainable development requires (i) a political system that secures effective citizen participation in decision-making; (ii) an economic system that is able to generate surpluses and technical knowledge on a self-reliant and sustained basis; (iii) a social system that provides solutions for the tensions arising from disharmonious development;

(iv) a production system that respects the obligation to preserve the ecological base for development; (v) a technological system that can search continuously for new solutions; (vi) an international system that fosters sustainable patterns of trade and finance; and (vii) an administrative system that is flexible and has the capacity for self-correction.

The same WCED report then raises the question: "[h]ow are individuals in the world to be persuaded or made to act in the common interests?" It says, "The answer lies partly in education, institutional development and environmental legislation."

Viewed from another angle, sustainable development rests on three pillars: economic growth, social development and environmental quality (UNDP/UNESCAP 2002). Economic growth provides resources for consumption, social services and improving the environment, and is a prerequisite for improving human development and alleviating poverty. Growth by itself, however, is not sufficient. It needs to be pro-poor in that, while increasing income-entitlement and capability, it also reduces inequity and deprivation. This, in turn, requires the promotion of the second element, social development and well-being, through the provision of health services, access to education and skills formation, provision of public goods, and the establishment of safety nets that empower the poor by giving them options. Without an equitable social framework, development cannot be sustainable. The third pillar, which is maintenance of environmental quality, refers to environmental services which are critical for many production processes and for human well-being without which long-term development cannot be sustained.

The following simple dicta have been presented to explain sustainable development vis-à-vis ecological sustainability: species extinction cannot exceed evolution; soil erosion cannot exceed soil formation; forest destruction cannot exceed forest regeneration; carbon emissions cannot exceed carbon fixation; fish catches cannot exceed the regenerative capacities of fisheries; and human births cannot exceed human deaths (Brown, 1994).

IV Environmental Law *vis-à-vis* Sustainable Development

The Stockholm Conference on the Human Environment (1972) which led to the Rio Summit on Environment and Development (1992) and onwards to the Johannesburg Summit on Sustainable Development (2002) and the recently concluded Rio+20 Earth Summit (2012) all represent an important shift from environmental protection to sustainable development as a central global agenda to realize the future we all want. They all exhorted Governments to establish an effective legal and regulatory framework in order to improve national capacities to respond to the challenges of sustainable development by adjusting or fundamentally reshaping the decision-making process relating to environment and development.

There have been significant changes in environmental legislation since those historic environmental summits before Rio+20. Among the several emerging trends in the evolution of environmental law *vis-à-vis* sustainable development are: crystallization of environmental issues in constitutional and policy documents (*e.g.* right to a healthy environment; sustainable use of natural resources); more comprehensive coverage of environmental issues (*e.g.* biodiversity conservation; management of hazardous wastes); establishment of environmental standards and norms (*e.g.* national air, water and noise quality standards; maximum level of emission of air-borne pollutants; maximum noise levels); use of economic instruments for environmental management (*e.g.* tax incentives for installation of anti-pollution devices not locally available; natural-resource-user-pays schemes; environment funds; polluter-pays principle); recognition of international environmental norms (*e.g.* legislative and institutional arrangements to give effect to multilateral environmental agreements; financial obligations required under some conventions/treaties); environmental impact assessment (EIA) (*e.g.* review of environmental impact statements); effective coordination of environmental management (*e.g.* ministries responsible for the environment; high level advisory councils dealing with environmental and developmental issues); efforts towards coherence of legislative framework (*e.g.* institutional mechanisms like inter-agency committees for cross-sectoral coordination and harmonization of policies and programmes); establishment of mechanisms for facilitating compliance with environmental regulations and measures for more effective environmental law implementation, compliance and enforcement (*e.g.* environmental law compliance guidelines; enforcement procedures); and provisions for public participation and review (*e.g.* public consultation in the EIA process; legal standing to sue/public interest litigation) (Wilson, 2000).

At the international level, multilateral environmental agreements (MEAs) have taken into consideration the socio-economic dimension which is what sustainable development is all about. Examples are the Convention on Biological Diversity and the Climate Change Convention which not only set rights and obligations for environmental protection but also take into account the associated development concerns. Furthermore, ways have been found in developing international legal instruments that are sufficiently flexible and capable of accommodating change as the scientific evidence becomes clearer. For instance, the concept of common but differentiated responsibilities where each State could act according to its capability and capacity is embodied in the Climate Change Convention and the Montreal Protocol on Substances that Deplete the Ozone Layer. The kind of differentiation of obligations is an important factor in the development of the law of sustainable development.

With regard to the unique nature of the implementation process of international law in the field of sustainable development, there is a history of introducing innovative means and mechanisms of implementation. What can be seen in recent environmental treaties is not only the setting of ambitious goals but also the provision of supportive means for the achievement of those goals, be they financial mechanisms, provisions for the transfer of resources or the transfer of technology. These facilitating and supportive means of environmental law will continue to develop, complementing the prohibitive mechanisms that have so long characterized legal regimes (UNDP/UNESCAP, 2002).

Be that as it may, for national environmental legislation, apart from establishing appropriate legal and institutional frameworks, effective implementation and enforcement remain the most daunting challenges especially for developing countries. How the matter is resolved will largely determine the capacity of the legal arrangements effectively to contribute towards the realization of the objectives of sustainable development. For, in the final analysis, ineffective law may be worse than no law at all. Its existence may satisfy political and administrative conscience or a formal international obligation, but it has no effective impact on the problems with which it is supposed to deal. It may have some initial deterrent effect, but this will disappear as soon as it becomes evident that the law will not be enforced. It gives the impression that something is being done whereas the existing legal arrangements are contributing little in terms of practical environmental management. In fact, the lack of ability to enforce the legislation will have promoted in its continued breach an undesirable disrespect towards an important state policy.

Sustainable development requires not only appropriate and adequate legal and institutional regimes for environmental management, but, even more importantly, effective environmental law.

v   Sustainable Development Law

So, at this point in the history of its evolution, what is the direction of environmental law?

From its beginning as natural resources law which, as mentioned above, was use-oriented to its transformation into the present environmental law which is resource-oriented, the newly emerged branch of law is fast becoming referred to also as the law of sustainable development. That is because the post-Johannesburg (2002 World Summit on Sustainable Development) environmental law calls for the integration of environmental protection measures and economic development activities. The goal of this integration is to raise living standards while preserving the environmental potential of the future to bring about sustainable development. For developing countries, in particular, a sound economy is a social and governmental precondition to environmental commitment.

The transition of environmental law to a law of sustainable development can best be made by organizing the reform agenda around human activities, thus infusing the main body of development law with ecological principles. This calls for a re-examination of property rights and principles, investment and banking operations, the tax laws, and the conduct of a sector-by-sector revision of the laws governing agriculture, energy, transportation and manufacturing, among others. By tailoring environmental law more closely to the patterns of human behaviour, law administration and enforcement will be more efficient, and environmental law will blend with other areas of law, thus strengthening respect for the rule of law and effectiveness of the law as a tool for the attainment of social justice.

It should be noted that all the efforts exerted in the recent past under the command-and-control regulation to protect the environment produced a lot of legal response to curb pollution and conserve natural resources which focused almost exclusively either on pollution control laws or on resource management laws, seldom on the interface between the two. Specifically, pollution control laws focus primarily on processing and recovering resources for disposal, while natural resources laws focus mainly on resource extraction. The laws in both areas concentrate on consequences but not causes, on water purification, for example, but not on pollution prevention; or on saving protected areas but not checking on soil erosion; on protecting endangered species but not on biological diversity. This piecemeal reaction in law-making even resulted to piecemeal emergency response (chemical-related industrial accidents, oil spills, *etc.*) not joined into a coherent environmental management system. Worst is the regulation of the same activity by many government agencies like pollution from mining by the mining agency, pollution from industry by the environment agency, coastal pollution by the coast guard, *etc.* (Futrell, 1994). To be more specific, the law on environment and development has not been integrated into a purposeful whole.

To illustrate the expectation on interface between environment and development in the context of the new law on sustainable development, let us take as an example the human activity associated with forestry. The formulation of sustainable development legislation would require analysis of the economic aspect of the activity from the time resources are extracted, processed and disposed of, showing how each stage of each economic activity affects the environment. Using the resource-to-recovery analysis of an examination centred on forest products, for instance, starts with the natural resource laws and regulations affecting timber harvesting and goes through the air, water and waste regulation of pollution control laws affecting milling operations, and ends with laws dealing with the manufacture, recycling and ultimate disposal of wood products.

The resource-to-recovery analysis will help point out the pollution control and natural resources laws that must be integrated with property and other development laws to create a system that promotes sustainability. It will expose those areas where development and environmental regulation clash and help to modify the provisions that undermine sustainability. Let us take as an example a resource threatened by overuse anywhere in the world – groundwater. In developing countries in particular, groundwater is being withdrawn for irrigation much faster than it can be recharged, and whole watersheds face shortages in a short time span. The need to control groundwater pollution and its conservation is an intricate policy and regulatory challenge for which revision of agricultural law could be the solution. Be that as it may, there are instances when agriculture law entangles with pollution control and resource laws with tax measures and, in this connection, reform should be one which could lead to an integrated scheme aimed at sustainable economy and ecology.

Perhaps, a simpler example would be land use laws *vis-à-vis* pollution control legislation. Command-and-control regulation might be lighter on industry if land use laws effectively directed factory location in a manner aimed at sustainable development, meaning that land use planning should balance environmental and developmental interests by incorporating the air and water pollution control aspects at the outset. Indeed, the transition to sustainable development law will require a move beyond the command-and-control regulation to the satisfactory use of all legal tools.

As mentioned above, the transition envisages an examination of the 'non-environmental laws' on agriculture, public works, transport, banking, taxation, *etc*. Analysis of the laws should proceed natural resource by natural resource, industry sector by industry sector based on the total cycle resource-to-recovery, being careful to keep the fundamental structure of the law in place. As the transition to a sustainable development law is effected, the pollution control laws can be simplified and the burden of command-and-control regulation will ease. Furthermore, the integration of development and environmental laws can lead to increased use of other, more effective tools such as planning methods and strategies, process changes for pollution prevention, and economic incentives, all encouraging sustainability. This will in turn lead to better law by infusing the old environmental movement with economic realism and a commitment to social justice.

VI Conclusion

The Rio Declaration, Agenda 21, the Johannesburg Plan of Implementation and, of late, the Rio+20 final output document 'The World We Want' call for further efforts at sustainable development. This requires a normative framework for economic relations conducive to sustainable development. In the field of legislation, this would comprise not only the rules which constitute environmental law but also elements of development law which necessarily encompass the economy. Special attention has to be focussed on the delicate balance between environment and development concerns, including experiences about the effectiveness of existing legal instruments and institutions as well as priorities for future law-making on sustainable development.

Illustration of sustainable development *vis-à-vis* environmental law can be likened to 'Matrushka', the Russian grandmother doll. When opening the doll, one finds inside a smaller doll, and then again a smaller one and still another smaller doll and so on. Proceeding in the reverse or opposite direction starts naturally with the smallest one to reach the biggest at the end. Following this pattern, one could begin with sustainable utilization of a natural resource backed up by appropriate and effective legislation. The whole series of legislation is then to be placed in the general framework of sustainable development such that wherever one starts there is sustainable development as the overall theme to appreciate the law for sustainable development fully.

As changes are made, sustainable development can help to define the path towards increasing preservation of the dignity of nature and of the dignity of humanity within it. Ultimately, the passage from environmental law to sustainable development law becomes complete.

References

L. Brown et al., *Vital Signs*, Norton and Co., New York, 1994.
D. Craig, N. Robinson, K.L. Koh, *Capacity Building for Environmental Law in the Asian and Pacific Region*, Asian Development Bank, Manila, 2002.

W. Futrell, *The Transition to Sustainable Development Law*, Environmental Law Institute, Washington, D.C., 1994.

UNDP/UNESCAP, *Environmental Governance for Sustainable Development in Asia and the Pacific*, New York, 2002.

UNEP, *The World We Want, Rio+20 Final Document Output*, Rio de Janeiro, 2012.

UNESCAP, *State of the Environment in Asia and the Pacific*, Bangkok, 2005.

P. Wilson et al., *Emerging Trends in National Environmental Legislation in Developing Countries*, UNEP, Nairobi, 2000.

World Commission on Environment and Development (WCED), *Our Common Future*, Oxford University Press, New York, 1987.

Printed in the United States
By Bookmasters